MindTap™

QUICK START

1. To get started, navigate to www.cengagebrain.com and select "Register a Product."

A new screen will appear prompting you to add a Course Key. A Course Key is a code given to you by your instructor — this is the first of two codes you will need to access MindTap. Every student in your course section should have the same Course Key.

2. Enter the Course Key and click "Register."

If you are accessing MindTap through your school's Learning Management System, such as BlackBoard or Desire2Learn, you may be redirected to use your Course Key/Access Code there. Follow the prompts you are given and feel free to contact support if you need assistance.

3. Confirm your course information above and proceed to the log in portion below.

If you have a CengageBrain username and password, enter it under "Returning Students" and click "Login." If this is your first time, register under "New Students" and click "Create a New Account."

4. Now that you are logged in, you can access the course for free by selecting "Start Free Trial" for 20 days or enter in your Access Code.

Your Access Code is unique to you and acts as payment for MindTap. You may have received it with your book or purchased separately in the bookstore or at www.cengagebrain.com. Enter it and click "Register."

NEED HELP?

For CengageBrain Support: Login to **Support.Cengage.com**. Call **866-994-2427** or access our **24/7 Student Chat!** Or access the **First Day of School PowerPoint Presentation** found at **www.cengagebrain.com**.

Western Civilization

Ideas, Politics, and Society

Western Civilization

Ideas, Politics, and Society

Eleventh Edition

Marvin Perry
Baruch College, City University of New York

Myrna Chase
Baruch College, City University of New York

James R. Jacob
John Jay College of Criminal Justice, City University of New York

Margaret C. Jacob
University of California, Los Angeles

Jonathan W. Daly
University of Illinois, Chicago

Theodore H. Von Laue
Late of *Clark University*

George W. Bock, *Editorial Associate*

CENGAGE
Learning®

Australia • Brazil • Mexico • Singapore • United Kingdom • United States

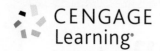

Western Civilization: Ideas, Politics, and Society, Eleventh Edition

Marvin Perry, Myrna Chase, James R. Jacob, Margaret C. Jacob, Jonathan W. Daly, Theodore H. Von Laue

Product Manager: Brooke Barbier

Content Developer: Lauren Floyd

Associate Content Developer: Cara Swan

Product Assistant: Andrew Newton

Media Developer: Kate MacLean

Market Development Manager: Kyle Zimmerman

Senior Content Project Manager: Jane Lee

Senior Art Director: Cate Rickard Barr

Manufacturing Planner: Sandee Milewski

IP Analyst: Alexandra Ricciardi

IP Project Manager: Amber Hosea

Production Service: Lumina Datamatics

Cover Designer: Faith Brosnan

Cover Image: *L'Audition*, detail, Forain, Jean Louis (1852–1931)

Credit: Harper Collins Publishers/ The Art Archive at Art Resource, NY

Compositor: Lumina Datamatics

Library of Congress Control Number: 2014938881

ISBN: 978-1-305-09139-9

Cengage Learning
20 Channel Center Street
Boston, MA 02210

Cengage Learning is a leading provider of customized learning solutions with office locations around the globe, including Singapore, the United Kingdom, Australia, Mexico, Brazil and Japan. Locate your local office at **international.cengage.com/region.**

Cengage Learning products are represented in Canada by Nelson Education, Ltd.

For your course and learning solutions, visit **www.cengage.com.**

Purchase any of our products at your local college store or at our preferred online store **www.cengagebrain.com.**

Instructors: Please visit **login.cengage.com** and log in to access instructor-specific resources.

Printed in the United States of America
Print Number: 01   Print Year: 2014

Brief Contents

v

Contents

Part Four

An Age of Revolution: Liberal, National, Industrial 1789–1848   450

Maps

Chronologies

Preface

Western civilization is a grand but tragic drama. The West has forged the instruments of reason that make possible a rational comprehension of physical nature and human culture, conceived the idea of political liberty, and recognized the intrinsic worth of the individual. But the modern West, though it has unraveled nature's mysteries, has been less successful at finding rational solutions to social ills and conflicts between nations. Science, the great achievement of the Western intellect, while improving conditions of life, has also produced weapons of mass destruction. Though the West has pioneered in the protection of human rights, it has also produced totalitarian regimes that have trampled on individual freedom and human dignity. Although the West has demonstrated a commitment to human equality, it has also practiced brutal racism.

Despite the value that Westerners have given to reason and freedom, they have shown a frightening capacity for irrational behavior and a fascination for violence and irrational ideologies, and they have willingly sacrificed liberty for security or national grandeur. The world wars and totalitarian movements of the twentieth century have demonstrated that Western civilization, despite its extraordinary achievements, is fragile and perishable. Yet the West has also shown the capacity to reassert its best values and traditions.

Western Civilization: Ideas, Politics, and Society examines the Western tradition—those unique patterns of thought and systems of values that constitute the Western heritage. While focusing on key ideas and broad themes, the text also provides a balanced treatment of economic, political, and social history for students in Western civilization courses.

The text is written with the conviction that history possesses profound meaning. Without a knowledge of history, men and women cannot fully know themselves, for all human beings have been shaped by institutions and values inherited from the past. Without an awareness of the historical evolution of reason and freedom, the dominant ideals of Western civilization, commitment to these ideals will diminish. Without knowledge of history, the West cannot fully comprehend or adequately cope with the problems that burden its civilization and the world.

In attempting to make sense out of the past, the authors have been careful to avoid superficial generalizations that oversimplify historical events and arrange history into too neat a structure. But they do strive to interpret and to synthesize in order to provide students with a frame of reference with which to comprehend the principal events and eras in Western history.

CHANGES IN THE ELEVENTH EDITION

For the eleventh edition, every chapter has been reworked to some extent. The hundreds of carefully selected modifications and additions significantly enhance the text. Some changes deepen the book's conceptual character while others provide useful and illustrative historical detail. In several chapters the concluding essays, which strive for meaning and significance, have been enlarged and improved. We have been particularly careful to strengthen chapters dealing with intellectual history, the text's distinguishing feature. Each chapter continues to contain a profile of a significant historical figure, as well as a primary source that illuminates the narrative and includes questions for analysis of the documents.

In Chapter 1, "The Ancient Near East," brief inserts strengthen the treatment of prehistory, Mesopotamian medicine, Phoenicia, and Persia. In Chapter 2, "The Hebrews," we expanded the discussion of Hebrew law. Several judicious inserts improve the narrative in Chapter 3, "The Greek City-State," and a discussion of the significance of Greek politics for the Founding Fathers of the United States enriches the concluding section, "The Dilemma of Greek Politics." In Chapter 4, "Greek Thought," here too judicious additions improve the account of Greek philosophers, Thucydides, and Sophocles; and, as in past editions, we have strengthened the end piece, "The Greek Achievement: Reason, Freedom, and Humanism." The most important changes in Chapter 5, "The Hellenistic Age," are a fuller treatment of Alexander the Great and Hellenistic society. In Chapter 6, "The Roman Republic," we have improved the discussion of slavery and culture in the Republic; also noteworthy is the expanded treatment of Julius Caesar. Among the changes made in Chapter 7, "The Roman Empire," are a fuller treatment of the reign of Augustus and the status of slaves. And consistent with the text's approach, we have strengthened the end piece, "The Roman Legacy." In Chapter 8, "Early Christianity," among the improvements made is a fuller discussion of the Dead Sea Scrolls and Christianity's appeal in the Roman world, particularly among women.

Most of the changes in Chapter 9, "The Heirs of Rome," deal with the Koran, Islamic interpretations of jihad, and Muslim science. The discussion of medieval towns has been enhanced in Chapter 10, "The High Middle Ages." In Chapter 11, "The Flowering of Medieval Culture," we have enriched the introduction, deepened the treatment of the medieval university, inserted a passage from the writings of Adelard of Bath as the Primary Source feature, broadened the treatment of Abelard in the section on philosophy, and briefly discussed Chaucer's *Canterbury Tales*. A major improvement is the transfer of the section, "The Medieval Worldview" to the end of the chapter where it

serves as a fitting interpretive statement. The treatment of the Black Plague has been broadened in Chapter 12, "The Late Middle Ages," and the concluding end piece, "The Middle Ages and the Modern World: Continuity and Discontinuity," has been somewhat expanded.

In Chapter 13, "The Renaissance: Transition to the Modern Age," there is a new Primary Source, namely, selections from the "Oration on the Dignity of Man" by Pico della Mirandola, showing both his radical humanistic outlook and his fundamental break with medieval tradition. The treatment of women in the Renaissance has also been expanded. Chapter 14, "The Reformation," has had added emphasis placed upon the Council of Trent in the light of new research. In Chapter 15, "European Expansion," we have strengthened the Profile of Bartolomé de Las Casas, the treatment of slavery, and the concluding section, "Economic and Social Transformations." Chapter 16, "The Rise of Sovereignty," lays additional emphasis on international competition between states for overseas conquest and exploitation. Chapter 17, "The Scientific Revolution" now better shows the connections between it and the first Industrial Revolution. Chapter 18, "The Age of Enlightenment," renews the emphasis upon its international character.

In Chapter 19, "The French Revolution," the insertion of a quotation expressing enthusiasm for the Revolution enriches the introduction. Major additions to the chapter are the discussion of the Jacobin policy of de-Christianization and statements by Napoleon illustrating his attitude toward women, religion, and his pursuit of glory. In Chapter 20, "The Industrial Revolution," the revisions have focused on the uneven economic and social development in Western Europe and America in the eighteenth and early nineteenth centuries. The treatment of conservatism and nationalism in Chapter 21, "Thought and Culture in the Early Nineteenth Century," benefits from the inclusion of quotations from contemporaries. The major change in the chapter is the new Primary Source, an excerpt from the writings of Benjamin Constant, the French liberal theorist. The changes in Chapter 22, "Revolution and Counterrevolution, 1815–1848," include a passage from Alexis de Tocqueville analyzing the June Days, and several other insertions dealing with the revolutions in France and Germany in 1848.

The new Primary Source is an excerpt from Carl Schurz's *Reminiscences* in which he recalls the expectations of German liberal-nationalists after the February Revolution in Paris.

The few lines added to Chapter 23, "Thought and Culture in the Mid-Nineteenth Century," enhance the treatment of Realism, Social Darwinism, Proudhon, and the evolution of liberalism. The section on anti-Semitism has been expanded and deepened in Chapter 24, "The Surge of Nationalism." In Chapter 25, "The Industrial West," the updates have focused on the responses to modernization in each of the great powers as the political rulers attempted to include, absorb, and control masses of citizen-subjects. Chapter 26, "Imperialism," now includes enhanced discussion of the revolutionary and nationalistic responses in Latin America, Asia, and Africa. In Chapter 27, "Modern Consciousness," we have enriched the treatment of Nietzsche, literary modernism, and the section on social thought, and inserted a new Profile, Gaetano Mosca, the influential social theorist.

The principal changes in Chapter 28, "World War I," are telling examples of the enthusiasm German theologians and intellectuals displayed when war broke out, and a fuller discussion of Germany's last offensive in 1918. The concluding section, "The War and European Consciousness" provides a deeper analysis of the impact of the war on European thought and attitudes. Also added to the section is a discussion of how the war impacted on women. In Chapter 29, "An Era of Totalitarianism," we have expanded the discussion of Stalin's war on the kulaks and his drive for unchallenged personal power. Also expanded is the treatment of the ordeal faced by German Jews in the new Nazi regime. An eyewitness report describes the frenzied adoration shown by the German people for their führer. A new profile, Charlie Chaplin's, has been inserted in Chapter 30, "Thought and Culture in an Era of World Wars." Two significant changes have been made in Chapter 31, "World War II"—new material on the war in Russia and a discussion of war criminals in the concluding section, "The Legacy of World War II."

Chapters 32 and 33 have been heavily revised. In Chapter 32, "Europe After World War II," we have laid greater stress on the role of ideology in the development of the Cold War, increased our coverage of the Brezhnev era, and significantly reformulated and enhanced the discussion of Gorbachev and the collapse of the Soviet Union. Important changes to Chapter 33, "The Troubled Present," are updates to recent events in individual countries and in the European Union more broadly—in particular the continuing economic travails of the region. We nevertheless also emphasized the continuing economic and political vibrancy of the EU and the continuing relevance of Western ideals in the contemporary world. The treatment of terrorism, the strife in Afghanistan and Iraq, and the Arab Spring has all been updated. A new section, "Our Global Age: Promise and Problems," has been added. It discusses the themes of globalization, human rights (including the growing persecution of Christians in Muslim lands), the problem of transferring Western democracy to the developing world, the specter of wars, and the march of science and technology. The Epilogue, "Reaffirming the Core Values of the Western Tradition," is now the concluding section of Chapter 33.

The text represents the efforts of several authors. Marvin Perry, general editor of the project, wrote Chapters 1–12, 19, 21–24, 27–31, some of the material in Chapter 32, and half of Chapter 33. James R. Jacob is the author of Chapters 13 and 15. Margaret C. Jacob wrote Chapters 14 and 16–18. Myrna Chase is the author of Chapters 20, 25, and 26. Jonathan Daly, a new addition to the team, is responsible for Chapter 32 and half of Chapter 33. The late Theodore H. Von Laue, who had been with the project since its inception, had written on the Soviet Union and Europe since World War II. After his death Marvin Perry and Angela Von Laue had revised and updated his material. Although much of T. H. Von Laue's material has been reworked, his insights continue to enrich certain chapters. Over the years Marvin Perry and George Bock edited the manuscript for continuity and clarity. Unfortunately, George Bock, my good friend and a superb reader of manuscript, passed away. I shall miss him.

DISTINCTIVE FEATURES

The text contains several pedagogical features. Chapter outlines and introductions provide comprehensive overviews of key themes and give a sense of direction and coherence to the flow of history. Most chapters contain concluding essays that treat the larger meaning of the material. Facts have been carefully selected to illustrate key relationships and concepts and to avoid overwhelming students with unrelated and disconnected data. Appropriate quotations, many not commonly found in texts, have been integrated into the discussion. Each chapter begins with focus questions to aid students' reading of the chapter, and concludes with chapter notes. An annotated bibliography for each chapter, along with a glossary, is provided online.

Western Civilization: Ideas, Politics, and Society is available in both one- and two-volume editions, and in a third edition, *Since 1400*. *Since 1400* (twenty-two chapters) has been prepared for those instructors whose courses begin with the Renaissance or the Reformation.

Volume I of the two-volume edition covers the period from the first civilizations in the Near East through the Age of Enlightenment in the eighteenth century (eighteen chapters). Volume II covers the period from the growth of national states in the seventeenth century to the contemporary age (nineteen chapters). Because some instructors start the second half of their course with the period prior to the French Revolution, Volume II incorporates the last three chapters of Volume I: "The Rise of Sovereignty," "The Scientific Revolution," and "The Age of Enlightenment." Volume II also contains a comprehensive introduction that surveys the ancient world, the Middle Ages, and the opening centuries of the modern era; the introduction is designed particularly for students who did not take the first half of the course. *Since 1400* also contains an introduction that covers the ancient world and the Middle Ages.

ANCILLARIES

We are pleased to introduce an expanded ancillary package that will help students in learning and instructors in teaching.

Instructor Resources

Mind Tap™. MindTap for *Western Civilization: Ideas, Politics, and Society* is a personalized, online digital learning platform providing students with an immersive learning experience that builds critical thinking skills. Through a carefully designed chapter-based learning path, MindTap allows students to easily identify the chapter's focus questions, complete readings activities organized into short, manageable blocks, and test their content knowledge with Aplia™ Critical Thinking Activities developed for the most important concepts in each chapter.

- *Setting the Scene:* Each chapter of the MindTap begins with a brief activity that introduces the chapter's major themes in a compelling, visual way that encourages students to think critically about the subject matter.
- *Aplia:* The Aplia Critical Thinking assignments will include at least one map-based exercise, one primary source–based exercise, and an exercise summarizing the content and themes of the chapter.
- *Reflection Activity:* Every chapter ends with an assignable, gradable reflection activity, intended as a brief writing assignment to be shared with the class as an online discussion, through which students can apply a theme or idea they've just studied.

MindTap for *Western Civilization: Ideas, Politics, and Society* goes well beyond an eBook, a homework solution/digital supplement, a resource center website, or a Learning Management System. It is truly a Personal Learning Experience that allows you to synchronize the text reading and engaging assignments. To learn more, ask your Cengage Learning sales representative to demo it for you—or go to www.Cengage.com/MindTap.

Instructor Companion Website. This website is an all-in-one resource for class preparation, presentation, and testing for instructors. Accessible through Cengage.com/login with your faculty account, you will find an Instructor's Manual, Powerpoint presentations (descriptions below), and test bank files (please see Cognero description).

Instructor's Manual. Prepared by Janet Jenkins of Arkansas Tech University, this manual contains for each chapter instructional objectives, chapter outlines, lecture suggestions, group learning projects, primary source analysis, audiovisual bibliographies, suggested readings, and Internet resources.

PowerPoint® Lecture Tools. Prepared by Janet Jenkins of Arkansas Tech University, these presentations are ready-to-use, visual outlines of each chapter. They are easily customized for your lectures. There are presentations of only lecture or only images, as well as combined lecture and image presentations. Also available is a per chapter JPEG library of images and maps.

Cengage Learning Testing, powered by Cognero®. This test bank for *Western Civilization: Ideas, Politics, and Society* was prepared by Jennifer McNabb of Western Illinois University and is accessible through Cengage.com/login with your faculty account. This test bank contains multiple-choice and essay questions for each chapter. Cognero® is a flexible, online system that allows you to author, edit, and manage test bank content for *Western Civilization*, 11e. Create multiple test versions instantly and deliver through your LMS from your classroom, or wherever you may be, with no special installs or downloads required.

The following format types are available for download from Instructor Companion Site: Blackboard, Angel, Moodle, Canvas, Desire2Learn. You can import these files directly into your LMS to edit, manage questions, and create tests. The test bank is also available in PDF format from the Instructor Companion Website.

MindTap Reader for Western Civilization. MindTap Reader is an eBook specifically designed to address the ways students assimilate content and media assets. MindTap Reader combines thoughtful navigation ergonomics, advanced student annotation, note-taking, and search tools, and embedded media assets such as video and MP3 chapter summaries, primary source documents with critical thinking questions, and interactive (zoomable) maps. Students can use the eBook as their primary text or as a multimedia companion to their printed book. The MindTap Reader eBook is available within the MindTap found at www.cengagebrain.com.

CourseReader. CourseReader is an online collection of primary and secondary sources that lets you create a customized electronic reader in minutes. With an easy-to-use interface and assessment tool, you can choose exactly what your students will be assigned—simply search or browse Cengage Learning's extensive document database to preview and select your customized collection of readings. In addition to print sources of all types (letters, diary entries, speeches, newspaper accounts, and more), the collection includes a growing number of images, and video and audio clips. Each primary source document includes a descriptive headnote that puts the reading into context. In addition, each document is further supported by both critical thinking and multiple-choice questions designed to reinforce key points. For more information, visit www.cengage.com/coursereader.

Reader Program. Cengage Learning publishes a number of readers, some containing exclusively primary sources, others a combination of primary and secondary sources, and some designed to guide students through the process of historical inquiry. Visit Cengage.com/history for a complete list of readers.

Cengagebrain.com. Save your students time and money. Direct them to www.cengagebrain.com for a choice in formats and savings and a better chance to succeed in your class. Cengagebrain.com, Cengage Learning's online store, is a single destination for more than 10,000 new textbooks, eTextbooks, eChapters, study tools, and audio supplements. Students have the freedom to purchase a-la-carte exactly what they need when they need it. Students can save 50 percent on the electronic textbook and can purchase an individual eChapter for as little as $1.99.

Custom Options. Nobody knows your students like you, so why not give them a text that is tailor-fit to their needs? Cengage Learning offers custom solutions for your course—whether it's making a small modification to Western Civilization, 11e, to match your syllabus or combining multiple sources to create something truly unique. You can pick and choose chapters, include your own material, and add additional map exercises along with the Rand McNally Atlas to create a text that fits the way you teach. Ensure that your students get the most out of their textbook dollars by giving them exactly what they need. Contact your Cengage Learning representative to explore custom solutions for your course.

Student Resources

Student Companion Site. This website features an assortment of resources to help students master the subject matter. It includes chapter outlines, glossary, flashcards, and focus questions.

MindTap Reader. MindTap Reader is an eBook specifically designed to address the ways students assimilate content and media assets. MindTap Reader combines thoughtful navigation ergonomics, advanced student annotation, note-taking, and search tools, and embedded media assets such as video and MP3 chapter summaries, primary source documents with critical thinking questions, and interactive (zoomable) maps. Students can use the eBook as their primary text or as a multimedia companion to their printed book. The MindTap Reader eBook is available within the MindTap found at www.cengagebrain.com.

Reader Program.   Cengage Learning publishes a number of readers. Some contain exclusively primary sources, others are devoted to essays and secondary sources, and still others provide a combination of primary and secondary sources. All of these readers are designed to guide students through the process of historical inquiry. Visit www.cengage.com/history for a complete list of readers.

Cengagebrain.com.   Save time and money! Go to www.cengagebrain.com for choice in formats and savings and a better chance to succeed in your class. Cengagebrain.com, Cengage Learning's on-line store, is a single destination for more than 10,000 new textbooks, eTextbooks, eChapters, study tools, and audio supplements. Students have the freedom to purchase a-la-carte exactly what they need when they need it. Students can save 50 percent on the electronic textbook and can pay as little as $1.99 for an individual eChapter.

Writing for College History, 1e [ISBN: 9780618306039].   Prepared by Robert M. Frakes, Clarion University. This brief handbook for survey courses in American history, Western Civilization/European history, and world civilization guides students through the various types of writing assignments they encounter in a history class. Providing examples of student writing and candid assessments of student work, this text focuses on the rules and conventions of writing for the college history course.

The History Handbook, 2e [ISBN: 9780495906766].   Prepared by Carol Berkin of Baruch College, City University of New York and Betty Anderson of Boston University. This book teaches students both basic and history-specific study skills such as how to read primary sources, research historical topics, and correctly cite sources. Substantially less expensive than comparable skill-building texts, The History Handbook also offers tips for Internet research and evaluating online sources.

Doing History: Research and Writing in the Digital Age, 2e [ISBN: 9781133587880].   Prepared by Michael J. Galgano, J. Chris Arndt, and Raymond M. Hyser of James Madison University. Whether you're starting down the path as a history major, or simply looking for a straightforward and systematic guide to writing a successful paper, you'll find this text to be an indispensable handbook to historical research. This text's "soup to nuts" approach to researching and writing about history addresses every step of the process, from locating your sources and gathering information, to writing clearly and making proper use of various citation styles to avoid plagiarism. You'll also learn how to make the most of every tool available to you—especially the technology that helps you conduct the process efficiently and effectively.

The Modern Researcher, 6e [ISBN: 9780495318705].   Prepared by Jacques Barzun and Henry F. Graff of Columbia University. This classic introduction to the techniques of research and the art of expression is used widely in history courses but is also appropriate for writing and research methods courses in other departments. Barzun and Graff thoroughly cover every aspect of research, from the selection of a topic through the gathering, analysis, writing, revision, and publication of findings, presenting the process not as a set of rules but through actual cases that put the subtleties of research in a useful context. Part One covers the principles and methods of research; Part Two covers writing, speaking, and getting one's work published.

Rand McNally Historical Atlas of the World, 2e [ISBN: 9780618841912].   This valuable resource features over 70 maps that portray the rich panoply of the world's history from preliterate times to the present. They show how cultures and civilization were linked and how they interacted. The maps make it clear that history is not static. Rather, it is about change and movement across time. The maps show change by presenting the dynamics of expansion, cooperation, and conflict. This atlas includes maps that display the world from the beginning of civilization; the political development of all major areas of the world; expanded coverage of Africa, Latin America, and the Middle East; the current Islamic World; and the world population change in 1900 and 2000.

Acknowledgments

The authors would like to thank the following instructors for their critical reading of sections of the manuscript: Stephen Balzarini, Gonzaga University; James Burns, Clemson University; Edward Doherty, Queensborough Community College; Brian Hilly, Suffolk Community College; Brian McKnight, University of Virginia's College at Wise; Pedro Meza, Queensborough Community College; Nathan Orgill, Georgia Gwinnett College; David White, McHenry County College; and Jason Wojcik, Pennsylvania Highlands Community College. Several of their suggestions were incorporated into the final version.

We are grateful to the staff of Cengage Learning who lent their considerable talents to the project. In particular, we would like to thank Content Developer Lauren Floyd for her conscientiousness and superb administrative skills, Associate Content Developer Cara Swan, who capably assumed Lauren Floyd's responsibilities during her maternity leave, and Jane Lee, Senior Content Project Manager, for her careful supervision. Over the years, both Jean Woy, who had been affiliated with the text since the first edition published in 1981, and Nancy Blaine, who had worked with us for ten years, continued to recognize and support what we are trying to do—and for this we remain grateful. Although Nancy Blaine is no longer with Cengage Learning, her contribution to the project endures. In addition, we would like to thank Cate Barr, Senior Art Director, and Faith Brosnan, Cover Designer, for their creativity and artistic vision in updating the cover and interior design for this edition. A special thanks to Valarmathy Munuswamy, Senior Project Manager at Lumina Datamatics, who managed the overall production with skill and dedication. Reba Frederics, the photo researcher, deserves praise for her fine eye and enthusiasm for the project. So too do Kristine Janssens, text researcher, who managed the difficult task of obtaining permissions smoothly, and Paula Pyburn, the copy editor, for her careful eye for detail.

Angela Von Laue, who had assisted me after the death of her husband, Theodore Von Laue, in 2000, retired from the project after the ninth edition. I remain grateful for her aid on past editions. I also remain grateful to my good friend George Bock, who passed away in 2012. His creative insights in previous editions continue to contribute to the text's distinguishing character—a concern for crucial concepts and essential relationships. Our often heated but always fruitful discussions demonstrate to me the intrinsic value of the Socratic dialogue. And, as always, I am grateful to my wife, Phyllis Perry, for her encouragement and computer expertise, which has saved me much time and frustration.

M.P

Geography of Europe

The map on the following pages features the continent of Europe and parts of North Africa and the Middle East. Like most maps, it contains a selected combination of physical and political information. The physical part pertains to the natural world—the shapes of landmasses, mountains, and bodies of water—and serves as a kind of background or screen onto which the political information is projected. Categories of political information commonly featured on historical maps include the location and names of important cities and states, the changing borders of countries and empires, and the routes people traveled as they explored, migrated, traded, and fought with one another.

Europe is one of seven continents; the others are Africa, Asia, North America, South America, Australia, and Antarctica. Europe is bounded in the north by the Arctic Sea, in the west by the Atlantic Ocean, in the south by the Mediterranean Sea, and in the southeast by the Black Sea and the Caspian Sea. Off the mainland but traditionally considered a part of Europe are thousands of islands, from those of the United Kingdom, Ireland, and Iceland in the northwest, to Crete, Sicily, and Sardinia in the southeast.

Europe is quite distinctive in shape. The first thing to notice is that there is no natural border between Europe and Asia. The traditional eastern boundary is the Ural River, but looked at from a purely geographic standpoint, Europe might simply be called western Asia. The second thing to notice is how much of Europe is made up of peninsulas. In fact, Europe itself is one gigantic peninsula, with a coastline equal in distance to one and a half times around the equator (37,877 miles).

North Americans are often surprised to discover the small size of the European continent. The geographic area of France, for example, is less than that of Texas; Britain is similar in size to Alabama. The distance from London to Paris is about the same as from New York to Boston, while the distance from Berlin to Moscow is comparable to that of Chicago to Denver.

Major Peninsulas and Islands There are six major European peninsulas: the Iberian (comprising Portugal and Spain); the Apennine (Italy); the Balkan (Slovenia, Croatia, Bosnia-Herzegovina, Serbia and Montenegro, Albania, Greece, Bulgaria, and Macedonia); the Anatolian (Turkey); the Scandinavian (Norway, Sweden, and Finland); and the Jutland or Danish peninsula. The islands of Iceland, Ireland, and the United Kingdom lie to the Atlantic west, while to the east lie some of the major islands of the Mediterranean, such as Corsica, Sardinia, Sicily, Crete, and Cyprus.

Seas, Lakes, and Rivers Europe's irregular coastline encloses large areas of water into bays, gulfs, and seas. Moving from west to east in the Mediterranean, we have the Tyrrhenian Sea (between Italy and the islands of Sicily, Sardinia, and Corsica), the Adriatic (between Italy and the nations of the western Balkan peninsula), the Ionian (between Italy and Greece), and the Aegean (between Greece and Turkey). The Baltic Sea is bordered on the east (moving clockwise from the north) by Finland, Russia, Estonia, Latvia, Lithuania, Poland, Germany, and Sweden. It is connected by narrow channels to the North Sea, which lies (moving clockwise from the north) between Norway, Denmark, Germany, the Netherlands, and Belgium in the east and south, to the United Kingdom in the north and west. The English Channel separates England and France; the Bay of Biscay lies between southwestern

Elevation

Meters	Feet
4,000	13,120
2,000	6,560
500	1,640
200	656
Sea level	Sea level
Below sea level	Below sea level

⊛ National capital
• Other city

Reykjavik ⊛

ICELAND

Faroe Islands (Den.)

Arctic Circle

SWEDEN

NORWAY

Shetland Islands (U.K.)

Oslo ⊛

Stoc •

North Sea

NORTHERN IRELAND

Edinburgh •

DENMARK

Baltic Sea

LITH

Belfast •

Copenhagen ⊛

IRELAND

Kaliningrad •

Dublin ⊛

UNITED KINGDOM

NETHERLANDS

Hamburg •

Gdansk •

POLAN

Cardiff •

Amsterdam ⊛

Elbe R.

Berlin ⊛

London ⊛

GERMANY

Warsav •

English Channel

Brussels ⊛

ATLANTIC OCEAN

Bonn •

Leipzig •

BELGIUM

Frankfurt •

Prague •

Seine R.

Paris •

LUX.

Luxembourg ⊛

CZECH REPUBLIC

CARPA

Loire R.

Stuttgart •

SLOV

Bay of Biscay

FRANCE

Munich •

LIECH.

Vienna ⊛

Bratislava ⊛

Zurich •

Bern ⊛

Vaduz ⊛

Bud •

Geneva •

AUSTRIA

HUNGA

SWITZ.

ALPS

Ljubljana ⊛

Lyons •

SLOVENIA

Zagreb ⊛

Porto •

Rhône R.

Turin •

Milan •

Po R.

CROATIA

PORTUGAL

SPAIN

PYRENEES

Monaco ⊛

San Marino ⊛

SAN MARINO

BOSNIA & HERZEGOVINA

SE KO

Lisbon ⊛

Andorra la Vella ⊛

MONACO

Sarajevo •

Madrid •

ANDORRA

Corsica (Fr.)

Adriatic Sea

MONT.

Tagus R.

Barcelona •

APENNINES

Podgorica ⊛

Balearic Islands (Sp.)

Rome ⊛

ITALY

ALBANIA

MAC

Sardinia (It.)

VATICAN CITY

Naples •

Tiranë ⊛

Gibraltar (U.K.)

Mediterranean

Tyrrhenian Sea

Ionian Sea

G

Rabat ⊛

Algiers ⊛

Sicily (It.)

MOROCCO

ALGERIA

Tunis ⊛

Valletta ⊛ MALTA

ATLAS MTS.

0   200   400 Km.

0   200   400 Mi.

Sea

UNISIA

France and northern Spain. The Black Sea, on the southern border of Russia and Ukraine, is connected by two straits—the Bosphorous and the Dardanelles—to the Aegean Sea. The Caspian Sea, bordered in the north by Russia and Kazakhstan, is the world's largest saltwater lake and, at 92 feet below sea level, the lowest point in Europe.

Several of Europe's major rivers flow across the Russian plain. At 2,194 miles, the Volga is the longest river in Europe. Linked by canals and other river systems to the Arctic Ocean in the north and the Baltic Sea in the south, the Volga originates west of Moscow and empties into the Caspian Sea after flowing some 2,194 miles. At 1,777 miles, the Danube is Europe's second longest river and the principal waterway in the central part of the continent. It originates in southern Germany and flows through Austria, Slovakia, Hungary, Croatia, Serbia and Montenegro, Bulgaria, Moldova, Ukraine, and Romania, before reaching the Black Sea. The Rhine river comes next, at 766 miles, winding its way from the Swiss Alps to the Netherlands and the North Sea. Other prominent riverways in Europe include the Elbe (678 miles), which originates in the Czech Republic and passes through Germany before it, too, empties into the North Sea, and the Rhône (505 miles), which runs from Switzerland, through France, and into the Mediterranean Sea. The proximity of most areas of the European landmass to the coastline and to major river systems greatly affected the Continent's history.

LAND REGIONS Despite its relatively small size, the European continent presents a wide range of landforms, from rugged mountains to sweeping plains. These can be separated into four major regions: the Northwest Mountains, the Great European Plain, the Central Uplands, and the Alpine Mountain System. The mountains of the Northwest Region cover most of the region, running through northwestern France, Ireland, northern Great Britain, Norway, Sweden, northern Finland, and the northwest corner of Russia. The Great European Plain covers almost all of the European part of the former Soviet Union, extending from the Arctic Ocean to the Caucasus Mountains. This belt stretches westward across Poland, Germany, Belgium, the western portion of France, and southeastern England. The Central Uplands is a belt of high plateaus, hills, and low mountains. It reaches from the central plateau of Portugal, across Spain, the central highlands of France, to the hills and mountains of southern Germany, the Czech Republic, and Slovakia. The Alpine Mountain System is made up of several mountain ranges, including the Pyrenees between Spain and France, the Alps in southeastern France, northern Italy, Switzerland, and western Austria, and the Apennine range in Italy. Also included are the mountain ranges of the Balkan Peninsula, the Carpathian Mountains in Slovakia and Romania, and the Caucasus Mountains between the Black and Caspian Seas.

When studying the map of Europe, it is important to notice the proximity of Central Asia, the Middle East, and North Africa. Interaction with the peoples and cultures of these regions has had a profound impact on the course of European history.

Western Civilization

Ideas, Politics, and Society

Part One

The Ancient World: Foundation of the West

to A.D. *500*

3000
B.C.

2000
B.C.

1000
B.C.

500
B.C.

100
B.C.

A.D.
200

Politics and Society

Rise of civilization in Sumer (c. 3200)
Union of Upper and Lower Egypt (c. 2900)
Rise of Minoan civilization (c. 2600)

Rise of Mycenaean civilization (c. 2000)
Hammurabi of Babylon builds an empire
    (1792–1750)

Creation of a unified Hebrew monarchy
    under David (1000–961)
Dark Age in Greece (c. 1100–800)
Hellenic Age (c. 800–323)
Fall of Assyrian empire (612)
Persian conquest of Near East (550–525)
Formation of Roman Republic (509)

Persian Wars (499–479)
Peloponnesian War (431–404)
Conquest of Greek city-states by Philip of
    Macedon (338)
Conquests of Alexander the Great (336–323)
Hellenistic Age (323–330)
Roman conquest of Carthage and
    Hellenistic kingdoms (264–146)

Political violence and civil wars in Rome
    (88–31)
Assassination of Julius Caesar (44)
Octavian takes the title Augustus and
    becomes the first Roman emperor (27)
Greco-Roman Age (30 B.C.–C. A.D. 500)
Pax Romana—the height of Roman Empire
    (27 B.C.–A.D. 180)

Military anarchy in Rome (235–285)
Goths defeat Romans at Adrianople (378)
End of Roman Empire in the West (476)

Thought and Culture

Cuneiform writing in Sumer; hieroglyphics
    in Egypt

Epic of Gilgamesh (c. 1900)
Code of Hammurabi (c. 1790)
Amenhotep IV and a movement toward
    monotheism in Egypt (c. 1369–1353)
Moses and the Exodus (1200s)

Homer's *Iliad* and *Odyssey* (700s)
Age of classical prophecy: flowering of
    Hebrew ethical thought (750–430)

Law of the Twelve Tables (c. 450)
Rise of Greek philosophy: Ionians, Pythag-
    oreans, Parmenides (500s and 400s)
Greek dramatists: Aeschylus, Sophocles,
    Euripides, Aristophanes (400s)
Greek philosophers: Socrates, Plato,
    Aristotle (400s and 300s)
Hellenistic philosophies: Epicureanism,
    Stoicism, Skepticism, Cynicism

Roman philosophers during the Republic:
    Lucretius, Cicero (1st cent. B.C.)
Rise and spread of Christianity: Jesus
    (d. A.D. 29); Paul's missionary activity
    (c. 34–64)
Gospel According to Mark (c. 66–70)
Roman historians, poets, and philosophers
    during the Pax Romana: Livy, Tacitus,
    Virgil, Horace, Ovid, Juvenal, Seneca,
    Marcus Aurelius

Church fathers: Jerome, Ambrose,
    Augustine (300s and 400s)

The Ancient Near East: The First Civilizations

With the body of a lion and the face of a man, the Sphinx watches over Giza as a testament to the divine kingship of the pharaohs. (©dgmata/Shutterstock.com)

Focus Questions

1. What is meant by the term *civilization*? Under what conditions did it emerge?

2. What did Mesopotamian and Egyptian civilizations have in common? How did they differ?

3. In what ways did mythopoeic thought characterize Near Eastern civilization? How does this type of thinking differ from that of science?

4. What elements of Near Eastern civilization were passed on to Western civilization?

Civilization was not inevitable; it was an act of human creativity. The first civilizations emerged about five thousand years ago, in the Near Eastern river valleys of Sumer and Egypt. Before that time stretched the vast ages of prehistory, when our ancestors did not dwell in cities and knew nothing of writing; some 99 percent of human history took place before the creation of civilization. Today, when human beings have the capacity to destroy civilization, we might reflect on humanity's long and painful climb to a civilized state.

PREHISTORY

The period called the **Paleolithic Age,** or Old Stone Age, began with the earliest primitive tool-making human beings who inhabited East Africa some 2.5 million years ago. It ended ten thousand years ago in parts of the Near East when people discovered how to farm. Our Paleolithic ancestors lived as hunters (no doubt also as scavengers) and food gatherers. Because they had not learned how to farm, they did not establish permanent villages. When their food supplies ran short, they abandoned their caves or tentlike structures of branches and searched for new dwelling places.

Human social development was shaped by this 2.5 million-year experience of hunting and food gathering. Based on fossil evidence found in Ethiopia, it appears that *homo sapiens*, our species, first appeared some 190,000 years ago; it also seems certain that the common ancestor of modern humans originated in Africa and that some 40,000 years ago modern humans began to migrate into Europe and Asia. For survival, groups of families formed bands consisting of around thirty people; members learned how to plan, organize, cooperate, trust, and share. The men hunted for meat, and the women cared for the young, tended the fires, and gathered fruits, nuts, berries, and grain. Hunters assisted one another in tracking and killing game, finding cooperative efforts more successful than individual forays. By sharing their kill and bringing some back to their camp for the rest of the group, they reinforced the social bond. So, too, did women who gathered food for the group.

Chronology 1.1 ❖ The Near East

3200 B.C.*	Rise of civilization in Sumer
2900	Union of Upper and Lower Egypt
2686–2181	Old Kingdom: essential forms of Egyptian civilization take shape
2180	Downfall of Akkadian empire
1792–1750	Hammurabi of Babylon brings Akkad and Sumer under his control and fashions a code of laws
1570	Egyptians drive out Hyksos and embark on empire building
1369–1353	Reign of Amenhotep IV: a movement toward monotheism
1200	Fall of Hittite empire
612	Fall of Assyrian empire
604–562	Reign of Nebuchadnezzar: height of Chaldean empire
550–525 B.C.	Persian conquests form a world empire

*Most dates are approximations.

Bands that did not cooperate in the hunt, in food gathering, or in food distribution were unlikely to survive.

Hunting and food gathering also stimulated mental and physical development. Food gatherers had to know which plants were safe to eat and where to find them. Hunting required strength, speed, good eyesight and hearing, and mental ability. Hunters had to study and analyze the habits of their prey, judge weather conditions, recall the location of dens and watering places, and make better tools and weapons. The physically weak and mentally deficient, unable to track animals and to cope with new problems, did not survive long. Individuals with superior intelligence and physical attributes lived longer and had more opportunities to produce offspring, passing on their characteristics and gradually improving the human species.

Although human progress was very slow during the long centuries of the Paleolithic Age, advances occurred that influenced the future enormously. Paleolithic people developed spoken language and shaped bone, wood, and stone tools that corresponded to ideas in their minds. They preserved their creations and taught other people how to use them. Succeeding generations improved on what they had learned from their ancestors. With these simple but useful tools, Paleolithic human beings dug up roots; peeled the bark off trees; trapped, killed, and skinned animals; made clothing; and fashioned fish nets. They also discovered how to control fire, which allowed them to cook their meat. By killing microbes, fire made meat safer to eat. Fire also provided warmth and protection against predators—lions and leopards, for example—that feared fire. From evidence discovered in caves, it is certain that Paleolithic people had domesticated fire about 500,000 years ago. Some evidence points to fire use as far back as 1.5 million years.

Like toolmaking and the control of fire, language was a great human achievement. Language enabled individuals to acquire and share with one another knowledge, skills, experiences, and feelings. Thus, language was the decisive factor in the development of culture and its transmission from one generation to the next. Language helped parents teach their children rules of conduct and religious beliefs, as well as how to make tools and light fires.

Most likely, our Paleolithic ancestors developed mythic-religious ideas to explain the mysteries of nature, birth, sickness, and death. They felt that living powers operated within and beyond the world that they experienced, and they sought to establish friendly relations with these powers. To primitive peoples, the elements—sun, rain, wind, thunder, and lightning—were alive. The natural elements were spirits; they could feel and act with a purpose. To appease these forces of nature, hunters and gatherers made offerings to them. Gradually, there emerged shamans, medicine men, and witch doctors, who, through rituals, trances, and chants, seemed able to communicate with these spirits. Paleolithic people also began the practice of burying their dead, sometimes with offerings, which suggests belief in life after death. Corpses were sometimes dusted with red ocher, which represented blood, a source of life. Another belief is revealed in the many small statues of women, made between forty thousand and twenty-five thousand years ago, that have been found by archaeologists in Europe and Asia. Fashioned from ivory, wood, and clay and often marked by huge breasts and distended stomachs, these fertility figurines represent a mother goddess who gave life, food, and protection.

Between thirty thousand and twelve thousand years ago, Paleolithic people sought out the dark and silent interior of caves, which they probably viewed as sanctuaries, and, with only torches for light, they painted remarkably skillful and perceptive pictures of animals on the cave walls. Even prior to civilization, human beings demonstrated artistic talent, an esthetic sense. When these prehistoric artists drew an animal with a spear in its side, they probably believed that this act would make them successful in hunting; when they drew a herd of animals, they probably hoped that this would cause game to be plentiful. This belief that something done to an image of an animal or a person will produce the same effect on the being itself is called *sympathetic magic*. Hunting societies that endured into the modern world still engage in rituals designed to protect the hunter and to ensure a kill.

Some ten thousand years ago, the New Stone Age, or **Neolithic Age**, began in the Near East. During the Neolithic Age, human beings discovered farming, domesticated animals, established villages, polished stone tools, made pottery, and wove cloth. So important were these achievements that they are referred to as the Neolithic Revolution.

Agriculture—the deliberate planting and cultivation of crops—first developed in the hilly regions of the Near East, where rainfall was plentiful and wheat and barley grew abundantly in the wild. It is likely that women engaged in gathering plant food discovered how to cultivate plants. People there also began to domesticate the sheep and wild goats that roamed the hills. In other parts of the world, farming and the domestication of animals developed independently.

Agriculture and the domestication of animals revolutionized life. Whereas Paleolithic hunters and food gatherers had been forced to use whatever nature made available to them, Neolithic farmers altered their environment to satisfy human needs. Instead of spending their time searching for grains, roots, and berries, women and children grew crops near their homes; instead of tracking animals over great distances, men could slaughter domesticated goats or sheep nearby. (Later, horses, camels, and donkeys were tamed, providing people with a means of transportation.) Since farmers had to live near their fields and could store food for the future, farming led to the rise of permanent settlements. Villages containing as many as two hundred or three hundred people had occasionally emerged in late Paleolithic times, before the discovery of agriculture. Hunter-gatherers built such villages in areas that had an abundant, stable food supply—near a river or lake well stocked with fish, or in a valley with plenty of wild wheat and barley and herds of gazelles or goats. The development of farming greatly speeded the shift to villages. It is likely that trade also impelled people to gather in village communities. Herdsmen, hunters, and food gatherers living in regions rich in salt (needed for preserving food), volcanic glass (used for mirrors, blades, and spearheads), or hematite (an iron ore that was a source of red coloring for pottery) formed trading settlements, which exchanged raw materials for food.

Villages changed the patterns of life. A food surplus freed some people to devote part of their time to sharpening their skills as basket weavers or toolmakers. The demand for raw materials and the creations of skilled artisans fostered trade, sometimes across long distances, and the formation of trading settlements. An awareness of private property emerged. Hunters had accumulated few possessions, since belongings presented a burden in moving from place to place. Villagers, however, acquired property and were determined to protect it from one another and from outsiders—nomadic herdsmen who might raid the village. Hunting bands were egalitarian; generally, no one member had more possessions or more power than another. In farming villages, a ruling elite emerged that possessed wealth and wielded power.

No doubt farming also affected our emotional development. Human beings who had evolved as hunters and foragers, enjoying considerable leisure, personal freedom, independence, and equality, were now forced to adjust to a different tempo of life—unending toil, stifling routine, and the need to obey the commands of the elites. Scholars ponder the psychological dimensions of this shift from the hunter's way of life to sedentary farming.

In recent years, archaeologists have uncovered several Neolithic villages, the oldest of which was established before 8000 B.C. Among the most famous of these sites are Çatal Hüyük in Anatolia (Turkey), Jericho in Palestine, and Jarmö in eastern Iraq. Scholars disagree on whether these communities were just highly developed villages or the first cities. The traditional view is that cities arose about 3000 B.C. in Sumer, the home of the earliest civilization. Some scholars argue that five thousand years before the Sumerian cities Jericho's two thousand inhabitants had created urban life by engaging in trade and embarking on public works. Jericho's walls were six feet, six inches thick at the base and in some places twenty feet high. Their construction required cooperation and a division of labor beyond the capacity of an agricultural village. Similar communities, or primitive cities, spread throughout much of the Near East in late prehistoric times.

Neolithic people made great strides in technology. By shaping and baking clay, they made pottery containers for cooking and for storing food and water. The invention of the potter's wheel enabled them to form bowls and plates more quickly and precisely. Stone tools were sharpened by grinding them on rock. The discoveries of the wheel and the sail improved transportation and promoted trade, and the development of the plow and the ox yoke made tilling the soil easier for farmers.

The Neolithic period also marked the beginning of the use of metals. First used was copper, which was easily fashioned into tools and weapons. Copper implements lasted longer than those made of stone and flint, and they could be recast and reshaped if broken. In time, artisans discovered how to make bronze by combining copper and tin in the proper ratio. Bronze was harder than copper, a characteristic that made a sharper cutting edge possible.

During the Neolithic Age, the food supply became more reliable, village life expanded, and the population increased. Families that acquired wealth gained a higher social status and became village leaders. Religion grew more formal and structured; nature spirits evolved into deities, each with specific powers over nature or human life. Altars were erected in their honor, and ceremonies were conducted by priests, whose power and wealth increased as people gave offerings to the gods. Neolithic society was growing more organized and complex; it was on the threshold of civilization.

THE RISE TO CIVILIZATION

What we call **civilization** arose some five thousand years ago in the Near East (in Mesopotamia and Egypt) and then later in the Far East (in India and China). The first civilizations began in cities, which were larger, more populated, and more complex in their political, economic, and social structure than Neolithic villages. Because the cities depended on the inhabitants of adjacent villages for their food, farming techniques must have been developed sufficiently to produce food surpluses. Increased production provided food for urban inhabitants who engaged in nonagricultural occupations; they became merchants, craftsmen, bureaucrats, and priests.

The invention of writing enabled the first civilizations to preserve, organize, and expand knowledge and to pass it on to future generations; it also allowed government officials and priests to conduct their affairs more efficiently. Moreover, civilized societies possessed organized governments, which issued laws and defined the boundary lines of their states. On a scale much larger than Neolithic communities, the inhabitants erected buildings and monuments, engaged in trade and manufacturing, and used specialized labor for different projects. Religious life grew more organized and complex, and a powerful and wealthy priesthood emerged. These developments—cities, specialization of labor, writing, organized government, monumental architecture, and a complex religious structure—differentiate the first civilizations from prehistoric cultures.

Religion was the central force in these primary civilizations. It provided satisfying explanations for the workings of nature, helped ease the fear of death, and justified traditional rules of morality. Law was considered sacred, a commandment of the gods. Religion united people in the common enterprises needed for survival—for example, the construction and maintenance of irrigation works and the storage of food. Religion also promoted creativity in art, literature, and science. In addition, the power of rulers, regarded as gods or their agents, derived from religion.

The emergence of civilization was a great creative act and not merely the inevitable development of agricultural societies. Many communities had learned how to farm, but only a handful made the leap into civilization. How was it possible for Sumerians and Egyptians, the creators of the earliest civilizations, to make that breakthrough? This question has intrigued and baffled historians, and no single explanation is entirely convincing. Most scholars stress the relationship between civilizations and river valleys. Rivers deposited fertile silt on adjoining fields, provided water for crops, and served as avenues for trade. But environmental factors alone do not adequately explain the emergence of civilization. What cannot be omitted is the human contribution: capacity for thought and cooperative activity.

Both the Tigris and Euphrates Rivers in Mesopotamia and the Nile River in Egypt deposited fertile soil when they overflowed their banks. But before these rivers could be of any value in producing crops, swamps around them had to be drained; jungles had to be cleared; and dikes, reservoirs, and canals had to be built—activities that required the cooperation of large numbers of people. Learning to work together for the good of the community was an indispensible requirement for civilization. In the process of constructing and maintaining irrigation networks, people learned to formulate and obey rules and developed administrative, engineering, and mathematical skills. The need to keep records stimulated the invention of writing. These creative responses to the challenges posed by nature spurred the early inhabitants of Sumer and Egypt to make the breakthrough to civilization, thereby altering the course of human destiny. By the time the Hebrews and the Greeks, the spiritual ancestors of Western civilization, appeared on the stage of history, civilizations had been in existence for some two thousand years.

Civilization also had its dark side. Epidemic disease thrived in urban centers, where people lived close together in unsanitary conditions, drinking contaminated water and surrounded by rotting garbage. Slavery was an essential and accepted feature of early civilizations. The authority wielded by rulers and their officials and the habits of discipline acquired by the community's members made possible the construction of irrigation works, but they were also harnessed for destructive conflicts between states. Such warfare, which involved managing large numbers of combatants, was far more lethal than the sporadic and generally disorganized acts of violence that occurred in Neolithic times. A hostile and aggressive attitude toward members of alien groups has plagued human beings since the rise of civilization. Warfare fascinated the people who created the first civilizations: scribes recounted battle after battle, warrior-kings boasted of their military conquests, and military heroes were held in the highest esteem. Cultural historian Lewis Mumford observes:

> War was not a mere residue of more common primitive forms of aggression. . . . In all its typical aspects, its discipline, its drill, its handling of large masses of men as units, in its destructive assaults en masse, in its heroic sacrifices, its final destructions, exterminations, seizures, enslavements, war was rather the special invention of civilization: its ultimate drama.[1]*

---

*Numbered source notes appear at the end of each chapter.

MESOPOTAMIAN CIVILIZATION

Mesopotamia is the Greek word for "land between the rivers." It was here, in the valleys of the Tigris and Euphrates Rivers, that the first civilization began. The first to develop an urban civilization in Mesopotamia (present-day Iraq) were the Sumerians, who colonized the marshlands of the lower Euphrates, which, together with the Tigris, flows into the Persian Gulf. The Sumerians' origin is obscure, although scholars speculate that they migrated from the East, perhaps northern India. They spoke a language unrelated to the tongues of their Semitic neighbors, who had migrated from Arabia into Mesopotamia and adjacent regions.

Through constant toil and imagination, the Sumerians transformed the swamps into fields of barley and groves of date palms. Around 3000 B.C., their hut settlements gradually evolved into twelve independent city-states, each consisting of a city and its surrounding countryside. Among the impressive achievements of the Sumerians were a system of symbol writing (*cuneiform*), in which pictograms and signs for numbers were engraved with a reed stylus on clay tablets to represent ideas; elaborate brick houses, palaces, and temples; bronze tools and weapons; irrigation works; trade with other peoples; an early form of money; religious and political institutions; schools; religious and secular literature; varied art forms; codes of law; medicinal drugs; and a lunar calendar.

Map 1.1 MESOPOTAMIAN AND EGYPTIAN CIVILIZATIONS The first civilizations emerged in river valleys: Mesopotamia in the valleys of the Tigris and Euphrates Rivers, Egypt in the Nile Valley. (© 2016 Cengage Learning.)

The history of Mesopotamia is marked by a succession of conquests. To the north of Sumer was a Semitic city* called Akkad. About 2350 B.C., the people of Akkad, led by Sargon the Great, the warrior-king, conquered the Sumerian cities. Sargon built the world's first empire, which extended from the Persian Gulf to the Mediterranean Sea. Establishing a pattern that future despotic rulers would emulate, Sargon stationed garrisons in conquered lands and appointed governors and officials to administer the territories, as well as additional bureaucrats to register and parcel out the precious metals, horses, grain, and other commodities exacted from conquered peoples. He also retained a large standing army to quell revolts and to launch new imperialist ventures. The Akkadians adopted Sumerian cultural forms, including cuneiform, and spread them beyond the boundaries of Mesopotamia with their conquests. Mesopotamian religion became a blend of Sumerian and Akkadian elements. Illustrating the confluence of Akkadian and Sumerian culture was Sargon's daughter, Enheduanna, the world's oldest known poet. Serving as high priestess in the Sumerian city of Ur, Enheduanna wrote numerous poems and hymns to temple deities. In one of her hymns to the Sumerian goddess Ianna, she depicts Ianna as a fierce warrior; in a second, Ianna emerges as an overseer of home and children; and in the third surviving hymn, the poetess appeals to Ianna to help her regain her position as temple priestess after it was taken from her by a male enemy.

In succeeding centuries, the Sumerian cities were incorporated into various kingdoms and empires. The Sumerian language, which was replaced by a Semitic tongue, became an obscure language known only to priests and scholars, and the Sumerians gradually disappeared as a distinct people. But their cultural achievements endured. Akkadians, Babylonians, Elamites, and others adopted Sumerian religious, legal, literary, and art forms. The Sumerian legacy served as the basis for a Mesopotamian civilization that maintained a distinct style for three thousand years.

---

*Semites included Akkadians, Hebrews, Babylonians, Canaanites, Assyrians, and Aramaeans. Hebrew and Arabic are Semitic languages.

COUPLE FROM NIPPUR, 2500 B.C. Large eyes and geometrical beard and hair characterize Sumerian figures. Note the intimacy and informality of the pose.
(Courtesy of the Oriental Institute, University of Chicago)

Religion: The Basis of Mesopotamian Civilization

Religion lay at the center of Mesopotamian life. Every human activity—political, military, social, legal, literary, artistic—was generally subordinated to an overriding religious purpose. Religion was the Mesopotamians' frame of reference for understanding nature, society, and themselves; it dominated and inspired all other cultural expressions and human activities. Wars between cities, for instance, were interpreted as conflicts between the gods of those cities, and victory ultimately depended on divine favor, not on human effort. **Myths**—narratives about the activities of the gods—explained the origins of the human species. According to the earliest Sumerian myths, the first human beings issued forth from the earth like plant life, or were shaped from clay by divine craftsmen and granted a heart by the goddess Nammu, or were formed from the blood of two gods sacrificed for that purpose.

The Mesopotamians believed that people were given life so that they could execute on earth the will of the gods in heaven. No important decisions were made by kings or priests without first consulting the gods. To discover the wishes of the gods, priests sacrificed animals and then examined their livers; or the priests might find their answers in the stars or in dreams.

The cities of Mesopotamia were sacred communities dedicated to serving divine masters, and people hoped that appeasing the gods would bring security and prosperity to their cities. The Sumerians erected ziggurats—huge multilevel mounds—on which temples were built. The ziggurat in Ur measured 205 feet by 140 feet at the base and was about 70 feet high; staircases connected its levels and led to the top platform, on which stood a majestic temple.

The ziggurat was surrounded by low walls enclosing offices and houses for the priests and shops where potters, weavers, carpenters, and tanners performed their crafts. The temple was the religious and economic heart of the city. A particular city belonged to a god, who was the real owner of the land and the real ruler of the city; often a vast complex of temples was built for the god and the god's family. In the temple, the god was offered shelter, food, clothing, and the homage of dutiful servants. Temple priests collected rents, operated businesses, and received contributions for festivals. Female priestesses also served the temple. Most inhabitants of the city worked for the temple priests as tenant farmers, agricultural laborers, or servants. Anxious to curry favor with the gods and goddesses who watched over the fields, peasants surrendered part of their crops to the temple. Priests coordinated the city's economic activity, supervising the distribution of land, overseeing the irrigation works, and storing food for emergencies. Temple scribes kept records of expenditures and receipts. By serving as stewards of the city's deities and managing their earthly estates, the priests sustained civilized life.

The gods and goddesses, invisible to human eyes but omnipresent, controlled the entire universe and everything in it. The moon, the sun, the storm, the city, the irrigation works, and the fields—each was directed by a god. Mesopotamians saw gods and demons everywhere in nature. There was a god in the fire and another in the river; evil demons stirred up sandstorms, caused disease, and endangered women in childbirth. To shield themselves from hostile forces, Mesopotamians wore charms and begged their gods for help. Each Mesopotamian offered prayers and sacrifices to a personal god or goddess, who provided protection against evil spirits.

Mesopotamians believed that they were manipulated by divine beings. When misfortune befell them, people attributed it to the gods. Even success was not due to their own efforts but to the intervention of a god who had taken a special interest in them. Compared with the gods, an individual was an insignificant and lowly creature.

Uncertainty and danger filled life in Mesopotamia. Sometimes, the unpredictable waters of the rivers broke through the dikes, flooding fields, ruining crops, and damaging cities. At other times, an insufficient overflow deprived the land of water, causing crops to fail. Great windstorms left the countryside covered with a layer of sand, and heavy thunderstorms turned fields into a sea of mud that made travel impossible. Unlike Egypt, which was protected by vast deserts, Mesopotamia had no natural barriers to invasion. Feeling themselves surrounded by unfathomable and often hostile forces, Mesopotamians lived in an atmosphere of anxiety, which permeated their civilization.

Contributing to this sense of insecurity was the belief that the gods had little love for humanity. They had created a "savage, 'man' shall be his name . . . [who] shall be charged with the service of the gods that they might be at ease."[2] Toward humans the gods behaved capriciously, maliciously, and vindictively, and it was difficult to please them.

What do the gods demand of me? Is it ever possible to please them? To these questions Mesopotamians had no reassuring answers, for the gods' behavior was a mystery to mere human beings.

> *What is good for oneself may be offense to*
>   *one's god,*
> *What in one's own heart seems despicable*
>   *may be proper to one's god.*
> *Who can know the will of the gods in*
>   *heaven?*
> *Who can understand the plans of the*
>   *underworld gods?*
> *Where have humans learned the way of*
>   *a god?*
> *He who was alive yesterday is dead today.*[3]

A Mesopotamian man or woman hoped to experience the good life by being obedient to his or her older brother, father, foreman, priest, and king and to a personal deity, who could influence the decisions of the other gods. The rewards for obedience were long life, health, and worldly success. Nevertheless, the feeling persisted that happiness was either transitory or beyond reach—a pessimism that abounded in Mesopotamian literature.

A mood of uncertainty and anxiety, an awareness of the cosmos as unfathomable and mysterious, a feeling of dread about the fragility of human existence and the impermanence of human achievement—these attitudes are as old as the first civilization. The *Epic of Gilgamesh*, the finest work of Mesopotamian literature, masterfully depicts this mood of pessimism and despair. The epic deals with a profound theme: the human protest against death. The death of his close friend causes Gilgamesh to face the reality of his own death. "Despair is in my heart. What my brother is now that shall I be when I am dead. . . . I am afraid of death."[4] Gilgamesh yearns for eternal life, but he learns that when the gods created human beings, they allotted to them only death. "Where is the man who can clamber to heaven? Only the gods live forever . . . but as for us men, our days are numbered, our occupations are a breath of wind."[5]

And in contrast to the Egyptians, the Mesopotamians had little to look forward to after death. They believed that they would either be confined to a dreary underworld whose rulers would inflict pain on them or be transformed into spirits, flying about and tormenting the living.

Government, Law, and Economy

Kingship, bestowed on a man by the gods, was the central institution in Mesopotamian society. Unlike Egyptian pharaohs, Mesopotamian kings saw themselves not as gods but rather as great men selected by the gods to represent them on earth. Gods governed through the kings, who reported to the gods about conditions in their land (which was the gods' property) and petitioned the gods for advice. To honor the gods, kings built magnificent temples and adorned sacred statues with lavish dress and fine jewelry.

The king administered the laws, which came from the gods. Like everyone else in the land, the king had to obey divine laws. These laws provided Mesopotamians with a measure of security. The principal collection of laws in ancient Mesopotamia was the famous code of Hammurabi (c. 1792–c. 1750 B.C.), the Babylonian ruler. Unearthed by French archaeologists during 1901–1902, the code has provided invaluable insights into Mesopotamian society. The laws were inscribed on a stone slab (*stele*), near the top of which Hammurabi was depicted, standing reverently before the throne of Shamash, the sun god and patron of justice. In typical Mesopotamian fashion, Hammurabi claimed that his code rested on the authority of the gods; to violate it was to contravene the divine order.

The code reveals social status and mores in that area and time. Men were the heads of the family, although efforts were made to protect women and children from mistreatment and poverty. Thus, if a man divorced his wife because she did not bear him a son, he had to provide her with money. Punishments were generally severe—"an eye for an eye and a tooth for a tooth." The code prescribed death for housebreaking, kidnapping, aiding the escape of slaves, receiving stolen goods, and bearing false witness; however, it allowed consideration of extenuating circumstances. Being forgiven by the wronged party could also mitigate the penalty. For example, a wife who committed adultery could be spared execution if pardoned by her husband. Class distinctions were expressed in the code. Penalties varied with the status of both the wrongdoer and the victim. For instance, a person received a harsher punishment for harming a noble than for harming a commoner. Government officials engaging in extortion or bribery were punished severely. The code's many provisions relating to business transactions show the importance of trade to Mesopotamian life.

The economy of Mesopotamian cities depended heavily on foreign and domestic trade. Whereas trade in Egypt was conducted by the state bureaucracy, in Mesopotamia there was greater opportunity for private enterprise. Besides merchants, temple priests engaged in trade because they possessed surplus produce collected as rents from farmers using temple land. Early in Mesopotamian history, merchants were subservient to the king and the temple priests. Over the centuries, however, merchants began to behave as professionals—not just as agents of the palace or temple, but as private entrepreneurs.

Because of trade's importance to the life of the city, governments instituted regulations to prevent fraud. Business transactions had to be recorded in writing, and severe punishments were imposed for dishonesty. A system of weights and measures facilitated trade, and efforts were made to prevent excessive interest rates for loans.

Mesopotamians imported resources not found at home—stone, silver, and timber. In exchange, they exported textiles, fine handicrafts, and (less often because of difficulty in transporting them by donkey) agricultural products. They also imported copper from the Persian Gulf, precious metals from Afghanistan, ivory from Africa and the west coast of India, and cedar and cypress woods, oils, and essences from the Mediterranean coastal areas. Enterprising businessmen set up trading outposts in distant lands, making the Mesopotamians pioneers in international trade.

Writing, Mathematics, Astronomy, and Medicine

The Sumerians established schools, which trained the sons of the upper class in the art of cuneiform writing. Hundreds of tablets on which Sumerian students practiced their lessons have been discovered, testifying to the years of disciplined and demanding work required to master the scribal art. Virtually all scribes were men, but female scribes are at times mentioned in Mesopotamian writings. A literate woman was almost always a noble.

To assist their pupils, teachers prepared textbooks of word lists and mathematical problems with solutions. In translating Sumerian words into the Akkadian language, they compiled what was probably the world's first dictionary. Students who completed the course of study successfully were employed as archivists, secretaries, or accountants by the temple, the palace, the law

courts, or merchants. The Sumerian system of cuneiform writing spread to other parts of the Near East.

The Mesopotamians made some impressive advances in mathematics. They devised multiplication and division tables, including even cubes and cube roots. They determined the area of right-angle triangles and rectangles, divided a circle into 360 degrees, and had some understanding of the principles that centuries later would be developed into the Pythagorean theorem and quadratic equations. But the Babylonians, who made the chief contribution in mathematics, barely advanced to the level of theorizing; they did not formulate general principles or furnish proofs for their mathematical operations.

By carefully observing and accurately recording the positions of planets and constellations of stars, Babylonian sky watchers took the first steps in developing the science of astronomy, and they devised a calendar based on the cycles of the moon. As in mathematics, however, they did not form theories to coordinate and illuminate their data. Believing that the position of the stars and planets revealed the will of the gods, astronomers did not examine the heavens to find what we call cause-and-effect connections between the phenomena. Rather, they sought to discover what the gods wanted. With this knowledge, people could organize their political, social, and moral lives in accordance with divine commands and escape the terrible consequences that they believed resulted from ignoring the gods' wishes. Thus, despite its impressive achievements, Babylonian astronomy remained essentially a mythical interpretation of the universe.

As was consistent with their religious worldview, the Mesopotamians believed that disease was caused by gods or demons. To cure a patient, priest-physicians resorted to magic; through prayers and sacrifices, they attempted to appease the gods and eject the demons from the sick body. Nevertheless, in identifying illnesses and prescribing appropriate remedies, Mesopotamians demonstrated some accurate knowledge of medicine and pharmacology. Physicians most likely utilized splints to set broken bones, lancets to pierce abscesses, and bandages to protect wounds.

EGYPTIAN CIVILIZATION

During the early period of Mesopotamian civilization, the people of another river valley, to the west, put themselves on the path toward civilization. The Egyptians developed their civilization in the fertile valley of the Nile. For good reason, the Greek historian Herodotus called Egypt "the gift of the Nile," for without this mighty river, which flows more than four thousand miles from central Africa northward to the Mediterranean, virtually all of Egypt would be a desert. When the Nile overflowed its banks, as it did reliably and predictably, the floodwaters deposited a layer of fertile black earth, which, when cultivated, provided abundant food to support Egyptian civilization. The Egyptians learned how to control the river—a feat that required cooperative effort and ingenuity, as well as engineering and administrative skills.

Nature favored Egypt in a number of ways. Besides water, fish and fowl, and fertile land, the Nile also provided an excellent transportation link between Upper (southern) and Lower (northern) Egypt. Natural barriers—mountains, deserts, cataracts (rapids) in the Nile, and the Mediterranean—protected Egypt from attack, allowing the inhabitants to enjoy long periods of peace and prosperity. Gold, copper, and stone abounded, along with other natural resources. In addition, the climate of Egypt is dry and salutary. To the Egyptians, nature seemed changeless and beneficent. Hence, unlike Mesopotamians, Egyptians derived a sense of security from their environment.

From the Old Kingdom to the Middle Kingdom

About 2900 B.C., a ruler of Upper Egypt, known as Narmer or Menes, conquered the Nile Delta and Lower Egypt. By 2686 B.C., centralized rule had been firmly established, and great pyramids, tombs for the pharaohs, were being constructed. The pyramids required rigorous central planning to command and coordinate the tens of thousands of Egyptian laborers drafted to build these immense monuments. During this Pyramid Age, or Old Kingdom (2686–2181 B.C.), royal power reached its height and the essential forms of Egyptian civilization crystallized.

The Egyptians believed the pharaoh to be both a man and a god, the earthly embodiment of the deity Horus; he was an absolute ruler of the land and held his court at the city of Memphis. The Egyptians regarded the pharaoh as a benevolent protector who controlled the floodwaters of the Nile, kept the irrigation works in order, maintained justice in the land, and expressed the will of heaven. They expected that when the pharaoh died and joined his fellow gods, he would still help his living subjects.

In time, the nobles who served as district governors gained in status and wealth and gradually came to undermine the divine king's authority. The nobles' growing power and the enormous expenditure of Egypt's human and material resources on building pyramids led to the decline of the Old Kingdom. From 2181 to 2040 B.C.—a time called the First Intermediate Period—rival families competed for the throne, thus destroying the unity of the kingdom. The civil wars and the collapse of central authority required to maintain the irrigation system cast a pall over the land, as illustrated in this ancient Egyptian poem:

> *The wrongdoer is everywhere. . . .*
> *Plunderers are everywhere. . . .*
> *Nile is in flood, yet none plougheth for*
>   *him. . . .*
> *Laughter hath perished and is no longer*
>   *made.*
> *It is grief that walketh through the land,*
>   *mingled with lamentations. . . .*
> *The storehouse is bare.*[6]

During what is called the Middle Kingdom (2040–1786 B.C.), strong kings reasserted pharaonic rule and reunited the state. The restoration of political stability reinvigorated cultural life and revived economic activity. Pharaohs extended Egyptian control south over the land of Nubia, which became a principal source of gold. A profitable trade was carried on with Palestine, Syria, and Crete.

About 1800 B.C., central authority again weakened. In the era known as the Second Intermediate Period (1786–1570 B.C.), the nobles regained some of their power, the Nubians broke away from Egyptian control, and the Hyksos (a mixture of Semites and Indo-Europeans) invaded Egypt. For centuries, desert and sea had effectively guarded Egypt from foreign invasion, but the Hyksos invaders, using horse and chariot and body armor, ended Egyptian complacency. The Hyksos succeeded in dominating Egypt for about a hundred years. Resentful of foreign rule, the Egyptians became more militant and aggressive; they learned to use the Hyksos' weapons and drove out the invaders in 1570 B.C. The period of empire building known as the New Kingdom (1570–1085 B.C.) then began.

The basic features of Egyptian civilization had been forged during the Old and Middle Kingdoms. The Egyptians looked to the past, believing that the ways of their ancestors were best. For almost three thousand years, Egyptian civilization sought to retain a harmony with the order of nature instituted at creation. Believing that the universe was changeless, the Egyptians did not value change or development—what we call progress—but venerated the institutions, traditions, and authority that embodied permanence.

Religion: The Basis of Egyptian Civilization

Religion was omnipresent in Egyptian life and accounted for the outstanding achievements of Egyptian civilization. Religious beliefs were the basis of Egyptian art, medicine, astronomy, literature, and government. The great pyramids, which took decades to finish and required the labor of thousands of people, were tombs for the pharaohs, man-gods. Magical utterances pervaded medical practices, for disease was attributed to the gods. Astronomy evolved to determine the correct time to perform religious rites and sacrifices. The earliest examples of literature dealt wholly with religious themes. The pharaoh was a sacrosanct monarch who served as an intermediary between the gods and human beings. Justice was conceived in religious terms, something bestowed by a creator-god. Egyptians appealed to the gods to grant victory in war, provide a bountiful harvest, and protect them from illness and misfortune. The Egyptians developed an ethical code, which they

believed the gods had approved. In a number of treatises compiled by high officials, now called *Books of Instruction*, Egyptians were urged to tell the truth and to treat others fairly. In one *Book of Instruction* prepared at the end of the second millennium, the author, in a high ethical tone, enjoined Egyptians to express compassion for the poor, widows, and the handicapped.

Egyptian **polytheism** took many forms, including the worship of animals, for the Egyptians believed that gods manifested themselves in animal shapes. Certain gods were conceived by the Egyptians as taking various forms. Thoth, for example, was represented as the moon, a

AKHENATON. A bas-relief found in Tell el-Amarna shows Akhenaton and his family sacrificing to Aton, the sun god. (Erich Lessing/Art Resource, N.Y.)

baboon, an ibis, and an ibis-headed man. The god Amon was depicted both in human form and as a ram. To the Egyptians, these different representations were not contradictory, for they did not seek logical consistency in religion. The Egyptians also believed great powers in nature—sky, sun, earth, the Nile—to be gods or the abodes of gods. Thus, the universe was alive with divinities—there were about two thousand gods in the Egyptian pantheon—and human lives were tied to the movements of the sun and the moon and to the rhythm of the seasons. In the heavens the Egyptians found answers to the great problems of human existence. In their temples, Egyptians prayed and dedicated offerings to their gods. During temple rituals, women chanted and played musical instruments.

A crucial feature of Egyptian religion was the afterlife. Through pyramid-tombs, mummification to preserve the dead, and funerary art, the Egyptians showed their yearning for eternity and their desire to overcome death. Mortuary priests recited incantations to ensure the preservation of the dead body and the continuity of existence. Inscribed on the pyramids' interior walls were so-called pyramid texts, written in *hieroglyphics*—a form of picture writing in which figures such as crocodiles, sails, eyes, and so forth represented words or sounds that would be combined to form words. The texts contained fragments from myths, historical annals, and magical lore and provided spells to assist the king in ascending to heaven.

At first, the Egyptians believed that only the pharaoh and the royal family were immortal. In time, the nobility and then the commoners claimed that they, too, could share in the blessings of the "other world." Prayers hitherto reserved for the pharaoh were, for a fee, recited by priests at the burial of commoners. Egyptians believed that their deceased relatives would intercede with the gods in their behalf. They wrote letters to these spirits, petitioning them for help for such problems as infertility, inheritance of property, and family quarrels. Widows and widowers placed letters in the tomb of a deceased spouse in which they expressed their grief, often with great tenderness. To the Egyptians, the other world contained the same pleasures as those enjoyed on earth—friends, servants, fishing, hunting, paddling a canoe, picnicking with family members, entertainment by musicians and dancers, and good food.

However, because earthly existence was not fundamentally unhappy, Egyptians did not yearn for death. Unlike early Christians, they did not reject this world or willingly endure martyrdom in order to enter a higher and better world. The following song, inscribed in a pharaoh's tomb, reveals the Egyptians' relish for life.

> *Enjoy yourself while you live,*
> *put on fine linen*
> *anoint yourself with wonderful ointments,*
> *multiply all your fine possessions on earth,*
> *follow your heart's command on earth*
> *be joyful and make merry.*[7]

Divine Kingship

"What is the king of Upper and Lower Egypt? He is a god by whose dealings one lives, the father and mother of men, alone by himself, without an equal."[8] Divine kingship was the basic institution of Egyptian civilization. Perhaps the requirements of the Egyptian environment helped forge the idea of the pharaoh as a living god because a ruler with supernatural authority, held in favor by the gods, could hold together the large kingdom and draft the mass labor required to maintain the irrigation system. Both the priesthood and a standing army answered to the pharaoh and enhanced his authority.

Through the pharaoh, the gods made known their wishes for the Egyptian people. As kingship was a divine, not a manmade, institution, it was expected to last for eternity. The Egyptians rejoiced in the rule of an all-powerful, all-knowing **god-king** who controlled the Nile, bringing fertility to the land, and could intercede in their behalf with the other deities. Even after death, when the pharaoh joined the other gods in the otherworld, he would still assist his subjects. To the Egyptians, the pharaoh was "the herdsman of everyone without evil in his heart."[9] They believed that divine kingship, which was instituted by a creator-god, was the only acceptable political arrangement, that it was in harmony with the order of the universe, and that it brought stability and authority to the nation.

The power of the pharaoh extended to all sectors of society. Peasants were drafted to serve in labor corps as miners or construction workers. Foreign trade was a state monopoly. The pharaoh authorized commercial ventures—caravan expeditions south to Nubia for ivory, gold, and ebony and sailing expeditions east to Lebanon for timber. Profits from foreign trade enriched the royal treasury. Although private ownership of land was recognized in practice, in theory, all land belonged to the pharaoh. As the supreme overlord, the pharaoh oversaw an army of government officials, who collected taxes, managed construction projects, checked the irrigation works, surveyed the land, kept records, and supervised government warehouses, where grain was stored as insurance against a bad harvest. All Egyptians were subservient to the pharaoh, and there was no conception of political liberty.

Egyptian rulers, like their Mesopotamian counterparts, believed that they had an obligation to render justice. Injustice was seen as an offense against the gods. Most pharaohs took their responsibilities seriously and tried to govern as benevolent protectors of the people as instructed by Egyptian wisdom literature.

> *Be not evil, it is good to be kindly. . . . Do right so long as thou abidest on the earth. Calm the weeper, oppress no widow, expel no man from the possessions of his father. . . . Take heed lest thou punish wrongfully. . . . Slay not a man whose good qualities thou knowest. . . . Exalt not the son of one of high degree more than him that is of lowly birth, but take to thyself a man because of his actions.*[10]

Egyptians derived a sense of security from the concept of divine kingship. It meant that earthly government and society were in harmony with the cosmos, a divine order that provided justice and security. The Egyptians believed that the institution of kingship dated from the creation of the universe, that as part of the rhythm of the universe kingship was necessary and beneficial to human beings.

The pharaoh was seen as ruling in accordance with Ma'at, which means justice, law, right, and truth. The pharaoh embodied Ma'at; his divinity assured that he would correctly determine which

STROLL IN THE GARDEN, EIGHTEENTH DYNASTY, C. 1350 B.C. This relief portrays members of the Egyptian royal family. (Aegyptisches Museum, SMPK, Berlin/Ancient Art and Architecture Collection Ltd./The Bridgeman Art Library)

actions accorded with Ma'at and which did not. To oppose the pharaoh was to violate the universal and divinely ordained order of Ma'at and to bring disorder to society. Because the Egyptians regarded Ma'at, which had been established with the creation of the universe, as the right order of nature, they believed that its preservation must be the central object of human activity—the guiding norm of the state and the standard by which individuals conducted their lives. Those who did Ma'at and spoke Ma'at would be justly rewarded. Could anything be more reassuring than this belief that divine truth was represented in the person of the pharaoh, who guaranteed and defended the sacred order of the universe?

Science and Mathematics

Like the Mesopotamians, the Egyptians made practical advances in mathematics and science. They demonstrated superb engineering skills in building pyramids. For example, the pyramid of Khufu, still the largest stone building ever constructed, contains 2.3 million stone blocks, each averaging 2.5 tons. The Egyptians fashioned an effective system of mathematics, including geometry for measurements, that enabled them to solve relatively simple problems.

Controlling the floodwaters of the Nile required careful planning. Therefore, it was vital to know when the Nile would begin to overflow. Noting that the Nile flooded after the star Sirius appeared in the sky, the Egyptians developed a calendar by which they could predict the time of the flood. Eventually, they fashioned a calendar of twelve months, each having thirty days. To complete the solar year, they added a separate period of five days after the last month. The Egyptian calendar based on the sun was more accurate than the Babylonian lunar calendar.

In the area of medicine, Egyptian doctors were more capable than their Mesopotamian counterparts. They were able to identify illnesses; they recognized that uncleanliness encouraged contagion; they had some knowledge of anatomy and performed operations—circumcision and perhaps the draining of abscessed teeth. Sick people were instructed to recite an incantation designed to free their body from the demon's hold and to perform a ritual act such as being burned with hot irons. Although the progress of medicine was handicapped by the belief that supernatural forces caused illnesses, nevertheless, there is evidence that some Egyptian doctors examined the body in a scientific way. In a scroll, the Edwin Smith Surgical Papyrus (named after the nineteenth-century American Egyptologist who acquired it), the writer omitted all references to divine intervention in his advice for treating wounds and fractures. He described fractures in a matter-of-fact way and recommended healing them with splints and casts. In another papyrus document (papyrus is a writing material made from the stalks of the papyrus plant), the writer identified the various snakes, analyzed the effects of their

bites, and listed treatments, including the use of specific drugs—and he did so with only minimum references to magical incantations.

Egyptian Literature

Generally only a small percentage of the population, the elite, was literate. Egyptian literature took a wide variety of forms: hymns and other religious texts; love poems; tales of adventure, romance, and fantasy; and collections of maxims prepared by elderly sages for the benefit of young rulers.

Containing hymns, litanies and other religious texts, the *Book of the Dead* was written to guide the deceased person safely between this world and the afterlife. In the Judgment Hall, before Osiris and other gods who assisted him in the judgment of souls, deceased individuals proclaimed that they did not commit violence against others, utter evil words, or enrich themselves unjustly.

The New Kingdom and the Decline of Egyptian Civilization

The New Kingdom began in 1570 B.C. with the war of liberation against the Hyksos. This war gave rise to an intense militancy, which found expression in empire building. Aggressive pharaohs conquered territory that extended as far east as the Euphrates River. From its subject states, Egypt acquired tribute and slaves. Conquests led to the expansion of the bureaucracy, the creation of a professional army to protect the new territorial acquisitions, and the increased power of priests, whose temples, which grew larger and more lavish, shared in the spoils. Foreign slaves acquired from imperial conquests provided much of the labor for the construction of new shrines and temples. The formation of the empire ended Egyptian isolation and accelerated commercial and cultural intercourse with other peoples. During this period, Egyptian art, for example, showed the influence of foreign forms.

A growing cosmopolitanism was paralleled by a movement toward **monotheism** during the reign of Pharaoh Amenhotep IV (C. 1369–1353 B.C.). Amenhotep sought to replace traditional polytheism with the worship of Aton, a single

Hatchepsut

Hatchepsut, daughter of Thutmose I (reigned, 1493–1482 B.C.), was an exceptional figure in Egyptian history—a female pharaoh. As the wife of her half brother, Thutmose II, she did not produce a male heir. When Thutmose II died after a three-year reign, his infant son by a secondary wife inherited the throne. But because of his tender years, Hatchepsut served as regent. By the seventh year of the regency, Hatchepsut had assumed the royal title of king of Egypt. Although females were not officially barred from becoming pharaohs, it was an unchallenged tradition that this revered position was reserved for men. To legitimize her rule, Hatchepsut had a sequence of pictures carved on the porch of her mortuary temple that told the story of her divine birth. She was conceived when the god Amon-Re, disguised as Thutmose I, visited her mother's boudoir. Amon indicated that he intended to father a female, who one day would rule Egypt. "Come to me in peace, daughter of my loins, . . . thou art the king who takes possession of the diadem [crown] on the Throne of Horus of the Living, eternally."*

Hatchepsut came to be depicted with male attire and a male body. Apparently, by casting off her female appearance, she aimed to be seen as a king, the equal of all other pharaohs, and not as a queen, who was not regarded as divine. Hatchepsut, says Egyptologist Joyce Tyldesley, "needed to make a sharp and immediately obvious distinction between her former position as queen regent and her new role as pharaoh. The change of dress was a clear sign of her altered state."φ

During her twenty-year reign, from about 1479 to 1458, Hatchepsut promoted extensive building projects, including her royal tomb, and trading expeditions, particularly to the land of Punt, in present-day Eritrea and Djibouti. From Punt the Egyptians obtained myrrh and frankincense, precious resins used for making incense that was burned in temple rituals and perfumes and for the mummification of bodies. It was an arduous journey to Punt; the return of the expeditions with these treasures must have greatly increased the prestige of the female pharaoh.

After Hatchepsut's death, her monuments were mutilated and her name and image deleted in a deliberate attempt to obliterate her memory. The campaign was probably initiated by Thutmose III, but his motivation is not clear. Was he demonstrating hatred for his stepmother, who had relegated him to a subordinate role for so many years? Did he try to erase the memory of Hatchepsut in order to prevent the succession in the future of still another female pharaoh in the belief that such a situation was a grave violation of tradition and Ma'at?

---

*Quoted in Joyce Tyldesley, *Hatchepsut: The Female Pharaoh* (New York: Penguin Books, 1998), 105.
φIbid., 133.

god of all people, a supreme force in nature represented as the sun disk. Amenhotep took the name Akhenaton ("Servant of Aton") and moved the capital from Thebes to a newly constructed holy city called Akhetaten ("Horizon of Aton," which is near present-day Tell el-Amarna). The city had palaces, administrative centers, and a temple complex honoring Aton. Akhenaton and his wife, Nefertiti, who played a prominent role in his court, dedicated themselves to Aton—the creator of the world, the maintainer of life, and the god of love, justice, and peace. Akhenaton (or Ikhnaton) dispensed with the worship of Egypt's traditional deities and ordered his officials to remove the names and images of other gods from temples and monuments. With awe, Akhenaton celebrated Aton's power and magnificence.

> *How manifold are thy works!*
> *They are hidden from man's sight.*
> *O sole god, like whom there is no other.*
> *Thou hast made the earth according to thy*
> *desire.*[11]

Akhenaton's monotheism had little impact on the masses of Egyptians, who remained devoted to their traditional gods and ancient beliefs, and was resisted by priests, who resented his changes. The new religion could not survive the death of its founder. Akhenaton's successor, Tutankhamen (1352–1344 B.C.), abandoned the capital at Amarna and returned to Thebes. Tutankhamen was succeeded by an elderly relative, who reigned briefly. In 1340, Horemheb (1340–1315 B.C.), an army commander, seized power and had the monuments to Aton destroyed, along with records and inscriptions bearing Akhenaton's name. The great visionary was vilified as "The Blasphemer."

Historians are not certain why Akhenaton made such a radical break with tradition by propagating the worship of a single god. Was he trying to strike at the priests, whose wealth and prestige had increased considerably with Egypt's conquests? Did the break stem essentially from the vision of a great prophet? But the most significant historical questions concerning Akhenaton are these: First, was Akhenaton's religion genuine monotheism, which pushed religious thought in a new direction? And second, if this was the case, did it influence the ancient Hebrews who, according to the Old Testament, left Egypt about a century later?

These two questions have aroused controversy among historians. The principal limitation on the monotheistic character of Atonism is that there were really two gods in Akhenaton's religion—Aton and the pharaoh himself, who was still worshiped as a deity. Egyptologist John A. Wilson sheds light on this notion. Because Egyptians could not break with the central idea of their civilization, divine kingship, "one could say that it was the closest approach to monotheism possible within the thought of the day. That would still fall short of making it a belief in and worship of only one god."[12] Regarding the relationship of Atonism to a later Hebrew monotheism, Wilson says, "The mechanism of transmission from the faith of Akhenaton to the monotheism of Moses is not

apparent."[13] Moreover, the Hebrews never identified God with the sun or any other object in nature.

Reigning almost sixty-seven years from 1279 B.C. to 1213 B.C., Ramesses II is considered one of Egypt's greatest pharaohs. He campaigned to the south in Nubia, to the west in Libya, and to the east in Canaan and Syria against the Hittite empire. His inconclusive struggles with the Hittites resulted in the signing of a peace treaty, copies of which survive both in hieroglyphics and cuneiform. In order to honor Ramesses II, the Egyptian version of the treaty falsely claims that the Hittites had begged for peace. Ramesses II is most noted for the construction of numerous huge monuments, statues of himself, and temples whose walls contain extravagant glorifications of his person and achievements. Two pairs of colossal statutes of Ramesses flank the entrance to a temple at Abu Simbel in Lower Nubia.

Late in the thirteenth century B.C., Libyans, probably seeking to settle in the more fertile land of Egypt, attacked from the west, and the Peoples of the Sea, as unsettled raiders from the Aegean Sea area and Asia Minor were called, launched a series of strikes at Egypt. A weakened Egypt abandoned its empire. In the succeeding centuries, Egypt came under the rule of Libyans, Nubians, Assyrians, Persians, and finally Greeks, to whom Egypt lost its independence in the fourth century B.C. Egyptian civilization had flourished for nearly two thousand years before it experienced an almost one-thousand-year descent into stagnation, decline, and collapse. During its long history, the Egyptians tried to preserve its ancient forms, revealed to them by their ancestors and representing for all time those unchanging values that they believed to be the way of happiness.

EMPIRE BUILDERS

The rise of an Egyptian empire during the New Kingdom was part of a wider development in Near Eastern history after 1500 B.C.—the emergence of international empires. Empire building led to the intermingling of peoples and cultural traditions and to the extension of civilization well beyond the river valleys.

One reason for the growth of empires was the migration of peoples known as Indo-Europeans. Originally from a wide area ranging from southeastern Europe to the region between the Caspian and Black Seas, Indo-Europeans embarked, around 2000 B.C., on a series of migrations, which eventually brought them into Italy, Greece, Asia Minor, Mesopotamia, Persia, and India. From a core Indo-European tongue emerged the Greek, Latin, Germanic, Slavic, Persian, and Sanskrit languages.

Hittites

Several peoples established strong states in the Near East around 1500 B.C.—the Hurrians in northern Mesopotamia, the Kassites in southern Mesopotamia, and, most important, the Hittites in Asia Minor.

Penetrating Asia Minor, Indo-Europeans coalesced with native Hattic-speaking peoples to create the Hittite empire (1450–1200 B.C.). The Hittites ruled Asia Minor and northern Syria, raided Babylon, and challenged Egypt for control of Syria and Palestine.

The Hittites wanted to control the trade routes that ran along the Euphrates River into Syria. In the 1300s, the Hittite empire reached its peak and included much of Asia Minor and northern Syria. The Hittites succeeded because of their well-trained army. Mass attacks by light, horse-drawn chariots demolished enemy lines, while foot soldiers made effective use of the battle-ax and a short curved sword.

The Hittites borrowed several features of Mesopotamian civilization, including cuneiform, legal principles, and literary and art forms. Hittite religion blended the beliefs and practices of Indo-Europeans, native inhabitants of Asia Minor, and Mesopotamians. The Hittites were probably the first people to develop a substantial iron industry. Initially, they apparently used iron just for ceremonial and ritual objects and not for tools and weapons. However, because iron ore was more readily available than copper or tin (needed for bronze), after 1200 B.C. iron weapons and tools spread throughout the Near East, although bronze implements were still used. Around 1200 B.C., the Hittite empire fell, most likely to Indo-European invaders from the north.

Small Nations

During the twelfth century B.C., a temporary lull in empire building permitted a number of small nations in Syria and Palestine to assert their sovereignty. Three of these peoples—the Phoenicians, the Aramaeans, and the Hebrews*—were originally Semitic desert nomads. The Phoenicians were descendants of the Canaanites, a Semitic people who had settled Palestine about 3000 B.C. The Canaanites who had migrated northwest into what is now Lebanon were called Phoenicians.

Settling in the coastal Mediterranean cities of Tyre, Byblos, Berytus (Beirut), and Sidon, the Phoenicians were naturally drawn to the sea. These daring explorers established towns along the coast of North Africa, on the islands of the western Mediterranean, and in Spain, and they became the greatest sea traders of the ancient world. Phoenician merchants exported lumber, glass, copper and bronze utensils, and the purple dye produced from the murex, a mollusk that was plentiful in the coastal waters. In the ninth and eighth centuries, Phoenicians established colonies in Sardinia, Sicily, Malta, Spain, and North Africa; Carthage, in modern day Tunisia, was founded around 750 B.C. and became a great power in the western Mediterranean. The Phoenicians (or their Canaanite forebears) devised the first alphabet—a monumental contribution to writing. Since all words could be represented by combinations of letters, it saved memorizing thousands of diagrams and aided the Phoenicians in transmitting the cultural achievements of the Near East to the western Mediterranean. Adapted by the Greeks, who added vowels, the phonetic alphabet became a crucial component of European languages.

The Aramaeans, who settled in Syria, Palestine, and northern Mesopotamia, performed a role similar to that of the Phoenicians. As great caravan traders, they carried both goods and culture to various parts of the Near East. The Hebrews and the Persians, for example, acquired the Phoenician alphabet from the Aramaeans.

Assyria

In the ninth century B.C., empire building resumed with the Assyrians, a Semitic people from the

*The Hebrews are discussed in Chapter 2.

Map 1.2 **Kingdoms and Peoples of the Ancient World** In addition to the Sumerians and Egyptians, founders of the first civilizations, other peoples contributed to the development of civilization in the Near East. The Hebrews conceived the idea of the one God, the Phoenicians invented the alphabet, and the Hittites developed a substantial iron industry. (© 2016 Cengage Learning.)

region around the upper Tigris River. The Assyrians carefully planned their military campaigns and excelled in siege weapons—battering rams built on massive wheeled frames—which pulverized city walls that had hitherto resisted attackers. Their soldiers wore armor and wielded iron swords, and charging chariots terrorized the foe's infantry, which generally consisted of farmer-soldiers armed with little more than bows and arrows.

Although they had made forays of expansion in 1200 and 1100 B.C., the Assyrians began their march to "world" empire three centuries later. In the eighth and seventh centuries, the Assyrians became a ruthless fighting machine that stormed through Babylonia, Syria, Palestine, and Egypt. Assyrian kings believed that their gods commanded them to conquer and assisted them in their campaigns. At its height, the Assyrian empire extended from the Iranian plateau in the east to the Egyptian city of Thebes.

How did the Assyrians administer such a vast empire? An Assyrian king, who was the representative and high priest of the god Ashur, governed absolutely. Nobles appointed by the king kept order in the provinces and collected tribute, which they probably used for building palaces, temples, and canals. The Assyrians improved roads, established messenger services, and engaged in large-scale irrigation projects to facilitate effective administration of their conquered lands and promote prosperity. To keep their subjects obedient, the Assyrians resorted to terror and to deportation of troublesome subjects from their home territories. (It is also likely that masses of people were moved around for economic reasons—to replenish a diminishing labor supply.) Assyrian kings boasted of their ruthlessness toward rebellious subjects.

> *13,000 of their warriors I cut down with the sword. Their blood like the water of a stream I caused to run through the squares of their city. The corpses of their soldiers I piled in heaps. . . . [The Babylonian king's] royal bed, his royal couch, the treasure of his palaces, his property, his gods and everything from his palace without number, I carried away. His captive warriors were given to the soldiers of my land like grasshoppers. The city I destroyed, I devastated, I burned with fire.*[14]

Despite an almost all-consuming concern for war, the Assyrians maintained and spread the culture of the past. They copied and edited the literary works of Babylonia, adopted the old Sumerian gods, and used Mesopotamian art forms. The Assyrian king Ashurbanipal (669–626 B.C.) maintained a great library, which contained thousands of clay tablets.

"The king knows that all lands hate us," wrote an official to King Esarhaddon (680–669 B.C.).[15] After a period of wars and revolts weakened Assyria, a coalition of Medes, or Indo-Europeans from Iran, and the Semitic Chaldeans, or Neo-Babylonians, sacked the Assyrian capital of Nineveh in 612 B.C. The conquerors looted and destroyed the city, and the surviving Assyrians fled. Assyrian power was broken.

The Neo-Babylonian Empire

The destruction of the Assyrian empire made possible the rise of a Chaldean empire, which included Babylonia, Assyria, Syria, and Palestine. Under Nebuchadnezzar, who ruled from 604 to 562 B.C., the Chaldean, or Neo-Babylonian, empire reached its height. A talented general and statesman and a brilliant administrator, Nebuchadnezzar had Babylon rebuilt. The new Babylon that arose on the shore of the Euphrates had magnificent procession-ways that led to palaces and temples. On his palace grounds, Nebuchadnezzar created the famous Hanging Gardens for his

Median wife, according to legend. The 350-foot building was a series of vaulted terraces and was surrounded by a moat of flowing water. Trees, shrubs, and flowers decorated each terrace. In the interior, vaulted halls were stocked with vessels, fabrics, ornaments, and wines gathered from different regions of the empire. Here guests reclined on divans and were attended by slaves.

Persia: Unifier of the Near East

After Nebuchadnezzar's death, the Chaldean empire was torn by civil war and threatened by a new power—the Persians, an Indo-European people who had settled in southern Iran. (Iranians today are descendants of the ancient Persians.) Under Cyrus the Great and his son and successor, Cambyses, the Persians conquered all lands between the Nile in Egypt and the Indus River in India. This conquest took twenty-five years, from 550 to 525 B.C. The Near Eastern conception of absolute monarchy justified by religion reached its culminating expression in the person of the Persian king, who, with divine approval, ruled a vast empire, "the four quarters of the earth." Persian kings developed an effective system of administration—based in part on an Assyrian model—which gave stability and a degree of unity to their extensive territories. In so doing, they performed a creative act of statesmanship. The Persian empire was divided into twenty provinces (satrapies), each administered by a governor (satrap) responsible to the emperor. To guard against subversion, the king employed special agents—"the eyes and ears of the emperor"—who supervised the activities of the governors. Persian kings allowed the provincials a large measure of self-rule, and local elites continued to function in the province administered by a Persian satrap. They also respected local laws and traditions, particularly in matters of religion, as long as subjects paid their taxes, served in the royal army, and refrained from rebellion; and they deliberately tried to win the goodwill of priests in conquered lands. These policies served to minimize opposition to Persian rule. But the Persians could also be brutal, impaling and mutilating opponents.

The empire was bound together by a uniform language, Aramaic (the language of the Aramaeans

Map 1.3 THE ASSYRIAN AND PERSIAN EMPIRES In the last part of the sixth century B.C., the Persians established the greatest empire of the ancient Near East, conquering all the lands between the Nile in Egypt and the Indus River in India. (© 2016 Cengage Learning.)

of Syria), which was used by government officials and merchants. Aramaic was written in letters based on the Phoenician alphabet. By making Aramaic a universal language, the Persians facilitated written and oral communication within the empire. The empire was further unified by an elaborate network of roads, an efficient postal system, a common system of weights and measures, and an empire-wide coinage, based on an invention of the Lydians from western Asia Minor. The Persian military was a multinational force recruited and conscripted from numerous lands, and the official bureaucracy was also staffed by a wide range of peoples.

Besides providing impressive political and administrative unity and promoting international trade, the Persians fused and perpetuated the various cultural traditions of the Near East. Persian palaces, for example, boasted the terraces of Babylon, the colonnades of Egypt, the winged

bulls that decorated Assyrian palace gates, and the craftsmanship of Median goldsmiths and Greek stonemasons.

The political and cultural universalism of the Persian empire had its counterpart in the emergence of an ethically oriented religion, Zoroastrianism. Named for its founder, the Persian prophet Zarathustra (Zoroaster in Greek), who probably lived in the sixth century B.C. (some scholars place him much earlier), this religion taught belief in Ahura Mazda—the Wise Lord—the eternal god of light, the creator of the universe, the embodiment of justice, wisdom, goodness, and immortality. In addition to the Wise Lord, there also existed Ahriman, the spirit of darkness, who was evil and destructive. Ahriman was in conflict with Ahura Mazda. People were free to choose whom they would follow. By choosing Ahura Mazda, they chose good over evil. To serve Ahura Mazda, one had to speak the truth and be good to

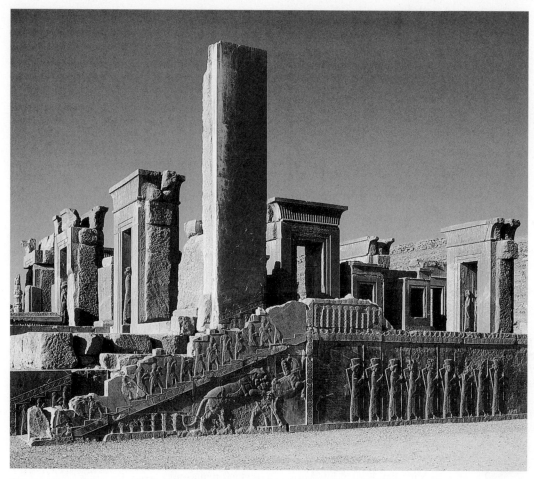

PERSEPOLIS, IRAN, C. 500 B.C. The Persian ruler Darius (522–486 B.C.) constructed a thirty-acre earthen terrace almost fifty feet above the plain and built there a complex of palaces, reception halls, a treasury, and barracks for his royal guards. Persepolis became the ceremonial center of the vast Persian empire until it was destroyed by Alexander the Great's soldiers. (©George Holton/Science Source)

others; the reward for such behavior was life eternal in paradise, the realm of light and goodness. Followers of the evil spirit could be cast into a realm of darkness and torment. In contrast to the traditional religions of the Near East, Zoroastrianism rejected magic, polytheism, and blood sacrifices and instead stressed ethics.

Persia unified the nations of the Near East into a world-state, headed by a divinely appointed king, and synthesized the region's cultural traditions. Soon it would confront the city-states of

Greece, whose political system and cultural orientation differed from that of the Near East.

THE RELIGIOUS ORIENTATION OF THE NEAR EAST

Religion dominated, suffused, and inspired all features of Near Eastern society—law, kingship, art, and science. In the first civilizations, the deepest thoughts of human beings were expressed in the form of religious myths. They were the source of the vitality and creativity of Mesopotamian and Egyptian civilizations. Near Eastern art derived from religion, and science was permeated with it; literature and history dealt with the ways of the gods; and priest-kings or god-kings, their power sanctioned by divine forces, furnished the necessary authority to organize large numbers of people in cooperative ventures. Near Eastern kings sought revelations—through oracles, observations, dreams and interpreting organs of sacrificed animals—from the gods before making decisions. Religion also encouraged and justified wars—including enslavements and massacres—which were seen as conflicts between the gods. Religious beliefs and values served as a powerful social force uniting people into a cohesive community.

A Mythmaking Worldview

A religious or **mythopoeic** (mythmaking) **view** of the world gives Near Eastern civilization its distinctive form and allows us to see it as an organic whole. Mesopotamians and Egyptians inherited from their prehistoric ancestors a great variety of communally produced imagery, rituals, and tales accounting for the origin of the world and human life. Giving free play to their imagination, they altered the old myths and elaborated new ones to resolve questions that today we try to answer with science. Mythmaking was humanity's first way of thinking; it was the earliest attempt to explain the beginnings of the universe and human history, to make nature's mysteries and life's uncertainties comprehensible. Appealing primarily to the imagination and emotions, rather than to reason, mythical thinking, as expressed in language, art, poetry, and social organization, has been a fundamental formative element of human culture.

Originating in sacred rites, ritual dances, feasts, and ceremonies, myths narrated the deeds of gods, who, in some remote past, had brought forth the world and human beings. Holding that human destiny was determined by the gods who interceded in earthly events, Near Eastern people interpreted their experiences through myths. Myths also enabled Mesopotamians and Egyptians to make sense out of nature, to explain the world of phenomena.

Through myths, the Near Eastern mind sought to give coherence to the universe, to make it intelligible. Mesopotamian myths, for example, attributed personal misfortune and the catastrophes that afflicted a city to supernatural forces displeased with people's behavior. These myths gave Near Eastern peoples a framework with which to pattern their experiences into a meaningful order, justify their rules of conduct, and help them to overcome the uncertainty of existence.

The civilizations of the ancient Near East were based on a way of thinking fundamentally different from the modern scientific outlook. The difference between scientific and mythical thinking is profound. The scientific mind views physical nature as an *it*—inanimate, impersonal, and governed by universal law. The mythmaking mind of the Near East saw every object in nature as a *thou*—personified, alive, with an individual will. It saw gods or demons manipulating things. The world was enchanted, imbued with mysterious spirits. The sun and stars, the rivers and mountains, the wind and lightning were either gods or the dwelling places of gods. Live agents were the forces behind natural events. An Egyptian or a Mesopotamian experienced natural phenomena—a falling rock, a thunderclap, a rampaging river—as life facing life. If a river flooded the region, destroying crops, it was because it wanted to; the river or the gods desired to punish the people. A drought was caused by the hot breath of the Bull of Heaven. Relief came when the gigantic bird Imdugud devoured the bull and released storm clouds from her wings.

The Egyptians believed that Nut, the sky goddess, gave birth to the sun, a deity who sailed west across the celestial sea before descending into his mother's womb to be reborn again in the morning. For the Egyptians, the rising and setting of the sun were not natural occurrences—a celestial body obeying an impersonal law—but a religious drama.

The scientific mind holds that natural objects obey universal rules; hence, the location of planets, the speed of objects, and the onset of a hurricane can be predicted. The mythmaking mind of the ancient Near East had no conception of natural causes or natural law; nor was it troubled by contradictions. It did not seek logical consistency and had no awareness of repetitive laws inherent in nature. Rather, it attributed all occurrences to the actions of gods, whose behavior was often erratic and unpredictable. Shamans employed magic to protect people from evil supernatural forces that surrounded them. The scientific mind appeals to reason—it analyzes nature logically and systematically and searches for general principles that govern phenomena. The mythmaking mind appeals to the imagination and feelings and proclaims a truth that is emotionally satisfying, not one that has been arrived at through intellectual analysis and synthesis. Thus, mythical explanations of nature and human experience made life seem less overwhelming and death less frightening.

Of course, Near Eastern people did engage in rational forms of thought and behavior. They certainly employed reason in building irrigation works, calculating the rise of the Nile, preparing a calendar, and performing mathematical operations. Moreover, in their daily life, men and women were often driven by purely pragmatic concerns. Fields had to be planted, goods sold, and household chores attended to. In dealing with these concerns, people did what had to be done in commonsense ways. They planned and prepared; they weighed actions as either beneficial or harmful and behaved accordingly. However, because rational or logical thought remained subordinate to a mythic-religious orientation, they did not arrive at a *consistently* and *self-consciously* rational method of inquiring into physical nature and human culture.

Thus, Near Eastern civilization reached the first level in the development of science—observing nature, recording data, and improving technology in mining, metallurgy, and architecture. But it did not advance to the level of self-conscious philosophical and scientific thought—that is, logically deduced abstractions, hypotheses, and generalizations. Mesopotamians and Egyptians did not fashion a body of philosophical and scientific ideas that were logically structured, discussed, and debated. They had no awareness of general laws that govern particular events. These later developments were the achievement of Greek philosophy. It gave a "rational interpretation to natural occurrences which had previously been explained by ancient mythologies. . . . With the study of nature set free from the control of mythological fancy, the way was opened for the development of science as an intellectual system."[16]

Near Eastern Achievements

Sumerians and Egyptians demonstrated enormous creativity and intelligence. They built irrigation works and cities, organized governments, charted the course of heavenly bodies, performed mathematical operations, constructed large-scale monuments, engaged in international trade, established bureaucracies and schools, and considerably advanced the level of technology and engineering skills. Without the Sumerian invention of writing—one of the great creative acts in history—what we mean by *civilization* could not have emerged.

Many elements of ancient Near Eastern civilization were passed on to the West. The wheeled vehicle, the plow, coinage, and the phonetic alphabet—all important to the development of civilization—derive from the Near East. In the realm of medicine, the Egyptians knew the value of certain drugs, such as castor oil; they also knew how to use splints and bandages. The innovative divisions that gave 360 degrees to a circle and 60 minutes to an hour originated in Mesopotamia. Egyptian geometry and Babylonian astronomy were utilized by the Greeks and became a part of Western knowledge. The belief that a king's power came from a heavenly source, a key idea in historic Western political thought, also derived from the Near East. In Christian art, too, one finds connections to the Mesopotamian art forms—for example, the Assyrians depicted winged angel-like beings.

Both the Hebrews and the Greeks borrowed Mesopotamian literary themes. For example, some biblical stories—the Flood, the quarrel between Cain and Abel, and the Tower of Babel—stem from Mesopotamian antecedents. A similar link exists between the Greek and the earlier Mesopotamian mythologies.

Thus, many achievements of the Egyptians and the Mesopotamians were inherited and assimilated by both the Greeks and the Hebrews, the principal founders of Western civilization. Even more important for an understanding of the essential meaning of Western civilization are the ways in which the Greeks and Hebrews rejected or transformed elements of the older Near Eastern traditions to create new points of departure for the human mind.

Mythical Thinking

Mesopotamians and Egyptians believed that their destinies were determined by the gods. Drought, hurricanes, sickness, and foreign invasion were all attributed to divine intervention. In the "Lament for Ur" the assembly of gods decides to punish the Sumerian city-state of Ur. The execution of the assembly's command is left to Enlil.

To the evil storm Enlil gave (his) order;
   The people groan.
To the storm that annihilates the land he called;
   The people groan.
To all the evil winds he called.
   The people groan.
Enlil brings Gibil to his aid;

To the great storm of heaven he called.
   The people groan.
The great storm howls above;
   The people groan.
The land-annihilating storm roars below.
   The people groan.
The evil wind like the rushing torrent cannot be restrained;
The boats of the city it attacks (and) *devours.* . . .
In front of the storm *it made fire burn;*
   The people groan. . . .

The destructive storm makes the land tremble and quake;

Like the storm of the flood it destroys the cities.
The land-annihilating storm set up (its) decrees in the city;
The all-destroying storm came doing evil. . . .
The evil, afflicting storm, the command of Enlil, the storm unceasingly undermining the land
Covered Ur like a garment, enveloped it like linen. . . .
On its walls *they lay prostrate.*
   The people groan.
In its lofty gates where they were won't to promenade dead bodies were lying about;

In its boulevards where the feasts were celebrated they were *viciously attacked.*
In all its streets where they were wont to promenade dead bodies were lying about;
In its places where the festivities of the land took place the people were *ruthlessly laid low.*

Questions for Analysis

1. How does mythical thinking differ from scientific thinking?
2. It has been said that humans are myth-making animals and that all human societies sustain themselves by creating myths. Discuss.

Samuel N. Kramer, "Lamentation Over the Destruction of Ur," Assyriological *Studies,* The Oriental Institute of the University of Chicago (University of Chicago Press, 1940), vol 12, pp. 35–41.

NOTES

1. Lewis Mumford, *Transformation of Man* (New York: Harper Torchbooks, 1972), 46–47.
2. Excerpted in James B. Pritchard, ed., *Ancient Near Eastern Texts Relating to the Old Testament,* 3rd ed., with supplement (Princeton, N.J.: Princeton University Press, 1969), 67.
3. Excerpted in James B. Pritchard, ed., *The Ancient Near East: A New Anthology of Texts and Pictures* (Princeton, N.J.: Princeton University Press, 1975), 154.
4. *The Epic of Gilgamesh,* with an introduction by N. K. Sandars (Baltimore: Penguin Books, 1960), 94.

5. Ibid., 69, 104.

6. Excerpted in Adolf Erman, ed., *The Ancient Egyptians: A Sourcebook of Their Writings* (New York: Harper Torchbooks, 1966), 94, 97, 99.

7. Quoted in Eugen Strouhal, *Life of the Ancient Egyptians* (Norman: University of Oklahoma Press, 1992), 41.

8. Quoted in Henri Frankfort, *Ancient Egyptian Religion* (New York: Harper Torchbooks, 1961), 43.

9. Quoted in John A. Wilson, "Egypt," in Henri Frankfort et al., *Before Philosophy* (Baltimore: Penguin Books, 1949), 88.

10. Excerpted in Erman, *The Ancient Egyptians*, 76–78.

11. Quoted in John A. Wilson, *The Culture of Ancient Egypt* (Chicago: University of Chicago Press, Phoenix Books, 1951), 227.

12. Ibid., 225.

13. Ibid., 226.

14. Quoted in Joan Oates, *Babylon* (London: Thames and Hudson, 1979), 110–111.

15. Quoted in Georges Roux, *Ancient Iraq* (Harmondsworth, England: Penguin Books, 1966), 278.

16. S. Sambursky, *The Physical World of the Greeks* (New York: Collier Books, 1962), 18–19.

Chapter 2

The Hebrews:
A New View of God
and the Individual

A sculptured relief from the triumphal Arch of Titus showing Jewish captives bearing the menorah and vessels from the holy temple burned by the Romans at the end of the Jewish revolt, first century A.D. (Vanni Archive/Art Resource, N.Y.)

Focus Questions

1. In what ways did the Hebrew view of God mark a revolutionary break with Near Eastern thought?

2. How did Hebrew religious thought promote the ideas of moral autonomy?

3. What were the distinguishing features of Hebrew law?

4. What were the unique achievements of the Hebrew prophets?

5. Why are the Hebrews regarded as a principal source of the Western tradition?

Ancient Mesopotamia and Egypt, the birthplace of the first civilizations, are not the spiritual ancestors of the West. For the origins of the Western tradition, we must turn to the Hebrews and the Greeks. Both the Greeks and the Hebrews, of course, absorbed elements of the civilizations of Mesopotamia and Egypt, but even more significant is how they transformed this inheritance and shaped worldviews that differed markedly from the outlooks of these first civilizations. As Egyptologist John A. Wilson writes,

> The Children of Israel built a nation and a religion on the rejection of things Egyptian. Not only did they see God as one, but they ascribed to him consistency of concern for man and consistency of justice to man. . . . Like the Greeks, the Hebrews took forms from their great neighbors; like the Greeks, they used those forms for very different purposes.[1]

In this chapter, we examine one source of the Western tradition, the Hebrews, whose conception of God broke with the outlook of the Near East and whose ethical teachings helped fashion the Western idea of humanity and the dignity of the individual.

OUTLINE OF HEBREW HISTORY*

The Hebrews (Israelites or Jews) originated in Mesopotamia and migrated to Canaan, a portion of which was later called Palestine. The Hebrew patriarchs—Abraham, Isaac, and Jacob, so prominently depicted in the Old Testament—were chieftains of seminomadic clans that roamed Palestine and occasionally journeyed to Mesopotamia and Egypt. The early Hebrews absorbed some features of Mesopotamian civilization. For example, there are parallels between biblical law and the Mesopotamian legal

---

*Since there is a paucity of references to the early Hebrews in nonbiblical sources, scholars have to rely almost entirely on the Hebrew Bible for reconstructing much of the history of the ancient Israelites. The divergence of scholarly opinion regarding the Bible's accuracy and reliability creates additional uncertainty for the historian.

Chronology 2.1 ❖ The Hebrews

1250 B.C.*	Hebrew Exodus from Egypt
1024–1000	Reign of Saul, Israel's first king
1000–961	Creation of a united monarchy under David
961–922	Reign of Solomon: construction of the first temple
750–430	Age of classical prophecy
722	Kingdom of Israel falls to Assyrians
586	Kingdom of Judah falls to Chaldeans; the temple is destroyed
586–539	Babylonian exile
538	Cyrus of Persia allows exiles to return to Judah
515 B.C.	Second temple is dedicated

*Most dates are approximations.

tradition and between Mesopotamian creation stories and the book of Genesis. Several biblical stories, including the Garden of Eden and the Flood, derive from Mesopotamian sources. The wise sayings of Egyptian teachers have parallels in Hebrew wisdom literature.

The biblical account tells us that some Hebrews, seeking relief from drought and famine, journeyed from Canaan to Egypt to be herdsmen and farmers, but they eventually became forced laborers for the Egyptians. Fearful of remaining permanent slaves of the pharaoh, the Hebrews yearned for an opportunity to escape. In the early thirteenth century B.C., an extraordinary leader rose among them, called Moses, who came to his people as a messenger of God. Leading the Hebrews in their Exodus from Egypt, Moses transformed them during their wanderings in the wilderness of Sinai into a nation, welded together and uplifted by a belief in Yahweh, the one God. The inspiring biblical narrative of God's liberation of the Hebrews from slavery is the fulcrum of Jewish history.

Arguing that there is no extrabiblical evidence for the Exodus or even for the presence of Jews in Egypt, some scholars dismiss the Exodus as fiction; although numerous Egyptian hieroglyphics detail events at the time, none of them refers specifically to Israelites in Egypt. Certainly, say these scholars, the flight of thousands of foreigners would have attracted notice. Moreover, it is highly unlikely that an escape by a large group of slaves could have succeeded when Egypt was at the peak of its power. The biblical account says that Israelites wandered in the Sinai desert for forty years, but archaeologists, who have excavated a number of sites in the Sinai mentioned in the book of Exodus, have uncovered no traces of Israelite campsites. These scholars, known as biblical minimalists, deny the Exodus from Egypt ever occurred. Other scholars reject this position, holding that there is evidence of Semitic forced laborers toiling in Egypt, some of whom might have been Hebrews. Moreover, assert these scholars, ancient Hebrew scribes would not have concocted and faithfully preserved such an inglorious history of enslavement unless the biblical account contained a core historical truth along with legend, folklore, and mythic imagery.

The Israelite Kingdom

The wandering Israelites returned to Canaan to rejoin other Hebrew tribes that had not migrated to Egypt. The colonization of Canaan, a gradual process, took many generations. Threatened by the Philistines, originally from the islands of the

33

Wall Painting from the Synagogue of Dura-Europos, Roman Syria, Early Third Century A.D. Although a strict prohibition of the use of images inhibited representational art among the Hebrews, in Hellenistic times scenes from Hebrew history appeared on the walls and floors of Jewish synagogues. Here the prophet Samuel is depicted anointing David as king of Israel. (Art Resource, N.Y.)

Aegean Sea and the coast of Asia Minor, and from whom the name Palestine derives, the twelve tribes united under the leadership of Saul, a charismatic hero, whom they acclaimed as their first king. Under Saul's successor, David, a gifted warrior and a poet, the Hebrews (or Israelites) broke the back of Philistine power and subdued neighboring peoples.

David's son Solomon erected a royal palace in Jerusalem and beside it a splendid temple honoring God. Under Solomon, Israel experienced a cultural flowering: some magnificent sections of the Old Testament took form, and music flourished. Under Solomon, ancient Israel was at the height of its power and prosperity. However, opposition to Solomon's tax policies and his favored treatment

of the region of Judah in the south led to the division of the kingdom after his death in 922 B.C. The tribes loyal to Solomon's son belonged to the kingdom of Judah, whereas the other tribes organized the northern kingdom of Israel. Both second-rate powers, neither Judah nor Israel could hold on to earlier conquests.

Conquest, Captivity, and Restoration

In 722 B.C., Israel fell to the Assyrians, who deported many Hebrews to other parts of the Assyrian empire. These transported Hebrews—the so-called ten lost tribes—merged with neighboring peoples and lost their identity as the people

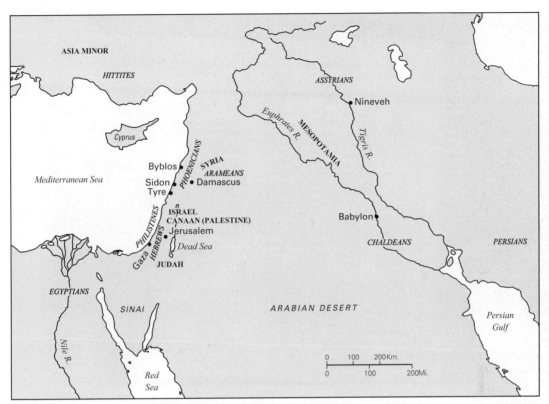

Map 2.1 **HEBREWS AND OTHER PEOPLES OF THE ANCIENT MIDDLE EAST** Despite conquest and exile, the Hebrews survived as a people, retained their faith, and remained devoted to their homeland, which, they believed, God had given them.
(© 2016 Cengage Learning.)

who had made a covenant with God. By 586 B.C., the Chaldeans had conquered Judah, destroyed Solomon's temple, devastated the land, and deported several thousand Hebrews to Babylon. The prophets Isaiah, Ezekiel, and Jeremiah declared that the destruction of Judah was a punishment that the Hebrews had brought on themselves by violating God's laws. This time was the darkest moment in the history of the Hebrews. Their state was gone, neighboring peoples had overrun their land, and their holy temple was in ruins. Thousands had died in battle, had been executed, or had fled to Egypt and other lands, and thousands more were in exile in Babylon. This exile is known as the Babylonian Captivity.

Still, in what is a marvel of history, the Hebrews survived as a people. Although many of the exiles in Babylon assimilated Babylonian

ways, some remained faithful to their God Yahweh and the Law of Moses and longed to return to their homeland. Priests struggled to understand the misfortunes that had befallen their people and to prevent the erosion of faith in a foreign environment. They codified ancient traditions, records, and practices, particularly laws, and in the process created the Torah (see next section). Thus, their faith enabled them to endure conquest and exile. When the Persians conquered Babylon, King Cyrus, in 538 B.C., permitted the exiles to return to Judah, now a Persian province, and to rebuild the temple. The majority of Judeans preferred to remain in prosperous and cosmopolitan Babylon. But some of them did return to Judah, and in 515 B.C. the Hebrews, now commonly called Jews, dedicated the second temple at Jerusalem.

A Dead Sea Scroll, Judea, Second Century b.c. God's law, as recorded in the Holy Scriptures, still remains a unifying force among Jews. Many ancient Hebrew scrolls were found in caves near the west bank of the Dead Sea beginning in the late 1940s. The scroll depicted here contains the earliest existing copy of a complete Hebrew text of the book of the prophet Isaiah. It barely differs from more modern manuscripts. (Israel images/Alamy Limited)

The Hebrew Scriptures

In the following centuries, the Jews would lose their independence to Rome and become a dispersed people. But they never relinquished their commitment to God and his Law as recorded in the Hebrew Scriptures. Called *Tanak* by Jews (and Old Testament by Christians), the Hebrew Scriptures consist of thirty-nine books* by several authors who lived in different centuries. Jews call the first five books of the Old

Testament—Genesis, Exodus, Leviticus, Numbers, and Deuteronomy—the Torah (which originally meant "teaching" or "instruction"). Often, the Torah is referred to as the Pentateuch, a Greek word meaning "five books."

The Hebrew Scriptures represent Jewish oral and written tradition dating from about 1250 to 150 b.c. Compiled by religious devotees, not research historians, they understandably contain factual errors, imprecisions, discrepancies, legends, and folklore. However, there are also passages that offer reliable history, and historians find the Old Testament an indispensable source for studying the ancient Near East. Literary scholars study it for its poetry, legends, and themes, all of which are an integral part of the Western

---

* In ancient times, the number of books was usually given as twenty-four. Certain books are now divided into two parts, and the twelve works by the minor prophets are now counted as individual books.

literary tradition. But it is as a work of religious inspiration that the Hebrew Scriptures attain their most profound importance.

The Old Testament is the record of more than a thousand years of ancient Jewish history. Containing Jewish laws, wisdom, hopes, legends, and literary expressions, it describes an ancient people's efforts to comprehend the ways of God. The Old Testament emphasizes and values the human experience; its heroes are not demigods but human beings. It depicts human strength as well as weakness. Some passages exhibit cruelty and unseemly revenge against the enemies of Israel and apostates, while others express the highest ethical values. As set forth in the Hebrew Scriptures, the Hebrew idea of God and his relationship to human beings is one of the foundations of the Western tradition.

GOD: ONE, SOVEREIGN, TRANSCENDENT, GOOD

The Hebrew view of God evolved through the history and experiences of the Hebrew people. In the days of the patriarchs, before the sojourn in Egypt, the Hebrews most likely were not monotheists. They probably devoted themselves to the god of their particular clan and expressed no hatred for the idolatrous beliefs of neighboring peoples. The chief of each clan established a special attachment to the god of his fathers, hoping that the deity would protect and assist the clan.

Some historians say that Moses' religion was not pure monotheism because it did not rule out the existence of other gods. According to this view, not until the prophets, centuries later, did the Hebrews explicitly deny that other gods existed and proclaim that Yahweh stood alone. Other scholars believe that Moses proclaimed a monotheistic idea, that this idea became the central force in the life of the Hebrews at the time of the Exodus from Egypt, and that it continues to be central today. John Bright, an American biblical scholar, suggests a judicious balance. The religion of Moses "did not deny the existence of other gods," says Bright, but it "effectively denied them status as *gods*."[2] The Hebrews could serve only Yahweh

and "accorded all power and authority to Him." Consequently, Israel was

> *forbidden to approach [other deities] as gods. . . . The gods were thus rendered irrelevant, driven from the field. . . . To Israel only the one God was God. . . . The other gods, allowed neither part in creation, nor function in the cosmos, nor power over events. . . . were robbed of all that made them gods and rendered non-entities, in short, were "undeified." Though the full implications of monotheism were centuries in being drawn, in the functional sense Israel believed in but one God from the beginning.*[3]

The Hebrew view of the one God marked a profound break with Near Eastern religious thought. The gods of other Near Eastern peoples were not truly free; their power was not without limits. Unlike Yahweh, Near Eastern gods were not eternal but were born or created; they issued from some prior realm. They also were subject to biological conditions, requiring food, drink, sleep, and sexual gratification. Sometimes they became ill or grew old or died. When they behaved wickedly, they had to answer to fate, which demanded punishment as retribution; even the gods were subject to fate's power.

The Hebrews regarded God as *fully sovereign*. He ruled all and was subject to nothing. Yahweh's existence and power did not derive from a preexisting realm, as was the case with the gods of other peoples. The Hebrews believed that no realm of being preceded God in time or surpassed him in power. They saw God as eternal and omnipotent, the source of all in the universe, and having a supreme will. He created and governed the natural world and shaped the moral laws that govern human beings. He was not subservient to fate but determined what happened.

Whereas Near Eastern divinities dwelt within nature, the Hebrew God was transcendent, above nature and not a part of it. Yahweh was not identified with any natural force and did not dwell in a particular place in heaven or on earth. Nature was God's creation but was not itself divine. Therefore, when the Hebrews confronted natural phenomena, they experienced God's magnificent handiwork, not objects with wills of their own. All natural phenomena—rivers, mountains, storms, stars—were divested of any supernatural quality. The stars and planets were creations of Yahweh, not divinities or the abodes of divinities. The Hebrews neither regarded them with awe nor worshiped them. This removal of the gods from nature is a necessary prerequisite for scientific thought.

The Hebrews demythicized nature, but concerned as they were with religion and morality, they did not create theoretical science. As testimony to God's greatness, nature inspired people to sing the praises of the Lord; it invoked worship of God, not scientific curiosity. When Hebrews gazed at the heavens, they did not seek to discover mathematical relationships but admired God's handiwork. The Hebrews did not view nature as a system governed by natural law. Rather, they saw the rising sun, spring rain, summer heat, and winter cold as God intervening in an orderly manner in his creation. The Hebrews, unlike the Greeks, were not philosophers. They were concerned with God's will, not with the human intellect; with the feelings of the heart, not the power of the mind; with righteous behavior, not abstract thought.

Unlike the Greeks, the Hebrews did not speculate about the origins of all things and the operations of nature; they knew that God had created everything. For the Hebrews, God's existence was based on religious conviction, not on rational inquiry; on revelation, not reason. It was the Greeks, not the Hebrews, who originated systematic rational thought. But Christianity, born of Judaism, retained the Hebrew view of a transcendent God and the orderliness of his creation—concepts that could accommodate Greek science.

The Hebrews also did not speculate about God's nature. They knew only that he was *good* and that he made ethical demands on his people who were obligated to imitate God's holiness. Unlike Near Eastern gods, Yahweh was not driven by lust or motivated by evil but was "merciful and gracious, long-suffering, and abundant in goodness and truth . . . forgiving iniquity and transgression and sin" (Psalm 145:8).[4]* In contrast to pagan gods, who were indifferent to human beings, Yahweh was attentive to human needs.

* The Bible passages in this chapter are quoted from *The Holy Scriptures* (published by the Jewish Publication Society of America).

By asserting that God was *one, sovereign, transcendent*, and *good*, the Hebrews effected a religious revolution that separated them entirely from the worldview held by the other peoples of the ancient Near East.

THE INDIVIDUAL AND MORAL AUTONOMY

This new conception of God made possible a new awareness of the individual, who was seen as the culmination and centerpiece of God's creation. Created in the image of God, the human being is unique, qualitatively different from the rest of animate nature. Only the human being has the power of volition, the power to make choices. The Hebrews believed that God, who possessed total freedom himself, had bestowed on his people moral freedom—the capacity to take responsibility for one's conduct and to choose between good and evil. Thus, in confronting God, the Hebrews developed an awareness of *self*, or *I*; the individual became conscious of his or her own person, moral autonomy, and personal worth.

Fundamental to Hebrew belief was the insistence that God did not create people to be his slaves. The Hebrews regarded God with awe and humility, with respect and fear, but they did not believe that God wanted people to grovel before him; rather, he wanted them to fulfill their moral potential by freely choosing to follow or not to follow God's Law. Thus, in creating men and women in his own image, God made them autonomous and sovereign. In God's plan for the universe, human beings were the highest creation, subordinate only to God. Of all his creations, only they had been given the freedom to choose between righteousness and wickedness, between "life and good, and death and evil" (Deuteronomy 30:15). But having the power to choose freely, men and women must bear the responsibility for their choice.

God demanded that the Hebrews have no other gods and that they make no images "nor any manner of likeness, of anything that is in heaven above, or that is in the earth beneath, . . . thou shalt not bow down unto them nor serve them" (Exodus 20:4–5). Breaking in a revolutionary way with their pagan surroundings, the Hebrews held that the one true God, both omnipotent and invisible, could not be represented in statues or other human creations. The Hebrews believed that the worship of **idols** deprived people of their freedom and dignity; people cannot be fully human if they surrender themselves to a lifeless idol. Hence, the Hebrews had to destroy images and all other forms of idolatry. A crucial element of Near Eastern religion was the use of images—art forms that depicted divinities—but the Hebrews believed that God, the Supreme Being, could not be represented by pictures or sculpture fashioned by human hands. The Hebrews rejected entirely the belief that an image possessed divine powers that could be manipulated for human advantage. Ethical considerations, not myth or magic, were central to Hebrew religious life.

By making God the center of life, Hebrews could become free moral agents; no person, no human institution, no human tradition could claim their souls. Because God alone was the supreme value in the universe, only he was worthy of worship. Thus, to give *ultimate* loyalty to a king or to a general violated God's stern warning against the worship of false gods. The first concern of the Hebrews was supposed to be righteousness, not power, fame, or riches, which were only idols and would impoverish a person spiritually and morally.

There was, however, a condition to freedom. For the Hebrews, people were not free to create their own moral precepts or their own standards of right and wrong. Freedom meant voluntary obedience to commands that originated with God. Evil and suffering were not caused by blind fate, malevolent demons, or arbitrary gods; they resulted from people's disregard of God's commandments. The dilemma is that in possessing freedom of choice, human beings also are free to disobey God, to commit a sin, which leads to suffering and death. Thus, in the Genesis story, Adam and Eve were punished for disobeying God.

For the Hebrews, to know God was not to comprehend him intellectually, define him, or prove his existence; to know God was to be righteous and loving, merciful and just. When men and women loved God, the Hebrews believed, they were uplifted and improved. Gradually, they learned to overcome the worst elements of human nature and to treat other people with respect and compassion. The Jews came to interpret the belief that man was created in God's image to mean that each human being has a divine spark in him or her, giving every person a unique dignity, which cannot be taken away.

By devotion to God, the Hebrews asserted the dignity and autonomy of human beings. Thus, the Hebrews conceived the idea of moral freedom, that each individual is responsible for his or her own actions. These concepts of human dignity and moral autonomy, which Christianity inherited, are at the core of the Western tradition.

THE COVENANT AND THE LAW

Central to Hebrew religious thought and decisive in Hebrew history was the covenant, God's special agreement with the Hebrew people. By this act, the Israelites as a nation accepted God's lordship.

> *And Moses went up unto God, and the Lord called unto him out of the mountain saying: "Thus shalt thou say to the house of Jacob and tell the children of Israel: Ye have seen what I did unto the Egyptians, and how I bore you on eagles' wings, and brought you unto Myself. Now therefore, if ye will hearken unto My voice indeed, and keep My covenant, then ye shall be Mine own treasure from all peoples; for all the earth is Mine; and ye shall be unto Me a kingdom of priests and a holy nation." (Exodus 19:3–6)*

The Hebrews came to see themselves as a unique nation, as a "chosen people," for God had given them a special honor, a profound opportunity, and (as they could never forget) an awesome responsibility. The Hebrews did not claim that God had selected them because they were better than other peoples or because they had done anything special to deserve God's election. They believed that God, in a remarkable manner, had rescued them from bondage in Egypt and had selected them to receive the Law so that their nation would set an example of righteous behavior— "a light to the nations," said the prophet Isaiah— and ultimately lead other peoples to acknowledge God, his greatness, and his moral commands.

This divinely assigned responsibility to be the moral teachers of humanity weighed

Judaea Capta S(enatus) C(onsulto). With a commander's baton in hand and his foot upon a helmet, a victorious centurion proclaims Rome's victory over Judea, personified weeping at the foot of the palm tree. The destruction of the city of Jerusalem under Titus was complete, but the ethics of Old Testament writing would become part of the foundation of Western civilization. (De Agostini/A. Rizzi/Getty Images)

the covenant was made with the entire Hebrew nation, society as a whole had a religious obligation to root out evil and make justice prevail. Duty to God demanded also a duty toward one's neighbor: "Thou shalt surely open thy hand unto thy poor and needy brother, in thy land" (Deuteronomy 15:11). Thus, there were laws to protect the poor, widows, orphans, resident aliens, hired laborers, and slaves. For example, in contrast to ancient Near Eastern law, which regarded slaves as property, biblical legislation emphasized the slave's humanity, although it acknowledged the slave's status as chattel and permitted masters to beat but not kill them. The law called for the punishment of masters who used excessive force against slaves, and it required masters to allow slaves to participate in religious observances and to rest on the Sabbath.

Israelite law incorporated many elements from Near Eastern legal codes and oral traditions. But by making people more important than property, by expressing mercy toward the oppressed, and by rejecting the idea that law should treat the poor and the rich differently, Israelite law demonstrated a greater ethical awareness and a more humane spirit than other legal codes of the Near East.

heavily on the Hebrews. They believed that God had revealed his Law—including the moral code known as the Ten Commandments—to the Hebrew people as a whole, and obedience to the Law became the overriding obligation of each Hebrew. The Law of the Torah—God's commands transmitted by Moses and others—provided Hebrews with normative guidelines for determining proper behavior for both individuals and the social community. Violating the Law meant breaking the sacred covenant—an act that could lead to national disaster. As the Law originated with the one God, the necessary prerequisite for understanding and obeying it was surrendering belief in other gods forever, since they were barriers to comprehending and carrying out God's universal Law.

Justice was the central theme of Old Testament ethics. The Israelites, liberated from slavery by a righteous and compassionate God, had a moral responsibility to overcome injustice, to care for the poor, the weak, and the oppressed. Because

> *And a stranger shalt thou not wrong, neither shalt thou oppress him; for ye were strangers in the land of Egypt. Ye shall not afflict any widow or fatherless child. (Exodus 22:20–21)*
>
> *If thy brother, a Hebrew man, or a Hebrew woman, be sold unto thee, he shall serve thee six years; and in the seventh year thou shalt let him go free from thee. And when thou lettest him go free from thee, thou shalt not let him go empty; thou shalt furnish him liberally. . . . (Deuteronomy 15:12–14)*
>
> *Thou shalt not curse the deaf, nor put a stumbling-block before the blind, but thou shalt fear thy God: I am the Lord. . . . Thou shalt love thy neighbor as thyself. (Leviticus 19:14, 18)*

While biblical law valued human life and was concerned with human welfare, it also contained provisions that shock us as cruel.

For example, verses in Deuteronomy warn that the Lord will smite those who disobey God's commandments with terrible curses: "ulcers and the scurvy. . . . madness and blindness and confusion of the mind; and you shall grope at noonday as the blind grope in darkness. . . . Your sons and daughters shall be given to another people" (Deuteronomy 27: 27-29, 32). In war, foreign enemies were perceived as sinners whose total annihilation was justified by God; God condemned to death by stoning family members who chose to serve other gods and ordered the execution of homosexuals. It is unknown to what extent these prescriptions were actually carried out, and over the centuries, there arose an oral and interpretive tradition that made the written law less rigid and enabled the Hebrews to adapt to changing cultural conditions.

Hebrew law regulated all aspects of daily life, including family relationships. The father had supreme authority in the family, and this authority extended to his married sons and their wives if they remained in his household. Although polygamy was permitted, monogamy was the general rule; adultery was punishable by death.

As in other Near Eastern societies, the Jews placed women in a subordinate position. The husband was considered his wife's master, and she often addressed him as a servant or subject would speak to a superior. A husband could divorce his wife, but she could not divorce him. Only when there was no male heir could a wife inherit property from her husband or a daughter inherit from her father. Women were not regarded as competent witnesses in court and played a lesser role than men in organized worship.

On the other hand, the Jews also showed respect for women. Wise women and prophetesses such as Judith and Deborah were respected by the community and were consulted by its leaders. Also honored were women who served the community. Prophets compared God's love for the Hebrews with a husband's love for his wife. Jewish law regarded women as persons, not as property who could be bartered, and women were never barred from worshipping God. Even female captives taken in war were not to be abused or humiliated. The law required a husband to respect and support his wife and never to strike her. One of the Ten Commandments called for honoring both father and mother.

THE HEBREW IDEA OF HISTORY

Their idea of God made the Hebrews aware of the crucial importance of historical time. Holidays commemorating specific historical events such as the Exodus from Egypt, the receiving of the Ten Commandments on Mount Sinai, and the destruction of Solomon's temple kept the past alive and vital. Egyptians and Mesopotamians did not have a similar awareness of the uniqueness of a given event: to them, today's incident merely reproduced events experienced by their ancestors. To the Jews, the Exodus and the covenant at Mount Sinai were singular, nonrepetitive occurrences, decisive in shaping their national history. This historical uniqueness and importance of events derived from the idea of a universal God profoundly involved in human affairs—a God who cares, teaches, and punishes.

The Jews valued the future as well as the past. Regarding human history as a process leading to a goal, they envisioned a great day when God would establish on earth a glorious age of peace, prosperity, happiness, and human brotherhood. This utopian notion has become deeply embedded in Western thought.

The Hebrews saw history as the work of God; it was a divine drama filled with sacred meaning and moral significance. Historical events revealed the clash of human will with God's commands. Through history's specific events, God's presence was disclosed and his purpose made known. When the Hebrews suffered conquest and exile, they interpreted these events as divine retribution for violating the covenant and the Law, sinful acts that brought down the wrath of God upon them. For the Hebrews, history also revealed God's compassion and concern. Thus, the Lord liberated Moses and the Israelites at the Red Sea and appointed prophets to plead for the poor and the oppressed. Because historical events revealed God's attitude toward human beings, these events possessed spiritual meaning and were worth recording, evaluating, and remembering.

THE PROPHETS

Jewish history was marked by the emergence of spiritually inspired individuals called prophets who felt compelled to act as God's messengers. The prophets believed that God had commanded

WALL PAINTING FROM THE SYNAGOGUE IN DURA-EUROPOS, ROMAN SYRIA, EARLY THIRD CENTURY A.D. This painting shows a Hebrew prophet reading from an open scroll. (Art Resource, N.Y.)

them to speak and had legitimated their words. The prophets cared nothing for money or possessions, feared no one, and preached without invitation. Often emerging in times of social distress and moral confusion, the prophets pleaded for a return to the covenant and the Law. Speaking in God's name, they exhorted the entire nation to make God's religious-moral commands central to its existence. One's evil acts, they said, harm not only the intended victim, but also oneself and the entire nation. Believing that they had been dispatched by God to rescue the disobedient Hebrews from their headlong rush to destruction, the prophets reminded their brethren that because of their moral

deterioration, God, who rules history, would inflict swift and terrible punishment on them. The prophets were remarkably courageous people who did not quake before the powerful. Among the prophets were Amos, a shepherd from Judea in the south; his younger contemporary, Hosea, from Israel in the north; Isaiah of Jerusalem; and Jeremiah, who witnessed the siege of Jerusalem by the Chaldeans in the early sixth century B.C.

Social Justice

The flowering of the prophetic movement—the age of classical, or literary, prophecy—began in the eighth century B.C. In attacking oppression, cruelty, greed, and exploitation, the classical prophets added a new dimension to Israel's religious development. These prophets were responding to problems emanating from Israel's changed social structure. The general lack of class distinctions characterizing a tribal society had been altered by the rise of Hebrew kings, the expansion of commerce, and the growth of cities. By the eighth century, there was a significant disparity between the wealthy and the poor. Small farmers in debt to moneylenders faced the loss of their land or even bondage; the poor and their families were often dispossessed and enslaved by the greedy wealthy. To the prophets, these social evils were religious sins that would bring ruin to Israel, for God, who intervenes in human affairs, punishes the unjust community. Amos, a mid-eighth-century prophet, felt a tremendous compulsion to speak out against these injustices. In the name of God, he denounced the pomp of the heartless rich and the hypocrisy of pious Jews who worshiped God in the prescribed manner but neglected their social obligations to their neighbors, and he demanded that the Hebrews

> Hate the evil and love the good,
> And establish justice in the gate. (Amos 5:15)

For Amos, the pursuit of justice was the most important requirement of the Law. The purpose of worship and ritual was to instill in human beings a passion for justice.

> I hate, I despise your feasts,
> And I will take no delight in your solemn
>   assemblies.
> Yea, though ye offer me burnt-offerings and
>   your meal-offerings,

Isaiah and Social Justice

The prophets' insistence that rituals were not the essence of the Law and their passion for righteousness are voiced in the Scriptures by Isaiah of Jerusalem, who lived in the mid-eighth century B.C. Scholars agree that Isaiah of Jerusalem did not write all sixty-six chapters that make up the book of Isaiah. Some material appears to have been written by his disciples and interpreters, and Chapters 40 to 55, which were composed two centuries later, are attributed to a person given the name Second Isaiah. The following verses come from Isaiah of Jerusalem.

11"What to me is the multitude of your
    sacrifices?
  says the LORD;
I have had enough of burnt offerings of rams
  and the fat of the fed beasts;
I do not delight in the blood of bulls, or of
  lambs, or of he-goats....
13Bring no more vain offerings;
  incense is an abomination to me.
New moon and sabbath and the calling of
    assemblies—
  I cannot endure iniquity and solemn
  assembly.
14Your new moons and your appointed feasts
  my soul hates;
they have become a burden to me,
  I am weary of bearing them.
15When you spread forth your hands,
  I will hide my eyes from you;
even though you make many prayers,

I will not listen;
  your hands are full of blood.
16Wash yourselves; make yourselves clean;
  remove the evil of your doings
  from before my eyes;
cease to do evil,
17 learn to do good;
seek justice,
  correct oppression;
defend the fatherless,
  plead for the widow.
  (Isaiah 1)

Isaiah denounces the rich and the powerful for exploiting the poor.

13The Lord has taken his place to contend,
  he stands to judge his people.
14The Lord enters into judgment
  with the elders and princes of his people:
"It is you who have devoured the vineyard,
  the spoil of the poor is in your houses.
15What do you mean by crushing my people,
  by grinding the face of the poor?"
  says the Lord God of hosts.
  (Isaiah 3)

Question for Analysis

1. Discuss the following statement: For Isaiah, ethical conduct was preferable to ritual acts as a way to worship God.

Scripture quotations are from the *Revised Standard Version of the Bible*, copyright © 1946, 1952, and 1971, National Council of the Churches of Christ in the USA.

I will not accept them;
Neither will I regard the peace offerings of
    your fat beasts.
Take thou away from Me the noise of thy
    songs;
And let Me not hear the melody of the
    psalteries.

But let justice well up as waters,
And righteousness as a mighty stream.
    (Amos 5:21–24)

Justice and righteousness are God's principal concerns and his supreme commandments, said the prophets. God's injunctions, declared Isaiah, were to

Jeremiah

In 597 B.C., the Babylonians, under King Nebuchadnezzar, captured Jerusalem, looted the temple, removed many leading citizens to Babylon, and placed Zedekiah on the throne of David as a puppet ruler. In 589 B.C., Zedekiah, ignoring the warnings of the prophet Jeremiah (born C. 645 B.C.), rebelled against Babylonian rule.

Jeremiah began prophesying when still in his teens, exhorting the Hebrews to avoid the evils of idol worship and mistreatment of their fellows. If the people did not change their ways, he warned, a "foe from the north"—clearly, he meant the Babylonians—would devastate the land and even destroy the temple. After the Babylonian conquest, Jeremiah warned Zedekiah to accept Babylonian dominion. Nebuchadnezzar, he said, was fulfilling God's purpose. God imposed the Babylonian yoke on Judah to provide the people with an opportunity for true contrition and spiritual renewal. To oppose Babylon was to contravene God's plan and bring down his wrath on Judah. Jeremiah told King Zedekiah: "Why should you and your people die by the sword, by famine, and by pestilence, as the Lord has spoken concerning any nation that will not serve the king of Babylon?" (27:12).

Jeremiah's political advice angered royal officials and popular prophets, who urged a war of liberation. When Zedekiah rebelled, Nebuchadnezzar responded with force. The enemies of Jeremiah demanded his execution as a traitor, and he was left to die in a deep cistern. However, Zedekiah allowed the prophet to be rescued but placed him under court arrest. Shortly afterward, the Babylonians poured through Jerusalem's breached walls; they burned the city, destroyed the temple, slaughtered nobles, and forcibly removed many

---

Seek justice, relieve the oppressed,
Judge the fatherless, plead for the widow.
   (Isaiah 1:17)

Prophets also denounced people whose principal concern was the accumulation of possessions and wealth. These objects are only transient, said Isaiah, "but the word of God will stand forever" (Isaiah 40:8).

Prophets stressed the direct spiritual-ethical encounter between the individual and God. Their concern was the inner person rather than the outer forms of religious activity. They criticized priests whose commitment to rites and rituals was not supported by a deeper spiritual insight or matched by a zeal for morality in daily life. To the prophets, an ethical sin was far worse than a ritual omission.

The prophets thus helped shape a social conscience that has become part of the Western tradition. This revolutionary social doctrine states that everyone has a God-given right to social justice and fair treatment; that each person has a religious obligation to denounce evil and oppose the mistreatment of others; and that the community has a moral responsibility to assist the unfortunate. The prophets held out the hope that life on earth could be improved, that poverty and injustice need not be accepted as part of an unalterable natural order, and that the individual was capable of elevating himself or herself morally.

Universalism

Hebrew thought displayed two tendencies: **parochialism** and universalism. Parochial-mindedness stressed the special nature, destiny, and needs of the chosen people—a nation set apart from others—for from among all the nations, God had chosen to give it his Law, the Torah. This narrow, tribal outlook was offset by **universalism**, a concern for all humanity, which found expression in the prophets who envisioned the unity of all people under God. Those prophets told of a great day when God, for whom all people were equally precious, would people to Babylon. King Zedekiah met a dreadful end. After being forced to watch the execution of his sons, he was blinded and taken in chains to Babylon.

For Jeremiah's support, Nebuchadnezzar ordered his release from prison. Remaining in Jerusalem, the prophet sent out a message of hope to the survivors. God had punished you, he told them, because "your guilt is great, because your sins are so numerous" (30:15). But God, who loved the people of Israel "with an everlasting love" (31:3) and also recognized his abiding commitment to them, will one day "restore the fortunes of my people" (30:3). The exiles will be returned, Jerusalem rebuilt, and the temple restored, he prophesied.

---

establish everlasting justice and peace among all nations.

> *In that day shall there be a highway out of Egypt to Assyria, and the Assyrian shall come into Egypt, and the Egyptian into Assyria; and the Egyptians shall worship with the Assyrians. In that day shall Israel be the third with Egypt and with Assyria. . . . For that the Lord of hosts hath blessed him saying: "Blessed be Egypt My people and Assyria the work of My hands, and Israel Mine inheritance." (Isaiah 19:23–24)*

Israel was charged with a sacred mission: to lead in the struggle against idolatry and to set an example of righteous behavior for all humanity.

The prophets were not pacifists, particularly if a war was being waged against the enemies of Yahweh. But some prophets denounced war as obscene and looked forward to its elimination. In a world where virtually everyone glorified the warrior, the prophets of universalism envisioned the day when peace would reign over the earth, when nations

> *shall beat their swords into plowshares, And their spears into pruning-hooks; Nation shall not lift up sword against nation, Neither shall they learn war any more. (Isaiah 2:4)*

These prophets maintained that when people glorify force, they dehumanize their opponents, brutalize themselves, and dishonor God. When violence rules, there can be no love of God and no regard for the individual.

Individualism

The prophets' universalism was accompanied by an equally profound awareness of the individual and his or her worth to God. Before Moses and the later prophets, virtually all religious tradition had been produced communally and anonymously. The prophets, however, spoke as fearless individuals who, by affixing their signatures to their thoughts, fully bore the responsibility of their religious inspiration and conviction. The prophets' emphasis on the individual's responsibility for his or her own actions is a key component of Western thought. In coming to regard God's Law as a *command to conscience, an appeal to the inner person*, the prophets heightened the awareness of the human personality. They enjoined individuals to be introspective, to examine their inner selves—their thoughts and feelings. They indicated that the individual could not know God by merely following edicts and by performing rituals; the individual must experience God. Precisely this *I-Thou* relationship could make the individual fully conscious of self and could deepen and enrich his or her personality. During the Exodus, the Hebrews were a tribal people who obeyed the Law largely out of awe and group compulsion. By the prophets' time, the Jews appeared to be autonomous individuals who heeded the Law because of a deliberate, conscious, inner commitment.

The ideals proclaimed by the prophets helped sustain the Jews throughout their long and often painful historical odyssey, and they remain a vital force for Jews today. Incorporated into the teachings of Jesus, these ideals, as part of Christianity, are embedded in the Western tradition.

45

THE LEGACY OF THE ANCIENT JEWS

For the Jews, monotheism had initiated a process of self-discovery and self-realization unmatched by other peoples of the Near East. The great value that Westerners give to the individual and to human dignity derives in part from the ancient Hebrews, who held that human beings were created in God's image and possessed free will and a conscience answerable to God. Inherited by Christianity, the prophets' teachings constitute the core principles of Western morality, and their command to the power structure not to abuse their authority but to pursue justice continues to inspire reformers.

Throughout the centuries, the Jewish Bible, with its view of God, human nature, divine punishment, the pursuit of righteousness, and social justice, has played a pivotal and profound role in Jewish life. Moreover, its significance has transcended the Jewish experience; it is also a cornerstone of Western civilization.

Christianity, the essential religion of Western civilization, emerged from ancient Judaism, and the links between the two, including monotheism, moral autonomy, prophetic values, and the Hebrew Scriptures as the Word of God, are numerous and strong. The historical Jesus cannot be understood without examining his Jewish background, and his followers appealed to the Hebrew Scriptures in order to demonstrate the validity of their beliefs. For these reasons, we talk of a Judeo-Christian tradition as an essential component of Western civilization.

The Hebrew vision of a future **messianic age**, a golden age of peace and social justice, is at the root of the Western idea of progress—that people can build a more just society, that there is reason to be hopeful about the future. This way of perceiving the world has greatly influenced modern reform movements. People longing to escape from oppression—African Americans in particular—have found inspiration in the Hebrews' deliverance from bondage in Egypt, the theme of Exodus.

In seeking to comprehend their relationship to God, the writers of the Hebrew Scriptures produced a treasury of themes, stories, and models of literary style and craftsmanship that have been a source of inspiration for Western religious thinkers, novelists, poets, and artists to the present day. Historians and archaeologists find the Hebrew Scriptures a valuable resource in their efforts to reconstruct ancient Near Eastern history.

❖   ❖   ❖

NOTES

1. John A. Wilson, "Egypt—the Kingdom of the 'Two Lands,'" in *The World History of the Jewish People*, vol. 1, *At the Dawn of Civilization*, ed. E. A. Speiser (New Brunswick, N.J.: Rutgers University Press, 1964), 267–268.

2. John Bright, *A History of Israel* (Philadelphia: Westminster Press, 1972), 154.

3. Ibid.

4. From *The Holy Scriptures* (Philadelphia: The Jewish Publication Society of America, 1917).

Chapter 3

The Greek City-State: Democratic Politics

The Acropolis of Athens. (John Elk III/Alamy Limited)

Focus Questions

1. What were the basic features and limitations of Greek democracy?

2. How did the Greek city-state differ from Near Eastern governments?

3. What were the causes and consequences of the Peloponnesian War?

4. How did Greek political life demonstrate both the best and the worst features of freedom as well as both the capabilities and the limitations of reason?

5. Why is the Greek political experience crucial to the shaping of the Western tradition?

*T*he Hebrew conception of ethical mono-theism, with its stress on human dignity, is one principal source of the Western tradition. The second major source is ancient Greece. Both the Hebrews and the Greeks absorbed the achievements of Near Eastern civilizations, but they also developed their own distinctive viewpoints and styles of thought that set them apart from the Mesopotamians and Egyptians. The great achievements of the Hebrews lay in the sphere of religious-ethical thought; those of the Greeks lay in the development of rational thought. As Greek society evolved, says British historian James Shiel, there

> was a growing reliance on independent reason, a devotion to logical precision, progressing from myth to logos [reason]. Rationalism permeated the whole social and cultural development. . . . Architecture. . . . developed from primitive cultic considerations to sophisticated mathematical norms; sculpture escaped from temple image to a new love of naturalism and proportion; political life proceeded from tyranny to rational experiments in democracy. From practical rules of thumb, geometry moved forward in the direction of the impressive Euclidian synthesis. So too philosophy made its way from "sayings of the wise" to the Aristotelian logic, and made men rely on their own observation and reflection in facing the unexplained vastness of the cosmos.[1]

The Greeks conceived of nature as following general rules, not acting according to the whims of gods or demons. They saw human beings as having a capacity for rational thought, a need for freedom, and a worth as individuals. Although the Greeks never dispensed with the gods, they increasingly stressed the importance of human reason and human decisions. They came to assert that reason is the avenue to knowledge and that people—not the gods—are responsible for their own behavior. In this shift of attention from the gods to human beings, the Greeks broke with the mythmaking orientation of the Near East and created the rational outlook that is a distinctive feature of Western civilization.

Chronology 3.1 ❖ The Greek City-State

1700–1450 B.C.*	Height of Minoan civilization
1400–1230	Height of Mycenaean civilization
1100–800	Dark Age
750–550	Age of Colonization
C. 700	Homer
621	Draco's code of law
594	Solon is elected chief executive
546–527	Under Pisistratus, tyranny replaces oligarchy
507	Cleisthenes broadens democratic institutions
499	Ionians revolt against Persian rule
490	Athenians defeat Persians at battle of Marathon
480	Xerxes of Persia invades Greece; Greek naval victory at Salamis
479	Spartans defeat Persians at Plataea, ending Persian Wars
478–477	Formation of Delian League
431	Start of Peloponnesian War
429	Death of Pericles
413	Athenian defeat at Syracuse
404	Athens surrenders to Sparta, ending Peloponnesian War
399	Execution of Socrates
387	Plato founds a school, the Academy
359	Philip II becomes king of Macedonia
338	Battle of Chaeronea: Greek city-states fall under the dominion of Macedonia
335 B.C.	Aristotle founds a school, the Lyceum

*Some dates are approximations.

EARLY AEGEAN CIVILIZATIONS

Until the latter part of the nineteenth century, historians placed the beginning of Greek, or Hellenic, history in the eighth century B.C. Now it is known that two related civilizations preceded Hellenic Greece: the Minoan and the Mycenaean.

Although the ancient Greek poet Homer had spoken of an earlier Greek civilization in his works, historians believed that Homer's epics dealt with myths and legends, not with a historical past. In 1871, however, a successful German businessman, Heinrich Schliemann, began a search for earliest Greece. Having been enthralled by Homer's epics as a youth, Schliemann was convinced that they referred to an actual civilization. In excavating several sites mentioned by Homer, Schliemann discovered tombs, pottery, ornaments, and the remains of palaces of what hitherto had been a lost Greek civilization. The ancient civilization was named after Mycenae, the most important city of the time. Mycenaean civilization pervaded the Greek mainland and the islands of the Aegean Sea for much of the second millennium B.C.

In 1900, Arthur Evans, a British archaeologist, made an equally extraordinary discovery. Excavating on the island of Crete, southeast of the Greek mainland, he unearthed a civilization even older than that of the Mycenaean Greeks. The Cretans, or Minoans, were not Greeks and did not speak a Greek language, but their influence on mainland Greece was considerable and enduring. Minoan civilization lasted about 1,350 years (2600–1250 B.C.) and reached its height during the period from 1700 to 1450 B.C.

The centers of Minoan civilization were magnificent palace complexes whose construction was evidence of the wealth and power of Minoan kings. That the architects of these palaces and the artists who decorated the walls were sensitive to beauty is shown in the ruins uncovered at various Cretan sites. The palaces housed royal families, priests, and government officials and contained workshops that produced decorated silver vessels, daggers, and pottery for local use and for export. Numerous Cretan artifacts have been found in Egypt, Syria, Asia Minor, and Greece, attesting to a substantial export trade.

Judging by the archaeological evidence, the Minoans seemed peaceful. Minoan art did not generally depict military scenes, and Minoan palaces, unlike the Mycenaean ones, had no defensive walls or fortifications. Thus, the Minoans were vulnerable to the warlike Mycenaean Greeks, who invaded and conquered Knossos, the Minoan capital. The Minoans never recovered from this blow, and within two centuries Minoan civilization faded away.

Who were these Mycenaeans? Around 2000 B.C., Greek-speaking tribes moved southward into the Greek peninsula, where, together with the pre-Greek population, they fashioned the Mycenaean civilization. In the Peloponnesus, the Mycenaeans built palaces that were based in part on Cretan models. In these palaces, Mycenaean kings conducted affairs of state, and priests and priestesses performed religious ceremonies; potters, smiths, tailors, and chariot builders practiced their crafts in the numerous workshops, much like their Minoan counterparts. Mycenaean arts and crafts owed a considerable debt to Crete. A script that permitted record keeping probably also came from Crete. The Mycenaeans were traders, too, exchanging goods with the peoples of Egypt, Phoenicia, Sicily, southern Italy, Macedonia, and the western coast of Asia Minor.

At the apex of Mycenaean society was the king, who headed the armed forces, controlled production and trade, and was the highest judicial authority. Assisting the king were aristocrats, who were officers in the army and held key positions in the administration. The priestesses and priests were also in the upper echelons of the society; they supervised sanctuaries and other properties of the gods. Farmers, stockbreeders, and craftsmen constituted the bulk of the free population. At the bottom of the social pyramid were the slaves—mostly foreign prisoners of war.

Mycenaean civilization, which consisted of several small states, each with its own ruling dynasty, reached its height in the period from 1400 to 1230 B.C. Following that, constant warfare between the Mycenaean kingdoms (and perhaps foreign invasions) led to destruction of the palaces and the abrupt disintegration of the Mycenaean civilization about 1100 B.C. But to the later Greek civilization the Mycenaeans left a legacy of religious forms, pottery making, metallurgy, agriculture, language, a warrior culture and code of honor immortalized in the Homeric epics, and myths and legends, which offered themes for Greek drama.

THE RISE OF HELLENIC CIVILIZATION

From 1100 to 800 B.C., the Greek world passed through the Dark Age, an era of transition between a dead Mycenaean civilization and a still unborn Hellenic civilization. The Dark Age saw the migration of Greek tribes from the barren mountainous regions of Greece to more fertile plains, and from the mainland to Aegean islands and the coast of Asia Minor. One group of invaders, the Dorians, penetrated the Peloponnesian peninsula in the south and later founded Sparta. Another group, the Ionians, settled in Attica, where Athens is located, and later crossed to Asia Minor. During this period, the Greeks experienced insecurity, warfare, poverty, and isolation. The bureaucratic system of Mycenaean government had disappeared, extensive trade had ceased, the art of writing had been forgotten, the palace workshops no longer existed, and art had reverted to primitive forms.

After 800 B.C., however, town life revived. Writing again became part of the Greek culture, this time with the more efficient Phoenician script. (Other borrowings from the Near East included artistic imagery and motifs, religious practices, craft skills, and mythological tales that were adapted and transformed by Greek poets.) The population increased dramatically, there was a spectacular rise in the use of metals, and overseas trade expanded. Gradually, Greek cities founded settlements on the islands of the Aegean, along the coast of Asia Minor and the Black Sea, and to the west in Sicily and southern Italy. These colonies, established to relieve overpopulation and land hunger, were independent, self-governing city-states, not possessions of the homeland city-states, although close ties were maintained between the two. During the two hundred years of colonization (750–550 B.C.), trade and industry expanded, the pace of urbanization quickened, and a new class emerged: the merchants, whose wealth derived from goods and money rather than from land. In time, this middle class would challenge the landholding aristocracy.

Homer, Shaper of the Greek Spirit

The poet Homer lived during the eighth century B.C., just after the Dark Age. His great narrative epics, the *Iliad* and the *Odyssey,** helped shape

---

*Although scholars agree that Homer composed the *Iliad*, some of them hold that the *Odyssey* was probably the work of an unknown poet who lived sometime after Homer; some say that Homer composed both epics, most likely utilizing oral poetic traditions already in circulation, in their earliest forms and that others altered them.

the Greek spirit and Greek religion. Homer was the earliest molder of the Greek outlook and character. For centuries, Greek youngsters grew up reciting the Homeric epics and admiring the Homeric heroes, who strove for honor and faced suffering and death with courage. Greek thinkers quoted Homer to illustrate moral truths.

In contrast to earlier works of mythology, Homer dealt not just with a hero's actions but also with what the hero thought and felt about his behavior. Homer was a poetic genius who could reveal a human being's deepest thoughts, feelings, and conflicts in a few brilliant lines. His characters, complex in their motives and expressing powerful human emotions—wrath, vengeance, guilt, remorse, compassion, and love—would intrigue and inspire Western writers down to the present.

The *Iliad* deals, in poetic form, with a small segment of the tenth and last year of the Trojan War, which had taken place centuries before Homer's time, during the Mycenaean period. At the very beginning, Homer states his theme.

> The Wrath of Achilles is my theme, that fatal wrath which, in fulfillment of the will of Zeus, brought the Achaeans [Greeks] so much suffering and sent the gallant souls of many noblemen to Hades, leaving their bodies as carrion for the dogs and passing birds. Let us begin, goddess of song, with the angry parting that took place between Agamemnon King of Men and the great Achilles Son of Peleus.[2]

The story goes on to reveal the cause and tragic consequences of this wrath. In depriving "the swift and excellent" Achilles of his rightful war-prize (the captive young woman Briseis), King Agamemnon has insulted Achilles' honor and has violated the solemn rule that warrior heroes treat each other with respect. His pride wounded, Achilles refuses to rejoin Agamemnon in battle against Troy and plans to affirm his honor by demonstrating that the Achaeans need his valor and military prowess. Not until many brave men have been slain, including his dearest friend Patroclus, does Achilles set aside his quarrel with Agamemnon and enter the battle.

Homer employs a *particular* event, the quarrel between an arrogant Agamemnon and a

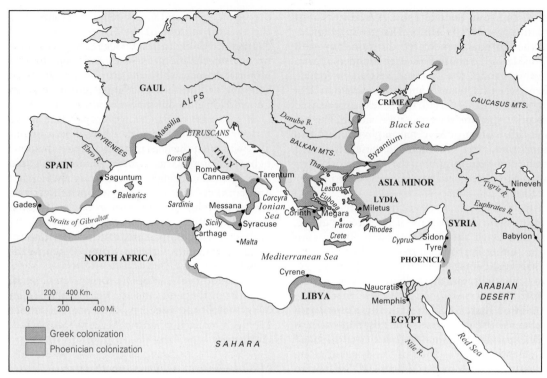

Map 3.1 Greek Colonization of the Mediterranean Basin From 750 to 550 B.C., the Greeks colonized the islands of the Aegean, the coasts of Asia Minor and the Black Sea, and, to the west, Sicily and southern Italy. (© 2016 Cengage Learning.)

revengeful Achilles, to demonstrate a *universal* principle: that "wicked arrogance" and "ruinous wrath" will cause much suffering and death. Homer grasps that there is an internal logic to existence. For Homer, says British classicist H. D. F. Kitto, "actions must have their consequences; ill-judged actions must have uncomfortable results."[3] People, and even the gods, operate within a certain unalterable framework; their deeds are subject to the demands of fate, or necessity. With a poet's intuition, Homer sensed what would become a fundamental attitude of the Greek mind: there is a universal order to things. Later Greeks would formulate Homer's poetic insight in philosophical terms.

Although human life is governed by laws of necessity, the Homeric warrior expresses a passionate desire to assert himself, to demonstrate his worth, to gain the glory that poets would immortalize in their songs—that is, to achieve **aretē**, excellence. In the *Iliad*, Hector, prince of Troy, does battle with Achilles, even though defeat and death seem certain. He fights not because he is a fool rushing madly into a fray nor because he relishes combat, but because he is a prince bound by a code of honor and conscious of his reputation and of his responsibility to his fellow Trojans. In the code of the warrior-aristocrats, cowardice brought unbearable shame, and honor meant more than life itself. When Hector knows that he is going to be slain by Achilles, he expresses this overriding concern with heroism and glory: "So now I meet my doom. Let me at least sell my life dearly and have a not inglorious end, after some feat of arms that shall come to the ears of generations still unborn."[4]

Heroism, the pursuit of glory and fame, and war's exhilaration are central to the *Iliad*, but

Homer is also sensitive to the suffering caused by war. Battlefields littered with dead and maimed warriors fill soldiers with tears, and the grief of widows, orphans, and parents is unremitting.

Homer grasped war's tragic character: it confers honor and dignity on the victorious, but suffering, grief, enslavement, and death on the defeated. And one day, the hero, who had been lauded for his courage and prowess and had brought glory to his family and city, will also perish by the sword. This is his destiny. Homer's insights into life's tragic nature instructed the great Greek dramatists (see Chapter 4) and future Western writers.

In the warrior-aristocrat world of Homer, aretē was principally interpreted as bravery and skill in battle. Homer's portrayal also bears the embryo of a larger conception of human excellence, one that combines thought with action. A man of true worth, says the wise Phoenix to the stubborn Achilles, is both "a speaker of words and a doer of deeds." In this passage, we find the earliest statement of the Greek educational ideal: the molding of a man who, says classicist Werner Jaeger, "united nobility of action with nobility of mind," who realized "the whole of human potentialities."[5] Thus, in Homer we find the beginnings of Greek humanism—a concern with the individual and his achievements.

To Mesopotamian and Egyptian minds, the gods were primarily responsible for the good or evil that befell human beings. In Homer's work, the gods are still very much involved in human affairs, but Homer also makes the individual a decisive actor in the drama of life. Human actions and human personality are very important. Homer's heroes demonstrate a considerable independence of will. Human beings pay respect to the gods but do not live in perpetual fear of them; they choose their own way, at times even defying the gods. As British classicist C. M. Bowra notes, "the human actors . . . pursue their own aims and deal their own blows; the gods may help or obstruct them, but success or failure remains their own. The gods have the last word, but in the interval men do their utmost and win glory for it."[6] Homer's view of the eternal order of the world and his conception of the individual striving for excellence that brought honor and esteem form the foundations of the Greek outlook.

Greek Religion

During the Dark Age, Greek religion was a mixture of beliefs and cults of gods and goddesses inherited from the Mycenaean past and from an even older Indo-European past imported from Asia Minor and from the early civilizations of the Near East. The Greeks had no prophets or works of scripture like the Hebrews, but Homer's epics and Hesiod's poetry (see profile in next chapter) gave some clarity and structure to Greek religion. They were not intended to have any theological significance, but their treatment of the gods had important religious implications for the Greeks. In time, Homer's epics formed the basis of the Olympian religion accepted throughout Greece. The principal gods were said to reside on Mount Olympus in northern Greece, and on its highest peak was the palace of Zeus, the chief deity. Although all Greeks recognized the Olympian gods, each city retained local gods and rituals that had been transmitted through generations by folk memory.

Many Greeks found an outlet for their religious feelings in the sacred ceremonies of mystic cults. Devotees of the cult of Dionysus, the god of wine and agricultural fertility, engaged in ecstatic dances and frenzied prayers for abundant harvests. Participants in the Eleusinian cult felt purified and reborn through their rituals and believed in a happy life after death. The Orphic cult, which was popular in the sixth century B.C., taught the unimportance of earthly life and the need to prepare for life after the grave. The Orphics believed that the soul, which once had enjoyed a happy existence in another world, was imprisoned in the body for an unknown fault, and that if the individual controlled his or her bodily desires, the soul would be liberated after death.

In the early stages of Greek history, most people sought to live in accordance with the wishes of the gods. Through prayer, offerings, and ritual purification, they tried to appease the gods and consulted oracles to divine the future. Although religion pervaded daily life, the Greeks had no official body of priests who ruled religious matters and could intervene in politics. Instead, religious ceremonies were conducted by citizens chosen to serve as priests. Nor was there an official creed with established doctrines. Religion was more social than spiritual; that is, it was more a way of expressing attachment to the community than finding inner peace through personal communion with a higher reality. In time, traditional religion would be challenged and undermined by a growing secular and rational spirit.

THE EVOLUTION OF THE CITY-STATE

The Break with Theocratic Politics

From 750 B.C. to the death of Alexander the Great in 323 B.C., Greek society consisted of independent city-states. The city-state based on tribal allegiances was generally the first political association during the early stages of civilization. Moreover, Greece's many mountains, bays, and islands—natural barriers to political unity—favored this type of political arrangement.

The scale of the city-state, or *polis*, was small; most city-states had fewer than 5,000 male citizens. Athens, which was a large city-state, had some 35,000 to 40,000 (some estimates are as high as 55,000) adult male citizens; the rest of its population of 350,000 consisted of women, children, resident aliens, and slaves, none of whom could participate in lawmaking. The citizens of the polis, many of whom were related by blood, knew one another well, and together they engaged in athletic contests and religious rituals. The polis gave individuals a sense of belonging, for its citizens were intimately involved in the political and cultural life of the community.

In the fifth century B.C., at its maturity, the Greeks viewed their polis as the only avenue to the good life—"the only framework within which man could realize his spiritual, moral, and intellectual capacities," in the words of Kitto.[7] The mature polis was a self-governing community that expressed the will of free citizens, not the desires of gods, hereditary kings, or priests. In the **theocracies** of the Near East, religion dominated political activity, and to abide by the mandates of the gods was the ruler's first responsibility. The Greek polis also had begun as a religious institution, in which the citizens sought to maintain an alliance with their deities. But gradually the

citizens deemphasized the gods' role in political life and based government not on the magic powers of divine rulers, but on human intelligence as expressed through the community. Seers, purported to have supernatural skills, might offer advice but could not override the rulings of the Assembly. The great innovation introduced by the Greeks into politics and social theory, says classicist Mason Hammond, was "the view that law did not emanate from gods, or divine rulers, but from the human community."[8] The evolution of the Greek polis from a tribal-religious institution to a secular-rational institution was only a part of the general transition of the Greek mind from myth to reason.

The emergence of rational attitudes did not, of course, spell the end of religion, particularly for the peasants, who remained devoted to their ancient cults, gods, and shrines. Greek commanders and statesmen, at times, were not beyond consulting omens and oracles before making decisions, and considerable public revenue went to the construction of temples and the observance of religious festivals. The Greeks were careful to show respect for the gods, for many believed that these deities could aid or harm a city. Paying homage to the god of the city remained a required act of patriotism, to which Greeks unfailingly adhered.

Thus, the religious-mythical tradition never died in Greece but existed side by side with a growing **rationalism**. As Greek rationalism gained influence, traditional religious beliefs and restrictions either were made to comply more with the demands of reason or grew weaker through neglect and disuse. When Athenian **democracy** reached its height in the middle of the fifth century B.C., religion was no longer the dominant factor in politics. For many Athenians, religion had become largely ceremonial, a way of expressing loyalty to the city. They had come to rely on human reason, not divine guidance, in their political and intellectual life.

Greek political life was marred by violent party conflicts, demagoguery, intercity warfare, and the exploitation of weak states by stronger ones. Nevertheless, the Greek political achievement was extraordinary. What made Greek political life different from that of earlier Near Eastern civilizations, and also gave it enduring significance, was the Greeks' gradual realization that community problems are caused by human beings and require human solutions. Thus, the Greeks came to understand law as an achievement of the rational mind rather than as an edict imposed by the gods; law was valued because it expressed the will and needs of the community, not out of fear of the divine. The Greeks also valued free **citizenship**. An absolute king, a tyrant who ruled arbitrarily and by decree and who was above the law, was abhorrent.

The ideals of political freedom are best exemplified by Athens. Before turning to Athens, however, let us examine another Greek city, which followed a different political course.

Sparta: A Garrison State

Situated on the Peloponnesian peninsula, farther inland than most Greek cities, Sparta had been settled by Dorian Greeks. The Greek city-states dealt with overpopulation and the need for new agricultural land by founding colonies. Sparta, however, established only one colony, Tarentum, in southern Italy. Sparta's chief means of expansion was to conquer, in the eighth century B.C., its neighbors on the Peloponnesian peninsula, including Messenia. Instead of selling the Messenians abroad, the traditional Greek way of treating a defeated foe, the Spartans kept them as state serfs, or *Helots*. Helots were owned by the state rather than by individual Spartans. Enraged by their enforced servitude, the Messenians, also a Greek people, desperately tried to regain their freedom. After a bloody struggle, the Spartans suppressed the uprising, but the fear of a Helot revolt became indelibly stamped on Spartan consciousness.

To maintain their dominion over the Messenians, who outnumbered them ten to one, the Spartans—with extraordinary single-mindedness, discipline, and loyalty—transformed their own society into an armed camp. Agricultural labor was performed by Helots; trade and crafts were left to the *perioikoi*, conquered Greeks who were free but were not citizens and had no political rights. The Spartans learned only one craft, soldiering, and were inculcated with only one conception of excellence: fighting bravely for their city.

The Spartans were trained in the arts of war and indoctrinated to serve the state. Military training for Spartan boys began at age seven; they exercised, drilled, competed, and endured physical hardships. Other Greeks admired the Spartans for their courage, obedience to law, and achievement in molding themselves according to an ideal. Spartan soldiers were better trained and disciplined and were more physically fit than other Greeks. But the Spartans were also criticized for having a limited conception of aretē.

Before Sparta converted itself into a military state, its cultural development had paralleled that of the other Greek cities. By isolating itself economically and culturally from the rest of Greece, however, Sparta became a closed provincial town and did not share in the cultural enlightenment that pervaded the Greek world. Sparta paid a heavy price for its militaristic outlook.

By 500 B.C., Sparta had emerged as the leader of the Peloponnesian League, an alliance of southern Greek city-states whose land forces were superior to those of any other combination of Greek cities. Sparta, though, was concerned with protecting its position, not with expansion. Cautious by temperament and always fearful of a Helot uprising, Spartans viewed the Peloponnesian League as an instrument for defense rather than aggression.

Athens: The Rise of Democracy

The contrast between the city-states of Athens and Sparta is striking. Whereas Sparta was a land power and exclusively agricultural, Athens, located on the peninsula of Attica near the coast, possessed a great navy and was the commercial leader among the Greeks. Reluctant to send soldiers far from home, where they were needed to control the Helots, Sparta's leaders pursued an isolationist foreign policy. The daring and ambitious Athenians, on the other hand, endeavored to extend their hegemony over other Greek cities. Finally, Athenians and Spartans differed in their concept of freedom. To the Spartans, freedom meant preserving the independence of their fatherland; this overriding consideration demanded order, discipline, and regimentation. The Athenians also wanted to protect their city from enemies, but, unlike the Spartans, they valued political freedom and sought the full development and enrichment of the human personality.

Thus, while authoritarian Sparta became culturally sterile, Athens, with its relatively free and open society, emerged as the cultural leader of Hellenic civilization.

Greek city-states generally moved through four stages: rule by a king (monarchy), rule by landowning aristocrats (oligarchy), rule by one man who seized power (tyranny), and rule by the people (democracy). During the first stage, monarchy, the king, who derived his power from the gods, commanded the army and judged civil cases.

Oligarchy, the second stage, was instituted in Athens during the eighth century B.C. when aristocrats (*aristocracy* is a Greek word meaning "rule

of the best") usurped power from hereditary kings. In the next century, aristocratic regimes experienced a social crisis. There was tension between the land-holding nobles, who dominated the government, and the newly rich and ambitious merchants, who wanted a share in governing Athens. Furthermore, peasants who borrowed from the aristocracy, pledging their lands as security, lost their property and even became enslaved for nonpayment of their debts. Merchants and peasants also protested that the law, which was based on oral tradition and administered exclusively by aristocrats, was unjust. The embittered and restless middle and lower classes were granted one concession.

ZEUS, C. 460 B.C. This bronze statue was found off the Greek coast in 1926. Although his face is still stylized, his athletic body pulsates with life, capturing the essence of Zeus as the omnipotent ruler of the gods. (National Archaeological Museum Athens/ Gianni Dagli Orti/The Art Archive/Picture Desk)

Detail of Greek Kylix (Cup), c. 490–480 b.c. The frenzied dancing of the Bacchantes, worshippers of the god Dionysius, is depicted by the vase painter Macron. Maenads (mad ones) dressed in fawn skins and carrying the thrysos, a wand made of vine leaves, leap and carouse in ecstatic orgies with satyrs in worship of the god of wine and sexual liberation. (The Metropolitan Museum of Art/Art Resource, N.Y.)

In 621 b.c., the aristocrats appointed Draco to draw up a code of law. Although Draco's code let the poor know what the law was and reduced the possibilities of aristocratic judges behaving arbitrarily, penalties were extremely severe (hence the word *draconian*), and the code provided no relief for the peasants' economic woes. As the poor began to organize and press for the cancellation of their debts and the redistribution of land, Athens was moving toward civil war.

Solon, the Reformer.

In 594 b.c., Solon (c. 640–559 b.c.), a traveler and poet with a reputation for wisdom, was elected chief executive. Although he came from a noble family, Solon maintained that the wealthy landowners, through their greed, had disrupted community life and brought Athens to the brink of civil war. Solon initiated a rational approach to the problems of society by deemphasizing the gods' role in human affairs and attributing the city's ills to the specific behavior of individuals; he sought practical remedies for these ills; and he held that written law should be in harmony with **Dikē**, the principle of justice that underlies the human community. The concept of a just city, a unifying principle of Solon's reforms, became a formative ideal of Greek political thought. At the same time, he wanted to instill in Athenians of all classes a sense of working for the common good of the city.

Solon aimed at restoring a sick Athenian society to health by restraining the nobles and improving the lot of the poor. To achieve this goal, he canceled debts, freed Athenians enslaved for debt, and brought back to Athens those who had been sold abroad; however, he refused to confiscate and redistribute the nobles' land as the extremists demanded. He permitted all classes of free men, even the poorest, to sit in the Assembly, which elected magistrates and accepted or rejected legislation proposed by a new Council of Four Hundred. He also opened the highest offices in the state to wealthy commoners, who had previously been excluded from these positions because they lacked noble birth. Thus, Solon undermined the traditional rights of the hereditary aristocracy and initiated the transformation of Athens from an aristocratic oligarchy into a democracy.

Solon also instituted ingenious economic reforms. Recognizing that the poor soil of Attica was not conducive to growing grain, he urged the cultivation of grapes for wine and the growing of olives, whose oil could be exported. To guard against food shortages and the resultant higher prices, Solon prohibited the export of food products with the exception of olives. To encourage industrial expansion, he ordered that all fathers teach their sons a trade and granted citizenship to foreign craftsmen who were willing to migrate to Athens. These measures and the fine quality of the native reddish-brown clay allowed Athens to become the leading producer and exporter of pottery. Solon's economic policies transformed Athens into a great commercial center. However, Solon's reforms did not eliminate factional disputes among the aristocratic clans or relieve much of the discontent of the poor.

Pisistratus, the Tyrant. In 546 B.C., Pisistratus (c. 605–527 B.C.), an aristocrat, took advantage of the general instability to become a one-man ruler, driving into exile those who had opposed him. Tyranny thus replaced oligarchy. Tyranny occurred frequently in the Greek city-states. Almost always aristocrats themselves, tyrants generally posed as champions of the poor in their struggle against the aristocracy. Pisistratus sought popular support by having conduits constructed to increase the Athenian water supply; like tyrants in other city-states, he gave to peasants land confiscated from exiled aristocrats and granted state loans to small farmers.

Pisistratus' great achievement was the promotion of cultural life. He initiated grand architectural projects, encouraged sculptors and painters, arranged for public recitals of the Homeric epics, and founded festivals, which included dramatic performances. In all these ways, he made culture, formerly the province of the aristocracy, available to commoners. Pisistratus thus launched a policy that eventually led Athens to emerge as the cultural capital of the Greeks.

Cleisthenes, the Democrat. Shortly after Pisistratus' death, a faction headed by Cleisthenes, an aristocrat sympathetic to democracy, assumed leadership. By an ingenious method of redistricting the city, Cleisthenes ended the aristocratic clans' traditional jockeying for the chief state positions, which had caused much divisiveness and bitterness in Athens. Cleisthenes replaced this practice, rooted in tradition and authority, with a new system that was rationally planned to ensure that historic allegiance to tribe or clan would be superseded by loyalty to the city as a whole.

Cleisthenes hoped to make democracy the permanent form of government for Athens. The power to govern Athens, he believed, should rest with male citizens acting as a body and not with aristocratic factions or a tyrant. To safeguard the city against tyranny, he utilized (or perhaps introduced) the practice of **ostracism**. Once a year, Athenians were given the opportunity to inscribe on a fragment of pottery (*ostracon*) the name of anyone who, they felt, endangered the state. An individual against whom six thousand votes were cast was ostracized, that is, forced to leave Athens for ten years.

Cleisthenes firmly secured democratic government in Athens. The Assembly, which Solon had opened to all male citizens, was in the process of becoming the supreme authority in the state. But the period of Athenian greatness lay in the future; the Athenians first had to fight a war of survival against the Persian empire.

ATHENIAN GREATNESS

The Persian Wars

In 499 B.C., the Ionian Greeks of Asia Minor rebelled against their Persian overlord. Sympathetic to the Ionian cause, Athens sent twenty ships to aid the revolt, an act that the Greek historian Herodotus said "was the beginning of trouble not only for Greece, but for the rest of the world as well."[9] Bent on revenge, Darius I, king of Persia, sent a small detachment to Attica. In 490 B.C., on the plains of Marathon, the citizen army of Athens defeated the Persians—for the Athenians, one of the finest moments in their history. Ten years later, Xerxes, Darius' son, organized a huge invasion force—some 250,000 men and more than 500 ships—with the aim of reducing Greece to a Persian province. Setting aside their separatist instincts, many of the city-states united to defend their independence and their liberty. Herodotus viewed the conflict as an ideological clash between Greek freedom and Asian despotism.

The Persians crossed the waters of the Hellespont (Dardanelles) and made their way into northern Greece. Herodotus describes their encounter at the mountain pass of Thermopylae with three hundred Spartans, who were true to their training and ideal of aretē and "resisted to the last with their swords if they had them, and if not, with their hands and teeth, until the Persians, coming on from the front over the ruins of the wall and closing in from behind, finally overwhelmed them."[10] Northern Greece fell to the Persians, who continued south, pillaging and burning a deserted Athens.

When it appeared that the Greeks' spirit had been broken, the Athenian statesman and general Themistocles (c. 527–460 B.C.), demonstrating in military affairs the same rationality that Cleisthenes had shown in political life, lured the Persian fleet into the narrowest entry to the Bay of Salamis. In this cramped space, the Persians were unable to deploy their more numerous ships. Excelling in ramming maneuvers and knowing what was at stake, the Athenian crews picked off the jammed Persian ships in a decisive victory. In 479 B.C., a year after the Athenian naval victory at Salamis, the Spartans defeated the Persians in the land battle of Plataea. The inventive intelligence with which the Greeks planned their military operations and a fierce desire to preserve their freedom—which, the war made them realize, was their distinguishing attribute—enabled them to defeat the greatest military power the Mediterranean world had yet seen.

The Persian Wars were decisive in the history of the West. Had the Greeks been defeated, it is very likely that their cultural and political vitality would have been aborted. The confidence and pride that came with its astonishing victory, however, propelled Athens into a golden age, which became marred by the Athenian urge for dominance in Greece.

The Persian Wars ushered in an era of Athenian imperialism, which had drastic consequences for the future. Immediately after the wars, more than 150 city-states organized a confederation, the Delian League (named after its treasury on the island of Delos), to protect themselves against a renewed confrontation with Persia. Because of its wealth, its powerful fleet, and the restless energy of its citizens, Athens assumed leadership of the Delian League. Largely thanks to the Athenian fleet, the league was able to drive both pirates and Persians from the Aegean Sea.

Although it had been conceived as a voluntary association of independent Greek states seeking protection against Persia, the league gradually came under the domination of Athens. The Athenians, seeing no contradiction between imperialism and democracy, also manipulated the league for their own economic advantage. They believed that their freedom and prosperity required subduing, exploiting, and enslaving others, and they adhered to the principle that strong states had a natural right to dominate weaker ones. They relished the empire that gave them wealth, power, and honor; in the Greek view, power was the principal determiner of a city's glory. Moreover, the Athenians claimed that the other city-states benefited from Athenian hegemony. Athens forbade member states to withdraw, crushed revolts, and stationed garrisons on the territory of confederate states. It used both tribute from members and the league's treasury to finance public works in Athens.

Although member states did receive protection, were not overtaxed, and enjoyed increased trade, they resented Athenian domination. As the Persian threat subsided, hatred for Athenian imperialism grew. In converting the Delian League into an instrument of Athenian imperialism, Athens may have lost an opportunity to perform a great creative act—forming a broad voluntary confederation that might have forestalled the intercity warfare that gravely weakened Hellenic civilization.

The Mature Athenian Democracy

Athenian imperialism was one consequence of the Persian Wars; another was the flowering of Athenian democracy and culture. The Athenian state was a direct democracy, in which the citizens themselves, not elected representatives, made the laws. In the Assembly, which was open

***Map 3.2* THE AEGEAN BASIN** This map shows major battle sites. Note also the Hellespont, where Xerxes' forces crossed into Greece, and Ionia, the coast of Asia Minor, where Greek philosophy was born. (© 2016 Cengage Learning.)

to all adult male citizens and that met some forty times a year, Athenians debated and voted on key issues of state; they declared war, signed treaties, and spent public funds. All decisions were arrived at after public discussion, in which all citizens had a right to speak. It is likely that on most occasions farmers did not journey into the city to attend a meeting of the Assembly. By the middle of the fifth century B.C., the will of the people, as expressed by a majority vote in the Assembly, was supreme. Rejecting the arbitrary rule of tyrants and domination by a small circle of nobles, the Athenians conceived the idea of **isonomy**—equality of political rights for citizens of the polis, that is, the right to vote, to speak before and submit motions to the Assembly, to hold the highest public positions, and to receive equal treatment before the law.

The Council of Five Hundred (which had been established by Cleisthenes to replace Solon's Council of Four Hundred) managed the ports, military installations, and other state properties and prepared the agenda for the Assembly. Because its members were chosen annually by lot and could not serve more than twice in a lifetime, the Council could never supersede the Assembly. Chosen at random, its membership could not become a cabal of the most powerful and ambitious citizens. Some 350 magistrates, also chosen by lot, performed administrative tasks: collecting fines, policing the city, repairing streets, inspecting markets, and so forth. Because of the special competence that their posts required, the ten generals who led the army were, for obvious reasons, not chosen by lot but were elected annually by the Assembly.

The introduction of pay for government officials marked a great democratic advance. It meant that an average person could afford to leave his job for a year in order to serve on the Council of Five Hundred, on a commission overseeing the administration of the city, or in the law courts.

Athens has been aptly described as a government of amateurs. There were no professional civil servants, no professional soldiers and sailors, no state judges—all legal cases were decided by juries chosen by lot—and no elected lawmakers. The duties of government were performed by ordinary citizens. Such a system rested on the assumption that the average citizen was capable of participating intelligently in the affairs of state and that he would, in a spirit of civic patriotism, carry out his responsibilities to his city. In fifth-century Athens, excellence was equated with good citizenship—a concern for the good of the community that outweighed personal aspirations. Indeed, to a surprisingly large number of Athenians, politics was an overriding concern, and they devoted considerable time and thought to civic affairs. Those who allowed private matters to take precedence over the needs of the community were denounced as useless people living purposeless lives.

Although Athens was a democracy in form, in practice aristocrats continued to dominate political life for most of the fifth century. Generals came from noble houses, as did the leading voices in the Assembly. This situation was not surprising, for aristocrats took for granted a responsibility to exercise leadership and acquired the education, particularly in public speaking and debate, needed to perform this role. The economic expansion after the Persian Wars produced a wealthy class of tradesmen, who eventually challenged aristocratic dominance in the Assembly during the last third of the fifth century B.C.

Judged by modern standards, Athenian democracy undoubtedly had its limitations and weaknesses. Modern critics point out that resident aliens were almost totally barred from citizenship and therefore from political participation. Slaves, who constituted about one-fourth of the Athenian population, enjoyed none of the freedoms that Athenians considered so precious. The Greeks regarded slavery as a necessary precondition for civilized life; for some to be free and prosperous, they believed, others had to be enslaved. The large number of slaves available for labor,

they believed, permitted free citizens to devote themselves to civic affairs and to fight for the city when needed.

Slaves usually did the same work as Athenian citizens: farming, commerce, manufacturing, domestic chores. Some slaves—the three hundred Scythian archers who made up the police force and those sufficiently educated to serve the state as clerks—enjoyed a privileged position. However, slaves, including preadolescent children, who toiled in the mines suffered a grim fate. In Athens, some slaves were Greeks, but most were foreigners. Slaves were generally prisoners of war and captives of pirates. Sometimes they were foreign children sold by their parents or abandoned infants left to die, a not uncommon practice in ancient Greece and Rome. A person finding the infant might eventually sell the child into slavery.

Athenian women were another group denied legal or political rights. Most Greeks, no doubt, agreed with Aristotle, who said: "[T]he male is by nature superior, and the female inferior; and . . . the one rules and the other is ruled."[11] A girl usually was married at fourteen to a man twice her age, and the marriage was arranged by a male relative. The wedding day might be the first time that the young bride saw her future husband. Although either spouse could obtain a divorce, the children remained with the father after the marriage was dissolved. Wives did not dine with their husbands and spent much of their time in the women's quarters.

Athenian women were barred from holding public office and generally could not appear in court without a male representative. They could not act in plays, and, when attending the theater, they sat in the rear, away from the men. Greek women received no formal education, although some young women learned to read and write at home. Training in household skills was considered the only education a woman needed. Since it was believed that a woman could not act independently, she was required to have a guardian—normally her father or husband—who controlled her property and supervised her behavior. Convinced that financial dealings were too difficult for women and that they needed to be protected from strangers, men, not women, did the marketing. When a woman left the house, she was usually accompanied by a male. The Athenian wife was treated as a minor; in effect, she was her husband's ward.

Modern critics also point out the failure of Hellenic Greeks to arrive at a conception of what seventeenth- and eighteenth-century liberal thinkers were to call natural or inalienable rights and what are now generally known as human rights. The Greeks limited rights to members of a particular community; they had no awareness of the modern idea that all individuals possess as a birthright basic rights that government must respect.

Ancient critics, too, attacked Athenian democracy. Having no confidence in the ability of the common people to govern, these aristocratic critics equated democracy with mob rule. In a democracy, they said, the envious, volatile, and incompetent poor tyrannize the rich; make unwise, impetuous decisions; and are easily manipulated by clever demagogues. A political system that gives power to people of limited ability, knowledge, and experience is destined to fail. The Assembly did at times make rash and foolish decisions and was swayed by the oratory of demagogues. For the most part, however, as British historian A. H. M. Jones concludes,

> the Assembly seems to have kept its head, and very rarely to have broken its rules of procedure. . . . Moreover, the people demanded high standards of its advisors. . . . It was informed advice, and not mere eloquence, that the people expected from rising politicians, and they saw to it that they got it.[12]

That the Athenians found democracy an indispensable form of government is proved by the paucity of revolts. In the almost two hundred years after Cleisthenes, there were only two attempts to undo the democracy, both made under the stress of the Peloponnesian War and both were short-lived.

The flaws in Athenian democracy should not cause us to undervalue its extraordinary achievement. The idea that the state represents a community of free, self-governing citizens remains a crucial principle of Western civilization. Athenian democracy embodied the principle of the legal state—a government based not on force but on laws debated, devised, altered, and obeyed by free citizens.

This idea of the legal state could have arisen only in a society that was aware of and respected the rational mind. In the same way that the Greeks demythicized nature, they also removed myth from the sphere of politics. Holding that government was something that people create to satisfy human needs, the Athenians regarded their leaders neither as gods nor as priests but as men who had demonstrated a capacity for statesmanship. Athens was unique, writes Italian historian Mario Attilio Levi, for Athenians "had the audacity to maintain that human reason is itself the source of legitimacy and therefore of the right to govern and command, in a world in which the only recognized source of legitimacy was the gods."[13]

Both democratic politics and systematic political thought originated in Greece. There people first asked questions about the nature and purpose of the state, rationally analyzed political institutions,

ATTIC BLACK-FIGURE HYDRIA, c. 510 This hydria, or water jug, shows women drawing water from a fountainhouse. Trips to the fountainhouse provided one of the few opportunities for women to socialize outside the home. (Photograph © 2016 Museum of Fine Arts, Boston/William Francis Warden Fund, 61.195.)

Pericles on Athenian Greatness

During the Peloponnesian War, Pericles delivered a funeral oration that eloquently expressed the ideals of Athenian society. Reconstructed by Thucydides, the oration is regarded as one of the finest speeches in world history.

"Let me say that our system of government does not copy the institutions of our neighbours. It is more the case of our being a model to others, than of our imitating anyone else. Our constitution is called a democracy because power is in the hands not of a minority but of the whole people. When it is a question of settling private disputes, everyone is equal before the law; when it is a question of putting one person before another in positions of public responsibility, what counts is not membership of a particular class, but the actual ability which the man possesses. No one, so long as he has it in him to be of service to the state, is kept in political obscurity because of poverty. And, just as our political life is free and open, so is our day-to-day life in our relations with each other. We do not get into a state with our next-door neighbour if he enjoys himself in his own way, nor do we give him the kind of black looks which, though they do no real harm, still do hurt people's feelings. We are free and tolerant in our private lives; but in public affairs we keep to the law. This is because it commands our deep respect.

"We give our obedience to those whom we put in positions of authority, and we obey the laws themselves, especially those which are for the protection of the oppressed, and those unwritten laws which it is an acknowledged shame to break.

"And here is another point. When our work is over, we are in a position to enjoy all kinds of recreation for our spirits. There are various kinds of contests [in poetry, drama, music, and athletics] and sacrifices regularly throughout the year; in our own homes we find a beauty and a good taste which delight us every day and which drive away our cares. Then the greatness of our city brings it about that all the good things from all over the world flow in to us, so that to us it seems just as natural to enjoy foreign goods as our own local products. . . .

"Our love of what is beautiful does not lead to extravagance; our love of the things of the mind does not make us soft. We regard wealth as something to be properly used, rather than as something to boast about. As for poverty, no one need be ashamed to admit it: the real shame is in not taking practical measures to escape from it. Here each individual is interested not only in his own affairs but in the affairs of the state as well: even those who are mostly occupied with their own business are extremely well-informed on general politics—this is a peculiarity of ours: we do not say that a man who takes no interest in politics is a man who minds his own business; we say that he has no business here at all. We Athenians, in our own persons, take our decisions on policy or submit them to proper discussions: for we do not think that there is an incompatibility between words and deeds; the worst thing is to rush into action before the consequences have been properly debated."

Questions for Analysis

1. According to Pericles, what are the chief characteristics of a democratic society?
2. Of what was Pericles most proud regarding Athens?

Thucydides, *History of the Peloponnesian War*, trans. Rex Warner (New York: Penguin Books, 1972), 145–147.

speculated about human nature and justice, and discussed the merits of various forms of government. It is to Greece that we ultimately trace the idea of democracy and all that accompanies it: citizenship, constitutions, equality before the law, government by law, reasoned debate, respect for the individual, and confidence in human intelligence.

Nevertheless, there is a fundamental difference between the Greek concept of liberty and our own. We are concerned with protecting the individual from the state, which we often see as a threat to personal freedom and a hindrance to the pursuit of our personal lives. Identifying the good of the individual with the good of the community, the Greeks were not concerned with erecting safeguards against the state; they did not view the state as an alien force to be feared or to be protected against. Rather, they saw it as a moral association, a second family, which taught proper conduct and enabled them to fulfill their human potential. Given this orientation, they were not much interested in universal human rights.

Pericles: Symbol of Athenian Democracy

Pericles (c. 495–429 B.C.), a gifted statesman, orator, and military commander, was the central figure in Athenian life during the middle of the fifth century. So impressive was his leadership that this period is called the Age of Pericles. During these years, Athenians achieved greatness in politics, drama, sculpture, architecture, and thought.

In the opening stage of the monumental clash with Sparta, the Peloponnesian War (431–404 B.C.), Pericles delivered an oration in honor of the Athenian war casualties (see Primary Source box). The oration, as reconstructed by Thucydides, the great Athenian historian of the fifth century B.C., contains a glowing description of the Athenian democratic ideal, which encompassed both civic and personal freedom. In Athens, he said, the many are not ruled by the few. All citizens share in governing the city.

Throughout the speech, Pericles contrasted the narrow Spartan concept of excellence with the Athenians' humanistic ideal of the full development of the human personality. Unlike Sparta, Athens valued both political freedom and cultural creativity; indeed, as Pericles recognized, freedom released an enormous amount of creative energy, making possible Athens's extraordinary cultural accomplishments. "Our love of what is beautiful does not lead to extravagance, our love of the things of the mind does not make us soft," continued Pericles in praise of Athenian society.[14]

THE DECLINE OF THE CITY-STATES

Although the Greeks shared a common language and culture, they remained divided politically. A determination to preserve city-state sovereignty prevented them from forming a larger political grouping, which might have contained the inter-city warfare that ultimately cost the city-state its vitality and independence. But the creation of a Pan-Hellenic union would have required a radical transformation of the Greek character, which for hundreds of years had regarded the city-state as the only suitable political system.

The Peloponnesian War

Athenian control of the Delian League engendered fear in the Spartans and their allies in the Peloponnesian League. Sparta and the Peloponnesian states decided on war because they felt that a dynamic and imperialistic Athens threatened their independence. At stake for Athens was hegemony over the Delian League, which gave Athens political power and contributed to its economic prosperity. Neither Athens nor Sparta anticipated the catastrophic consequences that the war would have for Greek civilization.

The war began in 431 B.C. and ended in 404 B.C., with a temporary and uneasy interlude of peace from 421 to 414 B.C. Possessing superior land forces, the Peloponnesian League invaded Attica and set fire to the countryside. In 430 B.C., a plague, probably coming from Ethiopia by way of Egypt, ravaged Athens, killing about one-third of the population, including its leader, Pericles (in 429 B.C.). Because of Athenian sea power and Spartan inability to inflict a crushing defeat on Athenian ground troops, the first stage of the war ended in stalemate. In 421 B.C., the war-weary combatants concluded a peace treaty.

What led to the resumption of the war and the eventual defeat of Athens was the

WRESTLERS: RELIEF FROM A STATUE BASE, ATHENIAN, LATE SIXTH CENTURY B.C.
Physical fitness and athletics were highly prized by the Greeks. Poets sang the praise of Olympic champions, and sculptors captured the beauty of athletic physiques for an admiring public. (National Archaeological Museum, Athens, Greece/The Bridgeman Art Library)

Athenian expedition against Sicily and its largest city, Syracuse. Athenians were intoxicated by an imperialist urge to extend the empire in the west and by prospects of riches. Swayed by speeches that stirred the emotions, the Athenian populace, believing disaster to be impossible and forsaking caution and reason, approved the Sicilian venture.

Launched with extravagant expectations, the Sicilian expedition ended in dismal failure. Athens and its allies lost fifty thousand men and two hundred ships in the venture; the expedition also cost Athens all hope of victory in the struggle with Sparta. Fearful that victory in Sicily would increase Athenian manpower and wealth, Sparta in 414 B.C. had again taken up the sword. Strengthened by financial support from Persia and by the defection of some Athenian allies, Sparta moved to end the war. Finally, with its navy decimated and its food supply dwindling, besieged Athens surrendered in 404 B.C. Sparta dissolved the Delian League, left Athens with only a handful of ships, and forced the city to pull down its long walls—ramparts designed to protect it against siege weapons. But the Spartans refused to massacre Athenian men and enslave the women and children, as some allies had urged.

The Peloponnesian War shattered the spiritual foundations of Hellenic society. During the course of the long war, men became brutalized—cities were sacked and captives murdered—selfish individualism triumphed over civic duty, moderation gave way to extremism, and politics degenerated into civil war. Thucydides tells us that civil war which broke out in city after city produced extravagances of revolutionary zeal, expressed by an elaboration in the methods of seizing power and unheard-of-atrocities in revenge. To fit in with the change of events, words too had to change

> their usual meanings. . . . [A]ny idea of moderation was just an attempt to disguise one's unmanly character; ability to understand a question from all sides meant that one was totally unfitted for action. Fanatical enthusiasm was the mark of a real man. . . . Anyone who held violent opinions could always be trusted, and anyone who objected to them became a suspect. . . . Family relations were a weaker tie than party membership, since party members were more ready to go to any extreme for any reason whatever. . . .[15]

The deterioration of Greek political life was exemplified by conflicts between oligarchs and democrats. Oligarchs, generally from the wealthier segments of Greek society, wanted to concentrate power in their own hands by depriving the lower classes of political rights. Democrats, generally from the poorer segment of society, sought to preserve the political rights of adult male citizens. Strife between oligarchs and democrats was quite common in the Greek city-states even before the Peloponnesian War. Both sides sought to dominate the Assembly and to manipulate the courts; both resorted to bribery and at times even assassinated opponents. During the Peloponnesian War, in many cities, including Athens, these party conflicts erupted into savage civil wars marked by fanaticism and vengeance. The moral basis of Hellenic society was wrecked. In the words of Thucydides,

> *Love of power, operating through greed and through personal ambition, was the cause of all these evils. To this must be added the violent fanaticism which came into play once the struggle had broken out. Leaders of parties in professing to serve the public interest . . . were seeking to win the prizes for themselves. In their struggle for ascendancy nothing was barred; terrible indeed were the actions to which they committed themselves, and in taking revenge they went further still. Here they were deterred neither by the claims of justice nor by the interests of the state. . . . Thus neither side had any use for conscientious motives; more interest was shown in those who could produce attractive arguments to justify some disgraceful action. As for the citizens who held moderate views, they were destroyed by both the extreme parties. . . . As the result of these revolutions, there was a general deterioration of character throughout the Greek World.*[16]

Athens shared the political problems of the Greek world during the war. Pericles had provided Athenians with effective leadership in the three decades prior to the war; when the Assembly seemed to support unwise policies, he had won it over with sound arguments. After his death

in 429 B.C., the quality of leadership deteriorated. Succeeding statesmen were motivated more by personal ambition than by civic devotion; instead of soberly examining issues, they supported policies that would gain them popularity. Without Pericles' wise statesmanship, the Assembly at times acted rashly, as it did in the case of the Sicilian expedition.

Taking advantage of the decline in morale after the failure of this expedition, oligarchs gained control of Athens in 411 B.C.; a body of citizens, known as the Four Hundred, wielded power. Seeking to deprive the lower classes of political influence, the Four Hundred restricted citizenship to four thousand men. But the crews of Athenian ships, loyal to democracy, challenged the authority of the Four Hundred, who were forced to flee.

After the defeat of Athens in 404 B.C., oligarchs again gained control, this time with the support of Sparta. A ruling council of thirty men, the so-called Thirty Tyrants, held power. Led by Critias, an extreme antidemocrat, the Thirty Tyrants trampled on Athenian rights, confiscating property and condemning many people to death. In the winter of 404–403 B.C., returned exiles led an uprising against the Thirty Tyrants, who were unseated.

The Fourth Century

The Peloponnesian War was the great crisis of Hellenic history. The golden age of Athenian culture came to an end, and the city-states never fully recovered from their self-inflicted spiritual wounds. The civic loyalty and confidence that had marked the fifth century B.C. waned, and the fourth century was dominated by a new mentality, which the leaders of the Age of Pericles would have abhorred. A concern for private affairs superseded devotion to the general good of the polis. Increasingly, professionals, rather than ordinary citizens, administered the tasks of government, and mercenaries began to replace citizen soldiers.

The political history of the fourth century can be summed up briefly. Athens, the only state that might have united the Greek world, had lost

Profile

Demosthenes

Debates in the Assembly stimulated the development of oratory as an art form in Athens and other city-states. Demosthenes (384–322 B.C.), the greatest of the Greek orators, earned his reputation through disciplined effort, for he was not a naturally gifted speaker. When he first addressed the Assembly, wrote Plutarch, the second-century biographer, he was "derided for his strange and uncouth style, which was cumbered with long sentences and tortured with formal arguments to a most harsh and disagreeable excess. Besides, he had, it seems, a weakness in his voice, a perplexed and indistinct utterance, and a shortness of breath, which, by breaking and disjointing his sentences, much obscured the sense and meaning of what he spoke."[*] But the very determined Demosthenes practiced constantly until he perfected his enunciation and delivery.

Demosthenes' fame rests mainly on his Philippics—speeches delivered over a ten-year period warning Greeks of the threat posed by Philip of Macedon. He urged the city-states of Greece to unite against the common enemy and lamented the deterioration of the Greek character since the heroic struggle against Persia.

> *And we, the Greek community . . . instead of sending embassies to one another about [the danger] and expressing indignation, are in such a miserable state, so intrenched in separate towns, that to this day we can attempt nothing that interest or necessity requires; we cannot combine, or form any association for succour and alliance; we look unconcernedly on the man's growing power, . . . not caring or striving for the salvation of Greece.[φ]*

A passionate patriot, Demosthenes warned his fellow citizens that Philip, an autocratic king, wanted to conquer Athens and put an end to Athenian democracy.

> *There is nothing which [Philip] strives and plots against so much as our constitution, nothing in the world he is so anxious about, as its destruction. . . . First then you must assume that he is an irreconcilable enemy of our constitution and democracy; secondly, you must be convinced that all his operations and contrivances are designed for the injury of our state.[†]*

Demosthenes negotiated an alliance between Thebes and Athens, but the two were defeated by Philip at Chaeronea in 338 B.C. Demosthenes, who witnessed the battle, delivered a funeral oration for the Greek dead, but the speech is lost. After the death of Alexander the Great in 323 B.C., Demosthenes helped organize Greek resistance to Macedonian rule. The Greeks were defeated the following year, and Antipater, the Macedonian governor of Greece, ordered the execution of Demosthenes and other orators who had urged war. The aging orator and passionate patriot took poison.

Demosthenes' speeches served as a model for subsequent orators, including Cicero, Rome's greatest orator. In modern times, patriots and lovers of freedom have evoked Demosthenes' devotion to his city and its free institutions.

---

[*]Plutarch, *The Lives of Noble Grecians and Romans*, trans. John Dryden, rev. A. H. Clough (New York: Modern Library, n.d.), 1025.

[φ]*Demosthenes' Orations*, intro. by John Warrington (London: Dent, Everyman's Library, 1954), Third Philippic, 195–196.

[†]Ibid., Fourth Philippic, 209.

its chance. A culturally sterile, provincial-minded, and heavy-handed Spartan government lacked the talent to govern the Greeks. In many cities, Sparta replaced democratic governments with pro-Spartan oligarchies under the supervision of a Spartan governor. But Spartan hegemony was short-lived; before long, the Greek city-states had thrown off the Spartan yoke. The quarrelsome city-states formed new systems of alliances and persisted in their ruinous conflicts. Some Greek thinkers, recognizing the futility of constant war, argued that peace should be the goal of Greek politics. However, their efforts were in vain.

In addition to wars between city-states, fourth-century Greece experienced a new outbreak of civil wars between rich and poor. Athens largely escaped these ruinous conflicts, but they engulfed many other cities. With good reason, Greek thinkers regarded social discord as the greatest of evils.

While the Greek cities battered one another in fratricidal warfare, a new power was rising in the north—Macedonia. To the Greeks, the Macedonians, a wild mountain people who spoke a Greek dialect and had acquired a sprinkling of Hellenic culture, differed little from other non-Greeks, whom they called barbarians. In 359 B.C., at the age of twenty-three, Philip II (382–336 B.C.) ascended the Macedonian throne. Having spent three years as a hostage in Thebes, Philip had learned the latest military tactics and had witnessed firsthand the weaknesses of the warring Greek states. He converted Macedonia into a first-rate military power and began a drive to become master of the Greeks.

Patient, deceitful, clever, and unscrupulous, Philip gradually extended his power over the Greek city-states. The Greeks did not correctly assess Philip's strength and were slow to organize a coalition against Macedonia, despite the efforts of Demosthenes, the Athenian orator and patriot, who urged the Greeks to unite against this threat to their freedom. In 338 B.C., at Chaeronea, Philip's forces inflicted a decisive defeat on the Greeks, and all of Greece was his. The city-states still existed, but they had lost their independence. The world of the small, independent, self-sufficient polis was drawing to a close, and Greek civilization was taking a different shape.

THE DILEMMA OF GREEK POLITICS

Philip's conquest of the city-states points to fundamental weaknesses of Greek politics. Despite the internal crisis and persistent warfare, the Greeks were unable to fashion any other political framework than the polis. The city-state was fast becoming an anachronism, but the Greeks were unable to see that, in a world moving toward larger states and empires, the small city-state could not compete. An unallied city-state, with its small citizen army, could not withstand the powerful military machine that Philip had created. A challenge confronted the city-states: the need to shape some form of political union, a Pan-Hellenic federation, that would end the suicidal internecine warfare, promote economic well-being, and protect the Greek world from hostile states. Because they could not respond creatively to this challenge, the city-states ultimately lost their independence to foreign conquerors. Learning from the Greek experience, after the American Revolution the Founding Fathers sought to establish a central government strong enough to prevent warfare between the states. Moreover, if the American states remained a weak and disunited assortment of republics, they could lose their independence to a foreign power, duplicating the experience of the Greek city-states with Macedonia.

The waning of civic responsibility among the citizens was another reason for the decline of the city-states. The vitality of the city-state depended on the willingness of its citizens to put aside private concerns for the good of the community. However, although Athens had recovered commercially from the Peloponnesian War, its citizens had suffered a permanent change in character; the abiding devotion to the polis, which had distinguished the Age of Pericles, greatly diminished during the fourth century. The factional strife, the degeneration of politics into personal ambition, the demagoguery, and the fanaticism that Thucydides had described persisted into the fourth century and were aggravated by the economic discontent of the poor. The Periclean ideal of citizenship dissipated as Athenians neglected the community to concentrate on private affairs or sought to derive personal profit from public office. The decline in civic responsibility could be seen in the hiring of mercenaries to replace citizen soldiers and in the indifference and hesitancy with which the Athenians confronted Philip. The Greeks did not respond to the Macedonian threat as they had earlier rallied to fight off the Persian menace because the quality of citizenship had deteriorated.

Greek political life demonstrated the best and the worst features of freedom. On the one hand, as Pericles boasted, freedom encouraged active citizenship, reasoned debate, and government by law. On the other hand, as Thucydides lamented, freedom could degenerate into factionalism, demagoguery, unbridled self-interest, and civil war. Because monarchy deprives people of freedom and self-rule, the Greeks regarded monarchy as a form of government appropriate for uncivilized barbarians. Nevertheless, their political experience showed that free men in a democracy are susceptible to demagogues, will base political decisions on keyed-up emotions rather than on cool reasoning, and are capable of behaving brutally toward political opponents. Moreover, Greek democracy, which valued freedom, was unable to overcome a weakness that has afflicted despotic rulers: an incautious attitude toward power that causes the state to overreach itself. Such an attitude demonstrated a self-destructive **hubris**, excessive pride or arrogance, which Greek moralists warned against. This is how Thucydides interpreted Athens's disastrous Sicilian expedition during the Peloponnesian War. Driven by a mad passion to possess what was beyond their reach, the Athenians brought ruin to their city.

The Athenians, who saw no conflict between imperialism and democracy, considered it natural for stronger states to dominate weaker ones, an attitude that helped precipitate the destructive Peloponnesian War. A particularly egregious example of this outlook occurred during that war when Athenians decided to invade the island of Melos despite the assurances of the Melians that they represented no threat to Athens. As reported by Thucydides, the Athenian envoys told the Melians that "the strong do what they have the power to do, and the weak accept what they have to accept."[17] When the Melians resisted, the Athenians slaughtered the men, enslaved the women and children, and colonized the territory.

Greek politics also revealed both the capabilities and the limitations of reason. Originally, the polis was conceived as a divine institution in which the citizen had a religious obligation to obey the law. As the rational and secular outlook became more pervasive, the gods lost their authority. When people no longer regarded law as an expression of sacred traditions ordained by the gods but saw it as a merely human contrivance, respect for the law diminished, weakening the foundations of the society. The results were party conflicts, politicians who scrambled for personal power, and moral uncertainty. Recognizing the danger, conservatives insisted that law must again be conceived as issuing from the gods and that the city must again treat its ancient traditions with reverence. Although the Greeks originated the lofty ideal that human beings could regulate their political life according to reason, their history, marred by intercity warfare and internal violence, demonstrates the extreme difficulties involved in creating and maintaining a rational society.

❖   ❖   ❖

NOTES

1. James Shiel, ed., *Greek Thought and the Rise of Christianity* (New York: Barnes and Noble, 1968), 5–6.

2. Homer, *The Iliad*, trans. E. V. Rieu (Baltimore: Penguin Books, 1950), 23.

3. H. D. F. Kitto, *The Greeks* (Baltimore: Penguin Books, 1957), 60.

4. Homer, *The Iliad*, 405.

5. Werner Jaeger, *Paideia: The Ideals of Greek Culture*, trans. Gilbert Highet (New York: Oxford University Press, 1945), 1:8.

6. C. M. Bowra, *Homer* (London: Gerald Duckworth, 1972), 72.

7. Kitto, *The Greeks*, 78.

8. Mason Hammond, *The City in the Ancient World* (Cambridge, Mass.: Harvard University Press, 1972), 189.

9. Herodotus, *The Histories*, trans. Aubrey de Sélincourt (Baltimore: Penguin Books, 1954), 350.

10. Ibid., 493.

11. Aristotle, *Politics*, in *Basic Works of Aristotle*, ed. Richard McKeon (New York: Random House, 1941), 1132.

12. A. H. M. Jones, *Athenian Democracy* (Oxford: Basil Blackwell, 1969), 132–133.

13. Mario Attilio Levi, *Political Power in the Ancient World* (New York: Mentor Books, 1968), 122–123.

14. Thucydides, *History of the Peloponnesian War*, trans. Rex Warner (Baltimore: Penguin Books, 1954), 147.

15. Ibid., 242–243.

16. Ibid., 243–244.

17. Ibid., 402.

Chapter 4

Greek Thought:
From Myth to Reason

Theater at Epidaurus, Greece, c. 350 B.C. (©DUSAN ZIDAR/Shutterstock.com)

- **Philosophy**
- **Art**
- **Poetry and Drama**
- **History**
- **The Greek Achievement: Reason, Freedom, Humanism**

Focus Questions

1. How did the Pre-Socratic thinkers make the transition from myth to reason?
2. How did the Sophists and Socrates advance the tradition of reason and humanism?
3. Why is Plato's *Republic* considered a milestone in the emergence of political thought?
4. What do Plato and Aristotle have in common? How do they differ?
5. How did Greek drama, art, and historiography contribute to the tradition of reason and humanism?
6. Why is ancient Greek civilization considered a cornerstone of the Western tradition?

The Greeks broke with the mythopoeic outlook of the Near East and conceived a new way of viewing nature and human society, which is the basis of the Western scientific and philosophical tradition. After an initial period of mythical thinking, by the fifth century B.C. the Greek mind had gradually applied reason to the physical world and to all human activities. This emphasis on reason marks a turning point for human civilization.

The development of rational thought in Greece was a process, a trend, not a finished achievement. The process began when some thinkers rejected mythical explanations for natural phenomena. The nonphilosophical majority never entirely eliminated the language, attitudes, and beliefs of myth from their lives and thought. For them, the world remained controlled by divine forces, which were appeased through cultic practices. Even in the mature **philosophy** of Plato and Aristotle, mythical modes of thought persisted. What is of immense historical importance, however, is not the degree to which the Greeks successfully integrated the norm of reason, but the fact that they originated this norm, defined it, and consciously applied it to their intellectual and social life.

PHILOSOPHY

The first theoretical philosophers in human history emerged in the sixth century B.C., in the Greek cities of Ionia in Asia Minor. Curious about the essential composition of nature and dissatisfied with earlier creation legends, the Ionians sought physical, rather than mythic-religious, explanations for natural occurrences. In the process, they arrived at a new concept of nature and a new method of inquiry. They maintained that nature was not manipulated by arbitrary and willful gods, nor was it governed by blind chance. The Ionians said that there is an intelligible pattern to nature; that nature contains a hidden structure—principles of order or general laws—that governs phenomena; and that these fundamental rules were ascertainable by the human mind. They implied that the origin, composition, and structure of the world can be investigated rationally and systematically. Thus, in seeking to account for rainbows, earthquakes, and eclipses, the Ionians posited entirely naturalistic explanations that relied on observation, had an awareness of cause and effect, and excluded the gods. This new outlook marks the beginning of scientific thought.

What conditions enabled the Greeks to make this breakthrough? Perhaps their familiarity with Near Eastern achievements in mathematics and science stimulated their ideas. But this influence should not be exaggerated, says Greek scholar John N. Theodorakopoulos, for Egyptians and Mesopotamians "had only mythological systems of belief and a knowledge of practical matters. They did not possess those pure and crystal clear products of the intellect which we call science and philosophy. Nor did they have any terminology to describe them."[1] Rooted in mythological thinking, the ancient Near East experienced no eruption of theorizing about nature in pristine philosophical and scientific terms as Greece did beginning in the sixth century B.C. Perhaps the poets' conception of human behavior as subject to universal destiny was extended into the philosophers' belief that nature was governed by law. Perhaps the breakthrough was fostered by the Greeks' freedom from a priesthood and rigid religious doctrines that limit thought. Or perhaps Greek speculative thought was an offspring of the city, because if law governed human affairs, providing balance and order, should not the universe also be regulated by principles of order?

The Cosmologists: A Rational Inquiry into Nature

The first Ionian philosophers are called cosmologists because they sought to discover the underlying principles of the universe: how nature came to be the way it was. They held that some single, eternal, and imperishable substance, which underwent various modifications, gave rise to all phenomena in nature.

Ionian philosophy began with Thales (C. 624–548 B.C.) of Miletus, a city in Ionia. He was a contemporary of Solon of Athens and concerned himself with understanding the order of nature. Thales said that water was the basic element, the underlying substratum of nature, and that through some natural process—similar to the formation of ice or steam—water gave rise to everything else in the world.

Thales revolutionized thought because he omitted the gods from his account of the origins of nature and searched for a natural explanation of how all things came to be. He broke with the commonly held belief that earthquakes were caused by Poseidon, god of the sea, and offered instead a naturalistic explanation for these disturbances: that the earth floated on water and when the water experienced turbulent waves, the earth was rocked by earthquakes. Thales was the first person to predict an eclipse of the sun. To do this, he had to dismiss traditional mythical explanations and to grasp a crucial scientific principle—that heavenly objects move in regular patterns, which can be known.

Anaximander (C. 611–547 B.C.), another sixth-century Ionian, rejected Thales' theory that water was the original substance. He rejected any specific substance and suggested that an indefinite, undifferentiated substance, which he called the Boundless, was the source of all things. He believed that from this primary mass, which contained the powers of heat and cold, there gradually emerged a nucleus, the seed of the world. According to Anaximander, the cold and wet condensed to form the earth and its cloud cover, while the hot and dry formed the rings of fire that we see as the moon, the sun, and the stars. The heat from the fire in the sky dried the earth and shrank the seas. From the warm slime on earth arose life, and from the first sea creatures there evolved land animals, including human beings. Anaximander's account of the origins of the universe and nature understandably contained fantastic elements. Nevertheless, by offering a natural explanation for the origin of nature and life and by holding that nature was lawful, it surpassed the creation myths.

Like his fellow Ionians, Anaximenes, who died around 525 B.C., made the transition from myth to reason. He also maintained that a primary substance, air, underlay reality and accounted for nature's orderliness. Air that was rarefied became fire, whereas wind and clouds were formed from condensed air. If the process of condensation continued, it produced water, earth, and eventually stones. Anaximenes also rejected the old belief that a rainbow was the goddess Iris; instead, he saw it as the consequence of the sun's rays falling on dense air.

The Ionians have been called matter philosophers because they held that everything issued from a particular material substance. Other sixth-century B.C. thinkers tried a different approach. Pythagoras (C. 580–507 B.C.) and his followers, who lived in the Greek cities in southern Italy, found the nature of things not in a particular substance but in mathematical relationships. The Pythagoreans discovered that the intervals in the musical scale can be expressed mathematically. Extending this principle of structure and proportion found in sound to the universe at large, they concluded that the cosmos also contained an inherent mathematical order and harmony. Thus, the Pythagoreans shifted the emphasis from matter to form, from the world of sense perception to the logic of mathematics. The Pythagoreans were also religious mystics who believed in the immortality and transmigration of souls. Consequently, they refused to eat animal flesh, fearing that it contained former human souls.

Parmenides (C. 515–450 B.C.), a native of the Greek city of Elea in southern Italy, argued that the fundamental view of the Ionians that the universe underwent change and development over time was utterly mistaken. In developing his position, Parmenides applied to philosophical argument the **logic** used by the Pythagoreans for mathematical thinking. In putting forth the proposition that an argument must be consistent and contain no contradictions, Parmenides became the founder of formal logic.

Despite appearances, asserted Parmenides, reality—the cosmos and all that is within it—is one, eternal, and unchanging. It is made known not through the senses, which are misleading, but through the mind; not through experience, but through reason. Truth could be reached through abstract thought alone. Parmenides' concept of an unchanging reality apprehended by thought alone influenced Plato and is the foundation of **metaphysics**—the branch of philosophy that attempts to define ultimate reality, or Being.

Parmenides' thought also had religious implications. Although he did not refer to True Being as God, he did ascribe to it the attributes of oneness, transcendence, permanence, and perfection. Such a description of Being abounds with religious meaning. Particularly as developed by Plato, the quest for Being would greatly influence religious thought, including Christian theology, in the ancient world.

Democritus (C. 460–370 B.C.), from the Greek mainland, renewed the Ionians' concern with the world of matter and reaffirmed their confidence in knowledge derived from sense perception—and the senses indicated that change did occur in nature, in contrast to Parmenides' view. But Democritus also retained Parmenides' reverence for reason. His model of the universe consisted of two fundamental realities: empty space and an infinite number of atoms. Eternal, indivisible, and imperceptible, these atoms moved in the void. All things consisted of atoms, and combinations of atoms accounted for all change in nature. In a world of colliding atoms, everything behaved according to mechanical principles. (Of course, Democritus' atomic theory did not derive from any empirical evidence of atoms but was purely speculative.)

Concepts essential to scientific thought thus emerged in embryonic form with Greek philosophers: physical laws operate in nature and understanding them requires natural explanations (Ionians), the mathematical order of nature (Pythagoras), logical proof (Parmenides), and the mechanical structure of the universe (Democritus). By giving to nature a rational, rather than a mythical, foundation and by holding that theories should be grounded in evidence and that one should be able to defend them logically, the early Greek philosophers pushed thought in a new direction. This new approach allowed a critical analysis of theories, whereas myths, accepted unconditionally on faith and authority, did not promote discussion and questioning. Greek thinkers established the crucial principle that a proposition is not considered true unless it can be supported by logic or empirical evidence. For the most part, the early Greek philosophers rejected the old mythical explanations of nature. Nevertheless, when they proclaimed the unity and orderliness of nature and asserted that an ultimate reality underlies the finite world, they were also expressing ideas integral to religious thought.

Porch of the Maidens, Attic Sculpture from the Acropolis. The architect has incorporated the human form as a functional element in a rationally organized structure. The balance and harmony of the Porch of the Maidens weds humanity with art. (Vanni Archive/Art Resource, N.Y.)

These early philosophers made possible theoretical thinking and the systematization of knowledge—as distinct from the mere observation and collection of data. The disciplined acquisition and structuring of knowledge extended into several areas. Greek mathematicians, for example, organized the Egyptians' practical experience with land measurements into the logical and coherent science of geometry, in which each statement followed logically from given assumptions. They established mathematics as a body of theoretical knowledge, an ordered system based on fundamental premises and necessary connections, and they developed logical procedures for arriving at mathematical proofs. Both Babylonians and Egyptians had performed fairly complex mathematical operations, but unlike the Greeks, they made no attempt to prove underlying mathematical principles—to demonstrate that certain conclusions must flow from

certain hypotheses. In another area, Babylonian priests observed the heavens for religious reasons, believing that the stars revealed the wishes of the gods. The Greeks used the data collected by the Babylonians, but not for a religious purpose; rather, they sought to discover the geometrical laws that govern the motions of heavenly bodies.

A parallel development occurred in medicine. No Near Eastern medical text explicitly attacked magical beliefs and practices. In contrast, Greek doctors, because of the philosophers' work, were able to distinguish between magic and medicine. The school of the Greek physician Hippocrates (c. 460–c. 377 B.C.), located on the island of Cos, off the Asia Minor coast, was influenced by the thought of the early Greek cosmologists. Hippocratic physicians recorded in detail their observations of ill patients, classified symptoms, and predicted the future course of the disease. They also ruled out supernatural and magical explanations and cures. The following tract from the school of Hippocrates on epilepsy, which was considered a sacred disease, illustrates the development of a scientific approach to medicine.

> *I am about to discuss the disease called "sacred." It is not, in my opinion, any more divine or more sacred than any other disease, but has a natural cause, and its supposed divine origin is due to men's inexperience, and to their wonder at its peculiar character. Now . . . men continue to believe in its divine origin because they are at a loss to understand it. . . . My own view is that those who first attributed a sacred character to this malady were like the magicians, purifiers, charlatans, and quacks of our own day; men who claim great piety and superior knowledge. Being at a loss, and having no treatment which would help, they concealed and sheltered themselves behind superstition, and called this illness sacred, in order that their utter ignorance might not be manifest.*[2]

The Sophists: A Rational Investigation of Human Society

In their effort to understand the external world, the cosmologists had created the tools of reason. These early Greek thinkers were developing a new and profound awareness of the mind's capacity for theoretical thinking. And equally important, they were establishing the mind's autonomy—its ability to inquire into any subject, relying solely on its own power to think. Greek thinkers then turned away from the world of nature and attempted a rational investigation of people and society, dismissing efforts to explain the social world through inherited beliefs about the gods. The Sophists exemplified this shift in focus. They were professional teachers who wandered from city to city teaching rhetoric, grammar, poetry, gymnastics, mathematics, and music. The Sophists insisted that it was futile to speculate about the first principles of the universe, for such knowledge was beyond the grasp of the human mind. Instead, they urged that individuals improve themselves and their cities by applying

reason to the tasks of citizenship and statesmanship. The Western **humanist** tradition owes much to the Sophists who examined, at times with great insight, political and ethical concerns, cultivated the minds of their students, and invented formal secular education.

The Sophists answered a practical need in Athens, which had been transformed into a wealthy and dynamic imperial state after the Persian Wars. Because the Sophists claimed that they could teach *political* aretē—the skill to formulate the right laws and policies for cities and the art of eloquence and persuasion needed for success in public life—they were sought as tutors by politically ambitious young men, especially in Athens.

Traditionally, the Greeks had drawn a sharp distinction between Greeks, the bearers of an enlightened civilization, and uncivilized and immoderate non-Greeks, whom they called barbarians, and held that some people were slaves by nature. The dramatist Euripides expressed these sentiments: "It is natural for Hellenes to rule barbarians and not . . . for barbarians to rule Hellenes. They are a slave race, Hellenes are free."[3] Some Sophists in the fourth century B.C. arrived at a broader conception of humanity. They asserted that slavery was based on force or chance, that people were not slaves or masters by nature, and indeed that all people, Greek and non-Greek, were fundamentally alike.

The Sophists were philosophical **relativists**— that is, they held that no truth is universally valid. Protagoras, a fifth-century Sophist, said that "man is the measure of all things." By this he meant that good and evil, truth and falsehood, are matters of community and individual judgment; there are no universal standards that fit all people at all times. Human laws and ethical beliefs have evolved according to a particular community's needs; they are simply human contrivances and conventions, not objective truths or standards written into nature. While not based on moral absolutes, hopefully the city's laws derive from the judgment of wise and good men.

In applying reason critically to human affairs, the Sophists challenged the traditional religious and moral values of Athenian society. Some Sophists taught that speculation about the divine was useless. Others went further, asserting that religion was just a human invention to ensure obedience to traditions and laws. Thus, the Sophist Critias (c. 480–403 B.C.) argued that to deter people from committing "open crimes of violence, . . . a wise and clever man invented fear (of the gods) for mortals, that there might be some means of frightening the wicked, even if they do anything or say or think it in secret. Hence he introduced the Divine (religion), saying that there is a God flourishing with immortal life, . . . who will hear everything said among mortals, and will be able to see all that is done."[4]

The Sophists also applied reason to law, with the same effect: the undermining of traditional authority. The laws of a given city, they asserted, did not derive from the gods; nor were they based on any objective, universal, and timeless standards of justice and good, for such standards did not exist. Each community determined for itself what was good or bad, just or unjust. Beginning with this premise, some Sophists simply urged that laws be changed to meet new circumstances. Some radical Sophists argued that law was merely something made by the most powerful citizens for their own benefit. (Or they said that law was a clever invention of the weak in order to check the strong, who benefited from natural advantages.) This view had dangerous implications: first, law did not need to be obeyed since it rested on no higher principle than might; and second, the strong should do what they have the power to do, and the weak must accept what they cannot resist. Both interpretations were disruptive of community life, for they stressed the selfish interests of the individual over the general welfare of the city.

Some Sophists combined this assault on law with an attack on the ancient Athenian idea of **sophrosyne**—moderation and self-discipline— because it denied human instincts. Instead of moderation, they urged that individuals should maximize pleasure and trample underfoot the traditions that restricted them from fully expressing their desires. As these radical Sophists saw it, the concept of sophrosyne was invented by the weak to enslave nobler natures.

In subjecting traditions to the critique of reason, the radical Sophists triggered an intellectual and spiritual crisis. Their doctrines encouraged loss of respect for authority, disobedience to law, neglect of civic duty, and selfish individualism. These attitudes became widespread during and after the Peloponnesian War, dangerously weakening community bonds.

Socrates: The Rational Individual

In attempting to comprehend nature, the cosmologists had discovered theoretical reason. The Sophists then applied theoretical reason to society. In the process, they created a profound problem for Athens and other city-states: the need to restore the authority of law and a respect for moral values. Conservatives argued that the only way to do so was by renewing allegiance to the sacred traditions that the Sophists had undermined.

Socrates, one of the most extraordinary figures in the history of Western civilization, took a different position. Born in Athens, probably in 469 B.C., about ten years after the Persian Wars, he was executed in 399 B.C., five years after the end of the Peloponnesian War. His life spanned the glory years of Greece, when Athenian culture and democracy were at their height, as well as the tragic years of the lengthy and shattering war with Sparta.

Both the Sophists and Socrates continued the tradition of reason initiated by the cosmologists, but unlike the cosmologists, both felt that knowledge of the individual and society was more important than knowledge of nature. For both, the old mythological traditions, which had served as a foundation for religion and morality, were no longer valid. Socrates and the Sophists endeavored to improve the individual and thought that this could be accomplished through education. Despite these similarities, Socrates' teaching marks a profound break with the Sophist movement.

Socrates attacked the Sophists' relativism, holding that people should regulate their behavior in accordance with universal values. As he saw it, the Sophists taught oratorical and debating skills but had no insights into questions that really mattered: What is the purpose of life? What are the values by which man should live? How does man perfect his character? Here the Sophists failed, said Socrates; they taught the ambitious to succeed in politics, but persuasive oratory and clever reasoning—cunning Sophists taught how to argue an issue from both sides—do not instruct a man in the art of living. He felt that the Sophists had attacked the old system of beliefs but had not provided the individual with a satisfactory replacement.

Socrates' central concern was the perfection of individual human character, the achievement of moral excellence. Moral values, for Socrates, did not derive either from a transcendent God, as they did for the Hebrews, or from an inherited mythic-religious tradition. They were attained when the individual regulated his life according to objective standards arrived at through rigorous rational reflection: that is, when reason became the formative, guiding, and ruling agency of the soul. For Socrates, true education meant the shaping of character according to values discovered through the active use of reason.

Socrates wanted to subject all human beliefs and behavior to the scrutiny of reason and in this way remove ethics from the realm of authority, tradition, dogma, superstition, and myth. He believed that reason was the only proper guide to the most crucial problem of human existence: the question of good and evil. Socrates taught that rational inquiry—a questioning mind—was a priceless tool, allowing one to test opinions, weigh the merit of ideas, and alter beliefs on the basis of knowledge. To Socrates, when people engaged in critical self-examination and strove tirelessly to perfect their nature, they liberated themselves from prevailing opinions and conventions and based their conduct on convictions that they could rationally defend. Socrates believed that people with questioning minds could not be swayed by sophistic eloquence or delude themselves into thinking that they knew something when they really did not. Thus for Socrates, philosophy, with its analyses, questioning, and arguments, was not simply an intellectual exercise. Rather it was a way of life that enabled individuals to acquire the wisdom needed to achieve virtue and the good life. His famous words, "the unexamined life is not worth living," aptly expressed this outlook. And Socrates himself made a powerful personal commitment to this conception of philosophy.

Socrates' fundamental premise was that wrong thinking resulted in wrongdoing and, conversely, that knowledge of what is right gave one the strength of will to do what is right. Critics, including religious thinkers, have castigated this assumption as naïve, arguing that Socrates credited others with his own extraordinary inner strength and underestimated the immense power of instinct and passions, which drive people, even those who know better, to do what is wrong.

Dialectics. In urging Athenians to think rationally about the problems of human existence, Socrates offered no systematic ethical theory, no list of ethical precepts. What he did supply was a method of inquiry called **dialectics**, or logical discussion. As Socrates used it, a dialectical exchange between individuals (or with oneself), a *dialogue*, was the essential source of knowledge. It forced people out of their apathy and smugness and made them aware of their ignorance. It compelled them to examine their thoughts critically; confront illogical, inconsistent, dogmatic, and imprecise assertions; and express their ideas in clearly defined terms.

Dialectics affirmed that the acquisition of knowledge was a creative act. The human mind could not be coerced into knowing; it was not a passive vessel into which a teacher poured knowledge. The dialogue compelled the individual to play an active role in acquiring ideas and values by which to live. In a dialogue, individuals became thinking participants in a quest for knowledge. Through relentless cross-examination, Socrates induced his partner in discourse to explain and justify his opinions rationally, for only thus did knowledge become a part of one's being.

Dialogue implied that reason was meant to be used in relations between human beings and that they could learn from each other, help each other, teach each other, and improve each other. It implied further that the human mind could and should make rational choices. To deal rationally with oneself and with others is the distinctive mark of being human. Through the dialectical method, people could make ethical choices, impose rules on themselves, and give form to their existence.

For Socrates, the highest form of excellence was taking control of one's life and shaping it according to ethical values reached through reflection. The good life, the moral life, is attained by the exercise of reason; by rationally examining one's own thoughts and behavior and that of others—this precept that virtue requires knowledge is the essence of Socratic teaching. Socrates made the individual the center of the universe, reason central to the individual, and moral worth

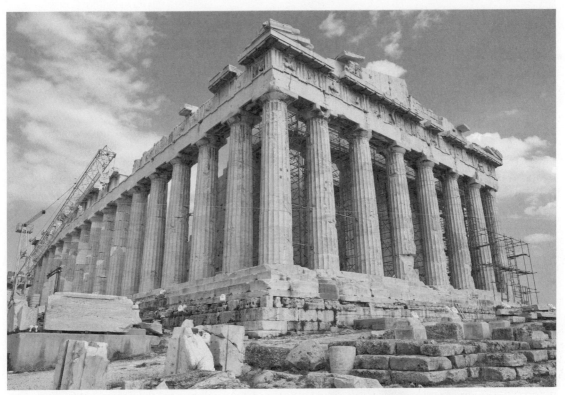

THE PARTHENON, ATHENS, 447–432 B.C. A masterpiece of the Doric style, the great temple dedicated to Athena Parthenos (the Maiden), the patron goddess of the city, was constructed through the efforts of Pericles. Its cult statue and the sculptural reliefs under its roofline were designed by the outstanding sculptor of the age, Phidias. In post-Hellenistic times, it served as a Christian church and then as a mosque, until it was destroyed in 1687. Between 1801 and 1812, the marble reliefs were removed by the Englishman Lord Elgin and now reside in the British Museum, in London. (©brannend/Shutterstock.com.)

the central aim of human life. In Socrates, Greek humanism found its highest expression.

Condemned to Death. Socrates devoted much of his life to what he believed was his mission: pricking the conscience of complacent Athenians and persuading them to think critically about how they lived their lives. "No greater good can happen to a man than to discuss human excellence every day,"[5] he said. Always self-controlled and never raising his voice in anger, Socrates engaged any willing Athenian in conversation about his values. Unlike the Sophists, who were paid professional teachers, Socrates never accepted a fee

for his instruction. Through probing questions, he tried to stir people out of their complacency and make them realize how directionless and purposeless their lives were.

For many years, Socrates challenged Athenians without suffering harm, for Athens was generally distinguished by its freedom of speech and thought. In the uncertain times during and immediately after the Peloponnesian War, however, Socrates made enemies. Several of the young men close to him were antidemocrats still mistrusted by some as a threat to the recently restored democracy. When Socrates was seventy, he was accused of corrupting the youth of the city and of

PHILOSOPHER (STATUETTE), C. 280 B.C. Greek artists were the first to excel in realistic portraiture. The philosopher is neither a divinely inspired seer nor a divine king, but a person in quest of knowledge. (Image copyright © The Metropolitan Museum of Art. Image source: Art Resource, N.Y.)

not believing in the city's gods but in other, new divinities. Underlying these accusations was the fear that Socrates was a troublemaker, a subversive, a Sophist who threatened the state by subjecting its ancient and sacred values to the critique of thought.

Socrates denied the charges and conducted himself with great dignity at his trial, refusing to grovel and beg forgiveness. Instead, he defined his creed:

> If you think that a man of any worth at all ought to . . . think of anything but whether he is acting justly or unjustly, and as a good or a bad man would act, you are mistaken. . . . If you were therefore to say to me, "Socrates, . . . we will let you go, but on the condition that you give up this investigation of yours, and philosophy. If you are found following these pursuits again you shall die." I say, if you offered to let me go on these terms, I should reply: . . . As long as I have breath and strength I will not give up philosophy and exhorting you and declaring the truth to every one of you whom I meet, saying, as I am accustomed, "My good friend, you are a citizen of Athens. . . . Are you not ashamed of caring so much for making of money and for fame and prestige, when you neither think nor care about wisdom and truth and the improvement of your soul?"[6]

Convicted by an Athenian court, Socrates was ordered to drink poison. Had he attempted to appease the jurors, he probably would have been given a light punishment, but he would not disobey the commands of his conscience and alter his principles even under threat of death. Socrates' friends wanted to arrange his escape from prison, but he refused, for this would mean violating the city's laws—an act he considered unconscionable.

Socrates did not write down his philosophy and beliefs. We are able to construct a coherent account of his life and ideals largely through the works of his most important disciple, Plato.

Plato: The Rational Society

Plato (C. 429–347 B.C.) used his master's teachings to create a comprehensive system of philosophy, which embraced both the world of nature and the social world. But Plato had a more ambitious goal than Socrates' moral reformation of the individual. He tried to arrange political life according to rational rules and held that Socrates' quest for personal morality could not succeed unless the community was also transformed on the basis of reason. In effect, Plato wanted to establish standards of thought and behavior for a city torn by moral and intellectual uncertainty. Many of the problems discussed by Western philosophers for the past two millennia were first raised by Plato. We focus on two of his principal concerns, the theory of Ideas and the theory of the just state.

Theory of Ideas. Socrates had taught that universal standards of right and justice exist and are arrived at through thought. Building on the insights of his teacher Socrates and of Parmenides, who said that reality is known only through the mind, Plato postulated the existence of a higher world of reality, independent of the world of things that we experience every day. This higher reality, he said, is the realm of Ideas, or Forms—unchanging, eternal, absolute, and universal standards of beauty, goodness, justice, and truth. To live in accordance with these everlasting standards constitutes the good life; to know these Forms is to grasp ultimate truth.

Truth resides in this world of Forms and not in the world made known through the senses. For example, a person can never draw a perfect square, but the properties of a perfect square exist in the world of Forms. Also, a sculptor observes many bodies, and they all possess some flaw; in his mind's eye, he tries to penetrate the world of Ideas and to reproduce with art a perfect body. Again, the ordinary person only forms an opinion of what beauty is from observing beautiful things; the philosopher, aspiring to true knowledge, goes beyond what he sees and tries to grasp with his mind the Idea of beauty. Similarly, the ordinary individual has only a superficial understanding of justice or goodness; a true conception of justice or goodness is available only to the philosopher, whose mind can leap from worldly particulars to an ideal world beyond space and time.

Plato saw the world of phenomena as unstable, transitory, and imperfect, whereas his transcendent realm of Ideas was eternal and universally valid. For him, true wisdom was to be obtained through knowledge of the Ideas, not the imperfect reflections of the Ideas perceived with the senses.

A champion of reason, Plato aspired to study human life and arrange it according to universally valid standards. In contrast to Sophist relativism, he maintained that objective and eternal standards do exist. Although Plato advocated the life of reason and wanted to organize society according to rational rules, his writing also reveals a religious-mystical side. At times, Plato seems like a mystic seeking to escape from this world into a higher reality, a realm that is without earth's evil and injustice.

Because Platonism is a two-world philosophy, which believes in a higher world as the source of values and in the soul's immortality, it has had an important effect on religious thought. Christian (as well as Jewish and Muslim) thinkers could harmonize Plato's stress on a higher nonmaterial reality and an immortal soul with their faith. In subsequent chapters, we examine the influence of Platonic otherworldliness on later philosopher-mystics and Christian thinkers.

The Just State. In adapting the rational legacy of Greek philosophy to politics, Plato constructed a comprehensive political theory. What the Greeks had achieved in practice—the movement away from mythic and theocratic politics—Plato accomplished on the level of thought: the fashioning of a rational model of the state.

Like Socrates, Plato attempted to resolve the problem caused by the radical Sophists: the undermining of traditional values. Socrates tried to dispel this spiritual crisis through a moral transformation of the individual, whereas Plato wanted the entire community to conform to rational principles. Plato said that if human beings are to live an ethical life, they must do so as citizens of a just and rational state. In an unjust state, people cannot achieve Socratic wisdom, for their souls will mirror the state's wickedness.

Plato had experienced the ruinous Peloponnesian War and the accompanying political turmoil. He saw Athens undergo one political crisis after another; most shocking of all, he had witnessed Socrates' trial and execution. Disillusioned by the corruption of Athenian morality and politics, Plato refused to participate in political life. He came to believe that under the Athenian constitution neither the morality of the individual Athenian nor the good of the state could be enhanced and that Athens required moral and political reform founded on Socrates' philosophy.

Like Socrates, and in contrast to the Sophists' relativism, Plato sought permanent truth and moral certainty.

In his great dialogue, *The Republic*, Plato devised an ideal state based on standards that would rescue his native Athens from the evils that had befallen it. *The Republic* attempted to analyze society rationally and to reshape the state so that individuals could fulfill the best within themselves and attain the Socratic goal of moral excellence. For Plato, the just state could not be founded on tradition (because inherited attitudes did not derive from rational standards) or on the doctrine of might being right (a principle taught by radical Sophists and practiced by Athenian statesmen). A just state, for Plato, based its laws on universally valid principles, on absolute moral norms, not on inherited custom; it aimed at the moral improvement of its citizens, not at increasing its power and material possessions. Such a state required leaders distinguished by their wisdom and virtue, rather than by sophistic cleverness and eloquence.

Fundamental to Plato's political theory as formulated in *The Republic* was his criticism of Athenian democracy. An aristocrat by birth and temperament, Plato believed that it was foolish to expect the common man to think intelligently about foreign policy, economics, or other vital matters of state. Yet the common man was permitted to speak in the Assembly, to vote, and to be selected, by lot, for executive office. A second weakness of democracy was that leaders were chosen and followed for nonessential reasons, such as persuasive speech, good looks, wealth, and family background.

A third danger of democracy was that it could degenerate into anarchy, said Plato. Intoxicated by liberty, the citizens of a democracy could lose all sense of balance, self-discipline, and respect for law.

> *The citizens become so sensitive that they resent the slightest application of control as intolerable tyranny, and in their resolve to have no master they end up by disregarding even the law, written or unwritten.*[7]

As liberty leads to license, Plato continued, the democratic society will deteriorate morally.

> *The parent falls into the habit of behaving like the child, and the child like the parent: the father is afraid of his sons, and they show no fear or respect for their parents, in order to assert their freedom. . . . To descend to smaller matters, the schoolmaster timidly flatters his pupils, and the pupils make light of their masters. . . . Generally speaking, the young . . . argue with . . . [their elders] and will not do as they are told; while the old, anxious not to be thought disagreeable tyrants, imitate the young and condescend to enter into their jokes and amusements.*[8]

As the democratic city falls into disorder, a fourth weakness of democracy will become evident. A demagogue—often a wealthy, handsome war hero of noble birth with an ability to stir the multitude with words—will be able to gain power by promising to plunder the rich to benefit the poor. Increasingly, the tyrant throws off all constraints and uses his authority to satisfy his desire for power and possessions. To retain his hold over the state, the tyrant

> *begins by stirring up one war after another, in order that the people may feel their need of a leader, and also be so impoverished by taxation that they will be forced to think of nothing but winning their daily bread, instead of plotting against him.*[9]

Because of these inherent weaknesses of democracy, Plato insisted that Athens could not be saved by more doses of liberty. He believed that Athens would be governed properly only when the wisest people, the philosophers, attained power.

> *Unless either philosophers become kings in their countries or those who are now called kings and rulers come to be sufficiently inspired with a genuine desire for wisdom; unless, that is to say, political power and philosophy meet together . . . there can be no rest from troubles . . . for states, nor yet, as I believe, for all mankind.*[10]

Plato rejected the fundamental principle of Athenian democracy: that the average person is capable of participating sensibly in public affairs. People would not entrust the care of a sick person to just anyone, said Plato, nor would they allow a novice to guide a ship during a storm. Yet in a democracy, amateurs were permitted to run the government and to supervise the education of the young. No wonder Athenian society was disintegrating. Plato felt that these duties should be performed only by the best people in the city, philosophers, who would approach human problems with reason and wisdom derived from knowledge of the world of unchanging and perfect Ideas. Only these possessors of truth would be competent to rule, said Plato. Whereas Socrates believed that all people could base their actions on reason and acquire virtue, Plato maintained that only a few were capable of philosophical wisdom and that these few were the state's natural rulers.

The organization of the state, as formulated in *The Republic*, corresponded to Plato's conception of the individual soul, of human nature. Plato held that the soul had three major capacities: reason (the pursuit of knowledge), spiritedness (self-assertion, courage, ambition), and desire (the "savage many-headed monster" that relishes food, sex, and possessions). In the well-governed soul, spiritedness and desire are guided by reason and knowledge—standards derived from the world of Ideas.

Plato divided people into three groups: those who demonstrated philosophical ability should be rulers; those whose natural bent revealed exceptional courage should be soldiers; and those driven by desire, the great masses, should be producers (tradespeople, artisans, or farmers). In what was a radical departure from the general attitudes of the times, Plato held that men and women should receive the same education and have equal access to all occupations and public positions, including philosopher-ruler.

Plato felt that the entire community must recognize the primacy of the intellect and sought to create a harmonious state in which each individual performed what he or she was best qualified to do and preferred to do. This would be a just state, said Plato, for it would recognize human inequalities and diversities and make the best possible use of them for the entire community. Clearly, this conception of justice was Plato's response to the radical Sophists, who taught that justice

consisted of the right of the strong to rule in their own interest or that justice was doing whatever one desired.

In *The Republic*, philosophers were selected by a rigorous system of education open to all children. Those not demonstrating sufficient intelligence or strength of character were to be weeded out to become workers or warriors, depending on their natural aptitudes. After many years of education and practical military and administrative experience, the philosophers were to be entrusted with political power. If they had been properly educated, the philosopher-rulers would not seek personal wealth or personal power; their only concerns would be pursuing justice and serving the community. To prevent the philosopher-rulers from pursuing their own interests rather than the good of the community, they would not be permitted to own property or to have families. Since the children they sired would come from a community of wives, no one would know which child was his.

The philosophers were to be absolute rulers. Although the people would lose their right to participate in political decisions, they would gain a well-governed state, whose leaders, distinguished by their wisdom, integrity, and sense of responsibility, would seek only the common good. Only thus could the individual and the community achieve well-being.

Plato repudiated the fundamental principles of a free community: the right to participate in government, equality before the law, and checks on leaders' power. Even freedom of thought was denied the great mass of people in Plato's state. Philosopher-rulers would search for truth, but the people were to be told clever stories—"noble lies," Plato called them—to keep them obedient. However, the philosopher-rulers, said Plato, would not be seekers of power or wealth. It would not be in their character as wise and virtuous people, the best products of polis education, to behave like ruthless tyrants.

The purpose of *The Republic* was to warn Athenians that without respect for law, wise leadership, and proper education for the young, their city would continue to degenerate. Plato wanted to rescue the city-state from disintegration by re-creating the community spirit that had vitalized the polis—and he wanted to re-create it not on the basis of mere tradition but on a higher level, with philosophical knowledge. The social and political institutions of Athens, Plato thought, must be reshaped according to permanent and unalterable ideals of truth and justice, and this could be done only when power and wisdom were joined. He aimed to fashion a just individual and a just state by creating conditions that permitted reason to prevail over the appetites, self-interest, and class and party loyalties.

Aristotle: A Synthesis of Greek Thought

Aristotle (384–322 B.C.) stands at the apex of Greek thought because he achieved a creative synthesis of the knowledge and theories of earlier thinkers. Aristotle studied at Plato's Academy for twenty years. Later, he became tutor to young Alexander the Great, the son of Philip of Macedon. Returning to Athens after Alexander had inherited his father's throne, Aristotle founded a school, the Lyceum.

The range of Aristotle's interests and intellect is extraordinary. He was the leading expert of his time in every field of knowledge, with the possible exception of mathematics. Even a partial listing of his works shows the universal character of his mind and his all-consuming passion to understand the worlds of nature and of humankind: *Logic, Physics, On the Heavens, On the Soul, On the Parts of Animals, Metaphysics, Nicomachean Ethics, Politics, Rhetoric, and Poetics.*

Aristotle undertook the monumental task of organizing and systematizing the thought of the Pre-Socratics, Socrates, and Plato. He shared with the natural philosophers a desire to understand the physical universe; he shared with Socrates and Plato the conviction that reason was a person's highest faculty and that the polis was the primary formative institution of Greek life. Out of the myriad of Aristotle's achievements, we discuss only three: his critique of Plato's theory of Ideas, his ethical thought, and his political thought.

Critique of Plato's Theory of Ideas. Like Democritus before him, Aristotle renewed confidence in **sense perception**, for which Plato had little respect; he wanted to swing the pendulum back from Plato's higher world to the material world. Possessing a scientist's curiosity to understand the facts of nature, Aristotle appreciated the world of phenomena, of concrete things. He respected knowledge obtained through the senses, as the following selection from his observations of a hen's embryo shows:

> *With the common hen after three days and three nights there is the first indication of the embryo. . . . Meanwhile the yolk comes into being . . . and, the heart appears, like a speck of blood, in the white of the egg. This point beats and moves as though endowed with life.*[11]

Aristotle retained Plato's stress on universal principles, but he wanted these principles to derive from human experience with the material world. To the practical and empirically minded Aristotle, the Platonic notion of an independent and separate world of Forms beyond space and time seemed contrary to common sense. To comprehend reality, said Aristotle, one should not escape into another world. For him, Plato's two-world philosophy suffered from too much mystery, mysticism, and poetic fancy; moreover, Plato undervalued the world of facts and objects revealed through sight, hearing, and touch, a world that was important to Aristotle. Like Plato, Aristotle desired to comprehend the essence of things and held that understanding universal principles is the ultimate aim of knowledge. But unlike Plato, he did not turn away from the world of things to obtain such knowledge.

For Aristotle, the Forms were not located in a higher world outside and beyond phenomena but existed in things themselves. He said that through human experience with such things as men, horses, and white objects, the essence of man, horse, and whiteness can be discovered through reason; the Form of Man, the Form of Horse, and the Form of Whiteness can be determined. These universals, which apply to all men, all horses, and all white things, were for both Aristotle and Plato the true objects of knowledge. For Plato, these Forms existed independently of particular objects; the Forms for men or horses or whiteness or triangles or temples existed, whether or not representations of these Ideas in the form of material objects were made known to the senses. For Aristotle, however, universal Ideas could not be determined without examination of particular things. Whereas Plato's use of reason tended to stress otherworldliness, Aristotle tried to bring philosophy back to earth.

By holding that certainty in knowledge comes from reason alone and not from the senses, Plato was predisposed toward mathematics and metaphysics—pure thought, which transcends the world of change and material objects. By stressing the importance of knowledge acquired through the rational examination of sense experience, Aristotle favored the development of empirical sciences—physics, biology, zoology, botany, and other disciplines based on the observation and investigation of nature and the recording of data. Aristotle maintained that theory must not conflict with facts and must make them more intelligible and that it was the task of science to arrange facts into a system of knowledge.

Ethical Thought. Like Socrates and Plato, Aristotle believed that a knowledge of **ethics** was possible and that it must be based on reason, for this is what distinguishes human beings from other forms of life. For him, ethical thought derived from a realistic appraisal of human nature and a commonsense attitude toward life. In *Nicomachean Ethics*, he offered this appraisal, as well as a practical guide to proper conduct. The good life, for Aristotle, was the examined life; it meant making intelligent decisions when confronted with specific problems. Individuals could achieve happiness when they exercised the distinctively human trait of reasoning, when they applied their knowledge relevantly to life, and when their behavior was governed by intelligence and not by whim, tradition, or authority.

Aristotle recognized that people are not entirely rational, that the human personality reveals a passionate element, which can never be eradicated or ignored. Aristotle held that surrendering completely to desire meant descending to the level of beasts, but that denying the passions and living as an ascetic was a foolish and unreasonable rejection of human nature. He maintained that by proper training people could learn to regulate their desires. They could achieve moral well-being, or virtue, when they avoided

extremes of behavior and rationally chose the way of moderation, which he defined as the mean between two extremes. For example, in one extreme, some people "become angry at the wrong things, more than is right, and longer, and cannot be appeased until they inflict vengeance or punishment." In the other extreme, foolish and slavish people endure every insult without defending themselves. Between these extremes is "the man who is angry at the right thing and with the right people, and, further as he ought, when he ought, and as long as he ought. . . . The good-tempered man tends to be unperturbed and not to be led by passion."[12] "Nothing in excess" is the key to Aristotle's ethics. Aristotle maintained that children reared and schooled with good habits are more likely to live virtuous lives, that is, to choose the path of moderation and to demonstrate self-mastery.

Aristotle believed that the contemplative life of the philosopher would yield perfect happiness. The pursuit of philosophical wisdom and beauty, he stated, offered "pleasures marvelous for their purity and their enduringness."[13] But Aristotle did not demand more from an individual than human nature would allow. He did not set impossible standards for behavior, recognizing that all persons cannot pursue the life of contemplation, of theoretical inquiry, for some lack sufficient leisure or intelligence. However, by applying reason to human affairs, all individuals could experience a good life.

Political Thought. Aristotle's *Politics* complements his *Ethics*. To live the good life, he said, a person must do so as a member of a political community. Only the polis—the only political order that develops free and equal citizens—would provide people with an opportunity to lead a rational and moral existence, that is, to fulfill their human potential. With this assertion, Aristotle demonstrated a typically Greek attitude. At the very moment when his pupil Alexander the Great was constructing a world-state that unified Greece and Persia, Aristotle defended the traditional system of independent city-states. Indeed, his *Politics* summed up the polis-centered orientation of Hellenic civilization.

Also in typically Greek fashion, Aristotle did not want women to participate in the political life of the city. Unlike Plato, who, in *The Republic*, gave women an equal opportunity with men to become philosopher-rulers, Aristotle, in his *Politics*, put women in an inferior category and maintained that the free male should rule over women. Though Aristotle taught that all human beings share in a rational soul, he felt that women, along with children and slaves, shared in it to a lesser degree.

> *Although the parts of the soul are present in all of them, they are present in different degrees. For the slave has no deliberative faculty at all; the woman has, but it is without authority, and the child has, but it is immature. . . . Clearly, then, moral virtue belongs to all of them; but the temperance of a man and of a woman, or the courage and justice of a man and of a woman, are not, as Socrates maintained, the same; the courage of a man is shown in commanding, of a woman in obeying. . . . All classes must be deemed to have their special attributes, as the poet says of women, "Silence is a woman's glory," but this is not equally the glory of man.*[14]

Like Plato, Aristotle presumed that political life could be rationally understood and intelligently directed. In *Politics*, as in *Ethics*, he adopted a commonsense, practical attitude. He did not aim at utopia but wanted to find the most effective form of government for most men in normal circumstances. Exemplifying the polis outlook, Aristotle held that enhancing the good of the community is nobler and more virtuous than doing good for oneself, however worthy the act.

Aristotle emphasized the importance of the rule of law. He placed his trust in law rather than in individuals, for they are subject to unruly passions. Aristotle recognized that at times laws should be altered, but he recommended great caution; otherwise, people would lose respect for law and legal procedure.

> *For the law has no power to command obedience except that of habit, which can only be given by time, so that a readiness to change from old to new laws enfeebles the power of the law.*[15]

Tyranny and revolution, Aristotle said, can threaten the rule of law and the well-being of the citizen. To prevent revolution, the state must maintain

> *the spirit of obedience to law, more especially in small matters; for transgression creeps in unperceived and at last ruins the state. [This cannot be done] unless the young are trained by habit and education in the spirit of the constitution. [To live as one pleases] is contradictory to the true interests of the state. . . .*
>
> *Men should not think it slavery to live according to the rule of the constitution, for it is their salvation.*[16]

Aristotle held "that the best political community is formed by citizens of the middle class [those with a moderate amount of property], and that those states are likely to be well-administered in which the middle class is large and stronger if possible than the other classes [the wealthy and the poor]." Both the rich, who excel in "beauty, strength, birth, [and] wealth," and the poor, who are "very weak or very much disgraced, [find it] difficult to follow rational principles. Of these two the one sort grow into violence and great criminals, the other into rogues and petty rascals." The rich are unwilling "to submit to authority . . . for when they are boys, by reason of the luxury in which they are brought up, they never learn even at school, the habit of obedience." Consequently, the wealthy "can only rule despotically." On the other hand, the poor "are too degraded to command and must be ruled like slaves."[17] Middle-class citizens are less afflicted by envy than the poor and are more likely than the rich to view their fellow citizens as equals.

ART

The classical age of Greek art spans the years from the end of the Persian Wars (479 B.C.) to the death of Alexander the Great (323 B.C.). During this period, standards were established that would dominate Western art until the emergence of modern art in the late nineteenth century.

Greek art coincided with Greek achievement in all other areas. Like Greek philosophy and politics, it too applied reason to human experience and made the transition from a mythopoeic-religious worldview to a world perceived as orderly and rational. It gradually transformed the supernatural religious themes with which it was at first preoccupied into secular human themes. Classical art was representational—that is, it strove to imitate reality, to represent the objective world realistically, as it appeared to the human eye.

Artists carefully observed nature and human beings and sought to achieve an exact knowledge of human anatomy; they tried to portray accurately the body at rest and in motion. They knew when muscles should be taut or relaxed, one hip lower than the other, the torso and neck slightly twisted—in other words, they succeeded in transforming marble or bronze into a human likeness that seemed alive. In addition to being realistic and naturalistic, Greek art was also idealistic, aspiring to a finer, more perfect representation of what was seen, depicting the essence and form of a thing more truly than it actually appeared. Thus, a Greek statue resembled no specific individual but revealed a flawless human form, without wrinkles, warts, scars, or other imperfections.

In achieving an accurate representation of objects and in holding that there were rules of beauty that the mind could discover, the Greek artist employed an approach consistent with the new scientific outlook. The Greek temple, for example, is an organized unity obeying nature's laws of equilibrium and harmony; classical sculpture captures the basic laws that govern life in motion. Such art, based on reason, which draws the mind's attention to the clear outlines of the outer world, also draws attention to the mind itself, making human beings the center of an intelligible world and the masters of their own persons.

Greek artists, just like Greek philosophers, proclaimed the importance and creative capacity of the individual. They exemplified the humanist spirit that characterized all aspects of Greek culture. Classical art placed people in their natural environment, made the human form the focal point of attention, and exalted the nobility, dignity, self-assurance, and beauty of the human being.

POETRY AND DRAMA

Through their awareness of human personality, poets and dramatists, like philosophers and artists, gave expression to the rise of the individual. One of the earliest and best of the Greek poets was Sappho, a woman who lived around 600 B.C. on the island of Lesbos. Sappho established a school to teach music and singing to well-to-do girls and to prepare them for marriage. With great tenderness, Sappho wrote poems of friendship and love: "Some say the fairest thing on earth is a troop of horsemen, others a band of foot-soldiers, others a squadron of ships. But I say the fairest thing is the beloved."[18] And of her daughter Cleïs, she wrote:

> *I have a child; so fair*
> *As golden flowers is she,*
> *My Cleïs, all my care.*
> *I'd not give her away*
> *For Lydia's* wide sway*
> *Nor lands men long to see.*[19]

Sappho's love poetry, addressed also to women, indicates that she was bisexual. This form of sexual behavior was tolerated in ancient Greece, says classicist Lyn Hatherly Wilson, "because it was not procreative, because it did not alter a woman's virginal status, or affect her entry into marriage and male/female relations, except in ways that were considered positive."[20] Sappho was the most prominent female poet in the ancient world. She was depicted on coins and in art, and Plato praised the beauty of her lyric poetry. Sometimes, however, she was treated in an uncomplimentary way by comic playwrights who thought it inappropriate for a woman to write poetry. Her influence endured for centuries: the Roman poets Catullus, Horace, and Ovid alluded to her.

Pindar (C. 518–438 B.C.) was another Greek lyric poet. In his poem of praise for a victorious athlete, Pindar expressed the aristocratic view of excellence. Although life is essentially tragic—triumphs are short-lived, misfortunes are many, and ultimately death overtakes all—man must still demonstrate his worth by striving for excellence.

---

*Ancient country in Asia Minor.

He who wins of a sudden, some noble prize
In the rich years of youth
Is raised high with hope; his manhood takes
  wings;
He has in his heart what is better than wealth
But brief is the season of man's delight.
Soon it falls to the ground;
Some dire decision uproots it.
—Thing of a day! such is man: a shadow in
  a dream.
Yet when god-given splendour visits him
A bright radiance plays over him, and how
  sweet is life![21]

The high point of Greek poetry is drama, an art form that originated in Greece. The Greek dramatist portrayed the sufferings, weaknesses, and triumphs of individuals. Just as a Greek sculptor shaped a clear visual image of the human form, so also a Greek dramatist brought the inner life of human beings, their fears and hopes, into sharp focus and tried to find the deeper meaning of human experience. Thus, both art and drama evidenced the growing self-awareness of the individual.

Drama originated in the religious festivals honoring Dionysus, the god of wine and agricultural fertility. A profound innovation in these sacred performances, which included choral songs and dances, occurred in the last part of the sixth century B.C. when Thespis, the first actor known to history, stepped out of the chorus and engaged it in dialogue. By separating himself from the choral group, Thespis demonstrated a new awareness of the individual.

With only one actor and a chorus, however, the possibilities for dramatic action and human conflicts were limited. Then Aeschylus introduced a second actor in his dramas, and Sophocles a third. Dialogue between individuals thus became possible. The Greek actors wore masks, and by changing them, each actor could play several roles in the same performance. This flexibility allowed the dramatists to depict the clash and interplay of human wills and passions on a greater scale. By the middle of the fifth century B.C., tragedies were performed regularly as civic festivals. The audience sat on wooden bleachers in an open-air, hillside theater (*theatron*). The acoustics of these stone theaters were so superb that a clear voice projected from the front could be heard, without amplification, in the last row. In the staging of these tragedies, the all-male chorus generally

danced and sang in a circular area called the *orchestra* ("dancing place"), which encircled an altar. Their costumes consisted of goat skins (only later did the costumes become elaborate), larger-than-life masks, and elevated shoes.

Because of the grandeur of the dramatists' themes, the eminence of their heroes, and the loftiness of their language, Greek spectators felt intensely involved in the lives portrayed. What they were witnessing in a **tragedy** went beyond anything in their ordinary lives, and they experienced the full range of human emotions.

A development parallel to Socratic dialectics—dialogue between thinking individuals—occurred in Greek drama. Through the technique of dialogue, early dramatists first pitted human beings against the gods and destiny. Later, by placing characters in conflict with one another, dramatists arrived at the idea of individuals as active subjects responsible for their behavior and decisions, which were based on their own feelings and thoughts. Greek tragedy evolved as a continuous striving toward humanization and individualization.

Like the natural philosophers, Greek dramatists saw an inner logic in the universe and called it Fate or Destiny. When people were stubborn, narrow-minded, arrogant, and immoderate, when their "word and deed" showed no respect for justice, when they dishonored the gods, they were punished. The order in the universe required it, said Sophocles.[22]

In being free to make decisions, the dramatist says, individuals have the potential for greatness, but in choosing wrongly, unintelligently, they bring disaster on themselves and others. Also like philosophy, Greek tragedy entailed rational reflection. Tragic heroes were not passive victims of fate. They were thinking human beings who felt a need to comprehend their position, explain the reasons for their actions, and analyze their feelings. The audience was prodded to think, for a tragedy depicted a clash of viewpoints that, as in the Assembly, the audience had to analyze before choosing sides.

The essence of Greek tragedy lies in the tragic hero's struggle against cosmic forces and insurmountable obstacles, which eventually crush him. But what impressed the Greek spectators (and impresses today's readers and viewers of Greek drama) was not the vulnerability or weaknesses of human beings, but their courage and determination in the face of these forces.

Hesiod

The poet Hesiod (eighth century B.C.) lived on a farm in Boetia, in central Greece, and wrote two major poems. *Theogony* deals with the formation of the universe, and *Works and Days* depicts the life of peasants.

Theogony is replete with mythical imagery, but for several reasons scholars regard it as a precursor of Greek philosophy. First, in explaining the origins of the world through the genealogy of the gods, Hesiod produced an ordered and structured mythology that can be interpreted as nascent rational speculation. Second, the gift of law bestowed by Zeus on humanity can be viewed as an early expression of natural law—the recognition of both a physical and a moral order inherent in the universe. Crucial for philosophical thought, the concept of natural law that Hesiod expressed in mythical-religious terms was explicitly formulated in the rational categories of philosophy by Greek thinkers after Hesiod.

Whereas Homer's epics concentrate on heroes striving to win honor as defined by a chivalric aristocratic ideal, Hesiod's later poem, *Works and Days*, describes the daily ordeal of common folk struggling to feed their families. A man of the soil, Hesiod maintains that honest labor promotes the good life.

Although he was generally pessimistic, Hesiod believed that human beings could improve their lot if they embraced justice, which "is proved the best thing they have." An awareness of justice is what distinguishes human beings from other creatures.

> You, Perses, should store away in your mind all
>   that I tell you,
> and listen to justice, and put away
>   all notions of violence.
> Here is the law, as Zeus established it
>   for human beings;
> as for fish, and wild animals, and the flying
>   birds,
> they feed on each other, since there is no idea of
>   justice among them;
> but to men he gave justice, and she in the end is
>   proved the best thing
> they have. If a man sees what is right and
>   is willing to argue it,
> Zeus of the wide brows grants him
>   prosperity.*

Human beings are faced with the choice between diké (straight judgment and justice), which safeguards society, and hubris (excessive pride), which destroys it. Honoring justice is what distinguishes a civilized society from a state of savagery.

Throughout *Theogony* and *Works and Days*, Hesiod used the language and imagery of myth to express curiosity about the genesis of the universe, concern for justice, and awareness of a universal moral order. In succeeding centuries, Greek thinkers would discuss these issues using the language and categories of philosophy.

---

*Hesiod, *Works and Days*, in *Hesiod*, trans. Richard Lattimore (Ann Arbor: University of Michigan Press, 1973), 51.

Aeschylus

Aeschylus (525–456 B.C.), an Athenian nobleman, had fought in the battle of Marathon. He wrote more than eighty plays, of which only seven survive. They have common themes. As an Athenian patriot, Aeschylus urged adherence to traditional religious beliefs and moral values. Like Solon, the statesman, Aeschylus believed that the world was governed by divine justice, which could not be violated with impunity; when individuals evinced hubris (overweening pride or arrogance), which led them to overstep the bounds of moderation and to set themselves above the gods, they must be punished. Another principal theme was that through suffering came knowledge: the terrible consequences of sins against the divine order should remind all to think and act with moderation and caution.

Aeschylus' play *The Persians* dealt with an actual event, the defeat of the Persian emperor Xerxes by the Greeks. Xerxes' intemperate ambition to become master of Asia and Greece conflicted with the divine order of the universe. For this hubris, Xerxes and his fellow Persians must pay.

> *A single stroke has brought about the ruin of great*
> *Prosperity, the flower of Persia fallen and gone.*[23]

The suffering of Xerxes should make people aware of what they can and cannot do.

> *And heaps of corpses even in generations hence*
> *Will signify in silence to the eyes of men*
> *That mortal man should not think more than mortal thoughts.*
> *For hubris blossomed forth and grew a crop of ruin,*
> *And from it gathered in a harvest full of tears.*
> *In face of this, when Xerxes, who lacks good sense, returns*
> *Counsel him with reasoning and good advice,*
> *To cease from wounding God with overboastful rashness.*[24]

Whereas Aeschylean drama dealt principally with the cosmic theme of the individual in conflict with the moral universe, later dramatists, while continuing to use patterns fashioned by Aeschylus, gave greater attention to the psychology of the individual.

Sophocles

Another outstanding Athenian dramatist was Sophocles (c. 496–406 B.C.). His greatness as a playwright lay in both the excellence of his dramatic technique and the skill with which he portrayed character. The people that he created possessed violent passions and tender emotions; they were noble in their nature, though their actions showed human frailty. Sophocles consciously formulated a standard of human excellence: individuals should shape their character in the way a sculptor shapes a form, according to laws of proportion. Sophocles felt that when these principles of harmony were violated by immoderate behavior, a person's character would be thrown off balance and misfortune would strike. The physical world and human activities obey laws, said Sophocles, and human beings cannot violate these laws with impunity.

Whereas Aeschylus concentrated on religious matters and Euripides (see the next section) dealt with social issues, Sophocles wrote about the perennial problem of well-intentioned human beings struggling valiantly, but unwisely and vainly, against the tide of fate. His characters, bent on some action fraught with danger, resist all appeals to caution and inescapably meet with disaster.

In *Oedipus Rex*, first performed about 429 B.C., Sophocles probes deeply into the human psyche. Oedipus is warned not to pursue the mystery of his birth but insists on searching for the truth about himself: "Nothing will move me. I will find the whole truth." (He had unsuspectingly killed his father and married his mother.*) For this determination, born more of innocence than arrogance, he will suffer. Events do not turn out, as Oedipus discovers, the way a person thinks and desires that they should; the individual is impotent before a relentless fate, which governs human existence. It seems beyond imagining that Oedipus, whom all envied for his intelligence, courage, and good works, would suffer such dreadful misfortune.

But tragedy also gives Oedipus the strength to assert his moral independence. Although struck down by fate, Oedipus remains an impressive figure. The tragedy's catharsis (the purging of the audience's emotions through a work of art) comes from Oedipus' choice of

---

*Sigmund Freud's interpretation of the Oedipus story has had a profound impact on psychoanalytic theory: "[Oedipus'] destiny moves us only because it might have been ours. . . . It is the fate of all of us, perhaps, to direct our first sexual impulse towards our mother and our first hatred and . . . murderous wish against our father. Our dreams convince us that this is so" (*The Interpretation of Dreams*).

SOPHOCLES. The great Athenian dramatist wrote 123 tragedies, only seven of which have survived.

his own punishment, self-inflicted blindness. Oedipus demonstrates that he still possesses the distinctly human qualities of choosing and acting, that he still remains a free man responsible for his actions. Despite his misery, Oedipus is able to confront a brutal fate with courage and to demonstrate nobility of character.

In *Antigone*, Sophocles deals with a theme that recurs in Western thought over the centuries: the conflict between individual morality and the requirements of the state, between personal conscience and the state's laws. Creon, king of Thebes, forbids the burial of Polyneikes, Antigone's brother, because he rebelled against the state. The body, decrees Creon, shall remain unburied, food for dogs and vultures, despite the fact that Antigone is his niece and betrothed to his son. Antigone believes that a higher law compels her to bury her brother, even though this means certain death for her. Both Antigone's defiance of unjust authority and her devotion to a higher cause continue to be cited by moralists and those engaged in political resistance.

Euripides

The rational spirit of Greek philosophy permeated the tragedies of Euripides (c. 485–406 B.C.). Like the Sophists, Euripides subjected the problems of human life to critical analysis and challenged human conventions. It was this critical spirit that prompted the traditionalist Aristophanes (see the next section) to attack Euripides for introducing the art of reasoning into tragedy. The role of the gods, women's conflicts, the horrors of war, the power of passion, and the prevalence of human suffering and weakness were carefully scrutinized in Euripides' plays. Euripides blends a poet's insight with a psychologist's probing to reveal the tangled world of human passions and souls in torment. Thus, in *Medea,* he presents the deepest feelings of a Greek woman (see Primary Source box).

Euripides recognized the power of irrational, demonic forces that seethe within people—what he called "the bloody Fury raised by fiends of Hell."[25] A scorned Medea, seeking revenge against her husband by murdering their children, says:

> *I know indeed what evil I intend to do,*
> *But stronger than all my afterthoughts is*
> *   my fury,*
> *Fury that brings upon mortals the greatest*
> *   evils.*[26]

In his plays, Euripides showed that the great tragedy of human existence is that reason can offer only feeble resistance against these compelling, relentless, and consuming passions. The forces that destroy erupt from the volcanic nature of human beings.

A second distinctive feature of Euripidean tragedy is its humanitarianism. No other Greek thinker expressed such concern for a fellow human being, such compassion for human suffering. In *The Trojan Women*, Euripides depicted war as agony and not glory, and the warrior as brutish and not noble. He described the torments of women, for whom war meant the loss of homes, husbands, children, and freedom. In 416 B.C., Athens massacred the men of the small island of Melos, sold its women and children into slavery, and sacked the city, actions that Euripides regarded as mindless savagery.

Euripides, *Medea*

The Greek dramatist Euripides applied a keen critical spirit to the great question of individual life versus the demands of society. His play Medea *focuses on a strong-willed woman whose despair at being cast off by her husband leads her to exact a terrible revenge. But in the following passage, Medea might speak for the deepest feelings of any Greek woman.*

It was everything to me to think well of one
  man,
And he, my own husband, has turned out
  wholly vile.
Of all things which are living and can form a
  judgement
We women are the most unfortunate creatures.
Firstly, with an excess of wealth it is required
For us to buy a husband and take for our bodies
A master; for not to take one is even worse.
And now the question is serious whether we
  take
A good or bad one; for there is no easy escape
For a woman, nor can she say no to her
  marriage.
She arrives among new modes of behaviour
  and manners,
And needs prophetic power, unless she has
  learnt at home,
How best to manage him who shares the bed
  with her.

And if we work out all this well and carefully,
And the husband lives with us and lightly bears
  his yoke,
Then life is enviable. If not, I'd rather die.
A man, when he's tired of the company in his
  home,
Goes out of the house and puts an end to his
  boredom
And turns to a friend or companion of his own
  age.
But we are forced to keep our eyes on one
  alone.
What they say of us is that we have a peaceful
  time
Living at home, while they do the fighting in
  war.
How wrong they are! I would very much rather
  stand
Three times in the front of battle than bear one
  child.

Questions for Analysis

1. According to this passage, what were the difficulties Greek women faced? What, do you think, was the likely response of a Greek male to Medea's grievances?
2. Do Medea's concerns in any way apply to women today?

Euripedes, *Medea*, trans. Rex Warner (London: The Bodley Head, 1944), 18.

The Trojan Women, performed a year later, warned Athenians:

> *How are ye blind,*
> *Ye treaders down of cities, ye that cast*
> *Temples to desolation, and lay waste*
> *Tombs, the untrodden sanctuaries where lie*
> *The ancient dead; yourselves so soon to die!*[27]

By exposing war as barbaric, Euripides was expressing his hostility to the Athenian leaders who persisted in continuing the disastrous Peloponnesian War.

Aristophanes

Greek dramatists often served as political and social critics, none more so than Aristophanes (c. 448–c. 380 b.c.), the greatest of the Greek comic playwrights. He lampooned Athenian statesmen and intellectuals, censured government policies, and protested against the decay of traditional Athenian values. Behind Aristophanes' sharp wit lay a deadly seriousness, for there was much in Athens during the Peloponnesian War that angered him. As an aristocrat, he was repelled by Cleon, the common tanner who succeeded Pericles. As an admirer of the ancient values of honor, duty, and moderation, he was infuriated by corruption, which he attributed to the Sophists. As a man of common sense, he recognized that the Peloponnesian War must end. In the process of serving as a social critic, Aristophanes wrote some of the most hilarious lines in world literature.

In *Lysistrata*, an antiwar comedy, the women of Greece agree to abstain from having sexual relations with their husbands to compel the men to make peace. Lysistrata reveals the plan.

> *For if we women will but sit at home,*
> *Powdered and trimmed, clad in our daintiest*
> *lawn,** *
> *Employing all our charms, and all our arts*
> *To win men's love, and when we've won it,*
> *then*
> *Repel them firmly, till they end the war,*
> *We'll soon get Peace again, be sure of that.*[28]

After the plan has been implemented, many women, now sexually frustrated, seek to desert the temple where they have gathered. But the men also suffer.

> *Oh me! these pangs and paroxysms of love,*
> *Riving my heart, keen as a torturer's wheel!*[29]

Through these unorthodox methods, the women achieve their goal, peace. Performed during the darkest days of the war, this play reminded its audiences to concentrate their efforts in the real world on securing peace.

In *The Clouds*, Aristophanes ridiculed the Sophist method of education both for turning the youth away from their parents' values and for engaging the youth in useless, hair-splitting logic. To Aristophanes, the worst of the Sophists was Socrates, who is depicted in *The Clouds* as a fuzzy-minded thinker with both feet planted

firmly in the clouds. Socrates is made to look ridiculous, a man who walks on air, contemplates the sun, and teaches such absurd things as "Heaven is one vast fire extinguisher" or "How many feet of its own a flea could jump." The Sophists in the play teach only how "to succeed just enough for my need and to slip through the clutches of the law." A student of these Sophists becomes "a concocter of lies . . . a supple, unprincipled, troublesome cheat."[30] To Aristophanes, Socrates was a subversive who caused Athenians to repudiate civil morality and to speculate about nonsense questions. Clearly, Aristophanes admired the Athens that had bested the Persians at the battle of Marathon and feared the rationalism that Euripides, the Sophists, and Socrates had injected into Athenian intellectual life.

HISTORY

The Mesopotamians and the Egyptians kept annals that purported to narrate the deeds of gods and their human agents, the priest-kings or god-kings. These chronicles, filled with religious sayings, royal records, and boastful accounts of military campaigns, are devoid of critical analysis and interpretation. The Hebrews valued history, but believing that God acted in human affairs, they did not remove historical events from the realm of religious-mythical thought. The Greeks initiated a different approach to the study of history. For the Greeks, history was not the record of God's wrath or benevolence—as it was for the Hebrews—but the actions solely of human beings. As the gods were eliminated from the natural philosophers' explanations for the origins of things in the natural world, mythical elements were also removed from the writing of history.

Greek historians asked themselves questions about the deeds of people, based their answers on available evidence, and wrote in prose, the language of rational thought. They not only narrated events but also examined them, says Italian historian Arnaldo Momigliano, with a "critical attitude . . . enabling [them] to distinguish between facts and fancies. To the best of my knowledge no historiography earlier than the Greek or independent of it developed these critical methods."[31]

*Fine linen dress

In the same spirit, British philosopher and historian R. G. Collingwood states:

> *The Greeks quite clearly and consciously recognized both that history is, or can be, a science, and that it has to do with human actions. Greek history is not legend, it is research; it is an attempt to get answers to definite questions about matters of which one recognizes oneself as ignorant. It is not theocratic, it is humanistic; the matters inquired into are not of gods, they are of men. Moreover, it is not mythical. The events inquired into are not events in a dateless past, at the beginning of things; they are events in a dated past, a certain number of years ago. This is not to say that legend, either in the form of theocratic history or in the form of myth, was a thing foreign to the Greek mind. . . . But what is remarkable about the Greeks was not the fact that their historical thought contained a certain residue of elements which we should call non-historical, but the fact that side by side with these, it contained elements of what we call history.*[32]

In several respects, however, the Greeks were unhistorical. To them, history moved in cycles; events and periods repeated themselves. Unlike the Hebrews, they had little awareness of historical uniqueness and progression. Nor was history as vital to the Greeks as it was to the Hebrews. Greek philosophers preferred fixing their minds on eternal and changeless truths rather than on the vicissitudes of history. Aristotle said that poetry (which also included drama) is "more philosophic and of greater import than history, since its statements are of the nature of universals," whereas histories deal only with particular events.[33]

Herodotus

Often called "the father of history," Herodotus (c. 484–c. 424 B.C.) wrote a history of the Persian Wars. Herodotus valued the present and recognized that it is not timeless but has been shaped by earlier happenings. To understand the conflict between Persia and Greece, the most important event during his lifetime, he first inquired into the histories of these societies. Much of his information was derived from posing questions to natives of the lands he visited. Interested in everything, Herodotus frequently interlaced his historical narrative with a marvelous assortment of stories and anecdotes.

The central theme of Herodotus' *Histories* is the contrast between Near Eastern despotism and Greek freedom and the subsequent clash of these two worldviews in the Persian Wars. Certain of their superiority, the Greeks considered the non-Hellenic world to be steeped in ignorance and darkness. Herodotus, however, was generally free of this arrogance. A fair-minded, sympathetic, and tolerant observer, he took joy in examining the wide range of human character and experience.

Though Herodotus found much to praise in the Persian empire, he was struck by a lack of freedom and by what he considered barbarity. Herodotus emphasized that the mentality of the free citizen was foreign to the East, where men were trained to obey the ruler's commands absolutely. Not the rule of law but the whim of despots prevailed in the East. When a Persian official urged some Greeks to submit to Xerxes, Herodotus wrote that the Greeks said: "You understand well enough what slavery is, but freedom you have never experienced, so you do not know if it tastes sweet or bitter. If you ever did come to experience it, you would advise us to fight for it not with spears only, but with axes too."[34] Of all the Greek city-states, Herodotus admired Athens most. Freedom had enabled Athens to achieve greatness, said Herodotus, and it was this illustrious city that had rescued the Greek world from Persia.

Another theme evident in Herodotus' work was punishment for hubris. In seeking to become king of both Asia and Europe, Xerxes had acted arrogantly; although he behaved as if he were superhuman, "he too was human, and was sure to be disappointed of his great expectations."[35] Like the Greek tragedians, Herodotus drew universal moral principles from human behavior.

In several ways, Herodotus was a historian rather than a teller of tales. First, he recognized that there is value in studying and preserving the past. Second, he asked questions about the past, instead of merely repeating ancient legends; he tried to discover what had happened, analyzed the motivations behind actions, and searched for cause-and-effect connections. Third, he demonstrated at times a cautious and critical attitude toward his sources, refusing to rely on legends based on little or no objective evidence.

> *The course of my story now leads me to Cyrus: who was this man who destroyed the empire of Croesus, and how did the Persians win their predominant position in Asia? I could, if I wished, give three versions of Cyrus' history, all different from what follows; but I propose to base my account on those Persian authorities who seem to tell the simple truth about him without trying to exaggerate his exploits.*[36]

Fourth, rising above inherited prejudices and a narrow parochialism, he attempted to examine disinterestedly and critically the histories of both the Greeks and the Persians. Fifth, although the gods appeared in Herodotus' narrative, they played a far less important role than they did in Greek popular mythology. Still, by retaining a belief in the significance of dreams, omens, and oracles and by allowing divine intervention, Herodotus fell short of being a thoroughgoing rationalist. Herodotus' writings contain the embryo of rational history; Thucydides brought it to maturity.

Thucydides

Thucydides (c. 460–c. 400 B.C.) also concentrated on a great political crisis confronting the Hellenic world: the Peloponnesian War. Living in Periclean Athens, whose lifeblood was politics, Thucydides regarded the motives of statesmen and the acts of government as the essence of history. He did not just catalogue facts but also sought those general concepts and principles that the facts illustrated. His history was the work of an intelligent mind trying to make sense of his times.

Thucydides applied to the sphere of political history a rationalist empiricism worthy of the Ionian natural philosophers. He strove for factual accuracy and drew conclusions based on a critical analysis of events and motives. He searched for the truth underlying historical events and attempted to present it objectively. From the Sophists, Thucydides learned that the motives and reactions of human beings follow patterns. Therefore, a proper analysis of the events of the

Peloponnesian War would reveal general principles that govern human behavior and relations between states. He intended his history to be a source of enlightenment for future ages, a possession for all time, because the kinds of behavior that caused the conflict between Sparta and Athens would recur regularly throughout history, for human nature is unchanging and predictable.

> *Of the events of the war I have not ventured to speak from any chance information, nor according to any notion of my own; I have described nothing but what I either saw myself, or learned from others of whom I made the most careful and particular inquiry. The task was a laborious one, because eyewitnesses of the same occurrences gave different accounts of them, as they remembered or were [partial to] one side or the other. And very likely the strictly historical character of my narrative may be disappointing to the ear. But if he who desires to have before his eyes a true picture of the events which have happened, and of the like events which may be expected to happen hereafter in the order of human things shall pronounce what I have written to be useful, then I shall be satisfied. My history is an everlasting possession, not a prize composition which is heard and forgotten.*[37]

In Thucydides' history, there was no place for myths, for legends, for the fabulous—all of which were hindrances to historical truth. He recognized that a work of history was a creation of the rational mind and not an expression of the poetic imagination. The historian seeks to learn and to enlighten, not to entertain.

Rejecting the notion that the gods interfere in history, Thucydides looked for the social forces and human decisions behind events. Undoubtedly, he was influenced by Hippocratic doctors, who frowned on divine explanations for disease and distinguished between the symptoms of a disease and its causes. Whereas Herodotus occasionally lapsed into supernatural explanations, Thucydides wrote history in which the gods were absent, and he denied their intervention in human affairs. For Thucydides, history was the work of human beings, and the driving force in history was men's will to power and domination.

In addition to being a historian who meticulously examined evidence, Thucydides was also an astute and innovative political thinker with a specific view of government, statesmen, and international relations. He warned against the dangers of extremism unleashed by the strains of war, and he believed that when reason was forsaken, the state's plight would worsen. He had contempt for statesmen who waged war lightly, acting from impulse, reckless daring, and an insatiable appetite for territory. Consequently, he regarded the decision to attack Syracuse in Sicily, which cost so many lives, as a gross political blunder. Although Thucydides admired Athens for its democratic institutions, rule of law, sense of civic duty, and cultural achievements, he recognized an inherent danger in democracy: the emergence of demagogues, who rise to power by stirring up the populace and abuse their power when in office. He extended to international relations the Sophists' insight that people tend to act out of self-interest; national interest, he maintained, was the motivating force in relations between states. Further, he explicitly formulated the principle of balance of power as a basic formula governing international relations. What caused the Peloponnesian War, he said, was the sudden and spectacular increase of Athenian power and the Spartans' fear that this would upset the balance. Finally, Thucydides left us with an enduring insight: extremism, which is often the cause of war, is exacerbated during the conflict; terrible passions are unleashed among ordinary people that culminate in slaughter and misery. Thucydides recognized the tragic nature of human existence. Despite their knowledge of those forces that undermine civilized life, human beings do not alter their behavior.

Political scientists, historians, and statesmen still turn to Thucydides for insights into the realities of power politics, the dangers of political fanaticism, the nature of imperialism, the methods of demagogues, and the effects of war on democratic politics.

THE GREEK ACHIEVEMENT: REASON, FREEDOM, HUMANISM

Like other ancient peoples, the Greeks warred, massacred, and enslaved; they could be cruel, arrogant, contentious, and superstitious; and they often violated their ideals. But their achievement was unquestionably of profound historical significance. Western thought essentially begins with the Greeks, who first defined the individual by the capacity to reason. It was the great achievement of the Greek spirit to rise above magic, miracles, mystery, authority, and custom and to discover the procedures and terminology that permit a rational understanding of nature and society. Every aspect of Greek civilization—science, philosophy, art, literature, politics, historical writing—showed a growing reliance on human reason and a diminishing dependence on the gods. For the Greeks, the pursuit of intellectual concerns was the supreme human activity. They expressed confidence in the mind's capacity to fathom the physical laws that governed nature and to comprehend and cope with the problems afflicting the human community. Fundamental to Greek reason was the conviction that objective standards, laws of proportion, governed the cosmos, art, architecture, and the just city, and that philosophical inquiry provides us with the knowledge and inner discipline to live a good life.

In Mesopotamia and Egypt, people had no clear conception of their individual worth and no understanding of political liberty. They were not citizens but subjects who marched to the command of a ruler whose power originated with the gods. Such royal power was not imposed on an unwilling population but was religiously accepted and obeyed. Observing Eastern despots, and from their own experience with tyranny, the Greeks learned that a just polis is not one ruled arbitrarily by a monarch.

Unlike in the Near East, monarchs were incidental to Greek political history, a development that enabled the Greeks to create both civic politics and political freedom. They saw the state as a community of free and equal citizens who made laws that served the common good. Disputes between citizens were decided by a jury of one's peers, not by the whims of a ruler or his officials. The citizens had no other masters but themselves. Denouncing arbitrary rule, they argued that power should be regulated by law and justice. The Greeks held that men are capable of governing themselves, and they regarded active participation in public affairs as a duty. For the Greeks, the state was a civilizing agent that permitted people to live the good life. Greek political thinkers arrived at a conception of the rational or legal state, in which law was an expression of reason, not of whim or divine commands; of justice, not of might; of the general good of the community, not of the self-interest of a particular class or individuals. And they admired statesmen like Solon and Pericles who unselfishly placed the good of the city ahead of their own. At the beginning of the fourth century B.C., an Athenian orator eloquently captured the meaning of his city's political achievement. The Athenians, he said, "deemed that it was the way of wild beasts to be held subject to one another by force, but the duty of men to delimit justice by law, to convince by reason, and to serve these two by submitting to the sovereignty of law and the instruction of reason."[38] The ideas and terminology of this statement were totally alien to the political experience of the ancient Near East and remain an integral component of the Western democratic tradition. An offshoot of the Greek democratic experience was the emergence of political thought. Greek thinkers' discussions of justice, power, freedom, and the strengths and weaknesses of democracy are the foundation of Western political theory.

The Greeks also gave to Western civilization a conception of inner, or ethical, freedom. People were free to choose between shame and honor, cowardice and duty, moderation and excess. The heroes of Greek tragedy suffered not because they were puppets manipulated by higher powers but because they possessed the freedom of decision. The idea of ethical freedom reached its highest point with Socrates, who shifted the focus of thought from cosmology to the moral life. To shape oneself according to ideals known to the mind, to develop into an autonomous and self-directed person, became for the Greeks the highest form of freedom.

Underlying everything accomplished by the Greeks was a humanist attitude toward life. The Greeks expressed a belief in the worth, significance, and dignity of the individual. They called for the maximum cultivation of human talent, the full development of human personality, and the deliberate pursuit of excellence. In valuing human personality, the Greek humanists did not approve of living without restraints; they aimed at creating a higher type of man. Such a man would mold himself according to worthy standards; he would make his life as harmonious and flawless as a work of art. This aspiration required effort, discipline, and intelligence. Fundamental to the Greek humanist outlook was the belief that human beings could master themselves. Although people could not alter the course of nature, for there was an order to the universe over which neither human beings nor gods had control, Greek humanists believed that people could control their own lives. Contemporary humanists continue to derive inspiration and guidelines from the literary, artistic, and philosophical creations of ancient Greece.

Despite their lauding of the human being's creative capacities, the Greeks were not naïve about human nature. Rather, intensely aware of the individual's inherent capacity for evil, Greek thinkers repeatedly warned that without the restraining forces of law, civic institutions, moral norms, and character training, society would be torn apart by the savage elements within human nature.

By discovering theoretical reason, conceiving political freedom, and affirming the worth and potential of human personality, the Greeks broke with the past and founded the rational and humanist tradition of the West. "Had Greek civilization never existed," wrote poet W. H. Auden, "we would never have become fully conscious, which is to say that we would never have become, for better or worse, fully human."[39]

❖　　❖　　❖

NOTES

1. John N. Theodorakopoulos, "The Origins of Science and Philosophy," in *History of the Hellenic World: The Archaic Period* (University Park: Pennsylvania State University Press, 1975), 438.

2. Quoted in George Sarton, *A History of Science* (Cambridge, Mass.: Harvard University Press, 1952), 1:355–356.

3. Euripides, *Iphigenia at Aulis*, in *Ten Plays by Euripides*, trans. Moses Hadas and John McClean (New York: Bantam Books, 1960), 348, lines 1400–1401.

4. Excerpted in Kathleen Freeman, *Ancilla to the Pre-Socratic Philosophers* (Cambridge, Mass.: Harvard University Press, 1957), 157–158.

5. Plato, *Apology*, trans. F. J. Church, rev. R. D. Cummings (Indianapolis: Bobbs-Merrill, 1956), sec. 28.

6. Ibid., secs. 16–17.

7. Plato, *The Republic*, trans. F. M. Cornford (New York: Oxford University Press, 1945), 289.

8. Ibid.

9. Ibid., 293.

10. Ibid., 178–179.

11. *Historia Animalium*, in *Works of Aristotle*, trans. D'Arcy Wentworth Thompson (New York: Oxford University Press, 1962), 4:561.

12. *Nicomachean Ethics*, in *Basic Works of Aristotle*, ed. Richard McKeon (New York: Random House, 1941), 996.

13. Ibid., 1104.

14. *Politics*, in *Basic Works of Aristotle*, ed. McKeon, 1144–45.

15. Ibid., 1164.

16. Ibid., 1246, 1251.

17. Ibid., 1220–21.

18. Cited in Werner Jaeger, *Paideia: The Ideals of Greek Culture*, trans. Gilbert Highet (New York: Oxford University Press, 1945), 1:135.

19. *The Oxford Book of Greek Verse in Translation*, ed. T.F. Higham and C.M. Bowra (1938), Sappho, "A Girl" (6 lines from 211). By Permission of Oxford University Press.

20. Lyn Hatherly Wilson, *Sappho's Sweet Bitter Songs* (London and New York: Routledge, 1966), 70.

21. Cited in H. D. F. Kitto, *The Greeks* (Baltimore: Penguin Books, 1957), 174–175.

22. See Sophocles, *Oedipus the King*, trans. Bernard M. W. Knox (New York: Washington Square Press, 1959), 61.

23. Aeschylus, *The Persians*, trans. Anthony J. Podlecki (Englewood Cliffs, N.J.: Prentice-Hall, 1970), 49, lines 250–251.

24. Ibid., 96–97, lines 818–822, 829–831.

25. *Medea*, trans. Rex Warner, in *Euripides*, vol. 3 of *The Complete Greek Tragedies*, ed. David Grene and Richard Lattimore (Chicago: University of Chicago Press, 1959–1960), 101, line 1260.

26. Ibid., 96, lines 1078–80.

27. Euripides, *The Trojan Women*, trans. Gilbert Murray (New York: Oxford University Press, 1915), 16, lines 95–97.

28. *Lysistrata*, in *Five Comedies of Aristophanes*, trans. Benjamin Bickley Rogers (Garden City, N.Y.: Doubleday Anchor Books, 1955), 292.

29. Ibid., 320.

30. *The Clouds*, in *Five Comedies of Aristophanes*, trans. Rogers, 156–157, 169–170.

31. Arnaldo Momigliano, *The Classical Foundations of Modern Historiography* (Berkeley: University of California Press, 1990), 30.

32. R. G. Collingwood, *The Idea of History* (New York: Oxford University Press, 1956), 17–18.

33. Poetics, in *Basic Works of Aristotle*, ed. McKeon, 1464.

34. Herodotus, *The Histories*, trans. Aubrey de Sélincourt (Baltimore: Penguin Books, 1954), 458.

35. Ibid., 485.

36. Ibid., 53.

37. Thucydides, *The Peloponnesian War*, trans. B. Jowett (Oxford: Clarendon Press, 1881), bk. 1, chap. 22.

38. Quoted in Jennifer Tolbert Roberts, *Athens on Trial: The Antidemocratic Tradition in Western Thought* (Princeton, N.J.: Princeton University Press, 1994), 46.

39. W. H. Auden, ed., *The Portable Greek Reader* (New York: Viking, 1952), 38.

Chapter 5

The Hellenistic Age: Cultural Diffusion

Alexander the Great on Horseback. In conquering the lands from Greece to India, Alexander the Great displayed a military genius that would fascinate commanders from Caesar to Napoleon. (Alinari/Art Resource, N.Y.)

- **Alexander the Great**
- **Hellenistic Society**
- **Hellenistic Culture**
- **The Hellenistic Legacy**

Focus Questions

1. What are the basic differences between the Hellenic and the Hellenistic Ages?
2. How did Alexander the Great contribute to the shaping of the Hellenistic Age?
3. Why are the terms *individualism, universalism,* and *cosmopolitanism* used to characterize the Hellenistic Age?
4. What prescriptions did each of the Hellenistic philosophies offer for achieving happiness?
5. What is the enduring significance of Stoicism for the modern world?

Greek civilization, or Hellenism, passed through three distinct stages: the Hellenic Age, the Hellenistic Age, and the Greco-Roman Age. The **Hellenic Age** began about 800 B.C. with the early city-states, reached its height in the fifth century B.C., and endured until the death of Alexander the Great in 323 B.C. At that time, the ancient world entered the **Hellenistic Age**, which ended in 30 B.C., when Egypt, the last major Hellenistic state, fell to Rome. The **Greco-Roman Age** lasted five hundred years, encompassing the period of the Roman Empire up to the collapse of the Empire's western half in the last part of the fifth century A.D.

Although the Hellenistic Age absorbed the heritage of classical (Hellenic) Greece, its style of civilization changed. During the first phase of Hellenism, the polis was the center of political life. The polis gave Greeks an identity, and only within the polis could Greeks live a good and civilized life. With the coming of the Hellenistic Age, this situation changed. Kingdoms and empires eclipsed the city-state in power and importance. Cities retained a large measure of autonomy in domestic affairs but lost their freedom of action in foreign affairs. Dominated by monarchs, cities were no longer self-sufficient and independent communities as they had been in the Hellenic period. Monarchy—the essential form of government in the Hellenistic world—had not been admired by the Greeks of the Hellenic Age. They agreed with Aristotle that monarchy was suitable only for non-Greeks, who lacked the capacity to govern themselves.

As a result of Alexander the Great's conquests of the lands between Greece and India, tens of thousands of Greek soldiers, merchants, and administrators settled in eastern lands. Their encounters with the different peoples and cultures of the Near East widened the Greeks' horizon and weakened their ties to their native cities. Because of these changes, the individual had to define a relationship not to the narrow, parochial society of the polis, but to the larger world. The Greeks had to examine their place in a world more complex, foreign, and threatening than the polis. They had to fashion a conception of a community that would be more comprehensive than the city-state.

Hellenistic philosophers struggled with these problems of alienation and community.

BATTLE OF ISSUS, ROMAN MOSAIC. The subject of the mosaic is believed to be Alexander's victory over the Persian king Darius III in 333 B.C. at the battle of Issus. On the right side of the mosaic, we see a realistic battle scene filled with both commotion and emotion. (Scala/Ministero per i Beni e le Attività culturali/Art Resource, N.Y.)

They sought to give people the inner strength to endure in a world where the polis no longer provided security. In this new situation, philosophers no longer assumed that the good life was tied to the affairs of the city. Freedom from emotional stress—not active citizenship and social responsibility—was the avenue to the good life. This pronounced tendency of people to withdraw into themselves and seek emotional comfort helped shape a cultural environment that contributed to the spread and triumph of Christianity in the Greco-Roman Age.

In the Hellenic Age, Greek philosophers had a limited conception of humanity, dividing the world into Greeks and barbarians. In the Hellenistic Age, the intermingling of Greeks and peoples of the Near East—the fusion of different ethnic groups and cultures scattered over great distances—caused a shift in focus from the city to the **oikoumene** (the inhabited world); parochialism gave way to **cosmopolitanism** and **universalism** as people began to think of themselves as members of a world community. Philosophers came to regard the civilized world as one city, the city of humanity. This new concept was their response to the decline of the city-state and the quest for an alternative form of community.

By uniting the diverse nationalities of the Mediterranean world under one rule, Rome gave political expression to the Hellenistic philosophers' longing for a world community. But the vast and impersonal Roman Empire could not rekindle the sense of belonging, the certainty of identity, that came with being a citizen of a small polis. In time, a resurgence of the religious spirit, particularly in the form of Christianity, helped overcome the feeling of alienation by offering an image of community that stirred the heart.

ALEXANDER THE GREAT

After the assassination of Philip of Macedon in 336 B.C., his twenty-year-old son, Alexander, succeeded to the throne. Alexander inherited a proud and fiery temperament from his mother. From his tutor Aristotle, Alexander gained an appreciation for Greek culture, particularly the Homeric epics. Undoubtedly, the young Alexander was excited by these stories of legendary heroes, particularly of Achilles, and their striving for personal glory. Alexander acquired military skills and qualities of leadership from his father.

Alexander also inherited from Philip an overriding policy of state: the invasion of Persia, the greatest power yet to emerge in the ancient world. Such an exploit attracted the adventurous spirit of the young Alexander. A war of revenge against the Persians, who were masters of the Greek city-states of Asia Minor, also appealed to his Pan-Hellenic sentiments. Alexander was heir to the teachings of the fourth-century orator Isocrates, who urged a crusade against Persia to unite the Greeks in a common cause. Philip had intended to protect his hold on Greece by driving the Persians from Asia Minor. But Alexander, whose ambition knew no bounds, aspired to conquer and extend his rule over the entire Persian Empire. He possessed the irrepressible energy of a romantic adventurer. Among his military virtues were audacity—he took risks that were almost always successful; bravery—a fearless warrior, he sustained several wounds in battle; military acumen—he quickly sized up battlefield situations and made the correct adjustments; and charisma—his men adored him and respected his leadership.

With an army of thirty-five thousand men, including highly skilled cavalrymen, Alexander crossed into Asia Minor in 334 B.C.; and with thousands of additional warriors, many recruited from conquered regions, advanced all the way to India. In his military campaigns, which covered about ten thousand miles, Alexander proved himself to be a superb strategist and leader of men. Winning every battle, Alexander's army had carved an empire that stretched from Greece to India. Future conquerors, including Caesar and Napoleon, would read of Alexander's career with fascination and longing.

The world after Alexander differed sharply from that existing before he took up the sword. His conquests brought West and East closer together, marking a new epoch. Alexander himself helped implement this transformation, whether intentionally or unwittingly. He took a Persian bride, arranged for eighty of his officers and ten thousand of his soldiers to marry Asian women, and planned to incorporate thirty thousand Persian youths into his army. Alexander founded Greek-style cities in Asia, where Greek settlers mixed with the native population.

As Greeks acquired greater knowledge of the Near East, the parochialism of the polis gave way to a world outlook. As trade and travel between West and East expanded, as Greek merchants and soldiers settled in Asiatic lands, and as Greek culture spread to non-Greeks, the distinctions between barbarian and Greek lessened. Although Alexander never united all the peoples in a world-state, his career pushed the world in a new direction, toward a fusion of disparate peoples and the intermingling of cultural traditions.

HELLENISTIC SOCIETY

Competing Dynasties

In 323 B.C., Alexander, not yet thirty-three years old, died after a sickness probably exacerbated by excessive drinking. He had built an empire that stretched from Greece to the Punjab of India, but he was denied the time needed to organize effective institutions to govern these vast territories. After Alexander's premature death, his generals engaged in a long and bitter struggle to see who would succeed the conqueror. Since none of the generals or their heirs had enough power to hold together Alexander's vast empire, the wars of succession ended in a stalemate. By 275 B.C., the empire was fractured into three dynasties: the Ptolemies in Egypt, the Seleucids in western Asia, and the Antigonids in Macedonia. Macedonia—Alexander's native country—continued to dominate the Greek cities, which periodically tried to break its hold. Later, the kingdom of Pergamum, in western Asia Minor, emerged as the fourth Hellenistic monarchy. These Hellenistic kings were not native rulers enjoying local support (except in Macedonia) but were foreign conquerors. Consequently, they had to depend on mercenary armies and loyal administrators.

In the third century B.C., Ptolemaic Egypt was the foremost power in the Hellenistic world. The Seleucid Empire, which stretched from the Mediterranean to the frontiers of India and encompassed many different peoples, defeated the Ptolemaic forces and established Seleucid control over Phoenicia and Palestine.

Rome, a new power, became increasingly drawn into the affairs of the quarrelsome Hellenistic kingdoms. By the middle of the second century B.C., it had imposed its will on them. From that time on, the political fortunes of the western and eastern Mediterranean were inextricably linked.

Cosmopolitanism and Urbanism

Hellenistic society was characterized by a growing cosmopolitanism—a mingling of peoples, an interchange of cultures, and a broad outlook. Greek traditions spread to the Near East, while Mesopotamian, Egyptian, Hebrew, and Persian traditions—particularly religious beliefs—moved westward. A growing cosmopolitanism replaced the parochialism of the city-state. Although the rulers of the Hellenistic kingdoms were Macedonians and their high officials and generals were Greeks, the style of government was modeled after that of the ancient Middle Eastern kingdoms. In the Hellenic Age, the law had expressed the will of the community, but in this new age of monarchy, the kings laid down the law. To promote loyalty, the Macedonian rulers encouraged the Near Eastern cultic practice of worshiping the king as a god or as a representative of the gods. In Egypt, for example, the priests conferred on the Macedonian king the same divine powers and titles traditionally held by Egyptian pharaohs. In accordance with ancient tradition, statues of the divine king were installed in Egyptian temples, suffusing political power with supernatural authority, in marked contrast to the democratic spirit of the Greek Assembly.

Following Alexander's lead, the Seleucids founded cities in the east patterned after the city-states of Greece. The cities, which were often founded to protect trade routes and as fortresses against hostile tribes, adopted the political institutions of Hellenic Greece, including a popular assembly and a council. Hellenistic kings generally did not intervene in the cities' local affairs. Thousands of Greeks settled in these cities, which were Greek in architecture and contained Greek schools, temples, costly constructed theaters where performances of classical plays were staged, and gymnasia. Gymnasia were essentially places to exercise, train in sports, and converse, but some had libraries and halls where public lectures and competitions of orators and poets were held. Hellenistic kings brought books, paintings, and statues from Greece to their cities. Hellenistic cities, inhabited by tens of thousands of people from many lands and dominated by a Hellenized upper class, served as centers and agents of Hellenism, which non-Greeks adopted. The ruling class in each Hellenistic city was united by a common Hellenism, which overcame national, linguistic, and racial distinctions. *Koine* (or shared language), a form of spoken Greek spread by soldiers, administrators, merchants, teachers, and others, became a common tongue throughout much of the Mediterranean world. Greek was the language both of government and culture.

Hellenistic cities engaged in economic activity on a much greater scale than the classical Greek city-states. Increased trade integrated the Near East and Greece into a market economy, and business methods became more developed and refined. The middle and upper classes enjoyed homes, furniture, and jewelry more elegant than those of Periclean Athenians, and some people amassed great fortunes. In contrast to the ideal of citizenship, which distinguished the fifth-century polis, many Greeks who settled in Egypt, Syria, and other eastern lands ran roughshod over civil law and moral values and engaged in competitive struggles for wealth and power.

The greatest city of the time and the one most representative of the Hellenistic Age was Alexandria, in Egypt, founded by Alexander. Strategically located at one of the mouths of the Nile, it became a hub of commerce and culture. The most populous city of the Mediterranean world, Alexandria had about 300,000 inhabitants fifty years after its founding. At the beginning of the Christian era, it contained perhaps a million people: Macedonians, Greeks, Romans, Jews, Syrians, Ethiopians, and Arabs.

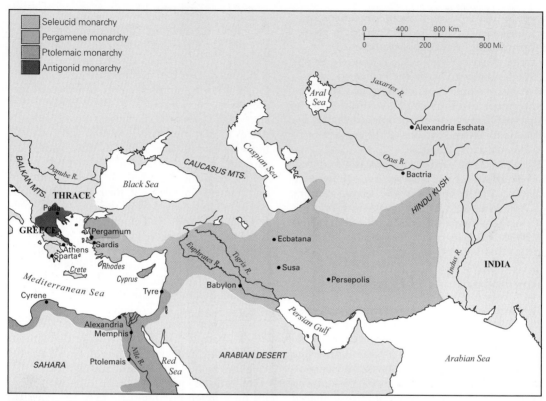

Map 5.1 THE DIVISION OF ALEXANDER'S EMPIRE AND THE SPREAD OF HELLENISM None of Alexander's generals could hold together the vast empire, which fractured into competing dynasties. (© 2016 Cengage Learning.)

Alexandria was an unrivaled commercial center; goods from the Mediterranean world, eastern Africa, Arabia, and India circulated in its marketplaces. Two handsome boulevards, squares, fountains, and great temples added to the city's beauty. Its library, created by the first two Ptolemies and often headed by distinguished scholars, had about half a million books. The library was part of a larger complex, the museum, which contained an astronomical observatory and botanical and zoological gardens. Some of the greatest poets, philosophers, physicians, and scientists of the Mediterranean world utilized these facilities. Athens and other classical Greek cities seemed like provincial towns compared to Alexandria, from which Hellenism radiated.

Aside from the proliferation of Greek urban institutions and ideas, Hellenistic cosmopolitanism expressed itself in an increased movement of peoples, the adoption of common currency standards, and an expansion of trade. International trade was made easier by improvements in navigation techniques, better port facilities, the extension of the monetary economy at the expense of barter, and the rapid development of banking. The makeup of Hellenistic armies also reflected the cosmopolitanism of the age. Serving the Hellenistic kings were men from lands stretching from India to the little-known areas north of the Danube. In Egyptian and Syrian cities, a native elite emerged who spoke Greek, wore Greek-style clothes, and adopted Greek customs. Cultural exchange permeated all phases of cultural life. Sculpture showed the influence of many lands. Historians wrote world histories, not just local ones. Greek astronomers worked with data collected over the centuries by the Babylonians. Greeks increasingly demonstrated a fascination with Near Eastern religious cults.

NIKE, THE GODDESS OF VICTORY, ON A GOLD EARRING, HELLENISTIC PERIOD. The calm, timeless, idealized forms of classical period sculpture gave way to a new style—the Hellenistic, marked by more dynamic, emotion-laden realism. This new aesthetic form reflected the cosmopolitan character of the Greek culture that emerged from Alexander's conquests.

(Photograph © 2016 Museum of Fine Arts, Boston/Henry Lillie Pierce Fund, 98.788.)

Like other Near Eastern people, the Jews—both those in Judea and the **Diaspora** (Jews who lived outside Palestine)—came under the influence of Hellenism. Some Jewish scholars, admiring Greek learning, expressed Jewish religious ideas in philosophical terms; God was identified with reason, and Moses' Law with the rational order of the universe. They wanted to show that Mosaic Law, revealed by God, was compatible with the truth discovered by natural reason. The Hebrew Scriptures were translated into Greek—the *Septuagint*—for use by Greek-speaking Jews living in Alexandria and other areas outside of Judea. Greek words entered the Hebrew language, and newly constructed synagogues employed Hellenistic architectural styles. Jews served in Hellenistic armies where they acquired Greek values and ways. Some Jews gave their children a Greek education. Clinging tenaciously to their ancient faith, many Jews rejected Greek learning and ways.

Philosophers helped break down the barriers between peoples by asserting that all inhabit a single fatherland. As the philosopher Crates said, "My fatherland has no single tower, no single roof. The whole earth is my citadel, a home ready for us all to live in."[1]

The spread of Greek civilization from the Aegean to the Indus River gave the Hellenistic world a cultural common denominator, but **Hellenization** did not transform the East and make it one with the West. Hellenization was limited almost entirely to the cities, and in many urban centers it was often only a thin veneer. Many non-Greeks learned Greek and received a Greek education, which was a necessity for advancement in the state bureaucracy, and some assumed Greek names. But for most, Hellenization did not go much deeper. The countryside lacked even the veneer of Greek culture. Retaining traditional attitudes, the countryside in the East resisted Greek ways. In the villages, local and traditional law, local languages, and family customs remained unchanged; religion, the most important ingredient of the civilizations of the Near East, also kept its traditional character, even if ancestral gods were given Greek names.

To be sure, Hellenistic society was male dominated, but the status of women did show some improvement over the classical period. Considerably more than Athenian women in the Hellenic Age, Alexandrian women were able to accumulate and dispose of property. Some royal mothers and daughters exercised political power, even if behind the scenes, and royal women had access to great wealth as indicated by their cash contributions to cities. Some nonroyal ladies held important priestly offices, and far more than in the classical era, women contributed to high culture as poets, harpists, artists, and architects. Two of the new schools of philosophy, Epicureanism and Cynicism, welcomed female participation.

HELLENISTIC CULTURE

Literature, History, and Art

The Hellenistic Age saw a great outpouring of literary works. Callimachus (C. 305–240 B.C.), an Alexandrian scholar-poet, felt that no one could duplicate the great epics of Homer or the plays of the fifth-century B.C. dramatists. He urged poets

OLD MARKET WOMAN, C. 2ND CENTURY B.C.
Hellenistic genre sculpture depicted people in
everyday situations as individuals, rather than as
types. Her stooped shoulders, weighed down by her
groceries, also suggest the harsh physical conditions
that have worn her down over the years. (© The Metropolitan
Museum of Art/Art Resource, N.Y.)

to write short, finely crafted poems instead of composing on a grand scale. A student of his, Apol-
lonius of Rhodes, took issue with him and wrote
the *Argonautica*. This Homeric-style epic tells the
story of Jason's search for the Golden Fleece.

The poet Theocritus (C. 315–250 B.C.), who
lived on the island of Sicily, wrote pastorals that
showed great sensitivity to natural beauty. He
responded with uncommon feeling to the sky and
wind, to the hills, trees, and flowers, and to the
wildlife of the countryside.

The Athenian playwright Menander (C. 342–
291 B.C.) depicted Athenian life at the end of the
fourth century. Menander's plays, unlike Aristophanes' lampoons of inept politicians, dealt little
with politics. Apparently, Menander reflected the
attitude of his fellow Athenians, who, bored with
public affairs, had accepted their loss of freedom

to Macedonia and were preoccupied with their
private lives. Menander dealt sympathetically
with human weakness and wrote about stock
characters: the clever slave, the young playboy,
bragging soldiers, compassionate prostitutes, the
elderly seducer, the heroine in trouble. Menander
also expressed a warm concern for people, urging
them to recognize the humanity of their fellows—
whether Greeks, barbarians, or slaves—and to
treat one another with kindness and respect.

The leading historian of the Hellenistic Age
was Polybius (C. 200–118 B.C.), a Greek, whose
history of the rise of Rome is one of the great
works of historical literature (see Primary Source
box). Reflecting the universal tendencies of the
Hellenistic Age, Polybius endeavored to explain
how Rome had progressed from a city-state to a
world conqueror.

Hellenistic art, like Hellenistic philosophy, expressed a heightened awareness of the individual.
Whereas Hellenic sculpture aimed to depict ideal
beauty—the perfect body and face—Hellenistic
sculpture, moving from idealism to realism, captured individual character and expression, often
of ordinary people—an old fisherman, a crippled
man, a drunken lady, a dwarf. Scenes of daily life
were realistically portrayed. Wealthy merchants
commissioned artists to embellish their private
homes. Monarchs, eager to glorify their reigns,
sought the services of eminent artists to produce
royal portraits, victory monuments, paintings of
great battles, temples, and tombs. Continuing a
practice initiated during the Hellenic Age, Hellenistic cities commissioned artists. What was new,
however, was the proliferation of portrait statues
honoring prominent civic leaders, orators, poets,
philosophers, and playwrights.

Science

During the Hellenistic Age, Greek scientific
achievement reached its height. When Alexander
invaded Asia Minor, the former student of Aristotle
brought along surveyors, engineers, scientists, and
historians, who continued with him into Asia. The
vast amount of data in botany, zoology, geography, and astronomy collected by Alexander's staff
stimulated an outburst of activity. To integrate
so much information, scientists had to specialize
in the various disciplines. Hellenistic scientists

preserved and expanded the tradition of science developed in the Hellenic Age. They attempted a rational analysis of nature; they engaged in research, organized knowledge in logical fashion, devised procedures for mathematical proof, separated medicine from magic, grasped the theory of experiment, and applied scientific principles to mechanical devices. Hellenistic science, says historian Benjamin Farrington, stood "on the threshold of the modern world. When modern science began in the sixteenth century, it took up where the Greeks left off."[2]

Although Alexandria with its Museum was the principal center of scientific research, Athens still retained some of its former luster in this area. After Aristotle died in 322 B.C., he was succeeded as head of the Lyceum by Theophrastus and then by Strato. Both wrote treatises on many subjects—logic, ethics, politics, physics, and botany. Theophrastus systematized knowledge of botany in a manner similar to Aristotle's treatment of animals. Strato is most famous for his study of physics. It is likely that Strato, in his investigation of physical problems, did not rely on logic alone but performed a series of experiments to test his investigations.

Because of its library, the finest in the ancient world, and its state-supported museum, Alexandria attracted leading scholars and superseded Athens in scientific investigation. The museum was really a research institute—the first institution in history specifically established for the purpose of scientific research—in which some of the best minds of the day studied and worked.

Alexandrian doctors advanced medical skills. They improved surgical instruments and techniques and, by dissecting bodies, added to anatomical knowledge. Through their research, they discovered organs of the body not known until then, made the distinction between arteries and veins, divided nerves into those comprising the motor and the sensory system, and identified the brain as the source of intelligence. Their investigations advanced knowledge of anatomy and physiology to a level that was not significantly improved until the sixteenth century A.D.

Knowledge in the fields of astronomy and mathematics also increased. Eighteen centuries before Copernicus, Alexandrian astronomer Aristarchus (310–230 B.C.) said that the sun was the center of the universe, that the planets revolved around it, and that the stars were situated at great distances from the earth. But these revolutionary ideas were not accepted, and the belief in an earth-centered universe persisted. In geometry, Euclid, an Alexandrian mathematician who lived around 300 B.C., creatively synthesized earlier developments. Euclid's hundreds of geometric proofs, derived from reasoning alone—his conclusions flowed logically and flawlessly from given assumptions—are a profound witness to the power of the rational mind.

Alexander's expeditions had opened the eyes of Mediterranean peoples to the breadth of the earth and had stimulated explorations and geographic research. Eratosthenes (c. 275–194 B.C.), an Alexandrian geographer, sought a scientific understanding of this enlarged world. He divided the planet into climatic zones, declared that the oceans are joined, and with extraordinary ingenuity and accuracy measured the earth's circumference.

Archimedes of Syracuse (c. 287–212 B.C.), who studied at Alexandria, was a mathematician, a physicist, and an ingenious inventor. His mechanical inventions, including war engines, dazzled his contemporaries. However, Archimedes dismissed his practical inventions, preferring to be remembered as a theoretician. In one treatise, he established the general principles of hydrostatics, a branch of physics that deals with the pressure and equilibrium of liquids at rest.

Philosophy

Hellenistic thinkers preserved the rational tradition of Greek philosophy. Like their Hellenic predecessors, they regarded the cosmos as governed by universal principles intelligible to the rational mind. For the philosophers of both ages, a crucial problem was the achievement of the good life. Also, both Hellenic and Hellenistic thinkers sought rules for human conduct that accorded with rational standards; both believed that individuals attain happiness through their own efforts, unaided by the gods. In the tradition of Socrates, Hellenistic thinkers taught a morality of self-mastery. But although they retained the inheritance of the classical age, they also transformed it, for they had to adapt thought to the requirements of a cosmopolitan society.

Profile

Polybius

Rome's expansion from a city-state to a world empire that embraced many different nationalities and the extension of citizenship to non-Romans exemplified the universalism and cosmopolitanism of the Hellenistic Age. So too did Polybius' Histories, which sought to account for Rome's unprecedented accomplishment.

In 168 B.C. at the battle of Pynda, the Romans defeated Macedonia, which ruled Greece, ending its independence. After the battle, Polybius, along with a thousand other Greeks who had shown sympathy for Macedonia, was deported to Rome to be questioned. Protected by an influential Roman family, no harm came to him.

In the tradition of Thucydides, Polybius believed that a historian had a duty to teach moral lessons and to enlighten by pointing to general principles governing the course of historical events. Like Thucydides, he believed that there are lessons to be learned from a study of history and that his work would instruct current and future officials regarding the proper course of action under given circumstances. But whereas Thucydides wrote about the Peloponnesian War, which involved the Greek city-states, Polybius, reflecting the spirit of the Hellenistic Age, took the entire Mediterranean world as his subject. His aim was to recount how "the Romans succeeded in less than fifty-three years in bringing under their rule the whole inhabited world, an achievement which is without parallel in human history."* No question was of greater importance, he said, than to understand how Rome acquired this supremacy. Polybius stated explicitly that, unlike his predecessors who wrote specialized narrow studies dealing with aspects of Greek or Persian history, he was attempting a unique project— a systematic world history that "examine[s] the general

In the Hellenic Age, the starting point of philosophy was the citizen's relationship to the city; in the Hellenistic Age, the point of departure was the solitary individual's relationship to humanity and the individual's personal destiny in a larger and more complex world. Philosophy tried to deal with the feeling of alienation—of not belonging—resulting from the weakening of the individual's attachment to the polis and to arrive at a conception of community that corresponded to the social realities of a world grown larger. Unlike Plato and Aristotle, Hellenistic philosophers were moralists, not great speculators and theorists. The Hellenistic schools of philosophy, in contrast to their predecessors, were far less concerned with the scientific understanding of nature. Also in contrast to earlier Greek thinkers, they were less concerned with political organization. Philosophy was now chiefly preoccupied with providing the individual with practical guidelines for living; it tried to alleviate spiritual uneasiness and loss of security. It aspired to make people ethically independent so that they could achieve happiness in a hostile and competitive world. As the philosopher Epicurus said: "Empty are the words of that philosopher who offers no therapy for human suffering. For just as there is no use in medical expertise if it does not give therapy for bodily disease, so too there is no use in philosophy if it does not expel the suffering of the soul."[3] To "expel the suffering of the soul"—to conquer fear and anxiety and to achieve happiness—said Hellenistic philosophers, people must not allow themselves to be troubled by cares and concerns that are ultimately trivial.

In striving for tranquility of mind and relief from conflict, Hellenistic thinkers reflected the general anxiety that pervaded their society. They retained respect for reason and aspired to the rational life, but by stressing peace of mind and the effort to overcome anxiety, they were performing a quasi-religious function. Philosophy was trying to provide comfort for the individual suffering from feelings of loneliness and insignificance. This attempt indicated that Greek and comprehensive scheme of events."⁺ Such a study, he held, was an avenue to a wisdom closed to historians who write monographs on parochial, insignificant, and obscure topics.

Among the reasons Polybius gave for Rome's success was its political system, which balanced aristocratic and democratic elements: the Senate, representing the aristocracy, wielded great power, but the Assembly, representing the commoners, also played an important role in political life. Polybius held that such a political balance promoted loyalty and effective government. Polybius was greatly impressed with the Roman army. The discipline and dedication of citizen soldiers, he said, help explain Rome's success in creating a world empire.

---

*Polybius, *The Rise of the Roman Empire*, trans. Ian Scott-Kilvert (New York: Penguin Classics, 1979), 41.
⁺Ibid., 44.

civilization was undergoing a spiritual transformation. (We examine the full meaning of this transformation in Chapters 7 and 8.) The gravitation toward religion in an effort to relieve despair gathered momentum in the centuries that followed. Thus, Hellenistic philosophies helped prepare people to accept Christianity, which promised personal salvation. Ultimately, the Christian answer to the problems of alienation and the need for community would predominate over the Greco-Roman attempt at resolution.

The Hellenistic world gave rise to four principal schools of philosophy: Epicureanism, Stoicism, Skepticism, and Cynicism.

Epicureanism. In the tradition of Plato and Aristotle, Epicurus (342–270 B.C.) founded a school in Athens at the end of the fourth century B.C. He broke with the attitude of the Hellenic Age in significant ways. Unlike classical Greek philosophers, Epicurus, reflecting the Greeks' changing relationship to the city, taught the value of passivity and withdrawal from civic life. To him, citizenship was not a prerequisite for individual happiness. Wise persons, said Epicurus, would refrain from engaging in public affairs, for politics is marred by clashing factions and treachery that deprive individuals of their self-sufficiency, their freedom to choose and to act. Nor would wise individuals pursue wealth, power, or fame, as the pursuit would only provoke anxiety. For the same reason, wise persons would not surrender to hate or love, desires that distress the soul. A wise person would also try to live justly, for one who behaves unjustly is burdened with troubles. Nor could there be happiness when one worried about dying or pleasing the gods.

To Epicurus, dread that the gods punished people in this life and could inflict suffering after death was the principal cause of anxiety. To remove this source of human anguish, which he regarded as pure superstition, he favored a theory of nature that had no place for supernatural intervention in nature or in people's lives. Therefore, he adopted the physics of Democritus, which taught that all things consist of atoms in motion. In a universe of colliding atoms, there could be no higher intelligence ordering things; there was no room for divine activity. Epicurus taught that the gods probably did exist but that they could not influence human affairs; hence, it was pointless to worry about them. Individuals should order their lives without considering the gods. Epicurus embraced atomism, not as a disinterested scientist aspiring to truth, but as a moral philosopher seeking to liberate emotional life from fear of the gods.

People could achieve happiness, said Epicurus, when their bodies were "free from pain" and their minds "released from worry and fear." Although Epicurus wanted to increase pleasure for the individual, he rejected unbridled hedonism—an accusation directed at him by his critics. Because he believed that pleasure and happiness must be pursued wisely, he thought that the merely sensuous pleasures with unpleasant aftereffects (such as overeating and excessive drinking) should be avoided. In general, Epicurus espoused the traditional Greek view of moderation and prudence. Most important for achieving the good life, said Epicurus, was the company of friends.

By opening his philosophy to men and women, slave and free, Greek and barbarian, and by separating ethics from politics, Epicurus fashioned

109

Epicureanism: Living Well

Epicureanism was named for its founder, Epicurus, who established a school at Athens in 307 or 306 B.C. To achieve peace of mind, taught Epicurus, one should refrain from worrying about death or pleasing the gods, avoid intense involvements in public affairs, cultivate friendships, and pursue pleasure prudently. The following excerpts from Epicurus' works reveal his prescription for living well in a world grown more complex.

. . . We must grasp this point, that the principal disturbance in the minds of men arises because they think that these celestial bodies are blessed and immortal, and yet we have wills and actions and motives inconsistent with these attributes; and because they are always expecting or imagining some everlasting misery (inflicted on them by the gods), such as is depicted in legends, or even fear the loss of feeling in death . . . and, again, because they are brought to this pass not by reasoned opinion, but rather by some irrational presentiment . . . and, by learning the true causes of celestial phenomena and all other occurrences that come to pass from time to time, we shall free ourselves from all which produces the utmost fear in other men.

It is vain to ask of the gods what a man is capable of supplying for himself.

But the many at one moment shun death as the greatest of evils, at another yearn for it as a respite from the evils of life. But the wise man neither seeks to escape life nor fears the cessation of life, for neither does life offend him nor does the absence of life seem to be any evil.

A man cannot dispel his fear about the most important matters if he does not know what is the nature of the universe but suspects the truth of some mythical story. So that without natural science it is not possible to attain our pleasures unalloyed.

When, therefore, we maintain that pleasure is the end, we do not mean the pleasures-of-profligates and those that consist in sensuality, as is supposed by some who are either ignorant or disagree with us or do not understand, but freedom from pain in the body and from trouble in the mind.

Of all the things which wisdom acquires to produce the blessedness of the complete life, far the greatest is the possession of friendship.

We must release ourselves from the prison of affairs and politics.

A free life cannot acquire many possessions, because this is not easy to do without servility to mobs or monarchs. . . .

The noble soul occupies itself with wisdom and friendship. . . .

Questions for Analysis

1. What did Epicurus believe were the chief causes of emotional distress among human beings?
2. What advice did he offer for achieving inner peace and happiness? Does his advice have any value for us today?

Epicurus: The Extant Remains translated by Cyril Bailey (1926), pp. 53–119, *passim.* By permission of Oxford University Press.

a philosophy adapted to the post-Alexandrian world of kingdoms and universal culture.

Stoicism. Around the time of the founding of Epicurus' school, Zeno (335–263 B.C.) also opened a school in Athens. Zeno's teachings, called Stoicism, became the most important philosophy in the Hellenistic world. Epicurus backed away

from civic participation and political life as snares that deprived the individual of self-sufficiency. Stoics, however, developed a new formula for the individual's membership in a political community. By teaching that the world constituted a single society, Stoicism gave theoretical expression to the world-mindedness of the age. By arriving at the concept of a world-state, the city of humanity,

Stoicism offered an answer to the problem of community and alienation posed by the decline of the city-state. By stressing gaining control over one's inner life in dealing with life's misfortunes, Stoicism offered an avenue to individual happiness in a world fraught with uncertainty.

At the core of Stoicism was the belief that the universe contained a principle of order, variously called Divine Reason (*Logos*), the Divine Fire, or God—more the fundamental force of the universe than a living being. This ruling principle underlay reality and permeated all things; it ordered the cosmos according to law. The Stoics reasoned that, being part of the universe, people too shared in the **Logos** that operated throughout the cosmos. Inherent in every human soul and discovered through reason, the Logos enabled people to comprehend the principles of order that governed nature and to act virtuously and intelligently. This **natural law** provides human beings with an awareness of what is and is not correct behavior, especially when dealing with other human beings. Living in accordance with natural law, that is, living in agreement with nature, is the avenue to both virtue and happiness; it is our highest good. Natural law alone commands our ultimate obedience, for it teaches us and gives us the discipline to regulate our lives in the right way. And it is our capacity to reason that enables us to govern our lives correctly.

Since reason was common to all, human beings were essentially brothers and fundamentally equal. Reason gave individuals dignity and enabled them to recognize and respect the dignity of others. To the Stoics, all people, Greek and barbarian, free and slave, rich and poor, were fellow human beings deserving of respect, and one law, the law of nature, applied to all of them. What people had in common as fellow human beings far outweighed differences based on culture. All rational human beings were fellow citizens of a cosmopolis, a world community. Thus, the Stoics, like the Hebrews, arrived at the idea of a common humanity subject to the same moral obligations.

Pericles had spoken of the Athenians' obligation to abide by the laws and traditions of their city; Stoics, viewing people as citizens of the world, emphasized the individual's duty to understand and obey the natural law that governed the cosmos and applied to all. Socrates had taught

a morality of self-mastery—reason exercising control over feelings; the Stoics spread Socrates' philosophy beyond Athens, beyond Greece, and enlarged it, offering it as a way of life for all. Like Socrates, the Stoics believed that a person's distinctive quality was the ability to reason and that happiness came from the disciplining of emotions by the rational part of the soul. Also like Socrates, the Stoics maintained that individuals should progress morally, thus perfecting their character.

In the Stoic view, wise persons ordered their lives according to the natural law—the Logos, or law of reason—that underlay the cosmos. To live

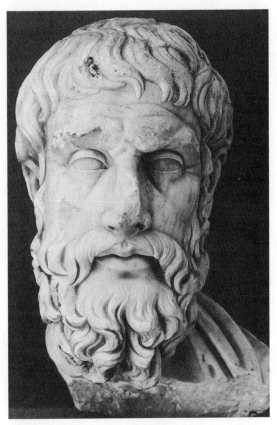

MARBLE PORTRAIT OF EPICURUS. The direct gaze and inner calm of the philosopher suggest the essence of his teachings. Epicurus believed that happiness came from a rationally ordered life. He urged his followers to disengage from the uncertainties and stress of politics, business, family, and religion. (The Metropolitan Museum of Art/Art Resource, N.Y.)

in agreement with nature—that is, to follow the dictates of reason—was the aim of moral activity. This harmony with the Logos would give these individuals the inner strength to resist the torments inflicted by others, by fate, and by their own passionate natures. Self-mastery and inner peace, or happiness, would follow. Such individuals would remain undisturbed by life's misfortunes, for their souls would be their own. Even slaves were not denied this inner freedom; although their bodies were subjected to the power of their masters, their minds still remained independent and free.

Stoicism had an enduring influence on the Western mind. To some Roman political and legal thinkers, the Empire fulfilled the Stoic ideal of a world community, in which people of different nationalities held citizenship and were governed by a worldwide law that accorded with the law of reason, or natural law—a moral order operating throughout the universe. Stoic beliefs—that by nature we are all members of one family, that each person is significant, that distinctions of rank and race are of no account, and that human law should not conflict with natural law—were incorporated into Roman jurisprudence, Christian thought, and modern liberalism. There is continuity between the Stoic idea of natural law and the principle of inalienable rights, rights to which all are entitled by nature, stated in the American Declaration of Independence. In the modern age, the principle of natural law provided theoretical justification for human rights that are the birthright of each individual.

Skepticism. The Epicureans tried to withdraw from the evils of this world and to attain personal happiness by reducing physical pain and mental anguish. The Stoics sought happiness by actively entering into harmony with universal reason, that is, with nature. Both philosophies sought peace of mind, but the Stoics did not disengage themselves from political life and often exerted influence over Hellenistic rulers. Skepticism, another school of philosophy, attacked the Epicurean and Stoic belief that there is a definite avenue to happiness. Skeptics held that one could achieve spiritual comfort by recognizing that none of the beliefs by which people lived were true or could bring happiness. Holding that human reason was grievously flawed, skeptics argued that nothing can be known with certainty. Therefore, suspending judgment—that is,

recognizing the existence of alternative viewpoints and disdaining a commitment to dogmatic beliefs—calms the mind and brings contentment.

Some Skeptics taught indifference to all theory and urged conformity to accepted views whether or not they were true. This attitude would avoid arguments and explanations. Gods might not exist, said the Skeptics, but to refuse to worship them or to deny their existence would only cause trouble; therefore, individuals should follow the crowd. The life of the mind—metaphysical speculation inquiring into the origin of things, and clever reasoning—did not bring truth or happiness, so why should one bother with it? Suspending judgment, recognizing the inability to understand, not committing oneself to a system of belief—by these means one could achieve peace of mind. Instead of embracing doctrines, said the Greek writer Lucian, individuals should go their way "with ever a smile and never a passion."[4] This was the position of those Skeptics who were suspicious of ideas, particularly all encompassing rational systems, and hostile to intellectuals.

The more sophisticated Skeptics did not run away from ideas but pointed out their limitations; they did not avoid theories but refuted them. In doing so, they did not reject reason. Rather, they focused on a problem of reason: whether indeed it could arrive at truth. Thus, Carneades of Cyrene (213–129 B.C.) insisted that all ideas, even mathematical principles, must be regarded as hypotheses and assumptions, not as absolutes. Just because the universe showed signs of order, Carneades argued, one could not assume that it had been created by God. Since there was never any certainty, only probability, morality should derive from practical experience rather than from dogma.

Cynicism. The Cynics were not theoretical philosophers but supreme individualists who rebelled against established values and conventions—against every barrier of society that restrained individuals from following their own natures. Cynics regarded laws and public opinion, private property and employment, and wives and children as hindrances to the free life. Extreme individualists, the Cynics had no loyalty to family, city, or kingdom and ridiculed religion, philosophy, and literature. They renounced possessions and showed no respect for authority. When Diogenes

AN ITINERANT CYNIC. Cynics renounced possessions, showed no loyalty to city or kingdom, dismissed philosophy and religion as nonsense, and lived ascetically, often wandering from place to place. The image shows an itinerant Cynic, lantern in hand.

(RMN-Grand Palais/Art Resource, N.Y.)

Of Sinope, a fourth-century B.C. Cynic, met Alexander the Great, he is supposed to have asked only that the great conqueror get out of his light.

Cynics put their philosophy into practice. They cultivated indifference and apathy and scorned wealth, fame, and noble birth. To harden themselves against life's misfortunes, they engaged in strenuous exercise, endured cold and hunger, and lived ascetically. Not tied down by property or employment, Cynics wandered shoeless from place to place, wearing dirty and ragged clothes and carrying staffs. To show their disdain for society's customs, Cynics grew long scraggly beards, used foul language, and cultivated bad manners. Diogenes supposedly said: "Look at me, . . . I am without a home, without a city, without property, without a slave; I sleep on the ground; I have neither wife nor children, no miserable governor's mansion, but only earth, and sky, and one rough cloak. Yet what do I lack? Am I not free from pain and fear, am I not free?"[5]

In their attack on inherited conventions, Cynics strove for self-sufficiency and spiritual security. Theirs was the most radical philosophical quest for meaning and peace of soul during the Hellenistic Age.

THE HELLENISTIC LEGACY

The Hellenistic Age encompassed the period from the death of Alexander to the formation of the Roman Empire. During these three centuries, Greek civilization spread eastward as far as India and westward to Rome. As Greeks settled in the Near East and intermingled with Egyptians, Syrians, Persians, and others, the parochialism of the Greek polis gave way to a new cosmopolitanism, an interest in the culture of other ethnic groups, and to universalism, an awareness that people were members of a world community that transcended citizenship in one's native city. Both philosophy and the arts reflected these new concerns.

Rome, conqueror of the Mediterranean world and transmitter of Hellenism, inherited the universalist tendencies of the Hellenistic Age and embodied them in its law, institutions, and art. So too did Christianity, which welcomed converts from every ethnic background and held that God loved all people and that Christ died for all humanity. The Stoic idea of natural law that applies to all human beings and its corollary that human beings are fundamentally equal were crucial to the formulation of the modern idea that the individual is endowed with **natural rights** that no government can violate. A parallel can be drawn between the Hellenistic Age, in which Greek civilization spread to the Near East and as far away as India and China, and our own age, in which the ideas, institutions, and technology of Western civilization have been exported throughout the globe.

❖   ❖   ❖

Notes

1. Quoted in John Ferguson, *The Heritage of Hellenism* (New York: Science History Publications, 1973), 30.

2. Benjamin Farrington, *Greek Science* (Baltimore: Penguin Books, 1961), 301.

3. Quoted in Anthony Gottlieb, *The Dream of Reason* (New York: W. W. Norton, 2000), 283–284.

4. Quoted in J. H. Randall Jr., *Hellenistic Ways of Deliverance and the Making of the Christian Synthesis* (New York: Columbia University Press, 1970), 74.

5. Epictetus, *The Discourses as Reported by Arrian, the Manual and Fragments*, trans. W. A. Oldfather (Cambridge, Mass.: Harvard University Press, 1966), 2:147.

Chapter 6

The Roman Republic:
City-State to World Empire

A Roman Warship with Legionnaires on a Relief from the Temple of Fortuna Primigenia, First Century B.C. Roman soldiers fought on sea as well as on land, conquering nations throughout the Mediterranean area during the eras of the Republic and the Empire. (Scala/Art Resource, N.Y.)

- **Evolution of the Roman Constitution**
- **Roman Expansion to 146 B.C.**
- **Culture in the Republic**
- **Collapse of the Republic**

Focus Questions

1. What was the significance of the conflict between plebeians and patricians?
2. What factors enabled the city-state of Rome to conquer Italy and the Mediterranean world?
3. What was the significance of Roman expansion?
4. What were the reasons for the collapse of the Roman Republic?

Rome's great achievement was to transcend the narrow political orientation of the city-state and to create a world-state that unified the different nations of the Mediterranean world. Regarding the polis as the only means to the good life, the Greeks had not desired a larger political unit and had almost totally excluded foreigners from citizenship. Although Hellenistic philosophers had conceived the possibility of a world community, Hellenistic politics could not shape one. Rome overcame the limitations of the city-state mentality and developed an empire-wide system of law and citizenship. The Hebrews were distinguished by their prophets and the Greeks by their philosophers. The Romans produced no Amos or Isaiah, and no Plato or Aristotle; their genius found expression in law and government and in the transmission of the Greek cultural achievement.

Historians divide Roman history into two broad periods: the period of the **Republic** began in 509 B.C. with the overthrow of the Etruscan monarchy; the period of the **Empire** began in 27 B.C., when Octavian (Augustus) became in effect the first Roman emperor, ending almost five hundred years of republican self-government. By conquering the Mediterranean world and extending Roman law and, in some instances, citizenship to different nationalities, the Roman Republic transcended the parochialism typical of the city-state. The Republic initiated the trend toward political and legal universalism, which reached fruition in the second period of Roman history, the Empire.

EVOLUTION OF THE ROMAN CONSTITUTION

By the eighth century B.C., peasant communities existed on some of Rome's seven hills near the Tiber River in central Italy. To the north stood Etruscan cities and to the south Greek cities. The more advanced civilizations of both Etruscans and Greeks were gradually absorbed by the Romans.

The origin of the Etruscans remains a mystery, although some scholars believe that they came from Asia Minor and settled in north-central Italy. From them, Romans acquired architectural

Chronology 6.1 ❖ The Roman Republic

509 B.C.	Expulsion of the Etruscan monarch
450	Law of Twelve Tables
287	End of the Struggle of the Orders
264–241	First Punic War: Rome acquires provinces
218–201	Second Punic War: Hannibal is defeated
149–146	Third Punic War: destruction of Carthage
133–122	Land reforms by the Gracchi brothers; they are murdered by the Senate
88–83	Conflict between Sulla and the forces of Marius; Sulla emerges as dictator
79	After restoring rule by Senate, Sulla retires
73–71	Slave revolt is led by Spartacus
58–51	Caesar campaigns in Gaul
49–44	Caesar is dictator of Rome
31 B.C.	Antony and Cleopatra are defeated at Actium by Octavian

styles and skills in road construction, sanitation, hydraulic engineering (including underground conduits), metallurgy, ceramics, and portrait sculpture. Symbols of authority and rule—purple robes, ivory-veneer chariots, thrones for state officials, and a bundle of rods and an ax held by attendants—were also borrowed from the Etruscans. Etruscan words and names entered into the Latin language, and Roman religion absorbed Etruscan gods.

The Etruscans had expanded their territory in Italy during the seventh and sixth centuries B.C., and they controlled the monarchy in Rome. However, defeated by Celts, Greeks, and finally Romans, the Etruscans had ceased to exercise any political power in Italy by the third century B.C.

Rome became a republic at the end of the sixth century B.C.—the traditional date is 509 B.C.—when the landowning aristocrats, or **patricians**, overthrew the Etruscan king. In the opening phase of republican history, religion governed the people, dictated the law, and legitimized the rule of the patricians—aristocrats by birth who regarded themselves as the preservers of sacred traditions. Gradually, the Romans loosened the ties between religion and politics

and hammered out a constitutional system that paralleled the Greek achievement of rationalizing and secularizing politics and law. In time, the Romans, like the Greeks, came to view law as an expression of the public will and not as the creation of god-kings, priest-kings, or a priestly caste.

The impetus for the growth of the Roman constitution came from a conflict—known as the Struggle of the Orders—between the patricians and the commoners, or **plebeians**. At the beginning of the fifth century B.C., the patrician-dominated government consisted of two annually elected executives called consuls, the Centuriate Assembly, and the Senate. Patricians owned most of the land and controlled the army. The two consuls, who came from the nobility, commanded the army, served as judges, and initiated legislation. To prevent either consul from becoming an autocrat, decisions had to be approved by both of them. In times of crisis, the consuls were authorized by the Senate to nominate a dictator; he would possess absolute powers during the emergency, but these powers would expire after six months. The consuls were aided by other annually elected magistrates and administrators. The Centuriate

117

Assembly was a popular assembly but, because of voting procedures, was controlled by the nobility. The Assembly elected consuls and other magistrates and made the laws, which also needed Senate approval. The Senate advised the Assembly but did not itself enact laws; it controlled public finances and foreign policy. Senators either were appointed for life terms by the consuls or were former magistrates. The Senate was the principal organ of patrician power.

The tension between patricians and commoners stemmed from plebeian grievances, which included enslavement for debt, discrimination in the courts, prevention of intermarriage with patricians, lack of political representation, and the absence of a written code of laws. Resenting their inferior status and eager for economic relief, the plebeians organized and waged a struggle for political, legal, and social equality. They had one decisive weapon: their threat to secede from Rome, that is, not to pay taxes, work, or serve in the army. Realizing that Rome, which was constantly involved in warfare on the Italian peninsula, could not endure without plebeian help, the pragmatic patricians begrudgingly made concessions. Thus, the plebeians slowly gained legal equality.

Early in the fifth century, the plebeians won the right to form their own assembly (the Plebeian Assembly, which was later enlarged and called the Tribal Assembly). This Assembly could elect tribunes, officials who were empowered to protect plebeian rights. As a result of plebeian pressure, in about 450 B.C., the first Roman code of laws was written. Called the Twelve Tables, the code gave plebeians some degree of protection against unfair and oppressive patrician officials, who could interpret customary law in an arbitrary way. Other concessions gained later by the plebeians included the right to intermarry with patricians; access to the highest political, judicial, and religious offices in the state; and the elimination of slavery as payment for debt. In 287 B.C., a date generally recognized as the termination of the plebeian–patrician struggle, laws passed by the Tribal Assembly no longer required Senate approval. Now the plebeians had full civil equality and legal protection, and their assembly had full power to enact legislation.

Despite these reforms, Rome was still ruled by an upper class. The oligarchy that now held power consisted of patricians and influential plebeians who had joined forces with the old nobility. Marriages between patricians and politically powerful plebeians strengthened this alliance. Generally only wealthy plebeians became tribunes, and they tended to side with the old nobility rather than defend the interests of poor plebeians. By using bribes, the ruling oligarchy of patricians and wealthy plebeians maintained control over the Assembly, and the Senate remained a bastion of aristocratic power.

A patron–client relationship extending back to the days of the monarchy reinforced upper-class rule. In early Rome, a plebeian seeking protection for himself and his family in the courts looked to a patrician for assistance. In return, the plebeian gave his patrician patron both military and political support. Enduring over the centuries, the patron–client relationship assured powerful nobles of their commoner clients' support in the Assembly, and it provided clients with food, money, and protection.

Thus, from beginning to end, an upper class—sometimes expanded to allow entry of new talent and wealth—governed the Roman Republic. This aristocracy's view of liberty always remained elitist: freedom for Rome's best men to achieve virtue (*virtus*), dignity (*dignitas*), and fame (*fama*) by competing with one another for political power and privilege. Cicero (see below), himself a member of the ruling elite, aptly summed up its outlook: "the safety of the State depends upon the wisdom of its best men, especially since Nature has provided not only that those men who are superior in virtue and in spirit should rule the weaker, but also that the weaker should be willing to obey the stronger."[1] Like others of the upper class, Cicero held that "the perversity and rashness of popular assemblies" precluded them from governing effectively.[2] In the Greek cities, tyrants had succeeded in breaking aristocratic dominance, thereby clearing a pathway for democratic government. But in the Roman Republic, the nobility maintained its tight grip on the reins of power until the civil wars of the first century B.C.

Deeming themselves Rome's finest citizens, the ruling oligarchy led Rome during its period of expansion and demonstrated a sense of responsibility and a talent for statesmanship. In noble families, parents and elders prepared the young for public service. They recounted the glorious deeds of ancestors who had served Rome, and they reminded youngsters of their responsibility to bring additional honors to the family by winning distinction as a commander, orator, or jurist. In this way, a son would prove his worth as a man and as a Roman.

During their two-hundred-year class struggle, the Romans forged a constitutional system based on civic needs rather than on religious mystery. The essential duty of government ceased to be the regular performance of religious rituals and became the maintenance of order at home and the preservation of Roman might and dignity in international relations. Although the Romans retained the ceremonies and practices of their ancestral religion—correct observance was a way of showing respect for tradition—public interest, not religious tradition, determined the content of law and was the standard by which all the important acts of the city were judged. When Romans chose a course of action in public life, they rarely took into consideration the fear of displeasing the gods. By the late Republic, Romans did not seem concerned about divine intervention in their daily lives; the prospect of divine punishment seemed quite remote. In the opening stage of republican history, law was priestly and sacred, spoken only by priests and known only to men of religious families. Gradually, as law was written, debated, and altered, it became disentangled from religion. Another step in this process of secularization and rationalization occurred when the study and interpretation of law passed from the hands of priests to a class of professional jurists, who analyzed, classified, systematized, and sought commonsense solutions to legal problems.

The Roman constitution was not a product of abstract thought, nor was it the gift of a great lawmaker such as the Athenian Solon. Rather, like the unwritten British constitution, the Roman constitution evolved gradually and empirically in response to specific needs. The Romans, unlike the Greeks, were distinguished by practicality and common sense, not by a love of abstract thought. In their pragmatic and empirical fashion, they gradually developed the procedures of public politics and the legal state.

Undoubtedly, the commoners' struggle for rights and power did arouse hatred on both sides. But in contrast to the domestic strife in Greek cities, Rome's class conflict did not end in civil war. This peaceful solution testifies to the political good sense of the Romans. Fear of foreign powers and the tradition of civic patriotism prevented the patrician–plebeian conflict from turning into a fight to the death. At the time of the class struggle, Rome was also engaged in the extension of its power over the Italian peninsula. Without civic harmony and stability, Rome could not have achieved expansion.

ROMAN EXPANSION TO 146 B.C.

By 146 B.C., Rome was the dominant state in the Mediterranean world. Roman expansion occurred in three main stages: the uniting of the Italian peninsula, which gave Rome the forces that transformed it from a city-state into a great power; the collision with Carthage, from which Rome emerged as ruler of the western Mediterranean; and the subjugation of the Hellenistic states, which brought Romans in close contact with Greek civilization. As Rome expanded territorially, its leaders enlarged their vision. Instead of restricting citizenship to people having ethnic kinship, Rome assimilated other peoples into its political community. Just as Roman law had grown to cope with the earlier grievances of the plebeians, so too it adjusted to the new situations resulting from the creation of a multinational empire. The city of Rome was evolving into the city of humanity—the cosmopolis envisioned by the Stoics.

The Uniting of Italy

During the first stage of expansion, Rome extended its hegemony over Italy, subduing in the process neighboring Latin kinsmen, semicivilized Italian tribes, the once-dominant Etruscans, and Greek city-states in southern Italy. At the beginning, Roman warfare was principally motivated by the hunger for more farmland. As Rome expanded and its territory and responsibilities increased, it was often drawn into conflict to protect its widened boundaries and its allies. Also fueling Roman expansion was an aristocratic ethos, which placed the highest value on glory and reputation. Demonstrating prowess in war, aristocrats believed, was the finest way to win the esteem of fellow Romans, bring honor to their families, and enhance their own political careers.

Rome's conquest of Italy stemmed in part from superior military organization, grueling training, and iron discipline. From the Greeks they acquired the most advanced methods of siege craft. Also copying the Greeks, the Romans organized their soldiers into battle formations; in contrast, their opponents often fought as disorganized hordes, which were prone to panic and flight. Fighting as part of a unit strengthened the courage and confidence of the Roman soldier, for he knew that his comrades would stand with him. Roman soldiers who deserted their posts or fled from battle were punished and disgraced, an ordeal more terrible than facing up to the enemy. The promise of glory and rewards also impelled the Roman soldier to distinguish himself in battle.

Ultimately, Rome's success was due to the character of its people and the quality of its statesmanship. The Roman farmer-soldier was dedicated, rugged, persevering, and self-reliant. He could march thirty miles a day laden with arms, armor, and equipment weighing sixty pounds. In the face of danger, he remained resolute and tenacious, obedient to the poet Virgil's maxim: "Yield you not to ill fortune, but go against it with more daring." Romans willingly made sacrifices so that Rome might endure. In conquering Italy, they were united by a moral and religious devotion to their city strong enough to overcome social conflict, factional disputes, and personal ambition.

Despite its army's might, Rome could not have mastered Italy without the cooperation of other Italian peoples. Like other ancient peoples, Rome plundered, enslaved, and brutalized, at times with great ferocity. But it also endeavored, through generous treatment, to gain the loyalty of those it had conquered. Some defeated Italian communities retained a measure of self-government but turned the conduct of foreign affairs over to Rome and contributed contingents to the army when Rome went to war. Other conquered people received partial or full citizenship. In extending its dominion over Italy, Rome displayed a remarkable talent for converting former enemies into allies and eventually into Roman citizens. No Greek city had ever envisaged integrating nonnatives into its political community.

The Italian Confederation formed by Rome was a unique and creative organization that

Polybius: The Roman Army

The discipline and dedication of the citizen soldiers help explain Rome's success in conquering a world empire. In the following account, Polybius (see Profile in Chapter 5) tells how the commanders enforced obedience and fostered heroism.

A court-martial composed of the tribunes immediately sits to try him [a soldier], and if he is found guilty, he is punished by beating (*fustuarium*). This is carried out as follows. The tribune takes a cudgel and lightly touches the condemned man with it, whereupon all the soldiers fall upon him with clubs and stones, and usually kill him in the camp itself. But even those who contrive to escape are no better off. How indeed could they be? They are not allowed to return to their homes, and none of their family would dare to receive such a man into the house. Those who have once fallen into this misfortune are completely and finally ruined. The *optio* [lieutenant] and the *decurio* [sergeant] of the squadron are liable to the same punishment if they fail to pass on the proper orders at the proper moment to the patrols and the *decurio* of the next squadron. The consequence of the extreme severity of this penalty and of the absolute impossibility of avoiding it is that the night watches of the Roman army are faultlessly kept. . . .

The Romans also have an excellent method of encouraging young soldiers to face danger. Whenever any have especially distinguished themselves in a battle, the general assembles the troops and calls forward those he considers to have shown exceptional courage. He praises them first for their gallantry in action and for anything in their previous conduct which is particularly worthy of mention, and then he distributes gifts such as the following: to a man who has wounded one of the enemy, a spear; to one who has killed and stripped an enemy, a cup if he is in the infantry, or horse-trappings if in the cavalry—originally the gift was simply a lance. These presentations are not made to men who have wounded or stripped an enemy in the course of a pitched battle, or at the storming of a city, but to those who during a skirmish or some similar situation in which there is no necessity to engage in single combat, have voluntarily and deliberately exposed themselves to danger.

At the storming of a city the first man to scale the wall is awarded a crown of gold. In the same way those who have shielded and saved one of their fellow-citizens or of the allies are honoured with gifts. . . . The men who receive these trophies not only enjoy great prestige in the army and soon afterwards in their homes, but they are also singled out for precedence in religious processions when they return. On these occasions nobody is allowed to wear decorations save those who have been honoured for their bravery by the consuls, and it is the custom to hang up the trophies they have won in the most conspicuous places in their houses, and to regard them as proofs and visible symbols of their valour. So when we consider this people's almost obsessive concern with military rewards and punishments, and the immense importance which they attach to both, it is not surprising that they emerge with brilliant success from every war in which they engage.

Question for Analysis

1. How did the Romans ensure good discipline and promote bravery among their soldiers?

Polybius, *The Rise of the Roman Empire*, trans. Ian Scott-Kilvert (New York: Penguin Books, 1984), 332–334.

conferred on Italians a measure of security and order previously unknown. Rome prevented internecine wars within the peninsula, suppressed internal revolutions within city-states, and protected the Italians from barbarians (Gallic invaders from the north). In the wars of conquest outside Italy, a share of the glory and plunder fell to all Italians, another benefit of the confederation.

By 264 B.C., Rome had achieved two striking successes. First, it had secured social cohesion by redressing the grievances of the plebeians. Second, it had increased its military might by conquering Italy, thus obtaining the human resources with which it would conquer the Mediterranean world.

Conquest of the Mediterranean World

When Rome finished unifying Italy, there were five great powers in the Mediterranean area: the Seleucid monarchy in the Near East, the Ptolemaic monarchy in Egypt, the kingdom of Macedonia, Carthage in the western Mediterranean, and the Roman-dominated Italian Confederation. One hundred twenty years later, by 146 B.C., Rome had subjected the other states to its dominion—"an event for which the past affords no precedent," said the contemporary Greek historian Polybius.

Roman expansion beyond Italy did not proceed according to predetermined design. Indeed, some Roman leaders considered involvement in foreign adventures a threat to both Rome's security and its traditional way of life. But it is difficult for a great power not to get drawn into conflicts as its interests grow, and, without planning it, Rome acquired an overseas empire.

Shortly after asserting supremacy in Italy, Rome engaged Carthage, the other great power in the western Mediterranean, in a prolonged conflict. Founded about 800 B.C. by Phoenicians, the North African city of Carthage had become a prosperous commercial center. Its wealth was derived from a virtual monopoly of trade in the western Mediterranean and along the western coasts of Africa and Europe. The Carthaginians (*Poeni* in Latin) had acquired an empire comprising North Africa and coastal regions of southern Spain, Sardinia, Corsica, and western Sicily.

War between the two great powers began because Rome feared Carthage's designs on the northern Sicilian city of Messana. Rome was apprehensive about the southern Italian city-states that were its allies, fearing that Carthage would use Messana either to attack them or to interfere with their trade. Rome decided that the security of its allies required intervention in Sicily.

The two powers had stumbled into a collision, the First Punic War (264–241 B.C.), that

neither had deliberately sought. Although Rome suffered severe losses—including the annihilation of an army that had invaded North Africa and the destruction of hundreds of ships in battle and storms—the Romans never considered anything but a victor's peace. Drawing manpower from loyal allies throughout Italy, Rome finally prevailed over Carthage, which had to surrender Sicily to Rome. Three years later, Rome seized the islands of Corsica and Sardinia from a weakened Carthage. With the acquisition of these territories beyond Italy, which were made into provinces, Rome had the beginnings of an empire.

Carthaginian expansion in Spain in order to recoup wealth—Spain was rich in metals—and to obtain manpower for the depleted Carthaginian forces precipitated the Second Punic War (218–201 B.C.). Coming from Spain, the Carthaginian army was commanded by Hannibal (247–183 B.C.), whose military genius astounded the ancients. Hannibal led a seasoned army, complete with war elephants for charging enemy lines, through passes in the Alps so steep and icy that men and animals sometimes lost their footing and fell to their deaths. Others died fighting hostile mountain tribes or succumbed to the cold, but desertion was the principal reason for the diminution of Hannibal's army. Some twenty-six thousand men survived the crossing into Italy; fifteen thousand more were recruited from Gallic tribesmen of the Po valley. At the battle of Cannae (216 B.C.), 50,000 Carthaginian, many of them mercenaries—principally Libyans, Numidians, Gauls, and Spaniards—faced some 80,000 Roman citizen-soldiers. In a brilliant encircling maneuver, the Carthaginian forces completely destroyed the largest army Rome had ever put into the field. The butchering by hand of the trapped Roman soldiers lasted for hours. Some 50,000 corpses littered the open plain, the most costly battle in the ancient world.

Romans were in a state of shock. Mixed with grief for the dead was the fear that Hannibal would crown his victory with an attack on Rome itself. To prevent panic, the Senate ordered women and children indoors, limited mourning to thirty days, and prepared to raise a new army. Adding to Rome's distress was the defection of many southern Italian allies to Hannibal.

These were the Republic's worst days. Nevertheless, says the Roman historian Livy, the Romans

CAST MADE FROM TRAJAN'S COLUMN. Emperor Trajan (A.D. 98–117) constructed a column to commemorate his campaigns. One of the reliefs depicts a Roman fleet landing at the port of Acona. During the First Punic War, Rome had become a naval power able to counter Carthage's fleet. (DeA Picture Library/Art Resource, N.Y.)

did not breathe a word of peace. Hannibal could not follow up his victory at Cannae with a finishing blow, for Rome wisely would not allow its army to be lured into another major engagement. Nor did Hannibal possess the manpower to capture the city itself, with its formidable fortifications. In addition, most of Rome's Italian allies remained loyal, although some south Italian cities went over to Hannibal. Rome quickly raised and equipped new legions, even enlisting seventeen-year olds and promising freedom to slaves and amnesty to criminals who volunteered to serve. To finance the army, taxes were doubled and women surrendered their jewelry to the state. Most important, the Roman fleet prevented supplies from reaching the Carthaginians.

When Rome invaded North Africa, threatening Carthage, Hannibal was forced to withdraw his troops from Italy in order to defend his homeland. Hannibal, who had won every battle in Italy, was defeated by Scipio Africanus at the battle of Zama in North Africa in 202 B.C., ending the Second Punic War. Carthage was compelled to surrender Spain and to give up its elephants and its navy. Sheer determination, its vast reserves of manpower, and the state's willingness to garner its wealth to strengthen its legions explain Rome's victory.

The Second Punic War left Rome as the sole great power in the western Mediterranean; it also hastened Rome's entry into the politics of the Hellenistic world. In the year after Cannae, during Rome's darkest ordeal, Philip V of Macedonia formed an alliance with Hannibal. Fearing that the Macedonian ruler might have intentions of invading Italy, Rome initiated the First Macedonian War and won it in 205 B.C. To end Macedonian influence in Greece, which Rome increasingly viewed as a Roman protectorate, the Romans fought two other wars with Macedonia. Finally, in 148 B.C., Rome created the province of Macedonia.

Intervention in Greece led to Roman involvement in the Hellenistic kingdoms of the Near East and Asia Minor—Seleucia, Egypt, and Pergamum. The Hellenistic states became client kingdoms of Rome and consequently lost their freedom of action in foreign affairs.

Roman imperialism is a classic example of a great power being snared into overseas adventures. To achieve security, Rome protected its allies, prevented endemic warfare, and thwarted any would-be conquerors of Italy. In the course of these actions came considerable spoils of war, but Rome's principal motives for expansion were strategic and political, not economic.

In 146 B.C., the same year that Rome's hegemony over the Hellenistic world was assured, Rome concluded an unnecessary Third Punic War with Carthage. Although Carthage was by then a second-rate power and no longer a threat to Rome's security, Rome had launched this war of annihilation against Carthage in 149 B.C. The Romans were driven by old hatreds and the traumatic memory of Hannibal's near conquest. In what could be called genocide, the Romans massacred the Carthaginians, sold survivors into slavery, obliterated the city by fire (which burned for seventeen days), and turned the territory into the Roman province of Africa. Rome's savage and irrational behavior toward a helpless Carthage was an early sign of the deterioration of senatorial leadership; there would be others.

Rome had not yet reached the limits of its expansion, but there was no doubt that by 146 B.C. the Mediterranean world had been subjected to its will. No power could stand up to Rome. From 220 B.C., the start of the Second Punic War to 167 B.C., wrote Polybius "the Romans succeeded in less than fifty-three years in bringing under their rule almost the whole of the inhabited world, an achievement which is without parallel in human history."[3]

Consequences of Expansion

As a result of Rome's eastern conquests, thousands of Greeks came to Rome; many were educated persons who had been enslaved because of the conquests. This influx accelerated the process of Hellenization—the adoption of Greek culture—which had begun earlier with Rome's contact with the Greek cities of southern Italy.

A crucial consequence of expansion was Roman contact with the legal experience of other peoples, including the Greeks. Roman jurists, demonstrating the Roman virtues of pragmatism and common sense, selectively incorporated into Roman law elements of the legal codes and traditions of these nations. Thus, Roman jurists empirically fashioned the *jus gentium*, the law of nations, or peoples, which gradually was applied throughout the Empire (see "Law," in Chapter 7).

Rome's conquests also contributed to the rise of a business class, whose wealth was derived from trade, army supply contracts, construction, and tax collecting in the provinces. Rome had no professional civil service, and the collection of public revenues was open to bidding—the highest bidder receiving a contract to collect customs duties, rents on public lands, and tribute in the provinces. The collector's profit came from milking as much tax money as he could from the provincials. These financiers belonged to a group called the Equites, which also included prosperous landowners. Generally, the interests of the Equites paralleled those of the ruling oligarchy. At times, however, they did support generals—notably Julius Caesar—who challenged senatorial rule.

The immense wealth brought to Rome from ransacked eastern cities and overworked Spanish silver mines gave the upper classes a taste for luxury. The rich built elaborate homes, which they decorated with fine furniture and works of art and staffed with servants, cooks, and tutors. They delighted in sumptuous banquets, which contained all types of delicacies. Wealthy matrons wore fancy gowns and elaborate hairstyles. These excesses prompted Roman moralists to castigate the people for violating traditional values. Moralists lamented that the new prosperity deteriorated the Roman character.

Roman conquerors had transported to Italy hundreds of thousands of war captives, including Greeks, from all over the Empire. The enslavement and deportations would continue in the first century B.C. (Julius Caesar, for example, enslaved some one million Gauls.) It is estimated that between 80 and 8 B.C. more than two million enslaved aliens were transported to Italy. By the middle of that century, slaves constituted about one-third of Italy's population, compared with about 10 percent before the Second Punic War. The wars of conquest had made the slave trade a vast and lucrative commercial venture. Increasing the number of slaves was the sale of people kidnapped by pirates and of children sold to slaver traders by poor parents. At slave markets, human chattel was auctioned off to the highest bidder.

Like the Greeks, Romans considered slavery indispensable for the preservation of civilized life. Roman jurists and intellectuals regarded the division of humanity into masters and slaves as a rule of nature and viewed the slave as an animate tool, an object that produced and served; like other forms of property, slaves could be sold or rented out by their masters. The more fortunate or more capable slaves worked as domestic servants, artisans, bookkeepers, scribes, and administrators; the luckless and more numerous, branded and chained, toiled from dawn to dusk on the growing number of plantations or died early laboring in mines under inhuman conditions. So brutal was their existence that they begged for death, reported a Roman observer. Except for the very poor, every free Roman owned at least one slave. Roman masters often treated their slaves brutally: torture was common, and masters sexually exploited both male and female slaves for their own pleasure or compelled them to work as prostitutes. But strong personal bonds between master and slave also existed—for example, there are accounts of slaves enduring torture and death to protect their masters from enemies.

Although slave uprisings were not common, their ferocity terrified the Romans. In 135 B.C., slaves in Sicily revolted and captured some key towns, defeating Roman forces before being subdued. In 73 B.C., gladiators led by Spartacus broke out of their barracks and were joined by tens of thousands of runaways. Spartacus aimed to escape from Italy to Gaul and Thrace, the homelands of many slaves. The slave army, which grew to some 150,000, defeated Roman armies and devastated southern Italy before the superior might of Rome prevailed. Some 6,000 of the defeated slaves were tortured and crucified on the road from Capua to Rome.

Republican Rome treated the people in overseas lands differently from its Italian allies. Italians were drafted into the Roman army, but provincials as a rule served only in emergencies, for Rome was not certain of their loyalty or of their readiness to meet Roman standards of discipline. Whereas Rome had been somewhat generous in extending citizenship to Italians, provincials were granted citizenship only in exceptional cases. All but some favored communities were required to pay taxes to Rome. Roman governors, lesser officials, and businessmen found the provinces a source of quick wealth; they were generally unrestrained by the Senate, which was responsible for administering the overseas territories. Exploitation, corruption, looting, and extortion soon ran rampant. "No administration in history has ever devoted itself so whole-heartedly to fleecing its subjects for the private benefit of its ruling class as Rome of the last age of the Republic," concludes E. Badian.[4] The Roman nobility proved unfit to manage a world empire.

Despite numerous examples of misrule in the provinces, Roman administration had many positive features. Rome generally allowed its subjects a large measure of self-government and did not interfere with religion and local customs. Usually, the Roman taxes worked out to be no higher, and in some instances lower, than those under previous regimes. Most important, Rome reduced the endemic warfare that had plagued these regions.

Caspian Sea

Volga R.

Don R.

PARTHIA

Euphrates R.

Tigris R.

Seleucia

ARABIAN DESERT

ARMENIA

Damascus

Red Sea

Antioch

SYRIA

Nile R.

CAPPADOCIA

PONTUS

Dnieper R.

Black Sea

CRIMEA

PHRYGIA

CILICIA

JUDEA

Jerusalem

Cyprus

ASIA

Pergamum

EGYPT

Alexandria

Rhodes

THRACE

DACIA

MOESIA

Athens

Crete

Mediterranean Sea

SAHARA

MACEDON

DALMATIA

Actium

Brundisium

LIBYA

Danube R.

PANNONIA

VINDELICIA

NORICUM

RAETIA

Adriatic Sea

Cannae

Tarentum

Messana

Sicily

400 Mi.

GERMANY

Elbe R.

GAUL

Po R.

CISALPINE GAUL

ETRUSCANS

Tiber R.

Rome

Corsica

400 Km.

200

Rhine R.

Rhône R.

Sardinia

Carthage

200

North Sea

NUMIDIA

0

0

NARBONENSIS

Ebro R.

Balearics

NORTH AFRICA

BRITAIN

GAUL

NEARER SPAIN

MAURETANIA

ATLANTIC OCEAN

FARTHER SPAIN

Roman territories c. 140 B.C.

Roman territories added by 44 B.C.

Major battle

126

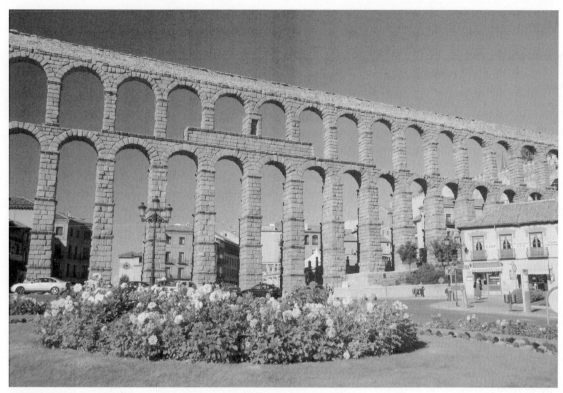

RUINS IN SPAIN. This Roman aqueduct in Spain stands as an impressive reminder of the ancient Romans' engineering skills. (© Alan Copson/JAI/Corbis.)

Essentially, Rome used its power for constructive ends: to establish order; to build roads, aqueducts, and public buildings; and to promote Hellenism. When Rome destroyed, it rebuilt creatively; when it conquered, it spread civilization and maintained peace. But no doubt its hundreds of thousands of prisoners of war, uprooted, enslaved, and degraded, did not view Roman conquest as beneficial; nor did the butchered Spanish tribesmen or the massacred Carthaginians. To these hapless victims, Rome appeared as an evil oppressor, not as the creator of a cosmopolis that brought order and security.

◀ *Map 6.1* ROMAN CONQUESTS DURING THE REPUBLIC The conquest of Italy gave Rome the manpower to expand throughout the Mediterranean world. In the Second Punic War, Rome defeated its greatest rival, Carthage. (© 2016 Cengage Learning.)

CULTURE IN THE REPUBLIC

One of the chief consequences of expansion was increased contact with Greek culture. During the third century B.C., Greek civilization started to exercise an increasing and fruitful influence on the Roman mind. Greek teachers, both slave and free, came to Rome, many of them as guests of the Roman aristocracy, and instructed Romans in Greek language, literature, philosophy, and art. As they conquered the eastern Mediterranean, Roman generals began to ship libraries and works of art from Greek cities to Rome. Roman sculpture and painting imitated Greek prototypes. In time, Romans acquired from Greece knowledge of scientific thought, philosophy, medicine, and geography. Roman writers and orators used Greek history, poetry, drama, and oratory as models. The Elder Pliny (A.D. 23–79), who wrote on many topics but is most famous for *Natural History*, refers to Homer's poetry as "the most valuable work of the human mind."[5] Cicero, Rome's greatest orator, tells us that ambitious young men eager to learn the art of oratory but unaware of the existence of any "course of training or any rules of art . . . attain[ed] what skill they could by means of their natural ability. . . . But later, having heard the Greek orators, gained acquaintance with their literature and called in Greek teachers, our people were fired with a really incredible enthusiasm for eloquence."[6]

Adopting the humanist outlook of the Greeks, the Romans came to value human intelligence and eloquent and graceful prose and poetry. Wealthy Romans retained Greek tutors, poets, and philosophers in their households and sent their sons to Athens to study. By the late Republic, educated Romans could speak and read Greek. Thus, Rome creatively assimilated the Greek achievement and transmitted it to others, thereby extending the orbit of Hellenism. To be sure, some conservative Romans were hostile to the Greek influence, which they felt threatened traditional Roman values that had accounted for Roman greatness. Cato the Elder (234–149 B.C.) and other Roman moralists denounced Socrates for undermining respect for Athenian law and warned that Greek philosophy might lure Roman youth into similar subversive behavior. Moreover, said these moralists, Greek philosophy, with its endless discussions of abstract themes, contrasted with the virtue most cherished by Romans—*gravitas*, or seriousness, which enabled Romans to conduct public affairs effectively. Philosophy seemed designed for a life of leisure and inaction, whereas a virtuous Roman was actively involved in practical civic matters. But the tide of Hellenism could not be stemmed.

Plautus (c. 254–184 B.C.), Rome's greatest playwright, adopted features of fourth- and third-century Greek comedy. His plays had Greek characters and took place in Greek settings; the actors wore the Greek style of dress. His characters resembled those found in Menander's comedies: a cunning slave, a lovesick youth, a foolish old man, a braggart soldier. The plots often consisted of a struggle between two antagonists over a woman or money, or both. The plays usually had the ending desired by the audience: the "good guy" won, and the "bad guy" received a fitting punishment. The pains of love were a common theme.

Not the throes of all mankind
Equal my distracted mind.
I strain and I toss
On a passionate cross;
Love's goad makes me reel,
I whirl on Love's wheel,
In a swoon of despair
Hurried here, hurried there—
Torn asunder, I am blind
With a cloud upon my mind.[7]

Terence (c. 185–159 B.C.), another playwright, was originally from North Africa and was brought to Rome as a slave. His owner, a Roman senator, provided the talented youth with an education and freed him. Terence demonstrated humaneness, a quality that can be seen in his attitude toward child rearing.

I give—I overlook; I do not judge it necessary to exert my authority in everything. . . . I think it better to restrain children through a sense of shame and liberal treatment than through fear. . . . This is the duty of a parent to accustom a son to do what is right rather of his own choice, than through fear of another.[8]

Catullus (c. 84–c. 54 B.C.) is generally regarded as one of the greatest lyric poets in world literature. He was a native of northern Italy whose father had provided him with a gentleman's education. In his early twenties, Catullus came to Rome and fell in love with Clodia; she was the wife of the governor of Cisalpine Gaul, who was away at the time. For the older Clodia, Catullus was a refreshing diversion from her many other lovers. Tormented by Clodia's numerous affairs, Catullus struggled to be "free from insane desire . . . Let me forget."[9]

Lucretius (c. 96–c. 55 B.C.), the leading Roman Epicurean philosopher, was influenced by the civil war fostered by two generals, Marius and Sulla, which is discussed later in this chapter. Distraught by the seemingly endless strife, Lucretius yearned for philosophical tranquility. Like Epicurus, he believed that religion prompted people to perform evil deeds and caused them to experience terrible anxiety about death and eternal punishment, a cruel feeling that precludes people from embracing life fully. In his work *On the Nature of Things*,

Lucretius expressed his appreciation of Epicurus. Like his mentor, Lucretius denounced superstition and religion for fostering psychological distress and advanced a materialistic conception of nature, one that left no room for the activity of gods—mechanical laws, not the gods, governed all physical happenings. (The rediscovery in the fifteenth century of Lucretius' great work helped to promote a secular and scientific outlook that is characteristic of the modern world.) To dispel the fear of punishment after death, Lucretius marshaled arguments to prove that the soul perishes with the body. He proposed that the simple life, devoid of political involvement and excessive passion, was the highest good and the path that would lead from emotional turmoil to peace of mind. Epicurus' hostility to traditional religion, disparagement of politics and public service, and rejection of the goals of power and glory ran counter to the accepted Roman ideal of virtue. On the other hand, his glorification of the quiet life amid a community of friends and his advice on how to deal with life's misfortunes with serenity had great appeal to first-century Romans like Lucretius, who were disgusted with civil strife.

Rome's finest orator, as well as a leading statesman, Cicero (106–43 B.C.) was an unsurpassed Latin stylist and a student of Greek philosophy. His letters, more than eight hundred of which have survived, provide modern historians with valuable insights into the politics of the late Republic. His Senate speeches have been models of refined rhetoric for all students of the Latin language. In the fifteenth century, Renaissance humanists idolized Cicero's elegant Latin style which they attempted to emulate. Cicero's discussion of such topics as republicanism, citizenship, friendship, virtue, duty, and justice had an enduring influence on Western moral and political thought. Dedicated to republicanism and public-spiritedness, Cicero sought to prevent one-man rule and in his writings exhorted fellow Romans to serve their city.

Cicero was drawn to Stoicism, the most influential philosophy in Rome. Stoicism's stress on virtuous conduct and performance of duty coincided with Roman ideals, and its doctrine of a natural law that applies to all nations, regardless of ethnicity or culture, harmonized with the requirements of a world empire. Cicero admired the Stoic goal of the self-sufficient sage who sought to accord his life with standards of virtue inherent in nature. Natural law commands people to do what is right and deters them from doing what is wrong, and our gift of reason enables us to abide by its commands. Thus, knowledge and virtue are closely linked. Cicero adopted the Stoic belief that the law of the state should conform to the rational and moral norms embodied in natural law, for adherence to such rationally formulated law creates a moral bond among citizens. All nations are subject at all times to natural law which is changeless and everlasting. No human legislation can override or supersede natural law. Implied in Cicero's Stoicism is the humanistic conviction that all human beings have dignity and value which should be respected.

He also shared the Stoic view that because natural law applies to all, we are all citizens of a single commonwealth and belong to a society of humanity. As he expressed it,

> *there is no difference in kind between man and man; for Reason, which alone raises us above the level of the beasts and enables us to draw inferences, to prove and disprove, to discuss and solve problems, and to come to conclusions, is certainly common to us all, and though varying in what it learns, at least in the capacity to learn it is invariable. . . . In fact, there is no human being of any race who, if he finds a guide, cannot attain virtue.*[10]

In the eighteenth century, the Founding Fathers of the United States praised Cicero's natural law philosophy, which coincided with their belief in inalienable rights; his condemnation of tyranny; and his advocacy of liberty, republicanism, and constitutional government.

COLLAPSE OF THE REPUBLIC

In 146 B.C., Roman might spanned the Mediterranean world. After that year, the principal concerns of the Republic were no longer foreign invasions but adjusting city-state institutions to the demands of empire and overcoming critical social and political problems at home. The Republic was unequal to either challenge. Instead of developing

Forum in Rome. The forum, a large rectangular space that served as a marketplace, was the center of a Roman city. In Rome itself, the forum evolved into a political center surrounded by large public buildings. (Hiroshi Higuchi/Getty Images.)

a professional civil service to administer the conquered lands, Roman leaders attempted to govern an empire with city-state institutions that had evolved for a different purpose. The established Roman administration proved unable to govern the Mediterranean world effectively. In addition, Rome's ruling elites showed little concern for the welfare of their subjects, and provincial rule worsened as governors, tax collectors, and soldiers shamelessly exploited the provincials.

During Rome's march to empire, all its classes had demonstrated a magnificent civic spirit in fighting foreign wars. With Carthage and Macedonia no longer threatening Rome, this cooperation deteriorated, as Cato the Elder had forewarned: "What was to become of Rome, when she should no longer have any state to fear?"[11] Internal dissension tore Rome apart as the drive for domination formerly directed against foreign enemies turned inward against fellow Romans. Civil war replaced foreign war.

The Romans had prevailed over their opponents partly because of their traditional virtues: resoluteness, frugality, and willingness to sacrifice personal interests for the good of Rome. But the riches flowing into Rome from the plundered provinces caused these virtues to decay, and rivalry for status and a frenzied pursuit of wealth overrode civic patriotism. This "perverted greed" and "lack of principle," said the poet Horace (65–8 B.C.), had caused "impious slaughter, . . . intestine [domestic] fury, . . . and lawless licence."[12] And the masses, landless and afflicted with poverty and idleness, withdrew their allegiance from the state.

In this time of agony, both great and self-seeking individuals emerged. Some struggled to restore the social harmony and political unity that had prevailed in the period of expansion. Others, political adventurers, attacked the authority of the Senate to gain personal power. The Senate, which had previously exercised leadership creatively and responsibly, degenerated into a self-serving oligarchy that resisted reform and fought to preserve its power and privilege.

Neither the Senate nor its opponents could rejuvenate the Republic. Eventually it collapsed, a victim of class tensions, poor leadership, power-hungry demagogues, and civil war. Underlying all these conditions were the breakdown of social harmony and the deterioration of civic patriotism. The Republic had conquered an empire only to see the character of its citizens decay. In a high moral tone, the historian Sallust (c. 86–34 B.C.) condemned the breakdown of republican values.

> *Growing love of money, and the lust for power which followed it, engendered every kind of evil. Avarice destroyed honor, integrity, and every other virtue, and instead taught men to be proud and cruel, to neglect religion, and to hold nothing too sacred to sell. Ambition tempted many to be false. . . . At first these vices grew slowly and some times met with punishments; later on, when the disease had spread like a plague, Rome changed: her government, once so just and admirable, became harsh and unendurable.*[13]

Crisis in Agriculture

The downhill slide of the Republic began with an agricultural crisis. During the long war with Hannibal in Italy, each side had tried to deprive the other of food supplies; in the process, they ruined farm land, destroyed farmhouses and farm equipment, and slaughtered animals. With many Roman soldier-farmers serving in the army for long stretches of time, fields lay neglected. Returning veterans with small holdings lacked the wealth to restore their land. They were forced to sell their farms to wealthy landowners at low prices.

Another factor that helped to squeeze out the owners of small farms was the importation of hundreds of thousands of slaves to work on large plantations called **latifundia**. This massive use of slaves was unprecedented in Roman history. Farmers who had formerly increased their meager incomes by working for wages on neighboring large estates were no longer needed. Sinking ever deeper into poverty and debt, farmers gave up their lands and went to Rome, seeking work. The dispossessed peasantry found little to do in Rome, where there was not enough industry to provide them with employment and where much of the work was done by slaves. Congregated in rundown, crime-ridden slums and chronically unemployed, the urban poor faced a daily struggle for survival. The once sturdy and independent Roman farmer, who had done all that his country had asked of him, was becoming part of a vast urban underclass—destitute, embittered, and alienated. The uprooting of a formerly self-reliant peasantry was Hannibal's posthumous revenge on Rome; severing the civic bond, it would prove even more deadly than Cannae.

The Gracchan Revolution

In 133 B.C., Tiberius Gracchus (163–133 B.C.), who came from one of Rome's most honored families, was elected tribune. Distressed by the injustice done to the peasantry and recognizing that the Roman army depended on the loyalty of small landowners, Tiberius made himself the spokesman for land reform. He proposed a simple and moderate solution for the problem of the landless peasants: implementing an old law barring any Roman from using more than 312 acres of the state-owned land obtained in the process of uniting Italy. For many years, the upper class had ignored this law, occupying vast tracts of public land. By reenacting the law, Tiberius hoped to free land for distribution to landless citizens.

Rome's leading families viewed Tiberius as a revolutionary threatening their property and political authority. They thought him a dangerous

Cleopatra

Cleopatra (69–30 B.C.), the Greek queen of Egypt, belonged to the Ptolemaic family, the Macedonian Greeks who ruled Egypt during the Hellenistic Age. Cleopatra spoke Greek, received a Greek education, and viewed herself as Greek, but in contrast to her Ptolemaic predecessors, she also learned to speak the Egyptian tongue. Aspiring to revive Ptolemaic power, which had once extended into Palestine and Lebanon, she had the political good sense to realize that this could not be accomplished by antagonizing Rome, which dominated the Mediterranean world.

Cleopatra became Julius Caesar's mistress when the Roman leader stopped at Alexandria. In 47 B.C., she bore a son, declaring that Caesar was the father, and in the next year she followed Caesar to Rome. Three years after Caesar's assassination, she became Mark Antony's lover and bore him twins. She worked closely with Antony, who competed with Octavian for control of the Roman world. At the naval battle of Actium in 31 B.C., Antony and Cleopatra escaped to Egypt, where Octavian pursued them. When Antony's forces either surrendered to Octavian without a fight or fled, Cleopatra barricaded herself inside her mausoleum. Thinking that she had killed herself, Antony plunged a sword into his body. A messenger told the dying Antony that Cleopatra was still alive and wished to see him. Slaves carried him to her. Because the mausoleum's doors were sealed, he had to be hoisted with great difficulty to an opening in the wall by Cleopatra

democrat who would undermine the Senate, the seat of aristocratic power, in favor of the Assembly, which represented the commoners. When Tiberius sought reelection as a tribune, a violation of constitutional tradition, the senators were convinced that he was a rabble-rouser who aimed to destroy the republican constitution and become a one-man ruler. To preserve the status quo, with wealth and power concentrated in the hands of a few hundred families, senatorial extremists killed Tiberius and some three hundred of his followers, dumping their bodies into the Tiber.

The cause of land reform was next taken up by Gaius Gracchus (153–121 B.C.), a younger brother of Tiberius. An emotional and gifted speaker, Gaius won the support of the city poor and was elected tribune in 123 B.C. A more astute politician than his brother, Gaius increased his following by favoring the Equites, the new class of plebeian businessmen, and by promising full citizenship to all Italians. He aided the poor by reintroducing his brother's plan for land distribution and by enabling them to buy grain from the state at less than half the market price. But like his brother, Gaius aroused the anger of the senatorial class. Fearing that he was stirring up a violent class struggle that would culminate in one-man rule, the senators ordered his murder. After his death, three thousand of his followers were executed without trial.

By killing the Gracchi, the Senate had substituted violence for reason and made murder a means of coping with troublesome opposition. Soon the club and the dagger became common weapons in Roman politics, hurling Rome into an era of political violence that ended with the destruction of the Republic. Though the Senate considered itself the guardian of republican liberty, in reality it was expressing the determination of a few hundred families to retain their control over the state. This is a classic example of a once-creative minority clinging tenaciously to power long after it has ceased to govern effectively or to inspire allegiance. The Senate, which had led Rome to world dominance, became a self-seeking, unimaginative, entrenched oligarchy that was dragging the Republic and the Mediterranean world into disaster.

Rome in the first century B.C. was very different from the Rome that had defeated Hannibal.

and her female servants. Plutarch, the ancient biographer, described the scene:

Those that were present say that nothing was ever more sad than this spectacle, to see Antony, covered all over with blood and just expiring, thus drawn up, still holding up his hands to her, and lifting up his body with the little force he had left. . . . When she had got him up, she laid him on the bed, tearing all her clothes, which she spread upon him; and beating her breast with her hands, lacerating herself, and disfiguring her own face with the blood from his wounds, she called him her lord, her husband, her emperor.*

Antony died shortly afterward. Captured by the Romans, Cleopatra feared that Octavian would parade her in a victory celebration at Rome. To avoid such a humiliation, the proud Cleopatra poisoned herself, ending the Ptolemaic dynasty in Egypt. In a last letter, she requested to be buried beside Antony.

Cleopatra's life and death have intrigued historians; writers, including Shakespeare; and Hollywood producers. Her true character remains elusive. She had sufficient allure to attract both Caesar and Antony and sufficient ruthlessness to murder her younger brother, and co-ruler, in order to make her son co-ruler. No doubt her determination and ambition made her an equal partner with Antony in their political quest.

---

*Plutarch, *The Lives of Noble Grecians and Romans*, trans. John Dryden, rev. A. H. Clough (New York: The Modern Library, n.d.), 1148.

Entranced by luxuries flowing into Rome from its eastern conquests and determined to retain oligarchic rule, the senatorial families neglected their responsibility to the state. Many upper-class Romans, burning to achieve the dignity and glory that would mark them as great men, tried to climb onto the crowded stage of Roman politics, but the best roles were already reserved for members of the senatorial families. With so few opportunities, aspirants to political power stopped at nothing.

Roman politics in the century after the Gracchi was bedeviled by intrigues, rivalries, personal ambition, and violence. Political adventurers exploited the issue of cheap grain and free land in order to benefit their careers. Whereas the Gracchi were sincere reformers, these later champions of social reform were unscrupulous demagogues who cleverly charmed and manipulated the city poor with bread and circuses: low-cost food and free admission to games. These demagogues aspired to the tribunate of the plebes, an office possessing powers formidable enough to challenge the Senate and not too difficult to obtain since ten tribunes were elected each year. By riding a wave of popular enthusiasm, these political adventurers hoped to sweep aside the Senate and concentrate power in their own hands. The poor, denied land and employment, demoralized, alienated, and lulled into political ignorance by decades of idleness, food handouts, and free entertainment, were ready to back whoever made the most glittering promises. The Senate behaved like a decadent oligarchy, and the Tribal Assembly, which had become the voice of the urban mob, demonstrated a weakness for demagogues, an openness to bribery, and an abundance of deceit and incompetence. The Roman Republic had passed the peak of its greatness.

Rival Generals

Marius (157–86 B.C.), who became consul in 107 B.C., adopted a military policy that eventually contributed to the wrecking of the Republic. Until about 100 B.C., soldiers served essentially at their own expense, paying for their arms, armor, and food. This meant that only men of some substance could serve. Short of troops for a campaign in Numidia in North Africa, Marius disposed of the traditional property requirement for entrance into the army and filled his legions with volunteers from the urban poor, a dangerous precedent. These new soldiers, disillusioned with Rome, served only because Marius held out the promise of pay, loot, and land grants after discharge. In effect, they were Marius's clients. Their loyalty was not to Rome but to Marius, and they remained loyal to their commander only as long as he fulfilled his promises.

Marius set an example that other ambitious commanders followed. They saw that a general could use his army to advance his political career, that by retaining the confidence of his soldiers he could cow the Senate and dictate Roman policy. The army, no longer an instrument of government, became a private possession of generals. Seeing its authority undermined by generals appointed by the Assembly, the Senate was forced to seek army commanders who would champion the cause of senatorial rule. In time, Rome would be engulfed in civil wars as rival generals used their troops to strengthen their political affiliations and to further their own ambitions.

Meanwhile, the Senate continued to deal ineffectively with Rome's problems. When Rome's Italian allies—who had provided the manpower needed to conquer the Empire—pressed for citizenship, the Senate refused to make concessions. The Senate's shortsightedness plunged Italy into a savage war known as the Social War. As it ravaged the peninsula, the Romans reversed their policy and conferred citizenship on the Italians. The unnecessary and ruinous rebellion petered out.

While Rome was fighting its Italian allies, Mithridates, king of Pontus in northern Asia Minor, invaded the wealthy Roman province of Asia. In 88 B.C., he incited the local population to massacre eighty thousand Italian residents of the province, a devastating blow to Rome's economy and prestige. Mithridates and his forces crossed into Greece and occupied Athens and other cities. Faced with this crisis, the Senate entrusted command to Sulla (138–78 B.C.), who had distinguished himself in the Social War. But supporters of Marius, through intrigue and violence, had the order rescinded and the command given to Marius.

Sulla refused to accept his loss of command, which deprived him of honor and opportunity for riches; with his loyal troops, he proceeded to the capital. This was a fateful moment in Roman history: the first march on Rome by a Roman legion, the first prolonged civil war, and the first time a commander and his troops defied the government. The competition for honor, the overriding concern of Roman aristocrats, had taken Rome down a perilous path. Sulla won the first round. But when Sulla left Rome to fight Mithridates in Greece, Marius and his troops retook the city and, in a frenzy, lashed out at Sulla's supporters. The killing lasted for five days and nights.

Marius died shortly afterward. Sulla, on his return, quickly subdued Marius's supporters and became dictator of Rome. He instituted a terror that far surpassed Marius's violence. Without legal sanction and with cold-blooded cruelty, Sulla marked his opponents for death; the state seized their property and declared their children and grandchildren ineligible for public office.

Sulla resolved to use his absolute power to revive the Senate's rule and make it permanent. He believed that only rule by an aristocratic oligarchy could protect Rome from future military adventurers and assure domestic peace. Therefore, he restored the Senate's right to veto acts of the Assembly, limited the power of the tribunes and the Assembly, and, to prevent any march on Rome, reduced the military authority of provincial governors. To make the Senate less oligarchic, he increased its membership to six hundred. Having put through these reforms, Sulla retired.

Julius Caesar

The Senate failed to wield its restored authority effectively. The Republic was still menaced by military commanders who used their troops for their own political advantage, and underlying problems remained unsolved. In 60 B.C., a triumvirate, a ruling group of three—consisting of Julius Caesar (c. 100–44 B.C.), a politician; Pompey, a general; and Crassus, a wealthy banker—conspired to take over Rome. The ablest of the three was Caesar. Descended from an ancient noble family, Caesar had first gained public recognition for his demonstration of conspicuous bravery in Rome's assault on the rebellious Greek city of Mytilene. Upon returning to Rome, he distinguished himself as an orator—his star was rising.

Recognizing the importance of a military command as a prerequisite for political prominence, Caesar gained command of the legions in Gaul in 59 B.C. The following year he began the conquest of the part of Gaul not under Roman control, bringing the future France, Belgium, Germany, west of the Rhine, southern Holland, and Switzerland into the orbit of Greco-Roman civilization. Lasting eight years, the Roman conquest of Gaul was marked by brutal mutilations and massacres. Hundreds of thousands of Gauls were killed and hundreds of thousands more enslaved. The campaign was brilliantly described in his *Commentaries*, although, to be sure, the work was a deliberate attempt to apprise the Roman public of his military prowess. The successful Gallic campaigns and the invasion of Britain revealed Caesar's exceptional talent for generalship: he acted decisively and demonstrated a superior intellect and a resolute will; moving troops rapidly, he surprised and panicked the enemy; he gained the respect, if not love, of his men, who admired his battlefield skills and courage and were grateful for the material awards he distributed to them. By plundering Gaul, he also acquired a fortune that would be used to further his political career, particularly bribing Roman officials. Indeed, Caesar's victories alarmed the Senate, which feared that the popular general would use his devoted troops and soaring reputation to seize control of the state.

Meanwhile, the triumvirate had fallen apart. In 53 B.C., Crassus had perished with his army in a disastrous campaign against the Parthians in the East. The bonds between Pompey and Caesar were weak, consisting essentially of Pompey's marriage to Caesar's daughter Julia. After her death in 54 B.C., Pompey and Caesar grew apart. Pompey, who was jealous of Caesar's success and eager to expand his own power, drew closer to the Senate. Supported by Pompey, the Senate ordered Caesar to relinquish his command. Caesar realized that without his troops he would be defenseless; he decided instead to march on Rome. After Caesar crossed the Rubicon River from Gaul into Italy in 49 B.C., civil war again ravaged the Republic. Pompey proved no match for so talented a general; the Senate acknowledged Caesar's victory and appointed him to be dictator, a legal office, for ten years.

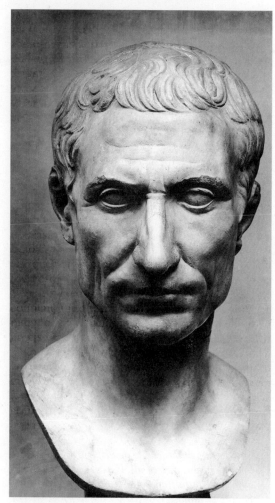

BUST OF CAESAR. Julius Caesar tried to rescue a dying Roman world by imposing strong rule. He paved the way for the transition from republican to imperial rule. (Scala/Art Resource, N.Y.)

Caesar realized that republican institutions no longer operated effectively and that only strong and enlightened leadership could permanently end the civil warfare destroying Rome. His reforms were designed to create order out of chaos. Caesar responded to the grievances of the provincial subjects by lowering taxes, making the governors responsible to him, restraining Roman businessmen from ruthlessly draining the provinces' wealth, and generously extending citizenship. To gain greater support for Rome, he also granted citizenship to more Italians. To aid the poor in Rome, he began a public works program, which provided employment and beautified the city. He also relocated more than a hundred thousand veterans and members of Rome's lower class to the provinces, where he gave them land. To improve administration, he reorganized town governments in Italy, reformed the courts, and planned to codify the law. He attempted to conciliate the senatorial class by treating former enemies with moderation and generosity.

In February 44 B.C., Rome's ruling class—jealous of Caesar's success and power and afraid of his ambition—became thoroughly alarmed when his temporary dictatorship was converted into a lifelong office. The aristocracy saw this event as the end of senatorial government and their rule, which they equated with liberty, and as the beginning of a Hellenistic type of monarchy. A fundamental principle of republican political thinking was that no one person, no tyrant, should ever rule Rome. On March 15 of that year, a group of aristocrats, regarding themselves as defenders of centuries-old republican traditions and institutions, assassinated Caesar. The group included the general and orator Marcus Junius Brutus. Cicero expressed the feeling that motivated the conspirators.

> Our tyrant deserves his death, [for his] was the blackest crime of all. [Caesar was] a man who was ambitious to be king of the Roman people and master of the whole world. . . . The man who maintains that such an ambition is morally right is a madman, for he justifies the destruction of law and liberty.[14]

The Republic's Last Years

The assassination of Julius Caesar did not restore republican liberty but plunged Rome into renewed civil war. Thousands more died in battle or were killed in the proscriptions—lists of Roman citizens declared by their political enemies to be outlaws. Those proscribed had their property confiscated and could be executed. Two of Caesar's trusted lieutenants, Mark Antony and Lepidus, joined with Octavian, Caesar's adopted son, and defeated the armies of Brutus and Cassius, two conspirators in the plot against Caesar. After Lepidus was forced into political obscurity, Antony and Octavian fought each other, with control of Rome as the prize. In 31 B.C., at the naval battle of Actium in western Greece, Octavian crushed the forces of Antony and his wife, Egypt's Queen Cleopatra (who had earlier borne Julius Caesar's son). Octavian emerged as master of Rome and four years later became, in effect, the first Roman emperor. The Roman Republic, whose death throes had lasted for decades and kept the Mediterranean world in turmoil, had finally perished.

The Roman Republic, which had amassed power to a degree hitherto unknown in the ancient world, was wrecked not by foreign invasion but by internal weaknesses: the personal ambitions of power seekers; the degeneration of senatorial leadership and the transformation of political rivalry into violence and terror, in which opponents were condemned to death and their property confiscated; the formation of private armies, in which soldiers gave their loyalty to their commander rather than to Rome; the transformation of a self-reliant peasantry into an impoverished and demoralized city rabble; and the deterioration of the ancient virtues that had been the source of the state's vitality. Before 146 B.C., the threat posed by foreign enemies, particularly Carthage, had forced Romans to work together for the benefit of the state, and the equilibrium achieved during the patrician–plebeian struggle was maintained. This social cohesion broke down when foreign danger diminished. In the ensuing century of turmoil, the apparatus of city-state government failed to function effectively.

Thus, the high point of Roman rule was not achieved under the Republic. The city-state constitution of the Republic was too limited to govern an immense empire. Rome first had to surpass the narrow framework of city-state government before it could unite the Mediterranean world in peace and law. The genius of Augustus (Octavian), the first emperor, made this development possible.

❖ ❖ ❖

Notes

1. Cicero, *De Republica*, trans. Clinton Walker. Keyes (Cambridge, Mass.: Harvard University Press, Loeb Classical Library, 1994), 79.

2. Ibid., 81.

3. Polybius, *The Rise of the Roman Empire*, trans. Ian Scott-Kilvert (New York: Penguin Books, 1979), 41.

4. E. Badian, *Roman Imperialism in the Late Republic* (Ithaca, N.Y.: Cornell University Press, 1971), 87.

5. Quoted in Alan Wardman, *Rome's Debt to Greece* (New York: St. Martin's Press, 1976), 62.

6. Cicero, *De Oratore*, trans. E. W. Sutton (Cambridge, Mass.: Harvard University Press, Loeb Classical Library, 1967), 14.

7. Quoted in J. Wright Duff, *A Literary History of Rome* (New York: Barnes and Noble, 1960), 136–137.

8. Terence, *The Brothers*, trans. H. T. Riley (London: Henry G. Bohn, 1853), 202–203.

9. Catullus, quoted in E. A. Havelock, *The Lyric Genius of Catullus* (New York: Russell and Russell, 1929), 63.

10. Cicero, *De Legibus*, trans. C. W. Keyes (Cambridge, Mass.: Harvard University Press, Loeb Classical Library, 1928), 329–330.

11. Quoted in Eli Sagan, *The Honey and the Hemlock* (New York: Basic Books, 1991), 25.

12. Horace, *The Odes and Epodes*, trans. C. E. Bennett (Cambridge, Mass.: Harvard University Press, 1988), ode 24, 255–256.

13. Sallust, *The Conspiracy of Catiline*, trans. S. A. Handford (Baltimore: Penguin Books, 1963), 181–182.

14. Cicero, *De Officiis*, trans. Walter Miller (Cambridge, Mass.: Harvard University Press, Loeb Classical Library, 1913), 357.

Chapter 7

The Roman Empire:
A World-State

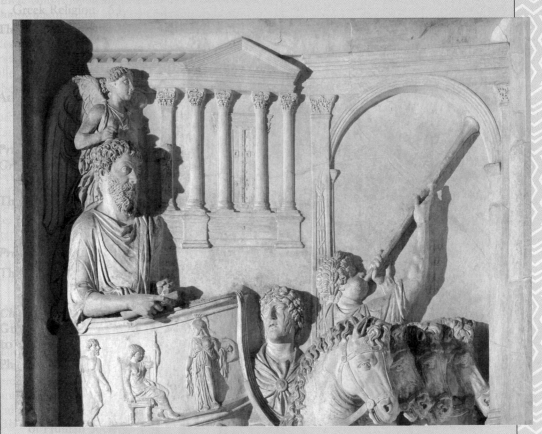

Marcus Aurelius, Roman Emperor (A.D. 161–180). *In this relief, Marcus rides through the Roman Forum in ceremonial triumph after defending the Empire against barbarian incursions.* (Alfredo Dagli Orti/© The Art Archive/Corbis.)

Focus Questions

1. What is the historical significance of Augustus?

2. Why is the Pax Romana regarded as one of the finest periods in world history? What continuity is there between the Pax Romana and the Hellenistic Age?

3. How did Roman law evolve? How did it incorporate Stoic principles?

4. Why is the third century regarded as an age of crisis?

5. What are the reasons for the decline of the Roman Empire?

6. Why do you think that over the centuries Rome's demise has intrigued historians?

7. What is Rome's legacy to Western civilization?

Rome's republican institutions, designed for a city-state, proved incapable of coping with the problems created by the conquest of a world empire. Invincible against foreign enemies, the Republic collapsed from within. But after Octavian's brilliant statesmanship brought order out of chaos, Rome entered its golden age under the rule of emperors. For more than two hundred years, from 27 B.C. to A.D. 180, the Mediterranean world enjoyed unparalleled peace and stability. The Roman world-state, erected on a Hellenic cultural foundation and cemented with empire-wide civil service, laws, and citizenship, gave practical expression to Stoic cosmopolitanism and universalism. Yet even this impressive monument had structural defects, and in the third century A.D. the Empire was wracked by crises from which it never fully recovered. In the fifth century, Germanic tribesmen overran the western half of the Empire, which had by then become a shadow of its former self.

During its time of trouble, Rome also experienced an intellectual crisis. Forsaking the rational and secular values of classical humanism, many Romans sought spiritual comfort in Near Eastern religions. One of these religions, Christianity, won out over its competitors and was made the official religion of the Empire. With the triumph of Christianity in the Late Roman Empire, Western civilization took a new direction. Christianity would become the principal shaper of the European civilization that emerged from the ruins of Rome.

AUGUSTUS AND THE FOUNDATIONS OF THE ROMAN EMPIRE

After Octavian's forces defeated those of Antony and Cleopatra at the battle of Actium in 31 B.C., no opponents could stand up to him. The century of civil war, political murder, corruption, and mismanagement had exhausted the Mediterranean world, which longed for order. Like Caesar before him, Octavian recognized that only a strong monarchy could rescue Rome from civil war and anarchy. But learning from Caesar's assassination, he also knew that republican ideals were far from dead. To exercise autocratic power openly, like a

Chronology 7.1 ❖ The Roman Empire

27 B.C.	Senate grants Octavian the title Augustus, and he becomes, in effect, the first Roman emperor; start of the principate and the Pax Romana
A.D. 14	Death of Augustus; Tiberius gains the throne
66–70	Jewish revolt: Romans capture Jerusalem and destroy the Second Temple
79	Eruption of Mount Vesuvius and destruction of Pompeii and Herculaneum
132–135	Hadrian crushes another Hebrew revolt
180	Marcus Aurelius dies: end of the Pax Romana
212	Roman citizenship is granted to virtually all free inhabitants of Roman provinces
235–285	Military anarchy; Germanic incursions
285–305	Diocletian tries to deal with the crisis by creating a regimented state
378	Battle of Adrianople: Visigoths defeat the Roman legions
406	Imperial borders collapse, and Germanic tribes move into the Empire
410	Rome is plundered by Visigoths
455	Rome is sacked by Vandals
476	End of the Roman Empire in the West

Hellenistic monarch, would have aroused the hostility of the Roman ruling class, whose assistance and goodwill Octavian desired.

Octavian demonstrated his political genius by reconciling his military monarchy with republican institutions: he held absolute power without abruptly breaking with a republican past. Magistrates were still elected, and assemblies still met; the Senate administered certain provinces, retained its treasury, and was invited to advise Octavian. With some truth, Octavian could claim that he ruled in partnership with the Senate. By maintaining the facade of the Republic, Octavian camouflaged his absolute power and contained senatorial opposition, which already had been weakened by the deaths of leading nobles in battle or in the purges that Octavian had instituted against his enemies. Moreover, Octavian's control over the armed forces made resistance futile, and the terrible violence that followed Caesar's assassination made senators amenable to change.

In 27 B.C., Octavian shrewdly offered to surrender his power, knowing that the Senate, purged of opposition, would demand that he continue to lead the state. By this act, Octavian could claim to be a legitimate constitutional ruler leading a government of law, not one of lawless despotism so hateful to the Roman mentality. In keeping with his policy of maintaining the appearance of traditional republican government, Octavian refused to be called king or even, like Caesar, *dictator*; instead, he cleverly disguised his autocratic rule by taking the inoffensive title *princeps* (first citizen). The Senate also honored Octavian by conferring on him the semireligious and revered name of *Augustus*—the Exalted One. (The rule of Augustus and his successors is referred to as the *principate*.)

The reign of Augustus signified the end of the Roman Republic and the beginning of the Roman Empire—the termination of senatorial rule and aristocratic politics and the emergence of one-man rule. The old Roman aristocracy, decimated by war and the proscriptions employed

THE PANTHEON, C. A.D. 125. The Pantheon, the most complete surviving building of Roman antiquity, was built by Emperor Hadrian in the second century A.D. In the temple, Greek forms of ornamentation are combined with Roman building techniques. The vast hemispherical dome was constructed by pouring concrete into great wooden forms; then the interior was faced with marble. In contrast to a Greek temple, where the exterior is paramount, the Roman temple emphasizes interior space. (©iStockphoto.com/OGphoto)

by Antony, Lepidus, and Octavian, had to adjust to a political situation in which they no longer predominated. As the historian Tacitus recognized, Augustus accomplished a profound revolution in Roman political life: "The country had been transformed, and there was nothing left of the fine old Roman character. Political equality was a thing of the past; all eyes watched for imperial commands."[1] Under Augustus, who ruled from 27 B.C. to A.D. 14, the power of the ruler was disguised; in ensuing generations, however, emperors would wield absolute power openly. As Rome became more autocratic and centralized, it took on the appearance of an oriental monarchy.

Augustus introduced the practice of emperor worship. In the eastern provinces, where Middle Eastern and Hellenistic monarchs had been traditionally regarded as divine, the person of Augustus was worshiped as a god. In Italy, where the deification of leaders was alien to the republican spirit, divine honors were granted to Augustus's genius, or spirit of leadership; once deceased, Augustus and his successors were deified. The imperial cult, with its ceremonies, processions, temples, and statues, strengthened the bonds of loyalty that tied subjects to the emperor. By the third century, Italians and other peoples in the western territories generally viewed the living emperor as a god-king.

Roman Empire under Augustus

Territory added by Hadrian's reign

Line dividing eastern and western parts of the Roman Empire

Major battle

ATLANTIC OCEAN

North Sea

BRITAIN

GERMANY

BELGIUM

GAUL

Elbe R.

Rhine R.

Seine R.

Rhône R.

NARBONENSIS

FARTHER SPAIN

NEARER SPAIN

Ebro R.

Balearics

Corsica

Sardinia

Sicily

Carthage

NUMIDIA

MAURETANIA

NORTH AFRICA

RAETIA

NORICUM

VINDELICIA

PANNONIA

Danube R.

Aquileia

Po R.

CISALPINE GAUL

Tiber R.

Rome

Pompeii

DALMATIA

Adriatic Sea

MOESIA

DACIA

MACEDON

ACHAEA

GREECE

Athens

Actium

Crete

Mediterranean Sea

SAHARA

Volga R.

Caspian Sea

Don R.

Dnieper R.

Black Sea

CRIMEA

Constantinople (Byzantium)

THRACE

PONTUS

PHRYGIA

ASIA

Pergamum

PISIDIA

CILICIA

Rhodes

Cyprus

ARMENIA

CAPPADOCIA

SYRIA

JUDEA

Jerusalem

EGYPT

Alexandria

Nile R.

LIBYA

Red Sea

ARABIAN DESERT

Babylon

PARTHIA

Tigris R.

Euphrates R.

0   200   400 Mi.

0   200   400 Km.

142

Despite his introduction of autocratic rule, Augustus was by no means a self-seeking tyrant, but a creative statesman. Heir to the Roman tradition of civic duty, he regarded his power as a public trust delegated to him by the Roman people. He was faithful to the classical ideal, which required that the state should promote the good life by protecting civilization from barbarism and ignorance; he sought to rescue a dying Roman world afflicted with assassinations, civil war, and anarchy. He aimed to restore political order and to revive the old moral values and civic spirit that had contributed to Rome's greatness.

To prevent a renewal of civil war and to safeguard the borders of the Empire, Augustus reformed the army. As commander in chief, he could guard against the reemergence of ambitious generals like those whose rivalries and private armies had wrecked the Republic. Augustus maintained the loyalty of his soldiers by ensuring that veterans, on discharge, would receive substantial bonuses and land in Italy or in the provinces. By organizing a professional standing army made up mostly of volunteers who generally served for twenty-five years, Augustus was assured a well-trained and loyal force capable of maintaining internal order, extending Roman territory, and securing the frontier.

For the city of Rome, Augustus had aqueducts and water mains built, which brought water to most Roman homes and, befitting Rome's revival under his rule, he beautified the city by restoring ancient monuments and temples and building new ones in gleaming marble. He created a fire brigade, which reduced the danger of great conflagrations in crowded tenement districts, and he organized a police force to contain violence. He improved the distribution of free grain to the impoverished urban masses and financed the popular gladiatorial combats out of his own funds.

◀ *Map 7.1* THE ROMAN EMPIRE UNDER AUGUSTUS AND HADRIAN During the Pax Romana, the Roman Empire expanded beyond the Rhine and Danube Rivers, the imperial boundary during the reign of Augustus. (© 2016 Cengage Learning.)

In Italy, Augustus had roads repaired, and he fostered public works. He arranged for Italians to play a more important role in the administration of the Empire. For the Italians' security, his army suppressed brigandage, which had proliferated in the countryside during the preceding century of agony, and he guarded the northern borders from barbarian incursions.

By ending the civil wars and their accompanying devastation and by ruling out forced requisition of supplies and extortion of money, Augustus earned the gratitude of the provincials. Also contributing to his empire-wide popularity were his efforts to correct tax abuse and to end corruption through improving the quality of governors and enabling aggrieved provincials to bring charges against Roman officials. An imperial bureaucracy, which enabled talented and dedicated men to serve the state, gradually evolved. In addition, Augustus continued the sensible practice of not interfering with the traditional customs and religions of the provinces. During his forty-year reign—the longevity itself was a stabilizing factor—Rome overcame the chaos of the years of revolution. The praise bestowed on him by grateful provincials was not undeserved. One decree from the province of Asia called Augustus

> *the savior of all mankind in common whose provident care has not only fulfilled but even surpassed the hopes of all: for both land and sea are at peace, the cities are teeming with the blessings of concord, plenty, and respect for law, and the culmination and harvest of all good things bring fair hopes for the future and contentment with the present.*[2]

THE PAX ROMANA

The brilliant statesmanship of Augustus inaugurated Rome's greatest age. For the next two hundred years, the Mediterranean world enjoyed the blessings of the **Pax Romana**, the Roman peace. The ancient world had never experienced such a long period of peace, order, efficient administration, and prosperity. Although both proficient and inept rulers succeeded Augustus, the essential features of the Pax Romana persisted.

Profile

Epictetus

Born a slave, Epictetus (C. A.D. 55–135) belonged to an official (himself a former slave) who served the emperors Nero and Domitian. Even before he was given his freedom, Epictetus received a good education from his master. In A.D. 89, Domitian, fearful that philosophers would cast doubt on the emperor's divinity, banished all philosophers from Rome and Italy. Epictetus moved to Epirus in Greece, where he attracted students. One student recorded and organized Epictetus's thoughts into eight books, four of which were lost. Epictetus presented his views in the form of maxims: admonitions from a teacher to his students to pursue the moral life. His ideas greatly influenced Marcus Aurelius, the Roman emperor and Stoic philosopher.

Like other Stoic philosophers, Epictetus was concerned with attaining peace of mind—an inner contentment that produces happiness. For Epictetus, happiness did not depend on material possessions, status, reputation, or the affection others have for us. By pursuing these externals, he said, we become subject to the people who are needed to procure them for us: "If you are absorbed in externals, you must necessarily be tossed up and down, according to the inclination of your master. Who is your master? Whosoever controls those things which you seek."*

Epictetus maintained that to achieve happiness we must reduce desires, shun things that are beyond our power to control, and deliberately strive for inner dignity and moral integrity. Human beings, said Epictetus, can shield themselves from life's uncertainties and misfortunes, even slavery, by taking control of the part of themselves that belongs to no one else: their minds. Epictetus defined man as a rational being. It is reason that

The Successors of Augustus

The first four emperors who succeeded Augustus were related either to him or to his third wife, Livia. They constituted the Julio-Claudian dynasty, which ruled from A.D. 14 to 68. Although their reigns were marked by conspiracies, summary executions, and assassinations, the great achievements of Augustus were preserved and strengthened. Direct control over wealthy provinces and the army—soldiers were promised pensions and farms at the end of their service—enabled emperors to crush provincial rebels and an occasional rebellious general.

The Julio-Claudian dynasty came to an end in A.D. 68, when the emperor Nero committed suicide. Nero had grown increasingly tyrannical and had lost the confidence of the people, the senatorial class, and the generals, who rose in revolt. In the year following his death, anarchy reigned as military leaders competed for the throne. After a

bloody civil war, the execution of two emperors, and the suicide of another, Vespasian gained the principate. Vespasian's reign (A.D. 69–79) marked the beginning of the Flavian dynasty. By rotating commanding officers and stationing native troops far from their homelands, Vespasian improved discipline and discouraged mutiny. By having the great Colosseum of Rome constructed for gladiatorial contests, he earned the gratitude of the city's inhabitants. Vespasian also had nationalist uprisings put down in Gaul and Judea.

In Judea, Roman rule clashed with Jewish religious-national sentiments. Recognizing the tenaciousness with which Jews clung to their faith, the Roman leaders deliberately refrained from interfering with Hebraic religious beliefs and practices. Numerous privileges, such as exemption from emperor worship because it conflicted with the requirements of strict monotheism, were extended to Jews not only in Judea but throughout the Empire. Sometimes, however, the Romans distinguishes man from wild beasts and cattle. He wrote:

> Take care, then to do nothing like a wild beast; otherwise you have destroyed the man; you have not fulfilled what your nature promises. Take care too, to do nothing like cattle; for thus likewise the man is destroyed. In what do we act like cattle? When we act gluttonously, lewdly, rashly, sordidly, inconsiderately, into what are we sunk? Into cattle. What have we destroyed? The rational being. When we behave contentiously, injuriously, passionately, and violently, into what we have sunk? Into wild beasts. . . . By all these means the nature of man is destroyed.[†]

---

*Epictetus, *Discourses*, based on translation of Thomas Wentworth Higginson (Roslyn, N.Y.: Walter J. Black, Classics Club, 1944), bk. 2, chap. 2, p. 92.
[†]Ibid, bk. 2, chap. 9, pp. 106–107.

---

engaged in activities that outraged the Jews. For example, Pontius Pilate, the Roman procurator in Judea from A.D. 26 to 36, at one point ordered a Roman army unit into Jerusalem with banners bearing the image of the emperor. The entire Jewish nation was aroused. To the Jews, this display of a pagan idol in their holy city was an abomination. Realizing that the Jews would die rather than permit this act of sacrilege, Pilate ordered the banners removed. Another explosive situation emerged when the emperor Caligula (A.D. 37–41) ordered that a golden statue of himself be placed in Jerusalem's temple. Again, the order was rescinded when the Jews demonstrated their readiness to resist.

Relations between the Jews of Judea and the Roman authorities deteriorated progressively in succeeding decades. Militant Jews, who rejected Roman rule as a threat to the purity of Jewish life, urged their people to take up arms. Feeling a religious obligation to reestablish an independent kingdom in their ancient homeland and unable to reconcile themselves to Roman rule, the Jews launched a full-scale war of liberation in A.D. 66. In A.D. 70, after a five-month siege had inflicted terrible punishment on the Jews, Roman armies captured Jerusalem and destroyed the temple, the central site and focus of Jewish religious life.

Vespasian was succeeded by his sons Titus (A.D. 79–81) and Domitian (A.D. 81–96). The reign of Titus was made memorable by the eruption of Mount Vesuvius, which devastated the towns of Pompeii and Herculaneum. After Titus's brief time as emperor, his younger brother Domitian became ruler. Upon crushing a revolt led by the Roman commander in Upper Germany, a frightened Domitian executed many leading Romans. These actions led to his assassination in A.D. 96, ending the Flavian dynasty. The Flavians, however, succeeded in consolidating and extending the borders of the Empire.

The Senate selected one of its own, Nerva, to succeed the murdered Domitian. Nerva's reign (A.D. 96–98) was brief and uneventful. But he introduced a wise practice that would endure until A.D. 180: he adopted as his son and designated as his heir a man with proven ability, Trajan, the governor of Upper Germany. This adoptive system assured a succession of competent rulers.

During his rule (A.D. 98–117), Trajan eased the burden of taxation in the provinces, provided for the needs of poor children, and had public works built. With his enlarged army, he conquered Dacia (parts of Romania and Hungary), where he seized vast quantities of gold and silver. He made the territory into a Roman province, adding to the large frontier Rome had to protect. The settlement of the region by many of Trajan's veterans led to its Romanization.

Trajan's successor, Hadrian (A.D. 117–138), abandoned what remained of Trajan's eastern conquests. He strengthened border defenses in Britain and fought the second Hebrew revolt in Judea (A.D. 132–135). After initial successes, including the capture of Jerusalem, the Jews were again defeated by superior Roman might. The majority of Palestinian Jews were killed, sold as slaves, or forced to seek refuge in other lands. The Romans renamed the province Syria Palestina; they forbade Jews to enter Jerusalem, except once a year, and encouraged non-Jews to settle the land. Although the Jews continued to maintain a presence in Palestine, they had become a dispossessed and dispersed people.

After Hadrian came another ruler who had a long reign, Antoninus Pius (A.D. 138–161). He introduced humane and just reforms. He set limits on the right of masters to torture their slaves to obtain evidence, and he established the principle that an accused person be considered innocent until proven guilty. During the reign of Antoninus, the Empire remained peaceful and prosperous.

Marcus Aurelius (A.D. 161–180), the next emperor, was also a philosopher whose *Meditations* eloquently expressed Stoic thought. Frequent strife marked his reign. Roman forces had to fight the eastern kingdom of Parthia. The Roman legions were victorious in this campaign but brought back from the East an epidemic that decimated the population of the Empire. Marcus Aurelius also had to deal with Germanic incursions into Italy and the Balkan Peninsula—incursions far more serious than any faced by previous emperors.

From the accession of Nerva in A.D. 96 to the death of Marcus Aurelius in A.D. 180, the Roman Empire was ruled by "the Five Good Emperors." During this period, the Empire was at the height of its power and prosperity, and nearly all its peoples benefited. The four emperors preceding Marcus Aurelius had no living sons, so they had resorted to the adoptive system in selecting successors, which served Rome effectively. But Marcus Aurelius chose his own son, Commodus, to succeed him. With the accession of Commodus—a misfit and a megalomaniac—in A.D. 180, the Pax Romana came to an end.

"The Time of Happiness"

The Romans called the Pax Romana "the Time of Happiness." They saw it as the fulfillment of Rome's mission: the creation of a world-state that provided peace, security, ordered civilization, and the rule of law. Roman legions defended the Rhine–Danube river frontiers from incursions by Germanic tribesmen, held the Parthians at bay in the east, and subdued the few uprisings that occurred. Nerva's adoptive system of selecting emperors provided Rome with internal stability and

a succession of emperors with exceptional ability. These Roman emperors did not use military force needlessly but fought for sensible political goals; generals did not wage war recklessly but tried to limit casualties, avoid risks, and deter conflicts by a show of force.

Constructive Rule. Roman rule was constructive. The Romans built roads—some fifty-three thousand miles of roads, from Scotland to the Euphrates—improved harbors, cleared forests, drained swamps, irrigated deserts, and cultivated undeveloped lands. The aqueducts they constructed brought fresh water for drinking and bathing to large numbers of people, and the effective sewage systems enhanced the quality of life. Goods were transported over roads made safe by Roman soldiers and across a Mediterranean Sea swept clear of pirates. A wide variety of goods from many lands circulated throughout the Empire. A stable currency, generally not subject to depreciation, contributed to the economic well-being of the Mediterranean world.

Scores of new cities sprang up, and old ones grew larger and wealthier. Although these municipalities had lost their power to wage war and had to bow to the will of the emperors, they retained considerable freedom of action in local matters. Imperial troops guarded against civil wars within the cities and prevented warfare between cities—two traditional weaknesses of city life in the ancient world. Some two thousand municipalities served as centers of Greco-Roman civilization, which spread to the farthest reaches of the Mediterranean, continuing a process initiated during the Hellenistic Age. Regions of North Africa, Gaul, Britain, and South Germany, hitherto untouched by Hellenism, were brought into the orbit of Greco-Roman civilization. Barriers between Italians and provincials broke down as Spaniards, Gauls, Africans, and other provincials rose to high positions in the army and in the imperial administration and even became emperors. Citizenship, generously granted, was finally extended to virtually all free people regardless of nationality by an edict of A.D. 212.

Improved Conditions for Both Slaves and Women. Conditions improved for those at the bottom of society, the slaves. At the time of

ARCH OF TITUS, C. A.D. 81, CONCRETE FACED WITH MARBLE, ROME. The arch stands at the crest of the Sacred Way to commemorate Titus's successful capture of Jerusalem in A.D. 70. It was dedicated in A.D. 81 by his brother, the Emperor Domitian. (Scala/ Art Resource, N.Y.)

BASALT BUST OF LIVIA. Octavian's third wife, Livia (58 B.C.–A.D. 29), was admired for her wisdom and dignity, and the emperor valued her counsel. (Alinari/Art Resource, N.Y.)

Augustus, slaves may have accounted for a quarter of the population of Italy. But their numbers declined as Rome engaged in fewer wars of conquest. The freeing of slaves also became more common during the Empire. Urban slaves, who were often skilled artisans, could be induced to work more effectively if there was the hope of **manumission**. Often, nobles liberated and set up in business skilled and enterprising slaves in return for a share of the profits. Freed slaves became citizens, with most of the rights and privileges of other citizens; their children suffered no legal disabilities. (The poet Terence, the Stoic philosopher Epictetus, and the father of the poet Horace were all freed slaves.)

During the Republic, slaves had been terribly abused; they were often mutilated, thrown to wild beasts, crucified, or burned alive. Several emperors issued decrees protecting slaves from cruel masters. Claudius forbade masters to kill sick slaves; Vespasian forbade masters to sell slaves into prostitution. Domitian prohibited the castration of slaves, and Hadrian barred the execution of slaves without a judicial sentence. But recaptured fugitive slaves could still be enchained, whipped, branded, and crucified. It was not uncommon for freed slaves to earn a respectable income as skilled artisans and shopkeepers. Some became wealthy and donated large sums to the city in which they dwelled or were born.

The status of women had been gradually improving during the Republic. In the early days of the Republic, a woman lived under the absolute authority first of her father and then of her husband. By the time of the Empire, a woman could own property and, if divorced, keep her dowry. A father could no longer force his daughter to marry against her will, although upper-class marriages were usually based on political and social considerations. Women could make business arrangements and draw up wills without the consent of their husbands. Roman women, unlike their Greek counterparts, were not secluded in their homes but could come and go as they pleased and participate in public spectacles and activities. Upper-class women of Rome had far greater opportunities for education than did those of Greece, and some formed groups that read and discussed poetry.

Supervising the household remained the principal responsibility of Roman women. The Romans regarded marriage as a sacred civic duty. Seeking to restore traditional values, Augustus issued decrees encouraging Romans to marry. Romans greatly admired the woman who loved only one man and had only one husband, but in reality promiscuity, adultery, divorce, and remarriage were quite common. A wife could obtain a divorce just as easily as her husband, but as a rule children remained with their father. Despite the frequency of divorce, there is evidence that husbands and wives held genuine affection for each other.

The history of the Empire, indeed Roman history in general, was filled with talented and influential women. Cornelia, the mother of Tiberius and Gaius Gracchus, influenced Roman politics through her sons. The historian Sallust said that Sempronia, the wife of a consul and the mother of Brutus, one of the assassins of Julius Caesar, was "well-educated in Greek and Latin literature. . . . She could write poetry, crack a joke, and converse at will. . . . She was in fact a woman of ready wit and considerable charm."[3] Livia, Augustus' dynamic wife, was a successful businesswoman, who accumulated estates, mines, granaries, and other properties throughout the empire and checked that they were properly managed. At times, Augustus consulted her on important government matters. During the third century there were times when women, operating behind the scenes as did Livia, controlled the throne.

An Orderly World Community. From Britain to the Arabian Desert, from the Danube River to the sands of the Sahara, some fifty to seventy million people with differing native languages, customs, and histories were united by Roman rule into a world community. Unlike officials of the Republic, when corruption and exploitation in the provinces were notorious, officials of the Empire felt a strong sense of responsibility to preserve the Roman peace, institute Roman justice, and spread Roman civilization.

In creating a stable and orderly political community with an expansive conception of citizenship, Rome resolved the problems posed by the limitations of the Greek city-state: civil war, intercity warfare, and a parochial attitude that divided people into Greek and non-Greek. Rome also brought to fruition an ideal of the Greek city-state—the protection and promotion of civilized life. By constructing a world community that broke down barriers between nations, by preserving and spreading Greco-Roman civilization, and by developing a rational system of law that applied to all humanity, Rome completed the trend toward universalism and cosmopolitanism that had emerged in the Hellenistic Age. The Roman world-state was the classical mind's response to the problem of community posed by the decline of the city-state in the era of Alexander the Great. Aelius Aristides, a second-century rhetorician (see Primary Source), although Greek, proudly considered himself a Roman and glowingly extolled the Roman achievement.

> *Neither sea nor any intervening distance on land excludes one from citizenship. No distinction is made between Asia and Europe in this respect. Everything lies open to everybody; and no one fit for office or a position of trust is an alien. . . . You have made the word "Roman" apply not to a city but to a universal people. . . . You no longer classify peoples as Greek or barbarian. . . . You have redivided mankind into Romans and non-Romans. . . . Under this classification there are many in each city who are no less fellow citizens of yours than those of their own stock, though some of them have never seen this city.*[4]

Bas-Relief from Constantine's Arch. Emperor Marcus Aurelius dispenses aid to needy citizens.

(Alinari/Art Resource, N.Y.)

Roman Culture and Law During the Pax Romana

During the late Roman Republic, Rome had creatively assimilated the Greek achievement (see Chapter 6) and transmitted it to others who had little or no contact with Hellenism. Rome had acquired Greek scientific thought, philosophy, medicine, and geography. Roman writers used Greek models; sharing in the humanist outlook of the Greeks, they valued human achievement and expressed themselves in a graceful and eloquent style. The diffusion of Hellenism throughout the Mediterranean world produced a cultural unity among elites that underlay the Pax Romana. Roman cultural life reached its high point during the reign of Augustus, when Rome experienced the golden age of Latin literature. While prose and poetry showed a Greek influence, they were not purely imitative, but expressed originality and creativity that derived from Rome's particular political and social history.

Literature and History. At the request of Augustus, who wanted a literary **epic** to glorify the Empire and his role in founding it, Virgil (70–19 B.C.) wrote the Aeneid, a masterpiece in world literature. The Aeneid is a long poem that recounts the tale of Aeneas and the founding of Rome. The first six books, which describe the wanderings of Aeneas, a survivor of Troy, show the influence of Homer's Odyssey; the last six, dealing with the wars in Italy, show the Iliad's imprint. Whereas Homer's epics focused on the deeds and misdeeds of heroic warriors, the Aeneid is a literary epic of national glory. The most profound ideas and feelings expressed in the Aeneid are Roman virtues—patriotism, devotion to the family, duty to the state, and a strong sense of religion. Intensely patriotic, Virgil ascribed to Rome a divine mission to bring peace and civilized life to the world, and he praised Augustus as a divinely appointed ruler who had fulfilled Rome's mission. The Greeks might be better sculptors, orators, and thinkers, said Virgil, but only the Romans knew how to govern an empire.

> *For other peoples will, I do not doubt,*
> *still cast their bronze to breathe with softer*
>   *features,*
> *or draw out of the marble living lines, plead*
>   *causes better,*
> *trace the ways of heaven with wands and tell*
>   *the rising*
> *constellations; but yours will be the rulership*
>   *of nations,*
> *remember, Roman, these will be your arts:*
> *to teach the ways of peace to those you*
>   *conquer, to spare*
> *defeated peoples, to tame the proud.*[5]

Aelius Aristides: The Blessings of the Pax Romana

In the following reading, Aelius Aristides (A.D. 117–187), a Greek intellectual, glowingly praises the Pax Romana in an oration that was probably delivered in Rome. In the tradition of Roman orators, Aristides used hyperbole and exaggeration. Nevertheless, the oration does capture the universalism and cosmopolitanism that characterized the Roman Empire.

"But the most marvelous and admirable achievement of all, and the one deserving our fullest gratitude, is this. . . . You alone of the imperial powers of history rule over men who are free. You have not assigned this or that region to [unscrupulous governors]. . . . Just as citizens in an individual city might designate magistrates, so you, whose city is the whole world, appoint governors to protect and provide for the governed, as if they were elective, not to lord it over their charges. As a result, so far from disputing the office as if it were their own, governors make way for their successors readily when their term is up, and may not even await their coming. Appeals to a higher jurisdiction are as easy as appeals from parish to county. . . .

"But the most notable and praiseworthy feature of all, a thing unparalleled, is your magnanimous conception of citizenship. All of your subjects (and this implies the whole world) you have divided into two parts: the better endowed and more virile, wherever they may be, you have granted citizenship and even kinship; the rest you govern as obedient subjects. Neither the seas nor expanse of land bars citizenship; Asia and Europe are not differentiated. Careers are open to talent. . . . Rich and poor find contentment and profit in your system; there is no other way of life. Your polity is a single and all-embracing harmony. . . .

. . . "[You] established cities in diverse parts. The cities you filled with colonists; you introduced arts and crafts and established an orderly culture. . . . Your military organization makes all others childish. Your soldiers and officers you train to prevail not only over the enemy but over themselves. The soldier lives under discipline daily, and none ever deserts the post assigned him.

"You alone are, so to speak, natural rulers. Your predecessors were masters and slaves in turn; as rulers they were counterfeits, and reversed their positions like players in a ball game. . . . You have measured out the world, bridged rivers, cut roads through mountains, filled the wastes with posting stations, introduced orderly and refined modes of life. . . .

"Be all gods and their offspring invoked to grant that this empire and this city flourish forever and never cease until stones float upon the sea and trees forbear to sprout in the springtide. May the great Ruler and his sons be preserved to administer all things well."

Question for Analysis

1. What did Aristides find so admirable in Rome's imperial system?

Moses Hadas, ed., *A History of Rome: From Its Origins to 529 A.D. as Told by the Roman Historians* (Garden City, N.Y.: Doubleday Anchor Books, 1956), 143–145.

In his *History of Rome,* the historian Livy (59 B.C.–A.D. 17) also glorified Roman virtues, customs, and deeds. He praised Augustus for attempting to revive traditional Roman morality, to which Livy felt a strong attachment. Modern historians criticize Livy for failing to utilize important sources of information in this work, for relying on biased authorities, and for allowing fierce patriotism to warp his judgment. Although Livy was a lesser historian than Thucydides or Polybius, his work was still a major achievement, particularly in its depiction of the Roman character, which helped make Rome great.

An outstanding poet, Horace (65–8 B.C.) was the son of a freed slave. He broadened his education by studying literature and philosophy in Athens, and Greek ideals are reflected in his writings. Horace enjoyed the luxury of country estates, banquets, fine clothes, and courtesans, along with the simple pleasures of mountain streams and clear skies. His poetry touched on many themes—the joy of good wine, the value of moderation, and the beauty of friendship. Desiring to blend reason and emotion, Horace urged men to seek pleasurable experiences but to avoid extremes and to keep desire under rational control. He also reminded Romans of the terrible civil wars that had ruined the Republic.

> *What plain is not enriched with Latin blood, to bear witness with its graves to our unholy strife. . . . What pool or stream has failed to taste the dismal war! What sea has Italian slaughter not discolored! What coast knows not our blood!*[6]

Unlike Virgil, Livy, or Horace, Ovid (43 B.C.–A.D. 17) did not experience the civil wars during his adult years. Consequently, he was less inclined to praise the Augustan peace. His poetry showed a preference for romance and humor, and he is best remembered for his advice to lovers contained in his most famous work, *The Art of Love.* Written when Ovid was fifty years old, the work deals with the art of seduction. Book I tells how to attract a woman who is the object of a man's desire; Book II explains how a man can keep a woman's love;

Book III advises women about men. To the man who wants to win a woman, Ovid gave this counsel:

> *First of all, be quite sure that there isn't a woman who cannot be won, and make up your mind that you will win her. Only you must prepare the ground.*
>
> *You must play the lover for all you're worth. Tell her how you are pining for her.*
>
> *Never cease to sing the praises of her face, her hair, her taper fingers, and her dainty foot.*
>
> *Tears too are a mighty useful resource in the matter of love. They would melt a diamond. Make a point, therefore, of letting your mistress see your face all wet with tears.*
>
> *Women are things of many moods. You must adapt your treatment to the special case.*[7]

The writers who lived after the Augustan age were of a lesser quality than their predecessors, although the historian Tacitus (A.D. 55–c. 118) was an exception. Sympathetic to republican institutions, Tacitus denounced Roman emperors and the imperial system in his *Histories* and *Annals.* In *Germania,* he turned his sights on the habits of the Germanic peoples. He described the Germans as undisciplined but heroic, with a strong love of freedom.

The satirist Juvenal (A.D. c. 55–138) attacked the evils of Roman society, such as the misconduct of emperors, the haughtiness of the wealthy, the barbaric tastes of commoners, and the failures of parents. He also described the noise, congestion, and poverty of the capital, as well as its criminal element.

> *But these aren't your only terrors. For you can never restrain*
> *The criminal element. Lock up your house, put bolt and chain*
> *On your shop, but when all's quiet, someone will rob you or he'll*
> *Be a cutthroat perhaps and do you in quickly with cold steel.*[8]

In addition, Juvenal expressed venomous views toward women. He describes the humiliations husbands must face—infidelity, poisonings, public harlotry, and being ignored, intimidated, and dominated. All of this, says Juvenal, is a consequence of a wife's failure to live up to the obligations of the married state—being silent, loyal, obedient, respectful of her husband, and caring for the children. He asks a friend who is contemplating marriage: "What Fury, what serpents are driving you mad?"[9] Suicide is preferable, he says sardonically.

After many years of teaching the children of the Roman elite, Quintilian (Marcus Fabius Quintilannua (c. A.D. 35–c. 90), the leading Roman rhetorician of his day, wrote a systematic treatise on education, *The Education of the Orator*, which provided astute insights into the learning process and emphasized the making of well-rounded, cultured orators and good citizens as important goals for the instructor. He recognized that instructors should praise young students for doing well, avoid talking over the heads of their students, and refrain from burdening them with tasks that are beyond their grasp. He also condemned flogging as a disgraceful form of punishment that unnerves and depresses the mind.

Philosophy. Stoicism was the principal philosophy of the Pax Romana, and its leading exponents were Seneca, Epictetus (A.D. c. 60–c. 117), and the emperor Marcus Aurelius. Perpetuating the rational tradition of Greek philosophy, Roman Stoics saw the universe as governed by reason, and they esteemed the human intellect. Like Socrates, they sought the highest good in this world, not in an afterlife, and envisioned no power above human reason. Moral values were obtained from reason alone. The individual was self-sufficient and depended entirely on rational faculties for knowing and doing good. Stoics valued self-sufficient persons who attained virtue and wisdom by exercising rational control over their lives. Roman thinkers also embraced the Stoic doctrine that all people, because of their capacity to reason, belong to a common humanity.

Lucius Annaeus Seneca (4 B.C.–A.D. 65), a student of rhetoric and philosophy, served the emperor Nero. After Nero accused him of participating in a conspiracy against the throne, Seneca was forced to commit suicide. Seneca's Stoic humanitarianism was expressed in his denunciation of the gladiatorial combats, which he labeled cruel and inhuman, and in his concern for slaves. He urged Romans "to consider, that he whom you call your slave, is sprung from the same origin, enjoys the same climate, breathes the same air, and is subject to the same condition of life and death as yourself."[10]

The emperor Marcus Aurelius, the last of the great Stoics, also had to deal with serious problems confronting the Empire. While commanding troops engaged in fighting plundering tribesmen in the Balkans, he wrote in Greek the *Meditations*, a classic work of Stoic thought. In Stoicism, he sought the strength to overcome the burdens of ruling an empire, the fear of death, and the injustices and misdeeds committed by his fellows.

> *Hour by hour resolve firmly, like a Roman and a man, to do what comes to hand with correct and natural dignity, and with humanity, independence, and justice. Allow your mind freedom from all other considerations. This you can do, if you will approach each action as though it were your last, dismissing the wayward thought, the emotional recoil from the commands of reason, the desire to create an impression, the admiration of self, the discontent with your lot. See how little a man needs to master, for his days to flow on in quietness and piety: he has but to observe these few counsels, and the gods will ask nothing more.[11]*

Musonius Rufus (c. A.D. 30–100) evidenced an enlightened view of women in his lectures. When asked if women should study philosophy, he replied:

> *[W]omen have received from the gods the same reasoning power as men—the power . . . according to which we consider whether each action is good or bad, honorable or shameful. . . . Since this is so, why would it be appropriate for men but not women to seek to live honorably and consider how to do so,*

*which is what studying philosophy is? . . .
[I]t is entirely appropriate for both men and
women to have the same upbringing and
education. . . . If men and women must be
equally good in virtue appropriate for a
human—must, that is, be wise and self controlled, and share in courage and justice—will
we not educate both alike, and teach both the
same way the art by which a human would
become good? We must do just that!*[12]

Science. The two most prominent scientists
during the Greco-Roman age were Ptolemy, the
mathematician, geographer, and astronomer, who
worked at Alexandria in the second century A.D.,
and Galen (A.D. C. 130–C. 201), who investigated
medicine and anatomy. Ptolemy's thirteen-volume
work, *Mathematical Composition*—more commonly known as the *Almagest*, a Greek-Arabic
term meaning "the greatest"—summed up antiquity's knowledge of astronomy and became the
authoritative text during the Middle Ages. In the
Ptolemaic system, a motionless, round earth stood
in the center of the universe, and the moon, sun,
and planets moved about the earth in circles, or
in combinations of circles. The Ptolemaic system
was built on a faulty premise, as modern astronomy eventually showed. However, it did work—
that is, it did provide a model of the universe that
adequately accounted for most observed phenomena. The Ptolemaic system would not be challenged until the middle of the sixteenth century.

As Ptolemy's system dominated astronomy, so
the theories of Galen dominated medicine down
to modern times. By dissecting both dead and living animals, Galen attempted a rational investigation of the body's working parts. Although his
work contains many errors, he made essential contributions to the knowledge of anatomy. Thanks
to Arab physicians who preserved his writings during the Middle Ages, Galen's influence continued
in the West into early modern times.

Art, Architecture, and Engineering. Romans
borrowed art forms from other peoples, particularly the Greeks, but they borrowed creatively,
transforming and enhancing their inheritance.
Roman portraiture continued trends initiated
during the Hellenistic Age. Imitating Hellenistic

models, Roman sculptors realistically carved every
detail of a subject's face: unruly hair, prominent
nose, lines and wrinkles, a jaw that showed weakness or strength. Sculpture also gave expression to
the imperial ideal. Statues of emperors conveyed
nobility and authority; reliefs commemorating
victories glorified Roman might and grandeur.

The Romans most creatively transformed the
Greek inheritance in architecture. The Greek
temple was intended to be viewed from the outside; the focus was exclusively on the superbly
balanced exterior. By using arches, vaults, and
domes, the Romans built structures with large,
magnificent interiors. The vast interior, massive walls, and overarching dome of the famous
Pantheon, a temple built in the early second century, during the reign of Hadrian, symbolizes the
power and majesty of the Roman world-state.

The Romans excelled at engineering. They
built amphitheaters, public baths, and aqueducts
that carried water to Roman cities—some still
survive. Roman engineers with an eye for natural
barriers and drainage problems carefully selected
routes and designed great embanked roads, the
finest in the ancient world.

Law. Expressing the Roman yearning for order
and justice, law was Rome's great legacy to Western
civilization. Roman law passed through two essential stages: the formation of civil law (*jus civile*)
and the formation of the law of nations (*jus gentium*). The basic features of the civil law evolved
during the two-hundred-year Struggle of the Orders, at the same time that Rome was extending
its dominion over Italy. The Twelve Tables, drawn
up in the early days of the patrician–plebeian
struggle (described at the beginning of Chapter 6),
established for the Roman state written rules of
criminal and civil law that applied to all citizens.
Over the centuries, the civil law was expanded
by statutes enacted by the assemblies, by the
legal decisions of jurisdictional magistrates, by the
rulings of emperors, and by the commentaries of
professional jurists, who, aided by familiarity with
Greek logic, engaged in systematic legal analysis.

During the period of the Republic's expansion
outside Italy, contact with the Greeks and other
peoples led to the development of the second
branch of Roman law, jus gentium, which combined Roman civil law with principles selectively

drawn from the legal tradition of Greeks and other peoples. Roman jurists identified the jus gentium with the natural law (*jus naturale*) of the Stoics. The jurists said that a law should accord with rational principles inherent in nature: uniform and universally valid standards that can be discerned by rational people. Serving to bind different peoples together, the law of nations harmonized with the requirements of a world empire and with Stoic ideals, as Cicero pointed out.

> True law is right reason in agreement with nature; it is of universal application, unchanging and ever lasting. . . . And there will not be different laws at Rome and at Athens or different laws now and in the future, but one eternal and unchangeable law will be valid for all nations and all times.[13]

The law of nations came to be applied throughout the Empire, although it never entirely supplanted local law. In the eyes of the law, a citizen was not a Syrian or a Briton or a Spaniard but a Roman. In effect, through jus gentium, an international law, Rome transformed what was a theoretical principle for the Stoics into a political reality.

After the fall of the Western Roman Empire, Roman law fell into disuse in Europe. Gradually reintroduced in the twelfth century, it came to form the basis of the common law in all Western European lands except Britain and its dependencies. Some provisions of Roman law are readily recognizable in modern legal systems, as the following excerpts illustrate:

> Justice is a constant, unfailing disposition to give everyone his legal due.
> No one suffers a penalty for what he thinks.
> In the case of major offenses it makes a difference whether something is committed purposefully or accidentally.
> The guilt or punishment of a father can impose no stigma upon the son, for every individual is subjected to treatment in accordance with his own action, and no one is made the inheritor of the guilt of another.
> In inflicting penalties, the age . . . of the guilty party must be taken into account.[14]

Entertainment.   Despite its many achievements, Roman civilization presents a paradox. On the one hand, Roman culture and law evidence high standards of civilization. On the other hand, the Romans institutionalized barbaric practices: battles to the death between armed gladiators and the tormenting and slaughtering of wild beasts.

The major forms of entertainment in both the Republic and the Empire were chariot races, wild animal shows, and gladiatorial combat. Chariot races were gala events in which the most skillful riders and the finest and best-trained stallions raced in an atmosphere of extreme excitement. The charioteers, many of them slaves hoping that victory would bring them freedom, became popular heroes. The rich staked fortunes on the races, and the poor bet their last coins.

The Romans craved brutal spectacles. One form of entertainment pitted wild beasts against each other or against men armed with spears. Another consisted of battles, sometimes to the death, between highly trained gladiators. The gladiators, mainly prisoners of war and condemned criminals, learned their craft at schools run by professional trainers. Some gladiators entered the arena armed with a sword, others with a trident and a net. The spectators were transformed into a frenzied mob that lusted for blood. If they were displeased with a losing gladiator's performance, they would call for his immediate execution.

Over the centuries, these spectacles grew more bizarre, brutal, and sadistic. Hundreds of tigers were set against elephants and bulls; wild bulls tore apart men dressed in animal skins; women battled in the arena; dwarfs fought each other. One day in the Colosseum, which could seat fifty thousand people, three thousand men fought one another; on the day the Colosseum opened in A.D. 80, nine thousand beasts were slaughtered.

Few Romans questioned these barbarities, which became a routine part of daily life. Occasionally, however, thoughtful Romans had strong doubts. After watching a public spectacle, the Stoic philosopher Seneca wrote in disgust: "There is nothing more harmful to one's character than attendance at some spectacle, because vices more easily creep into your soul while you are being entertained. When I return from some spectacle, I am greedier, more aggressive and . . . more cruel and inhuman."[15]

THE COLOSSEUM, ROME, A.D. 70–80. The joint work of the emperor Vespasian and his sons Titus and Domitian, this huge amphitheater was the largest in the ancient world. It was the site of innumerable spectacles, sham sea battles, gladiatorial games, wild beast hunts, and the deaths of Christian martyrs. (Scala/Art Resource, N.Y.)

SIGNS OF TROUBLE

The Pax Romana was one of the finest periods in ancient history. But even during the Time of Happiness, signs of trouble appeared that would grow to crisis proportions in the third century.

Internal Unrest

The Empire's internal stability was always subject to question. Were the economic foundations of the Empire strong and elastic enough to endure hard blows? Could the Roman Empire retain the loyalty of so many diverse nationalities, each with its own religious and cultural traditions? Were the mass of people committed to the values of Greco-Roman civilization, or would they withdraw their allegiance and revert to their native traditions if imperial authority weakened?

Most people in the Mediterranean world welcomed Roman rule and could not conceive of a world without the Empire that brought them peace and security. Nevertheless, during the Pax Romana, dissident elements did surface, particularly in Gaul, Egypt, and Judea. Separatist movements in Gaul were crushed by Roman forces. To provide free bread for Rome's poor, Roman emperors exploited the Egyptian peasantry. Weighed down by forced labor, heavy taxes, requisitions, and confiscations, Egyptian peasants frequently sought to escape from farm work. And the Romans suppressed two uprisings by the Jews of Judea.

The unrest in Egypt, Gaul, and Judea demonstrated that not all people at all times welcomed the grand majesty of the Roman peace and that localist and separatist tendencies persisted in a universal empire. In the centuries that followed, as Rome staggered under the weight of economic, political, and military difficulties, these native loyalties reasserted themselves. Increasingly, the masses, and even the Romanized elite of the cities, withdrew their support from the Roman world-state.

Social and Economic Weaknesses

A healthy world-state required empire-wide trade to serve as an economic base for political unity, expanding agricultural production to feed the cities, and growing internal mass markets to stimulate industrial production. But the economy of the Empire during the Pax Romana had serious defects. The means of communication and transportation were slow, which hindered long-distance commerce. Roman roads, built for military rather than commercial purposes, were often too narrow for large carts and in places were too steep for any vehicles. Consequently, transporting goods by land, even short distances, necessitated huge price increases that hampered trade. Many nobles, considering it unworthy for a gentleman to engage in business, chose to squander their wealth rather than invest it in commercial or industrial enterprises. Lacking the stimulus of capital investment, the economy could not expand.

Limited employment opportunities resulted from the Greco-Roman civilization's failure to improve its technology substantially and from reliance on slave labor. Also, because manual labor was considered degrading, fit only for a slave, there was little incentive for innovation that might have triggered economic growth and expanded employment opportunities. Because of these factors, millions of people simply did not engage in productive labor. Many unemployed inhabitants of Italian towns lived on free or cheap grain provided by the state. To feed this unemployed underclass, the government kept the price of grain artificially low. This practice discouraged farmers from planting more crops and expanding grain production and forced many of them to seek other livelihoods. As more farmers left the countryside, the towns became increasingly

swollen with an impoverished proletariat. Rural areas eventually faced a serious shortage of laborers due to this population migration.

Ultimately, only a small portion of the urban population—landlords whose estates were outside the city, merchants, and administrators—reaped the benefits of the Roman peace. They basked in luxury, leisure, and culture. The urban poor, on the other hand, derived few of the economic gains and shared little in the political and cultural life of the city. The privileged classes bought off the urban poor with bread and circuses, but occasionally mass discontent expressed itself in mob violence. Outside the cities, the peasantry—still the great bulk of the population—was exploited to provide cheap food for the city dwellers.

Such a parasitical, exploitative, and elitist social system might function in periods of peace and tranquility, but could it survive crises? Would the impoverished people of town and country—the overwhelming majority of the population—remain loyal to a state whose benefits barely extended to them and whose sophisticated culture, which they hardly comprehended, virtually excluded them?

Cultural Stagnation and Transformation

Perhaps the most dangerous sign for the future was the spiritual paralysis that crept over the ordered world of the Pax Romana. A weary and sterile Hellenism underlay the Roman peace. The ancient world was undergoing a transformation of values that foreshadowed the end of Greco-Roman civilization.

During the second century A.D., Greco-Roman civilization lost its creative energies, and the values of classical humanism were challenged by mythic-religious movements. The application of reason to nature and society, as we have seen, was the great achievement of the Greek mind. Yet despite its many triumphs, Greek rationalism never entirely subdued the mythic-religious mentality, which draws its strength from human emotion. The masses of peasants and slaves remained attracted to religious forms. **Ritual**, mystery, magic, and ecstasy never lost their hold on the ancient world—nor, indeed, have they on our own scientific and technological society. During the Hellenistic Age, the tide of rationalism gradually receded, and the nonrational, an ever-present undercurrent, showed renewed vigor. This resurgence of the mythical mentality could be seen in the popularity of the occult, magic, alchemy, and astrology. Feeling themselves controlled by heavenly powers, burdened by danger and emotional stress, and fearing fate as fixed in the stars, people turned for deliverance to magicians, astrologers, and exorcists.

They also became devotees of the many Near Eastern religious cults that promised personal salvation. More and more people felt that the good life could not be achieved by individuals through their own efforts; they needed outside help. Philosophers eventually sought escape from this world through union with a divine presence greater than human power. Increasingly, the masses, and then even the educated elite, came to believe that the good life could be found not on earth but only in a world beyond the grave. Seeing themselves as isolated souls wandering aimlessly in a social desert, people sought refuge in religion. Reason had been found wanting; the time for faith and salvation was at hand.

The Roman Empire had imposed peace and stability, but it could not alleviate the feelings of loneliness, anxiety, impotence, alienation, and boredom that had been gaining ground in the Mediterranean world since the fourth century B.C. A spiritual malaise descended on the Greco-Roman world. Among the upper classes, the philosophical and scientific spirit withered; rational and secular values were in retreat. Deprived of the excitement of politics and bored by idleness and pleasure, the best minds, says historian Michael Rostovtzeff,

> lost faith in the power of reason. . . . Creative genius dwindled; science repeated its previous results. The textbook took the place of research; no new artistic discoveries were made, but echoes of the past were heard. . . . [Writers] amuse[d] the mind but [were] incapable of elevating and inspiring it.[16]

The Spread of Mystery Religions

The proliferation of eastern mystery religions was a clear expression of this transformation of classical values. During the Hellenistic era, slaves, merchants, and soldiers brought many religious cults westward from Persia, Babylon, Syria, Egypt, and Asia Minor. The various mystery cults possessed many common features. Converts underwent initiation rites and were bound by oath to secrecy. The initiates, in a state of rapture, attempted to unite with the deity after first purifying themselves through baptism (sometimes with the blood of a bull), fasting, having their heads shaved, or drinking from a sacred vessel. Communion was achieved by donning the god's robe, eating a sacred meal, or visiting the god's sanctuary. This sacramental drama propelled initiates through an intense mystical experience of exaltation and rebirth. Cultists were certain that their particular savior-god would protect them from misfortune and ensure their soul's immortality.

Of special significance was the cult of Mithras, which had certain parallels with early Christianity and was its principal competitor. Originating in Persia, Mithraism spread westward into the Roman Empire. Because it stressed respect for the masculine virtues of bravery and camaraderie, it became particularly popular with the army. The god Mithras, whose birth date was celebrated on December 25, had as his mission the rescuing of humanity from evil. He was said to demand high standards of morality, to judge souls after death, and to grant eternal life to his faithful followers.

The popularity of magic and mystery demonstrates that many people in Roman society either did not comprehend or had lost faith in the rational and secular values of classical humanism. Religion proved more comforting to the spirit. People felt that the gods could provide what reason, natural law, and civic affairs could not: a sure way of overcoming life's misfortunes and discouragements, a guarantee of immortality, a sense of belonging to a community of brethren who cared, an exciting outlet for bottled-up emotions, and a sedative for anxiety at a time when dissatisfaction with the human condition showed itself in all phases of society and life.

The Spiritualization of Philosophy

The religious orientation also found expression in philosophy, which demonstrated attitudes markedly at odds with classical humanism. These attitudes, commonly associated with religion, included indifference to the world, withdrawal, and pessimism about the earthly state. From trying to understand nature and individuals' relationships to one another, the philosophers more and more aspired to a communion with a higher reality. Like the mystery religions, philosophy reached for something beyond this world in order to comfort the individual. In Neo-Platonism, which replaced Stoicism as the dominant school of philosophy in the late Roman Empire, religious yearnings were transformed into a religious system that transcended reason.

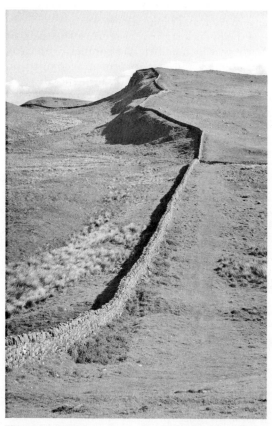

HADRIAN'S WALL. Between A.D. 122 and 127, the Romans constructed an elaborate defensive system in Britain consisting of a wall of solid masonry and a series of forts. Built on high ground, Hadrian's Wall extended from the estuary of the Solway to that of the Tyne, a distance of seventy-three miles. (Clearview/ Alamy Limited)

Plotinus (A.D. c. 205–c. 270), the most influential spokesman of Neo-Platonism, went far beyond Marcus Aurelius's natural religion; in aspiring to the ecstatic union of the soul with God, he subordinated philosophy to mysticism and the occult. Plato's philosophy, we have seen, contained both a major and a minor key. The major key stressed a rational interpretation of the human community and called for reforming the polis on the basis of knowledge, whereas the minor key urged the soul to rise to a higher world of reality. Plotinus was intrigued by Plato's otherworldliness.

What Plotinus desired was union with the One, or the Good, sometimes called God—the source of all existence. Plotinus felt that the intellect could neither describe nor understand the One, which transcended all knowing, and that joining with the One required a mystical leap, a purification of the soul that dispensed with logic, evidence, and proof. This vision, which induced the soul to return to its true home, was for Plotinus something greater and more compelling than reason. For Plotinus, philosophy became a religious experience, a contemplation of the eternal. His successors held that through acts of magic the soul can unite with the One. Compared with this union with the divine One, of what value was knowledge of the sensible world or a concern for human affairs? For Plotinus, the principal goal of life was not comprehension of the natural world or fulfillment of human potential or betterment of the human community but attaining spiritual truth—knowledge of the One—through a transrational experience. Neo-Platonism, concludes historian of philosophy W. T. Stace, "is founded upon . . . the despair of reason." It seeks to reach the Absolute not through reason but through "spiritual intoxication." This marks a radical transformation of philosophical thinking.

For philosophy is founded upon reason. It is the effort to comprehend, to understand, to grasp the reality of things intellectually. Therefore it cannot admit anything higher than reason. To exalt intuition, ecstasy, or rapture, above thought—this is the death of philosophy. . . . In Neo-Platonism, therefore, ancient philosophy commits suicide. This is the end. The place of philosophy is taken henceforth by religion.[17]

By the time of the late Roman Empire, mystery religions intoxicated the masses, and mystical philosophy beguiled the educated elite. Classical civilization was being transformed. Philosophy had become subordinate to religious belief; secular values seemed inferior to religious experience. The earthly city had raised its eyes toward heaven. The culture of the Roman world was moving in a direction in which the quest for the divine was to predominate over all human enterprises.

THE DECLINE OF ROME

Third-Century Crisis

At the death of Marcus Aurelius in A.D. 180, the Empire was politically stable, economically prosperous, and militarily secure. In the third century, the ordered civilization of the Pax Romana ended. Several elements caused this disruption. The Roman Empire was plunged into military anarchy, raided by Germanic tribes, and burdened by economic dislocations. During these critical times, effective leadership was lacking, for the adoptive system abandoned by Marcus Aurelius was not restored.

The degeneration of the army was a prime reason for the third-century crisis. During the great peace, the army had remained an excellent fighting force, renowned for its discipline, organization, and loyalty. In the third century A.D., however, there was a marked deterioration in the quality of Roman soldiers. Lacking loyalty to Rome and greedy for spoils, soldiers used their weapons to prey on civilians and to make and unmake emperors. Fearful of being killed by their unruly troops who wanted spoils or of being murdered by a suspicious emperor, generals were driven to seize the throne. Once in power, they had to buy the loyalty of their soldiers and guard against assassination by other generals. From A.D. 235 to 285, military mutiny and civil war raged as legion fought legion. During this period, there were twenty-six soldier-emperors, twenty-five of whom died violently. The once stalwart army neglected its duty of defending the borders against barbarian incursions and disrupted the internal life of the Empire.

Perhaps the degeneration of the army can be explained by the liberal granting of citizenship. In A.D. 212, citizenship was extended to virtually all freeborn inhabitants of the Empire. Previously, many army recruits had been drawn from among provincials, who were attracted by the promise of citizenship and its advantages. These recruits generally were men of a high caliber who were interested in bettering themselves and their families' lot. With citizenship no longer an inducement for enlistment, says Edward T. Salmon,

> *recruits were now only too likely to be drawn from the lowest and most primitive elements . . . men of the rough and reckless type, who were joining the army chiefly in order to get weapons in their hands with which they would be able to extort for themselves an even greater share of the Empire's collective wealth . . . men who knew little and cared less about Rome's mission and who, when not preying upon the civilians, had not the slightest compunction about preying upon one another.*[18]

During the third century, Rome also had to deal with a revived Persian Empire that forced the Romans to shift large contingents of legions eastward. Taking advantage of the weakened borders and military anarchy, Germanic tribesmen crossed the Rhine–Danube frontier to loot and destroy. The Goths raided coastal cities of Asia Minor and Greece and even burned much of Athens. In the Western Empire, other Germanic tribes penetrated Gaul, Spain, and Italy and engaged the Romans in a full-scale battle near Milan. At the same time that the European defense lines were being breached, a reborn Persian Empire, led by the Sassanid dynasty, attacked and at times conquered some Roman border lands in the east. Some sections of the Empire, notably in Gaul, attempted to break away; these moves reflected an assertion of local patriotism over Roman universalism. The "city of mankind" was crumbling.

These eruptions had severe economic repercussions. Cities were pillaged and destroyed, farmland ruined, and trade disrupted. To obtain funds and supplies for the military, emperors confiscated goods, exacted forced labor, and devalued the currency by reducing the gold and silver content of coins and adding base metals: zinc, tin, and lead. Cheap money caused a ruinous inflation, leading many people to turn to barter as a medium of exchange. These measures led many citizens to withdraw their loyalty from Rome.

Repeated invasions, civil war, pillage by Germanic tribes and by Roman soldiers, soaring prices, a debased coinage, declining agricultural production, disrupted transportation, and the excessive demands of the state caused economic havoc and famine in the cities. Compounding the problem was a great plague that spread across North Africa and the Balkans in midcentury. Driven to desperation by famine and plague, by invading barbarians and plundering Roman soldiers, and by the extortions and requisitions of government officials, many people fled the cities. The urban centers of the ancient world, creators and disseminators of high civilization, were caught in a rhythm of breakdown. As cities decayed, the center of life gravitated back to the countryside. Large, fortified estates, or villas, owned by the emperor or wealthy aristocrats, provided refuge for the uprooted and destitute of town and country. In the countryside, people had no deep commitment to classical civilization, which had made little headway against native languages, religions, and manners.

During the third century A.D., the spiritual crisis intensified as the rational foundations of Greco-Roman civilization eroded further. People turned increasingly to the mystery cults, which offered relief from earthly misery, a sense of belonging, and a promise of immortality. In philosophy, creative energies were directed not toward a greater understanding of nature or society but toward a knowledge of the divine, which, taught the philosophers, was the path to happiness. Hellenism was breaking down.

Diocletian and Constantine: The Regimented State

The emperors Diocletian (A.D. 285–305) and Constantine (A.D. 306–337) tried to contain the awesome forces of disintegration. At a time when agricultural production was steadily declining, they had to feed the city poor and an expanded army of more than 500,000, strung out over the Empire. They also had to prevent renewed outbreaks of military anarchy, drive the Germans back across the Danube frontier, and secure the eastern region against renewed aggression from Persia. Their solution was to weaken municipal institutions, tighten the reins of central government, and extort more taxes and requisitions from the citizens. In the process, they transformed Rome into a bureaucratic, regimented, and militarized state, which some historians refer to as "a vast prison."

Ruling like a Near Eastern despot, Diocletian completed a trend that had been developing for generations. He imitated the pomp of the East, wore magnificent robes and jewels, and demanded that subjects prostrate themselves in his presence. Cities lost their traditional right of local self-government—a loss that also culminated an earlier trend. To increase the size of the army, Diocletian drafted prisoners of war and hired German mercenaries. He also established, on vacant or deserted Roman lands, colonies of Germans from which soldiers could be recruited. To ensure continuous production of food and goods, as well as the collection of taxes, the state forced unskilled workers and artisans to hold their jobs for life and to pass them on to their children. For the same reasons, peasants were turned into virtual serfs, bound to the land that they cultivated. An army of government agents was formed to hunt down peasants who fled the land to escape crushing taxes and poverty.

Also frozen into their positions were city officials, or *curiales*. They often found it necessary to furnish from their own pockets the difference between the state's tax demands and the amount that they could collect from an already overtaxed population. This system of a hereditary class of tax collectors and of crippling taxes to pay for a vastly expanded bureaucracy and military establishment enfeebled urban trade and industry. Such conditions killed the civic spirit of townspeople, who desperately sought escape. By overburdening urban dwellers with taxes and regulations, Diocletian and Constantine helped shatter the vitality of city life, on which Roman prosperity and civilization depended. During the Pax Romana, municipal authorities had enjoyed considerable autonomy; now the state bureaucracy extended its often onerous and rapacious power everywhere.

Rome was governed by a despotism characteristic of the Near East—a highly centralized monarchy regimenting the lives of its subjects. Whereas Augustus had upheld the classical ideal that the commonwealth was a means of fostering the good life for the individual, Diocletian adopted the Eastern attitude that the individual lives for the state. The absolutism inherent in the concept of the principate had eclipsed the republican elements that had endured in the Augustan political settlement.

To guard against military insurrection, Diocletian appointed a loyal general as emperor to govern the western provinces of the Empire while he ruled the eastern regions; although both emperors bore the title Augustus, Diocletian remained superior. (Each emperor then chose an heir-designate, who received his own territory to govern. For a time, the Empire was a tetrarchy—a government by four.) By building an imperial capital, Constantinople, at the Bosporus, a strait where Asia meets Europe, Constantine furthered this trend of dividing the Empire into eastern and western halves. By winning major victories over Germanic tribes and regaining Dacia, which the Romans were forced to abandon in 271 A.D., Constantine did preserve the Empire.

Tribal Migrations and Invasions

Nearly two centuries after Diocletian's reign, the Roman historian Zosimus described the emperor's accomplishment.

> By the foresight of Diocletian the frontiers were everywhere studded with cities and forts and towers, and the whole army stationed along them. It was thus impossible for the barbarians to break through, since at every point they encountered an opposing force strong enough to repel them.[19]

By imposing some order on what had been approaching chaos, Diocletian and Constantine prevented the Empire from collapsing. Rome was given a reprieve. A long period of peace might have brought economic recovery, but misfortune continued to burden Rome, and the process of breakdown and disintegration resumed.

In the last part of the fourth century, the problem of guarding the frontier grew more acute. The Huns, a nomadic people from central Asia, swept across the plains of Russia. With their formidable cavalry—the Huns were expert riders and archers—they subdued the Ostrogoths, a Germanic tribe that had established itself in Ukraine, and forced

the Germanic Visigoths, who had migrated along the Danube in what is now Romania, to seek refuge within the eastern Roman Empire. Enraged by their mistreatment at the hands of Roman officials, the Visigoths took up arms. In A.D. 378, Goths and Romans fought each other in a historic battle at Adrianople. The Visigoths' cavalry cut to pieces the Roman forces, largely tribal mercenaries, and killed and captured perhaps as many as two-thirds of the Roman army. Emperor Valens perished in what was Rome's worst defeat since Cannae in the war with Hannibal. The Visigoths were on Roman territory to stay. The battle of Adrianople signified that Rome could no longer defend its borders. Since it was the Visigoth cavalry that prevailed over a Roman army composed mainly of foot soldiers, the battle also signified that cavalry had begun to supersede infantry as a principal instrument of warfare.

Other Germanic tribes increased their pressure on the Empire's borders. Attracted by Rome's riches and advanced civilization, they were also looking for new lands to farm and were frightened by the advent of the Huns. The borders finally collapsed at the very end of A.D. 406 as Vandals, Alans, Suebi, and other tribes joined the Goths in devastating and overrunning the Empire's western provinces. In A.D. 408–409, the Visigoths, led by Alaric, besieged Rome itself, extorting huge sums in return for permitting food to enter the city. Then, in A.D. 410, they rampaged through the city, which for eight hundred years had remained free of foreign occupation, slaughtering, destroying, and plundering. Saint Jerome lamented: "Who could believe that Rome, built upon the conquest of the whole world, would fall to the ground? that the mother herself would become the tomb of her peoples?"[20] Roman power continued to erode. The Vandals made inroads in Roman North Africa and conquered Carthage in A.D. 439.

Economic conditions continued to deteriorate. Cities in Britain, Gaul, Germany, and Spain lay abandoned. Other metropolises saw their populations dwindle and production stagnate. The great network of Roman roads was not maintained, and trade in the West almost disappeared or passed into the hands of Greeks, Syrians, and Jews from the East. Everywhere famine, the extortion of taxes by government officials, the proliferation of marauding outlaws (many of them driven from their homes by the excessive financial demands of the

Map 7.2 Incursions and Migrations, c. a.d. 300–500 In the fifth century, Germanic tribes, seeking land and desperate to escape the Huns, overran the weakened Roman borders. (© 2016 Cengage Learning.)

state bureaucracy), and murderous warfare added to the misery of the Roman populace and the decomposition and fragmentation of the Empire.

In a.d. 451, Attila (c. 406–453), who had united Mongol tribes, led his Huns into Gaul, where he suffered his only defeat at the hands of a coalition of Germans and remnants of the Roman army. He died two years later, having come within a hairsbreadth of turning Europe into a province of a Mongolian empire. But Rome's misfortunes persisted. In a.d. 455, Rome was again pillaged, this time by the Vandals. Additional regions fell under the control of Germanic chieftains, and increasingly the old Roman administration was collapsing. Germanic soldiers in the pay of Rome gained control of the government and dictated the choice of emperor.

In a.d. 476, Germanic officers overthrew the Roman emperor Romulus and placed a fellow German, Odoacer, on the throne. This act is traditionally regarded as the end of the Roman Empire in the West. By the end of the fifth century, the western empire had fragmented into separate Germanic kingdoms.

Reasons for Rome's Decline

What were the underlying causes of the decline and fall of the Roman Empire in the West? Surely, no other question has intrigued the historical imagination more than this one. Implicit in the answers suggested by historians and philosophers is a concern for their own civilization. Will it suffer the same fate as Rome?

To analyze so monumental a development as the fall of Rome, some preliminary observations are necessary. First, the fall of Rome was a process lasting hundreds of years; it was not a single event that occurred in A.D. 476. Second, only the western half of the Empire fell. The eastern half—wealthier, more populous, less afflicted with civil wars, and less exposed to barbarian invasions—survived as the Byzantine Empire until the middle of the fifteenth century. Third, no single explanation suffices to account for Rome's decline; multiple forces—internal problems and external threats—operated concurrently to bring about the fall.

The Role of the Germanic Tribes. Was Rome's fall suicide or murder? Did the Germans walk over a corpse, or did they contribute substantially to Rome's decline and fall? Undoubtedly, an empire enfeebled by internal rot succumbed to the Germanic migrations. Perhaps a stronger Rome might have secured its borders, as it had done during the Pax Romana. But attacks from increasingly better organized Germanic tribes occurred mainly in the west, and the western Empire, poorer and less populated than the eastern portion, reeled under these increasingly numerous and more severe barbarian onslaughts. The pressures exerted by the Germans along an immense frontier also aggravated Rome's internal problems. The barbarian attacks left border regions depopulated and impoverished, as expenditures for the military drained the western Empire's resources. The Empire imposed high taxes and labor services on its citizens in order to strengthen the armed forces, causing the overburdened middle and lower classes to hate the imperial government that took so much from them.

Moreover, as more and more territory fell to the barbarian invaders, the Roman state was deprived of badly needed tax revenues. Containing the threat from a revived Persian Empire made it more difficult for Rome to deal with the Germanic invaders: it necessitated stationing a large force on the eastern frontier that could have been deployed in the west, and it imposed a heavy financial burden on the Empire, preventing it from funding larger armies against the barbarians.

Spiritual Considerations. The classical mentality, once brimming with confidence about the potentialities of the individual and the power of the intellect, suffered a failure of nerve. The urban upper class, on whom the responsibility for preserving cosmopolitan Greco-Roman culture traditionally rested, became dissolute and apathetic and no longer took an interest in public life. The aristocrats secluded themselves behind the walls of their fortified country estates; many did not lift a finger to help the Empire. The townspeople demonstrated their disenchantment by avoiding public service and by rarely organizing resistance forces against the barbarian invaders. Hounded by the state and persecuted by the army, many farmers viewed the Germans as liberators. Focusing on the life to come, many Christians showed no interest in supporting the Roman legions charged with defending the empire. The great bulk of the Roman citizenry, disillusioned and indifferent, simply gave up, despite the fact that they overwhelmingly outnumbered the Germanic invaders.

Political and Military Considerations. The Roman government itself contributed to this spiritual malaise through its increasingly autocratic tendencies, which culminated in the regimented rule of Diocletian and Constantine. The insatiable demands and regulations of the state in the late Roman Empire sapped the initiative and civic spirit of its citizens. The ruined middle and lower classes withdrew their loyalty. For many, the state had become the enemy, and its administration was hated and feared more than the barbarians. Salvianus of Marseilles (c. A.D. 400–470), a monk from Gaul, described the disaffection toward Rome that led many to welcome the barbarians as liberators.

> *Meanwhile the poor are being robbed, widows groan, orphans are trodden down, so that many, even persons of good birth, who have enjoyed a liberal education, seek refuge with the enemy to escape death under the trials of general persecution. They seek among the barbarians the Roman mercy, since they cannot endure the barbarous mercilessness they find among the Romans. . . . So you find men passing over everywhere, now to the Goths . . ., or whatever other barbarians have established their power anywhere. . . . Hence the name of Roman citizen, once . . . much valued . . ., is now voluntarily repudiated and shunned, and is thought not merely valueless, but even almost abhorrent.*[21]

Related to the political decline was the government's inability to retain the allegiance of its armies and to control ambitious military commanders, who used their troops to seize the throne and its immense power. The internal security and stability of the Empire was thus constantly imperiled by army leaders more concerned with grandiose personal dreams than with defending the Empire's borders. These repeated civil wars imposed terrible financial burdens on the Empire and gravely weakened the frontier defenses—compounding the problem of forces spread thinly over thousands of miles and presenting an invitation to the Germans to increase their pressure.

During the Pax Romana, superior training and organization, rigorous discipline, a professional system of command, and a network of walls and forts enabled the Roman legions to protect the frontiers against incursions. The Roman soldier, for whom discipline was a deeply ingrained tradition, knew that his comrades would not desert the field, no matter how hard the fighting—an attitude that usually meant certain victory against untrained barbarian hordes. However, in the Late Roman Empire, the quality of Roman soldiers deteriorated, and the legions failed to defend the borders, even though the Germanic invaders were fewer numerically. During the third century, the army consisted predominantly of the provincial peasantry. These nonurban, non-Italian, semicivilized soldiers, often the dregs of society, were not committed to Greco-Roman civilization. They had little comprehension of Rome's mission and at times used their power to attack the cities and towns and to prey on hapless citizens. The emperors also recruited large numbers of Germans into the army—barbarians had been used as auxiliary troops since Julius Caesar—to fill depleted ranks. Ultimately, the army consisted predominantly of barbarians, as both legionnaires and officers. Although these Germans made brave soldiers, they too had little loyalty to Greco-Roman civilization and to the Roman state. This deterioration of the Roman army occurred in part because many young citizens evaded conscription. No longer imbued with patriotism, they considered military service a servitude to be shunned.

The deterioration of the Roman army is seen also on the level of tactics. Roman soldiers continued to fight in organized units, but the training and discipline required for fighting in close-order formations had lapsed. Barbarian units serving with the Roman army under their own commanders did not easily submit to traditional discipline. Thus, Rome lost the tactical superiority that it had once enjoyed over the barbarians.

Economic Considerations. Contributing to the decline of the Roman Empire in the west were population decline, the lack of technological advance, the heavy burden of taxation, and economic decentralization, which abetted political decentralization.

During the late Roman Empire, the population shrank. The epidemic during the reign of Marcus Aurelius, which might have been the bubonic plague, lasted fifteen years. A second plague struck the Empire during the reign of Commodus, Marcus Aurelius's son. Other plagues in the middle of the third century and constant warfare further reduced the population. The birth rate did not rise to compensate for these losses. Worsening economic conditions and lack of hope in the future apparently discouraged people from increasing the size of their families.

The decline in population adversely affected the Empire in at least three important ways. First, at the same time that the population was declining, the costs of running the Empire were spiraling, a situation that created a terrible burden for taxpayers. Second, fewer workers were available for agriculture, the most important economic activity of the Empire. Third, population decline reduced the manpower available for the army, forcing emperors to permit the establishment of Germanic colonies within the Empire's borders to serve as feeders for the army. This situation led to the barbarization of the army.

The Roman peace brought stability, but it failed to discover new and better ways of producing goods and agricultural products. To be sure, some advances in technology did take place during the Hellenistic Age and the Pax Romana: rotary mills for grain, screw presses, and improvements in glass-blowing and field-drainage methods. But the high intellectual culture of Greece and Rome rested on a meager economic and technological foundation. The widespread use of slave labor probably precluded a breakthrough in technology, for slaves had little incentive to invent more efficient ways of producing. The upper classes, identifying manual labor with slavery, would not condescend to engage in the mechanical arts. This failure to improve the level of technology limited employment opportunities for the masses. Because the masses could not increase their purchasing power, business and industry were without a mass internal market that might have acted as a continual stimulus for the accumulation of capital and for economic expansion.

Instead of expanding industry and trade, towns maintained their wealth by exploiting the countryside. The Roman cities, centers of civilized life and opulence, lacked industries. They spent but did not produce. Provided with food and entertainment—"bread and circuses"—the unproductive city dwellers, driven out of the labor force by slavery and economic stagnation, were a heavy burden for the state. The towns were dominated by landlords whose estates lay beyond the city and whose income derived from grain, oil, and wine. Manufacturing was rudimentary, confined essentially to textiles, pottery, furniture, and glassware. The methods of production rarely improved; the market was limited; the cost of transportation, particularly by land, was high; and agricultural productivity was low—the labor of perhaps nineteen peasants was required to support one townsman. Such a fundamentally unhealthy economy could not weather the dislocations caused by uninterrupted warfare and the demands of the military and a mushrooming bureaucracy.

With the barbarians pressing on the borders, the increased military expenditures overstrained the Empire's resources. To pay for the food, uniforms, arms, and armor of the soldiers, taxes were raised, growing too heavy for peasants and townspeople, particularly since the large landowners did not pay their fair share. The state also requisitioned wood and grain and demanded that citizens maintain roads and bridges. The government often resorted to force to collect taxes and exact services. Crushed by these demands, many peasants simply abandoned their farms and sought the protection of large landowners or turned to banditry.

Making the situation worse was the administrative separation of the Empire into eastern and western parts, undertaken by Diocletian and Constantine. As a result, western emperors could no longer rely on financial aid from the wealthier east to pay for the defense of the borders. Slow communications and costly transport continued to hamper the empire-wide trade, which was required to sustain political unity. Meanwhile, industries gravitated outward, to search for new markets in the frontier army camps and for new sources of slaves in border regions. This dispersion further weakened the bonds of economic unity. Gradually, trade became less international and more local, and provincial regions grew more self-sufficient. The strife of the third century intensified the drift toward economic self-sufficiency in the provinces, a condition that promoted localism and separatism.

Contributing to the economic decentralization was the growth of industries on latifundia, the large, fortified estates owned by wealthy aristocrats. Producing exclusively for the local market, these estates contributed to the impoverishment of urban centers by reducing the number of customers available to buy goods made in the cities. As life grew more desperate, urban craftsmen and small farmers, made destitute by the state, sought the protection of these large landlords, whose estates grew in size and importance. The growth of latifundia was accompanied by the decline of cities and the transformation of independent peasants into virtual serfs.

These great estates were also new centers of political power, which the imperial government could not curb. A new society was taking shape in the Late Roman Empire. The center of gravity shifted from the city to the landed estate, from the imperial bureaucrat to the local aristocrat. These developments epitomized the decay of ancient civilization and presaged a new era, the Middle Ages.

THE ROMAN LEGACY

Rome left the West a rich heritage, which endured for centuries. In admiration of the Roman Republic's good years, the Founding Fathers of the United States wanted their new country to be a free and self-governing republic in which citizens actively and responsibly participated in civic affairs. The idea of a world empire united by a common law and effective government never died. In the centuries following the collapse of Rome, people continued to be attracted to the idea of a unified and peaceful world-state. To this day, we ask what lessons we can learn from the Pax Romana that provided a multinational empire with two centuries of relative stability, order, and peace. Indeed the Roman conception of universal citizenship finds expression in European attempts at integration in the decades after World War II. By preserving and adding to the philosophy, literature, science, and arts of ancient Greece, Rome strengthened the basic foundations of the Western cultural tradition. Latin, the language of Rome, lived on long after Rome perished. The Western church fathers wrote in Latin, and during the Middle Ages, Latin was the language of learning, literature, and law. From Latin came Italian, French, Spanish, Portuguese, and Romanian. Roman law, the quintessential expression of Roman genius, influenced church law and

formed the basis of the legal codes of most European states. Finally, Christianity, the core religion of the West, was born within the Roman Empire and was greatly influenced by Roman law (the church's **canon law** owed much to Roman jurisprudence) and organization (the pope, head of the church and ruling from Rome, was the counterpart of the Roman emperor, and bishoprics were established in regions that coincided with the Empire's administrative structure). The ideal of a single Christian society embracing many different nationalities, so dear to medieval thinkers, was superimposed on the model of the Roman Empire.

Notes

1. Tacitus, *The Annals of Imperial Rome,* trans. Michael Grant (Baltimore: Penguin Books, 1959), 31.

2. Cited in David Magie, *Roman Rule in Asia Minor* (Princeton, N.J.: Princeton University Press, 1950), 490.

3. Sallust, *The Conspiracy of Cataline,* trans. S. A. Handford (Baltimore: Penguin Books, 1963), 193.

4. Excerpted in Naphtali Lewis and Meyer Reinhold, eds., *Roman Civilization, Sourcebook II: The Empire* (New York: Harper and Row, 1966), 136.

5. *From The Aeneid of Virgil,* trans. Allen Mandelbaum, copyright © 1971 by Allen Mandelbaum. Published by Bantam Books, division of Random House, Inc.

6. *The Odes and Epodes of Horace,* trans. C. E. Bennett (Cambridge, Mass.: Harvard University Press, Loeb Classical Library, 1914), 109.

7. *The Art of Love and Other Love Books of Ovid* (New York: Grosset and Dunlap, The Universal Library, 1959), 117–118, 130–132, 135.

8. *The Satires of Juvenal,* trans. Hubert Creekmore (New York: Mentor Books, 1963), 58–61.

9. Ibid., 83.

10. Adapted from Seneca, *The Epistles,* trans. Thomas Morell (London: W. Woodfall, 1786), vol. 1, epistle 47.

11. Marcus Aurelius, *Meditations,* trans. Maxwell Staniforth (Baltimore: Penguin Classics, 1964), bk. 2.

12. William B. Irvine, *Musonius Rufus Lectures and Sayings,* tr. Cynthia King (www.CreateSpace.com, 2011), 28, 32.

13. Cicero, *De Republica,* trans. Clinton Walker Keyes (Cambridge, Mass.: Harvard University Press, Loeb Classical Library, 1994), 211.

14. Excerpted in Lewis and Reinhold, eds., *Roman Civilization, Sourcebook II: The Empire,* 535, 539, 540, 547, 548.

15. Seneca, *The Epistles,* vol. 1, epistle 7.

16. Michael Rostovtzeff, *Rome* (New York: Oxford University Press, 1960), 322.

17. W. T. Stace, *A Critical History of Greek Philosophy* (London: Macmillan, 1924), 377.

18. Excerpted in Mortimer Chambers, ed., *The Fall of Rome* (New York: Holt, Rinehart and Winston, 1963), 45–46.

19. Quoted in Stephen Williams, *Diocletian and the Roman Recovery* (New York: Methuen, 1985), 101.

20. Excerpted in James Harvey Robinson, ed., *Readings in European History* (Boston: Ginn, 1904), 45.

21. Salvian, *On the Government of God,* trans. Eva M. Sanford (New York: Octagon, 1966), 141–142.

Chapter 8

Early Christianity: A World Religion

Christ Gives the Law to Saints Peter and Paul, fifth century, Santa Costanza, Rome. This mosaic portrays a haloed, beardless Christ bestowing the law in the manner of an emperor delivering an edict. (Vanni Archive/Art Resource, N.Y.)

Focus Questions

1. Why do you think that over the centuries there have been conflicting interpretations of Jesus' life, thought, and death?

2. How did Saint Paul transform a Jewish sect into a world religion?

3. What factors contributed to the triumph of Christianity in the Roman Empire?

4. How was early Christianity influenced by Judaism, Greek philosophy, and Hellenistic mystery religions?

5. What factors contributed to Christian anti-Judaism? What is the historical significance of the negative image of Jews and Judaism taught by early Christians?

6. What are the core features of Saint Augustine's theology?

7. What do the worldviews of Christianity and Greco-Roman humanism have in common? Why are they essentially different?

As confidence in human reason and hope for happiness in this world waned in the last centuries of the Roman Empire, a new outlook began to take hold. Evident in philosophy and in the popularity of Eastern religions, this viewpoint stressed escape from an oppressive world and communion with a higher reality. Christianity evolved and expanded within this setting of declining classicism and heightening otherworldliness. As one response to a declining Hellenism, Christianity offered a spiritually disillusioned Greco-Roman world a reason for living: the hope of personal immortality. The triumph of Christianity marked a break with classical antiquity and a new stage in the evolution of the West, for there was a fundamental difference between the classical and the Christian concepts of God, the individual, and the purpose of life.

THE ORIGINS OF CHRISTIANITY

A Palestinian Jew named Jesus was executed by the Roman authorities during the reign of Tiberius (A.D. 14–37), who succeeded Augustus. At the time, few people paid much attention to what proved to be one of the most pivotal events in world history. In the quest for the historical Jesus, scholars have stressed the importance of both his Jewishness and the religious ferment that prevailed in Palestine in the first century B.C. Jesus' ethical teachings are rooted in the moral outlook of the Old Testament prophets. Jesus, who prayed as a Jew, taught as a Jew to fellow Jews, and valued Jewish law and prophetic teachings, could only conceive of himself as a Jew. Hans Küng, the prominent Swiss student of religion, elaborates on this point.

> *Jesus was a Jew, a member of a small, poor, politically powerless nation living at the periphery of the Roman Empire. He was active among Jews and for Jews. His mother Mary, his father Joseph, his family, his followers were Jews. His name was Jewish (Hebrew Yeshu'a). . . . His Bible, his worship, his prayers were Jewish. In the situation at that time he could not have thought of any*

Chronology 8.1 ❖ Early Christianity

c. A.D. 29	Crucifixion of Jesus
c. 34–64	Missionary activity of Saint Paul
c. 66–70	The Gospel According to Mark is written
250–260	A decade of brutal persecution of Christians by the Romans
313	Constantine grants toleration of Christianity
c. 320	First convent is founded
325	Council of Nicaea rules that God and Christ are of the same substance, coequal and coeternal
391–392	Theodosius I prohibits public acts of pagan worship and the public profession of pagan religion; during his reign, Christianity becomes the state religion
430	Death of Saint Augustine
451	Council of Chalcedon rules that Christ is truly God and truly man
529	Saint Benedict founds monastery at Monte Cassino

proclamation among the gentiles. His message was for the Jewish people, but for this people in its entirety without any exception. From this basic fact it follows irrevocably that without Judaism there would be no Christianity. The Bible of the early Christians was the "Old Testament." The New Testament Scriptures became part of the Bible only by being appended to the Old. The gospel of Jesus Christ everywhere quite consciously presupposes the Torah and the Prophets.[1]

Judaism in the First Century B.C.

In the first century B.C., four principal social-religious parties, or sects, existed among the Palestinian Jews: Sadducees, Pharisees, Essenes, and Zealots. Composed of the upper stratum of Jewish society—influential landed gentry and hereditary priests, who controlled the temple in Jerusalem—the religiously conservative Sadducees insisted on a strict interpretation of **Mosaic Law** (Torah) and the perpetuation of temple ceremonies. Claiming to be the descendants of Sadok, the high priest of Solomon, Sadducees believed

that they were maintaining the ancient Hebrew teachings concerning the Torah, which they interpreted literally. Rejecting the concepts of the resurrection of the dead and of an afterlife, they held that God meted out rewards and punishments on earth. Challenging the aristocratic Sadducees, the Pharisees adopted a more liberal attitude toward Mosaic Law. They allowed discussion on varying interpretations of the Law and granted authority to oral tradition—an "oral Torah," which was communicated from one generation to another—as well as to written Scripture. Unlike the Sadducees, the Pharisees believed in life after death. The concept of personal immortality is barely mentioned in the Hebrew Scriptures. A later addition to Hebrew religious thought, probably acquired from Persia, the idea had gained wide acceptance by the first century A.D. The Pharisees had the support of most of the Jewish people. All later forms of Judaism developed from the Pharisees.

Besides the afterlife, another widely recognized idea in the first century B.C. was the belief in a **Messiah**, a redeemer chosen by God to liberate Israel from foreign rule. In the days of the Messiah, it was predicted, Israel would be free, the exiles would return, and the Jews would be blessed

169

SARCOPHAGUS OF BAEBIA HERTOFILA, LATE THIRD CENTURY, MUSEO DELLE TERME, ROME. Symbolizing the Christian Eucharist, Jesus distributes the bread and the wine of the Last Supper to his disciples. (Scala/Art Resource N.Y.)

with peace, unity, and prosperity. The Messiah, in contrast to wicked Roman rulers, would govern justly and righteously.

The third religious party, the Essenes, established a semimonastic community near the Dead Sea. Like the Sadducees, they considered themselves to be the true descendants of Sadok, but they rejected the temple priests as corrupt. Only those priests affiliated with their sect were deemed pure. In 1947, leather scrolls in hermetically sealed cylinders were found near the Essene community of Qumran, about fourteen miles from Jerusalem, close to the Dead Sea. Dated from between c. 200 B.C. and A.D. 66–70, the *Wady Qumran Manuscripts*, commonly called the Dead Sea Scrolls, contain the oldest extant Hebrew manuscripts and also documents that are unique to the sect of the Essenes, founded by a man they refer to as "the Teacher of Righteousness." The Essenes believed in the physical resurrection of the body, like the Pharisees, but gave this doctrine a more compelling meaning by tying it to the immediate coming of God's kingdom.

Certain that the Messiah was about to come, the Essenes saw themselves as the first generation of God's people.

By adding to our knowledge of Palestinian Judaism in the first century, the scrolls shed light on the period in which Christianity arose and the New Testament was written. Although the scrolls make no reference to Jesus or his followers, scholars do find parallels between the Qumran community and the Jesus movement. Like Jesus, for example, the community spoke of the end of days that they believed was imminent. Both the Qumran community and Jesus' early followers considered themselves the true Israel, referred to themselves as the "sons of light," and anticipated a coming messianic age. There is a similarity between many of the teachings of Jesus, particularly in the Sermon on the Mount, and the teachings of the Essenes' Teacher of Righteousness.

The fourth sect, the Zealots, demanded that the Jews neither pay taxes to Rome nor acknowledge the authority of the Roman emperor. Devoted patriots, the Zealots engaged in acts of resistance to Rome, which culminated in the great revolt of A.D. 66–70, discussed in Chapter 7.

Jesus (c. 4 B.C.–c. A.D. 29) practiced his ministry within this context of Jewish religious-national expectations and longings. The hopes of Jesus' early followers encompassed a lower-class dissatisfaction with the aristocratic Sadducees; a Pharisee emphasis on prophetic ideals and the afterlife; an Essene preoccupation with the end-of-days, the nearness of God, and the need for repentance; and a conquered people's yearning for a Messiah who would liberate their land from Roman rule and establish God's reign.

Jesus: The Inner Person

Historians are able to speak with greater certainty about social-religious developments in Judea at the time of Jesus than they can about Jesus himself. In reconstructing what Jesus did and believed, the historian labors under a handicap, for the sources are few. Jesus himself wrote nothing, and nothing was written about him during his lifetime. In the generations following his death, both Roman and Jewish historians paid him scant attention. Consequently, virtually everything known about Jesus derives from the Bible's New Testament, which was written decades after Jesus' death by devotees seeking to convey a religious truth and to propagate a faith.

Modern historians in quest of the historical Jesus have rigorously and critically analyzed the New Testament; their analyses have provided some insights into Jesus and his beliefs. Nevertheless, much about Jesus remains obscure. Very little is known about his childhood. Like other Jewish youths, he was taught Hebrew religious-ethical thought and the many rules that governed daily life. At about the age of thirty, no doubt influenced by John the Baptist, who likely was once part of the Essene community, Jesus began to preach the coming of the reign of God and the need for people to repent—undergo moral transformation—so that they could enter God's kingdom. "Now after John was arrested, Jesus came into Galilee, preaching the gospel of God, and

saying, 'The time is fulfilled, and the kingdom of God is at hand; repent, and believe in the gospel [good news]'" (Mark 1:14–15).[2]* This apocalyptic vision that the existing world was coming to an end and would be replaced by God's perfect kingdom had been preached by John the Baptist and other religious thinkers before him.

For Jesus, the coming of the kingdom was imminent; the process leading to the establishment of God's kingdom on earth had already begun. A new order would soon be established in which God would govern his people righteously and mercifully. Hence, the present moment became critical for him—a time for spiritual preparedness and repentance—because an individual's thoughts, goals, and actions would determine whether he or she would gain entrance into the kingdom. People had to radically change their lives. They had to eliminate base, lustful, hostile, and selfish feelings; stop pursuing wealth and power; purify their hearts; and show their love for God and their fellow human beings.

Most likely Jesus' early followers perceived him as a prophet. Like the Hebrew prophets, Jesus saw ethics as the core of Mosaic Law: "So whatever you wish that men would do to you, do so to them; for this is the law and the prophets" (Matthew 7:12). Like the prophets, he denounced injustice and oppression, urged mercy and compassion, and expressed a special concern for the poor and downtrodden.

Jesus did not intend to lead his fellow Jews, who called him rabbi, away from their ancestral religion: "'Think not that I have come to abolish the law and the prophets; I have come not to abolish them but to fulfil them'" (Matthew 5:17). Although Jesus did not negate the Law, some of his interpretations offended Jewish leaders.

While not seeking to break with his past or to reject Jewish law, Jesus was distressed by the Judaism of his day. Following the prophets, the rabbis taught the Golden Rule, as well as God's love and mercy for his children, but it seemed to Jesus that these ethical considerations were being undermined by an exaggerated rabbinical concern with ritual,

---

*The biblical quotations in this chapter are taken from the Revised Standard Version of the Holy Bible.

restrictions, and the fine points of the Law. Jesus believed that the center of Judaism had shifted from prophetic values to obedience to rules and prohibitions regulating the smallest details of daily life. (To Jewish leaders, of course, these detailed regulations governing eating, washing, Sabbath observance, family relations, and so forth were God's commands intended to sanctify all human activities.) To Jesus, such a rigid view of the Law distorted the meaning of prophetic teachings. Rules dealt only with an individual's visible behavior; they did not engage the person's inner being and lead to a moral transformation based on love, compassion, and selflessness. Observing the Lord's command to rest on the Sabbath—for example, by not eating an egg laid on Saturday or by not lifting a chair on that day—did not purify a person's heart.

For Jesus, the best way to realize the true meaning of Jewish law was through moral purity, which finds expression in a love for one's fellows. The inner person concerned Jesus, and it was an inner change that he sought: "For from within, out of the heart of man, come evil thoughts, fornication, theft, murder, adultery, coveting, wickedness, deceit, licentiousness, envy, slander, pride, foolishness. All these evil things come from within, and they defile a man" (Mark 7:21–23). To Jesus, the spirit of Mosaic Law was more important than the letter of the Law; for him, right living and a pure loving heart were Judaism's true essence. With the fervor of a prophet, he urged a moral transformation of human character through a direct encounter between the individual and God. By preaching active love for others and genuine compassion for sufferers and by stressing a personal and intimate connection between the individual and God, Jesus associated himself more with the Hebrew prophetic tradition than with the Hebrew rituals, rules, and prohibitions that served to perpetuate a national and cultural tradition of a distinct people.

It was inevitable that Jewish scribes and priests, guardians of the faith, would regard Jesus, who had become a popular preacher, as a threat to ancient traditions. To Jewish leaders, he was a troublemaker and a subversive. They accused him of associating with social outcasts, sinners, and imperial tax collectors; undermining respect for the Sabbath by violating God's strict command prohibiting any form of labor on this holy day; proclaiming spiritual truth in his own name and on his own authority; and claiming that he, above all other men, had a special and intimate relationship with God and that by associating with him a sinner would be forgiven. Stated succinctly, Jewish leaders believed that Jesus was setting the authority of his person over Mosaic Law—an unpardonable blasphemy in their eyes. They saw Jesus as a false prophet who was leading the people astray.

The Romans, who ruled Palestine, had little interest in Jewish intrareligious disputes. They feared Jesus as a political agitator, as a charismatic leader who could ignite Jewish messianic expectations into a revolt against Rome. After Jewish leaders turned Jesus over to the Roman authorities, the Roman procurator, Pontius Pilate, sentenced him to death by crucifixion, a customary punishment for someone guilty of high treason. Jesus' execution was consistent with Roman policy in Judea, for the Romans routinely arrested and executed Jews suspected of inciting unrest against Roman rule. Inscribed on the cross on which he was crucified were the words "King of the Jews," a seemingly clear indication of why Pilate ordered his death. Although it is questionable if Jesus ever intended to challenge Roman authority, Pilate was taking no chances. He wanted to eliminate this popular leader before he might ignite a popular uprising.

Some Jews, believing that Jesus was an inspired prophet or even the long-awaited Messiah, had become his followers; the chief of these were the Twelve Disciples. At the time of Jesus' death, Christianity was not a separate religion but a small Hebrew sect with dim prospects for survival. What established the Christian movement and gave it strength was the belief of Jesus' followers that he was raised from the dead on the third day after he was buried. The doctrine of the resurrection enabled people to regard Jesus as more than a superb ethical soul, more than a righteous rabbi, more than a prophet, more than the Messiah; it made possible belief in Jesus as a divine **savior-god** who had come to earth to show people the way to heaven. For early Christians, Jesus' death and belief in his resurrection took on greater importance than his life. For these believers, Jesus the savior-god became the center of their emerging church.

Map 8.1 **The Journeys of Saint Paul** Paul, a Greek-speaking citizen of Rome and thus free to travel throughout the Empire, won converts to the new religion. (© 2016 Cengage Learning.)

There is no evidence that Jesus, who never preached to Gentiles, intended to establish a new church; this was accomplished by his followers. In the years immediately following the crucifixion, the religion of Jesus was confined almost exclusively to Jews, who could more appropriately be called Jewish-Christians. The word *Christian* came from a name given Jesus: *Christ* (the Lord's Anointed, the Messiah). Missionaries of this dissenting Christian movement within Judaism were called Apostles—those sent out to preach the gospel about Christ. They addressed themselves to Jews and to converts to Judaism who, because they did not adhere fully to Mosaic Law, were not wholly accepted by the Jewish community.

Before this new Jewish messianic movement could realize the universal implications of Jesus' teachings and become a world religion, as distinct from a reformist Jewish sect, it had to separate itself both ideologically and socially from the corporate body of Judaism. Instrumental in this development was the work of a Hellenized Jew named Saul, known to the world as Saint Paul.

Saint Paul: From a Jewish Sect to a World Religion

Saint Paul (A.D. c. 5–c. 67) came from the Greek city of Tarsus in southeastern Asia Minor. Originally called Saul, he belonged to the Diaspora, or the "Dispersion"—the millions of Jews living outside Palestine. Though the Jews of the Diaspora retained their ancient faith, they were also influenced by Greek culture. An example is the Alexandrian Jew Philo (c. 20 B.C.–c. A.D. 50), who tried to demonstrate that Hebrew Scriptures could be explained and justified in terms of Greek philosophy.

SAINT PAUL MOSAIC FROM THE BAPTISTRY OF THE ARIANS, RAVENNA, ITALY. Inspired by Jesus' life and death, Paul taught that Jesus was a resurrected redeemer who held the promise of salvation for both Jews and Gentiles. (Scala/Art Resource N.Y.)

Non-Jews, or *Gentiles* (from Latin *gens*, or "nation"), who came into contact with Jews of the Diaspora were often favorably impressed by Hebrew monotheism, ethics, and family life. Some Gentiles embraced Hebrew monotheism but refused to adhere to provisions of the Law requiring circumcision and dietary regulations. Among these Gentiles and non-Palestinian Jews who were greatly influenced by the Greco-Roman milieu, Jesus' Apostles would find receptive listeners.

Reared in Tarsus, a stronghold of Greek culture, Saul knew Greek well, but it is unlikely, despite a respectable writing style, that he had great knowledge of Greek literature, philosophy, and science. Trained in the outlook of the Pharisees, the young Saul went to Jerusalem to study with Rabban Gamaliel, an outstanding Pharisee teacher. In Jerusalem, Saul persecuted Jesus' followers in the time after his crucifixion, but then Saul underwent a spiritual transformation and became a follower of Jesus. Serving as a zealous missionary of Jewish Christianity in the Diaspora, Saul, now called by his Roman name, Paul, preached to his fellow Jews in synagogues throughout the Roman Empire and wrote letters of advice back to the congregations he had started. Not having much success with his fellow Jews—he was at times beaten and stoned by them—and recognizing that the Christian message applied to non-Jews as well, Paul urged spreading it to the Gentiles. His knowledge of Greek was of inestimable value in his missionary work with both Diaspora Jews and Gentiles.

Although he was neither the first nor the only missionary to the Gentiles, Paul was without doubt the most important. In the process of his missionary activity—and he traveled extensively throughout the Roman Empire—he formulated doctrines that represented a fundamental break with Judaism and became the heart of this new religion. Paul taught that all people, both Jews and Gentiles, were sinners as a consequence of Adam's original defiance of God; that Jesus had come to earth to save all people from sin and death; that by suffering and dying on the cross he had atoned for the sins of all and made it possible for people to have eternal life in heaven; and that by believing in Jesus people could gain this salvation. Alone, one was helpless, possessed by sin, unable to overcome one's wicked nature. Jesus was the only hope, said Paul. "Wretched man that I am! Who will deliver me from this body of death? Thanks be to God through Jesus Christ our Lord!" (Romans 7:24–25).

Christ: A Savior-God.

To the first members of the Christian movement, Jesus was both a prophet who proclaimed the power and purpose of God and the Messiah, spoken of in the Hebrew scriptures, whose coming heralded a new age. To Paul, Jesus was a resurrected redeemer who offered salvation to all peoples. Paul taught that the crucified Messiah had suffered and died for the sins of human beings; that through Jesus God had shown his love of humanity and revealed himself to all people, both Jews and Gentiles; and that this revelation supplanted the earlier one to the Jewish people.

Increasingly Jesus' followers came to view the sacrificed Messiah as a savior-god, indeed, as God incarnate. This belief marked a dramatic break with Judaism, for to regard a man as divine, as God, was utterly unthinkable in the Jewish tradition. The idea of a slain savior-god was well known in the mystery religions of the eastern Mediterranean. Like these religions, Christianity initiated converts into the mysteries of the faith, featured a sacramental meal, and in time developed a priesthood. But the similarities between Christianity and the mystery cults should not be overstressed since the differences are more profound.

Unlike the cultic gods, Jesus had actually lived in history. Hence, people could identify with him, which enormously increased the appeal of this new religion. Moreover, the deities of the mystery religions were killed against their will by evil powers. In Jesus, it was said, God had become a man and suffered pain and death out of compassion for human beings, to show a floundering humanity the way that would lead from sin to eternal life. This suffering Savior evoked from distressed human beings deep feelings of love and loyalty. Adherents of the mystery cults were not required to undergo a profound moral transformation. Christian converts, however, felt a compelling obligation to make their behavior, in the words of Paul, "worthy of the God who calls you" (Thessalonians 2:12) and to obey Jesus' command: "Be perfect as your heavenly Father is perfect" (Matthew 5:48). Finally, Christians, with their Jewish heritage, would tolerate no other divinity but God. Pagans, on the other hand, often belonged to more than one cult, or at least recognized the divinity of gods in other cults.

The Break with Judaism.

In attempting to reach the Gentiles, Paul had to disentangle Christianity from a Jewish sociocultural context. Thus, he held that neither Gentile nor Jewish followers of Jesus were bound by the hundreds of rituals and rules that constitute Mosaic Law.* Paul saw no distinctive difference between Jew and Gentile; in his view, the ministry of Jesus was intended for all. As a consequence of Jesus' coming, Paul maintained, Mosaic regulations hindered missionary activity among the Gentiles. For Paul, not the Law of Moses but love of and faith in Christ were the new avenues to God and salvation. The followers of Jesus fulfilled Hebrew history; they were the new Israel.

To Paul, the new Christian community was the true fulfillment of Judaism: it was the means to moral transformation and eternal life. The Jews regarded their faith as a national religion, bound inseparably with the history of their people. Paul saw the new Christian community not as a nation but as an Oikoumene, a world community. Jesus fulfilled not only the messianic aspirations of the Jews but also the spiritual needs and expectations of all peoples. To this extent, Christianity shared in the universalism of the Hellenistic Age.

In preaching the doctrine of a risen Savior and insisting that Mosaic Law had been superseded, Paul (whatever his intentions) was breaking with his Jewish roots and transforming a Jewish sect into a new religion. Separating

---

*Paul's understanding of Mosaic Law is a matter of controversy. Some scholars argue that he regarded the Law as obsolete and broke with his ancestral faith. Other scholars, arguing that Paul did not forsake the Law, point to a famous passage: "Do we then nullify the law by this faith? Not at all! Rather we uphold the law" (Romans 3:31). Paul, who continually described himself as a Pharisee, lived an observant life and celebrated Jewish festivals. For these scholars, Paul never stopped revering the Torah but taught that Jesus, the Messiah, fulfilled the Torah's higher purpose—the biblical prophecy of the Messiah's coming.

Christianity from Judaism enormously increased its appeal for non-Jews, who were attracted to Hebrew ethical monotheism but repelled by practices such as circumcision, dietary regulations, and other strict requirements of Mosaic Law. Paul built on Jesus' appeal for individual spiritual renewal and his empathy for all humanity (both also concerns of the ancient Hebrew prophets) to create a religion intended not for a people with its own particular history, culture, and land, but for all humankind.

THE SPREAD AND TRIUMPH OF CHRISTIANITY

By establishing Christianity's independence from Judaism and its practices, Paul made the new religion attractive to the Greco-Roman world. Originating in the first century, Christianity took firm root in the second, grew extensively in the third, and became the official religion of the Roman Empire at the end of the fourth century.

The Appeal of Christianity

The triumph of Christianity was related to a corresponding decline in the vitality of Hellenism and a shift in cultural emphasis—a movement from reason to emotion and revelation. Offering comforting solutions to the existential problems of life and death, religion demonstrated a greater capacity than reason to stir human hearts. Hellenism had invented the tools of rational thought, but the power of mythical thought was never entirely subdued. By the Late Roman Empire, science and philosophy were unable to compete with mysticism, myth, and the divine.

This deterioration of the classical outlook was demonstrated by the growing popularity of Eastern religions and the spiritualization of philosophy. Mystery cults, which promised personal salvation, were spreading and gaining followers. Astrology and magic, which offered supernatural explanations for the operations of nature, were also popular. Stoicism and Epicureanism were performing a religious function by trying to help individuals overcome emotional stress, while Neo-Platonists yearned for a mystical union with the

One. This recoil from rational and worldly values helped prepare the way for Christianity. In a culturally stagnating and spiritually troubled Greco-Roman world, Christianity gave new meaning to life and offered new hope to disillusioned men and women.

During the Hellenistic Age, the individual had struggled with the problems of alienation and lack of community. With the decline of the independent city-state, the individual searched for a new frame of reference, a new form of attachment. The Roman Empire represented one possible allegiance. But for many people, it was not a satisfying relationship; the individual found it difficult to be devoted to a political organization so vast, remote, and impersonal. The Christian message of a divine Savior and a concerned Father, as well as of brotherly love, inspired men and women who were dissatisfied with the world of the here and now—who felt no attachment to city or empire, derived no inspiration from philosophy, and suffered from a profound sense of loneliness. Christianity offered the individual what the city and the Roman world-state could not: an intensely personal relationship with God, an intimate connection with a higher world, and membership in a community of the faithful who cared for one another.

Stressing the intellect and self-reliance, Greco-Roman thought did not provide for the emotional needs of many people. Christianity addressed itself to this deficiency in the Greco-Roman outlook. Particularly those who were poor, oppressed, or enslaved were attracted to the personality, life, death, and resurrection of Jesus, his love for all, and his concern for suffering humanity. They found spiritual sustenance in a religion that offered a hand in love and taught that a person need not be well-born, rich, educated, or talented to be worthy, that God draws no distinction between the lowly poor and enslaved and the mightiest aristocrats. To people burdened with misfortune and terrified by death, Christianity held the promise of eternal life, a kingdom of heaven where they would be comforted by God the Father. Thus, Christianity gave to the common person what the aristocratic values of Greco-Roman civilization generally did not: hope, a sense of dignity, and inner strength. By and large, classical philosophy offered little compassion for the sufferer, but the

Blandina

During the reign of the emperor Marcus Aurelius, a number of Christians in Lyons, Gaul, including Blandina, a frail young slave, were imprisoned and accused of engaging in cannibalism and incest. The Roman authorities tortured Blandina, hoping that she would implicate the Christian community in these abhorrent crimes. Despite the torments inflicted on her, Blandina would not speak falsely against her fellow Christians. The historian Eusebius described her terrible ordeal:

> Blandina was filled with such power that those who took it in turns to subject her to every kind of torture from morning to night were exhausted by their efforts and confessed themselves beaten—they could think of nothing else to do to her. They were amazed that she was still breathing, for her whole body was mangled and her wounds gaped; they declared that torment of any one kind was enough to part soul and body, let alone a succession of torments of such extreme severity.

> But the blessed woman, wrestling magnificently, grew in strength as she proclaimed her faith, and found refreshment, rest, and insensibility to her sufferings in uttering the words: "I am a Christian: we do nothing to be ashamed of."

> For several days Blandina had to watch other Christians being whipped, roasted, and set upon by wild beasts in the amphitheater. Finally, after surviving similar torments, she was "dropped into a basket and thrown to a bull. Time after time the animal tossed her, but she was indifferent now to all that happened to her, because of her hope and sure hold on all that her faith meant, and of her communing with Christ. Then she, too, was sacrificed, while the heathen themselves admitted that never yet had they known a woman suffer so much or so long."*

*Eusebius, *The History of the Church from Christ to Constantine*, trans. G. A. Williamson (New York: New York University Press, 1966), 196, 202.

cardinal principle of Christianity was that Jesus had endured earthly torments because of his love for all human beings and that even the lowliest could be redeemed.

Christianity succeeded not only through the appeal of its message but also through the power of its organization. To retain the devotion of the faithful, win new converts, protect itself from opponents, and administer its services, Christianity developed an organized body of followers. This body became the Christian church, which grew into a strong organization uniting the faithful. To city dwellers—lonely, alienated, disillusioned with public affairs; stranded mortals groping for a sense of community—the church that called its members "brother" and "sister" filled an elemental need of human beings to belong. Another attraction for Christian converts was the absence of painful or expensive initiation rites, such as those required for entrance into Mithraism, a leading rival (see "The Spread of Mystery Religions" in Chapter 7). Unlike Mithraism, the church also welcomed women converts, who were often the first to join and who brought their menfolk after them. Among the reasons that the church drew women was its command to husbands to treat their wives kindly, remain faithful, and provide for the children. Moreover, in the eyes of God, women were spiritually equal with men. The church also won new converts and retained the loyalty of its members by furnishing social services for the poor and infirm; welcoming slaves, criminals, sinners, and other outcasts; and offering community and comfort during difficult times. While there were some converts from the middle and even upper classes, the earliest

Christians came chiefly from the lower classes. Christian churches established in numerous cities insisted that their congregants evidence high moral standards in their daily lives. No doubt people impressed by the behavior of Christians were drawn to the new faith.

The ability of an evolving Christianity to assimilate elements from Greek philosophy and even from the mystery religions also contributed in no small measure to its growth. By becoming infused with Greek philosophy, Christianity could present itself in terms intelligible to those versed in Greek learning and thus attract educated people. Philosophers who converted to Christianity proved to be able defenders of their newly adopted faith. Because some Christian doctrines (the risen savior-god, the virgin and her child, life after death, communion with the divine), practices (purification through baptism), and holy days (December 25 was the birth date of the god Mithras) either paralleled or were adopted from the mystery religions, it became relatively easy to win converts from these rivals.

Christianity and Rome

At first, the Roman government, which was generally tolerant of religions, did not interfere much with the Christian movement. In fact, Christianity benefited in many ways from its association with the Roman Empire. Christian missionaries, among them some of the Twelve Disciples, who were the original followers of Christ, traveled throughout the empire over roads and across seas made safe by Roman arms. The common Greek dialect, Koine, spoken in most parts of the empire, facilitated the missionaries' task. Had the Mediterranean world been fractured into separate and competing states, the spread of Christianity might well have faced an insurmountable obstacle. The universalism of the Roman Empire, which made citizenship available to peoples of many nationalities, prepared the way for the universalism of Christianity, which welcomed membership from all nations. Early Christians grafted onto Rome's imperial mission a spiritual, evangelical cause: "Go ye therefore and teach all nations" (Matthew 28:19).

As the number of Christians increased, Roman officials began to fear the Christians as subversives, preaching allegiance to God and not to Rome, and as a self-absorbed sect that did not want to fit into the Empire. To many Romans, Christians were disloyal citizens, a loathsome cabal of enemies of Rome drawn from the dregs of society and ignorant women who attacked the state gods, would not engage in sacrifices to Roman divinities, scorned gladiatorial contests, stayed away from public baths, glorified nonviolence, refused to honor deceased emperors as gods, and worshiped a crucified criminal as Lord. Romans ultimately found in Christians a scapegoat for the ills burdening the Empire, such as famines, plagues, and military reverses. Were not these afflictions divine punishment for Christians' refusal to honor ancestral gods and traditions? Calumnies like the following were often directed against Christians: "An infant covered with spelt [wheat] . . . is set before the one to be initiated in the rites. The neophyte is induced to strike what seems to be harmless blows on the surface of the spelt, and this infant is killed . . . Its blood—oh, shocking!—they greedily lap up, the limbs they eagerly distribute."[3]

In an effort to stamp out Christianity, emperors occasionally resorted to persecution. Christians were imprisoned, beaten, starved, beheaded, burned alive, torn apart by wild beasts in the arena for the amusement of the Romans, and crucified. The authorities freed accused Christians who agreed to renounce their faith. But many Christians embraced the opportunity for martyrdom; they believed they were reenacting the passion of Jesus, who had sacrificed himself for humanity.

However, the early persecutions, beginning with those incited under Emperor Nero in A.D. 64, were local, did not cause much loss of life, and were too sporadic to impede the growth of Christianity. The persecutions in the mid-third century and during Diocletian's rule caused the brutal deaths of many Christians but did not last long enough to seriously threaten the new religion. Actually, they strengthened the determination of most of the faithful and won new converts, who were awed by the extraordinary courage of the martyrs willingly dying for their faith.

Unable to crush Christianity by persecution, Roman emperors decided to gain the support of the growing number of Christians within the Empire. In A.D. 313, Constantine issued the Edict of Milan, granting toleration to Christians. No doubt drawn to Christianity by its moral force, Constantine later was baptized. By allowing the free flow of Christian teachings and instituting legislation favorable to the church, Constantine and his successors accelerated the growth of Christianity and the Christianization of the Empire. By A.D. 392, Theodosius I had made Christianity the state religion of the Empire and declared the worship of pagan gods illegal.

With Christianity in power, persecution did not end, but its target shifted to pagans, Jews, and Christians with unorthodox views. The polytheistic religions of the Roman world did not claim to possess an exhaustive truth—they did not assert that a particular god or a particular form of worship should prevail over all others and that wrongful religious expressions should be rooted out. People were relatively free to select their own credo and engage in their own acts of worship. Christianity, in contrast, possessing an exclusive attitude toward truth, felt compelled to cleanse society of false gods and beliefs. Such an outlook often led Christians to view nonbelievers as enemies of God deserving of punishment. Thus, mobs, often driven by fanatic clergy, hurled non-Christian writings into bonfires, destroyed pagan altars and sacred images, and squelched pagan rites and festivals. Emperors, often pushed by the clergy, passed decrees calling for fining, imprisoning, torturing, and executing adherents of pagan cults.

Christianity and Greek Philosophy

Christianity synthesized both the Hebrew and the Greco-Roman traditions. Having emerged from Judaism, Christianity assimilated Hebrew monotheism and prophetic morality and retained the Old Testament as the Word of God. Without this Hebraic foundation, Christianity cannot be understood. As the new religion evolved, it also assimilated elements of Greek philosophy. The ability to combine a historic

Judaic monotheism, which had many admirers in the Gentile world, with Greek rational philosophy was a crucial reason for Christianity's triumph in the Roman Empire. But there was a struggle between conservatives, who wanted no dealings with pagan philosophy, and those believers who recognized the value of Greek thought to Christianity.

To conservative church fathers—early Christian writers whose works are accepted as authoritative by the church—classical philosophy erred completely because it did not derive from divine revelation. As the final statement of God's truth, Christianity superseded both pagan philosophy and pagan religions. According to the church fathers, the simple peasant who accepted Christ possessed more knowledge than the most learned philosopher who did not. These conservatives feared that studying classical authors would contaminate Christian morality (did not Plato propose a community of wives, and did not the dramatists treat violent passions?) and promote heresy (was not classical literature replete with references to pagan gods?). For these church fathers, there could be no compromise between Greek philosophy and Christian revelation. For them, faith was more reliable than all the demonstrations of human reason. "What indeed has Athens to do with Jerusalem?" asked Tertullian (A.D. 150–225). "With our faith, we desire no further belief. For this is our faith that there is nothing which we ought to believe besides."[4]

Some church fathers, including several who had a Greek education, resisted this anti-intellectualism. Defending the value of studying classical literature, they maintained that such literature, if properly taught, could aid in the moral development of children because it presented many examples of virtuous deeds. Some church fathers claimed that Greek philosophy contained a dim glimmer of God's truth, a pre-Christian insight into divine wisdom. Christ had corrected and fulfilled an insight reached by the philosophical mind; Christianity had perfected the ethical ideals of the philosophers. Knowledge of Greek philosophy, they also contended, helped Christians explain their beliefs logically and argue intelligently with pagan critics of Christian teachings.

***Map 8.2* THE SPREAD OF CHRISTIANITY** Aided by dedicated missionaries, Christianity expanded throughout the Mediterranean world and later into Germanic lands. (© 2016 Cengage Learning.)

Thus, Clement of Alexandria (c. A.D. 150–220) brought reason to the support of faith in his attempt to make Christianity more intellectually respectable in his world.

> *Rather, philosophy is a clear image of truth, a divine gift to the Greeks. Before the advent of the Lord, philosophy helped the Greeks to attain righteousness, and is now conducive to piety, it supplies a preparatory teaching for those who will later embrace the faith. God is the cause of all good things: some given primarily in the form of the Old and the New Testament; others are the consequence of philosophy. Perchance too philosophy was given to the Greeks pri*

> *marily till the Lord should call the Greeks to serve him. Thus philosophy acted as a schoolmaster to the Greeks, preparing them for Christ, as the laws of the Jews prepared them for Christ.[5]*

And Gregory of Nazianzus (c. 325–389) argued that it was an "ignorant view" to "despise [pagan culture] as hostile and erroneous and liable to remove people from God." He urged accepting "from pagan culture . . . whatever promotes enquiry and intellectual contemplation," and to reject "whatever leads towards evil spirits and error." Those people who "dishonour learning" should be regarded as "perverse and boorish, wanting everyone to be like themselves so as to conceal their own defects . . . and elude accusations of ignorance."[6]

Utilizing the language and categories of Greek philosophy, Christian intellectuals transformed Christianity from a simple ethical creed into a theoretical system, a theology. Greek philosophy enabled Christians to explain rationally God's existence and revelation in order to show that Christian teachings did not violate the laws of logic. Christ was depicted as the divine or incarnate Logos (reason) in human form. Educated believers could argue that the fundamental principles that Greek philosophers maintained operated in the universe were established by God the Father. The Stoic teaching that all people are fundamentally equal because they share in universal reason could be formulated in Christian terms: all are united in Christ. Christians could interpret the church to be the true fulfillment of the Stoic idea of a polity embracing the entire world. Stoic ethics, which stressed moderation, self-control, and brotherhood, could be assimilated by Christian revelation. Particularly in Platonism, which drew a distinction between a world perceived by the senses and a higher order—a transcendent world that should be the central concern of human existence—Christian thinkers found a congenial vehicle for expressing Christian beliefs. The perfect and universal Forms, or Ideas, which Plato maintained were the true goal of knowledge and the source of ethical standards, were held by Christians to exist in God's mind.

That Greek philosophy had a strong hold on church doctrine was immensely important, for it meant that rational thought, the priceless achievement of the Greek mind, was not lost. But Greek philosophy had to sacrifice its ability to think freely to the needs of Christian revelation: reason had to serve faith. And in any conflict between reason and faith, faith would prevail. Although Christianity made use of Greek philosophy, Christian truth ultimately rested on faith, not reason. As Tertullian stated, it is precisely because faith in a crucified Lord contradicted all human logic that he would believe: "And the Son of God died; it is by all means to be believed, because it is absurd. And He was buried, and rose again; the fact is certain because it is impossible."[7]

The Growth of Christian Organization, Doctrine, and Attitudes

Early in its history, the church gradually developed along hierarchical lines. Those members of the Christian community who had the authority to preside over the celebration of the Mass—breaking bread and offering wine as Christ had done in the Last Supper—were called either priests or bishops. Gradually, the designation *bishop* was reserved for the one clergyman in the community with the authority to resolve disputes over doctrines and practices. Regarded as the successors to Jesus' Twelve Disciples, bishops supervised religious activities within their regions. The most influential bishops ministered to the leading cities of the Empire: Rome, Alexandria, Antioch, and Milan. In creating a diocese that was supervised by a bishop and had its center in a leading city, the church adapted Roman administrative techniques.

The Primacy of the Bishop of Rome

The bishop of Rome, later called the *pope* ("father"), claimed primacy over the other bishops, maintaining that the Apostle Peter founded the Roman see (official seat of authority) and that both Peter and Paul were martyred in Rome. Moreover, as the traditional capital of the empire, Rome seemed the logical choice to serve as the center of the church.

In developing the case for their supremacy over the church organization, bishops of Rome increasingly referred to the famous New Testament passage in which Jesus says to his disciple Simon (also called Peter): "'And I tell you, you are Peter, and on this rock I will build my church'" (Matthew 16:18). Because *Peter* in Greek means "rock" (*petra*), it was argued that Christ had chosen Peter to succeed him as ruler of the universal church. It was commonly accepted that Saint Peter had established a church in Rome and was martyred there, so it was argued further that the Roman bishop inherited the power that Christ had passed on to Peter. Thus, the argument continued, the bishop of Rome held a unique office: of all the bishops, only he had inherited the powers originally granted by Christ to Peter. Because the Apostles had been subordinate to Peter, so too must the bishops defer to Peter's successor.

The Rise of Monasticism

Some devout Christians committed to living a perfect Christian life were distressed by the wickedness of the world about them, including the moral laxity of those clergy who chased after wealth and pomp. Seeking to escape from the agonies and corruptions of this world, some ardent Christians withdrew to deserts and mountains in search of solitude and spiritual renewal. In their zeal to emulate Jesus' self-denial, they sometimes practiced extreme forms of asceticism and self-mortification: self-flogging, wearing spiked corsets, eating only herbs, or living for years atop a column high above the ground. They believed that these ascetic practices would draw them closer to God.

Gradually, colonies of these hermits sprang up, particularly in Egypt and Syria; in time, the leaders of these monastic communities drew up written rules for prayer and work. Saint Basil (c. 329– c. 379), a Greek who was bishop of Caesarea in Cappadocia (eastern Asia Minor), established the rules that became the standard for monasteries in the East. Basil required monks to refrain from bodily abuses and to engage in manual labor. Through farming, weaving, and construction, monks could make a monastery self-supporting and have the means to assist the needy. Aware of the lure of materialism and selfishness, Basil forbade his monks to own personal property other than clothing and insisted that they spend much of their time in silence.

The monastic ideal spread from east to west. The principal figure in the shaping of **monasticism** in the West was Saint Benedict (c. 480–c. 543), who founded a monastery at Monte Cassino, Italy, in 529. The Rule of Saint Benedict (see Primary Source box) required the monks to live in poverty and to study, labor, and obey the abbot, the head of the monastery. They had to pray often, work hard, talk little, and surrender private property. In imposing discipline and regulations,

Benedict eliminated the excessive and eccentric individualism of the early monks. Benedict demonstrated the same genius for administration that the Romans had shown in organizing and governing their empire. Benedict's rule became the standard for monasteries throughout Western Europe.

Scriptural Tradition and Doctrinal Disputes

The earliest surviving Christian writings are Paul's Epistles, written some twenty-five to thirty years after the death of Jesus. Jesus' sayings were preserved by word of mouth. Sometime around A.D. 66–70, about forty years after the crucifixion, Saint Mark formulated the Christian message from this oral tradition and perhaps from some material that had been put in writing earlier. Later, Saint Matthew and Saint Luke, relying heavily on Mark's account, wrote somewhat longer Gospels. The Gospels of Mark, Matthew, and Luke are called *synoptic* because their approach to Jesus is very similar. The remaining Gospel, written by Saint John around A.D. 110, varies significantly from the synoptic Gospels. The Gospel of John uses the Stoic concept of Logos to present Jesus as the divine being. John identifies Jesus with the eternal word, or Logos, which became the incarnate Son of God: "In the beginning was the Word and the Word was with God, and the Word was God. . . . And the Word became Flesh and dwelt among us" (John 1:1, 14). The synoptic Gospels; the Gospel According to Saint John; Acts of the Apostles; the twenty-one Epistles, including those written by Saint Paul; and Revelation constitute the twenty-seven books of the Christian New Testament. Christians also accepted the Old Testament of the Hebrews as God's Word. The New Testament was written not by historians with the critical spirit of a Thucydides or a Polybius but by men moved by the fervor of faith. Under these circumstances, it is understandable that it contains discrepancies, some nonhistorical legends, and polemics.

The early Christians had a Bible and a clergy to teach it. But the Holy Writ could be interpreted differently by equally sincere believers, and controversies over doctrine threatened the loose unity of the early church. The most important controversy concerned how people viewed the relationship between God and Christ. Arius (250–336), a Greek priest in Alexandria, led one faction; he denied the complete divinity of Christ, one of the basic tenets of the church. To Arius, Christ was more than man but less than God; the Father and the Son did not possess the same nature, or essence. Arius said that there was no permanent union between God and Christ; the Father alone is eternal and truly God.

The Council of Nicaea (325), the first assembly, or ecumenical council, of bishops from all parts of the Roman world, was called to settle the controversy. The council condemned Arius and ruled that God and Christ were of the same substance, coequal and coeternal. The position adopted at Nicaea became the basis of the Nicene Creed, which remains the official doctrine of the church. Although Arianism, the name given the heresy of Arius, won converts for a time, it eventually died out, helped along by persecution. This meant that the Catholic church alone would shape the distinctive character of the new civilization that emerged in the Middle Ages.

Christianity and Society

Although salvation was their ultimate aim, Christians still had to dwell within the world and deal with its imperfections. In the process, Christian thinkers challenged some of the mores of Greco-Roman society and formulated attitudes that would endure for centuries.

Influenced by passages in the New Testament that condemned acts of revenge and the shedding of blood, and concerned only with the heavenly kingdom, some early Christians refused military service. Others, however, held that in a sinful world, defense of the state was necessary, and without concealment or apology they served in the army. With the barbarians menacing the borders, Christian officials could not advocate nonviolence. Christian theorists began to argue that under certain circumstances—to punish injustice or to restore peace—war was just. But even such wars must not entail unnecessary violence.

Christians denounced the gladiatorial combats and contests between men and beasts as bloodlust and murder, and regarded attendance at these spectacles as tantamount to participating in murder. Nevertheless, these spectacles persisted even after the majority of the population had converted to Christianity. When the games finally ended, it was probably due more to the growing poverty of the western Empire than to the Christian conscience.

Women were dedicated followers of Jesus in his ministry. He welcomed their devotion and at times confided in them. As the Christian movement gained momentum it attracted numerous women, and it is likely that more women than men attended church services and participated in church activities; a number of women suffered martyrdom. But positions of authority were reserved for men, including ordination as priests. The early Christian view of women was rooted in the patriarchal tradition of Jewish society. Paul subjected the wife to her husband's authority. "Wives, be subject to your husbands, as to the Lord. For the husband is the head of the wife as Christ is the head of the church" (Ephesians 5:22–23). Paul wanted women to remain quiet at church meetings. "If there is anything they desire to know, let them ask their husbands at home. For it is shameful for a woman to speak in church" (1 Corinthians 14:35). But Paul also held that all are baptized in Christ: "There is neither Jew nor Greek, there is neither slave nor free, there is neither male nor female; for you are all one in Christ Jesus" (Galatians 3:28). Consequently, both sexes were subject to divine law, and both possessed moral autonomy. The early church held to strict standards on sexual matters. It condemned adultery and esteemed virginity pledged for spiritual reasons.

Christians waged no war against slavery, which was widely practiced and universally accepted in the ancient world. Paul commanded slaves to obey their masters, and many Christians, including leaders of local churches, were slave owners. Although Christians did not try to alter the legal status of slaves, they did teach that slaves, too, were children of God; they sought their conversion; they urged owners not to treat slaves harshly; and they considered it a virtue for owners to free slaves. In the modern world, the

Saint Benedict of Nursia: The Christian Way of Life

In the following selection from his monastic book of rules, Saint Benedict of Nursia advises his monks on the attitudes and conduct necessary to live a virtuous Christian life.

What Are the Instruments of Good Works?

In the first place, to love the Lord God with the whole heart, whole soul, whole strength, then his neighbor as himself.

Then not to kill, not to commit adultery, not to steal, not to covet, not to bear false witness, to honor all men, and what anyone would not have done to him, let him not do to another. To deny himself, that he may follow Christ, to chasten the body, to renounce luxuries, to love fasting. To relieve the poor, to clothe the naked, to visit the sick, to bury the dead, to help in tribulation, to console the afflicted.

To make himself a stranger to the affairs of the world, to prefer nothing before the love of Christ, not to give way to anger, not to bear any grudge, not to harbour deceit in the heart, not to forsake charity. Not to swear, lest haply he perjure himself, to utter truth from his heart and his mouth. Not to return evil for evil, not to do injuries, but rather to bear them patiently, to love his enemies, not to curse against those that curse him, but rather to bless them, to endure persecution for righteousness' sake. Not to be proud, not given to wine, not gluttonous, not addicted to sleep, not slothful, not given to murmur, not a slanderer. To commit his hope to God; when he sees anything good in himself to attribute it to God, and not to himself, but let him always know that which is evil is his own doing; and impute it to himself. To fear the day of judgment, to dread hell, to desire eternal life with all spiritual longing . . . To watch over his actions at all times, to know certainly that in all places the eye of God is upon him; those evil thoughts which come into his heart to dash to pieces on Christ. . . . [T]o pray frequently every day, to confess his past sins to God, in prayer, with tears and groanings; from thence forward to reform as to those sins.

Not to fulfill the desires of the flesh, to hate his own will . . . to love charity, to hate no one, not to have jealousy or envy, not to love contention, to avoid self-conceit . . . to pray for enemies, . . . and never to despair of the mercy of God . . .

Question for Analysis

1. How might a Christian today react to Saint Benedict's approach to a virtuous life?

Oliver J. Thatcher, ed., *Library of Original Sources* (Milwaukee: University Research Extension, 1907), 4:133–134.

Christian teaching that all persons are spiritually equal before God would arouse some Christians to fight for the abolition of slavery.

Christian theorists condemned sex outside of marriage, adultery, prostitution, homosexuality, and abortion, and insisted that the sex drive should be confined to reproduction, as Clement of Alexandria wrote: "Yet marriage in itself merits esteem and the highest approval, for the Lord wished men to 'be fruitful and multiply.' He did not tell them, however, to act like libertines, nor did He intend them to surrender themselves to pleasure as though born only to indulge in sexual relations. . . . To indulge in intercourse without intending children is to outrage nature."[8]

Christianity and the Jews

Increasingly, Christians identified opponents—Jews, pagans, and heretics—with Satan, the fallen angel, and viewed conflicts in a moral context: a struggle between God's faithful and Satan's servants. Over the centuries, the view that they were participants in a cosmic struggle between good and evil led Christians to demonize adversaries, a practice that exacerbated hatred and justified mistreatment and even massacre. Christian attitudes and behavior toward Jews poignantly illustrate this point.

Numerous links connect early Christianity and Judaism. Jesus himself and his earliest followers, including the Twelve Disciples, were Jews who were faithful to Jewish law. Jesus attended synagogue and frequently quoted the Hebrew Scriptures, which to him and his disciples was the authoritative word of God, to support a particular viewpoint. Jesus' message was first spread in synagogues throughout the Roman Empire. Early Christianity's affirmation of the preciousness of the human being, created in God's image; its belief that God rules history; its awareness of human sinfulness; its call for repentance; and its appeal to God for forgiveness are rooted in Judaism. The Christian reference to God as a "merciful Father" derives from Jewish prayer. Also rooted in Judaism are the moral norms proclaimed by Jesus in the Sermon on the Mount and on other occasions. For example, "Thou shalt love thy neighbor as thyself" was the motto of the Jewish sage Hillel, a contemporary of Jesus, who founded a school. The great value that the Torah gives to charity was inherited by Christianity. Jesus' use of parables to convey his teachings, the concept of the Messiah, respect for the Sabbath, and congregational worship also stem from Judaism. Moreover, Christians viewed the Hebrew Scriptures as God's Word. In addition, a deep understanding of the New Testament requires knowledge of the Old Testament, for its thought and language permeate the Christian Gospels.

However, over the years, particularly after more and more non-Jews became followers of Christ, Christians forgot, devalued, or denied the Jewish roots of their faith, and some thinkers began to show hostility toward Judaism and Jews that had tragic consequences in later centuries. Several factors fueled this anti-Judaism: resentment against Jews for their refusal to embrace Jesus and their persecution of Jesus' first followers; the polemics of the Jewish establishment against followers of Jesus; the role in Jesus' death ascribed to Jews by the New Testament; resentment against those Christians who Judaized, that is, continued to observe Jewish festivals and the Jewish Sabbath, regard the synagogue as holy, and practice circumcision; and anger that Judaism remained a vital religion, for this undermined the conviction that Christianity was the fulfillment of Judaism and the one true faith.

What made Christian anti-Judaism particularly ominous was the effort of some theologians to **demonize** the Jewish people. The myth emerged that the Jews, murderers of the incarnate God who embodied all that was good, were a cursed people, children of the Devil, whose suffering was intended by God. Thus, Origen (c. 185–c. 251) maintained that "the blood of Jesus [falls] not only upon those who lived then but also upon all generations of the Jewish people following afterwards until the end of the world."[9] In the late fourth century, John Chrysostom described Jews as "inveterate murderers, destroyers, men possessed by the Devil. . . . [T]hey murder their offspring and immolate them to the devil." The synagogue, he said, was "the domicile of the devil as is also the soul of the Jews." Their rites are "criminal and impure," and their religion is "a disease." For the "odious assassination of Christ," there is "no expiation possible, . . . no pardon." Jews will live "under the yoke of servitude without end."[10] Since the Devil was very real to early and medieval Christians, the Jew became identified with evil. Christians developed a mindset, concludes the Reverend Robert A. Everett, that was "unable to see anything positive in Judaism. . . . Judaism and the Jewish people came to have no real value for Christians except as a negative contrast to Christianity."[11] Because of this "teaching of contempt" and the "diabolization of the Jew," the Christian ethic of love did not extend to Jews.

Once it is established that God has cursed the Jews, how can one argue that Christians should love them? If Jews have been fated by God to have . . . a long history of suffering, who are Christians to alter their history by doing anything to relieve Jewish suffering? The theology of victimization thus precludes Christian love as a basis of relating to Jews.[12]

The diabolization of the Jew, which bore no relationship to the actual behavior of Jews or to their highly ethical religion, and the "theology of victimization," which held that the Jews were collectively and eternally cursed for denying Christ, became powerful myths, which, over the centuries, poisoned Christians' hearts and minds against Jews, spurring innumerable humiliations, persecutions, and massacres by Christians who believed that their actions were pleasing to God. Alongside this hatred of Jews and antipathy to their suffering, there also evolved the belief that the Jews, faithless and perfidious though they were, should be permitted to survive, for their dispersal among the nations was evidence of divine punishment and the truth of Christianity. Moreover, one day the Jews would see the light and convert to the true faith.

SAINT AUGUSTINE: THE CHRISTIAN WORLDVIEW

During the early history of Christianity, learned fathers of the church explained and defended church teachings. Most of the leading early fathers wrote in Greek, but in the middle of the fourth century, three great Latin writers—Saint Jerome, Saint Ambrose, and Saint Augustine—profoundly influenced the course of Christianity in the West.

As a youth, Saint Jerome (c. 340–420) studied Latin literature in Rome. Throughout his life, he remained an admirer of Cicero, Virgil, Lucretius, and other great Latin writers, and he defended the study of classical literature by Christians. Criticized for attacking the luxurious living and laxness of the clergy, he left Rome and established a monastery near Bethlehem, where he devoted himself to prayer and study. His greatest achievement was the translation of the Old and New Testaments from Hebrew and Greek into Latin. Jerome's text, the common, or Vulgate, version of the Bible, became the official edition of the Bible for the Western church.

Saint Ambrose (340–397), bishop of Milan, Italy, urged clerics not to pursue wealth but to practice humility and avoid favoring the rich over the poor. Ambrose sought to defend the autonomy of the church against the power of the state. Emperors are not the judges of bishops, he wrote. His dictum that "the Emperor is within the church, not above it" became a cardinal principle of the medieval church.

The most important Christian theoretician in the Late Roman Empire was Saint Augustine (354–430), bishop of Hippo, in North Africa. Born in the North African province of Numidia, Augustine attended school at Carthage, where he studied the Latin classics. Struggling to find meaning in a world that abounded with evil, Augustine turned to Manichaeism, an Eastern religious philosophy whose central doctrine was the struggle of the universal forces of light and good against those of darkness and evil. But Augustine still felt spiritually restless. In Milan, inspired by the sermons of Ambrose, he abandoned Manichaeism and devoted his life to following Christ's teachings. After serving as a priest, he was appointed bishop of Hippo in 395. At the turn of the fifth century, when the Greco-Roman worldview was disintegrating and the Roman world-state was collapsing, Augustine wrote his greatest and most influential work, *The City of God*. He became the chief architect of the Christian outlook that succeeded a dying classicism.

In 410, when Augustine was in his fifties, Visigoths sacked Rome—a disaster for which the classical consciousness was unprepared. Throughout the Empire, people panicked. Non-Christians blamed the tragedy on Christianity, saying that the Christians had predicted the end of the world and by refusing to offer sacrifices to ancient gods had turned those deities against Rome. Even Christians expressed anxiety. Why

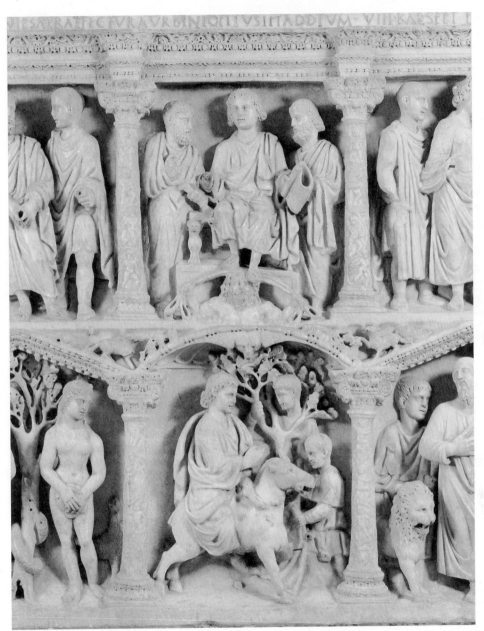

CHRIST ENTHRONED. This detail from the funerary sarcophagus of Junius Bassus, dating from A.D. 359, shows, among other scenes, Christ sitting on a throne (top middle). (Scala/Art Resource, N.Y.)

were the righteous also suffering? Where was the kingdom of God on earth that had been prophesied in the Scriptures?

Augustine's *City of God* was a response to the crisis of the Roman Empire, just as Plato's *Republic* had been a reaction to the crisis of the Athenian polis. Whereas Plato expressed hope that a state founded on rational principles could remedy the abuses of Athenian society, Augustine maintained that the worldly city could never be the central concern of a Christian. The ideal state, he wrote, could not be realized on earth; it existed only in heaven. The misfortunes of Rome, therefore, should not distress a Christian unduly, for Christianity belonged to the realm of the spirit and could not be identified with any state. The collapse of Rome did not diminish the greatness of Christianity because the true Christian was a citizen of a heavenly city that could not be pillaged by ungodly barbarians but would endure forever. Compared with God's heavenly city, Rome and its decline were unimportant. What really mattered in history, Augustine said, was not the coming to be or the passing away of cities and empires, but the individual's spiritual destiny, his or her entrance into heaven or hell.

Yet Augustine remained a man of this world. Although the earthly city was the very opposite of the heavenly city, he insisted that people must still deal with this earthly abode. Christians could not reject their city entirely but must bend it to fit a Christian pattern. The city that someday would rise from the ruins of Rome must be based on Christian principles. Warfare, economic activity, education, and the rearing of children should all be conducted in a Christian spirit. The church could not neglect the state but must guide it to protect human beings from their own sinful natures. The state must employ repression and punishment to restrain people, who were inherently sinful, from destroying one another. But the earthly city would never know tranquility, said Augustine, for it would always be inhabited predominantly by wretched sinners. People should be under no illusion that it could be transformed into the City of God. Because human beings are infected with sin, everywhere in human society we see

love for all those things that prove so vain and . . . breed so many heartaches, troubles, griefs, and fears; such insane joys in discord, strife, and war; such wrath and plots of enemies . . . such fraud and theft and robbery; such perfidy . . . homicide and murder, cruelty and savagery, lawlessness and lust; all the shameless passions of the impure— fornication and adultery . . . and countless other uncleannesses too nasty to be mentioned; the sins against religion—sacrilege and heresy . . . the iniquities against our neighbors—calumnies and cheating, lies and false witness, violence to persons and property . . . and the innumerable other miseries and maladies that fill the world, yet escape attention.[13]

Augustine did not hold that Christ, by his sacrificial death, had opened the door to heaven for all. Most of humanity remained condemned to eternal punishment; only a handful were blessed with the gift of faith and the promise of heaven. Whereas the vast majority of people, said Augustine, were citizens of a doomed earthly city, the small number endowed with God's grace constituted the City of God. These people lived on earth as visitors only, for they awaited deliverance to the Kingdom of Christ, where together with the good angels and God they would know perfect happiness. But the permanent inhabitants of the earthly city were destined for eternal punishment in hell. A perpetual conflict existed between the two cities and between their inhabitants; one city stood for sin and corruption, the other for God's truth and perfection. For Augustine, the highest good was not of this world but consisted of eternal life with God.

Augustine's distinction between this higher world of perfection and a lower world of corruption remained influential throughout the Middle Ages. But the church, rejecting Augustine's doctrine that only a limited number of people are predestined for heaven, emphasized that Christ had made possible the salvation of all who would embrace the precepts and injunctions of the church. Leading Protestant reformers of the sixteenth century, however, accepted Augustine's position.

Augustine repudiated the distinguishing feature of classical humanism: the autonomy of reason. For him, ultimate wisdom could not be achieved through rational thought alone. Reason had to be guided by faith. Without faith, there could be no true knowledge, no understanding. Philosophy had no validity if it did not first accept as absolutely true the existence of God and the authority of his revelation. Valid ethical standards could not be formulated by reason alone but were revealed to people by the living God. Christian truth did not rest on theoretical excellence or logical consistency; it was true because its source was God.

Augustine's belief contrasts with that of Socrates, who insisted that through rational reflection each individual could arrive at standards of good and evil. For the humanist Socrates, ultimate values were something that the individual could grasp through thought alone and could defend rationally. For Augustine, reason alone could not serve as a proper guide to life. He maintained that individuals, without divine guidance, lacked the capacity to comprehend ultimate truth or to regenerate themselves morally. Without God, they could not attain wisdom or liberate themselves from a wicked and sinful human nature: "the happiness of man can come not from himself but only from God, and . . . to live according to oneself is sin."[14]

Thus, in contrast to the classical view that asserted the primacy of reason, Augustine argued for the primacy of faith. He denied the classical view that reason *alone* could attain wisdom or could instruct people how to live. The wisdom that Augustine sought was Christian wisdom, God's revelation to humanity. The starting point for this wisdom, he said, was belief in God and the Scriptures. For Augustine, secular knowledge for its own sake had little value; the true significance of knowledge lay in its role as a tool for comprehending God's will. Let us utilize truths useful to the faith that pagan philosophers might have chanced upon, he said. Augustine adapted the classical intellectual tradition to the requirements of Christian revelation.

With Augustine, the human-centered outlook of classical humanism, which for centuries had been undergoing transformation, gave way to a

THE LADDER OF DIVINE ASCENT, TWELFTH-CENTURY ICON, ST. CATHERINE'S MONASTERY, MOUNT SINAI. Monks climbing a ladder to heaven, while demons are trying to prevent them from leaving earth. (Erich Lessing/Art Resource, N.Y.)

God-centered worldview. The fulfillment of God's will, not the full development of human talent, became the chief concern of life. The *City of God* encompassed several themes that would concern Christian thinkers for centuries: the meaning of history and the place of the individual, the state, and the church in God's plan.

Augustinian Christianity is a living philosophy because it still has something vital to say about the human condition. To those who believe that people have the intelligence and goodwill to transform their earthly city into a rational and just community that promotes human betterment, Augustine offers a reminder of human sinfulness, weakness, and failure. Nor will new and ingenious political and social arrangements alter a defective human nature. He cautions the optimist that progress is not certain; that people, weak and ever prone to wickedness, are their own worst enemies; that success is illusory; and that misery is the essential human reality.

CHRISTIANITY AND CLASSICAL HUMANISM: ALTERNATIVE WORLDVIEWS

Christianity and classical humanism are the two principal components of the Western tradition. The value that modern Western civilization places on the individual derives ultimately from classical humanism and the Judeo-Christian tradition. Classical humanists believed that human worth came from the capacity of individuals to reason and to shape their character and life according to rational standards. Christianity also places great stress on the individual. In the Christian view, God cares for each person; he wants people to behave righteously and to enter heaven; Christ died for all because he loves humanity. Christianity espouses active love and genuine concern for fellow human beings. Without God, people are as Augustine described them: "foul, crooked, sordid, . . . vicious." With God, the human personality can undergo a moral transformation and become loving, good, and free. The idea of a Christian conscience, prompted by God and transcending all other loyalties, reinforces respect for all human beings regardless of cultural and national differences. Also promoting respect for each person is the presupposition of natural equality stemming from the Christian belief that each individual, regardless of birth, wealth, or talent, is precious to God.

There are striking parallels between Christian and Stoic ethics. Both Christians and Stoics believed that there is an essential "brotherhood of man," that all human beings are related and possess a fundamental dignity. Both urged suppressing wild passions, expressing concern for others, living simply, and heeding the inner voice of conscience that commands human beings to do what is right.

But Christianity and classical humanism also represent two essentially different worldviews. The triumph of the Christian outlook signified a break with the essential meaning of classical humanism; it pointed to the end of the world of antiquity and the beginning of an age of faith, the Middle Ages. With the victory of Christianity, the ultimate goal of life shifted. Life's purpose was no longer to achieve excellence in this world through the full and creative development of human capacities, but to attain salvation in a heavenly city. A person's worldly accomplishments amounted to very little if he or she did not accept God and his revelation. The Christian ideal of the isolated and contemplative monk, who rejected the world in order to serve God, was alien to the spirit of classical humanism, which valued active citizenship and active participation in worldly activities. Equally foreign to the Greco-Roman mind was another idea introduced by Christianity: the need to escape from a sinful human nature, a consequence of Adam and Eve's defiance of God. This view of a corrupt human nature and an unclean human body, particularly in Augustine's formulation, became deeply embedded in the European mind during the Christian centuries—the Middle Ages.

In the classical view, history had no ultimate end, no ultimate meaning; periods of happiness and misery repeated themselves endlessly. In the Christian view, history is filled with spiritual meaning. It is the profound drama of individuals struggling to overcome their original sin in order to gain eternal happiness in heaven. History began with Adam and Eve's fall and would end when Christ returns to earth, evil is eradicated, and God's will prevails. For the Christian, Christ on the cross was both the central event and a turning point in world history.

Classicism held that there was no authority higher than reason, that individuals had within themselves, through unaided reason, the ability to understand the world and life. Christianity teaches that, without God as the starting point, knowledge is formless, purposeless, and prone to error. Classicism, unlike Judaism or Christianity, possessed no truths or moral precepts revealed by a divine power. Rather, classicism held that ethical standards were expressions of universal reason, laws of nature, which the human mind could discover. Through reason, individuals could discern the ethical norms by which they should regulate their lives. Reason would enable them to govern desires and will; it would show where their behavior was wrong and teach them how to correct it. Because individuals sought what was best for themselves, they would obey the voice of reason. Historically Christianity maintained that ethical standards emanate from the personal will of God. Without submission to God's commands, people remain wicked forever; the human will, essentially sinful, cannot be transformed by the promptings of reason. Only when individuals turn to God for forgiveness and guidance can they find the inner strength to overcome their sinful nature. People cannot perfect themselves through scientific knowledge; it is spiritual insight and belief in God that they require and that must serve as the first principle of their lives. For classicism, the ultimate good was sought through independent thought and action; for Christianity, the ultimate good comes through knowing, obeying, and loving God.

Although some Christian thinkers dismissed Greek philosophy as erroneous and useless, others respected the Greek intellectual tradition and rejected attempts to eradicate it. Rather, they sought to fit it into a Christian framework—that is, rational inquiry must be guided by and never conflict with Christian teachings that derive from an authoritative revelation. By holding that the mind is limited in its capacity to think for itself and must be guided by faith and clerical authority, Christianity contributed to the waning of the classical tradition in the Late Roman Empire. For centuries, articles of faith would predominate over empirical observation and logic. Nevertheless, by preserving the Greek philosophical tradition—even if it remained subordinate to the Christian outlook—Christian thinkers performed a task of immense historical significance.

PORTRAIT OF CHRIST. Painted on a ceiling in the Catacomb of Domitilla around the second century A.D., this is among the oldest surviving portraits of Jesus.

(Scala/Art Resource, N.Y.)

Christianity inherited the Hebrew view of the overriding importance of God for humanity: God, who is both lawgiver and judge, makes life intelligible and purposeful. For the Christian, God is a living being, loving and compassionate, in whose company one seeks to spend eternity; one knows God essentially through faith and feeling. Although the Greek philosophers had a conception of God, it was not comparable to the God of the Hebrews and Christians. For the Greeks, God was a logical abstraction, a principle of order, the prime mover, the first cause, the mind of the universe, pure thought, the supreme good, the highest truth; God was a concept, impersonal, unfeeling, and uninvolved with human concerns. The Greeks approached God through the intellect, not the heart; they neither loved nor worshiped God. In addition, because religion was at the periphery, not the center, of classical humanism, the idea of God did not carry the same significance as it did for Christianity.

Christianity maintained that there was a prescribed way to worship the one true God, that belief in other gods was an abomination, and that nonbelievers (or infidels) and heretics were wicked sinners hated by God. Over the centuries, this outlook sanctioned fanaticism, persecution, and holy war, with accompanying massacres—a terrible legacy that constitutes the dark side of monotheism. Unlike the monotheistic faiths—Judaism, Christianity, and Islam—Greek and Roman polytheism had no concepts of **martyrdom** for the true faith and holy war against the infidel and consistently tolerated many different religious beliefs and practices as long as they did not threaten the state.

In the classical world, the political community was the avenue to justice, happiness, and self-realization. In Christianity, the good life was identified not with worldly achievement but with life eternal, and the ideal commonwealth could only be one that was founded and ruled by Christ. It was entrance into God's kingdom that each person must make the central aim of life. Christian thinkers viewed the state as an inferior community to their own—the church of Christ, which had ties to the spiritual realm, the highest good. Therefore, they held that secular power should submit to ecclesiastical authority. For the next thousand years, this distinction between heaven and earth, this otherworldly, theocentric outlook, would define the Western mentality.

In the Late Roman Empire, when classical values were in decay, Christianity was a dynamic and creative movement. Possessing both institutional and spiritual strength, Christianity survived the fall of Rome. Because it retained elements of Greco-Roman civilization and taught a high morality, Christianity served as a civilizing agent in the centuries that followed Rome's collapse. Indeed, Christianity was the essential shaper of the European civilization that emerged in the Middle Ages.

❖   ❖   ❖

NOTES

1. Hans Küng, "Christianity and Judaism," in *Jesus' Jewishness,* ed. James H. Charlesworth (New York: Crossroad, 1991), 259.

2. The biblical quotations are from the Holy Bible, Revised Standard Version (New York: Thomas Nelson & Sons, 1952). The Revised Standard Version is the text used for biblical quotations throughout the chapter.

3. Naphtali Lewis and Meyer Reinhold, eds., *Roman Civilization: The Empire* (New York: Harper Torchbook, 1966), 585.

4. Tertullian, "On Prescription Against Heretics," chap. 7, in *The Ante-Nicene Fathers,* ed. Alexander Roberts and James Donaldson (New York: Charles Scribner's Sons, 1918), 3:246.

5. Clement of Alexandria, *Stromata (Miscellanies),* trans. William Wilson, in *Ante-Nicene Christian Library,* vol. 4, *The Writings of Clement of Alexandria,* ed. Alexander Roberts and James Donaldson (Edinburgh: T & T Clark, 1867–1872), 303–304.

6. James Shiel, ed., *Greek Thought and the Rise of Christianity* (New York: Barnes & Noble, 1968), 77.

7. Tertullian, "On the Flesh of Christ," in *The Ante-Nicene Fathers,* ed. Roberts and Donaldson, 525.

8. From Clement of Alexandria, *Christ the Educator,* trans. Simon P. Woo, C. P. (New York: Fathers of the Church, 1954), 175.

9. Quoted in Marvin Perry and Frederick M. Schweitzer, and Antisemitism: *Myth and Hate from Antiquity to the Present* (New York: Palgrave Macmillan, 2002), 75.

10. Quoted in Edward H. Flannery, *The Anguish of the Jews* (London: Macmillan, 1965), 48.

11. Randolph Braham, ed., *The Origins of the Holocaust: Christian Anti-Semitism* (Boulder, Colo: Social Science Monographs and Institute for Holocaust Studies of the City University of New York, 1986), 36.

12. Ibid., 37.

13. Saint Augustine, *The City of God,* trans. Gerald G. Walsh et al., abridged (Garden City, N.Y.: Doubleday Image Books, 1958), 519.

14. Ibid., 300.

Part Two

The Middle Ages: The Christian Centuries,

500 to 1400

500

600

700

800

900

1000

1100

1200

1300

Politics and Society	Thought and Culture
Germanic kingdoms established on former Roman lands (5th and 6th centuries)	Boethius, *Consolation of Philosophy* (523)
	Law code of Justinian (529)
	Byzantine church Hagia Sophia (532–537)
Saint Benedict founds monastery at Monte Cassino (529)	Cassiodorus establishes a monastic library at Vivarium (540)
Pope Gregory I sends missionaries to convert Anglo-Saxons (596)	
Spread of Islam (622–732)	The Koran
Charles Martel defeats Muslims at Tours (732)	Bede, *Ecclesiastical History of the English People* (c. 700)
	Muslim Golden Age (700s and 800s)
Charlemagne crowned Emperor of the Romans	Carolingian Renaissance (768–814)
Alfred the Great, ruler of Saxon kingdom of Wessex (871–899)	Alfred the Great promotes learning in England (871–899)
Muslim, Magyar, and Viking invasions of Latin Christendom (9th and early 10th centuries)	
Growth of feudalism (800–1100)	
German king Otto I becomes first Holy Roman Emperor (962)	
Split between the Byzantine and Roman churches (1054)	Romanesque style in architecture (1000s and 1100s)
Norman conquest of England (1066)	
Start of First Crusade (1096)	
Philip Augustus expands central authority in France (1180–1223)	Flowering of medieval culture (12th and 13th centuries): universities, Gothic architecture, scholastic philosophy, revival of Roman law
Development of common law and jury system in England (1100s)	
Pontificate of Innocent III: height of papal power (1198–1216)	
Magna Carta (1215)	Aquinas, *Summa Theologica* (1267–1273)
Destruction of Baghdad by Mongols (1258)	
Hundred Years' War (1337–1453)	Dante, *Divine Comedy* (c. 1307–1321)
Black Death (1347–1351)	Chaucer, *Canterbury Tales* (c. 1388–1400)
Great Schism of papacy (1378–1417)	

The Heirs of Rome:
Byzantium, Islam,
and Latin Christendom

Coronation of Charlemagne. (Scala/Art Resource, N.Y.)

Focus Questions

1. How did Latin Christendom blend Christian, Greco-Roman, and Germanic traditions?

2. In what ways were Greco-Roman ideas and institutions alien to Germanic traditions?

3. What was Byzantium's long-term influence on world history?

4. What does Islam have in common with Christianity? How do they differ?

5. What was the significance of medieval Muslim intellectual life?

6. Why is Charlemagne regarded as an important historical figure?

7. What conditions led to the rise of feudalism and manorialism?

The triumph of Christianity, the decay of the Roman Empire, and the establishment of Germanic kingdoms on once-Roman lands constituted a new phase in Western history: the end of the ancient world and the beginning of the Middle Ages, a period that spanned a thousand years. In the ancient world, the locus of Greco-Roman civilization had been the Mediterranean Sea; the heartland of Western medieval civilization gradually shifted to the north, to regions of Europe that Greco-Roman civilization had barely penetrated. **Latin Christendom** (Western and Central Europe) was only one of three new civilizations based on religion that emerged after the decline of the Roman Empire; Byzantium and Islam were the other two. Both of these Eastern civilizations influenced the emerging Europe in important ways.

BYZANTINE CIVILIZATION: THE MEDIEVAL CHRISTIAN EAST

Although the Roman Empire in the West fell to the Germanic tribes, the eastern provinces of the Empire survived. They did so because they were richer, more urbanized, and more populous and because the main thrust of the Germanic and Hunnish invaders had been directed at the western regions. In the eastern parts, Byzantine civilization took shape. Its religion was Christian, its culture Greek, and its machinery of administration Roman. The capital, Constantinople, was built on the site of the ancient Greek city of Byzantium, on a peninsula in the Straits of Bosporus—the dividing line between Asia and Europe. Constantinople was a fortress city perfectly situated to resist attacks from land and sea.

During the Early Middle Ages (500–1050), Byzantine civilization was economically and culturally far more advanced than the Latin West. At a time when few Westerners (Latin Christians) could read or write, Byzantine scholars studied the literature, philosophy, science, and law of ancient Greece and Rome. Whereas trade and urban life had greatly declined in the West, Constantinople was a magnificent Byzantine city of schools, libraries, open squares, and bustling markets.

197

Chronology 9.1 ❖ The Rise of Europe

496	Clovis adopts Roman Christianity
523	Boethius writes *Consolation of Philosophy*
540	Cassiodorus establishes a monastic library at Vivarium
596	Pope Gregory I sends missionaries to convert the Anglo-Saxons
717	Charles Martel becomes mayor of the palace under a weak Merovingian king
732	Charles Martel defeats the Muslims at Tours
751	Pepin the Short, with papal support, deposes the Merovingian ruler and becomes king of the Franks
755	Pepin donates to the papacy lands taken from the Lombards
768	Charlemagne becomes king of the Franks
774	Charlemagne defeats the Lombards
782	Alcuin of York heads Charlemagne's palace school
c. 799	Charlemagne subdues the Saxons
800	Charlemagne is crowned Emperor of the Romans by Pope Leo III
814	Charlemagne dies and is succeeded by his son, Louis the Pious
840	Death of Louis the Pious: the empire is divided among his sons
c. 840s	Height of Viking attacks
c. 890	Magyars invade Central Europe

Over the centuries, many differences developed between the Eastern church and the Roman church. The pope in Rome resisted domination by the Byzantine emperor, and the Byzantines denied the pope's claim to authority over all Christians. The two churches quarreled over ceremonies, holy days, and the display of holy images or icons. Fearing that some of his subjects were actually worshipping these images, in 726, Emperor Leo III ordered the destruction of all images of Christ, the Virgin, and the saints and persecuted monks who continued to venerate them. This decree greatly angered many Christians and the pope, who excommunicated Leo III. After a storm of protest convulsed the empire, the Empress Irene in 787 and the Empress Theodora in 843 restored the images. The iconoclastic struggle contributed to the rift between Byzantium and the papacy. The final break came in 1054 when the Christian church split into the Roman Catholic church in the West and the Eastern (Greek) Orthodox church in the East.

Political and cultural differences widened the rift between Latin Christendom and Byzantium. Latin Christians refused to recognize that the Byzantine emperors were, as they claimed, successors to the Roman emperors. In the Byzantine Empire, Greek was the language of religion and intellectual life; in the West, it was Latin.

Imperial Growth and Decline

Byzantine emperors were absolute rulers who held that God had chosen them to rule and to institute divine will on earth. As successors to the Roman emperors, they claimed to rule all the lands once

Map 9.1 **THE BYZANTINE EMPIRE** In the centuries after Justinian regained lands in the western Mediterranean that had been lost to Germanic invaders, the Byzantines faced attacks from Avars, Bulgars, Lombards, Persians, Arabs, Latin Christians, Seljuk Turks, and the Ottoman Turks, who captured Constantinople in 1453. (© 2016 Cengage Learning.)

part of the Roman Empire. The first great Byzantine ruler was Justinian, who reigned nearly forty years, from 527 to 565. Justinian often relied on the advice of his wife, Theodora. Theodora's background was unusual for an empress; she was not from the nobility but was the daughter of a bear trainer in the circus and had been an actress, a profession most people considered degrading. In a number of crises, the strong-willed and astute Theodora gave Justinian the courage to act decisively.

Justinian's most lasting achievement was the appointment of a commission of scholars to collect and codify Rome's ancient laws and the commentaries of learned jurists. The result was the *Corpus Juris Civilis*, a body of civil law, which

became the official body of law of the Byzantine Empire. In the twelfth century, it was gradually reintroduced into Western Europe, where it became the basis of civil law in many European lands.

Justinian sought to regain the lands in the western Mediterranean that had been conquered by Germanic invaders. During his reign, Byzantine forces retook North Africa from the Vandals, part of southern Spain from the Visigoths, and Italy from the Ostrogoths, establishing a western capital at Ravenna.

Besides draining the treasury, the long and costly wars led to the neglect of defenses in the Balkan Peninsula and the Near East. The Balkans were invaded by Slavic tribes from the Black Sea

RAVENNA MOSAICS. Theodora, Emperor Justinian's wife, was a strong-willed woman who exercised considerable authority and often advised her husband on matters of state. (INTERFOTO/Personalities /Alamy Limited.)

region and by Avars and Bulgars, originally from Central Asia; Syria was ravaged by the Persians. Nor were the conquered territories in the west secure. The Germanic Lombards, who had moved into northern Italy in the late sixth century, conquered much Byzantine territory that had been recently recovered from the Ostrogoths. By 629, the Visigoths had driven the Byzantines from Spain.

In the early seventh century, the Byzantines faced a renewed threat from the Persians, who seized the Byzantine provinces of Syria, Palestine, and Egypt. In an all-out effort, however, Emperor Heraclius (610–641) regained the provinces and in 627 crushed the Persians near the ruins of the ancient city of Nineveh. But the exhausted Byzantine Empire had become vulnerable to the Muslim Arabs, who had moved swiftly out of the Arabian Desert seeking to propagate Islam, their new faith (discussed later in this chapter).

By 642, the Arabs had stripped the Byzantine Empire of Syria, Palestine, and Egypt, and by the beginning of the eighth century, they had taken North Africa. Near the end of the seventh century and again in 717, the Muslims besieged Constantinople. But the Byzantine fleet was armed with a new weapon, "Greek fire"—a fiery explosive liquid shot from tubes—which set enemy ships aflame and made blazing pools on the water's surface. Thus, the light Byzantine ships were able to repulse the better-built Arabian ships.

The Arabs' failure to take Constantinople was crucial not only for the Byzantine Empire but also for the history of Christianity. Had this Christian fortress fallen in the eighth century, the Arabs would have been able to overrun the Balkan Peninsula and sail up the Danube River into the European heartland. After this defeat, however, Islamic armies largely concentrated their conquests outside Europe.

HAGIA SOPHIA, CONSTANTINOPLE. The largest church ever built in the Byzantine world, Hagia Sophia was constructed by Emperor Justinian. The extensive interior mosaics that once transformed the vaults of Hagia Sophia into the golden sky of heaven linked this Byzantine structure with early Christian architecture. But the heights and vast domed interior were new and became the hallmarks of the First Golden Age of Byzantine art. The emperors strongly identified themselves with Christ, and elaborate church ceremonies necessitated the presence of the emperor. Hagia Sophia provided the dramatic setting. (Wu Swee Ong/Flickr/Getty Images.)

But soon new enemies threatened. By 1071, the Normans from France had driven the Byzantines from Italy. In the same year, the Seljuk Turks, a people from Central Asia who had adopted Islam, defeated the Byzantines in Asia Minor and subjugated most of the peninsula, the heart of the Byzantine Empire. Internal dissension, however, led to the breakup of the Seljuk Empire.

Seeking to exploit Seljuk weakness and to regain lost territories, the Byzantines appealed to Latin Christians for help. Although European Christians had little love for the Byzantines, they did want to free Christian holy places from the Muslims. For this purpose, they undertook a series of Crusades, beginning in the late eleventh century (see Chapter 10). In 1204, during the Fourth Crusade, Latin Christian knights—greedy for riches—and Venetian merchants—eager to gain control of the rich Byzantine trade—decided to take Constantinople rather than fight the Muslims.

The Latin Christians looted the city, destroying sacred books, vandalizing churches, and carrying huge amounts of gold, jewels, Christian relics, and works of art back to Western Europe. They also set up kingdoms on Byzantine lands and tried to force Latin forms of Christianity on the Byzantine Greeks. Not until 1261 were the Westerners driven from Constantinople. The Byzantine Empire regained its independence, but its power was disastrously weakened. Crushing taxes, decreasing agricultural production, declining trade, and civil war continued to sap the tottering empire.

The deathblow to the empire was dealt by another group of Turks from central Asia. The Ottoman Turks had accepted Islam and had begun to build an empire. They drove the Byzantines from Asia Minor and conquered much of the Balkans. By the beginning of the fifteenth century, the Byzantine Empire consisted of only two small territories in Greece and the city of Constantinople. In 1453, the Ottoman Turks broke through Constantinople's great walls and plundered the city. After more than ten centuries, the Byzantine Empire came to an end.

The Bequest of Byzantium

During its thousand years, Byzantium made a significant impact on world history. First, it prevented the Muslim Arabs from advancing into Eastern Europe. Had the Arabs broken through Byzantine defenses, much of Europe might have been converted to the new faith of Islam. A far-reaching accomplishment was the codification of the laws of ancient Rome under Justinian. This monumental achievement preserved Roman law's principles of reason and justice. Today's legal codes in much of Europe and Latin America trace their roots to the Roman law recorded by Justinian's lawyers. The Byzantines also preserved the philosophy, science, mathematics, and literature of ancient Greece.

Contacts with Byzantine civilization stimulated learning in both the Islamic world to the east and Latin Christendom to the west. Speros Vryonis, a student of Byzantine civilization, states: "The Byzantines carried the torch of civilization unextinguished at a time when the barbarous Germanic and Slav tribes had reduced much of Europe to near chaos: and they maintained this high degree of civilization until Western Europe gradually emerged and began to take form."[1] Byzantium exerted an important religious, cultural, and linguistic influence on Latin Romanians, eastern Slavs (Russians and Ukrainians), and southern Slavs (Serbs and Bulgars). From Byzantium, the Slavs acquired legal principles, art forms, and an alphabet (the Cyrillic, based on the Greek) for writing their languages. (On the other hand, the western Slavs—Poles, Czechs, and Slovaks—came under the influence of Latin Christianity and Latin culture.)

ISLAMIC CIVILIZATION: ITS DEVELOPMENT AND DISSEMINATION

The Prophet: The Founding of a New Religion

The second Eastern civilization to arise after Rome's fall was based on the vital new religion of Islam, which emerged in the seventh century among the Arabs of Arabia. Its founder was Muhammad (c. 570–632), a prosperous merchant in Mecca, a trading city near the Red Sea. At times the introspective Muhammad withdrew from worldly affairs and devoted himself to meditation. He began to experience visions, which he interpreted as messages from God. When Muhammad was about forty, he believed that he was visited in his sleep by the angel Gabriel, who ordered him to "recite in the name of the Lord!" Transformed by this experience, Muhammad came to believe

that he had been chosen as a prophet, the carrier of God's revelation.

Although most desert Arabs worshiped tribal gods, many Arabs, including Muhammad, in the towns and trading centers were familiar with Judaism and Christianity, and some had accepted the idea of one God. Rejecting the many deities of the tribal religions, Muhammad offered the Arabs a new monotheistic faith, Islam, which means "surrender to Allah (God)."

Islamic standards of morality and rules governing daily life are set by the Koran, the holy book that Muslims believe contains the words of Allah as revealed to Muhammad. For Muslims, the Koran is both God's final word and infallible. Muslims see their religion as the completion and perfection of Judaism and Christianity; they believe both of those monotheistic predecessors were superseded by Allah's revelation to Muhammad. Muslims regard the ancient Hebrew prophets as sent from God and value their messages about compassion and the oneness of humanity. They also regard Jesus as a great prophet but do not consider him divine and view the Trinity as a form of polytheism. They see Muhammad as the last and greatest of the prophets and believe that he was entirely human, not divine. Muslims worship only Allah, the creator and ruler of heaven and earth, a single, all-powerful God who is merciful, compassionate, and just. According to the Koran, on the Day of Judgment, unbelievers and the wicked "shall dwell amidst scorching winds and seething water: in the shade of pitch-black smoke . . . sinners that deny the truth . . . shall eat . . . [bitter] fruit . . . [and] drink boiling water."[2] Faithful Muslims who have lived virtuously are promised paradise, which they believe to be a garden where they will experience bodily pleasures and spiritual delights.

An essential feature of Islam is the obligation of the faithful to obey the Five Pillars of the faith: (1) A Muslim must accept and repeat the statement of faith: "There is no God but Allah, and Muhammad is his Prophet." (2) At least five times a day, a believer must face the holy city of Mecca and pray. (3) Muslims have a religious duty to be generous to the poor. (4) During the holy month of Ramadan, believers should not eat or drink between sunrise and sunset. (5) Muslims are expected to make at least one pilgrimage to the holy city of Mecca. The Koran contains numerous other injunctions designed to promote righteous behavior, including strict modesty for females and the condemnation of polytheism as a vile sin.

Muhammad's religion began to win followers, but the ruling elite of Mecca would not accept this new faith. To escape persecution, Muhammad and his small band of followers left Mecca in 622 for Medina, a town about two hundred miles away. Their flight, known as the *Hegira*, or "emigration," is one of the most important events in Muslim history and is commemorated by yearly pilgrimages. The date of the Hegira became year one of the Muslim calendar.

In Medina, Muhammad gained converts and won respect as a judge, rendering decisions on such matters as family relations, property inheritance, and criminal behavior. Preaching a holy war against unbelievers, Muhammad urged followers to raid the trading caravans from Mecca and to subdue unfriendly Bedouin tribes. He tried to convert the Jews of Medina, but they would not accept him as a prophet and mocked his unfamiliarity with the Hebrew Scriptures and the learned writings of the rabbis. To a large extent, political considerations determined Muhammad's attitude toward Jews, who sided with his Meccan enemies. He expelled several thousand Jews from Medina, seized Jewish property, beheaded some six hundred Jewish men, and enslaved women and children. Later, he permitted the Arabian Jews the free exercise of their religion and guaranteed the security of their property. In 630, Mecca surrendered to a Muslim army virtually without a fight. Muhammad demonstrated leniency and forgiveness toward his former enemies and persecutors, a wise decision that helped gain him the support of the Meccans. Soon Bedouin tribes all over Arabia embraced Islam and recognized the authority of the Prophet Muhammad.

In a little more than two decades, Muhammad united the often feuding Arabian tribes into a powerful force dedicated to Allah and the spreading of the Islamic faith. After Muhammad's death in 632, his friend and father-in-law, Abu Bakr, became his successor, or caliph. Regarded as the defender of the faith, whose power derived from Allah, the caliph governed in accordance with Muslim law as defined in the Koran. Islam gave the many Arab tribes the unity, discipline, and

MOSQUE OF CÓRDOBA. The richness of Islamic culture and architecture is evident in Spain, where Muslim rule lingered until the conquest of Granada in 1492. The arch of alternating stone would find its way into Christian churches, most memorably at Vezelay in southern France. (Roger Viollet/Getty Images.)

organization to succeed in their wars of conquest. Under the first four caliphs, who ruled from 632 to 661, the Arabs, with breathtaking speed, overran Persia's empire, seized large parts of the Byzantine Empire, and invaded Europe.

Muhammad had conveyed to his followers their religious obligation to perform jihad, literally striving in the path of God. *Jihad* is a complex term whose two essential meanings are an internal striving by the individual for moral self-improvement and a collective military struggle to defend Islam against its enemies and to extend Muslim power over other lands so that all people will be subject to God's laws as revealed to Muhammad. Muhammad glorified jihad and criticized those who did not participate in it. Historically the doctrine of jihad held that the Islamic community (*umma*), the recipient of Allah's revelation, was commanded to make Allah's directives supreme over the whole world. Either by conversion through vigorous missionary activity or conquest, infidels were destined to submit to Islamic jurisdiction. Muslim theologians came to regard jihad as the finest religious act a man can perform.

Muslim warriors believed that they were required to engage in a holy war to spread Islam to nonbelievers and that those who died in the jihad were assured a place in paradise. A desire to escape from the barren Arabian Desert and to exploit the rich Byzantine and Persian lands was another compelling reason for expansion. Conflicts between Persia and Byzantium had greatly weakened both eastern empires, facilitating the Muslim conquest. By 750, Islam's territory in the east extended into India and to the borders of China; in the west, it encompassed North Africa and most of Spain. The Muslims' northward push lost momentum and was halted in 717 by the Byzantines at Constantinople and in 732 by the Franks at the battle of Tours, in central France.

The Muslim State and Society

After the death of Muhammad, Muslims sought authoritative guidance on religious, social, and moral questions that the Koran did not specifically address. The most important source for such guidance was the *Hadith*—a collection of sayings, stories, and actions of the Prophet on a wide range of topics. The Koran coupled with the Hadith provided directions for a complete way of life for Muslims.

The Islamic state was a theocracy: government and religion were inseparable; there could be no distinction between secular and spiritual authority. Muslims viewed God as the source of all law and political authority and the caliph as his earthly deputy. Divine law regulated all aspects of human relations. The ruler who did not enforce Koranic law failed in his duties. Thus, Islam was more than a religion; it was also a system of government, society, law, and thought that bound its adherents into an all-encompassing community. Muslim jurists called for the creation of a single society governed by Islamic law. And this world-state had a religious obligation to subdue the non-Muslim world. This goal, to be achieved by jihad, endured in the Muslim mind over the centuries and is a principal aim of Muslim extremists today. The separation of church and state, which became firmly rooted in the West in modern times, still remains an alien concept in much of the Muslim world.

Over the centuries, many Christians and Jews living in Muslim lands, for a variety of reasons, some of them economic and social, converted to the new faith. Those who retained their ancestral faith had to accept a subordinate status—they could not bear arms, were assessed a special tax, at times were barred from testifying in court against a Muslim, and were required to wear a distinguishing mark on their clothing, a sign of their humiliation. Over the years, thousands of Christian churches were demolished or converted into mosques. Nevertheless, as "people of the book," Jews and Christians were protected communities, and despite instances of loss of property and life, including massacres, the two groups generally went about their business and practiced their religions relatively free of persecution. Generally Jews were physically safer in Muslim than in Christian lands where Jews were treated as outsiders, legally and economically marginalized and subject to persecution, expulsion, and massacres. In contrast, Jews were more integrated into Muslim society as merchants and artisans. Moreover, unlike in Christian lands, Muslims did not perceive Jews as deicides—the killers of God.

Muslims perceived themselves as members of a single community of the faithful, but the emergence of sects ruptured the unity of Islam. The principal division—one that still incites bitter animosity—was between the Sunnis and the Shiites. The Sunnis, who were in the majority, followed traditional teachings and established practices as defined by the consensus of the Muslim community. The Shiites (*Shia* means "Party") maintained that not the existing caliphs but the descendants of Muhammad, starting with Ali, cousin and son-in-law of Muhammad and the fourth caliph, were the rightful rulers of the Islamic community.

Ali had been murdered in 661; his older son, in 669. The massacre in 680 of Ali's younger son, Husayn, and some of Husayn's followers and relatives gave rise to passionate devotion to the house of Ali, which is still expressed in processions, poetry, and self-mortification. To Shiites, the anniversary of Husayn's death remains the most important religious holiday in the Muslim calendar. Suffering and martyrdom are central to Shia.

Shiites viewed Ali and his descendants as *imams,* holy men, innocent of all sin, the most excellent of beings, selected by God to inherit Muhammad's spiritual and political powers. The imams linked the new generation with Muhammad's original inspiration. Shiites believed that without the imams' guidance, the true meaning of Islam could not be grasped.

The Muslim Golden Age

The Arabs who first burst into the Byzantine and Persian empires had no tradition of science or philosophy. But they were quick to absorb the learning of Byzantines and Persians who had preserved and studied ancient Greek works. In the eighth and ninth centuries, under the Abbasid caliphs based in Baghdad, Muslim civilization entered its golden age. Islamic civilization creatively integrated Arabic, Byzantine, Persian, and Indian cultural traditions. During the Early Middle Ages, when learning was at a low point in Western Europe, the Muslims forged a high civilization.

Muslim science, philosophy, and mathematics, based largely on the achievements of the ancient Greeks, made brilliant contributions to the sum of knowledge at a time when Latin Christendom had lost much of Greco-Roman thought and culture. The Muslims had acquired Greek learning from the older Persian and Byzantine civilizations, which had kept alive the Greek inheritance. By translating Greek works into Arabic and commenting on them, Muslim scholars performed the great historical task of preserving and expanding the philosophical and scientific heritage of ancient Greece. Muslim scholars, often affiliated with impressive universities, also creatively interpreted these Greek works and in some areas, particularly mathematics, pushed the frontiers of knowledge beyond what the Greeks had achieved. This intellectual heritage was passed on to Christian Europe, a transmission of immense historical significance

There are numerous examples of Muslim brilliance in mathematics, medicine, astronomy, optics, and philosophy. From India, the Muslims acquired the concept of zero and "Arabic" numerals, passing these ideas on to the West. Euclid's *Elements,* the creative synthesis of Greek geometry, was translated into Arabic and studied by Muslim scholars who produced numerous commentaries on the work. Muslim mathematicians also did original work in algebra and trigonometry. Also translated into Arabic was another important Greek writing, Ptolemy's *Almagest,* which synthesized astronomical knowledge. Muslim astronomers corrected some of Ptolemy's calculations, pointed out theoretical inconsistencies, and explored problems he had not considered. They were aided by the data collected in newly established observatories in Baghdad and Damascus. While a number of astronomers served as court astrologers, many more rejected astrology as unscientific. In physics, the Muslim Arabs' most significant contribution was in the field of optics. Rejecting Euclid's and Ptolemy's explanation that the eye emits visual rays, they recognized that vision is a consequence of rays of light.

Building on the medical knowledge of the Greeks, Muslim physicians became the best-trained and most skillful doctors of the time. Surgeons performed amputations, removed cancerous tissue, devised new medicines, and used anesthetics when performing operations. The best Muslim hospitals had separate wards for fevers, surgical cases, eye diseases, and dysentery. Well ahead of their time were those Muslim doctors who recommended humane treatment for the mentally ill. The Persian al-Razi, or Rhazes, who headed the hospital in Baghdad in the ninth century, wrote a medical encyclopedia in which he discussed measles, kidney stones, poisons, skin diseases, and ways of maintaining one's health. Al Razi emphasized an empirical approach—observation, diagnosis, and therapy—in determining the nature of an illness and its possible treatment. The works of Rhazes, translated into Latin, were widely consulted in Latin Christendom.

Muslim thinkers employed the categories of Greek philosophy to explain Islamic doctrine. Al-Farabi (c. 870–950), who wrote commentaries on Aristotle, offered proofs for God's existence based on Aristotelian logic that were later studied by medieval Christian philosophers. The most eminent Muslim thinker, Ibn-Sina, known to the West as Avicenna (980–1037), was a poet, doctor, scientist, and philosopher who wrote on every field of knowledge. His philosophical works, which relied heavily on Aristotle, had an important influence on medieval Christian thinkers. Another giant of Muslim learning was Ibn-Rushd, whom Westerners call Averroës (1126–1198). Averroës insisted that the Koran did not oppose the study of philosophy and held that the ancient Greeks—even though they were not Muslims—had discovered truth. His commentaries on Aristotle were studied in Western universities, where they sparked an important controversy (see page 261).

Greek philosophy and science had great appeal for Muslims; the same could not be said for Greco-Roman literature, Roman law, or Greek political thought. Islamic law and political theory derived from the Koran and the sayings of Muhammad. In such a religious intellectual setting, Roman legal strictures and Greek political speculation seemed both unnecessary and threatening.

Mongol Invasions and Ottoman Dominance

The Arab empire, stretching from Spain to India, was unified by a common language (Arabic), a common faith, and a common culture. By the eleventh century, however, the Arabs began losing their dominance in the Islamic world. The Seljuk Turks, who had taken Asia Minor from the Byzantines, also conquered the Arabic lands of Syria, Palestine, and much of Persia. Although the Abbasid caliphs remained the religious and cultural leaders of Islam, political power was exercised by Seljuk sultans. In the eleventh and twelfth centuries, the Muslims lost Sicily and most of Spain to Christian knights, and European Crusaders carved out kingdoms in the Near East.

In the thirteenth century came a new wave of invaders, the Mongols from central Asia. Led by Genghis Khan, Mongolian archers, mounted on fast-moving ponies, poured across Asia into Muslim lands. By 1227, when Genghis Khan died, the eastern part of the Muslim world had fallen to the Mongols. After the death of Genghis Khan, some Mongol forces swept across Russia

and threatened Central Europe; others continued to advance on Muslim lands in the Near East. Storming Baghdad in 1258, the Mongols burned, plundered, and killed with savage fury; among the fifty thousand people slaughtered was the last Abbasid caliph. The Mongols devastated the palaces, libraries, and schools that had made Baghdad the cultural capital of the Islamic world. A year later, they marched into Syria, again killing and looting. Their brutal advance westward was finally stopped in 1260 in Palestine by Egyptian forces.

By the beginning of the fourteenth century, the Mongols, who had by this time converted to Islam, remained in Persia and were unable to advance westward. In the late fourteenth century, however, the Mongols, under Tamerlane, again menaced the Near East. Another bloody conqueror, Tamerlane cowed opposition with huge pyramids built from the skulls of thousands of slaughtered victims. After Tamerlane's death in 1404, his empire disintegrated, and its collapse left the way open for the Ottoman Turks.

The Ottoman Empire reached its height in the sixteenth century with the conquest of Egypt, North Africa, Syria, and the Arabian coast. The Turkish conquest of much of Hungary in the 1520s and the siege of Vienna (1529) spread panic in Europe. The Ottomans developed an effective system of administration but could not restore the cultural brilliance, the thriving trade, or the prosperity that the Muslim world had known under the Abbasid caliphs of Baghdad. The vitality that had kept the Muslim world more advanced than Western Europe for most of the Middle Ages dissipated.

LATIN CHRISTENDOM: THE RISE OF EUROPE

The centuries of cultural greatness of the Islamic and the Byzantine civilizations enriched the Western world. They did not, however, produce the major breakthroughs in science, technology, philosophy, economics, and political thought that gave rise to the modern world. That process was the singular achievement of Europe. During the Middle Ages, a common European civilization— Latin Christendom—evolved. It integrated Christian, Greco-Roman, and Germanic elements.

Map 9.2 **The Expansion of Islam, 622–732** From 632 to 661, the Arabs, with breathtaking speed, overran the Persian Empire, seized some of Byzantium's provinces, and invaded southern Europe. Their northward momentum was halted in 717 by the Byzantines at Constantinople and in 732 by the Franks at the battle of Tours in central France. (© 2016 Cengage Learning.)

Christianity was at the center of medieval civilization, Rome was the spiritual capital and Latin the language of intellectual life, and Germanic customs pervaded social and legal relationships.

During the Early Middle Ages (500–1050), Latin Christendom was culturally far behind the two Eastern civilizations and did not catch up until the twelfth century. In succeeding centuries, however, it produced the movements that ushered in the modern age: the Renaissance, the Reformation, the Scientific Revolution, the Age of Enlightenment, the French Revolution, and the Industrial Revolution.

Political and Economic Transformation

From the sixth to the eighth century, Europeans struggled to overcome the disorder created by the breakup of the Roman Empire and the deterioration of Greco-Roman civilization. In the process, a new civilization, with its own distinctive style, took root. It grew out of the intermingling of Greco-Roman civilization, the Christian outlook, and Germanic traditions, although centuries would pass before it would come to fruition.

In the fifth century and after, Germanic invaders founded kingdoms in North Africa, Italy, Spain, Gaul, and Britain—lands formerly belonging to the Roman Empire. Even before the invasions, these Germanic tribes had acquired some knowledge of Roman culture and were attracted to it. Therefore, the new rulers sought not to destroy Roman civilization but to share in its advantages. For example, Theodoric the Great (474–526), the Ostrogoth ruler of Italy, retained the Roman Senate, civil service, and schools; and rich aristocratic Roman families continued to hold high government offices. The Burgundians in Gaul and the Visigoths in Spain maintained Roman law for their conquered subjects; and the Frankish ruler Clovis (c. 466–511) wore Roman imperial colors and took Roman titles. All the Germanic kingdoms tried to maintain Roman systems of taxation; furthermore, Latin remained the official language of administration.

However, torn by warfare, internal rebellion, and assassination, the Germanic kingdoms provided a poor political base on which to revive a decadent and dying classical civilization. Most of the kingdoms survived for only a short time and had no enduring impact. An exception to this trend occurred in Gaul and south-central Germany, where the most successful of the Germanic kingdoms was established by the Franks—the founders of the new Europe.

The Roman world was probably too far gone to be rescued, but even if it had not been, the Germans were culturally unprepared to play the role of restorer. By the end of the seventh century, the old Roman lands in Western Europe showed a marked decline in central government, town life, commerce, and learning. Though vigorous and brave, the Germanic invaders were essentially a rural and warrior people, tribal in organization and outlook. Their native culture, without cities or written literature, was primitive compared with the literary, philosophical, scientific, and artistic achievements of the Greco-Roman world. The Germans were not equipped to reform the decaying Roman system of administration and taxation or to cope with the economic problems that had burdened the Empire. Nor could they maintain roads and irrigation systems, preserve skills in the arts of stoneworking and glassmaking, or breathe new life into the dying humanist culture.

Roman ideas of citizenship and the legal state were totally alien to Germanic tradition. The Germans gave loyalty to their kin and to a tribal chief, not to an impersonal state that governed citizens of many nationalities. The king viewed the land he controlled as a private possession that could be divided among his sons after his death—a custom that produced numerous and devastating civil wars and partitions. Unlike the Romans, the Germanic invaders had no trained civil servants to administer the state and no organized system of taxation to provide a secure financial base for government.

The Germans also found Roman law strange, although the Germanic kingdoms did make attempts to retain Roman law codes. Roman law incorporated elements of Greek philosophy and was written, whereas Germanic law at the time of the invasions consisted of unwritten tribal customs. Roman law applied to all people throughout the Empire, regardless of nationality; a German could be judged only by the law of his own tribe. Roman judges investigated evidence and demanded proof; Germanic courts, in the absence of clear evidence, relied on trial by ordeal. In a typical ordeal, a bound defendant was thrown into a river. Sinking meant innocence; floating was interpreted as divine proof of guilt, because the pure water had "rejected" the evildoer. Although primitive by Roman standards, Germanic law did help lessen blood feuds between families. Before long, the Germanic kingdoms began to put customary tribal law, which had absorbed and continued to absorb elements from Roman law, into writing. Replacing Roman law and spreading throughout Europe, Germanic law became an essential element of medieval society.

The distinguishing feature of classical civilization, its vital urban institutions, had deteriorated in the Late Roman Empire. The shift from an urban to a rural economy accelerated under the kingdoms created by Germanic chieftains. Although the Germanic kings retained Roman cities as capitals, they did not halt the process of decay that had overtaken urban centers. These rulers settled their people in the countryside, not in towns; they did not significantly utilize cities as instruments of local government; and they failed to maintain Roman roads. Although towns did not vanish altogether, they continued to lose control over the surrounding countryside and to decline in wealth and importance. They were the episcopal seats (sees) of bishops, rather than centers of commerce and intellectual life. Italy remained an exception to this general trend. There, Roman urban institutions persisted, even during the crudest period of the Early Middle Ages. Italian cities kept some metal currency in circulation and traded with one another and with Byzantium.

Shrinking commerce during the Early Middle Ages was part of the process of decline begun in the Late Roman Empire. Although commerce never wholly disappeared, it was predominantly localized. Furthermore, it was controlled by colonies of Jews, Syrians, and Greeks—a sign of the economic inertia of Latin Christians. From the last decade of the fifth century to the middle of the seventh century, Byzantine merchants established themselves in the western lands and exchanged papyrus, spices, and textiles for European slaves. Then, in the second half of the seventh century, this trade dropped off greatly; as Muslim power expanded to control the Mediterranean, Byzantine merchants had to turn eastward for markets. Thus, the bonds between East and West weakened, and Europe shifted its axis northward, away from the Mediterranean. Few goods exchanged hands, and few coins circulated; people produced for themselves what they needed.

The Waning of Classical Culture

Greco-Roman humanism, in retreat since the Late Roman Empire, continued its decline in the centuries immediately following Rome's demise. The old Roman upper classes abandoned their heritage and absorbed the ways of their Germanic conquerors, the Roman schools closed, and Roman law faded into disuse. Aside from clerics, few people could read and write Latin, and even learned clerics were rare. Europeans' knowledge of the Greek language was almost totally lost, and the Latin rhetorical style deteriorated. Many literary works of classical antiquity were either lost or unread. Raids by Germanic tribes and later by Muslims, Magyars, and Vikings (see below) devastated libraries. Many works by great authors were lost forever. For example, only seven of the one hundred dramas written by Sophocles have survived. Gone were attempts to understand the natural world through reason; magic and the occult prevailed among both pagans and Christians. The literature of the seventh century, concerned principally with the lives of saints, was devoid of the humanist themes that had motivated Greek and Roman poets and dramatists. European culture was much poorer than the high civilizations of Byzantium, Islam, and ancient Rome.

During this period of cultural poverty, the few persons who were learned generally did not engage in original thought but salvaged and transmitted remnants of classical civilization. Given the context of the times, this was a considerable achievement. These individuals retained respect for the inheritance of Greece and Rome while remaining devoted to Christianity. In a rudimentary way, they were struggling to create a Christian culture that combined the intellectual tradition of Greece and Rome with the religious teachings of the Christian church.

An important figure in the intellectual life of this transitional period was Boethius (480–c. 525), a descendant of a noble family. Boethius had received a classical education at the Platonic Academy at Athens before Emperor Justinian closed it in 529. He was the last Latin-speaking scholar of the Roman world to have mastered the Greek language and to have intimate knowledge of Greek philosophy. Later, Boethius served the Ostrogoth Theodoric I, who ruled Italy. Recognizing that Greco-Roman civilization was dying, Boethius tried to rescue the intellectual heritage of antiquity. He translated into Latin some of Aristotle's treatises on logic and wrote commentaries on Aristotle, Cicero, and Porphyry (a Neo-Platonist philosopher). He also wrote treatises on theology and textbooks on arithmetic, astronomy, and music. A sudden turn of fortune deprived him of power, prestige, and possessions and confronted him with imminent death when Theodoric ordered him executed in 524 or 525 for allegedly participating in a plot against the throne.

While in prison awaiting execution, Boethius wrote *The Consolation of Philosophy,* which is regarded as one of the masterpieces of world literature. In it, Boethius pondered life's meaning: "Think you that there is any certainty in the affairs of mankind when you know that often one swift hour can utterly destroy a man?"[3] Alone in his dungeon, he turned for guidance and consolation to the philosophical training of his youth. He derived comfort from Lady Philosophy, who reassured him, in the tradition of Socrates and the Stoics, that "if then you are master of yourself, you will be in possession of that which you will never wish to lose, and which Fortune will never be able to take from you."[4] No tyrant can "ever disturb the peculiar restfulness which is the property of a mind that hangs together upon the firm basis of its reason."[5] In the life and thought of Boethius, the classical tradition lived on. He was a bridge between a classical civilization too weakened to be revived and a Christian civilization still in its embryonic stage.

Until the twelfth century, virtually all that Latin Christendom knew of Aristotle came from Boethius's translations and commentaries. Similarly, his work in mathematics, which contains fragments from Euclid, was the principal source for the study of that discipline in the Early Middle Ages. In his theological writings, he strove to demonstrate that reason did not conflict with orthodoxy—an early attempt to attain a rational comprehension of belief, or, as he expressed it, to join faith to reason. Boethius's effort to examine Christian doctrines rationally, a principal feature of medieval philosophy, would grow to maturity in the twelfth and thirteenth centuries. Writing in the sixth century, Boethius was a forerunner of this movement.

Cassiodorus (c. 490–575), a contemporary of Boethius, was born in southern Italy of a good family; he served three Ostrogoth kings. Although Cassiodorus wrote the twelve-volume *History of the Goths* and some theological treatises, his prime legacies were the establishment of a monastic library containing Greek and Latin manuscripts and his advocacy of higher education to improve the quality of the clergy. In his educational writings, he justified the importance of studying secular literature as an aid to understanding sacred writings. Even though his works were not original, they did rescue some ideas of the ancients from oblivion; these ideas would bear fruit again in later centuries. Cassiodorus's plans for founding a university in Rome modeled after the one in Alexandria did not materialize; in fact, six hundred years would elapse before universities would arise in Latin Christendom. Leaving political office, Cassiodorus retired to a monastery in southern Italy, where he helped initiate the monastic practice of copying ancient texts. Without this tradition, many key Christian and Greco-Roman works would undoubtedly have perished.

In Spain, Isidore of Seville (c. 576–636) compiled an encyclopedia, *Etymologiae,* covering a diversity of topics, from arithmetic and God to furniture. Isidore derived his information from many secular and religious sources. Quite understandably, his work contained many errors, particularly in its references to nature. For centuries, though, the *Etymologiae* served as a standard reference work and was found in every monastic library of note.

The translations and compilations made by Boethius, Cassiodorus, and Isidore, the books collected and copied by monks and nuns, and the schools established in monasteries (particularly those in Ireland, England, and Italy) kept intellectual life from dying out completely in the Early Middle Ages. Amid the deterioration of political authority, the stagnation of economic life, and the decline in learning, a new civilization was emerging. Germanic and Roman peoples intermarried, and Roman, Germanic, and Christian traditions intermingled. But it was the church more than anything else that gave form and direction to the emerging civilization.

THE CHURCH: SHAPER OF MEDIEVAL CIVILIZATION

The Church as Unifier

Christianity was the integrating principle and the church was the dominant institution of the Middle Ages. During the Late Roman Empire, as the Roman state and its institutions decayed, the church gained power and importance; its organization grew stronger, and its membership increased. Unlike the Roman state, the church was a healthy and vital institution. The elite of the Roman Empire had severed their commitment to the values of classical civilization, whereas church leaders were intensely devoted to their faith.

During the invasions of the fifth and sixth centuries, the church, retaining an effective administrative system, assumed many political functions formerly performed by the Roman state and continued to convert the Germanic tribes. By teaching a higher morality, the church tamed the warrior habits of the Germanic peoples. By preserving some of the high culture of Greece and Rome, it opened Germans' minds to new ideas. Missionaries actively propagated the faith in the newly established Germanic kingdoms, often first converting the rulers making it easier to reach the masses. However, despite the missionaries' best efforts, peasants continued to retain (and would for centuries) some deeply rooted pagan folk traditions, including divination and augury, that the clergy castigated as devil worship. But gradually the Christian outlook, rather than Germanic paganism, became the foundation of medieval civilization.

A unifying and civilizing agent, the church provided people with an intelligible and purposeful conception of life and death. In a dying world, the church was the only institution capable of reconstructing civilized life. During the course of the Middle Ages, people came to see themselves as participants in a great drama of salvation. There was only one truth: God's revelation to humanity. There was only one avenue to heaven, and it passed through the church. God had established the church to propagate his teachings and administer his rules. The church had the awesome responsibility of caring for human souls. Without the church, it was believed, people would remain doomed sinners. To the medieval mind, society without the church was inconceivable. Membership in a universal church replaced citizenship in a universal empire. Across Europe, from Italy to Ireland, a new society centered on Christianity was forming.

Monks and the Papacy

Monks helped construct the foundations of medieval civilization. During the seventh century, intellectual life on the European continent continued its steady decline. In the monasteries of Ireland and England, however, a tradition of learning persisted. Early in the fifth century, Saint Patrick began the conversion of the Irish to Christianity. In Ireland, Latin became firmly entrenched as the language of both the church and scholars at a time when it was in danger of disappearing in many parts of Europe. Irish monks preserved and cultivated Latin and even kept some knowledge of Greek alive. Irish scholars engaged in biblical analysis, and, besides copying manuscripts, they decorated them, with an exquisite eye for detail. In England, the Anglo-Saxons, both women and men, who converted to Christianity mainly in the seventh century, also established monasteries that kept learning alive. Double monasteries existed, in which monks and nuns obeyed a common rule and one superior, sometimes an abbess. The Venerable Bede

(673–735) wrote commentaries on Scripture and translated the fourth Gospel (Saint John's) into Anglo-Saxon. Bede is best known for his *Ecclesiastical History of the English People,* one of the finest medieval historical works.

In the sixth and seventh centuries, Irish and Anglo-Saxon monks and nuns built monasteries in continental Europe and converted people in the surrounding areas. They became the chief agents in Christianizing people in northern Europe. Thus, monks and nuns made possible a unitary European civilization based on a Christian foundation. By copying and preserving ancient texts, they also kept alive elements of ancient civilization.

During the Early Middle Ages, when cities were in decay, monasteries, whose libraries contained theological works and ancient Latin classics, were the main cultural centers; they would remain so until the rebirth of towns in the High Middle Ages. Monks instructed peasants in superior methods of farming and were partly responsible for the reclamation of lands that had been neglected or devastated during the great invasions and for the clearing of new lands. Monasteries also offered succor to the sick and the destitute and served as places of refuge for travelers. To the medieval mind, the monks' and nuns' selfless devotion to God, adoption of apostolic poverty, and dedication to prayer and contemplation represented the highest expression of the Christian way of life; it was the finest and most certain path to salvation. It was not uncommon for both men and women, with old age or even death approaching, to take the vows so that they might die as monks or nuns. Regarding the monks as soldiers in the war against paganism, unorthodoxy, and heresy, the popes protected monasteries and encouraged their spread.

The Early Middle Ages was a formative period for the **papacy**, as well as for society in general. The status of the papacy was closely tied to events in Italy. In the late sixth century, the papacy was compelled to protect Rome and the surrounding territory from the Lombards, the last Germanic people to settle in once-Roman lands. At this critical stage, Gregory I, the Great (590–604), became pope. A descendant of a prominent Roman family and a monk, Gregory turned out to be one of the ablest medieval popes. He used Roman methods

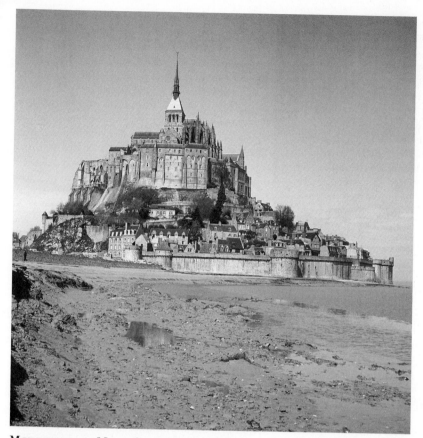

MONASTERY OF MONT ST. MICHEL. The monastic institutions throughout Western Europe stood firm amid the intellectual and cultural confusion of the Early Middle Ages. By copying ancient manuscripts and studying Latin, monks preserved elements of classical civilizations. (© Paul Almasy/CORBIS.)

of administration effectively to organize and administer papal property in Italy, Sicily, Sardinia, Gaul, and other regions. The papacy owned huge estates worked by serfs. It also owned timberlands and mines, which provided the income for maintaining the clergy, churches, monasteries, hospitals, and orphanages in Rome and other places. Because of Gregory's efforts, the papacy became the leading financial institution of the day.

Gregory tried to strengthen the pope's authority within the church, insisting that all bishops and the Byzantine church in Constantinople were subject to papal authority. Establishing monasteries, he tightened the bonds between the monks and the papacy, and it was he who dispatched Benedictine monks to England to win

over the Anglo-Saxons. The newly established Anglo-Saxon church looked to Rome for leadership. Gregory realized that to lead Christendom effectively the papacy must exercise authority over churches outside Italy—a policy adopted by popes who succeeded him.

He was also an intellectual who wrote commentaries on the books of the Bible and authored many works dealing with Christian themes: the duties of bishops, the lives of saints and monks, miracles, and purgatory. Because of his many writings, Gregory is regarded as the father of the Latin church. An astute diplomat, he knew that the papacy required the political and military support of a powerful kingdom to protect it from its enemies, especially the Lombards. Accordingly,

PAINTING OF SAINT MATTHEW FROM THE GOSPEL BOOK OF CHARLEMAGNE, c. 800–810. Handwritten and very costly, sacred books were often lavishly illustrated with miniature paintings. In this painting, Saint Matthew, wearing a Roman toga, is depicted with his pen poised, writing his Gospel. Because of the painting's clear Hellenistic style, scholars believe its artist was trained in an Italian or Byzantine school. (Kunsthistorisches Museum, Vienna.)

he set his sights on an alliance with the Franks. Finally materializing 150 years later, this alliance between the papacy and Frankish kings helped shape medieval history.

THE KINGDOM OF THE FRANKS

From their homeland in the Rhine River valley, the Frankish tribes had expanded into Roman territory during the fourth and fifth centuries. A Frankish leader, Childeric I, the son of Merovech, founded the Merovingian dynasty in the mid-fifth century. His successor, Clovis, united the various Frankish tribes and conquered most of Gaul. In 496, he converted to Roman Christianity. Clovis's conversion to Catholicism was an event of great significance. A number of other Germanic kings had adopted the Arian form of Christianity,

which the church had declared heretical. By embracing Roman Christianity, the Franks became a potential ally of the papacy.

Clovis's successors could not maintain control over their lands, and power passed to the mayor of the palace, the king's chief officer. Serving as mayor of the palace from 717 to 741, Charles Martel subjected all Frankish lands to his rule. In addition, at the battle of Tours in 732, he defeated the Muslims. Although the Muslims continued to occupy the Iberian Peninsula, they would advance no farther north into Europe.

Charles Martel was succeeded by his son, Pepin the Short, who in 751 deposed the king. With the approval of the papacy and his nobles, Pepin was crowned king by Boniface, a prominent bishop. Two years later, Pope Stephen II anointed Pepin again as king of the Franks and appealed to him to protect the papacy from the Lombards. Pepin crossed into Italy, defeated the Lombards, and turned over captured lands to the papacy. This famous Donation of Pepin made the pope ruler of the territory between Rome and Ravenna, which became known as the Papal States.

The Era of Charlemagne

The alliance between the Franks and the papacy was continued by Pepin's successor, Charlemagne (Charles the Great), who ruled from 768 to 814. Charlemagne continued the Carolingian policy of expanding the Frankish kingdom. He destroyed the Lombard kingdom, added Bavaria to his kingdom, and, after long, terrible wars, compelled the Saxons to submit to his rule and convert to Christianity—thousands were beheaded when they were slow to choose between baptism or execution. He also conquered a region in northern Spain, the Spanish March, which served as a buffer between the Christian Franks and the Muslims in Spain. At its height, Charlemagne's empire encompassed large parts of what is now France, Belgium, Switzerland, the Netherlands, western and central Germany, northern Italy, and northern Spain.

Immense difficulties arose in governing the expanded territories. Size seemed an insuperable obstacle to effective government, particularly since Charlemagne's administrative structure, lacking trained personnel, was primitive by

Map 9.3 The Carolingian World Resting more on the personal qualities of Charlemagne than on any firm economic or political foundation, the Carolingian Empire did not survive the emperor's death in 814. (© 2016 Cengage Learning.)

Islamic, Byzantine, or Roman standards. The empire was divided into about 250 counties administered by counts—nobles personally loyal to the ruler. Men from powerful families, the counts served as generals, judges, and administrators, implementing the king's decisions. To supervise the counts, Charlemagne created *missi dominici* (royal messengers)—generally two laymen and a bishop or abbot—who made annual journeys to the different counties. The purpose of the missi dominici was to prevent counts and their subordinates from abusing their power and undermining Charlemagne's authority.

On Christmas Day in Rome in the year 800, Pope Leo III crowned Charlemagne Emperor of the Romans. The initiative for the coronation probably came from the papacy, not from Charlemagne. The meaning of this event has aroused conflicting opinions among historians, but certain conclusions seem justified. The title signified that the tradition of a world empire still survived despite the demise of the western Roman Empire three hundred years earlier. But because it was the pope who crowned Charlemagne, this meant that the emperor had a spiritual responsibility to spread and defend the faith. Thus, Roman universalism was fused with Christian universalism.

The Frankish Empire, of course, was only a dim shadow of the Roman Empire. The Franks had no Roman law or Roman legions; there were no cities that were centers of economic and cultural activity; and officials were not trained civil servants with a world outlook, but uneducated war chieftains with a tribal viewpoint. Yet Charlemagne's empire did embody the concept of a universal Christian empire, an ideal that would endure throughout the Middle Ages.

The crowning of a Germanic ruler as emperor of the Romans by the head of the church represented the merging of Germanic, Roman, and Christian traditions, which is the essential characteristic of medieval civilization. This blending of traditions was also evident on a cultural plane, for Charlemagne, a Germanic warrior-king, showed respect for classical learning and Christianity, both non-Germanic traditions.

Carolingian Renaissance

Charlemagne felt that it was his religious duty to raise the educational level of the clergy so that they understood and could properly teach the faith. To do so required overcoming the illiteracy or semiliteracy of clergymen and preparing sacred Scriptures that were uniform, complete, and free of errors. Charlemagne also fostered education to train administrators who would be capable of overseeing his empire and the royal estates; such men had to be literate. He himself learned Latin and spoke it fluently.

To achieve his purpose, Charlemagne gathered some of the finest scholars in Europe. Alcuin of York, England (735–804), was given charge of the palace school attended by Charlemagne and his sons and daughters, high lords, and youths training to serve the emperor. Throughout France, Alcuin expanded schools and libraries, promoted the copying of ancient manuscripts, and imposed basic literary standards on the clergy.

The focus of the Carolingian Renaissance was predominantly Christian: an effort to train clergymen and improve their understanding of the Bible and the writings of the church fathers. This process raised the level of literacy and improved the Latin style. Most important, monastic copyists continued to preserve ancient texts, which otherwise might never have survived. Between the fifth and eighth centuries, as libraries degenerated and books vanished or were burned, most classical literature was lost forever. The oldest manuscripts of surviving ancient Greek and Roman works are Carolingian copies.

Compared with the Greco-Roman past, with the cultural explosion of the twelfth and thirteenth centuries, or with the great Italian Renaissance of the fifteenth century, the Carolingian Renaissance seems slight indeed. Although it did rediscover and revive ancient Roman works and adopt Roman architecture and artistic forms, it did not recapture the worldly spirit of Greece and Rome. Carolingian scholars did not seek to appreciate or replicate the humanist values of classical culture, which aspired to the full development of man's talents and worldly accomplishments; they did not engage in independent philosophical speculation or search for new knowledge, nor did they achieve that synthesis of faith and reason that would be constructed by the great theologians of the twelfth and thirteenth centuries. The Carolingian Renaissance did, however, reverse the process of cultural decay, which had characterized much of the Early Middle Ages. Learning would never again fall to the low level it had reached during the centuries following the decline of Rome.

During the era of Charlemagne, a distinct European civilization took root. It blended the Roman heritage of a world empire, the intellectual achievement of the Greco-Roman mind, Christian otherworldliness, and the customs of the Germanic peoples. This nascent civilization of Latin Christendom differed from Byzantine and Islamic civilizations, and Latin Christians were growing conscious of the difference. But the new medieval civilization was still centuries away from its high point, which would be reached in the twelfth and thirteenth centuries.

Charlemagne's empire also engendered the ideal of a unified Latin Christendom: a single Christian community under one government.

Saint Boniface

Of the many English monks and nuns who converted inhabitants of the Netherlands and Germany, none was more important than Saint Boniface (c. 680–754). In 716, Boniface, then a monk called Wynfrid who had earned a reputation as a Latin scholar, left England for Frisia in order to restore the churches that had been destroyed when the Frisians revolted against Frankish rule and Christian proselytizing. Consecrated bishop in 722, he extended his missionary activity into Bavaria and Thuringia. Working closely with the papacy, he founded monasteries, including the famous Abbey of Fulda; converted pagans; and imposed Christian standards of behavior on both clergy and laypeople. For example, he prohibited idol worship and the selling of slaves to heathens for sacrifices. In a letter to Pope Zacharias, he expressed his displeasure with deacons who "have four or five concubines in their beds, still read the Gospel and are not ashamed or afraid to call themselves deacons—nay rather, entering upon the priesthood, they continue in the same vices, add sin to sin, declare that they also have a right ... to celebrate mass."[*] He also denounced "any layman, be he emperor, king, official, or count [who] may capture a monastery from the power of a bishop, an abbot, or an abbess and begin to hold property bought by the blood of Christ—the ancient fathers called such a man a robber, sacrilegious, a murderer of the poor, a devil's wolf entering the sheepfold of Christ, to be condemned with the ultimate anathema before the judgment of Christ."[†]

Boniface maintained a correspondence with his cousin Lioba, an English-born nun, who became abbess of the convent Boniface founded at Tauberbischofsheim, near the Main River. Shortly before his death, Boniface visited with Lioba at her convent. He urged her not to "forsake the land of your pilgrimage.... Hold bravely to your course, carry on the good work

This new collectivity would supersede the separate Germanic tribal units. Over the centuries, the pursuit of this ideal of a Christian world-state, Christendom, would inspire many people, both clergy and laity.

The Breakup of Charlemagne's Empire

After Charlemagne's death in 814, his son, Louis the Pious, inherited the throne. Louis aimed to preserve the empire, but the task was virtually impossible. The empire's strength rested more on the personal qualities of Charlemagne than on any firm economic or political foundation. In particular, it never developed an empire-wide system of taxation and a professional bureaucracy, effective administrative procedures that had sustained the Roman Empire for centuries. Moreover, the empire was simply too large and consisted of too many diverse peoples to be governed effectively.

Besides Frankish nobles, who sought to increase their own power at the emperor's expense, Louis had to deal with his own rebellious sons. After Louis died in 840, the empire was divided among the three surviving sons.

The Treaty of Verdun in 843 gave Louis the German the eastern part of the empire, which marked the beginning of Germany; to Charles the Bald went the western part, which was the start of France; and Lothair received the Middle Kingdom, which extended from Rome to the North Sea. The Middle Kingdom would become a source of conflict between France and Germany into the twentieth century. As central authority waned, large landowners increasingly exercised authority in their own regions. Simultaneous invasions from all directions furthered this movement toward localism and decentralization.

In the ninth and tenth centuries, Latin Christendom was attacked on all sides. From bases day by day, and heed not the body's weakness. Time is not long, suffering is not hard, if your eyes are set upon eternity."[‡]

When Boniface died, Archbishop Cuthbert of Canterbury praised him for bringing "savage peoples from their long and devious wanderings in the wide abyss of eternal perdition into the glorious pathways of the heavenly fatherland by the inspiration of his holy words and by the example of his pious and gentle life."[§] When Lioba died in 780, she was buried at Fulda to be joined with Boniface.

---

[*]*The Letters of Saint Boniface*, trans. Ephraim Emerton (New York: Columbia University Press, 1940), 80.

[†]Ibid., 140.

[‡]Quoted in Eleanor Duckett, *The Wandering Saints of the Early Middle Ages* (New York: Norton, 1959), 227.

[§]*The Letters of Saint Boniface*, 184.

in North Africa, Spain, and Sicily, Muslims ravaged regions of southern Europe, even as far as the suburbs of Rome. They deported shiploads of Christians to North Africa to be sold in slave markets. The Magyars, originally from western Asia and linguistically related to Finns and Turks, crossed the Carpathian Mountains in the ninth century and established themselves on the plains of the Danube; their horsemen launched lightning raids into northern Italy, western Germany, and parts of France. Defeated in Germany in 933 and again in 955, the Magyars withdrew to what is now Hungary; they ceased their raids and adopted Christianity.

Still another group of invaders, the Northmen, or Vikings, sailed from Scandinavia in their long, open, wooden ships to raid the coasts and river valleys of Western Europe. Superb seamen, the Vikings crossed the North Atlantic and settled in Iceland and Greenland; from there, they almost certainly traveled to and landed on the coast of North America. In addition to their conquests and explorations, the Vikings also produced rich poetry, excelled at crafts, and contributed greatly to the revival of trade in the High Middle Ages.

In pursuit of slaves, jewels, and precious metals hoarded in monasteries, the Viking invaders plundered, destroyed, raped, and murdered. Villages were devastated, monasteries were looted and their libraries set ablaze, ports were ruined, and the population was decimated. People prayed to be delivered from the fury of the Northmen. Trade was at a standstill, coins no longer circulated, and farms were turned into wastelands. The European economy, already gravely weak, collapsed; the political authority of kings disappeared; and cultural life and learning withered.

These terrible attacks heightened political insecurity and accelerated anew the process of decentralization that had begun with the decline of Rome. During these chaotic times, counts came to regard as their own the land that they administered and defended for their king. At a time when monarchs could no longer guarantee the safety of their subjects, the inhabitants of a district looked on the count or local lord, frequently a former Carolingian official, as their ruler, for his men and fortresses protected them. In their regions, nobles exercised public power formerly held by kings, an arrangement later designated as *feudalism*.

Wherever great lords failed to protect their territories from neighboring counts or from invaders, political power was further fragmented. In other areas, local nobles chipped away at a count's authority in his county. In his region, the local lord, aided by warrior-knights, exercised virtually supreme authority; people turned to him for protection and for the administration of justice. Europe had entered an age of feudalism, in which the essential unit of government was not a kingdom but a local region, and political power lay in the hands of local lords.

MEDIEVAL SOCIETY

Arising during a period of collapsing central authority, invasion, scanty public revenues, and declining commerce and town life, feudalism attempted to provide some order and security.

217

Feudalism was not a planned system devised logically from general principles but rather an improvised response to the challenge posed by ineffectual central authority. Feudal practices differed from locality to locality and in some regions barely took root. Although it was only a stopgap means of government, feudalism did bring some order, justice, and law during an era of breakdown, localism, and transition. It would remain the predominant political arrangement until kings reasserted their authority in the High and Late Middle Ages.

Feudalism made an enduring impact on Western civilization. It contributed to Western notions about honor, the deportment of gentlemen, and romantic love (see Chapter 11). Most important, feudal traditions laid the groundwork for the principle of limiting a king's power and for the practice of parliamentary government (see Chapters 10 and 12).

Feudalism was built on an economic foundation known as *manorialism*. Although pockets of free peasantry remained, a village community, or manor, consisting of serfs bound to the land became the essential agricultural arrangement for much of the Middle Ages. The manorial village was the means of organizing an agricultural society with limited markets and money. Neither lords nor priests performed economically productive work. Their ways of life were made possible by the toil of serfs.

Manorialism and feudalism presupposed a stable social order: clergy who prayed, lords who warred, and serfs who toiled. People believed that society functioned smoothly when individuals accepted their status and performed their proper role. In the words of an eleventh-century cleric,

> *Mankind, since the beginning of time has been divided in three, those who pray, those who cultivate, those who fight, and each of the three is comforted on either side by the two others. He who, forsaking the world, gives himself to a life of prayer owes it to the warriors that he is able to carry out his holy task in safety, while he owes his bodily nourishment to the farmers. Similarly, the farmers ascend to God through the prayers of the ecclesiastics and are defended by the weapons of the warriors. So also, the warriors are fed*

> *by the produce of the fields and benefit from the income therefrom, while the holy prayers of the pious whom they protect will expiate the crimes which they commit in battle.[6]*

A person's rights, duties, and relationship to law depended on his or her ranking in the social order. To change position was to upset the organic unity of society. And no one, serfs included, should be deprived of the traditional rights associated with his or her rank. This arrangement was justified by the clergy.

> *God himself has willed that among men, some must be lords and some serfs, in such a fashion that the lords venerate and love God, and that the serfs love and venerate their lord following the word of the Apostle; serfs obey your temporal lords with fear and trembling; lords treat your serfs according to justice and equity.[7]*

Vassalage

Feudal relationships enabled lords to increase their military strength. The need for military support was the principal reason for the condition of vassalage. A vassal was a knight who in a solemn ceremony pledged loyalty to a lord. This feature of feudalism derived from an ancient Germanic ceremony during which warriors swore personal allegiance to the head of the war-band. Among other things, the vassal gave military service to his lord and received in return a *fief*, which was usually land sufficient to support his needs. This fief was inhabited by peasants, and the crops that they raised provided the vassal with his means of support.

Besides rendering military assistance and supplying knights, the vassal owed several other obligations to his lord in return for the fief and the lord's protection. These duties included sitting in the lord's court and judging cases, such as the breach of feudal agreements between the lord and his other vassals; providing lodgings when the lord traveled through the vassal's territory; offering a gift when the lord's son was knighted or when his eldest daughter married; and raising a ransom should the lord be captured by an enemy.

Bishop Adalbero of Laon: *The Tripartite Society*

Medieval thinkers came to see their society divided into three different but complementary groups: clergy, lords, and serfs. Each group had its own responsibilities—priests guided the souls of the faithful; lords protected society from its enemies; and the serfs' toil provided sustenance for everyone. Written in about 1020, the following statement by Bishop Adalbero of Laon, France, illustrates the tripartite nature of medieval society.

The community of the faithful is a single body, but the condition of society is threefold in order. For human law distinguishes two classes. Nobles and serfs, indeed, are not governed by the same ordinance. . . . The former are the warriors and the protectors of the churches. They are the defenders of the people, of both great and small, in short, of everyone, and at the same time they ensure their own safety. The other class is that of the serfs. This luckless breed possesses nothing except at the cost of its own labour. Who could, reckoning with an abacus, add up the sum of the cares with which the peasants are occupied, of their journeys on foot, of their hard labours? The serfs provide money, clothes, and food, for the rest; no free man could exist without serfs. Is there a task to be done? Does anyone want to put himself out? We see kings and prelates make themselves the serfs of their serfs; [but in truth] the master, who claims to feed his serf, is fed by him. And the serf never sees an end to his tears and his sighs. God's house, which we think of as one, is thus divided into three; some pray, others fight, and yet others work. The three groups, which coexist, cannot bear to be separated; the services rendered by one are a precondition for the labours of the two others; each in his turn takes it upon himself to relieve the whole. Thus the threefold assembly is none the less united, and it is thus that law has been able to triumph, and that the world has been able to enjoy peace.

Question for Analysis

1. According to Bishop Adalbero, what was the virtue of the tripartite society?

Jacques Le Goff, *Medieval Civilization*, trans. Julia Barrow (Oxford: Blackwell, 1990), 255.

Both lord and vassal felt honor-bound to abide by the oath of loyalty. It became an accepted custom for a vassal to renounce his loyalty to his lord if the latter failed to protect him from enemies, mistreated him, or increased the vassal's obligations as fixed by the feudal contract. Similarly, if a vassal did not live up to his obligations, the lord would summon him to his court, where the vassal would be tried for treachery. If found guilty, he could lose his fief and perhaps his life. Sometimes disputes between vassals and lords erupted into warfare. Because a vassal often held land from more than one lord and sometimes was himself a lord to vassals, situations frequently became awkward, complex, and confusing. On occasion, a vassal had to decide to which lord he owed *liege homage* (prime loyalty).

As feudalism evolved, the king came to be regarded as the chief lord, who had granted fiefs to the great lords, who in turn had divided them into smaller units and regranted them to vassals. Thus, all members of the ruling class, from the lowliest knights to the king, occupied a place in the feudal hierarchy. In theory, the king was the highest political authority and the source of land tenure, but in actual fact he was often less powerful than other nobles of the realm.

Feudalism would decline when kings converted their theoretical powers into actual powers. The decline of feudalism was a gradual process;

CHESS PIECES. These grim and foreboding chessmen depict the medieval nobility's concern with combat. (© The Trustees of the British Museum/Art Resource, N.Y.)

conflict between the crown and the aristocracy would persist, with varying degrees of intensity, for several centuries, but the future belonged to the centralized state being shaped by kings, not to feudal fragmentation.

Feudal Law

Feudal law, which incorporated many features of traditional Germanic law, differed markedly from Roman law. Roman law was universal, having been enacted by a central government for a world empire. It was also rational, for it sought to be in accord with natural law that applied to all; and it was systematic, for it offered a framework of standards that applied to individual cases. Feudal law, in contrast, was local, covering only a small region. Moreover, it was personal. In the Roman view, the individual as a citizen owed obligations to the state, whereas under feudalism, a vassal owed loyalty and service to a lord according to the terms of a personal agreement made between them.

In the feudal view, lords and kings did not make law; rather, they were guided by tradition and precedent. They discovered and confirmed law by examining ancient customs. Therefore, feudal patterns of landownership, military service, and wardship came to be regarded as an expression of ancient, unchanging, and inviolable custom. Consequently, if the vassal believed that his lord had violated the feudal agreement, that is, had broken faith with him and had transgressed tradition, the vassal would demand restoration of customary rights before an audience of his fellow vassals. Often lords battled one another, believing that they were defending their rights. Similarly, lords claimed the right to resist kings who did not honor their feudal agreements.

Feudal Warriors

Feudal lords viewed manual labor and commerce as degrading for men of their rank. They considered only one vocation worthy: that of warrior. Through combat, the lord demonstrated his valor, earned his reputation, measured his individual worth, derived excitement, added to his wealth, and defended his rights. Warfare was his whole purpose in life. During the twelfth century, to relieve the boredom of peacetime, nobles staged gala tournaments in which knights, fighting singly or in teams, engaged each other in battle to prove their skill and courage. The victors in these pageants gained prestige in the eyes of fellow nobles and admiring ladies and received prizes—falcons, crowns, and substantial amounts of money. The feudal glorification of combat became deeply ingrained in Western society and endured into the twentieth century. Over the centuries, a code of behavior, called *chivalry*, evolved for the feudal nobility. A true knight was expected to fight bravely, demonstrate loyalty to his lord, and treat other knights with respect and courtesy.

In time, the church interjected a religious element into the warrior culture of the feudal knight. It sought to use the fighting spirit of the feudal class for Christian ends: knights could assist the clergy in enforcing God's will. Thus, to the Germanic tradition of loyalty and courage was added a Christian component. As a Christian gentleman, a knight was expected to honor the laws of the church and to wield his sword in the service of God. He was supposed to protect women, children, and the weak and to defend the church against heretics and infidels. The very ceremony of knighthood was placed within a Christian framework. A priest blessed the future knight's arms and prayed that the knight would always "defend the Just and Right."

Regarding the private warfare of lords as lawless violence that menaced social life, the church, in the eleventh century, imposed strictures called the Peace of God and the Truce of God. These restrictions limited feudal warfare to certain days of the week and certain times of the year. Thus, the church tried to regulate warfare according to moral principles. Although only partially effective, these religious restraints did offer Christian society some respite from plundering and incessant warfare.

Noblewomen

Feudal society was very much a man's world. In theory, women were deemed to be physically, morally, and intellectually inferior to men; in practice, they were subjected to male authority. Fathers arranged the marriages of their daughters. Girls from aristocratic families were generally married at age sixteen or younger to a man often twice as old. The wife of a lord was at the mercy of her husband; if she angered him, she might expect a beating. A French law code of the thirteenth century stated: "In a number of cases men may be excused for the injuries they inflict on their wives, nor should the law intervene. Provided he neither kills nor maims her, it is legal for a man to beat his wife when she wrongs him."[8] Although the church taught that both men and women were precious to God and spiritual equals, church tradition also regarded women as agents of the Devil—evil temptresses who, like the biblical Eve, used their sexuality to lure men into sin—and church law also permitted wife beating.

In Mary, the mother of Jesus, however, Christians had an alternative image of women to the image suggested by Eve, one that placed women in a position of honor. Devotion to the Virgin Mary reached its high point in the twelfth and thirteenth centuries with the growing belief in the Immaculate Conception (the idea, which later became a doctrine, that Mary was conceived free of original sin and remained free of sin throughout her life).* Moreover, medieval Christians believed

*The Immaculate Conception did not become Roman Catholic dogma until 1854, when Pope Pius IX promulgated the bull *Ineffabilis Deus.*

NOBLEWOMEN. At times, medieval ladies joined their husband's hunting party. (akg-images)

goods, required by the convent for admission.) The nunneries provided an outlet for the talents of unmarried noblewomen. Abbesses demonstrated organizational skills in supervising the convent's affairs. Some nuns acquired an education and, like their male counterparts, copied manuscripts and thus preserved knowledge and ideas of the past. The nun Hroswitha (c. 935–c. 1001) of Gandersheim, in Saxony, Germany, produced poetry, history, and plays. Inspired by the Roman poet Terence, she wrote six dramas—the first since Roman times—along with a history of Germanic rulers and one of her own convent.

As the lady of the castle, the lord's wife performed important duties. She assigned tasks to the servants; made medicines; preserved food; taught young girls how to sew, spin, and weave (she was responsible for providing the lord and his companions with most of the clothes they required); and, despite her subordinate position, took charge of the castle when her husband was away. If the lord was taken prisoner in war, she raised the ransom to pay for his release. Sometimes she put on armor and went to war. For amusement, noblewomen enjoyed chess and other board games, played musical instruments, or embroidered tapestries to cover castle walls. A lady might also join her husband on the hunt, a favorite recreation of the medieval nobility.

Agrarian Life

The origins of manorialism can be traced in part to the Late Roman Empire, when peasants depended on the owners of large estates for protection and security. This dependence increased during the Early Middle Ages, especially during the invasions of Northmen, Magyars, and Muslims in the ninth and tenth centuries. Peasants continued to sacrifice their freedom in exchange for protection, or, in some cases, they were too weak to resist the encroachments of local magnates. Like feudalism, manorialism was not an orderly system but consisted of improvised relationships and practices that varied from region to region.

that Mary, by dedicating her entire life to Jesus in his work of redemption, cooperated with him in his ministry and could intercede with him in behalf of individual Christians. The numerous artistic depictions of Mary as the Mother of God and the Queen of Heaven, as well as the multitude of churches named after the Virgin, are evidence of the popular piety that the cult of Mary generated throughout the Middle Ages.

Aristocratic girls who did not marry often entered a convent. (Peasant daughters, because they were needed on the farm—they probably worked as hard and as well as men—rarely became nuns. Moreover, their parents could not afford the dowry, payable in land, cash, or

A lord controlled at least one manorial village; great lords might control hundreds. A small manor included a dozen families; a large one, as many as fifty or sixty. The manorial village was never completely self-sufficient because salt, millstones, and metalware were generally obtained from outside sources; it did, however, constitute a balanced economic setting. Peasants grew grain and raised cattle, sheep, goats, and hogs; blacksmiths, carpenters, and stonemasons built and repaired dwellings and implements; the village priest cared for the souls of the inhabitants; and the lord defended the manor and administered the customary law.

The serf and his family lived in a dismal, one-room cottage that they shared with chickens and pigs. In the center burned a small fire, the smoke escaping through a hole in the roof. In cold weather when the fire was strong, the room filled with smoke. When it rained, water came through the thatched roof and turned the earthen floor into mud. The odor from animal excrement was ever present.

Poor roads, few bridges, and dense forests made travel difficult; thieves and warring knights made it unsafe. Peasants generally lived, worked, and died on the lord's estate and were buried in the village churchyard. Few had any contact with the world beyond the village of their birth. When a manor was attacked by another lord, the peasants found protection inside the walls of their lord's house. In many places, by the twelfth century, this building had become a well-fortified stone castle.

In return for protection and the right to cultivate fields and to pass these holdings on to their children, serfs owed obligations to their lord, and their personal freedom was restricted in a variety of ways. Bound to the land, they could not leave the manor without the lord's consent. Before serfs could marry, they had to obtain the lord's permission and pay a fee. The lord could select a wife for his serf and force him to marry her. Sometimes a serf, objecting to the lord's choice, preferred to pay a fine: "Thomas of Oldbury came on summons and was commanded to take Agatha of Halesowen to wife; he said he would rather be fined."[9] These rules also applied to serfs' children, who inherited their parents' obligations. In addition to working their allotted land, the serfs had to tend the fields reserved for the lord. Other services exacted by the lord included digging ditches, gathering firewood, building fences, repairing roads and bridges, and sewing clothes. Probably somewhat more than half of a serf's workweek was devoted to these labor obligations. Serfs also paid a variety of dues to the lord, most notably for using the lord's mill, bake-oven, and winepress.

Serfs did derive some benefits from manorial relationships. They received protection from roving brigands and warring nobles, and they possessed customary rights, which the lord generally respected, to cottages and farmland. But in a world periodically threatened with famine and epidemics, serfs faced an unrelenting struggle to survive, a struggle made all the more difficult by the contempt lords had for them. Medieval literature often depicted peasants as repulsive creatures—ugly, dirty, cowardly, and uncouth.

If a lord demanded more services or dues than were customary, or if he interfered with their right to cottages or strips of farmland, the peasants might demonstrate their discontent by refusing to work for the lord. Up to the fourteenth century, however, open rebellion was rare because lords possessed considerable military and legal power. The manorial system promoted attitudes of dependency and servility among the serfs; their hopes for a better life were directed toward heaven.

Medieval agriculture suffered from several deficiencies. Among them was the short supply of fertilizer; farmers depended solely on animal manure. Inadequate wooden plows and primitive methods of harnessing draft animals resulted in low yields. Yet as the Middle Ages progressed, important improvements in agriculture (discussed in Chapter 10) took place and had wide ramifications for medieval economic and social life. In the High Middle Ages, the revival of an urban economy and the reemergence of central authority would undermine manorial (and feudal) relationships.

❖ ❖ ❖

Notes

1. Speros Vryonis Jr., *Byzantium and Europe* (New York: Harcourt, Brace and World, 1967), 193.

2. *The Koran*, trans. N. J. Dawood (Baltimore: Penguin Books, 1961), 108–109.

3. Boethius, *The Consolation of Philosophy*, trans. W. V. Cooper (New York: Modern Library, 1943), 26.

4. Ibid., 29.

5. Ibid., 34.

6. Quoted in Jean-Pierre Poly and Eric Bournazel, *The Feudal Transformation 900–1200*, trans.

Caroline Higgitt (New York: Holmes and Meier, 1991), 149.

7. Quoted in V. H. H. Green, *Medieval Civilization in Western Europe* (New York: St. Martin's Press, 1971), 35.

8. Cited in Frances Gies and Joseph Gies, *Women in the Middle Ages* (New York: Thomas Y. Crowell, 1978), 46.

9. Quoted in G. G. Coulton, *Medieval Village, Manor, and Monastery* (New York: Harper Torchbooks, 1960), 82.

The Art of the Ancient World and the Middle Ages

1. Praxiteles. *Hermes with Young Dionysus*, c. 350 B.C.

(Archaeological Museum, Olympia, Archaia, Greece/The Bridgeman Art Library.)

The art of the classical period (c. fifth century B.C.) was important not only to the ancient Greeks but also to the Romans and to later generations, from the Renaissance to the postmodern period of the late twentieth century. Through the ages, classical art has been kept alive—adopted, adapted, altered, and appreciated—by artists and craftspeople. Why has the classical style remained at the forefront of artistic endeavor?

The classical period has given us the first works of the Western world to represent the human form with accuracy. The body itself was the sculptors' subject. Their aim was to shape their marble so as to make a general and schematic figure lifelike. Classical sculpture has been a powerful learning device for aspiring artisans from Michelangelo to nineteenth-century artists such as Auguste Rodin. Ancient sculptures—and plaster casts made from them—have been used as teaching tools by educators since the Renaissance. Learning to draw from casts of ancient works was the traditional first step in an artist's education; even many abstract artists of the twentieth century had a solid grounding in works of the classical period.

2. Venus de Milo. Greek statue from the first century B.C., probably an imitation of a fourth-century work. (Vanni Archive/Art Resource, N.Y.)

The balanced, rhythmical composition of classical sculpture and architecture is another element that has influenced later artists. Earlier works—from the Greek Archaic period (sixth century B.C.) as well as from ancient Egypt and Mesopotamia—are solid, blocklike, and devoid of any sense of movement. Classical sculptors, by contrast, were able to bring the stone alive with innovative poses, luxuriant drapery, and a careful balancing between relaxation and tension.

The works of Praxiteles embody the ideal of classical sculpture and offer visual proof that the Greeks' search for beauty and truth extended beyond their literature and philosophy.

Praxiteles (fl. 375–330 B.C.) is renowned for the quality of his marble sculpture, such as *Hermes with Young Dionysus* (Figure 1), considered one of his finest works. Little is known of Praxiteles himself, but much has been written about his art.

3. Lysippos. Roman copy of *Apoxyomenos (Scrapers)*, original C. 325–300 B.C. (Apoxyomenos (marble), Roman, (1st century AD)/Vatican Museums and Galleries, Vatican City/Bildarchiv Steffens/Bildarchiv Steffens/Ralph Rainer Steffens/The Bridgeman Art Library.)

The Hermes statue has many of the attributes that distinguish the best classical sculpture. The stance is relaxed: an S-curve takes the weight off one leg and shifts it to the opposite hip. This *contrapposto*, or counterbalanced, pose draws attention to every part of the god's body. The turned and slightly tilted head is a departure from the fully frontal works of earlier periods. The drapery is a careful, three-dimensional rendering of drapery in vase painting from the same period. It is realistic and so fluid that viewers might forget they are looking at marble.

A roughly contemporary work, the *Venus de Milo* (Figure 2) by an unidentified artist, embodies many of the same principles as the Hermes figure. Venus puts her weight on one leg, tensing some muscles and relaxing others. Drapery loosely covers her waist and has the look of soft cotton.

A contemporary of Praxiteles, Lysippos (fl. fourth century B.C.) is credited with changing the "canon of proportions" established by his predecessor Polyclitus. The canon of proportions rules that earlier sculptors followed in carving their masterpieces assured a certain uniformity in the rendering of the human form. Heads were always a certain proportion of the whole, eyes were placed at a certain level within the face, and so on. But the work of Lysippos is notably different.

One of Lysippos' best-known works, the *Apoxyomenos (Scraper)* (Figure 3), shows a youthful athlete cleaning himself with a *strigyl* (scraper) after exercising. What distinguish this work from the works of other artists are the proportions. Lysippos' youth has a smaller head and a more slender body. Although he stands with his weight on one foot, his hips are not as sharply angled as the hips of other classical figures, in which the S-curve is more clearly pronounced. Even the face of the athlete foretells a new era in art. Unlike the serene, perfect faces of other classical figures, the Apoxyomenos' expression seems thoughtful and dreamy, not remote and dispassionate.

Distinguished by its portrayal of emotion and drama, *The Laocoön Group* (Figure 4) is one of the most famous works of Western art. Dated to the second century B.C., the work depicts the death of Laocoön, a priest of the god Apollo, and his twin sons, killed by sea serpents because they tried to prevent the entry into Troy of the huge wooden horse in which Greek warriors were concealed. The sculptors, Agesander, Atheodorou, and Polydoros of Rhodes, convey the violence and intensity of events through the exaggeration of facial features, musculature, and pose.

This work from the Hellenistic period differs from its classical predecessors in its emotionality and exaggeration of the human form. Laocoön's face shows anguish over the loss of his sons, and his muscles bulge as he strains to wrest himself

4. Hellenistic Sculpture. *The Laocoön Group*, second century B.C. (Scala/Art Resource, N.Y.)

from the serpent's grasp. Laocoön's children are depicted as smaller than their father yet as fully mature men.

Many historians have described the art of Rome as unoriginal and deriving from classical Greek works. The Romans did make multiple copies of many Greek prototypes, but they also excelled in areas of the decorative arts in which we have no evidence of Greek virtuosity. The Romans developed distinctive styles in wall painting (fresco), mosaic, and minor metal arts; their contributions to architecture are also noteworthy.

Frescoes are made by painting directly on wet or damp plaster. Some fresco painters limit their work to small scenes; others cover entire walls with landscapes, people, and architectural elements. Roman fresco painters were adept at reproducing the look of marble and other materials. The *trompe l'oeil* (literally "fool the eye") style of Roman fresco painters demonstrates their skill at reproducing the world around them.

As can be seen in Figure 5, Roman painters were able to convincingly present three-dimensional objects on a two-dimensional

5. Detail of a Pompeian Wall Fresco, *Lady Playing the Cithera*, first century B.C. (Roman/The Art Gallery Collection/Alamy Limited.)

surface. This first-century B.C. fresco, *Lady Playing the Cithera* (a harplike musical instrument), from a villa at Boscoreale, near Pompeii, is an excellent example of the fresco painter's art. Though painted on a flat surface, the chair is set at an angle and projects outward toward the viewer. The chair's three-dimensionality is further emphasized by the placement of the young attendant, who stands behind it, holding on to its back.

Roman sculptors tended to follow closely the classical Greek and Hellenistic traditions. Some art historians assert that originality in Roman sculpture is evident only in lifelike portrait busts of the emperors, often planted firmly on the necks of copies of Greek or Hellenistic gods and heroes. To an extent, this is the case with the life-size *Augustus of the Prima Porta* (Figure 6), a work probably completed during the reign of Augustus (27 B.C.–A.D. 14) or shortly after his death and deification. Many elements of this work are direct borrowings from classical and Hellenistic prototypes. It is the head, however, that sets this work apart from its forebears.

The face of Augustus is a lifelike representation of the emperor, if we assume that the great number of coins bearing Augustus's image offer an accurate likeness. Unlike Greek sculpture, which idealized the human form, this Roman work presents an image that would be recognized by all who viewed it.

Roman works such as the Augustus statue also served as illustrations of contemporary events. Carvings on the breastplate in *Augustus of the Prima Porta* portray the Romans' victory over the Parthians. Pictorial narratives of other Roman achievements were sculpted on free-standing columns and triumphal arches, as well as on the walls of buildings. In this way, Roman rulers were able to transmit news and information throughout their vast empire to people who could not read or who did not speak Latin.

The art and architecture of the Byzantine era and the Middle Ages show a transformation in subject matter. Christianity, with its theme of resurrection and salvation, dominated the period. Both Latin and Greek churches used art to spread Christian teachings and to buttress their authority. Because few people could read or write, both churches relied on sculpture, painting, and drawing to convey the essence of Christianity.

Figure 7, the mosaic *The Court of Justinian*, from the Church of San Vitale in the Italian city of Ravenna, shows the emperor Justinian and his attendants and dates to C. A.D. 547. The emperor stands in the center of the scene and is flanked by officials and local clergy. The contrast between this work and the Boscoreale fresco (Figure 5) is noteworthy. Here, the emphasis is on two-dimensionality and the vertical. All of the figures face front; there is little attempt to show depth or three-dimensionality, except for the somewhat unsuccessful overlapping of figures. These Byzantine figures, with small heads, tiny feet, and disproportionate arms, are elongated and slender, unlike the figures of the Roman painting or the Greek sculptures shown earlier.

As political and spiritual ruler of the Byzantine Empire, Justinian is flanked by twelve companions, drawing a parallel between him and Jesus Christ. His golden halo brings to mind the one usually shown around Christ's head; the attributes of Christianity, including a cross, a censer (incense burner), and a shield bearing a symbolic version of Jesus' name, remind viewers of Justinian's dual roles.

Easily recognized symbols and images such as the halo became part of a common language for transmitting the message of Christ and the church. This is exemplified by the *Enthroned Madonna and Child*, from the Byzantine school (Figure 8) in the thirteenth century, in which the Madonna is shown in what now seems to be a conventional pose—seated on an elaborate chair or throne, facing front, holding the child on her left knee, and supporting him with her left hand. The Madonna is heavily robed, but the artist was able to depict the clothes with the fluidity of the painter responsible for the Boscoreale fresco (Figure 5).

The *Enthroned Madonna and Child*'s origins are Eastern—the Byzantine school having developed in Byzantium, the capital of the eastern Roman Empire. Byzantium (renamed Constantinople in A.D. 330) had a certain sphere of influence in the West, attested to by the Ravenna mosaic (Figure 7), and, as a result, a fusion of Eastern and Western styles is evident in works such as the *Enthroned Madonna*. What is typically Byzantine about this work are the richness of color and the use of gold—in the background and in the Madonna's robes. The faces of the figures owe more to Western art, however. Soft modeling and careful shading make them look almost as if they were superimposed by another artist at another time.

The *Last Supper* of the thirteenth-century Magdalen Master (Figure 9) preserves the austere and otherworldly emphasis of the Eastern style exhibited by such works as the Ravenna Mosaic. It captures a pivotal moment, when Christ announces to his disciples that he will be betrayed by one of them, and instructs them to commemorate him by consuming bread and wine as his body and blood. (Compare with da Vinci's *Last Supper*, Figure 5 in the art essay "The Renaissance.") This event becomes the basis for the Christian sacrament of the Eucharist.

The painting is two-dimensional. There is no depth, no background, and no foreground. The table does not recede into the picture. The objects

6. *Augustus of the Prima Porta.* (Scala/Art Resource, N.Y.)

on its surface seem stacked vertically one on top of another. The tablecloth lacks texture. The figures seated at the table are immobile, rigid, lifeless, expressionless, severe, and monotonously spaced. There is a prevailing impersonality in the composition.

The painting perfectly exemplifies the characteristic style of Eastern and medieval art, which is nonperspectival, usually two-dimensional, and profoundly impersonal.

At this point, Western art begins to undergo another transformation. Styles and subject matter change, paralleling developments in politics and society. Artists working at the end of the Middle Ages and on the verge of the Renaissance

7. Mosaic. *The Court of Justinian*, C. A.D. 547. (Scala/Art Resource, N.Y.)

include the brothers Jan and Hubert van Eyck. Figure 10 shows *The Last Judgement* (C. 1420–1425), one panel of a diptych (a two-paneled work) painted by one or both of them (the other panel portrays the Crucifixion). *The Last Judgement* illustrates some of the stylistic elements that distinguish these artists. The image is divided in two horizontally. In the upper half, which represents heaven, the mood is one of calm and order; below, on earth and in hell, pandemonium reigns. This suggestion of the promise of heaven and the threat of hell was intended to motivate people to heed Christian teachings and clerical authority.

The van Eycks portrayed this idea with a clarity and realistic feeling unseen in other works. Their virtuosity is paralleled by the work of a slightly earlier Italian artist, Giotto di Bondone (1267–1337), whose style also marked a definite break with his peers, and whose work stands on the cusp between the Renaissance and what preceded it.

Giotto's *Kiss of Judas*, in the Scrovengi Chapel in Padua, dates from 1305 (Figure 11). A work of the Late Middle Ages, or Gothic period, it represents a major shift in artistic direction; its life-like depiction of the human figures seen in the foreground anticipates later perspectival painting. To understand this change in representational art in the fourteenth century, it is necessary to remember what was happening in Italy at the time. Although the art was meant to reflect the kingdom of heaven, actual events in the kingdom on earth played a great role.

As noted earlier, Byzantium and Byzantine art influenced Italian art and society in the medieval period. Images, symbols, and techniques that flourished in Eastern workshops took root in Italy, culminating in what art historians call a neo-Byzantine style in the early thirteenth century, soon after the Crusaders conquered Constantinople in 1204. Italian artists adopted the Byzantine style, which had its roots in classical Greek prototypes. The combination of Byzantine, Greek, and native Italian styles produced the new way of seeing epitomized by Giotto.

8. Byzantine School. *Enthroned Madonna and Child*, thirteenth century. (Virgin and Child (tempera on panel), Byzantine, (14th century)/Church of Sveti Kliment, Ohrid, Macedonia/Giraudon/The Bridgeman Art Library.)

9. Studio of Magdalen Master. *The Last Supper*, late thirteenth century. (© RMN-Grand Palais/Art Resource, N.Y.)

11. Giotto di Bondone. *Kiss of Judas*, c. 1305, Scrovengi Chapel, Padua, Italy. (Alinari/Art Resource, N.Y.)

10. Hubert or Jan van Eyck. *The Last Judgement*, c. 1420–1425. (© The Metropolitan Museum of Art/Art Resource, N.Y.)

The High Middle Ages: Vitality and Renewal

Miniature painting of Flemish citizens receiving a city charter, Chronique de Hainout, fifteenth century. (Bibliothèque Royale de Belgique.)

- **Economic Expansion**
- **The Rise of States**
- **The Growth of Papal Power**
- **Christians and Jews**

Focus Questions

1. What were the signs of vitality and recovery in European economic, political, and religious life during the High Middle Ages?

2. What factors contributed to the rise of towns? What was the significance of the medieval town?

3. Why was there a conflict between church and state during the Middle Ages?

4. What prompted lords and commoners to heed the papacy's call for a crusade?

5. What conditions led to the rise of states? What were the essential differences characterizing the development of medieval England, France, and Germany?

6. What factors led to the rise of anti-Semitism during the Middle Ages? How does anti-Semitism demonstrate the power of mythical thinking?

By the end of the eleventh century, Europe showed many signs of recovery and vitality. The invasions of Magyars and Vikings had ended, and powerful lords and kings imposed greater order on their territories. Improvements in technology and the clearing of new lands increased agricultural production. More food, the fortunate absence of plagues, and the limited nature of feudal warfare contributed to a population increase. The revival of long-distance trade and the emergence of towns were other visible signs of economic expansion. Offensives against the Muslims—in Spain, in Sicily, and (at the end of the century) in the Holy Land—demonstrated Europe's growing might and self-confidence. So too did the German conquest and colonization of lands on the northeastern frontier of Latin Christendom.

Reform movements strengthened the bonds between the church and the people and increased the power of the papacy. During the High Middle Ages (1050–1300), the pope, as Christ's deputy, sought to direct, if not rule, all Christendom. European economic and religious vitality was paralleled by a cultural flowering in philosophy, literature, and the visual arts. The civilization of Latin Christendom had entered its golden age.

ECONOMIC EXPANSION

A period of economic expansion, the High Middle Ages witnessed an agricultural revolution, a commercial revolution, the rebirth of towns, and the rise of an enterprising and dynamic middle class.

Agricultural Revolution

During the Middle Ages, important advances were made in agriculture. Many of these innovations occurred in the Early Middle Ages but were adopted only gradually and were not used everywhere. In time, however, they markedly increased production. By the end of the thirteenth century, medieval agriculture had reached a technical level far superior to that of the ancient world.

One innovation was a heavy plow that cut deeply into the soil. This new plow enabled

Chronology 10.1 ❖ The High Middle Ages

910	Founding of the Abbey of Cluny
962	Otto I crowned emperor of the Romans, beginning the Holy Roman Empire
987	Hugh Capet becomes king of France
1054	Split between the Byzantine and the Roman churches
1061–1091	Norman conquest of Sicily
1066	Norman conquest of England
1075	Start of the Investiture Controversy
1096	First Crusade begins
c. 1100	Revival of the study of Roman law at Bologna
1163	Start of the construction of the Cathedral of Notre Dame
1198–1216	Pontificate of Innocent III: height of the church's power
1267–1273	Saint Thomas Aquinas writes *Summa Theologica*
c. 1321	Dante completes *Divine Comedy*

farmers to work more quickly and effectively. As a result, they could cultivate more land, including the heavy, moist soils of northern Europe, which had offered too much resistance to the light plow. Another important advance in agricultural technology was the invention of the collar harness. The old yoke harness worked well with oxen but tended to choke horses, which, because they move faster and have greater stamina than oxen, are more valuable for agricultural work. The introduction of the horseshoe to protect the soft hooves of horses added to their ability to work on difficult terrain. The widening use of the water mill by the tenth century and the introduction of windmills in the twelfth century replaced ancient, less effective, hand-worked mills for grinding grain.

The gradual emergence of the three-field system of managing agricultural land, particularly in northern Europe, increased production. In the old, widely used two-field system, half the land was planted in autumn with winter wheat, while the other half was left fallow to restore its fertility. In the new three-field system, one-third of the land was planted in autumn with winter wheat, a second third was planted the following spring with oats and vegetables, and the last third remained fallow. The advantages of the three-field system were that two-thirds of the land were farmed and only one-third was left unused and that the diversification of crops made more vegetable protein available.

Greater agricultural production reduced the number of deaths caused by starvation and dietary disease and thus contributed to a population increase. Grain surpluses also meant that draft animals and livestock could survive the winter. The growing numbers of animals provided a steady source of fresh meat and milk and increased the quantity of manure for fertilizer.

Soon the farmland of a manorial village could not support the growing village population. Consequently, peasants had to look beyond their immediate surroundings and colonize trackless wasteland. Lords vigorously promoted this conversion of uncultivated soil into agricultural land because it increased their incomes. Monastic communities also actively engaged in this enterprise. Almost everywhere peasants were draining swamps, clearing forests, and establishing new villages. Their endeavors during the eleventh and twelfth centuries brought vast areas of Europe

227

A Painting from an Anglo-Saxon Calendar, Eleventh Century. The heavy, iron-pointed, wheeled plough was of immense importance in extending farming to the heavier wet soils of northern Europe's lowlands. It made possible the growing agricultural exploitation of lands recovered from floodplains, forests, and marshes. (akg-images/British Library/Newscom.)

under cultivation for the first time. New agricultural land was also acquired through expansion, the most notable example being the organized settlement of lands toward the east by German colonists.

The colonization and cultivation of virgin lands contributed to the decline of serfdom. Lords owned vast tracts of forests and swamps that would substantially increase their incomes if cleared, drained, and farmed. But serfs were often unwilling to move from their customary homes and fields to do the hard labor needed to cultivate these new lands. To lure serfs away from their villages, lords promised them freedom from most or all personal services. In many cases, the settlers fulfilled their obligations to the lord by paying rent rather than by performing services or providing foodstuffs, thus making the transition from serfs to freemen. In time, they came to regard the land as their own. As a result of these changing economic conditions, the percentage of French peasants who were serfs fell from 90 percent in 1050 to about 10 percent in 1350.

The improvement in agricultural technology and the colonization of new lands altered the conditions of life in Europe. Surplus food and the increase in population freed people to work at nonfarming occupations, making possible the expansion of trade and the revival of town life.

The Revival of Trade

Expanding agricultural production, the end of Viking attacks, greater political stability, the growth of a considerable money supply, and an increasing population produced a revival of commerce. During the Early Middle Ages, Italians and Jews kept alive a small amount of long-distance trade between Catholic Europe and the Byzantine and Islamic worlds. In the eleventh century, sea forces of Italian trading cities cleared the Mediterranean of Muslim fleets, which had blocked trade. As in Roman times, goods could circulate once again from one end of the sea to the other. The expanding population of northern Europe provided a market for Eastern silks, sugar, spices, and dyes, and Italian merchants were quick to exploit this demand.

By the start of the eleventh century, the European economy showed unmistakable signs of recovery from the disorders of the previous century. During the next two centuries, local, regional, and long-distance trade gained such momentum that some historians describe the period as a commercial revolution that surpassed the commercial activity of the Roman Empire during the Pax Romana. A class of traders emerged, many of them former serfs who had started trading by taking to the road as humble peddlers. Gradually they acquired business contacts in other lands, know-how, and ambition.

Crucial to the growth of trade were international fairs, where merchants and craftspeople set up stalls and booths to display their wares: swords, leather saddles, tools, rugs, shoes, silks, spices, furs, fine furniture, and other goods. Each fair lasted about three to six weeks; then the merchants would move on to another site. The Champagne region in northeastern France was the great center for fairs because the count of Champagne provided protection for merchants from thieves both en route to and at the fair, judges to guarantee the enforcement of contracts, and the necessary equipment, including covered stalls and accurate scales.

The principal arteries of trade flowed between the eastern Mediterranean and the Italian cities; between Scandinavia and the Atlantic coast; between northern France, Flanders, and England; and from the Baltic Sea in the north to the Black Sea and Constantinople via Russian rivers. The fine woolen cloth manufactured in Flanders provided the main stimulus for commerce along the Atlantic coast, and Flemish merchants prospered. In exchange for Flemish cloth, Scandinavians traded hunting hawks and fur; the English traded raw wools; and the Germans traded iron and timber. A wine trade also flourished between French vineyards and English wine merchants. Progress in navigation, including the use of the compass borrowed from the Arabs, and improvements in sails greatly aided long-distance commerce.

Because of their strategic position, Italian towns, which by the thirteenth century had become great trading cities, acted as intermediaries between the trade centers of the eastern Mediterranean and those of Latin Christendom. In Egyptian and North African ports, Italian merchants established enclaves where they set up permanent residence and conducted business. Luxury goods from as far away as India and China were transported to Italy by Italian ships and then taken overland to parts of Germany and France. In addition, the Italians extended their trade and increased their profits by sailing westward into the Atlantic Ocean and then north to the markets of Spain, the Netherlands, and England. On return voyages, they brought back wool and unfinished cloth, which in turn stimulated the Italian

textile industry. Because individual merchants often lacked sufficient capital for these large-scale enterprises, groups of merchants formed partnerships. By enabling merchants to pool their capital, reduce their risks, and expand their knowledge of profit-making opportunities, these arrangements furthered commerce. Italian businessmen, taking advantage of the income obtained from trade and their numerous business contacts in several lands, pioneered in the growth of banking practices, particularly access to credit that could finance the construction of large trading ships and trading expeditions. The accumulation of capital and the emergence of banking institutions provided a stimulus for the growth of capitalism.

Increased economic activity led to other advances in business techniques. The development of banking and credit instruments made it unnecessary for merchants to carry large amounts of cash. The international fairs not only were centers of international trade but also served as capital markets for international credit transactions. Fair-going merchants no longer had to carry with them large quantities of stealable coins or gold and silver bars; instead arrangements were made to settle debts through bills of exchange presented to business agents or factors who were able to convert one currency into another. The invention of double-entry bookkeeping gave merchants an overview of their financial situation: the value of their goods and their ready cash. Without such knowledge, no large-scale commercial activity could be conducted on a continuous basis. Another improvement in business techniques was the formation of commercial law, which defined the rules of conduct for debts and contracts. Finally, a system of insurance emerged to provide protection for merchants whose goods were in transit. For a fee, a syndicate of brokers—the risk was too great for a single broker—would compensate the merchant whose cargo was lost at sea due to storms or piracy.

The Rebirth of Towns

In the eleventh century, towns emerged anew throughout Europe, and in the next century, they became active centers of commercial and intellectual life. Towns were a revolutionary

LOCAL MARKET IN FLORENCE. The birth of towns in the eleventh and twelfth centuries was a revolutionary development. Towns gave rise to a middle class that moved away from the outlook of traditional medieval society—clergy, lords, and peasants. This picture depicts the commercial vitality of a market in Florence. (RMN-Grand Palais/Art Resource, NY.)

force—socially, economically, and culturally. Because they provided new opportunities, other than food production, for commoners, towns contributed to the decline of manorialism. A new class of merchants and craftspeople came into being. This new class—the middle class—comprised those who, unlike the lords and serfs, were not affiliated with the land. The townsperson was a new type of person, with a value system different from that of the lord, the serf, or the cleric.

What spurred town growth was the increased food supply resulting from advances in agricultural technology. Surplus farm production meant that the countryside could support an urban population of artisans and professionals. Expanding trade also fostered urbanization. Towns emerged in places that were natural for trade: seacoasts, riverbanks, crossroads, and market sites. They also sprang up outside fortified castles and monasteries and on surviving Roman sites.

The colonies of merchants who gathered at these locations were joined by peasants skilled in crafts or willing to work as laborers. From a medieval record comes this description of a town taking shape:

> *After this castle was built, certain traders began to flock to the place in front of the gate to the bridge of the castle, that is merchants, tavernkeepers, then other outsiders drifted in for the sake of food and shelter of those who might have business transactions with the count, who often came there. Houses and inns were erected for their accommodation, since there was not room for them within the chateau. These habitations increased so rapidly that soon a large ville came into being.[1]*

Medieval towns were protected from outside attack by thick, high walls, towers, and drawbridges. Most towns had a small population. The larger ones—Florence, Ghent, and Paris—had between fifty thousand and a hundred thousand inhabitants by the start of the fourteenth century; Venice and Milan had somewhat more than a hundred thousand. Covering only small areas, these walled towns were crowded with people. Booths and wares of merchants and artisans lined the narrow, unpaved, and crooked streets, which were strewn with refuse—animal blood and bones dumped by butchers, rotten fish discarded by fishmongers, and human waste thrown from windows. Such unsanitary conditions reeked with stench and were breeding grounds for contagious disease.

During the day the streets were jammed with merchants hawking their goods, women carrying baskets, men carting produce and merchandise, beggars pleading, children playing, and thieves lurking. Markets consisting of open stalls displaying a wide variety of goods—foodstuffs, linen, woolen cloth, jewelry— were a vital part of town life. A festive occasion, such as a procession honoring a patron saint, sometimes brought traffic to a standstill. A hanging—in Paris decomposing corpses on gallows were a permanent fixture—a beheading, or the burning of a heretic was looked upon as another festive occasion and always attracted a huge crowd. At night, the streets were deserted; few people ventured forth because the few elderly watchmen were no match for the numerous thieves. Even greater danger came from fires, which raged through overcrowded streets lined with wooden houses. Quarrels between individuals or groups were often settled violently.

Merchants and craftspeople organized guilds to protect themselves from outside competition. The merchant guild in a town prevented outsiders from doing much business. Craftsmen new to a town had to be admitted to the guild of their trade before opening a shop. Competition between members of the same guild was discouraged. To prevent any one member from making significantly more money than another, a guild required its members to work the same number of hours, pay employees the same wages, produce goods of equal quality, and charge customers a just price. These rules were strictly enforced. Guilds also performed social and religious functions.

Guild members attended meetings in the guildhall, celebrated holidays together, and marched in processions. The guilds cared for members who were ill or needy and extended help to widows and children of deceased members.

Women took an active part in the economic life of towns, working with men, usually their husbands, in the various crafts—as cobblers, tailors, hatters, bakers, goldsmiths, and so forth. Women brewed beer; made and sold charcoal; sold vegetables, fish, and poultry; and ran inns. In many towns, the wives and widows of master craftsmen were admitted to guilds. These guildswomen had many of the privileges of a master, including the right to train apprentices.

Because many towns were situated on land belonging to lords or on the sites of old Roman towns ruled by bishops, these communities at first came under feudal authority. In some instances, lords encouraged the founding of towns, for urban industry and commerce brought wealth to the region. However, tensions soon developed between merchants, who sought freedom from feudal restrictions that interfered with their pursuit of financial gain, and lords and bishops, who wanted to preserve their authority over the towns. Townspeople, or burghers (a *burg* is a fortified town), refused to be treated as serfs bound to a lord and liable for personal services and customary dues. The burghers wanted to travel, trade, marry, and dispose of their property as they pleased; they wanted to make their own laws and levy their own taxes. Sometimes by fighting, but more often by payments of money, townspeople obtained charters from the lords giving them the right to set up their own councils. These assemblies passed laws, collected taxes, and formed courts, which enforced the laws. Towns became more or less self-governing municipalities, the first since Greco-Roman days.

The leading citizens of the towns, the patricians, were members of the merchant guilds who engaged in commerce, industry, and banking. Some patricians in the prosperous Italian towns enjoyed great wealth, owned considerable real estate, and conducted business transactions involving large sums. These people generally dominated town politics; often they obtained country estates and intermarried with the feudal aristocracy. Successful doctors and lawyers also belonged to the urban elite. Below them on the social scale were master craftsmen in the more lucrative crafts (goldsmiths, for example) and large retailers. Then came small retailers, masters in the less profitable crafts, and journeymen training to be masters. At the bottom were the laboring poor—the bulk of the population—who had no special skills and were subject to unemployment.

In virtually every medieval city, the church was the largest property owner. Because the church frowned on the pursuit of wealth, many businessmen had guilt pangs, particularly in old age, about the way they had earned their livelihood. Compounding their guilt and fear of hellfire was an awareness of having violated the church's strict prohibitions against practicing usury. To allay these concerns about the destiny of their souls, businesspeople often bequeathed money and property to the church. These bequests helped to finance hospitals and schools, which were the church's responsibility.

In a number of ways, towns loosened the hold of lords on serfs. "City air makes a man free," went a medieval proverb. Seeking freedom and fortune, serfs fled to the new towns, where, according to custom, lords could no longer reclaim them after a year and a day. Enterprising serfs earned money by selling food to townspeople. When the serfs acquired a sufficient sum of money, they bought their freedom from lords, who needed cash to pay for goods bought from merchants. Lords increasingly began to accept fixed cash payments from serfs in place of labor services or foodstuffs. As serfs met their obligations to lords with money, they gradually became rent-paying tenants and, in time, were no longer bound to the lord's land. The manorial system of personal relations and mutual obligations was disintegrating.

The activities of townspeople made them a new breed; they engaged in business and had money and freedom. Their world was the market rather than the church, the castle, or the manor. Townspeople were freeing themselves from the prejudices both of feudal aristocrats, who considered trade and manual work degrading, and of the clergy, who cursed the pursuit of riches as sordid and shameful and an obstacle to salvation. They revived the Greco-Roman ideal of active citizens devoted to their city. Processions, celebrations, and feasts commemorating holy days or memorable events in the town's history strengthened civic bonds. An emerging secular civic life, combined with the new value given to business and the need for some secular education in order to handle business transactions, produced an ideological counterforce to Christian otherworldliness that would gain momentum in succeeding centuries. The townspeople were critical, dynamic, and progressive—a force for change.

THE RISE OF STATES

The revival of trade and the burgeoning of towns signaled a growing vitality in Latin Christendom. Another sign of strength was the greater order and security provided by the emergence of states. While feudalism fostered a Europe that was split into many local regions, each ruled by a lord, the church envisioned a vast Christian commonwealth, **Respublica Christiana**, governed by an emperor who was guided by the pope. During the High Middle Ages, the ideal of a universal Christian community seemed close to fruition. Never again would Europe possess such spiritual unity.

But other forces were propelling Europe in a different direction. Aided by educated and trained officials who enforced royal law, tried people in royal courts, and collected royal taxes—all of which served to reduce the power of local lords—kings expanded their territory and slowly fashioned strong central governments. Gradually, subjects began to transfer their prime loyalty from the church and the lords to the person of the king. These developments laid the foundations of European states. Not all regions followed the same pattern. Whereas England and France achieved a large measure of unity during the Middle Ages, the areas that later became Germany and Italy remained divided, with numerous independent territories.

England

After the Roman legions abandoned England in the fifth century, the Germanic Angles and Saxons invaded the island and established several small kingdoms. In the ninth century, the Danes—one group of the Northmen who raided Western Europe—conquered most of Anglo-Saxon

England. But the Saxon kingdom of Wessex, ruled by Alfred the Great (871–899), survived. To resist the Danes, Alfred strengthened his army and built a fleet. To stem the decline of learning that accompanied the Danish invasions, Alfred, like Charlemagne, founded a palace school, bringing to it scholars from other areas. Alfred himself studied Latin and translated a work of Pope Gregory I into Anglo-Saxon. He also had other works translated into Anglo-Saxon, including Boethius's *Consolation of Philosophy*. Alfred's descendants gradually regained land from the Danes and re-established Anglo-Saxon control over the island.

In 1066, the Normans—those Northmen who had first raided and then settled in France—defeated the Anglo-Saxons in the battle of Hastings and became masters of England. Normans replaced the Anglo-Saxon aristocracy and ecclesiastical hierarchy. Determined to establish effective control over his new kingdom, William the Conqueror (1027–1087), duke of Normandy (in western France), kept one-sixth of conquered England for himself. In accordance with feudal practice, he distributed the rest among his Norman nobles, who swore an oath of loyalty to him and provided him with military assistance. But William made certain that no feudal baron had enough land or soldiers to threaten his power. The Norman conquest strengthened the king's position as never before.

To tighten royal control, William retained some Anglo-Saxon administrative practices. The land remained divided into *shires* (counties) administered by *sheriffs* (royal agents). This structure gave the king control over local government. To determine how much money he could demand, William ordered a vast census taken of people and property in every village. Census data, compiled in the *Domesday Book*, indicated the number of tenants, cattle, sheep, and pigs and the quantities of farm equipment throughout the realm. Thus, better than any other monarch of his day, William knew what the assets of his kingdom were. Because William conquered England in one stroke, his successors did not have to travel the long, painful road to national unity that French monarchs had to take.

Crucial to shaping national unity was the development of common law. When Henry I became king in 1100, England had conflicting baronial claims and legal traditions, which were a barrier to unity. These legal traditions included Anglo-Saxon

law, feudal law introduced by the Normans from France, church law, and the commercial law emerging among the town businesspeople. During the reigns of Henry I (1100–1135) and Henry II (1154–1189), royal judges traveled to different parts of the kingdom. Throughout England, important cases began to be tried in the king's court rather than in local courts, thereby increasing royal power. The decisions of royal judges were recorded and used as guides for future cases. In this way, a law common to the whole land gradually came to prevail over the customary law of a specific locality. Because common law applied to all England, it served as a force for unity. It also provided a fairer system of justice. Common law remains the foundation of the English legal system and the legal systems of lands settled by English people, including the United States.

Henry II made an early form of trial by jury a regular procedure for many cases heard in the king's court, laying the foundations of the modern judicial system. Twelve men familiar with the facts of the case appeared before the king's justices and were asked under oath if the plaintiff's statement was true. The justices based their decisions on the answers. Henry II also ordered representatives of a given locality to report under oath to visiting royal judges any local persons who were suspected of murder or robbery. This indictment jury was the ancestor of the modern grand jury.

The growth of an efficient financial administration paralleled the development of a strong judicial system. The Exchequer, the royal accounting office, was formed during the early years of Henry I's reign. Its officials saw to the collection of all revenues owed the king. Like the judges, these officials formed a class of professional administrators who were personally loyal to the king.

King John (1199–1216) inadvertently precipitated a situation that led to another step in the political development of England. Fighting a costly and losing war with the king of France, John had coerced his vassals into giving him more and more revenue; he had also punished some vassals without a proper trial. In 1215, the angry barons rebelled and compelled John to fix his seal to a document called Magna Carta, or Great Charter. Magna Carta is celebrated as the root of the uniquely English respect for basic rights and liberties. Although essentially a feudal document directed against a king who had violated feudal barons' rights, Magna Carta stated certain principles that eventually could be interpreted more widely.

Over the centuries, these principles were expanded to protect the liberties of the English against governmental oppression. Magna Carta stated that no unusual feudal dues "shall be imposed in our kingdom except by the common consent of our kingdom." In time, this right came to mean that the king could not levy taxes without the consent of Parliament, the governmental body that represents the English people. Magna Carta also provided that "no freeman shall be taken or imprisoned . . . save by the lawful judgment of his peers or by the law of the land." The barons who drew up the document had intended it to mean that they must be tried by fellow barons. As time passed, these words were regarded as a guarantee of trial by jury for all men, a prohibition against arbitrary arrest, and a command to dispense justice fully, freely, and equally. Implied in Magna Carta is the idea that the king cannot rule as he pleases but must govern according to the law: not even the king can violate the law of the nation. Centuries afterward, when the English sought to limit the king's power, they would interpret Magna Carta in this way.

Anglo-Saxon England retained the Germanic tradition that the king should consider the advice of the leading men in the land. William the Conqueror continued this practice by seeking the opinions of leading nobles and bishops. In the thirteenth century, it became accepted custom that the king should not decide major issues without consulting these advisers, who assembled together as the Great Council. Lesser nobility and towns-people also began to be summoned to meet with the king. These two groups were eventually called the House of Lords (bishops and nobles) and the House of Commons (knights and burghers). Thus did the English Parliament evolve, and by the mid-fourteenth century, it was a permanent institution of government.

Frequently in need of money but unable to levy new taxes without the approval of Parliament, the king had to turn to that body for help. Parliament used this control over money matters to enhance its power. The tradition grew that the power to govern rested not with the king alone but with the king and Parliament together.

WOMEN WORKERS. At times noble ladies fought side by side with men when their castle was attacked. Here women hurl rocks and shoot arrows at the attackers. (Bibliotheque Royale de Belgique.)

During the Middle Ages, England became a centralized and unified state. But the king did not have unlimited power; he was not above the law. The rights of the people were protected by certain principles implicit in the common law and Magna Carta and by the power of Parliament.

France

In the 150 years after Charlemagne's death, the western part of his empire, which was destined to become France, faced terrible ordeals. Charlemagne's heirs fought one another for the crown; the Vikings raided everywhere their ships would carry them; Muslims from Spain plundered the southern coast; and strong lords usurped power for themselves. With the Carolingian family unable to maintain the throne, the great lords bestowed the title of king on one of their own. In 987, they chose Hugh Capet (987–996), the count of Paris. Because many great lords held territories far larger than those of Hugh, the French

Map 10.1 **THE KINGDOM OF FRANCE, 1180–1314** Through wars, alliances, and marriages, French kings expanded their territory. (© 2016 Cengage Learning.)

king did not seem a threat to noble power. But Hugh strengthened the French monarchy by having the lords also elect his son as his co-ruler. This practice continued until it became understood that the crown would remain with the Capetian family.

With the accession of Louis VI (1108–1137), a two-hundred-year period of steadily increasing royal power began. Louis started this trend by successfully subduing the barons in his own duchy.

A decisive figure in the expansion of French royal sway was Philip Augustus (1180–1223). Philip struck successfully at King John of England (of Magna Carta fame), who held more territory as feudal lord in France than Philip did. When William, duke of Normandy, conquered England in 1066, he became ruler of England and Normandy; William's great-grandson Henry II acquired much of southern France through his marriage to Eleanor of Aquitaine (c. 1122–1204) in 1152. Thus, as a result of the Norman Conquest and intermarriage, the destinies of France and England were closely intertwined until the end of the Middle Ages. By stripping King John of most of his French territory (Normandy, Anjou, and much of Aquitaine), Philip trebled the size of his kingdom and became stronger than any French lord.

Louis IX (1226–1270)—pious, compassionate, and conscientious and a genuine lover of peace—was perhaps the best-loved French monarch of the Middle Ages. Departing from feudal precedent, Louis issued ordinances for the entire realm without seeking the consent of his vassals. One ordinance prohibited private warfare among the nobility. Another promoted the nationwide circulation of coins produced by royal mints. These ordinances furthered royal power and promoted order.

Under Louis IX and his successors, the power of the French monarch continued to grow. Kings added to their lands by warfare and marriage; they devised new ways of raising money, including taxing the clergy. A particularly effective way of increasing the monarch's power was by extending royal justice. In the thirteenth century, the king's court, the *parlement*, became the highest court in France. Quarrels between the king and his vassals were resolved in the parlement, and many cases previously tried in lords' courts were transferred to the king's court. Moreover, because the decision of feudal courts could be appealed to the parlement, lords no longer had the last say on legal questions.

At the beginning of the fourteenth century, Philip IV (the Fair) engaged in a struggle with the papacy (see pages 277–278). Seeking to demonstrate that he had the support of his subjects, Philip summoned representatives of the church (First Estate), the nobility (Second Estate), and the townspeople (Third Estate) to meet in a national assembly known as the Estates General. This assembly would be called again to vote funds for the crown. Unlike the English Parliament, the Estates General never became an important body in French political life, and it never succeeded in controlling the monarch. Whereas the basis for limited monarchy had been established in England, no comparable checks on the king's power developed in France. By the end of the Middle Ages, French kings had succeeded in creating a unified state, but regional and local loyalties remained strong and persisted for centuries.

Germany

After the destruction of Charlemagne's empire, its German territories were broken into large duchies. Following traditional Germanic practice, the ruling dukes elected one of their own as king. The German king, however, had little authority outside his own duchy. Some German kings tried not to antagonize the dukes, but Otto the Great (936–973) was determined to control them. He entered into an alliance with German bishops and archbishops, who could provide him with fighting men and trained administrators—a policy continued by his successors.

In 951, Otto marched into northern Italy in an attempt to assert his influence. Ten years later,

Thirteenth-Century Politics. The representative assembly, antecedent of the modern parliament, was an original achievement of the Middle Ages. Here the king of Aragon presides over the *cortes*, an assembly representing clergy, nobles, and townspeople. (PRISMA ARCHIVO/Alamy Limited.)

he returned to protect the pope from his Italian enemies. In 962, emulating the coronation of Charlemagne, the pope crowned Otto "Emperor of the Romans" (later the title would be changed to "Holy Roman Emperor").

The revival of the empire meant that the history of medieval Germany was closely tied to that of Italy and the papacy. Otto and his successors wanted to dominate both Italy, which had been part of Charlemagne's empire, and the pope—an ambition that embroiled the Holy Roman Emperor in a life-and-death struggle with the papacy. The papacy allied itself with the German dukes and the Italian cities, enemies of the emperor. German intervention in papal politics and Italian lands was the principal reason that German territories did not achieve unity in the Middle Ages.

The Emergence of Representative Institutions

One great contribution of the Middle Ages to the modern world was the representative institution. Representative assemblies, or parliaments, had their beginnings at the end of the twelfth century in the Spanish kingdom of León. In the thirteenth century, they developed in other Spanish kingdoms—Castile, Aragon, Catalonia, and Valencia—as well as in Portugal, England, and the Holy Roman Empire. In the fourteenth century, parliaments formed in France and the Netherlands.

Kings generally came to accept the principles that parliamentary consent was required for levying taxes and that the king should consult parliament about important laws and obtain its approval. By and large, the parliaments had grown out of royal dependence on the nobility for military support. Because of this dependence, monarchs considered it wise to listen to the opinions of the lords. Consequently, it became customary for the king to summon councils to discuss matters of war and peace and other vital questions. Since the high clergy constituted an important group in the realm, they too were consulted. As towns gained in wealth and significance, townspeople were also asked to royal councils. Leading nobles came to represent the nobility as an order of society; members of the upper clergy—archbishops, bishops, and abbots—represented the entire clergy; and

deputies from the towns represented the townspeople. An important tradition had been established: the duty of the monarch to seek advice and consent on issues of concern to his subjects. Perhaps the practice of representative government was influenced by those church lawyers who held that the pope should seek the guidance of the Christian community as expressed in church councils—meetings of representatives of the clergy.

To be sure, in succeeding centuries, parliaments would be either ignored or dominated by kings. Nevertheless, the principle of constitutional government—government by consent—was woven into the fabric of Western society. The representative parliament is unique to Western civilization; it has no parallel in the political systems of the non-European world. Originating in the Middle Ages, the representative assembly is a distinct achievement and contribution of Western civilization.

THE GROWTH OF PAPAL POWER

In the High Middle Ages, a growing spiritual vitality accompanied economic recovery and increasing political stability. It was marked by several developments. The common people were showing greater devotion to the church. Within the church, reform movements were attacking clerical abuses, and the papacy was becoming more powerful. A holy war against the Muslims was drawing the Christian community closer together. During this period, the church tried with great determination to make society follow divine standards: it tried to shape institutions and cultural expressions according to a comprehensive Christian outlook.

The Sacraments

As the sole interpreters of God's revelation and the sole ministers of his sacraments—sacred rites—the clergy imposed and supervised the moral outlook of Christendom. Divine grace was channeled through seven sacraments, which could be administered only by the clergy, the indispensable intermediary between individuals and God. On persons who resisted its authority, the church could impose the penalty of excommunication—expulsion from the church and denial of the sacraments, without which there could be no salvation.

The seven sacraments involved the church in the lives of individuals from birth to death. Baptism cleansed individuals—usually infants—of the stain of original sin. Confirmation granted additional **grace** to previously baptized young adults. Matrimony made marriage a holy union. Extreme unction, administered to the dying, was intended to remove the remains of sin. The sacrament of the Eucharist, derived from Gospel accounts of Christ's Last Supper, took place within a liturgical service, the Mass. In a solemn ceremony, bread and wine were miraculously transformed into the substance of the body and blood of Christ, which the priest administered, allowing believers to partake of Christ's saving grace. The sacrament of penance required sinners to show sorrow for their sins, to confess them to a priest, and to perform an act of contrition: prayer, fasting, almsgiving, or a pilgrimage to a holy shrine. Through the priest, the sinner could receive absolution and be rescued from spending eternity in hell. This sacrament enabled the church to enforce its moral standards throughout Latin Christendom. The final sacrament, ordination, consecrated men to serve as clergy.

Gregorian Reform

By the tenth century, the church was Western Europe's leading landowner, owning perhaps a third of the land in Italy and vast properties in other lands. However, the papacy was in no position to exercise commanding leadership over Latin Christendom. The office of pope had fallen under the domination of aristocratic families; they conspired and on occasion murdered in order to place one of their own on the wealthy and powerful throne of Saint Peter. As the papacy became a prize for Rome's leading families, it was not at all unusual for popes themselves to be involved in conspiracies and assassinations. Also weakening the authority of the papacy were local lords, who dominated churches and monasteries by appointing bishops and abbots and by collecting the income from church taxes. These bishops and abbots, appointed by lords for political reasons, lacked the spiritual devotion to maintain high standards of discipline among the priests and monks.

What raised the power of the papacy to unprecedented heights was the emergence of a reform movement, particularly in French and German monasteries. High-minded monks called for a reawakening of spiritual fervor and the elimination of moral laxity among the clergy. They particularly denounced the concern for worldly goods, the taking of mistresses, and the diminishing commitment to the Benedictine rule. Of the many monasteries that took part in this reform movement, the Benedictine monks of Cluny, in Burgundy, France, were the most influential.

In the middle of the eleventh century, popes came under the influence of the monastic reformers. In 1059, a special synod, convened by the reform-minded Pope Nicholas II, moved to end the interference of Roman nobles and German Holy Roman Emperors in choosing the pope. Henceforth, a select group of clergymen in Rome, called *cardinals,* would be responsible for picking a new pontiff.

The reform movement found its most zealous exponent in the person of Hildebrand, who became Pope Gregory VII in 1073. Gregory insisted that human society was part of a divinely ordered universe, governed by God's universal law, and as the supreme spiritual leader of Christendom, the pope was charged with the mission of establishing a Christian society on earth. As successor to Saint Peter, the pope had the final word on matters of faith and doctrine. All bishops came under his authority; so too did kings, whose powers should be used for Christian ends. Disobeying the pope, God's viceroy on earth, constituted disobedience to God himself. The pope was responsible for instructing rulers in the proper use of their God-given powers, and kings had the solemn duty to obey these instructions. If the king failed in his Christian duty, the pope could deny him his right to rule. Responsible for implementing God's law, the pope could never take a subordinate position to kings.

Like no other pope before him, Gregory VII made a determined effort to assert the preeminence of the papacy over both the church hierarchy and secular rulers. This determination led to a bitter struggle between the papacy and the German monarch and future Holy Roman Emperor Henry IV. The dispute was a dramatic confrontation between two competing versions of the relationship between secular and spiritual authority.

Through his reforms, Gregory VII intended to improve the moral quality of the clergy and to liberate the church from all control by secular authorities. He forbade priests who had wives or concubines to celebrate Mass, deposed clergy who had bought their offices, excommunicated bishops and abbots who had received their estates from a lay lord, and expelled from the church lay lords who invested bishops with their office. The appointment of bishops, Pope Gregory insisted, should be controlled entirely by the church.

This last point touched off the conflict, called the Investiture Controversy, between King Henry and Pope Gregory. Bishops served a dual function. On the one hand, they belonged to the spiritual community of the church; on the other hand, as members of the nobility and holders of estates, they were also integrated into the feudal order. Traditionally, emperors had both granted bishops their feudal authority and invested them with their spiritual authority. In maintaining that no lay rulers could confer ecclesiastical offices on their appointees, Pope Gregory threatened Henry's authority.

In earlier times, seeking allies in the conflict with feudal nobility, German kings had made vassals of the upper clergy. In return for a fief, bishops had agreed to provide troops for a monarch in his struggle against the lords. But if kings had no control over the appointment of bishops—in accordance with Pope Gregory's view—they would lose the allegiance, military support, and financial assistance of their most important allies. To German monarchs, bishops were officers of the state who served the throne. Moreover, if they agreed to Gregory's demands, German kings would lose their freedom of action and be dominated by the Roman pontiff. Henry IV regarded Gregory VII as a fanatic who trampled on custom, meddled in German state affairs, and challenged legitimate rulers established by God, thereby threatening to subordinate kingship to the papacy.

With the approval of the German bishops, Henry called for Pope Gregory to descend from the throne of Saint Peter. Gregory in turn excommunicated Henry and deposed him as king. German lands were soon embroiled in a civil war as German lords used the quarrel to strike at Henry's power. Finally, Henry's troops crossed the Alps, successfully attacked Rome, and installed a new pope, who crowned Henry emperor of the Romans. Gregory died in exile in 1085.

In 1122, the papacy and Emperor Henry V reached a compromise. Bishops were to be elected exclusively by the church and invested with the staff and the ring—symbols of spiritual power— by the archbishop, not the king. This change signified that a bishop owed his role as spiritual leader to the church only. But the king would grant the bishop the scepter, to indicate that the bishop was also the recipient of a fief and the king's vassal, owing feudal obligations to the crown. This compromise, called the Concordat of Worms, recognized the dual function of the bishop as a spiritual leader in the church and a feudal landowner. Similar settlements had been reached with the kings of France and England several years earlier.

The conflict between the papacy and the German rulers continued after the Concordat of Worms—a contest for supremacy between the heir of Saint Peter and the heir of Charlemagne. German monarchs wanted to control the papacy and the prosperous northern Italian cities. When Frederick I (1152–1190), known as Frederick Barbarossa (Red Beard), tried to assert authority over these cities, they resisted. In 1176, the armies of an alliance of Italian cities, supported by the pope, trounced Frederick's forces at the battle of Legnano. The Italian infantry showed that it could defeat knights on horseback, and Frederick was compelled to recognize the independence of the Italian cities. His numerous expeditions to Italy weakened his authority. German princes strengthened themselves at the expense of the monarchy, thereby continuing to preclude German unity.

The Crusades

Like the movement for spiritual renewal associated with the Cluniac reformers, the Crusades—wars to regain the Holy Land from the Muslims—were an outpouring of Christian zeal and an attempt by the papacy to assert its preeminence. Along with the renewal of commerce and the growth of towns, the Crusades were a sign of vitality and self-confidence in Western Europe. The victims of earlier Muslim attacks, Latin Christians now took the offensive. Furthermore, the Crusades were part of a general movement of European expansion during the High Middle Ages. Latin Christians were venturing forth as pioneers to open new lands to cultivation and as conquerors to expand the borders of Christendom.

By the middle of the eleventh century, forces from the cities of Genoa and Pisa had driven the Muslims from Sardinia. By 1091, Normans had taken Sicily from the Muslims and southern Italy from Byzantium. With the support of the papacy, Christian knights engaged in the long struggle to drive the Muslims from Spain; by 1248, after more than two centuries of conflict, only the small southern kingdom of Granada remained in Muslim hands. Germans conquered and colonized lands south of the Baltic coast inhabited by non-Christian Slavs, Balts, and Prussians. German settlers brought with them Christianity and German language and culture. They cleared vast tracts of virgin land for farming and established towns, bishoprics, and monasteries in a region where urban life had been virtually unknown.

In the eleventh century, the Seljuk Turks, who had earlier embraced Islam, conquered vast regions of the Near East, including Anatolia, a province of the Byzantine Empire. With the death of the Turkish sultan in 1092, the Seljuk Empire broke up, which reduced the pressure on Byzantium. Seeking to strengthen his army

DEPICTION OF THE SIEGE OF TYRE IN 1124. The fall of the city gave Christians control of the Syrian coast. (William of Tyre (c.1130–85)/Bibliothèque Nationale, Paris, France/The Bridgeman Art Library.)

in preparation for the reconquest of Anatolia, Byzantine emperor Alexius appealed to Western rulers for mercenaries.

Pope Urban II, at the Council of Clermont (in France) in 1095, exaggerated the danger confronting Eastern Christianity. He called for a holy crusade against the heathen Turks, whom he accused of defiling and destroying Christian churches. Several months later, he expanded his objectives to include the conquest of Jerusalem. A Christian army, mobilized by the papacy to defend the faith and to regain the Holy Land from nonbelievers, accorded with the papal concept of a just war; it would channel the endemic violence of Europe's warrior class in a Christian direction. A crusade against the Muslims also held the promise of bringing the Eastern church, which had formally broken with Rome in 1054, under papal leadership. In organizing a crusade for Christian ends, Urban II, like Gregory VII in his struggle with Henry IV, sought to demonstrate the supremacy of the pope.

What motivated the knights and others who responded to Urban's appeal? To some younger sons with no hope of inheriting land at home, a crusade offered an opportunity to gain land by conquest. No doubt the Crusaders regarded themselves as armed and pious pilgrims dedicated to rescuing holy places from the hated Muslims. Through the years, Christian pilgrims had made the journey to Jerusalem to do penance for crimes against the church and to demonstrate their piety. These pilgrims and other devout Christians found it deplorable that Christian holy places were controlled by heathen Muslims. Moreover, Urban declared that participation in a crusade was itself an act of penance, an acceptable way of demonstrating sorrow for sin. In their eagerness to recruit warriors, popular preachers went even further: they promised cancellation of penalties for sin. To a knight, a crusade was no doubt a great adventure that promised land, glory, and plunder, but it was also an opportunity to remit

Map 10.2 **THE HOLY ROMAN EMPIRE, c. 1200** ▶
Unable to overcome the German princes, Holy Roman Emperors, unlike French and English rulers, could not build a unified state during the Middle Ages. Germany did not achieve unity until the late nineteenth century. (© 2016 Cengage Learning.)

sins by engaging in a holy war. The enthusiasm with which knights became Christian warriors demonstrated the extent to which the warrior mentality of the nobles had become permeated by Christian principles.

Stirred by popular preachers, the common people also became gripped by the crusading spirit. The most remarkable of the evangelists was Peter the Hermit, who rode his donkey through the French countryside arousing the religious zeal of plain folk. Swayed by the old man's eloquence, thousands of poor people abandoned their villages and joined Peter's march to Jerusalem. As this army of the poor crossed Germany, the credulous peasants expected to find Jerusalem just beyond the horizon; some thought that Peter was leading them straight to heaven. While Peter's army made its way to Constantinople, another army of commoners recruited in Germany sought to do God's work by massacring the Jews of the Rhineland, despite the efforts of bishops to protect them. Unlike Peter's army, these commoners never reached Constantinople; after plundering Hungary, they were slaughtered by Hungarians (Magyars). Camped in the suburbs of Constantinople, Peter's restless recruits crossed from Byzantine-controlled land into Turkish territory, where they too were massacred. Faith alone could not win Jerusalem.

Departing later than the commoners, an army of knights assembled at Constantinople in the spring of 1097. After enduring the long march through Anatolia, the Christian army arrived at Antioch in Syria, which it captured after a long siege. In June 1099, three years after Urban's appeal, the soldiers of the First Crusade (1096–1099) stood outside the walls of Jerusalem. Using siege weapons, they broke into the city and slaughtered Muslims and Jews. An eyewitness recorded the scene.

It was impossible to look upon the vast numbers of the slain without horror; everywhere lay fragments of human bodies, and the very ground was covered with the blood of the slain . . . headless bodies and mutilated limbs strewn in all directions. . . . The soldiers roved through the city in search of wretched survivors who might be hiding. . . . These were dragged out. . . . and slain like sheep. . . . Some. . . . broke into houses where they laid violent hands on heads of families, on

CAPTURE OF JERUSALEM. Gripped by religious frenzy, the Crusaders, "dripping with blood," massacred the Muslim and Jewish inhabitants of Jerusalem. (Snark/Art Resource, N.Y.)

their wives [and] children, these victims were either put to the sword or dashed headlong to the ground from some elevated place. . . . When at last the city had been set in order in this way, arms were laid aside. Then, clad in fresh garments, with clean hands and bare feet, in humility and contrition, [the victors] began to make the rounds of the venerable places which the Saviour had deigned to sanctify and make glorious with His bodily presence. With tearful sighs and heartfelt emotion they pressed kisses upon these revered spots.[2]

Weakened by local rivalries and religious quarrels, the Muslim world failed to unite against the Christian invaders, who, besides capturing

Map 10.3 THE ROUTES OF THE CRUSADES ▶
In 1291, almost two hundred years after Pope Urban II's appeal for a crusade, the last Christian stronghold in the Near East had fallen.

(© 2016 Cengage Learning.)

ISLAMIC

HOLY LAND

Manzikert 1071

Edessa 1044

Damascus

Antioch 1097

ISLAMIC

Jerusalem 1099, 1189

Acre 1191

Ascalon 1099

SELJUK TURKS

Iconium

Nicaea

Dorulaeum 1097

Tripoli

Cyprus

Damietta

KINGDOM OF THE
EGYPTIAN FATAMIDS

Red Sea

Nile R.

400 Mi.

400 Km.

200

200

Black Sea

Constantinople 1204

Smyrna

Louis VII

Conrad III

Alexandria

Dnieper R.

Danube R.

Frederick Barbarossa

HUNGARY

Belgrade

Vienna

Durazzo

Brindisi

Messina

GREEK
to
ORTHODOX

Richard the Lion-Hearted

Crete

Candia

Philip Augustus

ISLAMIC

Mediterranean Sea

NORTH AFRICA

Baltic Sea

HOLY ROMAN
EMPIRE

Ratisbon (Regensburg)

Rhine R.

Metz

LATIN
CHRISTIAN

Zara

Venice

Florence

Milan

Rome

Pisa

Sicily

Sardinia

Corsica

Marseilles

Tunis

North Sea

ENGLAND

London

Paris

Vezelay

Lyons

Clermont

FRANCE

Toulouse

Loire R.

Philip Augustus

Richard the Lion-Hearted

ATLANTIC
OCEAN

SPAIN

GRANADA

Lisbon

ISLAMIC

First Crusade, 1096–1099
Second Crusade, 1147–1149
Third Crusade, 1189–1192
Fourth Crusade, 1202–1204
Crusader kingdoms in the East
Major battle with date

243

Saladin

Salah al-Din Yusuf (1137–1193), known to the Western world as Saladin, recaptured Jerusalem from the Franks in 1187. Born into a prominent Kurdish family, Saladin served the emir of Syria, whose troops invaded Egypt in 1167. Rising quickly, Saladin was appointed vizier of Egypt and then confirmed as sultan of Egypt and Syria. After extending his authority over Muslim-controlled territories of Egypt, Syria, and Palestine, Saladin, deeply committed to jihad, turned against the Franks. In particular, he vowed to liberate Islamic holy places in Jerusalem from Christian control.

In 1187, Saladin lured the Franks into an engagement at Hittin, near Tiberias, in northern Palestine. Marching all day, the exhausted and thirst-crazed Franks suffered terrible losses when, in desperation, they threw themselves at the prepared Muslim lines, which blocked the Franks from reaching Lake Tiberias and its life-giving water. After the victory at Hittin, Saladin's forces took several Christian strongholds, most of which surrendered without a fight. Then Saladin turned on Jerusalem.

Living up to his reputation as a man of honor and magnanimity, Saladin made the Christian inhabitants of Jerusalem a generous proposal. If the Franks surrendered, Christians would be free to leave the city with their property, and Christian pilgrims would not be harmed. But the Frankish lords would not surrender without a fight the city where Jesus had been crucified. On September 20, 1187, Saladin's soldiers besieged Jerusalem and began battering its walls. A Muslim historian noted: "Then

Jerusalem, carved out four small states in Syria and Palestine. How long could these Christian states, islands in a Muslim sea, endure against a Muslim counteroffensive?

Never resigned to the establishment of Christian states in their midst, Muslim leaders called for a jihad, or holy war. In 1144, one of the Crusader states, the County of Edessa, in Syria, fell to the resurgent forces of Islam. Alarmed by the loss of Edessa, Pope Eugenius II called for the Second Crusade (1147–1149), which was a complete failure.

After 1174, Saladin, a brilliant commander, became the most powerful leader in the Muslim Near East. In 1187, he invaded Palestine, annihilated a Christian army near Nazareth, and recaptured Jerusalem. In contrast to Christian knights of the First Crusade, who filled Jerusalem with blood and corpses, Saladin permitted no slaughter. The capture of Jerusalem led to the Third Crusade (1189–1192), in which some of Europe's most prominent rulers participated—Richard I, the Lion-Hearted, of England; Philip Augustus of France; and Frederick Barbarossa of Germany.

The Crusaders captured Acre and Jaffa, but Jerusalem remained in Muslim hands.

Pope Innocent III, who called the Fourth Crusade (1202–1204), was enraged by the actions of the Crusaders. They had first attacked the Christian port of Zara, which was controlled by the king of Hungary, and then looted and defiled churches and massacred Byzantines in Constantinople. This shameful behavior, along with the belief that the papacy was exploiting the crusading ideal to extend its own power, weakened both the crusading zeal of Christendom and the moral authority of the papacy. It also left a legacy of bitterness and distrust that still taints relations between the Eastern Orthodox and other Christians.

Other Crusades followed, including even the Children's Crusade in 1212. Stirred by Stephen of Cloyes, a young shepherd boy who claimed that Christ had communicated with him, thousands of French peasant children, accompanied by priests, marched to Marseilles, where they expected the Mediterranean Sea to part, permitting them to continue their march to the Holy Land. When the began the fiercest struggle imaginable; each side looked on the fight as an absolute religious obligation. There was no need for a superior authority to drive them on."* On October 2, the Muslims rushed through the breached walls and captured the city. In stark contrast to the Christian conquest of Jerusalem in 1099, Saladin permitted no massacre and no plundering. The Franks could escape enslavement by paying a moderate ransom, and in an extraordinary display of tolerance, Saladin guarded Christian holy places from Muslims seeking revenge for earlier Frankish brutalities.

---

*Excerpted in Francesco Gabrieli, ed., *Arab Historians of the Crusades* (Berkeley: University of California Press, 1969), 130.

miracle did not occur, the children boarded seven ships offered to them by William the Pig and Hugo the Iron, two seemingly pious townsmen. Two of the ships were lost in a terrible storm, and the other five were captured by Muslim pirates, with whom William and Hugo had worked out a deal. The children were sold into slavery in North Africa, and as far as is known, none ever returned (one priest eventually did).

Despite other Crusades, the position of the Christian states in the Near East continued to deteriorate. In 1291, almost two centuries after Pope Urban's appeal, the last Christian strongholds in the Near East fell.

The Crusades had some immediate effects on Latin Christendom. They may have contributed to the decline of feudalism and the strengthening of monarchy because many lords were killed in battle or squandered their wealth financing expeditions to the Holy Land. The Crusades did foster trade between Latin Christendom and the East, but the revival of trade had already begun and would have proceeded without the Crusades.

The Crusades sparked an interest in geography and travel; introduced Westerners to new foods, clothing, and architecture; and became a theme in literature. Nevertheless, they did not significantly influence European intellectual progress. The Crusaders had no contact with Muslim centers of learning in the Near East; it was through Spain and Sicily that Muslim learning penetrated Latin Christendom and helped stimulate the cultural awakening of the twelfth and thirteenth centuries. Over the centuries, some have praised the Crusades for inspiring idealism and heroism. Others, however, have castigated the movement for corrupting the Christian spirit and unleashing intolerance and fanaticism in the name of God—including the massacre of Jews in the Rhineland and of Muslims and Jews in Jerusalem—which would lead to strife in future centuries. (It should be pointed out that none of Jesus' words as recorded in the New Testament could be used to justify these massacres.) The Crusades remain a crucial component of the ideology of contemporary Islamic extremists who denounce Israel as a hostile Crusader state and American forces in the Middle East as Christian Crusaders seeking once again to subjugate Muslim lands.

Dissenters and Reformers

Freedom of religion is a modern concept; it was totally alien to the medieval outlook. Regarding itself as the possessor and guardian of divine, and therefore ultimate, truth, the church felt a profound obligation to purge Christendom of **heresy**—beliefs that challenged Christian orthodoxy. To the church, heretics had committed treason against God and were carriers of a deadly infection. Heresy was the work of Satan; lured by false ideas, people might abandon the true faith and deny themselves salvation. The church could never create a Christian world community if heretics rebelled against clerical authority and created divisions among the faithful. In the eyes of the church, heretics not only obstructed individual salvation but also undermined the foundations of society. The church believed that it had a sacred duty to eradicate this moral defect.

To compel obedience, the church used its power of excommunication. An excommunicated person could not receive the sacraments or attend church services—fearful punishments in an age of faith. In dealing with a recalcitrant ruler, the church could declare an interdict on his territory, which in effect denied the ruler's subjects the sacraments (although exceptions could be made). The church hoped that the pressure exerted by an aroused populace would compel the offending ruler to mend his ways.

The church also conducted heresy trials. Before the thirteenth century, local bishops were responsible for locating heretics and putting them on trial. Gregory IX (1227–1241) started to use Franciscans and Dominicans (see next page) as official investigators, in effect creating a permanent tribunal, the Inquisition, directly under the pope's authority. An inquisitor and his staff established themselves in a region suspected of heresy. After taking testimony, often in secret, the inquisitors summoned suspects to answer accusations made against them. The accused were not told the names of their accusers, nor could they have legal defense or examine evidence of witnesses. They were tortured (torture had been sanctioned by Roman law), and those who persisted in their beliefs might be turned over to the civil authorities to be burned at the stake.

Religious dissent in the Middle Ages was often reformist in character. Inspired by the Gospels, reformers criticized the church for its wealth and involvement in worldly affairs. They called for a return to the simpler, purer life of Jesus and the Apostles. Reform movements drew support from the new class of town dwellers; the church often rebuked the way of life in towns and only slowly adjusted to the townspeople's spiritual needs.

The Waldensians. In their zeal to emulate the moral purity and material poverty of the first followers of Jesus, reform-minded dissenters attacked ecclesiastical authority. The Waldensians, followers of Peter Waldo, a rich merchant of Lyons, were a case in point. Peter was greatly moved by a passage in Matthew: "If thou wilt be perfect go sell what thou hast and give to the poor and thou shalt have treasure in heaven" (19:22). In the 1170s, Peter distributed his property to the poor and attracted both male and female supporters. Like their leader, they committed themselves to poverty and to preaching the Gospel in the vernacular, or native tongue, rather than in the church's Latin, which many Christians did not understand.

The Waldensians considered themselves true Christians, faithful to the spirit of the apostolic church. Repelled by Waldensian attacks against the immorality of the clergy and by the fact that these laypeople were preaching the Gospel without the permission of ecclesiastical authorities, the church condemned the movement as heretical. Despite persecution, however, the Waldensians continued to survive as a group in northern Italy.

The Cathari. Catharism was the most radical heresy to confront the medieval church. This belief represented a curious mixture of Gnosticism and Manichaeism—Eastern religious movements that had competed with Christianity in the days of the Roman Empire—and of doctrines condemned as heretical by the early church. Carried to Italy and southern France by Bulgarian missionaries, Catharism gained followers in regions where opposition to the worldliness and wealth of the clergy was already strong.

Cathari tenets differed considerably from those of the church. The Cathari believed in an eternal conflict between the forces of the god of good and those of the god of evil. Because the evil god, whom they identified with the God of the Old Testament, created the world, this earthly home was evil. The soul, spiritual in nature, was good but was trapped in wicked flesh. Because sexual activity was responsible for imprisoning the spirit in the flesh, the Cathari urged abstinence to avoid the birth of still another wicked human being. They also abstained from eggs, cheese, milk, and meat because these foods were the products of sexual activity. (This rigorous asceticism was demanded only of a select few, the *perfecti* [perfect ones]; simple believers could marry, and their diets were not restricted.) The Cathari taught that, since the flesh is evil, Christ would not have taken a human form; hence, he could not have suffered on the cross or have been resurrected. Nor could God have issued forth from the evil flesh of the Virgin. According to Catharism, Jesus was not God but an angel. In order to enslave people, the evil god created the church, which demonstrated its wickedness by pursuing power and wealth. They saw themselves as the true church, the successors of Jesus' apostles. Repudiating the existing church, the Cathari organized their own ecclesiastical hierarchy. People were impressed with the ascetic and moral lifestyle of the perfecti.

The center for the Catharist heresy was southern France, where a strong tradition of protest existed against the moral laxity and materialism of the clergy. When the Cathari did not submit to peaceful persuasion, Innocent III called on kings and lords to exterminate Catharism with the sword before the infection spread throughout Christendom. Lasting from 1208 to 1229, the war against the Cathari was marked by brutality and fanaticism. An army of crusading knights led by a papal legate assembled in northern France; it headed south, massacring heretics in the belief they were doing the work of God. Soon command of the crusading army passed to Simon de Montfort, a minor baron with great ambition. De Montfort slaughtered suspected heretics throughout the county of Toulouse, and for a short time he held the title of count of Toulouse. The crusading knights had effectively broken the power of the nobles who had protected the heretics. Innocent III sent legates to the region to arrest and try the Cathari. Under his successor, Dominican and Franciscan inquisitors completed the task of exterminating them virtually to the last person, a horrendous slaughter that some refer to as medieval genocide.

The Franciscans and the Dominicans.

Driven by a zeal for reform, devout laypeople condemned the clergy for moral abuses. Sometimes their piety and resentment exploded into heresy; at other times, it was channeled into movements that served the church. Such was the case with the two great orders of friars, the Franciscans and the Dominicans.

Like Peter Waldo, Saint Francis of Assisi (c. 1181–1226) came from a wealthy merchant family. After undergoing an intense religious experience, Francis abandoned his possessions and devoted his life to imitating Christ. Dressed as a beggar, he wandered into villages and towns preaching, healing, and befriending. Unlike the monks who withdrew into walled fortresses, Francis proclaimed Christ's message to the poor of the towns. Like Peter Waldo, he preached a religion of personal feeling; like Jesus, he stretched out a hand of love to the poor, to the helpless, to the sick, and even to lepers, whom everyone feared to approach. The saintly Francis soon attracted disciples, called Little Brothers, who followed in the footsteps of their leader.

To suspicious churchmen, the Little Brothers seemed to be another heretical movement protesting against a wealthy and worldly church. However, Francis respected the authority of the priesthood and the validity of the sacraments. Recognizing that such a popular movement could be useful to the church, Innocent III allowed Francis to continue his mission. Innocent hoped that the Franciscans would help keep within the church those members of the laity who had deep religious feelings but were dissatisfied with the leadership of the traditional hierarchy.

As the Franciscans grew in popularity, the papacy exercised greater control over their activities; in time, the order was transformed from a spontaneous movement of inspired laymen into an organized agent of papal policy. The Franciscans served the church as teachers and missionaries in Eastern Europe, North Africa, the Near East, and China. The papacy set aside Francis's prohibition against the Brothers owning churches, houses, and lands corporately. His desire to keep the movement a lay order was abandoned when the papacy granted the Brothers the right to hear confession. Francis's opposition to formal learning as irrelevant to preaching Gospel love was rejected when the movement began to urge university education for its members. Those who protested against these changes as a repudiation of Francis's spirit were persecuted, and a few were even burned at the stake as heretics.

The Dominican order was founded by Saint Dominic (c. 1170–1221), a Spanish nobleman who had preached against the Cathari in southern France. Believing that those well versed in Christian teaching could best combat heresy, Dominic, unlike Francis, insisted that his followers engage in study. In time, the Dominicans became some of the leading theologians in the universities. Like the Franciscans, they went out into the world to preach the Gospel and to proselytize. Dominican friars became the chief operators of the Inquisition. For their zeal in fighting heresy, they were known as "hounds of the Lord."

Innocent III: The Apex of Papal Power

During the pontificate of Innocent III (1198–1216), papal theocracy reached its zenith. More than any earlier pope, Innocent made the papacy the center of European political life. In the

Pope Innocent III: "Royal Power Derives Its Dignity from the Pontifical Authority"

In the tradition of Gregory VII, Innocent III (1198–1216), the most powerful of medieval popes, asserted the claim for papal supremacy.

The Creator of the universe set up two great luminaries in the firmament of heaven; the greater light to rule the day, the lesser light to rule the night. In the same way for the firmament of the universal Church, which is spoken of as heaven, he appointed two great dignities; the greater to bear rule over souls (these being, as it were, days), the lesser to bear rule over bodies (those being, as it were, nights). These dignities are the pontifical authority and the royal power. Furthermore, the moon derives her light from the sun, and is in truth inferior to the sun in both size and quality, in position as well as effect. In the same way the royal power derives its dignity from the pontifical authority; and the more closely it cleaves to the sphere of that authority the less is the light with which it is adorned; the further it is removed, the more it increases in splendour.

Question for Analysis

1. Why were papal claims likely to stir a conflict with royal rulers?

Henry Bettenson and Chris Maunder, eds., *Documents of the Christian Church* (New York: Oxford University Press, 1999), 123.

tradition of Gregory VII, he forcefully asserted the theory of papal monarchy. As head of the church, Vicar of Christ, and successor of Saint Peter, Innocent claimed the authority to intervene in the internal affairs of secular rulers when they threatened the good order of Christendom. According to Innocent, the pope, "lower than God but higher than man . . . judges all and is judged by no one."[3] Innocent demanded obedience to all his regulations, which he believed were the fulfillment of God's plans.

Innocent applied these principles of papal supremacy in his dealings with the princes of Europe. When King Philip Augustus of France repudiated Ingeborg of Denmark the day after their wedding and later divorced her to marry someone else, Innocent placed an interdict on France to compel Philip to take Ingeborg back. For two decades, Innocent III championed Ingeborg's cause until she finally became the French queen. When King John of England rejected the papal candidate for archbishop of Canterbury, Stephen Langton, Innocent first laid an interdict on the country. Then he excommunicated John, who expressed his defiance by confiscating church property and by forcing many bishops into exile. However, when Innocent urged Philip Augustus of France to invade England, John backed down. He accepted Innocent's nominee for archbishop, returned the property to the church, welcomed the exiles back, and, as a sign of complete capitulation, turned his kingdom over to Innocent to receive it back as a fief. Thus, as vassals of the papacy, John and his successors were obligated to pay homage to the pope and to pay him a feudal tribute. Innocent also laid interdicts on the Spanish kingdoms of Castile and León and on Norway and strove to make the Holy Roman Emperor subservient to the papacy.

Innocent called the Fourth Crusade against the Muslims and a crusade against the heretical Cathari. The culminating expression of Innocent's supremacy was the Fourth Lateran Council, summoned in 1215. Comprising some twelve hundred clergy and representatives of secular rulers, the council issued several far-reaching decrees. It maintained that the Eastern Orthodox church was subordinate to the Roman Catholic church, prohibited the state from taxing the clergy, and declared laws detrimental to the church null and void. The council made bishops responsible for ferreting out heretics in their dioceses and ordered secular authorities to punish convicted heretics. Insisting on high standards of behavior for the clergy, it also required each Catholic to confess his or her sins to a priest at least once a year and to perform the prescribed penance. Through this directive, the church tightened its control over the conscience of Europe. The council also decreed that in the sacrament of the Eucharist the body and blood of Christ are actually present in the bread and wine used in the sacrament. This meant that the priest at the altar was God's agent in the performance of a wondrous miracle.

CHRISTIANS AND JEWS

In their relations with heretics, pagans, and Muslims, medieval Christians demonstrated a narrow and hostile attitude that ran counter to the Gospel message that all human beings were children of God and that Christ had suffered for all humanity. Muslims were seen, in the words of Pope Urban II, as a "vile breed," "infidels," and "enemies of God." While the clergy denounced war among Christians, they considered it a duty to wage holy war against non-Christians. And knights regarded fighting the Muslims in Spain and the Holy Land as a heartfelt expression of their Christian ideals.

Medieval Christians also showed hatred for Jews—a visibly alien group in a society dominated by the Christian worldview. The First Crusade was a turning point for medieval Jews. Until then, there were few instances of organized violence against Jewish communities. If we are warring against God's enemies, reasoned zealous Crusaders, why not annihilate the Lord's enemies living in our midst? In 1096, bands of Crusaders, proclaiming that they were seeking vengeance against "Christ-killers," slaughtered Jews in French and German towns. The Crusaders were often aided by townspeople driven by hateful images of Jews and eager to seize Jewish property. The efforts of bishops to protect the Jews proved largely unsuccessful. In the German city of Mainz, more than a thousand Jews lost their lives. Some, in an act

of martyrdom, chose to kill themselves and their children rather than submit to forced baptism or face a crueler death at the hands of the Crusaders. One Latin contemporary wrote:

> *I know not whether by a judgment of the Lord, or by some error of mind, they rose in a spirit of cruelty against the Jewish people scattered throughout these cities and slaughtered them without mercy, . . . asserting it to be their duty against the enemies of the Christian faith. . . . The Jews of [Mainz], knowing of the slaughter of their brethren, . . . fled in hope of safety to Bishop Rothard. . . . He placed the Jews in the very spacious hall of his own house, [but the Crusaders] attacked the Jews in the hall with arrows and lances. Breaking the bolts and doors, they killed the Jews, about seven hundred in number, who in vain resisted the force and attack of so many thousands. They killed the women, also, and with their swords pierced tender children of whatever age and sex.*[4]

This venomous hatred of Jews unleashed by the First Crusade triggered numerous other massacres during the Middle Ages, at times fomented by clergy.

Viewing the Jews as possessions to be exploited, kings and lords taxed and fined them relentlessly and periodically expelled Jews from their territories in order to confiscate their property. In 1290, Jews were expelled from England, and in 1306, from France. Between 1290 and 1293, expulsions, massacres, and forced conversions led to the virtual disappearance of a centuries-old Jewish community life in southern Italy. In Germany, savage riots periodically led to the torture and murder of Jews. During 1348–1349, when the Black Death (see Chapter 12) raged across Europe, Jews were accused of spreading the plague by poisoning well water; thousands of them were burned alive in Basel, Freiburg, Strasbourg, Mainz, and other towns.

Several factors contributed to anti-Jewish feelings during the Middle Ages. To medieval Christians, the Jews' refusal to embrace Christianity was an act of wickedness, particularly since the church taught that the coming of Christ had been prophesied by the Old Testament. Related to this prejudice was the portrayal of the crucifixion

Anti-Semitism. Holding the Jews responsible for the Black Death, Christians committed mass murder. In Basel, several hundred Jews were herded into a wooden house and burned to death. Some six thousand Jews were burned alive in Mainz. Flames consumed another two thousand in a huge pyre outside Strasbourg, and their property was distributed to the local townspeople. In this picture depicting the slaughter of the Jews of Strasbourg, the townspeople evidently enjoy the spectacle. (Bibliothèque Royale de Belgique.)

in the Gospels. In the minds of medieval Christians, the crime of deicide—the killing of God— eternally stained the Jews as a people; medieval Christians saw Jews as dangerous, criminal people rejected by God and deserving of ceaseless punishment. Christian theologians taught that they were to remain forever in subjection to Christians. It was just such a view that led town magistrates and princes periodically to confiscate Jewish property, at times after burning the helpless Jews alive in a public spectacle. The flames of hatred were fanned by the absurd allegation that Jews, made bloodthirsty by the spilling of Christ's blood, tortured and murdered Christians, particularly children, to obtain blood for ritual purposes. Although some popes and emperors condemned the charges as groundless, it was propagated in vicious anti-Judaic sermons of itinerant friars;

this blood libel was widely believed by the credulous masses and incited numerous riots, which led to the torture, burning alive, and expulsion of countless Jews and the pillaging of their property.

The role of Jews as moneylenders also provoked animosity toward them. Jews were increasingly excluded from international trade and most professions and were barred from the guilds and in some areas from landholding as well. Hence, virtually the only means of livelihood open to them was moneylending—in reality an important activity in an expanding economy. This activity, which was in theory forbidden to Christians, aroused the hatred of the individual peasants, clergy, lords, and kings who did the borrowing.

The policy of the church toward the Jews was that they should not be harmed, and several medieval popes sought to protect Jewish life and property from wanton violence. But the church also wanted Jews to live in humiliation, a fitting punishment for their persumed act of deicide and continued refusal to embrace Christianity. Thus, the Fourth Lateran Council barred Jews from public office, ordered them to remain off the streets during Christian festivals, and required them to wear a distinguishing badge on their clothing, a symbol of their degradation. Christian art, literature, and religious instruction degraded Jews, depicting them as repulsive and grotesque and often identifying them with the Devil, who was very real and terrifying to medieval Christians. Such people deserved no mercy, reasoned medieval Christians. Indeed, nothing was too bad for them. Because Jews were seen as evil allies of Satan engaged in a diabolical plot against God and Christendom, Jew-hatred was regarded as an expression of Christian virtue, a message routinely spread by preachers. Deeply etched into the minds and hearts of Christians, the distorted image of the Jew as a contemptible creature persisted in the European mentality into the twentieth century.

Despite their precarious position, medieval Jews maintained their faith, expanded their tradition of biblical and legal scholarship, and developed a flourishing Hebrew literature. The work of Jewish translators, doctors, and philosophers contributed substantially to the flowering of medieval culture in the High Middle Ages. The foremost Jewish scholar of the Middle Ages was Moses ben Maimon (1135–1204), also called by the Greek name Maimonides (see profile in Chapter 11). In both Muslim and Christian lands Maimonides achieved fame during his lifetime as a philosopher, theologian, mathematician, and physician.

❖   ❖   ❖

NOTES

1. Quoted in J. W. Thompson, *Social and Economic History of the Middle Ages* (New York: Frederick Ungar, 1959), 2:772.

2. William of Tyre, *A History of Deeds Done Beyond the Sea*, trans. Emily Atwater Babcock and A. C. Krey (New York: Columbia University Press, 1943), 372, 373.

3. Excerpted in Brian Tierney, ed., *The Crisis of Church and State, 1050–1300* (Englewood Cliffs, N.J.: Prentice-Hall, 1964), 132.

4. Excerpted in A. C. Krey, ed., *The First Crusade: The Accounts of Eye-Witnesses and Participants* (Princeton, N.J.: Princeton University Press, 1921), 54–55.

Chapter 11

The Flowering of Medieval Culture: The Christian Synthesis

School of Bologna manuscript illumination. (Bildarchiv Preussischer Kulturbesitz/Art Resource, N.Y.)

Focus Questions

1. What conditions contributed to the revival of learning during the High Middle Ages?

2. What was the significance of medieval universities.

3. What were scholastic philosophers trying to accomplish?

4. How does the medieval view of the universe differ from the modern view?

5. How did religion pervade much of medieval philosophy, science, literature, art, and architecture?

Europe in the High Middle Ages showed considerable vitality. The population grew, long-distance trade revived, new towns emerged, states started to take shape, and papal power increased. The culminating expression of this recovery and resurgence was the cultural flowering in philosophy, the visual arts, and literature. Creative intellects achieved on a cultural level what the papacy accomplished on an institutional level: the integration of life around a Christian viewpoint. The High Middle Ages saw the restoration of some of the learning of the ancient world, the rise of universities, the emergence of an original form of architecture (the Gothic), and the erection of an imposing system of thought, called **scholasticism**. Medieval theologian-philosophers fashioned Christian teachings into an all-embracing philosophy, which represented the spiritual character of medieval civilization. They perfected what Christian thinkers in the Roman Empire had initiated and what the learned men of the Early Middle Ages were groping for: a synthesis of Greek philosophy and Christian **revelation**.

Not too long ago, some intellectuals viewed the Middle Ages as a period of ignorance and superstition, an era of cultural sterility that stood between the high civilizations of ancient Greece and Rome and the modern West. This view of the Middle Ages as a dark age has been abandoned, and quite properly so, for the High Middle Ages saw the crystallization of a rich and creative civilization. To be sure, its religious orientation sets it apart both from classical civilization and from our own modern secular and scientific civilization. But the *Summa Theologica* of Thomas Aquinas, *The Divine Comedy* of Dante, and the Gothic cathedral all attest to the creativeness and genius of the medieval religious spirit.

THE REVIVAL OF LEARNING

In the late eleventh century, Latin Christendom began to experience a cultural revival; all areas of life showed vitality and creativeness. In the twelfth and thirteenth centuries, a rich civilization with a distinctive style united the educated elite in the lands from England to Sicily. Gothic cathedrals,

253

Map 11.1 **MEDIEVAL CENTERS OF LEARNING** Medieval universities established in the West a tradition of learning that has never died. There is direct continuity between the universities of our own day and the medieval centers of learning.

(© 2016 Cengage Learning.)

an enduring testament to the creativeness of the religious impulse, were erected throughout Europe. Universities sprang up in several cities. Roman authors were again read, and their style was imitated. The quality of written Latin—the language of the church, learning, and education—improved, and secular and religious poetry, both in Latin and in the vernacular, abounded.

Roman law emerged anew in Italy, spread to northern Europe, and regained its importance (lost since Roman times) as worthy of study. Some key works of ancient Greece were translated into Latin and studied in universities. Employing the rational tradition of Greece, men of genius harmonized Christian doctrines and Greek philosophy. During this period, the status and influence of learned men grew considerably. The revival of classical works was accompanied by the increasing importance of vernacular literature.

Several conditions contributed to this cultural explosion, known as the Twelfth-Century Awakening. As attacks of Vikings, Muslims, and Magyars ended and kings and great lords imposed more order and stability, people found greater opportunities for travel and communication. The revival of trade and the growth of towns created a need for literacy and provided the wealth required to support learning. Increasing contact with Islamic and Byzantine cultures in Spain and Sicily led to the translation into Latin, often by learned Jews, of ancient Greek works preserved by these Eastern civilizations. By preserving Greek philosophy and science—and by commenting creatively on these classical works—Islamic civilization acted as a bridge between antiquity and the cultural revival of the High Middle Ages. The Twelfth-Century Awakening was also kindled by the legacy of the Carolingian Renaissance, whose cultural lights had dimmed but never wholly vanished in the period of disorder after the dissolution of Charlemagne's empire.

In the Early Middle Ages, the principal educational centers were the monastic schools. During the twelfth century, cathedral schools in towns gained importance. Paid a stipend by a local church, their teachers taught grammar, rhetoric, and logic. But the chief expression of expanding intellectual life was the university, a distinct creation of the Middle Ages.

The origins of the medieval university are obscure and varied. The first universities were not planned but grew spontaneously. They developed as students eager for knowledge and skills needed for high positions in government gathered around prominent teachers. The renewed importance of Roman law for business and politics, for example, drew students to Bologna to study with acknowledged masters. Some universities evolved from cathedral schools.

The university was really a guild or corporation of masters or students who joined together to defend their interests against church or town authorities or the townspeople. A university might emerge when students united because of common needs, such as protection against townspeople who overcharged them for rooms and necessities. Organized into a body, students could also make demands on their instructors. At Bologna, professors faced fines for being absent or for giving lectures that drew fewer than five students; they were required to leave behind a deposit as security to ensure their return if they took a journey. A corporation of students formed the University at Bologna. The University of Paris, which evolved from the Cathedral School of Notre Dame, was the creation of a corporation of masters.

University students attended lectures by masters, engaged in supervised disputations (*disputatio*) designed to strengthen their capacity to reason, prepared for examinations, and earned degrees. They studied grammar, rhetoric, logic, arithmetic, geometry, astronomy, music, medicine, and, when ready, church law and theology, which was considered queen of the sciences. The curriculum relied heavily on Latin translations of ancient texts, chiefly the works of Aristotle. In mathematics and astronomy, students read Latin translations of Euclid and Ptolemy, while students of medicine studied the works of two great medical men of the ancient world, Hippocrates and Galen. Latin was the language of instruction.

But sometimes students followed other pursuits. Instead of studying, they turned to drinking, gambling, and fighting. At Oxford University, it was reported that students "went through the streets with swords and bows and arrows and assaulted all who passed by."[1] Fathers complained that their sons preferred "play to work and strumming a guitar while the others are at their studies."[2] Students often faced financial problems, and they knew whom to ask for help: "Well-beloved father, to ease my debts . . . at the tavern, at the baker's, with the doctor . . . and to pay . . . the laundress and the barber, I send you word of greetings and of money."[3]

Universities performed a crucial function in the Middle Ages. Students learned the habit of reasoned argument. Universities trained professional secretaries and lawyers, who administered the affairs of church and state and of the growing cities; these institutions of learning also produced theologians and philosophers, who shaped the climate of public opinion. Since the curriculum and the texts studied were essentially the same in all lands, the learning disseminated by universities tightened the cultural bonds that united Christian Europe. Medieval universities established in the West a tradition of learning that has never died; there is direct continuity between the universities of our own day and the medieval ones.

PHILOSOPHY-THEOLOGY

In the universities the best minds studied theology, the queen of the sciences, which was closely linked with philosophy. Medieval philosophy, or scholasticism, applied reason to revelation. It explained and clarified Christian teachings by means of concepts and principles of logic derived from Greek philosophy. Scholastics struggled to accommodate Greek philosophy, particularly Aristotle's thought, which was the basis of higher education, to the requirements of Catholic doctrines. They tried to show that the teachings of faith, though not derived from reason, were not contrary to reason, that logic could confirm church dogma. They tried to prove through reason what they already held to be true through faith. For example, the existence of God and the immortality of the soul, which every Christian accepted as articles of faith, could also, they thought, be demonstrated by reason. In struggling to harmonize faith with reason, medieval thinkers constructed an extraordinary synthesis of Christian revelation and Greek thought.

The scholastic masters used reason not to challenge but to serve faith: to elucidate, clarify, and buttress it. They did not break with the central concern of Christianity, that of earning God's grace and achieving salvation. Although this goal could be realized solely through faith, scholastic thinkers insisted that a science of nature did not obstruct the pursuit of grace and that philosophy could assist the devout in the contemplation of God. They did not reject those Christian beliefs that were beyond the grasp of human reason and therefore could not be deduced by rational argument. Instead, they held that such truths rested entirely on revelation and were to be accepted on faith. To medieval thinkers, reason did not have

an independent existence but ultimately had to acknowledge a suprarational, superhuman standard of truth; Greek philosophy had to be interpreted to accord with Christian revelation. They wanted rational thought to be directed by faith for Christian ends and guided by scriptural and ecclesiastical authority. Ultimately, faith had the final word.

Not all Christian thinkers welcomed the use of reason. Regarding Greek philosophy as an enemy of faith (would not reason lead people to question belief in miracles?), a fabricator of heresies (would not reason encourage disbelief in essential church teachings?), and an obstacle to achieving communion of the soul with God (would not a deviation from church teachings, under the influence of pagan philosophy, deprive people of salvation?), conservative theologians opposed the use of reason to elucidate Christian revelation. For if reason could demonstrate the proof of Christian teachings, as its advocates insisted, it could also be used, warned conservatives, to challenge and reject those teachings. In a sense, the conservatives were right. By revitalizing Greek thought, medieval philosophy nurtured a powerful force that eventually would shatter the medieval concepts of nature and society and weaken Christianity. Modern Western thought was created by thinkers who refused to subordinate reason to religious authority. Reason proved to be a double-edged sword: it both ennobled and undermined the medieval worldview.

Saint Anselm and Abelard

An early scholastic, Saint Anselm (1033–1109) was abbot of the Benedictine monastery of Bec in Normandy. He used rational argument to serve the interests of faith. Like Augustine before him and other thinkers who followed him, Anselm said that faith was a precondition for understanding. Without belief, there could be no proper knowledge. He developed philosophical proof for the existence of God. Anselm argued as follows: We can conceive of no being greater than God. But if God were to exist only in thought and not in actuality, his greatness would be limited; he would be less than perfect. Hence, he exists. Anselm's motive and method reveal something about the essence of medieval philosophy. He does not begin as a modern might: "If it can be proven

Adelard of Bath: A Questioning Spirit

In the High and Late Middle Ages, ancient scientific texts, particularly the works of Aristotle, were translated from Greek and Arabic into Latin. Influenced by Aristotle's naturalistic and empirical approach, several medieval scholars devoted greater attention to investigating the natural world. An early exponent of this emerging scientific outlook was Adelard of Bath (c. 1080–c. 1145). Born in England, Adelard studied in France and traveled in Muslim lands, becoming an advocate of Arabic science.

Adelard's Natural Questions *was written before the major Greek works were translated into Latin and made available to Western European scholars. But it does show a growing curiosity and a questioning spirit, attitudes that are crucial to scientific thinking.* Natural Questions *is a dialogue between Adelard and his nephew; reproduced below are some of Adelard's responses to his nephew's queries.*

I take nothing away from God, for whatever exists is from Him and because of Him. But the natural order does not exist confusedly and without rational arrangement, and human reason should be listened to concerning those things it treats of. But when it completely fails, then the matter should be referred to God. Therefore, since we have not yet completely lost the use of our minds, let us return to reason. . . .

. . . I have learned one thing, under the guidance of reason, from Arabic teachers; but you, captivated by a show of authority, are led around by a halter. For what should we call authority but a halter? Indeed, just as brute animals are led about by a halter wherever you please, and are not told where or why, but see the rope by which they are held and follow it alone, thus the authority of writers leads many of you, caught and bound by animal-like credulity, into danger. Whence some men, usurping the name of authority for themselves, have employed great license in writing, to such an extent that they do not hesitate to present the false as true to such animal-like men. For why not fill up sheets of paper, and why not write on the back too, when you usually have such readers today who require no rational explanation and put their trust only in the ancient name of a title? For they do not understand that reason has been given to each person so that he might discern the true from the false, using reason as the chief judge. For if reason were not the universal judge, it would have been given to each of us in vain. It would be sufficient that it were given to one (or a few at most), and the rest would be content with their authority and decisions. . . . I will cut short this discussion of the fact that in my judgment authority should be avoided. But I do assert this, that first we ought to seek the reason for anything, and then if we find an authority it may be added. Authority alone cannot make a philosopher believe anything, nor should it be adduced for this purpose. . . .

I believe that man is dearer to the Creator than all the other animals. Nevertheless it does not happen that he is born with natural weapons or is suited for swift flight. But he has something which is much better and more worthy, reason I mean, by which he so far excels the brutes that by means of it he can tame them, put bits in their mouths, and train them to perform various tasks. You see, therefore, by how much the gift of reason excels bodily defenses.

Question for Analysis

1. In what ways does Adelard of Bath express a scientific attitude in this work?

Richard C. Dales, *The Scientific Achievement of the Middle Ages* (Philadelphia: University of Pennsylvania Press, 1973), pp. 40–44.

Maimonides

Moses ben Maimon, also called by the Greek name Maimonides (1135–1204), was recognized as the foremost Jewish sage of his day. His works were also read and respected by Muslim and Christian thinkers, including Thomas Aquinas and Albert the Great. Born in Córdoba, Spain, then under Muslim rule, his family was forced to flee the country when the Almohads, a fanatical fundamentalist group from North Africa, conquered Córdoba and demanded that Jews and Christians convert or face death. Maimonides' family went into exile, moving about Spain and then emigrating to Morocco and later to a suburb of Cairo. When his brother David, a merchant, perished

at sea with the family's fortune, Maimonides, who had read widely in Arabic translations of Greek and Muslim medical works, became a physician. Gaining a reputation, he served as court physician to Saladin and the Egyptian royal family.

During his lifetime, Maimonides achieved fame as a philosopher, theologian, mathematician, and physician. Maimonides was intimately familiar with the works of Arab philosophers and Arabic translations of ancient Greek philosophy, particularly Aristotle. Like Christian scholastics and Muslim philosophers, Maimonides tried to harmonize faith with reason, to reconcile the Hebrew Scriptures and the Talmud (Jewish biblical commentary) with the teachings of Aristotle.

---

that God exists, I will adopt the creed of Christianity; if not, I will either deny God's existence (atheism) or reserve judgment (agnosticism)." Rather, Anselm accepts God's existence as an established fact because he believes what Holy Scripture says and what the church teaches. He then proceeds to employ logical argument to demonstrate that God can be known not only through faith but also through reason. He would never use reason to subvert what he knows to be true by faith. In general, this attitude would characterize later medieval thinkers, who also applied reason to faith.

As a young teacher of theology at the Cathedral School of Notre Dame, Peter Abelard (1079–1142) acquired a reputation for brilliance and combativeness. His tragic affair with Héloise, whom he tutored and seduced, has become one of the great romances in Western literature. Héloise had a child and entered a nunnery; Abelard was castrated on orders of Canon Fulbert, Héloise's guardian, and sought temporary refuge in a monastery. After resuming his career as a teacher in Paris, Abelard again had to seek refuge, this time for writing an essay on the **Trinity** that church officials found offensive. After further difficulties and flights, he again returned to Paris to teach

dialectic—logical argument. Not long afterward, his most determined opponent, Bernard of Clairvaux, accused Abelard of using the method of dialectical argument to attack faith. To Bernard, a monk and a **mystic**, subjecting revealed truth to critical analysis was fraught with danger.

> The deepest matters become the subject of undignified wrangling. . . . Virtues and vices are discussed with no trace of moral feelings, the sacraments of the Church with no evidence of faith, the mystery of the Holy Trinity with no spirit of humility or sobriety: all is presented in a distorted form, introduced in a way different from the one we learned and are used to.[4]

Hearkening to Bernard's powerful voice, the church condemned Abelard and confined him to a monastery for the rest of his days.

Abelard believed that it was important to apply reason to faith and that careful and constant questioning led to wisdom. Since all knowledge derives from God, said Abelard, it is good to pursue learning. In *Sic et Non* (Yes and No), he took 150 theological issues and, by presenting passages from the Bible and the church fathers, showed

Reflecting the value that Jews gave to education, Maimonides insisted that every Jewish man, whether he be rich or poor, old or young, healthy or unhealthy, and even if burdened with family responsibilities, was obliged to study daily the Hebrew Scriptures. Drawing on the deeply ingrained Jewish tradition calling for care for the poor, Maimonides listed eight degrees of almsgiving. The highest was to help a needy person become self-supporting. Just below was giving charity in such a way that both the donor and the recipient are unknown to each other.

In his numerous medical writings, Maimonides displayed a scientific bent in treating the sick, and to preserve health he urged drinking clean water, breathing fresh air, and eating healthy foods.

that there were conflicting opinions. He suggested that the divergent opinions of authorities could be reconciled through proper use of dialectics. But like Anselm before him, Abelard did not intend to refute traditional church doctrines. Reason would buttress, not weaken, the authority of faith. After his condemnation in 1141, Abelard wrote:

> I will never be a philosopher, if this is to speak against St. Paul, I would not be an Aristotle if this were to separate me from Christ. . . . I have set my building on the cornerstone on which Christ has built his Church. . . . I rest upon the rock that cannot be moved.[5]

Although forced to quit his teaching post, the new scholastic rationalistic approach swept across the schools of Europe.

The Recovery of Aristotle

During the Early Middle Ages, scholars in the Muslim world translated the works of Aristotle into Arabic and wrote commentaries on them. The preservation of ancient Greek thought was a major contribution of Islamic civilization. During the High Middle Ages, these works were translated into Latin by learned Europeans.

The introduction into Latin Christendom of the major works of Aristotle created a dilemma for religious authorities. Aristotle's comprehensive philosophy of nature and man, a product of human reason alone, conflicted in many instances with essential Christian doctrine. For Aristotle, God was an impersonal principle that accounted for order and motion in the universe, the unmoved mover. For Christianity, not only was God responsible for order in the physical universe, but he was also a personal being—a loving Father concerned about the deeds of his children. Whereas Christianity taught that God created the universe at a specific point in time, Aristotle held that the universe was eternal. Nor did Aristotle believe in the personal immortality of the soul, another cardinal principle of Christianity. For Aristotle, it was impossible for the soul to exist independently of the body.

Some church officials feared that the dissemination of Aristotle's natural philosophy would endanger faith. Would the teachings of Christ and the church fathers have to answer to pagan philosophy? Would Athens prevail over Jerusalem? At various times in the first half of the thirteenth century, the teaching of Aristotle's scientific works was forbidden at the University of Paris. However, because the ban did not apply throughout Christendom and was not consistently enforced in Paris, Aristotle's philosophy continued to be studied.

Thomas Aquinas: The Synthesis of Faith and Reason

Rejecting the position of conservatives, who insisted that philosophy would contaminate faith, Saint Thomas Aquinas (c. 1225–1274) upheld the value of human reason and natural knowledge. He set about reconciling Aristotelianism with Christianity. Aquinas taught at Paris and at various institutions in Italy. His greatest work, *Summa Theologica*, is a systematic exposition of Christian thought and the crowning expression of the medieval attempt to integrate Aristotle with Christianity. As a devout Catholic and member of the Dominican order, he of course accepted the truth of revelation. He never used reason to undermine faith.

Aquinas divided revealed truth into two categories: beliefs whose truth can be demonstrated by reason and beliefs that reason cannot prove to be either true or false. For example, he believed that philosophical speculation could prove the existence of God and the immortality of the human soul but could not prove or disprove the doctrines of the Trinity, the **Incarnation**, and the **Redemption** because those articles of faith wholly surpassed the capacity of human reason. This fact, however, did not detract from their certainty. Doctrines of faith did not require rational proof to be valid. They were true because they originated with God, whose authority is unshakable.

Can the teachings of faith conflict with the evidence of reason? For Aquinas, the answer was emphatically no. He said that revelation could not be the enemy of reason because revelation did not contradict reason and reason did not corrupt the purity of faith. Revelation supplemented and perfected reason. If there appeared to be a conflict between philosophy and faith, it was certain that reason had erred somewhere, for the doctrines of faith were infallible. Since *both* faith and reason came from God, they were not in competition with each other but, properly understood, supported each other and formed an organic unity. Consequently, reason should not be feared, for it was another avenue to God. Because there was an inherent agreement between true faith and correct reason—they both ultimately stemmed from God—contradictions between the two were only a misleading appearance. Although philosophy had not yet been able to resolve the dilemma, for God no such contradictions existed. In heaven, human beings would attain complete knowledge, as well as complete happiness. While on earth, however, they must allow faith to guide reason; they must not permit reason to oppose or undermine faith.

Because reason was no enemy of faith, applying it to revelation need not be feared. As human reasoning became more proficient, said Aquinas, it also became more Christian, and apparent incompatibilities between faith and reason disappeared. Recognizing that both faith and reason point to the same truth, the wise person accepts the guidance of religion in all questions that relate directly to knowledge needed for salvation. There also existed a wide range of knowledge that God had not revealed and that was not required for salvation.

Into this category fell much knowledge about the natural world of things and creatures, which human beings had perfect liberty to explore.

Thus, in exalting God, Aquinas also paid homage to human intelligence, proclaimed the value of rational activity, and asserted the importance of physical reality revealed through human senses. Consequently, he valued the natural philosophy of Aristotle. Correctly used, Aristotelian thought would assist faith. Aquinas's great effort was to synthesize Aristotelianism with the divine revelation of Christianity. That the two could be harmonized he had no doubt. He made use of Aristotelian categories in his five proofs of God's existence. In his first proof, for example, Aquinas argued that a thing cannot move itself. Whatever is moved must be moved by something else, and that by something else again. "Therefore, it is necessary to arrive at a first mover, moved by no other; and this everyone understands to be God."[6]

Aquinas upheld the value of reason. To love the intellect was to honor God and not to diminish the truth of faith. He had confidence in the power of the rational mind to comprehend most of the truths of revelation, and he insisted that in nontheological questions about specific things in nature—those questions not affecting salvation—people should trust only to reason and experience.

Aquinas gave new importance to the empirical world and to scientific speculation and human knowledge. The traditional medieval view, based largely on Saint Augustine, drew a sharp distinction between the higher world of grace and the lower world of nature, between the world of spirit and the world of sense experience. Knowledge derived from the natural world was often seen as insignificant and an obstacle to true knowledge. Aquinas altered this tradition by affirming the importance of knowledge of the social order and the physical world. He gave human reason and worldly knowledge a new dignity. Thus, the City of Man was not merely a sinful place from which people tried to escape in order to enter God's city; it was worthy of investigation and understanding. But Aquinas remained a medieval thinker, for he always maintained that secular knowledge should be supervised and corrected by revealed truth, and he never questioned the truth of the medieval Christian view of the world and the individual. As historian Steven Ozment explains,

NOTRE-DAME DE CHARTRES, BEGUN C. 1194, CHARTRES, FRANCE. Because the two spires topping the west façade towers were constructed nearly four centuries apart, they provide an interesting contrast between early and late Gothic architecture. The simple north spire was built between 1160 and 1170; the south spire, constructed in the early sixteenth century, is a good example of the flamboyant Gothic style. (Nat Farbman/Time & Life Pictures/Getty Images.)

Aquinas brought reason and revelation together, but strictly as un-equals. . . . In this union, reason, philosophy, nature, secular man and the state ultimately had value only in subservience to the higher goals of revelation, theology, grace, religious man, and the church. . . . Thomist theology was the most sophisticated statement of the medieval belief in the secondary significance of the lay and secular world, a congenial ideology for a church besieged by independent and aggressive secular political powers.[7]

Strict Aristotelianism: The Challenge to Orthodoxy

Some teachers in the Faculty of Arts at Paris, relying heavily on the commentaries of Averroës, the great Muslim thinker (see page 206), found Aquinas's approach of Christianizing or explaining away Aristotle unacceptable. Unlike Aquinas, they did not seek to reconcile Aristotle's philosophy with Christian dogma. They held that certain Aristotelian propositions contradicting faith were philosophically true, or at least could not be proven false. These teachers maintained that it was impossible to refute these propositions by natural reason alone—that is, without recourse to faith. For example, by reason alone Aristotle had demonstrated that the world was eternal and that the processes of nature were unalterable. The first doctrine conflicted with the Christian belief that God created the universe at a point in time; the second conflicted with the belief that God could work miracles.

But these teachers did not take the next step and argue that Aristotle was correct and faith wrong. They maintained only that Aristotle's arguments could not be refuted by natural reason and that philosophers—as philosophers, not as Christians—should base their judgments on rational arguments only, not on miracles and revelation. These strict Aristotelians did not deny the truths of faith, but they did assert that natural reason could construct conclusive proofs for propositions that the church had explicitly stated to be false.

In 1277, the bishop of Paris condemned 219 propositions, many of them taught by these expositors of Aristotle at the University of Paris. Included in the condemnation were some propositions held by the great Aquinas. This move attempted to prevent Aristotle's philosophical naturalism from undermining Christian beliefs. Consequently, the condemnation was a triumph for conservative theologians, who had grown increasingly worried about the inroads made by Aristotelianism. To them, even the Christian Aristotelianism of Aquinas was suspect, for it could lead people astray, endangering their salvation.

Condemnations generally hinder the pursuit of knowledge, but, ironically, the condemnation of 1277 may have had the opposite effect. It led some thinkers to examine critically and reject elements of Aristotle's natural philosophy. This development may have served as a prelude to modern science, which, born in the sixteenth and seventeenth centuries, grew out of a rejection of Aristotelian physics.

SCIENCE

During the Early Middle Ages, few scientific works from the ancient world were available to Western Europeans. Scientific thought was at its lowest ebb since its origination more than a thousand years earlier in Greece. By contrast, both Islamic and Byzantine civilizations preserved and, in some instances, added to the legacy of Greek science. In the High Middle Ages, however, many ancient texts were translated from Greek and Arabic into Latin and entered Latin Christendom for the first time. The principal centers of translation were Spain, where Christian and Muslim civilizations intersected, and Sicily, which had been controlled by Byzantium up to the last part of the ninth century and then by Islam until Christian Normans completed the conquest of the island by 1091. Often learned Jews, who knew both Arabic and Latin, served as translators. These translations of ancient Greek scientific works and of Arabic commentaries stimulated interest in nature.

In the thirteenth and fourteenth centuries, a genuine scientific movement did occur. Impressed with the naturalistic and empirical approach of Aristotle, some medieval scholars spent time examining physical nature. Among them was the Dominican Albert the Great (Albertus Magnus). Born in Germany, Albert (c. 1206–1280) studied at Padua and taught at the University of Paris, where Thomas Aquinas was his student. To Albert, philosophy meant more than employing Greek reason to contemplate divine wisdom; it also meant making sense of nature. Albert devoted himself to mastering, editing, and commenting on the vast body of Aristotle's works.

While retaining the Christian stress on God, revelation, the supernatural, and the afterlife, Albert (unlike many earlier Christian thinkers) considered nature a valid field for investigation. In his writings on geology, chemistry, botany, and

zoology, Albert, like Aristotle, displayed respect for the concrete details of nature, utilizing them as empirical evidence.

> *I have examined the anatomy of different species of bees. In the rear, i.e. behind the waist, I discovered a transparent, shining bladder. If you test this with your tongue, you find that it has a slight taste of honey. In the body there is only an insignificant spiral-shaped intestine and nerve fibers which are connected with the sting. All this is surrounded with a sticky fluid.*[8]

Showing a modern-day approach, Albert approved of inquiry into the material world, stressed the value of knowledge derived from experience with nature, sought rational explanations for natural occurrences, and held that theological debates should not stop scientific investigations. He pointed to a new direction in medieval thought.

Robert Grosseteste (c. 1175–1253), chancellor of Oxford University, was also a scholar of the scientific movement. He declared that the roundness of the earth could be demonstrated by reason. In addition, he insisted that mathematics was necessary in order to understand the physical world, and he carried out experiments on the refraction of light.

Another Englishman, the monk and philosopher Roger Bacon (c. 1214–1294), foreshadowed the modern attitude of using science to gain mastery over nature. He recognized the practical advantages that might come and predicted these great changes.

> *Machines for navigation can be made without rowers so that the largest ships on rivers or seas will be moved by a single man in charge with greater velocity than if they were full of men. Also oars can be made so that without animals they will move with unbelievable rapidity. . . . Also flying machines can be constructed so that a man sits in the midst of the machine revolving some engine by which artificial wings are made to beat the air like a flying bird. Also a machine small in size can be made for walking in the sea and rivers, even to the bottom without danger.*[9]

Bacon maintained that mathematics was crucial for science and read Arabic works on the reflection and refraction of light. Among his achievements were experiments in optics and the observation that light travels much faster than sound. His description of the anatomy of the vertebrate eye and optic nerves was the finest of that era, and he recommended dissecting the eyes of pigs and cows to obtain greater knowledge of the subject.

The study of the ancient texts of Hippocrates and Galen and their Islamic commentators, particularly Avicenna's *Canon of Medicine*, which synthesized Greek and Arabic medicine, elevated medicine to a formal discipline. Although these texts contained numerous errors and contradictions, they had to be mastered, if only to be challenged, before modern medicine could emerge. In addition, medieval doctors dissected animals and, in the late fourteenth century, human bodies. From practical experience, medieval doctors, monks, and laypeople added to the list of plants and herbs that would ease pain and heal.

Medieval scholars did not make the breakthrough to modern science. They kept the belief that the earth was at the center of the universe and that different sets of laws operated on earth and in the heavens. Although some medieval thinkers explicitly urged seeking natural explanations to account for physical occurrences, medieval science was never wholly removed from a theological setting. Modern science self-consciously seeks the advancement of specifically scientific knowledge, but in the Middle Ages many questions involving nature were raised merely to clarify a religious problem.

Medieval scholars and philosophers, however, did advance knowledge about optics, the tides, and mechanics. They saw the importance of mathematics for interpreting nature, and they performed some experiments. By translating and commenting on ancient Greek and Arabic works, medieval scholars provided future ages with ideas to reflect on and to reject and surpass, a necessary precondition for the emergence of modern science.

Medieval thinkers also developed an anti-Aristotelian physics, which some historians of science believe influenced Galileo, the creator of modern mechanics, more than two centuries later.

To explain why heavy objects do not always fall downward—why an arrow released by a bow moves in a straight line before it falls—Aristotle said that when the arrow leaves the bow, it separates the air, which then moves behind the arrow and pushes it along. Aristotle, of course, had no comprehension of the law of inertia, which, as formulated by Isaac Newton in the seventeenth century, states that a body in motion will continue in a straight line unless interfered with. Unable to imagine that being in motion is as natural a condition as being at rest, Aristotle concluded that an outside force must maintain continual contact with the moving object. Hence, the flying arrow requires the "air-engine" to keep it in motion.

In the fourteenth century, Jean Buridan, a professor at the University of Paris, rejected Aristotle's theory. Buridan argued that the bowstring transmits to the arrow a force called impetus, which keeps the arrow in motion. Whereas Aristotle attributed the arrow's motion to the air, which was external to the arrow, Buridan found the motive force to be an agent imparted to the arrow by the bowstring. Though still far from the modern theory of inertia, Buridan's impetus theory was an advance over Aristotle's air-engine. In the impetus theory, a moving body requires a cause to keep it in motion. In the theory of inertia, as noted above, once a body is in motion, no force is required to keep it moving in a straight line.

Late medieval physics went beyond Aristotle in other ways as well, particularly in the importance given to expressing motion mathematically. The extent to which late medieval thinkers influenced the thinkers of the Scientific Revolution is a matter of debate. Some historians view modern science as a child of the Middle Ages. Other historians believe that the achievements of medieval science were slim and that modern science owes very little to the Middle Ages.

THE RECOVERY OF ROMAN LAW

During the Early Middle Ages, Western European law essentially consisted of Germanic customs, some of which had been written down. Although some elements of Roman law endured as custom, the formal study of Roman law disappeared. The late eleventh and the twelfth centuries saw the revival of Roman law, particularly in Bologna, Italy. Irnerius lectured on the *Corpus Juris Civilis*, Roman laws and judicial commentaries codified by Byzantine jurists in the sixth century by order of the emperor Justinian. He made Bologna the leading center for the study of Roman law. Irnerius and his students applied to the study of law the methods of organization and logical analysis that scholastic theologians used in studying philosophical texts.

Unlike traditional Germanic law, which was essentially tribal law, Roman law assumed the existence of universal principles, which could be grasped by the human intellect and expressed in the law of the state. Roman jurists had systematically and rationally structured the legal experience of the Roman people. The example of Roman law stimulated medieval jurists to organize their own legal tradition. Intellectuals increasingly came to insist on both a rational analysis of evidence and judicial decisions based on rational procedures. Law codes compiled in parts of France and Germany and in the kingdom of Castile were influenced by the recovery of Roman law.

Roman law also influenced church law, which was derived from the Bible, the church fathers, church councils, and the decisions of popes. In the last part of the eleventh century, church scholars began to codify church (or canon) law and were helped by the Roman legal tradition.

LITERATURE

Medieval literature was written both in Latin and in the vernacular—the normal spoken language, as distinct from the language of learning. Much of medieval Latin literature consisted of religious hymns and dramas depicting the life of Christ and saints.

Medieval university students, like their modern counterparts, lampooned their elders and social conventions, engaged in drinking bouts, and rebelled against the rigors of study. They put their feelings into poetry written in Latin. For them, youth and study did not mix. They wanted to "treasure all the pleasure of our youth." In later years, there was "time enough . . . to think on Truth."[10]

And, of course, their thoughts turned to romance. One poet described how pleasurable it was to gaze upon his lady, touch her hand, and kiss her "in modest measure." But the final act "of love's game/ Dream not of that pleasure."[11]

Poor or errant students who had given up their studies roamed the roads as free spirits. These vagabonds sometimes composed poetry that ridiculed clerics and sang the praises of wine, gambling, and women. They generally agreed with the poet who was "Avid for the world's delight/More than for Salvation."[12]

Vernacular literature emerged in the High Middle Ages. The French *chansons de geste*—epic poems of heroic deeds that had first been told orally—were written in the vernacular of northern France. The poems dealt with Charlemagne's battles against the Muslims, with rebellious nobles, and with feudal warfare. The finest of these epic poems, *The Song of Roland*, expressed the feudal ethic: loyalty to one's lord and devotion to Christianity were the highest virtues and treachery an unpardonable crime.

The *Nibelungenlied*, the best expression of the heroic epic in Germany, is often called "the *Iliad* of the Germans." Like its French counterpart, it dealt with heroic feats.

> In stories of our fathers, high marvels we are
> told
> Of champions well-approved in perils
> manifold.
> Of feasts and merry meetings, of weeping and
> of wail,
> And deeds of gallant daring I'll tell you in my
> tale.[13]

The *roman*—a blending of old legends, chivalric ideals, and Christian concepts—combined love with adventure, war, and the miraculous. Among the romans were the tales of King Arthur and his Round Table. Circulating by word of mouth for centuries, these tales spread from the British Isles to France and Germany.

Another form of medieval poetry spoken and written in the vernacular dealt with the romantic glorification of women. Known as courtly love, this form of poetry flourished particularly in Provence in southern France. Sung by troubadours, many of them nobles, the courtly love

MILLEFLEURS TAPESTRY: TWO MUSICIANS, SCHOOL OF THE LOIRE, FRANCE, C. 1500. The courtly love tradition, in which women were worshipped and untouchable, inspired poetry. Troubadours sang this poetry, which expressed a changing attitude toward women. By inviting poets to their courts and writing poetry themselves, noblewomen actively influenced the rituals and literature of courtly love. (DeAgostini/Getty Images.)

poetry expressed a changing attitude toward women. Although medieval men generally regarded women as inferior and subordinate, courtly love poetry ascribed to noble ladies superior qualities of virtue. To the nobleman, the lady became a goddess worthy of devotion, loyalty, and worship. He would honor her and serve her as he did his lord; for her love, he would undergo any sacrifice. Troubadours sang love songs that praised ladies for their beauty and charm and expressed both the joys and the pains of love.

> *I sing of her, yet her beauty*
> *is greater than I can tell,*
> *with her fresh color, lively eyes,*
> *and white skin, untanned*
> *and untainted by rouge.*
> *She is so pure and noble*
> *that no one can speak ill of her.*
> *But above all, one must praise,*
> *it seems to me, her truthfulness,*
> *her manners and her gracious speech*
> *for she never would betray a friend.*[14]

Noblewomen actively influenced the rituals and literature of courtly love. They often invited poets to their courts and wrote poetry themselves. Sometimes a lady troubadour expressed disdain for her husband and desire for the knight whom she truly loved.

> *I should like to hold my knight*
> *Naked in my arms at eve,*
> *That he might be in ecstasy*
> *As I cushioned his head against my breast,*
> *For I am happier far with him*
> *Than Floris with Blancheflor;*
> *I grant him my heart, my love,*
> *My mind, my eyes, my life.*
>
> *Fair friend, charming and good,*
> *When shall I hold you in my power?*
> *And lie beside you for an hour*
> *And amorous kisses give to you;*
> *Know that I would give almost anything*
> *To have you in my husband's place,*
> *But only if you swear*
> *To do everything I desire.*[15]

Ladies demanded that knights treat them with gentleness and consideration and that knights dress neatly, bathe often, play instruments, and compose (or at least recite) poetry. To prove worthy of his lady's love, a knight had to demonstrate patience, charm, bravery, and loyalty. It was believed that a knight would ennoble his character by devoting himself to a lady.

Courtly love involved not a husband–wife relationship but a noble's admiration and yearning for another woman of his class. Among nobles, marriages were arranged for political and economic reasons. The rituals of courtly love, it has been suggested, provided an outlet for erotic feelings condemned by the church. They also enhanced the skills and refined the tastes of the noble. The rough warrior acquired wit, manners, charm, and a facility with words. He was becoming a courtier and a gentleman.

The *Canterbury Tales* by Geoffrey Chaucer (c. 1340–1400, written in Middle English, is a masterpiece of English literature. Chaucer chose as his theme twenty-nine pilgrims en route from London to the religious shrine at Canterbury. In describing the pilgrims, Chaucer displayed humor, charm, an understanding of human nature, and a

THE VISITATION, WEST PORTAL, REIMS CATHEDRAL, c. 1225–1245. The reflection of Roman art exhibited by these statues of the expectant mothers (Mary and Elizabeth) of Jesus and John the Baptist suggests that the sculptor was well versed in the classical tradition. The carving of the draperies and the poses of the figures reveal classical traits, but instead of being idealizations, the figures display human warmth. (Scala/Art Resource, N.Y.)

superb grasp of the attitudes of the English. Few writers have pictured their times better.

The greatest literary figure of the Middle Ages was Dante Alighieri (1265–1321) of Florence. Dante appreciated the Roman classics and wrote not just in Latin, the traditional language of intellectual life, but also in Italian, his native tongue. In this respect, he anticipated the Renaissance. In the tradition of the troubadours, Dante wrote poems to his beloved Beatrice.

In *The Divine Comedy*, Dante synthesized the various elements of the medieval outlook and summed up, with immense feeling, the medieval understanding of the purpose of life. Written while Dante was in exile, *The Divine Comedy* describes the poet's journey through hell, purgatory, and paradise. Dante arranges hell into nine concentric circles; in each region, sinners are punished in proportion to their earthly sins. The poet experiences all of hell's torments—burning sand, violent storms, darkness, and fearful monsters that whip, claw, bite, and tear sinners apart. The ninth circle, the lowest, is reserved for Lucifer and traitors. Lucifer has three faces, each a different color, and two bat-like wings. In each mouth, he gnaws on the greatest traitors in history: Judas Iscariot, who betrayed Jesus, and Brutus and Cassius, who assassinated Caesar. Those condemned to hell are told: "All hope abandon, ye who enter in."

In purgatory, Dante meets sinners who, although they undergo punishment, will eventually enter paradise. He and Beatrice ascend to the highest heaven, a realm of light that radiates truth, goodness, and gentleness. In paradise, the poet meets the great saints and the Virgin Mary. He glimpses the Vision of God. In this mystical experience, the aim of life is realized.

ARCHITECTURE

Two styles of architecture evolved during the Middle Ages: Romanesque and Gothic. The **Romanesque** style dominated the eleventh century and the greater part of the twelfth. In imitation of ancient Roman structures, Romanesque buildings used massive walls to support stone barrel-and-groin vaults with rounded arches. Thick walls were needed to hold up the great weight of the roofs. Because the walls had few spaces for windows, little light entered the interior of Romanesque buildings.

The development of the pointed arch permitted supports that lessened the bearing pressure of the roof on the walls. This new style, called **Gothic**, allowed buildings to have lofty, vaulted ceilings and huge windows, which permitted sunlight to flood the interior. Whereas Romanesque buildings produced an impression of massive solidity, Gothic buildings created an illusion of lightness and upward motion. The Gothic cathedral gave visual expression to the medieval conception of a hierarchical universe. As the historian Joan Gadol puts it, "Inside and out, the Gothic cathedral is one great movement upward through a mounting series of grades, one ascent through horizontal levels marked by arches, galleries, niches, and towers. . . . [T]he material ascends to the spiritual, the natural is assumed into the supernatural—all in a graduated rise."[16] This illusion of upward reach to the heavens is created by the tall and narrow proportions of the interior spaces, the springing pointed arches, and the marching patterns of closely spaced columns and colonnettes.

The magnificently designed stained-glass windows and complex sculptural decoration of Gothic cathedrals depicted scenes from the Bible and the lives of saints, as well as scenes from daily life, for the worshipers, many of whom were illiterate. The reduction of wall space, which allowed these massive glass illustrations, was made possible by the flying buttresses on the buildings' exteriors. These great arcs of masonry carry the weight and thrust of the stone vaults out to the exterior walls. The light cage of buttresses surrounding the cathedral makes the exterior silhouette appear as airy and diffuse as the interior spaces. The architects and builders thought only of honoring God, not themselves; their identity remains a mystery.

Gothic cathedrals took many decades to complete and required donations from the devout. Only in an age of intense religious faith could such energy have been spent to glorify God. These vast building projects, many of them in northern France, were made possible by economic prosperity. Funds were raised from a variety of sources. Cathedrals owned income-producing properties, such as farmland, mills, and forests, and received donations from pilgrims visiting the relics of famous saints. Clerics also collected tolls and taxes on goods shipped to fairs through their region.

The Gothic style was to remain vigorous until the fifteenth century, spreading from France to England, Germany, Spain, and beyond. Revived from time to time thereafter, it has proved to be one of the most enduring styles in Western art and architecture.

THE MEDIEVAL WORLDVIEW

A distinctive worldview, based essentially on Christianity, evolved during the Middle Ages. This outlook differed from both the Greco-Roman and the modern scientific and secular views of the world. In the Christian view, not the individual but the Creator determined what constituted the good life. Thus, reason that was not illuminated by revelation was either wrong or inadequate, for God had revealed the proper rules for the regulation of individual and social life. Ultimately, the good life was not of this world but came from a union with God in a higher world. This Christian belief as formulated by the church made life and death purposeful and intelligible; it dominated the thought of the Middle Ages.

The Universe: Higher and Lower Worlds

Medieval thinkers sharply differentiated between spirit and matter, between a realm of grace and an earthly realm, between a higher world of perfection and a lower world of imperfection. Moral values derived from the higher world, which was also the final destination for the faithful. Two sets of laws operated in the medieval universe, one for the heavens and one for the earth. The cosmos was a giant ladder, with God at the summit; earth, composed of base matter, stood at the bottom, just above hell, where, farthest from God, dwelled Satan, his evil spirits, and the souls of the damned.

From Aristotle and Ptolemy, medieval thinkers inherited the theory of an earth-centered universe—the *geocentric theory*—which they imbued with Christian symbolism. The geocentric theory held that revolving around the motionless earth at uniform speeds were seven transparent spheres, in which were embedded each of the seven "planets"—the moon, Mercury, Venus, the sun, Mars, Jupiter, and Saturn. A sphere of fixed stars (that is, the stars, like chandeliers in a ceiling, stayed in a constant relationship to one another) enclosed this planetary system. Above the firmament of the stars were the three heavenly spheres. The outermost, the Empyrean Heaven, was the abode of God and the Elect. Through the sphere below—the Prime Mover—God transmitted

GOD AS ARCHITECT OF THE UNIVERSE, FRENCH OLD TESTAMENT MINIATURE PAINTING, THIRTEENTH CENTURY. To the medieval Christian, God was the creator of the world. The universe had a known hierarchical order—a "great chain of being"—extending from God downward to the lowest form of being. (Photos 12/Alamy Limited.)

motion to the planetary spheres. Underneath this was the lowermost sphere, the Crystalline Heaven, composed of a clear transparent substance.

An earth-centered universe accorded with the Christian idea that God created the universe for men and women and that salvation was the primary aim of life. Because God had created people in his image, they deserved this central position. Although they might be at the bottom of the cosmic ladder, only they, of all living things, had the capacity to ascend to heaven, the realm of perfection.

Also acceptable to the Christian mentality was the sharp distinction drawn by Aristotle between

the world above the moon and the one below it. Aristotle held that terrestrial bodies were made of four elements: earth, water, air, fire. Celestial bodies, which occupied the region encompassing the moon and the area above, were composed of a fifth element, the ether—too clear, too pure, and too perfect to be found on earth. The planets and stars existed in a world apart; they were made of the divine ether and followed celestial laws, which did not apply to earthly objects. Whereas earthly bodies underwent change—ice converting to water, a burning log converting to ashes—heavenly objects were incorruptible, immune to all change. Unlike earthly objects, they were indestructible.

Heavenly bodies also followed different laws of motion than earthly objects. Aristotle said that it was natural for celestial bodies to move eternally in uniform circles, such motion being considered a sign of perfection. According to Aristotle, it was also natural for heavy bodies (stone) to fall downward and for light objects (fire, smoke) to move upward toward the celestial world; the falling stone and the rising smoke were finding their natural place in the universe. This view of the universe would be shattered by the Scientific Revolution of the sixteenth and seventeenth centuries.

The Individual: Sinful but Redeemable

At the center of medieval belief was the idea of a perfect God, who had conceived and created the universe, and wretched and sinful human beings. God had given Adam and Eve freedom to choose; rebellious and presumptuous, they had used their freedom to disobey God. In doing so, they made evil an intrinsic part of the human personality. But God, who had not stopped loving human beings, showed them the way out of sin. God became man and died so that human beings might be saved. Men and women were weak, egocentric, and sinful. With God's grace, they could overcome their sinful nature and gain salvation; without grace, they were utterly helpless.

The medieval individual's understanding of self stemmed from a comprehension of the universe as a **hierarchy** instituted by and culminating in God. On earth, the basest objects were lifeless stones devoid of souls; higher than stones were plants, endowed with a primitive type of soul, which allowed for reproduction and growth. Still higher were animals, which had the capacity for motion and sensation. The highest of the animals were human beings; unlike other animals, they could grasp some part of universal truth. Far superior to them were the angels, for they apprehended God's truth without difficulty. At the summit of this graduated universe was God, who was pure Being, without limitation, and the source of all existence. God's revelation reached down to humanity through the hierarchical order. From God, revelation passed to the angels, who were also arranged hierarchically. From the angels, the truth reached men and women, grasped first by prophets and apostles and then by the multitudes. Thus, all things in the universe, from angels, men, and women to the lowest earthly objects, occupied a place peculiar to their nature and were linked by God in a great, unbroken chain.

Medieval individuals derived a sense of security from this hierarchical universe, in which the human position was clearly defined. Although they were sinners who dwelt on a corruptible earth, at the bottom of the cosmic hierarchy, they *could* ascend to the higher world of perfection above the moon. As children of God, they enjoyed the unique distinction that each human soul was precious; all Christians commanded respect, unless they were heretics. (A heretic forfeited dignity and could be justly executed.)

Medieval thinkers also arranged knowledge in a hierarchical order: knowledge of the spiritual surpassed all worldly knowledge, that is, all the sciences. Therefore, the true Christian understood that the pursuit of worldly knowledge could not proceed properly unless guided by divine revelation. To know what God wanted of the individual was the summit of self-knowledge and permitted entry into heaven. Thus, God was both the source and the end of knowledge. The human capacity to think and to act freely constituted the image of God within each individual; it ennobled man and woman and offered them the promise of associating with God in heaven.

True, human nobility derived from intelligence and free will. But if individuals disobeyed God, they brought misery on themselves. To challenge the divine will with human will constituted the sin of pride, contempt for God, and a violation of the divine order. Such sinful behavior invited self-destruction.

In the medieval view, neither nature nor the human being could be understood apart from God and his revelation. All reality emanated from God and was purposefully arranged in a spiritual hierarchy. Three great expressions of this view of life were scholastic philosophy, *The Divine Comedy* of Dante, and the Gothic cathedral.

❖　　❖　　❖

NOTES

1. Quoted in G. G. Coulton, *Life in the Middle Ages* (New York: Macmillan, 1928), 1:74.

2. Quoted in Charles Homer Haskins, *The Rise of Universities* (Ithaca, N.Y.: Cornell University Press, 1957), 79.

3. Quoted in Coulton, *Life in the Middle Ages*, 3:113.

4. Quoted in Anders Piltz, *The World of Medieval Learning* (Oxford: Blackwell, 1981), 83.

5. Quoted in David Knowles, *The Evolution of Medieval Thought* (New York: Vintage Books, 1964), 123.

6. *Summa Theologica*, excerpted in *Introduction to Saint Thomas Aquinas*, ed. Anton C. Pegis (New York: Modern Library, 1948), 25.

7. Steven Ozment, *The Age of Reform* (New Haven, Conn.: Yale University Press, 1980), 20.

8. Quoted in Piltz, *The World of Medieval Learning*, 176.

9. Quoted in A. C. Crombie, *Medieval and Early Modern Science* (Garden City, N.Y.: Doubleday Anchor Books, 1959), 1:55–56.

10. Quoted in Helen Waddell, ed. & trans., *Medieval Latin Lyrics*, originally published by Cambridge University Press in 1935; among the several new editions is Calender Press, 2013, located in Derry, Northern Ireland.

11. Excerpted in David C. Riede and J. Wayne Baker, eds., *The Western Intellectual Tradition* (Dubuque, Ia.: Kendall/Hunt, 1980), 1:62.

12. Excerpted in E. H. Zeydel, ed., *Vagabond Verse: Secular Latin Poems in the Middle Ages* (Detroit: Wayne State University Press, 1966), 61.

13. *The Fall of the Nibelungers*, trans. William Nanson Lettsom (London: Williams and Norgate, 1890), 1.

14. Excerpted in Anthony Bonner, ed., *Songs of the Troubadours* (New York: Schocken Books, 1972), 42–43.

15. Quoted in Frances Gies and Joseph Gies, *Women in the Middle Ages* (New York: T. Y. Crowell, 1978), 45.

16. Joan Gadol, *Leon Battista Alberti, Universal Man of the Early Renaissance* (Chicago: University of Chicago Press, 1969), 149–150.

Chapter 12

The Late Middle Ages: Crisis and Dissolution

The Jacquerie. Enraged French peasants attack the castle of a lord.

(© Mary Evans Picture Library/The Image Works.)

By the start of the fourteenth century, Latin Christendom had experienced more than 250 years of growth. On an economic level, agricultural production had expanded, commerce and town life had revived, and the population had increased. On a political level, kings had become more powerful, bringing greater order and security to large areas. On a religious level, the papacy had demonstrated its strength as the spiritual leader of Christendom, and the clergy had been reformed. On a cultural level, a unified worldview, blending faith and reason, had been forged.

During the Late Middle Ages, roughly the fourteenth and early fifteenth centuries, medieval civilization was in decline. The fourteenth century, an age of adversity, was marked by crop failures, famine, population decline, plagues, stagnating production, unemployment, inflation, devastating warfare, and abandoned villages. Violent rebellions by the poor of the towns and countryside were ruthlessly suppressed by the upper classes. The century witnessed flights into mysticism, outbreaks of mass hysteria, and massacres of Jews; it was an age of pessimism and general insecurity. The papacy declined in power, heresy proliferated, and the synthesis of faith and reason, erected by Christian thinkers during the High Middle Ages, began to disintegrate. These developments were signs that the stable and coherent civilization of the thirteenth century was drawing to a close.

But all was not decline and gloom. On the positive side, representative institutions developed, and thinkers showed a greater interest in the world of nature. And in Italy, the dynamic forces of urbanism and secularism were producing a period of cultural and humanistic flowering known as the Renaissance.

AN AGE OF ADVERSITY

Economic Problems, the Black Death, and Social Tension

In the Late Middle Ages, Latin Christendom was afflicted with severe economic problems. The earlier increases in agricultural production did not

Chronology 12.1 ❖ The Late Middle Ages

1303	The French attack papal summer palace at Anagni
1309–1377	Babylonian Captivity: the popes, all French, reside at Avignon and are influenced by the French monarchy
1323–1328	Peasants' Revolt in Flanders
1328	End of France's Capetian dynasty; Edward III of England tries to gain the French throne
1337–1453	Hundred Years' War between England and France
1346	Battle of Crécy: the English defeat the French
1347–1351	Black Death reaches Italian ports and ravages Europe
1356	Battle of Poitiers: the English defeat the French
1358	Jacquerie, the French peasants' revolt
1377	Pope Gregory XI returns papacy to Rome
1378	Florentine laborers revolt
1378–1417	Great Schism: Christendom has two and then three popes
1381	English peasants revolt
1382	Weavers revolt in Ghent
1415	Battle of Agincourt: Henry V of England defeats the French; Jan Hus, a Bohemian religious reformer, is burned at the stake
1429	Joan of Arc liberates Orléans
1431	Joan of Arc is condemned as a witch
1453	The English are driven from France, except Calais: end of the Hundred Years' War
1460	Pope Pius II condemns the Conciliar Movement as heretical

continue. Limited use of fertilizers and limited knowledge of conservation exhausted the topsoil. As more grazing land was converted to the cultivation of cereals, animal husbandry decreased, causing a serious shortage of manure needed for arable land. Intermittent bouts of prolonged heavy rains and frost also hampered agriculture. From 1301 to 1314, there was a general shortage of food, and from 1315 to 1317, famine struck Europe. People subsisted by scavenging. On roads and in villages, people died of starvation, and the dead remained unattended. Throughout the century, starvation and malnutrition were widespread. In Bruges, for example, two thousand of the town's thirty-five thousand inhabitants died of starvation.

Other economic problems abounded. A shortage of silver, caused by technical problems in sinking deeper shafts in mines, led to the debasement of coins and spiraling inflation, which hurt the feudal nobility in particular. Prices for manufactured luxury goods, which the nobility craved, rose rapidly. At the same time, the dues that the nobility collected from peasants diminished. To replace their revenues, lords and knights turned to plunder and warfare.

John Wycliff: Concerning the Pope's Power

John Wycliffe (c. 1320–1384), a respected English theologian, challenged the church's core doctrine that salvation was attainable only by adhering to its sacraments as administered by the clergy. Anticipating the Protestant Reformation of the sixteenth century, Wycliffe maintained that inspiration from Scripture, not obedience to the church, was the path to salvation. He specifically rejected the church doctrine that the clergy were indispensable intermediaries between human beings and God. In calling for a return to the spiritual purity of the early Christians, he attacked the luxurious life style of bishops and the pope. The following text, originally written in Middle English, was rendered into Modern English by Alfred J. Andrea.

Christ was a very poor man from His birth to His death and forswore worldly riches and begging . . . but Antichrist, in contrast to this, from the time that he is made pope to the time of his death, covets worldly wealth and tries in many shrewd ways to gain riches. Christ was a most meek man and urged that we learn from Him, but people say that the pope is the proudest man on earth, and he makes lords kiss his feet, whereas Christ washed His apostles' feet. Christ was a most unpretentious man in life, deeds, and words. People say that this pope is not like Christ in this way, for whereas Christ went on foot to cities and little towns alike, they say this pope desires to live in a castle in a grand manner. Whereas Christ came to John the Baptist to be baptized by him, the pope summons people to come to him wherever he might be, yea, as though Christ Himself, and not the pope, had summoned them to Him. Christ embraced young and poor in token of his humility; people say that the pope desires to embrace worldly prestige and not good people for the sake of God, lest he dishonor himself. Christ was busy preaching the Gospel, and not for worldly prestige or for profit; people say that the pope allows this, but he would

Compounding the economic crisis was the Black Death, or bubonic plague, a bacillus carried by fleas on black rats. The disease probably first struck Mongolia during 1331–1332, and from there it crossed into Russia. Carried back from Black Sea ports, the plague reached Sicily in 1347 and then spread swiftly throughout much of Europe through human contact. Some historians contend that the Black Death may have consisted of two diseases, the bubonic plague and anthrax, which was transmitted by eating meat from diseased cattle. The first crisis lasted until 1351, and other serious outbreaks occurred in later decades. Exiting from merchant ships docked in ports, the rats moved inland carrying the deadly fleas. The crowded cities and towns, where sewage made rats more fecund, had the highest mortality rate—as much as sixty percent. Perhaps twenty million people— about one-quarter to one-third of the European population—perished in the worst disaster in recorded history caused by natural forces. Contemporaries viewed the disaster as divine punishment for humanity's sins.

Overwhelmed by terror, people abandoned their sick children, spouses, and parents. Panic-stricken people drifted into debauchery, lawlessness, and frenzied forms of religious life. Confidence in the church declined as many priests fled, depriving the sick of spiritual comfort and the dying of last rites. Organized bands of flagellants marched from region to region beating themselves and one another with sticks and whips in a desperate effort to appease God, who, they believed, had cursed them with the plague. In churches they performed a scourging gladly make laws to which he gives more prestige and sanction than Christ's law. Christ so loved His flock that He laid down his life for them and suffered sharp pain and death in order to bring them to bliss. People say that the pope so loves the prestige of this world that he grants people absolution that guarantees a straight path to Heaven so that they might perform acts that redound to his honor. And so this foolishness could be the cause of the death, in body and soul, of many thousands of people. And how does he follow Christ in this way? Christ was so patient and suffered wrongs so well that He prayed for His enemies and taught His apostles not to take vengeance. People say that the pope of Rome wishes to be avenged in every way, by killing and by damning and by other painful means that he devises. Christ taught people to live well by the example of His own life and by His words, for He did what He taught and taught in a manner that was consonant with His actions. People say that the pope acts contrary to this. His life is not an example of how other people should live, for no one should live like him, inasmuch as he acts in a manner that accords to his high state. In every deed and word, Christ sought the glory of God and suffered many assaults on His manhood for this goal; people say that the pope, to the contrary, seeks his own glory in every way, yea, even if it means the loss of the worship of God. And so he manufactures many groundless gabblings.

If these and similar accusations are true of the pope of Rome, he is the very Antichrist and not Christ's vicar on earth.

Questions for Analysis

1. Why was John Wycliffe critical of the church?
2. Why did the church regard his teachings as a serious threat to its mission?

Source: From Alfred Andrea, *The Medieval Record*, 1E. © 1997 Wadsworth, a part of Cengage Learning, Inc. Reproduced by permission. www.cengage.com/permissions.

ceremony in which they used an instrument with iron spikes attached. "With such scourges," wrote a contemporary, "they beat themselves on their naked bodies so that they became swollen and blue, the blood ran down to the ground and bespattered the walls. . . . Occasionally they drove the spikes so deep into the flesh that they could only be pulled out by a . . . wrench."[1] Expressing the pervasive gloom and pessimism of these times, art concentrated on morbid scenes of decaying flesh, open graves laden with worm-eaten corpses—even the Madonna was represented as a corpse being eaten by snakes and frogs—dances of death, and the torments of hell. Sometimes this hysteria was directed against Jews, who were accused of causing the plague by poisoning wells. Terrible massacres of Jews, often by mass burnings, occurred despite the pleas of the papacy. Whole Jewish communities in Germany and Switzerland were exterminated. Invited by Duke Casimir II, who hoped they would stimulate economic activity, many Jews fled to Poland.

The millions of deaths caused production of food and goods to plummet. However, depopulation was a boon for surviving artisans, who found opportunities and higher wages in depopulated towns desperate for skilled workers. A diminishing labor pool also benefited peasants, who were able to attain lighter burdens from strapped lords, and free peasants who toiled as laborers demanded higher wages. The combination of lower agricultural prices and increasing wages hurt aristocratic landowners. As their agricultural income lessened, nobles tried to make peasants bear the brunt of the crisis. A law decreed in England in

THE GREAT PLAGUE. The Black Death, or bubonic plague, devastated Europe, carrying off entire villages. A new piety swept through European art in the plague's aftermath. The elegant French courtly love style was replaced by morbid scenes of decaying flesh and suffering saints. (Snark/Art Resource, N.Y.)

1349 required peasants to work for lords at fixed wages. Similar regulations of wages in German, Spanish, and Portuguese principalities aggravated tensions between peasants and nobles.

Economic and social tensions, some of them antedating the Black Death, escalated into rebellions. Each rebellion had its own specific causes, but a general pattern characterized the uprisings in the countryside. When kings and lords, breaking with customary social relationships, imposed new and onerous regulations, the peasants rose in defense of their traditional rights. No doubt their

revolt was also fueled by an instinctive hatred for the haughty lords, who, for centuries, had treated peasants with contempt. In 1323, the lords' attempt to reimpose old manorial obligations infuriated the free peasants of Flanders, whose condition had improved in earlier decades. The Peasants' Revolt lasted five bloody years. In 1358, French peasants took up arms in protest against the plundering of the countryside by soldiers. Perhaps twenty thousand peasants died in the uprising known as the Jacquerie. In 1381, English peasants revolted, angered over legislation that tied them to the land and imposed new taxes. John Ball, who claimed to be a priest, expressed egalitarian sentiments.

> *My good friends, things cannot go on well in England, nor ever will until everything shall be in common; when there shall neither be vassal nor lord, and all distinctions leveled; when the lords shall be no more masters than ourselves. But ill have they used us! and for what reason do they thus hold us in bondage? Are we not all descended from the same parents, Adam and Eve? and what can they show, or what reasons give, why they should be more the masters than ourselves? except, perhaps, in making us labor and work, for them to spend. . . . They have handsome manors, when we must brave the wind and rain in our labors in the field; but it is from our labor they have wherewith to support their pomp.*[2]

Like the revolts in Flanders and France, the uprising in England failed. To the landed aristocracy, the peasants were sinners attacking a social system ordained by God. Possessing superior might, the nobility suppressed the peasants, sometimes with savage cruelty.

Social unrest afflicted the towns as well as the countryside. The wage earners of Florence (1378), the weavers of Ghent (1382), and the poor of Paris (1382) rose up against the ruling oligarchy. These revolts were generally initiated not by the poorest and most downtrodden but by those who had made some gains and were eager for more. The rebellions of the urban poor were crushed just like the peasant uprisings.

The Hundred Years' War

In earlier centuries wars in medieval Europe had generally been short and small in scale with casualties limited; in the fourteenth century this trend changed dramatically. The most destructive war was the series of conflicts known as the Hundred Years' War (1337–1453). Because English kings ruled parts of France, conflicts between the two monarchies were common. In the opening phase of the war, the English inflicted terrible defeats on French knights at the battles of Crécy (1346) and Poitiers (1356). Using longbows, which allowed them to shoot arrows rapidly, English archers cut down wave after wave of charging French cavalry. The war continued on and off throughout the fourteenth century. During periods of truce, gangs of unemployed soldiers roamed the French countryside killing and stealing, actions that precipitated the Jacquerie.

After the battle of Agincourt (1415), won by the English under Henry V, the English controlled most of northern France. It appeared that England would shortly conquer France and join the two lands under one crown. At this crucial moment in French history, a young, illiterate peasant girl, Joan of Arc (1412–1431), helped rescue France. Believing that God commanded her to drive the English out of France, Joan rallied the demoralized French troops, leading them in battle. In 1429, she liberated the besieged city of Orléans. Later she was captured and imprisoned by the English, and in 1431 she was condemned as a heretic and a witch by a hand-picked church court and was burned at the stake. Inspired by Joan's death, the French drove the English from all French territory except the port of Calais.

During the Hundred Years' War, French kings introduced new taxes, which added substantially to their incomes. These monies furnished them with the means to organize a professional army of well-paid, loyal troops. By evoking a sense of pride and oneness in the French people, the war also contributed to a growing, but still incomplete, national unity. The English, too, emerged from the war with a greater sense of solidarity, and Parliament, because it had to finance the war, gained in stature. However, the war had horrendous consequences for the French peasants. Thousands of farmers were killed, and valuable farmland was destroyed by English armies and marauding bands of mercenaries. In a portentous development, the later stages of the Hundred Years' War saw the use of gunpowder and heavy artillery.

THE DECLINE OF THE PAPACY

The principal sign of breakdown in the Late Middle Ages was the waning authority and prestige of the papacy. In the High Middle Ages, the papacy had been the dominant institution in Christendom, but in the Late Middle Ages, its power disintegrated. The medieval ideal of a unified Christian commonwealth guided by the papacy was shattered. Papal authority declined in the face of the growing power of kings, who championed the parochial interests of states. The papacy's prestige and its capacity to lead diminished as it became more embroiled in European politics. Many pious Christians felt that the pope behaved more like a secular ruler than like an Apostle of Christ. Political theorists and church reformers further undermined papal authority.

Conflict with France

Pope Boniface VIII (1294–1303) vigorously upheld papal claims to supremacy over secular rulers. In the famous bull *Unam Sanctam* (1302), he declared:

> *If the earthly power errs, it shall be judged by the spiritual power . . . but [the pope] can be judged only by God not by man. . . . Whoever therefore resists this power so ordained by God resists the ordinance of God. . . . Therefore, we declare, state, define, and pronounce that it is altogether necessary to salvation for every human creature to be subject to the Roman Pontiff.[3]*

But in trying to enforce this idea of papal supremacy on proud and increasingly powerful kings, Boniface suffered defeat and humiliation.

Philip IV of France (1285–1314) taxed the church in his land to raise revenue for war. In doing so, he disregarded the church prohibition against the taxing of its property without papal permission. In 1296, in the bull *Clericis Laicos*, Pope Boniface VIII decreed that kings and lords who imposed taxes on the clergy and the clergy who paid them would be excommunicated. Far from bowing to the pope's threat, Philip acted forcefully to assert authority over the church in his kingdom. Boniface backed down from his position, declaring that the French king could tax the clergy in times of national emergency. Thus, the matter was resolved to the advantage of the state.

A DEAD MAN BEFORE HIS JUDGE: A MINIATURE PAINTING FROM THE ROMAN BOOK OF HOURS, FRANCE, C. 1420. God the Father, bearing the orb and sword of universal sovereignty, hears the final prayer of a dying man and sends an angel to liberate the man's soul from the clutches of a demon. A preoccupation with death and demons was characteristic of late medieval Christian art. (© Art Media/ HIP/The Image Works.)

A second dispute had more disastrous consequences for Boniface. Philip tried and imprisoned a French bishop despite Boniface's warning that this was an illegal act and a violation of church law and tradition, which held that the church, not the state, must judge the clergy. Philip summoned the first meeting of the Estates General to gain the backing of the nation. Shortly afterward, Boniface threatened to excommunicate Philip.

The outraged monarch raided the papal summer palace at Anagni in September 1303 and captured the pope. Although Boniface was released, this shocking event proved too much for him, and a month later he died.

Boniface's two successors, Benedict XI (1303–1304) and Clement V (1305–1314), tried to conciliate Philip. In particular, Clement decided to remain at Avignon, a town on the southeastern French frontier, where he had set up a temporary residence.

From 1309 to 1377, a period known as the Babylonian Captivity, the popes were all French and resided in Avignon, not Rome. During this time, the papacy, removed from Rome and deprived of revenues from the Papal States in Italy, was often forced to pursue policies favorable to France. The growing antipapalism among the laity further damaged the papal image. Laypeople were repelled by the luxurious style of living at Avignon and by the appointment of high churchmen to lands where they did not know the language and showed little concern for the local population. Criticism of the papacy increased.

The conflict between Boniface and Philip provoked a battle of words between proponents of papal supremacy and defenders of royal rights. The most important critique of clerical intrusion into worldly affairs was *The Defender of the Peace* (1324) by Marsiglio of Padua (c. 1290–c. 1343). Marsiglio held that the state ran according to principles that had nothing to do with religious commands originating in a higher realm. Religion dealt with a supernatural world and with principles of faith that could not be proved by reason, wrote Marsiglio. Politics, in contrast, dealt with a natural world and with the affairs of the human community. Political thinkers should not try to make the earthly realm conform to articles of faith. According to Marsiglio, the state was self-sufficient; it needed no instruction from a higher authority. Thus, Marsiglio denied the essential premises of medieval papal political theory: that kings received their power from God; that the pope, as God's vicar, was empowered to guide kings; that the state, as part of a divinely ordered world, must conform to and fulfill supranatural ends; and that the clergy were above the laws of the state. Marsiglio viewed the church as a spiritual institution with no temporal power. "Christ himself," said Marsiglio, "refuse[d] rulership in this world . . . and taught that all men, both priests and non-priests, should be subject . . . to the coercive judgment of the rulers of this world."[4] Marsiglio even went so far as to suggest that the church should be subordinate to the state; his concept of an autonomous state that did not answer to clerical authority anticipates modern political thought.

The Great Schism and the Conciliar Movement

The Avignon popes were often competent men who, despite the hard times that had overtaken the papacy, tried to bolster papal power. They tightened their hold over church administration by reserving for themselves certain appointments and collections of fees formerly handled by local bishops. Through a deliberate effort at financial centralization, including the imposition of new taxes and the more efficient collection of old ones, the Avignon popes substantially increased papal income.

Although Pope Gregory XI returned the papacy to Rome in 1377, the papacy was to suffer another humiliation: the Great Schism. Elected pope in 1378, Urban VI immediately displayed tactlessness, if not mental imbalance, by abusing and even imprisoning cardinals. Fleeing from Rome, the cardinals declared that the election of Urban had been invalid and elected Clement VII as the new pope. Refusing to step down, Urban excommunicated Clement, who responded in kind. To the utter confusion and anguish of Christians throughout Europe, there were now two popes: Urban ruling from Rome and Clement from Avignon.

Prominent churchmen urged the convening of a general council to end the disgraceful schism, which obstructed the papacy from performing its sacred duties. Held in 1409 and attended by hundreds of churchmen, the Council of Pisa deposed both Urban and Clement and elected a new pope. Since neither deposed pope recognized the council's decision, Christendom then had three popes.

PORTRAIT OF JOAN OF ARC: WITCH OR SAINT? Claiming that heavenly voices had called upon her to lead the armies of France to victory over the English, a young peasant girl, Joan of Arc, persuaded the French crown prince to give her command of the army. Victorious in battle, she fulfilled all that was required of her, including the crowning of the new King at Rheims. Captured soon after, she was tried as a witch by an English-dominated court and executed in Rouen in 1431. She has been a heroine and inspiration to many modern artists, poets, and dramatists. (The Art Archive/Archives Nationales Paris/CCI.)

A new council was called at Constance in 1414. In the struggle that ensued, each of the three popes either abdicated or was deposed in favor of an appointment by the council. In 1417, the Great Schism ended.

During the first half of the fifteenth century, church councils met at Pisa (1409), Constance (1414–1418), and Basel (1431–1449) in order to end the schism, combat heresy, and reform the church. The Conciliar Movement attempted to transform the papal monarchy into a constitutional system in which the pope's power would be regulated by a general council. Supporters of the movement held that the papacy could not reform the church as effectively as a general council representing the clergy. But the Conciliar Movement ended in failure. As the Holy Roman Emperor and then the French monarch withdrew their support from the councils, the papacy regained its authority over the higher clergy. In 1460, Pope Pius II condemned the Conciliar Movement as heretical.

Medieval popes claimed both spiritual and temporal powers. They saw this as a sacred duty, fulfilling the wishes of God who was working through them. This outlook deeply embroiled the papacy in European power politics and worldly life at the neglect of its spiritual and moral responsibilities. Many devout Christians longed for religious renewal and a return to simple piety; the papacy did not hear this cry for reform. The papacy's failure to provide creative leadership for reform made possible the Protestant Reformation of the sixteenth century. By splitting Christendom into Catholic and Protestant, the Reformation destroyed forever the vision of a Christian world commonwealth guided by God's vicar, the pope.

Fourteenth-Century Heresies

Another threat to papal power and to the medieval ideal of a universal Christian community guided by the church came from radical reformers who questioned the function and authority of the entire church hierarchy. These heretics in the Late Middle Ages were forerunners of the Protestant Reformation. The two principal dissenters were the Englishman John Wycliffe (c. 1320–1384) and the Czech Jan Hus (c. 1369–1415).

By stressing a personal relationship between the individual and God and by claiming that the Bible itself, rather than church teachings, is the ultimate Christian authority, Wycliffe, a respected English theologian teaching at the University of Oxford, challenged the fundamental position of the medieval church: that the avenue to salvation passed through the church alone. He argued that Scripture, which was the final authority, needed no further development by church authorities and that the sacraments are not necessary for salvation.

He denounced the wealth of the higher clergy and sought a return to the spiritual purity and material poverty of the early church. To Wycliffe, the wealthy, elaborately organized hierarchy of the church was unnecessary and wrong. The splendidly dressed and propertied bishops bore no resemblance to the simple people who first followed Christ. Indeed, these worldly bishops, headed by a princely and tyrannical pope, were really anti-Christians, the "fiends of Hell." Wycliffe wanted the state to confiscate church property and the clergy to embrace poverty. By denying that priests changed the bread and wine of Communion into the substance of the body and blood of Christ, Wycliffe rejected the special powers of the clergy.

In Bohemia, Wycliffe's ideas were enthusiastically received by Czech reformers led by Jan Hus. Like Wycliffe, Hus advocated vernacular translations of the Bible, which would be accessible to common people, and he upbraided the upper clergy for their luxury and immorality.

Both movements were declared heretical. The church deprived the Lollards—an order of poor priests that spread Wycliffe's teachings—of their priestly functions. In the early fifteenth century, some of Wycliffe's followers were burned at the stake, as was Jan Hus. Nevertheless, the church could not crush the dissenters' followers or eradicate their teachings. To some extent, the doctrines of the Protestant Reformation would parallel the teachings of Wycliffe.

THE BREAKUP OF THE THOMISTIC SYNTHESIS

In the Late Middle Ages, the papacy lost power as kings, political theorists, and religious dissenters challenged papal claims to supreme leadership. The great theological synthesis constructed by the scholastic theologians of the twelfth and thirteenth centuries was also breaking down. The process of fragmentation evident in the history of the church took place in philosophy as well.

Saint Thomas Aquinas's system culminated the scholastic attempt to show the basic agreement of philosophy and religion. In the fourteenth century,

a number of thinkers cast doubt on the possibility of synthesizing Aristotelianism and Christianity, that is, reason and faith. Consequently, philosophy grew more analytical and critical. Denying that reason could demonstrate the truth of Christian doctrines with certainty, philosophers tried to separate reason from faith. Whereas Aquinas had said that reason proved or clarified much of revelation, fourteenth-century thinkers asserted that the basic propositions of Christianity were not open to rational proof. Whereas Aquinas had held that faith supplemented and perfected reason, some philosophers were now proclaiming that reason often contradicted faith.

Duns Scotus (1265–1308), a Scottish Franciscan, held that human reason cannot prove that God is omnipotent, that he forgives sins, that he rewards the righteous and punishes the wicked, or that the soul is immortal. These Christian doctrines, which scholastic philosophers believed could be proven by reason, were for Scotus the province of revelation and faith, not reason.

To be sure, this new outlook did not urge abandoning faith in favor of reason. Faith had to prevail in any conflict with reason because faith rested on God, the highest authority in the universe. But the relationship between reason and revelation was altered. Articles of faith, it was now held, had nothing to do with reason; they were to be believed, not proved. Reason was not an aid to theology but a separate sphere of activity. This new attitude snapped the link between reason and faith that Aquinas had so skillfully forged. The scholastic synthesis was disintegrating.

The chief proponent of the new outlook was William of Ockham (c. 1285–1349). In contrast to Aquinas, Ockham insisted that natural reason could not prove God's existence, the soul's immortality, or any other essential Christian doctrine. Reason could say only that God probably exists and that he probably endowed humankind with an immortal soul. But it could not prove these propositions with certainty. The tenets of faith were beyond the reach of reason, said Ockham; there was no rational foundation to Christianity. For Ockham, reason and faith did not necessarily complement each other as they did for Aquinas; it was neither possible nor helpful to join reason to faith. Ockham, however, sought not to undermine faith—only to disengage it from reason.

Ockham's views had wide implications. He recognized the existence of divine law, which the pope was empowered to administer, but limited papal authority only to matters of faith. The pope's power did not extend into the arena of worldly politics. Ockham also furthered the use of reason to comprehend nature. His approach, separating natural knowledge from religious dogma, made it easier to explore the natural world empirically without fitting it into a religious framework. Thus, Ockham is a forerunner of the modern mentality, which is characterized by a separation of reason from religion and an interest in the empirical investigation of nature.

THE MIDDLE AGES AND THE MODERN WORLD: CONTINUITY AND DISCONTINUITY

Medieval civilization began to decline in the fourteenth century, but no "dark age" comparable to the three centuries following Rome's fall descended on Europe; its economic and political institutions and technological skills had grown too strong. Instead, the waning of the Middle Ages opened up possibilities for another stage in Western civilization: the modern age.

The modern world is linked to the Middle Ages in innumerable ways. European cities, the middle class, the state system, English common law, universities—all had their origins in the Middle Ages. During medieval times, important advances were made in business practices, including partnerships, systematic bookkeeping, and the bill of exchange, which paved the way for modern banking. By translating and commenting on the writings of Greek and Arabic thinkers, medieval scholars preserved a priceless intellectual heritage without which the modern mind could never have evolved. In the universities scholastic thinkers had established a tradition of critical thinking that in future centuries

would nurture intellectual activity in areas other than theology.

Feudal traditions lasted long after the Middle Ages. Up to the French Revolution, for instance, French aristocrats enjoyed special privileges and exercised power over local government. In England, the aristocracy controlled local government until the Industrial Revolution transformed English society in the nineteenth century. Retaining the medieval ideal of the noble warrior, aristocrats continued to dominate the officer corps of European armies through the nineteenth century and even into the twentieth. Aristocratic notions of duty, honor, loyalty, and courtly love have endured into our own day.

During the Middle Ages, Europeans began to take the lead over the Muslims, the Byzantines, the Chinese, and all other peoples in the use of technology. Medieval technology and inventiveness stemmed in part from Christianity, which taught that God had created the world specifically for human beings to subdue and exploit. Consequently, medieval people tried to employ animal power and labor-saving machinery to relieve human drudgery. Moreover, Christianity taught that God was above nature, not within it, so the Christians faced no spiritual obstacle to exploiting nature—unlike, for instance, the Hindus. In contrast to classical humanism, the Christian outlook did not consider manual work degrading; even monks combined it with study.

The Christian stress on the sacred worth of the individual (each person had an immortal soul that was God's concern), on human equality (differences in rank and birth were of no account to God on **Judgment Day**), and on the higher law of God (divine precepts had a greater pull on conscience than did the state's laws) has never ceased to influence Western civilization. Even though in modern times the various Christian churches have not often taken the lead in political and social reform, the ideals identified with the Judeo-Christian tradition have become part of the Western heritage. As such, they have inspired social reformers who may no longer identify with their ancestral religion.

In structuring canon (church) law into a coherent and rational system, church jurists provided a model for legal systems in emerging European states. Moreover, specific elements of canon law have become an integral part of modern Western law. Medieval jurists, for example, argued for the replacement of trials by ordeals of fire or water, which were central to ancient Germanic folk law, with rational trial procedures and insisted that marriages based on fraud or duress could be invalidated.

Believing that God's law was superior to state or national decrees, medieval philosophers provided a theoretical basis for opposing tyrannical kings who violated Christian principles. The idea that both the ruler and the ruled are bound by a higher law would, in a secularized form, become a principal element of modern liberal thought.

Feudalism also contributed to the history of liberty. According to feudal custom, the king, as a member of the feudal community, was duty-bound to honor agreements made with his vassals. Lords possessed personal rights, which the king was obliged to respect. Resentful of a king who ran roughshod over customary feudal rights, lords also negotiated contracts with the crown, such as Magna Carta (1215), to define and guard their customary liberties. To protect themselves from the arbitrary behavior of a king, feudal lords initiated what came to be called *government by consent* and the *rule of law*.

During the Middle Ages, then, there gradually emerged the idea that law was not imposed on inferiors by an absolute monarch but required the collaboration of the king and his subjects; that the king, too, was bound by the law; and that lords had the right to resist a monarch who violated agreements. A related phenomenon was the rise of representative institutions with which the king was expected to consult on the realm's affairs. The most notable of such institutions was the British Parliament; though subordinate to the king, it became a permanent part of the state. Later, in the seventeenth century, Parliament would successfully challenge royal authority. Thus, continuity exists between the feudal tradition of a king bound by law and the modern practice of limiting the authority of the head of state.

Although the elements of continuity are clear, the characteristic outlook of the Middle Ages is as different from that of the modern age as it was from the outlook of the Greco-Roman past.

Religion—often expressing a disdain of earthly pursuits and a preoccupation with the world to come—was the integrating feature of the Middle Ages, whereas science and secularism—a preoccupation with worldly life—determine the modern outlook. The period from the Italian Renaissance of the fifteenth century through the eighteenth-century Age of Enlightenment saw a gradual breaking away from the medieval worldview—a rejection of the medieval conception of nature, the individual, and the purpose of life. The transition from medieval to modern was neither sudden nor complete, for there are no sharp demarcation lines separating historical periods. Although many distinctively medieval ways endured in the sixteenth, seventeenth, and even eighteenth centuries, these centuries saw as well the rise of new intellectual, political, and economic forms, which marked the emergence of **modernity**.

Medieval thought began with the existence of God and the truth of his revelation as interpreted by the church, which set the standards and defined the purposes for human endeavor. The medieval mind rejected the fundamental principle of Greek philosophy: the autonomy of reason. Without the guidance of revealed truth, reason was seen as feeble. Philosophical inquiry was permissible only if the mind arrived at clerically approved conclusions.

Scholastics engaged in genuine philosophical speculation and demonstrated impressive signs of logical thinking, but they did not allow philosophy to challenge the basic premises of their faith. For them, the dissemination of views that contradicted church doctrine had to be prohibited lest they corrupt the mind of the faithful, endangering their salvation. Unlike either ancient or modern thinkers, medieval scholars ultimately believed that reason alone could not provide a unified view of nature or society. A rational soul had to be guided by a divine light. For all medieval philosophers, the natural order depended on a supernatural order for its origin and purpose. To understand the natural world properly, it was necessary to know its relationship to the higher world. The discoveries of reason had to accord with Scripture as interpreted by the church. In medieval thought, says the historian-philosopher Ernst Cassirer,

Wisdom Urges Medieval Scholars Forward. During the Middle Ages, Europeans made considerable advances in technology. The astrolabe, sundials, and mechanical clocks shown here exemplify medieval technical skills. (Master of Jean Rolin II/The Bridgeman Art Library/Getty Images.)

neither science nor morality, neither law nor state, can be erected on its own foundations. Supernatural assistance is always needed to bring them to true perfection. . . . Reason is and remains the servant of revelation; within the sphere of natural intellectual and psychological forces, reason leads toward, and prepares the ground for, revelation.[5]

In the modern view, both nature and the human intellect are self-sufficient. Nature is a mathematical system that operates without miracles or any other form of divine intervention. To comprehend nature and society, the mind needs no divine assistance; it accepts no authority above reason. The modern mentality finds it unacceptable to reject the conclusions of science on the basis of clerical authority and revelation or to ground politics, law, or economics on religious dogma. It refuses to settle public issues by appeals to religious belief, which is now seen as a strictly private concern.

The medieval philosopher understood both nature and society to be a hierarchical order. The heavens were qualitatively superior in purpose and substance to the earthly realm. God was the source of moral values, and the church was responsible for teaching and upholding these ethical norms. Kings acquired their right to rule from God. The entire social structure constituted a hierarchy: the clergy, the highest order, guided society according to Christian standards; lords defended Christian society from its enemies; and serfs, lowest in the social order, toiled for the good of all. In the hierarchy of knowledge, a lower form of knowledge derived from the senses, and the highest type of knowledge, theology, dealt with God's revelation. To the medieval mind, this hierarchical ordering of nature, society, and knowledge had a divine sanction.

Rejecting the medieval division of the universe into higher and lower realms and superior and inferior substances, the modern view postulated the uniformity of nature and of nature's laws: the cosmos knows no privilege of rank; heavenly bodies follow the same laws of nature as earthly objects. Space is geometric and homogeneous, not hierarchical, heterogeneous, and qualitative. The universe was no longer conceived as finite and closed but as infinite, and the operations of nature were explained mathematically. The modern thinker studies mathematical law and chemical composition, not grades of perfection. Spiritual meaning is not sought in an examination of the material world. Roger Bacon, for example, described seven coverings of the eye and then concluded that God had fashioned the eye in this manner in order to express the seven gifts of the Spirit. This way of thinking is alien to the modern outlook. So too is the medieval belief that natural disasters, such as plagues and famines, are God's punishments for people's sins.

The outlook of the modern West also broke with the rigid division of medieval society into three orders: clergy, nobles, and commoners. The intellectual justification for this arrangement, as expressed by the English prelate John of Salisbury (c. 1115–1180), has been rejected by modern Westerners: "For inferiors owe it to their superiors to provide them with service, just as the superiors in their turn owe it to their inferiors to provide them with all things needful for their protection and succor."[6] To be sure, Christian theorists also maintained that as God's children, all human beings are in principle equal in God's eyes. Opposing the feudal principle that an individual's obligations and rights are a function of his or her rank in society, the modern view stressed equality of opportunity and equal treatment under the law.

It rejected the idea that society should be guided by clergy who were deemed to possess a special wisdom, by nobles who were entitled to special privileges, and by monarchs who were thought to receive their power from God.

The modern West also rejected the personal and customary character of feudal law. As the modern state developed, law assumed an impersonal and objective character. For example, if the lord demanded more than the customary forty days of military service, the vassal might refuse to comply because he would see the lord's request as an unpardonable violation of custom and agreement, as well as an infringement on his liberties. In the modern state, with a constitution and a representative assembly, if a new law increasing the length of military service is passed, it merely replaces the old law. People do not refuse to obey it because the government has broken faith or violated custom.

In the modern world, the individual's relationship to the universe has been radically transformed. Medieval people lived in a geocentric universe that was finite in space and time. The universe was small, enclosed by a sphere of stars, beyond which were the heavens. The universe, it was believed, was some four thousand years old, and, in the not-too-distant future, Christ would return and human history would end. People in the Middle Ages knew why they were on earth and what was expected of them; they never doubted that heaven would be their reward for living a Christian life. Preparation for heaven was the ultimate aim of life. J. H. Randall Jr., a historian of ideas, eloquently sums up the medieval view of a purposeful universe in which the human being's position was clearly defined.

> *The world was governed throughout by the omnipotent will and omniscient mind of God, whose sole interests were centered in man, his trial, his fall, his suffering and his glory. Worm of the dust as he was, man was yet the central object in the whole universe. . . . And when his destiny was completed, the heavens would be rolled up as a scroll and he would dwell with the Lord forever. Only those who rejected God's freely offered grace and with hardened hearts refused repentance would be cut off from this eternal life.*[7]

Joan of Arc

A crucial phase in the Hundred Years' War occurred in 1415 when England inflicted an overwhelming defeat on the French at Agincourt. The victorious English imposed on the French the Treaty of Troyes (1420). Its terms stipulated that the daughter of Charles VI, the French monarch, would marry the English ruler, Henry V, and that their future son would reign over the dual monarchy of England and France. This provision deprived Charles VI's only living son, the dauphin Charles, from succeeding to the throne. From Bourges in central France, the dauphin continued the struggle against the English invaders and their Burgundian allies. In 1428, the English besieged Orléans in preparation for an attack on Bourges. The dauphin's position seemed hopeless.

At this critical moment, Joan of Arc appeared on the scene. Born to a peasant family in northern France, Joan very early demonstrated extreme piety. At age thirteen, she experienced revelations—voices from angels and saints who guided her behavior. When she was about sixteen, her voices instructed her to raise the siege of Orléans and have Charles anointed king of France at Rheims. Joan the maid, as she was called, attracted followers who believed that Joan was sent by God to rescue Orléans from the English.

Demonstrating great resolve, Joan, dressed in men's clothing and accompanied by believers in her mission, made the arduous journey to the dauphin's castle. Charles reluctantly granted an audience to Joan, whom some of his counselors considered mad. After listening to Joan detail her divine mission, Charles had her examined by his clerks and sages, who reported that the uneducated, but devout, peasant girl was neither a heretic nor a sorceress. With the military position worsening, the desperate dauphin provided Joan with an army—perhaps this religiously inspired maid had indeed been sent by God. Wearing a full set of armor and wielding a lance, Joan demonstrated remarkable leadership and courage, which inspired her troops. She also showed a facility for military planning. To the inhabitants of Orléans, it seemed that God had provided them with a deliverer. When she entered the city, crowds pressed to touch her. Aided by the citizens of Orléans, Joan's

This comforting medieval vision is alien to the modern outlook. Today, in a universe some thirteen to fourteen billion years old, in which the earth is a tiny speck floating in an endless cosmic ocean, where life evolved over tens of millions of years, many Westerners no longer believe that human beings are special children of God; that heaven is their ultimate goal; that under their feet is hell, where grotesque demons torment sinners; or that God is an active agent in human history. To many intellectuals, the universe seems unresponsive to the religious supplications of people, and life's purpose is sought within the limits of earthly existence. For many, science and secularism have driven Christianity and faith from their central position to the periphery of human concerns.

In the nineteenth and twentieth centuries, Christian thinkers lamented the waning of faith. Distressed by all-consuming secularism, crude materialism, and vicious class and national antagonisms, these thinkers attributed the ills of the modern West to a diminishing commitment to Christianity and called for spiritual renewal.

army attacked the English fortifications. Hit by an arrow above the breast, Joan had the wound dressed and immediately returned to the fray. In a decisive encounter, the maid grabbed her standard from a squire and led a successful assault on an English fortress. Soon after, the English abandoned the siege: the maid's forces had liberated the city. Several months later, Joan achieved her greatest victory, an open-field battle at Patay, which caught the English by surprise. Following the battle, the dauphin was crowned Charles VII at Rheims.

Meanwhile, in the ongoing conflict with the English and Burgundians, Joan could not escape a Burgundian siege and was taken prisoner. Charles VII made no effort to ransom Joan; he simply abandoned her. Purchasing the now-famous prisoner from the Burgundians, the English organized a show trial in Rouen, conducted by learned but hostile French clerics, to prove that the despised Joan was a heretic and a witch. The proceedings took about five months. During that time, Joan wore leg irons; at night in her dungeon, her jailers chained the leg irons to the foot of the bed. During the interrogation, Joan displayed remarkable self-control, dignity, cleverness, and even eloquence and humor, which often exasperated the inquisitors. The inquisitors asked Joan if she would defer to the church when told that her voices were illusions; Joan replied that her voices had not commanded her to disregard the church but she served the Lord first, a rebellious act that amounted to heresy.

When the judges accused her of lying and threatened to inflict torture unless she altered her statements, Joan replied: "Truly, though you were to have my limbs torn off and send the soul out of my body, I should not say otherwise; and if I did tell you otherwise, I should always thereafter say that you had made me speak so by force."*

After the judges ruled that she had been doing the work of the Devil, Joan was declared a heretic and condemned to burn at the stake. The sentence was carried out on May 30, 1431, and her ashes were thrown into the Seine. In 1456, the church nullified the condemnation, and in 1920 Joan was declared a saint.

---

*Quoted in Régine Pernoud, *Joan of Arc: By Herself and Her Witnesses*, trans. Edward Hyans (Lanham, Md.: Scarborough House, 1994), 206.

Some of them, looking back nostalgically to the Middle Ages, when life had an overriding religious purpose and few doubted the truth of Christian teachings, contended that the modern West would benefit from a reaffirmation of those Christian concerns and values that had energized medieval society.

The modern outlook developed gradually in the period from the Renaissance to the eighteenth-century Age of Enlightenment. Mathematics rendered the universe comprehensible. Economic and political thought broke free of the religious frame of reference. Science became the great hope of the future. The thinkers of the Enlightenment wanted to liberate humanity from superstition, ignorance, and traditions that could not pass the test of reason. They saw themselves as emancipating culture from theological dogma and clerical authority. Rejecting the Christian idea of a person's inherent sinfulness, they held that the individual was basically good and that evil resulted from faulty institutions, poor education, and bad leadership. Thus, the concept of a rational and free society in which individuals could realize their potential slowly emerged.

❖   ❖   ❖

NOTES

1. Quoted in Johannes Nohl, *The Black Death: A Chronicle of the Plague*, trans. C. H. Clarke (Yardley, Pennsylvania, 2006: originally published in 1926), 230.

2. Jean Froissart, *Chronicles of England, France, Spain* (London: Henry G. Bohn, 1849), 653.

3. Excerpted in Brian Tierney, ed., *The Crisis of Church and State*, 1050–1300 (Englewood Cliffs, N.J.: Prentice-Hall, 1964), 189.

4. Marsilius of Padua, *Marsilius of Padua: The Defender of the Peace*, trans. Alan Gewirth (New York: Columbia University Press, 1956), 2:119.

5. Ernst Cassirer, *The Philosophy of the Enlightenment* (Boston: Beacon Press, 1955), 40.

6. John of Salisbury, *Policraticus*, trans. John Dickinson (New York: Russell and Russell, 1963), 243–244.

7. J. H. Randall Jr., *The Making of the Modern Mind* (Boston: Houghton Mifflin, 1940), 34.

Part Three

Early Modern Europe: From Renaissance to Enlightenment

1350–1789

1300

1400

1500

1600

1700

Politics and Society

Hundred Years' War (1337–1453)

War of Roses in England (1455–1485)
Rule of Ferdinand and Isabella in Spain
  (1469–1516)
Charles VIII of France (1483–1498)
Henry VII; beginning of Tudor dynasty in
  England (1485–1509)
French invasion of Italy (1494)
Columbus reaches America (1492)

Henry VIII of England (1509–1547)
Francis I of France (1515–1547)
Charles V, Holy Roman emperor
  (1519–1556)
Henry VIII of England breaks with Rome
  (1529–1536)
Council of Trent (1545–1563)
Treaty of Augsburg in Germany (1555)
Philip II of Spain (1556–1598)
Elizabeth I of England (1558–1603)
Religious wars in France (1562–1598)
Revolt of the Netherlands from Spain
  (1566–1609)
Defeat of Spanish Armada (1588)

Thirty Years' War (1618–1648)
English revolutions (1640–1660,
  1688–1689)
Louis XIV of France (1643–1715)
Peter the Great of Russia (1682–1725)

War of Spanish Succession (1702–1714)
War of Austrian Succession (1740–1748)
Frederick the Great of Prussia (1740–1786)
Maria Theresa of Austria (1740–1780)
Seven Years' War (1756–1763)
Catherine the Great of Russia (1762–1796)
American Declaration of Independence
  (1776)
American Revolution (1776–1783)
Beginning of French Revolution (1789)

Thought and Culture

Italian Renaissance begins (c. 1350)

Early Renaissance artists: Brunelleschi,
  Masaccio, van Eyck
Printing with movable type (c. 1445)
Humanists: Valla, Pico della Mirandola
Late Renaissance artists: Botticelli, Leonardo
  da Vinci, Michelangelo, Raphael, Bellini,
  Giorgione, Titian
Renaissance spreads to northern Europe
  (late 15th–early 16th centuries)

Humanists: Castiglione, Erasmus,
  Montaigne, Rabelais, More, Machiavelli,
  Cervantes, Shakespeare
Luther writes Ninety-Five Theses (1517)
Calvin, *The Institutes of the Christian
  Religion* (1536)
Copernicus, *On the Revolution of the
  Heavenly Spheres* (1543)

Scientists: Kepler, Galileo, Newton
Philosophers: Bacon, Descartes, Spinoza,
  Hobbes, Bayle, Locke

Enlightenment thinkers: Voltaire,
  Montesquieu, Rousseau, Diderot, Hume,
  Adam Smith, Thomas Jefferson, Kant

Chapter 13

The Renaissance: Transition to the Modern Age

The School of Athens, *by Raphael (1483–1520). The ancient Greek philosophers, with Plato and Aristotle at the center, are depicted here, assembled in classical grandeur. Painted to decorate the Vatican, the papal palace in Rome, the picture exudes the Renaissance reverence for classical antiquity and reflects the widely held view that ancient philosophy represented a foreshadowing of Christianity and was essentially in harmony with it.* (PAINTING/Alamy Limited.)

- Italy: The Birthplace of the Renaissance
- The Renaissance Outlook: Humanism and Secular Politics
- The Spread of the Renaissance
- The Renaissance and the Modern Age

Focus Questions

1. What conditions gave rise to the Italian Renaissance?

2. What is the historical significance of Renaissance humanism?

3. How did Machiavelli's political thought mark a break with the medieval outlook?

4. What were the effects of the printing press on European civilization?

5. What were the essential features of the humanism of Erasmus, Montaigne, More, and Shakespeare?

6. Why do many historians view the Renaissance as the birth of modernity?

From the Italian Renaissance of the fifteenth century through the Age of Enlightenment of the eighteenth century, the outlook and institutions of the Middle Ages disintegrated and distinctly modern forms emerged. The radical change in European civilization could be seen on every level of society. On the economic level, commerce and industry expanded greatly, and capitalism in some countries largely replaced medieval forms of economic organization. On the political level, central government grew stronger at the expense of feudalism. On the religious level, the rise of Protestantism fragmented the unity of Christendom. On the social level, middle-class townspeople, increasing in number and wealth, were playing a more important role in economic and cultural life. On the cultural level, the clergy lost its monopoly on learning, and the otherworldly orientation of the Middle Ages gave way to a secular outlook in literature and the arts. Theology, the queen of knowledge in the Middle Ages, surrendered her crown to science. Reason, which in the Middle Ages had been subordinate to revelation, asserted its independence.

Many of these tendencies manifested themselves dramatically during the Renaissance. The word *renaissance* means "rebirth," and it is used to refer to the attempt by artists and thinkers to recover and apply the ancient learning and standards of Greece and Rome. In historical terms, the Renaissance is both a cultural movement and a period. As a movement, it was born in the city-states of northern Italy and spread to the rest of Europe. As a period, it ran from 1350 to 1600. Until the late fifteenth century, the Renaissance was restricted to Italy. What happened there in the fourteenth and fifteenth centuries sharply contrasts with civilization in the rest of Europe, which, until the end of the fifteenth century, still belonged to the Late Middle Ages.

The nineteenth-century historian Jacob Burckhardt in his classic study *The Civilization of the Renaissance in Italy* (1860) held that the Renaissance was the point of departure for the modern world. During the Renaissance, said Burckhardt, individuals showed increasing concern with worldly life and self-consciously aspired to shape their destinies—attitudes that are the key to modernity.

293

Chronology 13.1 ❖ The Renaissance

1200–1300	Bologna, Padua, and Ravenna become centers of legal studies
1300–1450	Republicanism reigns in northern Italian city-states
1304–1374	Petrarch, "father of humanism"
1378	Ciompi revolt in Florence
c. 1407–1457	Lorenzo Valla, author of *Declamation Concerning the False Decretals of Constantine*
c. 1445	Johann Gutenberg invents movable metal type
1454	Peace of Lodi is signed
1494	Charles VIII of France invades northern Italy; Pope Julius II commissions frescoes by Michelangelo for the Vatican's Sistine Chapel
1513	Machiavelli writes *The Prince*
1528	*The Book of the Courtier*, by Baldesar Castiglione, is published
1535	Sir Thomas More, English humanist and author of *Utopia*, is executed for treason

Burckhardt's thesis has been challenged, particularly by medievalists, who view the Renaissance as an extension of the Middle Ages, not as a sudden break with the past. These critics argue that Burckhardt neglected important links between medieval and Renaissance culture. One distinguishing feature of the Renaissance, the revival of classical learning, had already emerged in the High Middle Ages to such an extent that historians speak of "the renaissance of the twelfth century" and the "Twelfth-Century Awakening." The Renaissance owes much to the legal and scholastic studies that flourished in the Italian universities of Padua and Bologna before 1300. Town life and trade, hallmarks of Renaissance society, were also a heritage from the Middle Ages.

To be sure, the Renaissance was not a complete and sudden break with the Middle Ages. Many medieval ways and attitudes persisted. Nevertheless, Burckhardt's thesis that the Renaissance represents the birth of modernity has much to recommend it. Renaissance writers and artists themselves were aware of their age's novelty. They looked back on the medieval centuries as "the Dark Ages" that followed the grandeur of ancient Greece and Rome, and they believed that they were experiencing a rebirth of cultural greatness.

Renaissance artists and writers were fascinated by the cultural forms of Greece and Rome; they sought to imitate **classical** style and to capture the secular spirit of antiquity. In the process, they broke with medieval artistic and literary forms. They valued the full development of human talent and expressed fresh excitement about the possibilities of life in this world. This outlook represented a new trend in European civilization.

The Renaissance, then, was an age of transition that saw the rejection of certain elements of the medieval outlook, the revival of classical cultural forms, and the emergence of distinctly **modern** attitudes. As mentioned earlier, this rebirth began in Italy during the fourteenth century. It gradually spread north and west to Germany, France, England, and Spain during the late fifteenth and sixteenth centuries.

ITALY: THE BIRTHPLACE OF THE RENAISSANCE

The city-states of northern Italy that spawned the Renaissance were developed urban centers where the elite had the wealth, freedom, and inclination to cultivate the arts and to enjoy the fruits of worldly life. In Italy, moreover, reminders of ancient Rome's grandeur were visible everywhere. Roman roads, monuments, and manuscripts intensified Italians' links to their Roman past.

The Political Evolution of the City-States

During the Middle Ages, the feudal states of northern Italy had been absorbed into the Holy Roman Empire. They continued to owe nominal allegiance to the German emperor during the early Renaissance. But protracted wars with the papacy had sapped the empire's vitality. Its consequent weakness allowed the states of northern Italy to develop as autonomous political entities. The weakening of the papacy in the fourteenth century also promoted this development.

In their size and their varied types of governments, the city-states in northern Italy resembled those of ancient Greece. Among the more important were Rome, Milan, Florence, Venice, Mantua, Ferrara, Padua, Bologna, and Genoa. They differed markedly from most of Europe in two fundamental respects.

First, by the late eleventh and twelfth centuries, these city-states were flourishing commercial and banking centers and monopolized trade in Mediterranean areas, including trade between the East and the West. Merchant fleets, especially those of Venice and Genoa, carried goods from ports in the eastern Mediterranean westward into the Atlantic and from there north to the Baltic Sea. In contrast to the rest of Europe, the wealth of these cities lay not in land but in commerce and industry. When popes, monarchs, and feudal magnates of Europe needed money, they borrowed it from Italian, especially Florentine, merchant-bankers.

Second, the predominance of business and commerce within these city-states meant that the feudal nobility, which held the land beyond the city walls, played a much lesser role in government than they did elsewhere in Europe. By the end of the twelfth century, the city-states no longer were dominated by the feudal nobility, or landed aristocracy. The aristocracy and the rich merchants had to share power, and when their alliances broke down, as they often did, the two groups struggled for power based on their opposing interests and outlooks. The interests of the smaller merchants and the artisans in the towns also had to be catered to. When they were not, those groups rioted and rebelled, as they did, for instance, in 1378, during the revolt of the *Ciompi* (wool-workers) in Florence.

Politically, the city-states in northern Italy were inherently unstable. The instability had two sources: internal conflicts between merchants and nobles and external rivalries among the city-states themselves. The city-states managed to keep both the papacy and the Holy Roman Empire at bay, sometimes by playing one giant against the other. But the price of this continued independence was that the city-states, without any externally imposed power structure, had to seek their own solutions to their instability. Out of this situation came experiments in the form and technique of government. The origins of modern political thought and practice can be discerned in this experimentation, which is an important link between the Renaissance and the modern age.

The political experimentation in the northern Italian city-states can usefully, if only roughly, be divided into two periods: the first (1300–1450) marked by the defense of **republicanism**; the second (1450–1550), by the triumph of **despotism**. By the end of the twelfth century, the city-states had adopted a fairly uniform pattern of republican self-government built around the office of a chief magistrate. Elected by the citizens on the basis of a broad franchise, the chief magistrate ruled with the advice of two councils—a large public one and a small secret one. His powers were tightly circumscribed by the **constitution**; with his term of office restricted ordinarily to six months, he could be removed from government or punished at the end of his tenure.

The city-states not only developed republican institutions but also devised important theories to defend and justify their liberty and self-government in the face of their external enemies, the papacy and the empire. With the emperor, they argued that their customary feudal subjection to imperial authority must be radically adjusted to fit the changed reality that they were in fact self-governing. With the papacy, they contended that Christ had denied all political jurisdiction to the clergy, including the pope, and that this fact undercut the papal claim to political control in Italy and elsewhere.

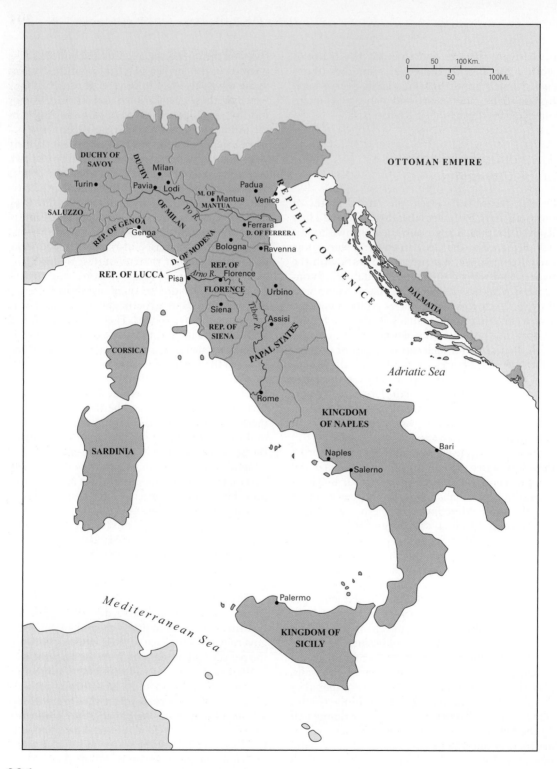

However, given the city-states' internal instability and rivalry, their republicanism proved precarious. During the fourteenth and early fifteenth centuries, the republican institutions in one city after another toppled in favor of despotic rule. Three conditions were responsible for this development. First, class war between rich merchants and nobles caused one group or the other, or both, to seek a resolution of the crisis by turning to one-person rule. Second, the economic disasters, famine, and disease of the period from 1350 to 1450 encouraged the drift toward despotism. Northern Italy was particularly hard hit by the bubonic plague. The citizenry lost faith in the ability of short-term republican governments to cope with such emergencies and put its trust in long-term, one-man rule. Third, and perhaps most important, the city-states, in wars with their rivals, had come to rely on mercenary troops. The leaders of those troops, the notorious *condottieri*—unschooled in and owing no loyalty to the republican tradition—simply seized power during emergencies.

Some city-states held out for a long time against the trend toward despotism. Among those that did, Florence was by far the most successful. In the process, the Florentines developed new arguments and theories for the maintenance of republicanism and liberty (discussed later in this chapter). But by the middle of the fifteenth century, even Florentine republicanism was giving way before the intrigues of a rich banking family, the Medicis. They had installed themselves in power in the 1430s, with the return of Cosimo de' Medici from exile. Cosimo's grandson, Lorenzo the Magnificent, completed the destruction of the republican constitution in 1480, when he managed to set up a government staffed by his own supporters.

The one city-state where republicanism survived until the advent of Napoleon was Venice.

◀ *Map 13.1* ITALIAN CITY-STATES, C. 1494 During the Renaissance, Italy was divided between large kingdoms in the south, dominated by the Spanish monarchy, and smaller city-states in the north, each with its own government and army and often hostile to one another. The French king Charles VIII took advantage of these divisions by invading and occupying much of northern Italy beginning in 1494.

(© 2016 Cengage Learning.)

PORTRAIT OF A MAN, CALLED THE SOLDIER, 1475, BY ANTONELLO DA MESSINA (D. 1479). This soldier could have been either a mercenary, hired to fight for pay, or a citizen-soldier who ideally would have fought not just for money but out of loyalty to his city-state, and who, as such, was thought to be the embodiment of civic virtue—honest, strong, and brave. (The Art Archive/Musée du Louvre Paris/Collection Dagli Orti.)

Protected from the rest of Italy by lagoons, Venice during the Middle Ages controlled a far-flung and exceptionally lucrative seagoing trade and a maritime empire stretching along the Adriatic and the eastern Mediterranean seas. Venetian maritime commercial successes were matched by political ones at home. For centuries, Venice managed to govern itself without a major upheaval; its republican constitution made this stability possible. Its chief executive offices, the Council of Ten, were elective, but after 1297 both these offices and the electorate were narrowly restricted by law to old patrician families. Venice was an aristocratic **republic**. The government proved remarkably effective because the ruling elite was able to instill in its young a sense of public duty that was passed on from one generation, and one century, to the next. Because Venetian government was at once stable and republican, it served as a model to republican theorists in seventeenth- and eighteenth-century Europe.

Aside from Venice, the city-states in northern Italy were not only internally unstable but also constantly warring with one another. By the middle of the fifteenth century, however, five major powers had emerged from the fighting: the kingdom of Naples and Sicily in the south; the Papal States, a papacy-controlled territory running across the center of the Italian peninsula; and the city-states of Florence, Venice, and Milan in the north. In 1454, these five powers, largely through the efforts of Cosimo de' Medici, concluded the Peace of Lodi. For the next forty years, they were relatively peaceful, until the French king Charles VIII invaded northern Italy in 1494.

The Peace of Lodi endured so long thanks to diplomacy. The essential techniques of modern diplomacy were worked out and applied in the second half of the fifteenth century in Italy. The practices of establishing embassies with ambassadors, sending and analyzing intelligence reports, consulting and negotiating during emergencies, and forming alliances all developed during this period. Some historians also see this time in Italian history as the seedbed for the notion of balance of power, which eventually became fundamental to the diplomacy of all Europe. Later, in the early modern period, European governments formed alliances so that no single state or group of allied states could dominate the Continent. Some elements of this balance of power were anticipated in the struggles among the Italian city-states.

Renaissance Society

The new way of life in the city-states paralleled developments in relations among them. Prosperous merchants played a leading role in the political and cultural life of the city. With the growth of commerce and industry, the feudal values of birth, military prowess, and a fixed hierarchy of lords and vassals decayed in favor of ambition and individual achievement, whether at court, in the counting-house, or inside the artist's studio. The old feudal chivalric code was not destroyed but transformed to serve different purposes.

The new urban, commercial **oligarchies** could not justify their power in the old way, through heredity. Moreover, they had to function within

the inherently unstable political climate of the city-states. Faced with this dual problem, the oligarchs fell back on the feudal idea of honor and developed elaborate codes. These codes differed in significant ways from their medieval antecedents. First came a depreciation (though never a complete elimination) of birth as a basis of merit and a corresponding emphasis on effort, talent, and (in the case of the artist) creative genius. Second, honor was no longer defined in narrow, largely military terms; it was expanded to include both the civic and courtly virtues of the worthy citizen and courtier and the artistic achievement of the painter, sculptor, architect, and poet.

The new code, however, did remain elitist and even aristocratic. Indeed, the new oligarchs of the Renaissance, because of their newness and insecurity, were all the more anxious to adopt the aristocratic outlook of the old nobility. The *nouveaux riches* (newly rich) aped the feudal aristocracy in dress and manners, even as they accommodated the code of knightly chivalry to the demands of a new urban and commercial culture. Renaissance society was a highly unstable compound of old and new.

Marriage and Family Life. City life profoundly altered family structures, marriage patterns, and relations between the sexes. Elsewhere in Europe, most people still lived on the land and tended to marry early in order to produce large families to work the fields. But in cities, early marriage could be a liability for a man who was attempting to make his fortune. The results were that older men married young brides and that wives usually outlived their husbands. Because a widow inherited her husband's property, she was not pressed to remarry and was likely to bring up her children in a single-parent household. According to the historian David Herlihy, the fact that so many women were responsible for nurturing their children may have encouraged the development of the Renaissance ideal of a gentleman, which emphasized civility, courtliness, and an appreciation of art, literature, and the feminine graces.

The large number of single, relatively prosperous, and leisured adults probably explains why Renaissance cities were reputed for sodomy, prostitution, and triangles involving an older husband, a young wife, and a young lover. Such sexual behavior was encouraged by the relative anonymity of the large cities and by the constant influx of young men of talent from the country districts.

Whatever the effect on their sons, upper-class women enjoyed greater freedom in greater numbers than they had since the fall of Rome. If they were married, they had the income to pursue pleasure in the form of clothes, conversation, and romance. If a well-to-do husband died while his wife was still young, she had no financial reasons to remarry and was free, to a degree previously unknown, to go her own way.

Patronage of the Arts.

Members of the urban upper class became patrons of the arts, providing funds to support promising artists and writers. Urban patricians, whose wealth was based on commerce and banking, not land, had become dominant in both republican Florence and despotic Milan. Unable to claim power by birth or to rely on traditional loyalties, they looked to culture to provide the trappings and justification of power.

For the newly rich, art could serve a political function. In its sheer magnificence, art could manifest power. Art, like literature, could also serve as a focus of civic pride and patriotism. Just as insecure rulers contended on the battlefield, they competed for art and artists to bolster their egos. Art became a desirable political investment, especially when, in the fifteenth century, economic investments were not offering as much return as they had a century or two before. The popes invested in art as well. Having lost the battle for temporal dominion in Europe, the papacy concentrated on increasing its direct dominion in Italy by consolidating and expanding the Papal States. As an adjunct to this policy, the popes heaped wealth on artists to enhance papal prestige. Indeed, the popes became the most lavish patrons of all, as the works of Michelangelo, Botticelli, and Raphael testify.

The result of this new patronage by popes and patricians was an explosion of creativity. The amount, and especially the nature, of this patronage also helped shape both art and the artist. For the first time since antiquity, portraiture became a separate genre and was developed much further than ever before. Patrician rivalry and insecurity of status, fed by the Renaissance ethic of achievement and reward, produced a scramble for honor and reputation. This fostered the desire to be memorialized in a painting, if not in a sculpture. A painter like Titian was in great demand.

Secularism.

Renaissance society was marked by a growing **secular** outlook. Intrigued by the active life of the city and eager to enjoy the worldly pleasures that their money could obtain, wealthy merchants and bankers moved away from the medieval preoccupation with salvation. Although they were neither nonbelievers nor atheists, for them religion increasingly had to compete with worldly concerns. Consequently, members of the urban upper class paid religion less heed or at least did not allow it to interfere with their quest for a full life. The challenge and pleasure of living well in this world seemed more exciting than the promise of heaven. This outlook found expression in Renaissance art and literature.

Individualism.

Individualism was another hallmark of Renaissance society. Urban life released people of wealth and talent from the old constraints of manor and church. The urban elite sought to assert their own personalities, discover and express their individual feelings, and demonstrate their unique talents. They strove to win fame and glory and to fulfill their ambitions. This Renaissance ideal was explicitly elitist. It applied only to the few, entirely disregarding the masses, and it valued what was distinctive and superior in an individual, not what was common to all. Concerned with the distinctions of the few, it did not consider the needs or rights of the many. Individualism became deeply embedded in the Western soul and was expressed by artists who sought to capture individual character, by explorers who ventured into uncharted seas, by conquerors who carved out empires in the New World, and by merchant-capitalists who amassed fortunes.

THE RENAISSANCE OUTLOOK: HUMANISM AND SECULAR POLITICS

Humanism

The most characteristic intellectual movement of the Renaissance was *humanism*, an educational and cultural program based on the study of ancient Greek and Roman literature. The humanist attitude toward antiquity differed from the attitude of medieval scholars, who had taken pains to fit classical learning into a Christian worldview. Renaissance

Giovanni Pico della Mirandola: Humanism and Man's Uniqueness and His Potential for Good and Evil

Giovanni Pico della Mirandola (1463–1494) was deeply educated in Christian theology, ancient Greek philosophy, and the cabala, a Jewish tradition of biblical interpretation. Oration on the Dignity of Man *was composed in 1486 but not printed until 1495–96, after Pico's death. Some of it was condemned by the pope as heretical, but it nevertheless became a highly influential statement and perhaps provides the most optimistic Renaissance expression of the power of human reason and the proper use of it. As such, it stands in sharp contrast to Machiavelli's deeply pessimistic views as set out in* The Prince *(see page 302–303).* Oration on the Dignity of Man *is excerpted here.*

At last it seems to me that I have understood why man is the most fortunate living thing worthy of all admiration and precisely what rank is his lot in the universal chain of being, a rank to be envied not only by the brutes but even by the stars and by minds beyond this world. It is a matter past faith and extraordinary! Why should it not be so? For it is upon this account that man is justly considered and called a great miracle and a truly remarkable being. . . . [God] accepted man as a work of indeterminate nature, and placing him in the center of the world, addressed him thus: . . .

. . . The nature of all other things in the universe is limited and constrained in accordance with the laws prescribed by us. Constrained by no limits, in accordance with your own free will, in whose hands we have placed you, you shall independently determine the bounds of your own nature. We have placed you at the world's center from where you may more easily observe whatever is in the world. We have made you neither celestial nor terrestrial, neither mortal nor immortal, so that with honor and freedom of choice, as though the maker and molder of yourself, you may fashion yourself in

humanists did not subordinate the classics to the requirements of Christian doctrines; rather, they valued ancient literature for its own sake—for its clear and graceful style and its insights into human nature. From the ancient classics, humanists expected to learn much that could not be provided by medieval writing: for instance, how to live well in this world and how to perform one's civic duties. For the humanists, the classics were a guide to the good life, the active life. To achieve self-cultivation, to write well, to speak well, and to live well, it was necessary to know the classics. In contrast to scholastic philosophers, who used Greek philosophy to prove the truth of Christian doctrines, Italian humanists used classical learning to nourish their new interest in a worldly life.

Whereas medieval scholars were familiar with only some ancient Latin writers, Renaissance humanists restored to circulation every Roman work that could be found. Similarly, knowledge of Greek was very rare in Latin Christendom during the Middle Ages, but Renaissance humanists increasingly cultivated the study of Greek in order to read Homer, Demosthenes, Plato, and other ancients in the original.

Although predominantly a secular movement, Italian humanism was not un-Christian. True, humanists often treated moral problems in a purely secular manner. Yet in dealing with religious and theological questions, they did not challenge Christian belief or question the validity of the Bible. They did, however, attack scholasticism for its hair-splitting arguments and preoccupation with trivial questions. They stressed instead a purer form of Christianity, based on direct study of the Bible and writings by the church fathers.

The early humanists, sometimes called the fathers of humanism, were Petrarch (1304–1374) and Boccaccio (1313–1375). Petrarch, Boccaccio, and their followers carried the recovery of the whatever form you prefer. You shall have the power to degenerate into the inferior forms of life which are brutish; you shall have the power, through your soul's judgment, to rise to the superior orders which are divine.

O supreme generosity of God the Father! O highest and most admirable felicity of man to whom it is granted to have whatever he chooses, to whatever he wills! . . .

Who would not admire this our chameleon? Or who could admire any other being more greatly than man? Asclepius the Athenian justly says that man was symbolized in the mysteries by the figure of Proteus, because of his ability to change his character and transform his nature. . . .

. . . . . .

But why do we reiterate all these things? To the end that from the moment we are born into the condition of being able to become whatever we choose, we should be particularly certain that it may never be said of us that, although born to a privileged position, we failed to realize it and became like brutes and mindless beasts of burden. . . . Otherwise, abusing the most in-dulgent generosity of the Father, we shall make that freedom of choice which He has given to us into something harmful rather than something beneficial.

Let some holy ambition invade our souls, so that, dissatisfied with mediocrity, we shall eagerly desire the highest things and shall toil with all our strength to obtain them, since we may if we wish. . . .

Questions for Analysis

1. How and why did God make men different from all other creatures in the universe?
2. God says that unlike others of his creation, man is "constrained by no limits." What opportunities and responsibilities does this create?
3. What is new about Pico's outlook that breaks in striking ways with the long medieval Christian tradition that preceded it?

Julia Conaway Bondanella and Mark Musa, eds., *The Italian Renaissance Reader* (New York: Meridian, 1987), 180–183.

classics further by making a systematic attempt to discover the classical roots of medieval Italian rhetoric. Petrarch's own efforts to learn Greek were largely unsuccessful, but by encouraging his students to master the ancient tongue, he advanced humanist learning. Petrarch was particularly drawn to Cicero, the ancient Roman orator. Following the example of Cicero, Petrarch insisted that education should consist not only of learning and knowing things but also of learning how to communicate one's knowledge and how to use it for the public good. Therefore, the emphasis in education should be on rhetoric and moral philosophy, wisdom combined with eloquence. As Bartolommeo della Fonte (1446–1513), professor of rhetoric at Florence, said, such a program of instruction would fit a man for effective rule: that is, "to punish the wicked, to care for the good, to embellish his native land and to benefit all mankind."[1] Thus, Petrarch helped make Ciceronian values dominant among the humanists. His followers set up schools to inculcate the new Ciceronian educational ideal.

Implicit in the humanist educational ideal was a radical transformation of the medieval (Augustinian) view of humanity. According to this view, since human beings were completely subject to divine will, not only were they incapable of attaining excellence through their own efforts and talents, but it was also wrong and sinful for them even to try. In contrast, the humanists, recalling the classical Greek concept of arête, made the achievement of excellence through individual striving the end not only of education but also of life itself. Moreover, because individuals were capable of this goal, it was their duty to pursue it as the end of life, although the pursuit was not effortless and indeed demanded extraordinary energy and skill.

People were deemed capable of excellence in every sphere and duty-bound to make the effort. This emphasis on human creative powers was one of the most characteristic and influential doctrines of the Renaissance. A classic expression of it is found in the *Oration on the Dignity of Man* (1486) by Giovanni Pico della Mirandola (1463–1494) (see Primary Source box). Man, said Pico, has the freedom to shape his own life. Pico has God say to man: "We have made you a creature" such that "you may, as the free and proud shaper of your own being, fashion yourself in the form you may prefer."[2]

Pico also spelled out another implication of man's duty to realize his potential: through his own exertions, man can come to understand and control nature. One of the new and powerful Renaissance images of man was as the *magus,* the magician. The vision of the mastery of nature would continue to inspire experimentalists, such as Francis Bacon, and natural philosophers, such as Robert Boyle and Isaac Newton, until at least the early eighteenth century. A major psychological driving force of the Scientific Revolution, this vision stemmed in large part from the philosophy of Italian humanists such as Pico.

The attack on the medieval scholastics was implicit in the humanist educational ideal. From the humanist perspective, scholasticism failed not only because its terms and Latin usage were barbarous but also because it did not provide useful knowledge. This humanist emphasis on the uses of knowledge offered an additional stimulus to science and art.

But the new humanist and heroic image of human beings was deeply compromised and conflicted in one major area: the subject of women and gender relations. The Renaissance humanists may have been, at least in Florence and Venice, staunch republican political idealists, but they were also, with some exceptions, decidedly antifeminist. Humanists did not object to barring educated and talented women from entering the professions, including law and teaching in universities.

During the Renaissance, there were a few powerful female rulers, such as Elizabeth I, queen of England (1558–1603), and Catherine de' Medici, who became the regent (ruler) of France after her husband Henri II's untimely death in 1559. However, they were the exceptions. Politics and especially monarchical rule were always considered a male monopoly from which women should be excluded because they were inferior beings unsuited to holding such power.

Some aristocratic women patronized humanist scholars. Margaret Beaufort (1443–1509), mother of an English king, founded two colleges that fostered the new learning in England. Catherine of Aragon (1485–1536), the first wife of Henry VIII, king of England (1512–1547), surrounded herself with leading humanists, such as Desiderius Erasmus (1466–1536) and Juan Vives (1492–1540). The latter wrote for her a book entitled *The Instruction of a Christian Woman* (1523), which summarized humanist teaching on the subject. Vives insisted that women should be educated so that they could read serious books on religion and philosophy. But for him, like so many others, the goals of female education should be very limited. Men, he said, must be educated to act in the world and to govern. In contrast, women should be taught virtue—that is, devotion to home and family—and cheerful obedience to their husbands. In particular, women, according to Vives, should never be taught rhetoric, which was thought to be the key discipline in training men to become strong and effective leaders. Such rhetorical training would be wasted on women because their place was in the home and not in public life.

Such split thinking was repeated over and over again throughout the Renaissance. For example, Erasmus, the foremost European humanist, advocated female education, not so that educated women could act in the world but because reading was a way to banish idleness at home and was preferable to such tasks as knitting and sewing. Erasmus's friend Sir Thomas More (1478–1535) insisted on educating his daughters to a high level, not so that they could cut a figure on the public stage, but to make them better wives and daughters, that is, more virtuous and obedient. As female humanists in England and Italy, if not elsewhere, said at the time, men were jealous of educated women and afraid of losing control over them.

There were, however, a very few exceptions to this cramped and hostile view of female potential. The German physician Heinrich Cornelius Agrippa von Nettesheim (1486–1535), for instance, wrote *On the Nobility and Excellence of Women* in 1529. In this work, he held that although women are biologically different from men, they are not intellectually inferior to them. He went on to argue for the full equality of the sexes, a radical claim very far from mainstream,

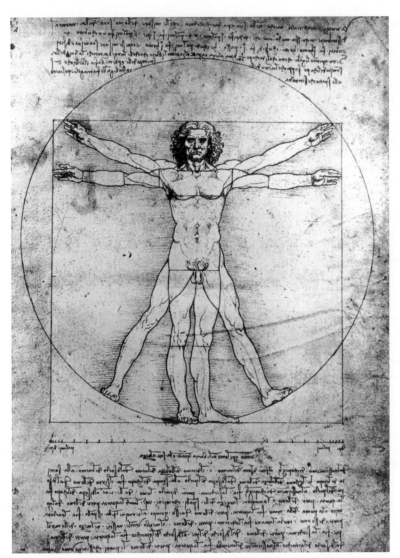

LEONARDO DA VINCI, *THE PROPORTIONS OF MAN.* Leonardo was fascinated by the human body. In his notebook, his written observations are accompanied by this marvelous drawing of the body, conceived and framed with realism and proportion. (Hulton Archive/Getty Images.)

and even educated, opinion. Long before Agrippa, Christine de Pizan (1364–c. 1430), an extraordinary French female humanist, attacked the ancient prejudice that men are by nature not only stronger but also wiser than women. As she said in her great book, *The City of Ladies*, written in 1404, "[N]either the loftiness nor the lowliness of a person lies in the body according to sex, but in the perfection of conduct and virtues."[3] In other words,

a person's worth is not about gender but about behavior. Despite this brilliant insight, which breaks through to an almost modern view of gender equality, even de Pizan could not hold her ground but fell back on the deep-seated prejudices of her time. She said that men and women from time immemorial have played distinctly different roles in society, and so it should ever be: men are ordained to rule; women, to follow and obey. This is God's will.

Another extraordinary female humanist was Moderata Fonte, a wealthy Venetian who completed the *Worth of Women* just before she died in childbirth in 1592 at the age of thirty-seven. The book's subtitle—*Wherein Is Clearly Revealed Their Nobility and Their Superiority to Men*—shows the author's intent. The work consists of a dialogue among intelligent and articulate noble Venetian ladies who rail against men's behavior, particularly their determination to subjugate women, as the following passage illustrates.

> *If men usurp our rights, should we not complain and declare that they have wronged us? For if we are their inferiors in status, but not in worth, this is an abuse that has been introduced into the world and that men have then, over time gradually translated into law and custom, and it has become so entrenched that they claim (and even actually believe) that the status they have gained through bullying is theirs by right. . . . Does this seem a matter of such little interest to us that we should be quiet and let things pass in silence?*[4]

In fourteenth- and fifteenth-century republican Florence, at least until the Medicis took control, Petrarchan humanism was not meant for a court elite. Humanism was a civic idea: to educate and inform citizens so that they could contribute to the common good to the greatest possible extent. In this sense, humanism was put in the service of republican values and the republican cause, and the mixture of the two is what has come to be called *civic humanism* by recent historians. This civic ideal developed furthest in the Florentine republic.

By the second half of the fifteenth century, as the Medicis gained increasing control, the civic ideal was being replaced by an ideal more fitting to the times, the ideal of princely rule. This ideal borrowed much from civic humanism, even though it was directed toward princes and courtiers and not toward citizens. The emphasis on the pursuit of virtue and honor continued. Like the ideal gentleman, the ideal prince would evolve through humanistic education, which would so prepare him for the struggle between virtue and fortune that virtue would prove victorious.

The similarities between the civic and princely ideals, however, were not as important as the differences. The aim of princely rule was not liberty but peace and security, and the best means to this end was not a republic but hereditary monarchy. This new princely ideal was reflected in a new spate of advice books, the most influential of which was *The Book of the Courtier*, written between 1513 and 1518 by Baldesar Castiglione (1478–1529). These books promoted the notion that the ideal ruler should be universally talented and skillful, equally commanding on the battlefield, at court, and in the state and virtuous throughout. These advice books, especially Castiglione's, were to serve as indispensable handbooks for courtiers and would-be gentlemen in Renaissance Italy and throughout the rest of Europe for centuries.

A Revolution in Political Thought

One advice book transcended all the others: *The Prince*, written in 1513 by the Florentine Niccolò Machiavelli (1469–1527). It offered an indictment of the humanist ideal of princely rule and in so doing made some fundamental contributions to political theory. Indeed, Machiavelli may be called the first major modern political thinker. To Machiavelli, the humanist ideal was naïve in its insistence on the prince's virtues and eloquence to the exclusion of all other considerations. He attacked the medieval and humanist tradition of theoretical politics.

> *Since my intention is to say something that will prove of practical use to the inquirer, I have thought it proper to represent things as they are in real truth, rather than as they are imagined. Many have dreamed up republics and principalities which have never in truth been known to exist; the gulf between how one should live and how one does live is so wide that a man who neglects what is actually done for what should be done learns the way to self-destruction.*[5]

Politics, Machiavelli argued, requires the rational deployment of force, as well as, and even prior to, the exercise of virtue.

On this point, Machiavelli's advice is quite specific. He wrote *The Prince* in part as a plea. Since 1494, Italy had fallen prey to France and Spain. Their great royal armies overpowered the mercenary armies of the city-states and

The Renaissance

1. Filippo Brunelleschi, Church of San Lorenzo, interior, looking toward the apse, Florence, Italy.
(Erich Lessing/Art Resource, N.Y.)

*T*he most vivid image of the Renaissance is conveyed through its architecture, sculpture, and painting. Renaissance examples of all three art forms display a style that stressed proportion, balance, and harmony. These artistic values were achieved through a new, revolutionary conceptualization of space and spatial relations. To a considerable extent, Renaissance art also reflects the values of Renaissance humanism in the use of classical models in architecture, in the rendering of the nude human figure, and in the heroic vision of human beings.

Medieval art sought to represent spiritual aspiration; the world was a veil merely hinting at the other, perfect, eternal world. Renaissance art expresses spiritual aspiration, but its setting and character differ altogether. This world is no longer a veil but the *place* where people live, act, and worship. The reference is less to the other world and more to this world, and people are treated as creatures who find their spiritual destiny as they fulfill their human one.

Renaissance artists produced revolutionary discoveries that served as the foundation of Western art up to the twentieth century. In art, as in philosophy, the Florentines played a leading role in this esthetic transformation. The first major contributor to Renaissance painting was the Florentine painter Giotto (c. 1276–1337). (See Figure 11 in the first art essay.) Giotto developed several techniques of perspective, representing three-dimensional figures and objects on two-dimensional surfaces so that they appear to stand in space. Giotto's figures look remarkably alive.

2. Donatello, *David*, c. 1425–1430. (Scala/Art Resource, N.Y.)

They are drawn and arranged in space to tell a story, and the expressions they wear and the illusion of movement they convey heighten the dramatic effect. The dramatic work of Giotto marked the end of the stiff, otherworldly style of the Middle Ages. The artists who followed Giotto diverged from his style and subject matter. Although Christianity was still an important theme, Renaissance artists also depicted subjects from Greek and Roman mythology as well as scenes from everyday life.

Painting, sculpture, architecture, and the minor arts evolved at a different pace throughout this period. It was not as if all artists declared themselves to be Renaissance figures simultaneously. Instead, styles changed with new artistic sensibilities, technological advances, and the requests of new patrons.

Rarely can one ascribe the development of an entire period of art to a single individual. Such is the case of Renaissance architecture, however. Filippo Brunelleschi (c. 1377–1446) began his career as a sculptor in Florence. He turned to architecture sometime after 1402 and traveled to Rome, where he studied the remains of imperial Roman buildings and monuments. Brunelleschi learned the theory of scientific perspective, perhaps while trying to draw on paper three-dimensional images of the monuments. He also developed a method of building double domes linked to reinforce each other. This lightened the weight of the dome, allowing the structure beneath to be built with fewer supporting elements.

One of the earliest expressions of his architectural skill can be seen in the Church of San Lorenzo in Florence (1421–1469) (Figure 1). Thanks to the benevolence of the Medici family, Brunelleschi was granted license to design an entire building himself. The Church of San Lorenzo was a new structure, not an adaptation of or an addition to an older, medieval building. Although some of its elements may have derived from earlier prototypes, the new building was distinct in its symmetry and regularity. Its floor plan shows a markedly regular repetition of equal-size squares to establish the nave, transept, and aisles. The centrally planned chapel, with its strict adherence to mathematical proportion, distinguishes the Church of San Lorenzo from the medieval Gothic cathedral. Brunelleschi's ability to grasp the concept of perspective in two dimensions is

3. Masaccio, *The Holy Trinity*, 1425. (Scala/Art Resource, N.Y.)

translated into three dimensions by the strong use of line and rhythmical arches that draw the eye to the altar.

Brunelleschi effected the same fusion of antique and Christian as his contemporaries did in other fields. Poets and writers experimented with classical and Christian styles; so too did Brunelleschi. Note, for example, the Corinthian capitals topping the San Lorenzo columns, whereas the floor plan is in the shape of a cross.

Architecture was not the only medium that combined experimentation and echoes of the past; sculpture did as well. Whereas Brunelleschi can be viewed as the father of Renaissance architecture, a host of sculptors advanced the Renaissance style in their medium. Prominent among them in the early Renaissance was Donatello (1386–1466), whose works distinguished him as a master even in his own time. The bronze *David* (c. 1425–1430) (Figure 2) is perhaps the most controversial of his best-known sculptures. The first life-size, freestanding nude sculpture since antiquity, this work is still something of an enigma.

Art historians assume that the statue was to have been exhibited outdoors, or at least in a central location, because it was meant to be viewed from all sides. The young David is wearing only a hat and high boots. Unlike the well-muscled athletes of the classical period, however, he is slender and slight, an adolescent instead of a developed adult. Donatello does pay homage to classical prototypes in the stance of his David— a *contrapposto,* or counterbalanced, pose, in which the weight on the legs is uneven (compare David's stance with Hermes's stance in Figure 1 of the first art essay).

Symbolic devices provide the key to the significance of the sculpture. David represents the city of Florence itself, and the helmet of Goliath under his feet represents the duchy of Milan, which at the time was at war with Florence. David's nudity may allude to the city's classical past, and the wreathed hat may suggest victory.

In painting, experiments in depth and linear perspective stand out as the major developments. Artists were seeking ways of making two-dimensional surfaces seem three-dimensional. Brunelleschi was the first to develop a system in which all parallel lines of a scene converge in one central point on the horizon; other artists adopted his scheme and carried it further.

4. Pietro Perugino, *The Delivery of the Keys*, 1481. (Scala/Art Resource, N.Y.)

The Holy Trinity (Figure 3), a fresco by Masaccio (1401–1428), a brilliant young artist who died at the age of twenty-seven, advanced further Brunelleschi's experiments with linear perspective. Masaccio takes a central Christian spiritual idea, the Trinity—God the Father, the Son, and the Holy Spirit—and materializes and humanizes it.

He depicts a crucified Christ on the cross with God the Father standing behind him, and the Holy Spirit descending as a dove on Christ's head. The figures of Christ, the onlooking Madonna, St. John, even the figure of God the Father, standing behind Christ on an elevated platform, are human, material figures in a three-dimensional space. The illusion of spatial depth is created by the architectural parameters of an overarching barrel-vaulted ceiling divided into squares diminishing in size.

Masaccio here provides a point of departure for subsequent art. Henceforth, artists will increasingly portray visual space within the three-dimensional perspectival format suggested by Masaccio, and human beings as real people, solid in form and realistic in anatomy, bones, muscles, and expressions.

Pietro Perugino's *The Delivery of the Keys* (1481) (Figure 4), a fresco from the Sistine Chapel in the Vatican, illustrates the enthusiasm with which other artists achieved perspective. Note that all the parallel lines in the foreground converge at the church in the center of the background. The viewer's eye is drawn into the painting, and figures seem real, not flat. Compare this

5. Leonardo da Vinci, *The Last Supper*, c. 1495–1498. (© The Gallery Collection/Corbis.)

portrayal with the flat and linear rendering of Justinian and his retinue in the mosaic from Ravenna. There, the effect is two-dimensional, and the viewer does not expect to see beyond the layer of figures. In the Perugino, by contrast, the figures are full and exist in a three-dimensional space.

The works of Leonardo da Vinci (1452–1519)—his drawings, paintings, sculpture, innumerable inventions, and copious writings—exemplify the Renaissance spirit. He expands the idea of three-dimensional, perspectival space to include the living form of things, their mathematical proportions. He announced a new way of looking at nature and the individual. For Leonardo, visual art offered a means of arriving at nature's truths. Truth was attained when the artist brought both human reason and creative capacity to bear on the direct experience of the senses. Leonardo examined objects in all their diversity and represented them realistically. He visually delineated the natural world with unprecedented scientific precision, and he asserted

his spiritual and intellectual freedom to do so. Through his art, Leonardo helped lay the foundations for modern science.

Leonardo's *The Last Supper* (Figure 5) affords a stark contrast to that of the Magdalen Master (compare with Figure 9 in the first art essay), providing a basis for gauging the distance traversed by Western art from the Middle Ages to modernity. Leonardo's version is explosive, and the scene is depicted vibrantly. The figures, in agitated motion, arranged in three-dimensional space, huddled into four groups, exhibit a wide range of postures, attitudes, and individual reactions to Christ's pronouncement that someone among them would betray him.

Leonardo has transformed medieval and Eastern two-dimensional space into the full-volumed three-dimensional space of the modern world and the lifeless, impersonal forms of medieval and Eastern art into unique individual personalities, their feelings captured at the very instant of their reaction to Christ's announcement.

6. Michelangelo Buonarroti, *Creation of Adam*, 1510. (Sistine Chapel Ceiling: Creation of Adam, 1510 (fresco) (post restoration), Buonarroti, Michelangelo (1475–1564)/Vatican Museums and Galleries, Vatican City/The Bridgeman Art Library.)

By the end of the fifteenth century, Renaissance art in Italy had reached its height. The High Renaissance flowered in the visual arts as well as in other areas of culture. Michelangelo, Titian, and Giorgione are among the best-known artists of this era.

The works of Michelangelo Buonarroti (1475–1564)—paintings, sculpture, literature, and architecture—epitomize the Renaissance. Looking at his paintings—for instance, *Creation of Adam* (1510) (Figure 6) on the ceiling of the Vatican's Sistine Chapel—a viewer is struck by the extent to which he learned from the art of the ancient world. Nevertheless, Michelangelo's reliance on the classical is subordinate to his Renaissance vantage point. Here, the figures float freely through a celestial landscape and depict the biblical story of creation.

But the artists of the Renaissance looked to the classical past not only for technique; they also borrowed and adapted subject matter. Unlike the art of the Middle Ages, which concentrated on Christian themes, Renaissance paintings also illustrated the myths of ancient Greece and Rome.

The Venetian artist Titian (1488/90–1576) was well known for his use of both mythology and biblical themes. His *Bacchus and Ariadne* (1523) (Figure 7) illustrates his independence from the stylistic conventions of other High Renaissance schools. Titian offers a sensual rendering of the classical tale, in which the young Ariadne marries Bacchus (Dionysus), the god of wine, after being abandoned by the Greek king Theseus. Titian's use of *chiaroscuro* (alternating areas of light and dark) is pronounced.

7. Titian, *Bacchus and Ariadne*, 1523. (FineArt/Alamy Limited.)

The general feeling of the work is much looser and freer than the feelings of the carefully constructed canvases produced by his contemporaries. The painting also has a roughness, as though it were unfinished—a quality that marks a departure from the meticulously realistic works of other High Renaissance artists.

As the artistic styles of the Italian Renaissance spread northward, they were adapted and superimposed on a different set of political and religious circumstances, resulting in a fusion of Renaissance method and local themes. Pieter Brueghel the Elder's (1525/30–1569) *Hunters in the Snow* (1565) (Figure 8) exemplifies this trend. The artist uses line and motion as Titian did. But the image he presents, although it contains many elements of the old style, looks ahead to the future.

Brueghel had spent almost two years studying in Italy, where he developed a technique for dealing with the problem of landscape. In his treatment of objects in three-dimensional space, he created a recessional movement that dominates the painting. The viewer's eye is drawn into the painting at an angle from the foreground to the background through myriad intermediate, diminishing shapes—dogs, human figures, trees, houses, a flying bird—all unified by one sweeping, sloping, downward motion. Brueghel thus achieves a perspectival depth that is entirely new, relying not on the correlation of stratified forms from left to right, but on the recession of

8. Pieter Brueghel the Elder, *Hunters in the Snow*, 1565. (Erich Lessing/Art Resource, N.Y.)

foreshortened forms. In this painting, the artist has surpassed the medieval representation of space in two dimensions and has produced a boundless three-dimensional space that belongs to the modern age.

By the late fifteenth and the sixteenth centuries, the styles of the Renaissance spread from Italy to the Low Countries (the Netherlands, Belgium, and Luxembourg), Germany, France, England, and Spain. These styles were not exported wholesale; rather, elements of the Renaissance fused with local traditions to produce new styles and variants of the Italian themes. What is consistent from one country to the next, however, is the extent to which Renaissance art really was a rebirth—a departure from the style of the medieval period.

proceeded to lay waste to Italy in their struggle for domination of the peninsula. To prevent this, Machiavelli said, the Italians should unite behind a leader—the prince—whose first act would be to disband the mercenaries and forge a new citizen army worthy of the glorious Roman past and capable of repelling the "barbarian" invasion. "Mercenaries," Machiavelli claimed, "are useless and dangerous." They are useless because "there is no . . . inducement to keep them on the field apart from the little they are paid, and this is not enough to make them want to die for you." And they are dangerous because their leaders, the infamous condottieri, "are anxious to advance their own greatness" at the expense of the city-state. Reliance on mercenaries was the sole cause of "the present ruin of Italy," and the cure lay in the creation of a national militia, led by a prince.[6]

This prince had to be both wily and virtuous, not just virtuous (as humanists had said): "The fact is that a man who wants to act virtuously in every way necessarily comes to grief among so many who are not virtuous." So Machiavelli scandalized Christian Europe by asserting that "if a prince wants to maintain his rule he must learn how not to be virtuous, and to make use of this or not according to his need."[7] Even more shocking, the prince must know how to dissemble, that is, to make all his actions appear virtuous, whether they are so or not. In ironic parody of conventional advice-book wisdom, Machiavelli argued that a ruler must cultivate a *reputation* for virtue rather than virtue itself. In this connection, Machiavelli arrived at a fundamental political truth: politics (and especially the relationship between the ruler and the ruled) being what it is, the road to success for the prince lies in dissimulation (the art of appearance and cover-up). As he put it, "Everyone sees what you appear to be, few experience what you really are. And those few dare not [contradict] the many who are backed by the majesty of the state."[8] Here again the Renaissance arrived at modernity.

Machiavelli broke with both the medieval and the humanist traditions of political thought. He was a secularist who tried to understand and explain the state without recourse to Christian teachings. Influenced by classical thought, especially the works of Livy, he rejected the prevailing view that the state is God's creation and the

NICCOLÒ MACHIAVELLI (1469–1527). Machiavelli looked back to the ancient Roman republic for his ideals and spent his life serving the city-state of Florence, but as the author of *The Prince*, his name became a byword for atheism and deceit. "Machiavellian" is still used to describe an unscrupulous politician. (Scala/Art Resource, N.Y.)

ruler should base his policies on Christian moral principles. For Machiavelli, religion was not the foundation for politics but merely a useful tool in the prince's struggle for success. The prince might even dissemble, if he thought he had to, in matters of faith, by appearing pious, whether he was or not, and by playing on and exploiting the piety of his subjects.

THE SPREAD OF THE RENAISSANCE

The Renaissance spread to Germany, France, England, and Spain in the late fifteenth and the sixteenth centuries. In its migration northward, Renaissance culture adapted itself to conditions unknown in Italy, such as the growth of the monarchical state and the strength of **lay piety**. In England, France, and Spain, Renaissance culture

A Renaissance Man

Leonardo da Vinci (1452–1519) is a supreme example of the so-called "universal man"—someone wonderfully gifted who excelled in many fields—so admired in the Renaissance. Because he was born illegitimate, he was disqualified from being trained in a learned profession such as law or medicine. But recognizing his immense talent, his father saw to it that he was apprenticed to Andrea del Verrocchio (1435–1488), the esteemed Florentine painter and sculptor, who carefully developed Leonardo's skills in the visual arts. Once Leonardo had been fully trained, it is said, Verrocchio was so struck by the beauty of his pupil's work that he decided never to paint again.

Given Leonardo's restless energy and insatiable curiosity, his genius could not be channeled in only one or a few directions. He quickly gained a reputation for tremendous skill in both science and art and was highly sought after. Florence was ruled by the Medicis, and Milan was ruled by the Sforzas. Leonardo worked for both, and briefly for the Medici pope Leo X (1513–1521) in Rome as well. He spent the last three years of his life in the pay of the French king Francis I (1515–1547), living in luxury at the French court and advising his patron on a variety of building projects.

Leonardo was a quick study and took advantage of opportunities for learning wherever he found them. At the Milanese court of the Sforzas, he met Luca Pacioli (1445–1517), the foremost Renaissance mathematician, who taught him geometry and the power of numbers to explain the world. Leonardo became committed to the view that mathematics provides the basis for true understanding in every field, not only in the physical and biological sciences but in painting and music as well. Leonardo had a large library and read widely, but he also believed that there was no substitute for studying nature first-hand and making experiments in order to obtain true and certain knowledge of things.

Leonardo was deeply interested in everything, and no subject was off limits. He studied human sexuality and, in his unpublished notebooks, made scientific drawings of a human fetus in the womb, male erections, and a couple having sex. One of his main fields of investigation

tended to be court centered and hence antirepublican, as it was, for instance, under Francis I in France and Elizabeth I in England. In Germany and the Rhineland, no monarchical state existed, but a vital tradition of lay piety was present in the Low Countries. For example, the Brethren of the Common Life was a lay movement emphasizing education and practical piety. Intensely Christian and at the same time anticlerical, the people in such lay movements found in Renaissance culture tools for sharpening their wits against the clergy—not to undermine the faith but rather to restore it to its apostolic purity.

Thus, northern humanists were profoundly devoted to ancient learning, just as the humanists in Italy had been. But nothing in northern humanism compares to the paganizing trend associated with the Italian Renaissance. The northerners were chiefly interested in the problem of the ancient church and, in particular, the question of what constituted original Christianity. They sought a model in the light of which they might reform the corrupted church of their own time.

Everywhere, two factors operated to accelerate the spread of Renaissance culture after 1450: growing prosperity and the printing press. Prosperity, brought on by peace and the decline of famine and plague, led to the founding of schools and colleges. The sons (women were excluded) of gentlemen and merchants were sent to school to receive a humanistic education imported from Italy. The purpose of such education was to prepare men for a career in the church or the civil service of the expanding state and for acceptance into higher social spheres.

was human anatomy, both for how it could inform his painting and for what it could tell him about the aging process. Once he discovered a one-hundred-year-old man in a hospital in Florence and waited expectantly for his death so that he could examine his blood vessels. By comparing the corpses of the very young and the very old, he was the first to describe the disease known as arteriosclerosis, the hardening of the arteries. At this time, the church took a dim view of the carving up of human remains.

Much of Leonardo's effort was spent on practical design projects, large and small. In the prosperous and warring Italian city-states, there was always a need for industrial machinery, military fortifications, and weapons, and he received as many commissions for engineering work as he did for works of art. In 1502, he served as a military engineer to the commander of the papal army, the ruthless Cesare Borgia (d. 1507). The next year the Florentine government hired him to divert the course of the River Arno in order to cut off access to the sea by the city-state of Pisa, with which Florence was then at war. On this project, which was not successful, he collaborated with another famous Florentine, Machiavelli (see the section "A Revolution in Political Thought").

The list of Leonardo's ideas for new mechanical devices is staggering. He made some four hundred detailed drawings of machines. A short list of his proposals gives a hint of the range of his inventiveness. He came up with suggestions for a robot, a lifting fork, various cranes, machinery for making cloth, improvements on the printing press, a prototype of a car powered by springs and gears, a bicycle, and a flying machine. And then there were his ideas for weapons, including armored tanks, battering rams, scaling ladders, cannons, catapults, crossbows, and a submarine.

For all his inventive energy, Leonardo was notorious for procrastinating and sometimes never finishing his commissions for artworks and building projects, so the number of his surviving paintings is very small. This meager output has always been looked on as a great loss because his finished work sets such a high standard, including such incomparable paintings as *The Last Supper, Mona Lisa*, and *St. John the Baptist*.

Printing with movable type, which was invented in the middle of the fifteenth century, quickened the spread of Renaissance ideas. Back in the Late Middle Ages, the West had learned, through the Muslims from the Chinese, of printing, paper, and ink. However, in this block printing process, a new block had to be carved from wood for each new impression, and the block was discarded as unusable as soon as a slightly different impression was needed. About 1445, Johann Gutenberg (c. 1398–1468) and other printers in Mainz in the Rhineland invented movable metal type to replace the cumbersome blocks. It was possible to use and reuse the separate pieces of type—as long as the metal in which they were cast did not wear down—simply by arranging them in the desired order.

With the advent of the printing press, the book-publishing industry began to develop. The first printed books were religious: Bibles, sermons, and prayer books. But other kinds soon followed because there was a ready market for books on a great variety of secular subjects. The market was enormous and continued to expand during the sixteenth century. Printed books were much cheaper than the earlier hand-copied ones, and many more people could now afford to buy them. Publishers catered to every taste in reading—learned and popular, technical and imaginative, serious and light. Books became big business, driven by both consumer demand and the profit motive. Fifteen or twenty million books had already been published by 1500, and another 150 million more a century later.

Not only were books cheaper and more numerous, but printing also made it easier to learn to read. Literacy rates were still very low, especially among women and the poor, but the clerical and genteel monopoly on reading had been broken. More and more books were also published in the **vernacular** (rather than Latin), which helped standardize written language and stimulated the development of national literatures all across Europe. Printing, moreover, provided a surer basis for scholarship and prevented the further corruption of texts through hand copying. By giving all scholars the same text to work from, it made progress in critical scholarship and science faster and more reliable.

But in early modern Europe, printing was not an unmixed blessing. Elite opinion was often divided, or at least ambivalent, on the issue. Printing was an obvious boon; the authorities, however, saw the need for censorship, for imposing controls on what was published. Today, ours is a **pluralistic** society that values new ideas and a variety of opinions, even differences of opinion, at least up to a point. Early modern Europeans were not so tolerant; in fact, they were suspicious of intellectual novelty and variety and sometimes downright hostile to **heterodox** thinking. For centuries, leaders in church and state had tried to build unity by enforcing Christian **orthodoxy** and punishing heresy. The motto of the French monarchy aptly sums up the point: "One king, one law, one faith." The Catholic church established an *Index of Prohibited Books* in the mid-sixteenth century, and books such as Machiavelli's *The Prince* were put on the list. Protestant authorities also set up machinery for regulating the book trade. Printers of "dangerous" books were punished, sometimes executed, and their book stocks confiscated. All intellectual life would be stifled by this atmosphere: the tension between the power of print and the desire to control opinion.

Erasmian Humanism

To Desiderius Erasmus (c. 1466–1536) belongs the credit for making Renaissance humanism an international movement. He was educated in the Netherlands by the Brethren of the Common Life, which was one of the most advanced religious movements of the age, combining mystical piety with rigorous humanist pedagogy. Erasmus traveled throughout Europe as a humanist educator and biblical scholar. Like other Christian humanists, he trusted the power of words and used his pen to attack scholastic theology and clerical abuses and to promote his philosophy of Christ. His weapon was satire, and his *Praise of Folly* and *Colloquies* won him a reputation for acid wit vented at the expense of conventional religion.

True religion, Erasmus argued, does not depend on dogma, ritual, or clerical power. Rather, it is revealed clearly and simply in the Bible and therefore is directly accessible to all people, from the wise and great to the poor and humble. Nor is true religion opposed to human nature. Rather, people are naturally capable of both apprehending what is good as set forth in the Scriptures and living in accordance with it. Perfect harmony between human nature and true religion allows humanity to attain, if not perfection, at least the next best thing, peace and happiness in this life.

This clear but quiet voice was drowned out by the storms of the Protestant Reformation (see Chapter 14), and the weight Erasmus gave to the individual's natural capacities could not hold its own before the renewed emphasis on human sinfulness and dogmatic theology. Erasmus was caught in the middle and condemned by both sides; for him, the Reformation was both a personal and a historical tragedy. He had worked for peace and unity and was treated to a spectacle of war and fragmentation. Erasmian humanism, however, survived these horrors as an ideal, and during the next two centuries, whenever thinkers sought toleration and rational religion (Rabelais and Montaigne, for instance), they looked back to Erasmus for inspiration.

French Humanism

German and French humanists pursued Christian humanist aims. They used humanist scholarship and language to satirize and vilify medieval scholastic Christianity and to build a purer, more scriptural Christianity. These northern humanists had great faith in the power of words. The discovery of accurate biblical texts, it was hoped, would lead to a great religious awakening. Protestant

Map 13.2 **THE GROWTH OF PRINTING IN EUROPE** The printing press was invented in the mid-fifteenth century, and its use had spread across Europe in less than a century. Even by 1500, some twenty million books had already been printed using the new technology. (© 2016 Cengage Learning.)

reformers, including Martin Luther, relied on humanist scholarship.

French thinkers of the next generation exploited and carried the humanist legacy in more radical directions. Among them, two were outstanding: Michel de Montaigne (1533–1592) and François Rabelais (c. 1494–1553). Both thought and wrote in reaction to the religious wars resulting from the Reformation. In the face of competing religious dogmatisms—Catholic, Protestant, and sectarian—Montaigne advanced a skepticism in which he maintained that one can know little or nothing with certainty. He therefore advocated political quietism and acceptance of Christianity on faith. This skepticism also entailed tolerance. An individual was not fully responsible for his or her beliefs, given that they were the product of frail reason and force of circumstance. Thus,

PORTRAIT OF ERASMUS (1523) BY HANS HOLBEIN THE YOUNGER. Erasmus was the leading early sixteenth-century Christian humanist. He insisted that all Christians should strive to think rationally and to live peacefully with one another, despite their differences. (© INTERFOTO/Alamy Limited.)

Montaigne argued, people should not be punished for their beliefs, and the only ones who deserved to be severely dealt with were the dogmatists in religion. These people deserved to be punished because their certainty and self-righteousness flew in the face of a fundamental epistemological fact: that reason cannot be relied on, especially in matters of religion.

Montaigne was not a systematic philosopher but devoted himself to what he could learn by Socratic self-examination, the results of which he set down in his *Essays*. In their urbane and caustic wit and their intense self-absorption, the *Essays* betray a crucial shift in humanist thought, which became more pronounced in the next century. Gone is the optimism and emphasis on civic virtue of the High Renaissance. In their place come skepticism and introspection, the attempt to base

morality on the self rather than on public values. As Montaigne says, "Let us learn to be no more avid of glory than we are capable of it."[9] This shift, produced by the increasing scale and violence of religious war, represented a retreat from the idealism of Renaissance humanism.

Rabelais took a different route from Montaigne's. In response to religious dogmatism, he asserted the essential goodness of the individual and the right to be free to enjoy the world rather than being bound down, as John Calvin later would have it, by fear of a vengeful God. Rabelais's folk-epic, *Gargantua and Pantagruel*, in which he celebrates earthly and earthy life, is the greatest French work of its kind and perhaps the greatest in any literature. Rabelais said that, once freed from dogmatic religion, people could, by virtue of their native goodness, build a paradise on earth and disregard the one dreamed up by theologians. In *Gargantua and Pantagruel*, he imagined a monastery where men and women spend their lives "not in laws, statutes, or rules, but according to their own free will and pleasure." They sleep and eat when they desire and learn to "read, write, sing, play upon several musical instruments, and speak five or six . . . languages and compose in them all very quaintly." They observe one rule: "do what thou wilt."[10]

Spanish Humanism

Spanish humanism represents a special case. The church hierarchy gained such a tight grip in Spain during the late fifteenth and early sixteenth centuries that it monopolized humanist learning and exploited it for its own repressive purposes. In contrast to Germany, France, and England, there was little or no room for a dissenting humanist voice. The mastermind behind this authoritarian Spanish humanism was Cardinal Francisco Jiménez de Cisneros (1436–1517). Jiménez founded the University of Alcalá, not far from Madrid, for the instruction of the clergy. He also sponsored and published the Complutensian Polyglot Bible, with Hebrew, Latin, and Greek texts in parallel columns. Jiménez, like Christian humanists elsewhere, sought to enlighten the clergy through a return to the pure sources of religion, and he saw his Polyglot Bible as one of the chief means of realizing that goal.

PORTRAIT OF SIR THOMAS MORE (1527) BY HANS HOLBEIN THE YOUNGER. In England, More and Erasmus were close friends and colleagues, united in their devotion to humanistic scholarship and a Christian idealism that preached rational religion and life lived in service to the larger community. (The Art Archive/Frick Collection, New York/Superstock.)

A century after Jiménez, Miguel de Cervantes Saavedra (1547–1616) produced his great novel, *Don Quixote,* in which he satirized the ideals of knighthood and chivalry. Don Quixote, the victim of his own illusions, roams the countryside looking for romance and an opportunity to prove his knightly worth. To Quixote's servant Sancho Panza, Cervantes assigned the role of pointing up the inanity of his master's quest by always acting prudently and judging according to common sense. Despite his earthy realism, however, Panza must share his master's misfortunes—so much for realism in a world run by men full of illusions. Cervantes's satire is very gentle. That knightly valor was still a valid subject for satire indicates how wedded Spain was even in the early seventeenth century to the conservative values of its crusading past.

English Humanism

Christian humanism in England sharply contrasted with that in Spain. It was developed by secular men in government as much as by clerics, and its objectives were often opposed to authority and tradition. Various Italian humanists came to England during the fifteenth century as bishops, merchants, court physicians, or artists. Englishmen also studied in Italy, especially in Florence, and introduced the serious humanistic study of the classics at Oxford University toward the end of the century.

The most influential humanist of the early English Renaissance was Sir Thomas More (1478–1535), who studied at Oxford. His impact arose from both his writing and his career. Trained as a lawyer, he became a successful civil servant and member of Parliament. His most famous book is *Utopia,* the major utopian treatise to be written in the West since Plato's *Republic* and one of the most original works of the entire Renaissance.

Many humanists had attacked private wealth as the source of pride, greed, and human cruelty. But in *Utopia,* More went further. He argued that an acquisitive society is by nature both unjust and unprosperous. "For, when everyone is entitled to get as much for himself as he can, all available property . . . is bound to fall into the hands of a small minority, which means that everyone else is poor." The unscrupulous few win out over the many who remain honest and decent. For More, the conclusion was inescapable: "I am quite convinced that you will never get a fair distribution of goods . . . until you abolish private property altogether."[11] But to balance things out, he stated the economic case against communism as well. In the absence of a profit motive, "there would always tend to be shortages because nobody would work hard enough. . . . Then when things really got short, the . . . result would be a series of murders and riots."[12] But More accused those who took this view of lacking the imagination to conceive of a truly just society. In *Utopia,* he set out to make up for this deficiency by inventing an ideal society in which private ownership was abolished and poverty eliminated because everyone had to work in order to eat. Such a system even produced surpluses, which allowed people the leisure for instruction and recreation.

More succeeded Cardinal Wolsey as lord chancellor under Henry VIII. But when the king broke with the Roman Catholic church, More resigned, unable to reconcile his conscience with the king's rejection of papal supremacy. Three years later, in July 1535, More was executed for treason for refusing to swear an oath acknowledging the king's ecclesiastical supremacy.

William Shakespeare (1564–1616), widely considered the greatest playwright the world has ever produced, gave expression to conventional Renaissance values: honor, heroism, and the struggle against fate and fortune. But there is nothing conventional about Shakespeare's treatment of characters possessing these virtues. His greatest plays, the tragedies (*King Lear, Julius Caesar,* and others), explore a common theme: men, even heroic men, despite virtue, are able only with the greatest difficulty, if at all, to overcome their human weaknesses. What fascinated Shakespeare was the contradiction between the Renaissance image of nobility, which is often the self-image of Shakespeare's heroes, and man's capacity for evil and self-destruction. Thus, Ophelia says of Hamlet, her lover, in the play of the same name:

> O, *what a noble mind is here o'erthrown!*
> *The courtier's, soldier's, scholar's, eye, tongue, sword;*
> *The expectancy and rose of the fair state,*
> *The glass of fashion and the mould of form,*
> *The observ'd of all observers, quite, quite down!*
> *[And] I, of ladies most deject and wretched,*
> *That suck'd the honey of his music vows,*
> *Now see that noble and most sovereign reason,*
> *Like sweet bells jangled, out of tune and harsh;*
> *That unmatch'd form and feature of blown youth*
> *Blasted with ecstasy. O, woe is me,*
> *T' have seen what I have seen, see what I see!*[13]

The plays are intensely human—so much so that humanism fades into the background. Thus, art transcends doctrine to represent life itself.

THE RENAISSANCE AND THE MODERN AGE

The Renaissance, then, marks the birth of modernity—in art, in the idea of the individual's role in history and nature, and in society, politics, war, and diplomacy. Central to this birth is a bold new view of human nature: individuals in all endeavors are free of a given destiny imposed by God from the outside—free to make their own destiny, guided only by the example of the past, the force of present circumstances, and the drives of their own inner nature. Individuals, set free from theology, are seen to be the products, and in turn the shapers, of history. Their future is not wholly determined by Providence but is partly the work of their own free will.

Within the Italian city-states, where the Renaissance was born, rich merchants were at least as important as the church hierarchy and the old nobility. The city-states were almost completely independent because of the weakness of church and empire. So the northern Italians were left free to invent new forms of government, in which merchant-oligarchs, humanists, and condottieri played a more important part than priests and nobles, who dominated politics in the rest of Europe. Along with the inventiveness, however, this newness and lack of tradition produced disorder and violence. Condottieri grabbed power from hapless citizens, and republics gave way to despotism.

But the problems created by novelty and instability demanded solutions, and the wealth of the cities called forth the talent to find them. Commercial wealth and the new politics produced a new culture: Renaissance art and humanism. Talented individuals—scholars, poets, artists, and government officials—returned to classical antiquity, which in any case lay near at hand in Italy and Greece. Ancient models in art, architecture, literature, and philosophy provided answers to their questions. This return to antiquity also entailed a rejection of the Middle Ages as dark, barbarous, and rude. The humanists clearly preferred the secular learning of ancient Greece and Rome to the clerical learning of the more recent past. The reason for this was obvious: the ancients had the same worldly concerns as the humanists; the scholastics did not.

The revival of antiquity by the humanists did not mean, however, that they identified completely with it. The revival itself was done too self-consciously for that. In the very act of looking back, the humanists differentiated themselves from the past and recognized that they were different. They were in this sense the first modern historians because they could study and appreciate the past for its own sake and, to some degree, on its own terms.

A Word of Caution

We have emphasized in this chapter that the Renaissance, especially in Italy, represented a sharp and deliberate break with medieval tradition. Thinkers crawled out from under that tradition and adopted striking new views in many fields, as, for instance, in art and science, philosophy and religion, politics and education. The result was the beginnings of a new kind of high culture, less religious and more secular, with more emphasis on individualism, artistic creativity, and political realism. The starting point for this development was to a large degree a rediscovery of the classics, that is, the writings of ancient Greek and Roman thinkers. These works were taught and translated as never before since the fall of the Roman Empire and the onset of the so-called Dark Ages a thousand years before. In other words, educated Europeans laid the foundations for a new Renaissance culture by reviving a once-powerful, dead culture and being inspired and instructed by it. Renaissance men and women undertook this project and saw it through more or less on their own initiative and without help from the outside. The Renaissance, in this view, was largely a European affair and the achievement of the northern Italian city-states in the first instance.

There is much to be said for this picture, but it is not the last word on the subject because, as historians are becoming more and more aware, southern Europe, including Italy, France and Spain, in the centuries before the Renaissance, was engaged in large-scale trade with a non-European culture, namely, the Muslim civilization stretching across the Middle East and Mediterranean. Based on Islam, this was a great civilization that had developed from the seventh century and that never experienced the long decline that Christian Europe suffered in the early Middle Ages. Instead, the Muslims conquered the Middle East

and North Africa and eventually Sicily and Spain. They built up great cities like Baghdad in the east, Cairo and Alexandria in Egypt, and Córdoba in southern Spain, all linked together by a flourishing trade throughout the Mediterranean. As prosperity increased in these cities, so did education, scholarship, and research. Schools and hospitals were founded for teaching and healing and large libraries created to facilitate study and learning. In the tenth century, the great library in Muslim Córdoba already had a collection of between 400,000 and 600,000 items, thus dwarfing the holdings of any library in Christian Europe at the time. As in Europe, much of this Muslim scholarship was based on ancient Greek and Latin manuscripts that were carefully preserved, translated into Arabic, and copied. But this educational tradition never died in Muslim lands as it had in Christian Europe. So when Europeans, led by the northern Italian city-states, rediscovered ancient literature and philosophy, they did not have to rely upon themselves alone but could also draw on Muslim sources for this ancient learning, where it was still being used and taught.

The Mediterranean was a "lake" in which goods like grain, oil, and wine were traded between Europeans in the north and Muslims in the south. Venice and Bologna in Italy established themselves as two of the principal hinges in this trade. Not only were goods and money exchanged, but also information, books, and knowledge. Much further west, scholars, Italian and otherwise, rushed to Spain, and especially to Córdoba, to use its great library and to get to know the works of antiquity, Aristotle especially (see pages 205–206).

During the Renaissance European scholars could draw upon texts, translations and scholarship made available to them over the centuries by contact between Europeans and Muslims, both through trade and by direct intellectual exchange. This is not to detract from the European Renaissance and its achievements, from which, after all, so much of the modern world emerged, including the very idea of modernity itself. This was in large part the invention of the northern Italian city-states, but it happened with considerable support from Muslim sources. To acknowledge this complicates matters somewhat and makes for a still unfinished, and less Eurocentric, story.

❖   ❖   ❖

Notes

1. Quoted in Quentin Skinner, *The Foundations of Modern Political Thought*, 2 vols. (Cambridge: Cambridge University Press, 1978), 1:89.

2. Giovanni Pico della Mirandola, *Oration on the Dignity of Man*, trans. A. Robert Caponigri (Chicago: Henry Regnery, 1956), 7.

3. Quoted in Margaret King, *Women of the Renaissance* (Chicago: University of Chicago Press, 1991), 221.

4. Moderata Fonte, *The Worth of Women*, ed. and trans. Virginia Cox (Chicago: The University of Chicago Press, 1997), 61.

5. Niccolò Machiavelli, *The Prince*, trans. George Bull (Harmondsworth, England: Penguin Books, 1961), 90–91.

6. Ibid., 77–78.

7. Ibid., 91.

8. Ibid., 101.

9. Quoted in Eugen Weber, ed., *The Western Tradition*, 2 vols., 4th ed. (Lexington, Mass., and Toronto: D. C. Heath, 1990), 1:395.

10. François Rabelais, *Gargantua and Pantagruel*, trans. Sir Thomas Urquhart (1883), bk. 1, chap. 57.

11. Thomas More, *Utopia*, trans. Paul Turner (Harmondsworth, England: Penguin Books, 1965), 66.

12. Ibid., 67.

13. From *Hamlet, Prince of Denmark*, in *The Complete Plays and Poems of William Shakespeare*, ed. William Allan Neilson and Charles Jarvis Hill (Boston: Houghton Mifflin, 1942), 1067.

Chapter 14

The Reformation: The Shattering of Christian Unity

St. Bartholomew's Day Massacre, *1572, by François Dubois (1529–1584).*

(St. Bartholomew's Day Massacre, 24th August 1572 (oil on panel), Dubois, Francois (1529–1584)/Musée d'Archéologie et d'Histoire, Lausanne, Switzerland/Giraudon/The Bridgeman Art Library.)

Focus Questions

1. What is a Protestant?
2. Why did the Protestant Reformation occur when it did?
3. What are the differences among a Lutheran, a Calvinist, and an Anglican?
4. What were the characteristics of the Radical Reformation?
5. Did Catholics and Protestants approach the modern world differently?

By the early sixteenth century, the only European institution that transcended geographic, ethnic, linguistic, and national boundaries was under severe attack from reformers. For centuries, the Catholic church, from its center in Rome, influenced every aspect of European society, culture, and politics. Reformers said that the church's desire to amass wealth and power appeared to outweigh its commitment to the search for holiness in this world and salvation in the next. Preoccupied by wealth, addicted to international power, and protective of their own interests, the clergy, from the pope down, took a battering from the church's critics. Humanists, made self-confident by the new learning and historical knowledge gathered during the Renaissance, called for reform and renewal, setting the stage for the Protestant Reformation. Eventually, though, the Reformation deviated significantly from what the Renaissance humanists had in mind. It brought into being a new form of Christianity, Protestantism, rather than reform of the Catholic church from within.

Schooled in new critical techniques, humanists used them to undermine the authenticity of documents that supposedly justified papal authority. Lorenzo Valla, for instance, disproved the validity of the Donation of Constantine (see "Humanism," in Chapter 13). But the fraud that especially vexed the humanists lay not on parchment but in the very practices by which the clergy governed the faithful.

The Protestant Reformation did not originate in elite circles of humanistic scholars. It began in German-speaking Europe with Martin Luther, an obscure monk and a brilliant theologian. Luther rejected the church's claim that it was the only vehicle for human salvation, and he defied the pope's right to silence, reprimand, and excommunicate any Christian who rejected papal authority or denied the truth of certain church teachings. After much soul-searching, in 1517 Luther proclaimed his *Ninety-Five Theses*. This set of short propositions started a public rebellion against the church's authority that in less than one decade shattered irrevocably the religious unity of Christendom. This rebellion also worked a quiet revolution in the lives of men and women. Marriage rather than celibacy for the clergy became an ideal, as did preaching, Bible-reading, and education. People felt less

Chronology 14.1 ❖ The Reformation

1381	English peasants revolt and support John Wycliffe, an early reformer
1414–1418	Council of Constance
1415	Hus burned at the stake
1431–1449	Council of Basel
1517	Martin Luther writes the *Ninety-Five Theses,* and the Reformation begins; thousands of printed copies circulate
1520	Pope Leo X excommunicates Luther
1524–1526	German peasants revolt
1526	Hungary falls to the Ottoman Turks, and its Diet is dissolved; it is powerless to stop the spread of Lutheranism
1529	English Parliament accepts Henry VIII's Reformation
1534	Henry VIII is declared head of the Church of England; Francis I of France declares Protestants heretics; Ignatius Loyola founds the Society of Jesus; Anabaptists, radical reformers, capture Münster in Westphalia
1536	John Calvin publishes *Institutes of the Christian Religion*
1536–1564	Calvin leads the Reformation in Geneva with William Farel
1545–1563	Council of Trent
1553–1558	Mary, Catholic queen of England, persecutes Protestants; many flee to Geneva
1555	Peace of Augsburg
1561	Scotland turns Presbyterian under John Knox
1562–1598	French wars of religion between Catholics and Protestants are settled by the Edict of Nantes in 1598; in the same period the Dutch revolt against Spain
1640–1660	English Revolution; rise and defeat of the Puritans

intimidated by clerical authority, but they were left to monitor their own behavior and to search for Godliness. For help they turned to the Bible. Pitted against the church, the Reformation and then the Catholic response dominated European history throughout much of the sixteenth century. They could be felt in religious antagonisms that lasted into the twentieth century.

THE MEDIEVAL CHURCH IN CRISIS

The fifteenth century in the church's history presented multiple and conflicting tendencies. Some theologians and political theorists rejected the pope's claim to supremacy over kings and to spiritual sovereignty over all of Western Christendom. They argued that the church had become inefficient and corrupt, and they blamed the papacy in Rome. They sought to wrest power from the pope and give it to a general council of the church's hierarchy. Before 1480, this was one of the aims of the Conciliar Movement. However, the Councils of Constance and of Basel failed to leave a meaningful inheritance to the church, largely because the special interests of kings and the papacy undercut the councils' authority. By 1500, the failure of the Conciliar Movement meant that reforming the church from within would be very difficult. A broader reformation required defiant action and outreach to the faithful. The recent invention of printing gave literate people access to the writings of the reformers and their Catholic adversaries. At the same time new reform movements sprang up in the Low Countries, Italy, and England and these were led by visionaries and mystics such as Catherine of Siena and the reclusive Julian of Norwich. Matching their zeal were two other earlier reformers.

Wycliffe and Hus

Prior to Luther, the two most significant attempts to reform the church occurred in the thirteenth century and late fourteenth century in England and Bohemia. In the fourteenth century, the leaders of two new movements, John Wycliffe in England and Jan Hus in Bohemia, were theologians who attacked vital church doctrines and practices. Wycliffe and Hus made heresy intellectually respectable. The influence of Wycliffe's and later Hus's movements also contributed to the long-term success of Protestantism in England and to its short-term success in portions of Eastern Europe. Hus laid the ground for the conversion of the Hungarian nobility. Even without access to printing, both Wycliffe and Hus appealed for mass support, prefiguring the populist quality of the Reformation.

John Wycliffe (c. 1320–1384), a master at Oxford University, attacked the church's authority by arguing simply that the worldly church did not control eternal destiny or the soul's access to grace. He said that salvation came only to those who possess faith, a gift freely given by God and not contingent on the church's rituals or sacraments. This position downgraded the clergy. Wycliffe attacked the church's wealth and argued that all true believers in Christ were equal and, in effect, Christ's priests. To make faith accessible to them, Wycliffe and his followers translated portions of the Bible into English. Wycliffe's preachings foreshadowed the teachings of Luther and the practices of the English Reformation.

Wycliffe received staunch support from some members of the English nobility. However, when his ideas were taken up by articulate peasants during an abortive peasants' revolt in 1381, Wycliffe lost many powerful backers. In the end, his attempt to reform the church by bringing it under secular control failed. Partly because he retained strong supporters and was more interested in scholarship than leadership, Wycliffe survived the failure of his movement and died a natural death. His ideas remained alive in popular religious beliefs, and his followers, called Lollards, have been credited with laying a foundation on which Protestant reformers of the sixteenth century could build.

A harsher fate awaited the Bohemian (Czech) reformer Jan Hus (c. 1369–1415): he was burned at the stake in 1415. Partly influenced by Wycliffe's writings, Hus, in his native Prague, attacked the sacramental system of the church, as well as its wealth and power. A popular preacher, he argued for Bohemian independence at a time when the Holy Roman Emperor had no intention of giving up his control over that territory. Hus was executed and his followers broke with the Roman Catholic church. In their independence from Rome, the Hussites prepared the ground for the success of the Protestant Reformation. Until well into the seventeenth century, Bohemia remained a battleground of popular Protestantism against the official church.

By and large the notable reform movements occurred outside of southern Europe. The one exception arose in southern France, where Waldo (d. 1218) led a band of reformers, the Waldensians, who wanted the Bible to be read in French and who laid emphasis on inner spirituality. As late as the 1680s, the French church, aided by the army, attempted to stamp out what it regarded as a form of Protestantism.

Mysticism and Humanism

Wycliffe's and Hus's reform attempts prefigured the new religiosity associated with mystics like Catherine of Siena and Julian of Norwich. They longed for an immediate and personal communication with God. Many late medieval mystics were women who, by virtue of their sex, were deprived of a clerical role in governing the church. First mysticism and then Protestantism offered women a way of expressing their independence in religious matters.

The church hierarchy had a deep distrust of mysticism. If people could experience God

THE SACRED HEART OF JESUS, A HAND-COLORED WOODCUT SOLD AS AN INDULGENCE, NUREMBERG, 1480s. The sale of indulgences to erase purgatory time disgusted Martin Luther. He also condemned the veneration of relics—objects associated with the life of Christ or his saints, even bones and hair. Rival churches often claimed to have "the only authentic" head of a certain saint. (Image copyright © The Metropolitan Museum of Art. Image source: Art Resource, N.Y.)

the Brethren embraced a practical piety intended to serve the needs of the entire community. With their teaching, they trained a new generation of urban-based scholars and humanists, including Erasmus, who were severe critics of the church. They also trained young men in administrative and accounting skills that would prove essential to the leadership of the Low Countries after their break with Spain. Their most famous pupil, the humanist Erasmus of Rotterdam, thought that satire should be enough to show the high and mighty the folly of their ways. In *The Praise of Folly* (1509), Erasmus has Folly herself proclaim, "I bring all things under the verge of my power, lording it over the greatest kings and potentates." But more was needed than wit and words.

Neither mysticism, with its emphasis on inner spirituality, nor humanism, with its stress on classical learning, captured the attention of ordinary Europeans. A successful reform movement required leaders with a common touch and an aggressive temperament. With actual political cunning, they could grapple with political realities and win lay support against the vast power of the church. Inspiration and urgency came from *millenarianism*, the belief that shortly Christ would come again and, after the Last Judgment, institute a thousand-year rule of saints on earth. Its believers found a radical and religious justification for attacking institutional corruption. The approaching end of the world allowed righteous reformers to believe their time had come.

The End of the World

In the movements inspired by Wycliffe and Hus, as well as in the peasant revolts often spurred by economic grievances, a sense of urgency became apparent. Millenarians, inspired by the biblical prophecies, looked forward to the moment of divine intervention when the world would be destroyed, sinfulness overwhelmed, and a paradise on earth created where God's chosen would rule. Millenarian reformists, some quite radical, took prophecies accepted but not promoted by the church and reinterpreted them to express their vision of a just society where religion aids the poor

directly, they would have little need for the church and its rituals. By the sixteenth and seventeenth centuries, radical reformers, some of them women preachers, often found in Christian mysticism a powerful alternative to the control and consolation offered by priests and sacraments. Mainstream Protestant reformers as well as the Catholic hierarchy took a dim view of what they deemed lawlessness posing as mystical piety.

In the Low Countries from the fifteenth century onwards, the Brethren of the Common Life propounded a religious movement known as the *devotiomoderna*, which was inspired by mysticism. A semimonastic order of laity and clergy, and oppressed. Protestant reformers reinterpreted Catholic millenarian doctrine. Some said that Christ would condemn the rich and propertied and establish a new society, not in heaven but on earth, which the poor would inherit, and for a thousand years—a millennium—the poor would rule in Christ's kingdom.

By 1500, the biblical concept of the Antichrist and the image of the whore of Babylon, both a part of **millenarian thinking**, became shorthand symbols for the corruption of the church. When Luther and other reformers in the early sixteenth century called the pope himself the Antichrist or the whore of Babylon, they drew upon the millenarian tradition of reform and protest.

THE LUTHERAN REVOLT

Only an attack on papal and clerical authority could strike at the church's power. To succeed, the attack had to address the multitudes while appealing to princes. Heresy had to be made respectable and compelling. Such a feat required someone whose inner spiritual struggle highlighted the church's failure to care for souls, someone who could translate the agony of the search for salvation into language accessible to all Christians. Martin Luther (1483–1546) had experienced a personal crisis of faith, and he possessed the will, the talent, and the intellectual vigor to offer it as an example for other Christians. Luther wrote voluminously and talked freely to his friends and students. Using this mass of recorded material, historians have been able to reconstruct the life and personality of this Augustinian friar and theologian who began the Reformation (see Primary Source feature).

Luther: Humanist, Prophet, and Conservative

Martin Luther was born in eastern Germany to relatively uneducated parents of humble origins. His strict father, Hans Luther, was exceptionally ambitious. Born a peasant, he left the land and became a miner and finally a manager of several mines in the booming late-fifteenth-century German mine industry. Like many of the newly rich, Hans Luther had ambitious plans for his son; he wanted Martin to attain the status of an educated man and become a lawyer. Luther's mother was intensely pious, thus putting Luther in close touch with German popular religion.

At the university, Luther's intellectual career was to make him one of the foremost theologians and biblical scholars of his day. At first, as his father wanted, he studied law, and of course he read the humanists, including Erasmus.

But a rebellious streak surfaced. In 1504, at the age of twenty-one, Luther suddenly abandoned his legal studies to enter the Augustinian monastery at Erfurt. The actual decision was made swiftly. In later life, Luther recounted that the decision had been made in fear, as a vow to Saint Anne in the midst of a fierce lightning storm, by a young man convinced that his death at that moment would bring him eternal damnation. Why Luther thought he was damned is not known, but his guilt conspired with his vivid imagination to kindle what must have been a growing resentment against his father's domination. Challenging authority became a habit for Luther.

Luther was also a millenarian; he thought that he was living in the last days of the world. Eventually, as he became the leader of an international religious movement, Luther grew convinced that he was the long-foretold, divinely ordained prophet chosen to announce the coming Final Judgment. When he became the strong leader of the German Reformation, he also had to make skillful political choices and pick his allegiances. Without hesitation and with deep conviction, Luther chose to preserve the social order, to support the power of princes and magistrates, and to maintain social hierarchy. Yet he took on papal authority and the power of the Holy Roman Emperor.

Luther's Break with Catholicism

As he prayed, Luther grew increasingly terrified by the possibility of his damnation. As a monk, he sought union with God, and he understood the church's teaching that salvation depended on faith, works (meaning acts of charity, prayer, fasting, and so on), and grace. He participated in the sacraments of the church, and through them sought God's grace. Indeed, after his ordination, Luther administered the sacraments. Yet he agonized over his sins, and the church seemed unable to relieve that burden.

Even the mystery of the Mass and the conversion of bread and wine into the body and blood of Christ brought Luther little inner peace. Seeking solace and salvation, he increasingly turned to reading the Bible. Two passages spoke directly to him: "For therein is the righteousness of God revealed from faith to faith: as it is written, 'He who through faith is righteous shall live'" (Romans 1:17); and "They are justified by his grace as a gift, through the redemption which is in Christ Jesus" (Romans 3:24).[1] In faith and grace, Luther found, for the first time in his adult life, some hope for his own salvation. These biblical passages said to him that faith, freely given only by God through Christ, gives salvation and that human beings, powerless because of their fallen and sinful nature, are rescued by divine mercy. Neither the pope nor the sacraments give what only God can provide—salvation.

The concept of salvation by faith alone satisfied Luther's spiritual quest. Practicing good works such as prayer, fasting, pilgrimages, and receiving the sacraments would not in themselves lead to grace. No amount of good works, however necessary for Christian unity, would bring salvation. Through reading the Bible and through faith alone, the Christian could find the purpose of earthly existence. For Luther, the true Christian was a courageous figure who faced the terrifying quest for salvation armed only with the hope that God had granted the gift of faith. The new Christian served others, not to bargain with good works for salvation, but solely to fulfill the demands of Christian love. Nuns left their convents and married in the belief that their faith and service to the community would save them. Priests also left the church to become, like Luther, leaders of their own churches. Luther's odyssey laid out a new Protestant piety that embraced activity in the world.

Pursuing his theological and biblical studies, Luther became a professor at the nearby university at Wittenberg, in Saxony, and a preacher in that city's church. He shared his personal struggle with his students and his congregations. At the University of Wittenberg and in the province of Saxony in general, Luther found an audience receptive to his views, and his popularity and reputation grew. Before 1517, he was considered a dynamic and controversial preacher, whose passionate interest lay in turning Christians away from their worldly pleasures and from reliance on good works while focusing their attention on Christ and the truth contained within Scripture. After 1517, Luther became internationally famous; eventually the church deemed him a heretic.

The Reformation began in 1517 with Luther's attack on the church's practice of selling indulgences. The church taught that some individuals go directly to heaven, some go directly to hell, and others go to heaven after spending time in purgatory. Punishment in purgatory is necessary for those who sinned excessively but had the good fortune to repent before death. Naturally, people worried about how long they might have to suffer in purgatory. Indulgences were intended to remit portions of that time and punishment and were granted by the church to those who prayed, attended Mass, and performed acts of charity—including making monetary offerings to the church itself. Could the church be selling, and people buying, admittance to heaven?

In the autumn of 1517, a friar named Tetzel was selling indulgences near Wittenberg. Some of the money went to rebuilding Saint Peter's Basilica in Rome, and the rest was for paying off debts incurred by a local archbishop when he purchased his office from the pope. Although Luther did not know about the purchase, he was incensed both by Tetzel's crude manner and by his flagrant exploitation of the people's ignorance and what Luther deemed his misuse of their money. Luther launched his attack on Tetzel and the selling of indulgences by tacking on the door of the Wittenberg castle church his *Ninety-Five Theses*.* He also sent a copy to the local archbishop. Luther's theses (propositions) challenged the entire notion of selling indulgences not only as a corrupt practice but also because it rested on a theologically unsound

---

*There is disagreement about whether or not the tacking to the door actually occurred.

Martin Luther: *Disputation of Doctor Martin Luther on the Power and Efficacy of Indulgences* (1517)

Out of love for the truth and the desire to bring it to light, the following propositions will be discussed at Wittenberg, under the presidency of the Reverend Father Martin Luther, Master of Arts and of Sacred Theology, and Lecturer in Ordinary on the same at that place. Wherefore he requests that those who are unable to be present and debate orally with us, may do so by letter.

In the Name our Lord Jesus Christ. Amen.

1. Our Lord and Master Jesus Christ . . . willed that the whole life of believers should be repentance.

2. This word cannot be understood to mean sacramental penance, i.e., confession and satisfaction, which is administered by the priests.

3. Yet it means not inward repentance only; nay, there is no inward repentance which does not outwardly work divers mortifications of the flesh.

4. The penalty [of sin], therefore, continues so long as hatred of self continues; for this is the true inward repentance, and continues until our entrance into the kingdom of heaven.

5. The pope does not intend to remit, and cannot remit any penalties other than those which he has imposed either by his own authority or by that of the Canons.

6. The pope cannot remit any guilt, except by declaring that it has been remitted by God and by assenting to God's remission; though, to be sure, he may grant remission in cases reserved to his judgment. If his right to grant remission in such cases were despised, the guilt would remain entirely unforgiven.

7. God remits guilt to no one whom He does not, at the same time, humble in all things and bring into subjection to His vicar, the priest.

8. The penitential canons are imposed only on the living, and, according to them, nothing should be imposed on the dying.

9. Therefore the Holy Spirit in the pope is kind to us, because in his decrees he always makes exception of the article of death and of necessity.

10. Ignorant and wicked are the doings of those priests who, in the case of the dying, reserve canonical penances for purgatory.

11. This changing of the canonical penalty to the penalty of purgatory is quite evidently one of the weeds that were sown while the bishops slept.

Questions for Analysis

1. What does it mean to say that the pope cannot remit our guilt? If not through the pope, then how will humans be forgiven?

2. What is Luther's view of the clergy?

Works of Martin Luther, trans. and ed. Adolph Spaeth, L. D. Reed, Henry Eyster Jacobs, et al. (Philadelphia: A. J. Holman, 1915), 1:29–38.

assumption—namely, that salvation could be earned by the good work of supporting the church. Luther was blunt with the church's hierarchy and, in particular, with the papacy: he challenged its sole authority to save souls and to guard

entrance into heaven. By his logic, indulgences were worthless.

Luther's argument rested on the belief that Christian salvation through personal piety requires contrition for sins and trust in God's mercy and grace. He also believed that no good work earned salvation. The church, in contrast, held that *both* faith and good works were necessary for salvation. Luther further insisted that every individual could discover the meaning of the Bible unaided by the clergy. The church maintained that only the clergy could read and interpret the Bible properly. Luther argued that in matters of faith there was no difference between the clergy and the laity; indeed, each person could receive faith directly and freely from God. The church held that the clergy through the sacraments were intermediaries between individuals and God: Christians reached eternal salvation only with the aid of the church and its clergy. For Luther, no priest, no ceremony, no sacrament, and certainly no confinement in convents or monasteries could bridge the gulf between the Creator and his creatures, and the possibility of personal damnation remained a distinct reality. Hope lay only in a personal relationship between the individual and God, as expressed through faith in God's mercy and grace. In Luther's view, no church could mediate that faith for the individual, and to that extent Luther's theology destroyed the foundations of the church's spiritual power. By declaring that clergy and church rituals do not hold the key to salvation, Luther rejected the church's claim that it alone offered the way to eternal life.

TETZEL SELLING LETTERS OF INDULGENCE. This engraving shows activities in the pope's audience-viewing room. Peasants and religious men are giving money to the church and receiving blessings after making their payments. (Kean Collection/Archive Photos/Getty Images.)

But Who Is Saved?

If faith alone, freely given by God, brings salvation to the believer, how can a person know whether he or she has faith? Luther seemed content to assert that the search itself by a pious and penitent supplicant implied God's favor. In Luther's doctrine of faith, the notion of *predestination* is barely beneath the surface. Luther never chose to bring forth the implications of his doctrine. His contemporary, the great French theologian John Calvin, however, made predestination central to his version of reformed Christianity. This belief made salvation an intensely personal matter—some might say an intensely terrifying or liberating matter.

Predestination is such a difficult doctrine that discussion about it continues today. Predestination rests on the assumption that God is all-knowing, eternal, his will absolute: he gives faith to whomever he chooses and does so for his own inscrutable reasons. Because God's existence and will are timeless, God knows the fate of every person even as individuals are searching for salvation. Given God's foreknowledge, it may be said that every person is predestined for either heaven or hell. But for believers, the question remains: how can individuals know whether God has chosen them for salvation?

Luther said simply that men and women should hope and trust in salvation but certainty would be granted only after death. For subsequent reformers predestination made Protestant doctrine logical and created an identifying experience for all true Christians. Calvin and his followers, who by 1650 became numerically the largest group of

European and American Protestants, believed firmly that some are chosen and others damned—but no one should presume one way or another.

The Creation and Spread of Lutheranism

In 1517, Luther could not foresee what he had started, that the Reformation was under way. Quickly translating his theses from Latin into German, his students printed and distributed them throughout Germany. Local church authorities recognized in Luther a serious threat and prepared to silence him. But Luther was tenacious; he began to write and preach his theology with increasing vigor. With the aid of the printing press, by 1525 there were probably three million Protestant pamphlets circulating in Germany. Students and well-wishers from Eastern Europe as well as Germany flocked to Wittenberg.

At this point, politics intervened. Recognizing that his life might be in danger if he continued to preach without a protector, Luther appealed for support to Prince Frederick, the elector of Saxony. The elector was a powerful man in international politics—one of the seven lay and ecclesiastical princes who chose the Holy Roman Emperor. Frederick's support for his most famous university professor convinced church officials, including the pope, that this friar had to be handled cautiously.

The years 1518 and 1519 were momentous ones for the Holy Roman Empire. Before his death in 1519, the Holy Roman Emperor Maximilian I wanted to see his grandson Charles, king of Spain, elected to succeed him. The papacy at first opposed Charles's candidacy, even looking to Frederick of Saxony as a possible alternative. Frederick wisely declined. However, because he was one of the seven electors, the contenders—Charles, Francis I of France, and Henry VIII of England—counted on him for his vote. Charles bribed the electors and won the title. Therefore, during this crucial period and for years afterward, he had to proceed cautiously on issues that might offend powerful German princes.

These political considerations explain the delay in Luther's official condemnation and excommunication by the pope. When in late 1520 the pope finally acted, it was too late; Luther had been given the time needed to promote his views. He proclaimed that the pope was the Antichrist and that the church was the "most lawless den of robbers, the most shameless of all brothels, the very kingdom of sin, death and Hell."[2] When the papal bull excommunicating him was delivered, Luther burned it.

Luther and his followers established congregations for Christian worship throughout Germany. To find protectors, in 1520 Luther published the *Address to the Christian Nobility of the German Nation*. In it, he appealed to the German princes to cast off their allegiance to the pope, who, he argued, had used taxes and political power to exploit them for centuries. His appeal tapped into the resentment against foreign papal intervention that had long festered in Germany. Luther also wrote to the German people about the meaning of his personal experience as a Christian. In *The Freedom of a Christian Man* (1520), he called on Germans to strive for true spiritual freedom through faith in Christ, to discipline themselves, to obey legitimate political authority, and to perform good works according to the dictates of Christian love. In these treatises, Luther made his political conservatism clear: he wanted to present no threat to legitimate authority, that is, to the power of German princes. Secular authority occupied a separate realm from the spiritual.

In 1521, Charles V, the Holy Roman Emperor and a devout Catholic, summoned Luther to Worms, giving him a pass of safe conduct. In that imperial city Luther faced the charge of heresy, both an ecclesiastical and a civil offense. As he traveled to Worms, crowds of well-wishers cheered his way. Then standing before the emperor and his court, Luther was supposed to recant. His careful and defiant reply became his most famous statement: "Unless I am convinced of error by the testimony of Scripture or by clear reason . . . I cannot and will not recant anything, for it is neither safe nor honest to act against one's conscience. God help me."

Shortly after this confrontation with the emperor, Luther went into hiding to escape arrest. In that one-year period, he translated the New Testament into German. With it, he offered literate Germans the opportunity to take the same arduous spiritual odyssey that he had undergone and to join him as a new type of Christian. These followers, or Lutherans, were eventually called *Protestants*, those who protested against the established church, and the term became generic for all supporters of the Reformation.

Religious Reform or Social Revolution?

Luther looked to every level of German society for support. In a country of many small towns with printing presses, the literate urban population responded dramatically to his call. Led by city fathers and preachers, individuals converted to the new Protestant churches or turned their own Catholic church into a Protestant one. The new faith made men and women bold. When a teenage boy married of his own will without consulting his family in Nuremberg, he defended his actions by saying that God "ordained that it happen this way by his divine will."[3] Priests were now expected to marry. Even though Protestants insisted that women marry and be silent and obedient, a Swiss Protestant woman who refused marriage justified her wanting to remain "masterless" by saying: "Those who have Christ for a master are not masterless."

Luther was a brilliant preacher, and clearly his message could inspire people to be defiant as well as devout. Protestantism came to be seen not only as a source of personal revitalization and salvation but also as a force that could renew society and government.

The same issues that moved Germans to leave the church appealed to people in towns and cities in Austria, Hungary, Poland, the Netherlands, and Switzerland. Even in Paris and London, as well as in northern Italy by the late 1520s, followers or readers of Luther could easily be found, and lives changed profoundly. Katharina von Bora, who married Martin Luther, was so devoted to the Lutheran cause that Luther called her his "Moses." There were thousands of devout and defiant Katharinas throughout Europe.

Despite repression by the Catholic church and the weight of habit and tradition, in 1550 Prot-estants were probably in the majority in some German towns, in much of Hungary and Bohemia, in Sweden, and in various Swiss cantons. In France, more than a million people converted to Calvin's version of Protestantism. Dutch city dwellers turned to it as well, much to the horror of their Spanish king. How could this have happened in one generation?

In the sixteenth century, any new religious or political movement needed the support of the nobility. Early on, Luther appealed to them, and they responded. Their motives ranged from piety to power and political ambition. The Reformation provided the nobility with the unprecedented opportunity to confiscate church lands, eliminate church taxes, and gain the support of their subjects by serving as leaders of a popular and dynamic religious movement. The Reformation also gave the nobles a way to resist the Catholic Holy Roman Emperor Charles V, who wanted to extend his authority over the German princes. Resenting Italian domination of the church, many other Germans who supported Martin Luther believed that they were freeing German Christians from foreign control. The same spirit motivated the nobility in France, the Low Countries, Poland, and Lithuania.

First and foremost, however, Lutheranism was a popular evangelical movement. Its battle cry became "The Word of God"; faith and the Bible were its hallmarks. Luther turned his wrath on the "detestable tyranny of the clergy over the laity; [the clergy] almost look upon them as dogs, unworthy to be numbered in the Church along with themselves. . . . They dare to command, exact, threaten, drive, and oppress, at their will."[4]

Those were fighting words—but uttered by a political conservative, who hesitated to challenge secular authority. To Luther, the good Christian must be an obedient citizen. The freedom of the Christian lay inward, a spiritual freedom. Yet Luther could not stop his ideas from spreading to the poor and the peasantry, often by word of mouth. The population of Germany was about 16 million, of which probably no more than 400,000 could read. For the illiterate and largely rural people, Lutheranism came to mean not only religious reform but also an evangelical social movement that would address their poverty.

Katharina von Bora

Katharina von Bora (1499–1552) and Martin Luther had a marriage that, though imperfect, well represents the Protestant model. Although Katharina came from a noble background, her family was not well-off. After a few years of religious education, she entered a nunnery—a common choice for women without dowries for marriage. Katharina and other women in the convent soon became disillusioned with the cloistered life. Somehow, Martin Luther learned of their plight and decided to help. In April 1523, he aided eleven nuns—among them Katharina—in their escape from the cloister. Legend has it that they hid in empty smoked herring barrels.

Two years later, Katharina and Martin were married. Their marriage became a love match that lasted all of their lives. Katharina and Martin became role models for other Protestant clergy. Protestant doctrine taught women that marriage and child-rearing, combined with obedience to one's husband, led to holiness. Katie, as Martin called her, ran a household with more than forty rooms, in addition to buying and running a farm. She raised six children and was a devoted Protestant wife. Her last recorded words are "I will stick to Christ as a burr to a topcoat." Beginning with Katharina and Martin, Protestant ministers married, raised families, and served their congregations who supported them.

In addition, the peasants believed that the end of the world was near and that God would soon impose justice. Millenarianism, poverty, and anti-clericalism inspired social revolution.

Although Luther had spoken forcefully about Christians' discontent with their church, he never understood that to the poor and socially oppressed, the church's abuses were visible signs of the poverty and exploitation they encountered in their daily lives. The wealthy feudal lords who dominated every aspect of their existence, as well as the prosperous townspeople who bought their labor for the lowest possible wages, seemed no different from the venal clergy; indeed, in some cases the lord was also a local bishop.

In the early sixteenth century, a rapid population explosion throughout Europe had produced severe inflation, high unemployment, and low wages. The poor got poorer. The peasantry in Germany was probably worse off than the peasantry in England and the Low Countries. In 1524, long-suffering peasants openly rebelled against their lords. The peasants' revolt spread to more than one-third of Germany; some 300,000 people took up arms against their masters. They were inspired by Luther's successful confrontation with the church. Had he not chastised the nobles for failing to care for the poor as commanded in the Gospel?

Luther, however, had no intention of associating his movement with a peasant uprising and thereby alienating the nobility from the Reformation. Luther virulently attacked the rebellious peasants, urging the nobility to become "both judge and executioner" and to "knock down, strangle, and stab . . . and think nothing so venomous, pernicious, Satanic as an insurgent. . . . Such wonderful times are these that a prince can merit heaven better with bloodshed than another with prayer."[5] During 1525–1526, the peasants had been put down by the sword. Thousands died or were left homeless, and many were permanently alienated from Lutheranism. Because of the failure of the revolt, the German peasantry remained relatively backward and oppressed well into the nineteenth century. In Germany, the Reformation meant religious reform, not social revolution or even social reform, and it became increasingly an urban phenomenon.

THE SPREAD OF THE REFORMATION

Lutheranism spread in waves and in every direction out from Wittenberg, the training ground for Luther's clergy. In northern Europe, cut off from the south by the Alps and the Pyrenees, the Reformation spread rapidly. In southern Europe, where the church and the Inquisition were strongest, the Reformation made fewer inroads in Italy or Spain. Thus, the spread of Protestantism had a pattern. It grew strong in northern Germany, Scandinavia, the Netherlands, Scotland, and England but failed in Ireland and the Romance countries, though not without a struggle in France.

Protestantism also appeared simultaneously in different places—a sure indication of its popular roots. For example, in the Swiss city of Zurich, the priest and reformer Ulrich Zwingli (1484–1531) preached faith and not good works and saw the Bible as the key to divine will and law. Like Luther, he looked for an alternative to the doctrine of *transubstantiation*—the priest's transformation of Communion bread and wine into the substance of Christ's body and blood. It gave enormous power to the priesthood. But the two reformers differed bitterly over the form and meaning of the ceremony. Zwingli radically altered the Communion service, and it became solely a commemoration of the Last Supper. Their quarrel highlights that the reformers, as predicted by the Catholic church, could not agree on the meaning of the Bible or on the ritual expressions they would give their new versions of Christianity.

ICONOCLAST FURY. In the sixteenth century, reformers tore out the statues and stained glass in Protestant, once Catholic, churches, arguing that decoration distracts from the Bible and the Word of God. To this day, Protestant churches remain less decorated than Catholic ones. (The Granger Collection, NYC.)

Zwingli died on the battlefield in a war to defend the Reformation. His teachings laid the foundation for a thorough reformation in Switzerland, and the major reform movement of the next generation, Calvinism, benefited from Zwingli's reforms. Both forms of the Reformation spread into Eastern Europe.

In Germany, the strife between Catholics and Protestants was settled, though not to everyone's satisfaction, by the Peace of Augsburg (1555). It decreed, by the famous dictum *cuius regio eius religio* ("whoever rules, his religion"), that each territorial prince should determine the religion of his subjects. Broadly speaking, northern Germany became largely Protestant, and Bavaria and other southern territories remained in the Roman Catholic church. The victors were the local princes. Toward the end of his life, Charles V expressed bitter regret for not intervening more forcefully in those early years. The decentralization of the empire and its division into Catholic and Protestant areas blocked German unity until the last part of the nineteenth century. In Eastern Europe, both forms of Christianity showed hostility to Islam, and it was returned in kind.

Calvin and Calvinism

The success of the Reformation outside Germany and Scandinavia derived largely from the theological rigor of John Calvin (1509–1564), a French scholar and theologian. By the 1530s, Lutheran treatises circulated widely in Paris. Some university students, including the young John Calvin, seized upon Luther's ideas.

Calvin was born into a French family of bourgeois status; his father, somewhat like Luther's, was self-made and ambitious. A lawyer and administrator, the elder Calvin served ecclesiastical authorities until a dispute led to his excommunication. He desired prosperous careers for his sons. John first studied to be a priest and then, at his father's insistence, took up the study of law at the University of Orléans. Unlike the rebellious Luther, Calvin waited until his father's death to return to Paris and resume his theological studies. Even more so than Luther, Calvin was trained as a humanist. He knew the ancient languages, as well as philosophy and theology, and he knew the Bible. From all those sources, Calvin fashioned

the most logically compelling version of Protestantism to come out of the Reformation.

Sometime in 1533 or 1534, Calvin met French followers of Luther and became convinced of the truth of the new theology. He took to the streets to spread his beliefs, and within a year he and his friends were in trouble with the authorities. Calvin was arrested but released because of insufficient evidence.

King Francis I, a bitter rival of the Holy Roman Emperor, could countenance Protestantism in Germany but would never permit disruptive religious divisions in France. Riots had already broken out in Paris between Catholics and supporters of the Reformation. In 1534, the French church, backed by a royal decree, declared the Protestants heretics and subjected them to arrest and execution.

Within a year, young Calvin abandoned his literary studies to become a preacher of the Reformation. Calvin explained his conversion as an act of God: "He subdued and reduced my heart to docility, which, for my age, was over-much hardened in such matters."[6] Calvin emphasized the power of God over sinful and corrupt humanity; his God thundered and demanded obedience, and only Christ mediated the terrible distance between God and the individual.

In his search for spiritual order and salvation, Calvin spoke to his age. His anxiety was widely shared. He feared disorder and ignorance, sinfulness, and simply the unpredictable quality of human existence. The only solution to anxiety lay in unshakable faith in God, knowledge of his laws, and absolute adherence to righteous conduct. We must see God's order everywhere, especially in nature, in "the symmetry and regulation" of the universe.[7] Faith in God is so obviously our salvation that, according to Calvin, only the damned, the reprobate, would turn their back on him and live in disorder. Calvin assured his congregations that God "will give a good result to everything we do. . . . God will cause our enterprises to prosper when our purpose is right and we attempt nothing except what he wills."[8] With Calvin, the doctrine of predestination became the centerpiece of Protestant theology: some people are saved, others damned at birth; inward belief and outward righteousness and integrity may signal a person's fate, but God alone knows what the future holds.

The social and political implications of predestination were immediate: Calvinists became militant Protestants capable of ruling their towns or cities with the same iron will they used to control their unruly passions. Like Luther, Calvin always stressed that Christians should obey legitimate political authority. But Calvinists were individuals who assumed that unfailing dedication to God's law could signal salvation; their obedience to human laws would always be contingent on their inner sense of righteousness. Thus, Calvinism made for stern followers, active

in their churches and willing to suppress vice in themselves and others. Calvinism also could produce revolutionaries willing to defy any temporal authorities seen to violate God's laws. Obedience to Christian law became the dominating principle of Calvin's life. Rigorous enforcement of the law ensured obedience to God's law; the local Calvinist church became an alternative to the power of the Catholic church.

The political situation in France forced Calvin to leave. After his flight from Paris, he finally sought safety in Geneva, a small, prosperous Swiss city near the French border. It was a logical choice. Before Calvin's arrival, Geneva's citizens

THE CHURCH OF ST. BAVO IN HAARLEM, PAINTED BY JOB BERCKHEYDE. This Protestant church in Haarlem in the Dutch Republic illustrates the aesthetics of the new version of Christianity—plain, undecorated, with emphasis on the importance of the pulpit. (Staatliche Kunstsammlungen Dresden/The Bridgeman Art Library.)

were in revolt against their Catholic bishops. The French-born reformer William Farel implored Calvin to stay to continue the work of the Reformation. Together, they became leaders of the Protestant movement in Geneva. After many setbacks, Calvin emerged as the most dynamic agent of reform in the city. Until his death in 1564, his beliefs and actions ruled Geneva's religious and social life.

Calvin established an unofficial Calvinist *theocracy*—a society in which Calvinist elders regulated citizens' personal and social lives and did so through church courts that were independent of state institutions. Older, pious, male members of the community governed the city. These elders of the Calvinist church imposed strict discipline in dress, sexual mores, church attendance, and business affairs; they severely punished irreligious and sinful behavior. This rigid discipline contributed to Geneva's prosperity; indeed, Calvin instituted the kind of social discipline that some of the merchants had always wanted. Prosperous merchants, as well as small shopkeepers, saw in Calvinism a series of doctrines that justified the self-discipline they already exercised in their own lives and wished to impose on the unruly masses. They particularly approved of Calvin's economic views, for Calvin, unlike the Catholic church, saw nothing sinful in commercial activities and even gave his assent to the practice of charging interest.

Geneva became the center of international Protestantism. Calvin trained a new generation of Protestant reformers of many nationalities who carried his message back to their homelands. Calvin's *Institutes of the Christian Religion* (1536), in its many editions, became (after the Bible) the leading textbook of the new theology. In the second half of the sixteenth century, Calvin's theology of predestination spread into France, England, Scotland, the Netherlands, and parts of the Holy Roman Empire.

Calvin opposed violence against the legitimate authority of magistrates. Yet when monarchy became a persecutor, his followers felt compelled to respond. Calvinist theologians became the first political theoreticians of modern times to publish cogent arguments for opposition to monarchy and eventually for political revolution. In France and later in the Netherlands, Calvinism became a revolutionary ideology, complete with an underground organization of dedicated followers who challenged monarchical authority. (In the seventeenth century, the English version of Calvinism—Puritanism—performed the same function.) In certain circumstances, Calvinism supplied the moral force to support the individual against the claims of the monarchical state.

France

Although Protestantism was illegal in France after 1534, its persecution was halfhearted and never systematic. The Calvinist minority in France, the Huguenots, became a well-organized underground movement that attracted nobles, city dwellers, some peasants, and especially women. Huguenot churches, often under the protection of powerful nobles, assumed an increasingly political character in response to the monarchy-sponsored persecution. By 1559, French Protestants had organized and challenged their persecutors, King Henry II and the Guise—one of the foremost Catholic families in Europe, tied by marriage and conviction to the Spanish monarchy and its rigorous form of Catholicism. Guise power in the French court meant that all Protestant appeals for lenient treatment went unheeded, and in 1562 civil war erupted between Catholics and Protestants. What followed was one of the most brutal religious wars in the history of Europe. In 1572, an effort at conciliation through the marriage of a Protestant leader into the royal family failed when Catholics, urged on by the queen mother, Catherine de' Medici, murdered the assembled Protestant wedding guests. Over the next week, a popular uprising left thousands of Protestants dead; the streets, according to eyewitness accounts, were stained red with blood. These murders and the ensuing slaughter, known as the Saint Bartholomew's Day Massacre, inspired the pope to have a Mass said in thanksgiving for a Catholic "victory." Such was the extent of religious hatred in late-sixteenth-century Europe.

After nearly thirty years of brutal fighting throughout France, victory went to the Catholic side—but just barely. Henry of Navarre, the Protestant bridegroom who in 1572 had managed to escape the fate of his supporters, became King Henry IV, but only after reconverting to Catholicism. He established a tentative peace by granting Protestants limited toleration. In 1598, he issued the Edict of Nantes, the first document in any nation-state that attempted to institutionalize a degree of religious toleration. In the seventeenth century, the successors of Henry IV (he was assassinated by a priest in 1610) gradually weakened the edict and then in 1685 revoked it. The foundations of toleration, in theory and practice, remained tenuous in early modern France. Every French king of the seventeenth century tried to decrease the number of Protestants. In 1685, more than 150,000 fled to the Protestant areas of Europe or the American colonies.

England

The Reformation in England differed profoundly from the Continental Reformations. The king, Henry VIII (1509–1547), and not clergymen in revolt, made it happen. The pope refused to grant Henry an annulment of his marriage to his first wife, who had failed to produce a male heir. So this self-confident Renaissance king, bent on having a new wife and new sources of revenue, removed the English church from papal jurisdiction.

Unlike the French and Spanish kings, the English Tudors never frightened the papacy. Henry VII (1485–1509), the first Tudor monarch, and his son, Henry VIII, enjoyed a good measure of control over the English church but never played a major role in European and papal politics. When Henry VIII decided that he wanted a divorce (he called it an annulment) from the Spanish princess Catherine of Aragon during 1527–1528, the pope in effect ignored his request. Henry had neither power nor theology on his side. As the pope stalled, Henry grew more desperate; he needed a male heir and arrogantly presumed that the failure to produce one lay with his wife. At the same time, he desired Anne Boleyn. But Spain's power over the papacy ensured that Henry's pleas for an annulment would go unheeded.

The English possessed a tradition of opposing the church that went back to Wycliffe in the

fourteenth century. Aware of that long tradition, Henry VIII arranged to grant himself a divorce by severing England from the Roman Catholic church. To do so, he summoned Parliament, which in turn passed a series of statutes drawn up at his initiative and guided through Parliament by his political adviser, Thomas Cromwell. Beginning in 1529, Henry convinced Parliament to accept his Reformation, and so began an administrative and religious revolution. In 1534, Henry had himself declared supreme head of the Church of England (also known as the Anglican church). In 1536, he dissolved English monasteries and seized their property, which was distributed or sold to his loyal supporters. In most cases, it went to the lesser nobility and landed gentry. By involving Parliament and the gentry, Henry VIII turned the Reformation into a national movement.

In the eleven years after Henry's death in 1547, three more Tudor monarchs ascended the throne of England. Henry was succeeded by his sickly son, Edward VI, a Protestant, who reigned from 1547 to 1553. On his death, Edward was succeeded by his Catholic half sister, Mary (1553–1558), the daughter of Henry VIII and Catherine of Aragon, the divorced first wife, who had been sent into exile. Allied with the remaining Catholic minority in England, Mary persecuted Protestants severely. On her death, she was succeeded by her Protestant half sister, Elizabeth I (1558–1603), Henry's daughter by Anne Boleyn, and England became a Protestant country again.

The Church of England as it developed in the sixteenth century differed only to a limited degree in its customs and ceremonies from the Roman Catholicism that it replaced. Sections of the English population, including aristocratic families, remained Catholic and even used their homes as centers for Catholic rituals performed by clandestine priests. Thus, the exact nature of England's Protestantism became a subject of growing dispute. Was the Anglican church to be truly Protestant? Was its hierarchy to be responsive to, and possibly even appointed by, the laity? Were its services and churches to be simple, lacking in "popish" rites and rituals and centered only on Scripture and sermon? Was Anglicanism to conform to Protestantism as practiced in

Switzerland, either in Calvinist Geneva or in Zwinglian Zurich? The clergy, especially the English bishops, would accept no form of Protestantism that might limit their ancient privileges, ceremonial functions, and power. Mary's persecutions, however, had forced leading English Protestants into exile in Geneva and into the arms of the Calvinist church.

Despite these religious issues, which were raised by the growing number of English Calvinists, or Puritans, as they were called, Elizabeth's reign was characterized by a heightened sense of national identity and by only the limited persecution of Catholics. At this same time, Calvinism flourished in Scotland. In Ireland, some elites and most peasants remained staunch Catholics.

Southern and Eastern Europe

In Spain and Italy, where the Inquisition was powerful, the Reformation struggled but failed to take hold. In Venice, as late as the 1560s, it was possible to find Protestants of all sorts—Lutherans, Calvinists, radical millenarians. We know about them from the interrogation reports filled out by their Catholic inquisitors. The Italian Inquisition had the backing of the papacy and the populace. Humanism, which might have given support to Protestantism, had never possessed a popular base in Italy, and the universities and printing presses, so vital to the Reformation north of the Alps, remained firmly under clerical control.

Luther's writings circulated in Spain for a time, but there, too, the authorities, both lay and clerical, quickly and thoroughly stamped out Protestantism. In the Middle Ages, the Spanish church and state had successfully joined in a religious and nationalist crusade to drive out the Muslims, and this effort forged strong links between the Spanish monarchy and the church. About a quarter of the Spanish population held a church office of one kind or another, and the church owned half of Spain's land. Allied with the state, the Inquisition enforced public and private morality. In southern Europe, the Reformation simply could not evade clerical authorities.

In Eastern Europe, the pattern was quite different and more complex than in Italy and Spain. In Hungary, warfare between Christians and Turks led to the collapse of the nobility, three-quarters of whom were killed in one battle in 1526. The weakness of Austrian Hapsburg authority in the country, coupled with the demise of the local elite, created a power vacuum into which the Reformation rushed.

Hungarian reformers such as Mathias Biró (1523–1545) and Stephen Kis (1505–1572) studied with Luther in Wittenberg and returned to Budapest to preach the Lutheran gospel. But as the number of their converts grew, Catholic and Turkish authorities became alarmed. They imprisoned Kis and Biró, confiscated their libraries, and fought the Reformation at every turn. Yet the Protestants did make converts among the Hungarian nobility, as well as among the townspeople. Not until the seventeenth century and the Hapsburg-led Counter-Reformation did Hungary return to the church. Even in the eighteenth century, during the Enlightenment, Hungarian Protestants were influential in the intellectual life of the country.

The pattern of the Reformation in Eastern Europe followed that in the rest of the continent. It began in the cities, succeeded where it was supported by the nobility or where traditional authority was weak, and lasted when it took root among the general population. In Poland, that pattern occurred; in neighboring Lithuania, only the nobility, already immensely powerful, took up Protestantism. When the church, led by the Jesuits, fought back, it easily triumphed in those areas where the Reformation lacked popular support. Very slowly, Poland was brought back into the church; in Lithuania, by the late sixteenth century, Protestantism had all but disappeared. The Catholic version of reformation had demonstrated its considerable appeal.

The Radical Reformation

The mainstream of the Protestant Reformation can be described as *magisterial* because the leading reformers generally supported established

***Map 14.1* THE PROTESTANT AND CATHOLIC ▶ REFORMATIONS** Europe fractured into competing camps, and religious warfare became a way of life.

(© 2016 Cengage Learning.)

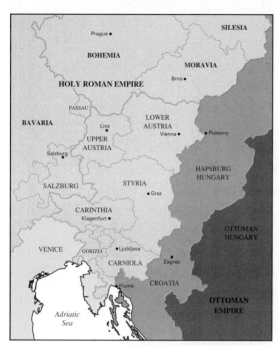

***Map 14.2* Inner Austria and Adjacent Territories** The Protestant Reformation sought converts throughout Hapsburg Europe and also confronted Islam in the Ottoman Empire. In both places, the Reformation was only minimally successful—Hungary is a major exception—and by the end of the century the Hapsburgs acquired a large portion of that country. (© 2016 Cengage Learning.)

political authorities, whether they were territorial princes or urban magistrates. For the reformers, human freedom was a spiritual, not a social, concept. Yet the Reformation did help trigger revolts among the artisan and peasant classes of Central and then Western Europe. Indications are that church doctrine had not made great inroads into the folk beliefs of large segments of the European masses. For example, some peasants held the very un-Christian beliefs that Nature was God or that witches had as much spiritual power as priests did. By the 1520s, several radical reformers arose, often from the lower classes of European society, and they channeled popular religion and folk beliefs into a new version of reformed Christianity

that spoke directly to the temporal and spiritual needs of the oppressed.

Some beliefs constituted what may be called the *Radical Reformation.* Appealing to the poor and oppressed, the radicals argued that ordinary men and women, even if illiterate, have certain knowledge of their salvation through an *inner light,* a direct communication from God to his chosen "saints"—men and women predestined for salvation. That knowledge makes the saint free. For the radicals, spiritual freedom paralleled their demands for social and economic freedom and equality. Protestantism, radically interpreted, proclaimed the righteousness and the priesthood of all believers. It said that all people can have faith if God wills it and that God would not abandon the wretched and humble of the earth.

The radicals said, as did the Bible, that the poor shall inherit the earth, which is ruled at present by the Antichrist, and that the end of the world had been proclaimed by Scripture. The saint's task was to purge this earth of evil to make it ready for Christ's Second Coming. For the radicals, the faith-alone doctrine meant certain salvation for the poor and lowly, and the Scriptures became an inspiration for social revolution. The doctrine could also inspire quietism, retreat from this world in anticipation of a better world to come. Luther, Calvin, and the other reformers vigorously condemned the social doctrines preached by the radical reformers, whether activist or quietist.

The largest group in the Radical Reformation prior to 1550 has the general name of Anabaptists. On receiving the inner light—the message of salvation—the Anabaptist felt born anew and yearned to be rebaptized. This notion had a revolutionary implication: the first infant baptism—thought to ensure allegiance to an established church (Protestant or Catholic)—did not count. The Anabaptist was a new Christian led by the light of conscience to seek the reform and renewal of all institutions in preparation for the Second Coming of Christ. Millenarian doctrines about the end of the world provided a sense of time and urgency.

In 1534, Anabaptists captured the city of Münster in Westphalia, near the western border of Germany. They seized the property of nonbelievers, burned all books except the Bible, and in a mood of jubilation and sexual excess openly practiced a repressive (as far as women were concerned) polygamy. All the while, the Anabaptists proclaimed that the Day of Judgment was close at hand. The radical leaders at Münster were men totally unprepared for power. They were defeated by the army led by a Lutheran prince, Philip of Hesse, and the local Catholic bishops brutally suppressed them. In early modern Europe, *Münster* became a byword for dangerous revolution. In Münster today, the cages still hang from the church steeple where the Anabaptist leaders were tortured and left to die as a warning to all would-be imitators.

By the late sixteenth century, many radical movements had either gone underground or grown quiet. But a century later, during the English Revolution of 1640 to 1660, the beliefs and political goals of the Radical Reformation resurfaced, threatening to push the political revolution in a direction that its gentry leaders desperately feared. Although the radicals failed in England, they left a tradition of democratic and antihierarchical thought. The radical assertion that saints led by their inner light are the equal of anyone, regardless of social status, helped shape modern democratic thought.

THE CATHOLIC RESPONSE

As late as the 1530s, the Catholic church hesitated, uncertain that the Protestant Reformation would gain strength or attract so many powerful noble families. Initially, the energy for reform came from ordinary clergy, as well as from laypeople such as Ignatius Loyola (1491–1556), rather than from the hierarchy or the established religious orders. Clergy and especially the laity gave renewed energy to Catholicism. Trained as a soldier, the Spanish reformer Loyola created a new religious order. He fused the intellectual rigor of humanism with a reformed Catholicism, forming a renewed spirituality with wide appeal. Founded in 1534, the Society of Jesus, commonly known as the **Jesuits**, became the backbone of the Catholic Reformation (also called the *Counter-Reformation*) in southern and Western Europe.

The Jesuits strove to bypass local corruption and appealed to the papacy to lead a truly international movement to revive Christian universalism. The Jesuits saw most clearly the bitter fragmentation produced by the Reformation. Moreover, they perceived one of the central flaws in Protestant theology. Predestination offered salvation to the literate and prosperous laity and, at least in theory, to the poor as well. However, it also included the possibility of despair for the individual and a life tormented by the fear of inescapable damnation. In response, the Jesuits offered hope: a religious revival based on ceremony, tradition, and the priestly power to offer forgiveness.

Jesuits became confessors to princes and urged them to strengthen the church in their territories. They developed a pragmatic theology that permitted "small sins" in the service of an ultimately just cause. Because of their erudition, the Jesuits, by the seventeenth century, became the greatest teachers in Europe and also the most controversial religious group within the church. Were they the true voice of a reformed church, or did they have nefarious intentions, as their critics claimed? Did they seek political power of their own, making themselves the Machiavellian servants of princes? It was a controversy that continued well into the eighteenth century. Urged on by Catholic reformers, the church finally convened a council at Trent. It tackled corrupt practices and renewed Catholic spirituality throughout the West. It took the Council of Trent over eighteen years to complete its work, and at no time did even a slim majority of European bishops attend its meetings.

As a result of this slow Catholic revival, new schools and universities appeared, as did newly designed churches. The revival even fostered a distinct style of art and architecture: cherubic angels grace the ornate decor of Counter-Reformation churches; heaven-bound saints beckon the penitent. This baroque style, so lavish and emotive, sought to move the heart, just as Protestant preachers sought to move the intellect. The baroque constituted a powerful response to the Protestant message that religion is ultimately a private, psychological matter;

instead, religion should move the emotions and inspire devotion to God and the church.

By the 1540s, the Counter-Reformation was well under way. The attempt to reform the church from within combined several elements—some benign, others bellicose. The leaders of this Catholic movement attacked many of the same abuses that Luther targeted, but they avoided a break with the doctrinal and spiritual authority of the pope and the clergy. They failed to undo clerical celibacy and to weaken the power of the Papacy.

At the same time, the Counter-Reformation also turned aggressive and hostile toward Protestants. The church tried to counter the popular appeal of Protestantism by offering dramatic, emotional, and even sentimental piety to the faithful.

For individuals who were unmoved by this appeal to sentiment or by the church's more traditional spirituality, and for those who allied themselves with Protestant heresy, the church resorted to sterner measures. The Inquisition expanded its activities, and wherever Catholic jurisdiction prevailed, unrepentant heretics—Protestants, especially Jews, and even Muslims—were subject to death or imprisonment. Catholics did not hold a monopoly on persecution: wherever Protestantism obtained official status—in England, Scotland, Ireland, and Geneva, for instance—Catholics or religious radicals also faced persecution. Calvin, for example, approved the execution in 1563 of the naturalist and skeptic Michael Servetus, who opposed the doctrine of the Trinity. (In 1600, the Catholic church in Italy burned Giordano Bruno for similar reasons.)

THE INQUISITION. This image of the Inquisition came from a French Protestant engraver who had been forced to flee France because of his religion. Clearly he saw the practices of the Inquisition as part of a continuous pattern of religious persecution by authorities with far too much power. (© Bettmann/Corbis.)

Aside from torture and imprisonment, one of the Catholic church's main tools was censorship. By the 1520s, the impulse to censor and burn dangerous books intensified as the church tried to prevent the rapid spread of Protestant ideas. In the rush to eliminate heretical literature, the church condemned the works of reforming Catholic humanists as well as those of Protestants. The *Index of Prohibited Books* became an institutional part of the church's life. Over the centuries, the works of many leading European thinkers were placed on the *Index*, which was abolished only in 1966.

The Counter-Reformation policies of education, vigorous preaching, church building, and self-reform but also torture, persecution, and censorship all succeeded in bringing thousands of people, Germans and Bohemians in particular, back into the church. Furthermore, the church implemented concrete changes in policy and doctrine. In 1545, the Council of Trent met to reform the church and strengthen it so as to better confront the Protestant challenge. Over the years, the council modified and unified church doctrine; abolished many corrupt practices, such as the selling of indulgences; and vested final authority in the papacy, thereby reasserting its power. The Council of Trent invigorated the church and gave it doctrinal clarity on such matters as the roles of faith and good works in attaining salvation. It made the church into the final arbiter of the Bible and demanded that texts be taken literally wherever possible. Galileo Galilei, the Italian physicist and astronomer, was to experience great difficulties in the next century because a literally read Bible implied that the motion of the earth contradicted Scripture.

After Trent, the church sought to offer a clear voice amid the babble of Protestant tongues. All compromise with Protestantism was rejected (not that Protestants were anxious for it). The Reformation had split Western Christendom irrevocably.

THE REFORMATION AND THE MODERN AGE

At first glance, the Reformation would seem to have renewed the medieval stress on otherworldliness and reversed the direction toward a secularized humanism that the Renaissance had taken. Yet a careful analysis shows decisively modern elements in Reformation thought, as well as antiauthoritarian tendencies in its political history. The Reformation shattered the religious unity of Europe, the cornerstone of medieval culture, and further weakened the principal authority in medieval society, the church. The political power of the church waned considerably. To this day, a deeply secular Western Europe nonetheless reveals aspects of both Catholic and Protestant traditions. Although doctrinal rigidity (and, in many places, church attendance) has largely disappeared, the split between the southern Catholic countries and the mostly Protestant north is still visible, if only in various customs and rituals. In Eastern European countries, where the churches, both Catholic and Protestant, emerged as powerful political forces, governments had to be cautious in dealing with them. During the 1980s, German Lutheran and Polish Catholic churches became focal points for anti-Soviet activities. Today, Northern Ireland stands as the sole reminder of the religious tensions that had once plagued the whole of Christian Europe. Even there, however, religious tensions appear to be waning. The challenge has now become to accept the Muslim minorities found in every European city, and to avoid a revival of anti-Semitism. The current financial problems of Southern Europe continue to remind us, however, that arriving late at industrial development can come back to haunt.

By strengthening the power of monarchs and magistrates at the expense of religious authority, the Reformation furthered the growth of the modern state. Protestant rulers completely repudiated the pope's claim to temporal power and extended their authority over Protestant churches in their lands. In predominantly Catholic lands, the church reacted to the onslaught of Protestantism by supporting the monarchies, but at the same time it preserved a significant degree of political independence. Protestantism did not create the modern secular state; it did, however, help free the state from subordination to religious authority. Such autonomy is an essential feature of modern and secular political life.

Indirectly, Protestantism contributed to the growth of political liberty: another ideal in the modern West. To be sure, neither Luther nor Calvin championed political freedom. Nevertheless, tendencies in the Reformation provided a basis for challenging monarchical authority. During the religious wars, both Protestant and Catholic theorists supported resistance to monarchs whose edicts, they believed, defied God's Law. Moreover, the Protestant view that all believers—laity, clergy, lords, and kings—were masters of their own spiritual destiny eroded hierarchical authority and became compatible with emerging constitutional government.

The Reformation also contributed to the creation of an individualistic ethic. Protestants sought an unmediated relationship with God and interpreted the Bible for themselves. Facing the prospect of salvation or damnation entirely on their own, without the church to provide sacramental aid, and believing that God had chosen them to be saved, Protestants developed inner confidence and assertiveness. This religious individualism was the counterpart of the intellectual individualism of the Renaissance humanists.

The Protestant ethic of the Reformation developed concurrently with a new economic system. Theorists have argued ever since about whether the new individualism of the Protestants brought on the growth of capitalism or whether the capitalistic values of the middle class gave rise to the Protestant ethic. In the middle of the nineteenth century, Karl Marx theorized that Protestantism gave expression to the new capitalistic values of the bourgeois: thrift, hard work, self-reliance, and rationality. Hence, Marx argued, the success of Protestantism can be explained by reference to the emergence of Western capitalism.

During 1904–1905, the German sociologist Max Weber argued that Marx had got it backward—that Protestantism enhanced the work ethic of capitalism, not vice versa.[9] Weber perceived in the Protestant ethic of the Reformation the spirit of a nascent capitalism. He saw the spirit of capitalism embodied in the entrepreneur, the parvenu, the self-made person. Such people strive for business success and bring to their enterprises self-discipline and self-restraint. They make profit not for pleasure but for the sake of more profit. They bring to their enterprises moral virtues of striving, frugality, and honesty. For Weber, Protestants made the best capitalists because predestination made them *worldly ascetics*: Christians forced to find salvation without clerical assistance and through activity in this world. The reformers had condemned the monastery as an unnatural life; their concomitant emphasis on human sinfulness established a psychology of striving that could be channeled only into worldly activity. The characteristics of the modern world—individual expression, economic development, and scientific learning—were to become most visibly present in Western European Protestant cities, such as London, Amsterdam, and Geneva. By 1700, both the Protestant entrepreneur and the Protestant intellectual began to endorse religious toleration, freedom in trade as well as learning, and scientific investigation.

The tension between the Roman church and Protestantism set the former in the direction of opposing modernity. By 1800, the papacy in Rome—but by no means all Catholics—viewed change with deep suspicion and came to believe that churches, whether Protestant or Catholic, had a right to interfere in the political process in order to stem the tide toward irreligion.

NOTES

1. The biblical quotations are from the Revised Standard Version of the Bible, copyright © 1946, 1952, 1971 the National Council of the Churches of Christ in the USA.

2. *The Freedom of a Christian Man* (1520), in *Martin Luther: Selections from His Writings*, ed. John Dillenberger (New York: Doubleday, 1961), 4.

3. Steven Ozment, ed., *Three Behaim Boys: Growing Up in Early Modern Germany* (New Haven, Conn.: Yale University Press, 1990), 79.

4. Martin Luther, *On the Babylonish Captivity of the Church*, quoted in Eugen Weber, ed., *The Western Tradition*, 2 vols., 4th ed. (Lexington, Mass.: D. C. Heath, 1990), 1:338. Interior of the Church of St. Bavo in Haarlem.

5. Martin Luther, *Luther's Works*, ed. Robert Schultz (Philadelphia: Fortress Press, 1967), 46:50–52.

6. François Wendel, *Calvin* (Paris: Presses Universitaires de France, 1950), 20.

7. Quoted in William J. Bouwsma, *John Calvin: A Sixteenth-Century Portrait* (New York: Oxford University Press, 1988), 104.

8. Ibid., 96.

9. See Max Weber, *Protestant Ethic and the Spirit of Capitalism*, trans. Talcott Parsons (New York: Charles Scribner's Sons, 1958).

Chapter 15

European Expansion: Economic and Social Transformations

The Blacksmith's Shop, *attributed to Antoine Le Nain or Louis Le Nain (both d. 1648). This is a portrait of a blacksmith at work with his family in his shop and, as such, offers a rare pictorial glimpse into the lives and work of the skilled men and women who played an important role in the early modern European economic expansion, brought on by the increase in population and rising consumer demand for goods. The painter invests the human subjects of this group portrait with a quiet dignity that also effectively dignifies the black-smith's skill and craft. Gravity and decorum have been achieved by framing the picture in a robustly neoclassical style that was usually reserved for depictions of the higher levels of society, namely, the church and the aristocracy.* (Alfredo Dagli Orti/© The Art Archive/Corbis.)

- **European Expansion**
- **The Price Revolution**
- **The Expansion of Agriculture**
- **The Expansion of Trade and Industry**
- **The Growth of Capitalism**
- **The Elite and the People**
- **Economic and Social Transformations**

Focus Questions

1. What were the new forces for expansion operating in early modern Europe?
2. How did the Spanish and Portuguese overseas expansion compare in terms of the motives, the areas of expansion, and the character of the two empires?
3. How did slavery in the future United States compare with slavery in South America and the Caribbean?
4. What was the price revolution, what caused it, and what were its effects on agriculture, trade, and industry?
5. How and why did the traditional relationship between the people and their rulers begin to change in the sixteenth century, and with what result?
6. What accounts for the witch craze and its subsequent decline? Why were most of its victims women?
7. What were the long-term effects of European expansion during this period?

During the period from 1450 to 1750, Western Europe entered an era of overseas exploration and economic expansion that transformed society. By 1450, Europe had recovered from the severe contraction of the fourteenth century, produced by plague and marginal agriculture, and was resuming the economic growth that had been the pattern in the twelfth and early thirteenth centuries. This new period of growth, however, was no mere extension of the earlier one but a radical departure from medieval economic forms.

Overseas exploration changed the patterns of economic growth and society. European adventurers discovered a new way to reach the rich trading centers of India by sailing around Africa. They also conquered, colonized, and exploited a new world across the Atlantic. These discoveries and conquests brought about an extraordinary increase in business activity and the supply of money, which stimulated the growth of capitalism. People's values changed in ways that were alien and hostile to the medieval outlook. By 1750, the model Christian in northwestern Europe was no longer the selfless saint but the enterprising businessman. The era of secluded manors and walled towns was drawing to a close. A world economy was emerging in which European economic life depended on the market in Eastern spices, African slaves, and American silver. During this age of exploration and commercial expansion, Europe generated a peculiar dynamism unmatched by any other civilization. A process was initiated that, by 1900, would give Europe mastery over most of the globe and wide-ranging influence over other civilizations.

The economic expansion from 1450 to 1650 or 1700 did not, however, raise the living standards of the masses. The vast majority of the people, 80 to 90 percent, lived on the land, and their main business was the production of primary goods: food, especially **grain production**, and wool. For most of these people, life hovered around the **subsistence level**, sometimes falling below subsistence during times of famine and disease. Whenever the standard of living improved, any surplus resources were soon taken up by the survival of more children and hence

Chronology 15.1 ❖ The Commercial Revolution

1394–1460	Henry the Navigator, prince of Portugal, encourages expansion into Africa for gold and for his anti-Muslim crusade
1430	The Portuguese expand into the Canaries and the Azores
1488	Bartholomeu Dias reaches the tip of Africa
1492	Christopher Columbus reaches the Caribbean island of Hispaniola on his first voyage; the Jews are expelled from Spain; Granada, the last Muslim kingdom in Spain, is conquered, completing the Reconquest
1497	Vasco da Gama sails around the Cape of Good Hope (Africa) to India
1509	The Portuguese defeat the Muslim fleet at Diu in the Indian Ocean
1513	Balboa discovers the Pacific Ocean at the Isthmus of Panama
1519–1521	Hernando Cortés conquers the Aztecs in Mexico
1520–1521	Magellan's soldiers circumnavigate the globe
1531–1533	Francisco Pizarro conquers the Incas in Peru
1545	Silver is discovered by the Spaniards at Potosí, Peru
1552	Silver from the New World flows into Europe via Spain, contributing to a price revolution
1590s	The Dutch develop shipping carriers for grain
1602–1609	Dutch East India Company is founded; Bank of Amsterdam is founded, expanding credit
1651	Navigation Act is passed in England to accomplish the goals of mercantilism
1694	Bank of England is founded

more mouths to feed. The beneficiaries of the commercial expansion, those whose income rose, were the rich, especially the *nouveaux riches* (newly rich).

In these respects, then, early modern Europe was comparable to an underdeveloped country today whose society consists of two main economic groups: a small, wealthy elite and a large and growing population that exists on the margin of subsistence and is racked by recurrent hunger and disease. Developments during overseas exploration and economic expansion should be viewed in the context of these social conditions.

EUROPEAN EXPANSION

During the Middle Ages, the frontiers of Europe had expanded, even if only temporarily in some instances. The Crusaders carved out feudal kingdoms in the Near East. Christian knights pushed back the Muslims on the Iberian Peninsula and drove them from Mediterranean islands. Germans expanded in the Baltic region at the expense of non-Christian Balts, Prussians, and Slavs. Genoa and Venice established commercial ports in the Adriatic Sea, the Black Sea, and the eastern Mediterranean. In the fifteenth and sixteenth centuries, Western Europeans embarked on a second and more lasting movement of expansion, which led them onto the uncharted waters of the Atlantic, Indian, and Pacific oceans. Combined forces propelled Europeans outward and enabled them to dominate Asians, Africans, and American Indians.

Forces Behind Expansion

The population of Western Europe increased rapidly between 1450 and 1600, at all levels of society. Among the gentry (hereditary landlords), population growth was translated into land hunger. As the numbers of those in the landed classes exceeded the supply of available land, the sons of the aristocracy looked beyond Europe for the lands and fortunes denied them at home. Nor was it unnatural for them to do so by plunder and conquest; their ancestors had done the same thing for centuries. Exploits undertaken and accomplished in the name of family, church, and king were deemed legitimate, perhaps the most legitimate, ways of earning merit and fame, as well as fortune. So the gentry provided the leadership—Hernando Cortés is an example—for the expeditions to the New World.

Merchants and shippers, as well as the sons of the aristocracy, had reason to look abroad. Trade between Europe, Africa, and the East had gone on for centuries, but always through intermediaries, who increased the costs and decreased the profits on the European end. Gold had been transported by Arab nomads across the Sahara from the riverbeds of West Africa. Spices had been shipped from India and the East Indies by way of Muslim and Venetian merchants. Western European merchants now sought to break those monopolies by going directly to the source: to West Africa for gold, slaves, and pepper, and to India for pepper, spices, and silks. Moreover, the incentive for such commercial enterprise grew because between 1450 and 1600 the wealth of prosperous Europeans increased dramatically. This wealth was translated into new purchasing power and the capacity to invest in foreign ventures that would meet the rising demand for luxury goods among the prosperous.

The centralizing monarchical state also played its part in expansion. Monarchs who, like Ferdinand and Isabella of Spain, had successfully established **royal hegemony** at home sought opportunities to extend their control overseas. The Spanish rulers looked over their shoulders at their neighbors, the Portuguese, and this competition spurred the efforts of both countries in their drive to the East. Later, the Dutch, the English, and the French engaged in a century-long rivalry. From overseas empires came gold, silver, and commerce that paid for ever more expensive royal government at home and for war against rival dynasties abroad.

Finally, religion helped the expansion. The crusading tradition was well established, especially on the Iberian Peninsula, where a five-hundred-year struggle known as the Reconquest had taken place to drive out the Muslims. Cortés, for example, saw himself as following in the footsteps of Paladin Roland, a medieval military hero who had fought to drive back Muslims and pagans. The Portuguese, too, were imbued with the crusading mission. Prince Henry the Navigator hoped that the Portuguese expansion into Africa would serve two purposes: the discovery of gold and the extension of Christianity at the expense of Islam. In this second aim, his imagination was fired by the legend of Prester John, which told of an ancient Christian kingdom of fabled wealth in the heart of Africa. If the Portuguese could reach that land, Prince Henry reckoned, the two kingdoms would join in a crusade against Islam.

Thus, expansion involved a mixture of economic, political, and religious forces and motives. The West had a crusading faith; divided into a handful of competing, warlike states, it expanded by virtue of forces built into its structure and culture. But besides the will to expand, the West also possessed the technology needed for successful expansion. This factor distinguished the West from China and the lands of Islam and helps explain why the West, rather than the Eastern civilizations, launched an age of conquest resulting in global mastery.

Not since the Early Middle Ages had there been such a rapid technological revolution as that which began in the fifteenth century. Europeans had already learned about gunpowder from the Chinese in the late thirteenth century, and by the fifteenth century, its military application had become widespread. The earliest guns were big cannons meant to knock holes in the walled defenses characteristic of the Middle Ages. In the sixteenth and seventeenth centuries, handheld firearms (particularly the musket) and smaller, more mobile field artillery were perfected. Dynastic and religious wars and overseas expansion kept demand for armaments high, and as a result, the armament industry was important to the growth of trade and manufacturing.

Another technological development during the period from 1400 to 1650 was the sailing ship. The vessels of the ancient world had been driven primarily by oars and human energy. Called galleys, they were suitable for the shorter distances, calmer waters, and less variable conditions of the Mediterranean and the Black and Red Seas—but not for the Atlantic and other great oceans, which Europeans began to ply in the early sixteenth century. Moreover, by the fifteenth century in Western Europe, labor was in short supply, making it difficult to recruit or condemn men to the galleys. For these reasons, the Portuguese, the Dutch, and the English abandoned the galley in favor of the sailing ship.

The sail and the gun were crucially important in allowing Europeans to overcome non-Europeans and penetrate and exploit their worlds. Western Europeans combined these devices in the form of the gunned ship. Not only was the sailing vessel more maneuverable and faster in the open seas than the galley, but the addition of guns gave it another tactical advantage over its rivals. The galleys of the Arabs in the Indian Ocean and the junks of the Chinese were not armed with guns below deck for firing at a distance to cripple or sink the enemy. In battle, they relied instead on the ancient tactic of coming up alongside the enemy vessel, shearing off its oars, and boarding to fight on deck.

The gunned ship gave the West naval superiority from the beginning. The Portuguese, for example, made short work of the Muslim fleet sent to drive them out of the Indian Ocean in 1509. That victory at Diu, off the western coast of India, indicated that the West not only had found an all-water route to the East but also was there to stay. Material and religious motives led Europeans to explore and conquer; superior technology ensured the success of their enterprises.

The Portuguese Empire

Several reasons account for Portugal's overseas success. Portugal's long Atlantic coastline ensured that its people would look to the sea—initially for fishing and trade and then for exploration. A sunny climate also spurred seafaring and commercial expansion. Portugal was northern Europe's closest supplier of subtropical products: olive oil, cork, wine, and fruit. The feudal nobility, typically antagonistic to trade and industry, was not as powerful in Portugal as elsewhere in Europe. Although feudal warriors had carved Portugal out of Moorish Iberia in the twelfth century, their descendants were blocked from further interior expansion by the presence of the strong Christian kingdom of Castile in the east. The only other outlet for expansion was the sea.

Royal policy also favored expansion. The central government promoted trading interests, especially after 1385, when the merchants of Lisbon and the lesser ports helped establish a new dynasty in opposition to the feudal aristocracy. In the first half of the fifteenth century, a younger son of the king, named Prince Henry the Navigator (1394–1460) by English writers, sponsored voyages of exploration and the nautical studies needed to undertake them. In these endeavors, he spent his own fortune and the wealth of the church's crusading order that he headed. Prince Henry sought to revive the anti-Muslim crusade, to which Portugal owed its existence as a Christian state. This connection between the medieval Crusades and the early modern expansion of Europe ran through Portuguese and Spanish history.

As early as the fifteenth century, the Portuguese expanded into islands in the Atlantic Ocean. In 1420, they began to settle Madeira and raise food there, and in the 1430s they pushed into the Canaries and the Azores in search of new farmland and slaves for their colonies. In the middle decades of the century, they moved down the West African coast to the mouth of the Congo

THE PORTUGUESE IN INDIA. A charming engraving by a Portuguese traveler in India, this painting mixes what to Western eyes was strange and foreign with the more familiar. The clothes and the elaborate parasols held high by turbaned servants may have seemed exotic, but the horse and the hunting dogs had their counterparts in Western European landed society. (akg-images/Newscom.)

River and beyond, establishing trading posts as they went.

By the last quarter of the century, they had developed a viable imperial economy among the ports of West Africa, their Atlantic islands, and Western Europe—an economy based on sugar, black slaves, and gold. Africans panned the gold in the riverbeds of central and western Africa, and the Portuguese purchased it at its source. They paid in cloth and slaves at a profit of at least 500 percent. Then the Portuguese transported the gold to Europe, where they sold it for even more profit. Slaves figured not only in the purchase of gold but also in the production of sugar. On their Atlantic islands, the Portuguese grew sugarcane and little else by the end of the century, as a cash crop for European consumption, and slaves were imported from West Africa to do the work. There was also

a lively trade in slaves to Portugal itself and elsewhere in southern Europe.

The Portuguese did not stop in western Africa. By 1488, Bartholomeu Dias had reached the southern tip of the African continent; a decade later, Vasco da Gama sailed around the Cape of Good Hope and across the Indian Ocean to India. By discovering an all-water route to the East, Portugal broke the **commercial monopoly** on Eastern goods that Genoa and Venice had enjoyed.

In search of spices, the Portuguese went directly to the source, to India and the East Indies. As they had done along the African coast, they established fortified trading posts—most notably at Goa, on the western coast of India (Malabar) and at Malacca (now Singapore), on the Malay Peninsula.

PORTRAIT OF A MAN, SAID TO BE CHRISTOPHER COLUMBUS (1519), BY SEBASTIANO DEL PIOMBO. Christopher Columbus was a Genoese navigator and explorer whose transatlantic voyages opened the way for European conquest and colonization of the Americas. (Metropolitan Museum of Art, New York, USA/Peter Newark Pictures/The Bridgeman Art Library.)

Demand for spices was insatiable. Pepper and other spices are relatively unimportant items in the modern diet, but in the era before refrigeration, fresh meat was available only at slaughtering time, customarily twice a year. The rest of the year the only meat available, for those who could afford it at all, was dried, stringy, and tough; spices made meat and other foods palatable.

The infusion of Italian, particularly Genoese, investment and talent contributed to Portuguese expansion. As Genoese trade with the Near East, especially the Black Sea, shrank due to the expansion of the Ottoman Empire, Genoese merchants shifted more and more of their capital and mercantile activities from the eastern to the western Mediterranean and the Atlantic—that is, to Spain and Portugal and their possessions overseas. This shift is evident in the life of Christopher Columbus (1451–1506), a Genoese sailor, who worked in Portugal before finally winning acceptance at the court of Castile in Spain for his scheme to find a westward route to the spices of the East.

The Spanish Empire

Spain stumbled onto its overseas empire, which nonetheless proved to be the biggest and richest of any until the eighteenth century. Columbus won the support of Isabella, queen of Castile. But on his first voyage (1492), he landed on a large Caribbean island, which he named Española (Little Spain), or Hispaniola. To the end of his life, even after subsequent voyages, Columbus believed that the West Indies were part of the East. Two forthcoming events would reveal that Columbus had discovered not a new route to the East but new continents: Vasco Nuñez de Balboa's discovery of the Pacific Ocean at the Isthmus of Panama in 1513 and Ferdinand Magellan's circumnavigation of the globe (1520–1521) through the strait at the tip of South America that now bears his name.

The Spanish and the Portuguese were not the first outsiders to explore and settle in the New World. Archaeological evidence indicates that there may have been several voyages undertaken from China, Ireland, Wales, and West Africa in the previous millennium. The Viking expeditions led by Leif Erikson and his brothers in the first decade of the eleventh century are well documented. The Vikings, originally from Scandinavia, sailed in small boats from Greenland and settled near

Map 15.1 **PORTUGUESE AND SPANISH EMPIRE** ▶ **BUILDING, 1415–1635** Not only did Spain and Portugal carve out empires in different parts of the world, but, as the map shows, they also built two different kinds of empires. Portugal established small colonies along the seacoast. Spain went in for conquering and governing large territories and large populations in the New World. (© 2016 Cengage Learning.)

ASIA

JAPAN
1542

CHINA

Macao 1517
Canton 1513

PHILIPPINES

NEW GUINEA

MOLUCCAS 1511

Malacca 1509

BORNEO

SUMATRA

JAVA

1521

AUSTRALIA

500 Mi.
250 500 Km.
250 500
0

1522

INDIA

CEYLON 1505

Calicut 1498

1498

Goa 1510

Ormuz 1507

PERSIA

Aden 1513

ARABIA
Muscat

MADAGASCAR
1500

Constantinople

1498

Malindi 1498

Mozambique

EUROPE

Amsterdam
Antwerp
Genoa Venice

AFRICA

Cape of Good Hope

ANTARCTICA

SPAIN
Seville

Lisbon

Timbuktu

PORTUGAL

CAPE VERDE 1445
Ceuta 1415

GUINEA

GOLD COAST

1522

1497

AZORES

MADEIRA

CANARY IS. 1492

CAPE VERDE IS. 1456

1519

NEWFOUNDLAND 1497

Rio de Janeiro 1516

St. Augustine 1565

SAN SALVADOR 1492

HISPANIOLA 1492

TRINIDAD 1498

SPANISH MAIN

BRAZIL

Straits of Magellan

NORTH AMERICA

CUBA 1492

HONDURAS

Cartagena

Quito 1534

SOUTH AMERICA

Potosí

Buenos Aires 1535

1535

Panama

PERU

Lima 1535

Santiago

Cape Horn

NEW SPAIN

Mexico City 1519

Vera Cruz 1519

1520

Columbus
Da Gama
Magellan and crew
Spanish holdings
Portuguese holdings

Profile

Bartolomé de las Casas

Bartolomé de las Casas (1474–1566), a Dominican friar excited in his youth by Columbus's discoveries, set out for the New World in 1502 and spent the rest of his life as a missionary to the American Indians. Not only did he preach to them and convert them to Christianity, but, appalled by the cruelty of the Spanish conquest, he also joined others in his order in defending the Indians against their oppressors. On the island of Hispaniola, he wrote, the Spaniards "began to carry out massacres and strange cruelties against [the Indians]. They . . . spared neither the children nor the aged, nor pregnant women nor women in childbed, not only stabbing them . . . but cutting them to pieces. . . . They laid bets as to who, with one stroke of the sword, could split a man in two or cut off his head."*

Some argued that the brutal treatment of the Indians, the confiscation of their lands, and even their enslavement were justified because the Indians fit Aristotle's definition of "natural slaves": people whose behavior and customs, such as human sacrifice, betrayed them as being less than rational and therefore subhuman. In book after book, de las Casas attacked such views. He pointed out that the Indians often lived up to a higher standard of civilized life than supposedly civilized European Christians—for example, in sexual conduct, choice of rulers, military discipline, child-rearing, and (something especially important to a monk) giving relief to the poor. In addition, de las Casas was impressed by the Incas' feats of engineering, especially the highways they had built through the Andes, which excelled anything he had seen that the Romans had done.

This radical champion of Indian rights also dreamed of building a New Jerusalem in the New World. He called for the creation of a new kind of empire, in which Philip II would still be emperor but most of the Spanish colonists would be forced to leave. The missionaries would stay on, protected by a small Spanish army, to guide the Indians toward realizing this millennial vision. For his contemporaries, the most extreme aspect of the view de las Casas propounded was that the Indians should regain possession of all the land the Spanish had taken, including rights to all the gold and silver that lay beneath.

---

*Bartolomé de Las Casas, *The Devastation of the Indies*, trans. Herma Briffault (Baltimore, Md.: The Johns Hopkins University Press, 1992), 33.

---

the mouth of the St. Lawrence River in what is now southeastern Canada. But these earlier expeditions all ended in failure due to war with native Indians, hunger, and disease. The factors that gave the Spanish and the Portuguese permanent success in the New World stand out in sharp relief against these earlier failures—guns, sails, horses, crusading and missionary zeal, and royal power capable of mobilizing enough men and resources for the long haul.

The Spanish found no spices in the New World, but they were more than compensated by the abundant land and the large quantities of precious metals. Stories of the existence of larger quantities of gold and silver to the west lured the Spaniards from their initial settlements in the Caribbean to Mexico. In 1519, Hernando Cortés landed on the Mexican coast with a small army. During two years of campaigning, he managed to defeat the native rulers, the Aztecs, and to conquer Mexico for the Spanish crown. A decade later, Francisco Pizarro achieved a similar victory over the mountain empire of the Incas in Peru. Both Cortés and Pizarro exploited the hostility that the subject tribes of Mexico and Peru felt toward their Aztec and Inca overlords, a strategy that accounts to some extent for the Spaniards' success. But the most important reason was probably the spread of infectious diseases among the native population, including the armies—diseases carried by the Europeans to which the Indians apparently had little or no resistance and that so weakened them that the Spanish forces could win despite being vastly outnumbered. This is one of the signal examples in world history where a non-human biological agency brought about a decisive turning point in the flow of events.

For good reasons, the Mexican and Peruvian conquests became the centers of the Spanish overseas empire. First, there were the gold hoards accumulated over the centuries by the rulers of these lands for religious and ceremonial purposes. Once these supplies were exhausted, the Spanish discovered silver at Potosí in Upper Peru in 1545 and at Zacatecas in Mexico a few years later. From the middle of the century, the annual treasure fleets sailing to Spain became the financial bedrock of Philip II's war against the Muslim Turks and the Protestant Dutch and English.

Not only gold and silver lured the Spanish to the New World. The crusading tradition also acted as a spur. Cortés, Pizarro, and many of their followers were *hidalgos*—lesser gentry whose status depended on the possession of landed estates and whose training and experience taught that holy war was a legitimate avenue to wealth and power. Their fathers had conquered Granada, the last Muslim kingdom in Spain, in 1492; they had expelled the Jews the same year and had carried the Christian crusade across to North Africa. The conquest and conversion of the peoples of the New World was an extension of the crusading spirit that marked the five previous centuries of Spanish history. The rewards were the propagation of the true faith, service to the crown, land grants, and control over the inhabitants, who would work the fields.

The conquerors initially obtained two kinds of grants from the crown: *encomiendas* and *estancias*. The latter were land grants, either of land formerly belonging to the native priestly and noble castes or of land in remoter and less fertile regions. Encomiendas were royal grants of authority over the natives. Those who received

such authority, the *encomenderos*, promised to give protection and instruction in the Christian religion to their charges. In return, they gained the power to extract labor and tribute from the peasant masses, who were worked beyond their capacity.

The royal grants of encomiendas during the first generation of Spanish settlement were partially responsible for the decimation of the native peoples in the New World within a century of European occupation. Between 1500 and 1600, the number of natives shrank from about twenty million to perhaps no more than two million. The major cause of this catastrophe, however, was not forced labor but the diseases introduced from Europe—dysentery, malaria, hookworm, and smallpox—against which the natives had little or no natural resistance. But syphilis was probably transmitted the other way, that is, from the New World to the Old. Beginning in the 1540s, the position of the natives gradually improved as the crown withdrew grants that gave authority over the natives and took increasing responsibility for controlling the Indians.

Power and wealth became concentrated in fewer and fewer hands. As the Spanish landholders lost authority over the native population to royal officials and their associates, the latter gained substantially in power and privilege. As recurrent depressions ruined smaller landowners, they were forced to sell out to their bigger neighbors. On their conversion to Christianity, the Indians were persuaded to give more and more land to the church. Thus, Spanish America became permanently divided between the privileged elite and the impoverished masses.

Black Slavery and the Slave Trade

One group suffered even more than the Indians: the black slaves originally brought over from West Africa. During the long period of their dominance in North Africa and the Middle East (from the seventh to the nineteenth century), the Muslim states relied on slave labor and slave soldiers from black Africa south of the Sahara. Blacks were captured and transported across the Sahara to be sold in the slave markets of North

Africa. It was common for such slaves, especially soldiers, to be eventually freed by their Muslim masters, a practice sanctioned by the Koran. Thus it was necessary to replenish the stock of slaves from south of the Sahara in every generation. At its height in the eighteenth century, this trans-Saharan trade may have risen to some ten thousand slaves a year.

But this annual traffic was eventually dwarfed by the slave trade between West Africa and the European colonies in the New World, which began in earnest in the early sixteenth century. The Portuguese dominated the Atlantic slave trade for a century and a half after 1450; during that time, it never rose beyond some five thousand black slaves a year. The Dutch edged out the Portuguese in the seventeenth century and competed with the French and the British for dominance. In the eighteenth century, the British gained control of at least 50 percent of the trade. As Roland Oliver notes in *The African Experience*, "By the end of the seventeenth century, stimulated by the growth of plantation agriculture in Brazil and the West Indies, Atlantic shipments had increased to about thirty thousand a year, and by the end of the eighteenth century they were nearly eighty thousand."[1]

Captured in raids by black African slavers, the victims were herded into specially built prisons on the West African coast. Those accepted for sale were "marked on the breast with a red-hot iron, imprinting the mark of the French, English or Dutch companies so that each nation may distinguish their own property."[2] Across the centuries, some 11 or 12 million blacks in all were exported to the New World. Of these, some 600,000 ended up in the thirteen colonies of British North America, forming the basis of the slave population of the new United States at the end of the American Revolution.

The conditions of the voyage from Africa, the so-called middle passage, were brutal. Crammed into the holds of ships, some 13 to 30 percent of blacks died on board. On arrival in the New World, slaves were greased with palm oil to improve their appearance and paraded naked into the auction hall for the benefit of prospective buyers, who paid top prices for "the strongest, youthfullest, and most beautiful."[3] The standard workload for slaves everywhere was ten or eleven hours a day, six days a week. But some distinction must be made between slavery in the American South and elsewhere in the New World. In Brazil and the West Indies, slaves were worked to exhaustion and death and then replaced. Slaves formed a large majority there and were concentrated on very large plantations. Revolts were frequent but were always crushed and savagely punished. In the American South, by contrast, slaves were a minority dispersed over relatively small holdings; large plantations were few. As a result, revolts and deadly epidemics were rare. After 1808, when the United States abolished the external slave trade, slaveholders could not ruthlessly exploit their slaves if they were to meet the growing need for workers caused by the increasing industrial demand for raw cotton. By 1830, the slave population of the southern states rose through natural increase to more than two million, which represented more than one-third of all slaves in the New World.

Slave traders grew rich; some of them invested their profits in banking, insurance, and plantations. Many slave traders were devout Christians who saw no conflict between trafficking in humans and their faith. In the eighteenth century, several Quaker and Methodist ministers, driven by a Christian conscience, worked tirelessly to get Britain to outlaw the slave trade.

Why had the Atlantic slave trade grown to such a large volume by the eighteenth century? On the American side, economics provide the answer. In the New World, fields and mines had to be worked, but since the native population had been decimated, an enormous labor shortage existed. Black slaves were imported to satisfy the demand. Not only were they plentiful and cheap to maintain, but they were also skilled in farming and mining and could withstand tropical heat, insects, and disease, including the infections brought over from Europe to which the Indians had succumbed.

On the African side, how did suppliers continue to meet this large and growing New World demand? First, the demand was greater for males than for females, and males constituted two-thirds of those transported. Since all African

Seventeenth-Century Slave Traders: Buying and Transporting Africans

Dealing in slaves was a profitable business that attracted numerous entrepreneurs. The following account was written by a slave trader in the seventeenth century.

As the slaves came down to Fida from the inland country, they are put into a booth, or prison, built for that purpose, near the beach, all of them together; and when the Europeans are to receive them, they are brought out into a large plain, where the surgeons examine every part of every one of them, to the smallest member, men and women being all stark naked. Such as are allowed good and sound, are set on the one side, and the others by themselves; which slaves so rejected are called Mackrons, being above thirty five years of age, or defective in their limbs, eyes or teeth; or grown grey, or that have venereal disease, or any other imperfection. These being so set aside, each of the others, which have passed as good, is marked on the breast, with a red-hot iron, imprinting the mark of the French, English, or Dutch companies, that so each nation may distinguish their own, and to prevent their being chang'd by the natives for worse, as they are apt enough to do. In this particular, care is taken that the women, as tenderest, be not burnt too hard.

The branded slaves, after this, are returned to their former booth, where the factor [agent] is to subsist them at his own charge, which amounts to about two-pence a day for each of them, with bread and water, which is all their allowance. There they continue sometimes ten or fifteen days, till the sea is still enough to send them aboard; . . . and when it is so, the slaves are carried off by parcels, in bar-canoes, and put aboard the ships in the road. Before they enter the canoes, or come out of the booth, their former Black masters strip them of every rag they have, without distinction of men or women. . . .

The Blacks of Fida are so expeditious at this trade of slaves that they can deliver a thousand every month. . . . If there happens to be no stock of slaves at Fida, the factor must trust the Blacks with his goods, to the value of a hundred and fifty, or two hundred slaves; which goods they carry up into the inland, to buy slaves, at all the markets, for above two hundred leagues up the country, where they are kept like cattle [are kept] in Europe; the slaves sold there being generally prisoners of war, taken from their enemies, like other booty, and perhaps some few sold by their own countrymen, in extreme want, or upon a famine; so also some as a punishment of heinous crimes: tho' many Europeans believe their parents sell their own children, men their wives and relations, which, if it ever happens, is so seldom, that it cannot justly be charged upon a whole nation, as a custom and common practice.

Questions for Analysis

1. How, why, and by whom are the slaves branded?
2. Who are those called "Black masters," and what role do they play in the slave trade?
3. Where do the slaves come from, and how do they initially come to be enslaved?

Elizabeth Donnan, ed., *Documents Illustrative of the Slave Trade* (Washington, D. C.: Carnegie Institution of Washington, 1935), 1:293–294.

peoples were polygynous (men might take more than one wife), the women and girls left behind in Africa continued to reproduce, so the population did not shrink, and there was always a supply of blacks to be captured and enslaved. Second, by 1700, a new factor was introduced, one that proved decisive: guns, imported from Europe, were now commonly traded for slaves. With the guns, the West African rulers built armies for capturing other peoples to sell to the Europeans, while protecting themselves from being enslaved by rival forces. The desire for profit led to the need for more captives to sell for still more firearms to take still more slaves. All the ingredients were now in place for a deadly arms race, and the result was "a spiral of mounting violence," which could not be broken.[4] But from the point of view of the Atlantic trade, this grisly scenario guaranteed a steady supply of human cargo to satisfy a steeply rising New World demand.

THE PRICE REVOLUTION

Linked to overseas expansion was another phenomenon: unprecedented inflation during the sixteenth century, known as the *price revolution*. Evidence is insufficient on the general rise in prices. Cereal prices, however, multiplied by eight times or more in certain regions during the sixteenth century and continued to rise, though more slowly, during the first half of the next century. After 1650, prices leveled off or fell in most places. This pattern continued throughout the eighteenth century in England and off and on in France up to the Revolution. Economic historians have generally assumed that the prices of goods other than cereals increased by half as much as grain prices. Because people at that time did not understand why prices rose so rapidly, inflation was not subject to control.

Like colonization, the price revolution played an enormous role in the commercial revolution and may have resulted partially from the silver mining conducted in New Spain. The main cause of the price revolution, however, was population growth during the late fifteenth and sixteenth centuries.

The population of Europe almost doubled between 1460 and 1620; then it leveled off and decreased in some places. The patterns of population growth and of cereal prices thus correspond in the sixteenth and seventeenth centuries. Before the middle of the seventeenth century, the number of mouths to feed outran the capacity of agriculture to supply basic foodstuffs, causing the vast majority of people to live close to subsistence. Until food production could catch up with the increasing population, prices, especially those of the staple food, bread, would continue to rise.

Why population grew so rapidly in the fifteenth and sixteenth centuries is not known, but we do know the reasons for the population decline in the seventeenth century. By then, the population had so outgrown the food supply that scarcity began to take its toll. Malnourishment, starvation, and disease pushed the death rate higher than the birth rate. With time, of course, prices decreased as population and hence demand declined in the 1600s.

The other principal cause of the price revolution was probably the flow of silver into Europe from the New World by way of Spain beginning in 1552. But as a cause, the influx of silver lies on shakier ground than the inflationary effects of an expanding population. Increases in production and consumption following the growth in population would, to some degree, have necessitated an increase in the money supply to accommodate the greater number of commercial transactions. At some point, it is assumed, the influx of silver exceeded the necessary expansion of the money supply and itself began contributing to the inflation. The most that can be said now is that the price revolution was caused by *too many people with too much money chasing too few goods*. The effects of the price revolution were momentous.

THE EXPANSION OF AGRICULTURE

The price revolution had its greatest effect on the land. Rising roughly twice as much as the prices of other goods, food prices spurred ambitious

A NEW WORLD SUGAR REFINERY, BRAZIL. Sugar was the main and most profitable crop of plantation agriculture until the late eighteenth century, when cotton took the lead, at least in some places. On the plantation, the cane was not only grown but also processed into a variety of products—sugar, molasses, and rum—that were exported to Europe to meet a rising demand. Black slaves did the work under efficient but brutal conditions and often at great profit to the plantation owners. (The Art Archive/Biblioteca Nacional Madrid/Gianni Dagli Orti.)

farmers to take advantage of the situation and produce for the expanding market. The opportunity for profit drove some farmers to work harder and manage their land better, and the impact of the price revolution came from that incentive. The most important changes occurred in England and the Netherlands.

The Old Pattern of Farming

All over Europe, landlords held their properties in the form of manors. A particular type of rural society and economy evolved on these manors in the Late Middle Ages. By the fifteenth century, much manor land was held by peasant-tenants according to the terms of a tenure known in England as *copyhold*. The tenants had certain hereditary rights to the land in return for the performance of certain services and the payment of certain fees to the landlord. Principal among these rights was the use of the commons—a tract of land consisting of pasture, woods, and a pond—by all tenants of a manor. For the copyholder, access to the commons often made the difference between subsistence and real want because the land tilled on the manor might not produce enough to feed a family.

Arable land was worked according to ancient custom. The land was divided into strips, and each peasant of the manor was assigned a certain number of strips. This whole pattern of peasant tillage and rights in the commons was known as the *open-field system*. After changing little for centuries, it was met head-on by incentives generated by the price revolution.

Enclosure

The open-field system, geared to providing subsistence for local villages, prevented large-scale farming for distant markets. The commons could not be diverted to the production of crops for sale, and the division of arable land into strips made it difficult to engage in profitable commercial agriculture. In the sixteenth century, English landlords aggressively pursued the possibilities for profit resulting from the inflation of farm prices and launched a two-pronged attack against the open-field system in an effort to transform their holdings into market-oriented, commercial ventures. First, they resorted to *enclosure*, fencing off the commons and thereby depriving their tenant peasantry of the use of the common land. Restriction of rights to the commons deprived tenants of critically needed produce. Then landlords changed the conditions of tenure from copyhold to leasehold. Copyhold was heritable and fixed; leasehold was not. When a lease came up for renewal, the landlord could raise the rent beyond the tenant's capacity to pay. Both acts of the landlord forced peasants off the manor or into the landlord's employ as

farm laborers. Rural poverty and violence increased because of the mass evictions of tenant farmers.

With tenants gone, fields could be incorporated into larger, more productive units. Subsistence farming gave way to commercial agriculture: the growing of a surplus for the marketplace. Landlords would either hire laborers to work recently enclosed fields or rent these fields to prosperous farmers in the neighborhood. Either way, landlords stood to gain. They could hire labor at bargain prices because of the swelling population and the large supply of peasants forced off the land by enclosure. If landlords chose to rent out their fields, they also profited. Prosperous farmers, who themselves grew for the market, could afford to pay higher rents than the previous tenants, the subsistence farmers, and they were willing to pay more because farm prices tended to rise even faster than rents.

The existence of prosperous farmers, known collectively as the *yeomanry*, was crucial to the commercialization of farming in England. Yeomen were men who might not own much land but rented enough to produce a marketable surplus, sometimes a substantial one. They emerged as a discernible rural group in the High Middle Ages and were a product of the unique English inheritance custom of *primogeniture*, observed by peasantry and gentry alike.

Because of the rights of primogeniture, the eldest son inherited his parents' entire estate, and younger sons had to fend for themselves. Thus, land remained undivided, and heirs often had enough land to produce a surplus for sale. Many a gentleman landowner enclosed his fields, not to work them himself, but to rent them to neighboring yeomen at rates allowing him to keep abreast of spiraling prices. Yeomen were better suited to work the land than the landlord, depending on it as they did for their livelihood.

One other process growing out of the price revolution promoted enclosure and the commercialization of farming. Rising prices forced less businesslike landlords, who did not take advantage of the profits to be made from farming, to sell property in order to meet current expenses.

***The Harvesters*, 1565, by Pieter Brueghel the Elder (d. 1569).** This painting shows crops being harvested by peasants in the Netherlands. Agriculture was the basis of all economic life in early modern Europe, and the Netherlands was one of the places where advanced farming techniques were applied to maximizing food production to feed a growing population. (Image copyright © The Metropolitan Museum of Art/Art Resource, N.Y.)

The conditions of the price revolution thus tended to put an increasing amount of land into more productive hands.

Convertible Husbandry

In the Netherlands, the effect of the price revolution on agriculture was as dramatic and important as in England. By the seventeenth century, the Dutch population had soared, and the majority of people had moved to the cities. As a result, a situation affecting all Europe—the problem of land use—became vitally important, especially as there was so little land to start with. The Dutch continued their efforts to reclaim land from the sea, as they had begun to do in the Middle Ages. More significant, however, was their development, in the fifteenth and sixteenth centuries, of a new kind of farming known as *convertible husbandry*. This farming system employed a series of innovations that replaced the old three-field system of crop rotation, which had left one-third of the land unplanted at any given time. The new techniques allowed farmers to cultivate all their land every year and diversified agriculture.

Convertible husbandry alternated the planting of soil-depleting cereals with the planting of soil-restoring legumes and grazing. For a couple of years, a field would be planted in cereals; in the third year, peas or beans would be sown to return essential nitrogen to the soil; then for the next four or five years, the field would become pasture for grazing animals, whose manure would further restore the soil for replanting cereals and restarting the cycle. Land thus returned to grain produced much more than land used in the three-field system. This method of increasing **productivity**, when exported from the Netherlands and applied in England and France between 1650 and 1750, played an essential role in the complicated process by which these countries eventually became industrialized, for industrialization requires agriculture productive enough to feed large, nonfarming urban populations.

THE EXPANSION OF TRADE AND INDUSTRY

The conditions of the price revolution also caused trade and industry to expand. Population growth, which exceeded the capacity of local food supplies, stimulated commerce in basic foodstuffs—for example, the Baltic trade with Western Europe. Equally important as a stimulus to trade and industry was the growing income of landlords, merchants, and, in some instances, peasants. This income created a rising demand for consumer goods, which helps explain several activities already mentioned. For example, the Portuguese spice trade with the East and the sugar industry in the Portuguese islands developed because prosperous people wanted such products. Higher income also created a demand for farm products other than cereals—meat, cheese, fruit, wine, and vegetables—and for fine cloth. The resulting land use reduced the area

available for grain production and contributed to the rise in bread prices, which meant even larger profits.

Another factor propelling commercial and industrial expansion was the growth of the state. With increasing amounts of tax revenue to spend, the expanding monarchies of the sixteenth and seventeenth centuries bought more and more supplies—ships, weapons, uniforms, paper—and so spurred economic development.

The Domestic System

Along with commercial and industrial expansion came a change in the nature of the productive enterprise. Just as the price revolution produced, in the enclosure movement, a reorganization of agriculture and agrarian society, it similarly affected trade and manufacturing. The reorganization there took place especially in the faster-growing industries—woolen and linen textiles—where an increasingly large mass market outpaced supply and thus made prices rise. This basic condition of the price revolution operated, just as it did in food production, to produce expansion. In the textile industries, increasing demand promoted specialization. For example, eastern and southwestern England made woolens, and northwestern France and the Netherlands produced linen.

Markets tended to shift from local to regional or even to international, a condition that gave rise to the merchant-capitalist. Merchant-capitalists' operations, unlike those of local producers, extended across local and national boundaries. Such mobility allowed these capitalists to buy or produce goods where costs were lowest and to sell where prices and volume were highest. Because of the size and range of a business, an individual capitalist could control the traditional local producers, who increasingly depended on the capitalist for the widespread marketing of their expanded output.

This procedure, which was well developed by the seventeenth century, gave rise to what is known as the domestic system of cottage industry. The manufacture of woolen textiles is a good example of how the system worked.

A merchant-capitalist would buy raw wool from English landlords, who had enclosed the common grazing land on their manors to take advantage of the rising price of wool. The merchant's agents collected the wool and took it (put it out) to nearby villages for spinning, dyeing, and weaving. The work was done in the cottages of peasants, many of whom had been evicted from the surrounding manors as a result of enclosure and therefore had to take whatever work they could get at whatever wages they were offered. When the wool was processed into cloth, it was picked up and shipped to market.

The domestic system represents an important step in the evolution of capitalism. It was not industrial capitalism, because there were no factories and the work was done by hand rather than by power machinery; nevertheless, the domestic system significantly broke with the medieval guild system. The new merchant-capitalists saw to it that the work was performed in the countryside, rather than in the cities and towns, to avoid guild restrictions on output, quality, pay, and working conditions. The medieval distinction between a master and an apprentice who would someday replace the master in the guild framework gave way to the distinction between the merchant-owner (the person who provided the capital) and the worker (the person who provided the labor in return for wages and would probably never be an owner).

Enclosure also served to capitalize industry. Mass evictions lowered the wages of cottage workers because labor was so plentiful. This condition provided an additional incentive for merchant-capitalists to invest in cottage industry. The changes in farming, however, were much more important to the economic development of Europe than the changes in industry because agriculture represented a much larger share of total wealth.

Innovations in Business

A cluster of other innovations in business life, some of them having roots in the Middle Ages, accompanied the emergence of the merchant-capitalist and the domestic system. Banking operations grew more sophisticated. It became possible for depositors to pay their debts by issuing written orders to their banks to make transfers to their creditors' accounts—the origins of the modern check. Accounting methods also improved. The widespread use of double-entry bookkeeping made errors immediately evident and gave a clear picture of the financial position of a commercial enterprise. Although known in the ancient world, double-entry bookkeeping was not widely practiced in the West until the fourteenth century. In this and other business practices, the lands of southern Europe, especially Italy, were the forerunners; their accounting techniques spread to the rest of Europe in the sixteenth century.

Business practices related to shipping also developed in the fourteenth century. A system of **maritime** insurance, without which investors would have been highly reluctant to risk their money on expensive vessels, evolved in Florence. By 1400, maritime insurance had become a regular item of the shipping business, and it was destined to play a major role in the opening of Atlantic trade. At least equally important to overseas expansion were business enterprises known as joint-stock companies, which allowed small investors to buy shares in a large venture. These companies made possible the accumulation of the huge amounts of capital needed for large-scale operations such as the building and deployment of merchant fleets—amounts quite beyond the resources of one person.

Patterns of Commercial Development

Responses to the price revolution in trade and industry hinged on social and political conditions and thus differed in various parts of Europe. In the United Provinces (the Netherlands) and England, there were far fewer strictures on trade and industry than in France and Spain, as will be explained later in this chapter. So in the sixteenth and seventeenth centuries, England and the United Provinces were better placed than

France and Spain to take advantage of conditions favorable for business expansion. In the United Provinces, favorable conditions resulted from the weakness of Dutch feudal culture and values in comparison with commercial ones, the small land area, and a far larger percentage of urban population than elsewhere in Western Europe.

England's advantage derived from another source: not the weakness of the landed gentry but its habits. Primogeniture operated among the owners of large estates just as it did among the yeomanry, with much the same effect. Younger sons were forced to make their fortunes elsewhere. Those who did so by going into business would often benefit from an infusion of venture capital that came from their elder brothers' landed estates. And, of course, capital was forthcoming from such quarters because of the profitable nature of English farming. In a reverse process, those who made fortunes in trade would typically invest money in land and rise gradually into landed society. The skills that had brought wealth in commerce would then be applied to new estates, usually with equal success.

England and the Netherlands.   In both England and the United Provinces, the favorable conditions led to large-scale commercial expansion. In the 1590s, the Dutch devised a new ship, the *fluit*, or flyboat, to handle bulky grain shipments at the lowest possible cost. This innovation permitted them to capture the Baltic trade, which became the main source of their phenomenal commercial expansion between 1560 and 1660. Equally dramatic was their commercial penetration of the East. Profits from the European carrying trade built ships that allowed the Dutch first to challenge and then to displace the Portuguese in the spice trade with the East Indies during the early seventeenth century. The Dutch chartered the United East India Company in 1602 and established trading posts in the islands—the beginnings of the Dutch empire, which lasted until World War II.

The English traded throughout Europe in the sixteenth and seventeenth centuries, especially with Spain and the Netherlands. The staples of this trade were raw wool and woolens, but increasingly the trade included such items as ships and guns.

The seventeenth century saw the foundation of a British colonial empire along the Atlantic seaboard in North America, from Maine to the Carolinas, and in the West Indies, where the English managed to dislodge the Spanish in some places.

In seventeenth-century England, the central government increasingly took the side of the capitalist producer. At the beginning of the century, the king had imposed feudal fees on landed property, acted against enclosures, and granted **monopolies** in trade and manufacture to court favorites, which restricted opportunities for investment. The king also spent revenues on maintaining an unproductive aristocracy. But by the end of the century, because of the revolutionary transfer of power from the king to Parliament, economic policy more closely reflected the interests of big business, whether agricultural or commercial. Landowners no longer paid feudal dues to the king. Enclosure went on unimpeded, and in fact was abetted, by parliamentary enactment.

The Navigation Act, first passed in 1651, allowed all English shippers to carry goods anywhere, replacing the old system that had restricted trade with certain areas to specific traders. The act also required that all goods be carried in English ships, enabling merchants, as Christopher Hill writes, "to buy English and colonial exports cheap and sell them dear abroad, to buy foreign goods cheap and sell them dear in England."[5] English shippers also gained the profits of the carrying trade, one factor leading to the displacement of the Dutch by the English as the leading power in international commerce after 1660.

France and Spain.   France benefited from commercial and industrial expansion, but not to the same degree as England. The principal reason for

Map 15.2 Industrial Centers in the Sixteenth ▶ Century This map of Europe (c. 1500) indicates the population of the most important cities (Naples is the largest). It also shows the centers of three kinds of industry: textiles, metals, and finance. Cloth making (textile production) was the most important industry in Europe in the early modern period. (© 2016 Cengage Learning.)

Moscow

Black Sea

Constantinople

Baltic Sea

Danzig

Adrianople

Sofia

Salonika

Lübeck

Hamburg

Vienna

Belgrade

Adriatic Sea

Messina

Prague

Nuremberg

Augsburg

Ulm

Verona Venice

Bologna

Rome

Naples

Cologne

Liège

Florence

Lucca

Palermo

Amsterdam
Leyden

Milan

Cremona

Haarlem

Antwerp

Genoa

Bruges Ghent

Brussels

Paris

Rouen

Lyon

Marseilles

North
Sea

London

Mediterranean Sea

Dublin

Bordeaux

Toulouse

Barcelona

Valencia

Valladolid

Madrid

Medina del
Campo

Granada

Seville Córdoba

ATLANTIC OCEAN

Lisbon

Towns of 200,000–500,000+ population

Towns of 30,000–100,000+ population

Centers of textile industry

Centers of metal industry

Centers of financial activity

○ •

▢ 〇 ▫

400 Mi.

400 Km.

200

200

0

0

the difference was the aristocratic structure of French society. Family ties and social intercourse between aristocracy and merchants, such as existed in England, were largely absent in France. Consequently, the French aristocracy remained contemptuous of commerce. Also inhibiting economic expansion were the guilds—remnants of the Middle Ages that restricted competition and production. In France, there was relatively less opportunity than in England for merchant-capitalists operating outside the guild structures.

Spain presents an even clearer example of the failure to grasp the opportunities afforded by the price revolution. By the third quarter of the sixteenth century, Spain possessed the makings of economic expansion: unrivaled amounts of capital in the form of silver, a large and growing population, rising consumer demand, and a vast overseas empire. These factors did not bear fruit because the Spanish value system regarded business as a form of social heresy. The Spanish held in high esteem gentlemen who possessed land gained through military service and crusading ardor, which enabled them to live on rents and privileges. Commerce and industry remained contemptible pursuits.

Numerous wars in the sixteenth century (with France, the Lutheran princes, the Ottoman Turks, the Dutch, and the English) increasingly strained the Spanish treasury, despite the annual shipments of silver from the New World. Spain spent its resources on maintaining and extending its imperial power and Catholicism rather than on investing in economic expansion. In the end, the wars cost even more than Spain could handle. The Dutch for a time, and the English and the French more permanently, displaced Spain as the great power. The English and the Dutch had taken advantage of the opportunities presented by the price revolution; the Spanish had not.

THE GROWTH OF CAPITALISM

What Is Capitalism?

The changes described—especially in England and the Netherlands—represent a crucial stage in the development of the modern economic system known as **capitalism**. This is a system of *private enterprise*: the main economic decisions (what, how much, where, and at what price to produce, buy, and sell) are made by private individuals in their capacity as owners, workers, or consumers. Capitalism is also said to be a system of *free enterprise*: the basic decisions are not left only to individuals; these decisions are also made in response to market forces. People are free, in other words, to obey the law of supply and demand. When goods and labor are scarce, prices and wages rise; when they are plentiful, prices and wages fall.

In the Middle Ages, capitalistic enterprise was not widespread because the market was severely restricted, and, consequently, so was the operation of market forces. The vast majority of people lived as self-sufficient subsistence farmers (peasants or serfs) on the land. In the High Middle Ages trade had greatly expanded and in cities, especially in Italy, capitalist enterprise was conducted. But this commerce was limited in comparison to the transoceanic trade during the Commercial Revolution. Moreover, capitalist forms of enterprise were hampered by guild restrictions, which set limits on production, wages, and prices without regard to market forces. In addition, the economic decay of the fourteenth and early fifteenth centuries did not predispose those who had surplus money to gamble on the future.

But conditions changed in certain quarters beginning in the fifteenth and sixteenth centuries, generating the incentive to invest—to take risks for future profit rather than to consume. This process was due, more than anything else, to the economic situation prevailing in Europe between 1450 and 1600.

The Fostering of Mercantile Capitalism

Several conditions sustained the incentive to invest and reinvest—a basic factor in the emergence of modern capitalism. One was the price revolution, stemming from a supply of basic commodities that could not keep pace with rising demand. Prices continued to climb, creating the most powerful incentive of all to invest rather than to consume. Why spend now, those with surplus wealth must have asked, when investment in commercial farming, mining, shipping, and publishing (to name a few important outlets) is almost certain to yield greater wealth in the future? The price revolution reduced the risk involved in investment, thus helping overcome the reluctance of the wealthy to engage in capitalistic enterprise.

Another condition that encouraged investment was the distribution of wealth in a way that promoted investment. Three distinct patterns of distribution worked to this effect. First, inflation widened the gap between the rich and the poor during the sixteenth century; the rich who chose to invest garnered increasing amounts of wealth, which probably added to their incentive to continue investing. Because of the growing population and the resulting shortage of jobs, employers could pay lower and lower wages; thus, again, their profits increased, encouraging reinvestment. Merchant-capitalists were an important group of investors who gained from these conditions. As they grew, they were able to exercise a controlling influence in the marketplace because they operated on a large scale, regionally to internationally; thus, they were able to dictate terms of production and employment, displacing the local guilds. This displacement was also favorable to investment and growth. Mercantile capitalism did not benefit everyone equally; in fact, it produced increasing inequities between rich and poor, owners and workers, and independent merchant-capitalists and members of local guilds.

The second pattern of wealth distribution that encouraged investment, especially in England, grew out of the practice of primogeniture. The concentration of inherited property in the hands of the eldest child (usually the oldest son) meant that he had sufficient wealth to be persuaded to invest at least part of it. Any younger sons were left to make their own way in the world and often turned their drive and ambition into profits.

Finally, a pattern of international distribution of wealth promoted investment in some lands. The classic example is that of Spain in relation, say, to England. Spain in the sixteenth century devoted its wealth and energies to religious war and empire and relied on producers elsewhere for many of its supplies. So Spanish treasure was exported to England to pay for imports, stimulating investment there rather than in Spain. Capitalism did not develop everywhere at the same pace, and as the Spanish case shows, the very conditions that discouraged it in one place encouraged it somewhere else.

Two additional stimuli for investment came from governments. First, governments acted as giant consumers, whose appetites throughout the early modern period were expanding. Merchants, who supplied governments with everything from guns to frescoes, not only prospered but reinvested as well because of the constancy and growth of government demand. Governments also sponsored new forms of investment, whether to satisfy the taste for new luxuries at the king's court or to meet the requirements of the military. Moreover, private investors reaped incalculable advantages from overseas empires. Colonies supplied cheap raw materials and cheap (slave) labor and served as markets for exports. They greatly stimulated the construction of ships and harbor facilities and the sale of insurance.

The second government stimulus comprised state policies meant to increase investment, which they no doubt sometimes did, though not always. Collectively, these policies constitute what is known as *mercantilism*: the conscious pursuit by governments of courses of action supposed to augment national wealth and power. One characteristic expression of mercantilism was the pursuit of a favorable balance of international payments. According to conventional wisdom, wealth from trade was measured in gold and silver, of which there was believed to be a more-or-less fixed quantity. The state's goal in international trade became to sell more abroad than it bought, that is, to establish a favorable balance of payments. When the amount received for sales abroad was greater than the amount spent for purchases, the difference would be an influx of precious metal into the state. By this logic, mercantilists were led to argue for the goal of national sufficiency: a country should try to supply most of its own needs to keep imports to a minimum. This argument, of course, ignored the fact that, in international trade, the more a country buys, the more it can sell because its purchases abroad create purchasing power for its goods overseas.

Mercantilism did have a positive side. Governments increased economic activity by employing the poor, subsidizing new industries, and chartering companies to engage in overseas trade. Particularly valuable were the steps taken by states to break down local trade barriers, such as guild regulations and internal tariffs, in an attempt to create national markets and internal economic unity.

The English, moreover, saw that mercantilistic calculations of national wealth should be made over the long run. For example, Thomas Mun (1571–1641) argued that a country might import more than it exported in the short run and still come out ahead in the end because raw materials that are imported and then reprocessed for export would eventually yield a handsome profit.

In addition, Mun was one of the first to discern the virtues of *consumerism*, a phenomenon that is still extremely important for achieving sustained economic growth. Speaking of foreign trade, he maintained that the more English merchants did to advertise English goods to potential customers, the greater the overseas market for those goods would be. In other words, demand can be *created*. Just as there is an urge to invest and make profits, so there is an appetite to consume and enjoy the products of industry, and both inclinations have played their part in the growth of capitalism. Nor was the message restricted to the foreign market. Between 1660 and 1750, England became the world's first consumer society: more and more people had more and more money to spend, and they acquired a taste for conspicuous consumption (which previously had always been confined to the aristocracy). Discretionary goods were available—lace, tobacco, housewares, flowers— and consumers wanted them. Concomitantly, just as today, the stronger the stimulus to buy, the harder the consumer worked, which induced further growth.

The price revolution, the concentration of wealth in private hands, and government activity combined to provide the foundation for sustained investment and for the emergence of mercantile capitalism. This new force in the world should not be confused with industrial capitalism. The latter evolved with the first Industrial Revolution in eighteenth-century England, but mercantile capitalism paved the way for it.

THE ELITE AND THE PEOPLE

Traditional Popular Culture

Europe's economic expansion was accompanied by equally important social and cultural changes in the relations between ordinary people and their rulers, whether kings, nobles, landlords, or clergy. Throughout the Middle Ages, there had always been two cultures: the elite culture of the royal court, the feudal lords, and the educated clergy, and the popular culture of largely illiterate peasants and artisans.

Over the centuries, the common people had evolved a distinctive culture, which their rulers patronized and, to some degree, participated in. This popular culture consisted of a mosaic of the customs of various groups of people—shepherds, peasants, cobblers, weavers, miners—each group with its own traditions. Even a youth culture of apprentices was to be found in the towns. Furthermore, besides the settled culture of the villages and towns, there was a vagabond culture of sailors, soldiers, beggars, thieves, and other "masterless men."[6]

The prosperous and the powerful called on the services of learned professionals—clergy, physicians, and lawyers. Ordinary people had their own humbler and cheaper equivalents— lay preachers, folk healers, and witches (that is, sorcerers and fortunetellers). The royal courts, manor houses, monasteries, and universities were centers of elite culture. Ordinary people worked, played, and worshiped in meaner settings: the village church, the tavern, the street, and especially the marketplace or village square. In the church and churchyard, they danced, feasted, and performed religious pageants; in the tavern and street, they gossiped, played games, watched puppet shows, staged cockfights, listened to folk preachers, and consulted healers, astrologers, and magicians.

Certain special occasions granted people the freedom to express themselves. Beginning in the thirteenth century, the most important of these occasions was the carnival, the three- to six-day festival preceding the onset of **Lent**. The carnival was a time of revelry and ritual processions through church and streets, excessive eating and drinking, and a sharp increase in sexual activity. It was also a time during which ordinary people, at least in their parades and public displays, engaged in what was called "turning the world upside down." So, for instance, in a procession a horse would be made to walk backward with its rider facing its tail. Popular illustrations of the era show a son beating his father, a pupil beating his teacher, servants giving orders to their masters, the laity preaching to the clergy, the husband minding the baby, and the wife smoking and holding a gun. What does all this mean? Was it a safety valve, allowing the people to blow off the steam generated by an otherwise oppressive and monotonous existence? Perhaps, but it sometimes led to real violence, and the elite, by the sixteenth century at any rate, looked on such behavior as subversive and fraught with danger. As a noble said on the occasion of the carnival at Palermo in 1648, "On the pretext of these assemblies of the people for these ridiculous spectacles, factious spirits would be able . . . to encourage some new riot."[7]

Nor was the carnival the only occasion for this ritual mockery of authority. The calendar year was punctuated by the observance of religious feast days on which similar behavior took place. So, for instance, in France, on the Feast of Fools (the Innocents) on December 28, an abbot or bishop of fools was elected, and a mock Mass took place in which the clergy dressed in women's clothes, played cards, ate sausages, sang ribald songs, and cursed their congregations instead of blessing them.

Among the most prevalent popular traditions was the ritual mockery of marriage known as the *charivari*. Only unconventional marriages qualified for such rude treatment at the hands of one's neighbors: an old man and a young wife, a second marriage, a husband beaten or cuckolded by his wife. The charivari consisted of a ritual procession in which the victim or his effigy would be mounted backward on an ass and drawn through the streets accompanied by "rough music" (the beating of pots and pans). Charivaris were sometimes conducted at the expense of tax collectors, preachers, and landlords. Here then was a kind of popular justice, another version of the world turned upside down.

The Reform of Popular Culture

Throughout the Middle Ages and until the early sixteenth century, elite culture and popular culture existed in more-or-less stable balance. Indeed, the two worlds, high and low, occupied considerable common ground. Landlords and clergy took part in village games and feasts and shared with their "inferiors" an outlook that stressed communal values: pulling together in a subsistence world, making sure that everyone had enough for survival, and extending relief to those in need. The emphasis was on communalism, not individualism, especially in the countryside.

In the sixteenth century, however, a drastic change took place in the attitude of the elite toward ordinary people. No longer willing to patronize and foster popular culture, the elite became increasingly suspicious of and hostile to it. This shift occurred for two reasons. The first was the elite's fear of the growing numbers of the poor and fear of the growing numbers of people, some poor and some not, who, inspired by the new religious movements and the new printed literature, were beginning to question the old authorities and sometimes even joined in rebellion against them. Encouraged by the greater accessibility of printed books and by the Protestant emphasis on Bible reading, more and more people became literate, and a popular literature of religious instruction, astrological almanacs, and chivalric romances poured from the presses to meet the growing demand. On this score, too, the authorities had their misgivings; books of the right sort were acceptable, even useful, but a little learning was thought to be a dangerous thing.

The second reason for the shift in elite attitudes toward ordinary people was not fear but hope. Not only were the elite alarmed by the growing

***Peasant Festival*, 1640, by David Teniers the Younger (1610–1690).** This scene depicts peasant revelry, the rural village at play. The common folk are eating, drinking, and dancing outside what looks like a country tavern. Hardworking farmworkers no doubt deserved their day off. Notice in the lower left of the picture a small group of gentry who owned the land on which the peasants worked. Such landlords indulged the peasants in their merrymaking, but warily and only up to a point because they feared the possibility of a riot and popular rebellion. (akg-images/ Joseph Martin.)

poverty and unrest among the people, but they also thought that they knew how to control the unrest and even perhaps in some measure overcome it. Just as religion inspired the people, so the Reformation, the Counter-Reformation, and the Christian humanism of the Renaissance inspired leaders to reform society and in particular to attack popular culture for being both too pagan and too disorderly. The customs of the people, it was thought, needed to be purified and made more decent and sober, and the people themselves needed to be disciplined so that they might become obedient subjects of king and church. Society came to be seen as divided between **the godly** (among whom the elite included themselves) and the ungodly multitude, who needed to be controlled and, if possible, educated for service in the Christian commonwealth.

What followed was a wide-ranging onslaught against all forms of traditional popular culture—what one historian has called "the triumph of Lent" over "the world of Carnival."[8] This reform movement included attacks on popular festivals, **lay preaching**, and "the world turned up side down." The Florentine ruler Girolamo Savonarola, a few days before the carnival of 1496, preached a sermon recommending that "boys should collect alms for the respectable poor, instead of mad pranks, throwing stones and making floats."[9] A century later, in England, Phillip Stubbe drew up a comprehensive indictment of May games, Lords of Misrule, Christmas feasting, church ales, wakes, bearbaiting, cockfighting, and dancing. Popular religious dramas disappeared in northern Italy during the third quarter of the sixteenth century and in England by the end of that century.

The new bureaucratic state joined the clergy in the reforming enterprise. In the sixteenth and seventeenth centuries, many forms of behavior that had been thought of as spiritual sins became secular crimes as well, subject to prosecution and punishment by the state. These newly criminalized activities included adultery, **blasphemy**, sodomy, infanticide, and witchcraft. In this period, too, public brothels, which had existed for centuries, were gradually shut down, a process beginning in Lutheran Germany between 1530 and 1560. The state enforced what the new moral puritanism decreed.

Witchcraft and the Witch Craze

The prosecution of witches constitutes a particularly important chapter in this attack on popular culture. Although it had always been suspect, witchcraft had been a part of traditional village culture for centuries. There were two kinds of witchcraft, known at the time as black and white. The white variety involved healing and fortunetelling. Black witchcraft conjured evil powers by a curse or by the manipulation of objects, such as the entrails of animals.

The medieval church developed a more theological and sinister interpretation of the phenomenon: that witches conspired with the Devil to work against God and human society, held secret meetings, and had carnal relations with the Devil. In the late twelfth century, Christian thinkers began to emphasize the idea of a Devil who roamed the world at the head of an army of demons, attempting to undermine the saving mission of Christ and tempting people to sin. Witches were regarded as those who had succumbed to temptation and entered into a pact to worship Satan in place of God. This worship was thought to take place at secret, nocturnal meetings (the legendary witches' Sabbats), during which witches and demons were supposed to engage in sexual orgies, sacrifice infants, and desecrate the Eucharist.

As early as the thirteenth century, bishops and popes prosecuted witches for heresy. Confessions were usually extracted by means of torture. Those found guilty were burned at the stake (on the Continent) or hanged (in England), and their property was confiscated by the authorities. The church held that a witch's "only hope of salvation was to be arrested and to recant before her execution. By such reasoning the torment and killing of witches was for their own good as well as that of God and society."[10]

The growth of printed literature on the subject of witchcraft was especially influential in the spread of the church's view that witchcraft involved a diabolical plot. In 1486, there appeared a handbook called *Malleus Maleficarum* (*The Hammer of Witches*) by two German Dominicans who claimed to show what witches did at the Devil's behest. These Dominicans had tried almost fifty people for witchcraft, all but two of them women.

By the sixteenth century, the linkage of women to witchcraft had been firmly established. Men could also be accused of the crime, but almost everywhere that witches were tried in the sixteenth and seventeenth centuries, more than 75 percent were women, often elderly widows and spinsters. The so-called witch craze is a phenomenon of these two centuries, when perhaps as many

WITCHES' SABBAT (1510) BY HANS BALDUNG GRIEN (1485–545). This woodcut depicts both learned and popular beliefs concerning witches. For example, the night ride through the air, the naked feasting, and orgiastic concourse with the Devil all reflect the view that witchcraft was an extremely dangerous heresy that sought to overthrow Christianity and put Devil worship in its place. (RMN-Grand Palais/Art Resource, N.Y.)

as 110,000 people were prosecuted and 60,000 executed all over Europe.

Why were most of the accused women? No doubt this pattern reflected an ancient prejudice that women were less rational and more lustful than men and so more susceptible to the Devil's wiles. As the authors of *The Hammer of Witches* declared, "Witchcraft comes from carnal lust, which is in woman insatiable."[11]

One view of English witch-hunts during the period may help explain the predominance of women among the accused. In traditional society, widows and the elderly were objects of local charity. An old woman, so the theory goes, would beg for alms and be rebuffed by a more prosperous neighbor; later, some misfortune would befall the neighbor, and he would blame it on the old woman, accusing her of witchcraft as a way of assuaging his guilt for having refused her request for help. According to this interpretation, such behavior characterizes a period of rapid transition from communal subsistence to an ethic of economic individualism that demanded that each person look out for himself or herself. Just such a period in England coincided with the large number of witchcraft prosecutions brought against poor old women.

By 1700, the witch craze had ended in Western Europe—first in Holland, the most tolerant country, and in Spain, the most intolerant because the Spanish Inquisition provided another focus for persecutions. Two factors probably helped put an end to the witch-hunts.

First, the religious turmoil unleashed by the Reformation, on which the witch craze fed, also triggered an intellectual backlash that led some to wonder whether **fanaticism** had not gotten the better of reason and to call for a tempering of inflamed passions and the exercise of a greater degree of skepticism in matters of faith. "It is rating our conjectures too high to roast people alive for them," the skeptic Michel de Montaigne exclaimed.[12] Thus, judges in seventeenth-century France imposed stricter tests and demanded that more conclusive evidence be presented before convicting people tried for witchcraft. In 1682, Louis XIV himself declared the phenomenon to be a kind of fraud.

Second, during the last half of the seventeenth century, another shift was taking place in relations between the elite and the common people. The elite began to associate belief in astrology, magic, and witches with the people. Both cultures had once shared these beliefs, but now the elite spurned them as representing so many vulgar superstitions. This shift owed something to the growth of **skepticism** and the impact of science. It also indicated a hardening of the lines drawn between the two cultures and a greater willingness by the elite to accept, if not foster, the resulting divisions. By the early eighteenth century, although almost nobody would admit to having given up the belief in the existence of witches, serious discussion, let alone prosecution, of witchcraft cases had been read out of polite society. The reason was not that the belief had been proved wrong, but that to talk about it, except by way of ridicule, was deemed unseemly. The belief in witchcraft declined in part by being rendered taboo in the upper reaches of society. It lost its appeal as much through social snobbery as through science and skepticism.

ECONOMIC AND SOCIAL TRANSFORMATIONS

The transformations considered in this chapter were among the most momentous in the world's history. In an unprecedented development that may never be repeated, one small part of the world, Western Europe, became lord of the sea-lanes, master of many lands throughout the globe, and banker and profit-taker in an emerging world economy. Western Europe's global hegemony was to last well into the twentieth century. By conquering and settling new lands, Europeans exported Western culture around the globe, a process that accelerated in the twentieth century.

The overseas expansion had profound effects. The native populations of the New World were decimated. To ease the labor shortage, millions of blacks were imported from Africa to work as slaves on plantations and in mines. Black slavery would produce large-scale effects on culture, politics, and society, which have lasted to the present day.

The widespread circulation of plant and animal life also had great consequences. Horses and cattle were introduced into the New World. (The Aztecs were so amazed to see a man on horse-back that they thought horse and rider were one demonic creature.) In return, the Old World sampled such novelties as corn, the tomato, and, most important, the potato, which was to become a staple of the northern European diet. Manioc, from which tapioca is made, was transplanted from the New World to Africa, where it helped sustain the population. Germs also traversed the Atlantic. Millions of Amerindians perished from disease carried by Europeans, and syphilis, brought back to Spain by Columbus' men, produced a fearsome outbreak of disease in Europe.

Western Europe was wrenched out of the subsistence economy of the Middle Ages and launched on a course of sustained economic growth. This transformation resulted from the grafting of traditional forms, such as primogeniture and holy war, onto new forces, such as global exploration, price revolution, and convertible husbandry. Out of this change emerged the beginnings of a new economic system, mercantile capitalism, which in large measure provided the economic thrust for European world predominance and paved the way for the Industrial Revolution of the eighteenth and nineteenth centuries.

Finally, these economic changes were accompanied by a major shift in relations between the rulers and the ruled. For centuries, the elite had tolerated and even patronized the culture of the common people. But under the impact of the commercial revolution and the Reformation, the authorities became increasingly suspicious of the people and undertook to purify and reform popular culture. The degree to which they succeeded remains an open question. But the gap between the elite and the people widened as the elite found less and less in popular culture to identify with and more and more to condemn or try to undo. The elite distanced themselves from ordinary people even as they attempted to impose their will. The result was the emergence of two separate cultures, divorced from and hostile to each other. Only in moments of mass hysteria, such as during the witch craze, could the people and their rulers join forces against a common and defenseless victim.

❖ ❖ ❖

NOTES

1. Roland Oliver, *The African Experience* (New York: HarperCollins, 1991), 123.

2. Quoted in Basil Davidson, *Africa in History* (New York: Collier Books, 1991), 215.

3. Quoted in Richard S. Dunn, *Sugar and Slaves* (Chapel Hill: University of North Carolina Press, 1972), 248.

4. Quoted in Davidson, *Africa in History*, 223.

5. Christopher Hill, *Reformation to Industrial Revolution* (Baltimore: Penguin Books, 1969), 159–160.

6. Christopher Hill, *The World Turned Upside Down* (New York: Viking, 1972), chap. 3.

7. Quoted in Peter Burke, *Popular Culture in Early Modern Europe* (New York: Harper and Row, 1978), 203.

8. Ibid., chaps. 7–8.

9. Ibid., 217.

10. Jeffrey B. Russell, *A History of Witchcraft* (London: Thames and Hudson, 1980), 78.

11. Quoted in Margaret L. King, *Women of the Renaissance* (Chicago: University of Chicago Press, 1993), 155.

12. Quoted in Russell, *A History of Witchcraft*, 73.

Chapter 16

The Rise of Sovereignty: Transition to the Modern State

Anton von Maron, Kaiser Joseph II (1741–1790). There is a standard pose intended to show the power of all absolute but reasonable monarchs. They live in elegant surroundings; they look earnest and strong. They use images to evoke their benevolence, hence the statue in back of Joseph II. (Imagno/Hulton Archive/Getty Images.)

Focus Questions

1. How did monarchs build strong states?
2. What enabled Spain to rise to greatness, and why was this greatness short-lived?
3. What were the achievements and failures of Louis XIV's reign?
4. What is the enduring historical significance of the English Revolution of the seventeenth century? How have historians quarreled about it?
5. What were the distinguishing features of Prussia and Russia by the early eighteenth century?
6. What was the role of the lesser nobility in the process of state formation?

From the thirteenth to the seventeenth century, a new and unique form of political organization emerged in the West: the **dynastic**, or national, **state**, which, through taxes and war, harnessed the power of its nobility and the material resources of its territory. The state was simply a large territory, generally with people speaking the same language who could very gradually imagine themselves as part of a community. Indeed, the European monarchs encouraged such thinking. Their right to rule had been established centuries earlier when a dynasty was founded, generally by the most militarily powerful nobleman. Under the laws and rights governing birth, the state became an entity inherited from generation to generation; thus, a dynasty was born. The power of the West to explore and dominate other lands and peoples would have been impossible without the backing provided by, and the competition between, the European states. They directed the energies of merchants and landed elites into national service and international competition. A degree of domestic stability ensued, and the states encouraged commerce and industry, which could in turn be taxed. Although they nurtured the aristocracy, many states also required that both lord and peasant serve in national armies bent upon foreign conquest as well as defense. States need not have been dynastic; witness, for example, the emergence of the Dutch Republic, which was led by elite families. But by the late fifteenth century, most of the European states became the inheritance of dynastic kings.

Monarchs and their courts became centers of gravity in the process of state formation. The centralized governments that emerged generally embraced a system best described as **absolutism**. Under the impact of absolutism, kings seemed invincible. Out of their courts came the administration of justice, the power to collect taxes, foreign policy, laws governing the content of books and the press, and even laws regulating the forms of dress permitted to various classes and occupations. Despite the appeal of such kingly power, one other form of government emerged in early modern Europe: *republican*, or *constitutional*, states. By 1800, the future lay with this other, more participatory system. Republican government gave

Chronology 16.1 ❖ The Rise of Monarchical Sovereignty

1469	Ferdinand and Isabella begin their rule of Castile and Aragon
1485	Henry VII begins the reign of the Tudor dynasty in England
1517	The Protestant Reformation starts in Germany
1519	Charles V of Spain becomes Hapsburg emperor of the Holy Roman Empire
1556–1598	Philip II of Spain persecutes Jews and Muslims
1559	Treaty of peace between France and Spain
1560–1609	The Netherlands revolts against Spanish rule
1562–1589	Religious wars in France
1572	Saint Bartholomew's Day Massacre: Queen Catherine of France thought to have ordered thousands of Protestants executed
1579	*Vindiciae contra Tyrannos*, published by Huguenots, justifies regicide; it will be translated and republished during the English Revolution
1588	English fleet defeats the Spanish Armada
1590s	A reaction in Russia against Ivan IV, the Terrible
1593	Henry IV of France renounces his Protestantism to restore peace in France
1598	French Protestants granted limited religious toleration by the Edict of Nantes
1630	King Charles I in England attempts to govern without Parliament
1640–1660	Revolution in England
1648	Treaty of Westphalia ends Thirty Years' War; guarantees the independence of the Dutch Republic
1649	Charles I, Stuart king of England, is executed by an act of Parliament
1649–1660	England is co-ruled by Parliament and the army under Oliver Cromwell
1660	Charles II returns from exile and becomes king of England
1683	Turks attack Vienna and are defeated
1685	Louis XIV of France revokes the Edict of Nantes
1688–1689	Revolution in England: end of absolutism; religious toleration for all Protestants
1699	Treaty of Karlowitz marks Austrians' victory over Turks and affirms Austria's right to rule Hungary, Transylvania, and parts of Croatia
1701	Louis XIV tries to bring Spain under French control
1702–1714	War of the Spanish Succession establishes a balance of power between England and France

more power to landed or mercantile elites than to kings and their courts.

Although kings in some medieval lands had begun to forge national states, medieval political forms differed considerably from the systems that developed in the early modern period. During the Middle Ages, feudal lords gave homage to their kings but ruled unencumbered over their local territories. Medieval representative assemblies, which met occasionally to give advice to kings, at times acted as a brake on the king's power. City-states enjoyed considerable autonomy. The clergy supported the monarch but governed in separate spiritual realms. The papacy challenged the authority of those monarchs who, it believed, did not fulfill their duty to rule in accordance with Christian teachings. In early modern times, powerful monarchs gradually subdued these competing systems of local authority and established strong central governments.

MONARCHS AND ELITES
AS STATE BUILDERS

At first, kings drove the development of states. European elites, whether landed or urban, grudgingly gave allegiance to these ambitious, and at times ruthless, authority figures. In general, a single monarch seemed the only alternative to the even more brutal pattern of war and disorder so basic to the governing habits of the feudal aristocracy. But it was essential that the kings of Europe subordinate the aristocracy to their needs and interests and gain firm control over the Christian churches in their territories. Gradually, religious zeal was made compatible with, and largely supportive of, the state's goals rather than with papal dictates or even universal Christian aspirations. The demise of medieval representative assemblies—with the notable exception of the English Parliament and the Dutch Estates General—is a dramatic illustration of how monarchs subjected to their will all other political authorities, whether local, regional, or national. Parliaments gave one representative one vote, whereas Estates General voted by a collective process whereby one social estate or one province cast only one vote (polling its members to do so). The actual votes cast

could be as few as three in the French case or seven for the number of Dutch provinces voting in The Hague. Few Estates General survived the seventeenth century. They were not in the monarch's interest.

Monarchs employed a variety of tools for extending their power. All encouraged the use of vernacular languages—English, French, or Spanish, for example—to foster a common identity, as well as to counteract the church's monopoly over the international language of the time, Latin. But more important than words were arms. The foundations of monarchical power lay in the standing army and the taxation that paid for the military. The goal of the monarch was to have independent wealth and power. In general, only war justified taxes. The rise and fall of the great European powers of the early modern period—first Spain and then the Dutch Republic, as well as France and England—can be traced directly in the fortunes of their armies on the battlefield and the fullness of the king's or state's treasury. Only the rise of the **Dutch Republic** broke with the pattern of king–army–taxes as the key to the creation of a centralized state. The Dutch case rested on local elites–army–taxes. The rich, urban, Protestant elite lent the state money at interest to wage a struggle for independence against Spain. In the process, the Dutch created the first system of national bonds and a citizen-financed national debt. A nation was created, but one without a king or a strong central government. Local elites held most of the power, just as they held the state bonds.

Where early modern monarchs succeeded in subduing, reconstituting, or destroying local aristocratic and ecclesiastical power systems, strong dynastic states emerged. Where the monarchs failed, as they did in the **Holy Roman Empire** and Italy, no viable states evolved until well into the nineteenth century. Those failures derived from the independent authority of local princes or city-states and, in the case of Italy, from the decentralizing influence of papal authority. In the Holy Roman Empire, feudal princes found allies in the newly formed Protestant communities, and in such a situation, religion worked as a decentralizing force. Once given the power to determine the local religion, many German princes also maintained their peasants as virtual serfs.

Early modern kings needed to gain control over religious authorities. They did not separate church and state (as was later done in the United States); rather they linked their subjects' religious identity with national identity. For example, in England, by the late seventeenth century, to be a true Protestant was to be a true English subject, while in Spain the same equation operated for the Catholic (as opposed to the Muslim or the Jew, who was discriminated against as non-Spanish). Even in the Dutch Republic, where a real, if limited, religious toleration prevailed, all the municipal, regional, and national offices were held by Protestants.

In the thirteenth century, most Europeans still identified themselves with their localities: their villages, manors, or towns. Their allegiance went to their local lord or bishop. They knew little, and probably cared less, about the activities of the king and his court, except when the monarch called on them for taxes or military service. By the late seventeenth century, in contrast, aristocrats in many European countries defined their political power in relation to king and court. By then, the lives of very ordinary people had been touched by national systems of tax collection, by the doctrines and practices of national churches, and by military conscription.

Increasingly, middle-class town dwellers, the **bourgeoisie**, also realized that their prosperity hinged, in part, on court-supported foreign and domestic policies. If the king assisted their commercial ventures, urban dwellers supported the growth of a strong central state. In only two states, England and the Dutch Republic, did landed and mercantile elites share in the process of governing by the late seventeenth century.

By that time commercial rivalry among states and colonial expansion were directly related to the ability of landed and commercial elites to protect their interests under the mantle of the state, and to the state's willingness to encourage world trade in order to enrich its own treasury. Monarchs and the states they helped create ushered in the modern world just as surely as did commercial expansion, capitalism, and science. They also enshrined political power as a masculine and familial preserve that could be inherited.

THE RISE AND FALL
OF HAPSBURG SPAIN

The Spanish political experience of the sixteenth century exemplifies the interconnectedness of king, army, church, and taxation. It was also one of the most spectacular examples in history of the rise and equally dramatic fall of a great power. The Spanish kings turned a dynastic state into an empire. First Spain burst through its frontiers and encompassed Portugal, part of Italy, the Low Countries, and enormous areas of the New World. Spain became an intercontinental empire—the first in the West since Roman times. Until 1469, however, although Spanish was widely spoken on the Iberian Peninsula, Spain did not exist as a political entity. Then in that year, Ferdinand, heir to the throne of Aragon, married his more powerful and prosperous cousin, Isabella, heiress of Castile. Yet even after the unification of Castile and the crown of Aragon (encompassing Catalonia, Aragon, and Valencia), relations among the fiercely independent provinces of Spain were often tense. Only through dynastic marriage of their offspring to a German-speaking family of central Europe, the Hapsburgs, did the Spanish monarchs emerge on the international scene. Marriage and inheritance were key pieces in the puzzle of state development.

Ferdinand and Isabella: Unity and Purity of "Blood" and Religion

During their rule (1479–1516), Ferdinand and Isabella put in place a dynastic state and laid the foundation for the Spanish Empire and Spanish domination of European affairs throughout the sixteenth century. Together, they built the army and consolidated the state by waging a campaign to reconquer Spanish territory still held by the Muslims. At the same time, they strove to bring the church into alliance with the state and forge a Spanish identity based on "blood" ancestry as well as religion. A person was considered Spanish only if no Jews or non-Spaniards could be found in the family lineage. The roots of racism lie deep in European religious and political history.

Map 16.1 Spain from the Ninth to the Sixteenth Century Spain became a nation gradually, and eventually Portugal split away to become a separate state.

(© 2016 Cengage Learning.)

Spanish rulers also had to bring the church's interests in line with their own. Whereas other Europeans, partly under the impact of the Renaissance, questioned the church's leadership and attacked its corruption, the Catholic Kings (as Ferdinand and Isabella were called) reformed the church and made it their servant. The crusade against the Muslims pleased the militant Spanish church. Popular piety and royal policy led in 1492 to a victory over Granada, the last Muslim-ruled territory of Spain. In the same year, the Spanish state expelled the Jews from its territory.

The five-hundred-year struggle for Christian hegemony in the Iberian Peninsula left the Spanish fiercely religious and strongly suspicious of foreigners. Despite centuries of intermarriage with non-Christians, by the early sixteenth century, purity of blood and orthodoxy of faith became necessary for, and synonymous with, Spanish identity. The Spanish state and church actively engaged in persecuting Muslims and Jews, who for centuries had contributed substantially to cultural and economic life.

In 1492, the crown expelled some 150,000 Jews (some estimates are considerably higher). The thousands of Jews who converted were watched by a church tribunal, **the Inquisition**, for signs of backsliding. The clerical inquisitors employed brutal means of interrogation and torture, such as waterboarding, to ferret out newly converted Christians and their descendants who were suspected of secretly practicing Judaism. Death by fire, sometimes in elaborate public ceremonies, was the ultimate penalty. Muslims also bore the pain of persecution: forced conversions, investigations, torture, and executions conducted by the Inquisition and, finally, mass expulsion in 1609 through 1614. The Inquisition represented the repressive side of the Spanish genius for conquest and administration, and its shadow stretched down through the centuries well into the twentieth, as witnessed by the support the Spanish clergy gave to the far-right regime of Francisco Franco (d. 1975). By contrast, today, Spain is a flourishing democracy.

The wars against the Muslims rendered the Spanish army one of the finest in Europe. With a superior army, the great magnates pacified, and the church and the Inquisition under monarchical control, the Catholic Kings expanded their interests and embarked on an imperialist foreign policy in Europe and the New World. It had extraordinary consequences. Ultimately, Spain became dominant in the Americas. Intent on expanding their territory, Ferdinand and Isabella gambled on Columbus's voyage to what he and they thought was a new passage to India. The gamble paid off in the discovery of what eventually came to be known as North and South America. Beginning in 1519 in Mexico, the conquistador Hernando Cortés, using only six hundred foot soldiers and sixteen horses, defeated the Aztec nation. This feat was partly due to the superiority of Spanish technology, but also to the condition of the Aztec nation, which was struggling to maintain a hold over its own people and over scores of other Mexican tribes that it had, in some cases, brutally subdued. *Hidalgos,* members of the minor aristocracy, led the Spanish forces. As younger sons of impoverished aristocrats, war was their means to riches and land. Unlike the great and wealthy aristocrats, they would serve the crown at home and abroad as soldiers and often as bureaucrats. Their loyalty to the king was matched only by their fierce ambition. The Spanish hidalgos had their counterparts in France and elsewhere. The bureaucracy and army of the early modern states were very important avenues for lesser nobles to obtain and keep elite status.

The Reign of Charles V: Hapsburg, King of Spain, and Holy Roman Emperor

Through a series of shrewd marriage agreements for their children, Ferdinand and Isabella laid the foundation of their dynasty while at the same time strengthening their international alliances. As a result, their grandson, Charles, who ruled from 1516 to 1556, inherited Spain, the Netherlands, Austria, Sardinia, Sicily, the kingdom of Naples, and Franche-Comté. In 1519, the same year as the conquest of Mexico, he was also elected Holy Roman Emperor (partly through bribery). Thus, he became the most powerful monarch in Europe. But in the course of his reign, problems emerged that would eventually lead to Spain's decline and weaken the Hapsburg dynasty, to which he had been heir through marriage.

Charles's inheritance was simply too vast to be governed effectively. The Lutheran Reformation in Germany proved to be the first successful challenge to Hapsburg power. It opened the first phase in the religious and political struggle between Catholic Spain and Protestant Europe. That struggle, which dominated the last half of the sixteenth century, ultimately reduced Spanish influence and led to the loss of the northern Low Countries and the further decentralization of the Holy Roman Empire.

The achievements of Charles V's reign rested on the army and bureaucracy. The Hapsburg Empire in the New World was vast and, on the whole, was effectively administered and policed, partly by the Catholic clergy. Out of a sprawling empire, with its exploited native populations, came the greatest flow of gold and silver the world had ever witnessed. Constant warfare in Europe, particularly in Italy and against the Turks in the Mediterranean, coupled with the immensity of the Spanish administrative network, required a steady intake of capital. But in the long run, this easy access to income was detrimental to the Spanish economy. There was no incentive for the development of domestic industry, entrepreneurship, or international commerce. Indeed, the influx of gold fostered an inflationary spiral. Constant war perpetuated a social order geared to the aggrandizement of a military class rather than to the development of a commercial class. Although war expanded Spain's power in the sixteenth century, it also sowed the seeds for the financial crises of the 1590s and beyond, and for the eventual decline of Spain as a world power.

Philip II

The reign of Philip II (1556–1598) was pivotal and exposed the strengths and weaknesses of the Spanish state. Philip II inherited the throne from his father, Charles V, who left his son with a large empire in both the Old World and the New. Philip II's zeal for Catholicism ruled his private conduct and infused his foreign policy. With the necessary revenue in hand, he launched an offensive against the Turks as well as international Protestantism.

To Philip II, being truly Spanish meant being Christian in faith and blood; the racist tendencies already evident in the later fifteenth century gained full expression during his reign. Increasingly, the country came to be ruled by an

ROMEYN DE HOOGHE, *ATROCITIES OF WAR,* **1673.** Nothing fueled Protestant zeal more than the history and images that depicted the Spanish assault on the Low Countries in the 1580s. Here, nearly one hundred years after the persecution of Dutch Protestants by the Spanish army, the most talented engraver of the late seventeenth century depicted the horrors inflicted on the Dutch during their revolt from Spain. (INTERFOTO/History/Alamy Limited.)

exclusive class of **Old Christians,** who claimed to be untainted because for centuries they had refused to marry Muslims or Jews, even if Jews were converts to Christianity—*New Christians,* as they were called. The Old Christians controlled the church, religious orders, and the Inquisition. Tradition enabled them to preserve an imperial system urgently in need of reform.

Morose and withdrawn, Philip II worked incessantly without any obvious pleasures. He took a fine comb to his ministers' reports, yet despite all the editing, he was strangely indecisive. Some problems remained unsolved for years; frustrated advisers begged the king to take action.

In the 1560s, Philip sent the largest land army ever assembled in Europe into the Netherlands in order to crush Protestant-inspired opposition to Spanish authority. The ensuing revolt of the Netherlands lasted until 1609, and in losing the Netherlands, Spain lost its industrial heartland. In 1576 and again in 1585, the Spanish army, in a desperate attempt to defeat the rebels, sacked Antwerp, the leading commercial and banking city in northern Europe. Within ten years, Antwerp's trade and many of its educated and commercial elite went to Amsterdam, a Protestant stronghold. Amsterdam replaced Antwerp as an international capital and became the center of the new Dutch Republic. Its stock exchange dominated global commerce into the late eighteenth century, when it was replaced by London.

By the 1580s, Philip's foreign policy followed his religious zeal. He intervened in the French religious wars on the Catholic side, although his intervention gave little to Spain in the way of power or influence. Philip's religious fervor also led to the disastrous attempt in 1588 to invade England with an armada of ships.

For Philip, an assault on Protestant England constituted a holy crusade against the "heretic and bastard" Queen Elizabeth; he particularly resented English assistance to Protestant rebels in the Dutch wars. Sailing from Lisbon in May, the Spanish Armada, twenty-two thousand men strong, met with humiliating defeat. Its large ships could not negotiate the treacherous English Channel, and the English ships easily outmaneuvered them, breaking their formation by crashing fire ships into them. Moreover, strong winds, typical for May, drove the Armada out of striking position.

The defeat had a psychological effect throughout Europe. The Spanish openly pondered what they had done to incur divine displeasure. Protestant Europe, however, hailed the victory as a sign of its election, and the "Protestant wind" stirred by divine intervention entered the mythology of English nationalism. In the rise and fall of nations, self-assurance has played a crucial, if inexplicable, role. The cultural renaissance associated with the England of Shakespeare owed its vigor and confidence in part to its pride at being Protestant and independent of Spanish influence.

The End of the Spanish Hapsburgs

After the defeat of the Armada, Spain gradually and reluctantly abandoned its imperial ambitions in northern Europe. By the first quarter of the seventeenth century, enormous weaknesses had surfaced in Spanish economic and social life. From the 1590s onward, bankruptcy reappeared while the agricultural economy, at the heart of any early modern nation, stagnated. At the height of its power, Spain had never devoted enough attention to increasing domestic production.

Despite these setbacks, Spain became an aggressor during the Thirty Years' War (1618–1648), at its heart a religious struggle for mastery over the Holy Roman Empire. The Austrian branch of the Catholic Hapsburg family joined forces with their Spanish cousins, and neither the Protestant Swedes and Germans nor the Dutch could stop them. Only French participation in the Thirty Years' War on the Protestant side tipped the balance decisively against the Hapsburgs. In the course of the war, large portions of what is today Germany were destroyed, and its population fled or was killed. Spanish aggression brought no victories, and with the Peace of Westphalia (1648), Spain officially recognized the independence of the Netherlands and cut its ties with the Austrian branch of the family.

By 1660, the domination of Europe by the Spanish Hapsburgs had come to an end. The rule of the Protestant princes had been secured in the Holy Roman Empire; the largely Protestant Dutch Republic flourished; Portugal and its slave colony of Brazil were independent of Spain; and dominance over European affairs had passed to France. The quality of material life in Spain deteriorated rapidly, and the ever-present gap between the rich and the poor widened. The traditional aristocracy and the church retained their land and power but failed conspicuously to produce effective leadership. With decline came rigidity of institutions and values. Spain remained authoritarian far longer than other European countries. Democratic revolutions did not occur in a country dominated exclusively by the landed elite and the church. The commercial elite became increasingly important in England, the Netherlands, and France, but failed to develop in monarchical and agricultural Spain.

The Spanish experience illustrates two aspects of the history of state formation. First, the state as empire can survive and prosper only if the domestic economic base continues to expand. Second, living off subjugated colonies ultimately means economic stagnation and can lead to technological backwardness at home.

In general, states with a vital and aggressive mercantile class generally prospered in the early modern period. In such states, the landed and commercial elites were complimentary. The latter comprised those who invested, or even participated, in the market and manufacturing, whether at home or abroad. In Spain, however, the old aristocracy and the church continued to dominate and control society and its mores. They not only despised manual labor and profit-taking through trade but also showed little interest in science and technology.

THE GROWTH OF FRENCH POWER

Two states in the early modern period succeeded most effectively in consolidating the power of their central governments: France and England. Each became a model of a very different form of statehood. The English model evolved into a constitutional monarchy. Parliament limited the king's power, and the rights of the English people were protected by law and tradition. The French model emphasized at every turn the glory of the king and, by implication, the **sovereignty** of the dynastic state and its right to stand above the interests of its subjects. France's monarchy became absolute, although very gradually. Only by the 1660s did the court and king achieve political hegemony.

When Hugh Capet became king of France in 987, as an aristocrat he was merely first among equals. From this small power base, more symbolic than real and centered in Paris, Hugh Capet's successors extended their territory and dominion at the expense of aristocratic power. To administer their territories, the Capetians established an efficient bureaucracy composed of townsmen and trustworthy lesser nobles who, unlike the great feudal lords, owed their wealth and status directly to the king. These royal officials, essential to monarchical power, collected the king's feudal dues and administered justice. At the same time, French kings emphasized that they had been selected by God to rule, a theory known as the *divine right of kings*. This theory conferred sanctity, and the French kings used it to enforce their commands over rebellious lords and to resist papal claims of dominance over the French church.

Yet medieval French kings never sought absolute power. Only during the reign of Louis XIV (d. 1715) did the power base of the French monarchy consolidate. The king and his court, as well as his representatives in the provinces, managed to rule without formal consultations with their subjects. In the Middle Ages, the French monarchs recognized the rights of, and consulted with, local representative assemblies, which represented the three estates, or orders, in society. These assemblies (whether regional or national) consisted of deputies drawn from the various elites: the clergy as the first estate, the nobility as the second estate, and the rest of the population as the third estate. The Estates met as circumstances—such as wars, taxes, or local disputes—warranted, and the king alone could summon the Estates General. Medieval French kings consulted these assemblies mainly to give legitimacy to their demands and credibility to their administration. They also recognized that the courts—especially the highest court, the *Parlement* of Paris—had the right to administer the king's justice with a minimum of royal interference. Medieval kings were never the originators of law; they were its guarantors and administrators.

In France, war served the interests of a monarchy bent on consolidating its power and authority. As a result of the Hundred Years' War (1337–1453), the English were eventually driven from France, their claims to the French throne dashed. In the process of war, the French monarchy grew richer. War enabled the French kings to levy new taxes, often enacted without the consent of the Estates General, and to maintain a large standing army under royal command. The Hundred Years' War also inspired allegiance to the king as the visible symbol of France. The war heightened the French sense of national identity; the English were a common enemy, discernibly different in manners, language, dress, and appearance.

Religion and the French State

In every emergent state, tension existed between the monarch and the papacy. At issue was control over the church within that territory—over its personnel, its wealth, and, of course, its pulpits, from which an illiterate majority learned what their leaders wanted them to know, religious doctrines but also obedience to civil authority. The monarch's power to make church appointments could ensure a complacent church, one that was willing to preach about the king's divine right to rule and that would offer no resistance to his authority. Centuries of tough bargaining with the papacy paid off when, in 1516, Francis I (1515–1547) concluded the Concordat of Bologna, by which Pope Leo X permitted the French king to nominate, and therefore effectively to appoint, his choice of bishops in the French church.

The Concordat of Bologna laid the foundation for the *Gallican church*—a term signifying the immense power and authority of the Catholic Church in France as sanctioned and overseen by the French kings. By the early sixteenth century, religious homogeneity had strengthened the central government at the expense of papal authority. This ecclesiastical and religious settlement lay at the heart of monarchical authority. Consequently, by the 1520s, the Protestant Reformation threatened the very survival of France as a unified state. Throughout the early modern period, French kings assumed that France must be governed by one king, one faith, and one set of laws. Any alternative to that unity offered the aristocracy or the clergy the opportunity to channel religious dissent into their service at the expense of royal authority. Once linked, religious and political opposition to any central government could be extremely dangerous.

During the decades that followed, partly through the efforts of the Huguenot (Protestant) underground and partly because the French king and his ministers vacillated in their attempts at persecution, the Protestant minority grew in strength and dedication. By challenging the authority of the Catholic Church, Protestants were also inadvertently challenging royal authority; the Gallican church and the French monarchy supported each other. Protestantism became the basis for a political movement of an increasingly revolutionary nature.

From 1562 to the final peace of 1598, France experienced waves of religious wars; the king lost control over vast areas of the kingdom. In 1579, extreme Huguenot theorists published the *Vindiciae contra Tyrannos*. This anonymous attack on the rights of kings, combined with a call to action, was the first of its kind in early modern times. It justified rebellion against, and even the execution of, an unjust king. European monarchs might claim power and divinely sanctioned authority, but by the late sixteenth century, their subjects had available the moral justification to oppose their monarch's will, by force if necessary. Significantly, this same treatise was translated into English in 1648, a year before Parliament publicly executed Charles I, king of England.

The French monarchy foundered in the face of a combined religious and political opposition. The era of royal supremacy ushered in by Francis I came to an abrupt end during the reign of his successor, Henry II (1547–1559). Wed to Catherine de' Medici, a member of the powerful Italian

banking family, Henry occupied himself not with the concerns of government but with the pleasures of the hunt. The sons who succeeded Henry—Francis II (1559–1560), Charles IX (1560–1574), and Henry III (1574–1589)—were uniformly weak. In this power vacuum, their mother, Catherine, emerged as virtual ruler—a queen despised as an Italian, a woman, and a backstairs intriguer. One of the most hated figures of her day, Catherine de' Medici defies dispassionate assessment. She or her son ordered the execution of Protestants by royal troops in Paris—the beginning of the infamous Saint Bartholomew's Day Massacre (1572). The massacre of more than five thousand Protestants became both a symbol and a legend in subsequent European history: a symbol of the excesses of religious zeal and a legend of Protestant martyrdom, which gave renewed energy to the cause of international Protestantism.

The civil wars begun in 1562 continued after the massacre. They dragged on until the death of the last Valois king in 1589. The Valois failure to produce a male heir to the throne placed Henry, duke of Bourbon and a Protestant, in line to succeed to the French throne. Realizing that the overwhelmingly Catholic population would not accept a Protestant king, Henry (apparently without much regret) renounced his adopted religion and embraced the church. His private religious beliefs may never be known, but outward conformity to the religion of the Catholic majority offered peace and the reestablishment of political stability. Under the reign of Henry IV (1589–1610), a form of religious toleration returned. Henry granted it to his Protestant subjects through the Edict of Nantes (1598), but they were never welcomed in significant numbers into the royal bureaucracy. Throughout the seventeenth century, every French king attempted to undermine the Protestants' regional power bases and ultimately to destroy their religious liberties.

Louis XIV: The Consolidation of French Monarchical Power

The defeat of Protestantism as a national force set the stage for the final consolidation of the French state under the great Bourbon kings, Louis XIII and Louis XIV. Louis XIII (1610–1643) depended

THE HALL OF MIRRORS IN THE ROYAL PALACE AT VERSAILLES. Immense and grand, Versailles was the wonder of the age. Like the person of the king, it said to his subjects: "I am grandeur incarnate." Even by today's standards, it was an impressive building, both inside and out. (© Massimo Listri/Corbis.)

on an efficient and trustworthy bureaucracy, a renewable treasury, and constant vigilance against the localized claims to power by the great aristocracy and Protestant cities and towns. Cardinal Richelieu, who served as the young Louis XIII's chief minister from 1624 to 1642, became the great architect of French absolutism.

Richelieu's political morality rested on one principle, embodied in a phrase he invented: *raison d'état*, reason of state. Richelieu applied the principle as he brought under the king's control the disruptive and antimonarchical elements within French society. He increased the power of the central bureaucracy; attacked the power of independent, and often Protestant, towns and cities; and harassed their Huguenot inhabitants. Above all, he humbled the great nobles by limiting their effectiveness as councilors to the king

and prohibiting their traditional privileges, such as using a duel rather than court action to settle grievances. Reason of state also guided Richelieu's foreign policy. It required that France turn against Catholic Spain and join the Protestant, and hence anti-Spanish, side in the Thirty Years' War. This led to a decisive victory for French power on the Continent.

Richelieu died in 1642, and Louis XIII the following year. Mazarin, a cardinal who had never been ordained a priest and was an Italian by birth, took charge during the minority of Louis XIV (he was five years old when Louis XIII died) and continued Richelieu's policies. Mazarin's heavy-handed actions produced a rebellious reaction, the *Fronde*, a series of street riots that eventually cost the government control over Paris and lasted from 1648 to 1653. Centered in Paris and supported by the great aristocracy, the courts, and the city's poorer classes, the Fronde threatened to develop into a full-scale uprising. It might have done so but for one crucial factor: its leadership was divided. Court judges (lesser nobles who had often just risen from the ranks of the bourgeoisie) deeply distrusted the great aristocrats and refused in the end to make common cause with them, and both groups feared disorders among the urban masses. Early modern states faced deep trouble only when the elites united against them.

When Louis XIV finally came to the throne in 1661, he vowed that what he had witnessed in Paris, when the Fronde brought street rioters to the palace windows, would never be repeated. Aided by his brilliant minister of finance, Jean Baptiste Colbert, Louis XIV crafted the absolutist state. He became the source of all power. Local elites or officials were expected to look to the central government for everything, from taxes to noble titles and exclusive privileges for perfume manufacturing or coal extraction. Provincial bureaucrats reported to ministers based in Paris. Indeed, even road engineers were sent out from Paris. The army was made larger and more professional, gaining, in addition, an architecture and engineering corps. The state also established a military school and sponsored academies for science, literature, and language. Intellectuals received court patronage and pensions, but only if they said what the crown wanted to hear. Colbert turned intelligence gathering into an art and put France on a firm financial footing. After his death thrift was replaced by royal excesses.

Under Louis XIV, the state became the major player in everything, from dredging the rivers to awarding manufacturing monopolies. No absolute monarch in Western Europe had ever before held so much personal authority or commanded such a vast and effective military and administrative machine. Louis XIV's reign finished the process of increasing monarchical authority. Intelligent, cunning, and possessing a unique understanding of the requirements of his office, Louis XIV became the envy of his age.

Perhaps the most brilliant of Louis XIV's many policies was his treatment of members of the aristocracy. He simply dispensed with their services as influential advisers. He treated them to elaborate rituals, feasts, processions, displays, and banquets,

but as they played, their power dwindled. The wiser aristocrats stayed home on their estates. For those who ventured to Versailles in search of power and glory, the possibility of financial ruin loomed. Few could keep up with the level of the king's spending.

Louis XIV's domestic policies, not surprisingly, centered on the incessant search for new revenues. Versailles and its banquets cost a fortune. So too did his wars, which Louis XIV waged to excess. He relied on Colbert, who improved methods of tax collecting, promoted new industries, and encouraged international trade. Such ambitious national policies were possible because Louis XIV inherited the efficient system of administration that had been introduced by Richelieu. Instead of relying on the local aristocracy to collect royal taxes and to administer royal policies, Richelieu had appointed the king's own men as *intendants*—functionaries with wide powers who were dispatched into the provinces. At first, their mission had been temporary and their success minimal, but gradually, they became a permanent feature of royal administration. During the reign of Louis XIV, the country was divided into thirty-two districts, controlled by intendants. Operating with a total bureaucracy of about a thousand officials and no longer bothering even to consult the parlements (courts of law) or the Estates, Louis XIV ruled absolutely.

Why did such a system of absolute authority work? The peasants occasionally revolted, but why did the old aristocracy not rise in rebellion? For the aristocrats, the loss of political authority was not accompanied by a comparable loss in wealth and social position; indeed, quite the contrary was true. During the seventeenth century, the French nobility—2 percent of the population—controlled approximately 20 to 30 percent of the total national income. The church, too, fared well under Louis, receiving good tax arrangements, provided it preached about the king's divinely given rights. Although there were peasant upheavals throughout the century, the sheer size of the royal army and police—more than 300,000 by the end of Louis's reign—made successful revolt nearly impossible. When, in the early 1700s, a popular religious rebellion led by Protestant visionaries broke out in the south, royal troops crushed it. Thus, absolutism rested

Louis XIV, *Instructions for the Dauphin*

In the Instructions for the Dauphin *of 1665, Louis XIV boasted to his heir that he understood the key to successful kingship.*

[Successful kingship lies in being] informed of everything, listening to the lowliest of my subjects, always knowing the number and character of my troops and the condition of my strongholds, constantly issuing orders for all their needs, dealing directly with foreign envoys, receiving and reading dispatches, drafting some of the replies personally and giving the substance of the others to my secretaries, regulating the collections and the expenditures of my state, having those whom I place in important positions report directly to me, maintaining greater secrecy in my affairs than any of my predecessors, distributing graces as I choose, and keeping my servants, unless I am mistaken—although showered with graces for themselves and their families—in modesty far removed from the loftiness and from the power of prime ministers.

Questions for Analysis

1. Could any one human being do all that Louis XIV claimed he was doing?
2. Why is Louis XIV concerned to keep his servants away from his prime ministers?

Jacob Soll, *The Information Master: The Rise and Fall of Jean-Baptiste Colbert's Secret State Library* (Ann Arbor: University of Michigan Press, 2010).

on the complicity of the old aristocracy, the self-aggrandizement of government officials, the church's doctrines, the revenues squeezed out of the peasantry, and the power of a huge military machine.

Yet Louis XIV's system was fatally flawed. Without any effective check on his power and on his dreams of international conquest, no limit was imposed on the state's capacity to make war or spend money. By the 1680s, his domestic and foreign policies turned violently aggressive. In 1685, he revoked the Edict of Nantes, and thousands of French Protestants fled or were imprisoned. In 1689, he embarked on a military campaign to gain territory from the Holy Roman Empire. And in 1701, he tried to bring Spain under the control of the Bourbon dynasty. Louis XIV, however, underestimated the strength of his northern rivals, England and the Dutch Republic. Their combined power, in alliance with the Holy Roman Empire and the Austrians, defeated Louis XIV's ambitions and left his treasury empty. In the winter of 1709–1710, famine stalked the land but no publications were permitted to discuss it.

The War of the Spanish Succession was fought on the battlefields of northern Europe. Out of it, the Austrians acquired the southern Netherlands (Belgium) and thus a buffer against the possibility of a French overrun of the Low Countries. Most dramatically, however, the war created a balance of power in Europe. Britain emerged as a major force in European affairs, the counterweight against the French colossus. Anglo-French rivalry dominated the international politics of the eighteenth century, creating a fragile balance of power in the Atlantic world.

These long wars emptied the royal treasury. By the late seventeenth century, taxes had risen intolerably and were levied mostly on those least able to pay: the peasants. In the early 1700s, the combination of taxes, bad harvests, and plague led to widespread poverty, misery, and starvation in large areas of France. Thus, for the great majority of French people, absolutism meant a decline in living standards and a significant increase in mortality rates. Absolutism also required surveillance of the population. Royal authorities censored books; spied on heretics, Protestants,

LOUIS XIV. By every gesture and pose, Louis XIV sought to display grandeur and to embody monarchy. His dress and affect were meant to awe and intimidate. (Masterpics/Alamy Limited.)

and freethinkers; and even tortured and executed opponents of state policy.

By 1715, France was a tightly governed society whose treasury was bankrupt. Protestants had been driven into exile or forced to convert. Strict censorship laws closely governed publishing, causing a brisk trade in clandestine books and manuscripts. Direct taxes burdened the poor and were legally evaded by the aristocracy. Critics of state policy within the church had been effectively marginalized. And over the long run, foreign wars had brought no significant gains.

In the France of Louis XIV, the dynastic and absolutist state reached maturity and began to display some of its classic characteristics: centralized bureaucracy; royal patronage to enforce

allegiance; a system of taxation universally but inequitably applied; and suppression of political opposition, either through the use of patronage or, if necessary, through force. On a more positive note, the state cultivated the arts and sciences as a means of increasing national power and prestige. Together, these policies enabled France and its monarchs to achieve political stability, enforce a uniform system of law, and channel the country's wealth and resources into the service of the state as a whole (see Primary Source box).

Nonetheless, at his death in 1715, Louis XIV left a bureaucracy and onerous taxation that were vastly in need of overhaul. But because this system favored the church and the nobility, reforming it was virtually impossible. The pattern of war, excessive taxation of the lower classes, and spending beyond revenues had damaged France's finances. Yet the bureaucracy of the absolutist state continued to grow and extend its influence into every area of trade. To this day, perfectly preserved pieces of silk and cotton cloth from every French province sit in the Parisian archives of the government. They had been sent there for inspection. Only when the king's ministers had approved the samples could the cloth from which they had been cut be sold in the open market, with the king's seal. By the 1780s, manufacturers clamored for freer markets; fewer, or at least faster, inspections; and more freedom to experiment. They smuggled and cheated the inspectors while looking across the Channel with envy at the power, wealth, and freedom of England's industry and its merchants. The discontent of French manufacturers contributed to the causes of the French Revolution of 1789.

THE GROWTH OF LIMITED MONARCHY AND CONSTITUTIONALISM IN ENGLAND

England achieved national unity earlier than any other major European state. Its island geography freed it from the border disputes that plagued emerging states in Continental Europe. By an accident of fate, its administrative structure also developed in such a way as to encourage centralization. In 1066, William, duke of Normandy and vassal

ENGRAVING OF THE FRENCH INVASION OF THE DUTCH REPUBLIC IN 1672, BY
BERNARD PICART. France's bellicosity against its neighbors was graphically
depicted in this engraving, which depicts a scene from the French invasion of
the Dutch Republic in 1672. This image may have been propaganda, but it was
effective in branding the French king, Louis XIV, as a tyrant. (Fine Arts Museum of San
Francisco, Achenbach Foundation for Graphic Arts A059746.)

to the French king, had invaded and conquered
England, acquiring at a stroke the entire kingdom.
In contrast, the French kings took centuries to
make the territory of France their domain.

As conquerors, the Norman kings intermarried
with their powerful subjects, such as earls and
barons, and consulted with the church and the
nobility. By the middle of the thirteenth century,
these consultations, or *parlays*, came to be called
parliaments. Increasingly, kings invited parliament's representatives from the counties—knights
and burgesses. Gradually, these lesser-than-noble

but landed and prominent representatives came
to regard Parliament as a means of redressing
their grievances. In turn, the later medieval kings
saw Parliament as a means of exercising control
and raising taxes. By 1297, the Lords (the upper house) and the Commons (the lower house)
had obtained the king's agreement that no direct
taxes could be levied without their consent. By the

Map 16.2 EUROPE, 1648 ▶
By 1648, Europe was exhausted by war.

(© 2016 Cengage Learning.)

RUSSIA

Black Sea

FINLAND

ESTONIA

LIVONIA

•Vilna

POLAND

•Warsaw

MOLDAVIA

WALLACHIA

TRANSYLVANIA

OTTOMAN EMPIRE

Crete
(To Rep. of Venice)

Athens

Lepanto

NORWAY

SWEDEN

Baltic Sea

PRUSSIA

Danzig

POMERANIA

Belgrade

Copenhagen

DENMARK

JUTLAND

SCHLESWIG

Hamburg

MECKLEN-BURG

Berlin•

BRANDENBURG

SAXONY

SILESIA

BOHEMIA

Prague•

MORAVIA

Vienna•

AUSTRIA

REPUBLIC OF VENICE

PAPAL STATES

NORTH SEA

North Sea

SCOTLAND

Edinburgh•

Durham•

ENGLAND

London•

English Channel

IRELAND

Dublin•

UNITED NETHERLANDS

Amsterdam•

Antwerp•

SPANISH NETHERLANDS

Cologne•

WEST-PHALIA

HESSE

Mainz•

Worms•

BAVARIA

Augsburg•

SWITZERLAND

FRANCHE-COMTÉ

Geneva•

SAVOY

MILAN

PIEDMONT

GENOA

Genoa•

Rome•

Naples•

FLORENCE

Corsica
(to Genoa)

Sardinia

NAPLES

Palermo•

Sicily

Paris•

FRANCE

Nantes•

ATLANTIC OCEAN

PORTUGAL

Lisbon•

SPAIN

Madrid•

CASTILE

ARAGON

CATALONIA

VALENCIA

ANDALUSIA

Granada•

Mediterranean Sea

400 Mi.

400 Km.

200

200

0   0

Austrian Hapsburg lands

Spanish Hapsburg lands

Prussian lands

German states

Swedish lands

Boundary of Holy Roman Empire

385

fourteenth century, Parliament had become a permanent institution of government. Its power was entirely subservient to the crown, but its right to question royal decisions had been established.

The English Parliament and Constitution

The medieval English Parliament possessed two characteristics that distinguished it from its many Continental counterparts, such as the various French Estates. The English Parliament was national, not provincial; more important, its representatives were elected across caste lines, with voting rights dependent on property, not on noble birth or status. These representatives voted as individuals rather than collectively as clergy, nobles, or commoners—that is, as Estates. In the Middle Ages, Parliament and the monarchy were interdependent; they were seen not as rivals but as complementary forms of centralized government. That very interdependence, however, would ultimately lead to conflict.

The constitution, too, emerged during the Middle Ages in England. It comprised unwritten and written precedents, laws, and royal acts that came to embody the basic principles of government. In contrast to the French model, England developed into a *constitutional* monarchy. The most famous document, Magna Carta (1215), guaranteed certain aristocratic privileges and was read at the opening meeting of almost every Parliament the king called. The theoretical foundation for the constitution—which was never a written document—grew out of legal practices and customs described under the generic term *common law*. Whereas feudal law applied only to a local region, common law extended throughout the realm and served as a unifying force.

The Tudor Achievement

Despite having a Parliament and constitution, England in the fifteenth century could be a lawless place where local noblemen made war on their neighbors largely unchecked by central government. One such war, the War of the Roses (1455–1485), pitted two noble families against

HENRY VIII. Although the ruler of a second-rate power, Henry VIII sought to impress upon his subjects that he was a new and powerful monarch. He sought to compete in style, if not in power, with the French and the Spanish kings. (GL Archive/Alamy Limited.)

each other in a struggle for domination. Out of it, the Tudors emerged triumphant, in the person of Henry VII (1485–1509), who spent much of his reign consolidating and extending his authority. He revitalized and remade the institutions of central government. Henry VII's goal was to check the unruly nobility. Toward this end, he brought commoners into the government. These commoners, unlike the great magnates, could be channeled into royal service because they craved what the king offered: financial rewards and elevated social status. Although they did not fully displace the aristocracy, commoners were brought into Henry VII's inner circle, into the Privy Council, into the courts, and eventually into all the highest offices of the government. The strength and efficiency of Tudor government were shown during the Reformation, when Henry VIII (1509–1547) made himself head of the English church. This giant step toward increasing royal power grew out of the restored order and stability imposed by his father.

The Henrican and Protestant Reformation in England was a revolution in royal, as well as ecclesiastical, government. It defeated a main obstacle to monarchical authority: the power of the papacy. At the same time, the Reformation greatly enhanced the power of Parliament. Henry VIII used Parliament to consolidate the Reformation because he knew that he needed the support of the lords, the country gentry, and the merchants. Parliament's participation in the Reformation gave it a greater role and sense of importance than it had ever possessed in the past. Nonetheless, the final outcome of this administrative revolution enhanced monarchical power. By the end of his reign, Henry VIII easily possessed as much power as his French rival, Francis I. Indeed, until the early seventeenth century, the history of monarchical power in England, with its absolutist tendencies, was remarkably similar to the Continental pattern. No one could imagine the instability that lay ahead.

At Henry's death, the Tudor bureaucracy and centralized government were strained to the utmost, yet they survived. The government weathered the reign of Henry's sickly son, Edward VI (1547–1553), and the extreme Protestantism of some of his advisers, and it survived the brief and deeply troubled reign of Henry's first daughter, Mary (1553–1558), who brutally tried to return England to Catholicism. At Mary's death, England stood dangerously close to the religious instability and sectarian tension that would undermine the French kings during the final decades of the sixteenth century.

Henry's second daughter, Elizabeth I (1558–1603), initiated a period of peace and religious stability. The Elizabethan period brought a heightened sense of national identity. The English Reformation enhanced that sense, as did the increasing fear of foreign invasion by Spain. The fear was real enough

and lessened only with the defeat of the Spanish Armada in 1588. For the English, the victory seemed like that of David over Goliath, and its value was both symbolic and real. Just as the Spanish agonized about what they had done to offend God, the English smugly concluded that they had pleased him. In the seventeenth century, the English would look back on Elizabeth's reign as a golden age. It was the calm before the storm. In the seventeenth century, a prosperous commercial class emerged, and it would demand a greater say in government.

The social and economic changes of the Elizabethan age can be seen, in microcosm, by looking at the Durham region in northern England. From 1580 to 1640, a new coal-mining industry developed there through the efforts of entrepreneurs—gentlemen with minor lands who, with the aid of engineers, exploited their mineral resources. The wool trade also prospered in Durham. By 1600, social and political tensions had developed. The wool merchants and the entrepreneurial gentry were demanding a greater say in governing the region. They were opposed by the traditional leaders of Durham society: the bishops and the dozen or so aristocratic families with major landholdings and access to the court in London.

This split can be described as one between "court" and "country." In this context, *court* refers to the traditional aristocratic magnates, the church hierarchy, and royal officialdom, and *country* denotes a loose coalition of merchants and rising agricultural and industrial entrepreneurs from the prosperous gentry class, whose economic worth far exceeded their political power. The pattern found in Durham was repeated in other parts of England, generally where industry and commerce grew and prospered. The gentry gained social status and wealth. In the seventeenth century, these social and economic tensions between court and country would help foment revolution. Indeed, English historians have argued that one needs look no further than the new merchant class for the roots of the civil wars of the 1640s.

By the early seventeenth century in England, the descendants of the old feudal aristocracy differed markedly from their Continental counterparts. Isolation from the great wars of the Reformation had produced an aristocracy less militaristic and more ceremonial and commercial in orientation.

Furthermore, the lesser ranks of the landowning aristocracy, gentlemen without titles (the gentry), had prospered significantly in Tudor times. In commercial matters, they were often no shrewder than the great landed magnates, but they had in Parliament, as well as in their counties, an effective and institutionalized means of expressing their political interests. The great nobles, in contrast, had largely abandoned the sword as the primary expression of their political authority without putting anything comparable in its place. Gradually, political initiative was slipping away from the great lords and into the hands of a gentry that was commercially and agriculturally innovative as well as fiercely protective of its local base of political power.

At Elizabeth's accession, male contemporaries worried in print whether she would be up to the task of ruling and urged her court and Privy Council to keep her in line. They were in for a shock as Elizabeth proved to be one of the most able monarchs; she did not hesitate to set policy as she saw fit, much to the annoyance of her advisers. Even the earl of Leicester, widely regarded as one of her suitors, said in 1578 that "our conference with her Majesty about affairs is both seldom and slender."

Elizabeth faced the possibility of rebellion led by her Catholic cousin, Mary Queen of Scots, and in the end, Elizabeth saw to her execution. Elizabeth's greatest test came in 1588 when the Spanish king, Philip II, sent his Armada to invade England for the purpose of restoring it to Catholicism. Consulting her astrologers but armed for battle, Elizabeth rallied the country, and the English fleet got very lucky. A gale-force wind blew the Spanish ships out of striking distance of the mouth of the Thames River, and the Armada was virtually destroyed. The wind that blew that day became known as "the Protestant wind," and Elizabeth went down in history as "good Queen Bess."

Even more so than her father, Elizabeth secured England, though not Ireland, for the Protestant cause. She also gave her name to the age, and Elizabethan England flourished culturally. During her reign, William Shakespeare wrote many of his greatest plays and the London theatre blossomed.

Religion played a vital role in this realignment of political interests and forces. Many of the old aristocracy clung to the Anglicanism of the Henrican Reformation, with bishops and liturgy intact, and some even clung to Catholicism. The newly risen members of the gentry found in the Protestant Reformation a form of religious worship more suited to their independent spirit. They felt that it was their right to appoint their own preachers and that the church should reflect local tastes and beliefs rather than doctrines and ceremonies inherited from a discredited Catholicism. In late Tudor times, gentry and merchant interests fused with Puritanism—the English variety of Calvinism—to produce a political-religious vision with ominous potential. Some historians have argued that, not a new merchant class, but religious tensions account for the civil wars. They add to that argument the errors in judgment made by Charles I.

The English Revolutions, 1640–1660 and 1688–1689

The religious and political forces threatening the monarchy were dealt with ineffectively by the first two Stuart kings: James I (1603–1625) and Charles I (1625–1649). Like their Continental counterparts, both believed in royal absolutism. Essentially, these Stuart kings tried to do in England what Louis XIV later did in France: establish crown and court administrators as the sole governing bodies within the state. The Stuarts, however, lacked an adequate financial and institutional base for absolutism, not least of all a standing army. Nor did they possess the vast independent wealth of the French kings.

Through the established church, the Stuarts preached the doctrine of the divine right of kings. James I, an effective and shrewd administrator, conducted foreign policy without consulting Parliament. In a speech before Parliament, he stated that "it is sedition in subjects to dispute what a king may do in the height of his power. . . . I will not be content that my power be disputed upon."[1]

James I made the standard moves toward creating an absolute monarchy: he centralized and consolidated the power of the government and tried to win over the aristocracy by giving them new offices and titles. To merchants, he gave royal monopolies for everything from soap to coal. James I did not have a sufficient economic base to pay for his largesse. His son and successor, Charles I, had the same problem. But Charles suspended Parliament in 1629 and attempted to rule through his advisers. He had two major goals: to rid the nation of Puritans and to root out the "country" opposition.

Elizabeth I, Queen of England (1558–1603)

Born in 1533, Elizabeth, the daughter of Henry VIII and his second wife, Anne Boleyn, was raised as a Protestant by her father. Fidelity to the Anglican Church may have been basic to Henry's interests, but fidelity to his marriage vows was not. He put Anne Boleyn to death on charges of treason. His marriage to her had led to England's break with the Roman Catholic Church, which would not grant him a divorce from his first wife, Catherine of Aragon, with whom he had failed to produce a male heir. When Henry's second marriage also did not produce the male heir he so deeply desired, he tired of Elizabeth's mother. Hence her tragic end.

The church of Rome regarded Elizabeth as a bastard and never accepted Henry's self-decreed divorce from his first wife. Not surprisingly, in her youth, Elizabeth came to fear marriage and to regard her claim to the English throne as precarious. She became queen in 1558—after the deaths of her half sister, Mary, and half brother, Edward, each of whom had short, tumultuous reigns.

Elizabeth watched and waited, knowing that unless assassinated she would someday be queen. She saw that intervention into the private religious beliefs of her subjects would lead to turmoil and persecution. She vowed never to repeat the mistakes especially of her half-sister, Mary, who persecuted and executed Protestant leaders.

With Elizabeth's accession to the throne, England and Wales returned to the fold of the Henrican Reformation, repudiating the efforts of Queen Mary to force them to revert to Roman Catholicism. Because Mary executed Protestant leaders, she went down in history as "Bloody Mary." Elizabeth recognized that as a woman, she would have to make alliances and never allow herself to be perceived as weak. Yet the obvious form of alliance, marriage to a foreign prince, made her hesitate, probably out of fear that she too would somehow meet the sad fate of her mother. Her steady hand gave England an era of relative peace complete with a flourishing of the arts and letters. By the end of her reign, many courtiers were discontent, but not the mass of population who had come to revere her.

Charles also tried to collect taxes without Parliament's consent. These policies ended in disaster; by 1640, the Puritans and the gentry opposition had grown closer together.

The first English Revolution began in 1640 because Charles I needed money to defend the realm against a recent Scottish invasion. Being staunch Calvinists, the Scots had rebelled against Charles's religious policies and thought that his Anglicanism was a barely concealed Catholicism. Moreover, their clan leaders saw rebellion as a way to get back at the Stuart kings, who long had been a thorn in their side, first when they ruled in Edinburgh and now from their base in London. Charles had no alternative but to call Parliament, and it could now dictate the terms: if Parliament received no concessions from Charles, then it would raise no money to fight the Scots, who

were also demanding payment for every day they occupied the northern territory. Parliament countered the king's requests with demands for rights: consultations with Parliament in matters of taxation, trial by jury, habeas corpus, and a truly Protestant church responsive to the beliefs and interests of its laity. Charles refused these demands, viewing them as an assault on royal authority. He even tried to arrest the leaders of Parliament. In 1642, civil war began. Directed by Parliament and financed by taxes and the merchants, the war was fought by the New Model Army, led by Oliver Cromwell (1599–1658), a Puritan squire with a gift for military leadership.

The two English revolutions became part of a constitutional crisis that lasted two generations. The crisis began in 1640, degenerated into civil war in 1642, and culminated in regicide in 1649.

After the restoration of monarchy in 1660, the crisis flared up again in 1679 through 1681 and was finally resolved by the revolution of 1688–1689—sometimes called the Glorious Revolution. The crisis affected England, Scotland, Ireland, and Wales differently, but in all cases, it led to the consolidation of English power over these territories. Perhaps the native Irish fared worst of all as Cromwell drove thousands to the barren western part of the island.

The civil wars of the 1640s generated a new type of military organization. The New Model Army was financed by Parliament's rich supporters and led by gentlemen farmers. Religious zealots dominated its ranks, along with the usual cross section of poor artisans and day laborers. This citizen army defeated the king, his aristocratic followers, and the Anglican Church's hierarchy. After his defeat, Charles refused to compromise with his Parliamentary captors.

In January 1649, Charles I was publicly executed by order of Parliament. During the interregnum (time between kings) of the next eleven years, Parliament joined with the army to govern the country as a republic. As power was distributed between the army and Parliament, Cromwell proved to be the key player. He had the support of the army's officers and some of its rank and file, and he had been a member of Parliament for many years. However, he gained control over the army only after it was purged of radical groups. Some of these radicals, known as Levellers, wanted to level society, that is, to redistribute property by ending monopolies and to give the vote to all male citizens. In the context of the 1650s, Cromwell was a moderate republican who also believed in limited religious toleration for Protestants, yet history has painted him, somewhat unjustly, as a military dictator.

Both English revolutions were led by a loose coalition of urban merchants and landed gentry imbued with the strict Protestantism of the Continental Reformation. In the 1650s, their success was jeopardized by growing discontent from the poor, who made up the rank and file of the army and demanded that their grievances be rectified. The radicals of the first English Revolution—men such as Gerrard Winstanley, the first theoretician of social democracy in modern times, and John Lilburne, the Leveller—demanded redistribution of property, even communal property; voting rights for the majority of the male population;

and abolition of religious and intellectual elites, whose power and ideology supported the interests of the ruling classes. The radicals rejected Anglicanism and moderate Puritanism; they opted instead for radical politics and free lifestyles. They spurned marriage, and the Quakers even allowed women to preach. They, in effect, created a revolution within the revolution. The radicals terrified devoted Puritans such as Cromwell. By 1660, two years after Cromwell's death, the country was adrift, without effective leadership.

Parliament, having secured the economic interests of its constituency (gentry, merchants, and some small landowners), chose to restore court and crown and invited the exiled son of the executed king to return to the kingship. Having learned the lesson his father had spurned, Charles II (1660–1685) never instituted royal absolutism, although he did try to minimize Parliament's role in the government. His court was a far more open institution than his father's had been, for Charles II feared a similar death.

Charles's brother James II (1685–1688), however, was a foolishly fearless Catholic and an admirer of French absolutism. Having gathered at his court a coterie of Catholic advisers (among them Jesuits) and supporters of royal prerogative, James attempted to bend Parliament and local government to the royal will. James's Catholicism, modeled on French Gallicanism, was the crucial element in his failure. The Anglican Church would not back him, and political forces similar to those that had gathered against his father, Charles I, in 1640 descended on him. But back in the 1650s, the ruling elites had learned their lesson: civil war would produce social discontent among the masses. The upper classes wanted to avoid open warfare and to preserve the monarchy as a constitutional authority but not as an absolute one. Puritanism, with its sectarian fervor and its dangerous association with republicanism, was allowed to play no part in the second English Revolution of 1688–1689.

In early 1688, Anglicans, some aristocrats, and opponents of royal prerogative (members of the Whig party, along with a few Tories) formed a conspiracy against James II. Their purpose was to invite his son-in-law, William of Orange, *stadholder* (head) of the Netherlands and husband of James's Protestant daughter Mary, to invade England and rescue its government from James's control. William and his conspirators, in conjunction with a freely elected Parliament, brought this revolution to a swift conclusion. This dangerous plan succeeded for three main reasons: William and the Dutch desperately needed English support against the threat of a French invasion; James had lost the loyalty of key men in the army, powerful gentlemen in the counties, and the Anglican Church; and the political elite was committed and united in its intentions. William and Mary were declared king and queen by act of Parliament, and William defeated James II's army in Ireland. The last revolution in English history defeated royal absolutism forever. Ironically, while political freedom increased in England, Scotland soon lost its parliament, and Catholics in Ireland were systematically repressed.

This bloodless revolution—the Glorious Revolution—created a new political and constitutional reality. Parliament gained the rights to assemble regularly and to vote on all matters of taxation; the rights of habeas corpus and trial by jury (for men of property and social status) were also secured. These rights were in turn legitimated in a constitutionally binding document, the Bill of Rights (1689). All Protestants, regardless of their sectarian bias, were granted toleration.

The Revolution Settlement of 1688–1689 resolved the profound constitutional and social tensions of the seventeenth century and laid the foundations of the English government that exists today. The year 1688 saw the creation of a new public and political order that would become the envy of enlightened reformers. The Glorious Revolution, says the historian Steve Pincus, succeeded when popular uprisings "that involved the spectrum of English society, from humble men and women who volunteered with their pitchforks . . . to wealthy businessmen and aristocratic landowners" drove out James II and his version of monarchical absolutism.[2] Throughout the eighteenth century, England was ruled by kings and Parliaments that represented the interests of the mercantile and the landed whose prosperity ensured social and political stability. While religion had been important, the English Revolution gave legitimacy to monied and landed interests.

In the end, the English revolutions established English parliamentary government and the rule of law; they also provided a degree of freedom for the propertied. In retrospect, we can see that absolutism according to the French model probably never had a chance in England. England had too

OLIVER CROMWELL. Cromwell wore the simple black of the Puritan gentry and sought to portray himself as a pious warrior. Yet in this portrait, he does have a somewhat regal bearing, and his task demanded that he act like a king without ever becoming one.
(Equestrian Portrait of Oliver Cromwell (1599–1658) (engraving) (b/w photo), English School, (17th century)/Private Collection/The Bridgeman Art Library.)

many gentlemen who possessed enough land to be independent of the crown, yet not so much that they could control whole sections of the kingdom. In addition, monarchs had no effective standing army. But to contemporaries, the issues seemed different: English opponents of absolutism spoke of their rights as granted by their ancient constitution and feudal law, of the need to make the English church truly Protestant, and, among the radicals, of the right of lesser men to establish their property. These opponents possessed an institution—Parliament—through which they could express their grievances. In 1689, the propertied classes invented limited monarchy and a constitutional system based on laws made by Parliament and sanctioned by the king. Very gradually, the monarchical element in that system would yield to the power and authority of parliamentary ministers and state officials. 1688–1689 has been called the "bloodless revolution," but that vastly underestimates the level of violence that gripped the country.

In the nineteenth and twentieth centuries, parliamentary institutions would be gradually and peacefully reformed to express a more democratic social reality. The events of 1688 and 1689 have rightly been described as "the year one," for they fashioned a system of government that operated effectively in Britain and could also be adopted elsewhere with modification. The British system became a model for other forms of representative government that were adopted in France and in the former British colonies, beginning with the United States. It was the model that offered a viable alternative to absolutism.

THE NETHERLANDS: A BOURGEOIS REPUBLIC

One other area in Europe developed a system of representative government that also survived until late in the eighteenth century. The Netherlands (the Low Countries, that is, the seven Dutch provinces and Belgium) had been part of Hapsburg territory since the fifteenth century. When Charles V ascended the Spanish throne in 1516, the Netherlands emerged as the economic linchpin of the Spanish empire. Spain exported wool and bullion to the Low Countries in return for manufactured textiles, hardware, grain, ships, and naval stores. Flanders, with Antwerp as its capital, was the manufacturing and banking center of the Spanish empire.

To the north, cities such as Rotterdam and Amsterdam built and outfitted the Spanish fleet. In The Hague, printers published the Bible in Spanish and in Dutch or Flemish (actually the same language). But in the north, too, Protestantism made significant inroads.

During the reign of Charles V's successor, Philip II, a tightly organized Calvinist minority, with its popular base in the cities and its military strategy founded on sea raids, at first harassed and then aggressively challenged Spanish power. In the 1560s, the Spanish responded by sending the Inquisition into the Netherlands supported by an enormous standing army under the duke of Alva. It was a classic example of overkill; thousands of once-loyal Flemish and Dutch subjects turned against the Spanish crown. The people either converted secretly to Calvinism or aided the revolutionaries. Led by William the Silent (1533–1584), head of the Orange dynasty, the seven northern provinces (Holland, Zeeland, Utrecht, Gelderland, Overijssel, Friesland, and Groningen) joined in the Union of Utrecht (1579) to protect themselves against Spanish aggression. Their determined resistance, coupled with the serious economic weaknesses of the overextended Spanish empire, eventually produced unexpected success for the northern colonies. They also formed the first state to articulate the notion that the government should leave people to their religious preferences.

By 1609, the seven northern provinces were effectively free of Spanish control and loosely tied together under a republican form of government. Seventeenth-century Netherlands (that is, the Dutch Republic) became a prosperous bourgeois state. Rich from the fruits of manufacture and trade in everything from tulip bulbs to ships—and, not least, slaves—Dutch merchants ruled their cities and provinces with a fierce pride. By the early seventeenth century, this new, highly urbanized nation of only 1.2 million people was practicing the most innovative commercial and financial techniques in Europe.

In this fascinating instance, capitalism and Protestantism fused to do the work of princes; the Dutch state emerged without absolute monarchy, and indeed in opposition to it. From that experience, the ruling Dutch oligarchy retained a deep distrust of hereditary monarchy and of central government. The exact position of the House of Orange remained a vexing constitutional question until well into the eighteenth century. The oligarchs and their party, the Patriots, favored a republic without a single head, ruled by them locally and in the Estates General. The Calvinist clergy, old aristocrats, and a vast section of the populace—all for very different reasons—wanted the head of the House of Orange to govern as stadholder of the provinces—in effect, as a limited monarch in a republican state. These unresolved political tensions between the center and the localities prevented the Netherlands from developing a form of republican government to rival the stability of the British system of limited monarchy.

The Dutch achievement came in other areas, particularly in art and technological innovation.

Calvinism had provided the ideology of revolution and national identity. Capital, in turn, created a unique cultural milieu in the Dutch urban centers of Amsterdam, Rotterdam, Utrecht, and The Hague. Wide toleration without a centralized system of censorship made the Dutch book trade, which often disseminated works by refugees from the Spanish Inquisition and later by French Protestants, the most vital in Europe right up to the French Revolution. By 1700, half the books published in Europe were printed in the Dutch Republic. And the sights and sounds of a prosperous population, coupled with a politically engaged and rich bourgeoisie, fed the imagination, as well as the purses, of various artistic schools. Rembrandt van Rijn, Jan Steen, Frans Hals, Jan Vermeer, and Jan van de Velde are at the top of a long list of great Dutch artists—many of them also refugees. They left timeless images portraying the people of the only republican state to endure in the course of the seventeenth century. By 1650, the Dutch Republic had become the richest state in Europe, possibly in the world. Only after invasion by the French revolutionaries in 1795 did the Dutch Republic confront the weaknesses of highly localized government and adopt a national constitution.

THE HOLY ROMAN EMPIRE:
THE FAILURE TO UNIFY GERMANY

In contrast to the English, French, Spanish, and Dutch experiences in the early modern period, the Germans failed to achieve national unity. This failure to unify is tied to the history of the Holy Roman Empire. That union of various central European territories was created in the tenth century, when Otto I, in a deliberate attempt to revive Charlemagne's empire, was crowned "emperor of the Romans" by the pope. Later, the title was changed to "Holy Roman Emperor." The empire consisted of mostly German-speaking principalities.

Otto and his medieval successors busied themselves not with administering their territories but with attempting to gain control over the rich Italian peninsula and dealing with the challenges presented by powerful popes. Meanwhile, members of the German nobility extended and consolidated their rule over their peasants and over various towns and cities within the empire. Their aristocratic power remained a constant obstacle to German unity. Only by incorporating the nobility into the fabric of the state's power, court, and army and by sanctioning their oppressive control of the peasants would Holy Roman Emperors very gradually manage to create a unified German state.

In the medieval and early modern periods, the Holy Roman Emperors depended on powerful noble lords—including archbishops and bishops—for support because the office of emperor was elective, not hereditary. German noble princes—including the archbishops of Cologne and Mainz, the Hohenzollern ruler of Brandenburg, and the duke of Saxony, electors responsible for choosing the Holy Roman Emperor—were fiercely independent. All regarded themselves as autonomous powers. These decentralizing tendencies were highly developed by the thirteenth century, and the emperors gradually realized that they were losing control of the outer frontiers of the empire. The French had conducted a successful military incursion into northern Italy and on the western frontier of the empire. Hungary had fallen to the Turks, and the Swiss, given their terrain, were impossible to beat into submission. At the same time, the Hapsburgs maneuvered themselves into a position from which they could monopolize the imperial elections.

The Holy Roman Empire in the reigns of the Hapsburg emperors Maximilian I (1493–1519) and Charles V (1519–1556) might have achieved a degree of cohesion comparable with that in France and Spain. Certainly, the impetus of war—against France and against the Turks—required the creation of a large standing army and the taxation to maintain it. Both could have worked to the benefit of a centralized, imperial power. But the Protestant Reformation, which began in 1517, meshed with already well-developed tendencies toward local independence and destroyed the last hope of Hapsburg domination and German unity. Members of the German nobility used the Reformation as a vindication of their local power, and indeed, Martin Luther made just such an appeal to their interests.

At precisely the moment in the 1520s when Charles V had to act with great determination to stop the spread of Lutheranism, he was at war with France over its claims to Italian territory. Charles had no sooner won his Italian territories, in particular the rich city-state of Milan, than he had to make war against the Turks, who in 1529 besieged Vienna. Not until the 1540s was Charles V in a position to attack the Lutheran princes. By then, they had solidified their position and united for mutual protection.

War raged in Germany between the Protestant princes and the imperial army led by Charles V. In 1551, Catholic France entered the war on the Protestant side, and Charles had to flee for his life. Defeated, Charles later abdicated and retired to a Spanish monastery. The Treaty of Augsburg (1555) gave every German prince the right to determine the religion of his subjects. The princes had won their local territories, and a unified German state was never constructed by the Hapsburgs.

When Charles V abdicated in 1556, he divided his kingdom between his son Philip and his brother Ferdinand. Philip inherited Spain and its colonies, as well as the Netherlands. Ferdinand acquired the Austrian territories. The Spanish and Austrian branches of the Hapsburg family defined their interests in common and often waged war accordingly. The enormous international power of the Hapsburgs faltered only in the German states within the Holy Roman Empire. Throughout the sixteenth century, the Austrian Hapsburgs barely managed to control these sprawling and deeply divided German territories. Protestantism, as protected by the Treaty of Augsburg, and the powerful German nobility continued to prevent the creation of a German state.

The Austrian Hapsburg emperors always sought to enhance the power of the Catholic Church and to court the favor of local interests opposed to the nobility. No Hapsburg was ever more fervid in that regard than the Jesuit-trained Archduke Ferdinand II, who ascended the throne of the Holy Roman Empire in Vienna in 1619. He immediately embarked on a policy of Catholic revival and used Spanish officials as his administrators. His policies provoked within the empire a thirty-year-long war that engulfed the whole of Europe.

The Thirty Years' War (1618–1648) began when the Bohemians attempted to put a Protestant king on their throne. The Austrian and Spanish Hapsburgs reacted by sending an army into Bohemia, and suddenly the whole empire was forced to take sides along religious lines. The Bohemian nobility, after centuries of enforcing serfdom, failed to rally the rural masses behind them, and victory went to the emperor. Bohemia and the German states suffered almost unimaginable devastation; ravaging Hapsburg armies sacked and burned three-fourths of each kingdom's towns and practically exterminated its aristocracy.

Until the 1630s, it looked as though the Hapsburgs would succeed in enhancing their power and promoting centralization. But the intervention of Lutheran Sweden, led by Gustavus Adolphus and encouraged by France, wrecked Hapsburg ambitions. The ensuing military conflict devastated vast areas of northern and central Europe. The civilian population suffered untold hardships: soldiers raped women and pillaged the land, and thousands of refugees fled. Partly because the French finally intervened directly, the Spanish Hapsburgs emerged from the Thirty Years' War with no benefits. At the Treaty of Westphalia (1648), their Austrian cousins reaffirmed their right to govern the eastern states of the kingdom, with Vienna as their capital. Austria took shape as a dynastic state, and the German territories in the empire remained fragmented by the independent interests of their largely recalcitrant feudal nobility. In consequence, the Thirty Years' War shaped the course of German history into the late nineteenth century.

THE EMERGENCE OF AUSTRIA AND PRUSSIA

Austria

As a result of the settlement at Westphalia, the Austrian Hapsburgs gained firm control over most of Hungary and Bohemia, where they installed a virtually new and foreign nobility. At the same time, they strengthened their grip on Vienna. In one of the few spectacular successes achieved by the Counter-Reformation, the ruling elites in all three territories were forcibly, or in many cases willingly, converted back to Catholicism. At long last, religious predominance could be used as a force—long delayed by the pull of the Protestant Reformation—for the creation of the Austrian dynastic state.

One severe obstacle remained: the military threat posed by the Turks, who sought to control much of Hungary. In 1683, the Turks again besieged Vienna, but a Catholic and unified Austrian army, composed of a variety of peoples and assisted by the Poles, managed to defeat the Turks and recapture the whole of Hungary and Transylvania and part of Croatia. Austria's right to govern these lands was firmly accepted by the Turks at the Treaty of Karlowitz (1699). Islam had been beaten back to the frontiers of Eastern Europe.

The Austrian Hapsburgs and their victorious army emerged into the larger arena of European power politics. In 1700, at the death of the last Spanish Hapsburg, Leopold I sought to place his second son, Archduke Charles, on the Spanish throne. But this attempt brought Leopold into a violent clash with Louis XIV. Once again, Bourbon and Hapsburg rivalry, a dominant theme in early modern history, provoked a major European war.

In the War of the Spanish Succession (1702–1714), the Austrians joined forces with the English and the Dutch against the French. The allies gained much: Austria acquired what is now Belgium as a colony and pieces of Italy, including Milan. The Austrians did not capture the Spanish throne, but they did become a major force in European power politics, later to be challenged by Prussia. The English and Dutch subdued French ambitions and formed an alliance that lasted for fifty years. In retrospect, we can see the war as the beginning of England's rise to the status of a world power; ironically, by the 1730s, the Dutch Republic had entered a period of economic decline.

Prussia

Prussia was a state within the Holy Roman Empire, and its territorial ambitions could be checked by the other princely states or the empire. Although Prussia developed an absolute monarchy like France's, its powerful aristocracy acquiesced to monarchical power only in exchange for guarantees of their feudal power over the peasantry. In 1653, the Prussian nobility granted the Hohenzollern ruler of Prussia power to collect taxes for the maintenance of a strong army, but only after he issued decrees rendering serfdom permanent.

The Hohenzollerns, the ruling dynasty of Prussia, had had a most inauspicious beginning in the later Middle Ages. These rulers were little more than dukes in the Holy Roman Empire until 1415,

MARIA THERESA AND JOSEPH. By the middle of the eighteenth century, the nuclear family was being valorized even among the monarchs of Europe. Here Maria Theresa and Joseph pose with their family. (RMN-Grand Palais/Art Resource, N.Y.)

when Holy Roman Emperor Sigismund made one of them an imperial elector with the right to choose imperial successors. For centuries, the Hohenzollerns had made weak claims to territory in northern Germany. They finally achieved control over Prussia and certain other smaller principalities by claiming the inheritance of one wife (1608) and by single-minded, ruthless aggression.

The most aggressive of these Hohenzollerns was the elector Frederick William (1640–1688), who played a key role in forging the new Prussian state. Frederick William inherited the territories of the beleaguered Hohenzollern dynasty, whose main holding, Brandenburg in Prussia, was very poor in natural resources. Indeed, Prussia barely survived the devastation wreaked by the Thirty Years' War, especially the Swedish army's occupation of the electorate.

Distaste for foreign intervention in Prussia, and for the accompanying humiliation and excessive taxes, prompted the Junker class (the landed Prussian nobility) to support national

Map 16.3 **THE GROWTH OF AUSTRIA AND BRANDENBURG-PRUSSIA, C. 1650–1750**
This growth laid the foundation for modern Germany and also for tension
between Christianity and Islam. (© 2016 Cengage Learning.)

unity and strong central government. However, they would brook no threat to their economic control of their lands and peasants. Frederick William's policy of foreign war, taxes, and military conscription led to an increase in the power of the central government. But in Prussia, in contrast to lands to the west, the bureaucracy was entirely military. No clerics or rich bourgeois shared power with the Junkers. The pattern initiated by the Great Elector (Frederick William) would be continued in the reigns of his successors: Frederick I (d. 1713), Frederick William I, and Frederick the Great.

In the older dynastic states, absolute monarchs tried to dispense with representative institutions once the monarchy had grown strong enough. So too did Frederick William I (1713–1740) finally undercut the Prussian provincial assemblies, the *Landtage*, which still had some power over taxation and army recruitment. He was able to do so only by integrating the landowning Junker class into the government and the army by keeping the taxpaying peasants in the status of serfs. A military elite with little interest in reform and a landed nobility supported by the labor of its serfs lay at the heart of the Prussian state.

Russia: Great Nobles and Starving Peasants

Though remote from developments in Western Europe, Russia in the early modern period possessed characteristics remarkably similar to those of Western European states. It relied on absolute monarchy reinforced by a feudal aristocracy. As in Europe, the power of the aristocracy to wreak havoc had to be checked and its energies channeled into the state's service. But the Russian pattern of absolutism broke with the Western model and resembled that adopted in Prussia, where serfdom increased as the power of centralized monarchy grew. The monarchy secured aristocratic cooperation in the state's growth by enforcing serfdom.

Late in the sixteenth century, Ivan the Terrible (1547–1584) sought to impose a tsarist autocracy. He waged a futile war against Sweden and created an internal police force, which he entrusted with the administration of central Russia. His failure in war and an irrational policy of repression (fueled in part by his mental instability) doomed his attempt to impose absolutism. Much of Ivan's state building was undone with his death, which launched the Time of Troubles, a period of foreign invasion and civil warfare that endured for years.

Order was restored in 1613, when the Romanovs gained the support of the aristocracy. The accession of Michael Romanov as tsar marks the beginning of the Romanov dynasty and the emergence of a unified Russian state. Of that dynasty, by far the most important ruler was Peter the Great (1682–1725). He journeyed throughout Western Europe and sought to imitate its political and cultural institutions. He ruthlessly suppressed the independent aristocrats while inventing new titles and ranks for his supporters. He reformed the army in accordance with military standards in Western Europe and he made the peasants into the personal property of their lords. From 1700 to 1707, taxes on the peasants multiplied fivefold. Predictably, the money went toward the creation of a professional army along European lines and toward making war. The preparation led this time to victory over the Swedes. Finally, Peter brought the Russian Orthodox Church under the control of the state by establishing a new office, called the Holy Synod; its head was a government official. He built St. Petersburg in imitation of Western cities and endowed its cultural institutions.

Peter managed to wed the aristocracy to the absolutist state, and the union was so successful that strong Russian monarchs in the eighteenth century, such as Catherine the Great, could embrace enlightened reforms without jeopardizing the stability of their regimes. Once again, repression and violence in the form of taxation, serfdom, and war led to the creation of a dynastic state—one that proved least susceptible to reform and was eventually dismantled in 1917 by the Russian Revolution.

The State and Modern Political Development

By the early seventeenth century, Europeans had developed a sophisticated concept of the *state:* an active political entity to which its subjects owed duties and obligations. That concept became the foundation of the modern science of politics. The one essential ingredient of the Western concept of the state, as it emerged in the early modern period, was the notion of *sovereignty:* the state defined itself as supreme within its borders and over other institutions and organizations. By implication, even the church was allowed to exist only if it recognized the state's authority. The art of government thus entailed molding powerful elites into service to the state. The sovereign state, its power enhanced by war and taxation, became the basic unit of political authority in Europe and eventually the American republic.

Interestingly, the concept of human liberty, now so basic to global human rights, was not articulated first in the sovereign states of Europe. Rather, the idea was largely an Italian creation, discussed with great vehemence by Italian theorists of the later Middle Ages and the Renaissance. These humanists lived and wrote in the independent city-states, and they often aimed their treatises against the encroachments of the Holy Roman Emperor—in short, against princes and their search for absolute power. In the sixteenth and seventeenth centuries, the idea of liberty was rarely discussed and was generally found only in the writings of Dutch and French Calvinist opponents of absolutism.

Not until the mid-seventeenth century in England did a body of political thought emerge that placed human liberty as a central political value within the state—a state governed by mere mortals and not by divinely sanctioned and absolute kings. In general, despite the English and Dutch developments, absolutism in its varied forms (Spanish, French, Prussian, Russian), often supported by national churches, dominated the political development of early modern Europe.

Although first articulated in the Italian republics and then enacted briefly in England and more durably in the Netherlands, the republican ideal did not gain acceptance as a viable alternative to absolutism until the European Enlightenment of the eighteenth century. In essence, the republican ideal placed the state in the service of those who support and create it. In the democratic and republican revolutions of the late eighteenth century, Western Europeans and Americans repudiated monarchical systems of government and opted for republics. By then, princes and military elites had outlived their usefulness in many parts of Europe. The states they had created, mostly to further their own interests, had become larger than their creators. Eventually, the national states of Western Europe, as well as of the Americas, proved able to survive and prosper without kings or aristocrats, although they retained the administrative and military mechanisms so skillfully and relentlessly developed by early modern kings and their court officials.

By the eighteenth century, the state, not the locality, had become the focal point of Western political life. Peace in Europe and its colonies depended on the art of balancing the powers of the various states so that no single state could expect to win domination, or *hegemony*, over all the others. Whenever a European state believed that it could dominate in Europe or expand its colonies abroad, war resulted. In early modern times, first the Spanish under Charles V and Philip II and

PETER THE GREAT. Peter the Great looked westward and outward and sought to modernize Russia. (The Art Archive/Russian Historical Museum Moscow/Collection Dagli Orti.)

then the French under Louis XIV sought, and for a brief time achieved, hegemony over European politics. Ultimately, however, these great states with inadequate taxing powers faltered because of the internal financial pressures that warmaking created. Nonetheless, the belief persisted, until 1945, that one state could dominate Western affairs. In the twentieth century, that belief produced not simply war but world war. By then, the power of Western states and, among others, their Japanese imitators had overtaken vast areas of the world, and the ability to impose a balance of power became a matter of world survival. The militarism at the basis of globally ambitious state power produced the nuclear age.

❖ ❖ ❖

NOTES

1. Quoted from *True Law of Free Monarchies,* excerpted in Marvin Perry et al., *Sources of the Western Tradition* (Boston: Houghton Mifflin, 1999), 358–359.

2. Steve Pincus, *1688. The First Modern Revolution* (New Haven, CT: Yale University Press, 2009), 483.

Chapter 17

The Scientific Revolution: The Universe Seen as a Mechanism

The late-eighteenth-century poet and engraver, William Blake, imaged Newton as the "first man" who followed the laws of geometry to fashion the world. Here Newton uses the simple compass of the mason to put his design onto the world. (Tate, London/Art Resource, N.Y.)

Focus Questions

1. What were the basic features of the medieval view of the universe?

2. Who were the leading figures of the Scientific Revolution, and what were their accomplishments?

3. What was the relationship between science and alchemy during this period?

4. Why was the Scientific Revolution a decisive force in the shaping of the modern approach to industry?

*I*n the fifteenth century, the medieval view of the world began to disintegrate. By the late seventeenth century, educated Europeans no longer believed in it. Thus, the collapse of medieval institutions such as feudalism and serfdom had an intellectual parallel. No set of ideas were as important in shaping the modern worldview as those associated with Scientific Revolution of the seventeenth century. They made physical nature a valid object for experimental and empirical inquiry and mathematical calculation. For the new science to arise, a philosophical break with the medieval conception of nature had to occur. The medieval approach to nature sought to explain nature's appearances. To the naked eye, the earth seems to be in the center of our universe. Medieval philosophy explained how and why the earth was in the center, and how and why heavy bodies fell toward it and light ones rose away from it. The philosophical revolution of the seventeenth century demolished such explanations. At the heart of the Scientific Revolution lay the assumption that appearances could lie, that truth depended upon seeing the universe as an abstract entity: as matter in motion, as geometrical shapes, and as weight and number. The universe became a mechanism.

The Scientific Revolution brought a new, **mechanical conception of nature** that enabled Westerners to discover and explain the laws of nature mathematically. Nature came to be composed solely of matter, whose motion, occurring in space and measurable by time, is governed by the push and pull of bodies and by laws of force. This philosophically elegant construction unified nature as composed of atoms, knowable and even possibly manageable. It led to the formulation of a unified science of mechanics that could be employed in an industrial setting.

The new science rested on a distinctive and replicable methodology. First, it was empirical, and gradually it became experimental. Because of successful observations and experiments performed by scientists and natural philosophers such as Galileo Galilei, William Harvey, Robert Boyle, and Isaac Newton, science acquired its still-characteristic methods of observation, experimentation, and replication. By the late seventeenth century, a serious interest in the physical order required actually doing—and recording—rigorous

Art of the Seventeenth and Eighteenth Centuries

1. Peter Paul Rubens, *The Betrothal of Saint Catherine*, sketch for a large altar painting, c. 1628.

(Enthroned Madonna with Child, Encircled by Saints, c.1627–28 (oil on canvas), Rubens, Peter Paul (1577–1640)/Staatliche Gemaldegalerie, Berlin, Germany/The Bridgeman Art Library.)

The influence of political, economic, and social change permeates the visual arts of the seventeenth and eighteenth centuries. Perhaps most significant to the artists who made their living by providing paintings with religious themes for churches, as well as for private patrons, were the religious conflicts that split apart European society. Catholics and Protestants quarreled and openly fought over doctrine and dogma; as a result of the struggles, artists had to decide how best to please patrons whose religious sympathies may have changed or developed in new directions. Politically, the seventeenth and eighteenth centuries are also marked by the emergence of new sovereign states and by a change in the nature of artistic patronage.

Although a number of terms are used to describe the seventeenth and eighteenth centuries, the one most commonly applied by art historians is *baroque*. The word literally means irregularly shaped, whimsical, grotesque, or odd. Its origin is French, but it is generally agreed that the baroque style of art originated in Rome.

Baroque art is hard to explain within the context of the social and political changes that were sweeping over Europe. Some historians see it as illustrative of the Counter-Reformation; others point out that the style was equally appealing to Catholics and Protestants. Nor was the baroque style favored only by the absolute rulers of France or other monarchs; it was also a style of the bourgeois.

2. Giovanne Benedetto Castiglione, *Melancholia*, Mid-Seventeenth Century. (Philadelphia Museum of Art: The Muriel and Philip Berman Gift, acquired from the Matthew Carey Lea Bequest of 1898 to the Pennsylvania Academy of Fine Arts.)

One of the most famous baroque painters was Peter Paul Rubens (1577–1640) of Flanders, which, prospering from its commercial connections, was home to many successful artists and patrons in this period. To study painting, Rubens traveled to Rome in 1600 and spent many years visiting other artistic centers in Italy. There he learned to paint on large-scale canvases and play with the size and weight of his subjects. Despite the influence of his southern contemporaries, however, his style remained essentially Flemish.

In his painting *The Betrothal of Saint Catherine* (Figure 1), we immediately sense the energy and fullness of the figures typical among Italian artists. But we also notice that Rubens's palette is much lighter than theirs, and consequently, the figures of Saint Catherine and the saints who surround her seem to move lightly as well.

Noteworthy, too, in this canvas is the depiction of the figures, whose hairstyles and mode of dress are contemporary rather than suggestive of biblical times. This juxtaposition of scenes from the Bible with the flavor of everyday life in the seventeenth century reveals much about the connection between the artist and his own surroundings.

The baroque style of highly finished, realistic works is very familiar to us. But we must also recall that baroque artists were skilled draftsmen. As an example, there is Giovanne Benedetto Castiglione's *Melancholia* (mid-seventeenth century) (Figure 2), a brush drawing in oil with added red chalk. Works on paper do not always survive as well as those on board or canvas. The drawings we do have attest to the artistic skill of seventeenth-century artists, who used line and shadow as well as did their Renaissance predecessors.

Melancholia is an allegory about the human dilemma of choosing among the worlds of art, religion, science, and learning. Symbols from each of these worlds—scientific tools, musical instruments, a globe, and the like—surround the figure of Genius, who sits in a contemplative pose.

Although by and large the artists of the baroque period were not well-rounded humanists like those of the Renaissance, some of them could work in a variety of art forms. For example, Gian Lorenzo Bernini (1598–1680) distinguished himself as a sculptor as well as an architect.

Bernini was responsible for the sculptural program of Saint Peter's Basilica in the Vatican. He also completed sculptures in other Roman churches, including the Cornaro Chapel in the Church of Santa Maria della Vittoria. His *The Ecstasy of Saint Teresa* (1644–1647) (Figure 3) is a remarkable work that tells a dramatic story. The heart of Saint Teresa of Avila was said to have been pierced by an angel's golden arrow; the pain was exquisite, for not only was it the pain of death but also the pleasure of everlasting life in the arms of God. Bernini skillfully portrays the exact moment of Saint Teresa's ecstasy, in a theatrical setting using not only sculpture but also the architectural elements of the chapel.

The saint and the angel are carved of white marble and seem to be floating on a cloud. The sculpted golden rays, which descend from a point above the figures, are bathed in light by a window hidden behind the frame that surrounds the two figures. Bernini decorated the entire chapel to follow the theme of Saint Teresa; ceiling frescoes show clouds of angels celebrating the event.

While Bernini was gaining fame in Italy, a French painter—one who spent almost his entire career in Rome—was winning an international reputation. Nicolas Poussin (1593/4–1665) relied strongly on the art of the classical and especially the Hellenistic periods for his inspiration. His *The Rape of the Sabine Women* (c. 1636–37) (Figure 4), a lavish and richly painted canvas, captures action like a carefully posed photograph. Indeed, if Bernini was theatrical in his portrayal of Saint Teresa, one could say that Poussin is cinematographic.

The story depicted in *The Rape of the Sabine Women* is derived from classical mythology; the poses of the figures hark back to the Hellenistic

3. Gian Lorenzo Bernini, *The Ecstasy of Saint Teresa*, 1644–1647. (Scala/Art Resource, Inc.)

period. Compare the positioning of the arms of the women on the left of the canvas with the tortured stance of Laocoön in the sculpture shown in Figure 4 of the first art essay. Other groups in the Poussin canvas are also reminiscent of that sculpture. As another bow to the ancient past, Poussin paints in the background buildings that are faithful to Roman prototypes. Such reliance on archaeology and mythology are typical of his work.

While paintings depicting mythological, historical, or religious themes dominated the major art markets during the baroque era, patrons in Holland sought paintings that related more to their own experience. For that reason, the genre of the still life—paintings of flowers, fruit, dishes,

4. Nicolas Poussin, *The Rape of the Sabine Women*, c. 1636–1637. (Image copyright © The Metropolitan Museum of Art/Art Resource, N.Y.)

food, and other familiar objects—reached its zenith in that country.

Willem Kalf (1622–1693), among the most skilled of Dutch still-life masters, was able to take a collection of objects and turn it into an object of art. His *Still Life* (Figure 5) showcases his meticulous, almost photorealistic style. In particular, it focuses on the way in which glass reflects light and on the juxtaposition of different textures. Although modern art historians view some still lifes as merely ornamental displays of technical skill, there was a reason for them. The popularity of still lifes and of landscapes probably has to do with the human desire for reassurance that "things are as they should be," that the status quo is being maintained, regardless of the religious or political turmoil affecting other aspects of life.

No matter what was going on politically, no matter what religious dispute was being negotiated, people could find a degree of comfort in being surrounded by familiar objects or scenes.

While Kalf distinguished himself as a still-life painter, another Dutch master, Rembrandt van Rijn (1606–1669), gained fame for his historical and religious canvases. Rembrandt was influenced in his early years by Italian painters, especially by their use of light. But that was not his only strength. His reputation as a portrait painter made him renowned and made his fortune in Amsterdam.

Even more impressive were his self-portraits, which he painted not for the commissions of patrons but entirely for himself in the pursuit of truth. For an artist to paint as many self-portraits as Rembrandt did in the seventeenth century was very unusual. Self-portraits are analogous to autobiographies: in both, the artist examines himself because he believes his own self is worthy of self-examination.

Rembrandt's quest for the meaning of the inner life is compatible with the growing introspectiveness of the seventeenth century, an age that also produced Descartes's dictum that to think is to be, the soliloquies of Shakespeare's Hamlet, and the hallucinations of Cervantes' Don Quixote.

Rembrandt produced a series of sixty-two self-portraits during the course of his lifetime, an exhaustive autobiography in pictures in which he seemed to engage in a dialogue with himself in a variety of attitudes and poses: vigorous, youthful, heroic, flamboyant, melodramatic, enigmatic, aging, distraught, struggling with despair, grimly resolved, disdainful, strong, weak. Rembrandt completed *Self-Portrait at Old Age*, 1669 (Figure 6), the fifty-fifth in a corpus of sixty-two self-portraits, in the last year of his life. It is among a cluster of self-portraits in which he appears to have "pulled himself together" and defined his identity. In it, we find Rembrandt staring back at us with the calm assurance of a man who has mastered his art and life, and surpassed his time and place.

The later part of the eighteenth century marks the beginning of the rococo and neoclassical periods in art history. Especially popular in France, the rococo and neoclassical movements owed much to political and social forces. The term *rococo* describes a style that is frothy and frivolous and compatible with the peripheral concerns of royalty. In 1698, King Louis XIV ordered the redecoration of his palace at Versailles with works that were lighthearted and youthful instead of stodgy and serious. His dabbling with artistic matters led to quarrels and esthetic disagreements in the artistic community.

An example of the rococo is François Boucher's (1703–1770) *The Toilet of Venus* (1751) (Figure 7). Although some art historians describe his work as slick and artificial, Boucher became the darling of the French court. In his *The Toilet of Venus,* the goddess is full figured and lush, surrounded by all the sensual accouterments that the goddess of love and erotic pleasure should have. Given her appearance

5. Willem Kalf, *Still Life,* C. 1660. (Scala/Art Resource, N.Y.)

and her surroundings, Boucher's Venus looks as though she would have been comfortable in period dress, supervising the decor of her boudoir at the palace at Versailles. Clearly, Boucher understood his audience well.

While Boucher exemplified the light and airy sentiment of the rococo style, Jacques Louis David (1748–1825) typified the neoclassical. The neoclassical style represents a return to the rationality and harmony of the classical past; many of the works from this period also reflect contemporary political events.

Justice, honor for one's country, and the need to portray inspirational themes were the guideposts of the neoclassical artists. Their training ground was Italy, primarily because it was the source of the classical prototypes from which they could learn. Jacques Louis David's *The Death of Marat* (1793) (Figure 8) captures the essence of that event in a manner that combines the best of Poussin and Rubens.

6. Rembrandt van Rijn, *Self-Portrait at Old Age*, 1669. (Fine Art/Corbis.)

The subject matter is important because it illuminates the neoclassical concept of virtue, represented by the martyrdom of Marat, a revolutionary. The style borrows from Poussin's ability to capture a scene with photographic stillness, rendering the figures in an almost sculptural way.

But David has also appropriated Rembrandt's technique of skillfully juxtaposing light and shadow. While the neoclassicists sometimes paid homage to the distant past in their subject matter, they also showed their reverence for the revolutionary ideals of their own time.

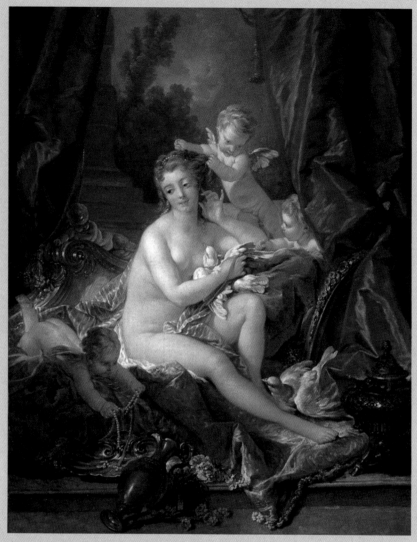

7. François Boucher, *The Toilet of Venus*, 1751.

8. Jacques Louis David, *The Death of Marat*, 1793.

and systematic experiments or, at the least, observing the behavior of physical phenomena. Regularity and order appeared to be embedded in nature, measurable and quantifiable.

Mathematics increasingly became the language of the new science. For centuries, Europeans had used first geometry and then algebra to explain certain physical phenomena. With the Scientific Revolution came a new mathematics, the infinitesimal **calculus**. Even more important, philosophers became increasingly convinced that all nature—moving physical objects, as well as invisible forces—could be described mathematically. By the late seventeenth century, even geometry had become so complex that the gifted philosopher John Locke (1632–1704), a friend of Isaac Newton, could not understand the sophisticated mathematics used in the *Principia*. A new scientific culture had been born. During the eighteenth-century Enlightenment (Chapter 18), the model of nature offered by science implied progress. If physical nature could be known, why not human nature and human institutions?

MEDIEVAL COSMOLOGY

The unique character of the modern scientific outlook contrasts sharply with the medieval understanding of the natural world and its physical properties. It rested on Christian thought combined with theories derived from ancient Greek writers, such as Aristotle and Ptolemy.

Aristotle (384–322 B.C.) had argued that nature possessed inherent, purposeful tendencies. A stone falls because it is absolutely heavy; fire rises because it is absolutely light. Weight is an inherent property of a physical thing; therefore, motion results from the properties of bodies, and not from the forces that impinge on them. It follows (logically but incorrectly) that if the medium through which a body falls is taken as a constant, then the speed of its fall could be doubled if its weight were doubled. Only rigorous experimentation refuted this erroneous, but commonsensical, concept of motion.

Aristotle's physics complemented his *cosmology*, or world picture. The earth, being the heaviest object, lay stationary and suspended at the center of the universe. The sun, planets, and moon revolved

in perfect circles around the earth. Aristotle presumed that because the planets were perfectly round, always in motion, and seemingly never altered, the most natural movement for them should be circular.

Aristotle could put the earth at the center of the universe and make it stationary because he presumed its absolute heaviness; all other heavy bodies that he had observed fell toward it. Aristotle believed that everything in motion had been moved by another object that was itself in motion—a continuing chain of movers and moved. By inference, this belief led back to some object or being that began the motion. Christian philosophers of the Middle Ages argued that Aristotle's Unmoved Mover must be the God of Christianity. Aristotle, a pagan Greek, knew nothing of a personal God nor an afterlife of rewards or punishments. He believed that the universe was eternal rather than created at a specific point in time, and he would have found the Christian identification of God as the Mover meaningless.

Although Aristotle's cosmology never gained the status of orthodoxy among the ancient Greeks, by the second century C.E. in Alexandria, Greek astronomy became codified and then rigid. Ptolemy of Alexandria produced the *Almagest* (C.E. 150), a handbook of Greek astronomy based on the theories of Aristotle. The crucial assumption in the *Almagest* was that a motionless earth lay at the center of the universe and that the planets moved about it in a series of circular orbits, interrupted by smaller circular orbits, called epicycles. The epicycles explained why at certain times a planet was visibly closer to the earth. As Ptolemy put it, if the earth moved, "living things and individual heavy objects would be left behind . . . [and] the earth itself would very soon have fallen completely out of the heavens."[1] By the Late Middle Ages, Ptolemy's handbook contained standard astronomical wisdom. As late as the 1650s, more than a hundred years after the Polish astronomer Nicolaus Copernicus had argued mathematically that the sun was the center of the universe, educated Europeans in most universities still believed that the earth held the central position. By 1750, the earth-centered universe had fallen to the status of a superstition.

In the thirteenth century, mainly through the philosophical efforts of Thomas Aquinas

(1225–1274), Aristotle's thought was adapted to Christian beliefs, often in ingenious ways. Aquinas emphasized that order pervaded nature and that every physical effect had a physical cause. Aquinas and his followers, who were called **scholastics**, searched for causes—again, to ask *why* things move, rather than *how* they move. Aquinas insisted that nature proves God's existence; God is the First Cause of all physical phenomena. The world picture taught by the scholastics in their schools affirmed the earth and humankind as the center of the Christian drama of birth, death, and salvation.

Medieval thinkers integrated the cosmology of Aristotle and Ptolemy into a Christian framework that drew a sharp distinction between the world beyond the moon and the earthly realm. Celestial bodies were composed of the divine ether, a substance too pure and too spiritual to be found on earth; heavenly bodies, unlike earthly bodies, were immune to all change and obeyed different laws of motion. The universe was divided into a higher world of the heavens and a lower world of earth. Earth could not compare with the heavens in spiritual dignity, but God had nevertheless situated it in the center of the universe. Earth deserved this position of importance; only here did Christ live and die for humankind. This concept of the physical universe collapsed under the impact of the new science.

Also shattered by the new **natural philosophy** was the belief that all reality, natural as well as human, could be described as consisting of *matter* and *form*. Following Aristotle, the scholastics argued that matter was inchoate, lifeless, and indistinguishable. Only form gave it shape and identity. A table, for instance, possessed a recognizable shape and could be identified as a table because it possessed the form of tableness. A human being existed only because the matter of the body was given life by the soul, by its form. This doctrine was central to medieval philosophy and theology. Important beliefs were justified by it. For example, the church taught that the priest, when performing the sacrament of the **Eucharist**, had the power to transform bread and wine into the body and blood of Christ. This was possible because, theologians argued, the matter of the bread and wine looked the same, but their form was changed by the power of the priest. Consequently, the Mass could be explained without

recourse to blind faith, or worse, magic. Similarly, medieval people believed that the king's power resided within him; kingness was part of his essence. Likewise, nobility was a quality said to be inherent in the person of the nobleman or noblewoman. The mechanical philosophy of Galileo, Boyle, and Newton, which was central to the Scientific Revolution, denied the very existence of forms. Matter was simply composed of tiny **corpuscles**, or **atoms**, hard and impenetrable, governed by the laws of impact or force. Such a conception of nature threatened whole aspects of medieval and even Christian doctrine; ultimately, in social terms, the implications of the mechanical and atomic philosophy proved to be democratic.

A NEW VIEW OF NATURE

Renaissance Neo-Platonism

Italian Renaissance thinkers rediscovered the importance of the ancient Greek philosopher Plato (c. 429–347 B.C.E.). Plato taught that the philosopher must look beyond the appearances of things to an invisible reality, which is abstract, simple, rational, and best expressed mathematically. For Plato, the greatest achievements of the human mind were mathematics and music; both revealed the inherent harmony and order within nature.

Renaissance Platonists interpreted Plato from a Christian perspective, and they believed that the Platonic search for truth about nature, about God's work, was but another aspect of the search for knowledge about God. The Italian universities and academies became centers where the revival of Plato flourished among teachers and translators, who came to be known as **Neo-Platonists**. Central to their humanist curriculum was the study of philosophy, mathematics, music, Greek and Latin, and in some cases Arabic. Those languages made available the world of pagan, pre-Christian learning and its many different philosophies of nature. The leading thinkers of the Scientific Revolution were all influenced by Renaissance Neo-Platonism. They revered Plato's search for an abstract and mathematically elegant truth. They returned to other ancient thinkers for an alternative to Aristotle. Some of the ancients had been atomists; a few had even argued that the sun might be at the center of the universe. They had also invented geometry.

With the impulse to mathematize nature came the desire to measure and experience it. The rediscovery of nature found expression in the study of human anatomy, as well as in the study of objects in motion. Renaissance art shows the fruits of this inquiry, for artists tried to depict the human body as exactly as possible and yet to give it ideal form. The revival of artistic creativity associated with the Renaissance is linked to an interest in the natural world and to Neo-Platonism.

Magic, Alchemy, and the Search for Nature

One other body of thought and practice had been available in European civilization for centuries. Derived from Arabic sources, alchemy taught a basic pharmacology that depended upon the constant distillation of common substances to produce more pure and powerful remedies. Alchemists were needed in the study of minerals, in agriculture, and of course most importantly in medicine. Alchemy also had its critics, who were irritated by the claim made by some alchemists that it was possible to turn base metals into gold. Only the truly pious practitioner could unlock the mysteries of gold or find an elixir of life that would ensure longevity. But critics cast a cold eye on such claims.

Isaac Newton for much of his life saw no contradiction in searching for the mathematical laws of nature while practicing alchemy—the search for a way to transform ordinary metals into gold—which was also the origin of modern chemistry. Gradually, the emphasis on the search for gold fell by the wayside, in part because the small amounts of gold that could be extracted from a large quantity of earth were irrelevant to the expanding early modern economy. Alchemy, more than any other natural practice, assumed that matter possessed a corpuscular structure and that by distillation it could be made purer, closer to what we would describe as a pure element. The alchemical literature became an important source for the theory of atoms. Alchemists had no need for the scholastic notion of forms, and among all the natural practitioners in early modern Europe they came closest to delivering useful remedies for pain, fevers, infertility, infections, and potions to poison vermin (not to mention one's enemies). Their practices were suspect to church and state, yet they could be found everywhere in Western and Eastern Europe and the American colonies.

In early modern Europe, the practitioners of alchemy and astrology could also be mathematicians and astronomers, and the sharp distinction drawn today between magic and science—between the irrational and the rational— would not have made sense to many of the leading natural philosophers who lived in the sixteenth and seventeenth centuries. Copernicus knew both astronomy and astrology and many an astronomer made his living by casting horoscopes.

The Renaissance revival of ancient learning contributed a new approach to nature, one that was simultaneously mathematical, experimental, and magical. Although the achievements of modern science depend on experimentation and mathematics, the impulse to search for nature's secrets presumes a degree of self-confidence best exemplified and symbolized by the seeker after gold or the elixir of life.

The Copernican Revolution

Nicolaes Copernicus was born in Poland in 1473. As a young man, he enrolled at the University of Kraków, where he may have come under the influence of Renaissance Platonism, which was spreading outward from the Italian city-states. Copernicus also journeyed to Italy, and in Bologna and Padua he might have encountered ancient Greek texts containing arguments for the sun being the center of the universe. We know very little about his early education.

Copernicus's interest in mathematics and astronomy was stimulated by contemporary discussions of the need for calendar reform, which required a thorough understanding of Ptolemaic astronomy. The mathematical complexity of the Ptolemaic system troubled Copernicus, who believed with the Neo-Platonists that truth was the product of elegance and simplicity. In addition, Copernicus knew that Ptolemy had predecessors among the ancients who philosophized about a heliocentric universe or who held Aristotle's cosmology and physics in little regard. Thus, a Renaissance education gave

COPERNICAN SYSTEM. In his *On Revolutions of the Heavenly Spheres,* Copernicus proposed a heliocentric model in which the planets orbit around the sun. (The Granger Collection New York.)

proposed a heliocentric model of the universe that was mathematically simpler than Ptolemy's earth-centered universe. His model eliminated some of Ptolemy's epicycles and cleared up various problems that had troubled geocentric astronomers.

Copernicus's genius lay in the pursuit of an idea—the concept of a sun-centered universe—and he pursued it with a lifelong dedication as well as considerable brilliance in mathematics. By removing the earth from its central position and by giving it motion—that is, by making the earth just another planet—Copernicus undermined the system of medieval cosmology and made possible the birth of modern astronomy.

Most thinkers of the time were committed to the Aristotelian-Ptolemaic system and to biblical statements that they thought supported it, and they rejected Copernicus's conclusions. They also raised specific objections. The earth, they said, is too heavy to move. How, some of Copernicus's colleagues asked, can an object falling from a high tower land directly below the point from which it was dropped if the earth is moving so rapidly?

The Laws of Planetary Motion: Tycho and Kepler

Copernicus laid the foundation for the intellectual revolution that gradually overturned the medieval conception of the universe and ushered in modern cosmology. But it fell to other observers to fill in the important details. Tycho Brahe (1546–1601) never accepted the Copernican system, but he saw it as a challenge to astronomers. Aided by the king of Denmark, Tycho built the finest observatory in Europe. In 1572, he observed a new star in the heavens. Its existence offered a direct and serious challenge to the Aristotelian and scholastic assumption of unalterable, fixed, and hence perfect heavens. To this discovery of what eventually proved to be an exploding star, Tycho added his observations

Copernicus an outlook that enabled him to break with traditional astronomical truth taught in the universities.

Copernicus became convinced that the sun was at the center of the universe. So he began a lifelong task to work out mathematical explanations of how a heliocentric universe operated. Unwilling to engage in controversy with the followers of Aristotle, Copernicus did not publish his findings until 1543, the year of his death, in a work titled *On the Revolutions of the Heavenly Spheres.* Legend says that his book, which in effect began the Scientific Revolution, was brought to him on his deathbed. Copernicus died as he lived, a Catholic priest, hoping only that his book would be read sympathetically.

The treatise retained some elements of the Aristotelian-Ptolemaic system; for example, Copernicus kept Aristotle's basic idea of the perfect circular motion of the planets and the existence of crystalline spheres within which the stars revolved. He also retained many of Ptolemy's epicycles—orbits within the circular orbits of the sun and planets. But Copernicus on the comet of 1577. He demonstrated that it moved unimpeded through the areas between the planets and passed right through the crystalline spheres. This finding raised the question of whether such spheres existed, but Tycho himself remained an Aristotelian. Although his devotion to a literal reading of the Bible led Tycho to reject the Copernican sun-centered universe, he did propose an alternative system, in which the planets revolved around the sun but the sun moved about a motionless earth.

Ultimately, Tycho's fame rests on his skill as a practicing astronomer. He bequeathed to future generations precise calculations about the movements of heavenly bodies. These calculations proved invaluable. They were put to greatest use by Johannes Kepler (1571–1630), a German who collaborated with Tycho during the latter's final years. Tycho bequeathed his astronomical papers to Kepler, who brought to the data a scientific vision that was both experimental and mystical.

Kepler searched persistently for harmonious laws of planetary motion. He did so because he believed profoundly in the Platonic ideal. It proclaimed that a spiritual force infuses the physical order, beneath appearances are harmony and unity, and the human mind can begin to comprehend that unity only through *gnosis*—a direct and mystical realization of unity—and through mathematics. Kepler believed that both approaches were compatible, and he managed to combine them. He believed in and practiced astrology (as did Tycho) and throughout his lifetime tried to contact an ancient but lost and secret wisdom.

In the course of his observations of the heavens, Kepler discovered the three basic laws of planetary motion. First, the orbits of the planets are elliptical, not circular as Aristotle and Ptolemy had assumed, and the sun is one focus of the **ellipse**. Unlike Tycho, Kepler accepted Copernicus's theory and provided proof for it. Kepler's second law—the line joining a planet to the sun sweeps out equal areas in equal times as the planet travels around the ellipse—demonstrated that the velocity of a planet is not uniform, as had been believed, but increases as its distance from the sun decreases. Kepler's third law—that the squares of the times taken by any two planets in their revolutions around the sun are in the same ratio as the cubes of their average distances from the sun—brought the planets into a unified mathematical system.

Kepler's work possessed immense significance. He gave sound mathematical proof to Copernicus's theory; forever eliminated the use of epicycles, which had saved the appearance of circular motion; and demonstrated that mathematical relationships can describe the planetary system. But Kepler left a significant question unresolved: What kept the planets in their orbits? Why did they not fly out into space or crash into the sun? Isaac Newton supplied the answer and synthesized the astronomy of Copernicus and Kepler with the new physics developed by Galileo.

Galileo: Experimental Physics

At the same time that Kepler was developing a new astronomy, his contemporary, Galileo Galilei (1564–1642), was breaking with the older physics of Aristotle. A citizen of Pisa by birth, Galileo lived for many years in Padua, where he conducted some of his first experiments on the motion of bodies. Guided by the dominant philosophy of the Italian Renaissance—the revived doctrines of Plato—Galileo believed that beyond the visible world lay certain universal truths, subject to mathematical verification. Galileo insisted that the study of motion entails not only the use of logic (as Aristotle had believed) but also the application of mathematics. For this Late Renaissance natural philosopher, mathematics became the language of nature. Galileo also believed that only after experimenting can the philosopher formulate harmonious laws and give them mathematical expression. Moreover, Galileo was trained in the practices of Renaissance art, in using shades and shadows to represent the placing of bodies relative to one another. When he first looked at the moon through his telescope, that training became very important.

In his mechanical experiments, Galileo discovered that, all other things being equal, bodies of unequal weight will experience a uniform acceleration (due to gravity). He demonstrated that bodies fall with arithmetic regularity. Motion, therefore, obeys laws that can be expressed mathematically.

Galileo established a fundamental principle of modern science: the order and uniformity of nature. No distinctions in rank or quality exist between the heavens and earth; heavenly bodies

NOTEBOOK SKETCHES OF THE PHASES OF THE MOON, BY GALILEO GALILEI, 1609–1610. Galileo saw only shadows when he looked into his telescope. But because he was trained as an artist in the principles of light and dark coloring to emphasize or shorten distance, he knew that what he saw represented real objects, in this case mountains and valleys. Somewhat satirically, he compared the moon to Bohemia. (Scala/Art Resource, N.Y.)

are not perfect and changeless as Aristotle had believed. In 1609, Galileo built a telescope through which he viewed the surface of the moon. The next year, in a treatise called *The Starry Messenger*, he proclaimed that the moon "is not smooth, uniform, and precisely spherical as a great number of philosophers believe it and the other heavenly bodies to be, but is uneven, rough, and full of cavities . . . being not unlike the face of the earth, relieved by chains of mountains and deep valleys."[2] In addition, Galileo noticed spots on the sun, providing further evidence that heavenly

objects, like earthly objects, are physical bodies susceptible to change. Nature is the same throughout. When he saw shadows through his telescope, he assumed that actual bodies were casting them, just as they do on an earthly landscape. Galileo's art and science were of a piece. Galileo would be pleased and not surprised that contemporary moon expeditions cannot locate a single element unknown on earth.

Through his telescope, Galileo also observed moons around Jupiter—a discovery that supported the Copernican hypothesis. If Jupiter had moons, then all heavenly bodies did not orbit the earth. The moons of Jupiter removed a fundamental criticism of Copernicus and opened up the possibility that the earth, with its own moon, might be just like Jupiter, and that both might in turn revolve around a central point—the sun.

With Galileo, the science of Copernicus and the assault on Aristotle entered a new phase. Scholastic priests began to attack Galileo from their pulpits in Florence. In Galileo's public notoriety and his popularity among the laity, they saw a threat to their own power. A secret group of priests and academics, named the Liga, formed with the express purpose of silencing Galileo; they used Aristotle and the Bible to attack him. But Galileo was also a courtier with friends in high places, so he dared to challenge the clergy and to offer his science directly to the laity. He argued publicly with the theologians. In the early seventeenth century, the Catholic Church saw danger on every front: Protestants in Germany, Jews and Muslims in the East, and a laity demanding new schools that would provide practical education for their children. Now Galileo offered a view of the universe that conflicted with certain scriptural texts. He was in a bad place at a bad time.

The church attacked Galileo because he was a Copernican, that is, because he believed the sun to be at the center of the universe. There were other reasons. New evidence from the recently opened Vatican archives suggests that the church also may have worried about his corpuscular theory of matter and his abandonment of the scholastics' view of the relationship between matter and form. That view went to the heart of the doctrine of the Eucharist, and the church saw, rightly, that the new science threatened the philosophical foundations of certain key doctrines.

MAPPING THE HEAVENS AND THE EARTH. Contemporaries of Galileo knew that the discovery of the heavens was tied to the discovery of the New World, the exploration of the globe, and the mapping of the seas. Simultaneously, in the period from 1500 to 1700 Westerners found two new worlds, one in the heavens, the other very much on earth. (AbleStock.com (RF)/Hemera Technologies/© Getty Images/Jupiter Images.)

In 1632 and 1633, Galileo's teachings were condemned, and he was placed under house arrest. This act of repression cut short the open pursuit of science in many Catholic countries of the seventeenth century. Wherever the Inquisition was strong, the new science would be viewed as subversive. Censorship worked to stifle public intellectual inquiry. By midcentury, science had become an increasingly Protestant and northern European phenomenon.

THE NEWTONIAN SYNTHESIS: EXPERIMENT, MATHEMATICS, AND THEORY

By 1650, the works of Copernicus and especially of Galileo had dethroned the physics and astronomy of Aristotle and Ptolemy. A new philosophy of nature tied to empirical observation

and Neo-Platonism had come into existence; its essence lay in the mathematical expression of physical laws that describe matter in motion. Yet no single overriding law had been articulated that would bring together the experimental successes of the new science, its mathematical sophistication, and its philosophical revolution. Isaac Newton supplied the new law of universal gravitation.

Newton was born in 1642, in Lincolnshire, England, the son of a modest yeoman. Because of his intellectual promise, he obtained a place at Trinity College, Cambridge, and there he devoted himself to natural philosophy and mathematics. Newton's student notebooks survive and show him mastering philosophical texts while also trying to understand the fundamental truths of Protestant Christianity as taught at Cambridge. Combining Christian Neo-Platonism with a genius for mathematics, Newton produced a coherent synthesis of the science of Kepler and Galileo, which eventually captured the imagination of European intellectuals.

In 1666, Newton formulated the mathematics for the universal law of gravitation, and in the same year, after rigorous experimentation, he determined the nature of light. The sciences of physics and optics were transformed. However, for many years, Newton did not publish his discoveries, perhaps because he feared controversy. Finally, another mathematician and friend, Edmund Halley, persuaded him to publish under the sponsorship of the Royal Society. The result was the *Principia Mathematica* of 1687. In 1704, Newton published his *Opticks* and revealed his theory that light was corpuscular or atomic in nature and that it emanated from luminous bodies in a way that scientists later described as waves.

Of the two books, both monumental achievements in the history of science, the *Principia* made the greater impact on contemporaries. Newton offered universal mathematical laws, as well as a philosophy of nature that sought to explain the essential structure of the universe: matter is always the same; it is atomic in structure, in its essential nature it is dead or lifeless; and it is acted on by immaterial forces that are placed in the universe by God. Newton said that the motion of matter could be explained by three laws: inertia, that a body remains in a state of rest or continues its motion in a straight line unless impelled to change by forces impressed on it; acceleration, that the change in the motion of a body is proportional to the force acting on it; and that for every action there is an equal and opposite reaction. The notion of form disappeared entirely from his theoretical and practical science.

Newton applied his laws to observable matter on earth and to the motion of planets in their orbits. He showed that planets remain in their orbits not because circular motion is natural or because crystalline spheres keep them in place. Rather, said Newton, planets keep to their orbits because every body in the universe exercises a force on every other body, a force that he called *universal gravitation*. Gravity is proportional to the product of the masses of two bodies and inversely proportional to the square of the distance between them. It is operative throughout the universe, whether on earth or in the heavens, and it is capable of mathematical expression. Newton built his theory on the work of other scientific giants, notably Kepler and Galileo. No one before him, however, had possessed the breadth of vision, mathematical genius, and dedication to rigorous observation to combine this knowledge into one grand synthesis.

Atomic in structure, the universe now became matter in motion; governed by invisible forces that operate everywhere, both on earth and in the heavens, and these forces could be expressed mathematically. The medieval picture of the universe as closed and earth centered gave way forever to a universe seen to be infinite and governed by universal laws. The earth became simply another moving planet, and bodies in the heavens were seen to be uniform in composition.

Newtonian principles were taught by generations of Newton's followers as, in effect, applied mechanics. A revolution in thought changed Western ideas about nature forever and also created a body of knowledge that could be practically applied to everyday bodies. But what was God's role in this new universe? Newton and his circle labored to create a mechanical worldview dependent on the will of God. At one time, Newton

believed that gravity was simply the will of God operating on the universe. As he wrote in the *Opticks,* the physical order "can be the effect of nothing else than the wisdom and skill of a powerful ever-living agent."[3] Because of his strong religious convictions, Newton allowed his science to be used in the service of the established Anglican Church, and his followers argued for social stability anchored in an ordered universe and an established church. Newton, a scientific genius, was also a deeply religious thinker committed to the maintenance of Protestantism in England. Among his contemporaries, however, freethinkers such as John Toland (see "Skeptics, Freethinkers, and Deists" in Chapter 18) used his ideas to argue that nature can operate on its own, without the assistance of a providential God.

BIOLOGY, MEDICINE, AND CHEMISTRY

The spectacular advances in physics and astronomy in the sixteenth and seventeenth centuries were not matched in the biological sciences. Indeed, the day-to-day practice of medicine throughout Western Europe changed little in the period from 1600 to 1800, for much of medical practice relied, as it had since the Middle Ages, on astrology, alchemy and on the necessity for bloodletting.

Doctors clung to the teachings of the ancient practitioners Galen and Hippocrates. In general, Galenic medicine paid little attention to the discovery of specific cures for particular diseases. As a follower of Aristotle, Galen emphasized the elements that make up the body; he called their manifestations *humors*. A person with an excess of blood was sanguine; a person with too much bile was choleric. Health consisted of a restoration of balances among these various elements, so Galenic doctors often prescribed purges of one sort or another. The most famous of these was bloodletting, but sweating was also a favorite remedy. Taught devotedly in the medical schools of Europe, these methods were often as dangerous as the diseases they sought to cure.

Despite the tenacity of Galenic medicine, sixteenth- and seventeenth-century innovators and reformers challenged and eventually overturned medical orthodoxy. With an almost

SCIENCE AND BLOOD. For centuries, it was believed that blood carried character traits as well as nobility. The English experimenter William Harvey viewed blood as simply a liquid that circulated in the body in a uniform way. Illustrations such as this one made the point graphically. (© Bettmann/CORBIS.)

missionary zeal, Paracelsus (1493–1541), a Swiss-German physician and mystical Neo-Platonist, introduced the concept of diagnostic medicine and relied heavily on alchemy. He argued that particular diseases can be differentiated and are related to chemical, not humoral, imbalances. His treatments relied on chemicals and not on bloodletting or the positions of the stars (although he did not discount such influences), and he proclaimed an almost ecstatic vision of human vitality and longevity. In most universities, the faculties of medicine bitterly opposed his views, but by 1650 in England and later in that century in France, Paracelsian ideas had many advocates. Support for Paracelsian medicine, often combined with alchemy, invariably accompanied an attack on the

traditional medical establishment and its professional monopoly, and it often signaled an interest in the new science. The struggle between Galenists and Paracelsians quickly took on a social dimension; the innovators saw themselves pitted against a medical elite, which, in their opinion, had lost its commitment to medical research and existed solely to perpetuate itself. In the eighteenth century, Paracelsian ideas, stripped of their alchemical associations, became commonplace.

The medical reforms of the eighteenth century did not rest solely on the Paracelsian approach; they also relied heavily on the experimental breakthroughs made in the science of anatomy. A pioneer in this field was the Belgian surgeon Andreas Vesalius (1515–1564), who published *The Structure of the Human Body* in 1543. Opposing Galenic practice, Vesalius argued for observation and anatomical dissection as the keys to knowing how the human body works. By the late seventeenth century, doctors had learned a great deal about the body, its structure, and its chemistry.

The study of anatomy yielded dramatic results. In 1628, William Harvey (1578–1657) announced that he had discovered the circulation of blood. Harvey compared the functioning of the heart to that of a mechanical pump, and once again the tendency to mechanize nature, so basic to the Scientific Revolution in physics, led to a significant discovery. Yet the acceptance of Harvey's work was very slow, and the practical uses of his discovery were not readily perceived.

The experimental method in medicine produced other innovations, among them systematic examination not only of corpses but also of patients. In the late 1600s, the finest doctor of the age, Herman Boerhaave, taught his students in Leiden, in the Dutch Republic, by taking them on house calls, arguing that nothing in medicine can be known without a careful and rigorous examination of the body. He proclaimed that he was trying to bring the methods and philosophy of the new science to medicine, and he pioneered hands-on medical techniques.

Just as Newton applied the theory and method of science to the heavens, his contemporaries on both sides of the English Channel sought to utilize science to illuminate every object we experience. Protestantism inspired them to be aggressive in their assault on scholasticism. Indeed, the most original experimenter of the age, who codified the experimental method as we know it, was a devout English Protestant. Robert Boyle (1627–1691) believed that Aristotle's physics and the philosophy that supported it promoted Catholic teachings and thus amounted to little more than magic. At a time when English Protestants feared a revival of Catholic and absolutist monarchy, Boyle wanted to abolish the invisible forces on which Catholic theology rested. He also wished to defeat the magic of what he called "the vulgar," that is, the beliefs of the populace, whose disorder and tendencies to rebellion he feared.

To accomplish these aims, Boyle urged scientists to adopt the zeal of the magicians and alchemists, but without their secretive practices and their conjuring with spirits. As an alternative to spirits or scholastic forms, Boyle advocated the atomic explanation of matter: it consists of small, hard, indestructible particles that behave with regularity. According to Boyle, the existence of these corpuscles explained the changes in gases, fluids, and solids.

Boyle pioneered the experimental method with such exciting and accurate results that by the time of his death no serious scientist could attempt chemical experiments without following his guidelines. Thus, the science of chemistry acquired its characteristic experimentalism; it was also based on an atomic theory of matter. But only late in the eighteenth century was chemistry applied to medical research, particularly in an effort to cure tuberculosis.

Bacon and Descartes: Prophets of the New Science

The new science needed prophets and social theorists to give it direction and to assess its implications. During the early modern period, two major reformers tried, in disparate ways, to channel science into the service of specific social programs: Francis Bacon (1561–1626) and René Descartes (1596–1650).

Bacon

The decidedly practical and empirical Francis Bacon stands as the most important English proponent of the new science, though not its most important practitioner. Bacon was lord chancellor

PORTRAIT, FRANCIS BACON. Francis Bacon is seen as a prophet of the new science. Witness to the extraordinary scientific energy visible in Elizabethan England, Bacon wrote in order to urge Elizabeth's successor, James I, to embrace science and make it a state priority. Bacon also turned science into an activity of the pious; doing God's work with nature became as important as knowing God's biblical word. (© Historical Picture Archive/CORBIS.)

of England under James I, and he wrote about the usefulness of science partly in an effort to convince the crown of its advantages. He wanted science to serve the interests of strong monarchy and also to improve the human condition through better medicine and application. Partly inspired by alchemy, Bacon brought notions of progress to the enterprise of science.

No philosopher of modern science has surpassed Bacon in elevating the study of nature to a humanistic discipline. In the *Advancement of Learning* (1605), Bacon argued that science must be open and that all ideas must be allowed a hearing. Science must have human goals: the improvement of humanity's material condition and

RENÉ DESCARTES
Né à La Haye en 1596.

PORTRAIT, RENÉ DESCARTES. If the Scientific Revolution had a revolutionary, it was Descartes. Trained by the Jesuits and a devout Christian, Descartes nevertheless turned his back on scholasticism and based learning on the power of the individual mind. "Cogito ergo sum"—"I think, therefore I am"—rallied generations of inquirers, as did Descartes's mechanical understanding of matter in motion. (© Chris Hellier/Corbis.)

***FONTENELLE*, PORTRAIT BY BERNARD PICART.** Fontenelle understood the new science, but most important, he could make it understandable to those less learned than himself. He gave a eulogy on the death of Newton that was read throughout the century, and he also worked tirelessly for the French Academy of Sciences. (© CORBIS.)

the advancement of trade and industry. Bacon also saw the need for science to possess an inductive methodology grounded in experience; the scientist should first of all be a collector of facts.

Although Bacon was rather vague about how the scientist actually works, he knew that preconceived ideas imposed on nature seldom yield positive results. An opponent of Aristotle, Bacon argued that university education should be taken out of the hands of the scholastics and based upon the new learning. A powerful civil servant, he was not afraid to attack the guardians of tradition. The Baconian vision of progress in science leading to better lives and the security of the state inspired much scientific

activity in the seventeenth century, particularly in England. Bacon also benefited from the vibrancy of London's scientific community, one of the largest in Europe.

Descartes

René Descartes, a French philosopher, went to the best schools run by the Jesuits, and he knew the mathematics and scholastic philosophy of his day. Yet in his early twenties, he experienced a crisis of confidence and came to the conclusion that everything he had been taught was irrelevant and meaningless.

Descartes began to search within himself for what he could be sure was clear and distinct knowledge. All he could know with certainty was the fact of his existence, and even that he knew only because he experienced, not his body, but his mind: "I think, therefore I am." From this point of

René Descartes: *Discourse on Method* (1637)

René Descartes gave a meaning to the new science that validated human courage to think for one's self. He grounded everything that could be learned about nature on the individual's capacity to reason and to discover truth.

Part One

Good sense is, of all things among men, the most equally distributed; for everyone believes himself so well provided with it that even those who are the most difficult to please in everything else, do not usually desire a larger measure of this quality than they already have. It is not likely that they are deceived in this. It indicates rather that the power of judging well, and of distinguishing the true from the false, what is properly called good sense or reason, is by nature equal in all men. . . . For it is not enough to have a vigorous mind; but the main thing is to apply it well. . . .

I have been brought up on books from my childhood, and as I was persuaded that by their help I might acquire a clear and certain knowledge of all that is useful in life, I had an extreme desire to learn them. But as soon as I had finished the entire course of study, at the close of which one is normally admitted into the ranks of the learned, I completely changed my opinion. For I found myself so encumbered by doubts and errors that it seemed to me I had advanced no further in all my attempts at learning, than the discovery at every turn of my own ignorance. And yet I was studying at one of the most famous schools in Europe, where I thought that there must be learned men if there were any of them anywhere on earth. I had been taught all that others learned there; and not contented with the sciences actually taught us, in addition I read all the books I had been able to get my hands on . . . ones . . . most curious and most rare.

I was especially pleased with mathematics, on account of the certitude and evidence of its reasoning; but I did not as yet notice its true use, and thinking that it only served the mechanical arts, I was astonished thereby that its foundations being so firm and so solid, that no one had built anything lofty upon them. On the other hand, I compared the writings of the ancient pagans that deal with morals and found them to be towering and magnificent palaces with no better foundation than sand and mud. They extol the virtues so highly, and make them appear more valuable than anything in the world.

I revered our theology, and aspired, as much as anyone else, to reach heaven; but I came to understand that the way is not less open to the most ignorant than to the most learned, and that the revealed truths that guide us there are beyond our comprehension. I would not have dared to submit them to my feeble reasoning, and I thought that in order to undertake to examine them and to succeed in it, one would need to have some extraordinary help from heaven and need to be more than a mere man. . . . And finally, considering that all the same thought that we have when we are awake can also come to us when we are asleep, without there being any of them at that time that be true, I resolved to feign that all the things that had ever entered my mind were no more true than the illusions of my dreams. But, immediately afterward, I took note that, while I wanted thus to think that everything was false, it necessarily had to be that I, who was thinking this, were something. And, noticing that this truth—*I think, therefore I am*—was so firm and so assured that all the most extravagant suppositions of the skeptics were not capable of shaking it, I judged that I could accept it, without scruple, as the first principle of the philosophy that I was seeking.

Questions for Analysis

1. Why is Descartes so eager to find a new way of knowing?
2. What does the statement "I think, therefore I am" proclaim?

Margaret C. Jacob, *The Scientific Revolution: A Brief History with Documents* (Boston: Bedford/St. Martin's, 2009).

certitude, Descartes deduced the existence of God and of nature. He argued that science should be grounded on the human mind's ability to arrive at clear and distinct ideas, to think for itself and not slavishly follow tradition or doctrine.

God exists because Descartes had in his mind an idea of a supreme, perfect being, and, Descartes reasoned, this idea must have come from such a being, not from any ordinary mortal. Therefore, God's existence means that the physical world must be real, for no Creator would invent a vast hoax.

For Descartes, the new science meant confidence: in his own mind, and in the intelligibility of the physical world approached through mathematics and reason. Scientific thought meant an alternative to everything he associated with the medieval: confusion, disorder, conflict between church and state, fear of the unknown, and magic. Turning his back on the centuries immediately preceding his own, Descartes, possibly as a result of knowing Bacon's ideas for practical science, proclaimed that "it is possible to attain knowledge which is very useful in life, and that, instead of that speculative philosophy which is taught in the schools [that is, scholasticism], we may find a practical philosophy by means of which . . . we can . . . render ourselves the masters and possessors of nature."[4] Descartes was among the first to dream about the capacity of science to control and dominate nature, though he never could have imagined its modern potential to destroy nature.

Affirming existence of anything other than the abstractions of mathematics required that Descartes proclaim the existence of God and the physical world. He radically separated matter from spirit and mind from nature, and in the process, he widened a gap in Western thought that would haunt philosophers for centuries. What if a thinker who understood the implications of Descartes's separation of matter from spirit was to argue that only matter existed? Within the mechanical understanding of nature lurked the possibility of materialism.

Benedict de Spinoza (1632–1677) brought that possibility out into the open. Born in Amsterdam of recently immigrated Jewish parents, he was trained in classical languages and Hebrew thought. His genius drew him to the new science, and he became an early explicator of Descartes's philosophy, in which he spied a central weakness: its inability to explain the linkage between matter and spirit or to connect God to nature in any meaningful way. Spinoza's solution was radical, logical, and thoroughly heretical to monotheistic thinkers: he argued that God is, as it were, Nature, that matter and spirit in effect are one.

To this day, philosophers dispute Spinoza's purpose. Was he an atheist who wanted to do away with the monotheistic conception of God, or was he a mystic who wished to infuse God into Nature? His contemporaries of every religious persuasion (he was expelled from his Amsterdam synagogue) deemed him an atheist and thought that he had become one by reading too much science. Their condemnation made "spinozism" a byword for atheism and freethinking, and it flourished largely in anonymous and clandestine literature. In the Enlightenment, freethinkers and materialists would claim to have been inspired by Spinoza.

The philosophies of Bacon, Descartes, and Spinoza revealed the power and importance of scientific knowledge. Science could promote human well-being, as Bacon insisted; it could

La Vérité, **by Bernard Picart.** In the early eighteenth century, French critics of the existing order in church and state used Descartes as a symbol. Here he is pointing to the slaying of error and ignorance by truth. The engraver who created this picture fled France and settled in the Dutch Republic. (Teylers Museum Haarlem, The Netherlands.)

make human beings and nature the foundation of all meaningful knowledge, as Descartes assumed; science could express pantheism or justify a belief in Nature as God, as Spinoza suggested. Whichever position educated westerners embraced by the late 1600s, science would be used to challenge the traditional authority of the clergy, whether Catholic or Protestant. Why believe in dogmas and texts when nature offered another kind of truth—universal and, just as important, applicable to human problems? For good or ill, the Scientific Revolution gave its followers a sense of power and self-confidence unimagined even by Renaissance proponents of individualism or by the theorists of absolute state power.

THE SOCIAL IMPLICATIONS OF THE SCIENTIFIC REVOLUTION

Among the critical factors in the success of the Scientific Revolution lay the acceptance and use of the new science by artisans as well as educated elites. Without such acceptance, the science of Galileo, Kepler, Descartes, Boyle, and Newton would have remained the specialized knowledge of the few—or, worse still, a suspect, even heretical, approach to nature. Galileo could not have succeeded as much as he did in disseminating his theories (despite the hostility of the church) without his large European reading public and his many aristocratic patrons, particularly in Florence.

Access to the printing press in Europe promoted the acceptance of the new mechanical understanding of nature. Descartes understood that fact when he left France, after the condemnation of Galileo, and published and lived in the Netherlands. Persecution and censorship meant that the new science made far less of an impact in Catholic than in Protestant Europe. It is not accidental that most of the leaders within the scientific movement wrote and published in their native languages, not in Latin.

Equally important, the new science offered the dream of power to both governments and early promoters of industry. In the seventeenth century, this dream enticed monarchs and statesmen to give their patronage to scientific academies and projects. The achievements of the new science were quickly institutionalized in academies

BENEDICT SPINOZA. Spinoza lived most of his life in Amsterdam, but was expelled from his synagogue. We do not know why, but it may very well have had something to do with his radical understanding of nature as the only substance in the world. His closest friends were a Dutch sect of devout Protestants who deeply believed in the freedom to think for one's self.
(Archive Photos/Getty Images.)

dominated either by the state, as in France, or by the landed and commercial elite, as in England. Founded in the 1660s, scientific academies such as the Royal Society in England became centers for the dissemination of science at a time when many universities, still controlled by the clergy, were hostile to its attack on scholasticism. In Paris, the new French academy devoted its time to the study of mathematics, mechanics, and alchemy.

The new mechanical learning—not easily grasped from Newton's *Principia*, which was far too technical for most people—required elementary handbooks and lectures in mechanics. This newly systematized science came to be applied in Britain and Scotland during the second half of the eighteenth century. Applied mechanics improved the steam engine and utilized it in coal mining and water engineering. The knowledge of mechanics stemmed from Newtonian lectures and books, which proliferated in Britain during the 1700s. The road from the Scientific Revolution leads more directly to the Industrial Revolution than is often realized. James Watt, who perfected the steam engine, had been tutored in Newtonian mechanics. His engine revolutionized the manufacturing of cotton and the draining of coal mines. In the same period, the scientific gentleman and woman became fashionable, and elite and mildly prosperous families brought microscopes and globes into their homes. Owning these objects caused the family's status to rise, even if no one in the family became an engineer or doctor. Science had captured the Western imagination, and in Birmingham, Leeds, and Manchester, the new industrial centers, applied science became all the rage.

THE MEANING OF THE SCIENTIFIC REVOLUTION

The Scientific Revolution decisively shaped the modern mentality; it shattered the medieval view of the universe and replaced it with a wholly different worldview. Gone was the belief that a motionless earth lay at the center of a universe that was finite and enclosed by a ring of stars. Gone, too, was the belief that the universe was divided into higher and lower worlds and that the laws of motion operating in the heavens were different from those working on earth. Nature became uniform and could be mastered conceptually and mathematically.

The experimental methodology of the new science played a crucial historical role in reorienting Western thought away from theology and metaphysics and toward the study of physical and human problems. In the Late Middle Ages, most men of learning were Aristotelians and theologians. By the mid-eighteenth century, knowledge of Newtonian science and the dissemination of useful learning had become the goal of the educated classes. All knowledge, it was believed, could emulate scientific knowledge: based on observation, experimentation, or rational deduction, learning could be systematic, verifiable, progressive, and useful. This new approach to knowledge referenced the scientists of the sixteenth and seventeenth centuries as proof that no institution

JAMES WATT (1736–1819). This engraved portrait of James Watt comes from his successful years. His somewhat grim affect is consonant with the depression he often described in his letters.
(The Granger Collection New York.)

or dogma had a monopoly on truth. The scientific approach would yield knowledge that might, if properly applied for the good of all people, produce a new and better age. Such an outlook gave thinkers new confidence in the power of the human mind to master nature and led them to examine European institutions and traditions with an inquiring, critical, and skeptical spirit. Scientific societies and academies sprang up all over Europe. In the Dutch Republic in 1785, women founded a society where they received a scientific education. Most scientific academies, however, excluded women into the twentieth century.

The Scientific Revolution ultimately weakened traditional Christianity. God's role in a mechanical universe was not clear. Newton had argued that God not only set the universe in motion but still intervened in its operations, thus leaving room for miracles. Others retained a place for God as Creator but regarded miracles as limitations on nature's mechanical perfection. Applied to religious doctrines, Descartes's reliance on methodical doubt and clarity of thought and Bacon's

Sir Isaac Newton (1642–1727)

Today we know much more about Sir Isaac Newton, about his beliefs and life, than did his contemporaries. Newton was very private, even secretive. He wanted to appear to the world solely as a natural philosopher interested in local motion and the motions of the heavenly bodies. He said sternly, "I do not frame hypotheses," when asked to explain what universal gravitation actually is. In his heart, he believed it to be the will of God operating in the universe. This deeply religious man devoted as many hours of his working week to theology and biblical prophecy as he did to experiments. Perhaps most surprising of all his labors are his alchemical pursuits. Like the magicians of old, he wanted to understand the secret workings of chemical action, and he believed that someday the truly pious natural philosopher would be able to transform ordinary metals into gold. Evidence of the private Newton sits amid his vast manuscript collections, which are now dispersed all over the world. On the Internet, the Newton Project has succeeded in putting many of these manuscripts online so that everyone can read them. Go to http://www.newtonproject.sussex.ac.uk/prism.php?id=1.

insistence on careful observation led thinkers to question the validity of Christian teachings. Theology became a separate, and for some an irrelevant, area of intellectual inquiry, not fit for the interests of practical, well-informed people. Not only Christian doctrines but also various popular beliefs grew suspect. Magic, witchcraft, and astrology, still widespread among the European masses, were regarded with disdain by elite culture. Large numbers of people remained devoted to some form of traditional Christianity, and the uncertainty of a universe governed by devils, witches, or the stars continued to make sense to the poor and oppressed.

In Catholic countries, where the Scientific Revolution began, hostility toward scientific ideas gathered strength after the condemnation of Galileo. The mentality of the Counter-Reformation enabled lesser minds to exercise their fears against any idea they regarded as suspicious. Galileo was caught in this hostile environment, and the church condemned the Copernican system in 1616. In Spain and Poland, it was not officially taught until the 1770s.

Gradually, the science of Newton became the science of Western Europe: nature mechanized, analyzed, regulated, and mathematized. As a result of the Scientific Revolution, learned westerners came to believe more strongly than ever that nature could be mastered. Mechanical science—applied to canals, engines, pumps, and levers—became the science of industry. Thus, the Scientific Revolution, operating on both intellectual and commercial levels, laid the groundwork for two major developments of the modern West: the Age of Enlightenment and the Industrial Revolution.

❖   ❖   ❖

NOTES

1. Quoted in Jean D. Moss, *Novelties in the Heavens* (Chicago: University of Chicago Press, 1993), 33.

2. Excerpted in *Discoveries and Opinions of Galileo,* ed. Stillman Drake (Garden City, N.Y.: Doubleday, 1957), 28.

3. Excerpted in *Newton's Philosophy of Nature,* ed. H. S. Thayer (New York: Hafner, 1953), 177.

4. Excerpted in *Descartes' Philosophical Writings,* ed. Norman Kemp Smith (New York: Modern Library, 1958), 130–131.

Chapter 18

The Age of Enlightenment: Reason and Reform

Engraving by William Hogarth. During the eighteenth century it became fashionable to make fun of the clergy and their privileges. Here William Hogarth, the most brilliant engraver of the period, has the congregation in a bedlam-like state while the preacher invokes hellfire and brimstone. (© Roger-Viollet/The Image Works.)

Focus Questions

1. What does it mean to say that someone in the eighteenth century was "enlightened"?

2. Who were the Freemasons, and what role did they play in the eighteenth century?

3. What is a freethinker? A deist? An atheist? A pantheist?

4. With what economic doctrines do we associate Adam Smith?

5. To whom did Adam Smith's theories appeal? Why?

6. What is the enduring legacy of the Enlightenment? What were its political implications?

7. What do we mean by the Radical Enlightenment?

The eighteenth century's most exciting intellectual movement is called the Enlightenment. So powerful was its dedication to toleration and rational thought that until quite recently the era was sometimes characterized as the Age of Reason. It is more accurately described as an age of criticism, civility, and agitation for reform. What by 1750 came to be known as the Enlightenment began in the late seventeenth century. Three factors were critically important in this new intellectual ferment: revulsion against monarchical and clerical absolutism, especially as practiced by Louis XIV in France; a new freedom of publishing and with it the rise of a new public and a secular culture, especially in England and the Dutch Republic; and, not least, the impact of the Scientific Revolution, particularly the excitement generated by Newton's *Principia* (1687).

When Newton's great work appeared, censorship or imprisonment for ideas disliked by church or state was still commonplace. In France in 1685, the revocation of the Edict of Nantes left Protestants with few choices: they could either convert to Catholicism, go to prison, or try to find a way out of the country, an illegal act that often separated families. More than 150,000 French Protestants—many of them highly literate and all of them deeply angry—were forced to leave for the Dutch Republic, England, or Geneva or to journey to the American colonies. Others languished in French prisons. In the Dutch Republic, opponents of the Calvinist clergy who were deemed heretics could be detained indefinitely; one man died after three years in jail without a trial, probably a suicide. In England, Oxford University routinely expelled students whose ideas were seen to be heretical or unorthodox. In the papal territories, Jewish children were still forcibly baptized and then removed from their homes. By 1750, such extreme measures were rare anywhere north of the Alps or in the American colonies. A new set of values had come to prevail.

Rationality and order—imitative of the order found in Newton's universe—seemed to be gaining momentum. Proponents of enlightened values sought to grant an ordered freedom to social and political institutions. They were prepared to attack in print, though sometimes anonymously,

Chronology 18.1 ❖ The Enlightenment

1685	Revocation of the Edict of Nantes; persecution of Protestants in France
1687	Publication of Newton's *Principia*
1688–1689	Revolution in England: the clergy's power is weakened and censorship loosened; James II, a king with absolutist ambitions, is sent into exile in France
1690	Publication of Locke's *Two Treatises of Government*
1695	Publication of Locke's *Reasonableness of Christianity*
1696	Toland's *Christianity Not Mysterious* makes the case for deism
1717	Founding of the Grand Lodge, London; the beginning of organized Freemasonry
1719	Anonymous publication of the *Treatise on the Three Impostors*, the most radical text of the period
1733	Voltaire publishes *Letters Concerning the English Nation*
1740	Frederick the Great invades Silesia; the War of the Austrian Succession ensues
1748	Hume publishes *An Enquiry Concerning Human Understanding*; Montesquieu publishes *The Spirit of the Laws*
1751	Publication of the first volumes of Diderot's *Encyclopedia* in Paris
1756–1763	Seven Years' War
1762	Rousseau publishes *Émile* and *The Social Contract*
1775	American Revolution begins
1776	Adam Smith publishes *The Wealth of Nations*
1785	Russian Charter of Nobility; the servitude of the peasants is guaranteed
1787	Dutch Revolution begins
1789	French Revolution begins

the attitudes and beliefs that stood in the way of tolerance, freedom, and rationality. As combative intellectuals and pundits, they earned the name *philosophes*—simply the French word for "philosophers"—now used in many languages to describe the bold and witty satirists of clergymen, courtiers, and the pious in general. Thinkers as diverse as Voltaire in France, Benjamin Franklin and Thomas Jefferson in America, and Immanuel Kant (1724–1804), an abstract philosopher in Germany, may be labeled *philosophes*.

Late in the eighteenth century, Kant gave a succinct definition of enlightenment: bringing "light into the dark corners of the mind," dispelling ignorance, prejudice, and superstition. Kant went to the heart of one aspect of the Enlightenment: its insistence that each individual dare to think independently, without recourse to the authority of schools, churches, or clergymen.[1]

Being a political moderate and living in authoritarian Prussia, Kant called for self-education and critical thought without any disruption of the political order, at least at home. In his moderation, he was similar to most philosophes. Distrusting the uneducated people, these intellectual leaders sought a gradual transformation of the human condition.

Radicals could also be found amid the enlightened. Often publishing anonymously they advocated pantheism or materialism, railed against the power of the clergy, and attacked the power of monarchies. Such thinking was visible as early as the 1690s. During the late eighteenth century, there were radical thinkers, such as the American revolutionary Thomas Jefferson (1743–1826) and the feminist Mary Wollstonecraft (1759–1797), who were prepared to endorse an immediate political disruption of the traditional authority of monarchy, aristocracy, fathers, and churchmen. Whether radical or moderate, the philosophes were united by certain key ideas. They believed in the **new science**, were critical of clergy and all rigid dogma but tolerant of people's right to worship freely, and believed deeply in freedom of the press. They were also willing to entertain, though not necessarily accept, new heresies such as **pantheism**, which equated nature with God; or the belief that the earth had gradually evolved; or the view that the Bible was a series of wise stories but not the literal word of God.

Philosophes thrived in the major European cities, where they clubbed and socialized in literary and philosophical societies. By the 1770s, Paris was the center of the Enlightenment, but circles of philosophes could be found in Berlin, Moscow, Budapest, London, The Hague, and, across the Atlantic, in Philadelphia. Their writings spread far and wide because they adopted a new style for philosophical discussion: clear, direct, witty, satirical, even naughty and audacious. At times, they sounded like journalists, propagandists, writers of fiction, even pornographers, who sought to live by their pens. Their success owed much to the growing literacy of urban men and women, a new prosperity that made books affordable and a fashionable sociability where new ideas could be discussed. The philosophes' readers, too, were fed up with all vestiges of medieval culture. They resented priestly and aristocratic privileges, monarchical decrees in place of deliberation in representative assemblies, and

restrictions on who could manufacture what and where. It also helped that the printing presses were relatively free to publish what they pleased in both England and the Dutch Republic.

Appealing to the professional classes, literate merchants, and women with leisure to read, the philosophes opposed the old scholastic learning of the universities, mocked the clergy, and denied the Christian mysteries. They expressed confidence in science and reason, called for humanitarian treatment of slaves and criminals, and played a cat-and-mouse game with censors. Dedicated to freedom of thought and person, they combined these liberal values with a secular orientation and a belief in future progress. The philosophes helped shape, if not define, modern beliefs in tolerance, human rights, and free speech. They also put into print some of the most outrageous writings ever seen in the West; one of these, published in 1719, even labeled Jesus, Moses, and Muhammad as the three great impostors.

THE FORMATION OF A PUBLIC AND SECULAR CULTURE

In England and the Dutch Republic, by 1700 freedom of the press was a practical or a legal reality. During the same period, in 1685, Louis XIV outlawed Protestants from France. In exile, they set up journals and newspapers, formed new clubs, and began a vast international discussion—conducted in French, the language of all well-educated Europeans—aimed against the injustices of monarchical absolutism and the evils of religious persecution. In journals and newspapers, the reformers endorsed the need for political change, the end of clerical privileges, and the wisdom of Newtonian science.

At the same time, relative freedom of assembly in the cities of Western Europe (even in Paris, which was too big to police) gave rise to a new public and secular sphere: a zone for social life outside the family but not attached to churches or courts. The new public sphere, found in *salons* (gatherings in private homes), coffeehouses, and Masonic lodges, as well as in academies for scientific learning such as the Royal Society of London, provided the social space wherein the Enlightenment emerged.

All these autonomous and voluntary groups helped create a new secular and public culture. In this new and free mental space, what we now call *civil society*, people mingled with strangers, politeness and conviviality became norms of behavior, and informal learning flourished. Lecturers gave scientific demonstrations, ordinary men learned to vote for their leaders or to debate publicly, and women met outside the home to discuss novels or politics. Indeed, in some of the Parisian salons, women were often the key organizers. By the 1780s, throughout Western Europe, no town of any size was without a private association, club, and newspaper. In the Dutch Republic in 1785, the first scientific society founded by and for women met in the town of Middelburg (located in the province of Zeeland and no larger than about 17,000 souls).[2] The women chose a Freemason and follower of Voltaire to give scientific demonstrations, and they set about learning Newtonian mechanics with such dedication that their society lasted for more than a hundred years.

Men and women met at these sociable gatherings out of a common interest in politics, science, the new novels, or self-improvement. Members shared certain characteristics: they were highly literate; they possessed some surplus wealth and leisure time; and, if titled aristocrats, they were not opposed to mixing with bourgeois lawyers, doctors, civil servants, and merchants. Such cosmopolitan men and women made the theories of the philosophes come alive. The new societies thus became schools where the literate expanded their universe, learning about peoples of the East and the Americas and about the Newtonian heavens. In the words of Kant, they dared to think for themselves.

This training in self-governance, self-education, and social criticism helped prepare the way for the liberal revolutions that swept across America and Europe at the end of the eighteenth and during the first half of the nineteenth century. In the first years of the French Revolution, the revolutionaries set up clubs based on equality and fraternity and modeled after the clubs and lodges of the Enlightenment.

Salons

Perhaps the most famous of the many new forms of secular culture were the salons, often run by women and mostly found in Paris. Intellectually ambitious women, such as Madame Necker and Madame Geoffrin, organized regular evening receptions in their drawing rooms. There philosophes graced the tables of aristocrats and discussed ideas in an atmosphere that was civilized and open. Originally, the salon was an institution found only in noble homes, where the room designated for leisure activities gave the gathering its name. The habits of luxurious feasting and gaming soon were challenged by serious, if somewhat formal, egalitarian conversation. Salons also developed an international correspondence; letters from all over Europe were read to the assembled guests, many of whom were aristocrats. A new, cosmopolitan republic of letters could occasionally be experienced in the salons. Some salons, however, excluded women, who were attacked as frivolous and gossipy.

Freemasons

As the search for a new religiosity during the Enlightenment came to mean a striving after alternatives to traditional beliefs, private groups with a ritual and ethical component began to flourish. The most famous of these were the Freemasons, a fraternity that evolved in the late seventeenth century in England and Scotland. Originally guilds of working stonemasons, the Masonic lodges gradually admitted middle-class and aristocratic men (and some women). By the 1720s, they could be found in London and on the Continent. Keeping to the ideals of the older stonemasons, they said that all men should meet "upon the level." In practice, this meant calling one another "brother," holding elections for their leaders, and living under rules for correct behavior, all codified in a published book, *Constitutions* (1723). In Britain, after the Revolution of 1688–1689, lodges adhered to constitutional practices, religious toleration, charity, and self-education. The lodges sought to make their members virtuous, disciplined, and civilized. For some men, this experience came to

FREEMASON INITIATION CEREMONY. By the time this engraving was made (1805), freemasonry had become an accepted part of Western social life. But also by that year, the freemasons had been blamed for the French Revolution. They, along with the French philosophes, were said to be responsible for it. That was purely a myth, but it became a part of ultraconservative thought into the twentieth century. Here a blindfolded novice is being led to an initiation ceremony. This engraving is based on that of Gabanon on the same subject dated 1745. The costumes of the participants are changed to the English fashion at the start of the nineteenth century and the engraving is colored, but otherwise is that of 1745. (© P. Rotger/Iberfoto/The Image Works.)

rival that found in the churches. Philosophes such as Benjamin Franklin and, late in his life, Voltaire, joined lodges; in some cities, lodges became cultural centers. In Vienna, Mozart was a Freemason and wrote music for his lodge; in Berlin, Frederick the Great cultivated the lodges, which in turn became centers for the cult of enlightened monarchy. Both George Washington and Paul Revere were Freemasons.

By the middle of the eighteenth century, perhaps as many as fifty thousand men belonged to lodges in just about every major European city. British constitutionalism, as well as the old fraternal ideals of equality and liberty, took on new meaning in these private gatherings. In France in the 1780s, the national Grand Lodge instituted a general assembly of elected representatives from the entire country, as well as a monthly payment of charity for impoverished brothers. The lodges for women became places where women and men actually talked about the meaning of liberty and equality for their own lives. Many lodges were dominated by the most elite elements in Old Regime society (see Chapter 19), who found themselves giving allegiance, and often considerable financial support, to a new system of belief and governance—a system that was ultimately incompatible with the principles of birth and inheritance on which their power rested. In 1738, the pope condemned membership in the lodges. At the time of the French Revolution, its opponents claimed that the lodges were responsible for the uprising. There was no truth to the claim, but it turns up in right-wing rhetoric opposed to modernity and reform. The subversive quality of the lodges lay not in any conspiracy but rather in the freedom they allowed for thought, self-governance, and discussion.

Scientific Academies

By midcentury, in capitals as well as in provincial cities, scientific academies flourished. The first scientific societies had formed in the 1660s in London and Paris. They were imitated in Turin, Budapest, Berlin, and small cities of the Dutch Republic, such as Haarlem and Middelburg. Members of these societies performed experiments of greater or lesser sophistication, listened to learned papers, and searched for natural samples. Each society kept a cabinet of "rarities" containing everything from rocks to deformed animal bones. Anyone who possessed what the age called curiosity could join one of these groups and try to become proficient in the new science. Gradually, women were admitted—not as members but as spectators. By the 1770s, these scientific societies served as models for groups specifically interested in the application of scientific knowledge or in useful learning. The new groups became centers for the reformers and critics of the age, who sought to turn the Enlightenment into a movement for reform.

In Germany and France, where elites dominated the scientific societies, new societies with a utilitarian purpose were founded and had to compete with the older societies. The applied and the utilitarian were more visible in England and Scotland. In France, the academies became centers for abstract and advanced science and mathematics—for important and original contributions with little practical application. During the French Revolution, however, the academies were purged, and emphasis was then placed on applications of

mechanics and chemistry. In northern England during the 1790s, the Lunar Society provided a meeting place for some of the most important leaders of the new movement to apply power technology, like the steam engine, to industry. The application of scientific principles to technological innovation defined the industrial side of the British Enlightenment.

ALTERNATIVES TO ORTHODOXY

Christianity Under Attack

No single thread had united Western culture more powerfully than Christianity. Until the eighteenth century, educated people, especially rulers and state servants, had to give allegiance to one or another of the Christian churches—however un-Christian their political actions. The Enlightenment produced the first widely read, systematic assault on Christian doctrines launched from within the ranks of the educated. The philosophes argued that many Christian dogmas defied logic—for example, the conversion of the substance of bread and wine into the body and the blood of Christ called the Eucharist. They also ridiculed theologians for arguing about obscure issues that seemed irrelevant to the human condition and a hindrance to clear thinking. "Theology amuses me," wrote Voltaire. "That's where we find the madness of the human spirit in all its plenitude." In the same vein, the philosophes denounced the churches for inciting the fanaticism and intolerance that led to the horrors of the Crusades, the Inquisition, and the wars of the Reformation. They viewed Christianity's preoccupation with salvation and its belief in the depravity of human nature as barriers to social improvement and earthly happiness. Although liberal clerics led a moderate and religious Enlightenment, the secular-minded philosophes became far more famous and unorthodox.

Skeptics, Freethinkers, and Deists

An early attack on Christian dogma came from the skeptic and French Protestant refugee Pierre Bayle (1647–1706). He saw superstition as a social evil far more dangerous than atheism. Bayle had fled to the Dutch Republic as a result of Louis XIV's campaign against Protestants. Although a Calvinist in background, Bayle also ran into opposition from the strict Calvinist clergy, who regarded him as lax on doctrinal matters. He attacked his critics and persecutors in a new and brilliant form of journalism, his *Historical and Critical Dictionary* (1697), which was more an encyclopedia than a dictionary. Under alphabetically arranged subjects and in copious footnotes, Bayle discussed the most recent learning of the day and never missed an opportunity to ridicule the dogmatic, the superstitious, or the just plain arrogant. In Bayle's hands, the ancient philosophy of skepticism—the doubting of all dogma—was revived and turned into a tool; rigorous questioning of accepted ideas became a method for arriving at new truths. As Bayle noted in his *Dictionary*, "It is therefore only religion that has anything to fear from Pyrrhonism [that is, skepticism]."[3] In this same critical spirit, Bayle, in his dictionary article entitled "David," compared Louis XIV to Goliath. The message was clear enough: great tyrants and the clergy who prop them up should beware of self-confident, independently minded citizens who are skeptical of the claims of authority made by kings and churches and are eager to use their own intellects to search for truth.

Bayle's *Dictionary* had an enormous impact throughout Europe. Its alphabetical format captured the imagination of the philosophes. Here was a way of simply, even scientifically, classifying and ordering knowledge. Partly through Bayle's writings, skepticism became an integral part of an enlightened approach to religion. It taught its readers to question the clerical claim that God's design governs human events—that God "ordains" certain human actions. Skepticism dealt a serious blow to revealed religion and seemed to point in the direction of "natural" religion, that is, toward a system of beliefs and ethics designed by rational people on the basis of their own needs.

The religious outlook among the enlightened drew heavily on the writings of late-seventeenth- and early-eighteenth-century English freethinkers. These early proponents of the unorthodox used the term *freethinking* to signal their hostility to established church dogmas and their ability to think for themselves. They looked back to the English Revolution of 1640–1660 for their ideas about government; many English freethinkers were republicans in the tradition established in the 1650s. Indeed, the freethinkers of the 1690s and beyond helped popularize English republican ideas at home and in the American colonies, where in 1776 these views would figure prominently among American revolutionaries. French Protestant refugees also translated their writings and made them accessible to all who could read French.

The freethinkers had little use for organized religion or even for Christianity itself. In 1696, the freethinker John Toland (1670–1722) published *Christianity Not Mysterious*. In it, he argued that most religious doctrines seemed to contradict reason or common sense and such beliefs as the resurrection of Jesus and the miracles of the Bible should be dropped. Toland also attacked the clergy's power; in his opinion, the Revolution of 1688–1689 had not gone far enough in undermining the power of the established church and the king. Toland and his freethinking associates wanted England to be a republic governed by "reasonable" people who worshiped, as Toland proposed, not a mysterious God but intelligible nature. For Toland, Newton's science made nature intelligible, and he used it as a stick with which to beat at the doctrines of revealed religion. Toland went so far as to invent his own rituals for a private society of pantheists. It may never have met but by the 1770s liturgies celebrating nature and society were instituted by radical clergymen in London.

Combining science with skepticism, freethinking, and anticlericalism, critics found ample reason for abandoning all traditional authority. By 1700, the works of Bayle, the freethinkers, and philosophers such as Descartes provoked a general crisis of confidence in established authority. Once started in England and the Netherlands and broadcast via Dutch and French refugee printers, the Enlightenment quickly became international, with French as the language of choice.

Some of the early advocates of the Enlightenment were atheists. They often published clandestinely. A particularly early and outrageous example of their thinking appeared under the title *The Treatise of the Three Impostors* (1719). (See Primary Source box.) However, most of the philosophes were simply **deists**, who believed only those Christian doctrines that could meet the test

The Treatise of the Three Impostors

Never before in the Christian West had religion been attacked as forcefully as it was in the eighteenth century. Of course, there had been polemics among and between the various creeds, but the following document denounces all religion and even labels the founders of the three monotheistic religions as impostors. It is openly atheistic and advocates that people come out from under the influence of the clergy and simply worship Nature. To this day, we have only circumstantial evidence as to who wrote it, but we know the circle in the Dutch Republic where it originated. Predictably, it included book dealers (probably out to make some money) and angry French Protestants who had been persecuted and forced to flee their native country. They had also had contact with Toland. Sometimes anger and persecution beget renunciation and denunciation, in this case of the very impulse that caused such grief—namely, religion in general.

. . . One should therefore not be astonished that the world is filled with vain & ridiculous opinions; nothing is better able to give them currency than ignorance; it is the only source of the false ideas which men have of the Divinity, the Soul, Spirits, & of almost all the other objects which compose Religion. . . .

. . . The partisans of these absurdities have succeeded so well that it is dangerous to combat them. It matters too much to these impostors that the people be ignorant, to suffer that they be disabused.

If the people could understand into what an abyss ignorance throws them, they would soon shake off the yoke of unworthy leaders, for it is impossible to let reason act without its discovering the truth.

These impostors have sensed this so well, that to prevent the good effects which it [reason] would infallibly produce, they have had the idea of painting it to us as a monster . . . [and] they would nevertheless be much annoyed if the truth were listened to. . . .

Those who are ignorant of physical causes have a natural fear which proceeds from uneasiness & from the doubt they are in, if there exists a Being or a power which has the capacity to harm them or to preserve them. Thence the penchant which they have to feign [i.e., invent] invisible causes, which are only the Phantoms of their imagination, which they invoke in adversity & which they praise in prosperity. They make themselves Gods out of these in the end, & this chimerical fear of invisible powers is the source of the Religions. . . .

Questions for Analysis

1. What does the text say about the origin of the human impulse to have a religion? How does this text belong to the Radical Enlightenment?
2. Who are the imposters?

Margaret C. Jacob, *The Enlightenment: A Brief History with Documents* (Boston: Bedford/St. Martin's, 2009).

of reason. For example, they considered it reasonable to believe in God, for only with a creator, they said, could such a superbly organized universe have come into being. However, after God set the universe in motion, he in effect disappeared. Thus, although deists retained a belief in God the Creator, they rejected clerical authority, revelation, original sin, and miracles. They held that biblical accounts of the resurrection and of Jesus walking on water or raising the dead could not be reconciled with natural law. Deists viewed Jesus as a great moral teacher, not as the Son of God, and they regarded ethics, not faith, as the essence of religion. Rational people, they said, served God best by treating their fellow human beings justly. Early freethinkers, pantheists and deists in both England and the Dutch Republic constituted what historians now call the Radical Enlightenment.

David Hume (1711–1776), a Scottish skeptic, attacked both revealed religion and the deists' belief in order and design. He maintained that all religious ideas, including Christian teachings and even the idea of God, stemmed ultimately from human fears and superstitions. The universe, said Hume, might very well be eternal, and the seemingly universal order might simply be more in our heads than in reality. Hume laid great emphasis on social conventions, with which he associated religion. Reason should best be expressed through skepticism.

Voltaire the Philosophe

The French possessed a vital tradition of intellectual skepticism going back to the late sixteenth century, as well as a tradition of scientific rationalism exemplified by Descartes. In the early eighteenth century, however, French thinkers found it difficult to gain access to the new literature of the Enlightenment because Louis XIV controlled and censored the French printing presses. As a result, a brisk but risky traffic developed in clandestine books and manuscripts subversive of authority, and French-language journals poured from Dutch presses. *The Treatise of the Three Impostors*, written in French, was first circulated on this clandestine circuit.

As a poet and writer struggling for recognition in Paris, the young François Marie Arouet, known to the world as Voltaire (1694–1778), encountered some of the new ideas being discussed in Parisian salons. In the French capital, educated people interested in the new ideas, some hostile to the church or to the Sorbonne, the clerically controlled university, had to proceed with caution. Individuals had been imprisoned for writing, publishing, or owning books hostile to Catholic doctrine. Although Voltaire learned something of the new enlightened culture in Paris, it was in the early to mid-1720s, when he journeyed to the Dutch Republic and then to London, that Voltaire the poet became Voltaire the philosophe. Voltaire fled Paris after he was arbitrarily arrested when defending himself in a fight with a local aristocrat. His anger toward the French church came to resemble the hostility found among the exiled French Protestants.

In England, Voltaire became acquainted with the ideas of John Locke and Isaac Newton. From Newton, Voltaire learned the mathematical laws that govern the universe; he witnessed the power of human reason to establish general rules that seemed to explain the behavior of physical objects. From Locke, Voltaire learned that people should believe only the ideas received from the senses. Locke's theory of learning, his *epistemology*, impressed many of the philosophes. Again, the implications for religion were most serious: if people believed only what they experienced, they would not accept mysteries and doctrines simply because these concepts were taught by churches and clergy. Voltaire enjoyed considerable freedom

VOLTAIRE AND KING FREDERICK. The roundtable was beloved by the aristocracy because it claimed every one of them as equals. Here Voltaire visits with Frederick the Great and perhaps imagined himself as an equal. (Bildarchiv Preussischer Kulturbesitz/Art Resource, N.Y.)

of thought in England and witnessed social and religious toleration that was in sharp contrast with French absolutism and the power of the French clergy. He also witnessed a freer mixing of bourgeois and aristocratic social groups than was permitted in France at this time. He even went to the stock exchange and witnessed trading. Wittily he remarked that in this setting only the bankrupt are heretics.

Throughout his life, Voltaire fiercely supported toleration and free inquiry. He criticized churches and the Roman Catholic Inquisition. His books were banned in France, but he probably did more there than any other philosophe to popularize the Enlightenment. In *Letters Concerning the English Nation* (1733), Voltaire offered constitutional monarchy, Newtonian science, and religious toleration as models to be followed by all of Europe. In the *Letters*, he praised English society for its encouragement of these ideals. As he put it, "This is the country of sects. An Englishman, as a free man, goes to Heaven by whatever road he pleases."[4] Voltaire never ceased to ridicule the purveyors of superstition and blind obedience to religious authority, and in such works as *Candide* (1759) and *Micromegas* (1752), he castigated the clergy.

Voltaire, a practical reformer, campaigned for the rule of law, a freer press, religious toleration, humane treatment of criminals, and a more effective system of government administration. His writings constituted a radical attack on several aspects of eighteenth-century French society. Yet, like so many philosophes, Voltaire feared the power of the people, especially if goaded by the clergy. He was happiest in the company of the rich and powerful, provided they tolerated his ideas and supported reform. Not surprisingly, Voltaire was frequently disappointed by eighteenth-century monarchs, such as Frederick the Great in Prussia, who promised enlightenment but sought mainly to increase their own power and that of their armies.

Perhaps the happiest decision of Voltaire's life was to team up with the scientist and philosophe Madame du Châtelet (1706–1749). Together they read Newton, although she became the more proficient mathematician. Before her death during the birth of their child, Madame du Châtelet made the only French translation of the *Principia*,

explicated it, and trained scientists who took up Newtonian ideas and spread them throughout Western Europe.

POLITICAL THOUGHT

With the exception of Machiavelli in the Renaissance and Thomas Hobbes and the republicans during the English Revolution of 1640–1660, the Enlightenment produced the greatest originality in modern political thought witnessed in the West up to that time. Three major European thinkers and a host of minor ones wrote treatises on politics that remain relevant to this day: John Locke, *Two Treatises of Government* (1690); Baron de la Brède et de Montesquieu, *The Spirit of the Laws* (1748); and Jean Jacques Rousseau, *The Social Contract* (1762). All repudiated the divine right of kings and strove to check the power of monarchy; each offered different formulas for achieving that goal. These major political theorists of the Enlightenment were also aware of the writings of Machiavelli and Hobbes and, though often disagreeing with them, borrowed some of their ideas. They also made use of Spinoza (d. 1677), who argued that God and his creation are one substance and who deeply influenced what the freethinker John Toland first called *pantheism*.

During the Renaissance, Machiavelli (d. 1527) analyzed politics in terms of power, fortune, and the ability of the individual ruler; he did not call in God to justify the power of princes or to explain their demise. Machiavelli also preferred a republican form of government to monarchy, and his republican vision did not lose its appeal during the Enlightenment. Very late in the eighteenth century, most liberal theorists recognized that the republican form of government, or at least the virtues practiced by citizens in a republic, offered the only alternative to the corruption and repression associated with absolute monarchy assisted by the church.

Political thinkers of the Enlightenment were ambivalent toward much of the writing of Thomas Hobbes (1588–1679). All, however, liked his belief that self-interest is a valid reason for engaging in political activity and his refusal to bring God into his system to justify the power of kings. Hobbes said that power did not rest on divine right but arose out of a contract made among men who agreed to elevate the state, and hence the monarch, to a position of power over them. That contract, once made, could not be broken. As a consequence, the power of the government, whether embodied in a king or a parliament, was absolute.

Hobbes published his major work, *Leviathan,* in 1651, when England had just emerged from civil war; thus, he was obsessed with the issue of political stability. He feared that, left to their own devices, men would kill one another; the "war of all against all"[5] would prevail without the firm hand of a sovereign to stop it. Hobbes's vision of human nature was dark and forbidding. In the state of nature, people lived lives that could only have been "nasty, brutish, and short." Their sole recourse was to make a contract among themselves and establish a power that would restrain them. For Hobbes, the state was, as he put it, a "mortal god," the only guarantee of peace and stability. He was the first political thinker to realize the extraordinary power that had come into existence with the creation of strong centralized governments. Most Enlightenment theorists, however, beginning with John Locke, denied that governments possessed absolute power over their subjects, and to that extent they repudiated Hobbes. Many European thinkers of the eighteenth century, including Rousseau, also rejected Hobbes's gloomy view that human nature is greedy and warlike. Yet Hobbes lurks in the background of the Enlightenment. He is the first wholly secular political theorist, and he sounded the death knell for Christian political theology and the divine right of kings. The Enlightenment theorists started where he left off, and his notion that fear is the source of religious belief can be found in many enlightened texts.

Locke

Probably the most widely read political philosopher during the first half of the eighteenth century was John Locke (1632–1704). Locke came to maturity in the late 1650s, and like so many of his contemporaries, he was drawn to science. Although he was a medical doctor, his major interest lay in politics and political theory.

His *Two Treatises of Government* was seen as a justification for the English Revolution of 1688–1689 and the notion of government by consent of the people. (Although the treatises were published in 1690, Locke wrote them before the Glorious Revolution; that fact, however, was not known during the Enlightenment.)

Locke's theory, in its broad outlines, stated that the right to govern derived from the consent of the governed and was a form of contract. When people gave their consent to a government, they expected it to govern justly, protect their property, and ensure certain liberties for the propertied. If a government attempted to rule absolutely and arbitrarily—if it violated the natural rights of the individual—it reneged on its contract and forfeited the loyalty of its subjects. Such a

LOCKE ON THE CONTINENT. John Locke enjoyed an international reputation. This highly stylized portrait of him is adorned with French text. Locke had lived in the Dutch Republic, and his writings were promoted by French Huguenot refugees who hated the monarchy they left behind. (© Bettmann/CORBIS.)

government could legitimately be overthrown. Locke believed that a constitutional government that limited the power of rulers offered the best defense of property and individual rights. He also advocated religious toleration for religious groups whose beliefs did not threaten the state. Locke denied toleration to Catholics because of their association with the Stuarts and to atheists because their oaths to God could not be trusted. He also promoted the necessity for education, particularly for those who saw themselves as the natural leaders of society. And not least, he advocated commerce and trade as one of the foundations of England's national strength.

Late in the eighteenth century, Locke's ideas were used to justify liberal revolutions in both Europe and America. His *Two Treatises of Government* had been translated into French early in the century by Huguenot refugees. These Protestant victims of French absolutism, persecuted for their religion, saw that the importance of Locke's political philosophy was not simply in his use of contract theory to justify constitutional government; he also asserted that the community could take up arms against its sovereign in the name of the natural rights of liberty and property. Locke's ideas about the foundation of government had greater impact on the European Continent and in America during the eighteenth century than in England. The Dutch and American revolutions found their justification from reprinted editions of Locke's *Second Treatise*.

Montesquieu

Baron de la Brède et de Montesquieu (1689–1755) was a French aristocrat who, like Voltaire, visited England late in the 1720s and knew the writings of Locke. Montesquieu had little sympathy for revolutions, but he did approve of constitutional monarchy. His primary concern was to check the unbridled authority of the French kings. In opposition to the Old Regime, Montesquieu proposed a balanced system of government, with an executive branch offset by a legislature whose members were drawn from the landed and educated elements in society. From his writings we derive our notion of government divided into branches. Montesquieu genuinely believed that the aristocracy possessed

a natural and sacred obligation to rule and that their honor called them to serve the community. He also sought to fashion a government that channeled the interests and energies of its people, a government that was not bogged down in corruption and inefficiency.

In stressing the rule of law and the importance of nonmonarchical authority, Montesquieu became a source for legitimating the authority of representative institutions. Hardly an advocate of democracy, Montesquieu was nonetheless seen as a powerful critic of royal absolutism. His writings, particularly *The Spirit of the Laws*, established him both as a major philosophe who possessed republican tendencies and as a critic of the Old Regime in France. Once again, innovative political thinking highlighted the failures of absolutist government and pointed to the need for some kind of representative assembly in every European country. In addition, Montesquieu's ideas on a balanced system of government found favor in the new American republic.

Rousseau

Not until the 1760s did democracy find its champion: Jean Jacques Rousseau (1712–1778). Rousseau based his political philosophy on contract theory and his reading of Hobbes. For Rousseau, the people choose their government and, in so doing, effectively give birth to civil society. But he further demanded (in contrast to Hobbes) that the contract be constantly renewed and that government be made immediately and directly responsible to the will of the people. *The Social Contract* opened with this stirring cry for reform, "Man is born free; and everywhere he is in chains," and went on to ask how freedom could be attained. Freedom is in the very nature of man: "to renounce liberty is to renounce being a man, to surrender the rights of humanity and even its duties."[6] Human beings are born free and innocent in the state of nature; only society and government corrupt them.

Rousseau's political ideal was the city-state of ancient Greece, where men (but not women) participated actively and directly in politics and were willing to sacrifice self-interest to the community's needs. In the ancient republics, the state was a moral association that made people better and in which good citizenship was the highest form of excellence. In contrast, modern society was prey to many conflicting interests; Rousseau said that the rich and powerful used the state to preserve their advantages and power and that the poor and powerless viewed it as an oppressor. Consequently, obedience to law, devotion to the state, and freedom—the characteristics of the Greek city-state—had been lost.

In *The Social Contract*, Rousseau tried to resolve the conflict between individual freedom and the demands of the state. His solution was a small state, modeled after his native city of Geneva as well as after the Greek city-state. Such a state, said Rousseau, should be based on the *general will*: that which is best for the community and expresses its common interests. Rousseau wanted laws of the state to coincide with the general will. He believed in human beings' wisdom to arrive at laws that serve the common good, but to do so,

they must set aside selfish interests for the good of the community. For Rousseau, freedom consisted of obeying laws prescribed by citizens inspired by the general will. The citizens themselves must constitute the lawmaking body; lawmaking cannot be entrusted to a single person or a small group.

In Rousseau's view, those who disobey laws—who act according to their private will rather than in accordance with the general will as expressed in law—degrade themselves and undermine the community. Therefore, government has the right to force citizens to be obedient, to compel them to exercise their individual wills in the proper way. He left the problem of minority rights unresolved.

No philosopher of the Enlightenment was more dangerous to the Old Regime than Rousseau. His ideas were perceived as truly revolutionary—a direct challenge to the power of kings, churches, and aristocrats. Although Rousseau thought that the philosophes had been corrupted by easy living in the salons, he nevertheless earned an uneasy place in their midst. The French revolutionaries invoked his name to justify democracy, and of all the philosophes, Rousseau probably would have been the least horrified by the early phase of that revolutionary upheaval.

Social Thought

Rousseau looked on society as the corrupter of human beings, who, left to their own devices, were inherently virtuous and freedom loving. Many enlightened thinkers also viewed society, if not as corrupting, at least as needing constant reform. Some critics were prepared to work with those in power to bring about social reforms. Other philosophes believed that the key to reform lay not in social and political institutions but in changing the general mentality through education and knowledge. All developed new ideas about humankind as travelers told of new peoples and places where commonplace concepts, such as the Judeo-Christian God, had never existed. The societies of Native Americans fascinated Europeans, who vacillated between feeling superior and believing themselves mired in baroquely rigid customs. In general, the travel literature freed the European imagination to imagine new mores and to compare themselves with other peoples and their religions.

ROUSSEAU. Rousseau sought innocence and a return to nature. Here children lead the way.

(© Roger-Viollet/The Image Works.)

Profile

Mary Wollstonecraft

One of the founders of modern feminism and a deeply committed defender of liberty, human rights, and the French Revolution, Mary Wollstonecraft (1759–1797) came to maturity in a circle of English radicals. Her friends included the Unitarian ministers Richard Price and Joseph Priestley, and she knew the British-born American radical Thomas Paine. Although she received little formal education, she taught herself languages, made a living as a translator, read Rousseau critically, and began an intellectual odyssey that took her from liberal Protestantism to freethinking and possibly atheism. She went to France during its Revolution and wanted to raise her daughter there because she believed that in France she would be freer. By far her most famous book is *A Vindication of the Rights of Woman* (1792), a classic statement of women's rights and the causes of prejudice and inequality. Since the two hundredth anniversary of Wollstonecraft's famous book, her writings have been revived, and she has been placed at the center of the European Enlightenment as an embodiment of its belief in science and the possibility of human emancipation.

Epistemology and Education

Just as Locke's *Two Treatises of Government* helped shape the political thought of the Enlightenment, his *Essay Concerning Human Understanding* (1689) provided the theoretical foundations for an unprecedented interest in education. Locke's view that at birth the mind is blank—a clean slate, or **tabula rasa**—had two important implications. First, if human beings did not come into this world with innate ideas, then they were not, as Christianity taught, inherently sinful. Second, a person's environment was the decisive force in shaping his or her character and intelligence. Nine of every ten men, wrote Locke, "are good or evil, useful or not, [because of] their education." Such a theory was eagerly received by the reform-minded philosophes, who attributed wickedness to faulty institutions, improper rearing, and poor education rather than to a defective human nature.

In the Enlightenment view, the proper study of humanity addressed the process by which people can and do know. Locke had said that individuals take the information produced by their senses and reflect on it; in that way, they arrive at complex ideas. Education obviously requires the active participation of students. Merely receiving knowledge not tested by their own sense experience is inadequate.

More treatises were written on education during the eighteenth century than in all previous centuries combined. On the Continent, where the clergy controlled many schools and all the universities, the educated laity began to demand state regulation and inspection of educational facilities. This insistence revealed a growing discontent with the clergy and their independent authority. By the second half of the century, new schools and universities in Prussia, Belgium, Austria, Hungary, and Russia attempted to teach practical subjects suited to the interests of the laity. Predictably, science was given a special place. In France, for all the interest in education on the part of the philosophes, by 1789, probably only 50 percent of the men and about 20 percent of the women were literate.

The standards of education for girls and women were appalling. Only a few philosophes, mostly women, and the occasional clergyman who had seen firsthand the poor quality of female education called for reform. But reform did not come until after 1800, when industrialization put more women in the work force and required some literacy. As for higher education, women were excluded, with a few exceptions. Madame du Châtelet in France had studied mathematics with a private tutor; and in Italy, Laura Bassi became the first woman to teach in a European university, at Bologna. In the Netherlands, women founded a scientific academy in 1785. However, these were isolated waves in a sea of largely male and clerical indifference.

Generally, Protestant countries were better at ensuring basic literacy and numeracy for boys and probably also for girls. Lutheran Prussia and Presbyterian Scotland excelled in the field of education, but for very different reasons. In Prussia, Frederick the Great decreed universal public education for boys as part of his effort to surpass the level of technical expertise found in other countries. His educational policy was another example of his using the Enlightenment to increase the power of the central government. In Scotland, improvements in education were sponsored mainly by the established Presbyterian (Calvinist) church. The Protestant universities were by and large more progressive intellectually than their Catholic counterparts. The Jesuits, for instance, resisted teaching the new science. By contrast, medicine at the university of Edinburgh—along with medicine at the University of Leiden in the Netherlands—became the most advanced of the century. But ironically, the universities were never at the forefront of the Enlightenment. For the latest ideas, one went to the salons and not the professors.

That fact fitted in very well with Locke's doctrine that knowledge comes primarily through experience. Rousseau took it up and brought it to its logical conclusion. In *Émile* (1762), he argued that individuals learn from nature, from people, or from things. Indeed, Rousseau wanted the early years of a child's education to be centered on developing the senses and not spent with the child chained to a schoolroom desk. Later, attention would be paid to intellectual pursuits, and then finally to morality. Rousseau grasped a fundamental principle of modern psychology: the child is not a small adult, and childhood is not merely preparation for adulthood but a particular stage in human development with its own distinguishing characteristics.

Rousseau appealed especially to women to be virtuous and to protect their children from social convention, that is, to teach their children about honesty and sentiment. There were problems with Rousseau's educational system. He would make the family the major educational force, and he wanted the products of such education to be cosmopolitan and enlightened individuals, singularly free from superstition and prejudice. However, women (whom Rousseau would confine to the home) were to bear the burden of instilling enlightenment, although they had little experience of the world beyond the family, and in France their education was entirely in the hands of nuns.

Rousseau's contradictions, particularly about women, sprang in large measure from his desperate search for an alternative to aristocratic mores and clerical authority. He also shared in the gender bias of his age, although what may seem bias to us may also have reflected his belief that women sought the home as a solace and refuge. Certainly, many women read him critically, but essentially as an ally and defender.

Humanitarianism

Crime and Punishment. No society founded on the principles of the Enlightenment may condone the torture of prisoners and the inhumanity of a corrupt legal system. On those points, all the philosophes were clear, and they had plenty of evidence from their own societies on which to base their condemnation of torture and the inhumanity of the criminal justice system.

Whether an individual was imprisoned for unpaid debts or for banditry or murder, prison conditions differed little. Prisoners were often starved or exposed to disease, or both. In many Continental countries, where torture was still legal, prisoners could be subjected to brutal interrogation or to random torture such as waterboarding. In 1777, English reformer John Howard published a report in England and Wales that documented how prisoners went without food or medical assistance.

It was the reformers of the Enlightenment who began to agitate against the prison conditions of the day. Even if torture was illegal, as was the case only in England, prison conditions were often as harmful as torture to the physical and mental health of inmates. Conditions still present in some prisons and detention centers today would have been intolerable to the philosophe-reformers.

Although there is something particularly reprehensible about the torturer, his skills were consciously applauded in many countries during the eighteenth century. Fittingly, the most powerful critique of the European system of punishment came from Italy, where the Inquisition and its torture

THE INQUISITION. In one of the first histories of all the world's religions (published in 1723), the engraver Bernard Picart depicted the Inquisition as cold and ruthlessly interrogating (top panel), then as barbarous in its use of torture; at the bottom center is the practice of waterboarding. (Bibliotheque des Arts Decoratifs, Paris, France/Archives Charmet/The Bridgeman Art Library International.)

chambers had reigned with little opposition for centuries. In Milan, during the early 1760s, the Enlightenment had made very gradual inroads, and in a small circle of reformers, the methods of torture employed by the Inquisition and the relationship between church and state in the matter of criminal justice were avidly discussed.

Out of Milanese intellectual ferment came one of the most important books of the Enlightenment: *Of Crime and Punishment* (1764), by Cesare Beccaria (1738–1794). For centuries, sin and crime had been wedded in the eyes of the church; the function of the state was to punish crime because it was a manifestation of sin. Beccaria cut through that thicket of moralizing.

He argued that the church should concern itself with sin and should abandon its prisons and courts. Instead, the state should concern itself with crimes against society, and the purpose of punishment should be to reintegrate the individual into society. Punishment should be swift but intended to rehabilitate.

Beccaria also inquired into the causes of crime. Abandoning the concept of sin, Beccaria—rather like Rousseau, who perceived injustice and corruption in the very fabric of society—regarded private property as the root of social injustice and hence the root of crime. Pointedly, he asked, "What are these laws I must respect, that they leave such a huge gap between me and the rich? Who made these laws? Rich and powerful men. . . . Let us break these fatal connections. . . . Let us attack injustice at its source."[7]

Beccaria's attackers labeled him a *socialist*—the first time (1765) that term was used—by which they meant that Beccaria paid attention only to people as social creatures and that he wanted a society of free and equal citizens. In contrast, the defenders of the use of torture and capital punishment, and of the necessity of social inequality, argued that Beccaria's teachings would lead to chaos and to the loss of all property rights and legitimate authority. These critics sensed the utopian aspect of Beccaria's thought. His humanitarianism was not directed toward the reform of the criminal justice system alone; he sought to restructure society in such a way as to render crime far less prevalent and, whenever possible, to reeducate its perpetrators.

When Beccaria's book and then the author himself turned up in Paris, the philosophes greeted them with universal acclaim. All the leaders of the period—Voltaire, Rousseau, Denis Diderot, and the atheist d'Holbach—embraced one or another of Beccaria's views. But if the criminal justice system and the schools were subject to scrutiny by enlightened critics, what did the philosophes have to say about slavery, the most pernicious of all Western institutions?

Slavery. On both sides of the Atlantic during the eighteenth century, criticism of slavery was growing. At first, it came from religious thinkers such as the Quakers, whose own religious version of the Enlightenment predated the Europe-wide phenomenon by several decades. The Quakers were born out of the turmoil of the English Revolution, and their strong adherence to democratic ideas grew out of their conviction that the light of God's truth works in every man and woman. Many philosophes on both sides of the Atlantic knew Quaker thought, and Voltaire, who had mixed feelings about slavery, and Benjamin Franklin, who condemned it, admired the Quakers and their principles.

On the problem of slavery, some philosophes were strangely ambivalent. In an ideal world—just about all agreed—slavery would not exist. But the world was not ideal, and given human wickedness, greed, and lust for power, Voltaire thought that both slavery and exploitation might be inevitable. "The human race," Voltaire wrote in his *Philosophical Dictionary* (1764), "constituted as it is, cannot subsist unless there be an infinite number of useful individuals possessed of no property at all."[8] Diderot thought that slavery was probably immoral but concluded that, given the importance of slavery in the colonies and the fact that the French monarchy provided no leadership in changing the situation, there was no point in trying to abolish slavery at the time. Indeed, not until 1794, and only after agonized debate, did the French government, no longer a monarchy, finally abolish slavery in its colonies.

It must be remembered that political thinkers of the Enlightenment, among them Locke (who condoned slavery) and Montesquieu (whose ideas were used to condone it), rejected God-given political authority and argued for the rights of property holders and for social utility as the foundations of good government. Those criteria, property and utility, played right into the hands of the proslavery apologists. Montesquieu condemned slavery, but that did not stop its apologists from using his ideas about the relationship between hot climates and sloth to justify enslaving Africans. Even radicals inspired by the French Revolution, such as the British manufacturer Thomas Cooper, could emigrate to the Carolinas and become slave owners and apologists for the system.

Yet if the principle held, as so many philosophes argued, that human happiness was the greatest good, how could slavery be justified? In his short novel *Candide*, Voltaire has his title character confront the spectacle of a young African slave who has had his leg and arm cut off merely because it is the custom of a country. Candide's philosophical optimism is shattered as he reflects on the human price paid by this slave, who harvested the sugar that Europeans enjoyed so abundantly. Throughout the eighteenth century, the emphasis that the Enlightenment placed on moral sensibility produced a literature that used shock to emphasize over and over again, and with genuine revulsion, the inhumanity of slavery.

By the second half of the century, a new generation of philosophes launched bitter attacks on slavery. With Rousseau in the vanguard, they condemned slavery as a violation of the natural rights of man. The philosophes invented the concept of *human rights*. In a volume issued in 1755, the great *Encyclopedia* of the Enlightenment, edited by Diderot, condemned slavery in no uncertain terms: "There is not a single one of these hapless souls . . . who does not have the right to be declared free . . . since neither his ruler nor his father nor anyone else had the right to dispose of his freedom."[9] That statement appeared in thousands of copies and various editions of an encyclopedia that was probably the most influential publication resulting from the French Enlightenment. Indeed, French writers led the enlightened attacks on slavery. The Dutch novelist Betje Wolff had to translate French writers when, in 1790, she launched her attack on the Dutch slave trade.

These writers put the followers of the Enlightenment in the antislavery camp. But that victory was clouded by ambiguous language coming straight from the pens of some of Europe's supposedly most enlightened thinkers and by their prejudice against blacks as non-Europeans.

Social Equality.   The humanitarian impulse inevitably entailed taking a cold, hard look at social inequalities, very obvious in a century when dress, speech, body gestures, and even smell told all. The poor were visibly underfed; workers wore the costumes of their trade; aristocrats, both men and women, dressed in elaborate wigs, shoes, silks, jewels, and lace. Devout Calvinist women often wore black, and only their rings or headpieces betrayed their social status. How could the ideal of human equality be conceptualized in such a society?

Voltaire despised the lower classes. Kant said that women should feel and not reason: "her philosophy is not to reason, but to sense."[10] Women had

A Dutch Jewish Family Preparing for a Feast. Nothing makes the religious toleration advocated by enlightened critics more real than this portrait of a Jewish family in Amsterdam preparing for a religious feast day. They are made to resemble the Dutch in dress and interior design. In short they are being humanized, in contrast to the many anti-Semitic images to be seen in Europe well into the eighteenth century and beyond. (Gianni Dagli Orti/Galerie Saphir Paris/The Art Archive/The Picture Desk.)

few property rights, and the poor had even fewer; the Lockean contract seemed irrelevant to their circumstances. Yet in the American and French revolutions, the leaders proclaimed human equality as an ideal. But even though France freed the slaves in the colonies, the Jacobins closed down women's political clubs. In the new American republic, women began to take a more active role in civil society; slavery, however, remained (in every northern state, though, it was abolished by 1804). Modern critics condemn the

Enlightenment for being inconsistent, but imagine the alternatives: absolute monarchs, established churches, state-run torture chambers, and censorship of speech and writing. It is also the case that in 1785 a young philosopher, Jeremy Bentham, wrote, but did not publish, the first tract advocating the decriminalization of homosexuality and argued that the persecution of homosexuals performed no social usefulness. Blacks, women, gays, and all oppressed minorities can find solace in eighteenth-century social thought.

More than any other previous historical movement, the Enlightenment put human equality on the mental agenda of Western societies. Men and women could meet as equals at social gatherings, the new novels could depict the suffering of women at the hands of brutal men or describe the wretched life of the poor, women could travel abroad as never before, and traveling scientific lecturers frequently sought their tuition. Leisure, literacy, public and secular culture, fiery journalism, local newspapers, travelers' reports, even the new and naughty pornography—all attacked the superstitions and contradictions that centuries of custom had enshrined. The new science pointed to a universe where matter was everywhere the same—atoms are all equal—and it universally obeyed impersonal and impartial laws. The struggle to achieve democratic equality—the dilemma of modern life—first came to the surface in countless acts of reading and conversing in the new enlightened and urban culture. It continues to this day.

ECONOMIC THOUGHT

The Enlightenment's emphasis on property as the foundation for individual rights and its search for uniform laws inspired by Newton's scientific achievement led to the development of the science of economics. Appropriately, that intellectual achievement occurred in the most advanced capitalistic nation in Europe, Great Britain. Not only were the British in the vanguard of capitalist expansion, but by the 1770s that expansion had started the Industrial Revolution. Britain's new factories and markets for the manufacture and distribution of goods provided a natural laboratory where theorists schooled in the Enlightenment's insistence on observation and experimentation could watch the ebb and flow of capitalist production and distribution. In contrast to its harsh criticisms of existing institutions and old elites, the Enlightenment on the whole approved of the independent businessman—the entrepreneur. And there was no one more approving than Adam Smith (1732–1790), whose *Wealth of Nations* (1776) became a kind of bible for those who regarded capitalist activity as uniformly worthwhile and never to be inhibited by outside regulation.

Throughout the seventeenth century in England, there had been a long tradition of economic thought. The resulting ideology stressed independent initiative and the freedom of market forces to determine the value of money and the goods it can buy. By 1700, English economic thought was already well ahead of what could be found on the Continent, with the exception of some Dutch writings. That sophistication undoubtedly reflected the complexity of market life in cities such as London and Amsterdam.

One important element in seventeenth-century economic thought, as well as in the most advanced thinking on ethics, was the role of self-interest. Far from being considered crude or socially dangerous, it was seen as a good thing to be cautiously accepted. In the mid-seventeenth century, Hobbes took the view that self-interest lay at the root of political action. By the end of the century, Locke argued that government, rather than primarily restraining the extremes of human greed and the search for power, should promote the interests of its citizens. By the middle of the eighteenth century, enlightened theorists all over Europe—especially in England, Scotland, and France—had decided that self-interest was the foundation of all human actions and that at every turn government should aid people in expressing their interests and thus in finding true happiness.

Of course, the government had for centuries regulated most aspects of the economic life. The classic economic theory behind such regulation was mercantilism. Mercantilists believed that a constant shortage of riches—bullion, goods, whatever—existed and that governments must direct economic activity in their states so as to compete successfully with other nations for a share of the world's scarce resources.

It required faith in the inherent usefulness of self-interest to assert that government should cease regulating economic activity and that the market should be allowed to be free. The doctrine of **laissez faire**—leaving the market to its own devices—was the centerpiece of Adam Smith's massive economic study on the origins of the wealth of nations.

As a professor in Glasgow, Scotland, Smith actually went to factories to observe the work. He was one of the first theorists to see the importance of the division of labor in making possible the manufacture of more and cheaper consumer goods. Smith viewed labor as the critical factor in a capitalist economy: the value of money, or of an individual for that matter, rested on the ability to buy labor or the byproducts of labor, namely goods and services. According to *The Wealth of Nations,* "labor is the real measure of the exchangeable value of all commodities."[11] Market forces determine the value of labor; it is as simple as supply and demand. Before the invention of money or capital, labor belonged to the laborer, but in the money and market society, which had evolved since the Middle Ages, labor belonged to the highest bidder.

Smith was not bothered by the apparent randomness of market forces, although greed and exploitation angered him. Beneath the superficial chaos of commerce, he saw order—the same order that he saw in physical nature through his understanding of Newton's science. He used the metaphor of "the invisible hand" to explain the source of this order; by that he probably meant Newton's regulatory God, made very distant by Smith, who was a deist. That hand would invisibly reconcile self-interest to the common or public interest. With the image of the invisible hand, Smith expressed his faith in the rationality of commercial society and laid the first principle for the modern science of capitalist economics. He did not mean to license the oppression of the poor and the laborer. Statements in *The Wealth of Nations* such as "Landlords, like all other men, love to reap where they never sowed" or "Whenever there is great property, there is great inequality"[12] reveal Smith to be a moralist. Yet he knew of no means to stop the exploitation of labor. He believed that its purchase at market value ensured the working of commercial society, and he assumed that the supply of cheap labor was inexhaustible.

For all their differences, Smith and the French physiocrats shared certain characteristics common to enlightened economic theorists. Smith wanted to find the laws that regulated economic life; in that search, these economic theorists imitated the successes of the new science. In addition, they believed that progress was possible, resulting in wealth and well-being for all. Knowledge is progressive; hence, by implication, the human condition also yields to constant improvement. This vision sometimes made the advocates of laissez faire myopic when it came to poverty and the injustice of the market. What they bequeathed to the modern age was a belief in the inevitability of progress wedded to

capitalism and free trade—a belief that remains powerful to this day.

THE HIGH ENLIGHTENMENT

More than any other political system in Western Europe, the Old Regime in France was directly threatened by the doctrines and reforming impulse of the Enlightenment. The Roman Catholic Church was deeply entrenched in every aspect of life: landownership, control over the universities and the presses, and access to both the court and, through the pulpit, the people. For decades, the church had brought its influence to bear against the philosophes, yet by 1750, the Enlightenment had penetrated learned circles and academies in Paris and the provinces. After 1750, censorship of the press was relaxed by a new censor deeply influenced by Enlightenment ideals. In fact, censorship had produced the opposite of the desired effect: the more irreligious and atheistic the book or manuscript, the more attractive and sought after it became.

By the 1740s, the fashion among proponents of the Enlightenment was to seek an encyclopedic format for presenting their ideas. After Bayle's *Dictionary,* the first successful encyclopedia was published in England by Ephraim Chambers in 1728, and before too long, a plan was under way for its translation into French. A leading Freemason in France, the chevalier Ramsay, advocated that all the Masonic lodges in Europe should make a financial contribution to this effort, but few, if any, responded to the call.

Four aggressive Parisian publishers took up the task of producing the encyclopedia. One of them had had some shady dealings in clandestine literature, which had acquainted him with the more irreligious and daring philosophes in Paris. Hence, he knew the young Denis Diderot (1713–1784), who had spent six months in jail for his philosophical and pornographic writings. Out of that consortium of publishers and philosophes came the most important book of the Enlightenment, Diderot's *Encyclopedia.* Published in 1751 and in succeeding years and editions, the *Encyclopedia* initiated a new stage in the history of Enlightenment publishing. In the process, it brought to the forefront heretical ideas, which, until that time, only the most radical freethinkers in England and

PACIFIC
OCEAN

NEW
ZEALAND

NEW
GUINEA

NEW HOLLAND
(AUSTRALIA)

JAPAN

MANCHURIA

CHINA

ASIA

Formosa

Canton

Macao
(Port.)

DUTCH EAST INDIES

SOUTHEAST INDIES

Borneo

Timor

Philippine Is. (Sp.)

Java

Sumatra

Madras (Br.)

Pondicherry
(Fr.)

Calcutta

INDIA

Ceylon

Goa (Port.)

Cochin (Du.)

INDIAN
OCEAN

MADAGASCAR

Île de France (Fr.)

ARABIA

Mombasa

Zanzibar

EUROPE

NETHERLANDS

GREAT
BRITAIN

FRANCE

SPAIN

AFRICA

SENEGAL
(Fr.)

GUINEA

GOLD COAST
(Br.)

CAPE OF
GOOD HOPE
(Du.)

ICELAND

GREENLAND

PORTUGAL

Azores (Port.)

Madeira (Port.)

Canary Is. (Sp.)

Cape
Verde Is.
(Port.)

ATLANTIC
OCEAN

Recife

BRAZIL

Rio de Janeiro

Buenos Aires

PARAGUAY

CHILE

PATAGONIA

SOUTH
AMERICA

PERU

Lima

NEW
GRANADA

Quito

Caracas

GUIANA

Cartagena

West Indies

Bahamas (Br.)

GUATEMALA

Mexico City

MEXICO

NORTH
AMERICA

Quebec

Montreal

Boston

New York

Philadelphia

Williamsburg

Charles Town

St. Augustine

Hudson
Bay

NEWFOUNDLAND

PACIFIC
OCEAN

500Mi.

500Km.

250

250

0

0

British

French

Dutch

Portuguese

Spanish

DIDEROT AND ARTISANS. There are many extraordinary aspects of Diderot's great *Encyclopedia*. Among the most noted are the quality and precision of the engravings that depict workers at their crafts. To this day, the volumes remain important sources for knowledge about every craft of the age. (© Bettmann/CORBIS.)

the Netherlands had openly written about. The new era that resulted, called the *High Enlightenment*, was characterized by a violent attack on the church's privileges and the very foundations of Christian belief. From the 1750s to the 1780s, Paris shone as the capital of the Enlightenment. The philosophes were no longer a persecuted minority. Instead, they became cultural heroes. The *Encyclopedia* had to be read by anyone claiming to be educated.

In his preface to the *Encyclopedia*, Diderot's collaborator, Jean d'Alembert (c. 1717–1783), summed up the principles on which it had been compiled. In effect, he wrote a powerful summation of the Enlightenment's highest ideals. He also extolled Newton's science and gave a short description of its universal laws. The progress of geometry and mechanics in combination, d'Alembert wrote in his preface, "may be considered the most incontestable monument of the

◀ *Map 18.1* **EUROPEAN EXPANSION, 1715**
Globalization as a process began in the eighteenth century with European trade, exploration, and colonization. (© 2016 Cengage Learning.)

success to which the human mind can rise by its efforts."[13] In turn, he urged that revealed religion be reduced to a few precepts to be practiced; religion should, he implied, be made scientific and rational. The *Encyclopedia* itself explicitly followed Francis Bacon's admonition that the scientist should be first of all a collector of facts; in addition, it gave dozens of examples of useful new mechanical devices.

D'Alembert, in the preface, also praised the epistemology of Locke: all that is known is known through the senses. He declared that all learning should be catalogued and readily available, that the printing press should enlighten, and that literary societies should encourage men of talent. These societies, he added, "should banish all inequalities that might exclude or discourage men who are endowed with talents that will enlighten others."[14]

During the High Enlightenment, reformers dwelled increasingly on the Old Regime's inequalities, which seemed to stifle talent. The aristocracy and the clergy were not always talented, and seldom were they agitators for enlightenment and reform. Their privileges seemed increasingly less rational. By the 1780s, Paris had produced a new generation of philosophes, for whom Voltaire, Diderot, and Rousseau were aged or dead heroes. But these young authors found the life of the propagandist to be poor and solitary, and they looked at society's ills as victims rather than as reformers. They gained firsthand knowledge of the injustices catalogued so brilliantly by Rousseau in *The Social Contract*.

The High Enlightenment's systematic, sustained, and occasionally violent attacks on the clergy and the irrationality of privilege link that movement with the French Revolution. The link did not lie in the comfortable heresies of the great philosophes, ensconced as they were in the fashionable Parisian salons. Rather, it was to be found in the way those heresies were interpreted by a new generation of reformers—Marat and Robespierre among them—who in the early days of the Revolution used the Enlightenment as a mirror on which they reflected the evils of the old order.

EUROPEAN POLITICAL AND DIPLOMATIC DEVELOPMENTS

Warfare

The dreams of the philosophes seemed unable to forestall imperial developments in power politics, war, and diplomacy. The century witnessed two areas of extreme conflict: Anglo-French rivalry over control of territory in the New World and hegemony in northern Europe; and intense rivalry between Austria and Prussia over control of Central Europe. These major powers, with their imperialistic ambitions, were led by cadres of aristocratic ministers or generals. The Enlightenment did little to displace the warmaking role that had belonged to the aristocracy since the Middle Ages. In Berlin, some philosophes enjoyed the brilliance of court life and turned a blind eye to Prussian militarism.

France and England were the great rivals in the New World, although colonization had been well under way since the early sixteenth century. Spain had been the first sovereign state to establish an empire in America; located principally in South America and Central America, this empire was based on mining gold and silver, trade, and slaves. The English and the Dutch had followed, first as settlers and then also as slave traders, but their colonies lay

to the north—in Virginia, New Amsterdam (later to become New York), and New England. Farther north, the French explored and exploited Canada and the region now known as the midwestern United States. Early in the eighteenth century, the Dutch and the Spanish had largely dropped out of the race for colonies in North America, leaving the field to the French and the English.

By the middle of the eighteenth century, the rivalry of these two powers for territory in the New World increased tension in the Old World. Earlier, the British had sought to contain the French colossus and to ensure their historic trading interests in the Low Countries and the Rhineland by allying themselves with the Dutch Republic and the Austrians, who controlled what is today called Belgium. The alliance of the Maritime Powers (Britain and the Netherlands) with Austria tilted the balance of power against France for the entire first half of the eighteenth century.

Meanwhile, Prussia under Frederick the Great was entering the ranks of the major powers. In 1740, Frederick launched an aggressive foreign policy against neighboring states and ruthlessly seized the Austrian province of Silesia. The forces of the new Austrian queen, Maria Theresa, were powerless to resist this kind of military onslaught. Silesia augmented the Prussian population by 50 percent. The Austrians never forgave his transgression.

In 1756, Maria Theresa formed an alliance with France against Prussia; the ensuing Seven Years' War (1756–1763) involved every major European power. Austria's alliance with France in 1756, which ended the historic rivalry between France and the House of Hapsburg, is known as the *diplomatic revolution*. The Austrians had grown to fear Prussia in the north more than they feared the French. From the Austrian point of view, Prussia had stolen Silesia in 1740, and regaining it was more important than preserving historic rivalries with France. On the French side, King Louis XV longed for an alliance with a Roman Catholic power and for peace in Europe so that France would be better able to wage war against Britain in the New World.

For their part, the British sought an ally in the newer, stronger Prussia and reneged on their traditional ally, Austria. Frederick the Great stood at the head of a new state that was highly belligerent yet insecure, for all the European powers had reasons to want to keep Prussia weak and small.

The Seven Years' War—which seesawed between the opponents, with French, Austrian, and Russian forces ranged against Frederick's Prussians—changed things little in Europe but did reveal the extraordinary power of the Prussian war machine. Only gradually did Prussia join the ranks of the Great Powers, as did Russia.

Hostilities in North America tipped the balance of power there in favor of the English. From 1754 to 1763, the French and the English fought over their claims in the New World. England's victory in this conflict—which was also part of the Seven Years' War—led ultimately to the American Revolution. England secured its claim to control the colonies of the eastern seaboard, a market that would enrich its industrialists of the next generation enormously—though, from the colonists' point of view, unjustly. The French, having been pushed out of North America, tried without success to establish a colony in Guyana; thousands recruited by the French ministry died as a result of mismanagement and disease.

While the major Western European powers were growing stronger, some Eastern European countries were falling further under the domination of the Ottoman (Turkish) Empire as the result of warfare. Only Hungary decidedly benefited from the wars led by Austria against the Turks. With its new independence finally secured from the Turks in 1718, Hungary, now part of the Austrian Empire, entered an era of peace and enlightenment.

Empires and nation-states were the beneficiaries of eighteenth-century war and diplomacy. Only in the Dutch Republic did a little-noticed revolution in 1747 and 1748 provide any indication that the Great Powers or the merchant capitalists had anything to fear from their home populations. The Dutch Revolution was led by men who identified with the Enlightenment and who wanted to reform the institutions of government. Inspired by the restoration of the House of Orange, Amsterdam rose in a democratic rebellion headed by a coalition of small merchants and minor philosophes. In 1748, they failed to effect any meaningful changes, but the calls they made for reform and renewal would be heard again in Amsterdam in 1787 and in Paris in 1789. On the latter occasion, the world would listen. For most of the eighteenth century, however, warfare seemed only to confirm the internal security and stability of the ruling monarchs and elites controlling most European states.

Enlightened Despotism

Enlightened despotism, an apparent contradiction in terms, was a phrase used by the French philosophe Diderot as early as the 1760s. Wherever the philosophes used this term, it referred to an ideal shared by many of them: the strong monarch who would implement rational reforms, removing obstacles to freedom, ending book censorship, and allowing the laws of nature to work, particularly in trade and commerce. When historians use the term *enlightened despotism,* they generally are describing the reigns of specific European monarchs and their ministers: Frederick the Great in Prussia; Catherine the Great in Russia; Charles III in Spain; Maria Theresa and, to a greater extent, her son Joseph II in Austria; and Louis XV in France.

These eighteenth-century monarchs instituted specific reforms in education, trade, and commerce and against the clergy. This type of enlightened government must be understood in context: these countries developed late relative to the older states of Europe. Prussia, Austria, and Russia had to move very quickly if they were to catch up to the degree of centralization achieved in England and France. And when monarchies in France and Spain also occasionally adopted techniques associated with enlightened despotism, they generally did so to compete against a more advanced rival—for example, France against England or Spain against France.

Austria. In the course of the eighteenth century, Austria became a major centralized state through the administrative reforms of Charles VI and his successors. Though Catholic and devout at home, Charles allied himself abroad with Protestant Europe against France. In the newly acquired Austrian Netherlands, he supported the progressive and reforming elements in the nobility, which opposed the old aristocracy and clergy. His daughter Maria Theresa (1740–1780) continued this pattern, and the Austrian administration became one of the most innovative and progressive on the Continent. Many of its leading ministers—such as the Comte du Cobenzl in the Netherlands or Gerard van Swieten, Joseph II's great reforming minister—were Freemasons. This movement often attracted progressive Catholics (as well as Protestants and freethinkers), who despised what they regarded as the medieval outlook of the traditional clergy.

Dynastic consolidation and warfare did contribute decisively to the creation of the Austrian state. But in the eighteenth century, the intellectual and cultural forces of the Enlightenment enabled the state to establish an efficient system of government and a European breadth of vision. With these attributes, Austria came to rival (and, in regard to Spain, surpass) older, more established states in Europe. Frustrated in their German territories, the Austrian Hapsburgs concentrated their attention increasingly on their eastern states. Vienna gave them a natural power base, and Catholic religiosity gradually united the ruling elites in Bohemia and Hungary with their Hapsburg kings. Hapsburg power created a dynastic state in Austria, yet all efforts to consolidate the German part of the empire and to establish effective imperial rule met with failure. Also problematic were Joseph II's interventions in the southern Netherlands. He offended the clergy without winning liberal support. Revolution erupted in Brussels in 1787.

Prussia. German unification proceeded very slowly, and even enlightened despotism could not achieve it. Under the most famous and enlightened Hohenzollerns of the eighteenth century, Prussian absolutism acquired some unique and resilient features. Frederick II, the Great (1740–1786), pursued a policy of religious toleration and, in so doing, attracted French Protestant refugees who had manufacturing and commercial skills. Intellectual dissidents such as Voltaire also were attracted to Prussia. Voltaire eventually went home disillusioned with this new Prussian "enlightened despotism," but not before Frederick had used him and in the process acquired a reputation for learning. By inviting various refugees from French clerical oppression, Frederick gave Berlin a minor reputation as a center for Enlightenment culture. But alongside Frederick's courtship of the French philosophes, with their enlightened ideals, there remained the reality of Prussia's militarism and the serfdom of its peasants.

Enlightened despotism was, in reality, the use of Enlightenment principles by monarchs to enhance the central government's power and thereby their own. These eighteenth-century monarchs knew, in

ways their predecessors had not, that knowledge is power; they saw that application of learned theories to policy can produce useful results.

But did these enlightened despots try to create more humanitarian societies in which individual freedom would flourish on all levels? In this area, enlightened despotism must be pronounced a shallow deployment of Enlightenment ideals. For example, Frederick the Great decreed the abolition of serfdom in Prussia, but he had no means to force the aristocracy to conform because he desperately needed their support. In the 1780s, Joseph II instituted liberalized publishing laws in Austria; but when artisans began reading pamphlets about the French Revolution, the state quickly retreated and reimposed censorship. In the 1750s, Frederick the Great too had loosened the censorship laws, and writers were free to attack traditional religion; however, they were never allowed to criticize the army, the key to Frederick's aggressive foreign policy. Although Catherine the Great gave Diderot a pension, she was uncompromising about her political power, and her ministers were expected to give her unquestioning service.

Finally, if the Enlightenment means the endorsement of reason over force, and peace and cosmopolitan unity over ruthless competition, then the foreign policies of these enlightened despots were uniformly despotic. There were no major philosophes who did not grow disillusioned with enlightened monarchs on the rare occasions when their actions could be observed at close range.

THE ENLIGHTENMENT
IN EASTERN EUROPE

The impact of the Enlightenment in the countries of Eastern Europe varied enormously. Where it made greatest inroads, we see the subsequent emergence of discernibly modern social and political ideas and aspirations. In Hungary, for example, independence from the Ottoman Empire

Map 18.2 EUROPE, 1789 ▶
The Hapsburgs had vast holdings, and this situation did not make the other German states feel secure. This entire map would change after 1800 as Napoleon swept through Europe.

(© 2016 Cengage Learning.)

CATHERINE THE GREAT. Catherine the Great adorned herself to show her aristocracy that she was its superior. (Photo by Popperfoto/Getty Images.)

in 1718 left a country that was still essentially feudal yet eager for reform and renewal. In the 1720s, peace brought regeneration. The population doubled in the course of the eighteenth century, agricultural techniques markedly improved, and by midcentury schools and universities had begun to teach the new science. Hungarian Protestants who had traveled and studied abroad came home with the ideas of the philosophes. A lay intelligentsia was created, and with it came new literature and drama, as well as Western-style civil society: lodges, salons, clubs, and societies. By 1790, the Enlightenment and the French Revolution had inspired a movement for Hungarian nationalism and against the control of the Austrians and Hapsburgs. Then, in 1795, its leaders were executed. However, their nationalistic ideals survived well into the nineteenth and twentieth centuries.

In Poland and Lithuania, the Jesuits remained strong even after they were expelled from other Eastern European countries, such as Hungary. In Poland, the Catholic clergy continued to control education, and the Enlightenment remained a deeply censored, almost underground movement. Yet it did exist and influence educational reform, especially after the expulsion of the Jesuits in 1773. Those who advocated the Enlightenment allied themselves with the monarchy, which they saw as the only force that might be strong enough to oppose the entrenched clergy and aristocracy. The power of the Polish nobility had dire historical consequences for the country. No central authority emerged in eighteenth-century Poland comparable in its unifying ability to the monarchs of Prussia, Austria, and Russia. Not once but three times, in 1772, 1793, and 1795, Poland was partitioned by these three potent neighbors, who took portions of it. Some Poles resisted; a Polish nobleman even appealed to Rousseau in 1771 to help draft a constitution for his beleaguered country. The document in which Rousseau expressed his thoughts on Polish government was cautious and judicious, giving power to all the various elements within Polish elite society. The last partition of Poland wiped it off the map of Europe for more than a hundred years.

The failure of the Enlightenment to take hold in parts of Eastern Europe had far-reaching consequences, with which the people of those countries continue to grapple. In the 1990s, those countries that had experienced the Enlightenment—such as Hungary and the Czech Republic—seemed to show the greatest cohesiveness in the struggle to create a unified, secular, tolerant, and independent state.

THE AMERICAN REVOLUTION

England's victory over France in the Seven Years' War set in motion a train of events that culminated in the American Revolution. The war drained the British treasury, and now Britain faced the additional expense of paying for troops to guard the new North American territories that it had gained in the war. Strapped British taxpayers could not shoulder the whole burden, so the members of Parliament thought it quite appropriate that American colonists should help pay the bill; they reasoned that Britain had protected the colonists from the French and was still protecting them in their conflicts with Indians. Thus, new

THE BOSTON TEA PARTY. The engraver chose to depict free blacks as well as whites applauding one of the early acts that led to the American Revolution. (akg-images.)

colonial taxes and import duties were imposed. Particularly galling to the colonists were the Stamp Act (which placed a tax on newspapers, playing cards, liquor licenses, and legal documents) and the Quartering Act (which required colonists to provide living quarters and supplies to English troops stationed in America).

Vigorous colonial protest against taxation for which no consent had been given compelled the British Parliament to repeal the Stamp Act, but new taxes were imposed, raising the price of many everyday articles, including tea. The stationing of British troops in Boston, the center of rebelliousness, worsened tensions. In March 1770, a crisis

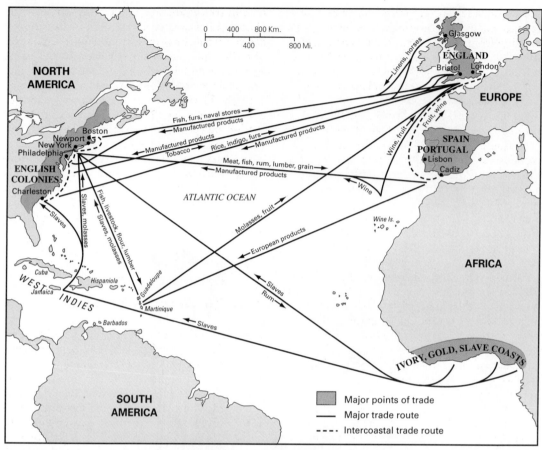

Map 18.3 TRADE ROUTES BETWEEN THE OLD AND NEW WORLDS The trade routes of the eighteenth century foreshadow the globalization of trade with which we are familiar. (© 2016 Cengage Learning.)

ensued after a squad of British soldiers fired into a crowd of Bostonians who had been taunting them and pelting them with rocks and snowballs. Five Bostonians died, and six were wounded. A greater crisis occurred in 1773, when Parliament granted the East India Company exclusive rights to sell tea in America. The colonists regarded this as yet another example of British tyranny. When a crowd of Bostonians dressed as Indians climbed aboard East India Company ships and dumped about ninety thousand pounds of tea overboard, the British responded with a series of repressive measures, which included suppressing self-government in Massachusetts and closing the port of Boston.

The quarrel turned to bloodshed in April and June 1775. On July 4, 1776, delegates from the thirteen colonies adopted the Declaration of Independence, written mainly by the philosophe Thomas Jefferson. Applying Locke's theory of natural rights, this document declared that government derives its power from the consent of the governed, that it is the duty of a government to protect the rights of its citizens, and that people have the right to "alter or abolish" a government that deprives them of their "unalienable rights."

Why were the American colonists so ready to revolt? For one thing, they had brought to North America a highly idealized understanding of English liberties. Long before 1776, they had extended representative institutions to include small property owners who probably could not have voted in England. The colonists had come to expect representative government, trial by jury, and protection from unlawful imprisonment. Each of the thirteen colonies had an elected assembly that acted like a miniature parliament; in these assemblies, Americans gained political experience and quickly learned self-government.

Familiarity with the thought of the Enlightenment and the republican writers of the English Revolution also contributed to the Americans' awareness of liberty. The ideas of the philosophes traversed the Atlantic and influenced educated Americans, particularly Jefferson and Benjamin Franklin. Like other philosophes, American thinkers expressed growing confidence in reason, valued freedom of religion and of thought, and championed the principle of natural rights.

Another source of hostility toward established authority among the American colonists was their religious traditions, particularly Puritanism, which viewed the Bible as infallible and its teachings as a higher law than the law of the state. Like their counterparts in England, American Puritans challenged political and religious authorities who, in their view, contravened God's law. Thus, Puritans acquired two habits that were crucial to the development of political liberty: dissent and resistance. When transferred to the realm of politics, these Puritan tendencies led Americans to resist authority that they considered unjust.

American victory came in 1783 as a result of several factors. George Washington proved to be a superior leader, able to organize and retain the loyalty of his troops. France, seeking to avenge its defeat in the Seven Years' War, helped the Americans with money and provisions, and then in 1778 entered the conflict. Britain had difficulty shipping supplies across three thousand miles of ocean, was fighting the French in the West Indies and elsewhere at the same time, and ultimately lacked commitment to the struggle.

Reformers in other lands quickly interpreted the American victory as a successful struggle of liberty against tyranny. During the Revolution, the various former colonies drew up constitutions based on the principle of popular sovereignty and included bills of rights that protected individual liberty. They also managed, somewhat reluctantly, to forge a nation. Rejecting both monarchy and

hereditary aristocracy, the Constitution of the United States created a republic in which power derived from the people. A system of separation of powers and checks and balances set safeguards against the abuse of power, and the Bill of Rights provided for protection of individual rights. To be sure, the ideals of liberty and equality were not extended to all people. Slaves knew nothing of the freedom that white Americans cherished, and women were denied the vote and equal opportunity; human equality remained an issue throughout the nineteenth and twentieth centuries, as it is today. To reform-minded Europeans, however, it seemed that Americans were fulfilling the promise of the Enlightenment. They were creating a freer and better society.

THE ENLIGHTENMENT AND THE MODERN WORLD

Enlightened thought culminated a trend begun by Renaissance humanists, who attacked medieval otherworldliness and gave value to individual achievement and the worldly life. It was a direct outgrowth of the Scientific Revolution, which provided a new method of inquiry and verification and demonstrated the power and self-sufficiency of the human intellect. If nature were autonomous—that is, if it operated according to natural laws without the need of divine intervention—then the human intellect also could be autonomous. Through its own powers, the mind could uncover the general principles that operate in the social world, as well as in nature.

The philosophes sought to analyze nature, government, religion, law, economics, and education by thinking for themselves, with little reference to Christian teachings, and they rejected completely the claims of clerics to a special wisdom. The philosophes broke decisively with the medieval view that the individual is naturally depraved, that heaven is the true end of life, and that human values and norms derive from a higher reality and are made known through revelation. Instead, they upheld the potential goodness of the individual, regarded the good life on earth as the true purpose of existence, and insisted that individuals could improve themselves and their society by the light of reason.

In addition, the political philosophies of Locke, Montesquieu, and Rousseau rested on an entirely new (and modern) concept of the relationship between the state and the individual: states should exist not simply to accumulate power but also to enhance human happiness. From that perspective, monarchy, and even oligarchy not based on merit, began to seem increasingly less useful. And if happiness is a goal, then it must be assumed that some sort of progress is possible in history.

When we observe societies that have never experienced their own version of enlightenment, oftentimes we see the oppression of women and authoritarian governments, sometimes run by clergymen. Religion can turn to intolerance or even the fanaticism of terrorists if unchecked by questions or doubt.

The philosophes wanted a freer, more humane, and more rational society, but they feared the people and their potential for revolutionary action. As an alternative to revolution, most philosophes offered science as the universal improver

of the human condition. Faith in reform without the necessity of revolution proved to be a doctrine for the elite of the salons. In that sense, the French Revolution can be said to have repudiated the essential moderation of philosophes such as Voltaire, d'Alembert, and Kant.

However, the Enlightenment established a vision of humanity so independent of Christianity and so focused on the needs and abuses of the society of the time that no established institution, once grown corrupt and ineffectual, could long withstand its penetrating critique. To that extent, the writings of the philosophes point toward the democratic revolutions of the late eighteenth century. To a lesser extent, the writers of the Enlightenment also point toward ideals that remain strong in most democratic Western societies: human rights in general, religious toleration, freedom from torture, a disdain for prejudice and superstition, a fear of unchecked political authority, and, of course, a belief in the power of the human mind to recognize the irrational and attempt to correct it.

❖ ❖ ❖

NOTES

1. "An Answer to the Question: 'What Is Enlightenment?'" in *Kant's Political Writings,* ed. Hans Reiss (Cambridge: Cambridge University Press, 1970), 54–60.

2. *Wetten van het Natuurkundig Genootschap, door eenige Dames opgericht, binnen Middelburg den 6 August. 1785* (Rules for the Scientific Society established by women within Middelburg on 6 August 1785) (Middelburg, 1785), 29. The only known copy is to be found in the Provincial Library in Zeeland, the Netherlands.

3. Pierre Bayle, *Historical and Critical Dictionary,* ed. Richard H. Popkin (New York: Bobbs-Merrill, 1965), 195.

4. Voltaire, *Philosophical Letters* (New York: Bobbs-Merrill, 1961), 22.

5. Thomas Hobbes, *Leviathan,* ed. C. B. Macpherson (Harmondsworth, England: Penguin, 1977), 189.

6. Jean Jacques Rousseau, *The Social Contract and Discourses* (New York: Dutton, 1950), 3, 9.

7. Quoted in Franco Venturi, *Utopia and Reform in the Enlightenment* (Cambridge: Cambridge University Press, 1971), 101.

8. Voltaire, *Philosophical Dictionary,* ed. Theodore Besterman (Harmondsworth, England: Penguin, 1974), 183.

9. Quoted in David B. Davis, *The Problem of Slavery in Western Culture* (Harmondsworth, England: Penguin, 1970), 449.

10. Immanuel Kant, *Beobachtungen,* in *Kants Werke,* ed. W. Dilthey Wilhelm (1900–1919), 2:230.

11. Adam Smith, *The Wealth of Nations,* ed. George Stigler (New York: Appleton, 1957), 3.

12. Ibid., 98.

13. Jean Le Rond d'Alembert, *Preliminary Discourse to the Encyclopedia of Diderot,* trans. Richard N. Schwab (New York: Bobbs-Merrill, 1963), 22.

14. Ibid., 101–102.

Part Four

An Age of Revolution: Liberal, National, Industrial

1789–1848

Politics and Society

French Revolution begins (1789)
Declaration of the Rights of Man and of
the Citizen (1789)

France declares war on Austria (1792)
Execution of Louis XVI (1793)
Reign of Terror (1793–1794)
Napoleon seizes power (1799)

Battle of Trafalgar: French and Spanish
fleets defeated by the British (1805)
Napoleon defeats Prussians at
Jena (1806)
Napoleon defeats Russians at
Friedland (1807)

Napoleon invades Russia (1812)
Napoleon defeated at Waterloo (1815)
Congress of Vienna (1814–1815)

Revolutions in Spain, Italy, Russia,
and Greece (1820–1829)

Revolutions in France, Belgium, Poland,
and Italy (1830–1832)
Reform in Britain: Reform Act of 1832;
slavery abolished within British Empire
(1833); Factory Act (1833)

Irish famine (1845–1849)
Revolutions in France, Germany, Austria,
and Italy (1848)

Thought and Culture

Kant, *Critique of Pure Reason* (1781)
Bentham, *Principles of Morals and
Legislation* (1789)

Burke, *Reflections on the Revolution in
France* (1790)
Wollstonecraft, *A Vindication of the Rights of
Woman* (1792)
De Maistre, *Reflections on the State of
France* (1796)
Wordsworth, *Lyrical Ballads* (1798)
Malthus, *Essay on the Principle of
Population* (1798)

Beethoven, *Fifth Symphony* (1807–1808)
Goethe, *Faust* (1808, 1832)

Byron, *Childe Harold* (1812)

Shelley, *Prometheus Unbound* (1820)
Ricardo, *Principles of Political
Economy* (1817)
Hegel, *The Philosophy of History*
(1822–1831)

Fourier, *Treatise on Agrarian Domestic
Fellowship* (1822)
Comte, *Course in Positive Philosophy*
(1830–1842)

Proudhon, *What Is Property?* (1840)
Tocqueville, *Democracy in America*
(1835–1840)
Gaskell, *Mary Barton* (1848)
Marx, *Communist Manifesto* (1848)

Chapter 19

The French Revolution: The Affirmation of Liberty and Equality

The Storming of Bastille, July 14, 1789. (Musée Carnavalet/akg-images.)

Focus Questions

1. What were the causes of the French Revolution?

2. How did the Enlightenment and the American Revolution influence the French Revolution?

3. Why are the reforms of the National Assembly described as the death warrant of the Old Regime?

4. Why and how did the French Revolution move from a moderate to a radical stage?

5. How do you evaluate the purpose and significance of the Terror?

6. What principles underlay Napoleon's domestic reforms?

7. How did Napoleon both preserve and destroy the ideals of the French Revolution?

8. Why is the French Revolution a decisive period in the shaping of the modern West?

The outbreak of the French Revolution in 1789 stirred the imagination of Europeans. Both participants and observers sensed that they were living in a pivotal age. On the ruins of the Old Order, founded on privilege and despotism, a new era was forming, and it promised to realize the ideals of the Enlightenment. These ideals included the emancipation of the human personality from superstition and tradition, the triumph of liberty over tyranny, the refashioning of institutions in accordance with reason and justice, and the tearing down of barriers to equality. It seemed that the natural rights of the individual, hitherto a distant ideal, would now become reality, and centuries of oppression and misery would end. Never before had people shown such confidence in the power of human intelligence to shape the conditions of existence. Never before had the future seemed so full of hope.

This lofty vision kindled emotions akin to religious enthusiasm and attracted converts throughout the Western world. "If we succeed," wrote the French poet André Chénier, "the destiny of Europe will be changed. Men will regain their rights and the people their sovereignty."[1] The editor of the Viennese publication *Wiener Zeitung* wrote to a friend: "In France a light is beginning to shine which will benefit the whole of humanity."[2] Friedrich von Gentz, who later turned against the Revolution, wrote in 1791: "The Revolution constitutes the first practical triumph of philosophy, the first example in the history of the world of the construction of government upon the principles of an orderly, rationally-constructed system. It constitutes the hope of mankind and provides consolation to men elsewhere who continue to groan under the weight of age-old evils."[3] The British reformer John Cartwright expressed the hopes of reformers everywhere: "Degenerate must be that heart which expands not with sentiments of delight at what is now transacting in . . . France. The French . . . are not only asserting their own rights, but they are asserting and advancing the general iberties of mankind."[4]

Chronology 19.1 ❖ The French Revolution

July 1788	Calling of the Estates General
May 5, 1789	Convening of the Estates General
June 17, 1789	Third Estate declares itself the National Assembly
July 14, 1789	Storming of the Bastille
Late July 1789	The Great Fear
August 4, 1789	Nobles surrender their special privileges
June 1791	Flight of Louis XVI
October 1791	Legislative Assembly succeeds the National Assembly
April 20, 1792	Legislative Assembly declares war on Austria
August 10, 1792	Parisians attack the king's palace
September 1792	September Massacres
September 20, 1792	Battle of Valmy
September 21–22, 1792	Abolition of the monarchy
January 21, 1793	Execution of Louis XVI
June 1793	Jacobins replace Girondins as the dominant group in the National Convention
July 28, 1794	Robespierre is guillotined
1795 and 1796	Failed insurrections by the poor of Paris
September 1797	Royalist coup d'état against the Directory is crushed
November 1799	Napoleon seizes power
December 2, 1804	Napoleon crowns himself emperor of the French
October–December 1812	Grand Army retreats from Russia
October 1813	Allied forces defeat Napoleon at Leipzig
1814	Paris is captured and Napoleon is exiled to Elba
March 20, 1815	Escaping, Napoleon enters Paris
June 1815	Defeated at Waterloo, Napoleon is exiled to Saint Helena

THE OLD REGIME

Eighteenth-century French society was divided into three orders, or **Estates**, which were legally defined groupings. The clergy constituted the First Estate, the nobility the Second Estate, and everyone else (about 96 percent of the population) the Third Estate. The clergy and nobility, totaling about 500,000 out of a population of 26 million, enjoyed special privileges, receiving pensions and profitable positions from the king. The social structure of the **Old Regime**, based on privileges and inequalities sanctioned by law, produced tensions that contributed to the Revolution.

The First Estate

The powers and privileges of the French Catholic church made it a state within a state. As it had done for centuries, the church registered births, marriages, and deaths; collected tithes (a tax on products from the soil); censored books considered dangerous to religion and morals; operated schools; and distributed relief to the poor. Because it was illegal for Protestants to assemble publicly for prayer, the Catholic Church enjoyed a monopoly on public worship. Although it owned an estimated 10 percent of the land, which brought in an immense revenue, the church paid no taxes. Instead, it made a "free gift" to the state (the church determined the amount), which was always smaller than direct taxes would have been. Critics denounced the church for promoting superstition and obscurantism, impeding reforms, and being more concerned with wealth and power than with the spiritual message of Jesus.

The clergy reflected the social divisions in France. The upper clergy shared the attitudes and way of life of the nobility from which they sprang. The parish priests, commoners by birth, resented the haughtiness and luxurious living of the upper clergy. In 1789, when the Revolution began, many priests sympathized with the reform-minded people of the Third Estate.

The Second Estate

Like the clergy, the nobility was a privileged order. Nobles held the highest positions in the church, army, and government. They were exempt from most taxes (or used their influence to evade taxes), collected manorial dues from peasants, and owned between one-quarter and one-third of the land. In addition to the income they drew from their estates, nobles were becoming increasingly involved in such nonaristocratic enterprises as banking, finance, commerce, and industry. Many key philosophes—Montesquieu, Condorcet, d'Holbach—were nobles, and nobles were the leading patrons of the arts. Most nobles, however, were suspicious and intolerant of the liberal ideas advanced by the philosophes.

All nobles were not equal; there were gradations of dignity among the 350,000 members of the nobility. Enjoying the most prestige were *nobles of the sword*: families that could trace their aristocratic status back several centuries. Many of these noblemen were officers in the king's army. The highest of the ancient nobles were engaged in the social whirl at Versailles and Paris, receiving pensions and sinecures from the king but performing few useful services for the state. Most nobles of the sword, unable to afford the gilded life at court, remained on their provincial estates, the poorest of them barely distinguishable from prosperous peasants.

Alongside this ancient nobility, a new nobility had arisen, created by the monarchy. To obtain money, reward favorites, and weaken the old nobility, French kings had sold titles of nobility to members of the **bourgeoisie** and had conferred noble status on certain government offices bought by wealthy bourgeois. Particularly significant were *nobles of the robe*, who had purchased judicial offices in the *parlements*—the high law courts—and whose ranks included many former bourgeois.

Opinion among the aristocrats was divided. Influenced by the liberal ideals of the philosophes, some nobles sought to reform France; they wanted to end royal despotism and establish a constitutional government. To this extent, the liberal nobility had a great deal in common with the bourgeoisie. These liberal nobles saw the king's difficulties in 1788 as an opportunity to regenerate the nation under enlightened leadership. When they resisted the king, they claimed that they were attacking despotic rule. But many nobles, concerned with preserving their privileges and honorific status, were hostile to liberal ideals and opposed reform.

The Third Estate

The Third Estate comprised the bourgeoisie, peasants, and urban laborers. Although the bourgeoisie provided the leadership for the Revolution, its success depended on the support given by the rest of the Third Estate.

The Bourgeoisie. The bourgeoisie consisted of merchant-manufacturers, wholesale merchants, bankers, master craftsmen, doctors, lawyers, intellectuals, and government officials below the top ranks. Although the bourgeoisie had wealth, it lacked social prestige. A merchant, despite his worldly success, felt that his occupation denied him the esteem enjoyed by the nobility. "There are few rich people who at times do not feel humiliated at being nothing but wealthy," observed an eighteenth-century Frenchman.[5]

Influenced by the aristocratic values of the day and envious of the nobility's lifestyle, the bourgeoisie sought to erase the stigma of common birth and to rise socially by becoming landowners. By 1789, the bourgeoisie owned about 20 percent of the land. Traditionally, some members of the bourgeoisie had risen socially either by purchasing a judicial or political office that carried with it a title of nobility or by gaining admission to the upper clergy and the officer ranks of the army. Access to the nobility remained open throughout the eighteenth century. Nevertheless, since the highest and most desired positions in the land were reserved for the nobility, able bourgeois were often excluded for a variety of reasons: the high cost of purchasing an office, the limited number of new offices created, the resistance of nobles to their advancement, or the hostility of the older nobility toward those recently ennobled. No doubt these men felt frustrated and came to resent a social system that valued birth more than talent. For most of the century, however, the bourgeoisie did not challenge the existing social structure, including the special privileges of the nobility.

By 1789, the bourgeois had many grievances. They wanted all positions in the church, army, and state to be open to men of talent regardless of birth. They sought a parliament that would make laws for the nation; a constitution that would limit the king's power and guarantee freedom of thought, a fair trial, and religious toleration; and administrative reforms that would eliminate waste, inefficiency, and interference with business.

The Peasantry. The condition of the more than 21 million French peasants was a paradox. On the one hand, they were better off than peasants in Austria, Prussia, Poland, and Russia, where serfdom still predominated. In France, serfdom had largely disappeared; many peasants owned land, and some were even prosperous. But most French peasants lived in poverty, which worsened in the closing years of the Old Regime.

Peasants owned between 30 and 40 percent of the land, but the typical holding was barely large enough to eke out a living. The rising birthrate (between 1715 and 1789, the population may have increased from 18 million to 26 million) led to the continual subdivision of farms among heirs. Moreover, many peasants did not own land but rented it from a nobleman or a prosperous neighbor. Others worked as sharecroppers, turning over to their creditors a considerable portion of the harvest.

Owning too little land to support themselves, many peasants tried to supplement their incomes. They hired themselves out for whatever employment was available in their region: as agricultural day laborers, charcoal burners, transporters of wine, or textile workers in their own homes. Landless peasants tried to earn a living in such ways. The increasing birthrate resulted in an overabundance of rural wage earners. This worsened the plight of small landowners and reduced the landless to beggary. "The number of our children reduces us to desperation"[6] was a common complaint of the peasants by 1789.

An unjust and corrupt system of taxation weighed heavily on the peasantry. Louis XIV had maintained his grandeur and financed his wars by milking ever more taxes from the peasants, a practice that continued throughout the eighteenth century. An army of tax collectors victimized the peasantry. In addition to royal taxes, peasants paid the tithe to the church and manorial dues to lords.

"LET'S HOPE THAT THE GAME FINISHES WELL." This political cartoon shows a laborer carrying smug representatives of the privileged orders on his back.
(Erich Lessing/Art Resource, N.Y.)

Although serfdom had ended in most parts of France, lords continued to demand obligations from peasants as they had done in the Middle Ages. Besides performing labor services on the lord's estate, peasants still had to grind their corn in the lord's mill, bake their bread in his oven, press their grapes in his winepress, and give him part of their produce in payment. (Their fees were called *banalities*.) In addition, the lord collected a land rent from peasant proprietors, levied dues on goods at markets and fairs, and exercised exclusive hunting rights on lands tilled by peasants. The last was a particularly onerous right, for the lord's hunting parties damaged crops. Lords were determined to hold on to these privileges, not only because of the income they brought but also because they were symbols of authority and social esteem. The peasants, however, regarded these obligations as hateful legacies of the past from which they derived no benefit.

Map 19.1 **THE FRENCH REVOLUTION, 1789–1793** French revolutionaries had to deal with both internal enemies and foreign invasion. (© 2016 Cengage Learning.)

In the last part of the eighteenth century, lords sought to exact more income from their lands by reviving manorial dues that had not been collected for generations, increasing the rates on existing dues, and contracting businessmen to collect payments from the peasants. These capitalists naturally tried to squeeze as much income as possible from the peasants, making them hate the whole system of manorial obligations even more.

Inefficient farming methods also contributed to the poverty of the French peasants. In the eighteenth century, France did not experience a series of agricultural improvements comparable to those in England. Failure to invest capital in modernizing agricultural methods meant low yields per acre and a shortage of farm animals.

A rise in the price of necessities during the closing years of the Old Regime worked hardship on those peasants who depended on wages for survival. With prices rising faster than wages, only the more prosperous peasants with produce to sell benefited. The great majority of peasants were driven deeper into poverty, and the number of beggars roaming the countryside increased. A poor harvest in 1788 and 1789 aggravated peasant misery and produced an atmosphere of crisis. The granaries were empty; the price of bread, the staple food of the French, soared; and starvation threatened. Hatred of the manorial order and worsening poverty sparked a spontaneous and autonomous peasant revolution in 1789.

Urban Laborers.   The urban laboring class in this preindustrial age consisted of journeymen working for master craftsmen, factory workers in small-scale industries, and wage earners such as day laborers, gardeners, handymen, and deliverymen, who were paid by those they served. The poverty of the urban poor, like that of the peasant wage earners, worsened in the late eighteenth century. From 1785 to 1789, the cost of living increased by 62 percent, while wages rose only 22 percent. For virtually the entire decade of the Revolution, urban workers struggled to keep body and soul together in the face of food shortages and rising prices, particularly the price of their staple food, bread. Material want drove the urban poor to acts of violence that affected the course of the Revolution.

Inefficient Administration and Financial Disorder

Eighteenth-century France was in theory an absolute monarchy. The king claimed that his power derived from God, and, unlike Britain, France had no parliament that represented the people and met as a continuous body. The administration of the country was complex, confusing, and ineffective. The practice of buying state offices from the king, introduced as a means of raising money, brought in many incompetent officeholders. "When his Majesty created an office," stated one administrator, "Providence called into being an imbecile to buy it."[7] Tariffs on goods shipped from one French province to another and differing systems of weights and measures hampered trade. No single law code applied to all the provinces; instead, there were overlapping and conflicting law systems based on old Roman law or customary feudal law, which made the administration of justice slow, arbitrary, and unfair. To admirers of the philosophes, the administrative system was an insult to reason. The Revolution would sweep the system away.

Financial disorders also contributed to the weakness of the Old Regime. In the regime's last years, the government could not raise sufficient funds to cover expenses. Servicing the debt incurred during the War of the Austrian Succession (1740–1748) and the Seven Years' War (1756–1763) placed an immense burden on the treasury. This burden reached crisis proportions when France incurred additional expenses by aiding the colonists in the American Revolution. The king's gifts and pensions to court nobles and the extravagant court life further drained the treasury.

Finances were in a shambles, not because France was impoverished but because it had an inefficient and unjust tax system. Few wealthy Frenchmen, including the bourgeois, paid their fair share of taxes. Because tax revenue came chiefly from the peasants, it was bound to be inadequate. Although serious, the financial crisis could have been solved if the clergy, nobility, and bourgeoisie paid their fair share of taxes. Some progressive ministers recognized the need for comprehensive reforms, but nobles and clergy resisted them, clinging tenaciously to their ancient privileges. The irresolution of the king and the intrigues, rivalries, and incompetence of his ministers also impeded reform.

The nobles were able to thwart royal will mainly through the parlements, the high law courts. Many parlementaires were originally wealthy bourgeois who had purchased their offices from the state (nobles of the robe). Both the office and status of nobility remained within the family. The Paris parlement and twelve provincial parlements reviewed the judgments of lower courts and registered royal edicts. The parlements had the right to *remonstrate*, that is, to pass judgment on the legality of royal edicts before registering them. If the courts considered the king's new laws at variance with previous legislation or ancient traditions, they would refuse to register them. (Generally, it was the Paris parlement that set the example.) The king could revise the edicts in accordance with the parlements' instructions or force their registration by means of a *lit de justice*: a solemn ceremony in which the monarch appeared before the court. If the parlementaires stood firm in their resistance, the king might order the arrest of their leaders. Although the king could force his will on the parlements, their bold opposition damaged royal prestige.

With France on the brink of bankruptcy, the king's ministers proposed that the nobility and the church surrender some of their tax privileges. The parlements protested and remonstrated. Some nobles resisted because they were steadfast defenders of noble prerogatives; the more liberal nobles resisted because they saw an opportunity to check absolutism and introduce fundamental reforms that would regenerate the nation.

The resistance of the nobility forced the government, in July 1788, to call for a meeting of the Estates General—a medieval representative assembly, which had last met in 1614—to deal with the financial crisis. The body was to convene in May 1789. Certain that they would dominate the Estates General, the nobles intended to weaken the power of the throne. Once in control of the government, they would introduce financial reforms. But the revolt of the nobility against the crown had unexpected consequences. It opened the way for revolutions by the Third Estate, which destroyed the Old Regime and with it the aristocracy and its privileges.

The Roles of the Enlightenment and the American Revolution

Revolutions are born in the realm of the spirit. Revolutionary movements, says George Rudé, a historian of the French Revolution, require "some unifying body of ideas, a common vocabulary of hope and protest, something, in short, like a common 'revolutionary psychology.'"[8] For this reason, many historians see a relationship between the Enlightenment and the French Revolution. Although the philosophes themselves were not revolutionaries, their attacks on the pillars of the established order and their appeals for a freer, more tolerant society helped create a revolutionary psychology. As Henri Peyre observes,

> *Eighteenth-century philosophy taught the Frenchman to find his condition wretched, or in any case, unjust and illogical and made him disinclined to the patient resignation to his troubles that had long characterized his ancestors. . . . The propaganda of the "Philosophes" perhaps more than any other factor accounted for the fulfillment of the preliminary condition of the French Revolution, namely discontent with the existing state of things.*[9]

As the Revolution progressed, its leaders utilized the philosophes' ideas and language to attack the foundations of the old order and to justify their own reform program.

The American Revolution, which gave practical expression to the liberal philosophy of the philosophes, also helped pave the way for the French Revolution. The Declaration of Independence, which proclaimed the natural rights of man and sanctioned resistance against a government that deprived men of these rights, influenced the framers of the Declaration of the Rights of Man and of the Citizen (see "The Reforms of the National Assembly" on pages 461–463). The United States showed that a nation could be established on the principle that sovereign power derived from the people. The Americans set an example of social equality unparalleled in Europe. In the United States, there was no hereditary aristocracy, no serfdom, and no state church. Liberal French aristocrats, such as the Marquis de Lafayette, who had fought in the American Revolution, returned to France more optimistic about the possibilities of reforming French society.

A Bourgeois Revolution?

Because the bourgeois were the principal leaders and chief beneficiaries of the French Revolution, many historians have viewed it, along with the English revolutions of the seventeenth century and the growth of capitalism, as "an episode in the general rise of the bourgeoisie."[10] Those who regard the Revolution as a bourgeois revolution argue that in the last part of the eighteenth century it became increasingly difficult for the bourgeoisie to gain the most honored offices in the land. According to this view, in the eighteenth century, a decadent and reactionary aristocracy sought to regain the powers that it had lost under Louis XIV. Through parlements, aristocrats blocked reforms proposed by the king that threatened their privileges, and they united to prevent commoners from entering their ranks. The nobility's determination to safeguard its power and social exclusiveness clashed head-on with the aspirations of a wealthy, talented, and progressive bourgeoisie. Finding the path to upward mobility and social dignity barred, the bourgeoisie, imbued with the rational outlook of the Enlightenment, came to perceive nobles as an obstacle to its advancement and the nation's progress. "The essential cause of the Revolution," concludes the French historian Albert Soboul, "was the power of a bourgeoisie arrived at its maturity and confronted by a decadent aristocracy holding tenaciously to its privileges."[11] Thus, when the bourgeois found the opportunity during the Revolution, they ended the legal division of France into separate orders.

In recent decades, some historians have challenged this interpretation. These revisionists argue that before 1789 France did not have a self-conscious bourgeois class aspiring to take control of the state in order to promote a capitalist economy, that the nobles and the bourgeoisie did not represent antagonistic classes divided by sharp differences. On the contrary, they were not clearly distinguishable from each other. The bourgeois aspired to noble status, and many nobles were involved in business enterprises—mining, metallurgy, textiles, and overseas trading

companies—traditionally considered the province of the bourgeoisie. Abandoning a traditional aristocratic disdain for business, many nobles had acquired the capitalist mentality associated with the middle class. Some nobles also shared with the bourgeois the liberal values of the philosophes and a desire to do away with monarchical despotism and reform France according to rational standards. Thus, French nobles, particularly those who lived in urban centers or had traveled to Britain and the American colonies, were receptive both to new means of livelihood and to progressive ideas. Moreover, the French nobility was constantly infused with new blood from below. During the eighteenth century, thousands of bourgeois, through marriage, the purchase of an office that carried with it a title of nobility, or service as local officials—mayors, for example—had some entitlement of nobility. As the British historian William Doyle puts it, "the nobility was an open elite, not a hereditary class apart. Nor is it now possible to maintain that this elite grew less open as the eighteenth century went on thanks to some exclusive 'aristocratic reaction.'"[12]

Just prior to 1789, revisionists contend, nobles and prosperous bourgeois were no longer clearly differentiated; the traditional distinctions that had set them apart were now obsolete. France's social elite actually consisted not of a hereditary nobility but of *notables*—both nobles and bourgeois—distinguished more by wealth than by birth. Bourgeois notables were essentially moderate; they did not seek the destruction of the aristocracy that was accomplished in the opening stage of the Revolution. The elimination of aristocratic privileges was not part of a preconceived bourgeois program, revisionists maintain, but an improvised response to the violent upheavals in the countryside in July and August 1789. Moreover, not until early 1789, when a struggle erupted over the composition of the Estates General (see the next section), did the bourgeoisie start to become conscious of itself as a class with interests that clashed with those of the aristocracy. Until then, both the bourgeoisie and many aristocrats were united around a common and moderate reform program.

Finally, revisionists argue that the nobility was not as decadent or reactionary as traditional accounts would have it. The nobles resisted the king's reforming ministers because they doubted the ability of a despotic and incompetent state to solve the financial crisis. To be sure, there were aristocrats who selfishly wanted to cling to their privileges, but many also aspired to serve the public good by instituting structural changes that would liberate the nation from despotic and inefficient rule and reform its financial and administrative system. It was this desire to institute crucial changes in French political life, say revisionists, that led nobles to press for the convening of the Estates General.

THE MODERATE STAGE, 1789–1791

The Clash Between the Nobility and the Third Estate

Frenchmen in great numbers met in electoral assemblies to elect deputies to the Estates General. Most deputies of the clergy were parish priests, many of them sympathetic to reform. Although the majority of deputies of the Second Estate were conservative country nobles, there was a sizable liberal minority (including some who had fought in the American Revolution) that favored reform; political liberalism was not a monopoly of the bourgeoisie. The delegates of the Third Estate consisted predominantly of bourgeois drawn from government service and the professions, including many articulate lawyers.

Each Estate drew up lists of grievances and suggestions (*cahiers de doléances*). The cahiers from all three orders expressed loyalty to monarchy and church. Many cahiers of the nobility insisted on the preservation of manorial rights and honorific privileges, whereas cahiers prepared by the urban bourgeoisie often demanded the abolition of serfdom, the fees paid by peasants to lords, the lords' courts, and the lords' exclusive hunting rights. On the other hand, cahiers drawn up by liberal nobles agreed with bourgeois demands on many crucial issues. Both groups called for the establishment of a national assembly that would meet periodically and consent to taxation. Both also wanted a written constitution; financial reforms, including the surrender of tax exemptions; a guarantee of personal liberty; and freedom of the press. There was general agreement that a constitutional government that met regularly to pass laws was preferable to absolute monarchy, which ruled by decree. Both reform-minded nobles and bourgeois held great hopes for the regeneration of France and the advancement of liberty.

At this stage, then, with a significant number of nobles sympathetic to reform, there was no inseparable gulf between the Second and the Third Estates. However, it soon became clear that the hopes of reformers clashed with the intentions of many aristocrats. What had started as a struggle between the crown and the aristocracy was turning into something far more significant: a conflict between the two privileged orders on one side and the Third Estate on the other. As one keen observer noted in early 1789, "The public debate has changed. Now the King, despotism, the constitution are merely secondary: it is a war between the Third Estate and the other two orders."[13] One pamphleteer, Abbé Sieyès (1748–1836), expressed the hatred that the bourgeoisie had for the aristocracy. "The privileged order has said to the Third Estate: 'Whatever be your services, whatever be your talents, you shall go thus far and no farther. It is not fitting that you be honored.'" The higher positions in the land, said Sieyès, should be the "reward for talents," not the prerogative of birth. Without the Third Estate, "nothing can progress"; without the nobility, "everything would proceed infinitely better."[14] What triggered the conflict between them was the issue of representation in the Estates General—a medieval assembly divided into the traditional orders of clergy, aristocracy, and commoners.

The Formation of the National Assembly

The Estates General convened at Versailles on May 5, 1789, but was stalemated by the question of procedure. Seeking to control the assembly, the nobility insisted that the three Estates follow the traditional practice of meeting separately and voting as individual bodies. Because the two privileged orders were likely to stand together, the Third Estate would always be outvoted, two to one. The delegates from the Third Estate, unwilling to allow the nobility and the higher clergy to dominate the Estates General, proposed instead that the three Estates meet as one body and vote by head. There were some 610 delegates from the Third Estate; the nobility and clergy together had an equivalent number. Since the Third Estate could rely on the support of sympathetic parish priests and liberal nobles, it would be assured a majority if all orders met together. As aristocrats and bourgeois became more polarized, antinoble rhetoric gained a growing audience among all segments of the Third Estate. Many commoners now saw the aristocracy as the chief obstacle to reform.

On June 17, the Third Estate made a revolutionary move. It declared itself the National Assembly. On June 20, locked out of their customary meeting hall (apparently by accident), the Third Estate delegates moved to a nearby tennis court and took a solemn oath not to disband until a constitution had been drawn up for France. By these acts, the bourgeois delegates demonstrated their desire and determination to reform the state.

Louis XVI commanded the National Assembly to separate into orders, but the Third Estate held firm. The steadfastness of the delegates and the menacing actions of Parisians who supported the National Assembly forced Louis XVI to yield. On June 27, he ordered the nobility (some had already done so) and the clergy (a majority had already done so) to join with the Third Estate in the National Assembly. The Third Estate had successfully challenged the nobility and defied the king.

But the victory of the bourgeoisie was not yet secure, for most nobles had not resigned themselves to a bourgeois-dominated National Assembly. Recognizing that France was on the threshold of a social revolution that jeopardized their power and status, many nobles now reversed their position of previous years and joined with the king in an effort to crush the National Assembly. Louis XVI, influenced by his wife, Queen Marie Antoinette, as well as his brother the Comte d'Artois and court aristocrats, ordered special foreign regiments to the outskirts of Paris and Versailles. He also replaced Jacques Necker, a reform-minded minister, with a nominee of the queen. It appeared that Louis XVI, overcoming his usual hesitancy and vacillation, had resolved to use force against the National Assembly and to stop the incipient revolution. At this point, uprisings by the common people of Paris and peasants in the countryside saved the National Assembly, exacerbated hostilities between the Third Estate and the nobility, and ensured the victory of the forces of reform.

The Storming of the Bastille

In July 1789, the level of tension in Paris was high for three reasons. First, the calling of the Estates General had aroused hopes for reform. Second, the price of bread was soaring: in August 1788, a Parisian laborer had spent 50 percent of his income on bread; by July 1789, he was spending 80 percent. The third element in the tension was the fear of an aristocratic plot to crush the National Assembly. Frightened that royal troops would bombard and pillage the city, Parisians searched for weapons.

On July 14, eight hundred to nine hundred Parisians gathered in front of the Bastille, a fortress used as a prison and a despised symbol of royal despotism. They gathered primarily to obtain gunpowder and to remove the cannons that threatened a heavily populated working-class district. Fearing an attack, the governor of the Bastille, Bernard Jordan de Launay, ordered his men to fire into the crowd; they killed ninety-eight and wounded seventy-three people. When the tables were turned and five cannons were aimed on the main gate of the Bastille, de Launay surrendered. Despite the promise that he would not be harmed, de Launay and five of his men were killed, and their heads were paraded on pikes through the city.

Historians hostile to the French Revolution have long depicted the besiegers of the Bastille as a destructive mob made up of the dregs of society—smugglers, beggars, bandits, and degenerates. However, more recent scholarship reveals that the Bastille crowd was not drawn from the criminal elements but consisted almost entirely of small tradesmen, artisans, and wage earners—concerned citizens driven by hunger, fear of an aristocratic conspiracy, and hopes for reform.[15] Whatever their social position, hopes, and fears, however, the commoners had displayed barbaric behavior that would be replicated in future incidents.

The fall of the Bastille had far-reaching consequences: a symbol of the Old Regime's darkness and despotism had fallen; some court nobles hostile to the Revolution decided to flee the country;

the frightened king told the National Assembly that he would withdraw all the troops ringing Paris. The revolutionary act of the Parisians had indirectly saved the National Assembly and with it the bourgeois revolution.

The Great Fear

The uprising of the Parisians strengthened the hand of the National Assembly. Revolution in the countryside also served the interests of the reformers. The economic crisis of 1788 and 1789 had worsened conditions for the peasantry; the price of bread soared, and the number of hungry beggars wandering the roads and spreading terror multiplied. Peasants feared that the beggars would seize their crops, which would soon be ready for harvest. Also contributing to the revolutionary mentality were the great expectations unleashed by the summoning of the Estates General, for like the urban poor, the peasants hoped that their grievances would be remedied. In the spring of 1789, peasants were attacking food convoys and refusing to pay royal taxes, tithes, and manorial dues. These revolutionary outbreaks intensified in the last weeks of July. Inflamed by economic misery and stirred by the uprisings of the Parisians, peasants began to burn manor houses and destroy the registers on which their obligations to the lords were inscribed.

The flames of the peasants' insurrection were fanned by rumors that aristocrats were organizing bands of brigands to attack the peasants. The large number of vagrants roaming the countryside helped trigger irrational fears among the peasantry. The mythical army of brigands never materialized, but the Great Fear, as this episode is called, led more peasants to take up arms against the lords. Convinced that aristocrats were plotting to block reforms, the peasants attacked the lords' chateaux with greater fury.

The peasant upheavals in late July and early August, like the insurrection in Paris, worked to the advantage of the reformers. The attacks provided the National Assembly with an opportunity to strike at noble privileges by putting into law what the peasants had accomplished with the torch—the destruction of feudal remnants. On the night of August 4, 1789, aristocrats, seeking to restore calm in the countryside, surrendered their special privileges: exclusive hunting rights, tax exemptions, monopoly on the highest offices, manorial courts, and the right to demand labor services from peasants.

In the decrees of August 5 and 11, the National Assembly implemented the resolutions of August 4. The Assembly also declared that the planned constitution should be prefaced by a declaration of rights. On August 26, it adopted the Declaration of the Rights of Man and of the Citizen.

October Days

Louis XVI, cool to these reforms, postponed his approval of the August Decrees and the Declaration of the Rights of Man and of the Citizen. It would require a second uprising by the Parisians to force the king to agree to the reforms and to nail down the victory of the reformers.

On October 5, 1789, Parisian housewives (and men) marched twelve miles to Versailles to protest the lack of bread to the National Assembly and the king. A few hours later, twenty thousand Paris Guards, a citizen militia sympathetic to the Revolution, also set out for Versailles in support of the protesters. The king had no choice but to promise bread and to return with the demonstrators to Paris. Two weeks later, the National Assembly abandoned Versailles for Paris.

Once again, the "little people" had aided the bourgeoisie. Louis XVI, aware that he had no control over the Parisians and fearful of further violence, approved the August Decrees and the Declaration of the Rights of Man and of the Citizen. Nobles who had urged the king to use force against the Assembly and had tried to block reforms fled the country in large numbers.

The Reforms of the National Assembly

With resistance weakened, the National Assembly continued the work of reform begun in the summer of 1789. By abolishing both the special privileges of the nobility and the clergy and the absolutism based on the divine right of kings, the National Assembly completed the destruction of the Old Regime.

Women's March to Versailles. A bread shortage and high prices sparked the protest march of thousands of women to Versailles in October 1789. The king was compelled to return to Paris, a sign of his diminishing power, and many aristocrats hostile to the Revolution fled the country. (RMN-Grand Palais/Art Resource, N.Y.)

Abolition of Special Privileges. By ending aristocratic and clerical privileges in the August Decrees, the National Assembly legalized the equality that the bourgeoisie had demanded. The aristocratic structure of the Old Regime, a remnant of the Middle Ages that had hindered the progressive bourgeoisie, was eliminated.

Statement of Human Rights. The Declaration of the Rights of Man and of the Citizen expressed liberal and universal goals of the philosophes and the particular interests of the bourgeoisie. To contemporaries, it was a refutation of the Old Regime, a statement of ideals that, if realized, would end longstanding abuses and usher in a new society. In proclaiming the inalienable rights to liberty of person, to freedom of religion and thought, and to equal treatment under the law, the declaration affirmed the dignity of the individual. It asserted that government belonged not to any ruler but to the people as a whole and that its aim was the preservation of the natural rights of the individual. Because the declaration contrasted sharply with the principles espoused by an intolerant

clergy, a privileged aristocracy, and a despotic monarch, it has been called the death warrant of the Old Regime.

The declaration expressed the philosophes' view that people need not resign themselves to the abuses and misfortunes of human existence: through reason, they can improve society. But in 1789, the declaration was only a statement of intent. It remained to be seen whether its principles would be achieved. A significant example of the new leadership's commitment to equality and religious toleration was the law passed in 1791 granting civil rights to Jews. In theory, Jews were now free to leave the ghetto, to which they had been forcibly confined for centuries in order to keep them apart from Christians, and to participate in French society as equal citizens.

Subordination of Church to State. The National Assembly also struck at the privileges of the Roman Catholic Church. The August Decrees declared the end of tithes, the church's principal source of income. To obtain badly needed funds, the Assembly in November 1789 confiscated church lands and put them up for sale. In 1790, the Assembly passed the Civil Constitution of the Clergy, which altered the boundaries of the dioceses, reducing the number of bishops and priests, and transformed the clergy into government officials elected by the people and paid by the state.

Almost all bishops and many priests opposed the Civil Constitution. When the Assembly required the clergy to take an oath that they would uphold the Civil Constitution, only about one-half would do so, and many believing Catholics supported the dissenting clergy. The Civil Constitution divided the French and gave opponents of the Revolution an emotional issue—resisting a godless regime—around which to rally supporters.

A Constitution for France.

In September 1791, the National Assembly achieved the goal at which it had been aiming since June 1789: a constitution limiting the power of the king and guaranteeing all French citizens equal treatment under the law. Citizens paying less than a specified amount in taxes could not vote. Probably about 30 percent of the males over the age of twenty-five were excluded by this stipulation, and only the more well-to-do citizens qualified to sit in the Legislative Assembly, a unicameral parliament created to succeed the National Assembly. The drafters of the constitution did not trust illiterate and propertyless men to vote and enact legislation. Nevertheless, the suffrage requirements under the constitution of 1791 were far more generous than those in Britain.

Administrative and Judicial Reforms.

The National Assembly sought to reform the chaotic administrative system of France. It replaced the patchwork of provincial units with eighty-three new administrative units, or departments, approximately equal in size. The departments and their subdivisions were allowed a large measure of self-government.

Judicial reforms complemented the administrative changes. A standardized system of courts replaced the innumerable jurisdictions of the Old Regime, and the sale of judicial offices was ended. All judges were selected from graduate lawyers, and citizen juries were introduced in criminal cases. In the penal code completed by the National Assembly, torture and barbarous punishments were abolished.

Aid for Business.

The National Assembly put an end to all tolls and duties on goods transported within the country, maintained a tariff to protect French manufacturers, and insisted that French colonies trade only with the mother country. The Assembly also established a uniform system of weights and measures, eliminated the guilds (medieval survivals that blocked business expansion), and forbade workers to form unions or to strike.

By ending absolutism, striking at the privileges of the nobility, and preventing the mass of people from gaining control over the government, the National Assembly consolidated the rule of the bourgeoisie. With one arm, it broke the power of the aristocracy and throne; with the other, it held back the common people. Although the reforms benefited the bourgeoisie, it would be a mistake to view them merely as a selfish expression of bourgeois interests. The Declaration of the Rights of Man and of the Citizen was addressed to all; it proclaimed liberty and equality as the right of all. These ideals became the core of the liberal-democratic credo that spread throughout the West in the nineteenth century.

THE RADICAL STAGE, 1792–1794

The Sans-Culottes

Pleased with their accomplishments—equality before the law, careers open to talent, a written constitution, parliamentary government—the men of 1789 wished the Revolution to go no further. But revolutionary times are unpredictable. Soon the Revolution moved in a direction neither anticipated nor desired by the reformers. A counter-revolution, led by irreconcilable nobles and alienated churchmen, gained the support of strongly Catholic peasants. It began to threaten the changes made by the Revolution, forcing the revolutionary leadership to resort to extreme measures.

The discontent of the *sans-culottes**—small shopkeepers, artisans, and wage earners—also propelled the Revolution toward **radicalism**. Although they had played a significant role in the

---

*Literally, *sans-culottes* means "without culottes" and refers to the people who wore the simple trousers of a laborer and not the knee breeches that aristocrats wore before the Revolution.

Revolution, particularly in the storming of the Bastille and the October Days, they had gained little. The sans-culottes, says the French historian Albert Soboul, "began to realize that a privilege of wealth was taking the place of a privilege of birth. They foresaw that the bourgeoisie would succeed the fallen aristocracy as the ruling class."[16] Inflamed by poverty and their hatred of the rich, the sans-culottes insisted that it was the government's duty to guarantee them the "right of existence"—a policy that ran counter to the economic individualism of the bourgeoisie. They demanded that the government increase wages, set price controls on food supplies, end food shortages, punish food speculators and profiteers, and deal severely with counterrevolutionaries.

Although most sans-culottes upheld the principle of private property, they wanted laws to prevent extremes of wealth and poverty. Socially, their ideal was a nation of small shopkeepers and small farmers. "No one should own more than one workshop or one store," read a sans-culotte petition.[17] Whereas the men of 1789 sought equality of rights, liberties, and opportunities, the sans-culottes expanded the principle of equality to include narrowing the gap between the rich and poor. To reduce economic inequality, the sans-culottes called for higher taxes for the wealthy and the redistribution of land. Politically, they favored a democratic republic in which the common man had a voice.

In 1789, the bourgeoisie had demanded equality with the aristocrats: the right to hold the most honored positions in the nation and an end to the special privileges of the nobility. By the close of 1792, the sans-culottes were demanding equality with the bourgeois. They wanted political reforms that would give the poor a voice in the government and social reforms that would improve their lot.

Foreign Invasion

Despite the pressures exerted by reactionary nobles and clergy on the one hand and discontented sans-culottes on the other, the Revolution might not have taken a radical turn had France remained at peace. The war that broke out with Austria and Prussia in April 1792 exacerbated internal dissensions, worsened economic conditions, and threatened to undo the reforms of the Revolution. It was in these circumstances that the Revolution moved from its moderate stage into a radical one, which historians refer to as the Second French Revolution.

In June 1791, Louis XVI and the royal family, traveling in disguise, fled Paris for the northeast of France to join with *émigrés* (nobles who had left revolutionary France and were organizing a counterrevolutionary army) and to rally foreign support against the Revolution. Discovered at Varennes by a village postmaster, they were brought back to Paris as virtual prisoners. The flight of the king turned many French people against the monarchy, strengthening the position of the radicals who wanted to do away with kingship altogether and establish a republic. But it was foreign invasion that ultimately led to the destruction of the monarchy.

In the Legislative Assembly, the lawmaking body that had succeeded the National Assembly in October 1791, one group, called the Girondins, urged an immediate war against Austria, which was harboring and supporting the émigrés. The Girondins believed that a successful war would unite France under their leadership, and they were convinced that Austria was already preparing to invade France and destroy the Revolution. Moreover, regarding themselves as crusaders in the struggle of liberty against tyranny, the Girondins hoped to spread revolutionary reforms to other lands to provoke a war of the people against kings. In the words of a leading Girondin: "Let us say to Europe that ten million Frenchmen, kindled by the fire of liberty, armed with the sword, with reason, with eloquence would be able . . . to change the face of the world and make the tyrants tremble."[18]

On April 20, 1792, the Legislative Assembly declared war on Austria. Commanded by the Duke of Brunswick, a combined Austrian and Prussian army crossed into France. French forces, short of arms and poorly led (about six thousand of some nine thousand officers had abandoned their command), could not halt the enemy's advance. Food shortages and a counterrevolution in western France led by aristocrats increased the unrest. In an atmosphere already charged with tension, the Duke of Brunswick issued a manifesto declaring that if the royal family were harmed, he would exact a terrible vengeance on the Parisians. On August 10, 1792, enraged Parisians and militia from other cities attacked the king's palace, killing several hundred Swiss guards, some of whom were summarily executed, and servants of the royal family, and they burned symbols of the monarchy removed from the palace. In the next few weeks, mobs killed hundreds of people suspected of counterrevolutionary activity.

In early September, as foreign troops advanced deeper into France, there occurred an event analogous to the Great Fear of 1789. As rumors spread that jailed priests and aristocrats were planning to break out of their cells to support the Duke of Brunswick, Parisians panicked. Driven by fear, patriotism, and murderous impulses, they raided the prisons and, after an improvised popular court determined the accused's fate—largely on the basis of appearance—hammered and hacked to death eleven hundred to twelve hundred prisoners, including more than two hundred priests. Most of the victims were not political prisoners but ordinary criminals.

On September 21 and 22, 1792, the National Convention (the successor to the Legislative Assembly) abolished the monarchy and established a republic. In December 1792, Louis XVI was placed on trial, and in January 1793 he was executed for conspiring against the liberty of the French people. The execution of Louis XVI intensified tensions between the revolutionaries and the crowned heads of Europe. The uprising of August 10, the September Massacres, the creation of a republic, and the execution of Louis XVI all confirmed that the Revolution was taking a radical turn.

Meanwhile, the war continued. Short of supplies, hampered by bad weather, and possessing insufficient manpower, the Duke of Brunswick never did reach Paris. Defeated by superior artillery—infantry played almost no role—at Valmy on September 20, 1792, the Prussians retreated to the frontier, and the armies of the new Republic took the offensive. By the beginning of 1793, French forces had overrun Belgium (then a part of the Austrian Empire), the German Rhineland, and the Sardinian provinces of Nice and Savoy. To the peoples of Europe, the National Convention solemnly announced that it was waging a popular crusade against privilege and tyranny, against aristocrats and princes.

THE EXECUTION OF LOUIS XVI. The king died with dignity. His last words were: "I forgive my enemies; I trust that my death will be for the happiness of my people, but I grieve for France, and I fear that she may suffer the anger of the Lord." (Bridgeman-Giraudon/Art Resource, N.Y.)

These revolutionary political and social ideas, the execution of Louis XVI, and, most important, French expansion that threatened the balance of power frightened the rulers of Europe. Urged on by Britain, by the spring of 1793, they formed an anti-French alliance. The allies' forces pressed toward the French borders, endangering the Republic.

Counterrevolutionary insurrections further undermined the fledgling republic. In the Vendée, in western France, peasants who were protesting against taxation and conscription and were still loyal to their priests and Catholic tradition, which the Revolution had attacked, took up arms against the Republic. Led by local nobles, the peasants of the Vendée waged a guerrilla war for religion, royalism, and their traditional way of life. In some provinces, federalists objecting to the power wielded by the centralized government in Paris also revolted. The Republic was unable to exercise control over much of the country.

The Jacobins

As the Republic tottered under the weight of foreign invasion, internal insurrection, and economic crisis, the revolutionary leadership grew still more radical; so too did commoners, the *petit peuple*, who sought vengeance against aristocrats accused of conspiring with foreign states against the Revolution. In June 1793, the Jacobins replaced the Girondins as the dominant group in the National Convention. The Girondins favored a government in which the departments would exercise control over their own affairs. The Jacobins wanted a strong central government, with Paris as the center of power. The Girondins also opposed government interference in business, whereas the Jacobins supported temporary governmental controls to deal with the needs of war and economic crisis. This last point was crucial; it won the Jacobins the support of the sans-culottes.

Both the Girondins and the Jacobins came from the bourgeoisie, but some Jacobin leaders were more willing to listen to the economic and political demands of the hard-pressed sans-culottes. Besides, the Jacobins wanted an alliance with the sans-culottes in order to defend the Revolution against foreign and domestic enemies. The Jacobins had a further advantage in the power struggle: they were tightly organized, well disciplined, and convinced that only they could save the republic. On June 2, 1793, some eighty thousand armed sans-culottes surrounded the Convention and demanded the arrest of Girondin delegates—an act that enabled the Jacobins to gain control of the government.

The problems confronting the Jacobins were staggering. They had to cope with civil war, particularly in the Vendée, economic distress, blockaded ports, and foreign invasion. They lived with the terrible dread that if they failed, the Revolution for liberty and equality would perish. Only strong leadership could save the Republic. It was provided by the Committee of Public Safety. Serving as a cabinet for the Convention, the Committee of Public Safety, composed of twelve ardent and able patriots, organized the nation's defenses, formulated foreign policy, supervised ministers, ordered arrests, and imposed the central government's authority throughout the nation.

Jacobin Policies

The Jacobins continued the work of reform. A new constitution, in 1793, expressed Jacobin enthusiasm for political democracy. It contained a new Declaration of Rights, which affirmed and amplified the principles of 1789. By giving all adult males the right to vote, it overcame sansculotte objections to the constitution of 1791. However, the threat of invasion and the revolts caused the implementation of the new constitution to be postponed, and it was never put into effect. Furthermore, by abolishing both slavery in the French colonies and imprisonment for debt and by making plans for free public education, the Jacobins revealed their humanitarianism and their debt to the philosophes.

Jacobin economic policies derived from the exigencies of war. To halt inflation and gain the support of the poor—both necessary for the war effort—the Jacobins decreed the *law of the maximum*, which fixed prices on bread and other essential goods. To win over the peasants, the Jacobins made it easier for them to buy the property of émigré nobles. To equip the Army of the Republic, the Committee of Public Safety requisitioned grain, wool, arms, shoes, and other items from individual citizens; required factories and mines to produce at full capacity; and established state-operated armament and munitions plants.

The Nation in Arms

For the war against foreign invaders, the Jacobins, in an act that anticipated modern conscription, drafted unmarried men between eighteen and twenty-five years of age. They mobilized all the resources of the nation, infused the army with a love for *la patrie* (the nation), and in a remarkable demonstration of administrative skill, equipped an army of more than 800,000 men. In creating the nation in arms, the Jacobins heralded the emergence of modern warfare. Inspired by the ideals of liberty, equality, and fraternity and commanded by officers who had proved their skill on the battlefield, the citizen soldiers of the republic won decisive victories. In May and June 1794, the French routed the allied forces on the vital northern frontier, and by the end of July, France had become the triumphant master of Belgium.

By demanding complete devotion to the nation, the Jacobin phase of the Revolution also heralded the rise of modern **nationalism**. In the schools; in newspapers, speeches, and poems; on the stage; and at rallies and meetings of patriotic societies, the French people were told of the glory won by republican soldiers on the battlefield and were reminded of their duties to *la patrie.* "The citizen is born, lives and dies for the fatherland."[19] These words were written in public places for all citizens to read and ponder. The soldiers of the Revolution fought not for money or for a king but for the nation. "When *la patrie* calls us for her defense," wrote a young soldier to his mother, "we should rush to her.... Our life, our goods, and our talents do not belong to us. It is to the nation, to *la patrie,* to which everything belongs."[20] Could this heightened sense of nationality, which concentrated on the special interests of the French people, be reconciled with the Declaration of the Rights of Man, whose principles were addressed to all humanity? The revolutionaries themselves did not understand the implications of the new force that they had unleashed.

The Republic of Virtue and the Reign of Terror

Robespierre. At the same time that the Committee of Public Safety was forging a revolutionary army to deal with external enemies, it was also waging war against internal opposition. The pivotal personality in this struggle was Maximilien Robespierre (1758–1794). Robespierre, who had served in the National Assembly and was an active Jacobin, was distinguished by a fervent faith in the rightness of his beliefs, a total commitment to republican democracy, and an integrity that earned him the appellation "the Incorruptible." In the early stage of the Revolution, Robespierre had strongly supported liberal reforms. He attacked,

at times with great fervor, slavery, capital punishment, and censorship; he favored civil rights for Jews; and, in what was considered a radical measure, he supported giving all men the vote regardless of how much property they owned.

Robespierre wanted to create a better society founded on reason, good citizenship, and patriotism. In his Republic of Virtue, there would be no kings or nobles; men would be free, equal, and educated; and reason would be glorified and superstition ridiculed. There would be no extremes of wealth or poverty; a person's natural goodness would prevail over vice and greed; and laws would preserve, not violate, inalienable rights. In this utopian vision, an individual's duties would be "to detest bad faith and despotism, to punish tyrants and traitors, to assist the unfortunate, to respect the weak, to defend the oppressed, to do all the good one can to one's neighbor, and to behave with justice towards all men."[21] Motivated by a sense of integrity, people would actively put the public good ahead of private interests.

Robespierre pursued his ideal society with religious zeal. Maintaining that the Republic of Virtue could not be established while France was threatened by foreign and civil war and certain that the counterrevolution was everywhere, Robespierre urged that enemies of the republic "be prosecuted by all not as ordinary enemies, but as rebels, brigands, and assassins."[22]

To preserve republican liberty, the Jacobins made terror a deliberate government policy. Robespierre declared:

> *Does not liberty, that inestimable blessing . . . have the . . . right to sacrifice lives, fortunes, and even, for a time, individual liberties? . . . Is not the French Revolution . . . a war to the death between those who want to be free and those content to be slaves? . . . There is no middle ground; France must be entirely free or perish in the attempt, and any means are justifiable in fighting for so fine a cause.*[23]

With Robespierre playing a key role, the Jacobin leadership executed those they considered enemies of the Republic: Girondins who challenged Jacobin authority, federalists who opposed a

Robespierre: The Necessity for Terror

In notes written in the style of a Catholic catechism, Robespierre advocated terror against the enemies of the Revolution.

What is our goal? The enforcement of the constitution for the benefit of the people.

Who will our enemies be? The vicious and the rich.

What means will they employ? Slander and hypocrisy.

What things may be favorable for the employment of these? The ignorance of the *sans-culottes*.

The people must therefore be enlightened. But what are the obstacles to the enlightenment of the people? Mercenary writers who daily mislead them with impudent falsehoods.

What conclusions may be drawn from this? 1. These writers must be proscribed as the most dangerous enemies of the people. 2. Right-minded literature must be scattered about in profusion.

What are the other obstacles to the establishment of liberty? Foreign war and civil war.

How can foreign war be ended? By putting republican generals in command of our armies and punishing those who have betrayed us.

How can civil war be ended? By punishing traitors and conspirators, particularly if they are deputies or administrators; by sending loyal troops under patriotic leaders to subdue the aristocrats of Lyon, Marseille, Toulon, the Vendée, the Jura, and all other regions in which the standards of rebellion and royalism have been raised; and by making frightful examples of all scoundrels who have outraged liberty and spilled the blood of patriots.

1. Proscription of perfidious and counterrevolutionary writers and propagation of proper literature.

2. Punishment of traitors and conspirators, particularly deputies and administrators.

3. Appointment of patriotic generals; dismissal and punishment of others.

4. Sustenance and laws for the people.

Question for Analysis

1. On what grounds did Robespierre justify terror?

E. L. Higgins, ed., *The French Revolution As Told By Contemporaries* (Boston: Houghton Mifflin, 1938), p. 301.

---

strong central government emanating from Paris, counterrevolutionary priests and nobles and their peasant supporters, and profiteers who hoarded food. The Robespierrists also executed Jacques Danton, a hero of the Revolution, who wished to end the Terror and negotiate peace with the enemy. The Jacobins even sought to discipline the ardor of the sans-culottes, who had given them power. Fearful that sans-culotte spontaneity would undermine central authority and promote anarchy, Robespierrists brought about the dissolution of sans-culotte societies. In addition, they executed radical revolutionaries known as the *enragés* (literally, madmen), who had considerable influence on the Paris sans-culottes. The leaders of the enragés threatened insurrection against Jacobin rule and pushed for more social reforms than the Jacobins would allow, including setting limits on incomes and on the size of farms and businesses.

Robespierre and his fellow Jacobins did not resort to the guillotine—the instrument used to behead victims of the Terror—because they were bloodthirsty or power mad. Instead, they sought to establish a temporary dictatorship in a desperate attempt to save the republic and the Revolution. Deeply devoted to republican democracy, the Jacobins viewed themselves as bearers of a higher faith. Like all true believers, Robespierre was convinced that he knew the right way and that the new society he envisaged would benefit all

M.M.J. ROBERSPIERRE

Député de l'Artois,
à l'Assemblée Nationale en 1789.

A Paris, chez l'AUTEUR, quay des Augustins Nº 71. au 3º

ROBESPIERRE, AN ENGRAVING BY FIÉSINGER AFTER A DRAWING BY PIERRE-NARCISSE GUÉRIN. To create a Republic of Virtue where men would be free and equal, Maximilien Robespierre considered terror necessary. Robespierre lost favor with his own party and was himself guillotined.

humanity. He saw those who impeded its implementation not just as opponents but as sinners who had to be liquidated for the general good.

Special courts were established in Paris and other cities to try suspects. The proceedings were carried on in haste, and most judgments called for either acquittal or execution. In the Vendée, where civil war raged, many of the arrested were executed by firing squads, without trial.

Ironically, most of the executions took place after the frontiers had been secured and the civil war crushed. In many ways, the Terror was less a means of saving the beleaguered republic and more a way of shaping the new republican society and the new individual in accordance with the radical Jacobin ideology. Of the 500,000 people imprisoned for crimes against the republic,

some sixteen thousand, including priests and nuns, were sentenced to death by guillotine and another twenty thousand perished in prison before they could be tried. More than 200,000 died in the civil war in the provinces, some 40,000 of whom were summarily executed by firing squad, guillotine, and mass drownings ordered by military courts authorized by the Convention.

The Terror was particularly brutal in the Vendée, where the counterrevolution was fought by deeply religious Catholic peasants, led by aristocrats, who wanted an end to conscription and the mistreatment of their priests. Although untrained and poorly armed, the Vendéans succeeded in capturing a major town in the Loire Valley; in the process, they killed some 150 republican soldiers and took 8,000 prisoners. The Republic was imperiled, but in June 1793, seasoned republican forces defeated the Vendéans in the port city of Nantes. This was followed in October by a crushing defeat in the town of Chalet. Then the mass murders began.

Regarding the Vendéans as superstitious fanatics who fought against the Revolution's ideals and as traitors in league with France's enemies, frenzied republican soldiers, under orders from their superiors, burned villages, slaughtered livestock, and indiscriminately killed tens of thousands of peasants. Some five thousand Vendéans were loaded onto barges that were then sunk in the middle of the Loire River. Perhaps one-quarter of the region's population, women and children included, perished during 1793–1794. (To this day, the Vendéans mourn these losses and express contempt for the Revolution.)

Anticlericalism reinforced by the exigencies of war fostered a phenomenon known as de-Christianization. In many regions, priests were dismissed and churches were closed, policies supported by the belief that the clergy helped instigate the counterrevolution. Removed from churches were items including metal crosses, which could be channeled into the war effort. One district decreed that "the throne of error and falsehood be overthrown at the same time as that of the tyrant, to be replaced by the eternal reign of reason and philosophy."[24]

To purge the Republic of Christianity, which many deputies regarded as superstition and fanaticism that undermined liberty, the Convention drew up a Republican calendar in which the year

LIBERTY ARMED WITH THE SCEPTER OF REASON STRIKES DOWN IGNORANCE AND FANATICISM, AN ENGRAVING BY JEAN-BAPTISTE CHAPUY, C. 1793. Using a scepter given to her by Reason (standing at the left), Liberty strikes down ignorance and fanaticism, usually identified with religion. Many of these prints were produced in 1793 and 1794, when there was a concerted effort to replace traditional Christianity with a civic religion, the Cult of Reason. (Liberty armed with the scepter of reason striking down Ignorance and Fanaticism, 1793 (engraving) (b/w photo), Boizot, Simon Louis (1743–1809) (after)/© Musee de la Ville de Paris, Musee Carnavalet, Paris, France/Giraudon/The Bridgeman Art Library.)

one started, not with Christ's birth, but with the founding of the French Republic on September 22, 1792. On November 10, 1793, a celebration honoring the goddess Reason took place in the cathedral of Notre Dame. Maintaining that belief in God strengthened civic order and that attacking the church drove people to support the counterrevolution, Robespierre was a staunch opponent of de-Christianization.

The Jacobins did save the Republic. Their regime expelled foreign armies, crushed the federalist uprisings, contained the counterrevolutionaries in the Vendée, and prevented anarchy. Without the discipline, order, and unity imposed on France by the Jacobins, it is likely that the Republic would have collapsed under the twin blows of foreign invasion and domestic anarchy.

Significance of the Terror. The **Reign of Terror** poses fundamental questions about the meaning of the French Revolution and the validity of the Enlightenment conception of the individual. To what extent was the Terror a reversal of the ideals of the Revolution as formulated in the Declaration of the Rights of Man? To what extent did the feverish passions and the lust for violence

Profile

François Dominique Toussaint L'Ouverture

In 1791, in the midst of the French Revolution, black slaves on San Domingo, the rich French sugar colony in the West Indies, revolted, murdering their masters, burning down plantations and crying "Vengeance! Vengeance!" Their hatred of servitude, which had ignited slave revolts in previous decades, was intensified by the ideals of liberty and equality reverberating across the Atlantic.

François Dominique Toussaint L'Ouverture (c. 1743-1803) joined the rebellion and quickly rose to a position of command. Toussaint was the son of a petty African chief from Dahomey who, like millions of other Africans, had been captured in war, sold to Westerners, and brought in chains to toil on plantations in the New World. Toussaint, the eldest of eight children, was born in captivity. A remarkable old black taught him French and some Latin and geometry, and his master, recognizing Toussaint's ability, made him first a coachman and then steward of the plantation's livestock, a position almost never held by a nonwhite.

At the time of the rebellion, 42,000 whites, employing brutal means of repression—whipping, chaining, roasting, and mutilation—dominated 500,000 black slaves, often working them like beasts. Complicating the social structure were mulattos, people of mixed race who were granted French citizenship in 1793 out of fear that they would side with the rebellious black slaves.

Aspiring to eliminate slavery entirely, Toussaint organized an army consisting mainly of illiterate slaves into a fighting force capable of defeating European-trained soldiers. In 1794, the Jacobins abolished slavery over the opposition of the white planters, and Toussaint, who had distinguished himself as a military commander, was appointed assistant governor. Toussaint was also a man of vision, deeply committed to the revolutionary ideals of liberty and equality and to introducing economic, administrative, and educational reforms in San Domingo.

In 1801, two years after he had seized power, Napoleon sent twenty thousand troops to San Domingo to restore slavery and to subdue Toussaint, whose power had increased considerably. The old warrior, having lost none of his skills in guerrilla warfare, was at the point of defeating the French when he proposed peace. The French commander tricked Toussaint into believing that if he retired, France would negotiate a favorable settlement with San Domingo. Shortly after he retired to his farm, Toussaint was arrested and sent to prison in France, where he suffered abuse and humiliation until his death in 1803. On January 1, 1804, revolutionaries on the island established the independent state of Haiti, whose foundation Toussaint L'Ouverture had laid.

demonstrated in the mass executions in the provinces and in the public spectacles in Paris—with vast crowds watching and applauding the beheadings—indicate a darker side of human nature, beyond the control of reason? Did Robespierre's religion of humanity revive the fanaticism and cruelty of the wars of religion, which had so disgusted the philosophes? Did the Robespierrists, who considered themselves the staunchest defenders of the Revolution's ideals, soil and subvert these ideals by their zeal? The Jacobins mobilized the might of the nation, created the mystique of *la patrie*, and imposed dictatorial rule in defense of liberty and equality; they also legalized and justified terror committed in the people's name, that is, in the cause of democracy. In so doing, were they unwittingly unleashing new forces that, in later years, would be harnessed by totalitarian ideologies consciously resolved to stamp out the liberal heritage of the Revolution?

The Fall of Robespierre

The Terror had been instituted during a time of crisis and keyed-up emotions. By the summer of 1794, with the victory of the Republic seemingly assured, fear of an aristocratic conspiracy had subsided, the will to punish "traitors" had slackened, and popular fervor for the Terror had diminished. As the need and enthusiasm for the Terror abated, Robespierre's political position weakened.

Opponents of Robespierre in the Convention, feeling the chill of the guillotine blade on their own necks, ordered the arrest of Robespierre and some of his supporters. On July 28, 1794, the tenth of Thermidor according to the new republican calendar, Robespierre was guillotined. And on the following day, the guillotine dispatched seventy-one of his followers.

After the fall of Robespierre, the machinery of the Jacobin republic was dismantled. Leadership passed to the property-owning bourgeois who had endorsed the constitutional ideas of 1789 through 1791, the moderate stage of the Revolution. The new leadership, known as Thermidoreans until the end of 1795, wanted no more of the Jacobins or of Robespierre's society. They had considered Robespierre a threat to their political power because he would have allowed the common people a considerable voice in the government. They had also viewed him as a threat to their property because he would have introduced some state regulation of the economy to aid the poor.

The Thermidorean reaction was a counterrevolution. The new government purged the army of officers who were suspected of Jacobin leanings, abolished the law of the maximum, and declared void the constitution of 1793. A new constitution, approved in 1795, reestablished property requirements for voting. The counterrevolution also produced a counterterror, as royalists and Catholics massacred Jacobins in the provinces.

At the end of 1795, the new republican government, the Directory, was burdened by war, a sagging economy, and internal unrest. The Directory crushed insurrections by Parisian sans-culottes, maddened by hunger and hatred of the rich (1795, 1796), and by royalists seeking to restore the monarchy (1797). As military and domestic pressures increased, power began to pass into the hands of generals. One of them, Napoleon Bonaparte, seized control of the government in November 1799, pushing the Revolution into yet another stage.

NAPOLEON AND FRANCE: RETURN TO AUTOCRATIC RULE

Napoleon was born on August 15, 1769, on the island of Corsica, the son of a petty noble. After finishing military school in France, he became an artillery officer. The wars of the French Revolution afforded him an opportunity to advance his career; in 1796, he was given command of the French Army of Italy. In Italy, against the Austrians, Napoleon demonstrated a dazzling talent for military planning and leadership, which earned him an instant reputation. Having tasted glory, he could never do without it. The pursuit of glory, he said, was "like the blood that circulates in my veins."[25] Since he had experienced only success, nothing seemed impossible; he sensed that he was headed for greatness; another Alexander, Caesar, or Charlemagne.

In 1799, Napoleon was leading a French army in Egypt when he decided to return to France and make his bid for power. He joined a conspiracy that overthrew the Directory and created an executive office of three consuls. As first consul, Napoleon monopolized power. In 1802, he was made first consul for life, with the right to name his successor. And on December 2, 1804, in a magnificent ceremony at the Cathedral of Notre Dame in Paris, Napoleon crowned himself "Emperor of the French." General, first consul, and then emperor—it was a breathless climb to the heights of power. Napoleon, who once said that he loved "power as a musician loves his violin," was determined never to lose it.

An Enlightened Despot

Napoleon did not identify with the republicanism and democracy of the Jacobins; rather, he belonged to the tradition of eighteenth-century enlightened despotism. Like the reforming despots, he admired administrative uniformity and efficiency; disliked feudalism and religious persecution; and favored government regulation of trade and industry. He saw in enlightened despotism a means of ensuring political stability and

CORONATION OF NAPOLEON AND JOSEPHINE, BY DAVID. Napoleon crowned himself emperor in a magnificent ceremony. To French émigrés and nobles throughout Europe, he was the "crowned Jacobin" who threatened aristocratic privileges and European stability. (Erich Lessing/Art Resource, N.Y.)

strengthening the state. But unlike the reforming despots, he had no intentions of shoring up an Old Regime based on privilege and inequality. Rather Napoleon aimed to preserve several gains of the Revolution: equality under the law, careers open to men of talent, promotion of secular education, and the weakening of clerical power. But he suppressed political liberty, which threatened his thirst for power and glory.

Napoleon succeeded in giving France a strong central government and administrative uniformity. An army of officials subject to the emperor's will reached into every village, linking together the entire nation. This centralized state suited Napoleon's desire for orderly government and rational administration, enabled him to concentrate power in his own hands, and provided him with the taxes and soldiers needed to fight his wars. To suppress irreconcilable opponents, primarily diehard royalists and republicans, Napoleon used the instruments of the police state—secret agents, arbitrary arrests, summary trials, and executions.

To prevent hostile criticism of his rule and to promote popular support for his policies and person, Napoleon also shaped public opinion. He was thus a precursor of twentieth-century dictators. Liberty of the press came to an end. Printers swore an oath of obedience to the emperor, and newspapers were converted into government mouthpieces. By repressing liberty, subverting republicanism, and restoring absolutism, Emperor Napoleon reversed some of the liberal gains of the Revolution.

Religion: Reconciliation with the Church

For Napoleon, who was a deist if not an atheist, the value of religion was not salvation but social and political cohesion. It promoted national unity and prevented class warfare. He stated:

> *Society cannot exist without inequality of fortunes and inequality of fortunes cannot exist*

without religion. When a man is dying of hunger alongside another who stuffs himself, it is impossible to make him accede to the difference unless there is an authority which says to him God wishes it thus; there must be some poor and some rich in the world, but hereafter and for all eternity the divisions will be made differently.[26]

This is what Napoleon probably had in when he said: "Men who do not believe in God—one does not govern them, one shoots them."[27]

Napoleon tried to close the breach between the state and the Catholic Church that had opened during the Revolution. Such a reconciliation would gain the approval of the mass of the French people, who still remained devoted to their faith, and would also reassure the peasants and bourgeois who had bought confiscated church lands. For these reasons, Napoleon negotiated an agreement with the pope. The Concordat of 1801 recognized Catholicism as the religion of the great majority of the French, rather than as the official state religion (the proposal that the pope desired). Napoleon had achieved his aim. The Concordat made his regime acceptable to Catholics and to owners of former church lands.

Legal, Educational, and Financial Policies

Under the Old Regime, France was plagued by numerous and conflicting law codes. Reflecting local interests and feudal traditions, these codes obstructed national unity and administrative efficiency. Efforts by the revolutionaries to draw up a unified code of laws bogged down. Recognizing the value of such a code in promoting effective administration throughout France, Napoleon pressed for the completion of the project. The Code Napoléon incorporated many principles of the Revolution: equality before the law, the right to choose one's profession, religious freedom, protection of property rights, the abolition of serfdom, and the secular character of the state.

The code also had its less liberal side, denying equal treatment to workers in their dealings with employers, to women in their relations with their husbands, and to children in their relations with their fathers. In making wives inferior to their husbands in matters of property, adultery, and divorce, the code reflected both Napoleon's personal attitude and the general view of the times toward women and family stability. The restoration of slavery in the French colonies—which the Jacobins had abolished—was another violation of equality.

Napoleon's educational policy was in many ways an elaboration of the school reforms initiated during the Revolution. Like the revolutionaries, Napoleon favored a system of public education with a secular curriculum and a minimum of church involvement. For Napoleon, education served a dual purpose: it would provide him with capable officials to administer his laws and trained officers to lead his armies, and it would indoctrinate the young in obedience and loyalty. He established the University of France, a giant board of education that placed education under state control. To this day, the French school system, unlike that in the United States, is strictly centralized, with curriculum and standards set for the entire country.

The emperor did not consider education for girls important, holding that "marriage is their whole destination."[28] In his view, whatever education girls did receive should stress religion. "What we ask of education is not that girls should think but that they should believe. The weakness of women's brains, the instability of their ideas, the place they fill in society, their need for perpetual resignation . . . all this can be met by religion."[29]

Napoleon's financial and economic policies were designed to strengthen France and enhance his popularity. To stimulate the economy and to retain the favor of the bourgeois who supported his seizure of power, Napoleon aided industry through tariffs and loans, and he fostered commerce (while also speeding up troop movements) by building or repairing roads, bridges, and canals. To protect the currency from inflation, he established the Bank of France, which was controlled by the nation's leading financiers. By keeping careers open to talent, he endorsed one of the key demands of the bourgeoisie during the Revolution. Fearing a revolution based on lack of bread, he provided food at low prices and stimulated employment for the laboring poor. He endeared himself to the peasants by not restoring feudal privileges and by allowing them to keep the land they had obtained during the Revolution.

NAPOLEON AND EUROPE: DIFFUSION OF REVOLUTIONARY INSTITUTIONS

Napoleon, the Corsican adventurer, realized Louis XIV's dream of French mastery of Europe. Between 1805 and 1807, he decisively defeated Austria, Prussia, and Russia, becoming the virtual ruler of Europe. In these campaigns, as in his earlier successes in Italy, Napoleon demonstrated his greatness as a military commander.

By 1810, Napoleon dominated the Continent, except for the Balkan Peninsula. The Grand Empire comprised lands annexed to France, vassal states, and cowed allies.

With varying degrees of determination and success, Napoleon extended the reforms of the Revolution to other lands. His officials instituted the Code Napoléon, organized an effective civil service, opened careers to talent, and equalized the tax burden. Besides abolishing serfdom, manorial payments, and the courts of the nobility, they did away with clerical courts, promoted freedom of religion, permitted civil marriage, pressed for civil rights for Jews, and fought clerical interference with secular authority. They also abolished the medieval guilds, introduced a uniform system of weights and measures, eliminated internal tolls, and built roads, bridges, and canals. They promoted secular education and improved public health. Napoleon had launched a Europe-wide social revolution that attacked the privileges of the aristocracy and the clergy—who regarded him as the "crowned Jacobin"—and worked to the advantage of the bourgeoisie. This diffusion of revolutionary institutions weakened the Old Regime irreparably in much of Europe and speeded up the modernization of nineteenth-century Europe.

Pleased by the overhaul of feudal practices and the reduction of clerical power, many Europeans, particularly the progressive bourgeoisie, welcomed Napoleon as a liberator. But there was another side to Napoleon's rule. Napoleon, the tyrant of Europe, turned conquered lands into satellite kingdoms and exploited them for the benefit of France—a policy that gained him the enmity of many Europeans.

THE FALL OF NAPOLEON

In addition to the hostility of subject nationals, Napoleon had to cope with the determined opposition of Great Britain, whose subsidies and encouragements kept resistance to the emperor alive. But perhaps Napoleon's greatest obstacle was his own boundless ambition, which warped his judgment. From its peak, the emperor's career soon slid downhill to defeat, dethronement, and deportation.

Failure to Subdue England

Britain was Napoleon's most resolute opponent. It could not be otherwise, for any power that dominated the Continent could organize sufficient naval might to threaten British commerce, challenge its sea power, and invade the island kingdom. Britain would not make peace with any state that sought European hegemony, and Napoleon's ambition would settle for nothing less.

Unable to invade Britain while British warships commanded the English Channel, Napoleon decided to bring what he called "the nation of shopkeepers" to its knees by damaging the British economy. His plan, called the *Continental System*, was to bar all countries under France's control from buying British goods. However, by smuggling goods onto the Continent and increasing trade with the New World, Britain, although hurt, escaped economic ruin. Besides, the Continental System also punished European lands that were dependent on British imports; the bourgeoisie, generally supportive of Napoleon's social and administrative reforms, turned against him because of the economic distress it caused. Furthermore, Napoleon's efforts to enforce the system enmeshed him in two catastrophic blunders: the occupation of Spain and the invasion of Russia.

The Spanish Ulcer

An ally of France since 1796, Spain proved a disappointment to Napoleon. It failed to prevent the Portuguese from trading with Britain, and it contributed little military or financial aid to France's war effort. Napoleon decided to incorporate Spain into his empire; in 1808, he deposed

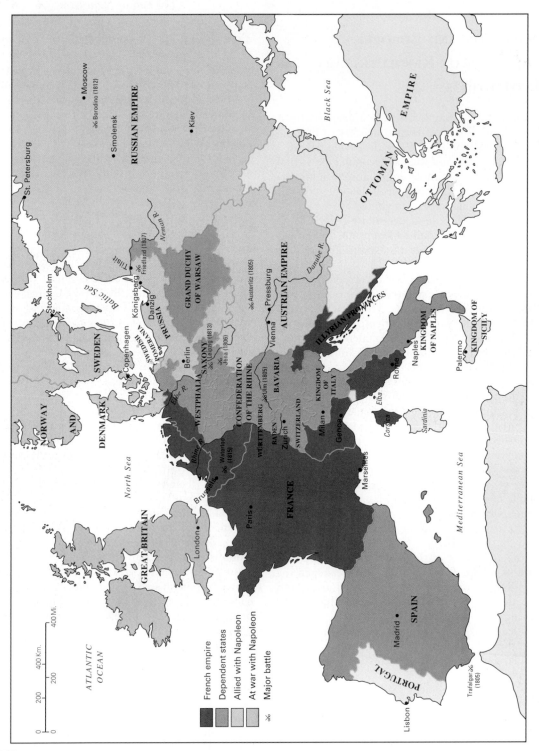

Major battle

At war with Napoleon

Allied with Napoleon

Dependent states

French empire

ATLANTIC OCEAN

400 M.

400 Km.

200

200

0

0

NORWAY AND

SWEDEN

DENMARK

GREAT BRITAIN

North Sea

London •

Brussels •

Waterloo (1815)

Paris •

FRANCE

SPAIN

Madrid •

PORTUGAL

Lisbon •

Trafalgar (1805)

Mediterranean Sea

St. Petersburg •

Stockholm •

Baltic Sea

Copenhagen •

SWEDISH POMERANIA

Berlin •

Königsberg •

Danzig •

Tilsit •

Friedland (1807)

PRUSSIA

GRAND DUCHY OF WARSAW

WESTPHALIA

SAXONY

Leipzig (1813)

Jena (1806)

CONFEDERATION OF THE RHINE

Elbe R.

Rhine R.

WÜRTTEMBERG

BADEN

Zurich •

SWITZERLAND

Milan •

KINGDOM OF ITALY

Genoa •

Marseilles •

Corsica

Sardinia

Elba

Neman R.

Ulm (1805)

BAVARIA

Vienna •

Pressburg •

Austerlitz (1805)

AUSTRIAN EMPIRE

Danube R.

ILLYRIAN PROVINCES

Rome •

Naples •

KINGDOM OF NAPLES

Palermo •

KINGDOM OF SICILY

RUSSIAN EMPIRE

Moscow •

Borodino (1812)

Smolensk •

Kiev •

Black Sea

OTTOMAN EMPIRE

478

the Spanish ruler and designated his own brother Joseph as king of Spain.

Napoleon believed that the Spanish would rally round the gentle Joseph and welcome his liberal reforms. This confidence was a fatal illusion. Spanish nobles and clergy feared French liberalism; the overwhelmingly peasant population, illiterate and credulous, intensely proud, fanatically religious, and easily aroused by the clergy, viewed Napoleon as the Devil's agent. Loyal to the Spanish monarchy and faithful to the church, the Spanish fought a "War to the Knife" against the invaders.

Seeking to keep the struggle against Napoleon alive, Britain came to the aid of the Spanish insurgents. The intervention of British troops, commanded by Sir Arthur Wellesley, the future Duke of Wellington, led to the ultimate defeat of Joseph in 1813. The "Spanish ulcer" drained Napoleon's treasury, tied down hundreds of thousands of French troops, enabled Britain to gain a foothold on the Continent from which to invade southern France, and inspired patriots in other lands to resist the French emperor.

Disaster in Russia

Deteriorating relations between Russia and France led Napoleon to his fatal decision to attack the Eastern giant. His creation of the Grand Duchy of Warsaw irritated the tsar, who feared a revival of Polish power and resented French influence on Russia's border. Another source of friction between the tsar and Napoleon was Russia's illicit trade with Britain, in violation of the Continental System. No doubt Napoleon's inexhaustible craving for glory and power also compelled him to strike at Russia.

In June 1812, the Grand Army, 614,000 men strong, crossed the Neman River into Russia. Fighting mainly rearguard battles and retreating according to plan, the tsar's forces lured the invaders into the vastness of Russia, far from their lines of supply. On September 14, the Grand Army, its numbers greatly reduced by disease, hunger,

◀ *Map 19.2* Napoleon's Europe, 1810
By 1810, Napoleon dominated much of the Continent. His Grand Empire comprised lands annexed to France, vassal states, and cowed allies.
(© 2016 Cengage Learning.)

exhaustion, desertion, and battle, entered Moscow, which the Russians had virtually evacuated. To show their contempt for the French conquerors and to deny the French shelter, the Russians set fire to the city, which burned for five days. Taking up headquarters in Moscow, Napoleon waited for Alexander I to admit defeat and come to terms. But the tsar remained intransigent.

Napoleon was in a dilemma: to penetrate deeper into Russia was certain death; to stay in Moscow with winter approaching meant possible starvation. Faced with these alternatives, Napoleon decided to retreat westward. On October 19, 1812, ninety-five thousand troops and thousands

Napoleon in Exile Dictating His Memoirs. While on Saint Helena, Napoleon prepared an account of his career that presented him in a most favorable light: a lover of peace who was forced to take up arms against the reactionary rulers of Europe in order to defend the gains of the Revolution. (Kean Collection/Archive Photos/Getty Images.)

of wagons loaded with loot left Moscow for the long trek back. In early November came the first snow and frost. Army stragglers were slaughtered by Russian Cossacks and peasant partisans. In the middle of December, with the Russians in pursuit, the remnants of the Grand Army staggered across the Neman River into East Prussia.

The German War of Liberation

Napoleon's disastrous Russian campaign helped to trigger uprisings in the German states, where anti-French feeling was high. Hatred of the French invaders evoked a feeling of national outrage among some Germans, who up to this time had thought only in terms of their own particular state and prince. Some German intellectuals, using the emotional language of nationalism, called for a war of liberation against Napoleon and, in some instances, for the creation of a unified Germany.

Besides kindling a desire for national independence and unity, the disastrous defeat of the Prussians at Jena (1806) and French domination of Germany stimulated a movement for reform among members of the Prussian high bureaucracy and officer corps. To survive in a world altered by the French Revolution, Prussia would have to learn the principal lessons of the Revolution: that aroused citizens fighting for a cause make better soldiers than mercenaries and oppressed serfs, and that officers selected for daring and intelligence command better than nobles possessing only a gilded birthright. The reformers believed that the elimination of social abuses would overcome defeatism and apathy and encourage Prussians to serve the state willingly and to fight bravely for national honor. A revitalized Prussia could then deal with the French.

Among the important reforms introduced in Prussia between 1807 and 1813 were the abolition of serfdom, the granting to towns of a large measure of self-administration, the awarding of army commissions on the basis of merit instead of birth, the elimination of cruel punishment in the ranks, and the establishment of national conscription. In 1813, the reform party forced King Frederick William III to declare war on France. The military reforms did improve the quality of the Prussian army. In the War of Liberation (1813), Prussian soldiers demonstrated far more enthusiasm and patriotism than they had at Jena in 1806, and the French were driven from Germany.

The German War of Liberation came on the heels of Napoleon's disastrous Russian campaign.

Final Defeat

After the destruction of the Grand Army, the empire crumbled. Although Napoleon raised a new army, he could not replace the equipment, cavalry horses, and experienced soldiers squandered in Russia. Now he had to rely on schoolboys and overage veterans. Most of Europe joined in a final coalition against France. In October 1813, allied forces from Austria, Prussia, Russia, and Sweden defeated Napoleon at Leipzig; in November, Anglo-Spanish forces crossed the Pyrenees into France. Finally, in the spring of 1814, the allies captured Paris. Napoleon abdicated and was exiled to the tiny island of Elba, off the coast of Italy. The Bourbon dynasty was restored to the throne of France in the person of Louis XVIII, younger brother of the executed Louis XVI and the acknowledged leader of the émigrés.

Only forty-four years of age, Napoleon did not believe that it was his destiny to die on Elba. On March 1, 1815, he landed on the French coast with a thousand soldiers, and three weeks later he entered Paris to a hero's welcome. Raising a new army, Napoleon moved against the allied forces in Belgium. There, the Prussians, led by Field Marshal Gebhard von Blücher, and the British, led by the Duke of Wellington, defeated Napoleon at Waterloo in June 1815. Napoleon's desperate gamble to regain power—the famous "hundred days"— had failed. This time the allies sent Napoleon to Saint Helena, a lonely island in the South Atlantic a thousand miles off the coast of southern Africa. On this gloomy and rugged rock, Napoleon Bonaparte, emperor of France and would-be conqueror of Europe, spent the last six years of his life. Napoleon's drive, military genius, and charisma had propelled him to the peak of power; his inability to moderate his ambition bled Europe, distorted his judgment, and led to his downfall.

THE MEANING OF THE FRENCH REVOLUTION

The French Revolution was a decisive period in the shaping of the modern West. It implemented the thought of the philosophes, destroyed

AND THERE IS NO REMEDY, ETCHING BY FRANCISCO GOYA (1746–1828). Spaniards resisted the installation of Joseph, Napoleon's brother, as king of Spain. Both sides engaged in terrible atrocities in the ensuing Peninsular War. The Spanish painter Francisco Goya captured the war's brutality. (Image copyright © The Metropolitan Museum of Art. Image source: Art Resource, N.Y.)

the hierarchical and corporate society of the Old Regime, which was a legacy of the Middle Ages, promoted the interests of the bourgeoisie, and quickened the growth of the modern state.

The French Revolution weakened the aristocracy. With their feudal rights and privileges eliminated, the nobles became simply ordinary citizens. Throughout the nineteenth century, France would be governed by both the aristocracy and the bourgeoisie; property, not noble birth, determined the composition of the new ruling elite.

The principle of careers being open to talent gave the bourgeois access to the highest positions in the state. Having wealth, talent, ambition, and now opportunity, the bourgeois would play an ever more important role in French political life. Throughout Continental Europe, the reforms of the French Revolution served as a model for progressive bourgeois, who sooner or later would challenge the Old Regime in their own lands.

The French Revolution transformed the dynastic state, on which the Old Regime was based, into the modern state: national, liberal, secular, and rational. When the Declaration of the Rights of Man and of the Citizen stated that "the source of all sovereignty resides essentially in the nation," the concept of the state took on a new meaning. The state was no longer merely a territory or a federation of provinces, nor was it the private possession of a king who claimed to be God's lieutenant on earth. In the new conception, the state belonged to the people as a whole. For a government to be legitimate it had to derive its power from the people. And the individual, formerly a subject, was now a citizen with both rights and duties and was governed by laws that permitted no legal distinction between commoners and nobles.

The liberal thought of the Enlightenment found practical expression in the reforms of the Revolution. Absolutism and divine right of monarchy, repudiated in theory by the philosophes, were invalidated by constitutions affirming that sovereignty resides with the people, not with a monarch, and setting limits to the powers of government and by elected parliaments that represented the governed. By providing for equality before the law and the protection of human rights—habeas corpus, trial by jury, civil rights for Protestants and Jews, and freedom of speech and the press—the Revolution struck at the abuses of the Old Regime. Because of violations and interruptions, these gains seemed at times more theoretical than actual. Nevertheless, these liberal ideals reverberated throughout the Continent. In the early nineteenth century, revolutionaries in France and other lands, aspiring for political and social change, took the French Revolution as their inspiration, and the pace of reform quickened.

Prior to the Revolution, religion was still closely linked to the state. As a general rule each state had an official religion, a state church that legitimated the ruling power. By disavowing any divine justification for the monarch's power, by depriving the church of its special position, and by no longer limiting citizenship to members of a state church, the Revolution accelerated the secularization of European political life.

Sweeping aside the administrative chaos of the Old Regime, the Revolution attempted to impose rational norms on the state. The sale of public offices, which had produced ineffective and corrupt administrators, was eliminated, and the highest positions in the land were opened to men of talent, regardless of birth. The Revolution abolished the peasantry's manorial obligations, which had hampered agriculture, and swept away barriers to economic expansion. It based taxes on income and streamlined their collection. The destruction of feudal remnants, internal tolls, and the guilds speeded up the expansion of a competitive market economy. In the nineteenth century, reformers in the rest of Europe would follow the lead set by France.

By spreading revolutionary ideals and institutions, Napoleon made it impossible for the traditional rulers to restore the Old Regime intact after the emperor's downfall. He had solidified in France what the Revolution had initiated—the destruction of a society based on orders and legal privileges and the opening of careers to talent regardless of birth. In conquered lands, his administrators undermined the authority of aristocrats and clergy. Napoleon's reforms furthered the rationalization and secularization of society and contributed to the transformation of the dynastic state into the modern national state and to the prominence of the bourgeoisie.

By showing that a decadent Old Order could be toppled and supplanted by a new one, the French Revolution inspired generations of revolutionaries aspiring to end longstanding abuses and to remodel society. In the process, it unleashed three potentially destructive forces identified with the modern state: total war, nationalism, and a fanatic utopian mentality. All these forces contradicted the rational and universal aims of the reformers as stated in the Declaration of the Rights of Man and of the Citizen. Whereas the restrained wars of the eighteenth century were fought by a limited number of professional soldiers for limited aims, the French Revolution brought conscription and the mobilization of all the state's resources for armed conflict, practices continued by Napoleon. The French emperor raised armies of unprecedented size and sought the complete destruction of the enemy force. The battle of Leipzig, for example, involved 500,000 combatants on both sides, of whom 150,000 were killed or wounded. Almost a million Frenchmen perished in Napoleon's wars. The world wars of the twentieth century were the terrible fulfillment of this new development in warfare.

The French Revolution also gave birth to modern nationalism. During the Revolution, loyalty was directed to the entire nation, not to a village or province or to the person of the king. The whole of France became the fatherland.

Under the Jacobins, the French became converts to a secular faith preaching total reverence for the nation. "In 1794 we believed in no supernatural religion; our serious interior sentiments were all summed up in the one idea, how to be useful to the fatherland. Everything else . . . was, in our eyes, only trivial. . . . It was our only religion."[30] Few suspected that the new religion of nationalism was fraught with danger. Louis-Antoine de Saint-Just, a young, ardent Robespierrist, was gazing into the future when he declared: "There is something terrible in the sacred love of the fatherland. This love is so exclusive that it sacrifices everything to the public interest, without pity, without fear, with no respect for the human individual."[31] The philosophes would have deemed nationalism, which demanded total dedication of body and soul to the nation and stifled clear thinking, to be a repudiation of their universalism and hopes for rational solutions to political conflicts. It was a new dogma capable of evoking wild and dangerous passions and a setback for the progress of reason.

The French Revolution gave rise to still another potentially destructive force: a revolutionary mentality that sought to demolish an unjust traditional society and create a new social order that would restore individuals to their natural goodness. The negative side of this lofty vision was its power to whip up an extremism that demonized opponents as irredeemably evil and that justified mass murder in the name of a supposedly higher good. Such was the case with Robespierre and other Jacobins. In the twentieth century, Nazis in Germany and radical socialists in Russia, China, and Cambodia, seeing themselves as idealists striving for a social regeneration of humanity, oppressed, terrorized, and murdered with intense dedication—and a clear conscience.

The Revolution attempted to reconstruct society on the basis of Enlightenment thought. The Declaration of the Rights of Man and of the Citizen, whose spirit permeated the reforms of the Revolution, upheld the dignity of the individual, demanded respect for the individual, attributed to each person natural rights, and barred the state from denying these rights. It insisted that society and the state have no higher duty than to promote the freedom and autonomy of the individual. "It is not enough to have overturned the throne," said Robespierre; "our concern is to erect upon its remains holy Equality and the sacred Rights of Man."[32] The tragedy of the Western experience is that this humanist vision, brilliantly expressed by the Enlightenment and given recognition in the reforms of the French Revolution, would be undermined in later generations. And, ironically, by its fanatical commitment to a seductive ideology that promised worldly salvation—the creation of a republic of virtue and truth—the French Revolution itself contributed to the shattering of this vision. It had spawned total war, including mass conscription, aggressive nationalism, terror as government policy, and a revolutionary mentality that sought to change the world through coercion and terror, including mass murder. In the twentieth century, these dangerous forces almost succeeded in crushing the liberty and equality so valued by the French reformers.

NOTES

1. Quoted in G. P. Gooch, *Germany and the French Revolution* (New York: Russell and Russell, 1966), 39.

2. Quoted in Ernst Wangermann, *From Joseph II to the Jacobin Trials* (New York: Oxford University Press, 1959), 24.

3. Quoted in Klaus Epstein, *The Genesis of German Conservatism* (Princeton: Princeton University Press, 1966), 436.

4. Excerpted in Alfred Cobban, ed., *The Debate on the French Revolution* (London: Adam and Charles Black, 1960), 41.

5. Quoted in Elinor G. Barber, *The Bourgeoisie in Eighteenth-Century France* (Princeton, N.J.: Princeton University Press, 1967), 57.

6. Quoted in C. B. A. Behrens, *The Ancien Régime* (New York: Harcourt, Brace and World, 1967), 43.

7. Quoted in Leo Gershoy, *The French Revolution and Napoleon* (New York: Appleton-Century-Crofts, 1933), 18.

8. George Rudé, *Revolutionary Europe, 1783–1815* (New York: Harper Torchbooks, 1966), 74.

9. Henri Peyre, "The Influence of Eighteenth-Century Ideas on the French Revolution," *Journal of the History of Ideas*, 10(1949): 73.

10. Georges Lefebvre, *The French Revolution from 1793 to 1799*, trans. John Hall Stewart and James Friguglietti (New York: Columbia University Press, 1964), 2:360.

11. Quoted in T. C. W. Blanning, *The French Revolution: Aristocrats Versus Bourgeois?* (Atlantic Highlands, N.J.: Humanities Press, 1987), 9.

12. William Doyle, *Origins of the French Revolution* (New York: Oxford University Press, 1980), 21.

13. Quoted in Blanning, *French Revolution*, 38.

14. Excerpted in John Hall Stewart, ed., *A Documentary Survey of the French Revolution* (New York: Macmillan, 1951), 43–44.

15. See George Rudé, *The Crowd in the French Revolution* (New York: Oxford University Press, 1959).

16. Albert Soboul, *The Parisian Sans-Culottes and the French Revolution, 1793–94*, trans. Gwynne Lewis (London: Oxford University Press, 1964), 28–29.

17. Quoted in ibid, 64.

18. Excerpted in Leo Gershoy, ed., *The Era of the French Revolution 1789–1799* (New York: D. Van Nostrand, 1957), 150.

19. Quoted in Hans Kohn, *Nationalism: Its Meaning and History* (Princeton, N.J.: D. Van Nostrand, 1965), 25.

20. Quoted in Carlton J. H. Hayes, *The Historical Evolution of Modern Nationalism* (New York: Richard R. Smith, 1931), 55.

21. Excerpted in George Rudé, ed., *Robespierre* (Engle wood Cliffs, N.J.: Prentice-Hall, 1976), 72.

22. Ibid., 57.

23. Excerpted in E. L. Higgins, ed., *The French Revolution As Told By Contemporaries* (Boston: Houghton Mifflin, 1938), 306–307.

24. Excerpted in Philip G. Dwyer and Peter McPhee, *The French Revolution and Napoleon: A Sourcebook* (London: Routledge, 2002), 88.

25. Excerpted in Maurice Hunt, ed., *Napoleon* (Englewood Cliffs, N.J.: Prentice Hall, 1972), 3.

26. Quoted in Robert B. Holtman, *The Napoleonic Revolution* (Philadelphia: J. B. Lippincott, 1967), 121.

27. Quoted in Felix Markham, *Napoleon and the Awakening of Europe* (New York: Collier Books, 1965), 97.

28. Holtman, *The Napoleonic Revolution*, 143.

29. Hunt, *Napoleon*, 49–50.

30. Quoted in Carlton J. H. Hayes, *The Historical Evolution of Modern Nationalism* (New York: Richard R. Smith, 1931), 55.

31. Quoted in Hans Kohn, *Making of the Modern French Mind* (New York: D. Van Nostrand, 1955), 17.

32. Quoted in Christopher Dawson, *The Gods of Revolution* (New York: New York University Press, 1972), 83.

Chapter 20

The Industrial Revolution: The Great Transformation

Railroad line from Nuremberg to Furth. The spectacle of the arrival and departure of the train attracts townspeople of all classes. Central Europe followed England and France in railroad mania. (Snark/Art Resource, N.Y.)

- **The Origins of the Industrial Age**
- **Society Transformed**
- **Relief and Reform**
- **Industrialism in Perspective**

Focus Questions

1. Why did England industrialize before the rest of Europe?

2. What political and social factors influenced British industrialization?

3. How did political and social factors affect industrialization in France, in the German states, and in the Netherlands?

4. Why did cities grow so rapidly between 1800 and 1860? How did that rapid industrialization influence politics?

5. How did the law discriminate against and punish the working class during the early stages of industrialization? How did it try to protect this class?

*I*n the second half of the eighteenth century, there were significant changes in the ways Western Europeans labored and traded; historians call the total process the Industrial Revolution. Although this revolution had no start, no single set pattern, little planning, and no organizers, its effects dominated the nineteenth and twentieth centuries, changing the lives of mankind today.

The term *Industrial Revolution* refers to the shift from an agrarian, handicraft, local, labor-intensive economy to one dominated by machine manufacture, specialization of tasks or division of labor, factories and cities, and a worldwide market for goods, services, and capital. These changes began in England in the eighteenth century where simple on-the-job changes made by workers "revolutionized" human tasks. Today, we find the causes of the Industrial Revolution in increased agricultural productivity, population growth, the rapid development of cities, new and more efficient ways of organizing tasks to use plentiful labor and stretch limited natural resources, and innovative ways of expanding capital.

Progress that spanned a century in Britain and as much as two centuries in the rest of the developed world hardly seems revolutionary. Our view of revolution is less than a generation, perhaps a decade. Yet the transformation of human existence in Western Europe from 1750 to 1850 is so great that no term other than *revolution* seems appropriate. In fact, historians see multiple industrial revolutions: one from 1750 to 1850 in Western Europe, one from the mid-nineteenth century that included the United States, another in the first half of the twentieth century that some call *modernization,* and yet another within the last fifty years that many refer to as *globalization.*

Industrial development did not proceed at the same pace everywhere. The changes begun in England in the mid-1700s were delayed in France by political and social revolution, and in the German and Italian states political disunity slowed the growth of industry. The German states began to industrialize in the 1840s, nearly a century after England. With German unification in 1870, industry grew phenomenally, but much of the traditional economy persisted alongside the new. In Italy, industrialization began slowly. The sharp economic divisions between north and south and a comparative lack of natural resources and political unity hampered industrial growth. Eastern Europe did not start industrializing until the 1890s, and in some cases not until the twentieth century.

Britain stepped out ahead. Europeans, Americans, and eventually other peoples around the globe, driven to adopt changes in agriculture and industry, copied Britain's techniques, borrowed its plans, imported its engineers as advisers, borrowed its capital, and studied English politics and society searching for the essentials of economic growth. By the end of the nineteenth century, Germany, France, and the United States were competitive with Britain; Italy, Russia, and Austria-Hungary raced to catch up. Everywhere, the conditions of labor and life were altered profoundly.

THE ORIGINS OF THE INDUSTRIAL AGE

From the fifteenth to the eighteenth century, Western Europe accumulated substantial wealth, much of it from trade with the Ottomans, the Chinese, and Mogul India, as well as the New World. This wealth was spread across more classes of people than ever before. In the Late Middle Ages, improved agriculture made possible the increase of the total population. Diverse rural handicrafts provided the foundation for the relatively rapid expansion of trade, both overseas and on the Continent, in the next two centuries. This expansion explains the aggressive search for new markets for handicraft products; it was built on the capitalist practices of medieval and Renaissance bankers and merchants. Expansion tapped the wealth of a much larger world than Mediterranean lands that were accessible to earlier generations. Thus, the resources of the New World and of Africa, both human and material, fueled Europe's accumulation of wealth.

The centralized states' strong monarchs—England, Spain, Portugal, and France, as well as the much less centralized Netherlands—competed for markets, territory, and prestige. These states engaged in fierce military and commercial rivalries. They actively promoted the manufacture of weaponry, uniforms, and ships, and also encouraged commerce for tax revenues. This commerce nurtured a greatly expanded economy involving many levels of society—owners of large estates, merchant princes, entrepreneurs, innovative artisans, sugar plantation colonials, slave traders, sailors, and even peasant farmers.

Europe's Population Explosion

Several factors, each linked to the increase in the European labor supply, contributed to industrialization. In the eighteenth century, the rural population grew enormously. The population explosion did not bring famine, disease, and misery to Europe as it had so many times before and as it has in so many other regions since. This increase led to the breakup of traditional farming and, in Western Europe, to capitalist farming for the market. Even the strong monarchs of Western Europe were not powerful enough to keep labor tied to the land. In labor-scarce areas, such as Russia, the United States, and much of Latin America, however, labor remained in serfdom, slavery, and peonage well into the nineteenth century.

The rapidly growing population provided both the laborers and the consumers of the products of economic development. In 1800, Europe had about 190 million people; by 1850, 260 million. By 1914, it had 460 million, and some 200 million other Europeans had settled throughout the world. Virtually simultaneous with this population boom, there were two major changes in agriculture: a "green revolution" of new crops, and new and different ways of utilizing land and labor. Productivity rose sufficiently to feed the increasing population and actually to improve the diet of Europeans. Better nutrition meant better health, more births, and fewer deaths of both young and old. Surviving children grew stronger and taller (the average European man was five foot six in 1900, but a mere five feet in 1800). They worked harder and longer and were more intellectually able. Girls menstruated earlier and married at a younger age, which meant more births. Greater demand meant higher prices for food and profits for land entrepreneurs—the development of a kind of capitalist agriculture for some but the impoverishment of the rural poor.

M'CORMICK'S AMERICAN REAPING MACHINE.

THE AGRICULTURAL REVOLUTION: THE McCORMICK REAPER. Harvesting grain with a horse-drawn machine released great numbers of laborers from farms to work in factories or cities. The great demand for labor may explain, in part, the constant search for and investment in mechanical devices for farm and factory in the United States, a major food exporter even today. (© Mary Evans Picture Library/The Image Works.)

Agricultural Revolution

Capitalist agriculture—production for the market, not for family or village consumption—was born in England and the Netherlands. Many people, aristocrats as well as peasants, persisted in traditional ways of mutual obligations, but powerful forces gradually drew most farmers to the marketplace, first in Western, then in Central, and finally in Eastern and Southern Europe. Land freed from traditional obligations became private property, just another commodity to be bought, sold, traded, and managed for profit.

Peasants who were no longer protected or obligated by manorial customs joined the ranks of entrepreneurs, tenants, or wage laborers—all farming for the market. Undeveloped land was cultivated; common land for animal grazing became private property of great landowners whose political power gave them legal advantages. This process, known as *enclosure*, took place over much of Europe. In England, most enclosure had occurred two centuries earlier, but the much

smaller number of enclosures in the 1700s was nonetheless responsible for much rural poverty. Dispossessed farmers tried to eke out a living as day laborers for the commercial farming land-owners. Entrepreneurs "farmed out" some manufacturing processes to poor men, women, and children "cottagers" for spinning or weaving. Ultimately, the new trends forced farmers to emigrate either to cities or to the Americas or Australia.

The agricultural revolution of the 1700s changed everything—landholding, soil usage, and animal husbandry, as well as the relations between master and man. Land use grew more efficient. Convertible husbandry—the term given to innovation in farming—cycled land from grain production to soil-restoring crops of legumes, then pasturage, and back to grain production. These methods were developed by landlords but gradually they were adopted by the peasantry. In some areas, however—within every country, and particularly in Southern and Eastern Europe—the old practices continued well into the nineteenth century.

After two centuries of increasing agricultural productivity with little change in technology, the application of technical ingenuity to farming brought steel plows, improved reapers, horse-drawn rakes, and threshers. (The Americans were very inventive in this area; agricultural machinery formed a substantial part of their manufacturing exports.) These changes greatly increased efficiency and production; fewer men and women could produce more food and raw materials.

Britain First?

In the early eighteenth century, Britain's competitive advantage was not obvious. The Netherlands and France were as wealthy, if not more so. They possessed a trading empire equal to England's, and their populations were equally skilled and industrious. Their scientific and intellectual life rivaled that of England. The French government, if anything, was even more responsive than Britain's to the need for transportation and communication; it subsidized innovation, established schools for technicians and trained civil engineers for public works such as waterworks, canals, roads, and bridges.

The French people, however, seemed less willing than the British to change the traditional ways of agriculture or craft production. Peasant landholdings, smaller than in England, may have discouraged experimentation. Pride of craft meant that the French produced fine goods by hand for the few, rather than cheap machine goods for the many. A number of serious obstacles—internal tariffs, government monopolies, and strong craft guilds—hampered industrialization in France and in Central Europe. In England, obstacles to the free flow of goods were less powerful or nonexistent. As a result of these commercial and cultural differences, French industrialization was slow.

The French Revolution, which gave so much political freedom and economic opportunity, perpetuated some traditional agricultural and commercial practices and attitudes. Peasants who acquired land in the Revolution often gained plots so small that new farming methods were difficult to apply. For more than a generation French resources went to building armies and the revenues of the state. Political instability made the French less willing to take risks that contributed to economic development.

The Netherlands, too, had more than sufficient wealth for industrialization. As early as the seventeenth century, the Dutch had developed techniques of finance and commerce that every nation tried to imitate. The Dutch capitalized the economic development of other states by offering capital at the lowest interest rate in Europe. They had a good transportation system, a fine navy, and technical know-how. The Dutch were well educated, and their government, like the French, fostered science and invention. They were Europe's most skilled farmers, but they lacked natural resources, particularly coal, forests, and iron deposits.

Thus Britain possessed several advantages enabling it to become the workshop of the world. First, it had a labor pool of hardworking, skilled farmers who could no longer earn a living on the land. Britain also possessed large and easily developed supplies of coal and iron, and a long tradition of metallurgy and mining. Britain's transportation system of canals and toll roads (turnpikes) were built for profit by private entrepreneurs; no other country relied as completely on private capital resources and individual entrepreneurs for development. Small wonder, then, that free trade and economic individualism had many champions there.

The state did contribute to Britain's Industrial Revolution. Though the aristocracy dominated the legislature, the courts, and all of society, there was greater freedom for business and industry than anywhere in Europe. No other country possessed as strong a legal system protecting private property (including invention as intellectual property). Laws allowed the enclosure of common lands, pushing small farmers off the land, permitting the aristocrats to consolidate large holdings, and providing cheap labor for mines and factories. Parliament fostered enterprise that expanded trade routes and enriched the British economy—toll bridge and canal builders and the East India Company. Most importantly, Parliament reshaped the electoral system with the Reform Bill of 1832, allowing middle-class subjects to gain the right to vote (and thereby be elected to sit in the House of Commons) based on the amount of property they owned and the taxes they paid. In the

Chronology 20.1 ❖ The Industrial Revolution

1764–1767	Hargreaves invents the spinning jenny
1769	Watt invents the modern steam engine
1785	Cartwright develops a power loom
1830	First railway line is built in England
1832	Reform Bill of 1832 expands British voting rights

eighteenth century, a British entrepreneur had remarkable freedom of entry into the economy, unrestricted by the monopolies and guilds that other Europeans faced. By the early nineteenth century, business people could actually shape the political and legal environment of business and commerce. Britain's culture spurred industrialization because it encouraged consumption and permitted social mobility. The British aspired to the consuming habits of their social superiors. Consumption was a great incentive to production and trade. Debt carried little of the social stigma that it did in other cultures. The upper class was prejudiced against trade, but those who gained a fortune from trade, commerce, investment, or even through marriage were soon accepted socially.

Technological Advance

Industrial Revolution for most people means inventions of machines to make goods using sources of energy other than human and animal power. Most people think of innovation and the development of new products, trades, and occupations. In the long run, inventions did have revolutionary implications for politics, society, and the economy, but the early stages of technological development grew from the simple changes workers made as they worked. Eager artisans quickly picked up on small improvements to increase their productivity and profits. Examination of some key industries indicates how the process took off, that is, how some technological and social changes pushed others.

Cotton Textiles. Cotton production was actually the first industry to grow at unprecedented rates, expanding tenfold between 1760 and 1785, and another tenfold between 1785 and 1825. In 1733,

long before expansion started, a simple invention—John Kay's flying shuttle—allowed wool weavers to double their output and to work at home. Weavers produced faster than spinners until James Hargreaves's spinning jenny (1768) enabled the operator to work several spindles at once powered only by human energy. Within five years, Richard Arkwright powered a spinning machine by water or animal energy. Six years later (1779), Samuel Crompton's spinning mule powered many spindles, first by human and later by animal and water energy. These changes improved spinning so much that there were shortages in weaving until Edmund Cartwright developed a power loom in 1787. To the end of the century, there was a race to speed up first the spinning and then the weaving by changing the power to looms or to new, larger devices for the jenny.

These inventions drastically altered the social conditions of the workplace. At first, families worked in their cottages; women and children spun while men wove. When more than human strength was needed to power the looms, the water frame made it more efficient to bring workers together near water. Later, steam meant factories could be built anywhere, preferably near coal to cut costs, which were higher than for water-powered factories. Power-driven weaving was primarily men's work; spinning, women's. Odd jobs were for children. Within two or three generations, the factory system revolutionized labor, changing family relations and urbanizing production and labor.

These were major social changes in a short space of time. The invention of Whitney's cotton gin in 1793 brought another social revolution. The machine removed seeds from raw cotton quickly and cheaply, leading farmers in the new world to devote more land and slave labor to production. Technology fostered slavery just as other

490

WOMAN AT HARGREAVES'S SPINNING JENNY. The cotton textile trade was one of the first to be mechanized. In cottage industries, the whole family contributed to the making of thread and cloth. James Hargreaves's spinning jenny, one of the early inventions made by the workers themselves, was an adaptation of his wife's thread-spinning tool. (ARPL/Topham/The Image Works.)

inventions moved farm-laboring men, women, and children from home to factory assembly lines, from women's work to men's labor.

Weavers and spinners—not technicians, engineers, or scientists—invented simple devices modeled after machines already in use. These inventions did not cause the cotton industry's expansion; social and economic demand did that. Once begun, the expansion was so great, the demand so urgent, and the potential profits so huge that more and more complicated technology developed. A role emerged for the engineer, not an on-the-job laborer but an expert in building or adapting machines utilizing different sources of power.

Steam Power. Roughly the same process took place in steam. James Watt's steam engine dates from the 1760s, but it was too expensive to be widely adopted. Women, children, and even men laborers were cheaper than steam-powered machinery. By the 1830s in England, there was rapid expansion as engines and fuel became cheaper. Coal or wood, not water, powered steam engines, so factories could be anywhere. Steam also

powered trains and carts but costs might maintain use of canal transportation. By the midcentury, steam was widely applied, causing the incredible rate of change generally identified with the Industrial Revolution. In the two previous centuries, increasing productivity, the accumulation of capital, and the provisioning of a growing population had been powered by people, animals, and water—an extraordinary feat. With steam, weaker, younger, and even less-skilled workers could perform the few simple, necessary tasks. As steam took hold, engines replaced people, and workers became "hands" that drove machines.

The New Iron Age. Steam power might mean the weak could operate machinery, but it required strong machines to withstand its force. As with textiles and power, the history of the search for better iron illustrates how developments in one industry prompted change in related industries and ultimately in society.

Until the eighteenth century, ironmaking had not changed much since the Middle Ages. By trial-and-error methods, entrepreneurs the Darbys in

The Darby Family

By trial and error, three generations of an English family of iron manufacturers developed new ways of producing the precious metal of industrialization.

Abraham Darby (1677–1717), a workman in Coalbrookdale, England, built a blast furnace for casting iron. He is believed to be the first to use coke in iron smelting to replace expensive charcoal. His improved iron was used for Royal Navy cannons, but the workman-inventor did not patent his process. By the time of his son Abraham II (1711–1763) coke smelting dominated the making of cast iron, but the industry still was one of small, competing firms concentrated near coal-rich regions such as Coalbrookdale.

Third generation Abraham III (1750–1791) was the pride of the family and of England. In 1779, he built the first cast-iron bridge, a semicircular arch across the Severn River.

The Severn bridge was a major technological feat. Darby rebuilt his grandfather's furnaces to cast large enough pieces—378 tons of interlocking iron pieces—for a bridge that is one hundred feet long with forty-five-foot-high castings, held together by bolts or rivets. Engineers and travelers from all over Europe came to see this marvel.

The story of the Darbys and the Severn bridge symbolizes English industrialization. When John Wilkinson, another small ironmonger, failed to get together the capital for the bridge, Darby designed, cast, and built it in his small enterprise. Darby also financed the bridge. He laid out half of the total funds and got the other half from private funds—none came from government. A technological marvel, the bridge was a financial one as well, capitalized by a workman-entrepreneur who wasn't even incorporated. He took all the risk; he and his family gained a reputation and built their firm on it.

England, replaced the burning of scarce and valuable wood with coal or coke to make cast iron and later wrought iron. Coal made brittle metal until Henry Cort copied the French practice of using a furnace with two separate compartments, one for the coke and one for the iron ore. By the 1780s, trial and error, copying, and adapting had perfected wrought iron so that it became the most widely used metal for construction and machinery. In the 1860s, Henry Bessemer converted pig iron into steel by removing impurities in the iron. William Siemens and Pierre and Émile Martin developed the open-hearth process, which could handle much greater amounts of metal than Bessemer's converter. Steel quickly replaced iron.

The new iron age became the age of steel and coal. Sixteen million tons were mined at the end of the Napoleonic wars; thirty million in 1836; and sixty-five million in 1856. Human beings mined this coal—entire families, whole villages. Steam engines were too expensive to replace human labor, so they pumped water and hauled carts and miners up the main shaft to the surface. Once steam engines became cheaper than human or animal labor, they were applied to mining itself, opening rich veins in existing mines, thus stoking this early industrialization.

Transportation and Communication. Creating the network to support expansion also revolutionized transportation. Major road building took place in the eighteenth century in England and in France, and later in the rest of Europe. Both Britain and the United States experienced a boom in canal construction between 1760 and 1820. But canals were outmoded fairly quickly by railroads, which, though they were much more expensive, were more flexible. Railroads also caught the public imagination much as automobiles, airplanes, and space ships would in the twentieth century. Steam-powered engines replaced horse-powered railroads in the 1820s.

Thinking railroads were essential for defense and fostered national unity, Continental governments expended major efforts to develop rail networks.

Communication changed as spectacularly as transportation. Britain inaugurated the penny post in 1840, making it possible to send a letter to any part of the kingdom for about half an American penny. But elsewhere the cost of postage was so high that letters were rare. The first telegraphic message was sent from Baltimore to Washington, D.C., in 1844, but businesses' demand for cheap, fast communication meant rapid development. Within seven years, the first undersea cable was laid under the English Channel, and by 1866, the transatlantic cable was operating, and though certainly not cheap, the telegraph was employed quickly by ever-expanding business.

Unprecedented amounts of private British capital built Britain's system of roads, canals, railways, and steamships. Continental states were slower to adopt steam transport because they lacked capital and skilled civil engineering. Only France invested a great percentage of private capital in building a Europe-wide transportation system, but ultimately the French government was forced to take control of its railroads. In most of Europe, government construction and control was the rule. In the United States, Congress gave enormous grants of land to railroad companies to encourage building. Everywhere during the railroad-building boom, financiers invested heavily. The flow of capital from Western Europe, particularly Britain and France, to other lands in Europe and America was an awe-inspiring achievement. The spectacular flow of finance across borders and oceans was more than matched by the flow of labor, as Europeans and Asians built railroad networks on every continent.

The Power of Finance

The first stages of industrialization—the use of new crop mixes and tools in agriculture and the first changes in spinning and weaving—did not require much capital. Neither did the early adaptations in the iron industry. However, subsequent growth—from the spread of factories and the extensive application of machinery in agriculture to the expansion of mining, transportation and the construction of cities—required enormous capital. Railroads and steamship lines were so expensive that only governments could finance them; even in Belgium, where they were privately financed at first, the king was the major investor. Large capital infusions were also needed to fund the steel industry.

In the beginning, the owning family was the source of a company's financing, its management, and even its technical innovation. Family firms dominated industry. But outside investment grew steadily from 1860 to World War I (1914). In Britain, wealthy merchants and landlords invested, borrowing at low interest rates. On the Continent, where the supply of capital was limited, the British became international investors of the first rank, furnishing much of the capital for the industrialization of other nations. French investors, who were often reluctant to invest at home for fear of political instability, financed railroads in Central Europe. They were the major investors in the Suez Canal and in the first Panama Canal project, which failed. Among banking families—including the Barings of London and the Rothschilds of France, England, and Germany—kinship ties joined together large amounts of investment capital. People of the same religion or region would often band together to gather capital for development, as the Protestant and Jewish bankers of France did. These investor groups fueled European industrialization.

Banking was risky business; dozens of banks failed in every nineteenth-century financial crisis. Lacking insurance for deposits and possessing only limited resources, banks tended to be cautious. They diversified their investments, fearing to lose everything in the failure of a single industry. Thus, in any given country, there was a limit to the number of industries able to borrow substantial amounts of capital. In most countries, bankers preferred safe investments in government debt, a preference that slowed the development of industry.

Financing industry was difficult until there was some organization to enable a number of people to pool their capital safely. In the existing joint-stock companies, individuals could be held responsible for all the debts of the enterprise. England was innovative in finance, permitting incorporation as early as 1844. Investors were liable for a corporation's debts only in proportion to the number of shares they owned. This legal change meant that investors endangered only the amount that they had paid for their stock, and not all the funds that they or their family possessed. In 1844, after nearly a century of industrial progress, England had almost 1,000 such companies, compared with only 260 in France. In the 1850s, limited liability was applied to the stock of most English businesses, and a little later it was extended to banking and insurance companies. By the 1860s, France, Germany, and the United States permitted limited liability, which released a flow of savings into industry.

Like so much of the Industrial Revolution, solving the problems of organizing, structuring, and managing firms and of acquiring funds for the development of industry was a matter of trial and error, experiment, and innovation. These inventions of the mind and culture were as important to the expanding revolution as were the inventions of machines.

SOCIETY TRANSFORMED

European society remained overwhelmingly rural; much of the old life continued even while the new society developed in its midst. Landed property remained the principal form of wealth and the source of social and political power. From England to Russia large landowners, usually aristocratic leaders of families and kinship groups, continued to exert political and social influence on the local or regional level if not the national.

Industrialization brought a new world, with many forms of property and power. Individuals became increasingly important—before the law, in trade, in political thought, and in politics. Ultimately, the nation became more important than the province, region, or local area, but even in Western Europe, this did not happen until the last quarter of the nineteenth century.

Contemporaries viewed the growth of cities and industrial towns as they did so many aspects of industrialization—as a sudden and complete break with the past. For them, it was the shattering of traditional moral and social patterns. Some people remembered the past clearly and were enthusiastically "progressive." Others idealized the past as a golden age in which the relations between master and worker had been based on values of respect and industriousness, not the cash nexus of wages, hours, and production.

Urbanization

The nineteenth century was a period of astounding urbanization; cities became places of manufacture and industry, growing in number, size, and population. Before 1800, about 10 percent of the European population lived in cities (20 percent in Great Britain and the Netherlands, the leading urban centers). A mere forty-five cities in the *world* had more than 100,000 people. Halfway through the nineteenth century, when 52 percent of the English lived in cities, just 25 percent of the French, 36 percent of the Germans, 7 percent of the Russians, and 10 percent of U.S. inhabitants were urban dwellers. In some regions (the Midlands in England, the Lowlands in Scotland, the northern plains in France, the German Rhineland, the northeastern United States, and parts of northern Italy), the urbanization seemed to occur overnight, even if the overall numbers were not in the millions until the twentieth century.

Most of the shift from rural to urban living in the West actually occurred in the twentieth century. Unlike capital cities, industrial ones, particularly in England, grew rapidly, without planning or much regulation by local or national governments. So much growth with so little planning or government led to cities with minimal sanitation, no street lighting, wretched housing, poor transportation, and scant security. Cities had grown without planning before, but they had not been home and workplace for such large numbers of people, many of them new arrivals. Rich and poor alike suffered in this environment of disease, crime, and ugliness, although the poor obviously bore the brunt of these evils.

Government and businesses were reluctant to finance remedies for poor working and living conditions. Those were workers' problems, or perhaps the responsibility of a particular industry or group of businessmen, but not of taxpayers as a whole. Private funders were too weak, and unwilling, to combat the effects of unregulated private enterprise. In the rest of Europe, where industrialization came later and laissez-faire beliefs

Map 20.1 **Industrial Growth on the Continent, Mid-1800s** Industry created a market and production unit in northwestern Europe even before Germany and Italy were unified states. (© 2016 Cengage Learning.)

were less dominant, states were more willing to regulate industrial and urban development. They also had a bureaucracy for planning and regulation, although such efforts were still woefully inadequate.

Major industrial cities developed similar housing patterns, reflecting the wide disparity in economic and social power between the classes. By the middle of the nineteenth century, the wealthiest inhabitants circled the city's edge and were close to the country, living in suburbs, which were roomier and cleaner than the city proper. As a general rule, the farther one lived from the central

city, the wealthier one was. Suburban houses were not row houses; they stood alone and usually had gardens, a carriage house, and horses. In an inner ring were artisans' dwellings, ranging from small detached middle-class residences to one-and two-story row houses, perhaps with small yards. In the center of industrial towns were workers' row houses, several stories high, jammed together as close to the factories as possible, separated from each other by a strip of mud or cobblestones with a pump in the middle that served all the residents in the surrounding buildings. When public transportation developed in the second half of the

LONDON ROW HOUSES. This painting by the French artist Gustave Doré depicts the overcrowded and unsanitary conditions in industrial London. Workers and their families lived in row houses, each just one room wide with a tiny yard in back. (© Hulton-Deutsch Collection/CORBIS.)

century, workers' districts dispersed, usually to the outskirts of the city.

Almost universally, those who wrote about industrial cities—England's Manchester, Leeds, and Liverpool and France's Lyon—described the stench, the filth, the inhumane crowding, the poverty, and the immorality. The novelists Charles Dickens, George Sand, and Émile Zola captured the horrors of urban industrial life and the plight of the poor. In *Bleak House*, Dickens, referring to one of the characters in the novel, warned about the effects of such wretchedness: "There is not an atom of Tom's slime . . . not a wickedness, not a brutality of his committing, but shall work its retribution, through every order of society, up to the proudest of the proud and the highest of the high."[1] Factual parliamentary reports read like the novels when describing a London row with its lack of toilets and its "undrained, unpaved, unventilated, uncared-for" streets.

Some reports indicated landlords' responsibility; others blamed the new arrivals from rural areas in Scotland and Ireland. The parliamentary reports and the press shaped English public opinion, forcing some regulation of urban building, transportation, sanitation, and public health. On the Continent, where the state was less committed to laissez-faire ideology, it took a much more active role in controlling urban conditions.

Changes in Social Structure

The Industrial Revolution destroyed forever the old division of society into clergy, nobility, and commoners. The development of industry and commerce created a bourgeoisie of middle-class people of common birth who engaged in trade and other capitalist ventures. Usually referred to as the middle classes (plural) because of the several

James Phillips Kay: Moral and Physical Dissipation

In 1832 James Phillips Kay, a physician, published a pamphlet describing the moral and physical condition of the working class in Manchester. His study, excerpted below, provided additional evidence of the painful effects industrialization had on factory workers and their families.

The township of Manchester chiefly consists of dense masses of houses, inhabited by the population engaged in the great manufactories of the cotton trade. . . . Prolonged and exhausting labour, continued from day to day, and from year to year, is not calculated to develop the intellectual or moral faculties of man. The dull routine of a ceaseless drudgery, in which the same mechanical process is incessantly repeated, resembles the torment of Sisyphus[1]—the toil, like the rock, recoils perpetually on the wearied operative. The mind gathers neither stores nor strength from the constant extension and retraction of the same muscles. The intellect slumbers, in supine inertness; but the grosser parts of our nature attain a rank development. To condemn man to such severity of toil is, in some measure, to cultivate in him the habits of an animal. He becomes reckless. He disregards the distinguishing appetites and habits of his species. He neglects the comforts and delicacies of life. He lives in squalid wretchedness, on meagre food, and expends his superfluous gains in debauchery. . . .

[T]he population . . . is crowded into one dense mass, in cottages separated by narrow, unpaved, and almost pestilential streets; in an atmosphere loaded with the smoke and exhalations of a large manufacturing city. The operatives are congregated in rooms and workshops during twelve hours in the day, in an enervating, heated atmosphere, which is frequently loaded with dust or filaments of cotton, or impure from constant respiration, or from other causes. They are engaged in an employment which absorbs their attention, and unremittingly employs their physical energies. They are drudges who watch the movements, and assist the operations, of a mighty material force, which toils with an energy ever unconscious of fatigue. The persevering labour of the operative must rival the mathematical precision, the incessant motion, and the exhaustless power of the machine.

Hence, besides the negative results—the total abstraction of every moral and intellectual stimulus—the absence of variety—banishment from the grateful air and the cheering influences of light, the physical energies are exhausted by incessant toil, and imperfect nutrition. Having been subjected to the prolonged labour of an animal—his physical energy wasted—his mind in supine inaction—the artisan has neither moral dignity nor intellectual nor organic strength to resist the seductions of appetite. His wife and children, too frequently subjected to the same process, are unable to cheer his remaining moments of leisure. Domestic economy is neglected, domestic comforts are unknown. A meal of the coarsest food is prepared with heedless haste, and devoured with equal precipitation. Home has no other relation to him than that of shelter—few pleasures are there—it chiefly presents to him a scene of physical exhaustion, from which he is glad to escape. Himself impotent of all the distinguishing aims of his species, he sinks into sensual sloth, or revels in more degrading licentiousness. His house is ill furnished, uncleanly, often ill ventilated, perhaps damp; his food, from want of forethought and domestic economy, is meagre and innutritious; he is debilitated and hypochondriacal, and falls the victim of dissipation. . . .

The absence of religious feeling, the neglect of all religious ordinances, we conceive to afford substantive evidence of so great a moral degradation of the community, as generally to ensure a concomitant civic debasement. . . .

Questions for Analysis

1. What is Doctor Kay's description of the mental and physical health of a worker in a Manchester cotton mill?
2. Kay does not seem to think the employer, the machines, or the society are responsible for the workers' misery. What do you think?

---

[1] This refers to the myth of Sisyphus, a cruel king of Corinth, who was condemned in Hades to push a big rock up to the top of a hill, only to have it roll back down again.

James Phillips Kay, M.D., *Moral and Physical Condition of the Working Classes Employed in the Cotton Manufacture in Manchester* (London: James Ridgway, 1832), pp. 6–8, 10–11, 39.

economic layers, the wealthiest bourgeois were bankers, factory and mine owners, and merchants, but shopkeepers, managers, lawyers, and doctors were also included. The middle classes stressed the virtues of work, thrift, ambition, and caution. Their critics believed they perverted these virtues into materialism, selfishness, and callousness.

The Industrial Revolution began in an agrarian society dominated by landowning and labor-controlling aristocracy. From the eighteenth century on, as industry and commerce developed, the middle class grew in size, first in England and then throughout Western Europe. Its larger size did not automatically bring greater power. The middle class struggled to end the political, economic, and social discrimination against it. Wherever industrial wealth became more important, the middle class gained political power and social respectability. The bourgeoisie was indeed able to force important changes, but its members still functioned in a political and social world that had existed long before they gained power and influence.

By the end of the century, bourgeois politicians held the highest offices in much of Western Europe, sharing power with aristocrats, but in Central and Eastern Europe, aristocrats remained dominant into the twentieth century. Wealthy bourgeois emulated the aristocracy—buying great estates, marrying their daughters to sons of aristocrats—but they were the elite of the new industrial age, not of the Old Regime.

Although some barriers may have diminished between the landed elites and the middle class, industrialization sharpened distinctions between the middle and laboring classes. Equally as diverse as the middle class, laborers encompassed different economic levels—rural laborers, miners, and city workers. Rural laborers included farmers and cottage workers and those who were both. In the 1700s and 1800s, much production took place in the villages, usually in the home, hence the term *domestic system*. A middleman supplied materials to a farming family, who wove or spun them at piecework rates. This system, which preceded factory production, undercut workers' livelihoods and ultimately forced their children or grandchildren into urban labor.

In the first years of the Industrial Revolution, rural workers responded to the harsh conditions and low wages by destroying machinery and engaging in other acts of violence. In England, they were called Luddites (*Ludd* was the name they gave to their Robin Hood, who probably did not exist). They raided farms in the night, breaking the machines or burning effigies of the farmers who they thought caused their misery. In all of Europe, peasants and artisans responded in that way to the introduction of machinery. In France, angry workers dropped wooden shoes (*sabots*) into the works to slow the machinery, giving us the word *sabotage*.

Three broad distinctions existed among city workers; there were artisans, factory workers, and servants. Factory workers were the newest and most rapidly growing social group. At midcentury, however, they did not constitute a majority of laboring people in any large city. For example, as late as 1890, they made up only one-sixth of London's population.

The artisans were the largest group of city workers until the 1850s, and in some places for much longer. Some of them worked in construction, printing, small tailoring or dressmaking establishments, food preparation, and food processing. Others were craftspeople who produced such luxury items as furniture, jewelry, lace, and velvet. As a group, artisans were distinct from factory workers; their technical skills were difficult to learn, and traditionally their crafts were regulated by guilds, which still served both social and economic functions. Artisans were usually educated; they could read and write and generally shared technical knowledge and political discussion. They lived in a city or village for generations and maintained stable families, often securing places for their children in their crafts.

As the Industrial Revolution progressed, artisans faced competition from cheap, factory-produced goods. They began to downgrade their skills by dropping apprenticeship training, forcing journeymen to work longer hours with shoddy materials, and loosening the rules of the guilds. They were the supports of the Chartists in England. In 1848, artisans, rather than factory workers, were at the forefront of the revolutionary movement (see Chapter 22) as they tried to save themselves from the effects of the Industrial Revolution.

Servants, the third group of urban workers, were especially numerous in the capitals. During the first half of the nineteenth century, in cities such as Paris and London, servants outnumbered factory workers. The great increase in domestic labor—a middle-class family employed at least one servant—changed the daily life of middle-class women, who supervised the household or, if truly prosperous, educated the smallest children.

Working in a middle- or upper-class household, urban servants lived in a world apart from factory workers and artisans. Sometimes a husband and wife were "in service," but generally servants were young women. They were completely at the mercy of their employers. They might be treated decently or exploited, but they had little recourse when they were abused. Some worked their entire lives as servants; some women left service to marry working-class men. (Domestic help could not keep their jobs when they married.) Servants usually had some education. If they married and had a family, they taught their children to read and write and sometimes the manners and values of the household in which they had worked. Sometimes these servants taught their children their own deference to authority and their aspirations to bourgeois status.

Working-Class Life

Life was difficult for the early factory workers, who were recent arrivals from the country. They had no special skills or traditions of working with others in a craft. Frequently, male factory workers moved to the city without their families, leaving wives and children behind until they could support them. Other workers were single men or women who could find no jobs as servants or farm laborers in their villages. These people entered rapidly growing industries, where long hours—sometimes fifteen a day—were common. Farming had meant long hours, too, as had the various forms of home-based labor for piecework rates, but the pace and routine of the machine made factory work oppressive. Machines required highly regulated, repetitive human labor, generally menial and often dangerous.

In the mines, men, women, and small children hacked out the coal and sorted it, while horses and mules—and sometimes humans—pulled coal wagons on rails to the main shaft, where steam-powered engines lifted the coal to the surface.

The miners labored to keep pace with the machines. They faced cave-ins, explosions, and deadly fumes. Deep under the earth's surface, life was dark, cold, wet, and uncertain. Their bodies stunted and twisted, their lungs wrecked, miners labored their lives away in "the pits." Technological advances, such as special lamps that would not ignite underground gases, saved their lives, but almost a century passed before working conditions improved, sometimes as a result of unions or government regulation and sometimes because laborsaving machinery became affordable.

Factory workers fared a little better than miners. Sometimes workers' standards of living rose when they moved from farms to cities, particularly if all family members found work together. The pay earned by a family might exceed what they could have earned for farm labor, but working and living conditions were terrible. Factories were dirty, hot, unventilated, and frequently dangerous. Housing was overcrowded, dirty, and badly built. Workers who were unmarried or had left their families in the country often lived in barracks. If they lost their jobs, they lost their shelter.

Factory workers had few links to their surroundings. Like immigrants to a new country, they lived with hardship and deprivation. In their villages, they had been poor but socially connected to family, to church, and even to local landlords. In the cities, they worked with twenty to a hundred others and had little contact with their employers; instead, foremen pushed them to work hard for long hours to keep up with the machines. They had little time to socialize; they were fined for talking to one another, as well as for lateness and petty infringements. To keep their jobs, they had to compete with each other. Lacking organization, comradeship, education, and experience of city life, they found little comfort when times were bad.

Yet factory workers did make lives for themselves. They married or entered into some relationship at a younger age than artisans and, on average, had more children than other classes. A wife and children were an economic asset because they worked. When workers grew old or were disabled, their children were their only "pension." As the introduction of machinery increased, women and children were generally driven out of the factory labor force, but in the early years they were the mainstay.

Many workers developed a life around the pub, the café, or some similar gathering place, where there were drinks and games and the gossip and news of the day. On Sundays, their one day off, workers drank and danced; absenteeism was so great on Monday that the day was called "holy Monday." Gin drinking was denounced on all sides; workers, their wives, and reformers alike urged temperance. Most workers did not attend church, but when they did, they frequented those churches that tried to reach them—usually not the established churches. In England, workers attended revivals; Methodists and others outside the established Church of England (Dissenters) welcomed them. The Catholic Church was particularly strong among Irish workers. Many workers played sports, and some social organizations grew up around their sporting games. In these and other ways, workers developed a culture of their own—a culture misunderstood and often deplored by middle-class reformers.

Industrial workers lacked political and economic rights, but they rarely protested their conditions with violence. They rarely broke machines—unlike country laborers. Unlike craftsmen, factory workers had few organizations. They did join artisans for political rights—the Chartists in England and the republicans in France. When workers protested, they were repressed. They lost their jobs and were "blacklisted" (employers circulated their names so that other employers would not hire them). Even a peaceful demonstration, during which they sang hymns and prayed, might be disrupted by soldiers and gunfire. The law might say that they were equal, but workers were neither wealthy enough nor sufficiently organized to take their mistreatment to court. Workers' political agitation did not achieve much in the first half of the nineteenth century, but they made some progress toward a minimum of economic security. They formed "friendly" or "mutual aid" societies and cooperatives to help themselves when they were out of work or sick. They paid some dues or took up special collections when one of their members died or was killed on the job. They also created clubs, where they could learn to read and write or someone could read to them or write a letter for them. Self-help organizations often developed into unions; sometimes they were unions in disguise to circumvent the law.

Many workers and radicals believed that the only hope for their class lay in unified action through trade unions, mutual aid societies, cooperatives, or political organizations. Workers developed a culture of solidarity, a sense of what was fair and unfair in relations with one another and with employers. In England and Western Europe, trade unions grew, even when they were illegal. Unions made some headway in protecting their members from unemployment and dangerous working conditions, but strikes were rarely successful. The general public, which was imbued with individualist and laissez-faire principles, saw strikes as an attack on the businessman's right to carry on trade. Not until the 1870s and 1880s was widespread discontent expressed by militant trade unions.

In England, unions were legalized in 1825 but were forbidden to strike. There were special protections for corporations but not for unions. If a union's officer ran away with its treasury, English law did not protect the workers' dues. Small unions were powerless. In 1834, there was an attempt to join all unions together in a Grand National Consolidated Trades Union. It failed. Measures that would help one trade would not necessarily help another. In the 1850s, highly skilled workers joined together in a single craft union, which was more successful because employers found it difficult to replace a skilled worker. Still, during much of the nineteenth century, the vast majority of workers were not organized.

RELIEF AND REFORM

If machines could produce so much wealth and so many products, why were there so many poor people in such misery? Why was the gap between the rich and poor so great, and what had happened to the bond between "master and man"?

Britain was the first nation to face the worsening condition of the poor. In the eighteenth century, English agricultural laborers had a higher standard of living than their counterparts in the rest of Europe. As Britain rapidly industrialized, the changing conditions convinced observers that all workers' lives had worsened. Parliamentary investigations by civic-minded citizens documented

ENGRAVING FROM THE ILLUSTRATED TIMES, 1859. As unemployed workers flooded into the great cities of Europe, homelessness became a pressing social problem. To keep dry and warm, homeless men sometimes slept in coffins made for the living and lined up in a factory or prisonlike building. These facilities were charitable institutions—not the poor-law workhouses—but they too reflected the common belief of the day that poverty was the fault of the poor, who should learn to help themselves. (Mansell/Time & Life Pictures/Getty Images.)

the suffering for all to read. Many leaders believed that only increasing economic capacity would end distress. But would the economy expand fast enough to benefit the lowliest workers through laissez faire, or did it need direction from the state? Socialists, utilitarians, and practical reformers urged better organization of industry and government.

The English Factory Acts were a series of measures, beginning in 1802, that limited the hours of women and children who labored in mines and factories. By 1833, children under thirteen could work no more than nine hours a day, and no one aged thirteen to eighteen could work more than twelve hours or at night.

The acts also required children to go to school for two hours a day. They did not create the schools. England was much slower than France or Germany to provide state schools; any education

initiative was taken by private enterprise and charities, not government. Controversy erupted among the religious sects about which of them should educate the children, who remained uneducated or self-educated amid the conflict. Sometimes there were schools for boys but not for girls. It was argued that for moral reasons the sexes should not mix in the classroom, even though they worked side by side in the factories and mines.

In 1847, English women and children were no longer permitted to work more than ten hours a day. A loophole in the Ten Hours Act allowed some employers to develop a "relay system," in which children worked intermittently during the day for a total of ten hours. Men still could work as much as sixteen hours but actually did not because it was difficult to organize many different shifts in a large factory. At first, workers resented the regulations because family income declined if children could not work. Gradually, they realized that the humanitarian protection of women and children might make their own lives easier and safer and their wages higher. A ten-hour day for adult male workers was not enacted until 1874, despite two generations of agitation.

In 1834, a reform of the Poor Law (which dated from the reign of Queen Elizabeth I) tried to differentiate between the "deserving" poor and the "undeserving" poor. The New Poor Law required anyone receiving assistance to live in a prisonlike workhouse. Legislators thought only those who were truly needy would submit to such conditions just to receive a meal and shelter. They were right. The poor and the unemployed working class hated the workhouse, where families were separated by age and sex, miserably fed, and hired out to manufacturers and farmers for less than the going wage. Nonetheless, in the "hungry forties," poverty was so widespread that there were not enough workhouses for the homeless and the jobless.

In contrast to Britain, people on the Continent more readily accepted the idea that the state could interfere with the market to protect labor. Most states in Europe had large bureaucracies to enforce regulations and to carry out relief measures. There was some concern that too much regulation of employers would handicap businesses competing with the English. Governments in Germany, France, and Belgium did not usually follow a laissez-faire policy, but sometimes they did, and when they did such policies deepened class bitterness and disaffection.

Historians still debate how bad workers' conditions were in the early stages of industrialization. Workers' testimony of acute distress, particularly from 1780 to 1830 and again in the 1840s, has left a powerful impression of their misery. Their champions—humanitarians, novelists, radicals, and socialists—protested their dreadful lives. However, from the limited statistics that are available and governmental and humanitarian reports, historians generally conclude that standards of living may actually have improved during the eighteenth and early nineteenth centuries. They stress the higher wages, greater opportunities, and more choices for men and women. The same argument exists with regard to developing countries today as they industrialize. Still, few would deny that the rapidity of change caused great hardship for the workers of all countries, who endured cruel conditions in factories and slums. Machines destroyed crafts and displaced the craftsmen. A million Irish farm laborers starved during the great famine of the 1840s. Those who emigrated to England, British colonies, or the United States may have escaped starvation but still lived desperately hard lives. As for the workers who did not emigrate, statistical evidence showing an increase in their living standard does not reveal much about the radically reduced quality of life that men, women, and children experienced as they moved from rural communities to urban factories and slums—and to daily insecurity. Their grim experiences were relived by workers in the rest of Europe and the United States later in the century and in much of the world in the twentieth and twenty-first centuries.

INDUSTRIALISM IN PERSPECTIVE

Like the French Revolution, the Industrial Revolution modernized Europe. Eventually, it transformed every facet of society and even the natural world. In preindustrial society—Europe in the mid-eighteenth century—agriculture was the dominant economic activity, and peasants were the most numerous class. Peasant life centered on the family and the village, which country folk rarely left. The new rational and critical spirit associated with the Enlightenment hardly penetrated rural Europe; there, religious faith, clerical authority, and ancient superstition remained firmly entrenched. The richest and most powerful class was the aristocracy, whose wealth stemmed from land and whose privileges were protected by custom and law. The French Revolution had undermined the traditional power structure of king, aristocracy, and clergy. The Industrial Revolution brought new groups to power, influence, and citizenship.

In time, cities and factories eclipsed agricultural villages and handicraft manufacturing. The very geography of the world changed with the construction of dams, canals, roads, railroads, cities, and factories. In the society fashioned by industrialization and urbanization, aristocratic political and social power and values declined. At the same time, the bourgeoisie increased in number, wealth, importance, and power. More and more, a person was judged by talent or income rather than by birth—although sometimes birth, talent, education, and income remained in the hands of the privileged—and opportunities for upward social mobility expanded.

In time and only in some places, the Industrial Revolution became a great force for democracy. During the nineteenth century, first the middle class and then the working class gained the vote, and with that privilege brought about legislation and policies which alleviated the misery of the early stages of industrialization. The Industrial Revolution also hastened the secularization of European life. In the cities, former villagers, separated from traditional communal ties, drifted away from their ancestral religion. Governments' power over individuals through public education and required military service contributed greatly to a secular, nationalistic society. Modernization did not proceed everywhere at the same pace or with the same thoroughness. Generally, in Eastern and Southern Europe and much of the rest of the world, traditional social and institutional forms remained deeply entrenched and persisted well into the twentieth century.

NOTE

1. Charles Dickens, *Bleak House* (Harmondsworth, England: Penguin, 1971), 683.

Chapter 21

Thought and Culture in the Early Nineteenth Century

Traveler Looking Over a Sea of Fog, *by Caspar David Friedrich.* (Bildarchiv Preussischer Kulturbesitz/Art Resource, N.Y.)

Focus Questions

1. How was the Romantic movement a reaction against the dominant ideas of the Enlightenment?

2. What was the impact of Romanticism on European life?

3. What was the attitude of conservatives and liberals toward the Enlightenment and the French Revolution?

4. How did early-nineteenth-century radicalism constitute an expansion of liberalism?

5. What did early socialists and liberals have in common? How did they differ?

6. What is the relationship between nationalism and liberalism? How do you explain nationalism's great appeal?

*I*n 1815, the armies of France no longer marched across Europe, and Napoleon was imprisoned on an island a thousand miles off the coast of Africa. The traditional rulers of the Continent, some of them recently restored to power, were determined to protect themselves and society from future Robespierres who organized reigns of terror and Napoleons who obliterated traditional states. As defenders of the status quo, they attacked the reformist spirit of the philosophes, which had produced the French Revolution. In *conservatism*, which championed tradition over reason, hierarchy over equality, and the community over the individual, they found a philosophy to justify their assault on the Enlightenment and the Revolution.

But the forces unleashed by the French Revolution had penetrated European consciousness too deeply to be eradicated. One of them was *liberalism*, which aimed to secure the liberty and equality proclaimed by the Revolution. Another was *nationalism*, which sought to liberate subject peoples and unify broken nations. Captivated by the dream to redeem humanity, idealistic youth and intellectuals joined in the revolutionary struggle for liberty and nationhood.

The early 1800s also saw the flowering of a new cultural orientation. **Romanticism**, with its plea for the liberation of human emotions and the free expression of personality, challenged the Enlightenment stress on rationalism. Though primarily a literary and artistic movement, romanticism also permeated philosophy and political thought, particularly conservatism and nationalism.

Still another force emerging in the post-Napoleonic period was *socialism*. Reacting to the problems spawned by the Industrial Revolution, socialists called for creating a new society based on cooperation rather than on capitalist competition. A minor movement in the era from 1815 to 1848, socialism in its Marxist version became a major intellectual and social force in the last part of the century.

ROMANTICISM: A NEW CULTURAL ORIENTATION

The Romantic Movement, which began in the closing decades of the eighteenth century, dominated European cultural life in the first half of the

505

nineteenth. Historians recognize the prominence of romanticism in nineteenth-century cultural life, but the movement was so complex and the differences among the various romantic writers, artists, and musicians so numerous that historians cannot agree on a comprehensive definition of romanticism. Romantics were both liberals and conservatives, revolutionaries and reactionaries; some were preoccupied with religion and God, while others paid little attention to faith.

Most of Europe's leading cultural figures came under the influence of the Romantic Movement. Among the exponents of romanticism were the poets Shelley, Wordsworth, Keats, and Byron in England; the novelist Victor Hugo and the Catholic novelist and essayist Chateaubriand in France; and the writers A. W. and Friedrich Schlegel, the dramatist and poet Schiller, and the philosopher Schelling in Germany. Caspar David Friedrich in Germany and John Constable in England expressed the romantic mood in art, and Beethoven, Schubert, Chopin, and Wagner expressed it in music.

Exalting Imagination, Intuition, and Feelings

Perhaps the central message of the romantics was that the imagination and emotions of the individual should determine the form and content of an artistic creation. This outlook ran counter to the rationalism of the Enlightenment, which itself had been a reaction against the otherworldly Christian orientation of the Middle Ages. The philosophes had attacked faith because it thwarted and distorted reason; romantic poets, philosophers, and artists now denounced the scientific rationalism of the philosophes because it crushed the emotions and impeded creativity.

According to the romantics, the philosophes had turned flesh-and-blood human beings into soulless thinking machines. The philosophes' geometric spirit, **mechanism**, which sought to fit all life into a mechanical framework, had diminished and demeaned the individual. Such shallow thinking had stifled imagination and spontaneity, preventing people from realizing their human potential. To be restored to their true nature and made whole again, human beings must be emancipated from the tyranny of excessive intellectualizing; their feelings must be nourished and expressed. Taking up one of Rousseau's ideas, romantics yearned to rediscover in the human soul the pristine freedom and creativity that had been squashed by habits, values, rules, and standards imposed by civilization.

Abstract reason and scientific knowledge, said the romantics, are insufficient guides to knowledge. They provide only general principles about nature and people; they cannot penetrate to what really matters—the uniqueness of each person, of each robin, of each tree, cloud, and lake. The philosophes had concentrated on people in general, focusing on the elements of human nature shared by all people. The romantics, in contrast, emphasized human uniqueness and diversity: the traits that set one person apart from others. Discover and express your true self, romantics commanded: cultivate your own imagination; play your own music; write your own poetry; paint your own personal vision of nature; live, love, and suffer in your own way. The philosophes had asserted the mind's autonomy—its capacity to think for itself and not depend on authority. Romantics gave primary importance to the autonomy of the personality—the individual's need and right to find and fulfill an inner self. This intense introspection, the individual's preoccupation with human feelings, is the distinguishing feature of romanticism. In the opening lines of his autobiography, *The Confessions,* Jean Jacques Rousseau, a romantic in an age of reason, expressed the passionate subjectivism that was to characterize the Romantic Movement.

> *I am commencing an undertaking, hitherto without precedent and which will never find an imitator. I desire to set before my fellows the likeness of a man in all the truth of nature, and that man myself. Myself alone! I know the feelings of my heart, and I know men. I am not made like any of those I have seen. I venture to believe that I am not made like any of those who are in existence. If I am not better, at least I am different.*[1]

Whereas the philosophes had regarded feelings as an obstacle to clear thinking, to the romantics they were the human essence. People could not live by reason alone, said the romantics. They

DANTE'S *INFERNO*: *THE WHIRLWIND OF LOVERS*, BY WILLIAM BLAKE (1757–1827). A radical romantic painter and poet, Blake totally rejected the artistic conventions of the past. His religious and political beliefs were as unique as his art; he spent his life trying to convey tormented inward visions. A prolific illustrator, his imaginative genius was stimulated by great literature such as Dante's *Divine Comedy*. (The Circle of the Lustful: Paolo and Francesca, Gift of W.G. Russell Allen. Image © 2011 Board of Trustees, National Gallery of Art, Washington D.C. Image courtesy Board of Trustees.)

agreed with Rousseau's words: "For us, to exist is to feel and our sensibility is incontestably prior to our reason."[2] For the romantics, reason was cold and dreary, its understanding of people and life meager and inadequate. Reason could not comprehend or express the complexities of human nature or the richness of human experience. By always dissecting and analyzing, by imposing deadening structure and form, and by demanding adherence to strict rules, reason crushed inspiration and creativity and barred true understanding. "The Reasoning Power in Man," wrote William

Blake, the British poet, artist, and mystic, is "an Incrustation [scab] over my Immortal Spirit."[3]

The avenue to truth for the romantics was spontaneous human emotion rather than the intellect. By cultivating emotions, intuition, and the imagination, individuals could experience reality and discover their authentic selves. The romantics wanted people to feel and to experience—"To bathe in the Waters of Life," said Blake.[4] Or as Johann Goethe, Germany's great poet, wrote in *Faust*, "My worthy friend, gray are all theories, And green alone Life's golden tree."[5]

Consequently, the romantics insisted that imaginative poets had a deeper insight into life than analytical philosophers. Poetry is a true philosophy, the romantics said; it can do what rational analysis and geometric calculations cannot do—speak directly to the heart, clarify life's deepest mysteries, participate in the eternal, and penetrate to the depths of human nature. To think profoundly, one has to feel deeply, said the romantics. For reason to function best, it must be nourished by the poetic imagination; that alone extricates and ennobles feelings hidden in the soul. "I am certain of nothing but of the holiness of the Heart's affections and the truth of Imagination," wrote John Keats. "O for a Life of Sensations rather than of Thoughts."[6] In his preface to *The Lyrical Ballads* (1798), often called the manifesto of romanticism, William Wordsworth (1770–1850) held that poetry—that is, imagination and feeling—not mathematics and logic, yielded the highest truth.

The Enlightenment mind had been clear, critical, and controlled. It had adhered to standards of esthetics, thought to be universal, that had dominated European cultural life since the Renaissance. It stressed technique, form, and changeless patterns and tended to reduce the imagination to mechanical relationships. "Analysis and calculation make the poet, as they make the mathematician," wrote Étienne Condillac, a prominent French philosophe. "Once the material of a play is given, the invention of the plot, the characters, the verse, is only a series of algebraic problems to be worked out."[7] Following in this tradition, Népomucène Lemercier determined that there were twenty-six rules for tragedy, twenty-three for comedy, and twenty-four for the epic; he proceeded to manufacture plays and epics according to this formula.

Romantic poets, artists, and musicians broke with the traditional styles and uniform standards, essentially those inherited from the classical tradition, and created new cultural forms and techniques. "We do not want either Greek or Roman Models," Blake declared, "but [should be] just & true to our own Imaginations."[8] Victor Hugo (1802–1885), the dominant figure among French romantics, urged: "Freedom in art! . . . Let us take the hammer to the theories, the poetics [the analysis of poetry] and the systems."[9] Yearning for unhindered self-expression and artistic subjectivity,

the romantics believed that one did not learn how to write poetry or paint pictures by following textbook rules, nor could one grasp the poet's or artist's intent by judging works according to fixed standards. Only by trusting their own feelings and intuition could individuals attain their creative potential and achieve self-realization. Hence, the most beautiful works of art were not photographic imitations of nature but authentic and spontaneous expressions of the artist's feelings, fantasies, intuitions, and dreams. It was the artist's inner voice that gave a work of art its supreme value. Caspar David Friedrich declared: "The artist should not only paint what he sees in front of him, but also what he sees inside himself."[10] Artists also sought to arouse the viewer's emotions by depicting nature in all its awesome glory and fury—majestic mountain peaks, raging storms and seas, thick woods, pounding waterfalls, and precipitous cliffs. Similarly, the romantics were less impressed by Beethoven's structure than by the intensity, power, and passion of his music, which expressed and touched every emotion. Thus, a contemporary of Beethoven's said that his "music moves the levers that open the floodgates of fear, terror, of horror, of pain and arouses the longing for the eternal which is the essence of Romanticism."[11]

The romantics explored the inner life of the mind, which Freud would later call **the unconscious**. "It is the beginning of poetry," wrote Friedrich Schlegel, "to abolish the law and the method of the rationally proceeding reason and to plunge us once more into the ravishing confusion of fantasy, the original chaos of human nature."[12] It was this dimension of the mind—mysterious, primitive, more elemental and more powerful than reason, the wellspring of creativity—that the romantics longed to revitalize and release. Some romantics had an intuitive awareness of the dark side of the unconscious. Buried there, they sensed, were our worst fears and most hideous desires. When we dig deeply into our "most cherished reveries," Hugo warned, we discover a spiral that

is deep, and when one descends into it
It continues ceaselessly and broadens out,
And because one has touched some fatal enigma,
One often returns pale from this dark journey.[13]

Nature, God, History

The philosophes had viewed nature as a lifeless machine, a giant clock, all of whose parts worked together in perfect precision and harmony. Nature's laws, operating with mathematical certainty, were uncovered by the methodology of science. The romantics rejected this impersonal, mechanical model. Inspired and awed by nature's beauty and majesty, they responded emotionally to nature and sought a mystical union with it. To the romantics, nature was alive and suffused with God's presence. Nature stimulated the creative energies of the imagination; it taught human beings a higher form of knowledge. As William Wordsworth wrote,

> One impulse from a vernal [springtime] wood
> May teach you more of man,
> Of moral evil and of good,
> Than all the sages can.[14]

Wordsworth felt that the poet had a unique capacity to know nature. Interaction with nature fostered self-discovery. Thus, Wordsworth saw in nature

> The anchor of my purest thoughts, the nurse,
> The guide, the guardian of my heart, and soul
> Of all my moral being.[15]

For the romantics, the poet's imagination unlocked nature's most important secrets. In perhaps the most impassioned application of this principle, English romantics decried their country's drab factories—the "dark satanic mills," which deprived life of its joy and separated people from nature.

Regarding God as a great watchmaker—a detached observer of a self-operating mechanical universe—the philosophes tried to reduce religion to a series of scientific propositions. Many romantics, on the contrary, viewed God as a spiritual force that inspired people and enriched life, and they deplored the decline of Christianity. The cathedrals and ceremonies, poetic and mysterious, satisfied the esthetic impulse; Christian moral commands, compassionate and just, elevated human behavior to a higher level. Consequently, the romantics condemned the philosophes for

weakening Christianity by submitting its dogmas to the test of reason, and they recoiled with anger at the philosophes' relegation of God to the status of a watchmaker. As Samuel Taylor Coleridge (1772–1834), poet and conservative political thinker, wrote, "What indeed but the wages of death can be expected from a doctrine which degrades the Deity into a bland hypothesis, and that the hypothesis of a clockwork-maker . . . a godless nature, and a natureless, abstract God . . . the Sunday name of gravitation."[16] The romantics' call to acknowledge the individual as a spiritual being and to cultivate the religious side of human nature accorded with their aim of restoring the whole personality, which had been fragmented by the philosophes' excessive emphasis on the intellect.

The Middle Ages, too, appeared as a very different era to the philosophes and the romantics. To the former, that period was a time of darkness, when superstition and fanaticism reigned; surviving medieval institutions and traditions served only to bar progress. The romantics, in contrast, revered the Middle Ages. The wars of the French Revolution, Napoleon, and the breakdown of political equilibrium had produced a sense of foreboding about the future. Some sought spiritual security by looking back to the Middle Ages, when Europe was united by a single faith and the fabric of society seemed intact and strong. To the romantic imagination, the Middle Ages, steeped in religious faith and spiritual sensitivity, had nurtured social harmony and abounded with heroic and chivalrous deeds as well as colorful pageantry.

The romantics and the philosophes also diverged in their conception of history. For the philosophes, history served a didactic purpose by providing examples of human folly. Such knowledge helped people prepare for a better future, and for that reason alone history should be studied. To the romantics, a historical period, like an individual, was a unique entity with its own soul. They wanted the historian to portray and analyze the variety of nations, traditions, and institutions that constituted the historical experience, always recognizing what is particular and unique to a given time, place, and people. The romantics' feeling for the uniqueness of phenomena and their appreciation of cultural differences laid the foundation of modern historical scholarship, for

LORD BYRON (1788–1824). One of the leading romantic poets, Byron created the "Byronic hero," a lonely and mysterious figure. His own short life exalted the emotions and the senses. He went to Greece in 1824 to aid the revolutionaries and died there from poor health. (© Bettmann/CORBIS.)

they sought to study the specific details of history and culture and to comprehend them in their own terms within the context of their own times.

Searching for universal principles, the philosophes dismissed folk traditions as peasant superstitions and impediments to progress. Rebelling against the standardization of culture, the romantics saw native languages, songs, and legends as the unique creations of a people; they were the deepest expression of national feeling, the wellspring of poetry and art, and the spiritual source of that people's cultural vitality, creativity, and identity. Hence, they examined these earliest cultural expressions with awe and reverence. They discovered the nation's past for their kinsmen. In this way, romanticism helped shape modern nationalism.

The Impact of the Romantic Movement

The romantic revolt against the Enlightenment had an important and enduring impact on European history. By focusing on the creative capacities inherent in the emotions—intuition, spontaneity, instinct, passion, will, empathy—the romantics shed light on a side of human nature that the philosophes often overlooked or undervalued. By encouraging personal freedom and diversity in art, music, and literature, they greatly enriched European cultural life. Future artists, writers, and musicians would proceed along the path cleared by the romantics. Modern art, for example, owes much to the Romantic Movement's emphasis on the legitimacy of human feeling and to its exploration of the hidden world of dreams and fantasies. The romantic emphasis on feeling sometimes found expression in humanitarian movements that fought slavery, child labor, and poverty. Romantics were among the first to attack the emerging industrial capitalism for subordinating individuals to the requirements of the industrial process and treating them as mere things. By recognizing the distinctive qualities of historical periods, peoples, and cultures, the romantics helped create the modern historical outlook. By valuing a nation's past, romanticism contributed to modern nationalism and conservatism.

However, the Romantic Movement had a potentially dangerous side: it served as background to the extreme nationalism of the twentieth century. As Ernst Cassirer points out, the romantics "never meant to politicize but to 'poeticize' the world," and their deep respect for human individuality and national diversity was not compatible with Hitler's racial nationalism. Yet by waging their attack on reason with excessive zeal, the romantics undermined respect for the rational tradition of the Enlightenment and thus set up a precondition for the rise and triumph of Fascist movements. Although their intention was cultural and not political, by idealizing the past and glorifying ancient folkways, legends, native soil, and native language, the romantics introduced a highly charged nonrational component into political life. In later generations, romanticism, particularly in Germany, fused with political nationalism to produce "a general climate of inexact thinking, an intellectual . . . dream world and an emotional approach to problems of political action to which sober reasoning should have been applied."[17]

The philosophes would have regarded the romantics' veneration of a people's history and traditions as a barbarous regression to superstition and a triumph of myth over philosophy. Indeed, when transferred to the realm of politics, the romantics' idealization of the past and fascination with inherited national myths as the source of wisdom did reawaken a way of thinking about the world that rested more on unrestrained feelings than on reason. In the process, people became committed to nationalist and political ideas that were fraught with danger. The glorification of myth and the folk community constitutes a link, however unintended, between romanticism and extreme nationalism, which culminated in the world wars of the twentieth century.

GERMAN IDEALISM

The romantics' stress on the inner person also found expression in the school of German philosophy called **idealism**. Idealists did not see the world as something objective, that is, existing independently of individual consciousness. Rather, they held that human consciousness, the knowing subject, builds the world and determines its form. German idealism arose in part as a response to the challenge posed by David Hume, the Scottish empiricist and skeptic.

The Challenge Posed by Hume's Empiricism

Enlightenment thinkers believed that physics and astronomy, epitomized by Newton, provided the kind of certainty that other forms of inquiry, notably theology, could not. But in his *Treatise of Human Nature* (1739–1740) and *Enquiry Concerning Human Understanding* (1748), Hume cast doubt on the view that scientific certainty was possible. He demolished the religious argument for miracles and the deist argument for a Creator; he also called into question the very notion of scientific law.

Science rests on the conviction that regularities observed in the past and the present will be repeated in the future: that there does exist an objective reality that rational creatures can comprehend. Hume, however, argued that science cannot demonstrate a *necessary connection* between cause and effect. Because we repeatedly experience a burning sensation when our fingers have contact with a flame, we assume a cause-and-effect relationship. This assumption is unwarranted, says Hume. All we can acknowledge is that there is a constant conjunction between the flame and the burning sensation.

According to Hume, a thoroughgoing **empiricist**, sense perception is the only legitimate source of knowledge, and our sense experiences can never prove a necessary connection between what we customarily perceive as cause and effect. We can see things happening, but we cannot see why they happen. Experience tells us only what happens at a particular moment; it cannot tell us with certainty that the same combination of events will be repeated in the future. Based on past experience, the mind expects the flame to burn, but we cannot prove that there is a law at work in nature guaranteeing that a specific cause will produce a specific effect. What we mean by cause and effect is simply something that the mind, through habit, imposes on our sense perceptions. For practical purposes, we can say that two events are in association with each other, but we cannot conclude with certainty that the second was caused by the first—that natural law is operating within the physical universe. Such a radical empiricism undermines the very foundations of science, so revered by progressive thinkers.

Immanuel Kant

In the *Critique of Pure Reason* (1781), Immanuel Kant, the German philosopher and proponent of Newtonianism and the scientific method, undertook the challenge of rescuing reason and science from Hume's empiricism. Kant rejected Hume's (and Locke's) underlying premise that all knowledge derives from sense experience, which imprints impressions on the mind. The mind, said Kant, is not a *tabula rasa*, a blank slate, passively receiving sense impressions, but an active instrument that structures, organizes, and interprets the multiplicity of sensations coming to it. The mind can coordinate a chaotic stream of sensations because it contains its own inherent logic; it is equipped with several categories of understanding, including cause and effect. These categories are *a priori* and universal: that is, they are necessary constituents of all human minds and exist independently of and prior to experience.

For Kant, the category of cause and effect has an objective existence; it exists as an a priori component of human consciousness. Because of the way the human mind is constituted, we presuppose a relationship of cause and effect in all our experiences with the objects of this world. The mind does not treat the physical world in an arbitrary or random way; it imposes structure and order on our sense experience. Cause and effect, space and time, and other categories of the mind permit us to attribute certainty to scientific knowledge. The physical world must possess certain definite characteristics because these characteristics conform to the categories of the mind. The object, said Kant, must "accommodate itself to the subject."

Kant rescued science from Hume's assault: the laws of science are universally valid. But in the process, Kant made scientific law dependent on the mind and its a priori categories. We see nature in a certain way because of the mental apparatus that we bring to it. The mind does not derive the laws of nature from the physical world. Indeed, the reverse is true. The mind imposes its own laws on nature—on the raw impressions received by the senses—giving the physical world form, structure, and order. By holding that objects must conform to the rules of the human mind, that it is the knowing subject that creates order within nature, Kant gave primacy to the knower rather than to the objects of knowledge. He saw the mind as an active agent, not a passive receptacle for sensations. This "turn in philosophy," which Kant considered as revolutionary as the Copernican theory had been for astronomy, gave unprecedented importance to the individual mind and its inherent capacity for knowing.

It is a fundamental principle of Kant's thought that we cannot know ultimate reality. Our knowledge is limited to the **phenomenal world**, the realm of natural occurrences. We can know only the things that we experience, that is, things we grasp through the active intervention of the mind's categories. We can have no knowledge of a thing-in-itself, that is, of an object's ultimate or real nature—its nature as it is independently of the way we experience it, apart from the way our senses receive it. The human mind can acquire knowledge only of that part of reality revealed through sense experience. We can say nothing about the sun's true nature but only describe the way the sun appears to us, that is, our impression of the sun formed by the mind's ordering of our sense experiences of it. Thus, at the same time that Kant reaffirmed the validity of scientific law, he also limited the range of science and reason.

G. W. F. Hegel

Kant had insisted that knowledge of what lies beyond the phenomena—knowledge of ultimate or absolute reality itself—is forever denied us. Georg Wilhelm Friedrich Hegel (1770–1831), another German philosopher, could not accept this. He constructed an all-embracing metaphysical system that attempted to explain all reality and uncover the fundamental nature and meaning of the universe and human history—to grasp the wholeness of life. In the process, he synthesized the leading currents of thought of his day: the rationalism of the Enlightenment, romanticism, and Kantian philosophy.

Adopting Kant's notion that the mind imposes its categories on the world, Hegel emphasized the importance of the thinking subject in the quest for truth. However, Kant held that we can have knowledge only of how a thing appears to us, not of the thing-in-itself. Hegel, in contrast, maintained that ultimate reality, total truth, is knowable to the human mind: the mind can comprehend the principles underlying all existence and can grasp the essential meaning of human experience.

Kant had asserted the essential idealist position that it is the knowing subject that organizes our experiences of the phenomenal world. Hegel went a giant step beyond that by positing the existence of a universal Mind—Absolute Spirit—that differentiates itself into the minds of thinking individuals. He saw Mind, the thing-in-itself, as a universal agent, whose nature can be apprehended through thought.

Percy Bysshe Shelley

Percy Bysshe Shelley (1792–1822) received a traditional classical education and was destined to follow his father into a parliamentary career. Flamboyantly imaginative, he had little in common with his peers and was tormented and bullied at school. This treatment resulted in a lifelong hatred of authority, combined with recklessness, intellectual brilliance, great personal charm, and a vivid emotional temperament.

Expelled from Oxford for writing a pamphlet advocating atheism, Shelley eloped with a sixteen-year-old bride and began a life of exile, shifting from place to place in England and Europe with an ever-changing number of family members and friends. His brief, stormy life—the suicide of his first wife, his marriage to Mary Godwin (the daughter of Mary Wollstonecraft and the author of *Frankenstein*), personal misfortunes, passionate friendships, financial problems, and bouts of depression—culminated in death by drowning in Italy. Throughout it all, he poured out an incessant stream of poetry, prose, and translations from five languages. Like his contemporaries in the Romantic Movement, he responded emotionally to politics, the natural world, love, and poetry. "A poem," he wrote, "is the very image of life expressed in its eternal truth."

A radical in politics, Shelley was inspired by the ideals of the French Revolution, abhorred the oppressive conservatism of English politics, and was frustrated by his inability to influence events. His sonnet "England in 1819" described his disgust with a country ruled by "an old, mad, blind, despised and dying king." His lyrical poetry was composed in a spontaneous rush of feeling. He celebrated the natural world, from the majesty of crashing waves and mountains to quietly radiant landscapes, and he identified himself in relation to the natural world. In "Ode to the West Wind," he compared himself to the driving wind: "A heavy weight of hours has chained and bowed / One too like thee: tameless, and swift, and proud."

Shelley was notorious for his irregular lifestyle and had little literary success in his lifetime; his life contained more pain than pleasure. In "Adonais," which he wrote on the death of fellow poet John Keats, who died in 1821 at the age of twenty-six, Shelley seemed to be prefiguring his own early death.

He has outsoared the shadow of our night;
Envy and calumny and hate and pain,
And that unrest which men miscall delight,
Can touch him not and torture not again;
From the contagion of the world's slow stain
He is secure, and now can never mourn
A heart grown cold, a head grown gray in vain;
Nor, when the spirit's self has ceased to burn,
With sparkless ashes load an unlamented urn. *

---

*From "Adonais," in *The Complete Works of Percy Bysshe Shelley*, ed. T. Hutchinson (London: Oxford University Press, 1945), 440.

Because Hegel viewed Absolute Spirit not as fixed and static but as evolving and developing, history plays a central role in his philosophical system. History is the development of Spirit in time. In the arena of world history, truth unfolds and makes itself known to the human mind. Like the romantics, Hegel said that each historical period has a distinctive character that separates it from every preceding age and enables us to see it as an organic whole. The art, science, philosophy, religion, politics, and leading events are sufficiently interconnected that the period may be said to possess an organic unity, a historical coherence.

Does history contain an overarching meaning? Are past, present, and future linked together by something more profound, more unifying than random chance? Hegel believed that world history reveals a rational process progressing toward a final destination. An internal principle of order underlies historical change. History has a purpose and an end: the unfolding of Absolute Spirit. In the course of history, an immanent Spirit manifests itself; gradually, progressively, and nonrepetitively, it actualizes itself, becoming itself fully. Nations and exceptional human beings, "world-historical" individuals—Alexander the Great, Caesar, Napoleon—are the vehicles through which Spirit realizes its potentiality and achieves self-consciousness. Hegel's philosophy of history gives meaning, purpose, and direction to historical events. Where is history taking us? What is its ultimate meaning? For Hegel, history is humanity's progress from lesser to greater freedom: "The History of the World is none other than the progress of the consciousness of Freedom . . . [It is] the absolute goal of history."[18]

According to Hegel, Spirit manifests itself in history through a **dialectical conflict** between opposing forces; the struggle between one force (thesis) and its adversary (antithesis) is evident in all spheres of human activity. This clash of opposites gains in intensity, ending eventually in a resolution that unifies and surpasses both opposing forces. Thought and history then enter a new and higher stage, that of synthesis, which, by absorbing the truths within both the thesis and the antithesis, achieves a higher level of truth and a higher stage of history. Soon this synthesis itself becomes a thesis that enters into another conflict with another opposing force. This conflict too is resolved by a still higher synthesis. Thus, the dynamic struggle between thesis and antithesis—sometimes expressed in revolutions and war, and sometimes in art, religion, and philosophy—and its resolution into a synthesis accounts for movement in history. Or, in Hegelian language, Spirit is closer to realization: its rational structure is progressing from potentiality to actuality. The dialectic is the march of Spirit through human affairs. Historical change is often instituted by world-historical individuals who, unknown to themselves, are agents of Spirit in its march through history. Since Hegel held that freedom is the essence of Spirit, it is

HEGEL IN HIS STUDY. Georg Wilhelm Friedrich Hegel (1770–1831) constructed a comprehensive philosophical system that sought to explain all reality. His philosophy of history, particularly the theories of dialectical conflict and of progress toward an ultimate end, greatly influenced Karl Marx. (Bildarchiv Preussischer Kulturbesitz/Art Resource, N.Y.)

through history that human beings progress toward consciousness of their own freedom. They become self-consciously aware of their own self-determination—their ability to regulate their lives rationally according to their own consciousness. For Hegel, two developments stand out in the evolution of individual freedom: Socrates, who taught people to examine inherited values with a critical spirit, and the Protestant Reformation, which held that salvation is a matter of personal conscience.

But for individual freedom to be realized, said Hegel, social and political institutions must be rationally determined and organized; that is, the will of the individual must be harmonized with the needs of the community. For Hegel, freedom is not a matter of securing abstract natural rights for the individual, which was the goal of the French Revolution. Rather, true freedom is attained only within the social group. Thus, in Hegel's view, human beings discover their essential character—their moral and spiritual potential—only as citizens of a cohesive political community. This view goes back to the city-states of ancient Greece, which Hegel admired.

Like Rousseau, Hegel sought to bring the individual's free choice into harmony with the needs of society as a whole. Hegel linked freedom to obedience to the state's commands. In the state's laws and institutions, which are manifestations of reason, the objectivization of Spirit, individuals find a basis for rationally determining their own lives. In this way, the private interests of citizens become one with common interests of the community. For Hegel, Absolute Spirit, which is also Ultimate Reason, realizes itself in the state, the highest form of human association. The state joins fragmented individuals together into a community and substitutes a rule of justice for the rule of instincts. It permits individuals to live the ethical life and to develop their human potential. An individual cannot achieve these goals in isolation.

The rationally organized community favored by Hegel was a constitutional monarchy. Yet he also reached the perplexing conclusion that the pinnacle of the consciousness of freedom was to be found in the Germany of his day. Germans recognized the value of monarchical leadership, he said, but also assimilated the Christian principle of the individual's infinite worth.

In deeming the Prussian state, which had an autocratic king, no constitution, no popularly elected parliament, and government-imposed censorship, to be the pinnacle of freedom and the goal for which history had been striving, Hegel's thought reveals a powerful undercurrent of statism—that is, the exaltation of the state and the subordination of the individual to it. For Hegel, the national state was the embodiment of Universal Reason and the supreme achievement of Absolute Spirit.

> It must . . . be understood that all the worth which the human being possesses—all spiritual reality, he possesses only through the State. . . . Thus only is he fully conscious; thus only is he a partaker of morality—of a just and moral social and political life. For Truth is the unity of the universal . . . and the Universal is to be found in the State, in its laws, its universal and rational arrangements. The state is the Divine Idea as it exists on Earth.[19]

German conservatives used Hegel's idea that existing institutions have a rational legitimacy to support their opposition to rapid change. Existing reality, even if it appears cruel and hateful, is the actualization of Absolute Spirit. Therefore, it is inherently necessary and rational and should not be altered.

Some of Hegel's followers, known as Young Hegelians, interpreted Hegel in a radical sense. They rejected his view that the Prussian state, or any German state, was the goal of world history, the realization of freedom. The Germany of their day, held the Young Hegelians, had not attained a harmony between the individual and society: it was not rationally organized and did not foster freedom. These Young Hegelians saw Hegel's philosophy as a means for radically altering the world to make existing society truly rational. The most important of the radical Young Hegelians was Karl Marx. Marx retained Hegel's overarching principles that history contains an inner logic, that it is an intelligible process, and that a dialectical struggle propels history from a lower stage to a higher stage.

CONSERVATISM: THE VALUE OF TRADITION

To the traditional rulers of Europe—kings, aristocrats, and clergy—the French Revolution was a great evil that had inflicted a near-fatal wound on civilization. As far as they were concerned, the revolutionaries heralded chaos when they executed Louis XVI, confiscated the land of the church, destroyed the special privileges of the aristocracy, and instituted the Reign of Terror. Then the Revolution gave rise to Napoleon, who deposed kings, continued the assault on the traditional aristocracy, and sought to dominate Europe. Disgusted and frightened by the revolutionary violence, terror, and warfare, the traditional rulers sought to refute the philosophes' worldview, which had spawned the Revolution. To them, natural rights, equality, the goodness of man, and perpetual progress were perverse doctrines that had produced the Jacobin "assassins." In conservatism, they found a political philosophy to counter the Enlightenment ideology.

Edmund Burke's *Reflections on the Revolution in France* (1790) was instrumental in shaping conservative thought. Burke (1729–1797), an Anglo-Irish philosopher and statesman, wanted to warn his countrymen of the dangers inherent in the ideology of the revolutionaries. Written during the early and still moderate stage of the Revolution, Burke astutely predicted that it would end with the murder of the king and queen, civil war, terror, and the seizure of power by a military leader. In Burke's view, fanatics armed with abstract ideas divorced from historical experience had dragged France through the mire of revolution. Burke developed a coherent political philosophy, which served as a counterweight to the ideology of the Enlightenment and the Revolution.

The leading conservative theorists on the Continent—more aptly called *reactionaries*—were Joseph de Maistre (1753–1821) and Vicomte Louis de Bonald (1754–1840). De Maistre, who fled his native Piedmont (northern Italy) in 1792 and again in 1793 after the invasion by the armies of the new French republic, vociferously denounced the philosophes for undermining belief and authority. He called their activity an "insurrection against God." In *Reflections on the State of France* (1796) and other works, he attacked the philosophes and the French Revolution, which he blamed them for inciting. Committed to authority and order, de Maistre fought any kind of political or religious liberalism. To him, the Revolution was a satanic evil; all its pronouncements must be totally condemned and its roots expunged from the soil of Christian Europe.

Like de Maistre, de Bonald, a French émigré, detested the French Revolution, staunchly defended monarchy, and attacked the rational spirit of the Enlightenment as an enemy of faith. His Catholicism and monarchism are summarized in his famous remark: "When God wished to punish France, he took away the Bourbon from her governance."

Hostility to the French Revolution

Entranced by the great discoveries in science, the philosophes and French reformers had believed that the human mind could also transform social institutions and ancient traditions according to rational models. Progress through reason became their faith. Intent on creating a new future, the revolutionaries abruptly dispensed with old habits, traditional authority, and familiar ways of thought. For them, these traditional ways were a form of bondage that stifled progress.

To conservatives who, like the romantics, venerated the past, this was supreme arrogance and wickedness. They regarded the revolutionaries as presumptuous men who recklessly severed society's links with ancient institutions and traditions and condemned venerable religious and moral beliefs as ignorance. De Maistre called Voltaire the man "into whose hands hell has given all its power."[20] Moreover, the revolutionaries forgot—or never knew—that the traditions and institutions that they wanted to destroy did not belong solely to them. Past generations and, indeed, future generations had a claim on these creations of French genius. By attacking time-honored ways, the revolutionaries had deprived French society of moral leadership and opened the door to anarchy and terror. "You began ill," wrote Burke of the revolutionaries, "because you began by despising everything that belonged to you. . . . When ancient opinions and rules of life are taken away, the loss cannot possibly be estimated. From that moment we have no compass to govern us; nor can we know distinctly to what port we steer."[21]

The philosophes and French reformers had expressed unlimited confidence in the power of human reason to understand and to change society. Although conservatives also appreciated human rational capacities, they recognized the limitations of reason. "We are afraid to put men to live and trade each on his own private stock of reason," said Burke, "because we suspect that this stock in each man is small, and that the individuals would do better to avail themselves of the general bank and capital of nations and of ages."[22] Conservatives saw the Revolution as a natural outgrowth of an arrogant Enlightenment philosophy that overvalued reason and sought to reshape society in accordance with abstract principles. An overly

Benjamin Constant: On the Limits of Popular Sovereignty

Benjamin Constant (1767–1830), a leading French liberal theorist, feared the danger posed to liberty by democratic revolutionaries like Robespierre and his fellow Jacobins, who would exercise unlimited authority to establish liberty. Constant embraced the principle of popular sovereignty (that government derives its legitimacy and authority from the people), but warned against the danger of unlimited popular sovereignty. Neither the people as a whole nor their delegated representatives, said Constant, can possess total authority over the lives of individuals. The following passage is taken from his book On the Sovereignty of the People, *published in 1815.*

When you establish that the sovereignty of the people is unlimited, you create and toss at random into human society a degree of power which is too large in itself, and which is bound to constitute an evil, in whatever hands it is placed. Entrust it to one man, to several, to all, you will still find that it is equally an evil. . . .

In a society founded upon the sovereignty of the people, it is certain that no individual, no class, is entitled to subject the rest to their particular will. But it is not true that society as a whole has unlimited authority over its members. . . .

There is, on the contrary, a part of human existence that by necessity remains individual and independent, and which is, by right, outside any [governmental authority]. Sovereignty has only a limited and relative existence. At the point where independence and individual existence begin, the jurisdiction of sovereignty ends. If society oversteps this line, it is as guilty as the despot who has, as his only title, his exterminating sword. . . .

When sovereignty is unlimited, there is no means of sheltering individuals from governments. . . .

This is what we must declare; this is the important truth, the eternal principle which we must establish.

No authority upon earth is unlimited, neither that of the people, nor that of the men who declare themselves their representatives. . . .

The citizens possess individual rights independently of all social and political authority, and any authority that violates these rights becomes illegitimate. The rights of the citizens are individual freedom, religious freedom, freedom of opinion, which includes the freedom to express oneself openly, the enjoyment of property, a guarantee against all arbitrary power. No authority can call these rights into question without destroying its own credentials. . . .

Let us now sum up the consequences of our principles. The sovereignty of the people is not unlimited: it is, on the contrary, circumscribed within the limits traced by justice and by the rights of individuals.

Questions for Analysis

1. What did Benjamin Constant mean by unlimited sovereignty? Why did he fear it?
2. Provide examples in American history when people protested that the government was interfering with their liberties.

Benjamin Constant Political Writings, translated and edited by Biancamaria Fontana (Cambridge: Cambridge University Press, 1988), pp. 176–177, 179–180, 182.

critical spirit promotes discontent, fosters atheism, and undermines established authority.

Conservatives did not regard human beings as good by nature. Human wickedness was not due to a faulty environment, as the philosophes had proclaimed, but was at the core of human nature, as Christianity taught. Evil was held in check not by reason but by tried and tested institutions—monarchy, church, and aristocracy—traditions, and beliefs. Without these habits inherited from ancestors, said conservatives, the social order was threatened by sinful human nature.

Because monarchy, aristocracy, and the church had endured for centuries, argued the conservatives, they had worth. The clergy taught proper moral values; monarchs preserved order and property; aristocrats guarded against despotic kings and the tyranny of the common people. All protected and spread civilized ways. By despising and uprooting these ancient institutions, the revolutionaries had hardened the people's hearts, perverted their morals, and caused them to commit terrible outrages on one another and on society.

Conservatives detested attempts to transform society according to a theoretical model, to experiment with people as if they were laboratory animals. They considered human nature too intricate and social relations too complex for such social engineering. In the conservatives' view, the revolutionaries had reduced people and society to abstractions divorced from their historical settings. They were fanatics who had destroyed ancient patterns that seemed to conflict with their metaphysical theories. They had drawn up constitutions based on the unacceptable principle that government derives its power from the consent of the governed.

The art of politics, argued Burke, entails practical reason: pursuing limited and realizable goals for a particular community at a particular time. The wise statesman, said traditionalists, abhors abstract principles and spurns ideal models. Rather, he values the historical experiences of his nation and is concerned with real people in specific historical situations. He recognizes that institutions and beliefs do not require theoretical excellence; they do not have to meet the test of reason or of nature in order to benefit society. Statesmen who ignore these truisms and strive to reform a commonwealth according to a priori models— political formulas that do not fit the realities of history and the social order—plunge the nation into anarchy. To Burke, the revolutionaries were zealots who, like the religious radicals during the Reformation, resorted to force and terror in order to create a new man and a new society. In politics, experience is the best teacher and prudence the best method of procedure. Burke warned:

It is with infinite caution that any man ought to venture upon pulling down an edifice which has answered in any tolerable degree for ages the common purposes of society, or on building it up again, without having models and patterns of approved utility before his eyes.[23]

For conservatives, God and history were the only legitimate sources of political authority. States were not made; rather, they were an expression of the nation's moral, religious, and historical experience. No legitimate or sound constitution could be drawn up by a group assembled for that purpose. Scraps of paper with legal terminology and philosophic visions could not produce an effective government. Instead, a sound political system evolved gradually and inexplicably in response to circumstances. For this reason, conservatives admired the English constitution. It was not a product of abstract thought; no assembly had convened to fashion it. Because it was an unwritten arrangement that grew imperceptibly out of the historical experience and needs of the English people, it was durable and effective.

Conservatives viewed society not as a machine with replaceable parts but as a complex and delicate organism. Tamper with its vital organs, as the revolutionaries had done, and it would die.

The Quest for Social Stability

The liberal philosophy of the Enlightenment and the French Revolution started with the individual. The philosophes and the revolutionaries envisioned a society in which the individual was free and autonomous. Conservatives, in contrast, began with the community; they believed that the individual could function well only as part of a social group: family, church, or state. Alone, a person would be selfish, unreliable, and frail. Through membership in a social group, however, individuals learned cooperation and manners. From the conservative perspective, by exalting the individual, the revolutionaries had threatened to dissolve society into disconnected parts. Individualism would imperil social stability, destroy obedience to law, and fragment society into self-seeking, isolated atoms.

Holding that the community was more important than the individual, conservatives rejected the philosophy of natural rights. Rights were not abstractions that preceded an individual's entrance into society and pertained to all people everywhere. Rather, the state, always remembering the needs of the entire community and its links to past generations, determined what rights and privileges its citizens might have. There were no "rights of man," only rights of the French, the English, and so forth, as determined and allocated by the particular state.

Conservatives viewed equality as another pernicious abstraction that contradicted all historical experience. For conservatives, society was naturally hierarchical, and so they believed that some men, by virtue of their intelligence, education, wealth, and birth, were best qualified to rule and instruct the less able. They blamed the revolutionaries for uprooting a long-established and divinely ordained ruling elite, thereby depriving society of effective leaders, causing internal disorder, and paving the way for a military dictatorship.

Whereas the philosophes had attacked Christianity for promoting superstition and fanaticism, conservatives agreed with de Maistre that religion is the basis of civil society. Without Christianity, he said, people become brutalized, and civilization degenerates into anarchy. "Religion alone civilizes nations. . . . [E]very educational system which does not have religion as its basis will . . . diffuse only poisons throughout the State. . . . [I]f the guidance of education is not returned to the priests, and if science is not uniformly relegated to a subordinate rank, incalculable evils await us. We shall become brutalized by science, and that is the worst sort of brutality."[24]

Conservatives were convinced that excess liberty and the weakening of religion had brutalized people and shattered the foundations of society. Conservatives denounced the Enlightenment for unshackling dangerous instincts that religion had held in check. Catholic conservatives, in particular, held that God had constituted the church and monarchy to rein in sinful human nature. "Christian monarchs are the final creation of the development of political society and of religious society," said Louis de Bonald. "The proof of this lies in the fact that when monarchy and Christianity are both abolished society returns to savagery."[25]

Conservatism exposed a limitation of the Enlightenment by pointing out that human beings and social relationships are far more complex than the philosophes had imagined. People do not always accept the rigorous logic of the philosopher and are not eager to break with ancient ways, however illogical they appear to the intellect. They often find familiar customs and ancestral religions more satisfying guides to life than the blueprints of philosophers. The granite might of tradition remains an obstacle to the visions of reformers. Conservative theorists warned that revolutionary violence in the pursuit of **utopian** dreams transforms politics into an ideological crusade that ends in terror and despotism. These warnings bore bitter fruit in the twentieth century.

LIBERALISM: THE VALUE OF THE INDIVIDUAL

The decades after 1815 saw a spectacular rise of the bourgeoisie. Talented and ambitious bankers, merchants, manufacturers, professionals, and officeholders wanted to break the stranglehold of the landed nobility, the traditional elite, on political power and social prestige. They also wanted to eliminate restrictions on the free pursuit of profits.

The political philosophy of the bourgeoisie was most commonly liberalism. While conservatives sought to strengthen the foundations of traditional society, which had been severely shaken in the period of the French Revolution and Napoleon, liberals strove to alter the status quo. Believing in the goodness of human nature and the capacity of individuals to control their own lives, they hoped to realize the promise of the Enlightenment and the French Revolution.

The Sources of Liberalism

In the long view of Western civilization, liberalism is an extension and development of the democratic practices and rational outlook that originated in ancient Greece. Also flowing into the liberal tradition was the Judeo-Christian affirmation of the worth and dignity of the individual endowed by God with freedom to make moral choices. But the immediate historical roots of nineteenth-century liberalism extended back to seventeenth-century England. At that time, the struggle for religious toleration by English Protestant Dissenters advanced the principle of freedom of conscience, which is easily transferred into freedom of opinion and expression in all matters. The Glorious Revolution of 1688 set limits on the power of the English monarchy. In that same century, John Locke's natural-rights philosophy proclaimed that the individual was by nature entitled to freedom, and it justified revolutions against rulers who deprived citizens of their lives, liberty, or property. The expansion of a market economy, particularly in Britain, the American colonies, and Holland, showed the virtues of individual initiative and voluntary human actions, uncoerced by the authority of government.

The French philosophes also helped shape liberalism. From Montesquieu, liberals derived the theory of the separation of powers and of checks and balances—principles intended to guard against autocratic government. The philosophes had supported religious toleration and freedom of thought, expressed confidence in the capacity of the human mind to reform society, maintained that human beings are essentially good, and believed in the future progress of humanity—all fundamental tenets of liberalism.

The American and French revolutions were crucial phases in the history of liberalism. The Declaration of Independence gave expression to Locke's theory of natural rights, the Constitution of the United States incorporated Montesquieu's principles and demonstrated that people could create an effective government, and the Bill of Rights protected the person and rights of the individual. In destroying the special privileges of the aristocracy and opening careers to talent, the French National Assembly of 1789 implemented the liberal ideal of equality under the law. It also drew up the Declaration of the Rights of Man and of the Citizen, which affirmed the dignity and rights of the individual, and a constitution that limited the king's power. Both revolutions explicitly called for the protection of property rights, another basic premise of liberalism.

Individual Liberty

The liberals' primary concern was the enhancement of individual liberty. They agreed with Kant that every person exists as an end in himself or herself and not as an object to be used arbitrarily by others. If uncoerced by government and churches and properly educated, a person could develop into a good, productive, and self-directed human being.

Liberals rejected a legacy of the Middle Ages, the classification of the individual as commoner or aristocrat on the basis of birth. They held that a man was not born into a certain station in life but made his way through his own efforts. Taking their cue from the French Revolution, liberals called for an end to all privileges of the aristocracy. In the tradition of the philosophes, liberals stressed the preeminence of reason as the basis of political life. Unfettered by ignorance and tyranny, the mind could eradicate evils that had burdened people for centuries and begin an age of free institutions and responsible citizens. For this reason, liberals supported the advancement of education.

Liberals attacked the state and other authorities that prevented the individual from exercising the right of free choice, interfered with the right of free expression, and impeded the individual's self-determination and self-development. They agreed with John Stuart Mill, the British philosopher, that "over his own body and mind, the individual is sovereign . . . that the only purpose for which power can be rightly exercised over any member of a civilized community, against his will, is to prevent harm to others."[26]

To guard against the absolute and arbitrary authority of kings, liberals demanded written constitutions that granted freedom of speech, of the press, and of religion; freedom from arbitrary arrest; and the protection of property rights. To prevent the abuse of political authority, liberals called for a freely elected parliament and the distribution of power among the various branches of government. Liberals held that a government that derived its authority from the consent of the governed, as given in free elections, was least likely to violate individual freedom. A corollary of this principle was that the best government is the one that governs least—that is, one that interferes as little as possible with the economic activities of its citizens and does not involve itself in their private lives or their beliefs.

Liberal Economic Theory

Bourgeois liberals thought that the economy, like the state, should proceed according to natural laws rather than the arbitrary fiat of rulers. Adopting the laissez-faire theory of Adam Smith, they argued that a free economy, in which private enterprise was unimpeded by government regulations, was as important as political freedom to the well-being of the individual and the community. When people acted from self-interest, the liberals said, they worked harder and achieved more. Self-interest and natural competitive impulses spurred economic activity and ensured the production of more and better goods at the lowest possible price, thereby benefitting the entire nation. For this reason, the government must neither block free competition nor deprive individuals of their property, which gave them the incentive to work hard and efficiently. The state contributed to the nation's prosperity when it maintained domestic order; it endangered economic development when it tampered with the free pursuit of profits.

Believing that individuals were responsible for their own misfortunes, liberals were often unmoved by the suffering of the poor. In their eyes, the poor suffered because of their own moral failings, laziness, and vice. Indeed, they used the principle of laissez faire—that government should not interfere with the market—to justify their opposition to humanitarian legislation intended to alleviate the misery of the factory workers. Liberals regarded such social reforms as unwarranted and dangerous meddling with the natural law of supply and demand.

One theorist upholding this view was Thomas R. Malthus (1766–1834), an Anglican cleric and professor of history and political economy. In his *Essay on the Principle of Population* (published in 1798 and then in a second, much-enlarged edition in 1803), Malthus asserted that population grows at a much faster rate than the food supply, resulting in food shortages, irregular employment, lower wages, and high mortality. The poor's distress, said Malthus, was not due to faulty political institutions

or existing social and property relations. Its true cause was the number of children they had.

> *When the wages of labour are hardly sufficient to maintain two children, a man marries and has five or six. He of course finds himself miserably distressed. . . . He accuses his parish. . . . He accuses the avarice of the rich. He accuses the partial and unjust institutions of society. . . . In searching for objects of accusation, he never alludes to the quarter from which all his misfortunes originate. The last person that he would think of accusing is himself.*[27]

The state cannot ameliorate the poor's misery, said Malthus; "the means of redress are in their own hands, and in the hands of no other persons whatever."[28] This "means of redress" would be a lowering of the birthrate through late marriages and chastity, but Malthus believed that the poor lacked the self-discipline to refrain from sexual activity. When they receive higher wages, they have more children, thereby upsetting the population–resource balance and bringing misery to themselves and others.* The view of poverty as an iron law of nature, which could not be undone by the good intentions of the state through philanthropy, buttressed supporters of strict laissez faire and eased the consciences of the propertied classes. Compassion for the poor was simply a misplaced emotion; government reforms were doomed to fail, and higher wages provided no relief. Malthus's theory also flew in the face of adherents of human perfectibility and inevitable progress. Poverty, like disease, was simply a natural phenomenon—a law of nature that could not be eliminated. No wonder his contemporaries called economics "the dismal science."

In *Principles of Political Economy* (1817), David Ricardo (1772–1823) gave support to Malthus's gloomy outlook. Higher wages, said Ricardo, lead workers to have more children, causing an increase in the labor supply. Competition for jobs by an expanding labor force brings down

---

*In later editions of his work, Malthus was more hopeful that checks on fertility through later marriage and "moral restraint" would lead to moderate improvements in the standard of living.

wages. This "iron law of wages" offered bleak prospects for the working poor.

> When, however, by the encouragement which high wages give to the increase of population, the number of labourers is increased, wages again fall to their natural price [to a subsistence level] and indeed from a reaction sometimes fall below it. . . . It is a truth which admits not a doubt, that the comforts and well-being of the poor cannot be permanently secured without some regard on their part, or some effort on the part of the legislature, to regulate the increase of their numbers, and to render less frequent among them early and improvident [imprudent] marriages.[29]

Liberals of the early nineteenth century saw poverty and suffering as part of the natural order and beyond the scope of government. They feared that state intervention in the economy to redress social ills would disrupt the free market, threatening personal liberty and hindering social well-being. Thus, on May 13, 1848, an editorial in the *Economist* protesting against a bill before Parliament that sought to improve housing and sanitation declared: "suffering and evil are nature's admonitions; they cannot be got rid of; and the impatient attempts of benevolence to banish them from the world by legislation . . . have always been productive of more evil than good." Government interference, liberals also argued, discouraged the poor from finding work and so promoted idleness. According to liberal political economy, unemployment and poverty stemmed from individual failings.

A particularly glaring example of the coldness and harshness of liberals toward suffering was their response to the Irish famine of 1845 through 1849. While the Irish were dying of starvation, the liberal leadership in Britain, fearing that government intervention would promote dependence, did little to lessen the suffering. "The more I see of government interference," wrote Sir Charles Wood, chancellor of the Exchequer, "the less I am disposed to trust it, and I have no faith in anything but private capital employed under the individual charge."[30] To some hardhearted liberals, the famine, which killed about 1.5 million people, was simply nature's way of dealing with Ireland's excess population. A dogmatic commitment to laissez faire discouraged British officials from coping humanely and creatively with this disaster.

In the last part of the century, liberals modified their adherence to strict laissez faire, accepting the principle that the state had a responsibility to protect the poor against the worst abuses of rapid industrialization.

Liberalism and Democracy

The French Revolution presented a dilemma for liberals. They supported the reforms of the moderate stage: the destruction of the special privileges of the aristocracy, the drawing up of a declaration of rights and a constitution, the establishment of a parliament, and the opening of careers to talent. But they repudiated Jacobin radicalism. Liberals were frightened by the excesses of the Jacobin regime: its tampering with the economy, which, to liberals, violated the rights of private property; its appeal to the "little people," which liberals saw as inviting mob rule; its subjection of the individual to the state, which they regarded as the denial of individual rights; and its use of terror, which awakened the basest human feelings.

To bourgeois liberals, the participation of commoners in politics meant a vulgar form of despotism and the end of individual liberty. They saw the masses—uneducated, unpropertied, inexperienced, and impatient—as lacking both the ability and the temperament to maintain liberty and protect property.

Few thinkers in the first half of the nineteenth century grasped the growing significance of the masses in politics as did Alexis de Tocqueville (1805–1859), the French political theorist and statesman. In the wake of the French Revolution, de Tocqueville, an aristocrat by birth but a liberal by temperament, recognized that the destruction of aristocracy—a system based on rank—and the march toward democracy could not be curbed. In *Democracy in America* (1835–1840), based on his travels in the United States, de Tocqueville analyzed, with cool detachment and brilliance, the nature, merits, and weaknesses of American democratic society.

In contrast to the France of the Old Regime, wrote de Tocqueville, American society had no hereditary aristocracy with special privileges; the avenues to social advancement and political participation were open to all. Arguing that democracy was more just than aristocratic government, de Tocqueville saw it as the political system of the future. But he also recognized the dangers inherent in democracy.

In a democratic society, he noted, people are willing to sacrifice political liberty to improve their material well-being. Consequently, democracies face an ever-present danger that people, craving equality, will surrender their liberty to a central government if it promises to provide them with property and other advantages.

According to de Tocqueville, democracy also spawns a selfish individualism, which could degenerate into vulgar hedonism. Driven by an overriding concern for possessions and profits, people can lose their taste for political participation and their concern for the public good. If narrow self-interest prevails over a sense of public duty, liberty cannot long endure.

Though recognizing the limitations of democracy, de Tocqueville did not seek to reverse its growth. In this new age that is dawning, he wrote,

> all who shall attempt . . . to base freedom upon aristocratic privilege will fail. . . . All who shall attempt to draw and to retain authority within a single class, will fail. . . . All . . . who would establish or secure the independence and the dignity of their fellow-men, must show themselves the friends of equality. . . . Thus the question is not how to reconstruct aristocratic society, but how to make liberty proceed out of that democratic state of society in which God has placed us.[31]

The problems of democracy, declared de Tocqueville, must be resolved without jeopardizing freedom. The task of a democratic society is to temper extreme individualism and unrestrained acquisitiveness by fostering public spirit. Without direct participation by cooperating citizens—that is, without a concern for the common good—democracy faces a bleak future. Freedom depends less on laws than it does on cultivating the sentiments and habits of civic virtue.

Because bourgeois liberals feared that democracy could quash personal freedom as ruthlessly as any absolute monarch, they called for property requirements for voting and officeholding. They wanted political power to be concentrated in the hands of a safe and reliable—that is, a propertied and educated—middle class. Such a government would prevent revolution from below, a prospect that caused anxiety among bourgeois liberals.

When liberals of the early nineteenth century engaged in revolutions, their aims were always limited. Once they had destroyed absolute monarchy and gained a constitution and a parliament or a change of government, they quickly tried to terminate the revolution. When the fever of revolution spread to the masses, liberals either withdrew or turned counterrevolutionary, for they feared the stirrings of the multitude.

Although liberalism was the political philosophy of a middle class generally hostile to democracy, the essential ideals of democracy flowed logically from liberalism. Eventually, democracy became a later stage in the evolution of liberalism because the masses, their political power enhanced by the Industrial Revolution, would press for greater social, political, and economic equality. Thus, by the early twentieth century, many European states had introduced universal manhood **suffrage**, abandoned property requirements for officeholding, and improved conditions for workers.

But the fears of nineteenth-century liberals were not unfounded. In the twentieth century, the participation of common people in politics indeed threatened freedom. The granting of political participation to the masses has not always made people freer. The confidence of liberal-democrats was shaken in the twentieth century. Growing impatient, in turbulent times, with parliamentary procedures, people in some European countries gave their support to demagogues who promised swift and decisive action. They were willing to trade freedom for economic security, state authority, and national power. Liberalism is based on the assumption that human beings can and do respond to rational argument and that reason will prevail over base human feelings. The history of the twentieth century shows that this may be an overly optimistic assessment of human nature.

RADICALISM AND DEMOCRACY: THE EXPANSION OF LIBERALISM

In the early 1800s, democratic ideals were advanced by thinkers and activists called *radicals*. Inspired by the democratic principles expressed in Rousseau's *Social Contract* and by the republican stage of the French Revolution, French radicals championed popular sovereignty—rule by the people. In contrast to liberals, who feared the masses, French radicals trusted the common person. Advocating universal manhood suffrage and a republic, radicalism gained the support of French workers in the 1830s and 1840s.

British radicals, like their liberal cousins, inherited the Enlightenment's confidence in reason and its belief in the essential goodness of the individual. In the 1790s, British radicals expressed sympathy for the French Revolution, approving its concern for natural rights and its attack on feudal privileges. In the first half of the nineteenth century, English radicals sought parliamentary reforms because some heavily populated districts were barely represented in Parliament, while lightly populated districts were overrepresented. They demanded payment for members of Parliament to permit the nonwealthy to hold office, they sought universal manhood suffrage to give the masses representation in Parliament, and they insisted on the secret ballot to prevent intimidation of and reprisals against voters. Radicals attacked the hereditary aristocracy and fought corruption. Some, such as William Cobbett, a crusading journalist, supported the struggle of the working class to improve its condition. He described the workers' penury.

> *A labouring man in England with a wife and only three children, though he never lose a day's work, though he and his family be economical, frugal and industrious in the most extensive sense of these words, is not now able to procure himself by his labour a single meal of meat from one end of the year into the other. Is this a state in which the labouring man ought to be?*[32]

English radicalism embodied the desires of parliamentary reformers for broader political representation and the hopes of the laboring poor for a better life. Two important theorists of the movement were Thomas Paine and Jeremy Bentham.

Thomas Paine

Thomas Paine (1737–1809), responding to Burke's *Reflections on the Revolution in France* with *The Rights of Man* (published in two parts in 1791 and 1792), denounced reverence for tradition, defended the principle of natural rights, and praised as progress the destruction of the Old Regime. Paine shared the conviction of other Enlightenment thinkers that superstition, intolerance, and despotism had interfered with human progress in the past, and he staunchly supported the American and French revolutions. To initiate a true age of enlightenment, he said, it is necessary to recognize that "all the great laws of society are laws of nature,"[33] and to reconstitute the social and political order in accordance with these principles inherent in nature. Paine denounced all hereditary monarchy and aristocracy as wretched systems of slavery, which deprived people of their inherent right to govern themselves and exploited them financially in order to raise money for war. The only legitimate government, he claimed, was representative democracy, in which the right of all men to participate was assured. Paine believed that republican governments would be less inclined than hereditary ones to wage war and more concerned with the welfare of the common person.

From Paine, the English radical tradition acquired a faith in reason and human goodness, a skeptical attitude toward established institutions, an admiration for the open and democratic society being shaped in the United States, and a dislike of organized religion. It also gained the belief that the goal of government was the greater happiness of ordinary people and that excluding common people from political participation was unjust.

Jeremy Bentham

Jeremy Bentham's (1748–1832) importance to the English radical tradition derives from the principle of **utility**, which he offered as a guide to reformers. The central fact of human existence, said Bentham, is that human beings seek to gratify their desires, that they prefer pleasure to pain, and that pleasure is intrinsically good and pain bad. In Bentham's view, human beings are motivated solely by self-interest, which they define in terms of pleasure and pain: "Nature has placed mankind under the governance of two sovereign masters, *pain and pleasure*. It is for them alone to point out what we ought to do, as well as to determine what we shall do."[34] Consequently, every political, economic, judicial, or social institution and all legislation should be judged according to a simple standard: Does it bring about the greatest happiness for the greatest number? If it does not, it should be swept away.

Bentham believed that he had found an objective and scientific approach to the study and reform of society. By focusing on the necessity for change and improvement on every level of society and by encouraging a careful and objective analysis of social issues, Bentham and his followers, called *philosophical radicals*, contributed substantially to the shaping of the English reform tradition.

According to Bentham, those in power had always used what they considered the highest principles—God's teachings, universal standards, and honored traditions—to justify their political and social systems, their moral codes, and their laws. On the basis of these principles, they persecuted and abused people, instituted practices rooted in ignorance and superstition, and imposed values that made people miserable because they conflicted with human nature and the essential needs of men and women. Bentham contended that the principle of utility—that one should act always to derive the greatest happiness for the greatest number of people—permits the reforming of society in accordance with people's true nature and needs. Utilitarianism, he declared, bases institutions and laws on an objective study of human behavior rather than on unsubstantiated religious beliefs, unreliable traditions, and mistaken philosophical abstractions. Its goal is to propose measures that augment rather than diminish the community's happiness.

Bentham's utilitarianism led him to press for social and political reforms. The aristocratic ruling elite, he said, were interested not in producing the "greatest happiness of the greatest number" but in furthering their own narrow interests. Only if the rulers came from the broad masses of people would government be amenable to reforms based on the principle of greatest happiness. Thus, he supported extension of the suffrage and a secret ballot and attacked political corruption and clerical control over education. Bentham wanted to do away with the monarchy and the House of Lords and to disestablish the Anglican Church. In contrast to laissez-faire liberals, Benthamites argued for legislation to protect women and children in the factories. They also sought to improve sanitation in the cities and to reform the archaic British prison system.

EARLY SOCIALISM: NEW POSSIBILITIES FOR SOCIETY

A new group, called *socialists*, went further than either the liberals or the radicals. Referred to as utopian socialists, they argued that the liberals' concern for individual freedom and the radicals' demand for extension of the suffrage had little impact on the poverty, oppression, and gross inequality of wealth that plagued modern society. Asserting that the liberals' doctrine of individualism degenerated into selfish egoism, which harmed community life, utopian socialists demanded the creation of a new society based on cooperation rather than on competition. Reflecting the spirit of the Enlightenment and the French Revolution, socialists, like liberals, denounced the status quo for perpetuating injustice and held that people could create a better world. Like liberals, too, they placed the highest value on a rational analysis of society and on transforming society in line with scientifically valid premises, whose truth rational people could grasp. Socialists believed that they had discerned a pattern in human society, which, if properly understood and acted upon, would lead men and women to an earthly salvation. Thus, early socialists were also romantics, for they dreamed of a new social order, a future utopia where each individual could find happiness and self-fulfillment. Although they sought to replace the existing social order with a more just arrangement, these early socialists, unlike Marx,

FOURIER: UTOPIAN SOCIALIST. French socialist Charles Fourier asserted that society's regulations and social arrangements conflicted with human nature and accounted for human misery. Fourier urged the reorganization of society, including work, in accordance with the needs of people for pleasure and satisfaction. To realize these aims, he proposed the creation of small communities where people would work at tasks that appealed to them, and marriage, which restricted a couple's sexual needs, would eventually disappear. In the 1840s twenty-nine communities based on Fourier's ideas were founded in the United States, but they all quickly disbanded. (Time Life Pictures/The LIFE Picture Collection/Getty Images.)

did not advocate class warfare. They aspired to create a new harmonious social order that would reconcile different classes; for Marx, by necessity a new social order entailed the destruction of the capitalist bourgeoisie.

Saint-Simon: Technocratic Socialism

Henri Comte de Saint-Simon (1760–1825) renounced his title during the French Revolution and enthusiastically preached the opportunity to create a new society. His mission, he believed, was to set society right by instilling an understanding of the new age that science and industry were shaping. He argued that just as Christianity had provided social unity and stability during the Middle Ages, so scientific knowledge would bind the society of his time. The scientists, industrialists, bankers, artists, and writers would replace the clergy and the aristocracy as the social elite and would harness technology for the betterment of humanity. Saint-Simon's disciples championed efforts to build great railway and canal systems, including the Suez and Panama canals. His vision of a scientifically organized society led by trained experts was a powerful force among intellectuals in the nineteenth century and is very much alive today among those who believe in a technocratic society.

Fourier: Psychological Socialism

Another early French socialist was Charles Fourier (1772–1837), who believed—like the romantics—that society conflicted with the natural needs of human beings and that this tension was responsible for human misery. Only the reorganization of society so that it would satisfy people's desire for pleasure and contentment would end that misery. Whereas Saint-Simon and his followers had elaborate plans to reorganize society on the grand scale of large industries and giant railway and canal systems, Fourier sought to create small communities that would let men and women enjoy life's simple pleasures.

These communities of about sixteen hundred people, called *phalansteries*, would be organized according to the unchanging needs of human nature. All the people would work at tasks that interested them and would produce things that brought them and others pleasure. Like Adam Smith, Fourier understood that specialization, with its deadening routine, bred boredom and alienation from work and life. Unlike Smith, he did not believe that vastly increased productivity compensated for the evils of specialization. In the phalansteries, money and goods would not be equally distributed; those with special skills and responsibilities would be rewarded accordingly, a system that conformed to nature because people have a natural desire to be rewarded.

Fourier thought that marriage distorted the natures of both men and women since monogamy restricted their sexual needs and narrowed the scope of their lives to just the family. Instead, people should think of themselves as part of the family of all humanity. Because married women had to devote all their strength and time to household and children, they had no time or energy left to enjoy life's pleasures. Fourier did not call for the abolition of the family, but he did hope that it would disappear on its own accord as society adjusted to his theories. Men and women would find new ways of fulfilling themselves sexually, and the community would be organized so that it could care for the children. Fourier's ideas found some acceptance in the United States, where in the 1840s at least twenty-nine communities were founded on Fourierist principles. None, however, lasted more than five or six years.

Owen: Industrial Socialism

In 1799, Robert Owen (1771–1858) became part owner and manager of the New Lanark cotton mills in Scotland. Distressed by widespread mistreatment of workers, Owen resolved to improve the lives of his employees and show that it was possible to do so without destroying profits. He raised wages, upgraded working conditions, refused to hire children under ten, and provided workers with neat homes, food, and clothing, all at reasonable prices. He set up schools for children and for adults. In every way, he demonstrated his belief that healthier, happier workers produced more than the less fortunate ones. Like Saint-Simon, Owen believed that industry and technology could and would enrich humankind if they were organized according to the proper principles. Visitors came from all over Europe to see Owen's factories.

Just like many philosophes, Owen was convinced that the environment was the principal shaper of character—that the ignorance, alcoholism, and crime of the poor derived from bad living conditions. Public education and factory reform, said Owen, would make better citizens of the poor. Owen came to believe that the entire social and economic order must be replaced by a new system based on harmonious group living

rather than on competition. He established a model community at New Harmony, Indiana, but it was shortlived.

NATIONALISM: THE SACREDNESS OF THE NATION

Nationalism is a conscious bond shared by a group of people who feel strongly attached to a particular land and who possess a common language, culture, and history marked by shared glories and sufferings. Nationalists contend that one's highest loyalty and devotion should be given to the nation. They exhibit great pride in their people's history and traditions and often feel that their nation has been specially chosen by God or history. They assert that the nation—its culture and history—gives meaning to an individual's life and actions. Like a religion, nationalism provides the individual with a sense of community and with a cause worthy of self-sacrifice. Identifying with the nation's collective achievements—with its past greatness—can enhance the feeling of self-worth.

In an age when Christianity was in retreat, nationalism became the dominant spiritual force in nineteenth-century European life. Nationalism provided new beliefs, martyrs, and "holy" days that stimulated feelings of reverence; it offered membership in a community, which satisfied an overwhelming psychological need of human beings for fellowship and identity. And nationalism supplied a mission—the advancement of the nation—to which people could dedicate themselves.

The Emergence of Modern Nationalism

The essential components of nationalism emerged during the French Revolution. The Revolution asserted the principle that sovereignty derived from the nation, from the people as a whole: the state was not the private possession of the ruler but the embodiment of the people's will. The nation-state was above king, church, estate, guild, or province, superseding all other loyalties. The French people must view themselves not as subjects of the king, not as Bretons or Normans, nobles or bourgeois, but as citizens of a united fatherland, *la patrie*. These two ideas—that the people possess unlimited sovereignty and that they are united in a nation—were crucial in fashioning a nationalist outlook.

As the Revolution moved from the moderate to the radical stage, French nationalism intensified. In 1793 and 1794, when the Republic was threatened by foreign invasion, the Jacobins created a national army, demanded ever greater allegiance to and sacrifice for the nation, and called for the expansion of France's borders to the Alps and the Rhine. With unprecedented success, the Jacobins used every means—press, schoolroom, and rostrum—to instill a love of country, to forge a sense of national loyalty that would supersede attachment to local regions.

The Romantic Movement also awakened nationalist feelings. By examining the language, literature, and folkways of their people, romantic thinkers instilled a sense of national identity and pride in their compatriots. Johann Gottfried Herder (1744–1803), a prominent German writer, conceived the idea of the *Volksgeist*—the spirit of the people. For Herder, each people was unique and creative; each expressed its peculiar genius in language, literature, monuments, and folk traditions. Herder did not make the theoretical jump from a spiritual or cultural nationalism to political nationalism; he did not call for the formation of states based on nationality. But his emphasis on the unique culture of a people and his assertion that an individual is defined as a member of a specific culture or nation stimulated a national consciousness among Germans and the various Slavic peoples who lived under foreign rule. Fascination with the Volksgeist prompted intellectuals to investigate the past of their own people, to rediscover their ancient traditions, and to extol their historic languages and cultures. From this cultural nationalism, it was only a short step to a political nationalism that called for national liberation, unification, and statehood.

The romantics were the earliest apostles of German nationalism. Resisting the French philosophes, who sought to impose universal norms on all peoples, German romantics stressed the uniqueness of the German nation and its history. They restored to consciousness memories of the German past, and they emphasized the distinct qualities of the German folk and the special destiny of the German nation. The romantics glorified medieval Germany and valued hereditary monarchy and aristocracy as vital links to the nation's past. They saw the existence of each individual as inextricably bound up with folk and fatherland, and they found the self-realization for which they yearned in the uniting of their own egos with the national soul. To these romantics, the national community was the source of artistic and spiritual creativity and the vital force that gave the individual both an identity and a purpose in life. The nation stood above the individual; the national spirit linked isolated souls into a community of brethren. In unmistakably romantic tones, poet Ernst Moritz Arndt (1769–1860) demonstrated this transition from cultural to political nationalism when he urged Germans to unite against Napoleon.

> *German man, feel again God, hear and fear the eternal, and you hear and fear also your Volk [people], you feel again in God the honor and dignity of your fathers, their glorious history rejuvenates itself in you, their firm and gallant virtue reblossoms in you, the whole German Fatherland stands again before you in the august halo of past centuries. No longer Catholics and Protestants, no longer Prussians and Austrians, Saxons and Bavarians, Silesians and Hanoverians, no longer of different faith, different mentality, and different will—be Germans, be one, will to be one by love and loyalty, and no devil will vanquish you.*[35]

In his appeal to German patriotism, Arndt peered into the future, grasping that devotion to the nation is "the religion of our times. . . . That is the ultimate religion, to hold the Fatherland more dearly than lords and princes, than father and mother, than wives and children."[36]

Most German romantics expressed hostility to the liberal ideals of the French Revolution. They condemned the reforms of the Revolution for trying to reconstruct society by separating individuals from their national past, for treating them as isolated abstractions. They held that the German folk spirit should not be polluted by foreign French ideas.

To the philosophes, the state was a human institution, a rational arrangement between individuals that safeguarded their rights and permitted them to realize their individual goals. To German romantics, such a state was an artificial and lifeless construction. The true German state was something holy, the expression of the divine spirit of the German people; it could not be manufactured to order by the intellect. The state's purpose was neither the protection of natural rights nor the promotion of economic well-being; rather, the state was a living organism that linked each person to a sacred past and reconciled and united heterogeneous wills, imbuing them with a profound sense of community, with which one entered into mystical communion. "This 'Romantic' image of a state founded not on any rational idea of the functions and purposes of a state but on love and perfect communion, is of course a formula for totalitarianism," observes R. J. Hollingdale, "and it was towards a state modeled on this formula that German nationalism continually moved."[37] Building on the romantics' views, radical German nationalists came to propound the dangerous racist idea that national identity was an inherited characteristic, that being and feeling German depended on birth—"on blood"—rather than acculturation. Holding this belief, some German nationalists maintained that Jews, no matter how many generations they had resided in Germany, could never be truly German.

Nationalism and Liberalism

In the early 1800s, liberals were the principal leaders and supporters of nationalist movements. They viewed the struggle for national rights—the freedom of a people from foreign rule—as an extension of the struggle for the rights of the individual. There could be no liberty, said nationalists, if people were not free to rule themselves in their own land.

Liberals called for the unification of Germany and Italy, the rebirth of Poland, the liberation of Greece from Turkish rule, and the granting of autonomy to the Hungarians of the Austrian Empire. Liberal nationalists envisioned a Europe of independent states based on nationality and popular sovereignty. Free of foreign domination and tyrant princes, these newly risen states would protect the rights of the individual and strive to create a brotherhood of nationalities in Europe.

In the first half of the nineteenth century, few intellectuals recognized the dangers inherent in nationalism or understood the fundamental conflict between liberalism and nationalism. For the liberal, the idea of universal natural rights transcended all national boundaries. Inheriting the cosmopolitanism of the Enlightenment, liberalism emphasized what all people had in common, called for all individuals to be treated equally under the law, and preached toleration. As they grew more extreme, nationalists increasingly regarded the nation as the essential fact of existence and manifested a narrow tribal outlook. Consequently, they often willingly subverted individual liberty for the sake of national grandeur. The liberal sought to protect the rights of all within the state, whereas the nationalist often ignored or trampled on the rights of individuals and national minorities. Liberalism grew out of the rational tradition of the West; nationalism derived from the emotions. Because it fulfilled an elemental yearning for community and kinship, nationalism exerted a powerful hold over human hearts, often driving people to political extremism. Liberalism demanded objectivity in analyzing tradition, society, and history, but nationalism evoked a mythic and romantic past, frequently a heroic golden age, that often distorted history.

"Nationalism requires . . . much belief in what is patently not so," wryly observes the British historian E. J. Hobsbawm.[38] Thus, nationalists inflated their people's past achievements and attributed to the nation a peculiar inner spirit that set it apart from others and accounted for its superiority. While constantly declaiming the wrongs that others had inflicted on them, they turned a blind eye to their own mistreatment of other nationalities. Nationalists interpreted history to serve political ends: the unity of their people and the forging of a powerful nation-state.

In the last part of the nineteenth century, the irrational and mythic quality of nationalism intensified. By stressing the unique qualities and history of a particular people, nationalism promoted hatred between nationalities. By kindling deep love for the past, for community, and for kinship, it often raised emotions to fever pitch. It shattered rational thinking, dragged the mind into a world of fantasy and myth, and introduced extremism into politics. Love of nation became an overriding passion, threatening to extinguish the liberal ideals of reason, freedom, and equality.

NOTES

1. Jean Jacques Rousseau, *The Confessions* (New York: Modern Library, 1950), 2.

2. Quoted in H. G. Schenk, *The Mind of the European Romantics* (Garden City, N.Y.: Doubleday, 1969), 4.

3. William Blake, "Milton," in *The Poetry and Prose of William Blake,* ed. David V. Erdman (Garden City, N.Y.: Doubleday, 1965), bk. 2, plate 40, lines 34–36, 141.

4. Ibid., plate 41, line 1.

5. Johann Goethe, *Faust,* trans. Bayard Taylor (New York: Modern Library, 1950), pt. 1, sec. 4.

6. Letter of John Keats, November 22, 1817, in *The Letters of John Keats,* ed. Hyder E. Rollins (Cambridge, Mass.: Harvard University Press, 1958), 1:184–185.

7. Quoted in John Herman Randall Jr., *The Career of Philosophy* (New York: Columbia University Press, 1965), 2:80.

8. Blake, "Milton," Preface, bk. 1, plate 1, 95.

9. Quoted in Robert T. Denommé, *Nineteenth-Century French Romantic Poets* (Carbondale: Southern Illinois University Press, 1969), 28.

10. Quoted in T. C. W. Blanning, ed., *The Oxford Illustrated History of Modern Europe* (New York: Oxford University Press, 1996), 124.

11. Quoted in Frederic Ewen, *Heroic Imagination* (Secaucus, N.J.: Citadel Press, 1984), 276.

12. Quoted in Ernst Cassirer, *An Essay on Man* (New York: Bantam Books, 1970), 178.

13. Victor Hugo, "La Pente de la Rêverie," *Les Feuilles d'Automne* (Paris: J. Hetzel, 1831), 157.

14. From "The Tables Turned," in *The Complete Poetical Works of Wordsworth,* ed. Andrew J. George (Boston: Houghton Mifflin, 1904, rev. ed. 1982), 83.

15. From "Lines Composed a Few Miles Above Tintern Abbey," in *The Complete Poetical Works of William Wordsworth* (Philadelphia: Porter and Coates, 1851), 194.

16. Quoted in R. W. Harris, *Romanticism and the Social Order, 1780–1830* (New York: Barnes and Noble, 1969), 223–224.

17. Horst von Maltitz, *The Evolution of Hitler's Germany* (New York: McGraw-Hill, 1973), 217.

18. G. W. F. Hegel, *The Philosophy of History,* trans. J. Sibree (New York: Dover, 1956), 19, 23.

19. Ibid., 39.

20. Quoted in George Brandes, *Revolution and Reaction in Nineteenth Century French Literature* (New York: Russell and Russell, reprint ed., n.d.), 106–107.

21. Edmund Burke, *Reflections on the Revolution in France* (New York: Liberal Arts Press, 1955), 40, 89.

22. Ibid., 99.

23. Ibid., 70.

24. Joseph de Maistre, *Essay on the Generative Principle of Political Constitutions and Other Human Institutions* in *Joseph de Maistre, On God and Society,* ed. Elisha Greifer, trans. Elisha Greifer and Laurence M. Porter (Chicago: Henry Regnery, 1959), 45, 51, 54.

25. Quoted in Frederick B. Artz, *Reaction and Revolution, 1814–1832* (New York: Harper Torchbooks, 1963), 73.

26. John Stuart Mill, *On Liberty,* ed. Currin V. Shields (Indianapolis: Bobbs-Merrill, 1956), chap. 1.

27. Thomas Robert Malthus, *First Essay on Population,* reprinted for the Royal Economic Society (London: Macmillan, 1926), 16.

28. Ibid., 17.

29. Excerpted in Allan Bullock and Maurice Shock, eds., *The Liberal Tradition from Fox to Keynes* (London: Adam and Charles Black, 1956), 31–32.

30. Quoted in Anthony Arblaster, *The Rise and Decline of Western Liberalism* (Oxford, England: Basil Blackwell, 1984), 258.

31. Alexis de Tocqueville, *Democracy in America*, trans. Henry Reeve (New York: Oxford University Press, 1924), 493–494.

32. Quoted in Raymond Williams, *Culture and Society, 1780–1945* (New York: Columbia University Press, 1983), 14.

33. Quoted in Francis Canavan, "Thomas Paine," in *History of Political Philosophy*, ed. Leo Strauss and Joseph Cropsey (Chicago: Rand McNally, 1963), 594.

34. Jeremy Bentham, *An Introduction to the Principles of Morals and Legislation*, together with *A Fragment on Government* (London: Basil Blackwell, 1948), chap. 1, sec. 1, 125.

35. Quoted in Hans Kohn, *Prelude to Nation-States* (Princeton, N.J.: D. Van Nostrand, 1967), 262.

36. Quoted in Michael Burleigh, *Earthly Powers: The Clash of Religion and Politics in Europe, from the French Revolution to the Great War* (New York: HarperCollins, 2007), 160.

37. R. J. Hollingdale, *Nietzsche* (London: Routledge and Kegan Paul, 1973), 25.

38. E. J. Hobsbawm, *Nations and Nationalism Since 1780* (Cambridge: Cambridge University Press, 1992), 12.

Chapter 22

Revolution and Counterrevolution, 1815–1848

The Uprising, *by Honoré Daumier.* (The Phillips Collection, Washington, D.C.)

Focus Questions

1. Why did Metternich fear liberalism and nationalism?

2. What were the accomplishments and failures of the Congress of Vienna?

3. What were the principal reasons for the revolutions that broke out in Europe in the decades after the Congress of Vienna?

4. What reforms were introduced in Britain between 1815 and 1848?

5. Why did the revolutions of 1848 essentially fail?

6. What were the liberal gains in 1848? Why were liberals and nationalists disappointed?

During the years 1815 through 1848, the forces unleashed by the French Revolution clashed with the traditional outlook of the Old Regime. The period opened with the Congress of Vienna, which drew up a peace settlement after the defeat of Napoleon, and closed with the revolutions that swept across much of Europe in 1848.

Much of the Old Regime outside France survived the stormy decades of the French Revolution and Napoleon. Monarchs still held the reins of political power. Aristocrats, particularly in Central and Eastern Europe, retained their traditional hold on the army and administration, controlled the peasantry and local government, and enjoyed tax exemptions. Determined to enforce respect for traditional authority and to smother liberal ideals, the conservative ruling elites resorted to censorship, secret police, and armed force.

The French Revolution, however, had shown that absolutism could be successfully challenged and feudal privileges abolished. Inspired by the revolutionary principles of liberty, equality, and fraternity, liberals and nationalists continued to engage in revolutionary action.

THE CONGRESS OF VIENNA, 1814–1815

Statesmen and Issues

After the defeat of Napoleon, representatives of European powers convened in Vienna to draw up a peace settlement. The pivotal figure at the Congress of Vienna was Prince Klemens von Metternich (1773–1859) of Austria, who had organized the coalition that triumphed over Napoleon.

A man of the Old Order, Metternich hated the new forces of nationalism and liberalism. He regarded liberalism as a dangerous disease carried by middle-class malcontents, and he believed that domestic order and international stability depended on rule by monarchy and respect for aristocracy. The misguided liberal belief that society could be reshaped according to the ideals of liberty and equality, said Metternich, had led to twenty-five years of revolution, terror, and war. In order

Chronology 22.1 ❖ Revolution and Reaction

1820	Revolt in Spain
1821	Austria crushes revolts in Italy
1823	French troops crush revolt in Spain
1825	Uprising in Russia crushed by Nicholas I
1829	Greece gains independence from the Ottoman Empire
1830	July Ordinances in France are followed by a revolution, which forces Charles X to abdicate
August 1830	Belgian revolution
October 1830	Belgians declare their independence from Holland, establishing a liberal government
1831	Polish revolution fails
1831–1832	Austrian forces crush a revolution in Italy
1832	Reform Act extends suffrage to the middle class in Britain
1848	Year of Revolution
February 1848	Revolution in Paris: Louis Philippe abdicates, and France becomes a republic
March 1848	Uprisings in capital cities of the German states lead to liberal reforms
March 18–22, 1848	"Five Glorious Days" in Milan
March 22, 1848	Citizens of Venice declare their freedom from Austria and establish a republic
June 1848	June Days of Paris: revolutionaries are beaten by professional soldiers
August 1848	Constitutional Assembly meets in Vienna and abolishes serfdom in the Austrian Empire
December 1848	Louis Napoleon is elected president of the Second Republic of France
August 1849	Hungarians' bid for independence is crushed by Hapsburg forces, aided by Russian troops

to restore stability and peace, the old Europe must suppress liberal ideas and quash the first signs of revolution. If the European powers did not destroy the revolutionary spirit, they would be devoured by it. Regarding all reformation as an invitation to radicalism and revolution, Metternich refused to make any concessions to liberalism.

Metternich also feared the new spirit of nationalism. Because Austria was a multinational empire, it was particularly vulnerable to nationalist unrest. If its many ethnic groups—Poles, Czechs, Magyars, Italians, South Slavs, and Romanians—became infected with the nationalist virus, they would shatter the Hapsburg Empire. Moreover, by arousing the masses and setting people against people, nationalism could undermine the foundations of the European civilization that he cherished.

CONGRESS OF VIENNA, 1815, BY JEAN BAPTISTE ISABEY (1767–1855). The delegates to the Congress of Vienna sought to reestablish many features of Europe that had existed before the French Revolution and Napoleon. They can be accused of shortsightedness; nevertheless, the balance of power that they formulated preserved international peace. Metternich is standing before a chair at the left. (Library of Congress Prints and Photographs division[LC-USZ62-101721])

Metternich wanted to return to power the ruling families deposed by more than two decades of revolutionary warfare. He also sought to restore the balance of power so that no one country could be in a position to dominate the European continent as France under Napoleon had done. Metternich was determined to end the chaos of the Napoleonic period and restore stability to Europe. There must be no more Napoleons who obliterate states, topple kings, and dream of European hegemony. Although he served the interests of the Hapsburg monarchy, Metternich also had a sense of responsibility to Europe as a whole. He sought a settlement that would avoid the destructiveness of another general war.

The other nations at the Congress of Vienna included Britain, Russia, France, and Prussia. Representing Britain was Robert Stewart, Viscount Castlereagh (1769–1822), the realistic British foreign secretary. Though an implacable enemy of Napoleon, Castlereagh demonstrated mature statesmanship by not seeking to punish France severely. Tsar Alexander I (1777–1825), steeped in Christian mysticism, wanted to create a European community based on Christian teachings. Alexander regarded himself as the savior of Europe, an attitude that caused other diplomats to view him with distrust. Representing France was Prince Charles Maurice de Talleyrand-Périgord (1754–1838). A devoted patriot, Talleyrand

Map 22.1 **Peoples of the Hapsburg Monarchy, 1815** In 1815, Austria was a multinational empire dominated by Germans. As nationalism among the various ethnic groups grew stronger, fear of dissolution became the principal concern of Hapsburg leaders. (© 2016 Cengage Learning.)

sought to remove the stigma of the Revolution and Napoleon from France. The aging Prince Karl von Hardenberg (1750–1822) represented Prussia. Like Metternich, Castlereagh, and Talleyrand, the Prussian statesman believed that the various European states, besides pursuing their own national interests, should concern themselves with the well-being of the European community as a whole.

Two interrelated issues threatened to disrupt the conference and enmesh the Great Powers in another war. One was Prussia's intention to annex the German kingdom of Saxony; the other was Russia's demand for Polish territories. The tsar wanted to combine the Polish holdings of Russia,

Austria, and Prussia into a new Polish kingdom under Russian control. Britain and Austria saw such an extension of Russia's power into Central Europe as a threat to the balance of power. Metternich declared that he had not fought Napoleon to prepare the way for the tsar. Britain agreed that Russia's westward expansion must be checked.

Prince Talleyrand of France suggested that Britain, Austria, and France form an alliance to oppose Prussia and Russia. Talleyrand's clever move restored France to the family of nations. Now France was no longer the hated enemy but a necessary counterweight to Russia and Prussia. Threatened with war, Russia and Prussia moderated their demands, and the crisis ended.

The Settlement

After months of discussion, quarrels, and threats, the delegates to the Congress of Vienna finished their work. Resisting Prussia's demands for a punitive peace, the allies did not punish France severely. They feared that a humiliated France would only prepare for a war of revenge. Moreover, Metternich continued to need France to balance the power of both Prussia and Russia. France had to pay a large indemnity over a five-year period and submit to allied occupation until the obligation was met.

Despite losing most of its conquests, France emerged with somewhat more land than it possessed before the Revolution. To guard against a resurgent France, both Prussia and Holland received territories on the French border. Holland obtained the southern Netherlands (Belgium); Prussia gained the Rhineland and part of Saxony, but not as much as the Prussians had desired. Nevertheless, Prussia emerged from the settlement significantly larger and stronger. Russia obtained Finland and a considerable part of the Polish territories, but not as much as the tsar had anticipated; the congress prevented further Russian expansion into Central Europe. The northern Italian province of Lombardy was restored to Austria, which also received adjacent Venetia. England obtained strategic naval bases: Helgoland in the North Sea, Malta and the Ionian Islands in the Mediterranean, the Cape Colony in South Africa, and Ceylon in the Indian Ocean. Germany was organized into a confederation of thirty-eight (later thirty-nine) states. Norway was given to Sweden. Legitimate rulers who had been displaced by the Revolution and Napoleon were restored to their thrones in France, Spain, Portugal, the Kingdom of the Two Sicilies, the Papal States, and many German states.

The conservative delegates at the Congress of Vienna have often been criticized for ignoring the liberal and nationalist aspirations of the different peoples and turning the clock back to the Old Regime. Critics have castigated the congress for dealing only with the rights of thrones and not the rights of peoples. But after the experience of two world wars in the twentieth century, some historians today are impressed with the peacemakers' success in restoring a balance of power that effectively stabilized international relations. No one country was strong enough to dominate the Continent; no Great Power was so unhappy that it resorted to war to undo the settlement. Not until the unification of Germany during 1870–1871 was the balance of power upset; not until World War I in 1914 did Europe have another general war of the magnitude of the Napoleonic wars.

REVOLUTIONS, 1820–1829

Russia, Austria, Prussia, and Great Britain agreed to act together to preserve the territorial settlement of the Congress of Vienna and the balance of power. After paying its indemnity, France was admitted into this Quadruple Alliance, also known as the Concert of Europe. Metternich intended to use the Concert of Europe to maintain harmony among nations and internal stability within nations. Toward this end, conservatives in their respective countries censored books and newspapers, imprisoned liberal activists, and suppressed nationalist uprisings.

But repression could not contain the liberal and nationalist ideals unleashed by the French Revolution. The first revolution after restoration of the legitimate rulers occurred in Spain in 1820. Fearing that the uprising, with its quasi-liberal overtones, would inspire revolutions in other lands, the Concert of Europe empowered France to intervene. In 1823, a hundred thousand French troops crushed the revolution in Spain.

Revolutionary activity in Italy also frightened the Concert of Europe. In 1821, it authorized Austria to extinguish a liberal uprising in the Kingdom of the Two Sicilies. The Austrians also crushed an uprising in Piedmont, in northern Italy. Rulers in other Italian states jailed and executed liberal leaders, and several thousand Italians went into exile.

In both instances, Britain strongly opposed the actions of the alliance. It interpreted the alliance differently from Austria, Prussia, and Russia. The three Eastern powers wanted the alliance to smother in the cradle all subversive movements that threatened the Old Order. To Metternich, the central problem of the age was suppressing revolutions, and he regarded the alliance as a means of preserving the status quo. Britain, however, viewed the alliance solely as a means of guarding

538

against renewed French aggression. It did not consider intervention in the domestic affairs of other nations to be in its own interest.

A revolution also failed in Russia. During the Napoleonic wars and the occupation of France, Russian officers were introduced to French ideas. Contrasting French liberal ideas and ways with Russian autocracy, some officers resolved to change conditions in Russia. Like their Western counterparts, they organized secret societies and disseminated liberal ideas within Russia. When Alexander I died, these liberal officers struck. But representing only a fraction of the aristocracy and with no mass following among the soldiers, they had no chance of success. Their uprising in December 1825 was easily smashed by the new tsar, Nicholas I, and the leaders were severely punished. To prevent Western ideas from infiltrating his realm, Nicholas imposed rigid censorship and organized the Third Section, a secret police force, which spied on suspected subversives.

The revolutions in Spain, Italy, and Russia failed, but the Metternich system also suffered setbacks. Stimulated by the ideals of the French Revolution, the Greeks revolted against their Turkish rulers in 1821. Although the Turkish sultan was the legitimate ruler, Russia, France, and Britain aided the Greek revolutionaries, for they were Christians and the Turks were Muslims. Moreover, pro-Greek sentiments were very strong among educated Western Europeans, who had studied the literature and history of ancient Greece and viewed the Greeks as struggling to regain their ancestral freedom. Not only the pressure of public opinion but also the fear of Russian motives led Britain to join in the intervention. If Russia carried out its intention of aiding the Greeks on its own, no doubt the Russian bear would never release Greece from its hug. Britain could not permit this extension of Russian power in the eastern Mediterranean. Despite Metternich's objections, Britain, France, and Russia took joint action against the Turks.

◀*Map 22.2* Europe, 1815 At the Congress of Vienna, Russia gained a considerable part of the Polish territories, Prussia acquired the Rhineland and part of Saxony, and Holland received Belgium. The northern Italian province of Lombardy was restored to the Hapsburg Empire, which also received adjacent Venetia. (© 2016 Cengage Learning.)

In 1829, Greece gained its independence. The Metternich system, which aimed to preserve the territorial settlements made at Vienna and to protect traditional and legitimate rulers against liberal and nationalist revolutions, had been breached. The success of the Greeks heartened liberals in other lands.

REVOLUTIONS, 1830–1832

After Napoleon's defeat, a Bourbon king, Louis XVIII (1814–1824), younger brother of the executed Louis XVI, ascended the throne of France. Recognizing that the French people would not accept a return to the Old Order, Louis pursued a moderate course. Although his pseudoconstitution, the Charter, declared that the king's power rested on divine right, it acknowledged that citizens possessed fundamental rights: freedom of thought and religion and equal treatment under the law. It also set up a two-house parliament. But peasants, urban workers, and most bourgeois could not meet the property requirements for voting. Louis XVIII was resisted by diehard aristocrats, or *ultras,* who wanted to erase the past twenty-five years of French history and restore the power and privileges of the church and the aristocracy. It was said of them that "they had forgotten nothing and learnt nothing." Their leader was the king's younger brother, the Comte d'Artois, who, after Louis's death in 1824, ascended the throne as Charles X (1824–1830).

The new government aroused the hostility of the bourgeoisie by indemnifying the émigrés for the property they had lost during the Revolution, censoring the press, and giving the church greater control over education. In the election of 1830, the liberal opposition to Charles X won a decisive victory. Charles responded with the July Ordinances, which dissolved the newly elected Chamber of Deputies; the ordinances also deprived rich bourgeois of the vote (less wealthy bourgeois did not have the vote) and severely curbed the press.

The bourgeoisie, students, and workers rebelled. Viewing themselves as heirs of the Jacobins, they hoped to establish a republic, but the wealthy bourgeois who took control of the revolution feared republican radicalism. They offered the throne to the Duc d'Orléans; Charles X abdicated and went into exile in Britain. The new king, Louis

THE BARRICADES. In February 1848, republican revolutionaries forced Louis Philippe to abdicate. This picture shows one of the barricades set up by the revolutionaries. (akg-images.)

Philippe (1830–1848), never forgot that he owed his throne to the upper bourgeois. And the Parisian workers who had fought for a republic and economic reforms to alleviate poverty felt betrayed by the outcome, as did the still-disenfranchised petty bourgeois.

The Revolution of 1830 in France set off shock waves in Belgium, Poland, and Italy. The Congress of Vienna had assigned Catholic Belgium to Protestant Holland. From the outset, the Belgians had protested. Stirred by the events in Paris, Belgian patriots proclaimed their independence from Holland and established a liberal government. Inspired by the uprisings in France and Belgium, Polish students, intellectuals, and army officers took up arms against their Russian overlords. The revolutionaries wanted to restore Polish independence, a dream that poets, musicians, and intellectuals had kept alive. Polish courage, however, was no match for Russian might, and Warsaw fell in

1831. The tsar took savage revenge on the revolutionaries. During 1831–1832, Austrian forces again extinguished a revolution in Italy. As in Poland, revolutionary leaders in Italy failed to stir the great peasant masses to the cause of Italian independence and unity.

THE RISE OF REFORM IN BRITAIN

Britain was the freest state in Europe in the early decades of the nineteenth century, but it was far from democratic. A constitutional monarchy, with many limits on the powers of king and state, Britain was nonetheless dominated by aristocrats. Landed aristocrats controlled both the House of Lords and the House of Commons—the Lords because they constituted its membership and the Commons because they patronized or sponsored men favorable to their interests. The vast majority of people, from the middle class as well as from the working class, could not vote. Many towns continued to be governed by corrupt groups. New industrial towns were not allowed to elect representatives to Parliament; often lacking a town organization, they could not even govern themselves effectively.

The social separation of noble and commoner was not as rigid in Britain as on the Continent. Younger sons of aristocrats did not inherit titles and were therefore obliged to make careers in law, business, the military, and the church. The upper and middle classes mingled much more freely than on the Continent, and the wealthiest merchants tended to buy lands, titles, and noble husbands for their daughters. Nonetheless, Parliament, the courts, local governments, the established Anglican Church, and the monarch were all part of a social and political system dominated by aristocratic interests and values. This domination had changed little despite the vast changes in social and economic structure that had taken place in the process of industrialization during the second half of the eighteenth century.

Some members of Parliament urged timely reforms. In 1828, Parliament repealed a seventeenth-century act that in effect barred Catholics and Nonconformists (non-Anglican Protestants) from government positions and from universities. In 1833, slavery was abolished within the British Empire. (The slave trade had been abolished earlier.) The Municipal Corporations Act (1835) granted towns and cities greater authority over their affairs; it created local governments that could begin to solve some problems of urbanization and industrialization. These municipal corporations could institute reforms such as sanitation, which Parliament encouraged by passing the first Public Health Act in 1848.

Increasingly, reform centered on extending suffrage and on enfranchising the new industrial towns. Middle-class men, and even workers, hoped to gain the right to vote. Because of population shifts, some sparsely populated regions, called *rotten boroughs*, sent representatives to the House of Commons, while many densely populated factory towns had little or no representation. Often a single important landowner controlled many seats in the Commons. Because voting was public, it made intimidation possible, and candidates frequently tried to influence voters with drinks, food, and even money.

Bitter feelings built up during the campaign for the Reform Bill of 1832. The House of Commons passed the bill to extend suffrage by some 200,000 men, almost double the number then entitled to vote. The House of Lords, however, refused to pass the bill. There were riots and strikes in many cities, and mass meetings, both of workers and of the middle class, took place all over the country. King William IV (1830–1837) became convinced, along with many politicians, that the situation was potentially revolutionary. To defuse it, he threatened to increase the number of the bill's supporters in the House of Lords by creating new peers. This threat brought reluctant peers into line, and the bill was passed. The Reform Act of 1832 extended the suffrage to the middle class and made the House of Commons more representative. The rotten boroughs lost their seats, which were granted to towns. Suffrage did not extend to workers, however, because there were high property qualifications.

During the 1830s and 1840s, reformers called *Chartists* agitated for democratic measures, such as universal manhood suffrage, the secret ballot, salaries and the abolition of property qualifications for members of Parliament, and annual elections for Parliament. The Chartists came from the ranks of both intellectual radicals and workers. Their platform remained the democratic reform program for the rest of the century, long after the death of Chartism itself at midcentury. All of the Chartists' demands, except annual elections for members of Parliament, were eventually realized.

The last political effort by the Chartists was led by Feargus O'Connor, a charismatic Irishman, who organized a mass demonstration to present a huge petition of six demands to Parliament in 1848. The cabinet ignored the great charter, which had the signatures of at least two million people. The movement died out just as most of Europe burst into revolution. The working-class leadership of Chartism turned away from political programs and focused almost exclusively on economic activity, such as trade unions, which could bring immediate benefits to workers.

Unlike the Continental states, England avoided revolution. British politicians held that the reason was that they had made timely reforms in the 1830s and 1840s, and this lesson should guide the state in the future. British parliamentary government came to be the model of liberal, progressive, and stable politics, a symbol for all those who

LIBERTY LEADING THE PEOPLE, 1830, BY EUGÈNE DELACROIX (1799–1863). Early-nineteenth-century reformers found their rallying cry in "liberty," a legacy of the French Revolution. In this painting, Delacroix, the leader of the French romantic artists, glorifies liberty. (RMN-Grand Palais/Art Resource, N.Y.)

argued for reform rather than revolution. In the rest of Europe in 1848, however, such arguments were meeting with little success.

THE REVOLUTIONS OF 1848:

FRANCE

In 1848, often called the Year of Revolution, uprisings for political liberty and nationhood took place throughout Europe. The economic crisis of the previous two years had intensified unrest. Food riots broke out in many places. The decimation of the potato crop by disease and of the grain harvest by drought had caused terrible food shortages. Furthermore, a financial crisis precipitated by overspeculation had caused business failures, unemployment, and reduced wages. The common people blamed their governments for their misery and sought redress. Doubtless, economic hardship aggravated discontent with the existing regimes.

But "it was the absence of liberty," concludes the historian Jacques Droz, "which . . . was most deeply resented by the peoples of Europe and led them to take up arms."[1]

The February Revolution

An uprising in Paris set in motion the revolutionary tidal wave that was to engulf much of Europe in 1848. The Revolution of 1830 had broken the back of the ultras in France. There would be no going back to the Old Regime. But King Louis Philippe and his ministers, moderates by temperament and philosophy, had no intention of going forward to democracy. A new law in 1831 broadened the franchise from fewer than 100,000 voters to 248,000 by 1846. Even so, only 3 percent of adult males qualified to vote.

The government of Louis Philippe was run by a small elite consisting of wealthy bourgeois bankers, merchants, and lawyers, as well as aristocrats who had abandoned the hope of restoring the Old Regime. This ruling elite championed the revolutionary ideas of equal treatment under the law and of careers open to talent, but, fearing democracy, it blocked efforts to broaden the franchise. When the less wealthy bourgeoisie protested against the limited franchise, which still excluded professionals and small tradesmen, François Guizot, the leading minister, arrogantly proclaimed: "Get rich, then you can vote." The ruling elite had become a selfish, entrenched oligarchy, unresponsive to the aspirations of the rest of the nation. Intellectuals denounced the government for its narrow political base and voiced republican sentiments. To guard against republicanism and as a reaction to repeated attempts to assassinate the king, the government cracked down on radical societies and newspapers.

Radical republicans, or democrats, wanted to abolish monarchy and grant all men the vote. They had fought in the Revolution of 1830 but were disappointed with the results. Patriots and romantics, who looked back longingly on the glory days of Napoleon, also hated Louis Philippe's government. These French nationalists complained that the king, who dressed like a businessman and pursued a pacifist foreign policy, was not fit to lead a nation of patriots and warriors. Under Louis Philippe, they said, France could not realize its historic mission of liberating oppressed nationalities throughout Europe.

The strongest rumblings of discontent, barely heeded by the ruling elite, came from the laboring poor. Many French workers, still engaged mainly in pre–Industrial Revolution occupations, were literate and concerned with politics; they read the numerous books and newspapers that denounced social injustice and called for social change. Artisans and their families had participated in the great revolutionary outbreaks of 1789 and had defended the barricades in 1830. Favoring a democratic republic that would aid the common people, they felt betrayed by the regime of Louis Philippe, which had brought them neither political representation nor economic reform.

The few factory workers and the artisans in small workshops were becoming attracted to socialist thinkers, who attacked capitalism and called for state programs to deal with poverty. Louis Blanc, a particularly popular socialist theorist, denounced capitalist competition

and demanded that the government establish cooperative workshops. Owned by the workers themselves, these workshops would ensure employment for the jobless.

A poor harvest in 1846 and an international financial crisis in 1847, which drastically curtailed French factory production, aggravated the misery of the laboring poor. Prevented by law from striking, unable to meet the financial requirements for voting, and afflicted with massive unemployment, the urban workers wanted relief. Alexis de Tocqueville, in a speech before the Chamber of Deputies on January 29, 1848, captured the mood of the working class.

> *Do you not hear them repeating unceasingly that all that is above them is incapable and unworthy of governing them; that the present distribution of goods throughout the world is unjust; that property rests on a foundation which is not an equitable foundation? And do you not realize that when such opinions take root, when they spread in an almost universal manner, when they sink deeply into the masses, they are bound to bring with them sooner or later, I know not when nor how, a most formidable revolution?*
>
> *This, gentlemen, is my profound conviction: I believe that we are at this moment sleeping on a volcano. I am profoundly convinced of it.*[2]

The government, however, steadfastly refused to pass reforms. Its middle-class opponents sidestepped regulations against political assemblies and demonstrations by gathering at large banquets to press for expansion of suffrage. When the government foolishly tried to block future banquets, students and workers took to the streets in February 1848, denouncing Guizot and demanding reforms. Barricades went up. Attempting to defuse an explosive situation, Louis Philippe dismissed the unpopular Guizot. But the barricades, commanded by republicans, stayed, and the antigovernment demonstrations continued. When soldiers, confused by a shot that perhaps had gone off accidentally, fired directly into a crowd and killed more than fifty men and women, the situation got out of hand. Unable to pacify the enraged Parisians, who had set up barricades in many parts of the city, Louis Philippe abdicated. France became a republic, and the people of Paris were jubilant.

The June Days: Revolution of the Oppressed

Except for one workingman, the leadership of the provisional government established in February consisted of bourgeois. The new leaders were committed to political democracy, but only some, notably the socialist Louis Blanc, favored social reforms. Most of the ministers had little understanding of or sympathy for the plight of the laboring poor, and they viewed socialist ideas as a threat to private property. Although they considered it a sacred duty to fight for the rights of the individual, they did not include freedom from hunger and poverty among these rights. The middle class saw itself as separate from the laboring poor by reason of occupation and wealth. To the bourgeoisie, the workers were dangerous creatures, "the wild ones," "the vile mob."

Meanwhile, workers who could find jobs labored twelve and fourteen hours a day under brutalizing conditions. In some districts, one out of three children died before the age of five. Everywhere in France, beggars, paupers, prostitutes, and criminals were evidence of the struggle to survive.

The urban poor were desperate for jobs and bread. Socialist intellectuals, sympathetic to the plight of the workers, proposed that the state organize producer cooperatives run by workers. Some wanted the state to take over insurance companies, railroads, mines, and other key industries. To the property owners of all classes, such schemes smacked of madness.

The middle-class leaders of the new republic gave all adult males the vote and abolished censorship; however, their attempts to ease the distress of the urban poor were insincere and halfhearted. The government limited the workday to ten hours and legalized labor unions, but it failed to cope effectively with unemployment. The socialist Louis Blanc called for the creation of producer cooperatives in order to guarantee employment for the city poor. The republic responded by establishing national workshops, which provided some employment on public works projects. Most workers, however, received

wages for doing nothing. Drawn by the promise of work, tens of thousands of laborers left the provinces for Paris, swelling the ranks of the unemployed. The national workshops provided work, food, and medical benefits for some of the unemployed. But to the workers, this was a feeble effort to deal with their monumental distress. To the property-owning peasantry and bourgeoisie, the national workshops were a waste of government funds. They viewed the workshops as nests of working-class radicalism, where plans were being hatched to change the economic system and seize their property.

For their participation in the February uprising against Louis Philippe, the workers had obtained meager benefits. When the government closed the workshops, working-class hostility and despair turned to open rebellion. Again, barricades went up in the working-class districts of Paris.

The June Revolution in Paris was unlike previous uprisings in France. It was a revolt against poverty, a cry for the redistribution of property, and a yearning to create a better society that would serve the common good; as such, it foreshadowed the great social upheavals of later generations. What distinguished the revolution, said Alexis de Tocqueville,

> is that it did not aim at changing the form of government, but at altering the order of society. It was not, strictly speaking, a political struggle . . . but a combat of class against class. . . . We behold in it nothing more than a blind and rude, but powerful, effort on the part of the workmen to escape from the necessities of their condition, which had been depicted to them as one of unlawful oppression. . . . These poor people had been told that the wealth of the rich was in some way the produce of a theft practised upon themselves. They had been assured that the inequality of fortunes was as opposed to morality and the welfare of society as it was to nature.[3]

The approximately ten thousand to fifteen thousand insurgents, most from the working class, stood alone. To the rest of the nation, they were barbarians attacking civilized society. Aristocrats, bourgeois, and peasants feared that no one's property would be safe if the revolution succeeded. From hundreds of miles away, Frenchmen

Carl Schurz: Revolution Spreads to the German States

The February Revolution in Paris was eagerly received by German liberals and nationalists who yearned for a Germany governed by a national parliament and a constitution that guaranteed basic liberties. In the following excerpt from his Reminiscences, *Carl Schurz (1829–1906), then a student at the University of Bonn, recalled the expectations of German liberal-nationalists. After the revolution failed, Schurz fled to Switzerland and eventually went to the United States, where he had a distinguished career as a senator, cabinet member, and journalist.*

Now had arrived in Germany the day for the establishment of "German Unity," and the founding of a great, powerful national German Empire. In the first line the convocation of a national parliament. Then the demands for civil rights and liberties, free speech, free press, the right of free assembly, equality before the law, a freely elected representation of the people with legislative power, responsibility of ministers, self-government of the communes, the right of the people to carry arms, the formation of a civic guard with elective officers, and so on—in short, that which was called a "constitutional form of government on a broad democratic basis." Republican ideas were at first only sparingly expressed. But the word democracy was soon on all tongues, and many, too, thought it a matter of course that if the princes should try to withhold from the people the rights and liberties demanded, force would take the place of mere petition. Of course the regeneration of the fatherland must, if possible, be accomplished by peaceable means. A few days after the outbreak of this commotion I reached my nineteenth birthday. I remember to have been so entirely absorbed by what was happening that I could hardly turn my thoughts to anything else. Like many of my friends, I was dominated by the feeling that at last the great opportunity had arrived for giving to the German people the liberty which was their birthright and to the German fatherland its unity and greatness, and that it was now the first duty of every German to do and to sacrifice everything for this sacred object. We were profoundly, solemnly in earnest. . . .

Great news came from Vienna. There the students of the university were the first to assail the Emperor of Austria with the cry for liberty and citizens' rights. Blood flowed in the streets, and the downfall of Prince Metternich was the result. The students organized themselves as the armed guard of liberty. In the great cities of Prussia there was a mighty commotion. Not only Cologne, Coblenz, and Trier, but also Breslau, Königsberg and Frankfurt-on-the-Oder, sent deputations to Berlin to entreat the king. In the Prussian capital the masses surged upon the streets, and everybody looked for events of great import.

Question for Analysis

1. What were the goals of Schurz and many of his colleagues? How did they seek to reconcile nationalism and liberalism?

Carl Schurz, *The Reminiscences of Carl Schurz* (New York: The McClure Co., 1907), Vol. I, see pp. 112–117.

flocked to Paris to crush what they considered to be the madness in their midst.

Although they had no leaders, the workers showed remarkable courage. Women and children fought alongside men behind the barricades. After three days of vicious street fighting and atrocities on both sides, the army, using cannon to demolish the barricades, extinguished the revolt. The government summarily executed in cold blood at least 1,500 suspected insurgents and eventually deported to Algeria many of the 12,000 it arrested. The June Days left deep scars on French society. For many years, workers would never forget that the rest of France had united against them; the rest of France would remain terrified of working-class radicalism.

In December 1848, the French people, in overwhelming numbers, elected Louis Napoleon—nephew of the great emperor—president of the Second Republic. They were attracted to the magic of Louis Napoleon's name, and they expected him to safeguard society and property from future working-class disorders. The election, in which all adult males could vote, demonstrated that most Frenchmen were socially conservative; they were unsympathetic to working-class poverty and deeply suspicious of socialist programs.

THE REVOLUTIONS OF 1848:
GERMANY, AUSTRIA, AND ITALY

Like an epidemic, the fever of revolution that broke out in Paris in February raced across the Continent. Liberals, excluded from participation in political life, fought for parliaments and constitutions; many liberals were also nationalists who wanted unity or independence for their nations. Some liberals had a utopian vision of a new Europe of independent and democratic states. In this vision, reactionary rulers would no longer stifle individual liberty; no longer would a people be denied the right of nationhood.

The German States:
Liberalism Defeated

After the Congress of Vienna, Germany consisted of a loose confederation of thirty-nine independent states, of which Austria and Prussia were the most powerful. Jealous of their states' independence and determined to preserve their absolute authority, the ruling princes detested liberal and nationalist ideals, which—urged on by Metternich—they tried to repress through censorship and the regulation of student associations. In the southern German states, which had been more strongly influenced by the French Revolution, princes did grant constitutions and establish

parliaments to retain the loyalty of their subjects. But even in these states, the princes continued to hold the reins of authority.

The German nationalism that had emerged during the French occupation intensified during the restoration (the post-Napoleonic period) as intellectuals, inspired in part by the ideas of the Romantic Movement, insisted that Germans, who shared a common language and culture, should also be united politically. During the restoration, the struggle for German unity and liberal reforms continued to be waged primarily by students, professors, writers, lawyers, and other educated people. The great mass of people, knowing only loyalty to their local prince, remained unmoved by appeals for national unity.

The successful revolt against Louis Philippe, hostility against absolute princes, and an economic crisis combined to produce uprisings in the capital cities of the German states in March 1848. Everywhere, liberals clamored for constitutions, parliamentary government, freedom of thought, and an end to police intimidation. Some called for the creation of a unified Germany governed by a national parliament and headed by a constitutional monarch. The poor joined the struggle. The Great Depression of the 1840s had aggravated the misery of the German peasants and urban masses, and as the pressures of hunger and unemployment worsened, their discontent exploded into revolutionary fervor.

In the spring of 1848, downtrodden artisans, facing severe competition from the new factories, served as the revolution's shock troops, setting up barricades along with students in Berlin and other cities. Unable to compete with the new machines, they saw their incomes fall and their work decrease. Skilled weavers working at home earned far less than factory hands, and some unemployed craftsmen were forced to take factory jobs, which they regarded as a terrible loss of status. These craftsmen wanted to restrict the growth of factories, curtail capitalist competition, and restore the power of the guilds, which had given them security and status.

Having lost hope that the absolute princes would aid them, craftsmen gave their support to bourgeois liberals, who, without this support, could not challenge the throne or wrest power from the aristocrats. In many German states, the actions of the embittered urban craftsmen determined the successful outcome of the insurrections.

(Factory workers in the emerging industries showed no enthusiasm for revolution, despite the appeals of radical socialists.) Adding to the discomfort of the ruling princes was rioting in the countryside by peasants, goaded by crop failure, debt, and oppressive demands from the aristocracy.

Terrified that these disturbances would lead to anarchy, the princes made concessions to the liberals, whom they previously had censored, jailed, and exiled. During March and April 1848, the traditional rulers in Baden, Württemberg, Bavaria, Saxony, Hanover, and other states replaced reactionary ministers with liberals, eased censorship, established jury systems, framed constitutions, formed parliaments, and ended peasant obligations to lords.

In Prussia, tensions between the army and Berliners exploded into violence. Unable to subdue the insurgents, the army urged bombarding the city with artillery. Frederick William IV opposed the idea and ordered the troops to leave Berlin. The insurgents had won the first round. The Prussian king, like the other German princes, had to agree to the formation of a parliament and the admission of prominent liberals into the government.

But the triumph of the liberals in Prussia and the other German states was not secure. Although reforms liberalized the governments of the German states, the insurrections had not toppled the ruling dynasties. Moreover, the alliance between the bourgeois and the artisans was tenuous. The artisans' violence frightened the property-owning middle class, which sought only moderate political reforms, preferably through peaceful means. In addition, the middle class saw restoration of the medieval guild system, with its restrictions on output and regulation of prices, as a reactionary economic measure.

Liberals took advantage of their successes in Prussia and other German states to form a national assembly charged with the task of creating a unified and liberal Germany. Representatives from all the German states attended the assembly, which met at Frankfurt. The delegates, including many articulate lawyers and professionals, came predominantly from the educated middle class; only a handful were drawn from the lower classes. After many long debates, the Frankfurt Assembly approved a federation of German states; it would have a parliament and would be headed by the Prussian king. Austria, with its many non-German nationalities, would be excluded from the federal union. Some radical democrats wanted to proclaim a German republic, but they were an ineffective minority. Most delegates were moderate liberals who feared that universal suffrage and the abolition of monarchy would lead to plebeian rule and the destruction of the social order. The deputies selected Frederick William as emperor of the new Germany, but the Prussian king refused; he would never wear a crown given to him by common people during a period of revolutionary agitation.

While the delegates debated, the ruling princes recovered from the first shock of revolution and ordered their armies to crush the revolutionaries. The February Revolution in Paris had shown European liberals that authority could be challenged successfully; the June Days, however, had shown the authorities that revolutionaries could be beaten by professional soldiers. Moreover, the German middle class, frightened by lower-class agitation and unsympathetic to the artisans' demands to restrict capitalism and restore guilds, was losing its enthusiasm for revolution, and so too were the artisans. The disintegration of the alliance between middle-class liberals and urban artisans deprived the revolutionaries of mass support. A revival of the Old Order would not face much resistance.

In Prussia, a determined Frederick William ordered his troops to reoccupy Berlin. In March, the citizens of Berlin had fought against the king's troops, but in November, no barricades went up in Berlin. Prussian forces also assisted the other German states in crushing the new parliaments. The masses of workers and peasants did not fight to save the liberal governments, which fell one by one. A small minority of democrats resisted, particularly in Baden; many of these revolutionaries died in the fighting or were executed.

The rulers of the various German states, supported by the army, the aristocracy, and the bureaucracy, retained their power. German liberalism had failed to unite Germany or to create a constitutional government dominated by the middle class. Liberalism, never securely rooted in Germany, was discredited. In the following decades, many Germans, identifying liberalism with failure, turned to authoritarian Prussia for leadership in the struggle for unification. The fact that authoritarians hostile to the spirit of parliamentary government eventually united Germany had deep implications for future German and European history.

Frantisek Palacky

Francis Palacky (1798–1876), Czech historian and statesman, is regarded by the Czech people as the founder of their nation. Palacky was a leader in the "Czech renaissance," a cultural revival in the first half of the nineteenth century. At that time, Czech writers began to use the Czech language as a vehicle of literary expression. (Until then, German had been the dominant literary language.) This facilitated the Czechs' discovery of their historical past and helped shape a national identity.

During the revolution of 1848, Palacky became the political spokesman for his people, advocating the right of the Czech nation to exist along with the other small nations of Austria in a federation of Danubian nations under the jurisdiction of the Hapsburg Empire. He participated in the Constitutional Assembly, which met in Vienna in 1848 to draft a constitution for the Empire. After months of deliberation, the assembly was disbanded by the emperor's army.

After the revolution, Palacky concentrated on completing his monumental *History of the Czech Nation*. The entire project occupied him over forty years. In the introduction, he wrote, "From my youth I have known no higher goal than to provide my beloved nation with a portrait of its past, in which, as in a mirror, it could recognize itself and remember what its needs are."

Palacky revered the ideals of the Enlightenment and supported the reforms of the French Revolution calling for constitutional government and protection of individual rights. The nationalism he advocated was liberal and cosmopolitan, not exclusive and intolerant. In contrast to many nineteenth-century nationalists who descended into a world of irrational and dangerous myths, Palacky's love of the Czech nation was circumscribed by a respect for humanity and reason. He wanted the Czechs, whom he regarded as being among the forerunners of the Enlightenment, to take their place in the modern age as an independent nation among the progressive nations of the world.

Palacky's liberal nationalism inspired twentieth-century Czech democrats, including Tomáš Masaryk, Eduard Beneš, and, more recently, Václav Havel.

In 1848, German political aspirations—the creation of a constitutional government—coincided with the goals of liberals in Western European lands. However, in the late nineteenth century, whereas Western European states were becoming more liberal, Germany moved in an authoritarian direction. The political systems that prevailed after 1848 stifled the growth of liberal-constitutional government.

Austria: Hapsburg Dominance

The Hapsburg Empire, the product of dynastic marriage and inheritance, had no common nationality or language; it was held together only by the reigning Hapsburg dynasty, its army, and its bureaucracy. The ethnic composition of the empire was enormously complex. Germans dominated; concentrated principally in Austria, they constituted about 25 percent of the empire's population. The Magyars predominated in the Hungarian lands of the empire. The great bulk of the population consisted of Slavs: Czechs, Poles, Slovaks, Slovenes, Croats, Serbs, and Ruthenians. There were also Italians in northern Italy and Romanians in Transylvania. The Hapsburg dynasty, aided by the army and the German-dominated civil service, prevented this multinational empire from collapsing into anarchy.

Metternich, it is often said, suffered from a "dissolution complex": he understood that the new forces of nationalism and liberalism could break up the Austrian Empire. Liberal ideas could lead Hapsburg subjects to challenge the authority of the emperor, and nationalist feelings could cause the different peoples of the empire to rebel against German domination and Hapsburg rule. To keep these ideas from infecting Austrian subjects, Metternich's police imposed strict censorship, spied on professors, and expelled from the universities students caught reading forbidden books. Despite Metternich's political police, the universities remained hotbeds of liberalism.

In 1848, revolutions spread throughout the Austrian Empire, starting in Vienna. Aroused by the abdication of Louis Philippe, Viennese liberals denounced Hapsburg absolutism and demanded a constitution, relaxation of censorship, and restrictions on the police. The government responded hesitantly and with limited force to the demonstrations of students and workers, and many parts of Vienna fell to the revolutionaries. The authorities used force that was strong enough to incense the insurrectionists and create martyrs but not strong enough to subdue them. Confused and intimidated by the revolutionaries, the government allowed freedom of the press, accepted Metternich's resignation, and promised a constitution. The Constitutional Assembly was convened and in August voted the abolition of serfdom. At the same time that the Viennese insurgents were tasting the heady wine of reform, revolts in other parts of the empire—Bohemia, Hungary, and northern Italy—added to the distress of the monarchy.

But the revolutionaries' victory was only temporary, and the defeat of the Old Order only illusory; the Hapsburg government soon began to recover its balance. The first government victory came with the crushing of the Czechs in Bohemia. In 1848, Czech nationalists wanted the Austrian Empire reconstructed along federal lines that would give Czechs equal standing with Germans. The Czechs called for a constitution for Bohemia and equal status for the Czech language in all official business. In June, students and destitute workers engaged in violent demonstrations, which frightened the middle and upper classes—both Czech and German. General Alfred zu Windischgrätz bombarded Prague, the capital of Bohemia, into submission and reestablished Hapsburg control.

In October 1848, Hapsburg authorities ordered the army to bombard Vienna. Against the regular army, the courageous but disorganized and divided students and workers had little hope. Imperial troops broke into the city, overcame resistance,

and executed several of the revolutionary leaders. In March 1849, the Hapsburg leadership replaced the liberal constitution drafted by the popularly elected Constitutional Assembly with a more conservative one drawn up by its own ministers.

The most serious threat to the Hapsburg realm came from the Magyars in Hungary. Some twelve million people lived in Hungary, five million of whom were Magyars. The other nationalities comprised South Slavs (Croats and Serbs) and Romanians. The upper class consisted chiefly of Magyar landowners, who enjoyed tax exemptions and other feudal privileges. Drawn to liberal and modern ideas and fearful of peasant uprisings, some Hungarian nobles pressed for an end to serfdom and the tax exemptions of the nobility. Louis Kossuth (1802–1894), a member of the lower nobility, called for both social reform and a deepening of national consciousness. The great landowners, determined to retain their ancient privileges, resisted liberalization.

Led by Kossuth, the Magyars demanded local autonomy for Hungary. Hungary would remain within the Hapsburg Empire but would have its own constitution and national army and would control its own finances. The Hungarian leadership introduced liberal reforms: suffrage for all males who could speak Magyar and owned some property, freedom of religion, freedom of the press, the termination of serfdom, and the end of the privileges of nobles and the church. Within a few weeks, the Hungarian parliament changed Hungary from a feudal to a modern liberal state.

But the Hungarian leaders' nationalist dreams towered above their liberal ideals. The Magyars intended to incorporate lands inhabited by Croats, Slovaks, and Romanians into their state (Magyars considered these lands an integral part of historic Hungary) and to transform these peoples into Hungarians. As the historian Hugh Seton-Watson has written,

> *Kossuth and his friends genuinely believed that they were doing the non-Hungarians a kindness by giving them a chance of becoming absorbed in the superior Hungarian culture. To refuse this kindness was nationalist fanaticism; to impose it by force was to promote progress. The suggestion that Romanians, Slovaks, or Serbs were nations, with a national culture of their own, was simply ridiculous nonsense.*[4]

In the spring of 1849, the Hungarians renounced their allegiance to the Hapsburgs and proclaimed Hungary an independent state, with Kossuth as president.

The Hapsburg rulers took advantage of the ethnic animosities inside and outside Hungary. They encouraged Romanians and Croats to resist the new Hungarian government. When Hapsburg forces moved against the Magyars, they were joined by an army of Croats, whose nationalist aspirations had been flouted by the Magyars. (The Slovaks fought alongside the Magyars.) Emperor Francis Joseph, who had recently ascended the Hapsburg throne, also appealed to Tsar Nicholas I for help. The tsar complied, fearing that a successful revolt by the Hungarians might lead the Poles to rise up against their Russian overlords. The Hungarians fought with extraordinary courage but were overcome by superior might. Kossuth and other rebel leaders went into exile; about one hundred rebel leaders were executed. Thus, through division and alliance, the Hapsburgs prevented the disintegration of the empire.

Italy: Continued Fragmentation

Italian nationalists, eager to end the humiliation of Hapsburg occupation and domination and to unite the disparate states into a unified and liberal nation, also rose in rebellion. Revolutions broke out in Sicily six weeks before the February Revolution in Paris. Bowing to the revolutionaries' demands, King Ferdinand II of Naples granted a liberal constitution. The Grand Duke of Tuscany, King Charles Albert of Piedmont-Sardinia, and Pope Pius IX, ruler of the Papal States, also felt compelled to introduce liberal reforms.

Then the revolution spread to the Hapsburg lands in the north. The citizens of Milan, in Lombardy, built barricades and stood ready to fight the Austrian oppressor. When the Austrian soldiers attacked, they were fired on from nearby windows. From rooftops, Italians hurled stones and boiling water. After "Five Glorious Days" (March 18 through 22) of street fighting, the Austrians withdrew. The people of Milan had liberated their city. On March 22, the citizens of Venice declared their city free of Austria and set up a republic. King Charles Albert, who hoped to acquire Lombardy and Venetia, declared war on Austria. Intimidated by the insurrections, the

ruling princes of the Italian states and Hapsburg Austria had lost the first round.

But soon everywhere in Italy the forces of reaction recovered and reasserted their authority. The Austrians defeated the Sardinians and reoccupied Milan, and Ferdinand II crushed the revolutionaries in the south. Revolutionary disorders in Rome had forced Pope Pius IX to flee in November 1848; in February 1849, the revolutionaries proclaimed Rome "a pure democracy with the glorious title of the Roman Republic." Heeding the pope's call for assistance, Louis Napoleon attacked Rome, destroyed the infant republic, and allowed Pope Pius to return. The last city to fall to the reactionaries was Venice, which the Austrians subjected to a merciless bombardment. After six weeks, the Venetians, weakened by starvation and cholera, surrendered. Reactionary princes still ruled in Italy; the Hapsburg occupation persisted in the north. Italy was still a fragmented nation.

THE REVOLUTIONS OF 1848: AN ASSESSMENT

The revolutions of 1848 in Central Europe and Italy began with much promise but ended in defeat. "We stood on the threshold of paradise—but the gates slammed in our faces," wrote one dejected intellectual.[5] The revolutionaries' initial success was due less to their strength than to the governments' hesitancy to use their superior force. The reactionary rulers overcame their paralysis, however, and moved decisively to smash the revolutions. The courage of the revolutionaries was no match for regular armies. Thousands were killed and imprisoned; many fled to America.

Class divisions weakened the revolutionaries in Central Europe. The union between middle-class liberals and workers, which brought success in the opening stages of the revolutions, was only temporary. Bourgeois liberals favoring political reforms—constitution, parliament, and protection of basic rights—grew fearful of the laboring poor, who demanded social reforms—jobs and bread. To the bourgeois, the workers were radical Jacobins, a mob driven by dark instincts that threatened property and social stability. When the workers engaged in revolutionary violence, a terrified middle class deserted the cause of revolution or joined the old elites in subduing the workers. These class

REVOLUTION IN VIENNA, MAY 1848. A student leads armed railway workers.
(Erich Lessing/Art Resource, N.Y.)

divisions showed that the liberals' concern for political reforms—the extension of suffrage and parliamentary government—did not satisfy workers who were mired in poverty. The events of 1848 also showed that social issues—the demands of the working class for an alleviation of their misery— would become a prime consideration of European political life in the generations to come.

Intractable nationalist animosities helped destroy all the revolutionary movements against absolutism in Central Europe. In many cases, the different nationalities hated each other more than they hated the reactionary rulers. Hungarian revolutionaries dismissed the nationalist yearnings of the South Slavs and Romanians living in Hungary, who in turn helped the Hapsburg dynasty extinguish the nascent Hungarian state. The Germans of Bohemia resisted Czech demands for self-government and the equality of the Czech language with German. When German liberals at the Frankfurt Assembly debated the boundary lines of a united Germany, the problem of Prussia's Polish territories emerged. In 1848, Polish patriots wanted to re-create the Polish nation, but German delegates at the convention, by an overwhelming majority, opposed returning the Polish lands seized by Prussia in the late eighteenth century. In addressing his fellow delegates, Wilhelm Jordan described the Poles as a people "which does not possess the same measure of human content as is given to the German kind" and denounced those Germans who would permit their kinsmen to live under Polish rule as traitors to their people. Then he justified Germany's claim to the Polish lands.

> *It is high time for us to wake up . . . to a healthy national egoism . . . which places the welfare and honor of the fatherland above everything else. . . . Frankly, the rules of theoretical justice never seem more pitiful to me than when they presume to fix the fate of nations. . . . No, I admit without blinking, our right is no other than the right of the stronger, the right of conquest.*[6]

Before 1848, democratic idealists envisioned the birth of a new Europe of free people and liberated nations. The revolutions in Central Europe showed that nationalism and liberalism were not natural allies and that nationalists were often indifferent to the rights of other peoples. Disheartened by these nationalist antagonisms, John Stuart Mill, the English liberal statesman and philosopher, lamented that "the sentiment of nationality

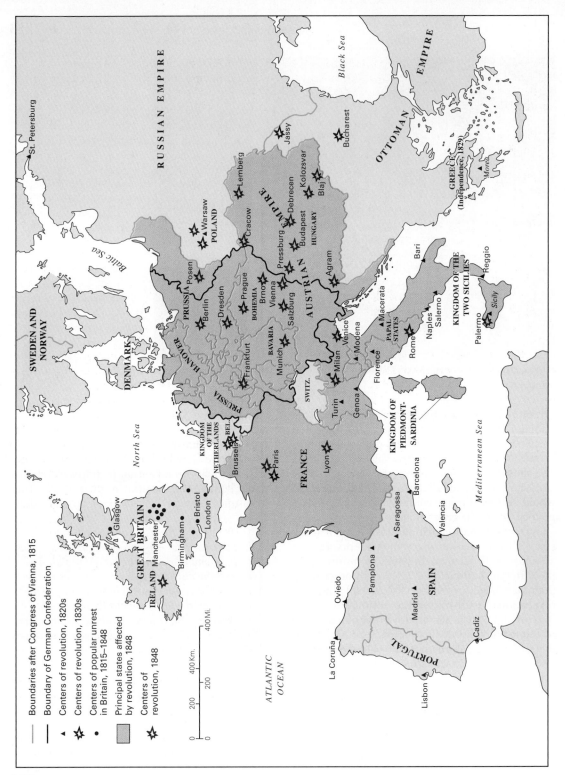

Boundaries after Congress of Vienna, 1815

Boundary of German Confederation

▲ Centers of revolution, 1820s

✪ Centers of revolution, 1830s

• Centers of popular unrest in Britain, 1815–1848

Principal states affected by revolution, 1848

✪ Centers of revolution, 1848

400 Mi.

400 Km.

200

200

RUSSIAN EMPIRE

Black Sea

OTTOMAN EMPIRE

St. Petersburg

Baltic Sea

SWEDEN AND NORWAY

DENMARK

North Sea

GREAT BRITAIN

Glasgow

Manchester

Birmingham

Bristol

London

IRELAND

KINGDOM OF THE NETHERLANDS

Brussels

BEL.

HANOVER

PRUSSIA

Berlin

Dresden

Frankfurt

Munich

BAVARIA

SWITZ.

Posen

PRUSSIA

Warsaw

POLAND

Cracow

Lemberg

Prague

BOHEMIA

Brno

Vienna

Salzburg

Pressburg

AUSTRIAN EMPIRE

Budapest

HUNGARY

Agram

Debrecen

Kolozsvar

Blaj

Jassy

Bucharest

GREECE
(Independence, 1829)

Morea

Paris

FRANCE

Lyon

Turin

Genoa

KINGDOM OF PIEDMONT-SARDINIA

Milan

Venice

Modena

Florence

PAPAL STATES

Macerata

Rome

Bari

Naples

Salerno

KINGDOM OF THE TWO SICILIES

Palermo

Sicily

Reggio

Mediterranean Sea

SPAIN

Madrid

Oviedo

Pamplona

Saragossa

Barcelona

Valencia

Cadiz

La Coruña

PORTUGAL

Lisbon

ATLANTIC OCEAN

◀ *Map 22.3* Europe's Age of Revolutions
In the decades after the Vienna settlement, Europe experienced a wave of revolution based chiefly on liberalism and nationalism. (© 2016 Cengage Learning.)

so far outweighs the love of liberty that the people are willing to abet their rulers in crushing the liberty and independence of any people not of their race or language."[7] In the revolutions of 1848, concludes the British historian Lewis Namier, "'nationality,' the passionate creed of the intellectuals, invades the politics of central and east-central Europe, and with 1848 starts the Great European War of every nation against its neighbors."[8]

Even though the liberal and nationalist aims of the revolutionaries were not realized, liberal gains were not insignificant. All French men obtained the right to vote. The new republican government abolished slavery throughout the French Empire. Peasant obligations to lords, a survival of medieval serfdom, were either abolished or greatly reduced in the German states and Austria; and parliaments were established in Prussia and other German states.

Despite the establishment of parliaments, however, the year 1848 represented a crucial defeat for German liberalism. Controlled by monarchs and aristocrats hostile to the democratic principles of 1848, the postrevolutionary governments, using the methods of a police state, intimidated and persecuted liberals, large numbers of whom were forced to emigrate. The failure of the revolution and the reactionary policies of the postrevolutionary governments thwarted the growth of a democratic parliamentary system in Germany. Discredited by the failure of 1848, weakened by government intimidation and the loss of many liberals to emigration, and less committed to liberal ideals—which brought no gains in 1848—the German middle class in the period immediately after 1848 became apolitical or was willing to sacrifice liberal principles in order to achieve a united and powerful Germany. Nationalism would supersede liberalism as the principal concern of the German middle class. The failure to unify Germany by liberal parliamentary methods in 1848 and the subsequent submission of liberals to an authoritarian Prussian-dominated Germany would have dire consequences in the early twentieth century.

In later decades, liberal reforms, including legal guarantees of basic rights, would be introduced peacefully in several European countries—in Germany too, but there power still remained in the hands of preindustrial semifeudal elites, not with the middle class—for the failure of the revolutions of 1848 convinced many people, including liberals, that popular uprisings were ineffective ways of changing society. The age of revolution, initiated by the French Revolution of 1789, had ended.

❖   ❖   ❖

Notes

1. Jacques Droz, *Europe Between Revolutions, 1815–1848* (New York: Harper Torchbooks, 1967), 248.

2. *The Recollections of Alexis de Tocqueville*, trans. Alexander Teixeira de Mattos (Cleveland, Ohio: Meridian Books, 1969), 11–12.

3. Ibid., 250.

4. Hugh Seton-Watson, *Nations and States* (Boulder, Colo.: Westview Press, 1977), 162.

5. Quoted in Adam Zamoyski, *Holy Madness: Romantics, Patriots, and Revolutionaries,* 1776–1871 (London: Weidenfeld and Nicolson, 1999), 356.

6. Quoted in J. L. Talmon, *Political Messianism: The Romantic Phase* (New York: Praeger, 1960), 482.

7. Quoted in Hans Kohn, *Nationalism: Its Meaning and History* (Princeton, N.J.: Van Nostrand, 1965), 51–52.

8. Lewis Namier, 1848: *The Revolution of the Intellectuals* (Garden City, N.Y.: Doubleday, Anchor, 1964), 38.

Part Five

An Age of Contradiction: Progress and Breakdown

1848–1914

1850

1860

1870

1880

1890

1900

Politics and Society

Second Empire in France (1852–1870)
Commodore Perry opens Japan to trade (1853)
Crimean War (1853–1856)
Unification of Italy (1859–1870)

Civil War in the United States (1861–1865)
Bismarck in power in Germany (1862–1890)
Unification of Germany (1866–1871)
Settlement of 1867 splits Hapsburg territories into Austria and Hungary
Reform Bill of 1867 in Great Britain
Opening of Suez Canal (1869)

Franco-Prussian War (1870–1871)
Third Republic in France (1870–1940)
Serbs gain independence from Ottoman Turks (1878)

French fight Chinese over Indochina (1883–1885)
Berlin Conference on Africa (1884)
Reform Bill of 1884 in Great Britain

Dreyfus affair in France (1894–1906)
Sino-Japanese War (1894–1895)
Spanish-American War (1898)
Battle of Omdurman in the Sudan (1898)
Boer War in South Africa (1899–1902)

Boxer Rebellion in China (1900)
Russo-Japanese War (1904–1905)
Anglo-French Entente Cordiale (1904)
Anglo-Russian Entente (1907)
Congo declared a Belgian colony (1908)
Mexican Revolution (1911)

Thought and Culture

Stowe, *Uncle Tom's Cabin* (1851–1852)
Dickens, *Hard Times* (1854)
Flaubert, *Madame Bovary* (1856)
Darwin, *Origin of Species* (1859)
Mill, *On Liberty* (1859)

Hugo, *Les Misérables* (1862)
Marx, *Capital* (1867)
Dostoyevsky, *The Idiot* (1868–1869)
Tolstoy, *War and Peace* (1863–1869)
Mill, *The Subjection of Women* (1869)

Impressionism in art (1860–1886): Manet, Monet, Pissarro, Degas, Renoir
Darwin, *The Descent of Man* (1871)
Nietzsche, *The Birth of Tragedy* (1872)
Ibsen, *A Doll's House* (1879)

Postimpressionism in art (1880s–1890s): Cézanne, Gauguin, van Gogh, Munch, Matisse
Zola, *The Experimental Novel* (1880)
Spencer, *The Man Versus the State* (1884)
Nietzsche, *The Anti-Christ* (1888)

Le Bon, *The Crowd* (1895)
Chamberlain, *The Foundations of the Nineteenth Century* (1899)
Bernstein, *Evolutionary Socialism* (1899)
Durkheim, *Suicide* (1897)

Freud, *The Interpretation of Dreams* (1900)
Cubism in art: Picasso, Braque
Abstract art: Mondrian, Kandinsky, Duchamp
Planck: quantum theory (1900)
Lenin, *What Is to Be Done?* (1902)
Einstein: theory of relativity (1905)
Weber, *The Protestant Ethic and the Spirit of Capitalism* (1904–1905)
Sorel, *Reflections on Violence* (1908)

Chapter 23

Thought and Culture in the Mid-Nineteenth Century: Realism and Social Criticism

The Stone Breakers *(1849), by Gustave Courbet. This painting illustrates the concern of realists for an accurate depiction of the details of everyday life.* (Foto Marburg/Art Resource, N.Y.)

- **Realism and Naturalism**
- **Positivism**
- **Darwinism**
- **Religion in a Secular Age**
- **Marxism**
- **Anarchism**
- **Liberalism in Transition**
- **Feminism: Extending the Principle of Equality**

Focus Questions

1. Why is the mid-nineteenth century described as an age of realism? How does realism differ from romanticism?

2. How did Darwin's theory affect conceptions of time, human origins, religious doctrines, and nationalism?

3. What did Marx have in common with the philosophes of the Enlightenment? What relationship did he see between economics and politics? Between economics and thought?

4. How has history treated Marx's claims and predictions?

5. How was the evolution of liberalism exemplified in the theories of Mill, Green, and Spencer?

6. How may the feminist movement be regarded as an outgrowth of certain ideals that had emerged during the course of Western history?

The second half of the nineteenth century was marked by great progress in science, a surge in industrialism, and a continuing secularization of life and thought. The principal intellectual currents of the century's middle decades reflected these trends. Realism, positivism, Darwinism, Marxism, and liberalism all reacted against romantic, religious, and metaphysical interpretations of nature and society and focused on the empirical world. In one way or another, each movement derived from and expanded the Enlightenment tradition. Adherents of these movements relied on careful observation and strove for scientific accuracy. This emphasis on objective reality helped stimulate a growing criticism of social ills; for despite unprecedented material progress, reality was often sordid, somber, and depressing. In the last part of the century, reformers, motivated by an expansive liberalism, a socially committed Christianity, or both, pressed for the alleviation of social injustice.

REALISM AND NATURALISM

Realism, the dominant movement in art and literature in the mid-1800s, opposed the romantic veneration of the inner life and romantic sentimentality. The romantics exalted passion and intuition; let their imaginations transport them to a medieval past, which they deemed idyllic; and sought subjective solitude amid nature's wonders. Realists, in contrast, turned their attention to the external world and concentrated on social conditions, contemporary manners, and the familiar details of everyday life. With clinical detachment and meticulous care, they analyzed how people actually looked, worked, and behaved.

Like scientists, realist writers and artists carefully investigated the empirical world in order to depict with unwavering frankness life as it actually is in all its nakedness, ugliness, and beauty. For example, Gustave Courbet (1819–1877), who exemplified realism in painting, sought to practice what he called a "living art." He painted common people and commonplace scenes: laborers breaking stones, peasants tilling the soil or returning from a fair, a country burial, wrestlers, bathers,

Profile

Charles Dickens

In his novels, Charles Dickens (1812–1870) blamed social institutions for the misery of the downtrodden. In doing so, he helped awaken the moral conscience of his day. In his early novels, Dickens deftly blends melodrama with playful humor and comedic characters, such as the Artful Dodger and Fagin, leaders of a den of pickpockets, prostitutes, and thieves in *Oliver Twist*. Dickens also demonstrates how uncaring adults mistreat children, and he evokes sympathy for society's youthful victims—the orphan Oliver Twist and his friend, Nancy, who is brutally murdered by her boyfriend, Sikes, when she tries to help Oliver escape from Sikes's gang. In *The Life and Adventures of Nicholas Nickleby* (1839), Dickens exposes the abusive treatment of children. In *Bleak House* (1853), he confronted the iniquities of the British judicial system which cried out for reform.

Hard Times, which takes place in an industrial town called Coketown, contains numerous and masterful examples of realist writing.

> It was a town of red brick, or of brick that would have been red if the smoke and ashes had allowed it; but, as matters stood it was a town of unnatural red and black like the painted face of a savage. It was a town of machinery and tall chimneys, out of which interminable serpents of smoke trailed themselves for ever and ever, and never got uncoiled. It had a black canal in it, and a river that ran purple with ill-smelling dye, and vast piles of buildings full of windows where there was a rattling and a trembling all day long, and where the piston of the steam-engine worked monotonously up and down, like the head of an elephant in a state of melancholy madness. It contained several large streets all very like one another, and many small streets still more like one another, inhabited by people equally like one another, who all went in and out at the same hours, with the same sound upon the same pavements, to do the same work, and to whom every day was the same as yesterday and tomorrow, and every year the counterpart of the last and the next.*

Dickens recognized that the monotony and stupefying conditions of industrial life crushed the spirit of the workers, curtailing both imagination and culture. Moreover, exploitation of the working class fostered class tensions because the workers viewed government institutions as being impervious to their needs and intent only on protecting the privileged status of the entrepreneurs and industrial elites. Dickens used *A Tale of Two Cities* (1859) to issue a warning: if the political elites of England did not effectively address the need for social reform, England, like France, would become embroiled in revolutionary violence.

---

*Charles Dickens, *Hard Times* (New York: Penguin Books, 1985), 65.

---

family groups. In a matter-of-fact style that sought to reproduce the environment just as it is, without any attempt at glorification or deviation, realist artists also depicted floor scrapers, rag pickers, prostitutes, and beggars. Gustave Flaubert (1821–1880) said of *Madame Bovary*, his masterpiece of realist literature: "Art ought . . . to rise above personal feelings and nervous susceptibilities! It is time to give it the precision of the physical sciences by means of a pitiless method."[1] Émile de Vogüé, a nineteenth-century French writer, described realism as follows:

> They [realists] have brought about an art of observation rather than of imagination, one which boasts that it observes life as it is in its wholeness and complexity with the least possible prejudice on the part of the artist. It takes men under ordinary conditions, shows characters in the course of their everyday

existence, average and changing. Jealous of the rigour of scientific procedure, the writer proposes to instruct us by a perpetual analysis of feelings and of acts rather than to divert us or move us by intrigue and exhibition of the passions. . . . The new art seeks to imitate nature.[2]

Romantic writers had written lyrics, for lyric poetry is the language of feeling. The realists' literary genre was the novel because it lends itself admirably to depicting human behavior and social conditions. Realist novels were often serialized in the inexpensive newspapers and magazines, which the many newly literate common people could read. Thus, the commoners' interests helped shape the novels' content. Seeking to portray reality as it is, realist writers frequently dealt with social abuses and the sordid aspects of human behavior and social life.

In his large output of novels, Honoré de Balzac (1799–1850) described how social and economic forces affected people's behavior. Another Frenchman, Eugène Sue, gave harrowing accounts of slum life and crime in his serialized novel, *Les Mystères de Paris* (1842–1843). George Sand (a woman writing under a male pen name) portrayed the married woman as a victim in *Indiana* (1832). A reviewer praised the book for presenting

a true, living world, which is our world . . . characters and manners just as we can observe them around us, natural conversations, scenes in familiar settings, violent, uncommon passions, but sincerely felt or observed and such as are still aroused in many hearts, under the apparent uniformity and monotonous frivolity of our lives.[3]

Many regard Gustave Flaubert's *Madame Bovary* (1856) as the quintessential realistic novel. It tells the story of Emma Bovary, a self-centered wife living in a drab French provincial town, who, interpreting the world from the prism of the romantic stories she reads, yearns for luxury, excitement, and romance. Disillusioned with her marriage to her devoted, hard-working, but dull husband, whom she detests, Emma commits adultery.

In this work, Flaubert strove to remain detached from his characters. Unlike romantics, he was concerned not with revealing his own emotions or opinions but with the accurate depiction of characters, situations, and dialogue. His goal, he said, was a book in which "the personality of the author is *completely* absent."[4] Commenting on the realism of *Madame Bovary*, a contemporary novelist noted that it "represents an obsession with description. Details are counted one by one, all are given equal value, every street, every house, every room, every book, every blade of grass is described in full."[5] Also described fully and in great clinical detail is Emma's death from poisoning.

Russian writers were among the leading realists. In *A Sportsman's Sketches* (1852), the novelist, dramatist, and short-story writer Ivan Turgenev (1818–1883) provided a true-to-life picture of Russian rural conditions, particularly the brutal life of serfs. In an unpolemic style, Turgenev showed that serfdom debased not only the serfs but also their masters, the rural nobility, who regarded serfs as barely human. In *War and Peace* (1863–1869), Leo Tolstoy (1828–1910) vividly described the manners and outlook of the Russian nobility and the tragedies that attended Napoleon's invasion of Europe. In *Anna Karenina* (1873–1877), he probed class divisions and the complexities of marital relationships. Anton Chekhov (1860–1904) was a physician who turned to literature. His major dramas concentrate on the realities of provincial life among ineffectual upper-class landowners, perennially short of money, who fritter away their lives and do nothing productive to better society. In essence, Chekhov was describing a decadent social order in its last throes. Fyodor Dostoyevsky (1821–1881), in his major novels *Crime and Punishment* (1866), *The Idiot* (1868), *The Possessed* (1871), and *The Brothers Karamazov* (1880), showed a superb ability to create memorable characters, to probe minds, and to describe vividly and perceptively.

Among English writers, Elizabeth Gaskell, the wife of a Unitarian minister in Manchester, dealt compassionately with the plight of industrial workers in *Mary Barton* (1848) and *North and South* (1855). The novels of Charles Dickens— *Bleak House* (1853), *Hard Times* (1854), and several others—detailed the squalor of life, the hypocrisy of society, and the drudgery of labor in British industrial cities. Dickens skillfully created characters who, concerned only with safeguarding their privileged way of life, ignore the misery of the working class. These people run the schools, prisons, law courts, and other government agencies that oppress the poor.

Literary realism evolved into **naturalism** when writers tried to demonstrate a causal relationship between human character and the social environment: that certain conditions of life produced predictable character traits in human beings. The belief that the law of cause and effect governed human behavior reflected the immense prestige attached to science in the closing decades of the nineteenth century.

The leading naturalist novelist, Émile Zola (1840–1902) had immense confidence in the scientific method and was convinced that it applied to literature. According to Zola, the novelist should proceed like a scientist performing an experiment. The "experimental novel," he wrote, shows "the reciprocal effect of society on the individual and the individual on society." It shows "man living in social conditions produced by himself, which he modifies daily, and in the heart of which he himself experiences a continual transformation." This type of novel, Zola claimed,

> is a consequence of the scientific evolution of the century; it continues and completes physiology, which itself leans for support on chemistry and medicine; it substitutes for the study of the abstract and the metaphysical man the study of the natural man, governed by physical and chemical laws, and modified by the influences of his surroundings; it is in one word the literature of our scientific age, as the classical and romantic literature corresponded to a scholastic and theological age.[6]

In his own novels, Zola probed the slums, brothels, mining villages, and cabarets of France, examining how people were conditioned by the squalor of their environment. *Germinal* (1885), his greatest novel, graphically renders the terrible toil and drudgery endured by coal miners.

Realism was not restricted to the novel alone. The leading realist playwright, Henrik Ibsen (1828–1906), a Norwegian, examined with clinical precision and uncompromising truth the commercial and professional classes, their personal ambitions, business practices, and family relationships; his dramas drew attention to bourgeois pretensions, hypocrisy, and social conventions that thwart individual growth. Although Ibsen wrote about profound social issues, he viewed himself as a dramatist relating a piece of reality and not as a social reformer agitating for reform.

In *Pillars of Society* (1877), Ibsen portrayed entrepreneurs who, aspiring for wealth and status, not only betray loved ones but also engage in unscrupulous business practices at the expense of their fellow citizens. The title is ironic, for the "pillars of society" are actually corrupt hypocrites.

In *A Doll's House* (1879), Ibsen took up a theme that shocked late-nineteenth-century bourgeois audiences: a woman leaving her husband and children in search of self-realization. Nora Helmer resents being a submissive and dutiful wife to a husband who does not take her seriously, who treats her like a child or a doll. Before walking out on Torvald, Nora tells him:

> In all these eight years—longer than that—from the very beginning of our acquaintance, we have never exchanged a word on any serious subject. . . . When I was at home with papa, he told me his opinion about everything, and so I had the same opinions; and if I differed from him I concealed the fact, because he would not have liked it. He called me his doll-child, and he played with me just as I used to play with my dolls. And when I came to live with you . . . I was simply transferred from papa's hands into yours. You arranged everything according to your own taste, and so I got the same tastes as you—or else I pretended to, I am really not sure which—I think sometimes the one and sometimes the other. . . . I have existed merely to perform tricks for you, Torvald. But you would have it so. You and papa have committed a great sin against me. It is your fault that I have made nothing of my life.[7]

By recognizing the truth about her life up to that point in time and then by resolving "to educate myself . . . to understand myself and everything about me," Nora now has the possibility of achieving individual freedom—of becoming a person in her own right.

INTERIOR, 1868–1869, BY EDGAR DEGAS. Set in a world of poor shopkeepers and clerks, *Thérèse Raquin* (1867) was Émile Zola's first great success as a naturalist novelist. This Degas painting depicts the sexual tension and violent emotions that Zola sought to uncover in his work. (Philadelphia Museum of Art: The Henry P. McIlhenny Collection in Memory of Francis P. McIlhenny, 1986, 1986-26-10.)

In striving for a true-to-life portrayal of human behavior and the social environment, realism and naturalism reflected attitudes shaped by science, industrialism, and secularism, all of which stressed the importance of the external world. The same outlook gave rise to positivism in philosophy.

POSITIVISM

Positivists viewed science as the highest achievement of the mind and sought to apply a strict empirical approach to the study of society. They believed that the philosopher must proceed like a scientist, carefully assembling and classifying data and formulating general rules that demonstrate regularities in the social experience. Such knowledge, based on concrete facts, would provide the social planner with useful insights. Positivists rejected metaphysics, which, in the tradition of Plato, tried to discover ultimate principles through reason alone rather than through observation of the empirical world. For positivists, any effort to go beyond the realm of experience to a deeper reality would be a mistaken and fruitless endeavor.

Auguste Comte (1798–1857), the father of positivism, called for a purely scientific approach to history and society: only through a proper understanding of the laws governing human affairs could society, which was in a state of intellectual anarchy, be rationally reorganized. Comte named his system *positivism* because he believed that it rested on sure knowledge derived from observed facts and was therefore empirically verifiable. Like others of his generation, Comte believed that scientific laws underlay human affairs and could be discovered through the methods of the empirical scientist— that is, through recording and systematizing observable data. "I shall bring factual proof," he said, "that there are just as definite laws for the development of the human race as there are for the fall of a stone."[8]

One of the laws that Comte believed he had discovered was the "law of the three stages." The human mind, he asserted, had progressed through three broad historical stages: the theological, the metaphysical, and the scientific. In the theological stage, the most primitive of the three, the mind found a supernatural explanation for the origins and purpose of things, and society was ruled by priests. In the metaphysical stage, which included the Enlightenment, the mind tried to explain things through abstractions, such as "nature," "equality," "natural rights," or "popular sovereignty," which rested on hope and belief rather than on empirical investigation. The metaphysical stage was a transitional period between the infantile theological stage and the highest stage of society, the scientific, or positive, stage. In this culminating stage, the mind breaks with all illusions inherited from the past, formulates laws based on careful observation of the empirical world, and reconstructs society in accordance with these laws. People remove all mystery from nature and base their social legislation on laws of society similar to the laws of nature discovered by Newton.

Because Comte advocated the scientific study of society, he is regarded as the principal founder of sociology; indeed, he coined the term. Comte's effort inspired many thinkers to collect and analyze critically all data pertaining to social phenomena.

DARWINISM

Many contributed to the steady advance of science in the nineteenth century. In 1808, John Dalton, an English chemist, formulated the modern atomic theory. In 1831, an English chemist and physicist, Michael Faraday, discovered the principle of electromagnetic induction, on which the electric generator and electric motor are based. In 1847, Hermann von Helmholtz, a German physicist, formulated the law of conservation of energy, which states that the total amount of energy in the universe is always the same; energy that is used up is not lost but is converted into heat. In 1887, another German physicist, Heinrich Hertz, discovered electromagnetic waves—a discovery

A CARICATURE OF DARWIN. Darwin's theory of evolution created much controversy and aroused considerable bitterness. In this caricature, the apelike Darwin, holding a mirror, is explaining his theory of evolution to a fellow ape. (Image Select/Art Resource, N.Y.)

that later made possible the invention of radio, television, and radar. Almost two decades earlier, in 1869, Dmitri Mendeleev, a Russian chemist, constructed a periodic table for the elements, which helped make chemistry more systematic and mathematical. In 1861, Louis Pasteur, a French scientist, initiated a revolution in medicine by proving that some diseases were caused by microbes, and he devised vaccines to prevent them.

Perhaps the most important scientific advance was the theory of **evolution** formulated by Charles Darwin (1809–1882). An English naturalist,

Darwin did for biology what Newton had done for physics: he made it an objective science based on general principles. The Scientific Revolution of the seventeenth century had given people a new conception of space; Darwin radically altered our conception of time and biological life, including human origins.

Natural Selection

During the eighteenth century, almost all people had adhered to the biblical account of creation contained in Genesis. God had instantaneously created the universe and the various species of animal and plant life. He had given every river and mountain a finished and permanent form and made each species of animal and plant distinct from every other species. God had designed the bird's wings so that it could fly, the fish's eyes so that it could see under water, and human legs so that people could walk. All this, it was believed, had occurred some five or six thousand years ago.

Gradually, this view was questioned. In 1794, Erasmus Darwin, the grandfather of Charles Darwin, published *Zoonomia, or The Laws of Organic Life*, which offered evidence that the earth had existed for millions of years before the appearance of people and that animals experienced modifications, which they passed on to their offspring. Nearly forty years later, Sir Charles Lyell published his three-volume *Principles of Geology* (1830–1833), which showed that the planet had evolved slowly over many ages.

In December 1831, Charles Darwin sailed as a naturalist on the HMS *Beagle*, which surveyed the shores of South America and some Pacific islands. During the five-year expedition, Darwin collected and examined specimens of plant and animal life; he concluded that many animal species had perished, that new species had emerged, and that there were links between extinct and living species.

Influenced by Lyell's achievement, Darwin sought to interpret distant natural occurrences by means of observable processes that were still going on. He could not accept that a fixed number of distinct and separate species had been instantaneously created a mere five thousand years ago. In the *Origin of Species* (1859) and the *Descent of Man* (1871), Darwin used empirical evidence to show that the wide variety of animal species was due to a process of development over many millennia, and he supplied a convincing theory that explained how evolution operates.

Darwin adopted the Malthusian idea that the population reproduces faster than the food supply, causing a struggle for existence. Not all infant organisms grow to adulthood; not all adult organisms live to old age. The principle of **natural selection** determines which members of the species have a better chance of survival in a world of myriad dangers and limited resources. The offspring of a lion, giraffe, or insect are not exact duplications of their parents. A baby lion might have the potential for being slightly faster or stronger than its parents; a baby giraffe might grow up to have a longer neck than its parents; an insect might have a slightly different color.

These small, random variations can give the organism a crucial advantage in the struggle for food and against natural enemies. The organism favored by nature is more likely to reach maturity, to mate, and to pass on its superior qualities to its offspring, some of which will acquire the advantageous trait to an even greater degree than the parent. Over many generations, the favorable characteristic becomes more pronounced and more widespread within the species. Over millennia, natural selection causes the death of old species that cannot adjust to a changing environment. It also leads to the creation of new species, for genetic changes within a segment of a species can so differentiate its members from the rest of the species that interbreeding is no longer possible. Very few of the species that dwelt on earth 10 million years ago still survive, and many new ones, including human beings, have emerged. People themselves are products of natural selection, evolving from earlier, lower, nonhuman forms of life.

Darwinism and Christianity

Like Newton's law of universal gravitation, Darwin's theory of evolution had revolutionary consequences in areas other than science. Evolution challenged traditional Christian belief. To some, it undermined the infallibility of Scripture and the

Charles Darwin,
The Descent of Man

In The Descent of Man *(1871), Charles Darwin argued that human beings have evolved from lower forms of life.*

The main conclusion here arrived at, and now held by many naturalists who are well competent to form a sound judgment, is that man is descended from some less highly organised form. The grounds upon which this conclusion rests will never be shaken, for the close similarity between man and the lower animals in embryonic development, as well as in innumerable points of structure and constitution, both of high and of the most trifling importance . . . are facts which cannot be disputed. They have long been known, but until recently they told us nothing with respect to the origin of man. Now when viewed by the light of our knowledge of the whole organic world, their meaning is unmistakable. The great principle of evolution stands up clear and firm, when these groups of facts are considered in connection with others, such as the mutual affinities of the members of the same group, their geographical distribution in past and present times, and their geological succession. It is incredible that all these facts should speak falsely. He who is not content to look, like a savage, at the phenomena of nature as disconnected, cannot any longer believe that man is the work of a separate act of creation. He will be forced to admit that the close resemblance of the embryo of man to that, for instance, of a dog—the construction of his skull, limbs and whole frame on the same plan with that of other mammals, independently of the uses to which the parts may be put—the

occasional reappearance of various structures, for instance of several muscles, which man does not normally possess, but which are common to the Quadrumana*—and a crowd of analogous facts—all point in the plainest manner to the conclusion that man is the co-descendant with other mammals of a common progenitor. . . .

Man may be excused for feeling some pride at having risen, though not through his own exertions, to the very summit of the organic scale; and the fact of his having thus risen, instead of having been aboriginally placed there, may give him hope for a still higher destiny in the distant future. But we are not only here concerned with hopes or fears, only with the truth as far as our reason permits us to discover it; and I have given the evidence to the best of my ability. We must, however, acknowledge, as it seems to me, that man with all his noble qualities, with sympathy which feels for the most debased, with benevolence which extends not only to other men but to the humblest living creature, with his god-like intellect which has penetrated into the movements and constitution of the solar system—with all these exalted powers—Man still bears in his bodily frame the indelible stamp of his lowly origin.

Question for Analysis

1. Why did Darwin's assertion that human beings have a "lowly origin" distress people?

---

*An order of mammals, Quadrumana includes all primates (monkeys, apes, and baboons) except human beings; the primates' hind feet and forefeet can be used as hands because they have opposable first digits.

Charles Darwin, *The Descent of Man* (New York: D. Appleton, 1976), 606–607.

conviction that the Bible was indeed the Word of God. Natural selection, which Darwin insisted was unplanned and undesigned, could explain the development of the organic world without

reference to any divine arrangement or ultimate purpose. Indeed, supernatural explanations of the origin of species now seemed superfluous and an obstacle to a scientific understanding of nature.

Darwin's theory touched off a great religious controversy between outraged fundamentalists, who defended a literal interpretation of Genesis, and advocates of the new biology. Humanity's brute origins seemed irreconcilable with the biblical assertion that man was created in the image of God. One theologian declared, "If the Darwinian theory is true, Genesis is a lie, the whole framework of the book of life falls to pieces, and the revelation of God to man, as we Christians know it, is a delusion and a snare."[9] A Methodist publication contended: "We regard this theory, which seeks to eliminate from the universe the immediate, ever-present, all pervasive action of a living and personal God, which excludes the possibility of the supernatural and the miraculous . . . as practically destructive of the authority of divine revelation, and subversive of the foundation of religion and morality."[10] In time, most religious thinkers tried to reconcile evolution with the Christian view that there was a creation and that it had a purpose. These Christian thinkers held that God created and then directed the evolutionary process, that he steered evolution so that it would culminate in the human being.

Darwinism ultimately helped end the practice of relying on the Bible as an authority in questions of science, completing a trend initiated by Galileo. Darwinism thus contributed to the waning of religious belief and to a growing secular attitude that dismissed or paid scant attention to the Christian view of a universe designed by God, a human being created in God's image, and a soul that rises to heaven. For many, the conclusion was inescapable: nature contained no divine design or purpose, and the human species itself, including its vaunted power of the mind, was a chance product of impersonal, mindless forces. The core ideas of Christianity—that all life was a product of God's intelligence and that people were children of God participating in a drama of salvation—rested more than ever on faith rather than reason. Some even talked openly about the death of God. The notion that people are sheer accidents of nature was shocking. Copernicanism had deprived people of the comforting belief that the earth had been placed in the center of the universe just for them; Darwinism deprived them of the privilege of being God's special creation.

Social Darwinism

Darwin's theories were extended by others beyond the realm in which Darwin had worked. Social thinkers, who recklessly applied his conclusions to the social order, produced theories that had dangerous consequences. Occasionally, Darwin himself departed from his rigorous empiricism and drew murky conclusions about the mentally and physically handicapped and what he termed the "savage races." But he never intended his discoveries, which applied to the natural world, to serve as a guide for a ruthless social policy that glorified war and justified genocide. **Social Darwinists**—those who transferred Darwin's scientific theories to social and economic issues—used the terms *struggle for existence* and *survival of the fittest* to buttress an often brutal economic individualism and political conservatism. Prosperous businessmen, they said, had demonstrated their superiority, their fitness to succeed in the competitive world of business. Their success accorded with nature's laws and therefore was beneficial to society. Thus, American industrialist Andrew Carnegie (1835–1919) wrote in *The Gospel of Wealth* (1900):

> We accept and welcome . . . the concentration of business, industrial and commercial, in the hands of a few and the law of competition . . . as being, not only beneficial, but essential to the future progress of the race. . . . We start, then, with a condition of affairs under which the best interests of the race are promoted, but which inevitably gives wealth to the few.[11]

According to Social Darwinists, those who lost out in the socioeconomic struggle demonstrated their unfitness. Traditionally, failure had been ascribed to human wickedness or to God's plan. Now, it was attributed to an inferior hereditary endowment.

Using Darwin's model of organisms evolving and changing slowly over tens of thousands of years, conservatives insisted that society, too, should experience change at an unhurried pace. Instant reforms conflicted with nature's laws and wisdom and resulted in a deterioration of the social body.

The loose application of Darwin's biological concepts to the social world, where they did not apply, also buttressed imperialism, racism, nationalism, and militarism—doctrines that preached relentless conflict. Social Darwinists insisted that nations and races were engaged in a struggle for survival in which only the fittest survive and deserve to survive. In their view, war was nature's way of eliminating the unfit. Karl Pearson, a British professor of mathematics, stated in *National Life from the Standpoint of Science* (1900):

> History shows me only one way, and one way only in which a higher state of civilization has been produced, namely the struggle of race with race, and the survival of the physically and mentally fitter race. . . . The path of progress is strewn with the wrecks of nations; traces are everywhere to be seen of the [sacrifice] of inferior races, and of victims who found not the narrow way to perfection. Yet these dead people are, in very truth, the stepping stones on which mankind has arisen to the higher intellectual and deeper emotional life of today.[12]

"We are a conquering race," said the U.S. senator Albert J. Beveridge. "We must obey our blood and occupy new markets, and if necessary, new lands."[13] "War is a biological necessity of the first importance," claimed the Prussian general Friedrich von Bernhardi in *Germany and the Next War* (1911).[14]

Darwinian biology was used to promote the belief in Anglo-Saxon (British and American) and Teutonic (German) racial superiority. Social Darwinists attributed to racial qualities the growth of the British Empire, the expansion of the United States to the Pacific, and the extension of German power. The domination of other peoples—American Indians, Africans, Asians, Poles—was seen as the natural right of the superior race. British naturalist Alfred Russel Wallace, who arrived at the theory of evolution independently of Darwin, wrote in 1864:

> The intellectual and moral, as well as the physical qualities of the European are superior; the same power and capacities which have made him rise in a few centuries from the condition of the wandering savage . . . to his present state of culture and advancement . . . enable him when in contact with savage man, to conquer in the struggle for existence and to increase at his expense.[15]

Several writers and supporters of their countries' expansion described Native Americans, Africans, and Pacific Islanders as low forms of humanity whose subjection, even extinction, would be beneficial to the progress of civilization. For them, the destruction of a "lower race" was justifiable, a biologically necessary and culturally worthy process. Thus, in 1912, Paul Rohrbach, a German colonial official in Southwest Africa, wrote:

> No false philanthropy or racial theory can convince sensible people that the preservation of a tribe of South Africa's kaffirs . . . is more important to the future of mankind than the spread of the great European nations and the white race in general.
>
> Not until the native learns to produce anything of value in the service of the higher race, i.e., in the service of its and his own progress, does he gain any moral right to exist.[16]

Social Darwinism also affected racial attitudes in the United States. Too willingly, scholars, joining antiblack polemicists, attributed an inferior biological inheritance to blacks, and some predicted their extinction, seeing them as losers in the Darwinian struggle for existence. Thus, in 1905, William B. Smith, a Tulane University professor, wrote: "The vision . . . of a race vanishing before its superior is not at all dispiriting, but inspiring. . . . The doom that awaits the Negro has been prepared in like measures for all inferior races."[17]

The theory of evolution was a great achievement of the rational mind, but in the hands of the Social Darwinists it served to undermine the Enlightenment tradition. Whereas the philosophes emphasized human equality, Social Darwinists divided humanity into racial superiors and inferiors. The philosophes believed that states would increasingly submit to the rule of law to reduce violent conflicts; Social Darwinists, in contrast, regarded racial and national conflict as a biological necessity, a law of history, and a means of progress. In propagating a tooth-and-claw version of human and international relations, Social Darwinists dispensed with the humanitarian and cosmopolitan sentiments of the philosophes and distorted the image of progress. Their views promoted territorial aggrandizement and military buildup and led many to welcome World War I. The Social Darwinist notions of the struggle of races for survival and of preserving racial purity became core doctrines of the Nazi Party after World War I and provided the "scientific" and "ethical" justification for genocide.

RELIGION IN A SECULAR AGE

In addition to Darwinism, other developments in the middle of the nineteenth century served to undermine traditional Christian belief. A growing secular attitude pushed religion to the periphery of human concerns for many people. Several intellectuals, in the tradition of the Enlightenment, attacked religion as an obstacle to progress. New trends in biblical scholarship questioned the established opinion about the authenticity of the text of the Bible. Fortified by the discoveries of anthropologists and psychologists, "higher critics" examined the Old and New Testaments and the rise of Christianity in a historical and critical way. Generally, Protestant scholars, particularly Germans or those trained in Germany, took the lead in the new biblical scholarship.

In his *Life of Jesus* (1835), David Friedrich Strauss (1808–1874), a German theologian, examined the Gospels in a critical spirit, attempting to discern what was historically valid. He maintained that the New Testament was replete with inherited legends and with myths—including the virgin birth and the resurrection—that were unconscious inventions by the Gospel writers, who embellished Jesus' life and words with their own messianic longings. The Gospels contain much mythical-religious content, Strauss said, but little history. Prior to the publication of Strauss's work, most students of religion had viewed the Gospels as a reliable historical source. But Strauss argued that the Jesus of faith is not the same as the Jesus of history. The belief that history, as presented in the Gospels, provided a firm basis for belief in

Christian teachings was permanently undermined. Strauss' work created an uproar, pitting religious authorities against secular-minded thinkers.

In *The Essence of Christianity* (1841), Ludwig Feuerbach (1804–1872), a German philosopher and theologian, argued that the starting point of philosophy should be the human being and the material world, not God. "Religion is the dream of the human mind," he said, and God is a human creation, a product of human feelings and wishes. Human beings believe in the divine because they seek assistance from it in life and fear death.

Feuerbach treated religion as an expression of mythical thinking and God as an unconscious projection of human hopes, fears, and self-doubts. Christianity diminishes human beings in order to affirm God, said Feuerbach; Christians deny their own worth and goodness that they might ascribe all value to God. The human being, weak and self-hating,

> sets God before him as the antithesis of himself.... God is the infinite, man the finite being; God is perfect, man imperfect; God eternal, man temporal; God almighty, man weak; God holy, man sinful. God and man are extremes: God is the absolutely positive, the sum of all realities; man the absolutely negative.[18]

Religion, said Feuerbach, is a form of self-alienation, for human beings diminish their humanity when they invest their finest qualities in a nonexistent God and reserve their worst qualities for themselves. God represents the externalization of an idealized human being. When individuals measure themselves against this God-ideal, they see only miserable, contemptible, and worthless creatures.

> To enrich God, man must become poor; that God may be all, man must become nothing.... Man is wicked, corrupt, incapable of good; but, on the other hand, God is the only good—the Good Being.[19]

Humanity liberates itself, said Feuerbach, when it rejects God's existence and religion's claim to truth. He declared that it was his aim to change the friends of God into friends of human beings and the seekers of heaven into active, productive, and life-affirming individuals.

Confronted by this assault on orthodox belief, some Christians continued to believe that the Bible was true in all its parts, that it was the divinely inspired storehouse of knowledge about God and the world. These defenders of traditional Christianity rejected evolution and any other scientific discovery that appeared to be in conflict with their reading of Scripture. The Danish philosopher and Lutheran pastor Søren Kierkegaard (1813–1855) argued that true Christians commit themselves to beliefs that are seemingly unintelligible. For Kierkegaard, truth is subjective and personal, reached through passion and commitment. To find a truth that has an all-consuming meaning, to find an idea for which one can live and die—this should be the individual's highest aim. According to Kierkegaard, all philosophical systems fail because they are concerned with objective certainty and humanity in general and not with what truly matters—the individual standing alone and making choices based on passionately held beliefs. It is this experience that brings the individual face-to-face with God.

For Kierkegaard, the highest truth is that human beings are God's creatures. However, God's existence cannot be demonstrated by reason; the crucial questions of human existence can never be resolved in a logical and systematic way. In Kierkegaard's view, the individual knows God through a leap of faith, not through systematic reasoning. In contrast to the Christian apologists who sought to demonstrate that Christian teachings did not conflict with reason, Kierkegaard denied that Christian doctrines were objectively valid. For him, Christian beliefs were absurd and irrational and could not be harmonized with reason. However, said Kierkegaard, true Christians confidently embrace beliefs that are incomprehensible, if not absurd.

Because Christian truths surpass reason, Kierkegaard said that true Christians, strengthened by faith, plunge with confidence into the absurd. But it is this leap of faith that enables Christians to conquer the agonizing feeling that life, in its deepest sense, means nothing and to give meaning to their own existence. Such a faith, based on total commitment, is thus the true avenue of self-discovery.

In the nineteenth century, the Catholic church felt threatened by the forces of modernity. The rational, skeptical, and secular outlook of the Enlightenment inherited by liberalism undermined traditional church beliefs. By examining the Bible and the rise of Christianity in a historical and critical way, scholars raised doubts about the clerically endorsed meaning of biblical texts. And Darwinism caused people to question the infallibility of Scripture and the conviction that the Bible was the word of God. These developments led Pope Pius IX to issue in 1864 "The Syllabus of Errors" that condemned many of the features of the modern world. Conservative Catholics praised the Syllabus for reaffirming basic Catholic principles. Those who wanted the church to adjust to modern civilization regarded the document's condemnation of religious freedom, Protestantism, civil marriage and divorce, and secular schools as a regrettable return to the Middle Ages.

In another encyclical, *Rerum Novarum* ("Of New Things") issued in 1891 by Pope Leo XIII, the church wrestled with the problems faced by the working class in the new industrial age, and showed a different side of the church. It supported state intervention when justice and social and individual well-being were threatened. The encyclical attacked the doctrine of class warfare, a core principle of Marxism, and defended private property. Pervaded with the Gospels' message, the ideals expressed in the encyclical formed the basis of Catholic social teachings in succeeding generations.

Modernism,* a movement of Catholic intellectuals, sought to liberalize the church, to make it more accepting of modern, liberal, political ideals and modern science, and to reexamine the Gospels and Catholic teaching in the light of modern biblical scholarship. In many of these instances, modernists took positions that directly challenged core Catholic principles. Thus, Alfred Firmin Loiry (1857–1940), a scholarly priest, questioned the historicity of the virgin birth and the bodily resurrection of Jesus, rejected the infallibility of papal and council pronouncements, and contended that Jesus did not impart God's permanent truths, that both he and the Gospels have to

*Not to be confused with cultural modernism, which is discussed in Chapter 27.

be interpreted within the context of their historical times.

Pope Pius X (1903–1914) strongly condemned Catholic modernists for undermining revelation and fostering agnosticism. The church also suppressed modernist journals, placed a number of modernist works on the *Index of Forbidden Books*, dismissed some modernist instructors, and excommunicated a number of the movement's staunchest supporters.

MARXISM

The failure of the revolutions of 1848 and growing fear of working-class violence led liberals to abandon revolution and to press for reforms through the political process. In the last part of the nineteenth century, Marxists and anarchists became the chief proponents of revolution. Both liberalism and Marxism shared common principles derived from the Enlightenment. Their adherents believed in the essential goodness and perfectibility of human nature and claimed that their doctrines rested on rational foundations. They wanted to free individuals from the accumulated superstition, ignorance, and prejudices of the past and to fashion a more harmonious and rational society. Both liberals and Marxists believed in social progress and valued the full realization of human talents.

Despite these similarities, the differences between liberalism and Marxism are profound. The goal of Marxism—the seizure of power by the working class and the destruction of capitalism—was inimical to bourgeois liberals; so too was the Marxist belief that violence and struggle were the essence of history, the instruments of progress, and the vehicle to a higher stage of humanity. Liberals, who placed the highest value on the individual, held that through education and self-discipline people could overcome inequality and poverty. Marxists insisted that without a transformation of the economic system, individual effort by the downtrodden would amount to very little.

Karl Marx (1818–1883) was born of German-Jewish parents (both descendants of prominent rabbis). To save his job as a lawyer, Marx's father converted to Protestantism. Enrolled at a university to study law, Marx switched to philosophy.

KARL MARX (LEFT) AND FRIEDRICH ENGELS (RIGHT) WITH MARX'S THREE DAUGHTERS, 1860S. Interpreting history in economic terms, Marx predicted that socialism would replace capitalism. He called for the proletariat to overthrow capitalism and to establish a classless society. (© Mary Evans/Marx Memorial Library/The Image Works.)

In 1842, he was editing a newspaper, which was soon suppressed by the Prussian authorities for its outspoken ideas. Leaving his native Rhineland, Marx went to Paris, where he met another German, Friedrich Engels (1820–1895), who was the son of a prosperous textile manufacturer. Marx and Engels entered into a lifelong collaboration and became members of socialist groups. In February 1848, they published the *Communist Manifesto*, which called for a working-class revolution to overthrow the capitalist system. Forced to leave France in 1849 because of his political views, Marx moved to London, where he spent the rest of his life.

Although supported by Engels, Marx was continually short of funds, and at times he and his wife and daughters lived in dreadful poverty. In

London, Marx spent years writing *Capital*—a study and critique of the modern capitalistic economic system, which, he predicted, would be destroyed by a socialist revolution.

A Science of History

Like other nineteenth century thinkers Marx believed that human history, like the operations of nature, was governed by scientific law. Marx was a strict materialist; rejecting all religious and metaphysical interpretations of both nature and history, he sought to fashion an empirical science of society. He viewed religion as a human creation—a product of people's imagination and feelings and a consolation for the oppressed. The happiness it brought he considered an illusion. Real happiness would come, said Marx, not by transcending the natural world but by improving it. Rather than deluding oneself by seeking refuge from life's misfortunes in an imaginary world, one must confront the ills of society and reform them. This last point is crucial. "The philosophers have only *interpreted* the world in different ways; the point is to *change it*."[20]

The world could be rationally understood and changed, said Marx. People were free to make their own history, but to do so effectively, they must comprehend the inner meaning of history: the laws governing human affairs in the past and operating in the present. Marx adopted Hegel's view that history was not an assortment of unrelated and disconnected events but a progressive development, which, like the growth of a plant, proceeded ineluctably according to its own inner laws. For both Hegel and Marx, the historical process was governed by objective and rational principles. Marx also adopted Hegel's view that history advanced dialectically: that the clash of opposing forces propelled history into higher stages.

However, Marx also broke with Hegel in crucial ways. For Hegel, it was the dialectical clash of opposing ideas that moved history into the next stage. For Marx, it was the clash of classes representing conflicting economic interests—what is called *dialectical materialism*—that accounted for historical change and progress. In Hegel's view, history was the unfolding of the Absolute Spirit, and a higher stage of development was produced by the synthesis of opposing ideas. According to Marx, Hegel's system failed because it was too metaphysical. It transcended the known world and downgraded reality to a mere attribute of Spirit. Marx saw Hegel's abstract philosophy as deflecting attention from the real world and its problems, which cried out for understanding and solution; it was a negation of life. For Marx, history was explainable solely in terms of natural processes—empirically verifiable developments.

Max valued Hegel's insight that history is a progressive and purposeful process, but he criticized Hegel for embedding this insight in metaphysical-theological fantasy. Hegel, said Marx, had made a mystical principle the real subject of history and thought. But, in truth, it is the "real man," the person who lives in and is conditioned by the objective world, the only true reality, who is the center of history. History is not Spirit aspiring to self-actualization but people becoming fully human, fulfilling their human potential. The moving forces in history, said Marx, were economic and technological factors: the ways in which goods were produced and wealth was distributed. They accounted for historical change and were the basis of all culture—politics, law, religion, morals, and philosophy. "The history of humanity," he concluded, "must therefore always be studied and treated in relation to the history of industry and exchange."[21]

According to Marx, material technology—the methods of cultivating land and the tools for manufacturing goods—determined society's social and political arrangements and its intellectual outlooks. For example, the hand mill, the loose yoke, and the wooden plow had given rise to feudal lords, whereas power-driven machines had spawned industrial capitalists.

Class Conflict

Throughout history, said Marx, there has been a *class* struggle between those who own the means of production and those whose labor has been exploited to provide wealth for this upper class. This dialectical, or opposing, tension between classes has pushed history forward into higher stages. In the ancient world, when wealth was based on land, the struggle was between master and slave, patrician and plebeian; during the Middle Ages, when land was still the predominant mode of production, the struggle was between lord and serf. In the modern industrial world, two sharply opposed classes were confronting each other: the capitalists owning the factories, mines, banks, and transportation systems and the exploited wage earners (the proletariat).

The class with economic power also controlled the state, said Marx and Engels. That class used political power to protect and increase its property and to hold down the laboring class. "Thus the ancient State was above all the slaveowners' state for holding down the slaves," said Engels, "as a feudal State was the organ of the nobles for holding down the . . . serfs, and the modern representative State is the instrument of the exploitation of wage-labor by capital."[22]

Furthermore, Marx and Engels asserted, the class that controlled material production also controlled mental production: that is, the ideas held by the ruling class became the dominant ideas of society. These ideas, presented as laws of nature or moral and religious standards, were regarded as the truth by oppressor and oppressed alike. In reality, however, these ideas merely reflected the special economic interests of the ruling class. Thus, said Marx, bourgeois ideologists would insist that natural rights and laissez faire were laws of nature having universal validity. But these "laws" were born of the needs of the bourgeoisie in its struggle to wrest power from an obsolete feudal regime and to protect its property from the state. Similarly, nineteenth-century slaveholders convinced themselves that slavery was morally right: that it had God's approval and was good for the slave. Slave owners and capitalist employers alike may have defended their labor systems by citing universal principles that they thought were true, but in reality their systems rested on a simple economic consideration: slave labor was good for the pocketbook of the slave owner, and wage labor was good in the same way for the capitalist. They were unaware of the real forces motivating their thinking.

The Destruction of Capitalism

Under capitalism, said Marx, workers knew only poverty. They worked long hours for low wages, suffered from periodic unemployment, and lived in squalid, overcrowded dwellings. Most monstrous of all, they were forced to send their young children into the factories.

Capitalism also produced another kind of poverty, according to Marx: poverty of the human spirit. Under capitalism, the factory worker was reduced to a laboring beast, performing tedious and repetitive tasks in a dark, dreary, dirty cave—an altogether inhuman environment that deprived people of their human sensibilities. Unlike the artisans in their own shops, factory workers found no pleasure and took no pride in their work; they did not have the satisfaction of creating a finished product that expressed their skills. Work, said Marx, should be a source of fulfillment for people. It should enable people to affirm their personalities and develop their potential. By treating people not as human beings but as cogs in the production process, capitalism alienated people from their work, from themselves, and from one another.

Marx further asserted that capitalism dehumanized not only the workers but the capitalists as well. Consumed by greed and a ruthless competitiveness, they abused workers and one another and lost sight of life's true meaning: the fulfillment of the individual's creative potential. Marx's view of the individual owed much to the Western humanist tradition, which aspired to shape self-sufficient and productive human beings who strive to develop their intellectual, esthetic, and moral capacities and relate to others as subjects, not as objects. By reducing people to commodities and human relations to a cash nexus, said Marx, capitalism thwarted the realization of this humanist vision.

Marx believed that capitalist control of the economy and the government would not endure forever; capitalist society produced its own gravediggers—the working class. The capitalist system would perish just as the slave society of the ancient world and the feudal society of the Middle Ages had perished. For Marx, the destruction of capitalism was inevitable; it was necessitated by the law of historical materialism. From the ruins of a dead capitalist society, a new socioeconomic system, socialism, would emerge.

Marx predicted how capitalism would be destroyed. Periodic unemployment would increase the misery of the workers and intensify their hatred of capitalists. Small businesspeople and shopkeepers, unable to compete with the great capitalists, would sink into the ranks of the working class, greatly expanding its numbers. Society would become polarized into a small group of immensely wealthy capitalists and a vast proletariat, poor, embittered, and desperate. The monopoly of capital by the few would become a brake on the productive process. Growing increasingly conscious of their misery, the workers—aroused, educated, and organized by Communist intellectuals—would revolt. "Revolution is necessary," said Marx, "not only because the *ruling* class cannot be overthrown in any other way, but also because only in a revolution *can the class which overthrows it* rid itself of the accumulated rubbish of the past and become capable of reconstructing society."[23] The working-class revolutionaries would smash the government that helped the capitalists maintain their dominance. Then they would confiscate the property of the capitalists, abolish private property, place the means of production in the workers' hands, and organize a new society. The *Communist Manifesto* ends with a ringing call for revolution.

> The Communists . . . openly declare that their ends can be attained only by the forcible overthrow of all existing social conditions. Let the ruling classes tremble at a Communist revolution. The proletarians have nothing to lose but their chains. They have a world to win. Workingmen of all countries, unite![24]

Marx did not say a great deal about the new society that would be ushered in by the socialist revolution. With the destruction of capitalism, the distinction between capitalist and worker would cease and with it the class conflict. No longer would society be divided into haves and have-nots, oppressor and oppressed. Since this classless society would contain no exploiters, there would be no need for a state, which was merely an instrument for maintaining and protecting the power of the exploiting class. Thus, the state would eventually wither away. The production and distribution of goods would be carried out through community planning and communal sharing, replacing the capitalist system of competition. People would work at varied tasks, rather than being confined to one form of employment, just as Fourier had advocated.

A revolutionary change in the conditions of life, Marx predicted, would produce a radical transformation of the human being. No longer debased by the self-destructive pursuit of profit and property and no longer victims of capitalist exploitation, people would become finer human beings—altruistic, sensitive, cooperative, and creative. United with others in a classless society free of exploitation and no longer divided by divergent interests, individuals would become truly communal and truly free beings (surpassing the merely political freedom achieved in the bourgeois state)—that is, they would become truly human.

Marxism had immense appeal for both the downtrodden and intellectuals. It promised to end the injustices of industrial society, it offered explanations that claimed the certainty of science for all the crucial events of history, and it assured adherents that history guaranteed the triumph of their cause. But far from being a scientific system, however, Marxism had the features of a religious myth, which, says Robert Tucker,

> appeal[ed] to some modern men in whom the hold of traditional religion has loosened but the craving for an all-inclusive world-view remains alive and strong.[25]

Marx's influence grew during the second wave of industrialization in the closing decades of the nineteenth century, when class bitterness between the proletariat and the bourgeoisie seemed to worsen. Many workers thought that liberals and conservatives had no sympathy for their plight and that the only way to improve their lot was through socialist parties.

Critics of Marx

Critics point out serious weaknesses in Marxism. The rigid Marxist who tries to squeeze all historical events into an economic framework is at a disadvantage. Economic forces alone will not explain the triumph of Christianity in the Roman Empire, the fall of Rome, the Crusades, the French Revolution, modern imperialism, World War I, the rise of Hitler, or the mindset of contemporary Islamic terrorists. Economic explanations fall particularly flat in trying to account for the emergence of modern nationalism, whose appeal, resting on deeply ingrained emotional needs, crosses class lines. The world wars of the twentieth century were not between classes but between nations, and today conflict is often fueled by religious and ethnic factors.

Many of Marx's predictions or expectations have not materialized. Workers in Western lands did not become the oppressed and impoverished proletariat that Marx had described in the mid-nineteenth century. Because of increased productivity and the efforts of labor unions and reform-minded governments, Western workers improved their lives considerably and totally abandoned revolution. The tremendous growth of a middle class of professionals, civil service employees, and small-business owners belies Marx's prediction that capitalist society would be polarized into a small group of very rich capitalists and a great mass of destitute workers. Marx believed that socialist revolutions would break out in the advanced industrialized lands. But the socialist revolutions of the twentieth century occurred in underdeveloped, predominantly agricultural states. The state in Communist lands, far from withering away, grew more centralized, powerful, and oppressive, inflicting much misery on millions of people. In no country where Communist revolutionaries seized power did people achieve the liberty that Marx desired. Nor, indeed, have orthodox Communists been able to sustain a viable economic system. The phenomenal collapse of Communist regimes in the former Soviet Union and Eastern Europe in recent years testifies to Marxism's failure. All of these failed predictions and expectations seem to contradict Marx's claim that his theories rested on an unassailable scientific foundation.

ANARCHISM

Anarchism was another radical movement that attacked capitalism. Like Marxists, anarchists denounced the exploitation of workers and the coercive authority of government and envisioned a stateless society. Only by abolishing the state, said anarchists, could the individual live a free and full life. To achieve these ends, a small number of anarchists advocated revolutionary terrorism; others, like the great Russian novelist Leo Tolstoy, rejected all violence. These anarchists sought to destroy the state by refusing to cooperate with it.

Anarchists drew inspiration from Pierre Joseph Proudhon (1809–1865), a self-educated French printer and typesetter. Proudhon criticized social theorists who devised elaborate systems that regimented daily life, conflicted with human nature, and deprived people of their personal liberty. He desired a new society that maximized individual freedom. He looked back longingly to preindustrial society, which he saw as free of exploitation and corruption, of great manufacturers and financiers, and of powerful governments that interfered in people's lives. Government, said Proudhon, only fosters privilege and suppresses freedom. It enables men without virtue or knowledge to spy on people and order them about.

Anarchism had a particular appeal in Russia. A repressive regime, economic backwardness, a youth movement passionately committed to improving the lives of the masses, and a magnetic leader, Mikhail Bakunin (1814–1876), all contributed to shaping the Russian anarchist tradition. Bakunin was a man of action who organized and fought for revolution and set an example of revolutionary fervor. The son of a Russian noble, he left the tsar's army to study philosophy in the West, where he was attracted to the ideas of Marx. He was arrested for participating in the German revolution of 1848 and was turned over to tsarist officials. He served six years in prison and was then banished to Siberia, from where he escaped in 1861.

Bakunin devoted himself to organizing secret societies that would lead the oppressed in revolt. Whereas Marx held that revolution would occur in the industrial lands through the efforts of a class-conscious proletariat, Bakunin wanted all oppressed people to revolt, including the peasants (the vast majority of the population in Central and Eastern Europe). Marx and Bakunin disagreed on one crucial issue of strategy. Marx wanted to organize the workers into mass political parties; Bakunin held that revolutions should be fought by secret societies of fanatic insurrectionists.

Bakunin feared that after the Marxists overthrew the capitalist regime and seized power, they would become the new masters and exploiters, using the state to enhance their own power. They would, said Bakunin, become a "privileged minority . . . of *ex-workers,* who, once they become rulers or representatives of the people, cease to be workers and begin to look down upon the toiling people. From that time on they represent not the people but themselves and their claims to govern the people."[26] Therefore, said Bakunin, once the workers capture the state, they should destroy it forever. Bakunin's astute prediction that a socialist revolution would lead state power to intensify rather than disappear was borne out in the twentieth century in all lands where Communists seized power.

Anarchists engaged in acts of political terrorism, including the assassination or attempted assassination of kings, presidents, and prime ministers, and tossed bombs into crowds, but they never waged a successful revolution. They failed to reverse the trend toward the concentration of power in industry and government, which would characterize the twentieth century.

LIBERALISM IN TRANSITION

In the early 1800s, European liberals were preoccupied with protecting the rights of the individual against the demands of the state. They championed laissez faire because they feared that state interference in the economy to redress social evils would threaten property rights and the free market, which they thought were essential to personal liberty. They also favored property requirements for voting and officeholding because they were certain that the unpropertied and uneducated masses lacked the wisdom and experience to exercise political responsibility.

In the last part of the century, liberals began—not without reservation and qualification—to support extended suffrage and government action to remedy the abuses of unregulated industrialization. This growing concern for the welfare of the laboring poor coincided with and was influenced by an unprecedented proliferation of humanitarian movements on both sides of the Atlantic. Nurtured by the Enlightenment as well as by Christian teachings, reform movements called for the prohibition of child labor, schooling for the masses, humane treatment for prisoners and the mentally ill,

equality for women, the abolition of slavery, and an end to war. By the beginning of the twentieth century, liberalism had evolved into liberal democracy, and laissez faire had been superseded by a reluctant acceptance of social legislation and government regulation. But from beginning to end, the central concern of liberals remained the protection of individual rights.

John Stuart Mill

The transition from laissez-faire liberalism to a more socially conscious and democratic liberalism is seen in the thought of John Stuart Mill (1806–1873), a British philosopher and statesman. Mill's *On Liberty* (1859) is the classic statement of individual freedom and minority rights: that the government and the majority may not interfere with the liberty of another human being whose actions do no injury to others.

Mill regarded freedom of thought and expression, the toleration of opposing and unpopular viewpoints, as a necessary precondition for the shaping of a rational, moral, and civilized citizen. Political or social coercion, said Mill, is also a barrier to the full development of individuality. Liberty is a supreme good that benefits both the individual and the community. When we silence an opinion, said Mill, we hurt present and future generations. If the opinion is correct, "we are deprived of the opportunity of exchanging error for truth." If the opinion is wrong—and of this we can never be entirely certain—we "lose the clearer perception and livelier impression of truth produced by its collision with error."[27] Therefore, government has no right to force an individual to hold a view

> because it will be better for him to do so, because it will make him happier, or because in the opinions of others, to do so would be wise, or even right. These are good reasons for remonstrating with him, or reasoning with him, or persuading him, or entreating him, but not for compelling him or visiting him with any evil in case he do otherwise.[28]

Mill would place limits on the power of government, for in an authoritarian state citizens cannot develop their moral and intellectual potential. Although he feared the state as a threat to individual liberty, Mill also recognized the necessity for state intervention to promote individual self-development: the expansion of individual moral, intellectual, and esthetic capacities. For example, he maintained that it was permissible for the state to require children to attend school against the wishes of their parents, to regulate hours of labor, to promote public health, and to provide workers' compensation and old-age insurance.

In *Considerations on Representative Government* (1861), Mill endorsed the active participation of all citizens, including the lower classes, in the political life of the state. However, he also proposed a system of plural voting in which education and character would determine the number of votes each person was entitled to cast. In this way, Mill, a cautious democrat, sought to protect the individual from the tyranny of a politically and intellectually unprepared majority.

Thomas Hill Green

The leading late-nineteenth-century figures in the shaping of a new liberal position in Britain were Thomas Hill Green (1836–1882), an Oxford University professor; D. G. Ritchie (1853–1903), who taught philosophy at Oxford and Saint Andrews; J. A. Hobson (1858–1940), a social theorist; and L. T. Hobhouse (1864–1929), an academic who also wrote for the *Manchester Guardian*. In general, these thinkers argued that laissez faire protected the interests of the economically powerful class and ignored the welfare of the nation. For example, Green valued private property but could not see how this principle helped the poor. "A man who possesses nothing but his powers of labor and who has to sell these to a capitalist for bare daily maintenance, might as well . . . be denied rights of property altogether."[29]

Green argued that the do-nothing state advocated by traditional laissez-faire liberalism condemned many citizens to destitution, ignorance, and despair. The state must preserve individual liberty and at the same time secure the common good by promoting conditions favorable for the self-development of the majority of the population. Liberalism, for Green, encompassed more than the protection of individual rights from an oppressive government. A truly liberal society, he said, gives people the opportunity to fulfill their moral potential and human capacities. And social reforms initiated by the state assisted in the realization of this broader conception of liberty. Green and other advocates of state intervention contended that the government has a moral obligation to create social conditions that permit individuals to make the best of themselves. Toward that end, the state should promote public health, ensure decent housing, and provide for education. The uneducated and destitute person cannot be morally self-sufficient or a good citizen, Green and other progressives argued.

Green and his colleagues remained advocates of capitalism but rejected strict laissez faire, which, they said, benefitted only a particular class at the expense of the common good. "If the ideal of true freedom is the maximum of power for all members of human society alike to make the best of themselves, we are right in refusing to ascribe the glory of freedom to a state in which the apparent elevation of the few is founded on the degradation of the many."[30] Overcoming a traditional liberal mistrust of state power, they viewed the state as an ethical institution, assigned it a positive role in improving social conditions, and insisted that state actions need not threaten individual freedom.

In general, by the beginning of the twentieth century, liberals in Britain increasingly acknowledged the need for social legislation. The foundations for the British welfare state were being laid. On the Continent, too, social welfare laws were enacted. To be sure, the motives behind such legislation were quite diverse and often had little to do with liberal sentiments. Nevertheless, in several countries liberalism was expanding into political and social democracy, a trend that would continue in the twentieth century.

Herbert Spencer: Rejection of State Intervention

Many traditional liberals regarded state intervention—"creeping socialism," they called it—as a betrayal of the liberal principle of individual freedom. They held to the traditional liberal view

CHILD LABOR. At times children were beaten by supervisors, as in this English cotton factory. (© Bettmann/ CORBIS.)

Spencer's extreme laissez faire and "rugged individualism" led him to oppose various forms of government intervention, including factory inspection, sanitary laws, pure food and drug requirements, a state postal system, compulsory public education, and public relief for the poor. "The function of Liberalism in the past was that of putting a limit to the powers of kings," he declared. "The function of true Liberalism in the future will be that of putting a limit to the powers of Parliament."[32]

A thoroughgoing individualist, Spencer saw the poor as incapable, weak, imprudent, and lazy—unfit to compete in the struggle for existence. For Spencer, state action was always misguided, for it tampered with nature's laws. "Instead of diminishing suffering, it eventually increases it. It favours the multiplication of those worst fitted for existence, and, by consequence, hinders the multiplication of those best fitted for existence—leaving, as it does, less room for them."[33] Government assistance creates an attitude of dependency among the poor; because they expect things to be done for them, they do not do things for themselves.

that the plight of the downtrodden was not a legitimate concern of the state. The new liberalism, they argued, would make people dependent on the state, thereby stifling industriousness, self-reliance, and thrift. Paternalistic government would cripple the working class morally by turning them into "grown-up babies."

In *The Man Versus the State* (1884), the British philosopher Herbert Spencer rejected the idea "that evils of all kinds should be dealt with by the State." The outcome of state intervention, he said, is that "each member of the community as an individual would be a slave to the community as a whole . . . and the slavery will not be mild."[31] Committed to a philosophy of extreme individualism, Spencer never abandoned the view that the state was an evil and oppressive institution. He favored a society in which government would play the smallest role possible and individual freedom would be maximized, for when the power of the state is extended, however well-intentioned the motive, the freedom of the individual is restricted.

FEMINISM: EXTENDING THE PRINCIPLE OF EQUALITY

Another example of the expansion of liberalism was the emergence of feminist movements in Western Europe and the United States. **Feminism** insisted that the principles of liberty and equality expressed by the philosophes and embodied in the French Declaration of the Rights of Man and of the Citizen (1789) and the American Declaration of Independence be applied to women. Thus, Olympe de Gouges's *Declaration of the Rights of Woman* (1791), modeled after the Declaration of the Rights of Man and of the Citizen, the French Revolution's tribute to Enlightenment ideals, stated: "Woman is born free and remains equal to man in rights. . . . The aim of every political association is the preservation of the natural . . . rights of man and woman."[34] Mary Wollstonecraft's *A Vindication of the Rights of Woman*, written under the influence of the French Revolution, protested against the prevailing subordination and submissiveness of women and the limited opportunities afforded them to cultivate their minds. She considered it an act of tyranny for women "to be excluded from participation [in] the natural rights of mankind."[35] And in 1837, the English novelist and economist Harriet Martineau observed: "One of the fundamental principles announced in the Declaration of Independence is that governments derive their just power from the consent of the governed. How can the political condition of women be reconciled with this?"[36]

In the United States, in the 1830s, Angelina and Sarah Grimké spoke in public—something women rarely did—against slavery and for women's rights. In 1838, Sarah Grimké published *Letters on the Equality of the Sexes and the Condition of Women*, in which she stated emphatically: "Men and women were Created Equal: they are both moral and accountable beings, and whatever is *right* for man to do is *right* for women. . . . How monstrous, how anti-Christian, is the doctrine that woman is to be dependent on man!"[37] The Woman's Suffrage Movement, holding its first convention in 1848 in Seneca Falls, New York, drew up a Declaration of Statements and Principles, which broadened the Declaration of Independence: "We hold these truths to be self-evident: that all men and women are created equal." The document protested "that woman has too long rested satisfied in the circumscribed limits which corrupt customs and a perverted application of the Scriptures have marked out for her" and called for the untiring effort of both men and women to secure for women "an equal participation with men in the various trades, professions, and commerce."[38]

In their struggle for equality, feminists had to overcome deeply ingrained premises about female inferiority and deficiencies. Even the philosophes, who often enjoyed the company of intelligent and sophisticated women in the famous salons, continued to view women as intellectually and morally inferior to men. Some philosophes, notably Condorcet, who wrote *Plea for the Citizenship of Women* (1791), argued for female emancipation, but they were the exception. Most philosophes concurred with Hume, who held that "nature has subjected" women to men and that their "inferiority and infirmities are absolutely incurable."[39]

Elizabeth Cady Stanton and Women's Rights

AN AMERICAN FEMINIST. Elizabeth Cady Stanton, who participated in the antislavery movement, was a key figure in the struggle for women's rights, including suffrage. (© Bettmann/Corbis.)

Rousseau, who believed that nature had granted men power over women, regarded traditional domesticity as a woman's proper role:

> *I would a thousand times rather have a homely girl, simply brought up, than a learned lady and a wit who would make a literary circle of my house and install herself as its president. A female wit is a scourge to her husband, her children, her friends, her servants, to everybody. From the lofty height of her genius, she scorns every womanly duty, and she is always trying to make a man of herself.*[40]

Nevertheless, by clearly articulating the ideals of liberty and equality, the philosophes made a women's movement possible. The growing popularity of these ideals could not escape women, who measured their own position by them. Moreover, by their very nature, these ideals were expansive. Denying them to women would ultimately be seen as an indefensible contradiction.

Opponents of women's rights argued that feminist demands would threaten society by undermining marriage and the family. An article in the *Saturday Review*, an English periodical, declared: "It is not the interest of States . . . to encourage the existence of women who are other than entirely dependent on man as well for subsistence as for protection and love. . . . Married life is a woman's profession."[41] And in 1870, a member of the House of Commons wondered "what would become, not merely of woman's influence, but of her duties at home, her care of the household, her supervision of all those duties and surroundings which make a happy home . . . if we are to see women coming forward and taking part in the government of the country."[42] This concern for the family combined with a traditional biased view of woman's nature, as one writer for the *Saturday Review* revealed.

> *The power of reasoning is so small in women that they need help, and if they have not the guidance and check of a religious conscience, it is useless to expect from them self-control on abstract principles. They do not calculate consequences, and they are reckless when they once give way, hence they are to be kept straight only through their [feelings], the religious sentiment and a well-educated moral sense.*[43]

No doubt the following comment of Jules and Edmond Goncourt, two prominent French writers, reflected the mood of many other French intellectuals.

> *Men like ourselves need a woman of little breeding and education who is nothing but gaiety and natural wit, because a woman of that sort can charm and please us like an*

> *agreeable animal to which we may become quite attached. But if a mistress has acquired a veneer of breeding, art, or literature, and tries to talk to us on an equal footing about our thoughts and our feeling for beauty; if she wants to be a companion and partner in the cultivation of our tastes or the writing of our books, then she becomes for us as unbearable as a piano out of tune—and very soon an object of dislike.*[44]

In contrast to most of their contemporaries, some prominent men did support equal rights for women. "Can man be free if woman be slave?"[45] asked Shelley, who favored female suffrage. So too did Bentham and the political economist William Thompson, who wrote *Appeal of One Half of the Human Race* (1825). John Stuart Mill thought that differences between the sexes (and between the classes) were due far more to education than to inherited inequalities. Believing that all people—women as well as men—should be able to develop their talents and intellects as fully as possible, Mill was an early champion of female equality, including women's suffrage. In 1867, Mill, as a member of Parliament, proposed that suffrage be extended to women (the proposal was rejected by a vote of 194 to 74).

In 1851, Mill had married Harriet Taylor, a longtime friend and a recent widow. An ardent feminist, Harriet Mill influenced her husband's thought. In *The Subjection of Women* (1869), Mill argued that male dominance of women constituted a flagrant abuse of power. He described female inequality as a single relic of an old outlook that had been exploded in everything else. It violated the principle of individual rights and hindered the progress of humanity.

> *The principle which regulates the existing social relations between the two sexes—the legal subordination of one sex to the other— is wrong in itself, and now one of the chief hindrances to human improvement. . . .*
>
> *It ought to be replaced by a principle of perfect equality, admitting no power or privilege on the one side, nor disability on the other.*[46]

Mill considered it only just that women be admitted to all the functions and occupations until then reserved for men. The struggle for female rights became a major issue in several lands at the end of the nineteenth century and the beginning of the twentieth.

Under the leadership of Emmeline Pankhurst (see "The Woman Question" in Chapter 25), agitation in Great Britain reached a peak during the turbulent years of parliamentary reform, 1909 to 1911. In 1913, Pankhurst carried her appeal to the United States, where she reiterated the anguish and logic of the feminists.

Now gentlemen, in your heart of hearts you . . . know perfectly well that if the situation were reversed, if you had no constitutional rights and we had all of them, if you had the duty of praying and obeying and trying to look . . . pleasant, and we were the proud citizens who could decide our fate and yours, because we knew what was good for you better than you knew yourselves, you know perfectly well that you wouldn't stand it for a single day, and you would be perfectly justified in rebelling against such intolerable conditions.[47]

NOTES

1. Quoted in George J. Becker, *Master European Realists of the Nineteenth Century* (New York: Ungar, 1982), 30–31.

2. Cited in Damian Grant, *Realism* (London: Methuen, 1970), 31–32.

3. Cited in F. W. J. Hemmings, ed., *The Age of Realism* (Atlantic Highlands, N.J.: Humanities Press, 1978), 152.

4. Quoted in Leonard J. Davis, "Gustave Flaubert," in *The Romantic Century*, vol. 7, *European Writers*, ed. Jacques Barzun and George Stade (New York: Charles Scribner's Sons, 1985), 1381.

5. Ibid., 1382.

6. Émile Zola, *The Experimental Novel*, trans. Belle M. Sherman (New York: Haskell House, 1964), 20–21, 23.

7. Henrik Ibsen, *A Doll's House*, in *Eleven Plays of Henrik Ibsen* (New York: Modern Library, n.d.), 85–87.

8. Quoted in Ernst Cassirer, *The Problem of Knowledge: Philosophy, Science, and History Since Hegel*, trans. William H. Woglom and Charles W. Hendel (New Haven, Conn.: Yale University Press, 1950), 244.

9. Quoted in Andrew D. White, *A History of the Warfare of Science with Theology in Christendom* (New York: Appleton, 1896), 1:71.

10. Excerpted in Richard Olson, ed., *Science as Metaphor* (Belmont, Calif.: Wadsworth, 1971), 124.

11. Andrew Carnegie, *The Gospel of Wealth* (New York: Century, 1900), 4, 11.

12. Karl Pearson, *National Life from the Standpoint of Science* (London: Adam and Charles Black, 1905), 21, 64.

13. Quoted in H. W. Koch, "Social Darwinism in the 'New Imperialism,'" in *The Origins of the First World War*, ed. H. W. Koch (New York: Taplinger, 1972), 341.

14. Ibid., 345.

15. Quoted in John C. Greene, *The Death of Adam* (New York: Mentor Books, 1961), 313.

16. Quoted in Sven Lindqvist, *Exterminate the Brutes*, trans. Joan Tate (New York: New Press, 1996), 150–151.

17. Quoted in George M. Fredrickson, *The Black Image in the White Mind* (New York: Harper Torch-books, 1972), 26–27.

18. Ludwig Feuerbach, *The Essence of Christianity*, trans. George Eliot (New York: Harper Torch-books, 1957), 33.

19. Ibid., 26–28.

20. Karl Marx, *Theses on Feuerbach*, excerpted in *Karl Marx: Selected Writings in Sociology and Social Philosophy*, ed. T. B. Bottomore and Maximilien Rubel (London: Watts, 1956), 69.

21. Karl Marx, *The German Ideology* (New York: International Publishers, 1939), 18.

22. Friedrich Engels, *The Origin of the Family, Private Property and the State*, in *A Handbook of Marxism*, ed. Emile Burns (New York: Random House, 1935), 330.

23. Marx, *German Ideology*, 69.

24. Karl Marx, *Communist Manifesto*, trans. Samuel Moore (Chicago: Henry Regnery, 1954), 81–82.

25. Robert Tucker, *Philosophy and Myth in Karl Marx* (Cambridge: Cambridge University Press, 1972), 22.

26. Excerpted in G. P. Maximoff, ed., *The Political Philosophy of Bakunin* (Glencoe, Ill.: Free Press, 1953), 287.

27. John Stuart Mill, *On Liberty* (Boston: Ticknor and Fields, 1863), 36.

28. Ibid., 22.

29. Thomas Hill Green, *Lectures on the Principles of Political Obligation* (Ann Arbor: University of Michigan Press, 1967), 219.

30. Thomas Hill Green, "Liberal Legislation or Freedom of Contract," a lecture given at Leicester, 1881, excerpted in Alan Bullock and Maurice Shock, eds., *The Liberal Tradition* (London: Adam and Charles Black, 1956), 181.

31. Herbert Spencer, *The Man Versus the State* (London: Watts, 1940), 34, 49–50.

32. Ibid., 152.

33. Quoted in Anthony Arblaster, *The Rise and Decline of Liberalism* (London: Basil Blackwell, 1984), 290.

34. Excerpted in Eleanor S. Riemer and John C. Fout, eds., *European Women: A Documentary History, 1789–1945* (New York: Schocken Books, 1980), 63–64.

35. Mary Wollstonecraft, *Vindication of the Rights of Woman* (London: Dent, 1929), 11–12.

36. Excerpted in Gayle Graham Yates, ed., *Harriet Martineau on Women* (New Brunswick, N.J.: Rutgers University Press, 1985), 134.

37. Excerpted in Miriam Schneir, ed., *Feminism: The Essential Historical Writings* (New York: Vintage Books, 1972), 40–41.

38. Ibid., 76, 82.

39. Quoted in Bonnie S. Anderson and Judith P. Zinsser, *A History of Their Own* (New York: Harper and Row, 1988), 2:113.

40. Jean Jacques Rousseau, *Emile*, trans. Barbara Foxley (London: Dent, Everyman's Library, 1974), 370.

41. Quoted in J. A. and Olive Banks, *Feminism and Family Planning in Victorian England* (Liverpool: Liverpool University Press, 1965), 43.

42. Ibid., 46.

43. Ibid., 47.

44. Robert Baldick, ed. and trans., *Pages from the Goncourt Journal* (New York: Penguin Books, 1984), 27.

45. Percy Bysshe Shelley, "The Revolt of Islam," canto 2, stanza 43, in *The Complete Poetical Works of Percy Bysshe Shelley*, ed. Thomas Hutchinson (London: Oxford University Press, 1929), 63.

46. John Stuart Mill, *The Subjection of Women*, in *On Liberty and The Subjection of Women* (London: Oxford University Press, 1924), 427.

47. Excerpted in Jane Marcus, ed., *Suffrage and the Pankhursts* (London: Routledge & Kegan Paul, 1967), 160–161.

Chapter 24

The Surge of Nationalism: From Liberal to Extreme Nationalism

Victor Emmanuel and Garibaldi at the Bridge of Teano (1860). The unification of Italy was the work of the romantic liberal Giuseppe Mazzini, the practical politician Count Cavour, and the seasoned revolutionary Giuseppe Garibaldi. Selflessly, Garibaldi turned over his conquests in the south to Victor Emmanuel in 1861. (Scala/Art Resource, N.Y.)

- **The Unification of Italy**
- **The Unification of Germany**
- **The Hapsburg Empire**
- **The Rise of Racial Nationalism**

Focus Questions

1. How did nationalism promote unity in some lands and division in others?
2. What was the historical significance of the unification of Germany under Prussian leadership?
3. Why did the expressions of extreme nationalism mark a repudiation of the Enlightenment tradition and a regression to mythical modes of thought?
4. What is the relationship between medieval and modern anti-Semitism? How does anti-Semitism demonstrate the immense power of mythical thinking?

The revolutions of 1848 ended in failure, but nationalist energies were too powerful to contain. In 1867, Hungary gained the autonomy it had sought in 1848, and by 1871 the unification of both Italy and Germany was complete. The leading architects of Italian and German unification were not liberal idealists or romantic dreamers of the type who had fought in the revolutions of 1848; they were tough-minded practitioners of **realpolitik**, "the politics of reality." Shrewd and calculating statesmen, they respected power and knew how to wield it; focusing on the actual world, they dismissed ideals as illusory, noble sentiments that impeded effective action. Realpolitik was the political counterpart of realism and positivism. All three outlooks shared the desire to view things coldly and objectively as they are, rather than as idealists would like them to be.

Nationalism, gaining in intensity in the last part of the nineteenth century, was to become the dominant spiritual force in European life. Once Germany was unified, Pan-Germans sought to incorporate Germans living outside the *Reich* (German Empire) into the new Germany and to build a vast overseas empire. Russian Pan-Slavs dreamed of bringing the Slavs of Eastern Europe under the control of "Mother Russia." Growing increasingly resentful of Magyar and German domination, the Slavic minorities of the Hapsburg Empire agitated for recognition of their national rights. In the late 1800s, nationalism became increasingly belligerent, intolerant, and irrational, threatening the peace of Europe and the liberal-humanist tradition of the Enlightenment.

THE UNIFICATION OF ITALY

In 1848, liberals failed to drive the Austrians out of Italy and to unite the Italian nation. By 1870, however, Italian unification was achieved despite many obstacles.

Forces for and Against Unity

In 1815, Italy consisted of separate states. In the south, a Bourbon king ruled the Kingdom

Chronology 24.1 ❖ The Unification of Italy

1821	Austria suppresses Carbonari rebellion
1831–1832	Austria suppresses another Carbonari insurrection
1832	Mazzini forms Young Italy
March 1848	Austrians are forced to withdraw from Milan and Venice
November 1848	Liberal revolution forces pope to flee Rome
1848–1849	Austria reasserts its authority in Milan and Venice; Louis Napoleon crushes revolutionaries in Rome
1858	Napoleon III agrees to help Piedmont-Sardinia against Austria
1859	War between Piedmont-Sardinia and Austria: Piedmont obtains Lombardy from Austria; Parma, Modena, Tuscany, and Romagna vote to join with Piedmont
1860	Garibaldi invades Kingdom of the Two Sicilies
March 17, 1861	Victor Emmanuel of Piedmont is proclaimed king of Italy
1866	Italy's alliance with Prussia against Austria results in annexation of Venetia by Italy
1870	Rome is incorporated into the Italian state, and unity is achieved

of the Two Sicilies; the pope governed the Papal States in central Italy; Hapsburg Austria ruled Lombardy and Venetia in the north; and Hapsburg princes subservient to Austria ruled the duchies of Tuscany, Parma, and Modena. Piedmont in the northwest and the island of Sardinia were governed by an Italian dynasty, the House of Savoy. Besides these political divisions, Italy was divided economically and culturally. Throughout the peninsula, attachment to the local region was stronger than the desire for national unity. Economic ties between north and south were weak; inhabitants of the northern Italian cities felt little closeness to Sicilian peasants. Except for the middle class, most Italians clung to the values of the Old Regime. Believing that society was ordered by God, they accepted without question rule by prince and pope and rejected the values associated with the French Revolution and the Enlightenment. To many traditionalists, national unity was also hateful. It would deprive the pope of his control over central Italy, introduce liberal ideas that would undermine clerical and aristocratic authority, and depose legitimate princes.

During the wars of the French Revolution, France had occupied Italy. The French eliminated many barriers to trade among the Italian states. They built roads, which improved links between the various regions, and they introduced a standard system of law over most of the land. The French also gave the Italian states constitutions, representative assemblies, and the concept of the state as a community of citizens.

The Italian middle class believed that expelling foreign rulers and forging national unity would continue the process of enlightened reform initiated by the French occupation and that this process would promote economic growth. Merchants and manufacturers wanted to abolish taxes on goods transported from one Italian state to another; they wanted roads and railways built to link the peninsula together; and they wanted to do away with the numerous systems of coinage and weights and measures, which complicated business transactions. Italians who had served Napoleon as local officials, clerks, and army officers resisted the restoration of clerical and feudal privileges, which denied them career opportunities.

583

Through works of history and literature, an intellectual elite awakened interest in Italy's glorious past. It insisted that a people who had built the Roman Empire and produced the Renaissance must not remain weak and divided, their land occupied by Austrians. These sentiments appealed particularly to university students and the middle class. But the rural masses, illiterate and preoccupied with the hardships of daily life, had little concern for this struggle for national revival.

Failed Revolutions

Secret societies kept alive the hopes for liberty and independence from foreign rule in the period after 1815. The most important of these societies was the Carbonari, which had clubs in every state in Italy. In 1820, the Carbonari, its members drawn largely from the middle class and the army, enjoyed a few months of triumph in the Kingdom of the Two Sicilies. Supported by the army and militia, they forced King Ferdinand I to grant a constitution and a parliamentary government. But Metternich feared that the germ of revolution would spread to other countries. Supported by Prussia and Russia, Austria suppressed the constitutional government in Naples and another revolution that broke out in Piedmont. In both cases, Austria firmly fixed an absolute ruler on the throne. During 1831–1832, the Austrians suppressed another insurrection by the Carbonari, in the Papal States. During these uprisings, the peasants had given little support; indeed, they seemed to side with the traditional rulers.

After the failure of the Carbonari, a new generation of leaders emerged in Italy. One of them, Giuseppe Mazzini (1805–1872), dedicated his life to the creation of a united and republican Italy—a goal he pursued with extraordinary moral intensity and determination. Mazzini was both a romantic and a liberal. As a liberal, he fought for republican and constitutional government and held that national unity would enhance individual liberty. As a romantic, he sought truth through heightened feeling and intuition and believed that an awakened Italy would lead to the regeneration of humanity. Mazzini believed that just as Rome had provided law and unity in the ancient world, and the Roman pope had led Latin Christendom during the Middle Ages, so a third Rome, a newly united Italy, would usher in a new age of free nations, personal liberty, and equality. This era would represent great progress for humanity: peace, prosperity, and universal happiness would replace conflict, materialism, and self-interest. Given to religious mysticism, Mazzini saw a world of independent states founded on nationality, republicanism, and democracy as the fulfillment of God's plan.

After his release from prison for participating in the insurrection of 1831, Mazzini went into exile and founded a new organization, Young Italy. Consisting of dedicated revolutionaries, many of them students, Young Italy was intended to serve as the instrument for the awakening of Italy and the transformation of Europe into a brotherhood of free peoples.

Mazzini believed that a successful revolution must come from below—from the people, moved by a profound love for their nation. They must overthrow the Hapsburg princes and create a democratic republic. This could be achieved only by a revolution of the masses. Mazzini had great charisma, determination, courage, and eloquence; he was also a prolific writer. His idealism attracted the intelligentsia and youth and kept alive the spirit of national unity. He infused the *Risorgimento*, the movement for Italian unity, with spiritual intensity.

Mazzini's plans for a mass uprising against Austria and the princes failed. In 1834, a band of Mazzini's followers attempted to invade Savoy. But everything went wrong, and the invasion collapsed. Other setbacks occurred in 1837, 1841, and 1843–1844. During the revolutions of 1848, however, Italian liberal-nationalists enjoyed initial successes. In Sicily, revolutionaries forced King Ferdinand to grant a liberal constitution. The rulers of Tuscany and Piedmont-Sardinia promised constitutions. After five days of fighting, revolutionaries drove the Austrians out of Milan in Lombardy. The Austrians were also forced to evacuate Venice, where a republic was proclaimed. The pope fled Rome, and Mazzini was elected to an executive office in a new Roman Republic. However, the forces of reaction, led by Hapsburg Austria, regained their courage and authority and crushed the revolutionary movements one by one. French troops dissolved the infant Roman Republic and restored Pope Pius IX to power. Italy remained divided, and Austria still ruled the north.

Cavour and Victory over Austria

The failure of the revolutions of 1848 contained an obvious lesson: Mazzini's approach, an armed uprising by aroused masses, did not work because the masses were not committed to the nationalist cause and the revolutionaries were no match for the Austrian army. Italian nationalists now hoped that the Kingdom of Piedmont-Sardinia, ruled by an Italian dynasty, would expel the Austrians and lead the drive for unity. Count Camillo Benso di Cavour (1810–1861), the chief minister of Piedmont-Sardinia, became the architect of Italian unity.

Unlike Mazzini, Cavour was neither a dreamer nor a speechmaker but a cautious and practical statesman who realized that mass uprisings could not succeed against Austrian might. Moreover, mistrusting the common people, he did not approve of Mazzini's goal of a democratic republic. Cavour had no precise plan for unifying Italy. His immediate aim was to increase the territory of Piedmont by driving the Austrians from northern Italy and incorporating Lombardy and Venetia into Piedmont-Sardinia. But this expulsion could not be accomplished without allies, for Austria was a great power and Piedmont a small state. To improve Piedmont's image in foreign affairs, Cavour launched a reform program to strengthen the economy. He reorganized the currency, taxes, and the national debt; in addition, he had railways and steamships built, fostered improved agricultural methods, and encouraged new businesses. Within a few years, Piedmont became a progressive, modern state.

In 1855, Piedmont joined England and France in the Crimean War against Russia. Cavour had no quarrel with Russia but sought the friendship of Britain and France and a chance to be heard in world affairs. At the peace conference, Cavour was granted an opportunity to denounce Austria for occupying Italian lands.

After the peace conference, Cavour continued to encourage anti-Austrian feeling among Italians and to search for foreign support. He found a supporter in Napoleon III (1852–1870), the French emperor, who hoped that a unified northern Italy would become an ally and client of France.

In 1858, Cavour and Napoleon III reached a secret agreement. If Austria attacked Piedmont, France would aid the Italian state. Piedmont would annex Lombardy and Venetia and parts of the Papal States. In return, France would obtain Nice and Savoy from Piedmont. With this agreement in his pocket, Cavour cleverly maneuvered Austria into declaring war (he did so by strengthening Piedmont's army and urging volunteers from Austrian-controlled Lombardy to join it), for it had to appear that Austria was the aggressor.

Supported by French forces and taking advantage of poor Austrian planning, Piedmont conquered Lombardy and occupied Milan. But Napoleon III quickly had second thoughts. If Piedmont took any of the pope's territory, French Catholics would blame their own leader. Even more serious was the fear that Prussia, suspicious of French aims, would aid Austria. For these reasons, Napoleon III, without consulting Cavour, signed an armistice with Austria. Piedmont would acquire Lombardy, but no more. An outraged Cavour demanded that his state continue the war until all northern Italy was liberated, but King Victor Emmanuel of Piedmont accepted the Austrian peace terms.

The victory of Piedmont-Sardinia, however, proved greater than Cavour had anticipated. During the conflict, patriots in Parma, Modena, Tuscany, and Romagna (one of the Papal States) had seized power. These new revolutionary governments voted to join with Piedmont.

Garibaldi and Victory in the South

Piedmont's success spurred revolutionary activity in the Kingdom of the Two Sicilies. In the spring of 1860, some one thousand red-shirted adventurers and patriots landed in Sicily. Led by Giuseppe Garibaldi (1807–1882), who, like Mazzini, was also a professional revolutionary, they were determined to liberate the land from its Bourbon ruler, and they succeeded.

An early supporter of Mazzini, Garibaldi had been forced to flee Italy to avoid arrest for his revolutionary activities. He spent thirteen years in South America, where he took part in revolutionary movements. There he learned the skills of the revolutionary's trade and toughened his body and will for the struggle that lay ahead.

Garibaldi held progressive views. He supported the liberation of all subject nationalities, female equality, the right of workers to organize, racial equality, and the abolition of capital punishment. But the cause of a unified Italy was his true religion.

Garibaldi returned to Italy just in time to fight in the revolution of 1848. He was a brilliant leader who captivated the hearts of the people and won the poor and illiterate to the cause of Italian nationalism. After the liberation of Sicily in 1860, Garibaldi invaded the mainland. He occupied Naples without a fight and prepared to advance on Rome. In this particular instance, Garibaldi's success confirmed Mazzini's belief that a popular leader could arouse the masses to heroic action.

Cavour feared that an assault on Rome by Garibaldi would lead to French intervention. Napoleon III had pledged to defend the pope's lands, and a French garrison had been stationed in Rome since 1849. Moreover, Cavour considered Garibaldi too impulsive and rash, too attracted to republican ideals, and too popular with the masses to lead the struggle for unification.

Cavour persuaded Napoleon III to approve an invasion of the Papal States by Piedmont to head off Garibaldi. A papal force offered only token opposition, and the Papal States of Umbria and the Marches soon voted for union with Piedmont, as did Naples and Sicily. Refusing to trade on his prestige with the masses to fulfill personal ambition, Garibaldi turned over his conquests to Piedmont's King Victor Emmanuel, who was declared king of Italy in 1861.

Italian Unification Completed

Two regions still remained outside the control of the new Italy: the city of Rome, ruled by the pope and protected by French troops; and Venetia, occupied by Austria. Cavour died in 1861, but the march toward unification continued. During the conflict between Prussia and Austria in 1866, Italy sided with the victorious Prussians and was rewarded with Venetia. During the Franco-Prussian War of 1870, France withdrew its garrisons from Rome; much to the anger of the pope, Italian troops marched in, and Rome was declared the capital of Italy.

THE UNIFICATION OF GERMANY

In 1848, German liberals and nationalists, believing in the strength of their ideals, naïvely underestimated the power of the conservative Old Order. After the failed revolution, some disenchanted revolutionaries retained only a half-hearted commitment to liberalism or embraced conservatism; others fled the country, weakening the liberal leadership. All liberals came to doubt the effectiveness of revolution as a way to transform Germany into a unified state; all gained new respect for the realities of power. Abandoning idealism for realism, liberals now thought that German unity would be achieved through Prussian arms, not liberal ideals.

Prussia, Agent of Unification

During the late seventeenth and eighteenth centuries, Prussian kings had fashioned a rigorously trained and disciplined army. The state bureaucracy, often staffed by ex-soldiers, perpetuated the military mentality. As the chief organizations in the state, the army and the bureaucracy drilled into the Prussian people a respect for discipline and authority.

The Prussian throne was supported by the Junkers. These powerful aristocrats, who owned vast estates farmed by serfs, were exempt from most taxes and dominated local government in their territories. The Junkers' commanding position made them officers in the royal army, diplomats, and leading officials in the state bureaucracy. The Junkers knew that a weakening of the king's power would lead to the loss of their own aristocratic prerogatives.

In France in the late 1700s, a powerful and politically conscious middle class had challenged aristocratic privileges. The Prussian monarchy and the Junkers had faced no such challenge, for the Prussian middle class at that time was small and ineffectual. The idea of individual rights did not deeply penetrate Prussian consciousness, nor

Chronology 24.2 ❖ The Unification of Germany

1815	German Confederation is formed
1834	Zollverein is established under Prussian leadership
1848	Liberals fail to unify Germany
1862	Bismarck becomes chancellor of Prussia
1864	Austria and Prussia defeat Denmark in a war over Schleswig-Holstein
1866	Seven Weeks' War between Austria and Prussia: Prussia emerges as the dominant power in Germany and organizes the North German Confederation
1870-1871	Franco-Prussian War
January 18, 1871	William I becomes German kaiser

did it undermine the Prussian tradition of obedience to military and state authority. Liberalism did not take firm root in Germany.

Reforms from Above. The reform movement that began after Napoleon completely routed the Prussians at Jena (in 1806) arose from distress at the military collapse and at the apathy of the Prussian population. High bureaucrats and military men demanded reforms that would draw the people closer to their country and king. These leaders had learned the great lesson of the French Revolution: a devoted citizen army fights more effectively than oppressed serfs. To imbue all classes with civic pride, the reformers abolished hereditary serfdom, gave the urban middle class a greater voice in city government, laid the foundations for universal education, and granted full citizenship to Jews. To improve the army's morale, they eliminated severe punishments and based promotions on performance rather than birth.

But the reformers failed to give Prussia a constitution and parliamentary institutions. The middle class still had no voice in the central government. Monarchical power persisted, and the economic, political, and military power of the Junkers remained unbroken. Thus, liberalism had an unpromising beginning in Prussia. In France, the bourgeoisie had instituted reforms based on the principles of liberty and equality; in Prussia,

the bureaucracy introduced reforms to strengthen the state, not to promote liberty.

In 1834, under Prussian leadership, the German states, with the notable exception of Austria, had established the *Zollverein*, a customs union, which abolished tariffs between the states. The customs union stimulated economic activity and promoted a desire for greater unity. Businessmen, particularly, felt that having thirty-nine states in Germany was an obstacle to economic progress. The Zollverein provided the economic foundations for the political unification of Germany, and it led many Germans to view Prussia, not Austria, as the leader of the unification movement.

Liberals' Failure. Influenced by the legacy of the French Revolution, the ideas of legal equality, political liberty, and careers open to talent found favor with the Prussian bourgeoisie. Like the French bourgeois of the Old Regime, Prussian bankers, manufacturers, and lawyers hated a system that denied them social recognition and political influence but rewarded idle sons of the nobility with the best positions. They also denounced government regulations and taxes, which hampered business, and they loathed the rigorous censorship, which stifled free thought. Peasants and artisans, concerned with economic survival, respectful of tradition, and suspicious of new ideas, did not identify with liberal principles.

Map 24.1 UNIFICATION OF GERMANY, 1866–1871 Between 1866 and 1871, Prussia fought wars against Denmark, Austria, and France, which resulted in the unification of Germany under Prussian leadership. Otto von Bismarck was the principal architect of German unification. (© 2016 Cengage Learning.)

During the revolution of 1848, liberals failed to wrest power from the monarchy and aristocracy and create a unified Germany. Frederick William IV (1840–1861) had refused the crown offered him by the Frankfurt Assembly. The Prussian monarch could not stomach German unity created by a revolution of commoners. But a German union fashioned and headed by a conservative Prussia was different and proved attractive to the Prussian monarchy.

Bismarck and the Road to Unity

Before Prussia could extend its hegemony over the other German states, Austrian influence in

German affairs would have to be eliminated. This was one reason why William I (1861–1888) called for a drastic reorganization of the Prussian army. But the liberals in the lower chamber of the Prussian Parliament blocked passage of the army reforms, for they feared that the reforms would greatly increase the power of the monarchy and the military establishment. Unable to secure passage, William withdrew the reform bill and asked the lower chamber for additional funds to cover government expenses. When Parliament granted these funds, he used the money to institute the army reforms. Learning from its mistake, the lower chamber would not approve the new budget in 1862 without an itemized breakdown.

A conflict had arisen between the liberal majority in the lower chamber and the crown. If the liberals won, they would, in effect, establish parliamentary control over the king and the army. At this critical hour, King William asked Otto von Bismarck (1815–1898) to lead the battle against Parliament.

Descended on his father's side from an old aristocratic family, Bismarck was a staunch supporter of the Prussian monarchy and the Junker class and a devout patriot. He yearned to increase the territory and prestige of his beloved Prussia and to protect the authority of the Prussian king, who, Bismarck believed, ruled by the grace of God. Liberals were outraged by Bismarck's domineering, authoritarian manner and his determination to preserve monarchical power and the aristocratic order. Set on continuing the reorganization of the army and determined not to bow to parliamentary pressure, Bismarck ordered the collection of taxes without Parliament's approval—an action that would have been unthinkable in Britain or the United States.

When the lower chamber continued to withhold funds, Bismarck dismissed the chamber, imposed strict censorship on the press, arrested outspoken liberals, and fired liberals from the civil service. The liberals protested against these arbitrary and unconstitutional moves, but they did not use force. Because the army fully supported the government and there was no significant popular support for challenging the government, an armed uprising would have failed. What led to a resolution of the conflict was Bismarck's extraordinary success in foreign affairs.

Wars with Denmark and Austria. To Bismarck, a war between Austria and Prussia seemed inevitable, for only by removing Austria from German affairs could Prussia extend its dominion over the other German states. Bismarck's first move, however, was not against Austria but against Denmark. The issue that led to the war in 1864 was enormously complex. Simplified, the issue was that Bismarck (and German nationalists) wanted to free the two duchies of Schleswig and Holstein from Danish control. Both territories, which contained a large number of Germans, had been administered by Denmark, but in 1863 Schleswig was incorporated into the Danish realm. Hoping to prevent Prussia from annexing the territories, Austria joined Prussia as an ally. After Denmark's defeat, Austria and Prussia tried to decide the disposition of the territories. Bismarck used the dispute to goad Austria into war. The Austrians, on their side, were convinced that Prussia must be defeated for Austria to retain its influence over German affairs.

In the Austro-Prussian War of 1866, Prussia, with astonishing speed, assembled its forces and overran Austrian territory. At the battle of Sadowa (or Königgrätz), Prussia decisively defeated the main Austrian forces, and the Seven Weeks' War ended. Prussia took no territory from Austria, but the latter agreed to Prussia's annexation of Schleswig and Holstein and a number of small German states. Prussia, moreover, organized a union of northern German states—the North German Confederation—that excluded Austria and was controlled by Prussia, now the dominant power in Germany.

The Triumph of Nationalism and Conservatism over Liberalism. The Prussian victory had a profound impact on political life within Prussia. Bismarck was the man of the hour, the great hero who had extended Prussia's power. Most liberals forgave Bismarck for his authoritarian handling of Parliament. The liberal press, which had previously denounced Bismarck for riding roughshod over the constitution, now lionized him. Prussians were urged to concentrate on the glorious tasks ahead and put aside the constitutional struggle, which, in contrast, appeared petty and insignificant.

Bismarck recognized the great appeal of nationalism and used it to expand Prussia's power

WILLIAM I OF PRUSSIA. In January 1871, while assembled in the Hall of Mirrors at Versailles, the German princes granted William the title of Kaiser (German emperor). (Three Lions/Getty Images)

over other German states and strengthen Prussia's voice in European affairs. By heralding his state as the champion of unification, Bismarck gained the support of nationalists throughout Germany. In the past, the nationalist cause had belonged to the liberals, but Bismarck appropriated it to promote Prussian expansion and conservative rule.

Prussia's victory over Austria, therefore, was a triumph for conservatism and nationalism and a defeat for liberalism. The liberal struggle for constitutional government in Prussia collapsed.

The Prussian monarch retained the right to override parliamentary opposition and act on his own initiative. In 1848, Prussian might had suppressed a liberal revolution; in 1866, liberals, beguiled by Bismarck's military triumphs, gave up the struggle for responsible parliamentary government. They had traded political freedom for Prussian military glory and power.

The capitulation of Prussian liberals demonstrated the essential weakness of the German liberal tradition. German liberals displayed

GAUL TO THE NEW CÆSAR.

"DEFIANCE, EMPEROR, WHILE I HAVE STRENGTH TO HURL IT!"

PRUSSIA'S GROWING MIGHT CONCERNS FRANCE. During the Franco-Prussian war, *Punch*, the humorist and satirical British weekly magazine, published this cartoon showing French fear of Prussia's growing might. It shows a woman, representing France, supplicating herself before Frederick William I, the ruler of Prussia. (Punch Limited.)

diminishing commitment to the principles of parliamentary government and growing fascination with power, military triumph, and territorial expansion. Bismarck's words, written in 1858, turned out to be prophetic: "Exalt his self-esteem toward foreigners and the Prussian forgets whatever bothers him about conditions at home."[1] The liberal dream of a united Germany had been preempted by conservatives. Enthralled by Bismarck's achievement, many liberals abandoned liberalism and threw their support behind the authoritarian Prussian state. Germans of all classes acquired an adoration for Prussian militarism and for the power state, with its Machiavellian guideline that

all means are justified if they result in the expansion of German power. In 1848, German liberals had called for "Unity and Freedom." What Bismarck gave them was unity and authoritarianism.

War with France. Prussia emerged from the war with Austria as the leading power in the North German Confederation; the Prussian king controlled the armies and foreign affairs of the states within the confederation. To complete the unification of Germany, Bismarck would have to draw the South German states into the new confederation. But the South German states, Catholic and hostile to Prussian authoritarianism, feared being absorbed by Prussia. Bismarck hoped that a war between Prussia and France would ignite the nationalist feelings of the South Germans, causing them to overlook the differences that separated them from Prussia.

Napoleon III, the emperor of France, was not averse to war either. The creation of a powerful North German Confederation had frightened the French, and the prospect that the South German states might one day add their strength to the new Germany was terrifying. Both France and Prussia had parties that advocated war.

A cause for war arose over the succession to the vacated Spanish throne. King William of Prussia discussed the issue with the French ambassador and sent Bismarck a telegram informing him of what had ensued. With the support of high military leaders, Bismarck edited the telegram. The revised version gave the impression that the Prussian king and the French ambassador had insulted each other. Bismarck wanted to inflame French feeling against Prussia and arouse German opinion against France. He succeeded. In both Paris and Berlin, crowds of people, gripped by war fever, demanded satisfaction. When France declared a general mobilization, Prussia followed suit; Bismarck had his war.

As Bismarck had anticipated, the South German states came to the aid of Prussia. Quickly and decisively routing the French forces and capturing Napoleon III, the Prussians went on to besiege Paris. Faced with starvation, Paris surrendered in January 1871. France was compelled to pay a large indemnity and to cede to Germany the border provinces of Alsace and Lorraine—a loss that French patriots could never accept.

OTTO VON BISMARCK. Bismarck (1815–1898), the Iron Chancellor, was instrumental in unifying Germany. A conservative, he resisted Parliament's efforts to weaken the monarch's power. Here he is portrayed in his youth, before becoming chancellor.
(akg-images/ullstein bild.)

The Franco-Prussian War completed the unification of Germany. On January 18, 1871, at Versailles, the German princes granted the title of German kaiser (emperor) to William I. A powerful nation had arisen in Central Europe. Its people were educated, disciplined, and efficient; its industries and commerce were rapidly expanding; its army was the finest in Europe. Vigorous, confident, and intensely nationalistic, the new German Empire would be eager to play a greater role in world affairs. No nation in Europe was a match for the new Germany. Metternich's fears had been realized: a Germany dominated by Prussia had upset the balance of power. The unification of Germany created fears, tensions, and rivalries that would culminate in world wars.

THE HAPSBURG EMPIRE

In Italy and Germany, nationalism had led to the creation of unified states; in Austria, nationalism eventually caused the destruction of the centuries-old Hapsburg dynasty. A mosaic of different nationalities, each with its own history and traditions, the Austrian Empire could not survive in an age of intense nationalism. England and France had succeeded in unifying peoples of different ethnic backgrounds, but they did so during the Middle Ages, when ethnic consciousness was still rudimentary. The Austrian Empire, in contrast, had to weld together and reconcile antagonistic nationalities when nationalistic consciousness was high. The empire's collapse in the final stages of World War I was the culmination of years of antagonism among its different peoples.

In the first half of the nineteenth century, the Germans, constituting less than one-quarter of the population, were the dominant national group in the empire. But Magyars, Poles, Czechs, Slovaks, Croats, Romanians, Ruthenians, and Italians were experiencing national self-awareness. Poets and writers who had been educated in Latin, French, and German began to write in their mother tongues and extol their splendors. By searching their past for glorious ancestors and glorious deeds, writers kindled pride in their native histories and folklore and aroused anger against past and present injustices.

During 1848–1849, the Hapsburg monarchy had extinguished the Magyar bid for independence, the Czech revolution in Prague, and the uprisings in the Italian provinces of Lombardy and Venetia. Greatly alarmed by these revolutions, the Austrian power structure resolved to resist pressures for political rights by strengthening autocracy and tightening the central bureaucracy. German and Germanized officials took over administrative and judicial duties formerly handled on a local level. An expanded secret police stifled liberal and nationalist expressions. The various nationalities, of course, resented these efforts at centralization and repression.

The defeats by France and Piedmont in 1859 and by Prussia in 1866 cost Austria its two Italian provinces. The defeat by Prussia also forced the Hapsburg monarchy to make concessions to the Magyars, the strongest of the non-German nationalities; for without a loyal Hungary, the Hapsburg monarchy could suffer other humiliations. The Settlement of 1867 split the Hapsburg territories into Austria and Hungary. The two countries retained a common ruler, Francis Joseph (reigned 1848–1916), who was emperor of Austria and king of Hungary. Hungary gained complete control over its internal affairs: the administration of justice and education. Foreign and military affairs, as well as common financial concerns, were dealt with by a ministry consisting of delegates from both lands.

With the Settlement of 1867, Magyars and Germans became the dominant nationalities in the empire. The other nationalities felt that the German-Magyar political, economic, and cultural domination blocked their own national aspirations. Nationality struggles in the half century following the Settlement of 1867 consumed the energies of the Austrians and Hungarians. In both lands, however, the leaders failed to solve the problem of minorities, a failure that helped precipitate World War I and led to the dissolution of the empire during the last weeks of the war.

THE RISE OF RACIAL NATIONALISM

In the first half of the nineteenth century, nationalism and liberalism went hand in hand. Liberals sought both the rights of the individual and national independence and unification. Liberal nationalists believed that a unified state free of foreign subjugation was in harmony with the principle of natural rights, and they insisted that love of country led to love of humanity. "With all my ardent love of my nation," said Francis Palacky, a Czech patriot, "I always esteem more highly the good of mankind and of learning than the good of the nation."[2] Addressing the Slavs, Mazzini declared: "We who have ourselves arisen in the name of our national right, believe in your right, and offer to help you to win it. But the purpose of our mission is the permanent and peaceful organization of Europe."[3] Liberals expected that nationalism would unite a people in freedom

and fellowship, foster a national cultural flowering, and promote idealism by leading people to set aside personal concerns for the good of the nation. They did not anticipate the emergence of an extreme nationalism that would subvert liberal values. The extreme nationalism of the late nineteenth and early twentieth centuries contributed to World War I and to the rise of Fascism after the war. It was the seedbed of totalitarian nationalism. Nationalism proved more successful than liberalism in attracting allegiance, which often was expressed by total commitment to the nation, and establishing cohesion—uniting the various classes in a common cause.

Concerned exclusively with the greatness of the nation, extreme nationalists rejected the liberal emphasis on political liberty. Liberals regarded the state as a community of individuals voluntarily bound by law and citizenship and entitled to the same rights. To extreme nationalists, however, the state was the highest development of a folkish-racial spirit inherited from their ancestors. In their eyes, profound and irreconcilable differences separated "their people" from those who did not share this ancestry. Even if they had dwelled in the land for centuries, such people were seen as dangerous aliens. Increasingly, they attacked parliamentary government as a barrier to national unity and greatness and maintained that authoritarian leadership was needed to meet national emergencies. The needs of the nation, they said, transcended the rights of the individual. Extreme nationalists also rejected the liberal ideal of equality. Placing the nation above everything, nationalists accused national minorities of corrupting the nation's spirit. In the name of national power and unity, they persecuted minorities at home and stirred up hatred against other nations. And they also glorified war as a symbol of the nation's resolve and will. At the founding of the Nationalist Association in Italy in 1910, one leader declared:

> *Just as socialism teaches the proletariat the value of class struggle, so we must teach Italy the value of international struggle. But international struggle is war? Well, then, let there be war! And nationalism will arouse the will for a victorious war, . . . the only way to national redemption.*[4]

Similar sentiments were voiced in 1913 by a German nationalist: "Let us regard war as holy, like the purifying force of fate, for it will awaken in our people all that is great and ready for selfless sacrifice, while it cleanses our soul of the mire of petty egotistical concerns."[5]

Interpreting politics with the logic of emotions, extreme nationalists insisted that they had a sacred mission to regain lands once held in the Middle Ages, to unite with their kinfolk in other lands, or to rule over peoples considered inferior. They organized patriotic societies; denounced national minorities, particularly Jews; and created a cult of ancestors and a mystique of blood, soil, and a sacred national past. In these ancestral traditions and attachments, the nationalists found a higher reality akin to religious truth. In the modern world, where traditional values were called into question, nationalism fulfilled a human need for identity and community. For many, it realized a yearning for meaning and transcendence. Loyalty to the nation-state was elevated above all other allegiances. The ethnic state became sanctified, a holy entity deserving of religious reverence, sacrifice, and even martyrdom; spiritual energies formerly dedicated to Christianity were now channeled into the worship of the nation-state, igniting primitive, dark, cruel feelings. In 1902, Friedrich Paulsen, a German philosopher, warned of the threat that this intense commitment to the nation-state posed to reason and morality.

> A supersensitive nationalism has become a very serious danger for all the peoples of Europe; because of it, they are in danger of losing the feeling for human values. Nationalism, pushed to an extreme, just like sectarianism, destroys moral and even logical consciousness. Just and unjust, good and bad, true and false, lose their meaning; what men condemn as disgraceful and inhuman when done by others, they recommend in the same breath to their own people as something to be done to a foreign country.[6]

By the beginning of the twentieth century, conservatives had become the staunchest advocates of nationalism, and the nationalism preached by conservative extremists was stripped of Mazzinian ideals of liberty, equality, and the fellowship of nations. In Germany, landholding aristocrats, generals, and clergy, often joined by big industrialists, saw nationalism as a convenient instrument for gaining a mass following in their struggle against democracy, social reform, and socialism. Championing popular nationalist myths and dreams and citing Social Darwinist doctrines, a newly radicalized Right, dominated by the elite of German society, hoped to harness the instinctual energies of the masses, particularly the peasants and the lower middle class—shopkeepers, civil servants, and white-collar workers—to conservative causes. Peasants viewed liberalism and a godless Marxism as threats to traditional values, while the lower bourgeoisie feared the power of the organized proletariat. These people were receptive to the rhetoric of ultranationalists, who denounced democracy and Marxism as threats to national unity and Jews as aliens who endangered the nation. Nationalism was presented as a victory of idealism over materialism and as the subordination of class and personal interests to the general good of the nation.

Volkish Thought

Extreme nationalism was a general European phenomenon, but it was especially dangerous in Germany. Bismarck's triumphs lured Germans into a dream world. Many started to yearn for the extension of German power throughout the globe. The past, they said, belonged to France and Britain; the future, to Germany.

The most ominous expression of German nationalism (and a clear example of mythical thinking) was **Volkish thought**.[7] (*Volk* means "folk" or "people;" in this context "ethnic" might be the best meaning.) German Volkish thinkers sought to bind together the German people through a deep love of their language, traditions, and fatherland. These thinkers felt that Germans were animated by a higher spirit than that found in other peoples. To Volkish thinkers, the Enlightenment and parliamentary democracy were foreign ideas that corrupted the pure German spirit. With fanatical devotion, Volkish thinkers embraced all things German: the medieval past, the German landscape, the simple peasant, and the village. They denounced the liberal-humanist tradition of the West as alien to the German soul.

Among the shapers of the Volkish outlook was Wilhelm von Riehl (1823–1897), a professor at the University of Munich. He contrasted the artificiality of modern city life with the unspoiled existence in the German countryside. Berthold Auerbach (1812–1882) glorified the peasant as the ideal German. Paul de Lagarde (1827–1891), a professor of Asian languages, called for a German faith, different from Christianity, that would unite the nation; he saw the Jews as enemies of Germany. Julius Langbehn (1851–1907) lauded a mystical and irrational life force as superior to reason and held that the Jews corrupted the German spirit.

Volkish thought attracted Germans frightened by all the complexities of the modern age: industrialization, urbanization, materialism, class conflicts, and alienation. Seeing their beloved Germany transformed by these forces of modernity, Volkish thinkers yearned to restore the sense of community, the spiritual unity, that they attributed to the preindustrial age. Only by identifying with their sacred soil and sacred traditions could modern Germans escape from the evils of industrial society. Only then could the different classes band together in an organic unity.

The Volkish movement had little support from the working class, which was concerned chiefly with improving its standard of living. It appealed mainly to farmers and villagers, who regarded the industrial city as a threat to native values and a catalyst for foreign ideas; to artisans and small shopkeepers, threatened by big business; and to scholars, writers, teachers, and students, who saw in Volkish nationalism a cause worthy of their idealism. The schools were leading agents for the dissemination of Volkish ideas.

Volkish thinkers looked back longingly to the Middle Ages, which they viewed as a period of social and spiritual harmony and reverence for ethnic traditions. They also glorified the ancient Germanic tribes that overran the Roman Empire; they contrasted their courageous and vigorous Germanic ancestors with the effete and degenerate Romans. A few tried to harmonize ancient Germanic religious traditions with Christianity.

Such attitudes led Germans to see themselves as a heroic people fundamentally different from and better than the English and the French. It also led them to regard German culture as unique—innately superior to and, indeed, contravening the humanist outlook of the Enlightenment. Like their romantic predecessors, Volkish thinkers claimed that the German people and culture had a special destiny and a unique mission. They pitted the German soul against the Western intellect—feeling, intuition, spirit, and idealism against a drab rationalism. To be sure, the Western humanist tradition had many supporters in Germany, but the counterideology of Volkish thought was becoming increasingly widespread. This murky, irrational, radically nationalist, and antiliberal outlook shaped by the Volkish thinkers in the late nineteenth century would later undermine support for the democratic Weimar Republic established in Germany after World War I and provide Hitler with receptive listeners. Many of Hitler's supporters hoped that he would transform these Volkish longings into political realities.

Racist doctrines had a special appeal for Volkish thinkers. Racist ideologues saw race as the key to history. They maintained that not only physical features but also moral, esthetic, and intellectual qualities distinguished one race from another. In their view, a race demonstrated its vigor and achieved greatness when it preserved its purity; intermarriage between races was contamination that would result in genetic, cultural, and military decline. Unlike liberals, who held that anyone who accepted German law was a member of the German nation, racists argued that a person's nationality was a function of his or her "racial soul" or "blood."

Like their Nazi successors, Volkish thinkers claimed that the German race was purer than, and therefore superior to, all other races. Its superiority was revealed in such physical characteristics as blond hair, blue eyes, and fair skin: all signs of inner qualities lacking in other races. German racists claimed that Germans were the purest descendants of the ancient Aryans.* They held that the Aryans were a superior race and the creators of European civilization and that the Germans had inherited their superior racial qualities.

Volkish thinkers embraced the ideas of Houston Stewart Chamberlain (1855–1927), an Englishman whose fascination with Germanism led him to adopt German citizenship. In *The Foundations of the Nineteenth Century* (1899), Chamberlain asserted in pseudoscientific fashion that races differed not only physically but also morally, spiritually, and intellectually and that the struggle between races was the driving force of history. He attributed Rome's decline to the dilution of its racial qualities through the intermixing of races. The blond, blue-eyed, long-skulled Germans, possessing the strongest strain of Aryan blood and distinguished by an inner spiritual depth, were the true ennoblers of humanity—both physically superior and bearers of a higher culture. Chamberlain denied that Christ was a Jew, saying that he was of Aryan stock. As agents of a spiritually empty capitalism and divisive liberalism, the Jews, said Chamberlain, were undermining German society. Materialistic, cowardly, and devious, they were the very opposite of the idealistic, heroic, and faithful Germans. Chamberlain's book was enormously popular in Germany. It was required reading in German schools and military academies, and Pan-German and other Volkish-nationalist organizations frequently cited it. Kaiser William II called *Foundations* a "Hymn to Germanism" and read it to his children.

Chamberlain's racist and anti-Semitic views make him a spiritual forerunner of Nazism, and he was praised as such by Alfred Rosenberg, the leading Nazi racial theorist in the early days of Hitler's movement. Joseph Goebbels, the Nazi propagandist, hailed Chamberlain as a "pathbreaker" and "pioneer" after meeting him in 1926. In 1923, Chamberlain, then sixty-eight years old, met Hitler, whose movement was still in its formative stage. Chamberlain subsequently praised Hitler as the savior of the Reich, and Hitler visited Chamberlain on his deathbed and attended his funeral.

German racial nationalists insisted that Germany had a unique mission; as a superior race, Germans had a right to dominate other peoples, particularly the "racially inferior" Slavs of Eastern Europe. The Pan-German League, whose membership included professors, schoolteachers, journalists, lawyers, and aristocrats, spread racial and nationalist theories and glorified war as an expression of national vitality. A statement from the association's journal sums up its philosophy.

> *The racial-biological ideology tells us that there are races that lead and races that follow. Political history is nothing but the history of struggles among the leading races. Conquests, above all, are always the work of the leading races. Such men can conquer, may conquer, and shall conquer.*[8]

Anti-Semitism: The Power and Danger of Mythical Thinking

German racial nationalists singled out Jews as a wicked race and a deadly enemy of the German people. **Anti-Semitism**, widespread in late-nineteenth-century Europe, affords a striking example of the perennial appeal, power, and danger of mythical thinking—of elevating to the level of objective truth ideas that have no basis in fact but provide all-encompassing, emotionally satisfying explanations of life and history. By manufacturing the myth of the wicked Jew, the radical Right confirmed the insight proffered by the political theorist Georges Sorel: people are moved and united by myths that offer simple, clear, and emotionally gratifying resolutions to the complexities of the modern world. Anti-Semitic organizations and political parties sought to deprive Jews of their civil rights, and anti-Semitic publications proliferated. The radical Right saw Jew-hatred as a popular formula for mobilizing and uniting all social classes—a precondition for strengthening the nation and subverting liberal democracy.

---

*The Aryans emerged some four thousand years ago, probably between the Caspian Sea and India. An Aryan tongue became the basis of most European languages. Intermingling with others, the Aryans lost their identity as a people.

The Pan-German League: Extreme Racial Nationalism

Organized in 1894, the ultranationalist and imperialist Pan-German League called for German expansion both in Europe and overseas. It often expressed blatantly Social Darwinist and racist views, as illustrated in the following article, which appeared in 1913 in the league's principal publication.

The historical view as to the biological evolution of races tells us that there are dominant races and subordinate races. Political history is nothing more than the history of the struggles between the dominant races. Conquest in particular is always a function of the dominant races. . . . Where now in all the world does it stand written that conquering races are under obligations to grant after an interval political rights to the conquered? Is not the practice of political rights an advantage which biologically belongs to the dominant races? . . . What are [these] rights? . . . In my opinion, the rights of men are, first, personal freedom; secondly, the right of free expression of opinion—as well as freedom of the press; . . . and, finally, the right to work, in case one is without means. . . .

The man with political rights sets up schools, and the speech used in the instruction is his speech. . . . The purpose must be to crush the [individuality of the] conquered people and its political and lingual existence. . . .

The conquerors are acting only according to biological principles if they suppress alien languages and undertake to destroy strange popular customs. . . . Only the conquering race must be populous, so that it can overrun the territory it has won. Nations that are populous are, moreover, the only nations which have a moral claim to conquest, for it is wrong that in one country there should be overpopulation while close at hand—and at the same time on better soil—a less numerous population stretches its limbs at ease.

[As to the inferior races:] From political life they are to be excluded. They are eligible only to positions of a non-political character, to commercial commissions, chambers of commerce, etc. . . . The principal thing for the conqueror is the outspoken will to rule and the will to destroy the political and national life of the conquered. . . .

Question for Analysis

1. Why is an ideology based on biological racism, as in the case of the Pan-German League, particularly dangerous?

Conquest and Kultur, compiled by Wallace Notestein and Elmer E. Stoll (Washington, D.C.: Government Printing Office, 1917), 90–91.

In 1886, Edouard Drumont, a French journalist, published *Jewish France*, which argued that the Jews, racially inferior and believers in a primitive religion, had gained control of France. The book sold more than a million copies. Drumont blamed the Jews for introducing capitalism, materialism, and greed into France. Like medieval Christian anti-Semites, Drumont accused Jews of murdering God and of using the blood of slaughtered Christian children for ritual purposes. (In rural France, the accusation of ritual murder, a deranged survival of the Middle Ages, still persisted, at times fomented by the clergy.) French politicians played the anti-Semitic card in order to gain popularity and votes. Fully one-third of the Chamber of Deputies wanted to deprive Jews of the civil rights that they had gained during the French Revolution. During the

Dreyfus affair (see Chapter 25), the xenophobic French Right—nationalists, the army, the church, royalists, and anti-republicans—stirred up hatred against Jews and in numerous anti-Semitic rallies and brawls (including the murder of Jews in pogroms in French Algeria) people shouted "Death to the Jews." Drumont's newspaper (founded with Jesuit funds) eagerly participated in the anti-Semitic tirades; in sensational polemics it blamed all the ills of France on the Jews, called for their expulsion from the country, and predicted that they would be massacred.

Romania barred most Jews from holding office and from voting, imposed various economic restrictions on them, and limited their admission into secondary schools and universities. The Romanian government even financed an international congress of anti-Semites, which met in Bucharest in 1886.

Russia placed a quota on the number of Jewish students admitted to secondary schools and higher educational institutions, confined Jews to certain regions of the country, and, "to purify the sacred historic capital," expelled around twenty thousand Jews from Moscow. Some government officials encouraged or did nothing to stop *pogroms* (mob violence) against Jews. Between 1903 and 1906, pogroms broke out in 690 towns and villages, most of them in Ukraine, traditionally a hotbed of anti-Semitism. (Ukrainian folk songs and legends glorified centuries-old massacres of Jews.) The attackers looted, burned, raped, and murdered, generally with impunity. In Russia and several other lands, Jews were put on trial for the old libel of ritual murder.

In Germany and Austria, hatred of the Jews developed into a systematic body of beliefs. As the historian Hans Kohn says, "Germany became the fatherland of modern anti-Semitism; there the systems were thought out and the slogans coined. German literature was the richest in anti-Jewish writing."[9] Like conservatives in other lands, German conservatives deliberately fanned the flames of anti-Semitism to win the masses over to conservative causes. The Christian Social Workers' Party, founded in 1878 by Adolf Stöcker, a prominent Protestant preacher, engaged in anti-Semitic agitation in order to recruit the lower bourgeoisie to the

THEODOR HERZL. Theodor Herzl is regarded as the founder of Zionism, the movement that called for Jews, the victims of persecution, to dwell once again in their ancient homeland. (© Bettmann/CORBIS.)

cause of the Protestant church and the Prussian monarchy. In German-speaking Austria, Karl Lueger, a leader of the Christian Social Party, founded by conservative German nationalists, exploited anti-Semitism to win elections in overwhelmingly Catholic Vienna. Georg von Schönerer, founder of the German National Party in Austria, wanted to eliminate Jews from all areas of public life.

Anti-Semitism and the success of the Italians, Germans, Serbians, and others in achieving political independence stirred nationalist feelings among Jews. Jewish nationalism took the form of **Zionism**—a movement advocating the return of Jews to Palestine, their historic homeland. A key figure in the emergence of Zionism was Theodor Herzl (1860–1904), an Austrian journalist, who was horrified by the anti-Semitism he witnessed in Paris during the Dreyfus trial. In *The Jewish State* (1896), he argued that the creation of a Jewish state was the best solution to the Jewish question.

We are a people—one people. We have honestly endeavored to merge ourselves in the social life of surrounding communities and to preserve only the faith of our fathers. We are not permitted to do so. In vain are we loyal patriots . . .; in vain do we strive to increase the fame of our native land in science and art, or her wealth by trade and commerce. In countries where we have lived for centuries we are still cried down as strangers. . . . I think we shall not be left in peace. . . . Old prejudices against us still lie deep in the hearts of people. . . . I say that we cannot hope for a change in the current . . . feeling. . . . The nations in whose midst Jews live are all either covertly or openly Anti-Semitic. . . . Palestine is our ever-memorable historic home. The very name of Palestine would attract our people with a force of marvellous potency.[10]

In 1897, in Switzerland, the first Zionist World Congress called for the establishment of a Jewish homeland in Palestine, which was then a province of the Ottoman Empire.

Anti-Semitism had a long and bloodstained history in Europe, stemming both from an irrational fear and hatred of outsiders with noticeably different ways and from the commonly accepted myth that the Jews as a people were collectively and eternally cursed for rejecting Christ. Christians saw Jews as the murderers of Christ—an image that provoked terrible anger and hatred.

During the Middle Ages, people believed and spread incredible tales about Jews. They accused Jews of torturing and crucifying Christian children in order to use their blood for religious ceremonies, poisoning wells to kill Christians, worshiping the Devil, and organizing a secret government that conspired to destroy Christianity. Jews were thought to be physically different from other people; they were said to have tails, horns, and a distinctive odor. Serving to propagate this myth was the decision of the Fourth Lateran Council (1215), which required Jews to wear a distinguishing mark on their clothing.

Although some medieval popes and bishops condemned these fables and sought to protect Jews from mob violence, the lower clergy and popular preachers spread the tales to the receptive masses. Periodically, mobs humiliated, tortured,

THE PROTOCOLS OF THE ELDERS OF ZION. This infamous forgery, commissioned by the Russian secret police, became an international bestseller and contributed to outrages against Jews. Anti-Semitic organizations continue to publish and circulate it today. The picture is the actual cover of a French edition of the *Protocols*. (Cover of an edition of "The Jewish Danger. The Protocols of the Learned Elders of Zion," c. 1940 (colour litho), French School, (20th century)/ Private Collection/Archives Charmet/The Bridgeman Art Library.)

and massacred Jews, and rulers expelled them from their kingdoms. Often barred from owning land and excluded from the craft guilds, medieval Jews concentrated in trade and moneylending— occupations that frequently earned them greater hostility. By the sixteenth century, Jews in a number of lands were forced by law to live in separate quarters of the town, called *ghettos*. Medieval Christian anti-Semitism, which depicted Jews as vile and Judaism as repulsive, fertilized the soil for modern anti-Semitism.

In the nineteenth century, under the aegis of the liberal ideals of the Enlightenment and the French Revolution, Jews gained legal equality in most European lands. They could leave the ghetto, vote, hold offices, and participate in many activities that had been closed to them. Traditionally an urban people, the Jews, who were concentrated in the leading cities of Europe, took advantage of this new freedom and opportunity. Motivated by the fierce desire of outsiders to prove their worth and aided by deeply embedded traditions that valued education and family life, many Jews achieved striking success as entrepreneurs, bankers, lawyers, journalists, doctors, scientists, scholars, and performers. For example, in 1880, Jews, who constituted about 10 percent of the Viennese population, accounted for 38.6 percent of the medical students and 23.3 percent of the law students in Vienna. Viennese cultural life before World War I was to a large extent shaped by Jewish writers, artists, musicians, critics, and patrons. All but one of the major banking houses were Jewish. By the early 1930s, German Jews, who constituted less than 1 percent of the population, accounted for 10.9 percent of the doctors, 10.7 percent of the dentists, 5.1 percent of the editors and authors, and 16.3 percent of the lawyers. Thirty percent of the Nobel Prize winners in Germany were Jews. Middle class Germans in particular resented Jewish success. For them, Jews were unscrupulous competitors in commerce, finance, and the professions. They saw themselves as powerless and the Jews privileged. A pamphlet published in 1912 by the nationalist Pan-German League represented an extremist position. It called for the state to impose the following restrictions on Jews:

> *All public appointments will remain barred to Jews. . . . They will not be allowed to serve in the army or in the navy. They will [be barred from voting]. The professions of law and teaching will be prohibited to them; as will be the management of theatres. Newspapers where Jews work, will be labeled as such; the others . . . will not be allowed to be owned by Jews or to have Jewish managers. Banks, which are not the purely personal businesses of individuals, will not be allowed to have Jewish managers. Landed property will not be allowed in the future . . . to be owned by Jews. . . . [Jews] will pay twice the tax Germans do.*[11]

But most European Jews—peasants, peddlers, and laborers—were quite poor. Many Russian Jews fled to the United States to escape from desperate poverty. But the anti-Semites saw only "Jewish influence," "Jewish manipulation," "Jewish conspiracy," and "Jewish domination." Aggravating anti-Semitism among Germans was the flight of thousands of Russian Jews into Austria and Germany. Poor, speaking Yiddish—a form of medieval German that sounded peculiar to nineteenth-century Germans—and having noticeably different customs, these Jews triggered primitive fears and hatreds among Germans.

Like other bourgeois, the Jews who were members of the commercial and professional classes gravitated toward liberalism. Moreover, as victims of persecution, they naturally favored societies that were committed to the liberal ideals of legal equality, toleration, the rule of law, and equality of opportunity. As strong supporters of parliamentary government and the entire system of values associated with the Enlightenment, the Jews became targets for those conservatives and Volkish thinkers who repudiated the humanist, tolerant, and cosmopolitan outlook of liberalism and professed a militant nationalism. To Volkish thinkers, the West represented an alien culture hostile to German racial-national identity, and the Jews, an alien race, symbolized the West. "Anti-Semitism was a manifestation of a rejection of the 'West' with which the Jews were identified," says the German historian Karl Dietrich Bracher, "because the Enlightenment and democracy were essential preconditions for their acceptance and progress."[12]

Anti-Semites invented a mythical evil to be blamed for all the social and economic ills caused by the rapid growth of industries and cities and for all the new ideas that were undermining the Old Order. Their anxieties and fears concentrated on the Jews, to whom they attributed everything they considered to be wrong with the modern age, all that threatened the German Volk.

The thought processes of Volkish anti-Semites demonstrate the mind's monumental capacity for self-delusion and irrational thinking. In the mythical world of Volkish thinkers, Jews were regarded as foreign intruders who could never be loyal to the fatherland; as a lower form of humanity that could infect and weaken the German race; as bearers of a racial soul that precluded them

Richard Wagner

Richard Wagner (1813–1883), Germany's most important musical composer, was also instrumental in giving German nationalism an irrational component that contributed to its dangerousness. Wagner's immensely popular operas glorified ancient, pre-Christian Germanic myths and warriors and heroines. To many Germans, his operas, particularly the Ring cycle, represented true German idealism, a heroic spirit now corrupted by materialism and greed. This hoary Teutonic past bound Germans together and set them apart from other Europeans; the Enlightenment and parliamentary democracy, associated with France and Britain, were foreign ideas that corrupted the true German spirit. Wagner also promulgated Jew-hatred, a central doctrine of militant German nationalists, who regarded Jews as an alien and dangerous element in their midst.

In his *Judaism in Music*, first published in 1850 under a pseudonym and republished in 1869 under his own name, Wagner, who resented the fame of the Jewish composers Felix Mendelssohn (who had converted to Lutheranism) and Giacomo Meyerbeer, asserted that Jews debased German music. They could not possess or express the feelings that animated the German soul; they had their own folk soul, which had been shaped by a degenerate culture. Devoid of a creative imagination and concerned only with self-centered materialist pursuits, said Wagner, Jews were incapable of making a creative contribution to European culture. The German people, he stated, have "the most profound repugnance for the Jewish nature." And in the concluding passage of the essay, Wagner wrote: "There is only one possible way of redeeming the Jews from the terrible curse that hangs over them—annihilation."*

In later essays published in the Wagnerian journal, the *Bayreuther Blätter*, and in private correspondence and conversations, Wagner's anti-Semitism grew even more vitriolic and racist. "I hold the Jewish race to be the born enemy of pure humanity and everything noble in it. It is certain that it is running us Germans to the ground."† Wagner and his immediate circle, including his wife Cosima, reviled Judaism as a curse, considered Jews inferior, and maintained that they were taking over Germany. They frequently referred to Jews as vermin, bacilli, and lice, the very language that Nazi mass murderers would employ. Holding that artistic creativity was a function of ethnicity, Wagner saw Jews as the deadly opponent of the German spirit, the contaminators of the arts in Germany, and rejected their participation in the regeneration of the nation's culture which he hoped to inspire. He also doubted that Jesus was Jewish and called for severing Christianity's relationship from its Jewish roots, believing that such a connection ruined it.

German anti-Semites regarded Wagner as their apostle: they sent him their anti-Semitic publications for approval and viewed the master's home as a shrine. A young Adolf Hitler was obsessed with Wagner's music, which he felt embodied the German soul; it may have inspired him to believe that he was the man of destiny needed to regenerate Germany and save it from the Jews, whom Wagner accused of dominating the country. Wagner's family and disciples viewed Hitler as the savior of the German soul. Once in power, the Nazis used the music and words of Wagner, whom they unreservedly revered, for propaganda purposes.

At the time that Wagner and many other German intellectuals were spreading their venomous anti-Semitic myths, Jews, who constituted less than 1 percent of Germany's population, considered themselves loyal Germans, were devoted to German culture, and were making immense contributions to medicine, science, the arts, and commerce.

---

*Quoted in Jacob Katz, *The Darker Side of Genius: Richard Wagner's Anti-Semitism* (Hanover, N.H.: Brandeis University Press and University Press of New England, 1986), 35–36.
†Ibid., 115.

from understanding and contributing to German culture, which they only debased; and as international conspirators who were plotting to dominate Germany and the world. That last accusation was an updated version of the medieval myth that Jews were plotting to destroy Christendom. In an extraordinary display of irrationality, Volkish thinkers held that Jews throughout the world were gaining control over political parties, the press, and the economy in order to dominate the planet.

The myth of a Jewish world conspiracy found its culminating expression in a notorious forgery, the *Protocols of the Elders of Zion*. The *Protocols*, written in France by someone in the service of the Russian secret police, sought to justify the tsarist regime's anti-Semitic policies. The forger concocted a tale of an alleged meeting of Jewish elders in the Jewish cemetery of Prague. In these eerie surroundings, the elders plot to take over the world. First published in Russia in 1903, the *Protocols* was widely distributed after World War I and widely believed. Influenced by the *Protocols*, Russian anti-Semites interpreted the Russian Revolution of 1917 as an attempt by Jews to subjugate Christian Russia. German anti-Semites regarded the *Protocols* as convincing evidence that the Jews were responsible for starting World War I, for Germany's defeat, and for the revolution that toppled the monarchy. Nazi propagandists exploited the *Protocols* to justify their quest for power. Even after the *Protocols* was exposed as a blatant forgery, it continued to be translated, distributed, and believed. For anti-Semites, the myth of a Jewish world-conspiracy had become an integrating principle; it provided satisfying answers to the crucial questions of existence.

In the Middle Ages, Jews had been persecuted and humiliated primarily for religious reasons. In the nineteenth century, national-racial considerations augmented the traditional, biased Christian perception of Jews and Judaism. Christian anti-Semites believed that, through conversion, Jews could escape the curse of their religion. Racial anti-Semites, however, used the language of Social Darwinism. They said that Jews belonged to a different species of the human race, that they were indelibly stained and eternally condemned by their biological makeup, and that their evilness and worthlessness derived from inherited racial characteristics, which could not be altered by conversion. As one anti-Semitic deputy stated in

a speech before the German Reichstag (the lower chamber of the German parliament) in 1895,

> If one designates the whole of Jewry, one does so in the knowledge that the racial qualities of this people are such that in the long run they cannot harmonize with the racial qualities of the Germanic peoples and that every Jew who at this moment has not done anything bad may nevertheless under the proper conditions do precisely that, because his racial qualities drive him to do it. . . . The Jews . . . operate like parasites. . . . The Jews are cholera germs.[13]

The Jewish population of Germany was quite small. In 1900, it was only about 497,000, or 0.98 percent of the total population of 50,626,000. Jews were proud of their many contributions to German economic and cultural life; they considered themselves patriotic Germans, relished German literature and music, and regarded Germany, a land of high civilization, as an altogether desirable place to live— a place of refuge in comparison with Russia, where Jews lived in terrible poverty and suffered violent attacks. German Jews, who felt that they already had a homeland, had little enthusiasm for Zionism.

German anti-Semitic organizations and political parties failed to get the state to pass anti-Semitic laws that would restrict both the Jews' civil liberties and their economic activities, and by the early 1900s, these groups had declined in political power and importance. But the mischief had been done. In the minds of many Germans, even in respectable circles, the image of the Jew as an evil and dangerous creature out to dominate Germany had been firmly planted. It was perpetuated by the schools, youth groups, the Pan-German League, and an array of racist pamphlets and books. Late-nineteenth-century racial anti-Semites had constructed an ideological foundation on which Hitler would later build his movement. In words that foreshadowed Hitler, Paul de Lagarde said of the Jews: "One does not have dealings with pests and parasites; one does not rear them and cherish them; one destroys them as speedily and thoroughly as possible."[14]

It is, of course, absurd to believe that a nation of 50 million was threatened by a half-million citizens of Jewish birth or that the 11 million Jews of the world (by 1900) had organized to rule the planet. The Jewish birthrate in Germany was low, the rate of intermarriage high, and the desire for complete assimilation into German life great. Within a few generations, the Jewish community in Germany might well have disappeared. Moreover, despite the paranoia of the anti-Semites, the German Jews and the Jews in the rest of Europe were quite powerless. There were scarcely any Jews in the ruling circles of governments, armies, civil services, or heavy industries. As events were to prove, the Jews, with no army or state and dwelling in lands where many despised them, were the weakest of peoples. But the race mystics, convinced that they were waging a war of self-defense against a satanic foe, were impervious to rational argument. Anti-Semites, said Theodor Mommsen, the great nineteenth-century German historian, would not listen to

> *logical and ethical arguments. . . . They listen only to their own envy and hatred, to the meanest instincts. Nothing else counts for them. They are deaf to reason, right, morals. One cannot influence them. . . .*

> *[Anti-Semitism] is a horrible epidemic, like cholera—one can neither explain nor cure it.*[15]

Racial nationalism, a major element in nineteenth-century intellectual life, attacked and undermined the Enlightenment tradition. Racial nationalists denied equality, scorned toleration, dismissed the idea of the oneness of humanity, and made myth and superstition vital forces in political life. They distorted reason and science to demonize and condemn an entire people and to justify humiliation and persecution. They presented a pathological racial ideology, fraught with unreason and hate, as something virtuous and idealistic. That many people, including the educated and the elite, embraced these racial doctrines was an ominous sign for Western civilization. It made plain the tenuousness of the rational tradition of the Enlightenment and showed how receptive the mind is to dangerous myths and how easily human behavior can degenerate into inhumanity.

❖   ❖   ❖

NOTES

1. Quoted in Otto Pflanze, *Bismarck and the Development of Germany: The Period of Unification* (Princeton, N.J.: Princeton University Press, 1963), 232.

2. Quoted in Hans Kohn, *Pan-Slavism* (Notre Dame, Ind.: University of Notre Dame Press, 1953), 66–67.

3. Quoted ibid., 44.

4. Cited in Edward R. Tannenbaum, *1900: The Generation Before the Great War* (Garden City, N.Y.: Doubleday, 1976), 337.

5. Quoted in Roger Chicklering, *Imperial Germany and the Great War, 1914–1918* (Cambridge: Cambridge University Press, 1998), 9.

6. Quoted in Friedrich Meinecke, *The German Catastrophe* (Boston: Beacon Press, 1963), 23–24.

7. This discussion is based largely on the works of George L. Mosse, particularly *The Crisis of German Ideology* (New York: Grosset and Dunlap Universal Library, 1964).

8. Cited in Horst von Maltitz, *The Evolution of Hitler's Germany* (New York: McGraw-Hill, 1973), 33.

9. Hans Kohn, *Nationalism: Its Meaning and History* (Princeton, N.J.: Van Nostrand, Anvil Books, 1955), 77.

10. Theodor Herzl, *The Jewish State* (New York: American Zionist Emergency Council, 1946), 76–77, 85, 96.

11. Excerpted in Ian Porter and Ian Armour, *Imperial Germany 1890–1918* (London: 1991), 89.

12. Karl Dietrich Bracher, *The German Dictatorship*, trans. Jean Steinberg (New York: Praeger, 1970), 36.

13. Quoted in Raul Hilberg, *The Destruction of the European Jews* (Chicago: Quadrangle, 1967), 10–11.

14. Quoted in Helmut Krausnick, Hans Buchheim, Martin Broszat, and Hans-Adolf Jacobsen, *Anatomy of the SS State*, trans. Richard Barry et al. (London: William Collins Sons, 1968), 9.

15. Quoted in Peter G. J. Pulzer, *The Rise of Political Anti-Semitism in Germany and Austria* (New York: Wiley, 1964), 299.

Chapter 25

The Industrial West: Responses to Modernization

Krupps metalworks factory. (© Bettmann/CORBIS.)

Focus Questions

1. Why was England considered the model liberal nation?
2. Why was it so difficult for French workers and employers to work together for reform?
3. What was the general crisis of liberalism after 1870?
4. How did the conservatives attempt to win over the mass support after 1870?
5. Why were liberal reforms and industrialization so difficult to achieve in tsarist Russia?

A "second industrial revolution" between 1870 and World War I forced rapid social and political change. Mechanized industry spread to all European states, though not evenly to all nor every region within them. This mechanization vastly increased the quantity of goods, making them available to many more people, not just to the wealthy. New groups rose to authority and to wealth; it was truly the golden age of the middle classes. They gained wealth, power, and influence; even the social discrimination against them steadily diminished. Dazzled by the material benefits of a mass-producing society, many Europeans saw progress as inevitable even though traditional society resisted the emerging forces and social groups that were reshaping fundamental institutions. Those who were still left out of the consuming society struggled for their share of the future.

To deal with the major changes wrought by industrialization, governments expanded their authority, strengthening central power over the diverse interests, regions, classes, and even nationalities. Civil wars, unification movements, and struggles for political representation usually ended with a stronger central government. Achieving the new balance of classes and regions meant repressing dissent, regionalism, and tradition—the American Civil War, the Irish struggle for home rule, and the subjugation of minorities in newly unified Germany, tsarist Russia, or Austria-Hungary are just some examples. Governments developed the machinery to control citizens: military **conscription**, public education, broad taxation, and, in some places, social legislation. Some governments encouraged nationalism, once thought dangerously democratic, enlisting the support of previously excluded people.

Industrialization affected international affairs as well. Population, area, and the size of the army were no longer adequate measures of national power. Coal and iron production, the mileage and tonnage of railways and navies, the mechanization of industry, even the skill of the populace became important components of military power. By 1914, production, trade, foreign markets, and political empires changed the positions of France, Russia, and Austria, tipping the scale toward the superior industrial might of Britain, Germany, and the United States.

Chronology 25.1 ❖ Europe in the Age of Industrialization

1845–1847	Great famine in Ireland
1851	Second French Republic overthrown; President Bonaparte becomes Emperor Napoleon III
1860s	Irish Republican Independence Movement (the Fenians); Civil War in the United States; unification movements in German and Italian states; Dual Monarchy declared for Austria-Hungary
1861	Kingdom of Italy is formed; Tsar Alexander II proclaims emancipation of serfs and other reforms in Russia
1863	Emancipation of slaves in the United States
1864	First International Workingmen's Association founded
1867	Second Reform Bill passes, doubling the English electorate
1870–1871	Franco-Prussian War; Paris Commune; German Empire declared
1873	The Great Depression; *Kulturkampf* in Germany
1875	German Social Democratic Party founded
1880s	Parnell leads the Irish home rule movement
1881	Tsar Alexander II assassinated
1884	Reform Bill grants suffrage to most English men
1889	Second International Workingmen's Association founded
1891	Trans-Siberian Railroad built
1894–1906	The Dreyfus affair in France
1903–1905	Russo-Japanese War; revolution of 1905 in Russia
1909	Lloyd George introduces "people's budget" in England
1911	House of Lords' power limited

THE ADVANCE OF INDUSTRY

Industry developed on the foundation of cheap labor and plentiful agricultural commodities, made easily and cheaply available by a relatively inexpensive transportation and communication system. It took a century to lay that foundation, but by midcentury it was in place for almost all of Europe and parts of the Americas. *Revolution* accurately describes the radically new forms of business and labor organization; the massive accumulation of capital; the scientific and technological advance; and the new modes of marketing, distribution, and production. The apparently limitless change assumed people could be replaced, raw materials replenished, nature rearranged, and even homelands exchanged.

Comparison with the midcentury quickly indicates the scope of the second industrial revolution. In 1850, most people were farmers, and much of industry produced tools and materials for farming. Even Britain had more domestic servants than factory hands and twice as many agricultural laborers as textile and clothing workers. Large factories were few; handicrafts still flourished. Electricity and steel were too expensive to use. Sailing ships still outnumbered steamships, and horses carried more freight than trains. On-the-job training was more common than schooling. Construction and machine making were trial-and-error practices, not the result of architectural and engineering knowledge.

This situation changed radically in two spurts: the first between 1850 and 1870; the second after the great depression of 1873, from the 1870s until World War I. During the first spurt, most of Europe and America extended earlier industrialization to previously untouched areas, shifting to machine production and harnessing steam power and other forms of energy. More sophisticated tools were introduced. The concentration of factory workers and production in industrial cities spurred many social changes: craftsmen organized unions; social legislation was passed protecting women and children; city governments struggled to control water pollution, improve sanitation, and regulate housing conditions; and unskilled male labor pushed women and children out of the workplace.

During the second spurt, from the late 1870s to 1890s, heavy industry in Germany and the United States concentrated in large firms, capitalized by specialist banks. Cartels and monopolies—groups of companies that joined together to fix prices—dominated national and international industries, drastically altering development. Monopolies, run by boards of directors, some professional managers, and financiers, operated far-flung enterprises of enormous mechanized factories staffed by unskilled, low-paid, often seasonal workers. These industrial giants controlled the output, price, and distribution of commodities; they dominated smaller firms, financed and controlled research and development, utilized scientific advances, and expanded far beyond national frontiers. The "captains of industry" often commanded political power as well. In much of Europe, such men were **ennobled**; Britain's railroad barons are early examples. In the United States, bankers and entrepreneurs, called "robber barons," ordered politicians to represent their interests as "the oil senator" or "the railroad senator." These industrial titans caused depressions or "owned" cities; they fascinated the public and obsessed their critics. The public focus on the titans overshadowed the fact

that the second industrial revolution was actually a very broad movement of thousands of small businesses and millions of workers.

Even in advanced industrial states economic development was extremely uneven, which intensified political conflicts and social animosities, which contributed to more uneven development. Industrialized Britain included rural, backward Ireland, which furnished foodstuffs and laborers but hardly shared in any benefits of industrialization. This, together with cultural and religious differences, fueled the Irish desire for autonomy. Until 1914, the central, southern, and eastern parts of Europe were also backwater areas. In these regions, economic oppression and repression of minorities went hand in hand. The lowest-paid workers and the poorest peasants were ethnic and national minorities. From these areas, hundreds of thousands of peasants and craftsmen immigrated to the Americas or British colonies. The movement from rural to urban areas was matched by an exodus from Europe on a scale hitherto unknown in history.

Britain alone developed industry according to free-trade principles. Other governments built or subsidized "essential" industries (transportation, communication, national banks, and, above all, the production of war goods). The eastern empires—Russia and Austria-Hungary—remained economically and socially backward: overwhelmingly agricultural, with craftspeople manufacturing in consumer-oriented, small-scale operations of textiles and food processing. Even in industrially advanced Germany, megacartels, such as the Krupp steelworks, existed alongside handicraft labor.

Industrial work and wealth were unevenly and unequally distributed. The bourgeoisie included families rich enough to be elevated to the House of Lords, to move in the German emperor's circle, or to marry the younger son of a noble family. The middle class also included white collar workers—the clerks in stores and government offices and poor but respected schoolteachers. In the second half of the century, middle-class values and interests provided standards of education, morality, and consumption for others to imitate. Traditional groups—artisans and peasantry—suffered considerable social dislocation as factory skills replaced craft skills and machinery revolutionized agriculture. Craftsmen and peasants became unskilled industrial laborers just when the introduction of heavy equipment replaced the total number of workers needed. Men replaced women and children. Cultural minorities replaced workers of the dominant groups.

Wages remained relatively stable after the 1870s, while the price of food and some other goods dropped. Employed workers could buy cheap consumer goods, but even the employed lost family income when the state required their children to attend school. Their wives' income was lost, too, unless the women could find low-paying work as domestics, pieceworkers, seamstresses, or laundresses. Married women would not be hired as domestics. Economic and social changes drastically altered the role of each of the family members. The ideal of women and children in the home (the "cult of domesticity") appealed even to the working class, but it depended on the worker's ability to support a family. To the degree that it could be achieved, it turned the world of work into a man's world.

The socioeconomic trends strongly affected political and social movements. As the middle class strove to control labor, labor responded by organizing. The rise in workers' standard of living and the improved working conditions did not narrow the gap between the workers and the owners. The gap between the poor and the well-off, the powerless and the powerful, widened immensely.

Technological Takeoff

Technology revolutionized production, multiplying rather than adding to the goods and services. At midcentury, the trial-and-error tinkering of the artisan or the inventor began to be replaced by practical applications of scientific research to engineering, production, transportation, and communication. By 1900, German electrical, chemical, and mechanical industries routinely hired engineers and applied scientists to solve technical problems and to produce new commodities, including artificial ones, such as dyestuffs, fertilizers, and fuels. Americans were early champions of "scientific management"—or "Taylorism," after Frederick Taylor, one of its

leading proponents. Americans taught management in schools of business, a new phenomenon. Even European socialist critics of capitalism talked of "Taylorizing" production and management to take the inefficiency out of capitalism. The result was a "takeoff" of technology, connecting industries to technological and scientific advances. A few key industries—railroads, communications, and especially energy—are illustrative.

Railroads thrilled the public as well as investors and politicians. Railroads had the aura of progress that the cheaper, equally efficient, and labor-intensive (rather than capital-intensive) canals and roads did not. Railroads were the engine of industrial growth in Britain, stimulating the demand for coal and iron, steel, gravel, wood, tar, engineering training, and electronic signaling. Processes developed by Bessemer and Siemens made quality steel cheaply and abundantly, and stronger steel machinery allowed a wider application of steam power to other industries, including mining.

From 1850 to the 1870s, many railroad firms competed with one another. Expansion required enormous capital so that the acquisition and use of funds was as innovative as the invention of better engines and cars. Railroad moguls who commanded the greatest amounts of capital defeated their rivals, acquiring immense personal and corporate fortunes. In countries without moguls, government stepped in with capital to build railroads, take over failing ones, and subsidize private builders by land or monopoly grants and contracts. It did so to foster commerce, maintain military power, and centralize by bringing regions and groups into the national market. Railroads transformed North America and Eurasia, opening up vast unsettled areas. In the United States by 1870, there were more miles of railway (176,000) than in all of Europe. British railroads linked India's diverse regions. In Russia, in the 1890s, the Trans-Siberian Railroad, a fledgling line reluctantly financed by French capital, carried millions of settlers eastward to central Asia.

The revolution in shipping paralleled the epic expansion of railroads, bringing distant parts of the world together making Europe the marketplace of the world. Applying steam power to ships was prohibitively expensive at first, just as

THE AGNEW CLINIC, BY THOMAS EAKINS. The great American painter has caught the atmosphere of medical school in the nineteenth century. Here, well-dressed, interested physicians observe a mastectomy operation. Note the female nurse! The combination of scientific study, expertise, and professional specialization lifted the practice of medicine from a trade to a science in the public's mind.

(CHARLES PHELPS CUSHING/ClassicStock/Alamy Limited.)

it was for railroads and mining. In 1870, sailboats carried 4.5 million tons of goods, and steamships less than a million tons; by 1913, steam carried 11 million tons of goods, and sail only 800,000. The whole world was open to cheap, plentiful goods.

Steam power replaced human and animal power as the major energy source for the first century of industrial revolution, fueling a massive increase in productivity, until the turn of the twentieth century when electricity became competitive, powering entire industries and lighting great cities. The internal combustion engine moved people and goods after two German engineers, Gottlieb Daimler and Karl Benz, applied it to a carriage, fathering the automobile age. Ultimately, petroleum power democratized many aspects of the industrial process, fostering changes in production, organization, and consumption, but it was a luxury in the beginning. The American Henry Ford

(1863–1947) produced his 1908 Model T for the "ordinary man." By 1914, Ford's **mass-production**, conveyer-belt assembly line techniques revolutionized industrial production. Another German developed the diesel engine, making the fuel for giant cargo ships, warships, and luxury liners much cheaper, more powerful, and more efficient. Steam, oil, gas, and electricity would power the twentieth century.

As they do today, communications pushed expansion, and industrial growth stretched communications. Then, the rapid improvement of everyday postal services was much more important than inventions of the telegraph, the telephone, and the radio. Development costs were so prohibitive for the telephone (invented by Alexander Graham Bell in 1876) and the wireless, or radio (invented by Guglielmo Marconi in 1895), that it took almost twenty-five years after invention for either device to be widely used even in industrial countries. Once costs were cut, communications grew exponentially.

By the end of the nineteenth century, the scientific and the industrial revolutions had joined forces. More than half a century elapsed between Michael Faraday and James Maxwell's discovery of the fundamentals of electricity and the practical applications of those fundamentals by Edison, Bell, and Marconi. In a much shorter time, electricity provided power for lights, for urban and suburban trains, and for some factory engines. This same trend was evident in industrial chemistry. In 1850, almost all industrial materials were the ones people had been using for centuries: wood, stone, cotton, wool, flax, hemp, leather, plant dyes, and the base metals such as copper, iron, lead, and tin and their various alloys. But within a generation, chemists discovered new elements and perfected formulas for

alloys, dyes, and coal-tar products. In medicine, too, the marriage of science and technology produced miraculous progeny—anesthetics, antiseptics, and the discovery and isolation of disease-causing bacteria by Louis Pasteur, a French chemist. By the end of the century, researchers had identified the causes of several killer diseases: typhoid, tuberculosis, cholera, tetanus, diphtheria, and leprosy. Science exposed poor sanitation and squalor as the breeders of disease, and industrialized countries worked harder to ameliorate those conditions. Life expectancy increased, the death rate decreased, and the population in the more advanced industrialized countries boomed.

In all, each advance—and we have discussed only a few key industries—brought changes in the political and social power of individuals, groups, and nations and pushed industrial and commercial development still further.

PAINTING OF THE BOWERY BY LOUIS SONTAG **(1895).** This New York City street scene bursts with commercial energy and activity lighted by blazing electricity. The artists puts pushcarts, trolleys, horse-drawn cabs, and trains side by side, as he does the classic architecture of the theater and the four-story buildings housing shops and families on the Bowery. The city throbs with the energy of modern technology. (Museum of the City of New York/Corbis.)

Map 25.1 EUROPEAN CITIES OF **100,000** OR MORE, **1800–1900** Within a century, industrialization brought about the urbanization of northwestern Europe, particularly England, Belgium, western Germany, and northern France.

(© 2016 Cengage Learning.)

Accelerated Urbanization

Rapid industrial development urbanized northwestern Europe and the United States. More densely populated cities drew people from rural life and labor to mix with those who were city-born and bred. Although the majority of England's population lived in cities of ten thousand as early as 1800, most other Europeans did not until the twentieth century. Most of the world waited in the countryside until after World War II. Though a commercial and not an industrial city, London was a megalopolis of 5 million people by 1880; it was home to 7 million by 1914. Between 1866 and 1914 Berlin grew from half a million to 2 million. At unification, Germany had just three cities of more than 100,000 inhabitants; by 1903, it had fifteen. Paris increased in population from 2 million to 3 million between 1850 and World War I. By 1900, the United States was more heavily urbanized than Europe and had more cities of a million inhabitants than any other nation. These millions were immigrants, recently European peasants, or the children of American farmers.

By the end of the century, most of Western Europe had taken some steps to provide sanitation, a public water supply, policing, and public transport. The draw of the factory, the drama of the train, and the squalor and poverty of rural life brought village and rural people to the city. The new professions of urban planner, transport and sanitation engineer, and social worker joined, then replaced, the well-meaning, civic-minded, urban-dwelling men and women volunteers who worked to alleviate the worst effects of urban industrial living.

Responding to the various pressures of education, the press, and patriotic campaigns, these urban immigrants became nationalistic. Maintaining traditional loyalties and minority identity became increasingly difficult, particularly for their children. There were exceptions: industrialization actually heightened minority identity among such industrially advanced peoples as the Czechs in Austria-Hungary and the Basques in Spain. Generally, however, if a minority culture managed to resist the pressures for integration, its success reflected the relative economic backwardness of the area. In Russia, the Austro-Hungarian Empire, the Iberian Peninsula, and southern

Italy, discontented peasants rejected pressures for national integration. There, the peasants barely eked out a living, often working on great estates for landlords who often spoke another language. The peasant's discontent stemmed from a mix of national or ethnic identity and economic woe.

Labor's Responses

Around the world, labor, too, was caught in the changing conditions of the second wave of industrialization. Giant enterprises required great armies of unskilled workers who toiled for low pay, usually by the day or by the job. Unskilled workers could not be fitted easily into craft unions. Technology increased the number of the unskilled, and it "deskilled" craft workers, often pitting the two groups against one another. Skilled craftspeople watched machines and unskilled workers—often foreigners, minorities, or displaced peasants—take their places. Labor standards, the quality of goods, and wages all declined. Rising wages in any industry became an incentive to invent a machine to drive them back down.

Where workers could vote, they pressed for government action against the social evils of industrialization and urbanization. In the United States, workers voted for the same political parties that other classes voted for. In Britain, at first workers did too, but then organized their own party. In France, Germany, and Italy, workers joined socialist parties calling for the end of capitalism; in Italy, Spain, and parts of France, even more radical, anarchist parties gained worker support. Beginning in the 1860s and 1870s, workers demanded union recognition, minimum wages, maximum hours, and better working conditions even for nonunion workers. Laborers had to win over the general public, which was imbued with individualist, property-protecting values as well as class prejudices. Labor first won public sympathy for the poorest of workers and for exploited women and children. In 1888, an English strike of women and girls who worked in match factories, where phosphorus endangered lives, drew public and press support, including "sympathy strikes" by other workers. The "match girls" made some limited gains.

But the next year, when impoverished British dockworkers struck, there was little public

"MATCH GIRLS." The "match girls" strike taught the public the human cost of cheap and dangerous products. Here the women pack phosphorus matches in a London factory. (Mary Evans Picture Library Ltd/AGE Fotostock.)

sympathy for these rough-and-ready men. Australian and American dockworkers rescued them from sure defeat. They knew the horrible conditions of the job and realized how vulnerable a union of unskilled day laborers actually was, even in England.

Between the "hungry forties" and the outbreak of World War I, the standard of living of many workers, both skilled craftspeople and factory hands, did improve, thanks to trade union organization, government intervention in the economy, and the general increase in productivity. Nevertheless, most workers—and their families—lived in overcrowded, bleak, cold tenements, without ventilation or running water. They worked long hours—as many as fifty-five per week in trades where governments restricted the length of the workweek, and from seventy to seventy-five in unregulated trades. Their jobs were exhausting, dangerous, and monotonous. Women workers had a particularly hard life, laboring the regulated number of hours in the factory and then doing piecework at home to make ends meet. In addition, they cared for the home and the children, of which there were usually five or more. Workers suffered from malnutrition, diseases (particularly tuberculosis), and lack of medical care for childbirth or accidents, even those that maimed and killed (for which there was usually no compensation other than the contributions of other workers who "passed the hat" if there were no "friendly society" dues).

Governments paid attention, taking the first steps to protect women and children and then extending reforms to men. Laborers were drawn to socialist or labor parties, which believed exploitation was built into the capitalist profit system. In the 1880s, Bismarck instituted reforms and by 1914, Britain, France, Austria, Italy, Denmark, Switzerland, and some state governments in the United States provided some benefits for sick, injured, and elderly workers. These social welfare measures offered only minimal assistance—much less than organized labor provided for itself from dues and welfare funds.

Socialist parties, which by the 1890s were often Marxist, grew phenomenally in Germany and rapidly in much of the rest of Europe. Even in England, where Marxism was unimportant and democracy was assumed, unionists organized the socialist Independent Labour Party. Even industrially backward Russia had a Marxist socialist party. Socialists did not always agree on tactics, depending on their ideology and their country's political environment. Some socialists—Wilhelm Liebknecht and August Bebel of Germany or Jules Guesde of France—insisted that only socialist revolution would improve workers' lives. Others—"revisionist" Marxists—argued that democracy could improve the standard of living and supported democratic measures.

In the decade before 1914, a wave of strikes swept through every industrial and industrializing country. Strikes were violently put down: the dock strikes in London and Liverpool, the railroad workers' strike in France, and the miners' strikes in England and France, for example. Strikes, violence, and the growth of socialist parties accentuated middle and upper class fear of class warfare.

GREAT BRITAIN: AN INDUSTRIAL MODEL

In 1850, foreigners and Englishmen alike believed England to be the most modern, progressive country in the world. It had made phenomenal industrial progress; it balanced an incomparable degree of political liberty with economic and social reforms, avoiding the continental extremes of revolution and reaction. Political parties competed to govern and in the process reformed evils and extended the political community to previously excluded groups, such as labor or the Irish. The reality was more complicated. "Country gentlemen" dominated British politics, with titled aristocrats staffing the cabinets and commanding the army and navy. Great social mobility existed, but wealthy entrepreneurs who wanted a public life had to conform to the ideal of the country gentleman. The existence and importance of its overseas empire challenged any view of Britain as a liberal state. How could a vast empire of subject and exploited peoples be reconciled with political liberty and social reforms in England?

A century of industrial and commercial changes brought prosperity and a sense of well-being. In parliament, the competition of two men of quite different personalities and values stimulated political reform: William E. Gladstone (1809–1898), a pious, sober man for whom politics was a way to do God's work; and the flamboyant Benjamin Disraeli (1804–1881), a novelist and a Conservative, who loved the game of politics. The rules of the parliamentary game required the prime minister, his cabinet, and his party to resign or call a new election if they failed to get a bill passed. The election would decide which party would govern.

In 1867, Gladstone's Liberals failed to pass a bill granting some working class men the vote. Disraeli countered, proposing suffrage for most city workers—not at all a Conservative measure. It carried, and suddenly, the electorate was doubled. Both parties actually feared democracy, yet in the competitive sport of politics democracy became a reality. Overnight, compulsory elementary education became a necessity (other European states had state schools and compulsory education). In 1884, Gladstone's party extended the vote to most Englishmen. Women and many

Irishmen still could not vote. Would "country gentlemen" admit women, the Irish, and labor into the political community? Would labor and women play by the "rules of the game?" On the eve of World War I, the demands for justice by each of these groups created a prolonged crisis for parliamentary government.

Labor Unrest

In the stable, prosperous middle decades of the nineteenth century, British workers created the strongest labor movement in Europe. The depression of 1873, which affected all of Europe, shook English self-confidence. Technology had altered entire industries, creating support in the 1880s for the more militant industrial unions. Unlike European workers, British labor had been relatively untouched by Marxism. In the 1880s, foreign competition brought a general industrial downturn, which led some labor leaders to advocate English socialism. In 1893, a colorful nonconformist who represented a poor Welsh mining district, J. Kier Hardie, formed the Independent Labour Party, which would ally with middle-class socialists, such as the Fabians, or with Liberals on political and economic programs.

The Labour Party might never have gotten off the ground if it had not been for the Taff Vale decision (1901). The courts awarded damages to an employer picketed by a union. If workers could be fined for "restraining trade," unions would be broken. This happened just as labor demanded protection against unemployment, accidents, sickness, and old age—benefits German workers obtained in the 1880s. By 1906, in a Liberal landslide, the new Labour Party gained twenty-nine seats so the Liberals, led by David Lloyd George (1863–1945) and the then-Liberal Winston Churchill (1874–1965), were able to introduce important social measures. They repealed the Taff Vale decision. They enacted a program of old-age pensions, labor exchanges to help the unemployed find work, minimum wages for certain industries, unemployment, and health insurance—a program deeply influenced by Bismarck's social legislation. The House of Lords rejected the budget, creating a constitutional crisis. The Lords took this extreme action because "the people's budget" financed the social legislation by taxes directed at the wealthy and the privileged—raising the income tax, levying inheritance taxes ("death duties") and "unearned income" taxes on rents, investments, and increases in the value of land.

The Liberals waged an all-out fight with the Lords, who saw their struggle as the defense of Britain and its empire against the Liberals' "socialist" campaign. Class hatreds, unacknowledged for a couple of generations, were bitterly and freely expressed. Britain's political balance ended. Miners, railway workers, and dockhands allied, calling a general strike of all labor. The people's budget ultimately passed.

Later, the Parliament Act of 1911 stipulated that the Lords could not prevent—only delay—a bill passed by the Commons. The machinery for democratic government in Britain was in place. Excluded groups had focused on democracy as the way to gain justice—democracy appeared able to bring social revolution! A long coal strike in 1912 involved 1.5 million workers; only government intervention could stop it. Could British liberal democracy survive this intense class conflict? There were several injustices ready to test that question.

The Irish Question

The Irish were a troublesome question for much of the nineteenth century. The great famine of 1845 through 1847 brought unparalleled suffering to the Irish: a million of them died, and another million emigrated. The sufferers saw England as the cause, or if not the cause, then as callously indifferent, to their plight. A revolutionary republican group, the Fenians, called for Irish independence. English Liberals thought that economic and religious reforms would placate Irish discontent; therefore, Gladstone ended the **tithe** that the mostly Catholic Irish paid to the Anglican Church. Liberals also passed land legislation for Irish tenant farmers. In the 1840s and 1850s, these reforms might have appeased Irish Catholics and farmers. By the 1880s, they were too little, too late—2 million dead or forced to leave with only this response? The issue had become independence or **home rule**—that is, self-government within the British Empire. In the Commons, the Irish, led by the Protestant Charles Stewart Parnell, formed a separate bloc to force the Conservatives and the Liberals to reckon with the issue of home rule. Parnell's supporters used every known parliamentary tactic, and invented some new ones, to secure their goals without violence. Others urged terrorist acts, which aroused public passions; Parliament enacted extreme measures, suspending trial by jury and many other liberties in Ireland, which only intensified the hostilities. Gladstone split his party and still failed to satisfy the Irish, who believed the question was a national one as well as a religious and class discrimination issue. Parnell failed as well; the Irish struggle had turned violent and revolutionary.

The ongoing bitter struggle for home rule made prewar British politics extremely volatile. Under the Parliament Act of 1911, the House of Lords, dominated by Tory imperialists (Conservatives), could not prevent the passage of home rule. Conservatives thought the empire more important than elections and majority rule. Militant groups took the law into their own hands. The Irish Republican Brotherhood and the Gaelic League pressed for full independence. Fearing Catholic domination, the Protestant Irish organized a private army, the Ulster Volunteers. Gangs smuggled guns (many from America), soldiers fired on demonstrators, and civil war seemed close. Some English Tory leaders threatened mutiny; one actually reviewed eighty thousand volunteer soldiers willing to fight against England for the Protestant cause in Ireland.

In 1914, when Great Britain declared war on Germany, Ireland was uppermost in British minds. On the day the archduke of Austria was assassinated, the front pages of the British papers were filled with news of Irish protest, not with foreign affairs. With the onset of war, women and labor suspended their militant campaigns, pledging their loyalty to king and country. Many Irish fought for Britain in World War I, but the deferred promise of home rule angered many others. Some, like Sir Roger Casement, joined the Germans to fight for Ireland's independence. In 1916, on Easter Sunday, a group of Irish nationalists seized the Dublin post office. The British army suppressed the uprising and its leaders were executed for treason. After the war, Lloyd George negotiated a settlement. Ireland was divided. The south gained self-government, and the predominantly Protestant northern six counties of Ulster remained part of the United Kingdom.

The Woman Question

The issue of women's equality was a much older struggle than that for the right to vote, but suffrage was the issue before World War I. The movement was strongest in England and America; elsewhere in Europe, in Scandinavia, Germany, and even Russia, the "new woman" demanded sexual freedom, the right of divorce, child custody, and property ownership, demands that would have been utopian dreams without the Industrial Revolution. Industrialization made it possible for women to work and to support themselves and their families. Nonetheless, husbands and fathers still had control of their children and the family property, education was unattainable for most women, and employment was scarce and low paying. On the eve of the World War I, the woman question was raised again. Artists and intellectuals, such as Henrik Ibsen, George Bernard Shaw, and H. G. Wells, supported women's emancipation. Others, such as August Strindberg, opposed it. Socialist feminists, such as the German Clara Zetkin, argued that only socialism could liberate women from responsibility for their children and from their lives of hard work. Conservatives, in contrast, thought that women's rights would destroy the family and undermine the nation. Paradoxically, radicals in France, Italy, and Spain, who ordinarily championed equality, opposed women's suffrage because they feared that priests and husbands would dominate the women. Finally, women themselves were torn between their role as wives and mothers and their desire for equality and some legal and social protection.

Women had greater freedom in England than in most countries; there they could vote for and serve on school and local government boards. Their volunteer work in schools and charity organizations was the backbone of the educational and social support system. But they could not vote for members of Parliament, their education was stunted, and they suffered from enormous social pressure to conform to traditional women's roles. The women's movement was far from united; middle-class and working-class women led very different lives. Many of the latter were much more concerned with economic security than with the right to vote.

Though no longer limited to the most miserable and sometimes degrading labor, working-class

POSTER PUBLISHED BY THE ARTISTS' SUFFRAGE LEAGUE, DESIGNED BY EMILY HARDING ANDERES, C. 1908. This suffragette poster illustrates the fact that British women could not vote in the early twentieth century. The cap and gown of the woman college graduate does not help her find the key that will release her from the imprisoning categorization with felons and the mentally ill, who couldn't vote for Parliament either. Women were leaders in local government—where they were in charge of schools, orphanages, and hospitals—but were unable to vote for members of the House of Commons until after World War I. (Library of Congress Prints and Photographs Division/LC-USZC4-6888.)

women were vulnerable to the ups and downs of the economy. Even middle-class women were divided. Some feminists—Millicent Fawcett and Josephine Butler, for instance—thought the focus on the vote a mistake, that women should concentrate on self-improvement and legal efforts to raise their status in society. Others proposed immediate radical action. Still others thought that the political road was the wrong road to take; women needed to liberate themselves economically and socially from their dependence on men.

Despite the many points of view, in England the "question" was a suffrage issue. It was posed in particularly vivid ways—ways that threatened the accepted forms and norms of liberal politics. In the campaign for women's suffrage, suffragist tactics and government repression steadily escalated in violence. Many Liberals and some Labourites supported women's suffrage; there were Conservatives who supported women's suffrage but feared that women would vote for Liberals and that working class women might vote "socialist" or Labour. A family of feminists called for an end to gentlemen's politics. Emmeline Pankhurst and her daughters Sylvia and Christabel urged demonstrations and disruptions of the House of Commons. When their petitions were ignored, they broke windows, started fires in mailboxes, tore up golf greens, and chained themselves to the gates of Parliament. In 1913, one militant protestor killed herself by jumping in front of the king's horse at the races. The suffragists' opponents argued that women were not rational enough to discuss politics. When lawbreaking feminists were arrested, they staged hunger strikes. The police force-fed the demonstrators and subjected them to ridicule and rough treatment. Often the police would release half-starved suffragists to recover their health and then reimprison them ("cat and mouse" it was called). Ridiculed, humiliated, and punished—but, above all, legally ignored—feminists refused to accept the passive role that Englishmen were willing to allow them.

Women played a major part on the home front during World War I, and in 1918 women over thirty years of age were enfranchised in Britain. In some colonies (Australia, New Zealand), women had the right to vote. Finally, in 1928, British women gained the right to vote on the same terms as men; that is, they had to be twenty-one years old and to have six months' residency. After the war, women gained the right to vote in the United States, Germany, and the Soviet Union, but they would have to wait a long time for this right in France, Spain, Italy, and Switzerland.

Britain on the Eve of War

The bitter conflicts of prewar Britain showed the cracks in the country's self-image as a stable, liberal, constitutional regime. The elite learned that the tactics of the new politics—strikes, demonstrations,

Hubertine Auclert:
La Citoyenne

The leading voice for women's rights in late-nineteenth-century France was the newspaper La Citoyenne *(The Female Citizen), started in 1881 by Hubertine Auclert (1848–1914). But in socially conservative France, women did not receive the vote until 1944. In the following passage, Auclert stated the case for female equality.*

Now, what do we mean by the political emancipation of woman? We mean women's receiving the right that confers the power to make laws. . . .

Thus, it is evident that political rights are for women the keystone that will give her all other rights.

When women are able to intervene in public affairs, their first concern will be to reform unjust legislation; their first act will be to use the right given them to change their situation.

But since woman does not have the power to weaken the laws that oppress her, whom can she count on to do it? On man? But it is man who has established the existing laws and these laws do not trouble him. On the contrary, they give him all the facilities to trouble us; thus, instead of suppressing these laws that enslave woman, man busies himself with creating laws that will further enlarge his horizons. In this country where there are seventeen million sovereigns—men—and more than seventeen million slaves—women—the reforms that men perceive as essential are the reforms that will grant them still more privileges. . . .

What women need to free themselves from masculine tyranny—made law—is the possession of their share of sovereignty; they need the title of *citoyenne française*; they need the ballot.

The French citizeness: this means that woman invested with the highest social rights will, by freedom, have her dignity restored; by the sense of responsibility, her character enlarged.

The French citizeness will promptly rise out of her distressing economic situation; the State and the laws will no longer render her inferior; the schooling of woman being, like that of man, essentially useful, every career, every profession will be open to her; and whatever her work, woman will no longer see it deprecated under the ridiculous pretext that it was done by a woman.

The French citizeness will quintuple the effectiveness of her maternal influence; she will raise the child not for herself alone, or for itself, but for society. She will inculcate those private and public virtues that will contribute to the child's happiness and that of his fellow-creatures.

The woman invested with the highest social rights, the French citizeness, will have the power to endow generations with such sweeping moral vision, that fraternity will replace egoism in human relationships, and harmony—the goal to which all aspire—will supplant the present conflict in society.

In as much as we believe that from the emancipation of woman will flow a source of good for all humanity, we can do no better than to consecrate all our efforts to this cause.

Questions for Analysis

1. What right does Hubertine Auclert believe is the fundamental requirement for the emancipation of women? What other rights will follow from that right, according to her?
2. In view of the fact that French women did not gain that right until the end of World War II (1944), was it as fundamental to female emancipation as she believed?

Hubertine Auclert, *La Citoyenne,* in *Victorian Women: A Documentary History of Women's Lives in Nineteenth Century England, France, and the United States,* trans. Karen M. Offen; ed. Erna Olafson Hellerstein, Leslie Parker Hume, and Karen M. Offen (Stanford, Calif.: Stanford University Press, 1981), 445–446.

passive resistance, and terrorism—would destroy the liberal parliamentary institutions that many saw as the basis of Britain's greatness. Parliamentary government proved able to win a grueling world war, but issues of empire and economic depression would test the constitution once again as excluded groups fought for full democracy.

FRANCE: THE NATION DIVIDED

The fortunes of France in the nineteenth century differed greatly from Britain's. Virtually each generation faced revolution and reaction, swinging from democratic revolution to authoritarian stability, from active participation of the people to rule by a single man or small group of men. France's slow and uneven industrialization greatly affected its national and international affairs.

Napoleon "le Petit"

At midcentury, the personality and politics of the great Napoleon's nephew Louis Napoleon Bonaparte (1808–1873) dominated France. In the elections (made possible by the democratic social revolution of 1848) in which all French males could vote, an overwhelming majority elected "little" Bonaparte ("le Petit") president of the Second French Republic. Bonaparte's imperialism, his support of Catholics in Rome and in France, and the end of the republic outraged liberals and republicans, including Alexis de Tocqueville and Victor Hugo, but the fear of revolution, particularly of working class republicanism, led most other Frenchmen to accept Bonaparte as second emperor in 1851.

Bonapartism was a mix of democratic, socialist, nationalist, and authoritarian ideas. It promised national glory, strong leadership, and social progress. Bonaparte combined the appearance of democracy—elections by universal manhood suffrage, plebiscites, a press, and intellectual debate—with economic expansion. At the same time, he suppressed opposition, censored the press, rarely convened the Parliament, and manipulated elections. Property owners, who liked stability at home, expansion abroad, railroad construction, and the rebuilding of Paris, liked him and tolerated foreign expansion in Mexico and Italy. He expressed concern for workers, whose suffering became acute

as industrialization took hold. After a decade of authoritarian rule, he loosened the controls on the press and the legislature, legalized strikes, and granted workers a limited right to unionize. In 1869, when members of the opposition were elected, they wrote a new constitution with liberal safeguards for individual liberties. The next year Bonaparte's foreign policy resulted in the Franco-Prussian War (1870–1871), in which France was defeated, occupied by Prussian troops, and the Prussian king was crowned emperor of united Germany in the Hall of Mirrors at Versailles, France.

After the Fall

As French armies collapsed, the people of Paris rose, refusing to accept defeat or the surrender to peace terms by France's provisional government. The Paris Commune (1871) simply refused to obey. The Communards included a wide range of opinion: the followers of anarchist Pierre Joseph Proudhon; groups of republican and socialist veterans of the revolution of 1848 suddenly and unexpectedly liberated from prisons, hiding, and exile; and many ordinary republicans and patriots. For two months, the revolutionaries ruled Paris, inspired by the Jacobins of 1793 and the radicals of June 1848. Then, Adolph Thiers, the man who had accepted Bismarck's peace terms, ordered French soldiers to attack Paris. The fighting was bitter and desperate, with many acts of terrorism and violence on both sides. The defeated Communards were treated as traitors, not as French patriots: twenty thousand men and women were executed without trial, and those who were tried received harsh sentences of death, life imprisonment, and transportation to prison colonies.

The Commune became legendary. It alarmed governing classes across Europe, who feared revolutionary socialism or anarchism. International revolutionaries, too, thought that the Communards were the radicalized masses, forgetting that they had risen to save their country. Convinced that political leaders everywhere would be just as brutal in defending private property as Thiers had been, Marx urged the masses to violent insurrection. Other radicals, appalled by the bloodbath, argued that the revolutionary days of 1789, 1830, and 1848 were over. The modern state was too powerful. Workers' protest had to be limited to votes and demonstrations.

The suppression of the Paris Commune marked a turning point in French political life. To French property owners, republican government meant radicalism, despite the fact that republicans had destroyed the Commune. Burdened by an indemnity and the loss of Alsace and part of Lorraine to Prussia, and embittered by the experience of war and civil war, republican France slowly rebuilt national unity and regained its place in Europe.

Threats to the Republic

The government born from the next few years of political crisis would be the longest-lasting republic in the history of France (1870–1940). Its birth was accidental; with no king willing to rule, republicans did. The Third Republic had a powerful bicameral legislature—a senate and a chamber of deputies, which resembled the House of Commons—and a prime minister, who had to have its support. The president was a figurehead; republicans wanted no new Napoleon. Unlike Britain, France had many political parties, which expressed the deep differences—regional, political, religious, economic, and historical—among the French but also exaggerated them. The republic faced many scandals; almost immediately, several republican deputies were involved in a giant stock swindle in the financing of the Panama Canal. Many viewed all politicians as immoral; politics seemed to consist of wheeling and dealing. Others thought democracy was particularly prone to corruption as it was in the United States and France. The Third Republic survived, but not without trouble; in the process, politics took to the streets and the press.

AFTER THE FALL: LaRoquette Prisoners Before the Firing Squad. The repression of the Paris Commune, which resisted peace with the Prussians, was a brutal bloodbath with atrocities on both sides. When it was over, almost eight thousand were sent into exile, five thousand imprisoned and fined, and many executed. Few could have predicted that the Third Republic would survive to World War II or that French culture and science of the Republic would make a major contribution to civilization. (© Bettmann/Corbis.)

Jean Jaurès

Jean Jaurès (1859–1914) was the most important socialist in the Third French Republic. A brilliant scholar who left the university for politics, he was the youngest member elected to the Chamber of Deputies. Deeply concerned about workers' problems, Jaurès believed that capitalism was a new feudalism in which the rich controlled society and only the working class struggled for justice.

Jaurès's message of justice brought liberal republicans and socialists together to work for social reforms. He championed Alfred Dreyfus, arguing that socialists had just as much at stake as liberals in questions of justice. Jaurès and French workers joined intellectuals and students demonstrating for a fair trial and freedom for the convicted Jewish officer. Many other socialists,

still embittered by the repression of the Paris Commune, refused to take any part in parliamentary politics, but Jaures brought wide support as he campaigned vigorously for reforms that French workers still had not won. In 1905, during a time of strikes and repression, the socialist parties of France joined together under his leadership, something most observers had thought impossible. On the international scene, in the Second International, Jaurès opposed war, calling all workers, not just French ones, to refuse to fight should their governments go to war.

In the last days before World War I, a French nationalist fanatic assassinated Jaurès convinced that the great speaker would lead his followers to resist the war. The assassin was wrong. French workers—even socialists—defended their country in 1914 because they believed in its democracy.

For more than a decade the Dreyfus affair tore France apart. In 1894, Captain Alfred Dreyfus, an Alsatian-Jewish artillery officer, was wrongly accused of selling military secrets to the Germans and condemned to life imprisonment on Devil's Island. Anti-Semitic elements joined the republic's opponents, including the army, the Catholic church, and monarchists, to block every attempt to clear Dreyfus. In the beginning, he had few champions; the vast majority distrusted the army, the church, and the monarchists, but they felt that the honor of France and the army was at stake. Then a few radical republicans, including socialists and celebrated writers Anatole France, Émile Zola, and the future war leader, Georges Clemenceau, came to Dreyfus's defense, mobilizing public opinion. University students demonstrated, insisting on a retrial. Dreyfus was finally cleared in 1906, but rather than healing the divisions in French society the case seemed to exacerbate them.

The radical republicans launched a fierce campaign to root out the anti-republican and anti-Semitic elements. **Anticlericalism** had been strong in France among certain groups ever since

the French Revolution. The radicals attacked the Catholic church, expelled religious orders, and confiscated their property. They tried to replace the influence of the parish priest with that of the district schoolmaster. Complete separation of church and state was ordered, making France a secular state.

France on the Eve of War

French economic development lagged; France had fewer and smaller industries than Britain or Germany, and more French people lived in rural areas or in small communities than in cities. In general, industry, trade unions, political parties, and socialist groups tended to be decentralized; artisans were much more influential than proletarians. For a generation after the Paris Commune, militants refused to cooperate with the republic or any bourgeois government. In the 1880s, however, trade unions and socialist political parties turned to democratic politics in an effort to gain pensions and regulations governing working conditions, wages, and hours. The ruling elite opposed any such measures that would tax the lives of ordinary people. Socialists were suspicious of such reforms as attempts to buy off workers; workers and intellectuals supported radical **syndicalism**, or worker control of industry and government.

The Third Republic was not popular; other institutions, the church, the army, socialism, and even the monarchy and the empire, inspired deeper passions than the republic but it survived because its enemies were divided. Yet, for all the political and social unrest, the "republic by default" was an era of genuine intellectual and cultural flourishing. It was a modern renaissance in which Paris was a pilgrimage site welcoming and nourishing Europe's greatest artists, intellectuals, and scientists. Few, who thought only of industry and politics, would have believed that France could fight and win the long, bloody, devastating World War I.

GERMANY: AN AUTHORITARIAN STATE?

Victory in the Franco-Prussian War (1870–1871) created a German empire with the Prussian king as emperor and the architect of the war Otto von Bismarck as chancellor. All roads led to Berlin's Brandenburg Gate, where Bismarck decided the great issues, shaping the political environment for the next generation for Germans and most of Europe.

Bismarck's constitution, like that of Napoleon III, granted universal manhood suffrage; both manipulated the votes and elections. The German government was federal, the twenty-four states having some powers, but foreign affairs and defense were in the hands of the emperor and his "iron chancellor." The German kaiser, unlike Britain's monarch, had considerable control over lawmaking, foreign affairs, and the military. Aristocrats held the important positions of government—in the military, the diplomatic corps, and the top echelon of the bureaucracy. The German Empire did not have Britain's two-party system, cabinet responsibility, or guarantees of civil liberties. Technically, the Reichstag could refuse to pass the budget, but politicians were usually unwilling to do that. Only the king-emperor could remove the chancellor or the cabinet members from office. Bismarck treated political parties as interest group lobbyists. He cared little

for liberal and democratic measures, maintaining an authoritarianism that would have significant consequences for Germany's future.

Bismarck's "Struggle for Culture"

To Bismarck, Catholics and socialists were both internationalists who did not put Germany's interests first. Taking advantage of prejudiced non-Catholics, who did not understand the declaration of papal infallibility of 1871, he passed discriminatory laws restricting the Jesuits, requiring government supervision of the church and the education of priests in state schools. All marriages had to be performed by state officials. Churchmen who rejected these laws were imprisoned or exiled. Almost 40 percent of Germany's people were Roman Catholic. Bismarck's persecution actually strengthened the German Catholics' loyalty to their church and to the Catholic Center Party. It weakened the liberals, who did not defend Catholic civil liberties. Prussian conservatives, though Protestant, actually resented Bismarck's anticlerical policy fearing it could be turned against Lutherans as well as Catholics. When Leo XIII became pope in 1878, Bismarck quietly ended the "struggle for culture" (**Kulturkampf**).

In the late 1870s, Bismarck attacked socialists—the other internationalists. The socialists were divided. Ferdinand Lassalle (1825–1864) led the German Workers' Association. Lassalle believed that if Germany enacted social reforms, workers would be just as patriotic as any other group. Marxists scoffed at his idealistic politics, but there were more Lassalleans than Marxists so they joined forces in 1875 to create a German Social Democratic Party, the SPD. Bismarck was sure that liberals would respond as they had when he attacked Catholics. When in 1878 two attempts were made on the emperor's life, Bismarck blamed the socialists, demanding the party be outlawed. The few socialists were not a threat; their immediate practical program called for civil liberties and democracy. Only those with narrow conservative views would think the socialists were dangerous, but many Prussian Junkers held such narrow views. The liberals scarcely objected when special legislation outlawed subversive organizations and authorized the police to ban meetings and newspapers.

The Social Democratic Party, like the Catholic Center Party before, survived discrimination and strengthened its disciplined organization. The liberals grew even weaker. Meanwhile, Bismarck wooed workers with social legislation to counter the effects of the rapid industrialization of the 1850s and 1860s. Germany was the first government to enact social legislation for its working people: insurance against sickness, disability, accidents, and old age. The employer, the state, and the worker each contributed small amounts to an insurance fund.

German socialists became the model for other socialists. There were more German workers; the organization and leadership were superior. Bismarck's social legislation gave German workers some protection. The Social Democratic Party seemed to have created a way of life, offering members political activities, youth and women's divisions, athletic leagues, and cultural societies. Before World War I, union membership stood at roughly 3 million, and the Social Democratic Party was the largest single party in Germany. The socialists talked revolution, but many members supported gradual reform. Most German workers were patriotic, even imperialistic.

Germany on the Eve of War

When Kaiser William II (1889–1918) ascended the throne, Germany possessed the most extensive sector of large-scale, concentrated industrial and corporate capitalist firms in the world. It also had the largest and most powerful unions and the strongest socialist party. Only the United States rivaled the scale and concentration of industry of Germany, but labor had very little influence in the United States.

Yet Germany's political regime preserved aspects of an absolute monarchy. The constitution was a peculiar mixture of aristocratic Prussian power in the upper house and, in the lower, democratic universal manhood suffrage that was manipulated to illiberal ends. The bureaucracy, the military, and the chancellor remained out of reach of the voting populace. Bismarck's hostility to liberalism and his authoritarian rule undermined the development of a democratic parliamentary government. The Social Democrats, ostensibly the party of revolution, were the only party that wanted the power of the Reichstag to reject the chancellor. In other European countries, such a measure was advocated by liberals, but in Germany democratic and liberal measures were part of the socialists' program.

ITALY: UNREALIZED AMBITIONS

Italian nationalists expected greatness when they unified their country, so long conquered, plundered, divided, and ruled by absolute princes. But the newly unified Italy faced serious problems. An overwhelmingly Roman Catholic country, like France, it was split by religious controversy. Liberals and republicans wanted a secular state, civil marriage, and public education, which was **anathema** to the church.

Another divisive factor was Italy's long tradition of separate and rival states—an extreme expression of the regional conflicts of other states. Unlike Germany and France few Italians could actually participate in the constitutional monarchy. Of the 27 million citizens, only about 2 million could vote, even after the reforms of 1881, which tripled the electorate. Liberals pointed out that almost every man who could read and write could vote, but this meant little to those, like Garibaldi, who had fought to unify but were denied the vote because they couldn't read or write.

Among Italian workers, cynicism was so deep that many turned to extreme radical movements, which advocated the rejection of authority and the tactics of terrorism, assassination, and general strikes. Disgust with parliamentary government led workers to favor direct action over elections and parties. Other alienated Italians included peasants from the poor rural south. Catholic, loyal to their landlords, and bitterly unhappy with their economic situation, they saw little of the new state aside from taxation and conscription.

The ruling elite brushed aside Italy's difficult social and economic problems. It concentrated instead on issues more easily expressed to an inexperienced political nation: nationalism, foreign policy, and military glory. The politicians trumpeted ambitions for Great Power status, justifying military expenditures beyond Italy's means. They advocated African and Mediterranean colonies as the solution to Italy's social ills, arguing that exploiting others would pay for badly needed social reforms, and the raw materials would fuel industry. The failure of these promises deepened the cynicism of a disillusioned people. Meanwhile, masses of Italians emigrated to North and South America. On the eve of World War I, Italy was deeply divided politically. A wave of strikes and rural discontent led political leaders to declare neutrality, deciding, unlike Russia, not to risk the shaky regime by entering the war. But the appeal of expansionism was too great for them to maintain this policy.

RUSSIA: TSARIST EMPIRE

The vast Russian empire differed fundamentally from Western Europe. Stretching through the Eurasian landmass from Germany to China and Japan and south through the Caucasus to the northern frontiers of India and Afghanistan, covering one-sixth of the world's land surface, the Russian empire suffered from incredible weaknesses. Large distances, an adverse climate, and poor communications, as well as extensive ethnic, religious, and cultural diversity held together by force, kept Russia a backward country. The great movements that had shaped the outlook of the modern West—the Renaissance, the Reformation, the Scientific Revolution, the Enlightenment, and the Industrial Revolution—had barely penetrated the lands to the east. Yet Russia's rulers and Western-educated elites were convinced that their country was part of Europe.

Russia's fortunes depended on its political order, which in the early eighteenth century centered on the commands of the ruler. Peter the Great reorganized the tsarist government, centralizing the administration, forcing the nobility to serve the state, building St. Petersburg on the Baltic and moving the capital from Moscow, and founding the Russian Academy of Sciences to bring western knowledge to the east. At the end of the century, an exceptionally energetic ruler, Catherine the Great, inspired by French intellectuals such as Voltaire, strengthened the authority of the tsarist regime. Her successors, however, had reason to fear the liberal views of the Enlightenment. Russian officers returning from Western Europe after the defeat of Napoleon, attempted an uprising in December 1825 at the accession of Nicholas I. Thereafter, fear of revolution haunted the tsarist government.

To counter the subversive influence of Western ideals and institutions, Nicholas I decreed an ideology of Russian superiority; called *official nationality*, it remained a policy until 1917. The government's version of Russian nationalism taught the Russian people that the Orthodox church, the autocratic rule of the tsar, and Russia's Slavic culture made the Russian Empire different from and superior to the West. The ideal was a monolithic regime, run like an army by a vigorous administration centered on the monarch; all Russians were to obey his wise and fatherly commands. But Nicholas's ambition to make Russia superior to Western Europe was thwarted in the Crimean War (1854–1856), fought on Russian soil. English and French expeditionary forces defeated the Russian efforts to gain political influence in the eastern Mediterranean area, areas they were interested in as well. A new regime began under Alexander II (1855–1881), who was determined to preserve autocratic rule but with the energetic support of all its subjects. Whether stimulating popular initiative was possible without undermining **autocracy** was the key puzzle for him and for his successors to the end of the tsarist regime.

Alexander's boldest reforms included the emancipation of the serfs in 1861. They were liberated from bondage to the nobility and given land of their own, but not individual freedom. They remained tied to their villages that owned the land collectively. Emancipation did not transform the peasants into enterprising and loyal citizens. For the nonpeasant minority, a package of other reforms brought new opportunities: limited self-government for selected rural areas and urban settlements, an independent judiciary, and the rule of law. Trial by jury was introduced, as well as the practice of law.

Meanwhile, Alexander lifted the restrictions on foreign travel, allowing closer ties with Europe. The rising class of businesspeople and professional experts looked to the West and conformed to Western European middle-class standards. There was some relaxation of the repression of non-Russian minorities. The construction of railroads facilitated agricultural exports to the West and permitted the importation of goods and capital from the West. For some years, the economy boomed.

More significant in the long run was the flowering of Russian thought and literature. Educated Russians were drawn to the ideas of the special nature of the "Russian soul" and an intensity of inward feeling unknown in Western society. They quarreled about whether Russia should pursue superiority by imitating the West or by cultivating its own Slavic genius, possibly through a Pan-Slavic movement. Pan-Slavism, which glorified the solidarity of Russians with other Slavic peoples of Eastern Europe, was a popular cause. The tsar, however, tried to control open discussion that seemed likely to provoke rebellion. Liberals advocating gradual change were thwarted by censorship and the police. The 1860s saw the rise of a fanatical intellectual opposition ready to foment social revolution. They organized a secret terrorist organization, and in 1881 they assassinated Alexander II. The era of reforms ended abruptly, but the revolutionary underground continued, soon led by intellectuals influenced by Marxist ideas.

Alexander III (1881–1894), a firm though unimaginative ruler, returned to the principles of Nicholas I. He perfected the police state, even enlisting anti-Semitism in its cause. He updated autocracy and stifled dissent at the same time that he also promoted economic development. Russia had relied too heavily on foreign loans and goods; it had to build up its own resources. It also needed more railroads to bind its huge empire together, so in 1891 the tsar ordered the construction of the Trans-Siberian Railroad. Soon afterward, Minister of Finance Sergei Witte used the railroad expansion to boost heavy industry and industrialization generally.

Forced industrialization brought perils. It propelled the country into alien, hated ways of life, created a discontented new class of workers, and impoverished agriculture. In addition, it promoted mobility, literacy, and even more contact with Western Europe. It helped increase political agitation among the professional classes, workers, peasants, and subject nationalities. Indispensable for national self-assertion and survival of the political system, industrialization strained the country's fragile unity.

The first jolt, the revolution of 1905, was the result of the Russo-Japanese War, in which Russia was defeated. Autocracy survived, although it was forced to accept a parliament, called the Imperial Duma, and political parties. The new regime, privately resisted by Nicholas II, started auspiciously. Russian art and literature flourished, and the economy progressed. Agrarian reforms introduced the incentives of private property and individual enterprise in the villages. Nevertheless, popular resentment against government-sponsored modernization festered, waiting for opportunities to explode.

PEASANTS IN RUSSIA. This photograph from the late nineteenth century shows Russian peasants in front of their home. (© Bettmann/CORBIS.)

The four imperial rulers of Russia between 1825 and 1914 labored under enormous difficulties in their efforts to match the power and prestige of the great states of Europe. Two of them met a violent end: Alexander II was assassinated, and Nicholas II was murdered. The other two died in weariness and failure. Russia as a world power was undermined by massive adversities: its enormous size and scarce means of communication, its ethnic, religious, and regional diversity, its poverty prevented the emergence of national identity. The country lacked an effective middle class, even the political means to address Russia's very real problems. Some of the intelligentsia, frustrated by their country's backwardness, became revolutionaries to bring about reforms; the majority of the educated and professional classes were deceived about their country's real needs; some even believed Russia was morally superior to the West. The abysmally backward peasant masses, scattered over the largest country in the world, were poor material for building a modern state. Outwardly impressive, the Russian empire faced a grim future as the international competition for power escalated during World War I.

THE UNITED STATES: DEMOCRATIC GIANT

Within a generation of its bloody Civil War (1861–1865), the United States moved into the ranks of giant industrial powers, then to the status of a Great Power, and, by the end of World War I, to world leadership. In the mid-nineteenth century, however, the United States was essentially a nation of farmers, producing primary goods or raw materials. In the northeastern part of the country, craft industries supplied consumer goods for a domestic market. Advancing beyond basic craft goods was just as slow a process as it was in France and most of Central Europe. Before the Civil War, the economy was primarily mercantile. Merchants were the commercial cement bonding the many small artisans, farmers, and exporters. Despite immigration from Europe and slavery, there was a steady demand for cheap labor. Capital was even scarcer than labor. Americans were inventive, competitive, and socially democratic.

In many ways, the early industrialization of the United States resembled that of Britain. Unskilled European immigrants and rural laborers furnished the manpower for New England textile mills, just as Irish and rural laborers had in England. Both shared the blessings of a single government, able to provide a stable framework for commerce, and, in the case of the United States, maintain tariffs against British competition. In both, government was noninterventionist—unwilling and unable to regulate private enterprise. In both, resources were exploited as private property, not as public social goods. Once a large internal market for cheap, standardized goods developed, entrepreneurs took the risks of investment and production on a large scale. Even more than the British, perhaps because of the much larger market for cheap goods, Americans took to machines that had standardized and interchangeable parts to produce such goods. (Eli Whitney, inventor of the cotton gin, began by producing interchangeable parts for handguns, for example.) Unlike Britain, however, the United States depended on an influx of capital, most of it English—a dependence that continued even after the Civil War, when great sectors of the American economy moved from the work of artisans to modern concentrated industry. American industrialization required substantial foreign investment in large-scale corporations in heavy industries such as coal mining and iron and steel manufacturing. This industrialization gained further momentum with the westward expansion.

The role of government is often underestimated in the United States. On both the regional and the national level, government encouraged free enterprise by allowing individuals and corporations to claim the nation's resources. It also fostered railroad building, tariff regulation, and free immigration—all of which contributed to the construction of an industrial giant. Government took a laissez-faire attitude toward social problems for a much longer time than England or Germany did. American politicians did much less than Europeans to support social legislation, such as pensions, minimum wages, or protection for women and children. There was no Bismarck, Lloyd George, or Churchill to write social legislation.

Yet until the end of the century, the United States had less labor strife than Europe and a relative absence of class conflict. Why? Did American workers share the dream of entrepreneurial success? Was the difficulty of forging class solidarity among varied ethnic groups of different cultures and languages decisive? Each new immigrant group (and later the rural blacks) entered at the bottom, supplying cheap and competitive labor and suffering violence at the hands of their fellow workers from other ethnic and racial groups. As an example, at the end of the century, assimilated and politically active workers agitated against Asian immigration. Congress closed the doors to Chinese workers *after* they had built the transcontinental railroad; a **gentleman's agreement** excluded the Japanese.

Labor conflict between workers and employers did flare up, however, in the decade before World War I. Generally, workers voted for one of the two major parties, but in the election of 1912, almost a million voted for the socialist candidate, Eugene Debs. In that election, about 70 percent of the votes cast were for either the Democratic or Progressive Party. Not all of these voters were "foreigners" or recent immigrants, as contemporaries pretended. Many Americans were critical of the money power of giant cartels and monopolies, and both Theodore Roosevelt of the Republicans and Woodrow Wilson of the Democrats called for restrictions on monopolies, or trusts. Unrestricted competition (which gave cartels and trusts an unfair advantage), corporate ethics, and "robber baron" businessmen upset many Americans who still believed in the American dream.

By 1914, the American market was the largest, most homogeneous, and most rapidly growing in the world. The United States was the largest industrial nation, producing more steel and coal than any other country. It was also the world's leader in automobiles, farming technology, electricity, and

A New York Sweatshop, Photo by Jacob Riis **(1849–1914).** The latter half of the nineteenth century saw a proliferation of sweatshops. Adults and children alike, usually immigrants, labored long hours in appalling conditions for little pay. (CORBIS.)

petroleum sectors. Its labor force was the most productive and had the highest standard of living. The United States had achieved this commanding position in a little more than a generation.

A GOLDEN AGE?

To thoughtful Europeans living in 1915, after a year of World War I, once the glow of national aura had diminished the nineteenth century must have seemed a golden era. They might have viewed it as a period of unparalleled peace and progress, full of the promise of all that well-meaning people considered modern: liberal institutions and democratic movements, autonomous nations, scientific and industrial progress, and individual human development. The century that had just ended seemed one of progress in the production of goods, the alleviation of want, the development of technology, and the application of science to industry and medicine. Part of that progress, in most minds, was the extension of constitutional and liberal government and the expression of humanitarian concern for others. Serfdom had been abolished in Europe; so had slavery in the United States and Brazil. Europeans spoke of self-government as a right. The importance of democracy had been acknowledged, and in most of Europe, universal manhood suffrage, if not universal suffrage, was in effect before the outbreak of the war.

The world had become smaller, more interdependent, and more cosmopolitan. Many Westerners were more educated and better fed, housed, and clothed than their immediate ancestors. Europe was at the height of its power in the nineteenth century. European productive capacities had reached out to most areas of the world. European culture was brilliant—whether considered in the aggregate or in the particular, as German, French, English, or Italian culture.

Yet people looking back from the vantage point of 1915 must have realized, too, that something had gone wrong in the nineteenth century. Authoritarian governments persisted in Central, Eastern, and Southern Europe; they chose war. Traditional institutions and groups still exercised their privileges at the expense of others, often by brutally repressing opposition, especially regional and minority loyalties. Some had begun to doubt when the revolutions of 1848 failed to reconcile national and class conflicts. Perhaps the bitter reaction to 1848, the harsh reality of the midcentury wars of unification, and the building of centralized states had perverted the ideals of liberal government and individual freedom. Many doubted democratic government when cynical leaders manipulated the passions of the masses. The ideals of liberal government, individual freedom, national autonomy, and economic progress struggled with authoritarianism, extreme nationalism, imperialism, class conflict, and racism.

Chapter 26

Imperialism: Western Global Dominance

Lithograph by Joseph Keppler, showing the Great Powers of the West fighting over China. (Library of Congress.)

- ■ **The Emergence of the New Imperialism**
- ■ **European Domination of Asia**
- ■ **The Scramble for Africa**
- ■ **Latin America**
- ■ **The Legacy of Imperialism**

Focus Questions

1. How did industrialization change European states' relations with China, India, the Ottoman Empire, and Japan?

2. How do historians explain the nineteenth century shift of European policies to imperialist domination?

3. How did Europeans and Americans justify their policies in non-Western areas of the world?

4. What were the obstacles to Indian national unity and independence?

5. How were China and Japan able to avoid dismemberment and rule by the Western powers?

6. Why was Africa divided by the Europeans in such a short time?

7. How did the relationship of the United States with Latin American states fit the picture of imperialism in the nineteenth and twentieth centuries?

8. What impact did European competition for empire have on European politics?

In the last decades of the nineteenth and the first of the twentieth century, European nations very rapidly laid claim to great portions of the world's surface. Russia and the United States pushed to the territorial limits of their continents and beyond. Westerners exploited weak Japanese and Chinese dynasties to gain economic and political advantage in the Far East. One by one they claimed the territories of the Ottoman Empire from its Turkish ruler. The British deprived India of any semblance of independence, ruling it directly or through puppet princes. Europeans grabbed most of Africa, seizing goods, annexing territories, and carving out empires when local rulers were too weak to prevent it. In Latin America, prosperity and stability seemed to depend on trade with Europe and the United States.

From about 1880 to 1914, Europeans confronted one another diplomatically and militarily, willing to fight over stretches of desert or rain forest that they could scarcely locate on the map. They colored the map red or blue to indicate British or French. Conflicts between Asian peoples or between Africans enabled Westerners to intervene to claim their lands and control their lives. Even those peoples who were united could not counter Western military and technological superiority.

Europeans continued to dominate most of the world until after World War II. The impact of **imperialism**—the domination by a country of the political, economic, or cultural life of another country, region, or people—contributed to both world wars involving far flung peoples and to the conflicting ideologies and crises of the Cold War. Today's interdependent global economy and intercultural conflicts and suspicions reflect the experience of more than a century of imperialism.

THE EMERGENCE OF THE NEW IMPERIALISM

From the long perspective, European history has been one of expansion. It has been a history of the struggle for domination of others—the sixteenth-century exploration, conquest, and settlement of the Americas, the aggressive inroads in Southeast Asia and Africa for lucrative trade in spices, silks,

Chronology 26.1 ❖ The Expansion of Western Power

1830	France moves into Algeria, North Africa
1839–1842	Opium War: Britain defeats China, annexing trading ports
1853	American naval Commodore Perry forces Japan open to trade with the West
1857–1858	British East India Company suppresses mutiny of native soldiers (sepoys); British government controls India
1867	Mexican revolt ends French dominance under Emperor Maximilian; Meiji Restoration in Japan
1869	Opening of the Suez Canal
1876	Stanley claims the Congo for Leopold II king of Belgium
1878	Congress of Berlin: great powers focus on overseas empire
1878–1881	Britain and Russia compete to control Afghanistan
1881	France controls Tunisia
1882	Britain occupies Egypt
1883–1885	France dominates Indochina, forcing China out
1884	Berlin Conference great powers focus on Africa
1894–1895	Sino-Japanese War: Britain, Russia, and France unite to prevent Japanese annexation of Chinese territory
1896	Ethiopians defeat Italy at Adowa
1898	Spanish-American War: the United States annexes the Philippines, Puerto Rico, and occupies Cuba. British massacre Muslim warriors at Omdurman in the Sudan
1899–1902	Britain defeats Dutch Afrikaners in South African Boer War
1900	Chinese rebel against foreigners: Great Powers' international army suppresses rebellion
1904–1905	Russo-Japanese War: Japan defeats European great power Russia
1911	Mexican Revolution; China's Manchu dynasty overthrown Sun Zhongshan (Sun Yat-sen) becomes president of Chinese republic
1919	British repress Indian protests at Amritsar. Gandhi's passive resistance nationalist movement broadens; Kemal Atatürk leads Turkey's nationalists; League of Nations establishes mandate system of colonies

luxury goods, and slaves, the seventeenth-century settlement of North America, the eighteenth-century wars for trade and colonies. By the early 1800s, however, the slaving stations in Africa had declined, along with the dominance of Caribbean sugar trade and mining in Central and South America. Revolutionary wars liberated the United States and Latin America, promising a new era of trade and investment without political control. For much of the nineteenth century, Europeans—at least those engaged in the growth of industry and the development of their nation—showed little interest in adding to the remnants of colonial empires. Advocates of free trade argued that commerce would go to the country that could produce the best goods most cheaply. In their minds, adding colonies wasted resources that could be better spent improving industry.

European influence over the rest of the world grew with the industrialization and strengthening of the European states. As European nations expanded world trade they drew previously untouched peoples into the network of supply and demand for raw materials, finished goods, and capital. Masses of European immigrants made new lives in North and South America, Australia, and New Zealand.

The expansion of world trade and the spread of Western ideas and technology did not require political empires. Suddenly, however, in the last decades of the century Europeans switched abruptly from commercial penetration to active conquest, political control, and exploitation of previously unclaimed and, in many ways, untouched territories. Why did Europeans strive to claim and control the entire world?

Conflicting Interpretations

Some historians suggest that the new imperialism (to differentiate it from the **colonialism** of settlement and trade of the 1500s and 1600s) was a direct result of industrialization. With intensified economic activity, Europeans competed for raw materials and markets for their manufactured goods, and for higher rates of return for their capital. In the late 1800s, many politicians and industrialists defended empire, believing the free market might allow competitor nations an advantage, and predicting dire economic consequences if their countries failed to get their share or a larger share of the world markets. Trade and commerce would spread culture, liberty, and political stability to "backward" areas of the world.

Historians today, however, point out that most of the areas claimed by Europeans and Americans were not profitable sources of raw materials or wealthy enough to be good markets. For Europeans and Americans, the primary trading and investment venues were Europe and America, not Asia or Africa. Some individual businesses made colonial profits, but most colonies burdened the Western taxpayer. Between 1865 and 1914, for example, only 39 percent of British investment went to the empire outside the British Isles, 28 percent of that amount going to the self-governing dominions, areas such as Australia, New Zealand, and Canada that were settled by British subjects. The average rate of return did not surpass that from home investments. In general, the colonies did not attract surplus European population that could contribute to the mother country's economy. The Americas and the British settlements drew most of the European emigrants, who also streamed to the dominions and South America—lands already dominated by Westerners. Two-thirds of British emigrants settled outside the empire, mostly in the United States. Italians certainly did not migrate to African territories. They and Germans went to the United States, and the French scarcely migrated at all.

The economic justifications of imperialism are inseparable from the intensely nationalistic ones. Policymakers hoped that empire would solve economic problems, which were particularly pressing after the crash of 1873. They hoped that class conflict would diminish when the different social groups took pride in national power. The newly unified states, Germany and Italy, demanded colonies as recognition of Great Power status. Leaders in those two nations were convinced that Britain's standing depended on colonies and naval power. They were aware of the expenses of empire, the heavy tax burden on British subjects. They knew that empire greatly increased the possibility of war with rival nations or resistant subjects, but these leaders chose an imperial course. Having lost ingloriously to Prussia in 1870 and having experienced bitter class war, France looked overseas, hoping to revitalize nationalism, recoup prestige, and add to its workforce and wealth for future European struggles. Some nations argued from strength: Americans, who built one of the world's great industrial powers after the Civil War, trumpeted their achievements by defeating the once-imperial Spain in Cuba and the Philippines. In the 1890s, Japan announced that it had joined the world's Great Powers by attacking China for control of Korea's raw materials and markets. Many political leaders hoped imperialism would win

Joseph Chamberlain: The Benefits of Empire

British imperialists argued that the welfare of Britain depended on the preservation and extension of the empire, for colonies fostered trade and served as a source of raw materials. Politician and business-man Joseph Chamberlain (1836–1914) asserted that Britain carried civilization, Christianity, and British law to the "backward" peoples of Africa and Asia.

June 10, 1896

. . . The Empire, to parody a celebrated expression, is commerce. It was created by commerce, it is founded on commerce, and it could not exist a day without commerce. (Cheers.) . . . The fact is history teaches us that no nation has ever achieved real greatness without the aid of commerce, and the greatness of no nation has survived the decay of its trade. Well, then, gentlemen, we have reason to be proud of our commerce and to be resolved to guard it from attack. (Cheers.) . . .

March 31, 1897

. . . We have suffered much in this country from depression of trade. We know how many of our fellow-subjects are at this moment un-employed. Is there any man in his senses who believes that the crowded population of these islands could exist for a single day if we were to cut adrift from us the great dependencies which now look to us for protection and assis-tance, and which are the natural markets for our trade? (Cheers.) . . .

January 22, 1894

. . . I am convinced that it is a necessity as well as a duty for us to uphold the domin-ion and empire which we now possess. (Loud cheers.) . . . I would never lose the hold which we now have over our great Indian dependency—(hear, hear)—by far the great-est and most valuable of all the customers we have or ever shall have in this country. For the same reasons I approve of the con-tinued occupation of Egypt; and for the same reasons I have urged upon this Government, and upon previous Governments, the neces-sity for using every legitimate opportunity to extend our influence and control in that great African continent which is now being opened up to civilisation and to commerce; and, lastly, it is for the same reasons that I hold that our navy should be strengthened—(loud cheers)—until its supremacy is so

them the loyalty of their own people. Some argued that the workers' well-being depended on colo-nies. Others urged imperialism from weakness. Economically backward Russia pushed east to the Pacific and south toward India for resources to develop its commerce and industry. Thus, both economically powerful states and struggling ones turned to imperialism.

On the eve of World War I, many socialists addressed the economic argument for imperi-alism. Vladimir Lenin, a revolutionary Marx-ist who would become one of the leaders of the Russian Revolution in 1917, argued that imperialism was inevitable in a highly advanced capitalist country. Many socialists asserted that capitalist nations maintained their mo-nopolistic economy and their political system by exploiting the less-developed world. The only way capitalism could deal with periodic depres-sions and ensure high wages and profits was imperialism. Lenin predicted that the Great Powers' conflicts over colonial territories and spheres of influence would lead to war and work-ing-class revolutions in those capitalist countries assured that we cannot be shaken in any of the possessions which we hold or may hold hereafter.

March 31, 1897

. . . We feel now that our rule over these territories can only be justified if we can show that it adds to the happiness and prosperity of the people—(cheers)—and I maintain that our rule does, and has, brought security and peace and comparative prosperity to countries that never knew these blessings before. (Cheers.)

In carrying out this work of civilisation we are fulfilling what I believe to be our national mission, and we are finding scope for the exercise of those faculties and qualities which have made of us a great governing race. (Cheers.) I do not say that our success has been perfect in every case, I do not say that all our methods have been beyond reproach; but I do say that in almost every instance in which the rule of the Queen has been established and the great *Pax Britannica** has been enforced, there has come with it greater security to life and property, and a material improvement in the condition of the bulk of the population. (Cheers.) No doubt, in the first instance, when these conquests have been made, there has been bloodshed, there has

been loss of life among the native populations, loss of still more precious lives among those who have been sent out to bring these countries into some kind of disciplined order, but it must be remembered that this is the condition of the mission we have to fulfil. . . .

. . . You cannot have omelettes without breaking eggs; you cannot destroy the practices of barbarism, of slavery, of superstition, which for centuries have desolated the interior of Africa, without the use of force. . . .

Questions for Analysis

1. How did Chamberlain justify imperialist politics to the British? What policies and costs followed from British general acceptance of such political beliefs?
2. Was Chamberlain's idea of civilization racist? Did the self-interested nature of his argument undermine any idealism that might have been present in British relations with the empire?

Pax Britannica means "British Peace" in the tradition of the *Pax Romana*, the peace, stability, and prosperity that characterized the Roman Empire at its height in the first two centuries A.D.

Joseph Chamberlain, *Foreign and Colonial Speeches* (London: G. Routledge and Sons, 1897).

---

which lagged the most in economic development (i.e., Russia and the Balkans). In general, socialists thought imperialism was one of the ways capitalists maintained control over their nations' workers. To many, the social and political facts about imperialism in the nineteenth and early twentieth centuries seemed to reinforce the socialists' critique.

Nationalistic competition among the Europeans led them to extend their power struggles to Africa and Asia. Far away from their European homelands, leaders acquired territories for strategic

reasons. Britons worked to keep the Germans out of the Middle East because influence there might open the Indian Ocean—and the British-dominated Indian subcontinent—to them. That thinking meant they had to keep Russians out of Afghanistan as well, and it meant that much of the world that bordered on the seas could call at some time or another for Britain to think it had to prevent another state from expanding trade there. Bismarck actually encouraged French expansion in Africa, betting on inevitable conflict with the Italians and the British distracting them from the loss of Alsace and Lorraine. Overseas expansion could create yet another political rift to weaken the French government; at the least it would be expensive for France to maintain. The strategy worked until Germany expanded its navy, threatening Britain enough to move it to ally with France.

The British liked to think that they were merely defending their empire, particularly India. They defined enormous territories and waterways as essential to that defense. Other nations saw Britain as their primary rival for the spoils of imperialism—for "a place in the sun," as the Germans liked to phrase it. In Russia, a small clique of nobles and officers urged expansion south, knowing that would threaten Britain. A move east would bring conflict with Japan, driving the British and Japanese together. Because the conflicts between Europeans were played out in Asia and Africa, Europe itself remained relatively peaceful after the Franco-Prussian War. In the long run, however, the tense atmosphere of imperialism—the **militarism** and the racism—contributed to a devastating conflict in Europe, during World War I. That war engaged the men and resources of empires as well.

The most extreme ideological expression of nationalism and imperialism was Social Darwinism. In the popular mind, the concepts of evolution justified the exploitation by the "superior races" of "lesser breeds without the law." This language of race and conflict, of superior and inferior people, had wide currency in the Western nations. Social

A German Missionary with Students. Throughout the nineteenth century, Christian missionaries went to Asia, Africa, and Latin America to preach and carry on the crusade against slavery. Many of these Christians devoted their lives to accomplishing their goals; at the same time, many carried with them the ethnocentric values and judgments of their compatriots who thought that non-Europeans were backward and uncivilized. (ullstein bild/The Granger Collection, NYC—All rights reserved.)

Darwinists vigorously advocated empires, saying strong nations—by definition, those that were successful at expanding industry and empire—would survive and others would not. To these elitists, all white peoples were more fit than nonwhites to prevail in the struggle for dominance. Even among Europeans, some nations were deemed more fit than others for the competition. Usually, Social Darwinists thought their own nation the best, an attitude that sparked their competitive enthusiasm. But some feared that their people were incapable of endurance and sacrifice. They hoped the struggle for colonies would strengthen the nation's biological inheritance, its racial stock.

Not all advocates of empire were Social Darwinists. Some did not think of themselves as racists; but when they believed that extending empire, law, order, and industry would raise "backward peoples" up the ladder of evolution to equality, they shared the assumptions and solutions of the Social Darwinists. In the nineteenth century, in contrast to the seventeenth and eighteenth centuries, Europeans, except for missionaries, rarely adopted the customs or learned the languages of local people. They had little sense that other cultures and other peoples deserved respect.

Many Westerners believed that it was their Christian duty to set an example and to educate others. Missionaries were the first to meet and learn about many peoples and the first to develop writing for those without a written language. Christian missionaries were ardently opposed to slavery. They went to unexplored African regions to preach against African and Arab slavery. Some, such as David Livingstone, the great explorer, hoped an expanding European economy would bring Africa to the world market which he believed would ultimately lead to freedom and progress.

Some of the passion for imperialism was sparked by interest in exotic places. At the end of the eighteenth century, the expeditions of Mungo Park, a Scottish explorer, on the Niger River in West Africa stimulated the romantic imagination. A half century later the explorations of Livingstone in the Congo Basin and of Richard Burton and John Speke (who raced with each other and with Livingstone to find the source of the Nile River) fascinated the public. In the early 1800s, expeditions were a matter of adventure and scientific curiosity; they often included explorers from

several countries. After the midcentury, national prestige became a goal in these forays. Sponsored by national geographic and exploratory societies and encouraged by their nation's military, explorers captured the public imagination, becoming celebrities in the popular press.

Individuals and nations competed to find the highest mountain, the longest river, the highest waterfall, and the land never before seen by white

LEOPOLD II OF BELGIUM. The Belgian king had such extravagant tastes and habits that he acted as a private entrepreneur in the Congo. His moneymaking, especially in the rubber plantations, created conditions that were so inhumane, akin to slavery, that Belgium's parliament took the territory away from him. His claim to the Congo, however, sparked the Great Powers into laying claim to much of Africa. (© Michael Nicholson/Corbis)

people. Such challenges called men and women away from their ordinary lives to dream of adventure. The mass press—the media of the day—spread stories of exotic peoples and customs, European bravery, and self-sacrificing heroes. The fiction of English authors Rudyard Kipling (1865–1936) and H. Rider Haggard (1856–1925) and their many inferior imitators stimulated the passion for faraway places and unknown peoples and helped shape the attitudes of the next generation. Kipling wrote: "Take up the White Man's Burden— / Send forth the best ye breed— / Go bind your sons to exile / To serve your captives' need." He also wrote of the Indian Gunga Din, whose death while serving his white masters won their respect. Authors usually depicted heroism and glory and rarely described the exploitation, cruelty, and abuses of empire—until twentieth-century writers such as Joseph Conrad, George Orwell, Olive Schreiner, and E. M. Forster began to probe imperialism's darker side of exploitation and racism.

A Global Economy

The Western economy became truly global by the end of the nineteenth century, thanks to new markets, new technology, and overseas trade and investment. As the Western powers industrialized, even small, underdeveloped European countries exploited raw materials and markets in the rest of the world. In many parts of Europe, even the working classes and the peasantry could buy goods from faraway places that previously had been available only to the very wealthy.

The underdeveloped areas of the world, in turn, found markets for their crops and were able to buy European goods—at least the wealthy could. But being part of the world economy also made these areas subject to the smallest tremors on the European and American stock exchanges and to changing fashions of consumption. Participation in the world market brought wealth to a few people but meant hardship for many. The world market also meant the loss of traditional crafts, customs, and social relationships.

Increasing crop production to satisfy European and American markets created problems too. Producing for the Western market meant turning land that had grown food for families over to export

crops such as coffee or **indigo**, thus reducing the local food supply. It often meant consolidation of small peasant holdings in the hands of richer peasants or landlords. Thus, market forces drove the poorer peasants off the land, into debt to the landlord or the usurer, and into cities. For most of the nineteenth century, the peasants felt bonded to their traditional masters, but in the twentieth century, they came to see themselves as enslaved by foreigners who either controlled the government or the world market. The passionate desire to escape this bondage fueled revolutionary and nationalist movements throughout the world.

Economic interdependence operated to the great advantage of Europeans and Americans, enriching the lives of consumers. Many Europeans and Americans dressed in Egyptian cotton, Australian wool, Chinese silk, and Argentinian leather and consumed Chinese tea or Colombian coffee; some had homes or offices furnished in hardwoods from Burma, Malaya, or Africa. Westerners could purchase all these goods and many more at prices so favorable that many luxury items became available even to those who were not rich. Europeans and Americans could travel anywhere, using gold or easily available foreign currency, exchanged at a rate almost always favorable to them. They could invest their money in the raw materials or the government bonds of virtually any area of the world and expect a good return. They also expected their investments to be secure and their property and themselves to be protected. Political authorities who were unable to guarantee that security, for whatever reason, risked intervention, perhaps occupation, by European or American forces. In some areas, the governors had to grant **extraterritoriality**, or the right of Europeans to trial by their own laws (or at the very least, special treatment) in foreign countries. Europeans also often lived a segregated and privileged life in quarters, clubs, and whole sections of foreign lands or cities that were closed to native inhabitants, sometimes by walls, always by mental boundaries.

Control and Resistance

Europeans possessed the enormous power of industry and of military technology. European nation-states could mobilize the support of all their citizens. These facts made it unlikely that a non-European country or people could successfully resist an industrialized European state intent on control or conquest. Yet there are examples of successful resistance. Ethiopia repelled Italy's incursions, North Africans kept the French on the defensive in Algeria and Morocco, and the Japanese held off potential invaders.

Europeans established varying degrees of political control over much of the rest of the world. Control meant Europeans had to have the help of native elites, which perpetuated traditional powers or created a new class of leaders. Control could mean outright annexation and the governing of a territory as a colony. In this way, Germany controlled Tanganyika (East Africa) after 1886, France governed Algeria, and Britain ruled much of India. Control could also mean status as a **protectorate**, in which the local ruler continued to rule but was directed, or "protected," by a Great Power. In this way, the British controlled Egypt after 1882 and maintained authority over dependent Indian princes, and France guarded Tunisia. There were also spheres of influence, where a European nation had special trading and legal privileges. The United States maintained its sphere of influence over Latin America, citing the Monroe Doctrine to any European would-be competitor. The Russians and the British, each recognizing the other's **sphere of influence**, divided Persia (Iran). Some peoples were so completely dependent for trade and finance that they seemed politically independent only in the most technical sense. Cuba and the Philippines, for example, dared take no action that might upset their economic connections to the United States in the 1930s, not even action that might ease their debt crisis.

Nevertheless, many non-Europeans resisted American and European economic and political control. Resistance shaped their history and their self-awareness. In many areas—the Ottoman Empire, China, and Japan—the rulers found ways of limiting the political influence of Western trading interests. Some countries—Japan, Egypt, and Turkey—defended their independence through modernization.

These forms of resistance were carried out by rulers who could command loyal subjects. Other resisters—individuals, groups, and regional communities—retained traditional ways, rejecting foreign education and **secularization**, even renewing institutions, particularly religious ones, that were falling into disuse when the Europeans arrived. Such resistance was a statement of both national and individual identity. One of the many instances of such resistance was the Sudanese Muslims' holy war led by the Mahdi Mohammed Ahmed. His followers attacked Egyptians who were fellow Muslims for being tools of the European nonbelievers. The Boxer Rebellion in China and the Sepoy Mutiny in India are other examples of traditionalist resistance to outsiders. Still other resisters reacted with strongly nationalistic feelings and fought to strengthen the nationalism of their people. Some attended European universities and military schools. Some observed factories to master technology and organization. Others, for example Mohandas Gandhi, opposed industrialization because it destroyed traditional industry. He, Jawaharlal Nehru, Sun Yat-sen (Sun Zhongshan), Chiang Kai-shek (Jiang Jieshi), and Kemal Atatürk are national heroes for their resistance to the West and its institutions.

In most cases, resistance brought non-European peoples even more firmly under Western control. Europeans generally responded by annexing the rebellious region or establishing a protectorate. Resistance continued nonetheless. Whole peoples in Africa moved from place to place to escape European religion, taxes, and laws; insurgent mountain people in Indochina and Algeria evaded French influence for generations, restricting it to the coastline.

Europeans might dominate the ruler and perhaps the ruling elite, and they might make entire sectors of the economy dependent on their trade. They could also see the influence of their ideas and language on the youth and observe the decline of local traditions. But the level of European power differed in each area, and in many places Europeans were never fully in control. Nevertheless, until the World War II, Western domination seemed, to Westerners and non-Westerners alike, a relentless and inevitable force.

EUROPEAN DOMINATION OF ASIA

India, China, and Japan were powerful kingdoms, advanced civilizations, when the first European traders arrived in the fifteenth and sixteenth centuries. For several hundred years, there were trading connections in which the European nation was the weaker party, dependent on the goodwill and interest of the rulers and traders. Generally, native craftspeople produced goods superior to European products, so they were sellers and the Europeans were buyers. By the nineteenth century, when many more and much more powerful Europeans came to Asia, they encountered Chinese and Mogul empires with internal problems. The situation gave Europeans an edge. Loyalties in the Asian kingdoms were cultural and religious, not nationalist as Europeans knew it. Cultural unity in Central Asia, the Middle East, India, and China was based on the great religious and ethical systems of Hinduism, Buddhism, Islam, and Confucianism. Within a short time, however, the resentment of European domination developed into a national feeling, unifying diverse social and religious communities.

India

From the Renaissance, European merchants had followed the Silk Road through the Middle East to India and China in search of fine goods. They marvelled at the Ottomans, the Moguls, and the Qings. When Italian, Portuguese, and Spanish merchants came as traders, admirers, and imitators of the Mogul Empire of India, they found it ruled by a dynasty of highly advanced, wealthy, and religiously tolerant Muslim princes. When British traders arrived in the eighteenth century, the empire was disintegrating. Emperor Aurangzeb Alamgir (1658–1707) had launched a Muslim holy war that would tear apart Hindus and Muslims, as well as Sikhs, for half a century. The rivalries of powerful native princes, each of whom wished to succeed the emperor, worked to foreign advantage. India fell prey to the Europeans, and by the end of the century, the British cleared out their rivals one by one. India became the jewel of the British Empire, the most completely governed Asian state.

British Rule. At first, Britain maintained **indirect rule**. Britain's East India Company was a regulated, chartered monopoly enterprise under the control of Parliament, which exercised little control until the Sepoy Mutiny of 1857–1858.

(The Indians call this massive act of resistance the *Great Rebellion.*) This major popular uprising joined Muslim and Hindu soldiers, some native princes and peasants, against the British. In a fierce war, the British troops from the Punjab repressed the uprising. After the rebellion about two-thirds of the subcontinent was ruled directly by about a thousand British officials.

The British community was so threatened that it took all the authority it could into its hands. The British segregated themselves socially and legally from Indians. The British civil service governed Indians according to English law and customs. Later, an elite of English-speaking Indians joined the Indian civil service. In 1900, about four thousand Europeans and half a million Indians governed some 300 million Indians of almost two hundred language groups and several religions, races, and cultures. The military was drawn from Indian warrior peoples; friendly native princes ruled. The British created a powerful state with a single system of law and administration, some political unity, and an English-educated elite with a common resentment of British control. The British created the state; the many Indian communities created a nation. (Today the territories that were once British India are India, Pakistan, Bangladesh, and Myanmar [Burma].)

The British imperialists pointed to the improvements they made—a modern railroad and communications system and an economy in which a segment was geared to meet the needs of the world market. The rest of the economy tried to supply local and regional demands. The railroad linked areas of food surplus with areas of need, reducing the incidence and impact of local famines, the plague of India's history. Fewer people starved and lives were saved with public projects of sanitation, hygiene, water and flood control, and Western medicine. British rule also ended the century of war and disorder that accompanied the disintegration of the Mogul Empire.

Map 26.1 Asia in 1914 ▶
This map of Asia is deceptive. There are no markings or colors that can indicate the level of influence and control European and U.S. powers exercised over the technically sovereign states of China, Siam (Thailand), and Persia (Iran).

(© 2016 Cengage Learning.)

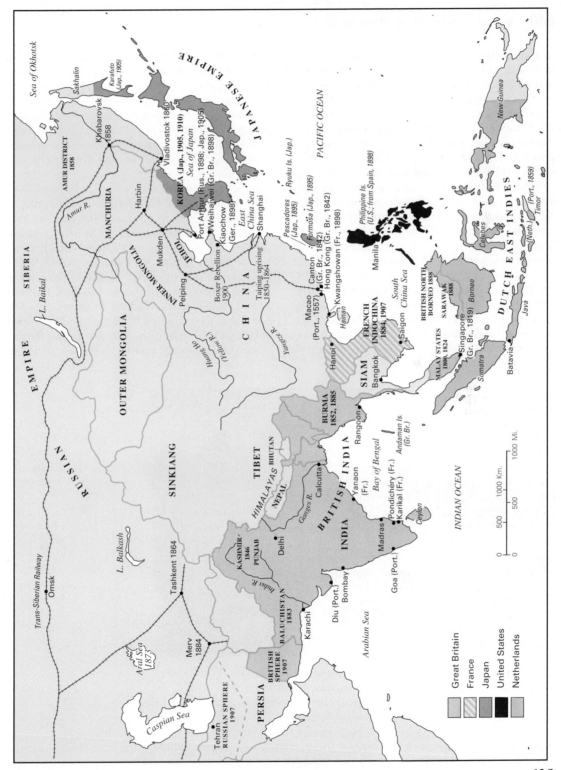

Sea of Okhotsk

Sakhalin   *Karafuto (Jap., 1905)*

RUSSIAN EMPIRE

JAPANESE EMPIRE

SIBERIA

AMUR DISTRICT 1858

Khabarovsk 1858

Amur R.

MANCHURIA

Harbin

Mukden

JEHOL

Peiping

Boxer Rebellion 1900

INNER MONGOLIA

OUTER MONGOLIA

Vladivostok 1860

Sea of Japan

KOREA (Jap., 1905, 1910)

Port Arthur (Rus., 1898; Jap., 1905)
Kiaochow (Ger., 1898)
Weihaiwei (Gr. Br., 1898)

Shanghai

East China Sea

Ryuku Is. (Jap.)

PACIFIC OCEAN

CHINA

Taiping uprising 1850–1864

Hoang Ho (Yellow R.)

Yangtze R.

Canton (Gr. Br., 1842)
Macao (Port., 1557)
Hong Kong (Gr. Br., 1842)
Kwangshowan (Fr., 1898)

Pescadores (Jap., 1895)
Formosa (Jap., 1895)

Hainan

Philippine Is. (U.S.; from Spain, 1898)

Manila

South China Sea

New Guinea

DUTCH EAST INDIES

Celebes

(Neth.)

Timor (Port., 1859)

BRITISH NORTH BORNEO 1888

SARAWAK 1888

Borneo

Java

Sumatra

Batavia

MALAY STATES 1800, 1824

Singapore (Gr. Br., 1819)

FRENCH INDOCHINA 1884, 1907

Saigon

Hanoi

SIAM

Bangkok

BURMA 1852, 1885

Rangoon

TIBET

HIMALAYAS

BHUTAN

NEPAL

SINKIANG

L. Baikal

RUSSIAN EMPIRE

L. Balkash

Trans-Siberian Railway

Omsk

Tashkent 1864

Merv 1884

Aral Sea 1873

Caspian Sea

Tehran

PERSIA

RUSSIAN SPHERE 1907

BRITISH SPHERE 1907

BALUCHISTAN 1883

Karachi

KASHMIR 1846

PUNJAB

Delhi

Indus R.

Diu (Port.)

Bombay

Arabian Sea

BRITISH INDIA

INDIA

Ganges R.

Calcutta

Yanaon (Fr.)

Pondichéry (Fr.)
Karikal (Fr.)

Madras

Goa (Port.)

Ceylon

Bay of Bengal

Andaman Is. (Gr. Br.)

INDIAN OCEAN

1000 Mi.

1000 Km.

500

500

0

0

Great Britain

France

Japan

United States

Netherlands

639

British rule did not end the control local landlords and usurers had over peasants. The Indian masses benefitted little from economic progress; landlords demanded payments that the poor could not afford. Moneylenders cheated the poor. The increase in population more than matched the increase in food. Even if they did not starve, most people suffered from malnutrition. The British flooded the Indian market with cheap, machine-produced English goods, driving native artisans out of business or even deeper into debt. Negative consequences were not unique to India. They could be found in many areas where the market economy and European rule disrupted traditional arrangements; their effect was most severe on the poorest and the weakest.

British racism excluded the Indian elite from clubs, hotels, and social gatherings. Top government positions were off-limits for Indians. Even traditional elites who profited from British connections resented the lack of respect for India's culture. In the 1880s, educated Indians demanded equality and self-government. They created the Indian National Congress, which was neither national, because its members were upper-class Hindus, nor a congress, because it had no power to represent. At first, the Congress Party sought home rule, or self-government within the empire. Eventually, it organized masses of Indians to gain independence.

The Anticolonial Campaign.

Resistance to colonialism grew in militancy throughout Asia when the Japanese defeated the Russians during 1904–1905 in the Russo-Japanese War. That victory inspired Indian nationalists. World War I brought greater solidarity among Indians, who, though opposed to British rule, had been far from united. Muslims founded the Muslim League to speak for their minority community. The Indian elite found grounds for cooperation among the disparate communities, but the masses continued to

THE SEPOY REBELLION: REPELLING A SORTIE BEFORE DELHI. When Indian troops (Muslims and Hindus) rebelled against foreigners in 1857–1858, the British presence was seriously threatened. Here British rifles defending Delhi sound the retreat. Thinking the troops had withdrawn, the Sepoys were badly defeated when they advanced. "The Mutiny," as the British saw it, or "the Great Rebellion," as the Indians saw it, was short-lived, but relations between Indians and Britons changed forever as the British segregated themselves socially from the people they governed. (© Bettmann/CORBIS.)

be divided by differences of religion, class, and culture. These differences made Indian self-government seem distant even to the Britons who wanted it.

In 1919, partly responding to Indian agitation and partly rewarding Indian loyalty during World War I, Britain granted India a legislative assembly. It would represent almost a million of the 300 million people in the subcontinent. Representation was by groups (Hindus, Muslims, Europeans, Anglo-Indians, and Sikhs) and by economic and social functions (that is, by rural, urban, university, landholding, and commercial classes). In the same year, agitation and unrest became most bitter. At Amritsar in the Punjab, a British officer commanded his Gurkha troops to fire into a peaceful demonstration until their ammunition was exhausted; 379 Indians died, and 1,200 were wounded. Women and children were among the victims. The government punished the officer, but the British community in India collected a fortune to honor him for what he had done. The massacre and British behavior stung Indians; even those Indians who had advocated self-government or home rule within the British Empire joined the protest.

Out of this feverish period emerged Mohandas K. Gandhi (1869–1948), a determined revolutionary leader. He preached **civil disobedience** and **nonviolent resistance**, a spiritually uplifting message and a shrewd political tactic as well. He called for the Indian elite to give up their privileges, resign their positions in British firms and government, and boycott British schools and all foreign goods. Gandhi rallied the masses, urging a mass refusal to pay taxes on salt, with "the march to the sea." Thrown in prison, Gandhi and his followers refused to eat, threatening the British with their possible starvation, which would set off more civil disturbances. For independence, he was even willing to oppose industrialization of India. He urged Indians to spin cotton and wear simple native dress to prohibit any dependence on British goods. He was able to join traditional religious and cultural beliefs into political tactics that inspired Indian nationalism.

World War II exhausted Britain's resources, reduced its power, and stirred much of the colonial world to struggle against racism, and for liberty, democracy, and self-government. There was no war between Britain and India, a fact that many credit to the strength of Gandhi's moral leadership. But even his leadership could not prevent the partition of the country into Muslim Pakistan and predominantly Hindu India, and the deaths of many in the resettlement according to the partition based on religious, cultural, and political power.

China

European intervention in China was a very different story. Westerners had admired China and Chinese culture for centuries. In an effort to preserve traditional beliefs and shield them from Christianity, Western science, and secular ideologies, China, unlike India, excluded foreigners, whether they were missionaries, traders, or soldiers and sailors.

The British forced the Manchu (Qing) dynasty to open trade to foreigners in the Opium War, from 1839 to 1842. When the Chinese destroyed the British East India Company's shipments, British ships seized several trading cities along the coast, including Hong Kong. By the Treaty of Nanking (1842), the British claimed the right to set tariffs on imported goods and the right of extraterritoriality (Britons in China would be tried for any crimes by British law). These provisions undermined the emperor's ability to control the foreigners in his country. Defeat forced the emperor to make reforms, but the dynasty was seriously threatened by economic discontents indicated by the Taiping Rebellion of 1850–1864. The emperor relied on Westerners to suppress the rebels. Britain and France extorted additional concessions for aiding the emperor.

For a time, the Europeans seemed content with trading rights in coastal towns and preferential treatment for their subjects, but Japan's easy victory in the Sino-Japanese War of 1894–1895 encouraged Europeans to mutilate China. Britain, France, Russia, and Germany all scrambled for concessions, protectorates, and spheres of influence. China might have been carved up like Africa. However, each Western nation resisted any partition that might give an advantage to a rival. To ensure American interests in China, the United States proclaimed the **"Open Door"** policy: that trade should be open to all and that the Great Powers should respect the territorial integrity of

Gandhi

Even before World War I, there was growing opposition in Asia and Africa to colonialism. A most unlikely leader emerged in India. A gentle pacifist, Mohandas Karamchand Gandhi (1869–1948), came to represent the most populous, most diverse, and largest colony in its struggle for independence. He devised the political tactics that would inspire peoples in their struggle for freedom around the world—marches, hunger strikes, passive resistance, civil disobedience, and boycotts.

Gandhi began in South Africa as a lawyer defending poor Indian immigrants against discrimination. In India, he joined the Congress Party, ultimately transforming it from an elite to a mass party whose leaders practiced *satyagraha,* or nonviolent resistance. It was a difficult political message to accept for people who were not yet one nation and who suffered repeated injustice and discrimination.

When in 1919, at Amritsar in the Punjab, the British brutally repressed a peaceful demonstration in which 1,500 Indians were killed or injured, Gandhi led thousands in a march to protest. Journalists and photographers from all over the world covered the protest. This simple man was turning the world of power and wealth upside down by refusing to accept the weapons of rulers. Throughout the 1930s, the British jailed demonstrators; Gandhi protested with hunger strikes and his followers rejected all things British. Finally, in 1935 and 1937, after a century of divide and conquer, Britain granted India provincial assemblies. But by then India's two main religious groups (Hindu and Muslim) were fragmented on every issue but independence.

When World War II broke out, the British declared war for India as well as for Britain.

China. American action protected its interests but hardly restrained the Western powers that had already apportioned the important treaty ports. Market capitalism, which Americans championed, was the most powerful threat to China's independence.

Chinese traditionalists organized secret societies to expel foreigners and punish Chinese who accepted any aspect of westernization. In 1900, encouraged by Empress Tzu-hsi, the Society of Righteous and Harmonious Fists (called the Boxers by Europeans) attacked foreigners throughout northern China. An international army of Europeans, Japanese, and Americans suppressed the rebellion, seized Chinese treasures, and forced China to pay an indemnity. They also made China accept foreign business and troops on Chinese soil.

Nationalistic opposition to the foreigners intensified. When Japan defeated Russia in 1905, many Chinese urged their country to imitate the Japanese and take up Western ways. Growing nationalism led to a boycott of American goods in 1905 to protest U.S. bans of Chinese immigrants. In 1911, nationalist revolutionaries (particularly strong among soldiers, workers, and students) overthrew the Manchu dynasty and declared a republic. Sun Zhongshan (Sun Yat-sen, 1866–1925) became president of the republic and head of the Nationalist Party.

Espousing the ideals of democracy, nationalism, and social welfare (the three principles of the people, as Sun called them), the republic struggled to establish its authority over a China torn by civil war and ravaged by foreigners. Russia claimed Mongolia; Britain, Tibet. Japan threatened as well. The northern warlords resisted any attempt to strengthen the republic's army because it might diminish their power. However, in the south, the republic more or less maintained control.

After Sun's death, the Guomindong (Kuomintang), under the **authoritarian** leadership of Jiang Jieshi (Chiang Kai-shek, 1887–1975), tried to modernize, using the military power of the state and introducing segments of a modern economic

Gandhi spent months striking and starving for "Independence Now." Although hundreds of thousands of Indian soldiers fought for their colonial rulers against Germany and Japan, India refused to put its demands on hold. At war's end, the British no longer had the power, the wealth, or even the will to hold on to India. In 1947, the promise to partition India in two states, Muslim Pakistan and Hindu India, brought uncontrollable violence to the subcontinent. Gandhi led his supporters to fast once again—to prevent civil war and bloody communal massacres. An angry Hindu nationalist who opposed the partition killed Gandhi as he walked to morning prayers. The world mourned.

India became the world's largest democracy under the leadership of the Congress Party and Jawaharlal Nehru (1889–1964). Congress Party and the Nehru family remains an important force in India to this day.

system. But faced with civil war and attacked from both the right and the Communist left under Mao Zedong (Mao Tsetung, 1893–1976), and by the Japanese after 1931, the Guomindong made slow progress. A divided China continued to be at the mercy of outside interests until after World War II.

Japan

Like China, Japan was forced open by the West. By the 1850s social dissension within Japan and foreign pressure combined to force the country to admit outside trade. In 1853, Commodore Matthew C. Perry sailed into Tokyo Bay, making a show of American strength. The Japanese signed treaties that granted Westerners extraterritoriality and control over tariffs.

A flood of violence ensued. The warrior nobility, the samurai, attacked foreigners and murdered members of their own government. They thought that trade would enhance the status of merchants, a social class they despised. In response to the

samurai actions, U.S. and European ships destroyed important Japanese fortresses. Samurai seized the government to preserve Japan's independence. This takeover—the Meiji Restoration of 1867—returned power to the emperor from the feudal aristocracy, which ruled in his name for almost seven hundred years.

The new government enacted a series of reforms, turning Japan into a powerful centralized state. Large landowners gave their estates to the emperor in exchange for compensation and high-level positions in the government. All classes were made equal before the law. As in France and Germany, universal military service was required, which diminished social privilege and helped imbue Japanese of all classes with nationalism. The Japanese modeled their constitution on Bismarck's: there was a **bicameral diet**, or parliament, but the emperor kept his spiritual authority. His advisers ruled in his name.

The Meiji regime introduced modern industry and economic competition. The Japanese visited factories all over the West and hired Westerners to teach industrial skills. The government, like Central and Eastern European governments, built defense industries, backed heavy industry and mining, and developed a modern communication system of railroads, roads, and telegraph lines. The government encouraged competitive consumer industries as well; it sold factories to wealthy family monopolies, the *zaibatsu*, which came to dominate the Japanese economy. Industry in Japan incorporated traditional Japanese values, emphasizing cooperation more than competition, paternalism rather than individualism, and deference rather than conflict. Westerners regarded the close cooperation of government and powerful families as something peculiar to the Japanese (neither capitalist nor socialist). Within little more than a generation of the Meiji Restoration, Japan moved from economic backwardness to a place among the top ten industrial nations. To underdeveloped countries, Japan became the model of a nation that borrowed from the West yet preserved its traditional values and social structure.

By 1900, Japan ended the humiliating treaties with the West and became an imperial power. Japan won Taiwan and Korea in its war with China during 1894–1895 despite Great Power intervention to gain even greater influence from the helpless Chinese. Japan joined the West in the suppression of the Boxer Rebellion. In 1904, conflict over which power was to have influence in Manchuria brought Japan and Russia to war, which Japan won. The victory of an Asian power over a European power had a tremendous impact, inspiring anti-imperialist nationalist movements throughout Asia as well as revolution in Russia.

In World War I, Japan fought with the Allies, emerging as the most powerful Asian state. It gained the former German holdings north of the equator, but was blocked in its ambitions for mainland Chinese outposts by the American president Woodrow Wilson at the Paris Peace Conference. In the 1920s, the prosperous economy strengthened the middle class and increased the importance of the working class, reinforcing democratic institutions. But the Great Depression of 1929 hit Japan hard because the major states blocked its trade. The Depression weakened elements that contributed to peace, stability, and democracy in Japan and strengthened militarist and imperialist groups, which were determined to control Manchuria and China.

In the 1930s, nationalists in Burma, India, Indochina, and Indonesia looked to Japan for support against Western imperialism. World War II, however, brought Japanese **occupation** and exploitation, not the independence and equality that these leaders hoped for. The defeat of Japan and the exhaustion of the Allies opened the way for nationalist struggles for independence in Asia.

The Ottoman Empire

In the eighteenth century, the philosophes idealized the Ottoman Empire, with its vast expanse of territory and the diversity of the peoples it ruled justly; in their view it was a great culture of unimaginable wealth. It was the force the Eastern European princes had had to reckon with for generations. For most of the nineteenth century, however, the Great Powers competed to inherit the estate of the "Sick Man of Europe," as Turkey was still a force in the Balkans and a rival to the Russians. The European competition ensured the "sick man's" demise as they claimed parts of the Balkans, Central Asia, North Africa, and the Middle East. In the early twentieth century, the longstanding rivalry between Russia and Britain in Central Asia took second place to the German and British conflict in the Middle East, a much wealthier and more vital sphere of influence. Conflicts in Ottoman territories reshaped European alliances and politics.

Not all conflicts were engineered by the diplomats and military leaders. A group of German financiers proposed a railroad from central Turkey to Baghdad with a connection down the Euphrates River to Basra and the Persian Gulf. Because the proposed new railroad would further open Turkey to the world market, the sultan offered to subsidize the project. The German investors offered British and French investment groups a 25 percent share each, with 25 percent control to the Turks; the Germans kept the final quarter for themselves. The deal seemed more than fair, but the British government refused to allow British investment for fear of German influence close to India and the Suez Canal. The Germans came to see the British as their number one rival. In World War I, the Ottomans sided with the Germans, led by a generation of German-educated Turkish elite. Other Ottomans feared a Russian presence in the Caucasus, the Balkans, and the Black Sea, territories with immediate impact on the Turkish homeland. In each of these moves, politics dominated economics.

Throughout World War I, the Allies secretly negotiated the division of the Ottoman Empire. To weaken the Turkish-German war effort, Britain sponsored Arab independence movements in the Arabian peninsula and in the territories that are today Iraq, Syria, Lebanon, Jordan, and Israel. In the 1917 Balfour Declaration, Britain promised Zionist Jews a place in Palestine, which Britain intended to control. The Allies also promised Turkish lands to Greece and Italy.

When the war was over, the Turks, led by Mustafa Kemal Atatürk, refused to honor any of the Allies' promises, which would dismember Turkish-speaking territory. Atatürk was willing to accept the loss of Arab lands. The Turks drove the Allies out of Anatolia, declared a republic in 1923 under Atatürk's presidency, and moved the capital to Ankara, far away from the cosmopolitan city of Constantinople (Istanbul). Turkey became a secular state, no longer claiming to be the spiritual leader of millions of Muslims throughout the world. During Atatürk's military-based presidency (1923–1938), the Turkish government banned traditional practices, such as veils for women, harems, and polygamy. European education and ideas flourished in the new republic. In Turkey, for at least a generation, the conflict between the modern and the traditional seemed resolved in favor of modern nationalism.

Arab nationalism, once encouraged against the Ottomans, could not be controlled by Europeans when the Turks ceased to be a power.

Several forces fostered the desire for **national self-determination** after World War I. The Arab chiefs welcomed British aid against the Turks but deeply resented any intervention in their spiritual and local political affairs. They suspected that the Europeans' real interest was oil. As nationalism developed, it sometimes joined with Islam to foment opposition to the imperialists. At other times, and in particular places, the nationalists rejected or controlled Islam because they hoped to secularize and modernize their states as Turkey had.

COMMODORE PERRY'S PADDLE-STEAMER ARRIVING IN A JAPANESE BAY. Matthew Perry opened Japan, against its will, to United States trade in 1853. With the Meiji Restoration of 1867, a strong central government pushed Japan until it became one of the top ten industrial nations by 1900. Japan's imperialistic expansion brought it into conflict with China, Russia, and the European and American imperialist powers. (Private Collection/J. T. Vintage/The Bridgeman Art Library.)

Southeast and Central Asia

The great power rush to claim territory was evident everywhere in Asia. When China, India, and the Ottoman Empire lost the ability to control border territories, European states tried to grab them. Indochina, Tibet, Korea, Burma, Afghanistan, and Persia were each the object of some power's design.

In Southeast Asia, the French claimed Indochina (Vietnam, Laos, and Cambodia today) and waged war with China (1883–1885) to gain it. The French parliament threw out the government that gained the faraway and not particularly valuable territory, but France annexed the land nonetheless. Indochina was a prosperous agricultural region trading with other Asians but hardly at all with France. Some French may have profited from the colony—merchants, civil servants, soldiers, priests, and scholars—but France as a whole was indifferent to its new acquisition.

From Indochina, the French might have expanded into Siam (Thailand), as might the British from their base in Burma (Myanmar). Neither power was willing to let the other take Siam. Like Turkey in the Middle East, Siamese rulers were able to play the powers against each other to preserve some territorial integrity. Only fear of German power in Europe led Britain and France to put colonial differences aside so long as the other state did not lay a claim for itself.

Elsewhere throughout Southeast Asia, Germany, the United States, Britain, and France competed for island naval stations and trading places. The Netherlands held on to a remnant of their seventeenth-century empire in the East Indies (Indonesia). Even colonies began to acquire colonies, as New Zealand and Australia pushed claims to Borneo and Tasmania. After World War I, they claimed German colonies south of the equator, perhaps for economic reasons but national prestige seems more likely.

Just as the French and British competed in Southeast Asia and the Japanese with each of the Great Powers in northern China and Korea, the Russians and the British confronted one another in Central Asia. Russia's moves south into Afghanistan and Persia (Iran), both of which bordered India, alarmed the British who were sure that hostile forces on the borders would inspire rebellious Indians. In Persia, the British and Russians vied with each other to lend money to the shah to build a railroad to Tehran. At that very moment, Russians were borrowing money from the French for their own industrialization, but to create a claim they were willing to borrow more. At stake was control of the "top of the world," the passages to India. British and Russian troops fought each other in Afghanistan. When Britain was fighting the Boer War in South Africa (see "Britain in Africa" later in this chapter), the Russians moved toward Persia, Tibet, and Afghanistan. These moves were for strategic control rather than economic benefit. The entire situation outside of Europe itself indicated the volatility of relations between the Great Powers in the era before World War I.

The rise of Germany made Britain and Russia, longtime foes, willing to compromise. The Russians agreed to a British puppet ruler in Afghanistan. They divided Persia into three zones: one in the north for the Russians, one in the south for the British, and in the middle the Persians to keep the Europeans apart. This resolution of difficulties made British and Russian cooperation in Europe possible. An important piece in the system of alliances that led to World War I was in place. Neither independent nor stable, Persia was torn between Britain and Russia. Its situation was further complicated after World War I, when its vast reserves of oil became valuable to the Great Powers. Reza Shah of the Pahlavi family gained control of Persia (Iran) in 1925, abolishing foreigners' special privileges. In 1934, the shah granted the concession of the Bahrain Islands to an American firm, Standard Oil, thinking that foreigners whose main interests were economic might be more easily controlled than foreigners with geopolitical designs. Yet as British power receded in the region during and after World War II, United States power took its place.

Nationalism was the response to European expansion and control throughout Asia before and after World War I. In a short time, in areas divided for centuries by ethnic and religious differences, states began organizing patriots into powerful movements to resist foreign domination. Those resistance movements would become nations in the aftermath of World War II.

THE SCRAMBLE FOR AFRICA

The most rapid European expansion took place in Africa. As late as 1880, European nations ruled only a tenth of the continent. Within a generation, by 1914, Europeans claimed everything except Liberia (a small territory of freed slaves from the United States) and the ancient empire of Abyssinia (Ethiopia).

In the early nineteenth century, European powers laid some claims to Africa. The French moved into Algeria in 1830, only to spend a generation trying to pacify the populace. Twenty years before, during the Napoleonic wars, Britain had gained Cape Town in South Africa, a useful provisioning place for ships bound for the East, particularly to India and in the service of the East India Company. The Boer cattlemen and farmers, who had migrated to South Africa from the Netherlands in the seventeenth century, refused to accept foreign rule and moved northward (the Great Trek, 1835–1837), warring with native tribes along the way. By 1880, the Boers were firmly established in the interior of South Africa, in the Transvaal and the Orange Free State. In general, though, until the 1870s, Europeans' interest in Africa was minimal, a way station on the way to the Far East.

Then Leopold II, the king of Belgium, changed the picture. Acting as a private entrepreneur, not as a monarch, he formed the International Association for the Exploration and Civilization of Central Africa. The title of the association sounds like a cultural, intellectual organization, but it was anything but that. Leopold intended to find a pot of gold, sending Henry Stanley (1841–1904) to the Congo River Basin to establish trading posts, sign treaties with the chiefs, and claim the territory for the association, that is, for Leopold and investors. Stanley, an adventurer and a newspaper reporter who had fought on both sides during the American Civil War, had earlier led an expedition to Central Africa in search of David Livingstone, the popular missionary-explorer who wasn't lost or captive or even in danger, as the public believed. But he was the object of public admiration, and through his human-interest adventure story Stanley's readers succumbed to the glamour of imperialism. Stanley and Leopold were pursuing profit and adventure. For the Congo the expedition was the beginning of brutal exploitation.

The French immediately declared the northern bank of the Congo under their protection.

The Berlin Conference

The scramble for African territory threatened European stability. Bismarck and Jules Ferry, the premier of France, called an international conference in Berlin in 1884 to lay some ground rules for the development of Africa south of the Sahara. Leopold (as businessman rather than as the king of Belgium) was declared the ruler of the Congo Free State. The Congo Basin was made a free-trade zone for every nation.

The conference agreed to stop slavery and the slave trade in Africa, which still engaged Arabs and Africans. The Congo Association adopted business practices as vicious as those of the African slave traders. It forced blacks into slavery to work for its rubber plantations, mutilating and murdering them if they refused. Humanitarians Edward D. Morel and Roger Casement—who later became an Irish national hero—waged a vigorous campaign against Leopold for the Aborigines' Protection Society. When the press printed photographs of the atrocities the Belgian parliament declared the territory a Belgian colony in 1908, ending Leopold's experiment in private enterprise.

Britain in Africa

Great Britain's activities in Africa exemplify the complicated motives, operations, and results of European imperialism. In the second half of the nineteenth century, Britain maintained only a few outposts along the coast of western Africa; even its hold on South Africa appeared to be loosening. From time to time, the British navy interfered with slave traders in Africa, but overall British interest seemed minimal. In principle, Britain rejected African empire. Its practice was another thing entirely.

Egypt. Local conditions in Egypt, which was part of the Ottoman Empire but was governed by strong *khedives* (Turkish governors), were complicated by the construction of the Suez Canal (1859–1869), leading to British occupation. For a generation (1805–1847), Mohammed Ali, governor of Egypt, had struggled for independence from the sultan of the Ottoman Empire. With British and French support, foreign investment and influence grew; successive khedives modernized. The building of the Suez Canal, in which the khedive and British and French capitalists were the principal stockholders, brought the country to the verge of bankruptcy. The promise of the canal was trade and contact with the world economy, but its cost brought immediate disaster. European creditors demanded that Egypt pay its debts, suggesting cuts in its army. Egyptian soldiers rebelled. National bankruptcy and the khedive's inability to keep law and order were sufficient pretext for the British to become "protectors" in 1882.

The canal was an important waterway to India for the British. When the British asked France to join the occupation, which was the way to "protect" investors, domestic politics prevented French participation; nevertheless the French resented that the British occupied without them. Meanwhile, British citizens hired ships to watch the naval bombardment of Egyptian ports as if war were a fireworks display.

Prime Minister William Gladstone, a "little Englander" (one who opposed empire), promised to withdraw British troops once order was established. Every day that the British remained, Egyptian discontent grew more violent. It threatened markets, investments, and even government. Order could not be restored by Egypt's leaders, and it seemed it couldn't be restored by the British either. Egyptian nationalism took two irreconcilable forms. Some Egyptians wanted a strong government and economy so that they could throw the British out. Others hated all modernization, and contact with the West, regarding it as a threat to Islam.

The British did not withdraw from Egypt; in fact, they moved farther south into the Sudan, where devout Muslims led by Mohammed Ahmed, the Mahdi ("divinely guided one"), were waging holy war against Egyptian authority. They resented foreign, non-Muslim influence over the khedive. The British, trying to strengthen the khedive's authority so that taxes would be collected, Egypt's budget balanced, and debts paid, were making the situation worse. An English general led ten thousand of the khedive's troops against the Sudanese Muslim followers of the Mahdi. The Egyptians were annihilated.

Gladstone's Liberal Party rejected costly occupation in the Sudan, but public opinion demanded action. In 1885, Gladstone sent General Charles "Chinese" Gordon, famous for suppressing the Taiping Rebellion, as an observer to the Sudan. At Khartoum, the garrison was killed, and Gordon's head was severed and placed on a pike. An enraged public accused Gladstone of having martyred the hero. Gladstone refused to annex the Sudan, losing the election. In 1898, a Conservative government sent General Herbert Kitchener to Africa. His men, armed with machine guns, mowed down charging Muslims at Omdurman. The casualties were ten thousand Sudanese killed and thirteen thousand wounded, forty-eight Britons killed and 382 wounded, and hundreds of Egyptians. The battle became noted as an example of the costs of conflict between forces with technology and those without.

The battle of Omdurman was an ugly victory; 1898 became a year of ugly confrontations and dubious victories for the British Empire. At Fashoda, also in the Sudan, British forces confronted a French exploratory mission under the command of Major Jean Baptiste Marchand. The French had marched from western Africa to the Sudan en route to Somaliland on the Red Sea to lay claim to territory from one side of Africa to the other. The British were moving south from Egypt and north from Kenya into the same territory. In the **diplomatic crisis** that followed, Britain and France were brought to the brink of war. Too divided by the Dreyfus affair at home (see Chapter 25) to risk a showdown with Britain, the French cabinet ordered Marchand to retreat. French public opinion was incensed. Behind the scenes, however, French diplomats began to negotiate with Britain to reconcile their two nations' ambitions. France could not challenge both Germany across the Rhine and Britain in Africa and Asia. The British, facing problems in Egypt and the Sudan as well as mounting troubles in

Map 26.2 Africa in 1914 ▶
Africa's rapid dismemberment is pictured in these two maps. In 1878, there were few enclaves of Europeans along the coasts. By 1914, Africa had been carved up, and all but Ethiopia and Liberia had been claimed. (© 2016 Cengage Learning.)

Madeira Is.
(Portugal)

Canary Is.
(Spain)

TANGIER
Casablanca
Algiers
TUNISIA
Tripoli
Mediterranean Sea
Cyrene

MOROCCO
Ifni (Sp.)

RIO DE ORO

ALGERIA
LIBYA
EGYPT
Cairo

Nile R.
Red Sea
ARABIA

FRENCH WEST AFRICA

SENEGAL
GAMBIA
Niger R.
L. Chad
ANGLO-EGYPTIAN
SUDAN
Khartoum
ERITREA
FRENCH
SOMALILAND

PORT.
GUINEA
BRITISH
SOMALILAND

SIERRA LEONE
IVORY
COAST
NIGERIA
TOGO
Fashoda
Adowa
ETHIOPIA

LIBERIA
GOLD
COAST
RIO MUNI
CAMEROONS
FRENCH EQUATORIAL AFRICA
Ubangi R.
UGANDA
ITALIAN
SOMALILAND

ATLANTIC OCEAN

CABINDA
(Port.)
Congo R.
BELGIAN
CONGO
BRITISH
EAST AFRICA
L. Victoria Nyanza
Mombasa

L. Tanganyika
GERMAN
EAST AFRICA
Zanzibar (Gr. Br.)

INDIAN
OCEAN

ANGOLA
NYASALAND

RHODESIA
MOZAMBIQUE

0   500   1000 Km.
0   500   1000 Mi.

GERMAN
SOUTHWEST
AFRICA
BECHUANALAND
MADAGASCAR

TRANSVAAL
SWAZILAND

ORANGE
FREE STATE
UNION OF
SOUTH AFRICA
NATAL
BASUTOLAND

Cape Town

ARAB AND BERBER PEOPLES

SAHARA
(Gr. Br.)

(Port.)
Sudanese Empires

(Gr. Br.)
(Sp.)
Swahili language

Bantu Kingdoms

AFRICA IN 1878

	British		Portuguese
	French		Belgian
	German		Spanish
	Italian		Independent African states

649

South Africa, also realized their limits. "Splendid isolation" was risky business if the whole world could be your battlefield and each of the Great Powers your enemy.

South Africa.

South Africa.   Nothing underlined Britain's isolation more than the Boer War, which began in 1899. British relations with the Boers had been difficult since the Great Trek. They were aggravated when rich deposits of gold and diamonds were discovered in Boer territory.

The opposing leaders in these territories were strong and unyielding. Paul Kruger (1825–1904), the Boer president of the Transvaal, wanted independence, power, and access to the sea. He aimed to restrict the foreign prospectors, who were flooding into Boer territory by the thousands. The prime minister of Cape Colony, Cecil Rhodes (1853–1902), had made a fortune in diamonds and gold in South Africa. He acquired Rhodesia (Zimbabwe), a sizable and wealthy territory, for Britain. He dreamed of British red coloring the map of Africa from Cape Town to Cairo.

In 1895, Rhodes's close friend Leander Jameson, expecting British support, led about 600 armed men into the Transvaal to spark an uprising against Kruger. The raid failed; both men were disgraced. Kaiser William II of Germany impetuously sent President Kruger a congratulatory telegram; the British took the diplomatic insult to heart. Accustomed to French opposition in every area of the globe, they now had to face the Germans.

Everything about the Boer War was unfortunate for the British. The Boers were formidable opponents—farmers by day and commandos by night, armed with the latest French and German rifles. Hatred for the British in the European press was almost universal. The war was exceptionally costly in both money and lives; it roused many Britons to a hysterical patriotism. Anti-imperialism gained strength, too. In London, humanitarians found British tactics shameful: for example, the British herded, or "concentrated," whole settlements of Boers into compounds surrounded by barbed wire. The British won the major battles but had to contend with bitter **guerrilla** resistance.

THE SECRET OF ENGLAND'S GREATNESS, BY THOMAS JONES BARKER. In this painting, Queen Victoria presents a Bible in the audience chamber at Windsor.

The nasty war ended in 1902. Hoping to live together in peace with the Boers, the British made many concessions to them, including the right to use their own language, Afrikaans (English remained the official language). They also offered amnesty to any Boer who would swear allegiance to the British king. The settlement, which appeared generous to the belligerents, boded ill for the majority black population of South Africa. Few safeguards for blacks were written into the treaty or the constitution of the new Union of South Africa, which developed into a rigidly segregated state.

The Costs of Colonialism

The cost of imperialism in Africa was high not just to the British and French but also to other Europeans. Italy's defeat at Adowa (1896) by Ethiopians belied dreams of empire and national glory. Victory would not have alleviated Italy's economic problems, although it might have reduced political discontent. Germans could take little heart from their African acquisitions—Southwest Africa (Namibia), Southeast Africa (Tanzania, but not Zanzibar, which was British), the Cameroons, and Togo. The German colonies were the most efficiently governed (critics said ruthlessly controlled) but yielded few benefits other than pride of ownership. The Belgians obviously gained no prestige from the horrors perpetrated in the Congo. Serious thinkers contemplating the depths to which Europeans would sink in search of fortune and fame suggested that the Europeans were more barbarous than the Africans.

For the most part, honor was fleeting and profits illusory in African empires. Yet it appeared that Europeans might go to war with one another for African lands with few people and fewer resources. War between Europeans promised to be more deadly than colonial conflicts with Africans and Asians. Only patient diplomacy and the growing threat of Germany kept England and France from coming to blows. Germany expressed its aggressive imperialism in a naval arms race with the British, which threatened the latter's power and national self-image. The "**Teutonic cousins**" eyed each other with deepening suspicion. This tension contributed to the alliances that the Great Powers made in the decade before World War I.

LATIN AMERICA

The growing European influence in Latin America in the nineteenth century was yet another variety of imperialism. Although it involved neither direct rule, as in Africa and parts of Asia, nor a foreign threat, as in China and Southeast Asia, it nonetheless gave Europeans and Americans control over much of Latin American life.

In the era of the American Revolution of 1776 and the French Revolution of 1789, Latin American colonists rebelled against Spain. Britain and the United States encouraged them, in part to gain a free hand for trade, which Spain did not allow. They successfully forestalled attempts of the other Great Powers to restore Spain or to extend colonies after Napoleon's fall. (Supported by the British the American president warned against intervention or colonization in the **Monroe Doctrine**.)

For the entire nineteenth century, European trade and immigration penetrated South America. Argentina, Brazil, Chile, and other countries took in Irish, Germans, Italians, Eastern Europeans, and Spaniards; like the United States, they became primarily immigrant nations. (A few countries—notably Mexico and Peru—attracted fewer Europeans, preserving an Amerindian or mestizo society.) Europeans also invested heavily. Britain and to a lesser degree France dominated the economy; they cooperated commercially with local merchants, loaned money, and negotiated favorable trade treaties for their citizens.

Both the Europeans and the local merchant and landowner elite exploited the lower classes. Brazil relied on African slave labor to produce for European markets; it was the last American nation to abolish slavery. Native Amerindians were pushed off their lands just as ruthlessly as they had been in North America.

The wealthy classes in Latin America depended on Europe for trade and investment. They became indebted to Europeans for funds to support their governments and build their railroads. For their part, the Europeans were content to gain the profits from commerce without direct colonization. If political dissension threatened to interfere with peaceful trade, Europeans had ways of letting the merchant class know the costs of that dissension. An exception to this general policy of nonintervention was Napoleon III's attempt in 1867 to conquer Mexico and to install an Austrian archduke (Maximilian) on a bogus throne. The Mexicans, led by Benito Juárez (1806–1872), resisted the French invasion; the United States threatened to intervene on the side of Juárez. Napoleon thought better of his dreams of easy glory and abandoned the campaign he had undertaken more to please members of his military than the French business community. The Mexicans executed Maximilian; the experience intensified Mexican nationalism.

Europe also dominated the Western Hemisphere culturally. In Latin America, a small, wealthy upper class imitated European culture. At Manaus in the Amazon region, using the profits of rubber farms worked by enslaved Indians, rich South Americans built an ornate opera house resembling Milan's La Scala. Using the profits of cotton or coffee labor, wealthy Latin Americans lived like the British gentry. In Buenos Aires, Rio de Janeiro, and Santiago, merchants discussed the latest European intellectual fads. Upper-class Latin Americans sent their children to Europe to attend school and to acquire "culture" before they entered business, agriculture, and government in their native lands. In these matters, the Latin American elite behaved much the same as westernizers among the elites of India, the Middle East, and Southeast Asia. Some people in both Latin and North America, however, felt that New World countries must develop their own cultures, not imitate Britain or France. Significant local cultures did evolve.

The business interests of Britain and the United States prevented other European interventions, but by the end of the century, the United States was able to energetically pursue its own interests, first in the Caribbean and Central America and then throughout Latin America. After the Spanish-American War (1898), the United States occupied Cuba and annexed Puerto Rico as well as the Philippines. It restated the Monroe Doctrine in 1904 insisting that Europeans could not intervene in the Western Hemisphere even to protect their citizens or their business interests.

U.S. citizens engineered Panama's secession from Colombia in 1903 in order to build the Panama Canal on favorable terms—a project that French capitalists had failed to complete. The United States intervened repeatedly in the Caribbean, sending United States marines to occupy the Dominican Republic, Haiti, Nicaragua, and the port of Veracruz in Mexico. Seizing customs revenues for payment of debts and threatening Latin American governments, American "**gunboat diplomacy**" replaced English and French commercial power. Like Britain, the United States used force to maintain its interests while at the same time articulating a policy of free competition for trade and commerce—of "open doors" around the world—but in Latin America the United States would guard the doorway.

In many ways, United States behavior resembled European imperialism. Like the European nations that acquired bases in China, the United States took Guantánamo Bay in Cuba, Fonseca in Nicaragua, and the Canal Zone in Panama. Like European businesses, U.S. entrepreneurs invested so heavily in underdeveloped areas that they frequently controlled governments and ruling elites. In 1923, 43 percent of all U.S. foreign investment went to Latin America, 27 percent to Canada, only 22 percent to Europe (at a time when the United States was underwriting German recovery from World War I), and 8 percent to Asia and Africa. Foreign investment may have been a mere fraction of total American wealth, but it was significant to important segments of the national economy.

The United States practiced "**dollar diplomacy**" in Latin America. It used its economic power to influence politics just as Europeans had in Morocco, Tunisia, Egypt, Persia, Turkey, and China. When corrupt members of dictatorial regimes borrowed money for national development or for their personal use and were unable to repay, the United States treated governments like private companies or private individuals in default. The Marines took customs, taxes, and treasuries until the debts were repaid. The customs revenues of Haiti (1915) and Santo Domingo (1904, 1916–1924) were collected for American bankers just as Britain and France had taken Egyptian revenues. Governments in Central America were U.S. puppets or clients just as European countries had controlled the Middle East or Central Asia. The influence of the United States on Mexico under Porfirio Díaz (1876–1880, 1884–1911) resembled that of Germany and Britain on the Ottoman Empire.

The Latin American response to imperialism was opposition and resistance. The strongest challenge to U.S. interests came with the Mexican Revolution of 1911. Mexican leaders—Emiliano Zapata, Victoriano Huerta, and Francisco "Pancho" Villa—had different motives for the overthrow of Díaz, but each saw the United States as part of the problem. Zapata wanted land reform, to break up the great estates and give land to the peasants; Huerta wanted to increase foreign investment in industry but keep Mexico, not the foreigners, in control. In 1916, Villa led a raid across the border. Woodrow Wilson ordered his troops to chase him into Mexico. At that very moment, Wilson was preaching self-determination for European nations and expressing concern about the wrongs done to the weak by the strong in Europe.

After World War I, relations between the United States and Latin America remained troubled, particularly during the Great Depression, which had devastating effects on the countries that had begun to industrialize and build an export market. Only very recently have U.S.–Latin American relations substantially improved.

THE LEGACY OF IMPERIALISM

World War I was a turning point in the history of imperialism, although neither mother countries nor colonies were aware of it at the time.

SLAVES CUTTING SUGAR CANE ON A PLANTATION IN TERREIROS, RIO DE JANEIRO (C. 1882). Brazilian slaves toiled to produce one of Brazil's main exports to the world market. The world economy, which developed during the commercial revolution, emerged full force with the age of imperialism as more and more resources of the non-European world were produced, bought, and sold for overseas consumption. (© Bettman/CORBIS.)

Britain and France divided the German colonial spoils and replaced Turkish power in the Middle East. Both empires were at their territorial peak in 1919. But the origins of **decolonization** also date from the postwar era. Wilson and Lloyd George championed national self-determination at the Paris Peace Conference. They meant their slogans to apply to Europeans, not to the colonial world, but many intellectuals, both in the colonies and in Europe, argued that the principle of self-determination should also apply to Asians and Africans. Liberal democrats began to talk of training the colonies for eventual self-government or independence. In the colonies, forces for independence grew. Colonial intellectuals thought the democrats' timetable for equality or for self-government was too slow. Some found leadership and inspiration in the anti-imperialist campaign of Lenin and the Bolsheviks.

Less than three decades later, World War II exhausted the European colonial powers. It depleted their soldiery, financial resources, and willingness to wage war against rebellious colonies. During the war, the Allies relied on colonies for labor, soldiers, bases, and supplies. Colonies and British Commonwealth states such as Australia made giant strides toward industrialization. At the very moment that colonies were most important to their mother countries, they were taking steps toward greater economic independence. Furthermore, after fighting against Nazi racism, it was difficult for Europeans to justify European rule over nations yearning for self-determination.

Today, almost a century after the rapid division of the world among the European and U.S. powers and decades after the decolonization of most of the world, the results of imperialism persist. Imperialism left a legacy of deep animosity toward the imperialists in the countries of Asia, Africa, and Latin America. Although most nations have political independence, Western economic and cultural domination still exists. Much of the world suffers from insufficient capital, unskilled leaders, and unstable governments. Many people believe that their countries' condition is the result of a century of colonial exploitation.

Imperialism has been a source of great bitterness to former colonial peoples, not just for economic exploitation but also for racism and callous disregard for other cultures. Thus, many non-Westerners see little to admire in the values of the imperialists. Their nationalism usually includes an intense suspicion of western motives, some of which is expressed in religious and cultural conservatism or fundamentalism. Politically, this anti-Western bent led some groups in some countries to pro-Communist or pro-Russian positions during the cold war or to the creation of their own versions of socialism, such as African socialism or Latin American revolutionary movements. In the aftermath of the cold war and decolonization, fundamentalism or traditionalism became a new political force opposing Western influence. This political opposition can be directed at the local elites as well. Local elites are thought corrupted by the profits and values of globalism, which threatens traditional values, particularly religious ones, and livelihoods.

In today's economically interdependent world, the influence of Western ideas, institutions, technologies, and economic practices is apparent everywhere. English is an international language. The languages of computer technology are universal. African and Asian lands have adopted and adapted democracy, parliamentary and party government, military strategy and technology, socialism, and national boundaries left by Western powers. Intellectuals speak of a global village; so closely connected is the community of ideas shared by leading Africans, Asians, and Latin Americans with Europeans and North Americans. At the same time, many countries are acutely conscious of their hard-won nationhood and of their dependence on shifts in the world markets and the economies of the Great Powers, over which they have little control.

Chapter 27

Modern Consciousness: New Views of Nature, Human Nature, and the Arts

Edvard Munch (1863–1944), The Scream, *1893. The dark forces of emotional torment and sexual aberration fill the canvases of the Norwegian postimpressionist Edvard Munch.*

Focus Questions

1. In what ways did late modern thought and the arts break with the Enlightenment tradition?

2. Why did Nietzsche disdain both Christianity and democracy?

3. How did the thought of Nietzsche, Dostoevsky, Bergson, and Sorel exemplify the growing power and appeal of irrationalism?

4. What did Freud contribute to an understanding of irrationalism? What is his relationship to the Enlightenment tradition?

5. How did the modernist movement in the arts break with the standards of esthetics that had governed European culture since the Renaissance?

6. How did modern physics alter the Newtonian conception of the universe?

7. In what ways was the Enlightenment tradition in disarray by the early twentieth century?

The modern mentality may be said to have passed through two broad phases: early modernity and late modernity. Formulated during the era of the Scientific Revolution and the Enlightenment, early modernity stressed confidence in reason, science, human goodness, and humanity's capacity to improve society for human betterment. Then in the late nineteenth and early twentieth centuries, a new outlook took shape. Late modern thinkers and scientists achieved revolutionary insights into human nature, the social world, and the physical universe; and writers and artists opened up hitherto unimagined possibilities for artistic expression.

These developments produced a shift in European consciousness. The mechanical model of the universe, which had dominated the Western outlook since Newton, was fundamentally altered. The Enlightenment view of human rationality and goodness was questioned, and the belief in natural rights and objective standards governing morality came under attack. Rules of esthetics that had governed the arts since the Renaissance were discarded. Shattering old beliefs, late modernity left Europeans without landmarks—without generally accepted cultural standards or agreed-on conceptions about human nature and life's meaning.

The late modern period was marked by extraordinary creativity in thought and the arts. Yet as imaginative and fruitful as these changes were for Western intellectual and cultural life, they also helped create the disoriented, fragmented, and troubled era that characterized the twentieth century.

IRRATIONALISM

While many intellectuals continued to adhere to the outlook identified with the Enlightenment, some thinkers in the late nineteenth century challenged the basic premises of the philosophes and their nineteenth-century heirs. In particular, they repudiated the Enlightenment conception of human rationality, stressing instead the irrational side of human nature. Regarding reason as sovereign, the philosophes had defined human beings by their capacity to think critically; now thinkers saw blind strivings and animal instincts as the primary fact of human existence. It seemed that reason exercised a very limited influence over human conduct, that impulses, drives, and instincts—all forces below the surface—determined behavior much more than did logical consciousness. Carrying this view further, intellectuals argued that the universal principles advanced by rational thought really masked an often disreputable self-interest.

The problem of **irrationalism** is manifold. Some thinkers, while recognizing the weakness of reason, continued to value it and sought to preserve it as an essential ingredient of civilized life. Some studied manifestations of the irrational in myth, religion, the arts, and politics in a logical and systematic way in order to gain understanding of human nature and human behavior. Others, concentrating on the creative potential of the irrational, urged nourishing the feelings, which they considered vital to artistic creativity and a richer existence. Still others celebrated violence as a healthy expression of the irrational.

The new insights into the irrational side of human nature and the growing assault on reason had immense implications for political life. In succeeding decades, these currents of irrationalism would become ideologized and politicized by unscrupulous demagogues who sought to mobilize and manipulate the masses. The popularity of Fascist movements, which openly denigrated reason and exalted race, blood, action, and will, demonstrated the naïveté of nineteenth-century liberals, who believed that reason had triumphed in human affairs.

Nietzsche

The principal figure in the dethronement of reason and the glorification of the irrational was the German philosopher Friedrich Nietzsche (1844–1900). Nietzsche's writings are not systematic treatises but rather collections of aphorisms, often containing internal contradictions. Consequently, his philosophy lends itself to misinterpretation and misapplication. Nazi theorists, for example, distorted Nietzsche to justify their notions of the German master race.

Nietzsche attacked the accepted views and convictions of his day as a hindrance to a fuller and richer existence. He denounced social reform, parliamentary government, and universal suffrage; ridiculed the vision of progress through science;

condemned Christian morality; and mocked the liberal belief in man's essential goodness and rationality. According to Nietzsche, man must understand that life, which is replete with cruelty, injustice, uncertainty, and absurdity, is not governed by rational principles. There exist no absolute standards of good and evil whose truth can be demonstrated by reflective reason. Nothing is true; there is no higher purpose or sense to the universe

FRIEDRICH NIETZSCHE (1844–1900). Possessing the intuitive genius of a great poet, Nietzsche grasped the crucial problem afflicting the modern European soul: What path should the individual take in a world where God is dead? Nietzsche's answer to this question—the superman who creates his own values—lent itself to considerable misinterpretation and distortion and had little constructive social value. (© Bettmann/Corbis.)

or human existence. There is only the naked individual living in a godless and absurd world.

Modern bourgeois society, said Nietzsche, is decadent and enfeebled—a victim of the excessive development of the rational faculties at the expense of will and instinct. Against the liberal-rationalist stress on the intellect, he urged recognition of the dark, mysterious world of instinctual desires, the true forces of life. If the human will is smothered with excessive intellectualizing, the spontaneity that sparks cultural creativity and ignites a zest for living is destroyed. The critical and theoretical outlook destroys the creative instincts. For man's manifold potential to be realized, he must stop relying on the intellect and nurture again the instinctual roots of human existence.

Christianity, with all its prohibitions, restrictions, and demands to conform, also crushes the human impulse for life, said Nietzsche, the son of a Lutheran pastor. Christian morality must be obliterated, for it is fit only for the weak, the slave. The triumph of Christianity in the ancient world, said Nietzsche, was a revolution of the lowest elements of society, the meek, the weak, and the ignoble, who sought to inherit the earth from their aristocratic superiors. It was nothing less than an attempt of resentful slaves and slave-like plebeians to prevent their aristocratic superiors from expressing their heroic natures and to strike back at the noble spirits whom they envied. They did so by condemning as evil the very traits that they themselves lacked—strength, power, assertiveness, and a zest for life—and by making their own base, wretched, and life-negating values—meekness, self-denial, humility, and compassion—the standard of all things. Then they saddled with guilt all those who deviated from the standard. This transvaluation of values engineered by Christianity, said Nietzsche, led to a deterioration of life and culture. In *The Anti-Christ* (1888), Nietzsche wrote:

> *Christianity has waged a war to the death against this higher type of man. . . . Christianity has taken the side of everything weak, base, ill-constituted, it has made an ideal out of opposition to the . . . instincts of strong life. . . . Christianity is a revolt of everything that crawls along the ground directed against that which is elevated.*[1]

The Christian virtues debilitate and cripple life. Moreover, added Nietzsche, they are really only a facade hiding Christians' true feelings of envy, resentment, hatred, and revenge against their superiors, betters, and tormentors and masking a desire for their own power.

Although the philosophes rejected Christian doctrines, they largely retained Christian ethics. Unlike the philosophes, Nietzsche did not attack Christianity because it was contrary to reason. He attacked it because, he said, it gave man a sick soul. It was life-denying. Blocking the free and spontaneous exercise of human instincts, it made humility, weakness, and self-abnegation virtues and pride a vice. In short, Christianity extinguished the spark of life. This spark of life, this inner yearning that fosters self-creation, must again burn.

"God is dead," Nietzsche proclaimed. God is man's own creation. Christian morality is also dead. Dead also are all the inherited truths based on nature and reason. There are no higher worlds, no transcendent or metaphysical truths, no morality derived from God or nature, and no natural rights, scientific socialism, or inevitable progress. We wander through an eternal nothing in which all the old values and truths have lost their intelligibility. This **nihilism**—the belief that moral and social values have no validity—had caused a crisis in European life. But the death of God and of all transcendental truths can mean the liberation of man, insisted Nietzsche. Man can surmount nihilism by adopting a new orientation that gives primacy to the superior man—the **overman** or **superman** who asserts his will, gives order to chaotic passions, makes great demands on himself, and lives life with a fierce joy. The overman aspires to self-perfection; without fear or guilt, he rejects traditional religion and morality and creates his own values and defines his own self, his own life. Such a man can overcome the deadening uniformity and mediocrity of modern civilization. He can undo democracy and socialism, which have made masters out of cattlelike masses, and surmount the shopkeeper's spirit, which has made man soft and degenerate. European society lacks heroic figures; everyone belongs to a vast herd, but there are no leaders.

According to Nietzsche, Europe could be saved only by the emergence of such a higher type of man, who would not be held back by the egalitarian rubbish preached by democrats and socialists. "A declaration of war on the masses by *higher* man is needed," said Nietzsche, to end "the dominion of *inferior* men." Europe required "the annihilation of *suffrage universal,* i.e., the system through which the lowest natures prescribe themselves as laws for the higher."[2] Europe needed a new breed of rulers, a true aristocracy of masterful men. The overman is a new kind of man who breaks with accepted morality and sets his own standards. He does not repress his instincts but asserts them. He destroys old values and asserts his prerogative as master. Free of Christian guilt, he proudly affirms his own being; dispensing with Christian "thou shalt not," he instinctively says, "I will." He dares to be himself. Because he is not like other people, traditional definitions of good and evil have no meaning for him. He does not allow his individuality to be stifled. He makes his own values, those that flow from his very being.

The overman understands and exemplifies the ultimate fact of life: that "the most fearful and fundamental desire in man [is] his drive for power,"[3] that human beings crave and strive for power ceaselessly and uncompromisingly. It is perfectly natural for human beings to want to dominate nature and other human beings; inherent in human nature is the desire "to overpower, overthrow, . . . to become master, a thirst for enemies and antagonisms and triumphs."[4] This will to power is not a product of rational reflection but flows from the very essence of human existence. As the motivating force in human behavior, it governs everyday life and is the determining factor in political life. The enhancement of power brings supreme enjoyment: "The love of power is the demon of men. Let them have everything— health, food, a place to live, entertainment—they are and remain unhappy and low-spirited; for the demon waits and waits and will be satisfied. Take everything from them and satisfy this and they are almost happy—as happy as men and demons can be."[5] The masses, cowardly and envious, will condemn the overman as evil; this has always been their way. Thus, Nietzsche castigated democracy because it "represents the disbelief in great human beings and an elite society,"[6] and Christianity because it imposes an unnatural morality, one that affirms meekness, humility, and compassion.

The German philosopher Arthur Schopenhauer (1788–1860) had declared that beneath the conscious intellect is the will, a striving, demanding, and imperious force, which is the real determinant of human behavior. Schopenhauer held that the intellect is merely a tool of an alogical and irrational will. Life is an endless striving to fulfill ceaseless desires. Blind animal impulses, not the capacity for rational choice, are a human being's true essence. Schopenhauer sought to repress the will. He urged people to stifle desires and retreat into quietude to escape from life's agonies.

Nietzsche learned from Schopenhauer to appreciate the power of unconscious strivings that dominate human behavior, but he rejected Schopenhauer's condemnation and negation of the will, his flight from life. Instead, Nietzsche called for the heroic and joyful assertion of the will and the affirmation of life in order to redeem life from nothingness.

Overmen cast off all established values. Free of all restrictions, rules, and codes of behavior imposed by society, they create their own values. They burst on the world propelled by that something that urges people to want, take, strike, create, struggle, seek, and dominate. They know that life is purposeless but live it laughingly, instinctively, and fully. Overmen are people of restless energy who enjoy living dangerously, have contempt for meekness and humility, and dismiss humanitarian sentiments; they are noble warriors, hard and ruthless. Only a new elite, which distanced itself from the masses and held in contempt the Christian belief that all people are equal before God, could save European society from decadence.

The influence of Nietzsche's philosophy is still a matter of controversy and conjecture. Perhaps better than anyone else, Nietzsche grasped the crucial problem of modern society and binding power. In a world where nothing is true, all is permitted. Nietzsche foresaw that the future, an age without values, would be violent and sordid, and he urged individuals to face themselves and life free of illusion, pretense, and hypocrisy. Nietzsche is also part of a general nineteenth-century trend that sought to affirm the human being and earthly aspirations rather than God or salvation.

But no helpful social policy could be derived from Nietzsche's heroic individualism, which

Friedrich Nietzsche: *The Will to Power*

First published in 1901, one year after Nietzsche's death, The Will to Power *consists of the author's notes written in the years 1883 to 1888. The following passages from this work show Nietzsche's contempt for democracy and socialism and proclaim the will to power.*

728 (March–June 1888)

. . . A society that definitely and *instinctively* gives up war and conquest is in decline: it is ripe for democracy and the rule of shopkeepers. . . .

752 (1884)

. . . Democracy represents the disbelief in great human beings and an elite society: "Everyone is equal to everyone else." "At bottom we are one and all self-seeking cattle and mob."

753 (1885)

I am opposed to 1. socialism, because it dreams quite naively of "the good, true, and beautiful" and of "equal rights"—(anarchism also desires the same ideal, but in a more brutal fashion); 2. parliamentary government and the press, because these are the means by which the herd animal becomes master.

765 (January–Fall 1888)

. . . Another Christian concept, no less crazy, has passed even more deeply into the tissue of modernity: the concept of the "equality of souls before God." This concept furnishes the prototype of all theories of equal rights: mankind was first taught to stammer the proposition of equality in a religious context, and only later was it made into morality: no wonder that man ended by taking it seriously, taking it practically!—that is to say, politically, democratically, socialistically. . . .

854 (1884)

In the age of *suffrage universel,* i.e., when everyone may sit in judgment on everyone and everything, I feel impelled to reestablish *order of rank.*

861 (1884)

A declaration of war on the masses by *higher men* is needed! Everywhere the mediocre are taught that "there are higher and lower men and that a single individual can . . . justify the existence of whole millennia."[7] Nietzsche thought only of great individuals, humanity's noblest specimens, who overcome mediocrity and the artificiality of all inherited values. The social community and social injustice did not concern him. "The weak and ill-constituted shall perish: first principle of our philanthropy. And one shall help them to do so."[8] Surely, these words offer no constructive guidelines for dealing with the problems of modern industrial civilization.

Likewise, Nietzsche had no constructive proposals for dealing with the disintegration of rational and Christian certainties. Instead, his vitriolic attack on European institutions and values helped erode the rational foundations of Western civilization. This assault appealed immensely to intellectuals in Central Europe, who saw Nietzsche's philosophy as liberating an inner energy. Thus, many young people, attracted to Nietzsche, welcomed World War I; they viewed it as a way of realizing Nietzsche's command to live dangerously; they saw it as a creative and aesthetic experience that would overcome bourgeois decadence and clear a path to a new heroic age. They took Nietzsche's words literally: "A society that definitely and *instinctively* gives up war and conquest is in decline."[9]

Nazi theorists tried to make Nietzsche a forerunner of their movement. They sought combining in order to make themselves master! Everything that makes soft and effeminate, that serves the ends of the "people" or the "feminine," works in favor of *suffrage universel*, i.e., the dominion of *inferior* men. But we should take reprisal and bring this whole affair (which in Europe commenced with Christianity) to light and to the bar of judgment.

862 (1884)

A doctrine is needed powerful enough to work as a breeding agent: strengthening the strong, paralyzing and destructive for the world-weary. The annihilation of the decaying races. Decay of Europe.—The annihilation of slavish evaluations.—Dominion over the earth as a means of producing a higher type.—The annihilation of the tartuffery [hypocrisy] called "morality." . . . The annihilation of *suffrage universel*; i.e., the system through which the lowest natures prescribe themselves as laws for the higher.—The annihilation of mediocrity and its acceptance. . . .

870 (1884)

The root of all evil: that the slavish morality of meekness, chastity, selflessness, absolute obedience, has triumphed. . . .

874 (1884)

The degeneration of the rulers and the ruling classes has been the cause of the greatest mischief in history! Without the Roman Caesars and Roman society, the insanity of Christianity would never have come to power.

997 (1884)

I teach: that there are higher and lower men, and that a single individual can under certain circumstances justify the existence of whole millennia—that is, a full, rich, great, whole human being in relation to countless incomplete fragmentary men.

Questions for Analysis

1. Why does Friedrich Nietzsche attack democracy, socialism, and Christianity?
2. Why did Nietzsche's philosophy appeal to some Nazis?

Friedrich Nietzsche, *The Will to Power*, trans. Walter Kaufmann and R. J. Hollingdale, ed. Walter Kaufmann (New York: Vintage Books, 1968), 386, 397, 401, 457–459, 465, 467, 518.

philosophical sanction for their own thirst for power, contempt for the weak, ruthlessness, and glorification of action, as well as for their cult of the heroic and their Social Darwinistic revulsion for human equality. Recasting Nietzsche in their own image, the Nazis saw themselves as Nietzsche's overmen: members of a master race, who, by force of will, would conquer all obstacles and reshape the world according to their own values. Some German intellectuals were drawn to Nazism because it seemed a healthy affirmation of life, the life with a new purpose, for which Nietzsche called.

Nietzsche himself, detesting German nationalism and militarism, scoffed at the notion of German racial superiority—his exceptional man could come from any ethnic group—disdained (despite some unfortunate remarks) anti-Semitism, and denounced state worship. He would have abhorred Hitler and been dismayed at the twisting of his idea of the will to power into a prototype Fascist principle. The men whom he admired were passionate but self-possessed individuals who, by mastering their own chaotic passions, would face life and death courageously, affirmatively, and creatively. Such men make great demands on themselves. Nevertheless, as Janko Lavrin points out, "practically all the Fascist and Nazi theories can find some support in Nietzsche's texts, provided one gives them the

661

required twist."[10] Nietzsche's extreme and violent denunciation of Western democratic principles, including equality; his praise of power; his call for the liberation of the instincts; his elitism, which denigrates and devalues all human life that is not strong and noble; and his spurning of humane values, provided a breeding ground for violent, antirational, antiliberal, and inhumane movements. His philosophy, which included loose talk about the virtues of pitiless warriors, the breeding of a master race, and the annihilation of the weak and the ill, is conducive to a politics of extremes that knows no moral limits.

Dostoevsky

Like Nietzsche, the Russian novelist and essayist Fyodor Dostoevsky (1821–1881) attacked the fundamental outlook of the Enlightenment, particularly as expressed by liberals and socialists. In contrast to their view that human beings are innately good, responsive to reason's promptings, and capable of constructing the good society through reason, Dostoevsky perceived human beings as inherently depraved, irrational, and rebellious. In contrast to Nietzsche's disdain of Christianity, Dostoevsky, who had a fervent and mystical attachment to Orthodox Christianity, maintained that loss of religious faith would lead to Russia's ruin.

In *Notes from Underground* (1864), the narrator (the Underground Man) rebels against the efforts of rationalists, humanists, positivists, liberals, and socialists to define human nature according to universal principles and to reform society so as to promote greater happiness. He rebels against science and reason, against the entire liberal and socialist vision. He does so in the name of human subjectivity: the uncontainable, irrepressible, whimsical, and foolish human will. Human nature, says the Underground Man, is too volatile, too diversified to be schematized by the theoretical mind; it will struggle against reason's yoke.

For the Underground Man, there are no absolute and timeless truths that precede the individual and to which the individual should conform. There is only a terrifying world of naked wills vying with one another. In such a world, people do not necessarily seek happiness,

prosperity, and peace—all that is good for them, according to "enlightened" thinkers. To the rationalist who aims to eliminate suffering and deprivation, Dostoevsky replies that some people freely choose suffering and depravity because it gratifies them—for some, "even in a toothache there is enjoyment"—and they are repelled by wealth, peace, security, and happiness. They do not want to be robots in a rigorously planned and regulated social order, which creates a slot for everything, and they consider excessive intellectualizing—"over-acute consciousness"—a disease that keeps them from asserting their autonomy, their "independent choice."

> *It seems that something that is dearer to almost every man than his greatest advantages must really exist . . . for which, if necessary, a man is ready to act in opposition to all laws, that is, in opposition to reason, honor, peace, prosperity. . . . One's own free unfettered choice, one's own fancy, however wild it may be, one's own fancy worked up at times to frenzy—why that is that very "most advantageous advantage" which we have overlooked, which comes under no classification and through which all systems and theories are continually being sent to the devil. . . . What man needs is simple independent choice, whatever that independence may cost and wherever it may lead.*[11]

It is this irrational will, Dostoevsky tells us, that defines the individual's uniqueness and leads him to resist the blueprints drawn up by social theorists. For such crystal palaces—secular utopias designed to satisfy all human needs—do not satisfy what the individual needs most: the expression of one's own desires, no matter how foolish or capricious they might appear to the rational mind. So much for any theory that tries to reduce human nature, which is essentially peculiar, irrational, and incomprehensible, to a formula. If Dostoevsky is right, if individuals do not act out of enlightened self-interest, if they are driven by instinctual cravings that resist reason's appeals, then what hope is there for social planners wishing to create the "good" society?

The Underground Man maintains that by following irrational impulses and engaging in irrational acts, human beings assert their individuality; they prove that they are free. The Underground Man is totally free. He struggles to define his existence according to his own needs rather than the standards and values created by others. For him, freedom of choice is a human being's most priceless possession, and it derives not from the intellect but from impulses and feelings that account for our essential individuality. He considers the "rational faculty" as "simply one-twentieth of all my faculties of life"; life is more than reasoning, more than "simply extracting square roots."[12]

In rejecting external security and liberal and socialist concepts of progress—in aspiring to assert his own individuality even if this means acting against his own best interests—the Underground Man demonstrates that a powerful element of irrationality underlies human nature, an element that reason cannot understand, control, or satisfy.

Bergson

Another thinker who reflected the growing irrationalism of the age was Henri Bergson (1859–1941), a French philosopher of Jewish background. Originally attracted to positivism, Bergson turned away from the positivistic claim that science could explain everything and fulfill all human needs. Such an emphasis on the intellect, said Bergson, sacrifices spiritual impulses, imagination, and intuition and reduces reality and the soul to mere mechanisms. The methods of science cannot reveal ultimate reality, Bergson insisted. European civilization must recognize the limitations of scientific rationalism. Our capacity for intuition, whereby the mind grasps the inner life of the object—participates in it—tells us more about reality than the method of analysis employed by science. The intuitive experience—something like the artist's instant comprehension of a natural scene—is a direct avenue to truth, which is closed to the calculations and measurements of science. Bergson's philosophy pointed away from science toward religious mysticism.

To his admirers, Bergson's philosophy liberated the person from the constraints of positivism, mechanism, and materialism. It also extolled the creative potential of intuition, the mystical experience, and the poetic imagination: those forces of life that resist categorization by the scientific mind. A protest against modern technology and bureaucracy—against all the features of mass society that seemed to stifle individual uniqueness and spontaneity—it sought to reaffirm the primacy of the individual in an increasingly mechanized and bureaucratic world. The popularity of Bergson's philosophy, with its depreciation of reason, symptomized the unsuspected strength and appeal of the nonrational—another sign that people were searching for new alternatives to the Enlightenment worldview.

Sorel

Nietzsche and Dostoevsky proclaimed that irrational forces constitute the essence of human nature; Bergson held that a nonrational intuition provides insights unattainable by the scientific mentality. The French social theorist Georges Sorel (1847–1922), who had given up engineering to follow intellectual pursuits, recognized the political potential of the nonrational. Like Nietzsche, Sorel was disillusioned with contemporary bourgeois society, which he considered decadent, unheroic, and life-denying. Like Nietzsche, he also denounced the liberal-democratic foundations of middle-class society. Whereas Nietzsche called for the overman to rescue society from decadence and mediocrity, Sorel placed his hopes in the workers, whose position made them courageous and virile. He saw them as bearers of higher values: as noble and determined producers struggling against exploiters and parasites.

Sorel wanted the proletariat to destroy the existing bourgeois-liberal-capitalist order and rejuvenate society by infusing it with dynamic and creative energy and a sense of moral purpose. The overthrow of decadent bourgeois society would be accomplished through a general strike: a universal work stoppage, which would bring down governments and give power to the workers. Sorel applauded violence, for it intensified the revolutionaries' dedication to the cause and spurred them to acts of heroism. It also accorded with his general conception that life is an unremitting battle and that history is a perpetual conflict between decay and vitality, between passivity and action. In his view, struggle purified, invigorated, and promoted creative change.

Sorel saw the general strike as having the appeal of a great mobilizing myth. What was important was not that the general strike actually takes place, but that its image stirs all the anticapitalist resentments of the workers and inspires them to carry out their revolutionary responsibilities. Sorel understood the extraordinary potency of myth: it structures and intensifies feelings, unifies people, and mobilizes and channels their energy into heroic action. Because they appeal to the imagination and the emotions, myths are an effective way of organizing the masses, buoying up their spirits, and moving them to revolt. By believing in the myth of the general strike, workers would soar above the moral decadence of bourgeois society and bear the immense sacrifices that their struggle called for.

Like Marx, Sorel believed that the goals of the worker could not be achieved through peaceful, parliamentary means. He, too, wanted no reconciliation between bourgeois exploiters and oppressed workers. The only recourse for workers was direct action and violence. However, Marx considered violence simply as a means to a revolutionary end and would dispense with it once the end was achieved. Regarding violence as sublime—a means of restoring grandeur to a flabby world—Sorel valued it as an end in itself.

Sorel's condemnation of liberal democracy and his conviction that fabricated myths could serve as a powerful political weapon found concrete expression in the Fascist movements after World War I. Sorel heralded the age of mass political movements committed to revolutionary violence and of myths manufactured by **propaganda** experts determined to destroy the liberal-rational tradition of the Enlightenment.

FREUD: A NEW VIEW OF HUMAN NATURE

In many ways, Sigmund Freud (1856–1939), an Austrian-Jewish physician who spent most of his adult life in Vienna, was a child of the Enlightenment. Like the philosophes, he identified

civilization with reason and regarded science as the avenue to knowledge. But in contrast to the philosophes, Freud focused on the massive power and influence of nonrational drives. Marx had argued that although people believe that they think freely, in truth their beliefs and thoughts reflect the interests and ideology of the ruling class. Freud, too, believed that our conscious thoughts are determined by hidden forces—namely, unconscious impulses.

Whereas Nietzsche glorified the irrational and approached it with a poet's temperament, Freud recognized its potential danger. He sought to comprehend it scientifically and wanted to regulate it in the interests of civilization. Unlike Nietzsche, Freud did not belittle the rational but always sought to salvage respect for reason. In a letter to the Austrian novelist Stefan Zweig, Freud wrote that the essential task of **psychoanalysis** was "to struggle with the demon" of irrationality in a "sober way," to make it "a comprehensible object of science."[13] By a "sober way," he meant the scientific method, not Bergson's intuition or Nietzsche's inspired insights. Better than anyone, Freud recognized reason's limitations and the power of the nonrational, but he never wavered in his support of reason.

> *We may insist as often as we like, that man's intellect is powerless in comparison with his instinctual life, and we may be right in this. Nevertheless, there is something peculiar about his weakness. The voice of the intellect is a soft one, but it does not rest until it has gained a hearing. Finally, after a countless succession of rebuffs, it succeeds. This is one of the few points on which one may be optimistic about the future of mankind.*[14]

Freud's explorations of the world of the unconscious had a profoundly upsetting impact on Western civilization's conception of the self. Freud himself viewed his theories as a great blow to human pride, to "man's craving for grandiosity."

> *Humanity has, in the course of time, had to endure from the hands of science two great outrages upon its naive self-love. The first was when it realized that our earth was not the*

FREUD AND HIS DAUGHTER ANNA (1912). Sigmund Freud, the father of psychoanalysis, penetrated the world of the unconscious in a scientific way. He concluded that powerful drives govern human behavior more than reason does. His explorations of the unconscious produced an image of the human being that broke with the Enlightenment's view of the individual's essential goodness and rationality.

(© Mary Evans/SIGMUND FREUD COPYRIGHTS/The Image Works.)

center of the universe, but only a tiny speck in a world-system of a magnitude hardly conceivable; this is associated in our minds with the name of Copernicus. . . . The second was when biological research robbed man of his peculiar privilege of having been specially created, and relegated him to a descent from the animal world, implying an ineradicable animal nature in him: this transvaluation has been accomplished in our own time upon the investigations of Charles Darwin. . . . But man's craving for grandiosity is now suffering

the third and most bitter blow from present-day psychological research which is endeavoring to show the "ego" of each of us that he is not even master in his own house, but that he must remain content with the veriest scrap of information about what is going on unconsciously in his own mind.[15]

Freud held that people are not fundamentally rational and that human behavior is governed primarily by powerful inner forces, which are hidden from consciousness. Within the human mind, intense mental activity takes place that is independent of and unknown to consciousness. Primitive drives, strivings, and thoughts influence our behavior, often without our awareness, so that we may not know the real reasons for our actions. Freud considered not just the external acts of a person but also the inner psychic reality underlying human behavior.

Freud, of course, did not discover the unconscious. Romantic poets had sought the wellspring of creativity in a layer of mind below consciousness. The Greek tragedians, Shakespeare, Schopenhauer, Nietzsche, and Dostoevsky, among others, had all penetrated the tangled world of the passions and marveled at its elemental power. Freud, who believed that artistic and literary creativity ultimately derives from primal instincts rooted in the unconscious, paid tribute to creative writers' intuition: "They are apt to know of a whole host of things between heaven and earth of which our philosophy has not yet let us dream. In their knowledge of the mind they are far in advance of us everyday people, for they draw upon sources which we have not yet opened up for science."[16] He described Nietzsche as a philosopher "whose guesses and intuitions often agree in the most astonishing way with the laborious findings of psychoanalysis."[17] Freud's great achievement was to explore the unconscious methodically and systematically with the tools and temperament of a scientist. He showed that the irrational contained a structure that could be empirically explained and rationally explored.

After graduating from medical school, Freud specialized in the treatment of nervous disorders. His investigations led him to conclude that childhood fears and experiences, often sexual in nature, accounted for neuroses: disorders in thinking, feeling, and behavior that interfere with everyday acts of personal and social life. Neuroses can take several forms, including hysteria, anxiety, depression, and obsessions. So painful and threatening were these childhood emotions and experiences that his patients banished them from conscious memory to the realm of the unconscious. To understand and treat neurotic behavior, Freud said, it is necessary to look behind overt symptoms and bring to the surface emotionally charged experiences and fears—childhood traumas—that lie buried in the unconscious, along with primitive impulses.

Freud probed the unconscious by urging his patients to say whatever came to their minds. This procedure, called *free association,* rests on the premise that spontaneous and uninhibited talk reveals a person's underlying preoccupations, his or her inner world, and the "demons" that are at the root of the person's emotional distress. A second avenue to the unconscious is the analysis of dreams. An individual's dreams, said Freud, reveal his or her secret wishes, often socially unacceptable desires, frightening memories, and suppressed childhood wishes. Finding them too painful to bear, we lock up these wishes and memories in the deepest dungeons of the unconscious. But repressed emotions do not disappear; even in their cages, the demons remain active, continuing to haunt us and to generate conflicts. Our distress is real and even excruciating, but we do not know its source.

The **id,** the subconscious seat of the instincts, said Freud, is "a cauldron full of seething excitations" that constantly demand gratification. The id is primitive and irrational. It knows no values; it has no awareness of good and evil. Unable to endure tension, it demands sexual release, the termination of pain, or the cessation of hunger. When the id is denied an outlet for its instinctual energy, people become frustrated, angry, and unhappy. Gratifying the id is our highest pleasure. But the full gratification of instinctual demands is detrimental to civilized life. That is why the **ego,** which stands for reason, seeks to hold the id in check, to bring it in line with reality.

Freud postulated a harrowing conflict between the relentless strivings of our instinctual nature and the requirements of civilization. In Freud's view, civilization requires the renunciation of instinctual gratification and the mastery of animal instincts, a thesis he developed in *Civilization and Its Discontents* (1930). Although Freud's thoughts in this work were, no doubt, influenced by the great tragedy of World War I and the rise of Fascist movements in several European lands, the main theme could be traced back to his earlier writings. Human beings derive their highest pleasure from sexual fulfillment, said Freud, but unrestrained sexuality drains off psychic energy needed for creative artistic and intellectual life and directs human energies away from work needed to preserve communal life. Hence, society, through the family, the priest, the teacher, and the police, imposes rules and restrictions on our animal nature. In effect, it implants a conscience in human beings that serves to check antisocial drives. But this is immensely painful. The human being is caught in a tragic bind. Society's demand to repress the instincts in the interest of civilization causes terrible frustration; equally distressing, the violation of society's rules under the pressure of instinctual needs evokes feelings of guilt. Either way, people suffer; civilized life simply entails too much pain for people. It seems that the price we pay for civilization is neurosis or mental distress. Most people cannot endure the amount of instinctual renunciation that civilization requires. There are times when our elemental human nature rebels against all the restrictions and "thou shalt nots" demanded by society, against all the misery and torment imposed by civilization.

"Civilization imposes great sacrifices not only on man's sexuality, but also on his aggressivity,"[18] said Freud. People are not good by nature, as the philosophes had taught, but are predisposed to behave cruelly and brutally. They are "creatures among whose instinctual endowments is to be reckoned a powerful share of aggressiveness." Their first inclination is not to love their neighbor but to "satisfy their aggressiveness on him, to exploit his capacity for work without compensation, to use him sexually without his consent, to seize his possessions, to humiliate him, to cause him pain, to torture and to kill him."[19] Man is wolf to man, concluded Freud. "Who has the courage to dispute it in the face of all the evidence in his own life and in history?"[20] Civilization "has to use its utmost efforts in order to set limits to man's aggressive instincts," but "in spite of every effort these endeavors of civilization have not so far achieved very much."[21] People find it difficult to do without "the satisfaction of this inclination to aggression."[22] When circumstances are favorable, this primitive aggressiveness breaks loose and "reveals man as a savage beast to whom consideration towards his own kind is something alien."[23] For Freud, "the inclination to aggression is an original self-subsisting disposition in man," and it "constitutes the greatest impediment to civilization." Civilization attempts "to combine single human individuals and after that families, then races, peoples and nations into one great unity. . . . But man's natural aggressive instinct, the hostility of each against all and of all against each, opposes this program of civilization."[24] Aggressive impulses drive people apart, threatening society with disintegration. For Freud, an unalterable core of human nature is ineluctably in opposition to civilized life. To this extent, everyone is potentially an enemy of civilization.

Freud's awareness of the irrational and his general pessimism regarding people's ability to regulate it in the interests of civilization did not lead him to break faith with the Enlightenment tradition, for Freud did not celebrate the irrational. He was too aware of its self-destructive nature for that. Civilization is indeed a burden, but people must bear it, for the alternative is far worse. In the tradition of the philosophes, Freud sought truth based on a scientific analysis of human nature and believed that reason was the best road to social improvement. Like the philosophes, he was critical of religion, regarding it as a pious illusion—a fairy tale in conflict with reason. Freud wanted people to throw away what he believed was the crutch of religion: to break away from childlike dependency and stand alone. Rules of morality, said Freud, can be formulated rationally without any dependence on religious beliefs.

Also like the philosophes, Freud was a humanitarian who sought to relieve human misery by making people aware of their true nature, particularly their sexuality. He wanted society to soften its overly restrictive sexual standards because they were injurious to mental health. As a practicing psychiatrist, he tried to assist his patients in dealing with emotional problems. Freud wanted to raise to the level of consciousness hitherto unrecognized inner conflicts that caused emotional distress. One enduring consequence of the Freudian revolution is the recognition of the enormous importance played by childhood in the shaping of the adult's personality. The neurotic disorders that burden adults begin in early childhood. Freud urged that we show greater concern for the emotional needs of children.

Yet Freud also differed from the philosophes in crucial ways. Dismissing the Christian doctrine of original sin as myth, the philosophes had believed human nature to be essentially good. If people took reason for their guide, evil could be eliminated. Freud, however, asserted, in secular and scientific terms, a pessimistic view of human nature. He saw evil as rooted in human nature rather than as a product of a faulty environment. Education and better living conditions would not eliminate evil, as the philosophes had expected, nor would the abolition of private property, as Marx had declared. In a socialist state where economic disparities have been eliminated, said Freud, people would lust after power and privilege. The philosophes venerated reason; it had enabled Newton to unravel nature's mysteries and would permit people to achieve virtue and reform society. Freud, who wanted reason to prevail, understood that its soft voice had to compete with the thunderous roars of the id. Freud broke with the optimism of the philosophes. His awareness of the immense pressures that civilization places on our fragile egos led him to be generally pessimistic about the future.

Unlike Marx, Freud had no vision of utopia. He saw the crude, untamable, and destructive character of human nature as an ever-present obstacle to harmonious social relations. That Freud was hounded out of Vienna by the Nazis just before World War II and his four sisters were later murdered by them simply for being Jewish is a telling footnote to his view of human nature, the power of the irrational, and the fragility of civilization.

SOCIAL THOUGHT: CONFRONTING THE IRRATIONAL AND THE COMPLEXITIES OF MODERN SOCIETY

The end of the nineteenth century and the beginning of the twentieth mark the great age of sociological thought. The leading sociological thinkers of the period all regarded science as the only valid model for correct thinking, and all claimed that their thought rested on a scientific foundation. They maintained that secular and scientific thinkers, not theologians, were best suited to comprehend the human condition; that in our new scientific age Christian dogma seemed implausible and Christian clergy irrelevant. They struggled with some of the crucial problems of modern society: How can society achieve coherence and stability when the customary associations and attachments that characterized village life are ruthlessly dissolved by the rapidly developing industrial-urban-capitalist order, which elevates often selfish individualism over integrative communal ties that had characterized preindustrial society, and when religion no longer unites people? What are the implications of the nonrational for political life? How can people preserve their individuality in a society that is becoming increasingly regimented? In many ways, twentieth-century dictatorships were responses to the dilemmas of modern society analyzed by these social theorists. And twentieth-century dictators would employ these social theorists' insights into group and mass psychology for the purpose of gaining and maintaining power.

Durkheim

Émile Durkheim (1858–1917), a French scholar of Jewish background and heir to Comte's positivism, was an important founder of modern sociology. Like Comte, he considered scientific thought to be the only valid model for modern society. Durkheim tried to show that the essential ingredients of modern times—secularism, rationalism, and individualism—threaten society with disintegration into a disconnected mass of self-seeking, antagonistic individuals. In traditional society, the social order was derived from God, and a person's place and function were assigned by God and determined by birth and custom. However, modern people, skeptical and individualistic, do not accept such restraints. Durkheim wanted to prevent the fragmentation of modern society and the alienation of the individual.

The weakening of those traditional ties that bind the individual to society constituted, for Durkheim, the crisis of modern industrial society. Without collective values and common beliefs, he felt, society was threatened with disintegration and the individual with disorientation. To a Western world intrigued by scientific progress, Durkheim emphasized the spiritual malaise of modern society. Modern people, said Durkheim, suffer from **anomie**—a collapse of values. They do not feel integrated into a collective community and find no purpose in life. In *Suicide* (1897), Durkheim maintained that "the exceptionally high number of voluntary deaths manifests the state of deep disturbances from which civilized societies are suffering and bears witness to its gravity."[25] The high level of boredom, anxiety, and pessimism also evidence the pathology of modern society. Modern people are driven to suicide by intense competition and the disappointment and frustration resulting from unfulfilled expectations and a lack of commitment to moral principles. People must limit their aspirations and exercise discipline over their desires and passions. They must stop wanting more. Religion once spurred people to view restraint and the renunciation of desires as virtues, but it could no longer do so.

Although Durkheim approved of modernity, he noted that modern ways have not brought happiness or satisfaction to the individual. Modern scientific and industrial society requires a new moral system, which would bind the various classes into a cohesive social order and help overcome the feelings of restlessness and dissatisfaction tormenting people. Like Saint-Simon (see Chapter 21), Durkheim called for a rational and secular system of morals to replace Christian dogma, which had lost its power to attract and to bind.

Durkheim focused on a crucial dilemma of modernity. On the one hand, modern urban civilization has provided the individual with unparalleled opportunities for self-development and material improvement. On the other, the breakdown of traditional communal bonds caused by the spread of rationalism and individualism has produced a sense of isolation and alienation. In modern mass society, the individual feels like an outsider, a condition that has been exacerbated by the decline of Christianity. Twentieth-century totalitarian movements sought to integrate these uprooted and alienated souls into new collectives: a proletarian state based on workers' solidarity or a racial state based on ethnic purity and nationalism (see Chapter 29).

Pareto

Like Comte, Vilfredo Pareto (1848–1923), an Italian economist and sociologist, aimed to construct a system of sociology on the model of the physical sciences. His studies led him to conclude that social behavior rests primarily not on reason but rather on nonrational instincts and sentiments. These deeply rooted and essentially changeless feelings are the fundamental elements in human behavior. Although society may change, human nature remains essentially the same. Whoever aims to lead and to influence people must appeal not to logic but to elemental feelings. Most human behavior is nonrational; nonlogical considerations also determine the beliefs that people hold. Like Marx and Freud, Pareto believed that we cannot accept a person's word at face value; we find the real cause of human behavior in human instincts and sentiments. People do not act according to carefully thought-out theories. They act first from nonlogical motivations and then construct a rationalization to justify their behavior. Much of Pareto's work was devoted to studying the nonrational elements of human conduct and the various beliefs invented to give the appearance of rationality to behavior that derives from feeling and instinct.

Pareto divided society into two strata: the elite and the masses. Elites have always existed, said Pareto, because human beings are unequal by nature and because the goods that all people seek cannot be shared equally. Because struggle is a general law of life, elites and masses will exist in all societies. The belief that a democracy constitutes rule by a people is a myth, said Pareto. In actuality, a small group of party leaders controls the political system. Pareto also rejected as naïve Marx's vision of the end of the class struggle under Communism.

In the tradition of Machiavelli, Pareto held that a successful ruling elite must exploit the feelings and impulses of the masses to its own advantage with cunning, and if necessary with violence. Democratic states, he said, delude themselves in thinking that the masses are really influenced by rational argument. A staunch opponent of parliamentary democracy, Pareto predicted that new political leaders would emerge who would master the people through propaganda and force, appealing always to sentiment rather than to reason. To this extent, Pareto was an intellectual forerunner of Fascism, which preached an authoritarian elitism (see Chapter 29). Mussolini praised Pareto and proudly claimed him as a source of inspiration.

Le Bon

Gustave Le Bon (1841–1931), a French social psychologist, concentrated on mass psychology as demonstrated in crowd behavior, a phenomenon of considerable importance in an age of accelerating industrialization and democratization. "The substitution of the unconscious action of crowds for the conscious activity of individuals is one of the principal characteristics of the present age,"[26] Le Bon declared in the preface to *The Crowd* (1895). In the past, said Le Bon, rivalries between monarchs dominated Europe's political stage; "the opinion of the masses scarcely counted, and most frequently did not count at all."[27] But Europe had experienced a great transformation. In this new age, he said, the masses organized in socialist parties, and unions were starting to determine the destinies of nations. Le Bon, who had contempt for democracy, intended his work to be a justification for rule by an authoritarian elite.

Le Bon applied the term *crowd* to a large group of people in which individuality is submerged in the mass and the individual loses control over his or her ideas and emotions. A psychological crowd could be a street mob, a political party, or a labor union. An agglomeration of individuals "presents new characteristics very different from those of the individuals composing it. The sentiments and ideas of all the persons in the gathering take one and the same direction, and their conscious personality vanishes."[28] The crowd acquires a collective mind, in which critical thinking is swamped and "unconscious qualities obtain the upper hand."[29]

Becoming increasingly intolerant and fanatical, the crowd member "descends several rungs in the ladder of civilization. Isolated, he may be a cultivated individual; in a crowd, he is a barbarian—that is, a creature acting by instinct."[30] Crowd behavior demonstrates convincingly that "the part played by the unconscious in all our acts is immense and that played by reason very small."[31] In a contest with aroused emotions, human reason is utterly powerless.

Le Bon also discussed the leaders of crowds and their means of persuasion. "A crowd is a servile flock that is incapable of ever doing without a master," he stressed. Leaders "are more frequently men of action than thinkers"; they are "morbidly nervous, excitable, . . . bordering on madness." Fanatically committed to their beliefs, they do not respond to logical argument. The masses, "always ready to listen to the strong-willed man,"[32] respond to the intensity of the leader's faith.

Both Mussolini and Hitler, who deliberately sought to seduce, manipulate, and dominate the masses, absorbed Le Bon's ideas, which had become commonplace in the early twentieth century. "I don't know how many times I have re-read *Psychologie des Foules* [*The Crowd*]," declared Mussolini. "It is an excellent work to which I frequently refer."[33] Hitler's analysis of the crowd—"sober reasoning determines their thoughts far less than emotion and feeling"[34]—restates many of Le Bon's observations.

Weber

Probably the most prominent social thinker of the age, the German academic Max Weber (1864–1920) was a leading shaper of modern sociology. In Weber's view, Western civilization, unlike the other civilizations of the globe, had virtually eliminated myth, mystery, and magic from its conception of nature and society—the "disenchantment of the world," Weber called it. Most conspicuous in Western science, this process of rationalization, or "calculated action," was also evident in politics, law, and economics. Weber considered Western science to be an attempt to understand and master nature through reason, and Western capitalism an attempt to organize work and production in a rational manner that achieved maximum efficiency. The Western state has a rational written constitution, rationally formulated law, and a bureaucracy of trained government officials who administer the affairs of state according to rational rules and regulations. Justice is not dispensed by wise elders but proceeds from codified law and established procedures. The question of why the West, and not China or India, engaged in this process of rationalization intrigued Weber, and much of his scholarly effort went into answering it.

Weber understood the terrible paradox of reason. Reason accounts for brilliant achievements in science and economic life, but it also despiritualizes life by ruthlessly eliminating centuries-old traditions, denouncing deeply felt religious beliefs as superstition, and regarding human feelings and passions as impediments to clear thinking. While giving people knowledge, the process of disenchantment has shattered the basis for belief in transcendental values; in a thoroughly disenchanted world, life is without ultimate purpose or intense meaning, and the individual is soulless. This is the dilemma of modern individuals, said Weber. Secular rationality is shaping a world in which standards cannot claim ultimate sanction. A disenchanted world contains no inherited truths, no God-given answers to the human being's desperate need for meaning. We are now confronted with an immense and unprecedented burden: how to create for ourselves values that give meaning to life in a world deprived of certainty.

Secular rationality has produced still another awesome problem, said Weber. It has fostered self-liberation, for it enables human beings to overcome illusions and take control of the environment and of themselves, but it is also a means of self-enslavement, for it produces institutions, giant public and corporate bureaucracies, that

Gaetano Mosca

Gaetano Mosca (1858–1941), an Italian social theorist, advanced the view that ruling elites are the basic feature of society. His principal work, *Elements of Political Science*, was first published in 1895; an enlarged third edition was issued in 1923 and later translated under the title *The Ruling Class*. Mosca argued that all societies are characterized by a minority that rules and a majority that is reduced to powerlessness. Members of the ruling minority possess wealth as well as superior intellectual and personal qualities—drive, ambition, and determination—that assist them in maintaining their dominance. Mosca held that the governing classes justify their power and privileges by finding a moral, religious, or legal basis for it, one that claims to rest on universal principles—for example, the will of God or the will of the people. Recently, said Mosca, Darwin's theory has provided a scientific justification for ruling elites which claim that they constitute a higher level in human evolution much superior to the lower classes. Both the rulers and the ruled believe that those in power govern not on the basis of force but on the basis of a moral principle.

Mosca contended that in a democratic society power is still exercised by a small minority. Therefore, the conviction that in a democracy the majority govern is an illusion. Those chosen to serve as representatives of the people in a democratic or socialist society soon transform themselves into a ruling elite determined to preserve and protect their own special interests. Through control of political parties and the press, this minority constitutes the real ruler in a democratic society. But Mosca did hold that in modern democracy the door should remain open for the ruled to enter the ruling class on the basis of ability. Mosca's ideas were used to undermine respect for democracy, particularly by apologists for Fascism.

in their relentless pursuit of efficiency encourage uniformity and depersonalization. Modern officials, said Weber, are emotionally detached. Concerned only with the efficient execution of tasks, they employ reason in a cold and calculating way; human feelings such as compassion and affection are ruled out as hindrances to effectiveness. In the name of efficiency, people are placed in "steel cages"—that is treated impersonally as mere objects—depriving them of their individuality, personal liberty, and humanity.

Like Freud, Weber was aware of the power of the nonrational in social life. One expression of the irrational that he analyzed in considerable depth was the charismatic leader who attracts people by force of personality. Charismatic leaders may be religious prophets, war heroes, or others who possess this extraordinary ability to attract and dominate others. People yearn for charismatic leadership, particularly during times of crisis, when they feel disoriented and helpless. The leader claims a mission—a sacred duty—to lead the people during the crisis. The leader's authority rests on the people's belief in the mission and their faith in the leader's extraordinary abilities that set him apart from ordinary people; a common allegiance to the charismatic leader unites the community. In an era that has seen its share of dictators and demogogues, the question of why people are drawn to the charismatic savior—why they succumb to his authority, and why they alter their lives in order to implement his vision—is of crucial concern to historians and social theorists.

THE MODERNIST MOVEMENT

Breaking with Conventional Modes of Esthetics

At the same time as Freud and social thinkers were breaking with the Enlightenment view of human nature and society, artists and writers sought to liberate the imagination from traditional forms of artistic and literary expression that had shaped European cultural life since the Renaissance. They adhered to Nietzsche's dictum: "What is needed above all is an absolute scepticism toward all inherited concepts."[35] Rejecting both classical and realist models, they subordinated form and objective reality to the inner life—to feelings, imagination, and the creative process. These avant-garde writers and artists found new and creative ways to express the explosive primitive forces within the human psyche that increasingly had become the subject of contemporary thinkers. Their experimentations produced a great cultural revolution, called **modernism**, which still profoundly influences the arts. In some ways, modernism was a continuation of the Romantic Movement, which had dominated European culture in the early nineteenth century. Both movements subjected to searching criticism cultural styles that had been formulated during the Renaissance and had roots in ancient Greece.

Even more than romanticism, modernism aspired to an intense introspection—a heightened awareness of self—and saw the intellect as a barrier to the free expression of elemental human emotions, the wellspring of creativity. Modernist artists and writers abandoned conventional literary and artistic models and experimented with new modes of expression. They liberated the imagination from the restrictions of conventional forms and enabled their audience, readers and viewers alike, to share in the process of creation, often unconscious, and to discover fresh insights into objects, people, and social conditions. They believed that there were further discoveries to be made in the arts, further possibilities of expression, that past masters had not realized. The consequence of their bold venture, wrote the literary critic and historian Irving Howe, was nothing less than the "breakup of the traditional unity and continuity of Western culture."[36]

Like Freud, modernist artists and writers probed beyond surface appearances for a more profound reality hidden in the human psyche. Writers such as Thomas Mann, Marcel Proust, James Joyce, August Strindberg, D. H. Lawrence, Joseph Conrad, and Franz Kafka explored the inner life of the individual and the psychopathology of human relations in order to lay bare the self. They dealt with the predicament of alienated and estranged men and women who rejected the values and customs of their day, and they depicted the anguish of people burdened by guilt, torn by internal conflicts, driven by inner self-destructiveness, and disfigured by moral collapse. Like Freud, several modernist writers explored the dark side of human nature. Besides showing the overwhelming might of the irrational and the seductive power of the primitive and the instinctual, they also broke the silence about sex that had prevailed in Victorian literature.

From the Renaissance through the Enlightenment and into the nineteenth century, Western esthetic standards had been shaped by the conviction that the universe embodied an inherent mathematical order. A corollary of this conception of the outer world as orderly and intelligible was the view that art should imitate reality. According to the sociologist Daniel Bell, from the Renaissance on, art was seen as "a mirror of nature, a representation of life. Knowledge was a reflection of what was 'out there' . . . a copy of what was seen."[37] Since the Renaissance, artists had deliberately made use of laws of perspective and proportion; musicians had used harmonic chords, which brought rhythm and melody into a unified whole; and writers had produced works according to a definite pattern, which included a beginning, middle, and end.

Modernist culture, however, acknowledged no objective reality of space, motion, and time that has the same meaning for all observers. Rather, reality can be grasped in a variety of ways; a multiplicity of frames of reference apply to nature and human experience. Consequently, reality is the way the viewer apprehends it to be through the prism of the imagination. "There is no outer reality," said the modernist German poet Gottfried Benn, but "only human consciousness, constantly building, modifying, rebuilding new worlds out of its own creativity."[38] Modernism

Art of the Late Nineteenth and Twentieth Centuries

During the late nineteenth century, a number of art movements emerged that redefined both the objectives and the techniques of painters, sculptors, architects, and artisans. What set nineteenth-century art apart from works that came before was the realization among artists that they did not need to devote themselves to capturing reality as it was. They began to move away from representational art, pursuing instead a course that would bring them far along the road to abstraction—so far that by the early twentieth century, images bore almost no resemblance to the objects from which they were drawn.

As a point of departure, it is useful to consider the work of Jean François Millet (1814–1875), a French realist who brought scenes from everyday life to his canvas. Like the neoclassicists, Millet aspired to visual accuracy. Nonetheless, his work was innovative, for he did not paint heroic, highly dramatic scenes but rather portrayed peasants and other common people at their usual tasks.

1. Jean François Millet, *The Gleaners*, 1857. (Erich Lessing/Art Resource, N.Y.)

2. Paul Cézanne, *Madame Cézanne in the Conservatory*, c. 1880. (Image copyright © The Metropolitan Museum of Art/Art Resource, N.Y.)

In *The Gleaners* (Figure 1), from 1857, Millet depicts, in a rhythmic composition, three heavy, slow-moving women harvesting a field of wheat. He uses color and light to convey their solid simplicity. In turning to everyday matters and bringing his canvas outside, Millet broke with tradition and set a precedent for the colorists of the later part of the century.

Art movements of the mid- and late nineteenth century include impressionism, a style that began in France and gained popularity both in Europe and in the newest emerging art center, the United States. A host of artists responded to the tenets of the impressionist movement, which heralded changes in color, line, and style. One hallmark of impressionists was their urge to paint *en plein air*, in nature—to take their easels out of the confining studio and set them down in fields, meadows, or anywhere else they could experience nature and put it on canvas, as Millet had done.

3. Georges Seurat, *The Seine at La Grande Jatte*, 1888. (World History Archive/Image Asset Management Ltd./Alamy Limited.)

Art historians describe the impressionist movement as a revolution in color, in part because impressionist painters did not laboriously mix their paints on palettes but rather mixed colors on the canvas itself. But the impressionist movement, and the postimpressionists who followed, also heralded a revolution in line, in dimension, and in painting itself. What impressionists had in common was the desire to record realistically their immediate visual impression of a subject—for example, how a landscape appeared in a fleeting moment when light and atmosphere randomly coalesced.

The artists who followed are loosely called postimpressionists. Generally speaking, the term *postimpressionist* can be applied to almost any artist who worked after the 1880s. Usually, the artist had an impressionist phase and then experimented further not only with color but with form and space as well.

The paintings of Paul Cézanne (1839–1906) are some of the finest work of the postimpressionist era. He is best known for still lifes, but his portraits are also important reminders of the developments in the visual arts during the nineteenth century. The portrait of his wife, *Madame Cézanne in the Conservatory* (c. 1880) (Figure 2),

illustrates many of the qualities of a postimpressionist work: overlapping brush strokes create depth and volume, and their rhythmic patterning adds texture to the flat canvas. Cézanne seems to be working at once in both a realistic and an impressionist genre. The face of the subject is rendered realistically, as are the tree behind her and some other elements of the composition. But her hands, her dress, and most aspects of the background are impressionistic. This blending of styles and the experimentation with different vantage points and different elements that go into the overall composition demonstrate the approach tried by many artists of this period.

In his brief career, Georges Seurat (1859–1891) was able to take the lessons of the impressionists and give them a new twist. He too shared the impressionists' love of color and worked at using color in a wholly new way. Called pointillism, the technique used by Seurat required meticulous brush control and a deep understanding of the mechanics of color. One of Seurat's pointillist works, *The Seine at La Grande Jatte* (1888) (Figure 3) illustrates the care with which the artist rendered his images.

Typically, a painting by Seurat, which more often than not was preceded by a great many

4. Vincent van Gogh, *Self-Portrait*, 1889. (The Gallery Collection/Corbis.)

preliminary sketches and drawings, comprises literally millions of tiny individual dots and strokes of pure color applied in such a way that the viewer's eye blends them into their final form. Thus, pointillism foreshadows the digitization used in electronic images today.

Seurat's contemporary, Vincent van Gogh (1853–1890), is one of the best-known painters. The subject of biography, music, and endless fascination, van Gogh could be classified as either a postimpressionist or an expressionist, although probably neither term would have found favor with the artist himself. Van Gogh's career spanned only ten years—even less time than that of Seurat—and some art historians call him the greatest Dutch artist since Vermeer and other painters of the seventeenth century.

Van Gogh's strengths lie in his use of color and his understanding of the medium of oil paint. His thickly applied brush strokes add light and shadow to his luminous canvases. He did not hesitate to depart from realism, to distort shape and exaggerate color to suggest energy and motion and to express feeling.

He painted a whole gamut of subjects from still lifes, to landscapes, to portraits and self-portraits. He was particularly fascinated by the human face. He said that there was something in the eyes—the soul, the inner life—whether those of a beggar or a streetwalker, that was more beautiful than a cathedral. His aim was to capture the human essence in such pictures.

In *Self-Portrait* (1889) (Figure 4), he scrutinized his own face one more time, shortly before his

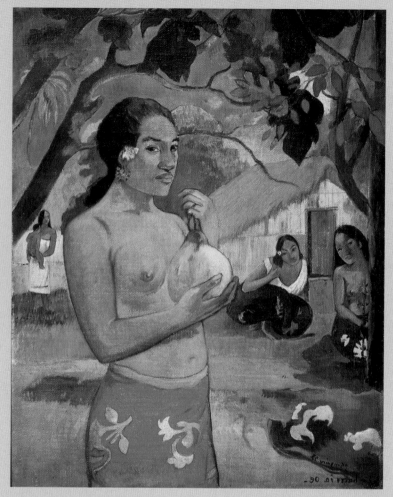

5. Paul Gauguin, *Ea Haere ia oe* (*Where Are You Going?*) (Scala/Art Resource, N.Y.)

suicide. It is a stark testament to a life tormented by mental illness yet driven to sublime heights of creative expression.

Among the other *-isms* that defined art in the late nineteenth century was primitivism, a movement "discovered" by progressive artists such as Pablo Picasso. Picasso looked to various sources for his inspiration, including Africa and the Far East. He also championed other artists who worked outside the mainstream.

In line with this tendency was the work of Paul Gauguin (1848–1903), who renounced not only impressionism but also the entire Western notion that a painter should reproduce the physical world as it actually appears. In 1891, attempting to escape what he viewed as a corrupt civilization, Gauguin abandoned France for the island of Tahiti, in the South Pacific. During his first two years in Tahiti, Gauguin painted sixty-six canvases, one of which was *Ea Haere ia oe* (*Where Are You Going?*) (Figure 5). In the two-dimensionality, intentional disproportion, rich coloration, and ambiguity of content of this painting, we see an attempt to revert to the pristine viewpoint of primitivism, in which the artist's work is predominated more by imagination and feeling than by the restraints of sensory perception.

6. Pablo Picasso, *Les Demoiselles d'Avignon*, 1907.

In the twentieth century, no single style prevailed. It was a period of great experimentation and great changes. One of the most important movements of the early decades was abstraction, more easily defined visually than in words. Pablo Picasso (1881–1974) was one of the champions of the abstract movement. His *Les Demoiselles d'Avignon* (1907) (Figure 6) redefines the female form. This is not Boucher's *Venus*. Picasso's female forms are reductive—angular distortions of female bodies—and they hint at a number of cultural influences. While some may see suggestions of the classical in the forms of the three women to the left, there are also echoes of African sculpture; indeed, Picasso was influenced by both. But he was also inventive and sophisticated. His work reduces the visual to its most abstract elements. Changes in his style over his long and productive career

indicate his receptiveness to influences from non-Western cultures as well as from his own Western heritage.

The genre of abstraction that Picasso pioneered is called *cubism*. Among the host of cubist followers, many developed their own distinct cubist subcategories. Marc Chagall (1887–1985), a Russian painter whose works often strongly reflected his Jewish roots, worked in a cubist style that combined fantasy and reality. In *The Fiddler* (1911) (Figure 7), he blends elements of Russian and Jewish folktales with cubist renderings of scenes from everyday life.

By World War I, avant-garde artists had experimented with a multitude of abstract styles. At the Armory Show in New York City in 1913, many abstract painters made their debut on the North American continent. Generally favorably received by the art community (though not as welcomed by the average viewer), abstract painting began to gain a foothold outside Europe. Given the disfavor with which the National Socialists in Germany viewed nonrepresentational art, it was a good thing that America was willing to welcome avant-garde artists and their work.

In 1939, the Nazis—either by auction or by destruction—got rid of many of the most famous abstract works in German museums. Some pieces were sold to museums or collectors in other European cities, only to fall victim once again to the strict anti-abstract sentiments of the Nazis as World War II progressed.

During and after World War II, art continued to be a compendium of various themes and movements. Not every artist worked in the abstract; some preferred to stick to realism. Still others painted in a style that came to be known as abstract expressionism.

The art of Wassily Kandinsky (1866–1944), a Russian who joined a group of avant-garde painters in Munich in 1896, summarizes the path taken by many abstract artists whose careers spanned both world wars. Between 1910 and 1914, Kandinsky painted a series of *Improvisations* and *Compositions* in which he

7. Marc Chagall, *The Fiddler*, 1911. (Erich Lessing/Art Resource, N.Y./© 2011 Artists Rights Society [ARS], New York/ADAGP, Paris.)

8. Wassily Kandinsky, *Composition Number 7*, 1913 (oil on canvas). (© Tretyakov Gallery, Moscow, Russia, © DACS/The Bridgeman Art Library/© 2011 Artists Rights Society [ARS], New York/ADAGP, Paris.)

9. Edward Hopper, *Hotel Lobby*, 1943. (Heritage Image Partnership Ltd./Alamy Limited.)

gradually abandoned representational subject matter, thus becoming the first abstract painter. In *Composition Number 7* (1913) (Figure 8), Kandinsky has removed all traces of the physical world, creating a nonobjective art that bears no resemblance to the natural world. In declaring that he "painted . . . subconsciously in a state of strong inner tension," Kandinsky explicitly expressed a distinguishing quality of modern Western art: the artist's private inner experience of the world.

Not all art of the twentieth century was abstract. Some of the best representational art of any era belongs to this period. This is exemplified by the work of the American painter Edward Hopper (1882–1967). His *Hotel Lobby* (1943) (Figure 9) shows the reality of loneliness. It placed Hopper in the school of social realists, who painted true-to-life images of the world around them. Hopper depicted not cathedrals or temples but diners, barber shops, and movie theaters, using light and shadow as skillfully as Rembrandt.

is concerned less with the object itself than with how the artist transforms it, with the sensations that an object evokes in the artist's inner being, and with the meaning that the artist's imagination imposes on reality. "Conscientious and exact imitation of nature does not create a work of art," wrote Emil Nolde, a German expressionist painter. "A work becomes a work of art when one re-evaluates the values of nature and adds one's own spirituality."[39] Bell makes this point in reference to painting.

> Modernism . . . denies the primacy of an outside reality, as given. It seeks either to rearrange that reality, or to retreat to the self's interior, to private experience as the source of its concerns and aesthetic preoccupations. . . . There is an emphasis on the self as the touchstone of understanding and on the activity of the knower rather than the character of the object as the source of knowledge. . . . Thus one discerns the intentions of modern painting . . . to break up ordered space . . . to bridge the distance between object and spectator, to "thrust" itself on the viewer and establish itself immediately by impact.[40]

Dispensing with conventional forms of esthetics, which stressed structure and coherence, modernism propelled the arts onto uncharted seas. Modernists abandoned the efforts of realists and naturalists to produce a clinical and objective description of the external world; instead they probed subjective views and visions and the inner world of the unconscious, searching within its primitive layer for an authentic inner self. Recoiling from the middle-class, industrial civilization, which prized rationalism, organization, clarity, stability, and definite norms and values, modernist writers and artists were fascinated by the bizarre, the mysterious, the unpredictable, the primitive, the irrational, and the formless. They gave expression to behavior driven by the unconscious and the human being's capacity to act absurdly and cruelly—the dark side of human nature.

Writers experimented with new techniques to convey the intense struggle between the conscious and the unconscious and to connote the aberrations and complexities of human personality and the irrationality and absurdity of human behavior.

In particular, they devised a new way, the **stream of consciousness**, to reveal the mind's every level—both conscious reflection and unconscious strivings—and to capture how thought is punctuated by spontaneous outbursts, disconnected assertions, random memories, undifferentiated and freely associated words and sounds, hidden desires, and persistent fantasies. The stream of consciousness is not narrated memory but a flow of feelings and thoughts in which the boundary between consciousness and unconsciousness is blurred. It attempts to reveal the mystery and complexity of the inner person, the hidden drives, desires, torments, and obsessions that intrigued Freud. This introspective turn was also expressed through *interior monologue,* in which a character's meandering and disconnected comments progressively penetrate deep into the unconscious, disclosing buried fears and torments.

Modernist writers also made use of symbols that convey larger implications about the human condition. A bird in a cage can represent entrapment and a bird spreading its wings symbolizes self-actualization. A fog can stand for confusion, a jungle for primal instincts, the ocean for escape and freedom, and the moon romantic and sexual notions.

Modern artists deliberately plunged into the world of the unconscious in search of the instinctual, the fantastic, the primitive, and the mysterious, which they believed yielded a truth higher than that given by analytical thought. They embarked on a voyage into the mind's interior in the hopes of finding stimulants that would spark the creative imagination. Composers engaged in open revolt against the conventional rules and standards of musical composition. For example, the Austrian composer Arnold Schönberg (1874–1951) purposefully abandoned traditional scale and harmonic chords to produce atonal music that "seeks to express all that swells in us subconsciously like a dream."[41] The Russian composer Igor Stravinsky (1882–1971) experimented with both atonality and primitive rhythms. When Stravinsky's ballet *The Rite of Spring* was performed in Paris in 1913, the theater audience rioted to protest the composition's break with tonality, its use of primitive, jazz-like rhythms, and its theme of ritual sacrifice.

The modernist movement, which began near the end of the nineteenth century, was in full

THE STARRY NIGHT **(1889), BY VINCENT VAN GOGH.** Van Gogh experienced wide mood swings—from extreme agitation to melancholy. His tumultuous temperament found expression in his paintings. The *Starry Night* conveys van Gogh's impression of a night sky. (Digital Image © The Museum of Modern Art/Licensed by SCALA/Art Resource, N.Y.).

bloom before World War I and would continue to flower in the postwar world. Probably the clearest expression of the modernist viewpoint is found in art.

Modern Art

In the late nineteenth century, artists began to turn away from the standards that had characterized art since the Renaissance. Increasingly, artists sought to penetrate the deepest recesses of the unconscious, which they saw as the source of creativity and the abode of a higher truth. Drawing inspiration from dreams, nightmares, and powerful emotions, they often represented the world in a startling manner that deviated from the Renaissance's search for precise form or the ideal. Paul Klee (1879–1940), a prominent twentieth-century artist, described modern art as

follows: "Each [artist] should follow where the pulse of his own heart leads. . . . Our pounding heart drives us down, deep down to the source of all. What springs from this source, whether it may be called dream, idea or phantasy—must be taken seriously."[42]

Between 1909 and 1914, a new style, called *cubism*, was developed by Pablo Picasso (1881–1973) and Georges Braque (1882–1963). They explored the interplay between the flat world of the canvas and the three-dimensional world of visual perception, to paint a reality deeper than what the eye sees at first glance. Cubist art presents objects from multiple viewpoints simultaneously. The numerous fragmentary images of cubist art make one aware of the complex experience of seeing. One art historian describes cubism as follows: "The cubist is not interested in usual representational standards. It is as if he were walking around the object he is analyzing, as one is free

***Street, Berlin* (1913), by Ernst Ludwig Kirchner.** This work is representative of Expressionism, an art style that emerged in Germany prior to World War I. Expressionists sought to break with both social conventions and academic standards that stifled personal expression in life and art. For them, a work of art should express the artist's inner voice, the intense feelings elicited by objects and events. (Digital Image © The Museum of Modern Art/Licensed by SCALA/Art Resource, N.Y.)

to walk around a piece of sculpture for successive views. But he must represent all these views at once."[43] The cubists' effort to depict something from multiple perspectives rather than from a single point in space and their need to deliberately deform objects in order to achieve this effect mark a radical break with artistic conventions.

Throughout the period 1890 to 1914, avant-garde artists were deemphasizing subject matter. It is not surprising that some artists, such as Piet Mondrian (1872–1944) and Wassily Kandinsky (1866–1944), finally created abstract art, a non-objective art totally devoid of reference to the visible world. In declaring that he "painted . . . subconsciously in a state of strong inner tension,"[44] Kandinsky explicitly expressed a distinguishing quality of modern Western art: the artist's private inner experience of the world.

The revolution in art that took place near the turn of the twentieth century is reverberating still. These masters of modern art continue to inspire with their passion and vision. By breaking with the Renaissance view of the world as inherently orderly and rational and by stressing the power of the imagination, modern artists opened up new possibilities for artistic expression. They also exemplified the growing power and appeal of the nonrational in European life.

MODERN PHYSICS

Until the closing years of the nineteenth century, the view of the universe held by the Western mind was based mainly on the classical physics of Isaac Newton (1642–1727). This view included the following principles: (1) Time, space, and matter are objective realities, existing independently of the observer. (2) The universe is a giant machine whose parts obey strict laws of cause and effect. (3) The atom, indivisible and solid, is the basic unit of matter. (4) Heated bodies emit radiation in continuous waves. (5) Through further investigation, it will be possible to gain complete knowledge of the physical universe. Between the 1890s and the 1920s, this view of the universe was shattered by a second scientific revolution.

The discovery of X-rays by Wilhelm Konrad Roentgen in 1895, of radioactivity by Henri Bequerel in 1896, and of the electron by J. J. Thomson in 1897 led scientists to abandon the concept of the atom as a solid and indivisible particle. Rather than resembling a billiard ball, they said, the atom consists of a nucleus of tightly packed protons, separated from orbiting electrons by empty space.

In 1900, Max Planck, a German physicist, proposed the quantum theory, which holds that a heated body radiates energy not in a continuous unbroken stream, as had been believed, but in intermittent spurts, or jumps, called quanta. Planck's theory of discontinuity in energy radiation challenged a cardinal principle of

***Ascet* (1903), by Pablo Picasso.** This depiction of a gaunt old man conveys a sorrowful if not tragic mood. (PAINTING/Alamy Limited.)

soon observed that radioactive atoms throw off particles and transform themselves from atoms of one element into atoms of an entirely different element. But the transformation of a single atom in a mass of radioactive material could not be predicted according to inexorable laws of cause and effect. For example, it is known that over a period of 1,620 years half the atoms of the element radium decay and transform into atoms of another element. It is impossible, however, to know when a particular atom in a lump of radium will undergo this transformation. Scientists can make accurate predictions only about the behavior of an aggregate of radium atoms. The transformation of any given radium atom is the result of random chance rather than of any known physical law. The fact that we cannot predict when a particular radioactive atom will decay calls into question the notion of classical physics that physical nature proceeds in an orderly fashion in accordance with strict laws of cause and effect.

Newtonian physics says that, given certain conditions, we can predict what will follow. For example, if an airplane is flying north at four

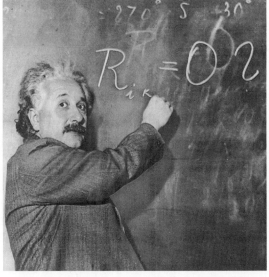

Albert Einstein (1879–1955), A Principal Architect of Modern Physics. Forced to flee Nazi Germany, Einstein became a U.S. citizen. He was appointed to the Institute for Advanced Study at Princeton, New Jersey. (AP Photos.)

classical physics: that action in nature was strictly continuous.

In 1905, Albert Einstein, a German-Swiss physicist of Jewish lineage, substantiated and elaborated Planck's theory by suggesting that all forms of radiant energy—light, heat, X-rays—move through space in discontinuous packets of energy. Then, in 1913, Niels Bohr, a Danish scientist, applied Planck's theory of energy quanta to the interior of the atom and discovered that the Newtonian laws of motion could not fully explain what happens to electrons orbiting an atomic nucleus.

As physicists explored the behavior of the atom further, it became apparent that its nature was fundamentally elusive and unpredictable. They hundred miles per hour, we can predict its exact position two hours from now, assuming that the plane does not alter its course or speed. Quantum mechanics teaches that in the subatomic realm we cannot predict with certainty what will take place; we can only say that, given certain conditions, it is probable that a certain event will follow. This principle of uncertainty was developed in 1927 by the German scientist Werner Heisenberg, who showed that it is impossible to determine at one and the same time both an electron's precise speed and its position. This means that the law of cause and effect does not apply to elementary particles such as electrons. We cannot describe an electron in terms of absolute certainties. In the small-scale world of the electron, we enter a universe of uncertainty, probability, and statistical relationships. No improvement in measurement techniques will dispel this element of chance and provide us with complete knowledge of the universe.

Einstein himself could not accept a core principle of modern physics—that complete comprehension of reality was unattainable. Nevertheless, his theory of relativity was instrumental in shaping modern physics, for it altered classical conceptions of space and time. Newtonian physics had viewed space as a distinct physical reality, a stationary and motionless medium through which light traveled and matter moved. Time was deemed to be a fixed and rigid framework, the same for all observers and existing independently of human experience. For Einstein, however, neither space nor time had an independent existence, and neither could be divorced from human experience. When asked to explain briefly the essentials of relativity, Einstein replied: "It was formerly believed that if all material things disappeared out of the universe, time and space would be left. According to the relativity theory, however, time and space disappear together with the things."[45]

Contrary to all previous thinking, relativity theory holds that time differs for two observers traveling at different speeds. Imagine twin brothers involved in space exploration, one as an astronaut, the other as a rocket designer who never leaves earth. The astronaut takes off in the most advanced spaceship yet constructed, one that achieves a speed close to the maximum attainable in our universe—the speed of light. After traveling several trillion miles, the spaceship turns around and returns to earth. According to the experience of the ship's occupant, the whole trip took about two years. But when the astronaut lands on earth, he finds totally changed conditions. For one thing, his brother has long since died, for according to earth's calendars some two hundred years have elapsed since the rocket ship set out on its journey. Such an occurrence seemed to defy all commonsense experience, yet experiments supported Einstein's claims.

Motion, too, is relative. The only way we can describe the motion of one body is to compare it with another moving body. This means that there is no motionless, absolute, fixed frame of reference anywhere in the universe.

In his famous equation, $E=mc^2$, Einstein showed that matter and energy are not separate categories but two different expressions of the same physical entity. The source of energy is matter, and the source of matter is energy. Tiny quantities of matter could be transformed into staggering amounts of energy. The atomic age was dawning.

The discoveries of modern physics transformed the world of classical physics. Whereas nature had been regarded as something outside the individual—an objective reality existing independently of ourselves—modern physics teaches that our position in space and time determines what we mean by reality and that our very presence affects reality itself. When we observe a particle with our measuring instruments, we are interfering with it, knocking it off its course; we are participating in reality. Nor is nature fully knowable, as the classical physics of Newton had presumed. Uncertainty, probability, and even mystery are inherent in the universe.

We have not yet felt the full impact of modern physics, but there is no doubt that it has been part of a revolution in human perceptions. That we cannot fully comprehend nature must inevitably make us less certain about our theories of human nature, government, history, and morality. That scientists must qualify and avoid absolutes has no doubt made us more cautious and tentative in framing conclusions about the individual and society. Like Darwin's theory of human origins, Freud's theory of human nature, and the transformation of classical space by modern artists, the modifications of the Newtonian picture by modern physicists contributed to the sense of uncertainty and disorientation that characterized the twentieth century.

THE ENLIGHTENMENT TRADITION IN DISARRAY

Most nineteenth-century thinkers carried forward the spirit of the Enlightenment, particularly in its emphasis on science and its concern for individual liberty and social reform. In the tradition of the philosophes, nineteenth-century thinkers regarded science as humanity's greatest achievement and believed that through reason society could be reformed. The spread of parliamentary government and the extension of education, along with the many advances in science and technology, seemed to confirm the belief of the philosophes in humanity's future progress.

But at the same time, the Enlightenment tradition was being undermined. In the early nineteenth century, the romantics revolted against the Enlightenment's rational-scientific spirit in favor of human will and feelings. Romantic nationalists valued the collective soul of the nation—ancient traditions rooted in a hoary and dateless past—over reason and individual freedom. Conservatives emphasized the limitations of reason and attacked the political agenda of the Enlightenment and the French Revolution.

In the closing decades of the nineteenth century, the Enlightenment tradition was challenged by Social Darwinists, who glorified violence and saw conflict between individuals and between nations as a law of nature and the avenue to progress. They considered domination by domestic elites and powerful states to be a right of nature beyond good and evil, and they castigated humanitarianism as weakness. Orthodox Marxists continued to teach that conflict between the proletariat and the industrial bourgeoisie was necessary for humanity's progress. Echoing Sorel, several thinkers trumpeted the use of force in social and political controversies. A number of thinkers, rejecting the Enlightenment view of people as fundamentally rational, held that subconscious drives and impulses govern human behavior more than reason

does. If this is so, then the individual is not essentially autonomous, master of his or her own self. Several of these thinkers urged celebrating and extolling the irrational, which they regarded as the true essence of human beings and life. They glorified an irrational vitality, or Nietzsche's will to power, which transcended considerations of good and evil. "I have always considered myself a voice of what I believe to be a greater renaissance—the revolt of the soul against the intellect—now beginning in the world," wrote the Irish poet William Butler Yeats.[46] German advocates of "life philosophy" explicitly called the mind the enemy of the soul.

Even theorists who studied the individual and society in a scientific way pointed out that below a surface of rationality lies a substratum of irrationality, which constitutes a deeper reality. The conviction was growing that reason was a puny instrument in comparison with the volcanic strength of nonrational impulses, that these impulses pushed people toward destructive behavior and made political life precarious, and that the nonrational did not bend very much to education. The Enlightenment's image of the autonomous individual who makes rational decisions after weighing the choices (a fundamental premise of liberalism and democracy) no longer seemed tenable. Often the individual was not the master of his or her own person; human freedom was limited by human nature.

Liberalism was also undermined by theorists who rejected the idea of natural rights. The view that all individuals are born with inalienable rights had provided the philosophical basis of classical liberalism. It was now argued, however, that natural rights were not a law of nature or a higher truth; rather, they were simply a human creation, a product of a specific set of circumstances at a particular stage in history, notably the emergence of the bourgeoisie. Could commitment to parliamentary government, the rule of law, and other liberal-democratic institutions and practices survive this assault on the core principle of liberalism?

Other theorists argued that ideas of right, truth, and justice do not have an independent value but are merely tools used by elites in their struggle to gain and maintain power. Opponents of liberalism and democracy utilized the theory of elites advanced by Pareto, as well as the new stress on human irrationality, as proof that the masses were incapable of self-government and that they had to be led by their betters. Many intellectuals of the Right employed the new social theories to devalue the individualist and rational bases of liberal democracy bequeathed by the Enlightenment.

A fundamental feature of European civilization was the conviction that the universe contained self-evident moral norms and that obedience to these laws promoted the good life. For Christians these moral imperatives were ordained by God and revealed to human beings. The philosophes, like the ancient Greeks, maintained that universal moral standards did indeed exist but that they were ascertained by reason, not by revelation. In the late nineteenth century, several thinkers, particularly Nietzsche, proclaimed that no such universal standards existed, that the foundational principles of religion and ethics have no ultimate validity. Could the Enlightenment's vision of a more humane and peaceful future be realized in a world where moral values had lost their authority, when neither religion nor reason could demonstrate their certainty?

At the beginning of the twentieth century, the dominant mood remained that of confidence in Europe's future progress and in the values of European civilization. However, certain disquieting trends were already evident; they would grow to crisis proportions in succeeding decades. Although few people may have realized it, the Enlightenment tradition was in disarray.

The thinkers of the Enlightenment believed in an orderly, machinelike universe; the operation of natural law and natural rights in the social world; objective rules that gave form and structure to artistic productions; the essential rationality and goodness of the individual; and science and technology as instruments of progress. This coherent worldview, which had produced an attitude of certainty, security, and optimism, was in the process of dissolution by the early twentieth century. The commonsense Newtonian picture of the physical universe, with its inexorable laws of cause and effect, was fundamentally altered; the belief in natural rights and objective standards governing morality was undermined; and rules and modes of expression that were at the very heart of Western esthetics were abandoned. Confidence in human rationality and goodness weakened. Furthermore, science and technology were accused of forging a mechanical, bureaucratic, and materialistic world that stifled intuition and feelings, thereby diminishing the self. To redeem the self, some thinkers urged a heroic struggle, which was easily channeled into primitive nationalism and martial crusades. They romanticized violence as a release of elemental and instinctual forces that liberated the human personality from unhealthy constraints imposed by traditional morality. Thus, the radical attack on the moral and intellectual values of the Enlightenment, as well as on liberalism and democracy, included the denunciation of reason, the exaltation of force, a quest for the heroic, and a yearning for a new authority. This critique constitutes the intellectual background of the Fascist movements that emerged after World War I. Holding the Enlightenment tradition in contempt and fascinated by power and violence, many people, including intellectuals, would exalt Fascist ideas and lionize Fascist leaders.

In the early twentieth century, then, the universe no longer seemed an orderly system, an intelligible whole; it seemed something fundamentally inexplicable. Human nature, too, seemed intrinsically unfathomable and problematic. To the question "Who is man?" Greek philosophers, medieval scholastics, Renaissance humanists, and eighteenth-century philosophes had provided a coherent and intelligible answer. By the early twentieth century, the old spiritual and intellectual certainties were rapidly eroding, and Western intellectuals no longer possessed a clear idea of who the human being was. Individuals had become strangers to themselves, and life seemed devoid of an overriding purpose. Nietzsche sensed this.

Disintegration characterizes this time, and thus uncertainty: nothing stands firmly on its feet or on a hard faith in itself; one lives for tomorrow as the day after tomorrow is dubious. Everything on our way is slippery and dangerous, and the ice that still supports us has become thin: all of us feel the warm, uncanny breath of the thawing wind; where we still walk, soon no one will be able to walk.[47]

This radical new disorientation led some intellectuals to feel alienated from Western civilization and even hostile toward it. At the beginning of the twentieth century, says the Dutch historian Jan Romein, "European man, who only half a century earlier had believed he was about to embrace an almost totally safe existence, and paradoxically enough did so in many ways, found himself before the dark gate of uncertainty."[48]

When the new century began, most Europeans were optimistic about the future, some even holding that European civilization was on the threshold of a golden age. Few suspected that European civilization would soon be gripped by a crisis that threatened its very survival. The powerful forces of irrationalism, which had been celebrated by Nietzsche, analyzed by Freud, and creatively expressed in modernist culture, would erupt with devastating fury in twentieth-century political life, particularly in the form of extreme nationalism and racism, which extolled violence. Disoriented and disillusioned people searching for new certainties and values would turn to political ideologies that openly rejected reason, lauded war, and scorned the inviolability of the human person. Dictators, utilizing the insights into the unconscious and the nonrational offered by Freud and social theorists, succeeded in manipulating the minds of people to an unprecedented degree.

These currents began to form at the end of the nineteenth century, but World War I brought them together in a tidal wave. World War I accentuated the questioning of established norms and the dissolution of Enlightenment certainties and caused many people to regard Western civilization as dying and beyond recovery. The war not only exacerbated the spiritual crisis of the preceding generation but also shattered Europe's political and social order. It gave birth to totalitarian ideologies that nearly obliterated the legacy of the Enlightenment. The world wars of the twentieth century, with their millions of dead and mutilated, and the totalitarian experiments, which trampled on human dignity, bore out Nietzsche's warning that in a nihilistic world all is permitted.

❖   ❖   ❖

NOTES

1. Friedrich Nietzsche, *Twilight of the Idols* and *The Anti-Christ,* trans. R. J. Hollingdale (New York: Penguin, 1972), 117–118.

2. Friedrich Nietzsche, *The Will to Power,* trans. Walter Kaufmann and R. J. Hollingdale, ed. Walter Kaufmann (New York: Vintage Books, 1968), 458–459.

3. Ibid., 383–384.

4. Friedrich Nietzsche, *The Genealogy of Morals,* Essay I, sec. 13 (New York: Modern Library, 1954), 656.

5. Quoted in R. J. Hollingdale, *Nietzsche* (London: Routledge and Kegan Paul, 1973), 82.

6. Nietzsche, *Will to Power,* 397.

7. Ibid., 518.

8. Nietzsche, *Anti-Christ,* 116.

9. Nietzsche, *Will to Power,* 386.

10. Janko Lavrin, *Nietzsche* (New York: Charles Scribner's Sons, 1971), 113.

11. Fyodor Dostoevsky, *Notes from Underground and The Grand Inquisitor,* trans. Ralph E. Matlaw (New York: Dutton, 1960), 20, 23.

12. Ibid., 25.

13. Quoted in Peter Gay, *Freud: A Life for Our Time* (New York: Norton, 1988), xvii.

14. Sigmund Freud, *The Future of an Illusion,* trans. W. D. Robeson-Scott, rev. James Strachey (Garden City, N.Y.: Doubleday, 1964), 87.

15. Sigmund Freud, *A General Introduction to Psychoanalysis,* trans. Joan Riviere (Garden City, N.Y.: Garden City Publishing, 1943), 252.

16. Sigmund Freud, "Delusions and Dreams in Jensen's 'Gradiva,'" trans. James Strachey, in *The Standard Edition of the Complete Psychological Work of Sigmund Freud,* 2nd ed. (London: Hogarth Press, 1959), 9:8.

17. Sigmund Freud, "An Autobiographical Study," ibid., 20:60.

18. Sigmund Freud, *Civilization and Its Discontents* (New York: Norton, 1961), 62.

19. Ibid., 58.

20. Ibid.

21. Ibid., 59.

22. Ibid., 61.

23. Ibid., 59.

24. Ibid., 69.

25. Émile Durkheim, *Suicide: A Study in Sociology*, trans. John Spaulding and George Simpson (New York: Free Press, 1951), 391.

26. Gustave Le Bon, *The Crowd: A Study of the Popular Mind* (New York: Viking, 1960), 3.

27. Ibid., 14–15.

28. Ibid., 23.

29. Ibid., 30.

30. Ibid., 32.

31. Ibid., 7.

32. Ibid., 118.

33. Quoted in Robert A. Nye, *The Origin of Crowd Psychology* (Beverly Hills, Calif.: Sage, 1975), 178.

34. Adolf Hitler, *Mein Kampf*, translated by Ralph Manheim (Boston, M. A.: Houghton Mifflin, 1962), 183.

35. Quoted in Christopher Butler, *Early Modernism: Literature, Music, and Painting in Europe, 1900–1916* (New York: Oxford University Press, 1994), 2.

36. Irving Howe, ed., *The Idea of the Modern in Literature and the Arts* (New York: Horizon Press, 1967), 16.

37. Daniel Bell, *The Cultural Contradictions of Capitalism* (New York: Basic Books, 1976), 110.

38. Quoted in Howe, *Idea of the Modern*, 15.

39. Excerpted in Herschel B. Chipp, ed., *Theories of Modern Art* (Berkeley: University of California Press, 1968), 146.

40. Bell, *Cultural Contradictions*, 110, 112.

41. Excerpted in Piero Weiss and Richard Taruskin, eds., *Music in the Western World: A History in Documents* (New York: Schirmer Books, 1984), 428.

42. Paul Klee, *On Modern Art*, trans. Paul Findlay (London: Faber and Faber, 1948), 51.

43. John Canaday, *Mainstreams of Modern Art* (New York: Holt, 1961), 458.

44. Quoted in G. H. Hamilton, *Painting and Sculpture in Europe, 1880–1940* (Baltimore: Penguin Books, 1967), 133.

45. Quoted in A. E. E. McKenzie, *The Major Achievements of Science* (New York: Cambridge University Press, 1960), 1:310.

46. Quoted in Roland N. Stromberg, *Redemption by War* (Lawrence: Regents Press of Kansas, 1982), 65.

47. Nietzsche, *Will to Power*, 40.

48. Jan Romein, *The Watershed of Two Eras*, trans. Arnold J. Pomerans (Middletown, Conn.: Wesleyan University Press, 1978), 658.

Part Six

World Wars and Totalitarianism: The West in Crisis

1914–1945

1910

1920

1930

1940

Politics and Society

World War I (1914–1918)
United States declares war on Germany (1917)
Bolshevik Revolution in Russia (1917)
Wilson announces his Fourteen Points (1918)
Treaty of Versailles (1919)

Mussolini seizes power in Italy (1922)
First Five-Year Plan starts rapid industrialization in the Soviet Union (1928)
Forced collectivization of agriculture in the Soviet Union (1929)
Start of the Great Depression (1929)

Hitler becomes chancellor of Germany (1933)
Hitler sends troops into the Rhineland (1936)
Rome–Berlin Axis (1936)
Stalin orders mass purges in the Soviet Union (1936–1938)
Spanish Civil War (1936–1939)
Franco establishes a dictatorship in Spain (1939)
Nazi–Soviet Non-Aggression Pact (1939)
German troops invade Poland: World War II begins (1939)

Germany invades Belgium, Holland, Luxembourg, and France (1940)
Japan attacks Pearl Harbor: United States enters war against Japan and Germany (1941)
War in Europe ends (1945)
United States drops atomic bombs on Japan; Japan surrenders (1945)

Thought and Culture

Bohr: Quantum theory of atomic structure (1913)
Stravinsky, *The Rite of Spring* (1913)
Pareto, *Treatise on General Sociology* (1916)
Spengler, *The Decline of the West* (1918, 1922)
Dadaism in art (1915–1924)
Barth, *The Epistle to the Romans* (1919)

Wittgenstein, *Tractatus Logico-Philosophicus* (1921–1922)
Eliot, *The Waste Land* (1922)
Cassirer, *The Philosophy of Symbolic Forms* (1923–1929)
Mann, *The Magic Mountain* (1924)
Surrealism in art (c. 1925)
Hitler, *Mein Kampf* (1925–1926)
Hemingway, *The Sun Also Rises* (1926)
Benda, *The Treason of the Intellectuals* (1927)
Heidegger, *Being and Time* (1927)
Whitehead, *Process and Reality* (1927–1928)
Lawrence, *Lady Chatterley's Lover* (1928)
Remarque, *All Quiet on the Western Front* (1929)

Freud, *Civilization and Its Discontents* (1930)
Ortega y Gasset, *The Revolt of the Masses* (1930)
Jaspers, *Man in the Modern Age* (1930)
Jung, *Modern Man in Search of a Soul* (1933)
Toynbee, *A Study of History* (1934–1961)
Keynes, *The General Theory of Employment, Interest, and Money* (1936)
Steinbeck, *The Grapes of Wrath* (1939)

Hemingway, *For Whom the Bell Tolls* (1940)
Koestler, *Darkness at Noon* (1941)
Fromm, *Escape from Freedom* (1941)
Camus, *The Stranger* (1942)
Sartre, *Being and Nothingness* (1943)
Orwell, *Animal Farm* (1945)

Chapter 28

World War I:
The West in Despair

For many people, the declaration of war was a cause for celebration. Few Europeans realized what a horror the war would turn out to be. (Archives Larousse, Paris, France/Giraudon/The Bridgeman Art Library International.)

Focus Questions

1. How did the nationality problem in Austria-Hungary contribute to the outbreak of World War I?

2. In assessing responsibility for the war, what arguments have historians advanced for each of the major countries involved?

3. Why did many Europeans celebrate the coming of war?

4. What was Wilson's peace program? What obstacles did he face?

5. Why did the Provisional Government and liberal democracy fail in Russia in 1917?

6. How did World War I transform the consciousness of Europeans?

rior to 1914, the dominant mood in Europe was one of pride in the accomplishments of Western civilization and confidence in its future progress. Advances in science and technology, the rising standard of living, the spread of democratic institutions, and Europe's position of power in the world all contributed to a sense of optimism, as did the expansion of social reform and the increase in literacy for the masses. Furthermore, since the defeat of Napoleon (1815), Europe had avoided a general war, and since the Franco-Prussian War (1870–1871), the Great Powers had not fought one another. Reflecting on the world he knew before World War I, the historian Arnold Toynbee recalled that his generation had

expected that life throughout the World would become more rational, more humane, and more democratic and that, slowly, but surely, political democracy would produce greater social justice. We had also expected that the progress of science and technology would make mankind richer, and that this increasing wealth would gradually spread from a minority to a majority. We had expected that all this would happen peacefully. In fact we thought that mankind's course was set for an earthly paradise, and that our approach towards this goal was predestined for us by historical necessity.[1]

Few people recognized that the West's outward achievements masked inner turbulence that was propelling Western civilization toward a cataclysm. The European state system was failing. By 1914, national states, fueled by explosive nationalism, were grouped into alliances that faced each other with ever-mounting hostility. Nationalist passions, overheated by the popular press and expansionist societies, poisoned international relations. Nationalist thinkers propagated pseudo-scientific racial and Social Darwinist doctrines, which glorified conflict and justified the subjugation of other peoples. Committed to enhancing national power, statesmen lost sight of Europe as a community of nations sharing a common civilization. Caution and restraint gave way to belligerency in foreign relations.

Chronology 28.1 ❖ World War I

June 28, 1914	Archduke Francis Ferdinand of Austria assassinated at Sarajevo
August 4, 1914	Germans invade Belgium
August 1914	Russians invade East Prussia and are defeated by Germans at the battle of Tannenberg
September 1914	The first battle of the Marne saves Paris
April 1915–January 1916	Gallipoli campaign: Allies withdraw after suffering 252,000 casualties
May 1915	Italy enters war on Allies' side
Spring 1915	Germany launches offensive that forces Russia to abandon Galicia and most of Poland
February 1916	General Pétain leads French forces at Verdun; Germans fail to capture the fortress town
June 1916	Russians suffer more than a million casualties in an offensive against Austrian lines
July–November 1916	Battle of the Somme: Allies suffer 600,000 casualties
January 1917	Germany launches unrestricted submarine warfare
March 1917	Tsarist regime is overthrown
April 6, 1917	United States declares war on Germany
May 1917	General Pétain restores French army's morale and discipline
July–November 1917	British defeat at Passchendaele
Fall 1917	Italian defeat at Caporetto
November 1917	Bolsheviks, led by Lenin, take command in Russia
January 1918	U.S. president Woodrow Wilson announces his Fourteen Points
1918–1920	Civil war and foreign intervention in Russia
March 1918	Russia signs Treaty of Brest-Litovsk, losing territory to Germany and withdrawing from the war
March 21, 1918	Germans launch a great offensive to end the war
June 3, 1918	Germans advance to within fifty-six miles of Paris
August 8, 1918	British victory at Amiens
October 1918	Turks are forced to withdraw from the war after several British successes
November 3, 1918	Austria-Hungary signs armistice with the Allies
November 11, 1918	Germany signs armistice with the Allies, ending World War I
January 1919	Paris Peace Conference
June 28, 1919	Germany signs Treaty of Versailles

Friedrich von Bernhardi: *Germany and the Next War*

A militaristic attitude that glorified war was widespread in Germany prior to World War I. The following excerpt comes from Friedrich von Bernhardi's work Germany and the Next War *(1911), which was immensely popular in his country.*

. . . War is a biological necessity of the first importance, a regulative element in the life of mankind which cannot be dispensed with, since without it an unhealthy development will follow, which excludes every advancement of the race, and therefore all real civilization. "War is the father of all things." The sages of antiquity long before Darwin recognized this.

The struggle for existence is, in the life of Nature, the basis of all healthy development. . . . The law of the stronger holds good everywhere. Those forms survive which are able to procure themselves the most favourable conditions of life, and to assert themselves in the universal economy of Nature. The weaker succumb. . . .

Struggle is, therefore, a universal law of Nature, and the instinct of self-preservation which leads to struggle is acknowledged to be a natural condition of existence.

Strong, healthy, and flourishing nations increase in numbers. From a given moment they require a continual expansion of their frontiers, they require new territory for the accommodation of their surplus population. Since almost every part of the globe is inhabited, new territory must, as a rule, be obtained at the cost of its possessors—that is to say, by conquest, which thus becomes a law of necessity.

The right of conquest is universally acknowledged. . . .

. . . Vast territories inhabited by uncivilized masses are occupied by more highly civilized States, and made subject to their rule. Higher civilization and the correspondingly greater power are the foundations of the right to annexation. . . .

Lastly, in all times the right of conquest by war has been admitted. It may be that a growing people cannot win colonies from civilized races, and yet the State wishes to retain the surplus population which the mother-country can no longer feed. Then the only course left is to acquire the necessary territory by war. Thus the instinct of self-preservation leads inevitably to war, and the conquest of foreign soil. It is not the possessor, but the victor, who then has the right. . . .

In such cases might gives the right to occupy or to conquer. Might is at once the supreme right, and the dispute as to what is right is decided by the judgment of war. War gives a biologically just decision, since its decisions rest on the very nature of things. . . .

The knowledge, therefore, that war depends on biological laws leads to the conclusion that every attempt to exclude it from international relations must be demonstrably untenable.

Question for Analysis

1. What conclusions did Friedrich Bernhardi draw from his premise that war was "a biological necessity"?

Friedrich von Bernhardi, *Germany and the Next War*, trans. Allan H. Fowles (New York: Longmans, Green, 1914), 18, 21–24.

The failure of the European state system was paralleled by a cultural crisis. Some European intellectuals attacked the rational tradition of the Enlightenment and celebrated the primitive, the instinctual, and the irrational. Increasingly, young people felt drawn to philosophies of action that ridiculed liberal bourgeois values and viewed war as a purifying and ennobling experience. Colonial wars, colorfully portrayed in the popular press, ignited the imagination of bored factory workers and daydreaming students and reinforced a sense of duty and an urge for gallantry among young men. These "splendid" little colonial wars helped fashion an attitude that made war acceptable, if not laudable. Yearning to break loose from their ordinary lives and to embrace heroic values, many Europeans regarded violent conflict as the highest expression of individual and national life.

"This peace is so rotten," complained a young German writer, George Heym, in 1912, longing for "a war, even an unjust one."[2] That same year, a survey of French students between the ages of eighteen and twenty-five showed that

> the most cultivated elite among [them] find in warfare an aesthetic ideal. . . . These young men impute to it all the beauty with which they are in love and of which they have been deprived in ordinary life. Above all, war, in their eyes is the occasion for the most noble of virtues . . . energy, mastery, and sacrifice for a cause which transcends ourselves.[3]

The popular historian Heinrich von Treitschke (1834–1896), whose lectures influenced many students who were to rise to positions of importance in the German army and administration, expressed the prevailing mood: "Those who preach the nonsense about everlasting peace do not understand the life of the [German] race. . . . [T]o banish war from history would be to banish all progress."[4] Friedrich von Bernhardi (1849–1930), a German general and influential military writer, considered war "a biological necessity of the first importance."

Although technology was making warfare more brutal and dangerous, Europe retained a romantic illusion about combat. "Even if we end in ruin it was beautiful," exclaimed General Erich von Falkenhayn, the future chief of the German general staff, at the outbreak of World War I.[5]

Although Europe was seemingly progressing in the art of civilization, the mythic power of nationalism and the primitive appeal of conflict were driving European civilization to the abyss. Few people recognized the potential crisis— certainly not the statesmen whose reckless blundering and horrific miscalculations allowed the Continent to stumble into war.

AGGRAVATED NATIONALIST TENSIONS IN AUSTRIA-HUNGARY

On June 28, 1914, a young terrorist, with the support of the secret Serbian nationalist society called Union or Death (more popularly known as the Black Hand), murdered Archduke Francis Ferdinand, heir to the throne of Austria-Hungary. Six weeks later, the armies of Europe were on the march; an incident in the Balkans had sparked a world war. An analysis of why Austria-Hungary felt compelled to attack Serbia and why the other powers became enmeshed in the conflict shows how explosive Europe was in 1914. And nowhere were conditions more volatile than in Austria-Hungary, the scene of the assassination.

With its numerous nationalities, each with its own history and traditions and often conflicting aspirations, Austria-Hungary stood in opposition to nationalism, the most powerful spiritual force of the age. Perhaps the supranational Austro-Hungarian Empire was obsolete in a world of states based on the principle of nationality. Dominated by Germans and Hungarians, the empire remained unable either to satisfy the grievances or to contain the nationalist aims of its numerous minorities, particularly the Czechs and South Slavs (Croats, Slovenes, and Serbs).

The more moderate leaders of the ethnic minorities did not call for secession from the empire. Nevertheless, heightened agitation among several nationalities, which increased in the decade before 1914, greatly perturbed Austrian leaders. The fear that the empire would be torn apart by rebellion caused Austria to react strongly to any country that fanned the nationalist feelings of its Slavic minorities. This policy increased the tensions between Austria and small Serbia, which had gained its independence from the Ottoman Empire in 1878.

Captivated by Western ideas of nationalism, the Serbs sought to create a Greater Serbia by uniting with their racial kin, the 7 million or so South Slavs living in the Hapsburg Empire. The shrill appeals by Serbian nationalists made Austrian leaders fear that the South Slavs might press for secession. Some of these leaders, notably Foreign Minister Count Leopold von Berchtold and Field Marshal Franz Conrad von Hötzendorf, urged the destruction of Serbia to eliminate the threat to Austria's existence.

Another irritant to Austria-Hungary was Russian Pan-Slavism, which called for the solidarity of Russians with their Slavic cousins in Eastern Europe—Poles, Czechs, Slovaks, South Slavs, and Bulgarians. Pan-Slavism was based on a mystic conception of the superiority of Slavic civilization to Western civilization and of Russia's special historic mission to liberate its kin from Austrian and Turkish rule. Although Russian Pan-Slavs were few and did not dictate foreign policy, they constituted a significant pressure group. Moreover, their provocative and semireligious proclamations frightened Austria-Hungary, which did not draw a sharp line between Pan-Slavic aspirations and official Russian policy.

The tensions stemming from the multinational character of the Austro-Hungarian Empire in an age of heightened nationalist feeling set off the explosion in 1914. Unable to solve its minority problems and fearful of Pan-Slavism and Pan-Serbism, Austria-Hungary felt itself in a life-or-death situation. This sense of desperation led it to lash out at Serbia after the assassination of Archduke Francis Ferdinand.

The German System of Alliances

Perhaps the war might have been avoided, or at least limited to Austria and Serbia, if Europe in 1914 had not been split into two hostile **alliance systems**. Such a situation contains inherent dangers. Counting on the support of its allies, a country might pursue a more provocative and reckless course and be less conciliatory during a crisis. Furthermore, a conflict between two states might spark a chain reaction that draws in the other powers, transforming a limited war into a general war. That is what happened after the assassination. This dangerous alliance system originated with Bismarck.

The New German Empire

With its unification in 1870–1871, Germany became an international power of the first rank, upsetting the balance of power in Europe. For the first time since the wars of the French Revolution, one nation was in a position to dominate the European continent. How a united and powerful Germany would fit into European life was the crucial problem in the decades following the Franco-Prussian War.

To German nationalists, unification both fulfilled a national dream and pointed to an even more ambitious goal: extending German power in Europe and the world. As the nineteenth century drew to a close, German nationalism became more extreme. Believing that Germany must either grow or die, nationalists pressed the government to build a powerful navy, acquire colonies, gain a much greater share of the world's markets, and expand German interests and influence in Europe. Sometimes these goals were expressed in the language of Social Darwinism: nations are engaged in an eternal struggle for survival and domination.

Militant nationalists preached the special destiny of the German race and advocated German expansion in Europe and overseas. Decisive victories against Austria (1866) and France (1871), the formation of the German Reich, rapid industrialization, and the impressive achievements of German science and scholarship had molded a powerful and dynamic nation. Imbued with great expectations for the future, Germans became increasingly impatient to see the fatherland gain its "rightful" place in world affairs—an attitude that alarmed non-Germans.

Bismarck's Goals

Under Bismarck, who did not seek additional territory but wanted only to preserve the recently achieved unification, Germany pursued a moderate and cautious foreign policy. One of Bismarck's goals was to keep France isolated and friendless. Deeply humiliated by its defeat in the Franco-Prussian War and the loss of Alsace and Lorraine, France found its nationalists yearning for a war of revenge against Germany. Victor Hugo expressed the "sacred anger" of the French: "France will have but one thought: to reconstitute her forces, gather her energy, . . . raise her young generation to form an army of the whole people. . . . Then one day she will be irresistible. Then she will take back Alsace-Lorraine."[6] Even though the French government, aware of Germany's strength, was unlikely to initiate a conflict, the issue of Alsace-Lorraine

increased tensions between the two countries. Annexing the French provinces proved to be a serious blunder by Germany, for it made reconciliation impossible.

Bismarck also hoped to prevent a war between Russia and Austria-Hungary since it could lead to German involvement, the breakup of Austria-Hungary, and Russian expansion in Eastern Europe. To maintain peace and Germany's existing borders, Bismarck forged complex alliances. In the 1880s, he created the Triple Alliance, consisting of Germany, Austria-Hungary, and Italy, as well as an alliance with Russia.

A major weakness marred Germany's alliance system, however, for Austria and Russia were potential enemies. Austria feared Russian ambitions in the Balkans and felt threatened by Russian Pan-Slavs. Bismarck knew that an alliance with Austria was essentially incompatible with Germany's treaty obligations to Russia. But he hoped that the arrangement would enable him to exercise a moderating influence over both eastern powers and prevent a war from erupting and upsetting the status quo. Besides, the treaty with Russia deprived France of a valuable ally.

Bismarck conducted foreign policy with restraint. He formed alliances not to conquer new lands but to protect Germany from aggression by either France or Russia. His aim was to preserve order and stability in Europe, not to launch war. However, when the young Kaiser William II (1888–1918) ascended the throne, he clashed with the aging prime minister, and in 1890 Bismarck was forced to resign. Lacking Bismarck's diplomatic skills, his cool restraint, and his determination to keep peace in Europe, the new German leaders pursued a belligerent and imperialistic foreign policy in the ensuing years.

The first act of the new leadership was to let the treaty with Russia lapse, allowing Germany to give full support to Austria, which was deemed a more reliable ally. Whereas Bismarck had warned Austria to act with moderation and caution in the Balkans, his successors not only failed to hold Austria in check but actually encouraged Austrian aggression. This proved fatal to the peace of Europe.

EMPEROR WILLIAM II OF GERMANY AND EMPEROR FRANZ JOSEPH OF AUSTRIA ATTENDING A PARADE IN BERLIN, 1889. (© Bettmann/CORBIS.)

THE TRIPLE ENTENTE

Fear of Germany

When Germany broke with Russia in 1890, France was quick to take advantage of the situation. Worried by Germany's increasing military strength, expanding industries, growing population, and alliance with Austria and Italy, France eagerly courted Russia as an ally. It urged its bankers to invest in Russia, supplied weapons to the tsar, and arranged for the French and Russian fleets to exchange visits. In 1894, France and Russia entered into an alliance; the isolation forced on France by Bismarck ended. France hoped that the alliance would deter German aggression, for Germany was now threatened with a two-front war.

Germany's growing military and industrial might also alarmed Great Britain. In addition, Germany had become a potent trade rival and strove to become a great colonial power as well—a goal demanded by German nationalists. But what troubled Britain most was Germany's decision to build a great navy. Germany was already the strongest land power on the Continent. Achieving naval parity with England would give Germany the potential to threaten Britain's overseas empire and to blockade the British Isles, depriving Britain of food and supplies. Germany's naval program was the overriding reason that Britain moved closer first to France and then to Russia. Germany's naval construction, designed to increase its stature as a Great Power but not really necessary for its security, was one indication that German leaders had abandoned Bismarck's policy of good sense. Eager to add the British as an ally and demonstrating superb diplomatic skill, France moved to end longstanding colonial disputes with Britain. The Entente Cordiale of 1904 accomplished this conciliation; England emerged from its self-imposed isolation.

Although the Franco-British understanding intensified German anxiety, Germany doubted that France and England, which had almost gone to war in 1898 in the Sudan, had overcome their deep animosities. Consequently, Chancellor Bernhard von Bülow (1849–1929) decided to test the Entente Cordiale by provoking a crisis; he chose Morocco because earlier the British had resisted French imperialist designs there. He prodded a reluctant Kaiser William II to visit the Moroccan port of Tangier, a sign that Germany would support the Moroccan sultan against France. In January 1906, however, at the conference held in Algeciras, Spain, to resolve the crisis, Britain sided with France, which was given special rights in Morocco. Germany's efforts to disrupt the Anglo-French Entente Cordiale had failed.

Eager to counter Germany's Triple Alliance with a strong alliance of their own, French diplomats sought to ease tensions between their Russian ally and their new British friend. Two events convinced Russia to adopt a more conciliatory attitude toward Britain: an unexpected and humiliating defeat in the Russo-Japanese War of 1904–1905 and a working-class revolution in 1905. Shocked by defeat, its army bordering on disintegration, its workers restive, Russia was receptive to settling its imperial disputes with Britain over Persia, Tibet, and Afghanistan—a decision encouraged by France. In the Anglo-Russian Entente of 1907, as in the Anglo-French Entente Cordiale of 1904, the former rivals conducted themselves in a conciliatory, if not friendly, manner. In both instances, what engendered this spirit of cooperation was fear of Germany; both agreements represented a triumph for French diplomacy. The Triple Entente, however, was not a firm alliance, for there was no certainty that Britain, traditionally reluctant to send its troops to the Continent, would give more than diplomatic support to France and Russia in case of a showdown with Germany.

Europe was now broken into two hostile camps: the Triple Entente of France, Russia, and Britain and the Triple Alliance of Germany, Austria-Hungary, and Italy. The costly arms race and the maintenance of large standing armies by all the states except Britain served to increase fear and suspicion between the alliances.

German Reactions

Germany denounced the Triple Entente as a hostile anti-German coalition designed to encircle and crush Germany. To survive, Germany must break this ring. In the past, German arms had achieved unification; German military might would also end this threat to the fatherland. Considering Austria-Hungary its only reliable ally, Germany resolved to preserve the power and dignity of the Hapsburg Empire. If Austria-Hungary fell from the ranks of the Great Powers, Germany would have to stand alone against its enemies. At all costs, Austria-Hungary must not be weakened.

This assessment, however, suffered from dangerous miscalculations. First, Germany overstressed the hostile nature of the Triple Entente. In reality, France, Russia, and Britain drew closer together not to wage aggressive war against Germany but to protect themselves against burgeoning German military, industrial, and diplomatic power. Second, by linking German security to Austria, Germany greatly increased the chance of war. Growing more and more fearful of Pan-Serbism and Pan-Slavism, Austria might well decide that only a war could prevent its empire from disintegrating. Confident of German support, Austria would be more likely to resort to force; afraid of any diminution of Austrian power, Germany would be more likely to support Austria. In contrast to Bismarck, the new leadership thought not of restraining Austria but of strengthening it, by war if necessary.

DRIFTING TOWARD WAR

The Bosnian Crisis

After 1908, several crises tested the competing alliances. Particularly significant was the Bosnian affair, for it contained many of the ingredients that eventually ignited the war in 1914. The defeat by Japan in 1905 had diminished Russia's stature as a Great Power. The new Russian foreign minister, Alexander Izvolsky, hoped to gain a diplomatic triumph by compelling the Ottoman Turks to allow Russian warships to pass through the Dardanelles, fulfilling a centuries-old dream of extending Russian power into the Mediterranean. Izvolsky hoped that England and France, traditional opponents of Russia's Mediterranean ambitions but now Russia's allies, would not block the move. But certainly Austria would regard it as a hostile act.

Russia made a deal with Austria: if Austria would support Russia's move to open the Dardanelles, Russia would permit Austrian annexation of the provinces of Bosnia and Herzegovina. Officially part of the Ottoman Empire, these provinces had been administered by Austria-Hungary since 1878. The population consisted mainly of ethnic cousins of the Serbs. A formal annexation would certainly infuriate the Serbs, who hoped one day to make the region part of Greater Serbia. In 1908, Austria proceeded to annex the provinces, but Russia met stiff resistance from England and France when it presented its case for opening the strait to Russian warships. Austria had gained a diplomatic victory, while Russia suffered another humiliation. Even more enraged than Russia, Serbia threatened to invade Bosnia to liberate its cousins from Austrian oppression. The Serbian press proclaimed that Austria-Hungary must perish if the South Slavs were to achieve liberty and unity. A fiery attitude also prevailed in Vienna: Austria-Hungary could not survive unless Serbia was destroyed.

During this period of intense hostility between Austria-Hungary and Serbia, Germany supported its Austrian ally. To keep Austria strong, Germany would even agree to the dismemberment of Serbia and to its incorporation into the Hapsburg Empire. The crisis led Austria and Germany to coordinate battle plans in case a conflict between Austria and Serbia involved Russia and France. Unlike Bismarck, who tried to hold Austria in check, German leadership now coolly envisioned an Austrian attack on Serbia, and just as coolly offered German support if Russia intervened.

Balkan Wars

The Bosnian crisis pushed Germany and Austria closer together, brought relations between Austria and Serbia to the breaking point, and inflicted another humiliation on Russia. The first Balkan War (1912) continued these trends. The Balkan states of Montenegro, Serbia, Bulgaria, and Greece attacked a dying Ottoman Empire. In a brief campaign, the Balkan armies captured the Turkish

Empire's European territory, with the exception of Constantinople. Because it was on the victorious side, landlocked Serbia gained the Albanian coast and thus a long-desired outlet to the sea. Austria, however, was determined to keep its enemy from reaping this reward, and Germany, as in the Bosnian crisis, supported its ally. Unable to secure Russian support, Serbia was forced to surrender the territory, which in 1913 became the state of Albania.

During a five-year period, Austria-Hungary had twice humiliated Serbia. Russia shared these humiliations, for it had twice failed to help its small Slavic friend and had been denied access to the Dardanelles at the time of the Bosnian crisis. Incensed Serbian nationalists accelerated their campaign of propaganda and terrorism against Austria. Believing that another humiliation would irreparably damage its prestige, Russia vowed to back Serbia in its next confrontation with Austria. And Austria, its patience exhausted and emboldened by German encouragement, wanted to end the Serbian threat once and for all. Thus, the ingredients for war between Austria and Serbia, a war that might easily draw in Russia and Germany, were present. Another incident might well start a war. It came on June 28, 1914.

The Assassination of Francis Ferdinand

On June 28, 1914, Archduke Francis Ferdinand (1863–1914), heir to the throne of Austria, was assassinated while making a state visit to Sarajevo, the capital of Bosnia. Young Gavrilo Princip, part of a team of Bosnian terrorists, fired two shots at close range into the archduke's car. Francis Ferdinand and his wife died within fifteen minutes. The conspiracy was organized by Dragutin Dimitrijevic, chief of intelligence of the Serbian army, who was linked to the Black Hand, a secret terrorist society. By killing the archduke, the terrorists hoped to bring to a boiling point tensions within the Hapsburg Empire and prepare the way for revolution.

Feeling that Austria's prestige as a Great Power and indeed its very survival as a supranational empire were at stake, key officials, led by the foreign minister, Count Leopold von Berchtold, decided to use the assassination as a pretext to crush Serbia. For years, Austrian leaders had yearned for war with Serbia in order to end agitation for the union of the South Slavs. Now, they reasoned, the hour had struck. But war with Serbia would require Germany's approval. Believing that Austria was Germany's only reliable ally and that a diminution of Austrian power and prestige threatened German security, German statesmen backed Austria, encouraging it to take up arms against Serbia. Both Germany and Austria wanted a quick strike, a localized conflict, to overwhelm Serbia before other countries were drawn in.

Germany Abets Austria

Confident of German backing, on July 23 Austria presented Serbia with an ultimatum and demanded a response within forty-eight hours. Serbia's reply seemed conciliatory, agreeing to virtually all Austria's demands. But Serbia refused Austrian officials entry to investigate the assassination and participate in the prosecution of those implicated in the assassination. To the Serbs this was a violation of their sovereignty and dignity. Moreover, assurance of Russian support dissuaded Serbian officials from doing all it could to avoid war.

This reaction was the one that Austria intended, as it sought a military solution to the crisis rather than a diplomatic one. But Russia feared that an Austrian conquest of Serbia was just the first step in an Austro-German plan to dominate the Balkans. Such an extension of German and Austrian power in a region close to Russia was unthinkable to the tsar's government. Moreover, after suffering repeated reverses in foreign affairs, Russia would not tolerate another humiliation. As Germany had resolved to back its Austrian ally, Russia determined not to abandon Serbia. Having already decided against a peaceful settlement, Austria insisted that rejecting one provision meant rejecting the entire ultimatum, and it ordered the mobilization of its army.

This was a crucial moment for Germany. Would it continue to support Austria, knowing that an Austrian attack on Serbia would most likely bring Russia into the conflict? Determined not to desert Austria and believing that a showdown with Russia was inevitable anyway, the German war party, with the military cajoling and persuading civilian authorities, continued to urge Austrian action against Serbia. They argued that it was better to fight Russia in 1914 than a few years later, when the tsar's empire, which already had a huge reserve of manpower and was rapidly building strategic railroads and expanding its Baltic fleet, would be stronger. The war party claimed that Germany's superior army could defeat both Russia and France, that Britain's army was too weak to make a difference, and that, in any case, Britain might remain neutral. Although Germany would have preferred a limited war involving only Austria and Serbia, the idea of a general war did not dismay it. Indeed, the prospect of a war with Russia and France exhilarated some military leaders and statesmen. The permanent weakening of Russia and France would break the ring of encirclement, increase German territory, and establish Germany as the foremost power in the world. The desire for territorial expansion and national self-assertion was widely expressed by German academics, journalists, and political figures in the years before 1914.

On July 28, 1914, Austria declared war on Serbia. Russia, with the assurance of French support, proclaimed partial mobilization aimed at Austria alone. But the military warned that partial mobilization would throw the slow-moving Russian war machine into total confusion if the order had to be changed suddenly to full mobilization. Moreover, the only plans, particularly railway schedules, the Russian general staff had drawn up called for full mobilization, that is, for war against both Austria and Germany. Pushed by his generals and nationalistic politicians, the tsar, who dreaded war that would disrupt his kingdom, succumbed to the pressure and gave the order for full mobilization on July 30. Russian forces would be arrayed against Germany as well as Austria.

Because the country that struck first gained the advantage of fighting according to its own plans rather than having to improvise in response to the enemy's attack, generals tended to regard mobilization by the enemy as an act of war. Therefore, when Russia refused a German warning to halt mobilization, Germany, on August 1, ordered a general mobilization and declared war on Russia. Two days later, Germany also declared war on France, believing that France would most likely support its Russian ally. Besides, German battle plans were based on a war with both Russia and France; therefore, a war between Germany and Russia automatically meant a German attack on France.

When Belgium refused to allow German troops to march through Belgian territory into France, Germany invaded the small nation, which brought Britain, pledged since 1839 to guarantee Belgian neutrality, into the war. Britain could never tolerate German troops directly across the English Channel in any case, nor could it brook German mastery of Europe. A century before, Britain had fought Napoleon to prevent France from becoming master of Europe; now it would fight Germany for the same reason. It was this fear that led Britain's military command to enter into joint planning with their French counterparts, which linked the two powers more closely. Should France be attacked, Britain would be unlikely to stay neutral.

The Question of Responsibility

The question of whether any one power was mainly responsible for the tragedy has intrigued historians. In assessing blame, historians have focused on Germany's role. The German historian Fritz Fischer argues that Germany's ambition to dominate Europe was the underlying cause of the war. Germany encouraged Austria to strike at Serbia, knowing that an attack on Serbia could mean war with Russia and its French ally. Believing that it had the military advantage, Germany was willing to risk such a war. Hence, "her leaders must bear a substantial share of the historical responsibility for the outbreak of general war in 1914."[7]

Attracted by Social Darwinist ideas that foresaw an inevitable racial struggle between Germans and Slavs, by militarist doctrines that glorified war, and by a nationalist drive for **Lebensraum**—more living space—continues Fischer, Germany sought to become the foremost economic and political power in Europe and to play

THE ASSASSINATION OF ARCHDUKE FRANCIS FERDINAND. Immediately after the assassination, Austrian authorities arrest one of the assassins. (©Bettmann/CORBIS.)

a far greater role in world politics; to achieve this goal, it was willing to go to war. Fischer supports his position by pointing to Germany's war aims, drawn up immediately after the outbreak of war, which called for the annexation of neighboring territories and the creation of satellite states, that is, imposing German hegemony over Europe. Fischer's thesis has distressed Germans, for it implies that there is continuity between Germany's territorial ambitions at the time of World War I and Hitler's territorial goals, that Nazi imperialism was not an aberration in German history but coincided with the wishes of Germany's traditional ruling elite.

Fischer's critics stress that Social Darwinism and militarism enthralled other European nations besides Germany. They argue further that Germany would have preferred a limited war between Austria and Serbia and before the war had no plans to dominate Europe. The plans for territorial acquisition, drawn up during the war, not before it, were not the reason that Germany went to war.

Historians also attribute blame to the other powers. Austria bears responsibility for its determination to crush Serbia and for its insistent avoidance of a negotiated settlement. Serbia's responsibility stems from pursuing an aggressive

Pan-Serbian policy and tolerating terrorist networks within the country, which set Serbia on a collision course with Austria-Hungary. In 1913, the British ambassador to Vienna warned: "Serbia will some day set Europe by the ears, and bring about a universal war on the Continent. I cannot tell you how exasperated people are getting here at the continual worry which that little country causes to Austria."[8] Russia bears responsibility for being the first country to institute general mobilization, a momentous decision that turned a limited war between Austria-Hungary and Serbia into a European war; France, for failing to restrain Russia and indeed for encouraging its ally to mobilize; and England, for failing to make clear that it would support its allies. Had Germany seen plainly that Britain would intervene, it might have been more cautious. Finally, blame falls on diplomats and statesmen for their ineptness and lack of imagination in dealing with a crisis that could have been resolved without war. Had Austro-Hungarian and Russian policymakers been more willing to compromise and less willing to risk war, and had German and French officialdom tried to restrain their allies, the tragedy could have been averted.

Some historians, dismissing the question of responsibility, regard the war as an obvious sign that European civilization was in deep trouble. Viewed in the broad perspective of European history, the war marked a culmination of dangerous forces in European life: the belief that violent conflict was a natural, inevitable, and worthy feature of human relations and a belligerent nationalism that pitted nation against nation in a struggle for survival. The war also pointed to the flaws and perils of the alliance system, which set off a chain reaction, and the failure of the European state system, which glorified national power at the expense of a common European civilization.

WAR AS CELEBRATION

When war was certain, an extraordinary phenomenon occurred. Crowds gathered in capital cities, demonstrating allegiance to the various fatherlands and readiness to fight. Particularly in Germany, clergy, theologians, scientists, scholars,

journalists, and literary figures justified the nation's participation in the war often claiming that God supported its virtuous cause. The sentiments of a German theologian voiced in the opening stage of the war were not uncommon: "Our battles are God's battles. Our cause is sacred. . . . We are God's chosen among the nations. That our prayers for victory will be heard is entirely to be expected, according to the religious and moral order of the world."[9] And Werner Sombart, a prominent sociologist and economist, wrote that "for us who are imbued with militarism, the war is holy, yes the most sacred thing on earth."[10]

In Germany and France, at first socialists organized antiwar demonstrations, but when war was declared all Social Democrat deputies in the Reichstag and all Socialist deputies in Paris voted to provide funds for a war in which workers would be killing workers. Patriotism won out over the socialist commitment to an international working class movement.

War and its violence seemed to offer an escape from the dull routine of classroom, job, and home and from the emptiness, drabness, mediocrity, and pettiness of bourgeois society—from "a world grown old and cold and weary," as Rupert Brooke, a young British poet, put it.[11] To some, war was a "beautiful . . . sacred moment" that satisfied an "ethical yearning."[12] To many people, especially youth and intellectuals, war seemed a healthy and heroic antidote to what they regarded as an unbearably decadent and soul-destroying machine age and to bourgeois preoccupation with work, profits, and possessions. More significantly, the outpouring of patriotic sentiments demonstrated the power that nationalism exerted over the European mind. Overcoming bitter class animosities, nationalism welded millions of people into a collective ready to commit body and soul to the nation, especially in its hour of need; all believed that their country was a victim of aggression. For decades, state-directed education had indoctrinated youth with nationalist attitudes, beliefs, and

***Map 28.1* WORLD WAR I, 1914–1918 ▶**
This map shows Europe divided into competing alliances and German advances into France and Eastern Europe once war broke out.

Inset map legend:

Germany, 1914

→ German offensive, 1914

Farthest German advance, Sept. 1914

— Front at beginning of 1915

- - - German offensive, summer 1918

—— Armistice line, November 1918

**Inset map labels:**

Cologne • Rhine R. • Strasbourg • ALSACE • Moselle R. • Saar R. • LORRAINE • LUXEMBOURG • NETHERLANDS • Liège • Nancy • Antwerp • Ardennes R. • Sedan • Verdun • BELGIUM • Meuse R. • Argonne Forest • Brussels • FLANDERS • Passchendaele • Reims • Ypres • Aisne R. • Marne R. • Ostend • Calais • Paris • Dover • Somme R. • Amiens • FRANCE • English Channel • Seine R.

**Main map labels:**

ICELAND • Triple Entente and its Allies • Central Powers • Neutral nations • Farthest German-Austrian advance • Major battle

400 Mi. • 400 Km. • 200 • 0

IRELAND • GREAT BRITAIN • London • Paris • NETH. • BELG. • LUX. • SWITZ. • FRANCE • SPAIN • PORTUGAL • ATLANTIC OCEAN • North Sea • British blockade line • Mediterranean Sea

NORWAY • SWEDEN • DENMARK • FINLAND • Helsinki • St. Petersburg • Moscow • RUSSIA • Baltic Sea • Riga • Tannenberg 1914 • Warsaw • POLAND • Brest-Litovsk • Kiev • Treaty of Brest-Litovsk, March 1918 • Armistice line, Dec. 1917 • GALICIA • Berlin • GERMANY • Vienna • AUSTRIA-HUNGARY • Caporetto 1917 • Danube R. • Rhine R. • ITALY • Rome • ROMANIA • Bucharest • Black Sea • Constantinople • BULGARIA • SERBIA • Sarajevo • MONTENEGRO • ALBANIA • GREECE • Dardanelles • Gallipoli 1915 • OTTOMAN EMPIRE

697

myths designed to promote social cohesion. This training proved extraordinarily successful as tens of thousands of young people, many of them students, volunteered to serve their country.

In Paris, men marched down the boulevards singing the stirring words of the French national anthem, "the Marseillaise," while women showered young soldiers with flowers. A participant recollected: "Young and old, civilians and military men burned with the same excitement. . . . [T]housands of men eager to fight would jostle one another outside recruiting offices, waiting to join up. . . . The word 'duty' had a meaning for them, and the word 'country' had regained its splendor."[13] These sentiments were echoed by another French soldier, Andre Fribourg, traveling to the front.

> Our hearts beat with enthusiasm. A kind of intoxication takes possession of us. My muscles and arteries tingle with happy strength. The spirit is contagious. Along the track walkers wave to us. Women hold up their children. We are carried away by the greeting of the land, the mystery that the future holds, the thought of glorious adventure, and the pride of being chosen to share it.[14]

The term *union sacrée* (sacred union) was coined to express the sense of oneness, inclusiveness, and devotion to the nation that gripped French men and women at the time. Similarly, in Germany, "flowers were thrown at [soldiers] from every window; everyone wanted to shake hands with the departing soldiers. . . . Musicians played. . . . People cried and sang at the same time. . . . Nobody could resist that ebullient feeling."[15] A German newspaper editorialized, "It is a joy to be alive. We wished so much for this hour. . . . The sword which has been forced into our hand will not be sheathed until our aims are won and our territory extended as far as necessity demands."[16] Writing about those momentous days, the British mathematician-philosopher Bertrand Russell (1872–1970) recalled his horror and "amazement that average men and women were delighted at the prospect of war. . . . [T]he anticipation of carnage was delightful to something like ninety per cent of the population. I had to revise my views on human nature."[17]

Soldiers bound for battle and wives and sweethearts seeing them off at train stations were in a euphoric holiday mood. "My dear ones, be proud that you live in such a time and in such a nation and that you . . . have the privilege of sending those you love into so glorious a battle," wrote a young German law student to his family.[18] The young warriors yearned to do something noble and altruistic, to win glory, and to experience life at its most intense. "There was only one thing we young men were afraid of," recalled a German veteran: "that it would be over before we had a chance to participate."[19]

The martial mood also captivated many of Europe's most distinguished intellectuals. They shared Rupert Brooke's sentiments: "Now God be thanked Who has matched us with His hour, / And caught our youth, and wakened us from sleeping."[20] In November 1914, Thomas Mann, the distinguished German writer, saw the war as "purification" and "liberation." "How could . . . the soldier in the artist," he asked, "not praise God for the collapse of a peaceful world with which he was fed up, so exceedingly fed up."[21] To the prominent German historian Friedrich Meinecke, August 1914 was "one of the great moments of my life which suddenly filled my soul with . . . the profoundest joy."[22]

Some intellectuals also welcomed the war because it unified the nation in a spirit of fraternity, which eliminated party squabbles and class differences and overcame individual isolation. Stefan Zweig (1881–1942), an Austrian writer, recalled how news of the war was greeted in Vienna.

> As never before, thousands and hundreds of thousands felt what they should have felt in peace time, that they belonged together. . . . All differences of class, rank, and language were flooded over at that moment by the rushing feeling of fraternity. Strangers spoke to one another in the streets, people who had avoided each other for years shook hands, everywhere one saw excited faces. Each individual experienced an exaltation of his ego. . . . He had been incorporated into the mass . . . and his person, his hitherto unnoticed person, had been given meaning.[23]

War, in the view of some intellectuals, would spiritually regenerate the nation. It would resurrect glory, honor, and heroism; it would awaken a spirit of self-sacrifice and dedication and give life an overriding purpose in a world suffocating from bourgeois materialism and drabness.

Thus, a generation of European youth—many of them eager volunteers—marched off to war joyously, urged on by their teachers and cheered by their delirious compatriots. It must be emphasized, however, that both the soldiers who went off to war singing and the statesmen and generals who welcomed war or did not try hard enough to prevent it expected a short, decisive, and gallant conflict. Few envisioned what World War I turned out to be: four years of barbaric, senseless slaughter in which there were no victors, only losers. The cheers of chauvinists, naïve and deluded idealists, and fools drowned out the words of those, principally socialists, labor leaders, pacifists, and left-leaning liberals, who realized that Europe was stumbling into darkness. "The lamps are going out all over Europe," said British Foreign Secretary Edward Grey. "We shall not see them lit again in our lifetime."

STALEMATE IN THE WEST

On August 4, 1914, the German army invaded Belgium. German war plans, drawn up years earlier, chiefly by General Alfred von Schlieffen, called

TROOPS LEAVING BERLIN, 1914. "The sword has been forced into our hand," said Germans at the outbreak of war. German troops mobilized eagerly and efficiently; here a trainload is leaving for the Western Front. (German soldiers leaving for the Western Front, Berlin, August 1914 (b/w photo), Haeckel, Georg (1873–1942) and Haeckel, Otto (1872–1945) /© SZ Photo/Scherl/The Bridgeman Art Library International.)

for the army to swing through Belgium to outflank French border defenses, envelop the French forces, and destroy the enemy by attacking its rear. With the French army smashed and Paris isolated, German railroads—an extensive system of tracks, carefully planned by the general staff, had been constructed in the previous decade—would rush the victorious troops to the Eastern front to bolster the small force that had been assigned to hold off the Russians. The German military felt certain that the spirit and skill of the German army would ensure victory over the much larger Russian forces. But everything depended on speed. France must be taken before the Russians could mobilize sufficient numbers to invade Germany. The Germans were confident that they would defeat France in two months or less.

French strategy called for a headlong attack into Alsace and Lorraine. Inspired by Napoleon's stress on offensive warfare and convinced of French soldiers' unconquerable will and irresistible nerve, the French army prepared its soldiers only for offensive warfare. The field regulations proclaimed: "Battles are . . . struggles of morale. Defeat is inevitable as soon as the hope of conquering ceases to exist. Success comes . . . to him whose will is firmest and morale strongest."[24]

The French doctrine proved an instant failure. Although bayonet charges against machine-gun emplacements demonstrated the valor of French soldiers, they also revealed the incompetence of French generals. Making no effort at concealment or surprise and wearing striking red and blue uniforms, French soldiers were perfect targets. Marching into concentrated fire, they fell like pins. Everywhere the audacious attack was failing, but French generals, beguiled by the mystique of the offensive, would not change their tactics. In the first six weeks of the war, the French suffered an astounding 385,000 casualties, including 100,000 dead. In the last days of August, it seemed that the Germans would duplicate their crushing defeat of the French army in the Franco-Prussian War forty-four years earlier.

German success was not complete, however. Moving faster than anticipated, the Russians invaded East Prussia. In response, General Helmuth von Moltke transferred troops from the French front, hampering the German advance.

By early September, the Germans had reached the Marne River, forty miles from Paris. With their capital at their backs, the regrouped French forces, aided by the British, fought with astounding courage and resolve. Meanwhile, the Germans were exhausted by long marches and had outrun their supplies. Moreover, in their rush toward Paris, they had unknowingly exposed their flank, which the French attacked. The British then penetrated a gap that opened up between the German armies, forcing the Germans to retreat. The first battle of the Marne had saved Paris. German military planners had been denied the quick victory that they had anticipated. With no side achieving a decisive victory, the war entered a new and unexpected phase: the deadlock of trench warfare.

For more than four hundred miles across northern France, from the Alps to the North Sea, the opposing sides constructed a vast network of trenches. These trenches had underground dugouts, and barbed wire stretched for yards before the front trenches as a barrier to attack. Behind the front trenches were other lines, to which soldiers could retreat and from which support could be sent. Between the opposing armies lay "no-man's-land," a wasteland of mud, shattered trees, torn earth, and broken bodies. In the trenches, soldiers were reduced to a primitive existence. Sometimes they stood knee-deep in freezing water or slimy mud; the stench from human waste, rotting corpses, and unwashed bodies overwhelmed the senses; rats, made more fecund and larger by easy access to food, including decaying flesh, swarmed over the dead and scampered across the wounded and the sleeping; and ubiquitous lice caused intense discomfort and disease, which frequently required hospitalization for several weeks. After days of uninterrupted, fearsome, earsplitting bombardment by artillery, even the most stouthearted were reduced to shivering, whimpering creatures. Unless the dugouts were fortified with concrete, soldiers rarely survived a direct hit; sometimes they were simply burned alive or torn apart and made unrecognizable by exploding shells. Artillery accounted for about 70 percent of casualties. The agonizing cries and pleas of the wounded, left to die on the battlefield because it was too dangerous to attempt a rescue, shattered the nerves

BRITISH MUNITIONS WORKERS. With millions of men in the military, women took jobs formerly held only by men. Women drove trucks and buses, operated cranes, and worked in armament factories. Resistance to granting them equal rights diminished, as politicians recognized the essential contribution of women to the war effort. (Hulton Archive/Stringer/Getty Images.)

of the men in the trenches. Trench warfare was a futile battle of nerves, endurance, and courage, waged to the constant thunder of heavy artillery, which from many miles away pulverized both ramparts and men. And in April 1915, the Germans introduced poison gas, which added to the war's horror.

But the most distinctive feature of trench warfare was butchery. As attacking troops climbed over their trenches and advanced bravely across no-man's-land, they were decimated by heavy artillery and chewed up by rapid machine-gun fire,

from weapons that could fire five hundred or more rounds a minute. If they did penetrate the front-line trenches of the enemy, they were soon thrown back by a counterattack.

Despite a frightful loss of life, little land changed hands in this war of attrition. So much heroism, sacrifice, and death achieved nothing. The Allied generals in particular, unfeeling and totally lacking in imagination, persisted in ordering greater but still ineffective frontal attacks by massed infantry, hoping to wear down German manpower, which was inferior to their own.

Once German reserves could not replenish losses, they reasoned, a breakthrough would be possible. But this strategy only increased the death toll, for the advantage was always with the defense, which possessed machine guns, magazine rifles, and barbed wire. Aided by radio, railroads, and aerial reconnaissance, the defense could rush reinforcements to thwart an enemy attack. Tanks could redress the balance, but the generals, committed to old concepts, did not make effective use of them. And whereas the technology of the machine gun had been perfected, the motorized tanks, a newly developed weapon, often broke down. Gains and losses of land were measured in yards, but the lives of Europe's youth were squandered by the hundreds of thousands. In 1915, for example, France launched numerous attacks against German lines but never gained more than three miles in any one place. Yet these small gains cost France 1,430,000 casualties.

In 1915, neither side could break the deadlock. Hoping to bleed the French army dry and force its surrender, in February 1916 the Germans attacked the town of Verdun, which was protected by a ring of forts. They chose Verdun because they knew the French could never permit a retreat from this ancient fortress. The Germans hoped that France, compelled to pour more and more troops into battle, would suffer such a loss of men that it would be unable to continue the war. However, the leadership of General Henri Philippe Pétain, the tenacity of the French infantry, and the well-constructed concrete and steel forts enabled the French to endure the ten-month siege, the longest battle of the war. The 40 million shells fired by German and French artillery left corpses, many of them horribly mutilated, everywhere. "One eats, one drinks beside the dead, one sleeps in the midst of the dying, one laughs and one sings in the company of corpses," wrote a French surgeon.[25] When the British opened a major offensive on July 1, the Germans had to channel their reserves to the new front, relieving the pressure on Verdun. Verdun was World War I's bloodiest battle. France and Germany together suffered perhaps a million casualties, including some 300,000 dead.

At the end of June 1916, the British, assisted by the French, attempted a breakthrough at the Somme River. On July 1, after seven days of intense, unprecedented bombardment intended to destroy German defenses, the British climbed out of their trenches and ventured into no-man's-land. But German positions remained largely undamaged. Emerging from their deep dugouts reinforced by concrete, German machine gunners fired repeatedly at the British, who had been ordered to advance in rows. So tightly packed were the advancing British infantry that German machine gunners hardly had to aim. Marching into this maelstrom of concentrated machine-gun fire and continuous artillery barrages while desperately searching for a way through the still-intact German wire, few British troops ever made it across no-man's-land. Out of 110,000 who attacked, some 57,000 fell dead or wounded—most in the first hour of the assault— "the heaviest loss ever suffered in a single day by a British army or by any army in the First World War," observes the British historian A. J. P. Taylor.[26] Some reached the German wire, only to become entangled in it. The Germans killed them with rifle fire and bayonets. For days, the wounded lay in no-man's-land, their shrieks unheeded. The Germans suffered only 8,000 casualties, another powerful sign that in trench warfare the advantage lay with the defense.

After this initial disaster, common sense and a concern for human life demanded that the attack be called off, but the generals, who rarely made an appearance at the front to observe the actual conditions of battle, continued to feed soldiers to the German guns. When the battle of the Somme ended in mid-November, Britain and France had suffered more than 600,000 casualties, yet the military situation remained essentially unchanged.

In December 1916, the new commander in chief of the French forces, General Robert Nivelle, ordered another mass attack for April 1917. The Germans discovered the battle plans on the body of a French officer and withdrew to a shorter line on high ground, constructing the strongest defense network of the war. Although Nivelle knew that the French had lost the element of surprise, he went ahead with the offensive, insisting that "the offensive alone gives victory; the defensive gives only defeat and shame."[27] The offensive proved to be another bloodbath; sometimes the fire was so intense that the French could not make it out of their own trenches. Although French soldiers fought with courage, the situation was hopeless. Still Nivelle persisted with the attack. After ten days, French casualties numbered 187,000.*

The soldiers could endure no more. Spontaneous revolts, born of despair and military failure, broke out in rest areas as soldiers refused to return to the slaughter ground. In some instances, they shouted "Peace" and "To hell with the war." Mobs of soldiers seized trains to reach Paris and stir up the population against the war. Mutineers took control of barracks and threatened to fire on officers who interfered. The mutiny spread to the front lines as soldiers told their officers that they would defend the trenches but not attack. The French army was disintegrating. "The slightest German attack would have sufficed to tumble down our house of cards and bring the enemy to Paris," recalled a French officer.[28]

General Pétain, the hero of Verdun, replaced the disgraced Nivelle. To restore morale, Pétain granted more leave, improved the quality of food, made the rest areas more comfortable, and ordered officers to show concern for their men. He visited the troops, listened to their complaints, and told them that France would engage in only limited offensives until the United States, which had just entered the war, reinforced the Allies in large numbers. These measures, combined with imprisonments and executions, restored discipline. The Germans, unaware of the full magnitude of the mutiny, had not put pressure on the front. By the time the Germans attacked, General Pétain had revitalized the army.

OTHER FRONTS

While the Western Front hardened into a stalemate, events moved more decisively on the Eastern front. In August 1914, according to plan, the bulk of the German army invaded France, hoping for a speedy victory, while a small force defended the eastern frontier against Russia. Responding to French requests to put pressure on Germany, the Russians, with insufficient preparation, invaded East Prussia. Defeated at the battle of Tannenberg (August 26–30, 1914), the Russians withdrew

*Thousands of troops recruited from French African colonies were among the victims. Some 164,000 West Africans served in the French army and more than 33,000 perished during the war.

from German territory, which remained inviolate for the rest of the war.

Meanwhile, Germany's ally Austria was having no success against Serbia and Russia. Germany had to come to Austria's rescue. In the spring of 1915, the Germans made a breakthrough that forced the Russians to abandon Galicia and most of Poland. But Germany did not gain the decisive victory it had sought. Although badly battered, Russia remained in the war, forcing Germany to fight on two fronts.

In June 1916, the Russians launched an offensive, opening a wide breach in the Austrian lines. However, a German counteroffensive forced a retreat and cost the Russians more than a million casualties. Russia's military position deteriorated, and its domestic unrest worsened.

In March 1917, food shortages and disgust with the great loss of life exploded into a spontaneous revolution. The tsar abdicated. Dominated by liberals, the new government opted to continue the war, despite the weariness of the Russian masses. In November 1917, a second revolution brought to power the Bolsheviks, or Communists. In March 1918, the Bolsheviks ended Russia's role in the war by signing the punitive Treaty of Brest-Litovsk, in which Russia surrendered Poland, Ukraine, Finland, and the Baltic provinces.

Some major battles involved belligerents who joined the conflict after August 1914—notably, the Ottoman Turks, who sided with the Germans, and the Italians, who joined the Allies. Intent on seizing the Dardanelles, the Allies met fierce Turkish resistance on the Gallipoli Peninsula. The Gallipoli campaign (1915–1916) cost the Allies 252,000 casualties, and they gained nothing. In 1917, the Italians were badly defeated by a combined German and Austrian force at Caporetto. Germany and Austria took some 275,000 prisoners.

THE COLLAPSE OF THE CENTRAL POWERS

American Entry

The year 1917 seemed disastrous for the Allies. The Nivelle offensive had failed, the French army had mutinied, a British attack at Passchendaele did

Manfred Freiherr von Richthofen ("the Red Baron")

During World War I, airplanes were first used to gather intelligence about enemy positions. To thwart these reconnaissance planes, the other side sent up its own planes, arming pilots first with revolvers and grenades and later with machine guns. Thus, aerial combat was born. The daredevil pilots who dueled in the air captured the imagination of the people back home, and their exploits were widely publicized in the press.

The most famous ace of the war was Manfred Freiherr von Richthofen (1892–1918). Known as "the Red Baron" because he painted his plane scarlet so that both friend and foe could identify it, Richthofen is credited with shooting down eighty Allied aircraft. Richthofen's parents were typical Junker landowners. As a young man, Manfred acquired a passion for hunting and later transferred his marksmanship skills to aerial combat. A fellow pilot said that Richthofen "has to thank his hunter's eye for his incredible success. Watching like an eagle, he spots the weakness of his opponent and like a bird of prey he dives on the victim, which is inescapably in his clutches."* Following in his father's footsteps, Manfred pursued a military career. Learning to fly in 1915, he soon was given command of a squadron of fighter pilots. An enthusiastic huntsman, Richthofen confessed that shooting down Allied planes satisfied his passion for the hunt and a compulsive need for glory.

In drawing comparisons between German and Allied pilots, he stressed the superiority of the Germans' "aggressive spirit," which he believed he exemplified. He noted some of that spirit in the English pilots as well, ascribing it to their "German blood."

The Frenchman lies in wait for his prey to surprise him in a trap. That is hard to do in the air. Only a beginner will let himself be taken unawares. Ambush does not work, for one cannot hide and the invisible airplane has not yet been invented. Now and then, however, the Gallic blood rages in him and he launches an attack, but it is comparable to carbonated soda. For a moment there is an awful lot of spirit that suddenly goes flat. He is lacking in tenacious endurance.

The Englishman, on the other hand, shows some of his Germanic blood. These sportsmen take readily to flying, but they lose themselves in sport. They have enough amusement looping, diving, flying upside-down and demonstrating similar stunts for our men in the trenches. This would make a good impression during the Johannistal Sportsweek, but the men in the trenches are not as appreciative.[†]

April 1917 was a particularly successful month for Richthofen. He shot down twenty-one British planes, including four in one day, and was promoted to captain. One year later, in a furious dogfight above the Somme involving more than twenty German and British planes, the Red Baron's plane was hit by a Canadian pilot. When Australian soldiers reached the crashed plane, they found the Red Baron dead, his nose and jaw crushed from having smashed into the machine-gun butts in front of him. (Since the Australians on the ground were also firing at his plane, it is not certain who inflicted the fatal bullet.)

---

*Quoted in Peter Kilduff, *The Red Baron: Beyond the Legend* (London: Cassell, 1999), 7.

[†]Manfred Freiherr von Richthofen, *The Red Baron*, trans. Peter Kilduff (Garden City, N.Y.: Doubleday, 1969), 67.

not bring the expected breakthrough and added some 300,000 casualties to the list of butchery, and the Russians, torn by revolution and gripped by war weariness, were close to making a separate peace. But there was one encouraging development for the Allies. In April 1917, the United States declared war on Germany.

From the outset, America's sympathies lay with the Allies. To most Americans, Britain and France were democracies threatened by an autocratic and militaristic Germany. These sentiments were reinforced by British propaganda, which depicted the Germans as cruel "Huns." Since most war news came to the United States from Britain, anti-German feeling gained momentum. What precipitated America's entry was the German decision in January 1917 to launch a campaign of unrestricted submarine warfare. To deprive Britain of war supplies and to starve it into submission, the Germans resolved to torpedo both enemy and neutral ships in the war zone around the British Isles. Because the United States was Britain's principal supplier, American ships became a target of German submarines.

Angered by American loss of life and materiel, as well as by the violation of the doctrine of freedom of the seas, and fearful of a diminution of prestige if the United States took no action, President Woodrow Wilson (1856–1924) pressed for American entry. Also at stake was American security, which would be jeopardized by German domination of Western Europe. As Secretary of State Robert Lansing wrote in a private memorandum just before the United States entered the war, "The Allies must not be beaten. It would mean the triumph of Autocracy over Democracy; the shattering of all our moral standards; and a real, though it may seem remote, peril to our independence and institutions."[29]

When Germany initiated unrestricted submarine warfare against merchant and passenger ships with a loss of American life, the United States strongly protested. For a while Germany suspended these attacks. When it resumed unrestricted submarine warfare around the British Isles in February 1917, Germany gambled that the United States, even if it became a belligerent, could not intervene in sufficient numbers quickly enough to make a difference. The Germans lost their gamble. The United States broke diplomatic relations with Germany immediately on learning of the submarine campaign. Three weeks later, the British gave the Americans a message sent by German foreign secretary Arthur Zimmermann to the German ambassador in Mexico City and deciphered by British code experts. In the Zimmermann telegram, Germany proposed that in case of war between Germany and the United States, Mexico should join Germany as an ally; in return, Mexico would receive Texas, New Mexico, and Arizona. This fantastic proposal further exacerbated anti-German feeling in the United States. As German submarines continued to attack neutral shipping, President Wilson, on April 2, 1917, urged Congress to declare war on Germany, which it did on April 6.

Although the United States may have entered the war to protect its own security, President Wilson told the American people and the world that the United States was fighting "to make the world safe for democracy." With America's entry, the war was transformed into a moral crusade: an ideological conflict between democracy and autocracy. In January 1918, Wilson enunciated American war aims in his "Fourteen Points," which called for territorial changes based on nationality and the application of democratic principles to international relations. An association of nations would be established to preserve peace; it would conduct international relations with the same respect for law as was evidenced in democratic states. Thus, Wilson placed his hope for the future peace of the world in liberal nationalism and democracy, the two great legacies of the nineteenth century.

Germany's Last Offensive

With Russia out of the war, the transfer of forty divisions from the east gave the Germans numerical superiority. General Erich Ludendorff prepared for a decisive offensive before the Americans could land sufficient troops in France to help the Allies. A war of attrition now favored the Allies, who could count on American supplies and manpower. Without an immediate and decisive victory, Germany could not win the war. Ludendorff hoped to drive the British forces back to the sea, forcing them to withdraw from the Continent. And by seizing the Channel ports, he would disrupt the arrival of American troops on the Continent. Then he would turn his full might against the French, including the several 100,000 troops that had been transferred from the Eastern front. The great offensive began on March 21, 1918. The Germans breached the enemy lines, and the British retreated. Expanding their offensive, the Germans sought to split the British and French forces by capturing Amiens, the Allies' major communications center, and to drive the British back to the channel ports.

Suddenly, the deadlock had been broken; it was now a war of movement. Within two weeks, the Germans had taken some 1,250 square miles. But British resistance was astonishing, and the Germans, exhausted and short of ammunition and food, called off the drive. A second offensive against the British in April also had to be called off as the British contested every foot of ground. Both campaigns depleted German manpower while the Americans were arriving in great numbers to strengthen Allied lines and uplift morale.

At the end of May, Ludendorff resumed his offensive against the French. Attacking unexpectedly, the Germans broke through and by June 3 advanced to within fifty-six miles of Paris. General John Pershing, head of the American forces, cabled Washington that "the possibility of losing Paris has become apparent."[30] But the offensive was already winding down as reserves braced the French lines. In the battle of Belleau Wood (June 6–25, 1918), the Americans checked the Germans. There would be no open road to Paris.

In mid-July, the Germans tried again, crossing the Marne River in small boats. By August 3, the second battle of the Marne ended with the Germans being forced back over the river. Although they had thrown everything they had into their spring and summer offensives, it was not enough. The Allies had bent, but reinforced and encouraged by American arms, they did not break. Now they began to counterattack. The tide had turned. Between March and July the Germans had suffered nearly 1 million dead, wounded, and missing. And there were signs—thousands deserting and surrendering—that morale at the front was breaking. On August 8, the British, assisted by the French and using tanks to great advantage, broke through east of Amiens. Ludendorff called August 8 "the black day of the German Army." The kaiser himself declared to his generals: "We have nearly reached the limit of our powers of resistance. The war must be ended."[31] The Allies, their confidence surging, continued to attack with great success in August and September.

Meanwhile, German allies, deprived of support from a hard-pressed Germany, were unable to cope. An Allied army of French, Britons, Serbs, and Italians compelled Bulgaria to sign an armistice on September 29. Shortly afterward, British successes in the Middle East forced the Turks to withdraw from the war. In the streets of Vienna, people were shouting, "Long live peace! Down with the monarchy!" The Austro-Hungarian Empire was rapidly disintegrating into separate states based on nationality.

By early October, the last defensive position of the Germans crumbled. The army's spirit collapsed as well; war-weary soldiers, sensing that the war was lost, surrendered in large numbers and refused orders to return to the front. Fearing an Allied invasion of Germany, Ludendorff wanted an immediate armistice. But he needed to find a way to obtain favorable armistice terms from President Wilson and to shift the blame for the lost war from the military and the kaiser to the civilian leadership. Cynically, he urged the creation of a popular parliamentary government in Germany. But events in Germany went further than the general had anticipated. Whereas Ludendorff sought a limited monarchy, the shock of defeat and hunger sparked a revolution that forced the kaiser to abdicate. Imperial Germany perished in the last days of the war.

On November 11, the new German republic signed an armistice ending the hostilities. At 11 a.m., soldiers from both sides walked into no-man's-land and into a new day. A newspaper correspondent with the British army in France wrote: "Last night for the first time since August in the first year of the war, there was no light of gunfire in the sky, no sudden stabs of flame through darkness, no spreading glow above black trees where for four years of nights human beings were smashed to death. The Fires of Hell had been put out."[32]

THE PEACE CONFERENCE

Wilson's Hope for a New World

In January 1919, representatives of the Allied powers assembled in Paris to draw up peace terms; President Wilson was also there. The war-weary masses turned to Wilson as the prophet who would have the nations beat their swords into plowshares. In Paris, 2 million people lined the streets to cheer Wilson and throw bouquets; his carriage passed under a huge banner proclaiming "Honor to Wilson the Just." In Rome, hysterical crowds called him the god of peace; in Milan, wounded soldiers sought to kiss his clothes; in Poland, university students spoke his name when they shook hands with each other.

For Wilson, the war had been fought against autocracy. He hoped that a peace settlement based on liberal-democratic ideals would sweep away the foundations of war. Wilson proclaimed his message with a spiritual zeal that expressed his Presbyterian background and his faith in American democracy.

None of Wilson's principles seemed more just than the idea of self-determination: the right of a people to have its own state, free of foreign domination. In particular, this goal meant (or was interpreted to mean) the return of Alsace and Lorraine to France, the creation of an independent Poland, readjustment of the frontiers of Italy to incorporate Austrian lands inhabited by Italians, and an opportunity for Slavs of the Austro-Hungarian Empire to form their own states. Although Wilson did not demand the liberation of all colonies, the Fourteen Points did call for "a free, open-minded and absolutely impartial adjustment of all colonial claims" and a territorial settlement "made in the interest and for the benefit of the population concerned."

Aware that a harshly treated Germany might well seek revenge, engulfing the world in another cataclysm, Wilson insisted that there should be a "peace without victory." A just settlement would encourage a defeated Germany to work with the victorious Allies in building a new Europe. But on one point he was adamant: Prussian militarism, which he viewed as a principal cause of the war, must be eliminated. To create a better world, Wilson urged the formation of a League of Nations, an international parliament to settle disputes and discourage aggression. Wilson wanted a peace of justice to preserve Western civilization in its democratic and Christian form.

The Problems of Peacemaking

But could such moralistic pronouncements translate into concrete peace provisions in a world of hostile, competing nations stirred by nationalist passions?

Wilson's negotiating position had been undermined by the Republican Party's victory in the congressional elections of November 1918. Wilson had appealed to the American people to elect Democrats as a vote of confidence in his diplomacy. But instead Americans sent twenty-five Republicans and fifteen Democrats to the Senate. Although the Republicans' success apparently stemmed from local and national, rather than international, issues, the outcome diminished Wilson's prestige at the conference table. In the view of his fellow negotiators, Wilson was trying to preach to Europe even though he lacked the support of his own country. Because the Senate had to ratify any American treaty, European diplomats worried that what Wilson agreed to the Senate might reject, which is precisely what happened.

Attending the conference in person also weakened Wilson's negotiating position. As leader of the nation that had rescued the Allies and as initiator of a peace program that held the promise of a new world, Wilson occupied a position of honor, from which he could exert considerable influence and authority. But by haggling with the other representatives, he was knocked from his lofty pedestal and became all too human.

A major obstacle to Wilson's peace program was France's demand for security and revenge. Nearly the entire war on the Western Front had been fought on French territory. France mourned the loss of half its young men, and the terrible atrocities committed on French citizens in parts of the country occupied by Germany stoked the fires of French anger. Many French industries and farms had been ruined. Particularly galling to the French was the flooding of mines and the general destruction of property carried out by the Germans in their retreat at the war's end. France's representative at the conference table, Georges Clemenceau (1841–1929), did not share Wilson's hope for a new world or his confidence in the future League of Nations. Instead, he demanded that Germany be severely punished and its capacity to wage war destroyed. Desperately fearing Germany's strength, he wanted guarantees that the wars of 1870–1871 and 1914–1918 would not be repeated. The latter war had shown that without the help of Britain and the United States, France would have been at the mercy of Germany. Because there was no certainty that these states would again aid France, Clemenceau wanted to use his country's present advantage to cripple Germany.

The intermingling of nationalities was another barrier to Wilson's program, for no one could create a Europe completely free of minority problems. Some nationalities would always feel that they had been treated shabbily, and the various nationalities were not willing to moderate their demands or lower their aspirations. For example, the Fourteen Points called for an independent Poland with secure access to the sea.

WILSON AND CLEMENCEAU ARRIVE AT VERSAILLES, JUNE 18, 1919. The idealism of President Wilson (center) clashed with Premier Clemenceau's (left) determination to enhance France's security. (Hulton Archive/Getty Images.)

But between Poland and the sea lay land populated by Germans. Giving this land to Poland would violate German self-determination; denying it to Poland would mean that the new country had little chance of developing a sound economy. No matter what the decision, one people would regard it as unjust. Similarly, to provide the new Czechoslovakia with defensible borders, it would be necessary to give it land inhabited principally by Germans. This, too, could be viewed as a denial of German self-determination, but not granting the area to Czechoslovakia would mean that the new state would not be able to defend itself against Germany.

Secret treaties drawn up by the Allies during the war also interfered with Wilson's program. These agreements, dividing up German, Austrian, and Ottoman territory, did not square with the principle of self-determination. For example, to entice Italy into entering the war, the Allies had promised it Austrian lands that were inhabited predominantly by Germans and Slavs. Italy was not about to repudiate its prize because of Wilson's principles.

Finally, the war had aroused great bitterness, which persisted after the guns had been silenced. Both the masses and their leaders demanded retribution and held exaggerated hopes for territory and reparations. In such an atmosphere of postwar enmity, the spirit of compromise and moderation could not overcome the desire for spoils and punishment.

The Settlement

After months of negotiations, often punctuated by acrimony, the peacemakers hammered out a settlement. Five treaties made up the Peace of Paris: one each with Germany, Austria, Hungary, Bulgaria, and Turkey. Of the five, the Treaty of Versailles, which Germany signed on June 28, 1919, was the most significant.

France regained Alsace and Lorraine, the territory lost to Germany in the Franco-Prussian War of 1870–1871. The Treaty of Versailles also barred Germany from placing fortifications in the Rhineland. The French military had wanted to take the Rhineland from Germany and break it up into one or more republics under French suzerainty. Under this arrangement, French control would extend to the Rhine River, which was a natural defensive border; French forces had only to destroy the bridges to prevent a German invasion of France. With Germany deprived of this springboard for invasion, French security would be immensely improved. Recognizing that the German people would never permanently submit to the amputation of the Rhineland, which was inhabited by more than 5 million Germans and contained key industries, Wilson and British prime minister David Lloyd George (1863–1945) resisted these French demands. They did not want to create an Alsace-Lorraine in reverse by awarding France a region that was overwhelmingly German. Nor could Wilson ever agree to such a glaring violation of the principle of self-determination.

Faced with the opposition of Wilson and Lloyd George, Clemenceau backed down and agreed instead to Allied occupation of the Rhineland for fifteen years, its demilitarization, and an Anglo-American promise of assistance if Germany attacked France in the future. This last point, considered vital by France, proved useless. The alliance went into effect only if both the United States and Britain ratified it. Because this so-called Security Treaty did not get past the U.S. Senate, Britain also refused to sign it. France had made a great concession on the Rhineland issue but received nothing in exchange. The French people felt that they had been duped and wronged.

A related issue concerned French demands for annexation of the coal-rich Saar Basin, which adjoined Lorraine. By obtaining this region, France would weaken Germany's military potential. France argued that this would be just compensation for the deliberate destruction of the French coal mines by the retreating German army at the end of the war. But here, too, France was disappointed. The final compromise called for a League of Nations commission to govern the Saar Basin for fifteen years, after which the inhabitants would decide whether their territory would be ceded to France or returned to Germany.

In eastern Germany, in certain districts of Silesia that had a large Polish population, a plebiscite determined the future of the region. As a result, part of Upper Silesia was ceded to Poland. The settlement also gave Poland a corridor cut through West Prussia and terminating in the Baltic port of Danzig, and Danzig itself was declared an international city to be administered by the League of Nations. The Germans would never resign themselves to this loss of territory that separated East Prussia from the rest of Germany.

The victorious nations were awarded control of German colonies and Ottoman lands. However, these nations held the colonies not outright but as mandates under the supervision of the League, which would protect the interests of the native peoples. Thus, the division of Ottoman lands and German colonies represented a compromise between traditional imperialism and Wilsonian idealism. The mandate system implied the ultimate end of colonialism, for it clearly opposed the exploitation of colonial peoples and asserted independence as the rightful goal for subject nations.

To strip Germany of any offensive capacity, the settlement abolished the German general staff and forbade military conscription in Germany. The German army was limited to 100,000 volunteers and deprived of heavy artillery, tanks, and warplanes. The German navy was limited to a token force, which did not include submarines.

The issue of war reparations caused great bitterness between Wilson and his French and British adversaries. The American delegation wanted the treaty to fix a reasonable sum that Germany would have to pay and specify the period of years allotted for payment. But, instead, the Treaty of Versailles left Germany with an open-ended bill, which would probably take generations to pay. Wilson had lost on the issue of reasonable reparations. Moreover, Article 231, which preceded the reparation clauses, placed sole responsibility for the war on Germany and its allies. The Germans responded to this accusation with contempt.

In separate treaties, the conference dealt with the dissolution of the Hapsburg Empire. In the closing weeks of the war, the Austro-Hungarian Empire had crumbled as the various nationalities proclaimed their independence from Hapsburg rule. In most cases, the peacemakers ratified with treaties what the nationalities had already accomplished in fact. Serbia joined with Austro-Hungarian lands inhabited by South Slavs to become Yugoslavia. Czechoslovakia arose from the predominantly Czech and Slovak regions of Austria.

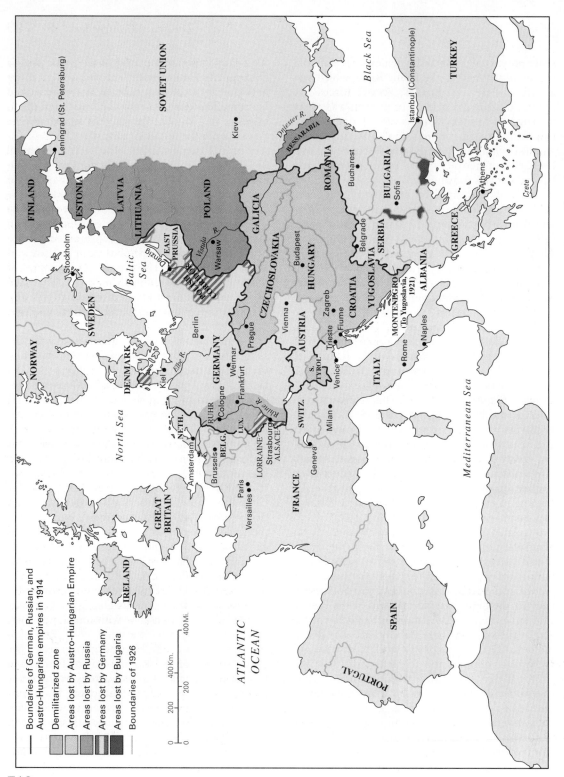

Black Sea

TURKEY

SOVIET UNION

Leningrad (St. Petersburg)

Kiev

Djiester R.

BESSARABIA

Istanbul (Constantinople)

FINLAND

ESTONIA

LATVIA

LITHUANIA

POLAND

GALICIA

ROMANIA

Bucharest

BULGARIA

Sofia

Athens

Crete

GREECE

Stockholm

Baltic Sea

EAST PRUSSIA

Danzig

Vistula R.

Warsaw

POLISH CORRIDOR

CZECHOSLOVAKIA

Budapest

HUNGARY

Belgrade

SERBIA

YUGOSLAVIA

CROATIA

Zagreb

MONTENEGRO (To Yugoslavia, 1921)

ALBANIA

SWEDEN

NORWAY

Berlin

DENMARK

Elbe R.

Kiel

GERMANY

Weimar

Frankfurt

Prague

Vienna

AUSTRIA

S. TYROL

Trieste

Fiume

Venice

ITALY

Rome

Naples

Mediterranean Sea

North Sea

NETH.

Amsterdam

BELG.

Brussels

LUX.

RUHR

Cologne

Rhine R.

LORRAINE

Strasbourg

ALSACE

SWITZ.

Milan

Geneva

FRANCE

Paris

Versailles

GREAT BRITAIN

IRELAND

ATLANTIC OCEAN

SPAIN

PORTUGAL

Boundaries of German, Russian, and Austro-Hungarian empires in 1914

Demilitarized zone

Areas lost by Austro-Hungarian Empire

Areas lost by Russia

Areas lost by Germany

Areas lost by Bulgaria

Boundaries of 1926

400 Mi.

400 Km.

200

200

0

0

710

Hungary, which broke away from Austria to become a separate country, had to cede a considerable amount of land to Romania and Yugoslavia. Austria had to turn over to Italy the South Tyrol, which was inhabited by 200,000 Austrian Germans. This clear violation of the principle of self-determination greatly offended liberal opinion. Deprived of its vast territories and prohibited from union with Germany, the new Austria was a third-rate power.

Assessment and Problems

The Germans unanimously denounced the Treaty of Versailles, for in their minds the war had ended not in German defeat but in a stalemate. They regarded the armistice as the prelude to a negotiated settlement among equals, based on Wilson's call for a peace of justice. Instead, the Germans were barred from participating in the negotiations. And they viewed the terms of the treaty as humiliating and vindictive—a peace of submission designed to keep Germany militarily and economically weak. What standard of justice, they asked, allowed the Allies to take the German colonies, reduce the German military to a pitiful size without disarming themselves, ban Germany from the League of Nations, and saddle the country with impossible reparations? Why should Germany lose approximately one-eighth of its territory and one-tenth of its population? Why should the Allies blame the war on Germany, provide for the self-determination of Poles while precluding the union of German-speaking Austria with Germany, hand over to Italy some 200,000 Austrian Germans, place Germans under Polish rule, and declare the German port of Danzig a free city?

The Germans protested that when the United States entered the war, Wilson had stated that the enemy was not the German people but their government. Surely, the Germans now argued, the new German democracy should not be punished for the sins of the monarchy and the military. To the Germans, the Treaty of Versailles was not the dawning of the new world that Wilson had promised but a vile crime.

Worn out by war, torn by revolutionary unrest, and desperately short of food, with its economy in disarray and with the Allies poised to invade, the new German republic had no choice but to sign the treaty. However, the sentiments of the German people were clearly and prophetically expressed by the Berlin *Vorwärts,* the influential Social Democratic newspaper: "We must never forget it is only a scrap of paper. Treaties based on violence can keep their validity only so long as force exists. Do not lose hope. The resurrection day comes."[33]

Critics in other lands also condemned the treaty as a punitive settlement, warning that it would only exacerbate old hatreds and enflame German nationalism. The treaty's defenders, however, insisted that had Germany won the war, it would have imposed a far harsher settlement on the Allies. They pointed to German war aims, which called for the annexation of parts of France and Poland, the reduction of Belgium and Romania to satellites, and German expansion in Africa. They pointed also to the Treaty of Brest-Litovsk, which Germany compelled Russia to sign in 1918, as an example of Germany's ruthlessness. An insatiable Germany deprived Russia of 34 percent of its population, 32 percent of its farmland, 54 percent of its industrial enterprises, and 89 percent of its coal mines. Furthermore, they noted that the peace settlement did reflect Wilson's principles: the new map of Europe was the closest approximation of the ethnic distribution of its peoples that Europe had ever known.

What is most significant about the Treaty of Versailles is that it did not solve the German problem. Germany was left weakened but unbroken— its industrial and military power only temporarily contained, and its nationalist fervor not only undiminished but stoked by a peace treaty that all political parties viewed as unjust, dictated, and offensive to national pride. The real danger in Europe was German unwillingness to accept defeat or surrender the dream of expansion.

◀ *Map 28.2* **Post–World War I: Broken Empires and Changed Boundaries** World War I led to the breakup of the Russian, Austro-Hungarian, and Ottoman Empires and the creation of several new countries, including Poland, Czechoslovakia, Yugoslavia, Lithuania, Latvia, and Estonia. (© 2016 Cengage Learning.)

Would France, Britain, and the United States enforce the treaty against a resurgent Germany? The war had demonstrated that an Allied victory depended on American intervention. But in 1920, the U.S. Senate, angry that Wilson had not taken Republicans with him to Paris and fearing that membership in the League of Nations would involve America in future wars, refused to ratify the Treaty of Versailles. Britain, feeling guilty over the treatment of Germany, lacked the will for enforcement and even came to favor treaty revision. The responsibility for preserving the settlement therefore rested primarily with France, which was not encouraging. Germany had greater industrial potential than France, and with Russia now Communist, France could not count on Russian manpower to balance Germany's much larger population. The Paris peace settlement left Germany resentful but potentially powerful—German industrial capacity was considerable, and only Russia had a larger population—and to the east lay small and weak states, some of them with sizable German minorities, that could not check a rearmed Germany. French general Ferdinand Foch commented prophetically: "This is not peace. It is an armistice for twenty years."[34]

THE RUSSIAN REVOLUTION OF 1917

One consequence of the war that influenced the course of European and world history in momentous ways was the Russian Revolution of 1917 and the resultant triumph of the Bolsheviks. The people of Russia had initially responded to the war with a show of patriotic fervor. But the realities of war quickly dimmed this ardor. The ill-equipped and poorly led Russian armies suffered huge losses. In July 1915, the minister of war wrote this dismal report:

The soldiers are without doubt exhausted by the continued defeats and retreats. Their confidence in final victory and in their leaders is undermined. Ever more threatening signs of impending demoralization are evident. Cases of desertion and voluntary surrender to the enemy are becoming more frequent. It

is difficult to expect enthusiasm and selflessness from men sent into battle unarmed and ordered to pick up the rifles of their dead comrades.[35]

By 1916, the home front began to fall apart. Shops were empty, money had no value, and hunger and cold stalked the working quarters of cities and towns. Factory workers, many of them women replacing husbands, brothers, and sons who were at the front, toiled long hours for wages that could not keep up with the accelerating inflation. When they protested, the government resorted to heavy-handed repression. By January 1917, nearly all Russians, soldiers and civilians alike, had lost trust in their autocratic government. But Tsar Nicholas II, determined to preserve autocracy, resisted any suggestion that he liberalize the regime for the sake of the war effort.

Autocracy was ready to collapse at the slightest blow. In early March (February 23 by the calendar* then in use), a strike, riots in the food lines, and street demonstrations in Petrograd (formerly Saint Petersburg) flared into sudden, unpremeditated revolution. The soldiers, who in 1905 had stood by the tsar, now rushed to support the striking workers. The Romanov dynasty, after three hundred years of rule (1613–1917), came to an end. A Provisional Government was set up—provisional until a representative Constituent Assembly, to be elected as soon as possible, could establish a permanent regime.

Problems of the Provisional Government

The collapse of autocracy was followed by what supporters in Russia and the West hoped would be a liberal, democratic regime pledged to give Russia a constitution. In reality, however, the course of events from March to November 1917 resembled a free-for-all—a no-holds-barred fight for the succession to autocracy, with only the fittest surviving. Events demonstrated the desperate state of the Russian Empire. Its vast size promoted internal disunity; increasing hardships

---

*Until March 1918, events in Russia were dated by the Julian calendar, thirteen days behind the Gregorian calendar used in the West. By the Julian calendar, the first revolution occurred in February, the second in October.

raised the fury of the accumulated resentments to raw brutality among the masses. National minorities took advantage of the anarchy to dismember the country.

Among the potential successors to the tsars, liberals of various shades seemed at first to enjoy the best chances. They represented the educated and forward-looking elements in Russian society that had arisen after the reforms of the 1860s: lawyers, doctors, professional people of all kinds, intellectuals, businesspeople and industrialists, many landowners, and even some bureaucrats. Liberals had opposed autocracy and earned a reputation for leadership.

Liberals had joined the March revolution reluctantly, for they were afraid of the masses and the violence in the streets. They dreaded social revolution that could result in the seizure of factories, dispossession of landowners, and tampering with property rights. Although most leaders of the Provisional Government had only modest means, they were capitalists, believing in private enterprise as the best way of promoting economic progress. Their ideal was a constitutional monarchy, its leadership entrusted to the educated and propertied elite familiar with the essentials of statecraft.

Unfortunately, the liberals misunderstood the mood of the people. Looking to the Western democracies—including, after April 1917, the United States—for political and financial support, the liberals decided to continue the war on the side of the Allies. Moreover, the new leadership considered it a matter of national honor to stand with their allies and to regain Russian land occupied by Germany. The decision antagonized the war-weary masses, along with the Russian soldiers, almost 2 million of whom had deserted. The liberals also antagonized the Russian peasants (by not confiscating and redistributing the landlords' lands free of charge) and industrial workers (whose economic conditions continued to deteriorate). As Russian nationalists who wanted their country to remain undivided, the liberals opposed national minorities—Finns, Ukrainians, Georgians, and others—who sought self-determination; hence, they lost the minorities' support.

Frustrated by the Provisional Government's inaction on the land question, peasants began taking matters into their own hands. They seized land and torched the estates of nobles, sometimes putting their owners to death. Seeking to claim a share of the confiscated land, more soldiers deserted. The breakdown of the railways stopped factory production; enraged workers ousted factory managers and owners. Consumer goods grew scarce and prices soared, and the peasants could see no reason to sell their crops if they could buy nothing in return. Thus, the specter of famine in the cities arose. Hardships and anger mounted. Adding to the disorder were the demands of the non-Russian nationalities for self-determination and even secession.

Freedom in Russia was leading to dissolution and chaos. The largely illiterate peasant masses had no experience with or understanding of the institutions, habits, and attitudes of a free society. Without their cooperation, Russian liberalism collapsed. This outcome demonstrated the difficulty of establishing Western liberal democratic forms of government in countries lacking a sense of unity, a strong middle class, or a tradition of responsible participation in public affairs.

By July 1917, when Aleksandr Kerensky (1881–1970), a radical lawyer of great eloquence, took over the leadership of the Provisional Government, it had become clear that law and order could be upheld only by brute force. In late August and early September, a conspiracy led by a right-wing general, Lavr Kornilov, sought to establish a military dictatorship. Kornilov had the support not only of the officer corps and the tsarist officials but also of many liberals fed up with anarchy. What stopped the general was not Kerensky's government (which had no troops) but the workers of Petrograd. Their agitators demoralized Kornilov's soldiers, proving that a dictatorship of the Right had no mass support. The workers also repudiated Kerensky and the Provisional Government, as well as their own moderate leaders; henceforth, they supported the Bolsheviks.

Lenin and the Rise of Bolshevism

Revolutionary movements had a long history in Russia, going back to the early nineteenth century, when educated Russians began to compare their country unfavorably with Western Europe. They, too, wanted constitutional liberty and free speech in order to make their country modern. Prohibited from speaking out in public, they went underground, giving up their liberalism as ineffective. They saw revolutionary socialism, with its idealistic vision and compassion for the multitude, as a better ideology in the harsh struggle with the tsar's police. By the 1870s, many socialists had evolved into austere and self-denying professional revolutionaries who, in the service of the cause, had no moral scruples, just as the police had no scruples in the defense of the tsars. Bank robbery,

STARVING CHILDREN IN A FAMINE REGION OF RUSSIA, 1921. The privations suffered by the Russian people in the years immediately following World War I and the Bolshevik Revolution are incalculable. The first four years of the new Communist regime (1917–1921) were marked by civil war and foreign invasion. Cities faced starvation, and food was taken from peasants at gunpoint. Several million lives were lost. (© Mary Evans Picture Library/The Image Works.)

murder, assassination, treachery, and terror were not seen as immoral if they served the revolutionary cause.

In the 1880s and 1890s, revolutionaries learned industrial economics and sociology from Marx; from Marxism they also acquired a vision of a universal and inevitable progression toward socialism and Communism, which satisfied their semireligious craving for salvation in this world, not the next. Marxism also allied them with socialist movements in other lands, giving them an internationalist outlook. History, they believed, was on their side, as it was for all the proletarians and oppressed peoples in the world.

By 1900, a number of able young Russians had rallied to revolutionary Marxism; almost all of them were educated or came from privileged families. The most promising was Vladimir Ilyich Ulyanov, known as Lenin (1870–1924), the son of a teacher and school administrator who had attained the rank of a nobleman. Lenin had studied law but practiced revolution instead. His first contribution lay in adapting Marxism to Russian conditions; to do so, he took considerable liberties with Marx's teaching. His second contribution followed from the first: outlining the organization of an underground party capable of surviving against the tsarist police. It was to be a tightly knit conspiratorial elite of professional revolutionaries. Its headquarters would be safely located abroad, and it would have close ties to the masses, that is, to the workers and other potentially revolutionary elements.

Two other prominent Marxists were Leon Trotsky (1879–1940) and Joseph Stalin (1879–1953). Trotsky, whose original name was Lev Bronstein, was the son of a prosperous Jewish farmer from southern Russia and was soon known for his brilliant pen. Less prominent until after the Revolution, Stalin (the man of steel) was originally named Iosif Dzhugashvili; he was from Georgia, beyond the Caucasus Mountains. Bright enough to be sent to the best school in the area, he dropped out for a revolutionary career. While they were still young, Lenin, Trotsky, and Stalin were all hardened by arrest, imprisonments, and exile to Siberia. Lenin and Trotsky later lived abroad, while Stalin, following a harsher course, stayed in Russia; for four years before 1917, he was banished to bleakest northern Siberia and conditioned to ruthlessness for life.

In 1903, the Russian Marxists split into two factions: the moderate Mensheviks, so named after finding themselves in a minority *(menshinstvo)* at a rather unrepresentative vote at the Second Party Congress, and the extremist **Bolsheviks**, who at that moment were in the majority *(bolshinstvo)*. They might more accurately have been called the "softs" and the "hards." The "softs" (Mensheviks) preserved basic moral scruples; they would not stoop to crime or undemocratic methods for the sake of political success. For that the "hards" (Bolsheviks) ridiculed them, noting that a dead, imprisoned, or unsuccessful revolutionary was of little use.

Meanwhile, Lenin perfected Bolshevik revolutionary theory. He violated Marxist tradition by paying close attention to the revolutionary potential of peasants (thereby anticipating Mao Zedong). Lenin also looked closely at the numerous peoples in Asia who had recently fallen under Western imperialist domination. These people, he sensed, constituted a potential revolutionary force. In alliance with the Western—and Russian—proletariat, they might overthrow the worldwide capitalist order. The Bolsheviks, the most militant of all revolutionary socialists, were ready to assist in that gigantic struggle.

Lenin was a Russian nationalist as well as a socialist internationalist; he had a vision of a modern and powerful Russian state destined to be a model in world affairs. Russian Communism was thus nationalist Communism. The Bolsheviks saw the abolition of income-producing property by the dictatorship of the proletariat as the most effective way of mobilizing the country's resources. Yet the Bolshevik mission was also internationalist. The Russian Revolution was intended to set off a world revolution, liberating all oppressed classes and peoples around the world, and achieving a higher stage of civilization.

Lenin's Opportunity

On April 16, 1917, Lenin, with German help, arrived in Petrograd from exile in Switzerland.

(The Germans provided Lenin with a secret train to take him to Petrograd; they hoped that the Bolshevik leader, who wanted Russia to withdraw from the "capitalist" war, would initiate a revolution and gain power.) The Provisional Government, he said, could not possibly preserve Russia from disintegration. Most of the soldiers, workers, and peasants would repudiate the Provisional Government's cautious liberalism in favor of a regime expressing their demand for peace and land. Nothing would stop them from avenging themselves for centuries of oppression. Lenin also felt that only complete state control of the economy could rescue the country from disaster. The sole way out, he insisted, was the dictatorship of the proletariat backed by *soviets* (councils) of soldiers, workers, and peasants, particularly the poorer peasants.

Lenin prepared his party for the second stage of the Revolution of 1917: the seizure of power by the Bolsheviks. His slogan, "Peace, Land, and Bread," held a magnetic attraction for the desperate Russian masses. The Bolsheviks' determined effort to win over the disheartened soldiers proved particularly effective. Many of the people who supported the Bolsheviks interpreted Lenin's other powerful slogan—"All Power to the Soviets"—to mean that the Bolsheviks aimed to create a democratic socialist state that would institute needed social reforms. They did not anticipate the creation of Bolshevik dictatorship.

Conditions favored the Bolsheviks, as Lenin had predicted. The Bolsheviks obtained majorities in the soviets. The peasants were in active revolt, seizing the land themselves. The Provisional Government lost all control over the course of events; three years of warfare had caused the disintegration of Russian society. On November 6 (October 24 by the old calendar), Lenin urged immediate action: "The government is tottering. It must be given the death blow at all costs."[36] On the following day, the Bolsheviks, meeting little resistance, seized power. Lenin permitted elections for the Constituent Assembly that had been scheduled by the Provisional Government. In a free election, the Bolsheviks received only 24 percent of the vote. After meeting once in

WOMEN DEMONSTRATE IN PETROGRAD, 1917. The collapse of the tsarist regime was followed by a period of political fermentation, meetings, and concern about food shortages. Women demonstrated for increased bread supplies. The poster reads, "Comrades, workers, and soldiers, support our demands!" (Everett Collection/ Newscom.)

January 1918, however, the Constituent Assembly was disbanded by the Bolsheviks.

The Bolsheviks Survive

Lenin contended that he was guiding the Russian proletariat and all humanity toward a higher social order, symbolizing—in Russia and much of the world—the rebellion of the disadvantaged against Western (or "capitalist") dominance. That is why, in 1918, he changed the name of his party from Bolshevik to Communist, which implied a concern for the human community. For Lenin, as

for Marx, a world without exploitation was humanity's noblest ideal.

But staggering adversity confronted Lenin after his seizure of power. In the prevailing anarchy, Russia lay open to the German armies. Under the Treaty of Brest-Litovsk, signed in March 1918—the lowest point in Russian history for more than two hundred years—Russia lost Finland, Poland, and the Baltic provinces, all regions inhabited largely by non-Russians. It also lost the rebellious Ukraine, its chief industrial base and breadbasket. Yet Lenin, with the country in shambles, had no choice but to accept the humiliating terms.

V. I. LENIN. Red Army soldiers leaving for battle in the civil war are addressed by Lenin in Moscow in May 1920. (SZ Photo/Scherl/DIZ Muenchen GmbH, Sueddeutsche Zeitung Photo/Alamy.)

THE WAR AND EUROPEAN CONSCIOUSNESS

"There will be wars as never before on earth," predicted Nietzsche. World War I bore him out. Modern technology enabled the combatants to kill with unprecedented efficiency; modern nationalism infused both civilians and soldiers with the determination to fight until the enemy was totally beaten. Exercising wide control over its citizens, the modern state mobilized its human, material, and spiritual resources to wage total war. As the war hardened into a savage stalemate, statesmen did not press for a compromise peace but rather demanded ever more mobilization, ever more escalation, and ever more sacrifices.

The Great War profoundly altered the course of Western civilization, deepening the spiritual crisis that had helped produce it. How could one speak of the inviolability of the individual when Europe had become a slaughterhouse, or of the primacy of reason when nations permitted the slaughter to go unabated for four years? How could the mind cope with this spectacle of a civilization turning against itself, destroying itself in an orgy of organized violence? How could it explain students leaving their schoolbooks to become, as one participant said, "nocturnal beasts of prey hunting each other in packs"?[37] A young French soldier, shortly before he was killed at Verdun, expressed the disillusionment that gripped the soldiers in the trenches: "Humanity is mad! It must be mad to do what it is doing. What a massacre! What scenes of horror and carnage, I cannot find words to translate my impressions. Hell cannot be so terrible. Men are mad!"[38] The war, said the British poet Robert Graves, provoked an "inward scream" that still reverberates. The agony caused by the astronomical casualty figures—some 9.4 million dead and 21 million wounded, many of them pathetically mutilated, disfigured, or mentally deranged—touched millions of homes. About 300,000 of French fatalities were unidentifiable, their bodies blown apart by artillery shelling. For a generation, millions of grieving widows and orphaned children were a tragic reminder of Europe's descent into savagery. Now only the naïve could believe in continuous progress, a principal dogma of nineteenth-century liberal culture. Western civilization had entered an age of violence, anxiety, and doubt.

World War I was a great turning point in the history of the West. The war left many with the gnawing feeling that Western civilization had lost its vitality and was caught in a rhythm of breakdown. It seemed that Western civilization was fragile and perishable, that Western people, despite their extraordinary accomplishments, were never more than a step or two away from barbarism. Surely, any civilization that could allow such senseless slaughter to last four years had entered its decline and could look forward to only the darkest of futures.

European intellectuals were demoralized and disillusioned. The orderly, peaceful, rational world of their youth had been destroyed, and they knew in their hearts that it would never be restored. Their foreboding was not misplaced, for without World War I it is doubtful that either the Communists in Russia or the Nazis in Germany would have gained power. The Enlightenment worldview, weakened in the nineteenth century by the assault of romantics, Social Darwinists, extreme nationalists, race mystics, and glorifiers of the irrational, was now disintegrating. The enormity of the war had shattered faith in the capacity of reason to deal with crucial social and political questions. It appeared that civilization was fighting an unending and seemingly hopeless battle against the irrational elements in human nature and that war would be a continuous phenomenon in the twentieth century.

Scientific research had produced more efficient weapons to kill and maim Europe's youth. The achievements of Western science and technology, which had been viewed as a boon for humanity and the clearest testament to the superiority of European civilization, were called into question. Confidence in the future gave way to doubt. The old beliefs in the perfectibility of humanity, the blessings of science, and ongoing progress now seemed an expression of naïve optimism, if not post-Christian myths that the war had exposed as fraudulent. As A. J. P. Taylor concludes,

> *The First World War was difficult to fit into the picture of a rational civilization advancing by ordered stages. The civilized men of the twentieth century had outdone in savagery the barbarians of all preceding ages, and their civilized virtues—organization, mechanical skill, self-sacrifice—had made war's savagery all the more terrible. Modern man had developed powers which he was not fit to use. European civilization had been weighed in the balance and found wanting.*[39]

Western civilization had lost its spiritual center. The French writer Paul Valéry summed up the mood of a troubled generation, for whom the sun seemed to be setting on the Enlightenment.

> *The storm has died away, and still we are restless, uneasy as if the storm were about to break. Almost all the affairs of men remain in a terrible uncertainty. We think of what has disappeared, and we are almost destroyed by what has been destroyed; we do not know what will be born, and we fear the future, not without reason. We hope vaguely, we dread precisely; our fears are infinitely more precise than our hopes; we confess that the charm of life is behind us. There is no thinking man . . . who can hope to dominate this anxiety, to escape from this impression of darkness. . . . But among all these injured things is the Mind. The Mind has indeed been cruelly wounded; its complaint is heard in the hearts of intellectual men; it passes a mournful judgment on itself. It doubts itself profoundly.*[40]

Having lost confidence in the power of reason to solve the problems of the human community, in liberal doctrines of individual freedom, and in the institutions of parliamentary democracy, many people turned to Fascism as a simple, saving faith. Far from making the world safe for democracy, as Wilson and other liberals had hoped, World War I gave rise to totalitarian movements, which would nearly destroy democracy.

The war produced a generation of young people who had reached their maturity in combat. Violence had become a way of life for millions of soldiers hardened by battle and for millions of civilians aroused by four years of war stories, the relentless massacre of Europe's young men had a brutalizing effect. Violence, cruelty, suffering, and even wholesale death seemed to be natural and acceptable components of human existence. The sanctity of the individual seemed to be liberal and Christian claptrap.

To be sure, many people, including veterans, repelled by the slaughter, abandoned the popular romantic view that war was glorious and heroic. But the fascination with, if not worship of, violence and contempt for life persisted in the postwar world. Many returned veterans yearned for the excitement of battle and the fellowship of the trenches—what one French soldier called "the most tender human experience." After the war, a young English officer reminisced: "There was an exaltation, in those days of comradeship and dedication, that would have come in few other ways."[41] A fraternal bond united the men of the trenches. Many veterans also shared a primitive attraction to war's fury. A Belgian veteran expressed it this way:

> The plain truth is that if I were to obey my native animal instincts—and there was little hope for anything else while I was in the trenches—I should enlist again in any future war, or take part in any sort of fighting, merely to experience again that voluptuous thrill of the human brute who realizes his power to take away life from other human beings who try to do the same to him. What was first accepted as a moral duty became a habit and the habit . . . had become a need.[42]

And no doubt Julian Grenfell spoke for many other combat soldiers when he declared in November 1914: "I adore war. I have never been so well or so happy. . . . The fighting excitement vitalizes everything, every sight and word and action."[43] The brutalizing effect of the war is evident in this statement by a German soldier, for whom the war never ended:

> People told us that the War was over. That made us laugh. We ourselves are the War. Its flame burns strongly in us. It envelops our whole being and fascinates us with the enticing urge to destroy. We . . . marched onto the battlefields of the postwar world just as we had gone into battle on the Western Front: singing, reckless, and filled with the joy of adventure as we marched to the attack; silent, deadly, remorseless in battle.[44]

The British novelist D. H. Lawrence (1885–1930) understood that the brutality and hate unleashed by the war had ruined old Europe and would give rise to even greater evils. On the day the armistice was signed, he warned prophetically:

> I suppose you think the war is over and that we shall go back to the kind of world you lived in before it. But the war isn't over. The hate and evil is greater now than ever. Very soon war will break out again and overwhelm you. . . . The crowd outside thinks that Germany is crushed forever. But the Germans will soon rise again. Europe is done for. . . . The war isn't over. Even if the fighting should stop, the evil will be worse because the hate will be dammed up in men's hearts and will show itself in all sorts of ways.[45]

Particularly in Germany, the veterans who aspired to recapture the exhilaration experienced in combat and men who had been too young to fight but were inspired by the heroic deeds of their elders made ideal recruits for extremist political movements that glorified action and brutality and promised to rescue society from a decadent liberalism. Hitler and Mussolini, both ex-soldiers imbued with the ferocity of the front, knew how to appeal to them. The lovers of violence and the harbingers of hate who took control of Fascist parties would come within a

THE SURVIVORS **(1922), BY KÄTHE KOLLWITZ.** With an estimated 9.4 million dead and 21 million wounded, World War I shattered the hope that Western Europe had been making continuous progress toward a rational and enlightened civilization. (Image © DeA Picture Library/Art Resource, N.Y. © 2011 Artists Rights Society (ARS), New York/VG Bild-Kunst, Bonn.)

hairbreadth of destroying Western civilization. The intensified nationalist hatreds following World War I also helped fuel the fires of World War II. The Germans vowed to regain lands lost to the Poles. Many Germans, like the embittered Hitler, were consumed by anguish over a defeat that they believed never should have happened and over the humiliating Treaty of Versailles. Many Germans also succumbed to the distortion of truth propagated by army leaders and nationalists that Germany had not been defeated on the battlefield but had been betrayed—stabbed in the back—at home by socialists and Jews. A desire for revenge festered in their souls. Italy, too, felt aggrieved because it had not received more territory from the dismembered Austro-Hungarian Empire. Mussolini would cleverly exploit these feelings in his bid for power.

Yet while some veterans clung to an aggressive militarism, others aspired to build a more humane world. Such veterans embraced democratic and socialist ideals and resolved that the bloodbath would never be repeated. Tortured by memories of war, European intellectuals wrote pacifist plays and novels and signed pacifist declarations. Indeed, in the 1930s, an attitude of "peace at any price" discouraged resistance to Nazi Germany in its bid to dominate Europe.

The war had a huge impact on women. In order to release men for military service, women in England, France, Germany, and later the United States responded to their countries' wartime needs. They took jobs in munitions factories; worked on farms; and drove ambulances, mail trucks, and buses. They worked as nurses, laboratory assistants, plumbers' helper, and bank clerks. By performing effectively in jobs formerly occupied by men, women demonstrated that they had an essential role to play in their countries' economic life. The employment of women in many areas of the workplace did encounter strong resistance, and after the war many female workers were dismissed from their new positions. Nevertheless, by the end of the war, little opposition remained to granting women political rights.

During World War I, new weapons were introduced, particularly the tank and the fighter plane, which revolutionized the future of warfare. Just before World War II, imaginative military planners recognized that planes and tanks, properly deployed, could penetrate and smash the enemy's defenses, circumventing the stalemate of trench warfare. Planes also meant terror from the skies, for bombs could pulverize a city, killing and maiming tens of thousands of civilians.

World War I was total war; it encompassed the entire nation and had no limits. States demanded total victory and total commitment from their citizens. They regulated industrial production, developed sophisticated propaganda techniques to strengthen morale, and exercised ever-greater control over the lives of their people, organizing and disciplining them like soldiers. This total mobilization of nations' human and material resources provided a model for future dictators. With ever-greater effectiveness and ruthlessness, dictators would centralize power and manipulate thinking. The ruthless dictatorships that emerged in Russia, Germany, and Italy were products of the war. The war gave Communists the opportunity to seize power in Russia, and the mentality of the front and dissatisfaction with the peace settlement helped to mold the Fascist movements that emerged in Italy and Germany. And both Hitler and Stalin drew a moral lesson from the immense loss of life in the trenches: a desired political end justifies vast human sacrifices. The barbarism of the trenches would be eclipsed by the horrors inflicted on people by totalitarian regimes and a second world war that was begotten by World War I. The noble sentiment, widely publicized during the war, that this was "the war to end all wars" proved to be another naïve fantasy.

❖   ❖   ❖

NOTES

1. Arnold Toynbee, *Surviving the Future* (New York: Oxford University Press, 1971), 106–107.

2. Quoted in Roland N. Stromberg, *Redemption by War* (Lawrence: Regents Press of Kansas, 1982), 24.

3. Excerpted in John W. Boyer and Jan Goldstein, eds., *Twentieth Century Europe*, vol. 9 of *University of Chicago Readings in Western Civilization*, ed. John W. Boyer and Julius Kirshner (Chicago: University of Chicago Press, 1987), 26.

4. Heinrich von Treitschke, *Politics*, excerpted in *Germany's War Mania* (New York: Dodd, Mead, 1915), 222–223.

5. Quoted in James Joll, "The Unspoken Assumptions," in *The Origins of the First World War*, ed. H. W. Koch (New York: Taplinger, 1972), 325.

6. Quoted in Barbara Tuchman, *The Guns of August* (New York: Macmillan, 1962), 46–47.

7. Fritz Fischer, *Germany's Aims in the First World War* (New York: Norton, 1967), 88.

8. Quoted in Joachim Remak, *The Origins of World War I* (New York: Holt, 1967), 135.

9. Quoted in Michael Burleigh, *Earthly Powers: The Clash of Religion and Politics in Europe, from the French Revolution to the Great War* (New York: HarperCollins, 2007), 445.

10. Quoted in Koppel S. Pinson, *Modern Germany: Its History and Civilization* (New York: Macmillan, 1954), 315.

11. Rupert Brooke, "Peace," in *Collected Poems of Rupert Brooke* (New York: Dodd, Mead, 1941), 111.

12. Quoted in Joachim C. Fest, *Hitler* (New York: Harcourt Brace Jovanovich, 1973), 66.

13. Roland Dorgelès, "After Fifty Years," in *Promise of Greatness*, ed. George A. Panichas (New York: The John Day Company, 1968), 14–15.

14. Excerpted in Joe H. Kirchberger, ed., *The First World War: An Eyewitness to History* (New York: Facts on File, 1992), 45.

15. Quoted in Joseph E. Persico, *Eleventh Month, Eleventh Day, Eleventh Hour: Armistice Day, 1918* (New York: Random House, 2004), 27.

16. Quoted in Tuchman, *The Guns of August,* 145.

17. Bertrand Russell, *The Autobiography of Bertrand Russell, 1914–1944* (Boston: Little, Brown, 1968), 4, 6.

18. Quoted in Robert G. L. Waite, *Vanguard of Nazism* (New York: Norton, 1969), 22.

19. Carl Zuckmayer, *A Part of Myself* (New York: Carroll and Graf, 1984; originally published by Harcourt Brace Jovanovich, 1970), 147.

20. Brooke, "Peace," 111.

21. Quoted in Peter Gay, *Freud: A Life for Our Time* (New York: Norton), 348.

22. Quoted in Koch, *Origins of the First World War,* 318.

23. Stefan Zweig, *The World of Yesterday* (New York: Viking, 1970), 223.

24. Quoted in Tuchman, *Guns of August,* 51.

25. Quoted in Jay Winter and Blaine Baggett, *The Great War and the Shaping of the Twentieth Century* (New York: Penguin Books, 1966), 165.

26. A. J. P. Taylor, *A History of the First World War* (New York: Berkeley, 1966), 84.

27. Quoted in Richard M. Watt, *Dare Call it Treason* (New York: Simon & Schuster, 1963), 69.

28. Ibid., 215.

29. Quoted in Daniel M. Smith, *The Great Departure* (New York: Wiley, 1965), 20.

30. Quoted in S. L. A. Marshall, *The American Heritage History of World War I* (New York: Dell, 1966), 334.

31. Quoted in John Terraine, *To Win a War: 1918, the Year of Victory* (Garden City, N.Y.: Doubleday, 1981), 102.

32. Excerpted in Louis L. Snyder, ed., *Historic Documents of World War I* (Princeton, N.J.: Van Nostrand, 1958), 183.

33. Quoted in Thomas A. Bailey, *Woodrow Wilson and the Lost Peace* (Chicago: Quadrangle Books, 1963), 303.

34. Peter Vansittart, *Voices from the Great War* (New York: Avon Books, 1985), 263.

35. Excerpted in Ronald Kowalski, *The Russian Revolution, 1917–1921* (New York: Routledge, 1997), 20.

36. From *Collected Works of V. I. Lenin*, Vol. 26, 4th edition (Moscow, 1960–1967), 235.

37. Quoted in Michael Adas, *Machines as the Measure of Man* (Ithaca, N.Y.: Cornell University Press, 1989), 376.

38. Quoted in Alistair Horne, *The Price of Glory* (New York: Harper, 1967), 240.

39. A. J. P. Taylor, *From Sarajevo to Potsdam* (New York: Harcourt, Brace and World, 1966), 55–56.

40. Paul Valéry, *Variety* (New York: Harcourt, Brace, 1927), 27–28.

41. Quoted in Modris Eksteins, *Rites of Spring: The Great War and the Birth of the Modern Age* (New York: Doubleday Anchor Books, 1989), 232.

42. Quoted in Eric J. Leed, *No Man's Land: Combat and Identity in World War I* (New York: Cambridge University Press, 1979), 201.

43. Quoted in Reginald Pound, *The Lost Generation of 1914* (New York: Coward-McCann, 1964), 80.

44. Quoted in Robert G. L. Waite, *Vanguard of Nazism* (New York: W. W. Norton, 1969), 42.

45. Quoted in Samuel Hynes, *A War Imagined* (New York: Atheneum, 1991), 266.

Chapter 29

An Era of Totalitarianism

Adolf Hitler before his Labor Army at Nuremberg, Germany, September 1938. (© Bettmann/CORBIS.)

Focus Questions

1. What are the distinctive features of a totalitarian state?

2. What motivated Stalin to make terror a government policy? What motivated Communist bureaucrats to participate in Stalin's inhumanities?

3. What were the essential features of the Fascist movements that arose in Europe after World War I?

4. What were Hitler's attitudes toward liberalism, war, race, the Jews, and propaganda?

5. In what ways did Nazism conflict with the core values of both the Enlightenment and Christianity? Why did the Nazi regime attract so many supporters?

6. What lessons might democratic societies draw from the Nazi experience?

*I*n the 1930s, the term **totalitarianism** was used to describe the Fascist regime in Italy, the National Socialist regime in Germany, and the Communist regime in the Soviet Union. To a degree that far exceeded the ancient tyrannies and early modern autocratic states, these dictatorships aspired to and, with varying degrees of success, attained control over the individual's consciousness and behavior and all phases of political, social, and cultural life. To many people it seemed that a crisis-riddled democracy was dying and that the future belonged to these dynamic totalitarian movements, an outlook that was an integral part of totalitarian ideologies.

Totalitarianism is a twentieth-century phenomenon, for such all-embracing control over the individual and society could be achieved only in an age of modern ideology, technology, and bureaucracy. The totalitarian state was more completely established in Germany and the Soviet Union than in Italy, where cultural and historic conditions impeded the realization of the totalitarian goal of monolithic unity and total control.

In *Totalitarian Dictatorship and Autocracy* (1956), Carl J. Friedrich and Zbigniew K. Brzezinski viewed Fascist and Communist dictatorships as "historically unique and *sui generic* [of its own kind]"[1]—different in nature from ancient Eastern despotisms, the Roman Empire, the tyrannies of the Renaissance city-states, or the absolute monarchies of modern Europe. "Broadly speaking, totalitarian dictatorship is a new development; there has never been anything quite like it before." They contended further that "fascist and communist totalitarian dictatorships are basically alike."[2] Even though the ideological aims and social and economic policies of Hitler and Stalin differed fundamentally, both Soviet Russia and Nazi Germany shared the totalitarian goal of total domination of the individual and institutions and employed similar methods to achieve it. Mussolini's Italy is more accurately called *authoritarian*, for the party-state either did not intend to control all phases of life or lacked the means to do so. Moreover, Mussolini hesitated to use the ruthless methods that Hitler and Stalin employed so readily.

725

Chronology 29.1 ❖ Totalitarianism

November 1917	Bolsheviks, led by Lenin, take command in Russia
1918–1920	Civil war and foreign intervention in Russia
March 1918	Treaty of Brest-Litovsk
July 1918	Nicholas II of Russia and his family are murdered
March 1919	Communist International is formed
1921–1928	New Economic Policy
1922	Stalin becomes general secretary of the Communist Party
1922	Mussolini rises to power
1923	Hitler's failed Beer Hall Putsch and subsequent imprisonment
January 1924	Lenin dies
1924	Constitution of the Union of Soviet Socialist Republics takes effect
1928	First Five-Year Plan starts rapid industrialization in Russia
October 1929	The Great Depression begins
1929	Stalin in sole command in Russia; collectivization of agriculture begins
1933	Hitler elected chancellor of Germany
1936	Stalin's constitution: socialism achieved
1936–1938	Stalin's terror purges
1936–1939	Spanish Civil War
November 1938	Nazi pogrom—*Kristallnacht*
1939	Hitler invades Poland; World War II starts
June 1941	Hitler invades the Soviet Union

THE NATURE OF TOTALITARIANISM

Striving for total unity, control, and obedience, the totalitarian dictatorship is the antithesis of liberal democracy. Seeking to obliterate the democratic state which preceded it (the short-lived Provisional Government in Russia and the Weimar Republic in Germany), both Communist Russia and Nazi Germany abolished all competing political parties, suppressed individual liberty, eliminated or regulated private institutions, and utilized the modern state's bureaucracy and technology to impose its ideology and enforce its commands. The one-party state determines what people should believe—what values they should hold. There is no room for individual thinking, private moral judgment, or individual conscience, all considered evils that threaten the totalitarian ideology and party. The individual possesses no natural rights that the state must respect. The state regards individuals merely as building blocks, human material to be hammered and hewed into a new social order. It seeks to create an efficiently organized and stable society—one whose members do not raise troublesome questions or hold unorthodox opinions.

Nevertheless, the totalitarian dictatorship is also an unintended consequence of liberal democracy. It emerged in an age in which, because of the French and Industrial Revolutions, the masses had become a force in political life. The totalitarian leader seeks to gain and preserve power by harnessing mass support. Hitler, in particular, built a party within the existing constitutional system and exploited the electoral process in order to overthrow the democratic government.

Unlike previous dictatorial regimes, the dictatorships of both the Left and the Right sought to legitimize their rule by gaining the masses' approval. They claimed that their governments were higher and truer expressions of the people's will. The Soviet and Nazi dictatorships established their rule in the name of the people—the German Volk or the Soviet proletariat.

A distinctive feature of totalitarianism is the overriding importance of the leader, who is seen as infallible and invincible. The masses' slavish adulation of the leader and their uncritical acceptance of the dogma that the leader or the party is always right promote loyalty, dedication, and obedience and distort rational thinking.

Totalitarian leaders want more than power for its own sake; they engage in vast projects of social engineering, intending to transform the world according to an all-embracing ideology, a set of convictions and beliefs that, says Hannah Arendt, "pretend[s] to know the mysteries of the whole historical process—the secrets of the past, the intricacies of the present, the uncertainties of the future."[3] The ideology constitutes a higher and infallible truth based on a law of history or social development that, says Karl Dietrich Bracher, "reduce[s] the past and the future to a single historical principle of struggle, no matter whether by state, nation, people, race, or class."[4] The ideology contains a dazzling vision of the future—a secular New Jerusalem—that strengthens the will of the faithful and attracts converts. "This utopian and **chiliastic** outlook of totalitarian ideologies," declare Friedrich and Brzezinski, "gives them a pseudoreligious quality. In fact, they often elicit in the less critical followers a depth of conviction and a fervor of devotion usually found only among persons inspired by a transcendent faith."[5] Like a religion, the totalitarian ideology provides its adherents with beliefs that make society and history intelligible, that explain all of existence in an emotionally gratifying way. A distinguishing feature of both Communist and Nazi ideologies was the dogmatic belief that

conflict—between classes for Marxists and between nations and races for Nazis—was the driving force in history.

The ideology—a "grand transcendent fiction [or] *metamyth*" in Brzezinski's apt phrase—promises to transform the social order in accordance with an ultimate and exclusive truth, a natural law, propagated by the party, thereby satisfying a human yearning for complete certitude.[6] Like a religion, it creates true believers, who feel that they are participating in a great cause—a heroic fight against evil—that gives meaning to their lives and justifies torture, deportation, and mass murder. During World War II, a German soldier fighting on the Eastern Front wrote to his brother that the battle "is for a new ideology, a new belief, a new life! I am glad that I can participate . . . in this war of light and darkness."[7]

Also like a religion, the totalitarian party gives isolated and alienated individuals a sense of belonging, a feeling of camaraderie; it enables a person to lose himself or herself in the comforting and exhilarating embrace of a mass movement. The radical Russian anarchist Bakunin had sensed the seductive power of the community when he stated: "I do not want to be I, I want to be We."[8]

Not only did the totalitarian religion-ideology supply followers with a cause that claimed absolute goodness; it also provided a Devil. For the Soviets, the source of evil and the cause of all the people's hardships were the degenerate capitalists, reactionary peasants who resisted collectivization, the traitorous Trotskyites, or the saboteurs and foreign agents who impeded the realization of the socialist society. For the Nazis, the Devil was the conspirator Jew. These "evil" ones must be eliminated in order to realize the totalitarian movement's vision of the future.

Thus, both the Nazis and the Soviets engaged in genocidal actions, liquidating large numbers of people designated as enemies of the race or enemies of the socialist state. Historical necessity or a higher purpose demanded and justified their liquidation. The appeal to historical necessity has all the power of a great myth. Presented as a world-historical struggle between the forces of good and the forces of evil, the myth incites fanaticism and numbs the conscience. Traditional rules of morality have no meaning; seemingly decent people, losing all regard for human life, engage in terrible acts of brutality with no remorse, convinced that they are waging a righteous war.

Totalitarians are utopians inspired by idealism; they seek the salvation of their nation, their race, or humanity. They believe that the victory of their cause will usher in the millennium, a state of harmony and bliss. Such a vision is attractive to people burdened by economic insecurity or spiritual disorientation. The history of the twentieth century demonstrates how easily utopian beliefs can be twisted into paranoid fantasies, idealistic sentiments transformed into murderous fanaticism, and destructive components of human nature mobilized and directed by demagogues who see themselves as possessors of an overarching historical truth.

Unlike earlier autocratic regimes, the totalitarian dictatorship is not satisfied with its subjects' outward obedience; it demands the masses' unconditional loyalty and enthusiastic support. It strives to control the inner person: to shape thoughts, feelings, and attitudes in accordance with the party ideology, which becomes an official creed. It does not rule by brute force alone but seeks to create a "new man," one who dedicates himself body and soul to the party and its ideology. Such unquestioning, faithful subjects can be manipulated by the party. The disinterested search for truth, justice, and goodness—the exploration of those fundamental moral, political, and religious questions that have characterized the Western intellectual tradition for centuries—is abandoned. Truth, justice, and goodness are whatever the party deems them to be, and ideological deviation is forbidden.

The totalitarian dictatorship deliberately politicizes all areas of human activity. Ideology pervades works of literature, history, philosophy, art, and even science. It dominates the school curriculum and influences everyday speech and social relations. The state is concerned with everything its citizens do: there is no distinction between public and private life, and every institution comes under the party-state's authority. If voluntary support for the regime cannot be generated by indoctrination, then the state unhesitatingly resorts to terror and violence to compel obedience. People live under a constant strain. Fear of the secret police is ever present; it produces a permanent state of insecurity, which induces people to do everything that the regime asks of them and to watch what they say and do.

COMMUNIST RUSSIA

In 1918, Lenin's infant Communist government was threatened with civil war. Tsarist officers had gathered troops in the south; other anti-Communist centers rose in Siberia, and still others in the extreme north and along the Baltic coast. The political orientation of these anti-Communist groups, generally called *Whites* in contrast to the Communist *Reds,* combined all shades of opinion, from moderate socialist to reactionary, the latter usually predominating. Generally the Whites were monarchists who identified with the old tsarist regime. The Whites received support from foreign governments, which freely intervened. Until their own revolution in November 1918, the Germans occupied much of southern Russia. England, France, and the United States sent troops to points in northern and southern European Russia; England, Japan, and the United States also sent troops to Siberia. At first, they wanted to offset German expansion, but later they hoped to overthrow the Communist regime. In May and June 1918, Czech prisoners of war, about to be evacuated, precipitated anti-Communist uprisings along the Trans-Siberian Railroad, bringing the civil war to fever pitch.

In July 1918, Communists murdered Nicholas II and his entire family. In August, a non-Communist socialist nearly assassinated Lenin, while White forces in the south moved to cut off central Russia from its food supply. In response, the Communists speeded the buildup of their own Red Army. Recruited from the remnants of the tsarist army and its officer corps, the Red Army was reinforced by compulsory military service and strict discipline, including execution of deserters. Threatened with death if they refused, many tsarist officers served in the Red Army. They were closely watched by Trotsky's ruthless political commissars, who were also responsible for the political reliability and morale of the troops. Trotsky ordered the formation of "blocking units" to machine-gun retreating soldiers. The civil war was brutal; both sides butchered civilians and their own comrades.

In November 1918, thanks to the Allied victory and the American contribution to it, the German menace in Russia ended. Yet foreign intervention stepped up in response to the formation of the Communist International (Comintern), an organization founded by Lenin to guide the international revolutionary movement that he expected to issue from the world war. Lenin sought revolutionary support from abroad for strengthening his hand at home; his enemies reached into Russia to defeat at its source the revolution that they feared in their own countries. At the same time, the civil war rose to its climax.

Hard-pressed as Lenin's party was, by the autumn of 1920 it had prevailed over its enemies. The Whites were divided among themselves and discredited by their association with the tsarist regime; the Communists had greater popular support, the advantage of interior communications, and superior political skills. The war-weary foreign interventionists called off their efforts to overthrow the Communist regime by force.

The Communist victory in the civil war exacted a staggering price. Reds and Whites alike carried the tsarist tradition of political violence to a new pitch of horror (some of it later described in novels by Boris Pasternak and Mikhail Sholokhov). The entire population, including the Communist Party and its leaders, suffered in the war. Some 1.2 million combatants on both sides perished. In addition, the Communists killed some 250,000 peasants who resisted grain requisitions. Adding to the death toll were some 100,000 Jews, victims of pogroms perpetrated largely by the Whites and Ukrainian nationalists, but also by the Red Army. Compounding the nation's anguish was the famine of 1921–1922, which claimed some 5 million victims.

War Communism and the New Economic Policy

Besides the extreme misery brought on by the world war and civil war, the Russian people had to endure the rigors of the policy known as War Communism. It was introduced in 1918 to deal with the plummeting agricultural and economic production, rampant inflation, and desperate hunger in the cities. Under War Communism,

the state took over the means of production and greatly limited private ownership; it conscripted labor and, in effect, confiscated grain from the peasants. War Communism devastated the economy even further and alienated workers and peasants. The state-run factories were mismanaged, workers stayed away from their jobs or performed poorly, and peasants resisted the food requisition detachments that the government sent to seize their grain.

There was even open rebellion. In March 1921, sailors at the Kronstadt naval base and workers in nearby Petrograd—people who in 1917 had been ready to give their lives for the Revolution—rose against the repression that had been introduced during the civil war; they called for the establishment of socialist democracy. Trotsky ruthlessly suppressed that uprising and ordered the execution of a large number of rebels. But the lesson was clear: the Communist regime had to implement a strategic retreat from War Communism and to restore a measure of stability to the country.

In 1921, the Communist Party adopted the New Economic Policy (NEP), which lasted until 1928. Under a system that Lenin characterized as "state socialism," the government retained control of finance, industry, and transportation— "the commanding heights" of the economy—but allowed the rest of the economy to return to private enterprise. Peasants, after giving part of their crops to the government, were free to sell the rest in the open market; traders could buy and sell as they pleased. With the resumption of small-scale capitalism, an air of normal life returned.

One-Party Dictatorship

While the Communists were waging a fierce struggle against the Whites, they instituted a militant dictatorship run by their party. The party's iron rule was profoundly influenced by the authoritarianism of tsarist Russia, which had conditioned many of the Bolsheviks. Numbering about 500,000 members in 1921, the Communist Party was controlled by a small, intimate group, the politburo (political bureau), which assumed a dictatorial role. The key leaders—Lenin, Trotsky, Stalin, and a few others—determined policy, assigned tasks, and appointed important officials. The party dominated all public agencies;

its leaders held the chief positions in government. No other political parties were tolerated, and trade unions became agents of the regime. Never before had the people of Russia been forced into such compulsory unity and abject dependence on their government.

Impatient with the endless disputes among righteous and strong-willed old revolutionaries, Lenin, in agreement with other top leaders, demanded unconditional submission to his decisions. He even ordered that dissidents within the party be disciplined and political enemies be terrorized. No price was too high to achieve monolithic party unity and total commitment to the party's policies. Believing that they were creating a new and better society that would serve as a model for the rest of humanity, the Communists felt no moral objection to the use of force or even terror, including executions and forced-labor camps. The dreaded Cheka, a ruthless secret police organization, executed some 200,000 people from 1919 to 1925. The means Lenin employed for ruling his backward country denied the human values that Marx had taken from the Enlightenment and put into his vision of a socialist society. Lenin was perfectly willing to use state terror to promote the class struggle.

The Communists abolished the power of the Orthodox church, which was the traditional ally of tsarism and the enemy of innovation. They were militant atheists, believing with Marx that religion was the "opium of the people"; God had no place in their vision of a better society. Above all, they wiped out—by expropriation, discrimination, expulsion, and execution—the educated upper class of bureaucrats, landowners, professional people, and industrialists.

The Communist Party promised "to liberate woman from all the burdens of antiquated methods of housekeeping, by replacing them by house-communes, public kitchens, central laundries, nurseries, etc."[9] But traditional values, particularly in the Asian parts of the Soviet Union, hardly favored equality between the sexes, especially in political work. The practical necessity of combining work with family responsibility, moreover, tended to keep women out of managerial positions in the party and the organizations of the state, but the ideal remained alive.

The Communists never ceased to stress that they worked strenuously for the welfare of the vast majority of the population. They received much acclaim for their emphasis on providing housing, food, and clothing and making education, theater, and other cultural activities, previously reserved for the elite, available to the masses. Although the Communists were not opposed to some private ownership of property, they outlawed income-producing property that enabled capitalists to employ (or exploit, as the Communists said) others for their own profit.

For Lenin, socialism meant reeducating the unruly masses to higher standards of individual conduct and economic productivity that would be superior to capitalism. In the spring of 1918, he complained that Russian workers had not yet matched capitalist performance: "The Russian worker is a bad worker compared with the workers of the advanced, i.e., western countries." To overcome this deficiency, Lenin urged competition—socialist competition—and hammered home the need for "iron discipline at work" and "un-questioning obedience" to a single will, that of the Communist Party. There was no alternative: "Large-scale machinery calls for absolute and strict unity of will, which directs the joint labors of hundreds and thousands and tens of thousands of people. A thousand wills are subordinated to one will."[10]

In those words lay the essence of subsequent Soviet industrialization. The economy was to be monolithic, rationally planned, and focused on pursuing a single goal: overcoming the weaknesses of Russia so disastrously demonstrated in the war. Allowing workers to make their own decisions, Lenin held, would perpetuate Russian backwardness. Instead, he called for a new "consciousness," a hard-driving work ethic expressed in the Russian Marxist revolutionary vocabulary.

In attempting to transform their Soviet Russia into a modern industrialized state that would serve as a model for the world, the Communists imposed a new autocracy even more authoritarian than that of the tsars. The minds of the people, therefore, came under unprecedented government control. In education, from kindergarten through university, in the press, on radio, and in literature and the arts, the Communist Party tried to fashion people's thoughts to create the proper "consciousness."

The party made Marxism-Leninism the sole source of truth, eliminating as best it could all rival creeds, whether religious, political, or philosophical. Thinking was to be as reliably uniform as a machine process and totally committed to the party. Moreover, thoughts were to be protected against subversive capitalist influences. Soviet Russia, the party boasted, had risen to a superior plane of social existence and would attract other revolutionary states to its federal union until eventually it covered the entire world. Lest Soviet citizens doubt their new superiority, the party prohibited all uncontrolled comparison with other countries.

Lenin molded Soviet Russia into an international revolutionary force, the champion of anticapitalism and of the liberation of colonial peoples. The Russian Revolution inspired nationalistic ambitions for political self-determination and cultural self-assertion among a growing number of peoples around the world, especially in Asia. It appealed particularly to intellectuals educated in the West (or in westernized schools) yet identifying themselves with their downtrodden compatriots.

To have a political tool for world revolution, Lenin created the Communist—or Third—International (Comintern). The most radical successor to earlier socialist international associations, it helped organize small Communist parties in Western Europe, which in time became dependable, though rather powerless, agents of Soviet Russia. In Asia, where no proletariat existed, Lenin tried to work closely with incipient nationalist movements. Lenin and the Bolshevik Revolution gained the admiration and instinctive loyalty of colonial and semicolonial people in what would come to be called the Third World.

In 1923, a new constitution laid down federal guidelines for Soviet Russia, henceforth officially known as the Union of Soviet Socialist Republics (USSR) or the Soviet Union. Having captured the attention of the world, the Soviet Union now stood out as the Communist alternative to the capitalist West.

The Stalin Revolution

Lenin died in 1924, and the task of achieving the goal that he had set was taken up by Stalin. The "man of steel" was crude and vulgar, toughened by the revolutionary underground and tsarist prisons and by the roughest aspects of Russian life. Relentlessly energetic but relatively inconspicuous

among key Bolsheviks, Stalin had been given, in 1922, the unwanted and seemingly routine task of general secretary of the party. He used this position to his own advantage, building up a reliable party cadre—apparatus men, or *apparatchiki,* as they came to be called—and dominating the party as not even Lenin had done. When he was challenged, particularly by Trotsky and his associates, in the protracted struggles for the succession to Lenin, it was too late to unseat him. None of Stalin's rivals could rally the necessary majorities at the party congresses; none could match Stalin's skill in party infighting or in making rough and anarchic people into docile members of the Communist Party apparatus.

Industrialization. To Stalin, Russia's most pressing need was not world revolution but the fastest possible buildup of Soviet power through industrialization. The country could not afford to risk near annihilation again, as it had done in the world war and then in the civil war. Soviet protection against capitalist encirclement and Communist pride dictated that the country be made as strong as possible. Stalin set forth the stark reckoning of Russian history in a speech delivered in 1931, three years after launching a program of massive industrialization.

> *Those who fall behind get beaten. But we do not want to be beaten. No, we refuse to be beaten. One feature of the history of old Russia was the continual beatings she suffered for falling behind, for her backwardness. All beat her—for her backwardness, for military backwardness, cultural backwardness, political backwardness, for industrial backwardness, for agricultural backwardness. She was beaten because to do so was profitable and could be done with impunity. . . . You are backward, you are weak—therefore you are wrong, hence you can be beaten and enslaved. You are mighty, therefore you are right, hence we must be wary of you. Such is the law of the exploiters. . . . That is why we must no longer lag behind.[11]*

Stalin decided on all-out industrialization at the expense of the toiling masses. Peasants and workers, already poor, would be required to make tremendous sacrifices of body and spirit to overcome the nation's weaknesses.

Abandoning the NEP, Stalin decreed a series of Five-Year Plans, the first and most experimental one commencing in 1928. The industrialization drive was heralded as a vast economic and social revolution, undertaken by the state according to a rational plan. The emphasis lay on heavy industry: the construction of railroads, power plants, steel mills, and military hardware, such as tanks and warplanes. Production of consumer goods was cut to the minimum, and all small-scale private trading, revived under the NEP, came to an end—with disastrous results for the standard of living. Having just come within sight of their pre-1914 standard of living, Russians now found their expectations dashed.

A new, grim age of drastic material hardships and profound anguish began. Harsh punishments, including denial of food cards and imprisonment, were meted out for lateness, slowness, or incompetence. Many people, however, particularly the young, were fired to heroic exertions. They were proud to sacrifice themselves for the building of a superior society. And many common factory workers had the opportunity to attend school and become engineers and administrators, tying them to the regime. When the Great Depression in the capitalist countries put millions out of work, no Soviet citizen suffered from unemployment; in the 1930s, gloom pervaded the West, but confidence and hope, artificially fostered by the party, buoyed up many people in Soviet Russia. The first two Five-Year Plans dramatically and rapidly increased Russia's industrial infrastructure as factories, mines, dams, and railroads were feverishly constructed. At no time, though, did the planning produce Western-style efficiency, and workers, who labored in a herculean way, actually suffered a decline in real wages. The regime concentrated on heavy industry, not consumer goods or improving the standard of living.

IDEALIZED PORTRAIT OF STALIN. Like Lenin, Stalin's public image was idealized, but the real man was ruthless. He was determined to reshape the Soviet people's consciousness through a totalitarian revolution. His policy of forced collectivization and his purges killed millions, many of them after being deported to the gulag. The father of the little girl shown on the banner here was assassinated by Stalin that very same year. Her mother was arrested and died under "mysterious" circumstances a few years later. (Sovfoto.)

Collectivization.

Meanwhile, a different and far more brutal revolution overtook Soviet agriculture: peasants were forcibly integrated into the planned economy through collectivization. Collectivization meant the pooling of farmland, animals, and equipment to achieve efficient, large-scale production. The Communist solution for the backwardness of Russian agriculture was for peasants to become organized like factory workers. But knowing the peasants' distaste for the factory, their attachment to their own land, and their stubbornness, the party had hesitated to carry out its ambitious scheme. In 1929, however, Stalin believed that, for the sake of industrialization, he had no choice. If the Five-Year Plan was to succeed, the government had to receive planned crops of planned amounts and quality at planned times. This could be accomplished, Stalin thought, only by destroying the independent peasantry and forcing millions of peasants into collective farms, huge agricultural factories. With collectivization, the ascendancy of the party over the people of Russia became almost complete.

The peasants paid a ghastly price. Stalin declared war on the Russian countryside. He ordered that the *kulaks,* the most enterprising and well-to-do peasants, be "liquidated as a class." Designated as "enemies of the people" and dehumanized as "swine," "scum," and "vermin," between late 1929 and 1932 some 10 million kulaks were forcibly removed from their homes and land. Large numbers were killed outright and millions were deported to forced-labor camps in the far north, where many ultimately perished from hunger, cold, or abuse. Their poorer and less-efficient neighbors were herded onto collective farms at the point of a bayonet.

The peasants struck back, sometimes in pitched battles. The horror of forced collectivization broke the spirit even of hardened officials. "I am an old Bolshevik," sobbed a secret police colonel to a fellow passenger on a train; "I worked in the underground against the Tsar and then I fought in the civil war. Did I do all that in order that I should now surround villages with machine guns and order my men to fire indiscriminately into crowds of peasants? Oh, no, no!"[12] Typically, however, the local officials and activists who stripped the peasants of their possessions and searched for hidden grain viewed themselves as idealists building a new society that was in the best interests of a suffering humanity; they infused their own ruthlessness into the official orders. Their dedication to the triumph of Communism overcame all doubts caused by the sight of starving people and the sounds of wailing women and children.

Defeated but unwilling to surrender their livestock, the peasants slaughtered their animals, gorging themselves in drunken orgies against the days of inevitable famine. The country's cattle herds declined by one-half, inflicting irreparable secondary losses as well. The number of horses, crucial for rural transport and farm work, fell by one-third. Crops were not planted or not harvested, the Five-Year Plan was disrupted, and from 1931 to 1933 millions starved to death.

The suffering was most cruel in Ukraine, where famine killed approximately 3 million people, many after extreme abuse and persecution. Desperate starving Ukrainians resorted to cannibalism, for which they were executed by the state. In order to buy industrial equipment abroad so that industrialization could proceed on target, the Soviet Union had to export food, as much of it as possible and for prices disastrously lowered by the Great Depression. Let the peasants in the Ukrainian breadbasket starve so that the country could grow strong! Moreover, Stalin relished the opportunity to punish the Ukrainians for their disloyalty during the civil war and their resistance to collectivization.

By 1935, practically all farming in Russia was collectivized. The kulaks had been wiped out as a class, and the peasants, ever rebellious under the tsars, had been cowed into obeying the directives handed down from the nearest party office. People grumbled about the rise of a new serfdom.

Stalin had hoped to create technically efficient "factory farms" that would provide inexpensive food for the massive industrial labor force. But in reality, collectivization stifled agricultural production. Resentful peasants had slaughtered livestock rather than turn it over to the state; mismanagement and unenthusiastic collective farmers resulted in a precipitous decline in agricultural production. For decades, collective farming failed to achieve the levels of production previously reached in the 1920s.

Total Control. To quash resistance and mold a new type of suitably motivated and disciplined citizen, Stalin unleashed a third revolution, the revolution of totalitarianism. Only Communist regimentation and monolithic control by the party over state and society, he believed, could liberate Russia from its historic inferiority. The Five-Year Plans obliterated private enterprise; virtually every worker and peasant was now an employee of the state. Moreover, the totalitarian state accorded with his desire to exercise total control over the party and the nation. Stalin's totalitarianism aimed at a complete reconstruction of state and society, down to the innermost recesses of human consciousness. It called for a "new man," suited to the needs of Soviet industrialism. In many ways Stalin's totalitarianism fulfilled Lenin's policies.

The revolution of totalitarianism encompassed all cultural activity. Religion, which offered an alternative worldview, came under attack. Priests were jailed, organized worship was

A *Collective Farm Festival* (1936–1937), by Sergei Gerasimov. This propaganda painting of a festival on a collective farm glorifies the new agricultural system that Stalin imposed on the Russian peasantry by force.
(Scala/Art Resource, N.Y.)

discouraged, and churches were converted into barns. All media of communication—literature, the arts, music, the stage—were forced into subservience to the Five-Year Plan and Soviet ideology. In literature, as in all art, an official style was promulgated. Called *socialist realism,* it was expected to describe the world as the party saw it or hoped to shape it. Novels in the social realist manner told how the romances of tractor drivers and milkmaids or of lathe operators and office secretaries led to new victories of production under the Five-Year Plan. Composers found their music examined for remnants of bourgeois spirit; they were to write simple tunes suitable for heroic times. Everywhere huge, high-color posters showed men and women hard at work with radiant faces, calling others to join them; often Stalin, the wise father and leader, was shown among them. In this way, artistic creativity was locked into a dull, utilitarian straitjacket of official cheerfulness; creativity was allowed only to boost industrial productivity. Behind the scenes, all artists were disciplined to conform to the will of the party or be crushed.

Education, from nursery school to university, was likewise harnessed to train dutiful and loyal citizens, and Soviet propaganda made a cult of

Stalin that bordered on deification. Thus, a writer declared in 1935:

> *Centuries will pass and the generations still to come will regard us as the happiest of mortals, as the most fortunate of men, because we . . . were privileged to see Stalin, our inspired leader. Yes, and we regard ourselves as the happiest of mortals because we are the contemporaries of a man who never had an equal in world history. The men of all ages will call on thy name, which is strong, beautiful, wise, and marvellous. Thy name is engraven on every factory, every machine, every place on the earth, and in the hearts of all men.*[13]

To break stubborn wills and compel conformity, Stalin—calculating, cunning, cold, cruel, and cynical—unleashed raw terror. Terror had been used as a tool of government ever since the Bolsheviks seized power. Lenin, who had provided theoretical justification for terror in the struggle against tsarism, employed it after the Revolution (and the tsars had also used it intermittently). After the start of the first Five-Year Plan, show trials were staged in which engineers

Map 29.1 Ethnic Groups and Forced Labor Camps in the Soviet Union
The Soviet Union consisted of many different nationalities whose nationalist
aspirations were held in check by the repressive regime. The map also designates
the forced labor camps to which millions of people were sent, many of whom
perished. (© 2016 Cengage Learning.)

who disagreed with Stalin's production timetable
were denounced as saboteurs. The terror used to
herd the peasants onto collective farms was even
greater. Stalin also used terror to crush opposition
and to instill abject fear in the ranks of the party
and in Russian society at large.

Purges had long been used to rid the party of
weaklings. After 1934, however, they became an
instrument of Stalin's drive for unchallenged personal power. Stalin's paranoia, which defied all
logic and morality, led him to see threats to his
rule everywhere and more enemies to be exterminated in ever increasing numbers. In 1936, his vindictive terror broke into the open. The first batch
of victims, including many founders of the Communist Party, were accused of conspiring with the
exiled Trotsky to set up a "terrorist center" and of

scheming to terrorize the party. After being sentenced to death, they were immediately executed.
Included among the millions that Stalin consigned
to death were close friends and comrades in the
Bolshevik Revolution. In 1937, the next group,
including prominent Communists of Lenin's day
and Stalin's old comrades, were charged with
cooperating with foreign intelligence agencies
and wrecking "socialist reconstruction," the term
for Stalin's revolution; they too were executed.
Shortly afterward, a secret purge decimated the
military high command, for which the country
paid a heavy price when Germany attacked in
1941. Almost half the country's seventy thousand
officers were either shot or sent to the camps—
after the Nazi invasion, many of these prisoners
were rehabilitated and restored to active duty.

In 1938, the last and biggest show trial advanced the most bizarre accusation of all: sabotage, espionage, and attempting to dismember the Soviet Union and kill all its leaders (including Lenin in 1918). In the public hearings, some defendants refuted the public prosecutor, but in the end all confessed, usually after torture and threats to their family, before being executed. Western observers were aghast at the cynical charges and at the physical and mental tortures used to obtain the confessions. Under Stalin, the revolution was devouring its own children at a rate that far surpassed earlier revolutions.

The great trials, however, involved only a small minority of Stalin's victims; many more perished in silence without benefit of legal proceedings. The terror first hit members of the party, especially the Old Bolsheviks, who had joined before the Revolution; they were the most independent-minded members and therefore the most dangerous to Stalin. But Stalin also decimated the cultural elite that had survived the Lenin revolution. Thousands of engineers, scientists, industrial managers, scholars, and artists disappeared; accused of counterrevolutionary crimes, they were shot or sent to forced-labor camps, where many of them perished. Their relatives also suffered, often fired from their jobs, evicted from their apartments, exiled to remote regions, and even sentenced to labor camps. No one was safe. To frighten the common people in all walks of life, men, women, and even children were dragged into the net of Stalin's secret police, leaving the survivors with a soul-killing reminder: submit or else. "In the years of the terror," recalled one victim, "there was not a house in the country where people did not sit trembling at night."[14]

The 476 forced-labor camps to which Stalin's victims were deported played an important role in the Soviet economy. Slave labor constructed the White Sea–Baltic Sea Canal, which the regime held up as a monument of Communist achievement. Mining, logging, and construction enterprises in remote parts of the country also depended on forced labor. It is estimated that from 1929 until the death of Stalin in 1953, some 18 million people were confined to the gulag, as Stalin's system of concentration camps came to be known. Many perished from abuse, starvation, and bone-crushing labor in freezing weather. Organized executions of vanloads of victims were common. As in Nazi concentration camps, administrators and guards deliberately dehumanized and brutalized the prisoners, whom the regime designated as "filth" and "enemies of the people."

Stalin may have orchestrated the terror, but large numbers of party members believed that terror, which was decimating their own ranks, was necessary. The memory of the vicious civil war, when domestic and foreign enemies sought to overthrow the new Bolshevik regime, and the resistance of the kulaks to collectivization created a siege mentality among the Communist leadership. Everywhere they saw anti-Soviets plotting against the party; they defined these enemies as Trotskyites, former kulaks, Whites who had fought in the civil war, members of outlawed anti-Soviet political parties, foreign agents, and criminals—cattle and horse thieves, contraband smugglers, bandits, and so on. Party officials saw terror as a legitimate way both of protecting the party to which they were ideologically committed—and from which they derived prestige, power, and material benefits—and of protecting the Soviet experiment, which they viewed as humanity's best hope.

The toll of the purges is reckoned in many millions; it included Trotsky, who in 1940 was murdered in Mexico. The bloodletting was ghastly, as Stalin's purge officials themselves followed each other into death and ignominy. Stalin, however, was untroubled by the waste of life. By showing party officials and the Russian masses how vulnerable they were, how dependent they were on his will, he frightened them into servility. No doubt the terror was also an expression of his craving for personal power and his cruel, vengeful, and suspicious, some say clinically paranoid, nature. He saw enemies everywhere, took pleasure in selecting victims, and reveled in his omnipotence. For good reason, Stalin has been called a twentieth-century Ivan the Terrible. Like the sixteenth-century tsar, for whom he expressed admiration, Stalin stopped at no brutality in order to establish personal autocracy. Although it might take decades for some to realize it, Stalin's criminal rule blackened the ideal of a humane socialist society.

But more than a craving for personal power motivated Stalin. He regarded himself as Lenin's heir, responsible for securing and expanding the Revolution and defending it against foreign and domestic enemies. The only way to do this was to create a powerful Soviet Union through rapid modernization. Stalin believed that without the total obedience of the Russian people, the Soviet state and society could not be effectively modernized and that terror was necessary to compel compliance. Stalin, as much a Russian patriot as a Marxist, did not forget the threat to Russia's survival after World War I. He was keenly aware of the expansionist ambitions of Japanese militarists in the Far East and eventually of German rearmament under Hitler. As he had said in 1931, if the Soviet Union did not make the utmost effort to strengthen itself within ten years, it could not withstand another attack; its people would perish under foreign domination. In Stalin's mind, totalitarianism was necessary to save Russia from foreign enemies that would devour it. Ten years after Stalin's warning of 1931, Hitler's armies invaded the Soviet Union, ready to exploit, enslave, and annihilate its citizens and seize its territory. The expansion of industrial capacity under Stalin was a key reason why Russia ultimately defeated the Nazi invaders.

THE NATURE OF FASCISM

Liberals viewed the Great War as a conflict between freedom and autocracy and expected an Allied victory to accelerate the spread of democracy throughout Europe. Right after the war, it seemed that liberalism would continue to advance as it had in the nineteenth century. The collapse of the autocratic German and Austrian empires had led to the formation of parliamentary governments throughout Eastern and Central Europe. Yet within two decades, in an extraordinary turn of events, democracy seemed in its death throes. In Spain, Portugal, Italy, and Germany, and in all the newly created states of Central and Eastern Europe except Czechoslovakia, democracy collapsed, and various forms of authoritarian government emerged. The defeat of democracy and the surge of authoritarianism were best exemplified by the triumph of Fascist movements in Italy and Germany; with brutal frankness, their leaders proclaimed that individual freedom, a relic of a dying liberal age and a barrier to national greatness, would be dispensed with.

The emergence of Fascist movements in more than twenty European lands after World War I was a sign that liberal society was in a state of disorientation and dissolution. The cultural pessimism, disdain for reason, elitism, romantic glorification of action and heroism, and contempt for liberal values voiced by many intellectuals and nationalists before the war found expression after the war in the antidemocratic and irrational Fascist ideologies that altered European political life. Fascism marked the culmination of the counter-Enlightenment mentality inherent in the extreme nationalism and radical conservatism of the late nineteenth century and in the repudiation of modern Western civilization by disenchanted intellectuals.

As a Europe-wide phenomenon, Fascism was a response to a postwar society afflicted with spiritual disintegration, economic dislocation, political instability, and thwarted nationalist hopes. A general breakdown of meaning and values led people to search for new beliefs and new political arrangements. Fascism was an expression of fear that the Bolshevik Revolution would spread westward. It was also an expression of hostility to democratic values and a reaction to the failure of liberal institutions to solve the problems of modern industrial society. Disillusioned with liberal governments that failed to cope with massive social and economic problems, particularly during the Depression, many Europeans were tempted by authoritarian alternatives that would dispense with parliamentary government and the protection of individual rights. Anything seemed better than the ineffectual parliaments that appeared helpless in the face of mounting misery. Moreover, in many European lands, democracy had shallow roots. Having little familiarity with or appreciation of the procedures and values of constitutional government, people were susceptible to antidemocratic ideologies.

Fascist movements were marked by a determination to eradicate liberalism and Marxism—to undo the legacy of the French Revolution of 1789 and the Bolshevik Revolution of 1917. Fascists believed that theirs was a spiritual revolution, that they were initiating a new era in history and building a new civilization on the ruins of liberal democracy. "We stand for a new principle in the world," said Mussolini. "We stand for the sheer, categorical, definitive antithesis to the world of democracy . . . to the world which still abides by the fundamental principles laid down in 1789."[15] The chief principle of Nazism, said Hitler, "is to abolish the liberal concept of the individual and the Marxist concept of humanity, and to substitute for them the Volk community, rooted in the soil and united by the bond of its common blood."[16] The Fascists' uniforms, songs, flags, parades, mass rallies, and cult of physical strength and violence all symbolized this call for a reawakened and reunited people.

Fascists accused liberal society of despiritualizing human beings and transforming them into materialistic creatures whose highest ideal was moneymaking. Regarding liberalism as bankrupt and parliamentary government as futile, Fascists yearned for a powerful military state. To Fascists and their sympathizers, democracy seemed an ineffective and enfeebled old order ready to be overthrown. Idealistic youth and intellectuals rejoiced in Fascist activism. They saw Fascism as a revolt against the mediocrity of the liberal state and modern mass society and a reaffirmation of the noblest human qualities: heroism and dedication to one's people. Fascists saw themselves as participants in a dynamic mass movement that would rectify the weaknesses and irresolution of parliamentary government and rid the nation of corrosive foreign influences. For them, the triumph of Fascism would mark a new beginning for their nation and a new era in world history.

The Fascist vision of a regenerated nation—a new order led by a determined and heroic elite—arising from the ruins of a decadent old order had the appeal of great myth; it evoked belief, commitment, and loyalty. The myth of rebirth—a nation cured of evil and building a new and vigorous society—had a profound impact on people dissatisfied with liberal society and searching for new beliefs. The myth of the nation reborn answered a metaphysical yearning to give meaning to life and history. It provided an emotionally gratifying worldview at a time when many people had lost confidence in liberal-democratic ideals and institutions.

Fascists regarded Marxism as another enemy, for class conflict divided and weakened the state.

To Fascists, the Marxist call for workers of the world to unite meant the death of the national community. Fascism, in contrast, would reintegrate the proletariat into the nation and end class hostilities by making people at all levels feel that they were a needed part of the nation. Fascism thus offered a solution to the problem of insecurity and isolation in modern industrial society.

Attacking the rational tradition of the Enlightenment, Fascism exalted will, blood, feeling, and instinct. Intellectual discussion and critical analysis, said Fascists, cause national divisiveness; reason promotes doubt, enfeebles the will, and hinders instinctive, aggressive action. Fascism made a continual appeal to the emotions as a means of integrating the national community. This flow of emotion fueled irrational and dangerous desires, beliefs, and expectations, which blocked critical judgment and responsible action. Glorifying action for its own sake, Fascists aroused and manipulated brutal and primitive impulses and carried into politics the combative spirit of the trenches. They formed private armies, which attracted veterans—many of them rootless, brutal, and maladjusted men who sought to preserve the loyalty, camaraderie, and violence of the front.

Fascist ideology exalted the leader, who, it was believed, intuitively grasped what was best for the nation. It also called for rule by an elite of dedicated party members. The leader and the party would relieve the individual of the need to make decisions. Convinced that the liberal stress on individual freedom promoted national divisiveness, Fascists pressed for monolithic unity: one leader, one party, one ideology, and one national will.

Fascism drew its mass support from the lower middle class: small merchants, artisans, white-collar workers, civil servants, and peasants of moderate means, all of whom were frightened both by big capitalism and by Marxism. They hoped that Fascism would protect them from the competition of big business and prevent the hated working class from establishing a Marxist state, which would threaten their property. The lower middle class saw in Fascism a non-Communist way of overcoming economic crises and restoring traditional respect for family, native soil, and nation. Furthermore, many of these people saw Fascism as a way of attacking the existing social order, which denied them opportunities for economic advancement and social prestige.

Although a radicalized middle class gave Fascist movements their mass support, the Fascists could not have captured the state without the aid of existing ruling elites: landed aristocrats, industrialists, and army leaders. In Russia, the Bolsheviks had to fight their way to power; in Italy and Germany, the old ruling order virtually handed power to the Fascists. In both countries, Fascist leaders succeeded in reassuring the conservative elite that they would not institute widespread social reforms or interfere with private property and would protect the nation from Communism. Even though the old elite often abhorred Fascist violence and demagoguery, it entered into an alliance with the Fascists to protect its interests. In Germany, the elite could not have installed Hitler in power had he not had the electoral backing of a significant number of Germans.

In their struggle to bring down the liberal state, Fascist leaders aroused primitive impulses and tribal loyalties; they made use of myths and rituals to mobilize and manipulate the masses. Organizing their propaganda campaigns with the rigor of a military operation, Fascists stirred and dominated the masses and confused and undermined their democratic opposition, breaking its will to resist. Fascists were most successful in countries with weak democratic traditions. When parliamentary government faltered, it had few staunch defenders, and many people were drawn to charismatic demagogues who promised direct action.

The proliferation of Fascist movements demonstrated that the habits of democracy are not quickly learned, easily retained, or even desired. Particularly during times of crisis, people lose patience with parliamentary discussion and constitutional procedures, sink into nonrational modes of thought and behavior, and are easily manipulated by unscrupulous politicians. For the sake of economic or emotional security and national grandeur, they will often willingly sacrifice political freedom. Fascism starkly manifested the immense power of the irrational; it humbled liberals, making them permanently aware of the limitations of reason and the fragility of freedom.

The Fascist goal of maximum centralization of power was furthered by developments during World War I: the expansion of bureaucracy, the concentration of industry into giant monopolies, and the close cooperation between industry and the state. The instruments of modern technology—radio, motion pictures, public address systems, telephones, and teletype—made it possible for the state to indoctrinate, manipulate, and dominate its subjects.

THE RISE OF FASCISM IN ITALY

Postwar Unrest

Although Italy was on the winning side in World War I, it resembled a defeated nation. Food shortages, rising prices, massive unemployment, violent strikes, workers occupying factories, and peasants squatting on the uncultivated periphery of large estates created a climate of crisis. These dismal conditions contrasted sharply with the vision of a postwar world painted by politicians during the war. Italy required effective leadership and a reform program, but party disputes paralyzed the liberal government. With several competing parties, the liberals could not organize a solid majority that could cope with the domestic crisis.

The middle class was severely stressed. To meet accelerating expenses, the government increased taxes, but the burden fell unevenly on small landowners, small business owners, civil service workers, and professionals. Moreover, the value of war bonds, purchased primarily by the middle class, declined considerably because of inflation. Instead of being able to retrieve the good old days and their former status once the war ended, these solid citizens found that their economic position continued to deteriorate.

Large landowners and industrialists feared that their nation was on the verge of a Bolshevik-style revolution. They took seriously the proclamations of the socialists: "The proletariat must be incited to the violent seizure of political and economic power and this must be handed over entirely and exclusively to the Workers' and Peasants' Councils."[17] In truth, Italian socialists had no master plan to seize power. Peasant squatters and urban strikers were responding to the distress in their own regions and did not significantly coordinate their efforts with those in other localities. Besides, when workers realized that they could not keep factories operating, their revolutionary zeal waned and they started to abandon the plants. The workers' and peasants' poorly led and futile struggles did not portend a Red revolution. Nevertheless, the industrialists and landlords, with the Bolshevik Revolution still vivid in their minds, were taking no chances.

Adding to the unrest was the national outrage at the terms of the peace settlement. Italians felt that despite their sacrifices—500,000 dead and 1 million wounded—they had been robbed of the fruits of their victory. Although Italy had received the Brenner Pass and Trieste, it had been denied the Dalmatian coast, the Adriatic port of Fiume, and territory in Africa and the Middle East. Nationalists blamed the liberal government for what they called a "mutilated victory." In 1919, a force of war veterans, led by the poet and adventurer Gabriele D'Annunzio (1863–1938), seized Fiume, to the delirious joy of Italian nationalists and the embarrassment of the government. D'Annunzio's occupation of the port lasted more than a year, adding fuel to the flames of Italian nationalism and demonstrating the weakness of the liberal regime in imposing its authority on rightist opponents.

Mussolini's Seizure of Power

Benito Mussolini (1883–1945) was born in a small village in east-central Italy. Proud, quarrelsome, violent, and resentful of the humiliation he suffered for being poor, the young Mussolini was a troublemaker and was often brought before school authorities. But he was also intelligent, ranking first on final examinations in four subjects. After graduation, Mussolini taught in an elementary school, but this work did not suit his passionate temperament. From 1902 to 1904, he lived in Switzerland, where he broadened his reading, lectured, and wrote. He also came under the influence of anarchists and socialist revolutionaries.

Returning to Italy, Mussolini was labeled a dangerous revolutionary by the police. As a reward for his zeal and political agitation, which led to five months in prison for inciting riots, in 1912 he was made editor of *Avanti,* the principal socialist newspaper. During the early days of World War I, he was expelled from the Socialist Party for advocating Italian intervention in the war. After Italy entered the war, Mussolini served

at the front and, during firing practice, suffered a serious wound, for which he was hospitalized.

In 1919, Mussolini organized the Fascist Party to realize his immense will to obtain political power. The quest for power and the yearning for action and a release of dynamic energy, more than a set of coherent doctrines, characterized the young movement. A supreme opportunist rather than an ideologist, Mussolini exploited the unrest in postwar Italy in order to capture control of the state. He attracted converts from among the discontented, the disillusioned, and the uprooted. Many Italians, particularly the educated bourgeois who had been inspired by the unification movement of the nineteenth century, viewed Mussolini as the leader who would gain Fiume, Dalmatia, and colonies and win Italy's rightful place of honor in international affairs.

MUSSOLINI WITH HIS TROOPS. The Italian dictator deliberately tried to sustain an image of a virile warrior. Although Mussolini established a one-party state, he was less successful than Hitler or Stalin in creating a totalitarian regime. (AP Photos.)

Hardened war veterans, who had been told that they would be rewarded for their sacrifices at the front but instead confronted unemployment and landlessness, were drawn to Fascism's dynamism. So too were veterans eager to escape the boredom and idleness of civilian life, which seemed so squalid in comparison with the high drama of battle. These demobilized soldiers welcomed an opportunity to wear the uniforms of the Fascist militia (Black Shirts), parade in the streets, and fight socialist and labor union opponents. Squads of Fascist Black Shirts (*squadristi*) raided socialist and trade union offices, destroying property and beating the occupants. As socialist Red Shirts responded in kind, it soon appeared that Italy was drifting toward civil war.

Hoping that Mussolini would rescue Italy from Bolshevism, industrialists and landowners contributed large sums to the Fascist Party. The lower middle class, fearful that the growing power of labor unions and the Socialist Party threatened their property and social prestige, viewed Mussolini as a protector. Middle-class university students, searching for adventure and an ideal, and army officers, dreaming of an Italian empire and hostile to parliamentary government, were also attracted to Mussolini's party. Intellectuals disenchanted with liberal politics and parliamentary democracy were intrigued by his philosophy of action. Mussolini's nationalism, activism, and anti-Communism gradually seduced elements of the power structure: capitalists, aristocrats, army officers, the royal family, and the church.

In 1922, Mussolini made his bid for power. Speaking at a giant rally of his followers in late October, he declared: "Either they will give us the government or we shall take it by descending on Rome. It is now a matter of days, perhaps hours." A few days later, thousands of Fascists began the March on Rome. Some members of the Chamber of Deputies demanded that the army defend the government against a Fascist coup. It would have been a relatively simple matter to crush the twenty thousand Fascist marchers, armed with little more than pistols and rifles, but King Victor Emmanuel III (1869–1947) refused to act. The king's advisers, some of them sympathetic to Mussolini, exaggerated the strength of the Fascists. Believing that he was rescuing Italy from terrible violence, the king appointed Mussolini prime minister.

Mussolini had bluffed his way to power. Fascism had triumphed not because of its own strength—the Fascists had only 35 of the 535 seats in Parliament—but because the liberal government, irresolute and indecisive, did not counter force with force. In the past, the liberal state had not challenged Fascist acts of terror; now it feebly surrendered to Fascist blustering and threats. No doubt liberals hoped that, once in power, the Fascists would forsake terror, pursue moderate aims, and act within the constitution. But the liberals were wrong; they had completely misjudged the antidemocratic character of Fascism.

THE FASCIST STATE IN ITALY

Consolidation of Power

In October 1922, when Italy's liberal government capitulated, the Fascists by no means held total power. Anti-Fascists still sat in parliament, and only four of the fourteen ministers in Mussolini's cabinet were Fascists. In this early stage of Fascist rule, when his position was still tenuous, Mussolini sought to maintain an image of respectability and moderation. He tried to convince the power structure that he intended to operate within the constitution, and he did not seek dictatorial power. At the same time, he gradually secured his position and turned Italy into a one-party state. In 1923, the Acerbo electoral law, approved by both chambers of parliament, decreed that the party with the most votes in a national election (provided that the figure was not less than 25 percent of the total votes cast) would be granted two-thirds of the seats in the Chamber of Deputies. In the elections of 1924, which were marred by Fascist terrorism, Mussolini's supporters received 65 percent of the vote. Even without the implementation of the new electoral law, the opponents of Fascism had been enfeebled.

When socialist leader Giacomo Matteotti protested Fascist terror tactics, Fascist thugs killed him in 1924. Although Mussolini had not ordered Matteotti's murder, his vicious attacks against his socialist opponent inspired the assassins. Repelled by the murder, some sincere democrats withdrew from the Chamber of Deputies in protest, and some influential Italians called for Mussolini's dismissal. But the majority of liberals, including the leadership, continued to support Mussolini. And the king, the papacy, the army, large landowners, and industrialists, still regarding Mussolini as the best defense against internal disorder and Marxism, failed to back an anti-Fascist movement.

Pressed by the radicals within the Fascist party, Mussolini moved to establish a dictatorship. During 1925–1926, he eliminated non-Fascists from his cabinet and dissolved opposition parties. He also smashed the independent trade unions, suppressed opposition newspapers, replaced local mayors with Fascist officials, and organized a secret police to round up troublemakers. Many anti-Fascists fled the country or were deported.

Mussolini was less successful than Hitler and Stalin in fashioning a totalitarian state. The industrialists, the large landowners, the church, and to some extent even the army never fell under the complete domination of the party. Nor did the regime possess the mind of its subjects with the same thoroughness as the Nazis did in Germany. Life in Italy was less regimented and the individual less fearful than in Nazi Germany or Communist Russia. The Italian people might cheer Mussolini, but few were willing to die for him.

Control of the Masses

Like Communist Russia and Nazi Germany, Fascist Italy used mass organizations and mass media to control minds and regulate behavior. As in the Soviet Union and Nazi Germany, the Fascist regime created a cult of the leader. "Mussolini goes forward with confidence, in a halo of myth, almost chosen by God, indefatigable and infallible, the instrument employed by Providence for the creation of a new civilization," wrote the philosopher Giovanni Gentile.[18] To convey the image of a virile leader, Mussolini had himself photographed bare-chested or in a uniform with a steel helmet. Other photographs showed him riding horses, driving fast cars, flying planes, and playing with lion cubs. Mussolini frequently addressed huge throngs of admirers from his balcony. His tenor voice, grandiloquent phrases, and posturing—jaw thrust out, hands on hips, rolling eyes—captivated audiences. Idolatry from the masses, in

turn, intensified Mussolini's feelings of grandeur. Elementary-school textbooks depicted Mussolini as the savior of the nation, a modern-day Julius Caesar.

Fascist propaganda urged that the grandeur of the Roman Empire be restored through conquest. It also inculcated habits of discipline and obedience: "Mussolini is always right." "Believe! Obey! Fight!" Propaganda also glorified war: "A minute on the battlefield is worth a lifetime of peace." It enticed Italians with a utopian vision—a proud, powerful, and vigorous nation imbued with the martial spirit of their Roman ancestors. The press, radio, and cinema idealized life under Fascism, implying that Fascism had eradicated crime, poverty, and social tensions. Schoolteachers and university professors were compelled to swear allegiance to the Fascist government and to propagate Fascist ideals, while students were urged to criticize instructors who harbored liberal attitudes. Millions of youths belonged to Fascist organizations, in which they participated in patriotic ceremonies and social functions, sang Fascist hymns, and wore Fascist uniforms. They submerged their own identities in the group.

Economic Policies

Fascists denounced economic liberalism for promoting individual self-interest and reviled socialism for instigating conflicts between workers and capitalists, which divided and weakened the nation. The Fascist way of resolving tensions between workers and employers was to abolish independent labor unions, prohibit strikes, and establish associations or corporations that included both workers and employers from a given industry. In theory, representatives of labor and capital would cooperatively solve labor problems in a particular industry. In practice, the representatives of labor turned out to be Fascists who protected the interests of the industrialists. Although the Fascists lauded the corporative system as a creative approach to modern economic problems, in reality it played a minor role in Italian economic life. Big business continued to make its own decisions, paying scant attention to the corporations.

Nor did the Fascist government solve Italy's longstanding economic problems. To curtail the export of capital and reduce the nation's dependence on imports in case of war, Mussolini sought to make Italy self-sufficient. To win the "battle of grain," the Fascist regime brought marginal lands under cultivation and urged farmers to concentrate on wheat rather than other crops. Although wheat production thus increased substantially, total agricultural output declined because wheat was planted on land better suited to animal husbandry and fruit cultivation. To make Italy industrially self-sufficient, the regime limited imports of foreign goods, with the result that Italian consumers paid higher prices for Italian-manufactured goods. Mussolini posed as the protector of the little people, but under his regime the power and profits of big business grew and the standard of living of small farmers and urban workers declined. Government attempts to grapple with the Great Depression (see "The Western Democracies" on page 760) were halfhearted. Aside from providing family allowances—an increase in income with the birth of each child—the Fascist regime did little in the way of social welfare.

The Church and the Fascist Regime

Although anticlerical since his youth, Mussolini practiced expediency. He recognized that coming to terms with the church would improve his image with Catholic public opinion. The Vatican regarded Mussolini's regime as a barrier against atheistic Communism and as less hostile to church interests and more amenable to church direction than a liberal government. Pope Pius XI (1922–1939) was an ultraconservative whose hatred of liberalism and secularism led him to believe that the Fascists would increase the influence of the church in the nation.

In 1929, the Lateran Accords recognized the independence of Vatican City, repealed many of the anticlerical laws passed under the liberal government, and made religious instruction compulsory in all secondary schools. The papal state, Vatican City, became a small enclave within Rome over which the Italian government had no authority. Relations between the Vatican and the Fascist government remained fairly good throughout the 1930s. One crisis arose in 1931 when Mussolini, pushed by militant anticlericals

within his party, dissolved certain Catholic youth groups as rivals to Fascist youth associations, but a compromise that permitted the Catholic organizations to function within certain limits eased tensions. When Mussolini invaded Ethiopia and intervened in the Spanish Civil War, the church supported him. Although the papacy criticized Mussolini for drawing closer to Hitler and introducing anti-Jewish legislation, it never broke with the Fascist regime.

THE NEW GERMAN REPUBLIC

In the last days of World War I, a revolution brought down the German government, a semi-authoritarian monarchy, and led to the creation of a democratic republic. In October 1918, the German admirals ordered the German navy to engage the British in the English Channel, but the sailors, anticipating peace and resentful of their officers (who commonly resorted to cruel discipline), refused to obey. Joined by sympathetic soldiers, the mutineers raised the red flag of revolution. The revolt soon spread as military men and workers demonstrated for peace and reform and in some regions seized authority. Reluctant to fire on their comrades and also fed up with the war, German troops did not move to crush the revolutionaries.

On November 9, 1918, the leaders of the government announced the end of the monarchy, and Kaiser William II fled to Holland. Two days later, the new German republic, headed by Friedrich Ebert (1871–1925), a Social Democrat, signed an armistice agreement ending the war. Many Germans remained unconvinced that they had lost the war on the battlefield. Rather, they blamed the creators of the new democratic republic for the defeat—a baseless accusation, for the German generals, knowing that the war was lost, had sought an armistice. This legend that traitors, principally Jews and Social Democrats—both strong supporters of the Weimar Republic—cheated Germany of victory was created and propagated by the conservative Right—generals, high-ranking bureaucrats, university professors, and nationalists—who wanted to preserve the army's reputation and bring down the new and hated democratic Weimar Republic. This "stab in the back" myth provided an effective weapon for the republic's enemies, including Hitler's movement.

In February 1919, the recently elected National Assembly met at Weimar and proceeded to draw up a constitution for the new state. The Weimar Republic—born in revolution, which most Germans detested, and military defeat, which many attributed to the new government—faced an uncertain future.

Threats from Left and Right

Dominated by moderate socialists, the infant republic faced internal threats from both the radical Left and the radical Right. In January 1919, the newly established German Communist Party, or Spartacists, disregarding the advice of their leaders, Rosa Luxemburg and Karl Liebknecht, took to the streets of Berlin and declared Ebert's government deposed. To crush the revolution, Ebert turned to the Free Corps: volunteer brigades of ex-soldiers and adventurers, led by officers loyal to the emperor, who had been fighting to protect the eastern borders from encroachments by the new states of Poland, Estonia, and Latvia. The men of the Free Corps—many of whom would later become prominent in Hitler's party—relished action and despised Bolshevism. They suppressed the revolution and murdered Luxemburg and Liebknecht on January 15. In May 1919, the Free Corps also marched into Munich to overthrow the soviet republic set up there by Communists a few weeks earlier.

The Spartacist revolt and the short-lived soviet republic in Munich (and others in Baden and Brunswick) had a profound effect on the German psyche. The Communists had been easily subdued, but fear of a Communist insurrection remained deeply embedded in the middle and upper classes—a fear that drove many into the ranks of the Weimar Republic's right-wing opponents.

In March 1920, the republic was threatened by the radical Right. Refusing to disband as the government ordered, detachments of the right-wing Free Corps marched into Berlin and declared the formation of a new government, headed by Wolfgang Kapp, a staunch German nationalist. President Ebert and most members of the cabinet and National Assembly fled to Stuttgart. Insisting that it could not fire on fellow soldiers, the German

THE GERMAN INFLATION, 1923. As the value of the mark plummeted, many Germans lost their entire savings, which had taken a lifetime to accumulate. Here children play with now worthless bank notes.
(© Hulton-Deutsch Collection/CORBIS.)

army, the Reichswehr, made no move to defend the republic. A general strike called by the labor unions and the socialist parties prevented Kapp from governing, and the coup collapsed. However, the Kapp Putsch demonstrated that the loyalty of the army to the republic was doubtful and that important segments of German society supported the overthrow, by violence if necessary, of the Weimar Republic and its replacement by an authoritarian government driven by a nationalist credo.

Economic Crisis

In addition to uprisings by the Left and Right, the republic was burdened by an economic crisis. During the war, Germany had financed its military expenditures not by increasing taxation but through short-term loans, accumulating a huge debt that now had to be paid. A trade deficit and enormous reparation payments worsened the nation's economic plight. Unable to meet the deficit in the national budget, the government simply printed more money, causing the value of the German mark to decline precipitously. In 1914, the mark stood at 4.2 to the dollar; in 1919, at 8.9 to the dollar; and in early 1923, at 18,000 to the dollar. In August 1923, a dollar could be exchanged for 4.6 million marks and in November, for 4 billion marks. Bank savings, war bonds, and pensions, representing years of toil and thrift, became worthless. Blaming the government for this disaster, the ruined middle class became more receptive to ultrarightist movements that aimed to bring down the republic.

With the economy in a shambles, the republic defaulted on reparation payments. Premier Raymond Poincaré (1860–1934) of France took a hard line. In January 1923, he ordered French troops into the Ruhr, the nerve center of German industry. Responding to the republic's call for passive resistance, factory workers, miners, and railroad workers in the Ruhr refused to work for the French. To provide strike benefits for the Ruhr workers, the government printed yet more money, making inflation even worse.

In August 1923, Gustav Stresemann became chancellor. The new government lasted only until November 1923, but during those one hundred days, Stresemann skillfully placed the republic on the path to recovery. He declared Germany's willingness to make reparation payments and issued a new currency backed by a mortgage on German real estate. To protect the value of the new currency, the government did not print another issue. Inflation receded, and confidence was restored.

A new arrangement regarding reparations also contributed to the economic recovery. Recognizing that in its present economic straits Germany could not meet its obligations to the Allies or secure the investment of foreign capitalists, Britain and the United States pressured France to allow a reparation commission to make new proposals. In 1924, the parties accepted the Dawes Plan, which reduced reparations and based them on Germany's economic capacity. During the negotiations, France agreed to withdraw its troops from the Ruhr—another step toward easing tensions for the republic.

From 1924 to 1929, economic conditions improved. Foreign capitalists, particularly Americans, were attracted by high interest rates and the low cost of labor. Their investments in German businesses stimulated the economy. By 1929, iron, steel, coal, and chemical production exceeded prewar levels. The value of German exports also surpassed that of 1913. This spectacular boom was partly due to more effective methods of production and management and the concentration of related industries in giant trusts. Real wages were higher than before the war, and improved unemployment benefits made life better for the workers. It appeared that Germany had also achieved political stability, as threats from the extremist parties of the Left and the Right subsided. And Weimar Germany was distinguished by a flourishing intellectual and cultural life unmatched in Europe. Given time and economic stability, democracy might have taken firmer root in Germany. But then came the Great Depression. The global economic crisis that began in October 1929 revealed how weak the Weimar Republic was.

Fundamental Weaknesses of the Weimar Republic

German political experience provided poor soil for transplanting an Anglo-Saxon democratic parliamentary system. Before World War I, Germany had been a semi-autocratic state ruled by an emperor who commanded the armed forces, controlled foreign policy, appointed the chancellor, and called and dismissed parliament. This authoritarian system blocked the German people from acquiring democratic habits and attitudes. Still accustomed to rule from above, still adoring the power state, many Germans sought the destruction of the Weimar Republic.

Traditional conservatives—the upper echelons of the civil service, judges, industrialists, large landowners, and army leaders—were contemptuous of democracy and were avowed enemies of the republic. They wanted to restore a pre-1914 authoritarian government, which would fight liberal ideals and protect the fatherland from Bolshevism. These traditional conservatives regarded the revolution against the monarchy in the last weeks of the war as a treacherous act and the establishment of a democratic republic as a violation of Germany's revered tradition of hierarchical leadership. Nor were many middle class Germans committed to the liberal-democratic principles

746 ♦ 29 An Era of Totalitarianism

on which the republic rested. The traditionally nationalistic middle class identified the republic with defeat in war and the humiliation of the Versailles treaty. Rabidly antisocialist, this class saw the leaders of the republic as Marxists who would impose a working-class state on Germany.

Right-wing intellectuals often attacked democracy as a barrier to the true unity of the German nation. In the tradition of nineteenth-century Volkish thinkers, they scorned reason and political freedom; glorified instincts, race, and action; and longed for a true German state that would embody order, discipline, and authority. In doing so, they turned many Germans against the republic, eroding the popular support on which democracy depends. As the German historian Kurt Sontheimer puts it,

> The submission of a large part of German intellectual society to the National Socialist Weltanschauung [worldview] . . . would have been inconceivable without the anti-democratic intellectual movement that preceded it and that, in its contempt for everything liberal, had blunted people's sensibilities to the inviolable rights of the individual and the preservation of human dignity. . . . Nothing is more dangerous in political life than the abandonment of reason. . . . The intellect must remain the controlling, regulating force in human affairs. The anti-democratic intellectuals of the Weimar period . . . despised reason and found more truth in myth or in the blood surging in their veins. . . . Had they a little more reason and enlightenment, these intellectuals might have seen better where their zeal was leading them and their country.[19]

The Weimar Republic also showed the weaknesses of the multiparty system. With the vote spread over a number of parties, no one party held a majority of seats in the parliament (Reichstag), and so the republic was governed by a coalition of several parties. But because of ideological differences, the coalition was always unstable and in danger of failing to function. This is precisely what happened during the Great Depression. When effective leadership was imperative, the government could not act. Political deadlock caused Germans to lose what little confidence they had in the democratic system. Support for the parties that wanted to preserve democracy

dwindled, and extremist parties that aimed to topple the republic gained strength.

Supporting the republic were Social Democrats, Catholic Centrists, and German Democrats; a coalition of these parties governed the republic during the 1920s.* Seeking to bring down the republic were the Communists, on the left, and two rightist parties, the Nationalists and the National Socialist German Workers' Party, the latter led by Adolf Hitler.

THE RISE OF HITLER

The Early Years

Adolf Hitler (1889–1945) was born in the town of Braunau am Inn, Austria, on April 20, 1889, the fourth child of a minor civil servant. Much of his youth was spent in Linz, a major city in Upper Austria. A poor student at secondary school, although by no means unintelligent, Hitler left high school and lived idly for more than two years. In 1907, the Vienna Academy of Arts rejected his application for admission. After the death of his mother in December 1907 (his father had died in 1903), Hitler drifted around Vienna, viewing himself as an art student. Contrary to his later description of these years, Hitler did not suffer great poverty, for he received an orphan's allowance from the state and an inheritance from his mother and an aunt. When the Vienna Academy again refused to admit him in 1908, he did not seek to learn a trade or to work steadily but earned some money by painting picture postcards.

Hitler was a loner, often given to brooding and self-pity. He found some solace by regularly attending Wagnerian operas (much admired

---

*The Social Democrats hoped one day to transform Germany into a Marxist society, but they had abandoned revolutionary means and pursued a policy of moderate social reform. The largest party until the closing months of the Weimar Republic, the Social Democrats were committed to democratic principles and parliamentary government. The Catholic Center Party opposed socialism and protected Catholic interests but, like the Social Democrats, supported the republic. The German Democratic Party consisted of middle-class liberals who also opposed socialism and supported the republic. Although the right-wing German People's Party was more monarchist than republican, on occasion it joined the coalition of parties that sought to preserve the republic.

by German nationalists for their glorification of German folk traditions and their stress on a savior, a heroic figure who rescues his people), by fantasizing about great architectural projects that he would someday initiate, and by reading. He read a lot, especially in art, history, and military affairs. He also read the racial, nationalist, anti-Semitic, and Pan-German literature that abounded in multinational Vienna. This literature introduced Hitler to a bizarre racial mythology: a heroic race of blond, blue-eyed Aryans battling for survival against inferior races. The racist treatises preached the danger posed by mixing races, called for the liquidation of racial inferiors, and marked the Jew as the embodiment of evil and the source of all misfortune, all themes that became core Nazi principles.

In Vienna, Hitler came into contact with Georg von Schönerer's Pan-German movement. For Schönerer, the Jews were evil not because of their religion, nor because they rejected Christ, but because they possessed evil racial qualities. Schönerer distributed a postcard carrying his signature, which read: "The Jew is the evil genius of the decline of civilization."[20] Schönerer's followers wore a watch chain with a picture of a hanged Jew attached. Hitler was particularly impressed with Karl Lueger, the mayor of Vienna, a clever demagogue who skillfully manipulated the anti-Semitic feelings of the Viennese for his own political advantage. In Vienna, Hitler also acquired a hatred for Marxism and democracy and the conviction that the struggle for existence and the survival of the fittest are the essential facts of the social world. His years in Vienna emptied Hitler of all compassion and scruples and filled him with a fierce resentment of the social order, which, he felt, had ignored him, cheated him, and condemned him to a wretched existence.

When World War I began, Hitler was in Munich. He welcomed the war as a relief from his daily life, which lacked purpose and excitement. "Overpowered by stormy enthusiasm," he later declared, "I fell down on my knees and thanked Heaven from an overflowing heart for granting me the good fortune of being permitted to live at this time."[21] Volunteering for the German army, Hitler found battle exhilarating, and he fought bravely, twice receiving the Iron Cross.

The experience of battle taught Hitler to prize discipline, regimentation, leadership, authority, struggle, and ruthlessness. The shock of Germany's

defeat and of revolution intensified his commitment to racial nationalism. To lead Germany to total victory over its racial enemies became his obsession. Like many returning soldiers, he required vindicating explanations for lost victories. His own explanation was simple and demagogic: Germany's shame was due to the creators of the republic, the "November criminals"; and behind them was a Jewish-Bolshevik world conspiracy.

The Nazi Party

In 1919, Hitler joined the German Workers' Party, a small right-wing group and one of the more than seventy extremist military-political-Volkish organizations that sprang up in postwar Germany. Displaying fantastic energy and extraordinary ability as a demagogic orator, propagandist, and organizer, Hitler quickly became the leader of the party, whose name was changed to the National Socialist German Workers' Party (commonly called Nazi). As leader, Hitler insisted on absolute authority and total allegiance—a demand that coincided with the postwar longing for a strong leader who would set right a shattered nation. Without Hitler, the National Socialist German Workers' Party would have remained an insignificant group of discontents and outcasts. Demonstrating a Machiavellian cunning in politics, Hitler tightened the party organization and perfected the techniques of mass propaganda.

Like Mussolini, Hitler incorporated military attitudes and techniques into politics. Uniforms, salutes, emblems, flags, and other symbols imbued party members with a sense of solidarity and camaraderie. At mass meetings, Hitler was a spellbinder who gave stunning performances. His pounding fists, throbbing body, wild gesticulations, hypnotic eyes, rage-swollen face, and repeated, frenzied denunciations of the Versailles treaty, Marxism, the republic, and Jews inflamed and mesmerized the audience. Many listeners—and his speeches generally attracted people already hostile to the Weimar Republic—were swayed by Hitler's earnestness, conviction, and self-confidence. They believed that Hitler and his movement could restore Germany's strength and pride; they would undo the injustices and humiliations that had been inflicted on Germany by the Allied powers. Hitler instinctively grasped the innermost feelings of his audience: its resentments and its longings. "The intense will of the man, the passion of his sincerity seemed to flow from him into me. I experienced an exaltation that could be likened only to religious conversion," said one early admirer.[22]

In November 1923, Hitler attempted to seize power in Munich, in the state of Bavaria, as a prelude to toppling the republic. The attempt, which came to be known as the Beer Hall Putsch, failed, and the Nazis made a poor showing; they quickly scattered when the Bavarian police opened fire. Ironically, however, Hitler's prestige increased, for when he was put on trial, he used it as an opportunity to denounce the republic and the Versailles treaty and to proclaim his philosophy of racial nationalism. His impassioned speeches, publicized by the press, earned Hitler a nationwide reputation and a light sentence: five years' imprisonment, with the promise of quick parole. While in prison, Hitler dictated *Mein Kampf*, a rambling and turgid work, which contained the essence of his **worldview.**

The unsuccessful Munich putsch taught Hitler a valuable lesson: armed insurrection against superior might fails. He would gain power not by force but by exploiting the instruments of democracy: elections and party politics. He would use apparently legal means to destroy the Weimar Republic and impose a dictatorship. As Nazi propaganda expert Joseph Goebbels would later express it, "We have openly declared that we use democratic methods only to gain power and that once we had it we would ruthlessly deny our opponents all those chances we had been granted when we were in the opposition."[23]

Hitler's Worldview

Hitler was concerned not with the objective truth of an idea but with its potential political usefulness. He was not a systematic thinker like Marx. Whereas Communism claimed the certainty of science and held that it would reform the world in accordance with rational principles, Hitler proclaimed the higher validity of blood, instinct, and will and regarded the intellect as an enemy of the soul. Hitler, nevertheless, possessed and was guided by a remarkably consistent ideology.

THE SPELLBINDER. Hitler was a superb orator who knew how to reach the hearts of his listeners. The masses, he said, are aroused by the spoken, not the written, word. (Roger Viollet/Getty Images.)

Hitler's thought comprised a patchwork of nineteenth-century anti-Semitic, Volkish, Social Darwinist, antidemocratic, and anti-Marxist ideas. From these ideas, many of which enjoyed wide popularity, Hitler constructed a worldview rooted in myth and race. Given to excessive daydreaming and never managing to "overcome his youth with its dreams, injuries, and resentments,"[24] Hitler sought to make the world accord with his fantasies—struggles to the death between races, a vast empire ruled by a master race, and a thousand-year Reich.

German thought, particularly after Nietzsche, was permeated by the idea of crisis: that Germany and Europe were experiencing a unique historical upheaval. The unexpected loss in World War I intensified the feeling among Germans that the nation required a radical transformation, a new beginning. Hitler conceived himself as a man of destiny leading a movement of world-historical significance; he had been chosen by fate to rescue the nation by imbuing Germans with a rejuvenating ideology, one that was inherent in their primordial past.

Racial Nationalism. **Nazism** was a radical rejection of both Judeo-Christian and Enlightenment traditions and sought to found a new world order based on racial nationalism. For Hitler, race was the key to understanding world history. He believed that Western civilization was at a critical juncture. Liberalism was dying, and Marxism, that "Jewish invention," as he called it, would inherit the future unless it was opposed by an even more powerful worldview. "With the conception of race National Socialism will carry its revolution and recast the world," said Hitler.[25] As the German barbarians had overwhelmed a disintegrating Roman Empire, a reawakened, racially united Germany, led by men of iron will, would undo the humiliation of the Versailles treaty, carve out a vast European empire, and deal a decadent liberal civilization its deathblow. It would conquer Russia, eradicate Communism, and reduce to serfdom the subhuman Slavs, "a mass of born slaves who feel the need of a master."[26]

In the tradition of crude Volkish nationalists and Social Darwinists, Hitler divided the world into superior and inferior races and pitted them against each other in a struggle for survival. For him, this fight for life, that is, for territory and resources, was a law of nature and of history. The Germans, descendants of ancient Aryans, possessed superior racial characteristics; a nation degenerates and perishes if it allows its blood to be contaminated by intermingling with lower races. Conflict between races was desirable, for it strengthened and hardened racial superiors. It made them ruthless—a necessary quality in this Darwinian world. As a higher race, the Germans were entitled to conquer and subjugate other races. Germany must acquire *Lebensraum* (living space) by expanding eastward at the expense of the racially inferior Slavs.

The Jew as Devil. An obsessive and virulent hatred of Jews dominated Hitler's mental outlook. In waging war against the Jews, Hitler believed that he was defending Germany from its worst enemy, a sinister force that stood in total opposition to the new world he envisioned. Many of his ideas had been advanced by German anti-Semites in the closing decades of the nineteenth century (see pages 594–601). In Hitler's mythical interpretation of the world, the Aryan was the originator and carrier of civilization. As descendants of the Aryans, the German race embodied creativity, bravery, and loyalty. In contrast, Jews, who belonged to a separate biological race, personified the vilest qualities. "Two worlds face one another," said Hitler in a statement that clearly reveals the mythical character of his thought, "the men of God and the men of Satan! The Jew is the anti-man, the creature of another god. He must have come from another root of the human race. I set the Aryan and the Jew over and against each other."[27] And because of the high rate of intermarriage, Jews were polluting the Germans' Aryan blood. Everything Hitler despised—liberalism, intellectualism, pacifism, parliamentarianism, internationalism, Communism, modern art, and individualism—he attributed to Jews.

For Hitler, the Jew was the mortal enemy of racial nationalism. The moral outlook of the ancient Hebrew prophets, which affirmed individual worth and made individuals morally responsible for their actions, was totally at odds with Hitler's morality, which subordinated the individual to the national community. Hitler once called conscience a Jewish invention. The Hebrew prophets' vision of the unity of humanity under God and the belief in equality, justice, and peace were also contrary to Hitler's creed that all history is a pitiless struggle between races and that only the strongest and most ruthless deserve to survive.

Hitler's anti-Semitism served a functional purpose as well. By concentrating all evil in one enemy, "the conspirator and demonic" Jew, Hitler provided true believers with a simple, all-embracing, and emotionally satisfying explanation for their misery. By defining themselves as the racial and spiritual opposites of Jews, true believers of all classes felt joined together in a Volkish union. By seeing themselves engaged in a heroic battle for self-preservation and racial survival against a demonic enemy that embodied evil, they strengthened their will. Even failures and misfits gained self-respect. Anti-Semitism provided insecure and hostile people with powerless but recognizable targets on whom to focus their antisocial feelings.

The surrender to myth served to disorient the intellect and unify the nation. When the mind accepts an image such as Hitler's image of Jews as vermin, germs, and satanic conspirators, it has lost all sense of balance and objectivity. Such a disoriented mind is ready to believe and to obey, to be manipulated and to be led, to brutalize and to tolerate brutality; it is ready to be absorbed into the collective will of the community. That many people, including intellectuals and members of the elite, accepted these racial ideas shows the enduring power of mythical thinking and the vulnerability of reason. In 1933, the year Hitler took power, Felix Goldmann, a German-Jewish writer, commented astutely on the irrational character of Nazi anti-Semitism: "The present-day politicized racial anti-Semitism is the embodiment of myth, . . . nothing is discussed . . . only felt, . . . nothing is pondered critically, logically or reasonably, . . . only inwardly perceived, surmised. . . . We are apparently the last [heirs] of the Enlightenment."[28]

The Importance of Propaganda. Hitler understood that in an age of political parties, universal suffrage, and a popular press—the legacies of the French and Industrial Revolutions—the successful leader must win the support of the masses. To do so, Hitler consciously applied and perfected elements of circus showmanship, church pageantry, American advertising, and the techniques of propaganda that the Allies had used to stir their civilian populations during the war. To be effective, said Hitler, propaganda must be aimed principally at the emotions. The masses are not moved by scientific ideas or by objective and abstract knowledge, but by primitive feelings, terror, force, and discipline. Propaganda must reduce everything to simple slogans incessantly repeated and must concentrate on one enemy. The masses are aroused by the spoken, not the written, word—by a storm of hot passion erupting from the speaker, "which like hammer blows can open the gates to the heart of a people."[29]

The most effective means of stirring the masses and strengthening them for the struggle ahead, Hitler had written in *Mein Kampf*, is the mass meeting. Surrounded by tens of thousands of

people, individuals lose their sense of individuality and no longer see themselves as isolated. They become members of a community bound together by an **esprit de corps** reminiscent of the trenches during the Great War. Bombarded by the cheers of thousands of voices, by marching units, by banners, by explosive oratory, individuals become convinced of the truth of the party's message and the irresistibility of the movement. Their intellects overwhelmed, their resistance lowered, they lose their previous beliefs and are carried along on a wave of enthusiasm. Their despair over the condition of their nation turns to hope, and they derive a sense of belonging and mission. They feel that they are participants in a mighty movement that is destined to regenerate the German nation and initiate a new historical age. "The man who enters such a meeting doubting and wavering leaves it inwardly reinforced; he has become a link to the community."[30]

Hitler Gains Power

When Hitler left prison in December 1924 after serving only nine months, he proceeded to tighten his hold on the Nazi Party. He relentlessly used his genius for propaganda and organization to strengthen the loyalty of his cadres and to instill in them a sense of mission. In 1925, the Nazi Party counted about 27,000 members; in 1929, it had grown to 178,000, with units throughout Germany. But its prospects seemed dim, for since 1925 economic conditions had greatly improved—Germany's exports had even surpassed those of Britain—and the republic seemed politically stable. In 1928, the National Socialist German Workers' Party (NSDAP) received only 2.6 percent of the vote. Nevertheless, Hitler never lost faith in his own capacities or his destiny. He continued to build his party and waited for a crisis that would rock the republic and make his movement a force in national politics.

The Great Depression, which began in the United States at the end of 1929, provided that crisis. Desperate and demoralized people lined up in front of government unemployment offices. Street peddlers, beggars, and youth gangs proliferated; suicides increased, particularly among middle-class people shamed by their descent into poverty, idleness, and uselessness. As Germany's economic plight worsened, the German people became more amenable to Hitler's radicalism. The Nazis tirelessly expanded their efforts. Everywhere, they staged mass rallies, plastered walls with posters, distributed leaflets, and engaged in street battles with their opponents of the Left. Hitler promised all things to all groups, avoided debates, provided simple explanations for Germany's misfortunes, and insisted that only the Nazis could establish domestic order, promote economic prosperity, and restore Germany's position as an international power. Nazi propaganda attacked the Communists, the "November criminals," the democratic system, the Versailles Treaty, reparations, and the Jews. It depicted Hitler as a savior. Hitler would rescue Germany from chaos; he understood the real needs of the Volk; he was sent by destiny to lead Germany in its hour of greatest need. These propaganda techniques worked. The Nazi Party went from 810,000 votes in 1928 to 6.4 million in 1930, and its representation in the Reichstag soared from 12 to 107.

The Social Democratic Party of Germany (SPD), the principal defenders of democracy, could draw support only from the working class; to the middle class, they were hated Marxists. Moreover, in the eyes of many Germans, the SPD was identified with the status quo, that is, with economic misery and national humiliation. Swallowing right-wing propaganda, they held the founders and leaders of the Weimar Republic responsible for the defeat in World War I and the diminution of Germany's power in world affairs. The SPD simply had no program that could attract the middle class or give it hope for a better future.

To the lower middle class, the Nazis promised effective leadership and a solution to the economic crisis. For this segment of society, the Great Depression was the last straw, the final evidence that the republic had failed and should be supplanted by a different kind of regime. Germans of the lower middle class craved order, authority, and leadership and abhorred the endless debates and factional quarrels of the political parties. To them, parliamentary government was fatally flawed. They wanted Hitler to protect Germany from the Communists who, they feared, would do to their country what the Bolsheviks had done in Russia. They also wanted him to

contain the power of organized labor and to revive the economy. The traumatic experience of the Great Depression caused many bourgeois—until then apathetic about voting—to cast ballots. The Depression was also severe in England and the United States, but the liberal foundations of these countries were strong. In Germany, they were not, because the middle class had not committed itself to democracy, nor indeed did it have any liking for it. Democracy endured in Britain and the United States; in Germany, it collapsed.

But Nazism was more than a class movement. It appealed to the discontented and disillusioned from all segments of the population: embittered veterans, romantic nationalists, idealistic intellectuals, industrialists and large landowners frightened by Communism and social democracy, rootless and resentful people who felt that they had no place in the existing society, the unemployed, lovers of violence, and newly enfranchised youth yearning for a cause. The Social Democrats spoke the rational language of European democracy. The Communists addressed themselves to only a part of the nation, the proletariat, and were linked to a foreign country, the Soviet Union. The Nazis reached a wider spectrum of the population, and their promise to unite the German people in a racial brotherhood dedicated to restoring German honor and power touched deeper feelings.

And always there was the immense attraction of Hitler, who tirelessly worked his oratorical magic on increasingly enthusiastic crowds, confidently promising leadership and national rebirth. Many Germans were won over by his fanatical sincerity, his iron will, and his conviction that he was chosen by fate to rescue Germany. What a new party member wrote after hearing Hitler speak expressed the mood of many Germans who yearned for leadership: "There was only one thing for me, either to win with Adolf Hitler or to die for him. The personality of the Fuehrer had me totally in its spell."[31] Many others, no doubt, voted for Hitler not because they approved of him or his ideas, but because he was a strong opponent of the Weimer Republic, which they viewed as weak and contemptible. What these people wanted, above all, was the end of the republic they hated.

Meanwhile, the parliamentary regime failed to function effectively. According to Article 48 of the constitution, during times of emergency the president was empowered to govern by decree, that is, without the Reichstag, the parliament. When President Paul von Hindenburg (1847–1934), the aging field marshal, exercised this emergency power, the responsibility for governing Germany was in effect transferred from the political parties and the Reichstag to the president and chancellor. Rule by the president, instead of by parliament, meant, for one thing, that Germany had already taken a giant step away from parliamentary government in the direction of authoritarianism.

In the election of July 31, 1932, the Nazis received 37.3 percent of the vote and won 230 seats, far more than any other party but still not a majority. Determined to become chancellor, Hitler refused to take a subordinate position in a coalition government. Franz von Papen, who had resigned from the chancellorship, persuaded Hindenburg, whose judgment was distorted by old age, to appoint Hitler chancellor. In this decision, Papen had the support of German industrialists, aristocratic landowners, and the Nationalist Party.

As in Italy, the members of the ruling elite were frightened by internal violence, unrest, and the specter of Communism. They had abhorred the creation of the Weimar Republic, and the government's ineffectiveness in coping with crises only confirmed their disdain for parliamentary democracy. They thought Hitler a vulgar man, a lowly corporal, and they detested his demagogic incitement of the masses. But they regarded him as a useful instrument to fight Communism, block social reform, break the back of organized labor, and rebuild the armament industry. They expected him to break the shackles of the hated Versailles treaty, which the Weimar Republic had passively accepted; restore the strength of the military; and in international affairs pursue a more assertive policy reminiscent of the days of the emperor. They also hoped that the charismatic Hitler would revive the nation's spirit and pride, which had eroded under the republic. And, traditionally anti-Semitic, they welcomed an opportunity to restrict the role of Jews in Germany's political, economic, and cultural life.

Hitler had cleverly reassured these traditional conservatives that the Nazis would protect private property and business, and go slow with social reform. They would have preferred a dictatorship under Hindenburg, a respected general who shared their views and upbringing, but a dictatorship under Hitler still seemed to them better than the Weimar Republic, which they had hated since its inception.

Like the Italian upper class, which had assisted Mussolini in his rise to power, the old conservative ruling elite intrigued to put Hitler in power. Ironically, this decision was made when Nazi strength at the polls was beginning to ebb. Expecting to control Hitler, conservatives calculated badly, for Hitler could not be tamed. They had underestimated his political skills, his ruthlessness, and his obsession with racial nationalism. Hitler had sought power not to restore the old order but to fashion a new one. The new leadership would be drawn not from the traditional ruling segments but from the most dedicated Nazis, regardless of their social background.

Never intending to rule within the spirit of the constitution, Hitler, who took office on January 30, 1933, quickly moved to assume dictatorial powers. In February 1933, a Dutch drifter with Communist leanings set a fire in the Reichstag. Hitler persuaded Hindenburg to sign an emergency decree suspending civil rights on the pretext that the state was threatened by internal subversion. The chancellor then used these emergency powers to arrest, without due process, Communist and Social Democratic deputies.

In the elections of March 1933, Nazi thugs broke up Communist Party meetings, and Hitler called for a Nazi victory at the polls to save Europe from Bolshevism. Intimidated by street violence and captivated by Nazi mass demonstrations and relentless propaganda, the German people elected 288 Nazi deputies in a Reichstag of 647 seats. With the support of 52 deputies of the Nationalist Party and in the absence of Communist deputies, who were under arrest, the Nazis now had a secure majority. Hitler then bullied the Reichstag into passing the Enabling Act (in March 1933), which permitted the chancellor to enact legislation independently of the Reichstag. With astonishing passivity, the political parties had allowed the Nazis to dismantle the government and make Hitler a dictator with unlimited power. Hitler had used the instruments of democracy to destroy the Weimar Republic, Germany's first liberal democracy, and create a dictatorship. And he did it far more thoroughly and quickly than Mussolini.

NAZI GERMANY

Mussolini's Fascism exhibited much bluster and bragging, but Fascist Italy did not have the industrial and military strength or the total commitment of the people necessary to threaten the peace of Europe. Nazism, in contrast, demonstrated a demonic quality, which nearly destroyed Western civilization.

Hitler's sinister, fanatical, and obsessive personality had a far greater impact on the German movement than Mussolini's character had on Italian Fascism. Also contributing to the demonic radicalism of Nazism were certain deeply rooted German traditions, which were absent in Italy: Prussian militarism, adoration of the power state, and belief in the special destiny of the German racial community. These traditions made the German people's attachment to Hitler and Nazi ideology much stronger than the Italian people's devotion to Mussolini and his party.

The Leader-State

The Nazis moved to subjugate all political and economic institutions and all culture to the will of the party. There could be no separation between private life and politics: ideology must pervade every phase of daily life, and all organizations must come under party control. There could be no rights of the individual that the state must respect. The party became the state, and its teachings the soul of the German nation. Joseph Goebbels (see "Shaping the 'New Man'" later in this chapter) summed up this totalitarian goal: "It is not enough to reconcile people more or less to our regime, to move them towards a position of neutrality towards us, we want rather to work on people until they are addicted to us."[32] An anonymous Nazi poet expressed the totalitarian credo in these words:

> *We have captured all the positions*
> *And on the heights we have planted*
> *The banners of our revolution.*
> *You had imagined that that was all that we*
>   *wanted*
> *We want more*
> *We want all*
> *Your hearts are our goal,*
> *It is your souls we want.*[33]

The Third Reich was organized as a leader-state, in which Hitler, the *führer* (leader), embodied and expressed the true will of the German people, commanded the supreme loyalty of the nation, and held omnipotent power. His authority was neither limited by constitutional checks or individual rights. Virtually all crucial decisions in foreign affairs were made by Hitler. Yet, at the same time, the Nazi state comprised organizations and individuals competing with one another for influence, power, and plunder.

To strengthen the power of the central government and coordinate the nation under Nazism, the regime abolished legislatures in the various German states and appointed governors who would make certain that Nazi directives were carried out throughout the country. The Nazis took over the civil service and used its machinery to enforce Nazi decrees. In this process of *Gleichschaltung* (coordination), the Nazis encountered little opposition. The political parties and the trade unions collapsed without a struggle.

In June 1933, the SDP was outlawed, and within a few weeks, the other political parties simply disbanded on their own. In May, the Nazis had seized the property of the trade unions, arrested the leaders, and ended collective bargaining and strikes. The newly established German Labor Front, an instrument of the party, became the official organization of the working class. Although there is evidence that the working class in 1933 would have resisted the Nazis, its leadership never mobilized proletarian organizations. With surprising ease, the Nazis imposed their will on the nation.

Hitler made strategic but temporary concessions to the traditional ruling elite. On June 30, 1934, Nazi executioners swiftly murdered the leaders of the *Sturmabteilung* or SA (Nazi storm troopers who had battled political opponents) to eliminate any potential opposition to Hitler from within the party. With this move, Hitler also relieved the anxieties of industrialists and landowners, who feared that Ernst Röhm, the head of the SA, would persuade Hitler to remove them from positions of power and to implement a program of radical social reform, threatening their property.

The execution of the SA leaders (including Röhm) was also approved by the generals, for they regarded the SA as a rival to the army.

Ernst Huber: "The Authority of the Führer Is . . . All-Inclusive and Unlimited"

In Verfassungsrecht des grossdeutschen Reiches (Constitutional Law of the Greater German Reich), *legal scholar Ernst Rudolf Huber (1903–1990) offered a classic explication of the basic principles of National Socialism. The following excerpts from that work describe the nature of Hitler's political authority.*

The Führer-Reich of the [German] people is founded on the recognition that the true will of the people cannot be disclosed through parliamentary votes and plebiscites but that the will of the people in its pure and uncorrupted form can only be expressed through the Führer. Thus a distinction must be drawn between the supposed will of the people in a parliamentary democracy, which merely reflects the conflict of the various social interests, and the true will of the people in the Führer-state, in which the collective will of the real political unit is manifested. . . .

It would be impossible for a law to be introduced and acted upon in the Reichstag which had not originated with the Führer or, at least, received his approval. The procedure is similar to that of the plebiscite: The lawgiving power does not rest in the Reichstag; it merely proclaims through its decision its agreement with the will of the Führer, who is the lawgiver of the German people.

The Führer unites in himself all the sovereign authority of the Reich; all public authority in the state as well as in the movement is derived from the authority of the Führer. We must speak not of the state's authority but of the Führer's authority if we wish to designate the character of the political authority within the Reich correctly. The state does not hold political authority as an impersonal unit but receives it from the Führer as the executor of the national will. The authority of the Führer is complete and all-embracing; it unites in itself all the means of political direction; it extends into all fields of national life; it embraces the entire people, which is bound to the Führer in loyalty and obedience. The authority of the Führer is not limited by checks and controls, by special autonomous bodies or individual rights, but it is free and independent, all-inclusive and unlimited.

Question for Analysis

1. Point out several ways that Ernst Rudolf Huber's views represent a rejection of the Western liberal-democratic tradition.

Raymond E. Murphy, et. al., *National Socialism: Basic Principles, Their Application by the Nazi Party's Organization and the Use of Germans Abroad for Nazi Aims* (Washington, D.C.: Government Printing office, 1943), 34, 36–38.

In August, all German soldiers swore an oath of unconditional allegiance to the führer, cementing the alliance between the army and National Socialism. The army tied itself to the Nazi regime because it approved of the resurgence of militaristic values and applauded the death of the Weimar Republic. As the German historian Karl Dietrich Bracher concludes, "Without the assistance of the Army, at first through its toleration and later through its active cooperation, the country's rapid and final restructuring into the total leader state could not have come about."[34]

Economic Life

Hitler had sought power not to improve the living standards of the masses but to convert

Germany into a powerful war machine. Economic problems held little interest for this dreamer, in whose mind danced images of a vast German empire. For him, the "socialism" in National Socialism meant not a comprehensive program of social welfare but the elimination of the class antagonisms that divided and weakened the fatherland and blocked the revitalization of German communal and racial ties. Radicals within the party wanted to deprive the industrialists and landowners of power and social prestige and to expropriate their property. The more pragmatic Hitler wanted only to deprive them of freedom of action; they were to serve, not control, the state. Germany remained capitalist, but the state had unlimited power to intervene in the economy. Unlike the Bolsheviks, the Nazis did not destroy the upper classes of the old regime. Hitler made no war against the industrialists. He wanted from them loyalty, obedience, and a war machine capable of waging total war. German businessmen prospered but exercised no influence on political decisions. The profits of industry rose, and workers lauded the regime for ending the unemployment crisis through an extensive program of public works, the restoration of conscription, and rearmament.

Nazism and the Churches

Nazism conflicted with the core values of Christianity. "The heaviest blow that ever struck humanity was the coming of Christianity," said Hitler to intimates during World War II.[35] Had Germany won the war, the Nazis would no doubt have tried to root Christianity out of German life. In 1937, the bishop of Berlin defined the essential conflict between Christianity and Nazism.

> *The question at stake is whether there is an authority that stands above all earthly power, the authority of God, Whose commandments are valid independent of space and time, country and race. The question at stake is whether individual man possesses personal rights that no community and no state may take from him; whether the free exercise of his conscience may be prevented and forbidden by the state.*[36]

Nazism could tolerate no other faith alongside itself. Recognizing that Christianity was a rival claimant for the German soul, the Nazis moved to repress the Protestant and Catholic churches. In the public schools, religious instruction was cut back and the syllabus changed to omit the Jewish origins of Christianity. Christ was depicted not as a Jew, heir to the prophetic tradition of Hebrew monotheism, but as an Aryan hero. The Gestapo (secret state police) censored church newspapers, scrutinized sermons and church activities, forbade some clergymen to preach, dismissed the opponents of Nazism from theological schools, and arrested some clerical critics of the regime.

The clergy were well represented among the Germans who resisted Nazism; some were sent to concentration camps or executed. But these courageous clergy were not representatives of the German churches, which, as organized institutions, capitulated to and cooperated with the Nazi regime. Both the German Evangelical (Lutheran) and German Catholic churches demanded that their faithful give Hitler their loyalty; both turned a blind eye to Nazi persecution of Jews. Even before World War II and the implementation of genocide, many Evangelical churches banned baptized Jews from entering their temples and dismissed pastors with Jewish ancestry. During the war, both Catholic and Evangelical churches condemned resistance and found much to admire in the Third Reich, and both supported Hitler's war. When Germany attacked Poland, starting World War II, the Catholic bishops declared: "In this decisive hour we encourage and admonish our Catholic soldiers, in obedience to the Füehrer, to do their duty and to be ready to sacrifice their whole existence."[37] Both churches urged their faithful to fight for fatherland and führer, pressured conscientious objectors to serve, and celebrated Nazi victories.

The German churches, which preached Christ's message of humanity, failed to take a stand against Nazi inhumanity for a variety of reasons. Many German church leaders feared that resistance would lead to even more severe measures against their churches. Traditionally, the German churches had bowed to state authority and detested revolution. Church leaders also found some Nazi ideas appealing. Intensely nationalistic, antiliberal, antirepublican, anti-Communist, and anti-Semitic, many members of the clergy were filled with hope when Hitler came to power. They anticipated that Hitler would restore respect for traditional Christian morality, which, they believed, had been undermined by the secularism, materialism, and vice rampant in the Weimar Republic. And he would declaw the Communists, who had declared war on Christianity. The prominent Lutheran theologian who "welcomed that change that came to Germany in 1933 as a divine gift and miracle"[38] voiced the sentiments of many members of the clergy. Such feelings encouraged prolonged moral nearsightedness, not a revolt of Christian conscience. When the war ended, the German Evangelical church leaders lamented:

> *We know ourselves to be one with our people in a great company of suffering and in a great solidarity of guilt. With great pain do we say: "Through us endless suffering has been brought to many people and countries. . . . We accuse ourselves for not witnessing more courageously, for not praying more faithfully, for not loving more ardently."*[39]

Shaping the "New Man"

Propaganda had helped the Nazis come to power. Now it would be used to consolidate their hold on the German nation and shape a "new man," committed to Hitler, race, and Volk. Hitler was a radical revolutionary who desired not only the outward form of power but also control over the inner person, over the individual's thoughts and feelings. The purpose of Nazi propaganda was to condition the mind to revere the führer and to obey the new regime. Its intent was to deprive individuals of their capacity for independent thought. By concentrating on myths of the race and the infallibility of the führer, Nazi propaganda sought to disorient the rational mind and give the individual new standards to believe in and obey. Propaganda aimed to mold the entire nation to think and respond as the leader-state directed. Even science had to conform to Nazi racial ideology. Thus, Johannes Stark, a Nobel Prize winner, declared that scientific thought is a function of race.

> *Natural science is overwhelmingly a creation of the Nordic-Germanic blood component of the Aryan peoples. . . . The Jewish spirit is wholly different in its orientation. . . . True, Heinrich Hertz made the great discovery of electromagnetic waves, but he was not a full-blooded Jew. He had a German mother, from whose side his spiritual endowment may well have been conditioned.*[40]

The Ministry of Popular Enlightenment, headed by Joseph Goebbels (1897–1945), controlled the press, book publishing, the radio, the theater, and the cinema. A holder of a doctoral degree in the humanities, Goebbels was intelligent and a master in the art of propaganda. Viewing Hitler as a Nietzschean overman, a man of destiny who was inculcating Germans with a saving faith, Goebbels was completely devoted to the führer. He was also vain, cynical, and contemptuous of the very masses he manipulated. But the German people were not merely passive victims of clever and ruthless leaders. "The effective spread of propaganda and the rapid regimentation of cultural life," says Bracher, "would not have been possible without the invaluable help eagerly tendered by writers and artists, professors and churchmen." And the manipulation of the minds of the German people "would not have been effective had it not been for profound historically conditioned relations based . . . on a pseudo-religious exaggerated nationalism and on the idea of the German mission."[41] Although some intellectuals showed their abhorrence of the Nazi regime by emigrating, the great majority gave their support and lent their talents, often with overt enthusiasm, to their leader and to Nazi ideology. Some individuals rejected Nazi propaganda, but the masses of German people came to regard Nazism as the fulfillment of their nationalist longings.

Nazi propaganda, especially when spread by radio, saturated the nation. The Nazis tried to keep the emotions in a state of permanent mobilization, for Hitler understood that the emotionally aroused are most amenable to manipulation. Goose-stepping SA and SS (elite military and police) battalions paraded in the streets; martial music quickened the pulse; Nazi flags decorated public buildings; loudspeakers installed in offices and factories blared the Nazi message, and all

NAZI CULTURE. The Nazis considered jazz to be racially degenerate Jewish and black music. (Bildarchiv Preussischer Kulturbesitz/Art Resource, N.Y.)

work stopped for important broadcasts. Citizens were ordered to greet each other with "Heil Hitler," a potent sign of reverence and submission. Nazi propaganda constructed a cult around the person of Hitler, who was portrayed as an inspired leader chosen by destiny to redeem the fatherland.

The regime made a special effort to reach young people. All youths between the ages of ten and eighteen were urged and then required to join the Hitler Youth, and all other youth organizations were dissolved. At camps and rallies, young people paraded, sang, saluted, and chanted: "We were slaves; we were outsiders in our own country. So were we before Hitler united us. Now we would fight against Hell itself for our leader."[42]

Nazification of Education. The schools, long breeding grounds of nationalism, militarism, anti-liberalism, and anti-Semitism, now indoctrinated the young in Nazi ideology. The Nazis instructed teachers in how certain subjects were to be taught; and to ensure obedience, members of the Hitler Youth were asked to report suspicious teachers. Portraits of Hitler, along with Nazi banners, were displayed in classrooms. War stories, adventures of the Hitler Youth, and ancient Nordic legends replaced fairy tales and animal stories in reading material for the young. The curriculum upgraded physical training and sports, curtailed religious instruction, and introduced many courses in "racial science." Decidedly anti-intellectual, the Nazis stressed character building over book learning. They intended to train young people to serve the leader and the racial community—to imbue them with a sense of fellowship for their Volkish kin, that sense of camaraderie found on the battlefield. Expressions of individualism and independence were suppressed.

The universities quickly abandoned freedom of the mind, scientific objectivity, and humanist values. "We repudiate international science, we repudiate the international community of scholars, we repudiate research for the sake of research. Sieg Heil!" declared one historian.[43] Even before the Nazi takeover, many university students and professors had embraced Volkish nationalism and antidemocratic right-wing radicalism. In their volatile lectures and writings, professors called for the destruction of the Weimar Republic, and two years before Hitler came to power, 60 percent of all undergraduates supported the Nazi student organization, and anti-Semitic riots broke out at several universities.

"From now on it will not be your job to determine whether something is true but whether it is in the spirit of the National Socialist revolution," the new minister of culture told university professors.[44] Numerous courses on Nazi ideology were introduced into the curriculum. In May 1933, professors and students proudly burned books, many of them written by Jews, considered a threat to Nazi ideology, a display of cultural barbarism that gave prophetic meaning to the famous words of Heinrich Heine, the great nineteenth-century German-Jewish poet: "wherever they burn books they will also, in the end, burn people." As books removed from public and private libraries were hurled into the flames, students danced and chanted.

YOUNG NAZIS BURNING BOOKS IN SALZBURG, AUSTRIA, IN 1938. "The age of extreme Jewish intellectualism has now ended," said Joseph Goebbels to cheering students. (© Topham/The Image Works.)

Many academics praised Hitler and the new regime. Some 10 percent of the university faculty, principally Jews, Social Democrats, and liberals, were dismissed, and their colleagues often approved. Many writers, scientists, and artists, the cream of European intellectual life, left Germany. Others served the regime, providing an intellectual justification for Hitler's dictatorship, Nazi racial theories, and the persecution of Jews. Physical anthropologists and biologists were instrumental in erecting a "scientific" foundation for Nazi racism. Many German academics, some of them noted scholars, willingly, if not enthusiastically, lent their talents and learning to the new regime.

Giant Rallies. Symbolic of the Nazi regime were the monster rallies staged at Nuremberg. Scores of thousands roared, marched, and worshiped at their leader's feet. These true believers, the end product of Nazi indoctrination, celebrated Hitler's achievements and demonstrated their loyalty to their savior. Everything was brilliantly orchestrated to impress Germans and the world with the irresistible power, determination, and unity of the Nazi movement and the greatness of the führer. Armies of youths waving flags, storm troopers bearing weapons, and workers shouldering long-handled spades paraded past Hitler, who stood at attention, his arm extended in the Nazi salute. The endless columns of marchers, the stirring martial music played by huge bands, the forest of flags, the chanting and cheering of spectators, and the burning torches and beaming spotlights united the participants into a racial community. "Wherever Hitler leads, we follow," thundered thousands of Germans in a giant chorus. The Nuremberg rallies were among the greatest theatrical performances of the twentieth century.

Terror. Another means of ensuring compliance and obedience was terror. Its instrument, the *Schutzstaffel* (SS), had been organized in 1925 to protect Hitler and other party leaders and to stand guard at party meetings. Under the leadership of Heinrich Himmler (1900–1945), a fanatical believer in Hitler's racial theories, the SS was molded into an elite force of disciplined, dedicated, and utterly ruthless men. Myopic, narrow-chested, and sexually prudish, Himmler contrived a cult of manliness. He envisioned the SS, who were specially selected for their racial purity and physical fitness, as a new breed of knights: Nietzschean supermen who would lead the new Germany.

The SS staffed the concentration camps established to deal with political prisoners. Through systematic terror and torture, the SS sought to deprive the inmates of their human dignity and to harden themselves for the struggles that lay ahead. The knowledge that these camps existed and that some prisoners were never heard from again was a strong inducement for Germans to remain obedient. Yet the vast majority of Germans had nothing to fear from the Gestapo, the security police, and even willingly cooperated with them. Recent research shows that the Gestapo, a relatively small organization, could not function effectively without the assistance of civilians willing to inform on their neighbors and even family members.

Anti-Semitic Legislation

The Nazis deprived Jews of their German citizenship and instituted many anti-Jewish measures designed to make them outcasts. Thousands of Jewish doctors, lawyers, musicians, artists, and professors—many of them prominent figures who had contributed enormously to German intellectual and cultural life—were barred from practicing their professions, and Jewish members of the civil service were dismissed. Many Germans supported eliminating Jews from the professions and from economic life; this opened up opportunities, they said, for true Germans. A series of laws tightened the screws of humiliation and persecution. To protect the purity of German blood, marriage or sexual encounters between Germans and Jews were forbidden. Universities, schools, restaurants, pharmacies, hospitals, theaters, museums, and athletic fields were gradually closed to Jews, who were now social pariahs. The propaganda

machine, including schools and the media, conditioned Germans to see the Jew as an evil, alien, and dangerous parasite. The Nazi state also expropriated Jewish property, an act of thievery from which individual Germans and business firms benefitted. As a rule, German academic and clerical elites did not protest; many agreed with the National Socialists' edicts. The Jews were simply abandoned.

In November 1938, using as a pretext the assassination of a German official in Paris by a seventeen-year-old Jewish youth whose family the Nazis had mistreated, the Nazis organized an extensive pogrom not seen in Germany since the Middle Ages. Nazi gangs murdered scores of Jews, destroyed 267 synagogues, and burned and vandalized 7,500 Jewish-owned businesses all over Germany—an event that became known as the Night of Broken Glass (*Kristallnacht*). In many communities local citizens joined the Nazis in the pogrom, often brutalizing neighbors. Many Germans were also shamed by this relapse into barbarism. Thirty thousand Jews were thrown into concentration camps where they were systematically humiliated and brutalized. The Reich then imposed on the Jewish community a fine of one billion marks. These measures were a mere prelude, however. During World War II, genocidal murder of European Jewry became a cardinal Nazi objective.

Mass Support

The Nazi regime became a police state, symbolized by arrests of innocents, the persecution of Jews, and concentration camps that institutionalized terror. But since the secret police arrested and incarcerated mainly Communists and Jews, average Germans had nothing to fear. In many ways life seemed normal. The Nazis established the totalitarian state without upsetting the daily life of the majority of the population. Moreover, Hitler, like Mussolini, was careful to maintain the appearance of legality. By not abolishing the Reichstag or repealing the constitution, he could claim that his was a legitimate government.

To people concerned with little but family, job, and friends—and this includes most people in any country—life in the first few years of the Third

Charles Maurras

Some historians view Action Française, an ultranationalist, antidemocratic, and anti-Semitic organization founded in 1898–1899 by Charles Maurras (1868–1952), as a forerunner of the Fascist movements that emerged in the aftermath of World War I. In the tradition of early-nineteenth-century French conservatives, Maurras held that the collective takes precedence over the individual: "The primary reality, more real than the individual and more real also than the world," he declared, "is *la patrie, the Country*."* He regarded the religious individualism of the Reformation, the political individualism of the French Revolution, and the cultural individualism of romanticism as forces of national division and discord. The principle of equality, he said, permitted rule by the mediocre and the incompetent.

To save France from class war, political factions, capitalist exploitation, and spiritual disintegration—all consequences of unbridled individualism, in his eyes—Maurras championed integral nationalism. Action Française sought the integration of the nation around Catholicism, France's ancestral religion; monarchy, a deeply rooted French tradition; and hierarchy, leadership based on birth and talent. Maurras valued the France of the Old Regime, for it was monarchical, hierarchical, and community minded. Hostile and foreign elements— Maurras meant specifically Masons, Protestants, Jews, alien residents, and recently naturalized citizens—must be deprived of political rights and influence. Such people, he argued, had no deep roots in the French nation; they could never be truly French. Maurras hoped that army leaders, inspired by the Action Française philosophy, would overthrow the Third Republic and reestablish monarchical rule.

Maurras was strongly anti-Semitic, holding that "Jewish capitalism" and "Jewish democracy" were corrupting the French soul. He attributed a destructive individualism to Judaism, for it had conceived the idea of one God who had endowed everyone with a conscience: "it is in the Law and the Prophets . . . that are to be found the first expressions in antiquity of the individualism, egalitarianism, humanitarianism, and social and political idealism that were to mark 1789."† He

Reich seemed quite satisfying. Most Germans believed that the new government was trying to solve Germany's problems in a vigorous and sensible manner, in contrast to the ineffective Weimar leadership. By 1936, the reinvigoration of the economy, stimulated in part by rearmament, had virtually eliminated unemployment, which had stood at 6 million jobless when Hitler took power. An equally astounding achievement in German eyes was Hitler's bold termination of the humiliating Versailles treaty, the rebuilding of the war machine, and the restoration of power in international affairs. It seemed to most Germans that Hitler had awakened a sense of self-sacrifice and national dedication among a people dispirited by military defeat, political weakness, and economic depression. He had united a country torn by class antagonisms and social distinctions and given people a sense of national pride. Workers had jobs, businessmen profits, and generals troops, and the bonds of community had been greatly strengthened—what could be wrong?

Many intellectuals, viewing Hitlerism as the victory of idealism over materialism and of community over selfish individualism, lent their talents to the regime and endorsed the burning of books and the suppression of freedom. To them, Hitler was a visionary, an agent for the rebirth and regeneration of the fatherland, who had shown Germany and the world a new way of life—a new creed.

Thus, having regained confidence in themselves and their nation, many Germans rejoiced in Hitler's leadership, did not regret the loss of saw the Jews as agents of revolution and as alien conspirators. Action Française waged a fierce campaign against a pardon for Dreyfus, the Jewish army officer who was falsely convicted of treason. At times, it engaged in organized vandalism and violence against his supporters. For decades, Maurras's paper fomented anti-Semitism with vicious editorials such as the following: "*Down with the Jews!* Those whom we make the mistake of treating as if they were our equals display a ridiculous ambition to dominate us. They shall be put in their place and it will be our pleasure to do so."

Student members of the Action Française joined with young royalists to form the Camelots du Roi (hawkers of the king), which sold the Action Française newspaper in the streets, acted as guards at the organization's meetings, and participated in antirepublican and nationalist demonstrations. The organized violence of Camelots du Roi presaged the Fascist terror tactics after World War I. In this sense, the Camelots could be viewed as the first storm troopers.

Support for the Action Française came principally from the army, the nobility, the clergy, and middle-class professionals. Between 1910 and 1926, Action membership ranged from thirty thousand to forty thousand. The group posed no threat to the state, but its cult of *la patrie,* condemnation of democracy, celebration of war, virulent anti-Semitism, employment of organized violence, and call for a leader to resurrect the nation anticipated and coincided with Fascism.

After France's defeat in World War II, Maurras supported the authoritarian Vichy regime and denounced the resistance movement. He applauded Vichy's laws that made Jews second-class citizens, and his paper published the hiding places of Jews so that they could be rounded up and sent to German concentration camps. After the liberation of France, Maurras was sentenced to life imprisonment but was released in 1951 for medical reasons.

---

*Quoted in Michael Sutton, *Nationalism, Positivism, and Catholicism: The Politics of Charles Maurras and French Catholics, 1890–1914* (Cambridge, England: Cambridge University Press, 1982), 26.
†Ibid., 8.

political freedom, and remained indifferent to the plight of the persecuted, particularly the Jews. Moreover, Hitler's popularity and mass support rested on something far stronger than propaganda and terror, for he had won the hearts of a sizable proportion of the German people. To many Germans, Hitler was exactly as Nazi mythology depicted him, a man of destiny and a savior of the nation who "stands like a statue grown beyond the measure of earthly man."[45] When Hitler rode into Nuremberg in preparation for a giant rally, observed American journalist William L. Shirer, "wildly cheering Nazis packed the streets. . . . [T]en thousand hysterics . . . jammed the moat in front of Hitler's hotel. . . . [When] Hitler appeared on the balcony for a moment . . . they looked at him as if he were a Messiah, their faces transformed into something positively inhuman."[46]

The frenzied adoration shown by the German people for Hitler both in peacetime and in war, and their faith in his mission to regenerate the German nation, is an extraordinary phenomenon that continues to intrigue historians and social psychologists and to astonish new generations of Europeans, including Germans. It was considerably different for other dictators of Hitler's generation. Whatever devotion the Italians felt for Mussolini quickly faded once he brought the country into war. And the Soviet people's bonds to Stalin, particularly for non-Russian ethnic groups, were often based more on fear than genuine adulation. The German people did not have to be terrorized to praise Hitler and his dictatorial rule. They did not have to be coerced to support and serve the Nazi state even as collaborators in persecutions and genocide during World War II. Rarely in history has a nation been so spellbound by a leader.

There was some opposition and resistance to the Hitler regime. Social Democrats and Communists organized small cells. Some conservatives, who considered Hitler to be a threat to traditional German values, and some clergy, who saw Nazism as a pagan religion in conflict with Christian morality, also formed small opposition groups. But only resistance from the army could have toppled Hitler. Some generals, even before World War II, urged such resistance. The overwhelming majority of German officers, however, either preferred the new regime—which had smashed Marxism within Germany, destroyed an ineffective democracy, restored Germany's military might and pride, and given them the opportunity for professional advancement—or considered it dishonorable to break their oath of loyalty to Hitler. And most of these officers would remain loyal until the bitter end. Very few Germans realized that they were ruled by evil men driven by an evil ideology, and that their country, an advanced industrial society with an impressive tradition of high culture, was passing through a long night of barbarism. Still fewer considered resistance. The great majority of Germans would remain loyal to their führer and would serve the Nazi regime until its final defeat.

LIBERALISM AND AUTHORITARIANISM IN OTHER LANDS

The Spread of Authoritarianism

After World War I, in country after country, parliamentary democracy collapsed, and authoritarian leaders came to power. In most of these countries, liberal ideals had not penetrated deeply; liberalism met resistance from conservative elites.

Spain and Portugal. In both Spain and Portugal, parliamentary regimes faced strong opposition from the church, the army, and large landowners. In 1926, army officers overthrew the Portuguese republic that had been created in 1910, and gradually, Antonio de Oliveira Salazar (1889–1970), a professor of economics, emerged as dictator. In Spain, after antimonarchist forces won the election of 1931, King Alfonso XIII (1902–1931) left the country, and Spain was proclaimed a republic. But the new government, led by socialists and liberals, faced the determined opposition of the traditional ruling elite. The reforms introduced by the republic—expropriation of large estates, reduction of the number of army officers, dissolution of the Jesuit order, and closing of church schools—only intensified the old order's hatred.

The difficulties of the new Spanish republic mounted: workers, near starvation, rioted and engaged in violent strikes; the military attempted a coup; and Catalonia, with its long tradition of separatism, tried to establish its autonomy. Imitating the example of France (described later in this chapter), the parties of the left, including the Communists, united in the Popular Front, which came to power in February 1936. In July 1936, General Francisco Franco (1892–1975), stationed in Spanish Morocco, led a revolt against the republic. He was supported by army leaders, the church, monarchists, landlords, industrialists, and the Falange, a newly formed Fascist party. Spain was torn by a bloody civil war. Aided by Fascist Italy and Nazi Germany, Franco won in 1939 and established a dictatorship.

Eastern and Central Europe. Parliamentary government in Eastern Europe rested on weak foundations. Predominantly rural, these countries lacked the sizable professional and commercial classes that had promoted liberalism in Western Europe. Only Czechoslovakia had a substantial native middle class with a strong liberal tradition. The rural masses of Eastern Europe, traditionally subjected to monarchical and aristocratic authority, were not used to political thinking or civic responsibility. Students and intellectuals, often gripped by a romantic nationalism, were drawn to antidemocratic movements.

Right-wing leaders also played on the fear of Communism. When parliamentary government failed to solve internal problems, the opponents of the liberal state seized the helm. Fascist movements, however, had little success in Eastern

Europe. Rather, authoritarian regimes headed by traditional ruling elites—army leaders or kings—extinguished democracy there.

With the dissolution of the Hapsburg Empire at the end of World War I, Austria became a democratic republic. From the start, it suffered from severe economic problems. The Hapsburg Empire had been a huge free-trade area. Food and raw materials had been permitted to circulate unimpeded throughout the empire. The new Austria lacked sufficient food to feed the population of Vienna and needed raw materials for its industries. Worsening its plight was the erection of tariff barriers by each of the states formerly part of the Hapsburg Empire. Between 1922 and 1926, the League of Nations had to rescue Austria from bankruptcy. The Great Depression aggravated Austria's economic position. Many Austrians believed that only *Anschluss* (union) with Germany could solve Austria's problems.

Austria was also burdened by a conflict between the industrial region, including Vienna, and the agricultural provinces. Factory workers were generally socialist and anticlerical; the peasants were strongly Catholic and antisocialist. The Social Democrats controlled Vienna, but the rural population gave its support to the Christian Social Party. Each party had its own private army: the workers had the *Schutzbund,* and the provincials the *Heimwehr.*

In the early 1920s, under the guidance of its Social Democratic mayor, Vienna introduced a number of social reforms—including free kindergartens, hospitals, and burials and subsidized housing projects—that significantly improved conditions for the working class. The middle class, which bore the brunt of the tax burden needed to pay for these reforms designed specifically for the working class, saw the Social Democrats, who dominated Vienna, as implacable enemies. During the Great Depression, Chancellor Engelbert Dollfuss (1892–1934) sought to turn the country into a one-party state. In February 1934, police and Heimwehr contingents raided Social Democratic headquarters. When the Social Democrats called a general strike, Dollfuss bombarded workers' strongholds, including huge municipal housing projects, killing 193 civilians. After the workers were subdued, the Dollfuss government tried and imprisoned more than one thousand socialists,

outlawed leftist trade unions, and disbanded the Social Democratic Party. Austria had joined the ranks of authoritarian states.

When Hitler came to power in Germany, Austrian Nazis pressed for Anschluss. In July 1934, a band of them assassinated Dollfuss, but a Nazi plot to capture the government failed. Four years later, however, Hitler would march into Austria, bringing about the Anschluss desired by many Austrians.

The new Hungary that emerged at the end of World War I faced an uprising by Communists inspired by the success of the Bolsheviks in Russia. Béla Kun (1885–1937), supported by Russian money, established a soviet regime in Budapest in March 1919. But Kun could not win the support of the peasants and was opposed by the Allies, who helped crush the revolutionary government. In 1920, power passed to Admiral Miklós Horthy (1868–1957), who instituted a brief White terror, which exceeded the Red terror of the Kun regime. During the Great Depression, the Horthy government, which favored the large landholders, was challenged by the radical Right, which preached extreme nationalism, anti-Semitism, and anticapitalism and tried to win mass support through land reform. Its leader, Gyula Gömbös (1886–1936), who served as prime minister from 1932 to 1936, sought to align Hungary with Nazi Germany. Wishing to regain territories lost as a result of World War I and aware of Hitler's growing might, Hungary drew closer to Germany in the late 1930s.

Poland, Greece, Bulgaria, and Romania became either royal or military dictatorships. In September 1940, a year after World War II started, the Fascist Iron Guard seized power in Romania and engaged in the mass murder of Jews. In January 1941, the Iron Guard was crushed by the military. The new state of Czechoslovakia, guided by President Tomás Masaryk (1850–1937) and Foreign Minister Eduard Benes (1884–1948), who were both committed to the liberal-humanist tradition of the West, preserved parliamentary democracy. Its most serious problem came from the 3.25 million Germans living within its borders, primarily in the Sudetenland. The German minority founded the Sudetenland German Party, which modeled itself after Hitler's Nazi Party. Hitler later exploited the issue of the Sudetenland Germans to dismember Czechoslovakia.

The Western Democracies

While liberal governments were failing in much of Europe, the great Western democracies—the United States, Britain, and France—continued to preserve democratic institutions. In Britain and the United States, Fascist movements were merely a nuisance. In France, Fascism was more of a threat because it exploited deeply ingrained hostility in some quarters to the liberal ideals of the French Revolution.

The United States. The central problem faced by the Western democracies was the Great Depression, which started in the United States. In the 1920s, hundreds of thousands of Americans had bought stock on credit; this buying spree sent stock prices soaring well beyond what the stocks were actually worth. In late October 1929, the stock market was hit by a wave of panic selling; prices plummeted. Within a few weeks, the value of stocks listed on the New York Stock Exchange fell by some $26 billion. A terrible chain reaction followed over the next few years. Businesses cut production, and unemployment soared; farmers unable to meet mortgage payments lost their land; banks that had made poor investments closed down. American investors withdrew the capital they had invested in Europe, causing European banks and businesses to fail. Throughout the world, trade declined and unemployment rose.

When President Franklin Delano Roosevelt (1882–1945) took office in 1933, more than 13 million Americans—one-quarter of the labor force—were out of work. Hunger and despair showed on the faces of the American people. Moving away from laissez faire, Roosevelt instituted a comprehensive program of national planning, economic experimentation, and reform known as the New Deal. Although the U.S. political and economic system faced a severe test, few Americans turned to Fascism or Communism. The government engaged in national planning but did not break with democratic values and procedures.

Britain. Even before the Great Depression, Britain faced severe economic problems. Loss of markets to foreign competitors hurt British manufacturing, mining, and shipbuilding; rapid development of water and oil power reduced the demand for British coal, and outdated mining equipment put Britain in a poor competitive position. To decrease costs, mine owners in 1926 called for salary cuts; the coal miners countered with a strike and were joined by workers in other industries. To many Britons, the workers were leftist radicals trying to overthrow the government. Many wanted the state to break the strike. After nine days, industrial workers called off their strike, but the miners held out for another six months, only to return to work with longer hours and lower pay. Although the general strike failed, it did improve relations between the classes, for the workers had not called for revolution, and they had refrained from violence. The fear that British workers would follow the Bolshevik path abated.

The Great Depression cast a pall over Britain. The Conservative Party leadership tried to stimulate exports by devaluing the British pound and to encourage industry by providing loans at lower interest rates, but in the main, it left the task of recovery to industry itself. Not until Britain began to rearm did unemployment decline significantly. Despite the economic slump of the 1920s and the Great Depression, Britain remained politically stable, a testament to the strength of its parliamentary tradition. Neither the Communists nor the newly formed British Fascist Party gained mass support.

France. In the early 1920s, France was concerned with postwar rebuilding. From 1926 to 1929, France was relatively prosperous. Industrial and agricultural production expanded, tourism increased, and the currency was stable. Although France did not feel the Great Depression as painfully as did the United States and Germany, the nation was hurt by the decline in trade and production and the rise in unemployment.

The political instability that had beset the Third Republic almost since its inception continued, and hostility to the republic mounted. The rift between liberals and conservatives, which had divided the country since the Revolution and grown worse with the Dreyfus affair, continued to plague France during the Depression. The French Right, whose numbers had been increasing since the 1880s, had traditionally rejected the ideals of liberty, equality, individual rights, and parliamentary government associated with the Enlightenment and the French Revolution and was violently anti-Marxist. Negating liberal ideals and democratic government, the right endorsed an authoritarian and hierarchical system, which would oppose social reform and protect right-wing interests, and extreme nationalism, which would integrate all classes and restore France's greatness. As the leading parties failed to solve the nation's problems, a number of Fascist groups gained strength. On February 6, 1934, right-wing gangs threatened to invade the Chamber of Deputies. What brought on the crisis was the exposure of the shady dealings of Alexander Stavisky, a financial manipulator with high government connections, including parliamentary deputies and a cabinet minister. Antirepublican forces on the Right, with their paramilitary units, saw the scandal as an opportunity to replace the Third Republic with an authoritarian regime. The resulting violence left hundreds wounded and several dead. The whole affair was too poorly organized to constitute a serious threat to the government. But to the parties of the Left, the events of February 6–7 constituted a rightist attempt to establish a Fascist regime.

Fear of growing Fascist strength at home and in Italy and Germany led the parties of the Left to form the Popular Front. In 1936, Léon Blum (1872–1950), a socialist, heir of Enlightenment humanism, and a Jew, became premier. Blum's Popular Front government instituted more reforms than any other ministry in the history of the Third Republic. At the time he took office, French workers in many industries were not unionized, worked ten or more hours a day six days a week without vacations, and were poorly compensated. To end a wave of strikes that tied up production, Blum gave workers a forty-hour workweek and holidays with pay, and guaranteed them the right to collective bargaining. He took steps to nationalize the armaments and aircraft industries. To reduce the influence of the wealthiest families, he put the Bank of France under government control. By raising prices and buying wheat, he aided farmers. Conservatives and Fascists denounced Blum as a Jewish socialist who was converting the fatherland into a Communist state. "Better Hitler than Blum," grumbled French rightists.

Despite significant reforms, the Popular Front could not revitalize the economy. In 1937, the Blum ministry was overthrown, and the Popular Front, always a tenuous alliance, fell apart. Through democratic means, the Blum government had tried to give France its own New Deal, but the social reforms passed by the Popular Front only intensified hatred between the working classes and the rest of the nation. France had preserved democracy against the onslaught of domestic Fascists, but it was a demoralized and divided nation that confronted a united and dynamic Nazi Germany.

❖   ❖   ❖

NOTES

1. Carl J. Friedrich and Zbigniew K. Brzezinski, *Totalitarian Dictatorship and Autocracy* (New York: Praeger, 1961), 5.

2. Ibid., 7.

3. Hannah Arendt, *The Origins of Totalitarianism* (New York: World, Meridian Books, 1958), 469.

4. Karl Dietrich Bracher, *The Age of Ideologies*, trans. Erwald Osers (New York: St. Martin's Press, 1984), 83.

5. Friedrich and Brzezinski, *Totalitarian Dictatorship and Autocracy*, 13.

6. Zbigniew Brzezinski, *Out of Control* (New York: Charles Scribner's Sons, 1993), 19.

7. Quoted in Omer Bartov, *Hitler's Army: Soldiers, Nazis, and War in the Third Reich* (New York: Oxford University Press, 1992), 166.

8. Quoted in Arendt, *Origins of Totalitarianism*, 330.

9. "All-Russian Communist Party (Bolsheviks), 1919," in *Soviet Communism: Programs and*

Rules. Official Texts of 1919, 1952, 1956, 1961, ed. Jan F. Triska (San Francisco: Chandler, 1962), 23.

10. V. I. Lenin, "The Immediate Tasks of the Soviet Government," in *The Lenin Anthology*, ed. Robert C. Tucker (New York: Norton, 1975), 448 ff.

11. J. V. Stalin, "Speech to Business Executives" (1931), in *A Documentary History of Communism from Lenin to Mao*, ed. Robert V. Daniels (New York: Random House, 1960), 2:22.

12. Quoted in Isaac Deutscher, *Stalin: A Political Biography* (New York: Oxford University Press, 1966), 325.

13. Excerpted in T. H. Rigby, ed., *Stalin* (Englewood Cliffs, N.J.: Prentice-Hall, 1966), 111.

14. Quoted in Jonathan Glover, *Humanity: A Moral History of the Twentieth Century* (New Haven, Conn.: Yale University Press, 1999), 241.

15. Quoted in Zeev Sternhill, "Fascist Ideology," in *Fascism: A Reader's Guide*, ed. Walter Laqueur (Berkeley: University of California Press, 1976), 338.

16. Quoted in John Weiss, *The Fascist Tradition* (New York: Harper and Row, 1967), 9.

17. Quoted in F. L. Carsten, *The Rise of Fascism* (Berkeley: University of California Press, 1969), 53.

18. Quoted in Max Gallo, *Mussolini's Italy* (New York: Macmillan, 1973), 218.

19. Kurt Sontheimer, "Anti-Democratic Thought in the Weimar Republic," in *The Path to Dictatorship, 1918–1933*, trans. John Conway, intro. Fritz Stern (Garden City, N.Y.: Doubleday Anchor Books, 1966), 47–49.

20. Quoted in Joachim Köhler, *Wagner's Hitler: The Prophet and His Disciple*, trans. Ronald Taylor (Cambridge: Polity Press, 2000), 68.

21. Adolf Hitler, *Mein Kampf*, trans. Ralph Mannheim (Boston: Houghton Mifflin, 1962), 161.

22. Quoted in Joachim C. Fest, *Hitler*, trans. Richard and Clara Winston (New York: Harcourt Brace Jovanovich, 1974), 162.

23. Quoted in Karl J. Newman, *European Democracy Between the Wars* (Notre Dame, Ind.: University of Notre Dame Press, 1971), 276.

24. Fest, *Hitler*, 548.

25. Quoted in Alan Bullock, *Hitler: A Study in Tyranny* (New York: Harper Torchbooks, 1964), 400.

26. *Hitler's Secret Conversations, 1941–1944*, with an introductory essay by H. R. Trevor Roper (New York: Farrar, Straus and Young, 1953), 28.

27. Quoted in Lucy S. Dawidowicz, *The War Against the Jews, 1933–1945* (New York: Holt, Rinehart and Winston, 1975), 21.

28. Quoted in Uri Tal, "Consecration of Politics in the Nazi Era," in *Judaism and Christianity Under the Impact of National Socialism*, ed. Otto Dov Kulka and Paul R. Mendes Flohr (Jerusalem: Historical Society of Israel, 1987), 70.

29. Adolf Hitler, *Mein Kampf*, 107.

30. Ibid., 479.

31. Cited in Ian Kershaw, "Hitler and the Germans," in *Life in the Third Reich*, ed. Richard Bessel (New York: Oxford University Press, 1987), 43–44.

32. Quoted in David Welch, ed., *Nazi Propaganda* (Totowa, N.J.: Barnes and Noble, 1983), 5.

33. Quoted in J. S. Conway, *The Nazi Persecution of the Churches* (New York: Basic Books, 1968), 202.

34. Karl Dietrich Bracher, *The German Dictatorship*, trans. Jean Steinberg (New York: Praeger, 1970), 243.

35. *Hitler's Secret Conversations*, 6.

36. Quoted in Hans Rothfels, "Resistance Begins," in *Path to Dictatorship*, 160–161.

37. Quoted in Guenter Lewy, *The Catholic Church and Nazi Germany* (New York: McGraw-Hill, 1965), 226.

38. Quoted in Hermann Graml et al., *The German Resistance to Hitler* (Berkeley: University of California Press, 1970), 206.

39. Quoted in Conway, *Nazi Persecution of the Churches*, 332.

40. Excerpted in George L. Mosse, ed., *Nazi Culture* (New York: Grosset and Dunlap, 1966), 206–207.

41. Bracher, *German Dictatorship*, 248, 251.

42. Quoted in T. L. Jarman, *The Rise and Fall of Nazi Germany* (New York: New York University Press, 1956), 182.

43. Quoted in Horst von Maltitz, *The Evolution of Hitler's Germany* (New York: McGraw-Hill, 1973), 433–434.

44. Quoted in Bracher, *German Dictatorship*, 268.

45. Quoted in Fest, *Hitler*, 532.

46. William L. Shirer, *Berlin Diary: The Journal of a Foreign Correspondent, 1934–1941* (New York: Galahad Books, 1945), 16–18.

Chapter 30

Thought and Culture in an Era of World Wars and Totalitarianism

Guernica, *by Pablo Picasso, a passionate protest against Fascism and the horrors of war.*

- **Intellectuals and Artists in Troubled Times**
- **Existentialism**
- **The Modern Predicament**

Focus Questions

1. Why and how did European intellectual and cultural life convey a mood of pessimism and disillusionment after World War I?

2. How did art and literature express a social conscience during the 1920s and 1930s?

3. What were the different ways that intellectuals struggled with the crisis of European society in an era of world war and totalitarianism?

4. What were some of the conditions that gave rise to existentialism? What are the basic principles of existentialism?

The presuppositions of the Enlightenment, already eroding in the decades before World War I, seemed near collapse after 1918—another casualty of trench warfare. Economic distress, particularly during the Great Depression, also profoundly disoriented the European mind. Westerners no longer possessed a frame of reference, a common outlook for understanding themselves, their times, or the past. The core values of Western civilization—the self-sufficiency of reason and the inviolability of the individual—no longer seemed inspiring or binding.

The crisis of consciousness evoked a variety of responses. Having lost faith in the purpose of Western civilization, some intellectuals turned their backs on it or found escape in their art. Others sought a new hope in the Soviet experiment or in Fascism; still others reaffirmed the rational-humanist tradition of the Enlightenment. Christian thinkers, repelled by the secularism, materialism, and rootlessness of the modern age, urged Westerners to find renewed meaning and purpose in their ancestral religion. A philosophical movement called existentialism, which rose to prominence after World War II, aspired to make life authentic in a world stripped of universal values.

INTELLECTUALS AND ARTISTS IN TROUBLED TIMES

Postwar Pessimism

After World War I, Europeans looked at themselves and their civilization differently. It seemed that in science and technology they had unleashed powers that they could not control, and belief in the stability and security of European civilization appeared to be an illusion. Also illusory was the expectation that reason would banish surviving signs of darkness, ignorance, and injustice and usher in an age of continual progress. European intellectuals felt that they were living in a "broken world." In a time of heightened brutality and mobilized irrationality, the values of old Europe seemed beyond recovery. "All the great words," wrote D. H. Lawrence, "were cancelled out for that generation."[1] The fissures discernible in European civilization before 1914 had grown wider and deeper. To be sure, Europe also had its optimists—those who found reason for hope in the League of Nations and in the easing of international tensions and improved economic conditions in the mid 1920s. However, the Great Depression and the triumph of totalitarianism intensified feelings of doubt and disillusionment.

The somber mood that gripped intellectuals in the immediate postwar period had been anticipated by Freud in a series of papers published in 1915 under the title "Thoughts for the Times on War and Death." The war, said Freud, stripped Westerners of those cultural restraints that had served to contain a murderous primeval aggressiveness, and it threatened to inflict irreparable damage on European civilization.

> We cannot but feel that no event has ever destroyed so much that is precious in the common possessions of humanity, confused so many of the clearest intelligences or so thoroughly debased what is highest. . . .
> The war in which we had refused to believe broke out, and it brought—disillusionment. . . .
> It tramples in blind fury on all that comes in its way, as though there were to be no future and no peace among men after it is over. It cuts all the common bonds between the contending peoples, and threatens to leave a legacy of embitterment that will make any renewal of these bonds impossible for a long time to come.[2]

Other expressions of pessimism abounded. In 1919, Paul Valéry stated: "We modern civilizations have learned to recognize that we are mortal like the others. We feel that a civilization is as fragile as life."[3] "We are living today under the sign of the collapse of civilization,"[4] declared the humanitarian Albert Schweitzer in 1923. In the midst of the Depression, Arnold Toynbee wrote: "The year 1931 was distinguished from previous years . . . by one outstanding feature. In 1931 men and women all over the world were seriously contemplating and frankly discussing the possibility that the Western system of Society might break down and cease to work."[5] The German philosopher Karl Jaspers noted in 1932 that "there is a growing awareness of imminent ruin

tantamount to a dread of the approaching end of all that makes life worthwhile."[6]

In *All Quiet on the Western Front* (1929), Erich Maria Remarque dealt with the horrors of the war and their impact. A German soldier in the novel ponders the war's effect on youth.

> I am twenty years old; yet I know nothing of life but despair, death, fear, and fatuous superficiality cast over an abyss of sorrow. I see how peoples are set against one another, and in silence, unknowingly, foolishly, obediently, innocently slay one another. I see that the keenest brains of the world invent weapons and words to make it yet more refined and enduring. . . . All my generation is experiencing these things with me. . . . What do they expect of us if a time ever comes when the war is over? Through the years our business has been killing. . . . Our knowledge of life is limited to death. What will happen afterwards?[7]

In the poem "The Second Coming" (1919), William Butler Yeats conveys his sense of the dark times.

> Mere anarchy is loosed upon the world,
> The blood-dimmed tide is loosed, and everywhere
> The ceremony of innocence is drowned;
> The best lack all conviction, while the worst
> Are full of passionate intensity.
> Surely some revelation is at hand;
> Surely the Second Coming is at hand.[8]

T. S. Eliot's "The Waste Land" (1922) also expresses a feeling of foreboding. In his image of a collapsing European civilization, Eliot creates a macabre scenario. Hooded hordes, modern-day barbarians, swarm over plains and lay waste cities. Jerusalem, Athens, Alexandria, Vienna, and London—each once a great spiritual or cultural center—are now collapsing.[9]

Other writers and thinkers also focused on the crises facing the Western world. Carl Gustav Jung, a Swiss psychologist, stated in *Modern Man in Search of a Soul* (1933):

> I believe I am not exaggerating when I say that modern man has suffered an almost fatal shock, psychologically speaking, and as a

result has fallen into profound uncertainty. . . . The revolution in our conscious outlook, brought about by the catastrophic results of the World War, shows itself in our inner life by the shattering of our faith in ourselves and our own worth. . . . I realize only too well that I am losing my faith in the possibility of a rational organization of the world, the old dream of the millennium, in which peace and harmony should rule, has grown pale.[10]

In *The Fate of Man in the Modern World* (1935) Nikolai Berdyaev, a Russian Orthodox Christian philosopher, who fled the Soviet Union, described how World War I and the totalitarian ideologies have devalued the individual.

Once the veil of civilization was torn aside by the war. . . . the faith in mankind, which had existed for nineteen hundred years was finally shattered. . . . Man appears unable to . . . defend his own value, to find support within himself, and he grasps as at a life-belt, at the collective, communist or national and racial State as the Absolute here on earth. . . . A bestial cruelty toward man is characteristic of our age. Over against man there rises a class or a race, a defied collective or state.[11]

In 1939, as the war clouds darkened, E. M. Forster, the distinguished British novelist, lamented:

During the present decade thousands and thousands of innocent people have been killed, robbed, mutilated, insulted, imprisoned. We, the fortunate exceptions, learn of this from the newspapers and from refugees, we realize that it may be our turn next, and we know that all these private miseries may be the prelude to an incalculable catastrophe, in which the whole of western civilization . . . may go down. Perhaps history will point to these years as the moment when man's inventiveness finally outbalanced his moral growth, and toppled him downhill.[12]

The most influential expression of pessimism was Oswald Spengler's *The Decline of the West.* The first volume was published in July 1918, as the war was drawing to a close, and the second

volume in 1922. The work achieved instant notoriety, particularly in Spengler's native Germany, which was shattered by defeat. Spengler viewed history as an assemblage of many different cultures that, like living organisms, experience birth, youth, maturity, and death. What contemporaries pondered most was Spengler's insistence that Western civilization had entered its final stage and that its death could not be averted.

According to Spengler, cultures had to pass through three necessary stages: a heroic youth, a creative maturity, and a decadent old age. In its youth, during the Renaissance, said Spengler, Western culture experienced the triumphs of Michelangelo, Shakespeare, and Galileo; in its maturity, during the eighteenth century, Western culture reached its creative height in the music of Mozart, the poetry of Goethe, and the philosophy of Kant. But now, Western culture, entering old age, was showing signs of decay: a growing materialism and skepticism, a disenchanted proletariat, rampant warfare and competition for empire, and decadent art forms. "Of great painting or great music there can no longer be, for Western people, any question," Spengler concluded.[13]

To an already troubled Western world, Spengler offered no solace. The West, like other cultures and like any living organism, was destined to die. Its decline was irreversible and its death inevitable; the symptoms of its degeneration were already evident. Spengler's gloomy prognostication buttressed the Fascists, who claimed that they were creating a new civilization on the ruins of the dying European civilization.

Literature and Art: Innovation, Disillusionment, and Social Commentary

Postwar pessimism did not prevent writers and artists from continuing the cultural innovations begun before the war. In the works of D. H. Lawrence, Marcel Proust, André Gide, James Joyce, Franz Kafka, T. S. Eliot, and Thomas Mann, the modernist movement achieved a brilliant flowering. Often these writers gave expression to the troubles and uncertainties of the postwar period.

Johan Huizinga, *In the Shadow of Tomorrow*

The memory of World War I, the rise of Nazism, and the Great Depression caused many European liberals to have grave doubts about the future of Western civilization. Dutch historian Johan Huizinga (1872–1945) wrote that European civilization was at the breaking point in his book In the Shadow of Tomorrow *(1936).*

We are living in a demented world. And we know it. It would not come as a surprise to anyone if tomorrow the madness gave way to a frenzy which would leave our poor Europe in a state of distracted stupor, with engines still turning and flags streaming in the breeze, but with the spirit gone.

Everywhere there are doubts as to the solidity of our social structure, vague fears of the imminent future, a feeling that our civilization is on the way to ruin. . . . How to avoid the recognition that almost all things which once seemed sacred and immutable have now become unsettled, truth and humanity, justice and reason? We see forms of government no longer capable of functioning, production systems on the verge of collapse, social forces gone wild with power. The roaring engine of this tremendous time seems to be heading for a breakdown. . . .

If, then, this civilization is to be saved, if it is not to be submerged by centuries of barbarism but to secure the treasures of its inheritance on new and more stable foundations, there is indeed need for those now living fully to realise how far the decay has already progressed.

It is but a little while since the apprehension of impending doom and of a progressive deterioration of civilization has become general. . . .

The first ten years of this century have known little if anything in the way of fears and apprehensions regarding the future of our civilization. . . . Friction and threats, shocks and dangers, there were then as ever. But except for the revolution menace which Marxism had hung over the world, they did

Franz Kafka (1883–1924), whose major novels, *The Trial* and *The Castle*, were published after his death, did not receive recognition until after World War II. Yet perhaps better than any other novelist of his generation, Kafka grasped the dilemma of the modern age. There is no apparent order or stability in Kafka's world. Human beings strive to make sense out of life, but everywhere ordinary occurrences thwart them. They are caught in a bureaucratic web they cannot control; they live in a nightmare society dominated by oppressive, cruel, and corrupt officials and amoral torturers. In Kafka's world, cruelty and injustice are accepted facts of existence, power is exercised without limits, and victims cooperate in their own destruction. Traditional values and ordinary logic do not operate. Our world, thought to be secure, stable, and purposeful, easily falls apart. Like Kierkegaard, Kafka understood the intense anxiety that torments modern people.

In *The Trial*, for example, Josef K., an ordinary man who has no consciousness of wrongdoing, is arrested. "K. lived in a country with a legal constitution, there was universal peace, all the laws were in force; who dared seize him in his own dwelling?"[14] Josef K. is never told the reason for his arrest, and he is eventually executed, a victim of institutional evil that breaks and destroys him "like a dog." In these not appear as evils threatening mankind with ruin. . . .

How naïve the glad and confident hope of a century ago, that the advance of science and the general extension of education assured the progressive perfection of society, seems to us today! Who can still seriously believe that the translation of scientific triumphs into still more marvelous technical achievements is enough to save civilization, or that the eradication of illiteracy means the end of barbarism! . . .

Delusion and misconception flourish everywhere. . . . The world is filled with hate and misunderstanding. . . . For the shallow, semi-educated person the beneficial restraints of respect for tradition, form and cult are gradually falling away. Worst of all is that widely prevalent indifference to truth which reaches its peak in the open advocacy of the political lie.

Barbarisation sets in when, in an old culture which once, in the course of many centuries, had raised itself to purity and clarity of thought and understanding, the vapours of the magic and fantastic rise up again from the seething brew of passions to cloud the understanding: when the *muthos* [myth] supplants the *logos* [reason].

Again and again the new creed of the heroic will to power, with its exaltation of life over understanding, is seen to embody the very tendencies which to the believer in the Spirit spell the drift towards barbarism. For the "life-philosophy" does exactly this: it extols *muthos* over *logos*. To the prophets of the life-philosophy barbarism has no deprecatory implications. The term itself loses its meaning. The new rulers desire nothing else.

Question for Analysis

1. What contrasts did Johan Huizinga draw between Europe at the turn of the century and the Europe of his day?

Johan Huizinga, *In the Shadow of Tomorrow* (London: Heinemann, 1936), pp. 1–3, 51, 194–195.

---

observations, Kafka anticipated the emerging totalitarian state. (Kafka's three sisters perished in the Holocaust.)

A German-speaking Jew in the alien Slav environment of Czechoslovakia, Kafka died of tuberculosis at an early age. In voicing his own deep anxieties, Kafka expressed the feelings of alienation and isolation that characterize the modern individual. He explored life's dreads and absurdities, offering no solutions or consolation. In Kafka's works, people are defeated and unable to comprehend the irrational forces that contribute to their destruction. Although the mind yearns for coherence, Kafka tells us that uncertainty, if not chaos, governs human relationships. We can be sure neither of our own identities nor of the world we encounter, for human beings are the playthings of unfathomable forces, too irrational to master.

A brooding pessimism about the human condition pervades Kafka's work. One reason for the intensified interest in Kafka after World War II, observes Angel Flores, "is that the European world of the late 30's and 40's with its betrayals and concentration camps, its resulting cruelties and indignities, bore a remarkable resemblance to the world depicted by Kafka in the opening decades of the century. History seems to have imitated the nightmarish background evoked by the dreamer of Prague."[15]

Before World War I, the German writer Thomas Mann (1875–1955) had earned a reputation for his short stories and novels, particularly *Buddenbrooks* (1901), which portrayed the decline of a prosperous bourgeois family. At the outbreak of the war, Mann was a staunch conservative who disliked democracy. After the war, he drew closer to liberalism, supporting the Weimar Republic and attacking the Nazi cult of irrationalism.

In *Mario and the Magician* (1930), Mann explicitly attacked Italian Fascism and implied that it would require armed resistance. In 1931, two years before Hitler took power, Mann, in an article entitled "An Appeal to Reason," described National Socialism and the extreme nationalism it espoused as a rejection of the Western rational tradition and a regression to primitive and barbaric modes of behavior. Nazism, he said, "is distinguished by . . . its absolute unrestraint, its orgiastic, radically anti-humane, frenziedly dynamic character. . . . Everything is possible, everything is permitted as a weapon against human decency. . . . Fanaticism turns into a means of salvation . . . politics becomes an opiate for the masses . . . and reason veils her face."[16]

After Hitler's seizure of power, Mann went to Switzerland and eventually to the United States, where he remained a resolute foe of totalitarianism. In 1938, he described the crisis of reason that afflicted his generation: "The twentieth century has in its first third taken up a position of reaction against classic rationalism and intellectualism. It has surrendered to admiration of the unconscious, to a glorification of instinct. And the bad instincts have accordingly been enjoying a heyday."[17]

In *The Magic Mountain*, begun in 1912 and completed in 1924, Mann had reflected on the decomposition of bourgeois European civilization. The novel is set in a Swiss sanatorium, just prior to World War I. The patients, drawn from several European lands, suffer from tuberculosis and are diseased in spirit as well as body. The sanatorium symbolizes Europe. It is the European **psyche** that is sick and rushing headlong into a catastrophe.

The Magic Mountain, which ends with the advent of World War I, raised, but did not resolve, crucial questions. Was the epoch of rational-humanist culture drawing to a close? Did bourgeois Europe welcome its spiritual degeneration in the same way that some of the patients in the sanatorium had a will to illness? How could Europe rescue itself from decadence?

D. H. Lawrence (1885–1930), the son of an illiterate British coal miner, was saddened and angered by the consequences of industrial society: the deterioration of nature, tedious work divorced from personal satisfaction, and a life-denying quest for wealth and possessions. He looked back longingly on preindustrial England and wanted people to reorient their thinking away from moneymaking and suppression of the instincts. In his works, he dealt with the clash between industrial civilization, which regiments human beings in the name of efficiency, and the needs of human nature. Thus, in *Women in Love* (1920), the new owner of the family coal mine, determined to utilize modern management techniques in order to extract greater wealth from the business, dismisses the human needs of the workers.

> *Suddenly he had conceived the pure instrumentality of mankind. There had been so much humanitarianism, so much talk of sufferings and feelings. It was ridiculous. The sufferings and feelings of individuals did not matter in the least. . . . What mattered was the pure instrumentality of the individual. As a man as of a knife: does it cut well? Nothing else mattered.*
>
> *Everything in the world has its function, and is good or not good in so far as it fulfills this function. . . . Was a miner a good miner? Then he was complete.*[18]

In *Lady Chatterly's Lover* (1928), a highly erotic novel, Lawrence affirmed sexual passion as both necessary and beneficial for human well-being and criticized cultural norms that disfigured it with distaste, shame, and guilt.

Like nineteenth-century romantics, Lawrence found a higher truth in deep-seated passion than in reason; this led him to rail against Christianity for stifling human sexuality. Like Nietzsche, he believed that excessive intellectualizing destroyed the life-affirming, instinctual part of human nature. In 1913, he wrote:

> *My great religion is a belief in the blood, the flesh, as being wiser than the intellect. We can go wrong in our minds. But what our blood feels and believes and says is always true. The intellect is only a bit and a bridle. What do I care about knowledge. All I want is to answer to my blood without fribbling intervention of mind, or moral, or what not. . . . We have got so ridiculously mindful, that we never know that we ourselves are anything.*[19]

Characteristic of the new developments in thought associated with Nietzsche, modernism, and the new physics, Lawrence rejected the notion of absolute truth.

> *We should ask for no absolutes, or absolute. Once and for all and for ever, let us have done with the ugly imperialism of any absolute. There is no absolute good, there is nothing absolutely right. All things flow and change, and even change is not absolute.*[20]

Shattered by World War I, disgusted by Fascism's growing strength, and moved by the suffering of the Depression, many writers became committed to social and political causes. Remarque's *All Quiet on the Western Front* was one of many antiwar novels. In *The Grapes of Wrath* (1939), John Steinbeck captured the suffering of American farmers losing their land when it became the Dust Bowl or driven from it by foreclosure during the Depression. George Orwell's *The Road to Wigan Pier* (1937) recorded the bleak lives of English workers. Few issues stirred the conscience of intellectuals as did the Spanish Civil War, and many of them volunteered to fight with the Spanish republicans against the Fascists. Ernest Hemingway's *For Whom the Bell Tolls* (1940) expressed the sentiments of these idealists.

New art trends emerged, mirroring the trauma of a generation that had experienced the war and lost its faith in Europe's moral and intellectual values. In 1915 in Zurich, artists and writers founded a movement, called *Dada*, to express their revulsion against the war and the civilization that spawned it. From neutral Switzerland, the

movement spread to Germany and Paris. Dadaists viewed artistic and literary standards with contempt, rejected God, and glorified unreason as a means to self-liberation. They celebrated nihilism for its own sake. "Through reason man becomes a tragic and ugly figure," said one Dadaist; "beauty is dead," said another. Dada shared in the postwar mood of disorientation and despair. Dadaists regarded life as essentially absurd (*Dada* is a nonsense term) and cultivated indifference. "The acts of life have no beginning or end. Everything happens in a completely idiotic way," declared the poet Tristan Tzara, one of Dada's founders. Tzara elevated spontaneity above reason.

> *What good did the theories of the philosophers do us? Did they help us to take a single step forward or backward? . . . We have had enough of the intelligent movements that have stretched beyond measure our credulity in the benefits of science. What we want now is spontaneity because everything that issues freely from ourselves, without the intervention of speculative ideas . . . represents us.*[21]

For Dadaists, the world was nonsensical, and reality disordered; hence, they offered no solutions to anything. "Like everything in life, Dada is useless," said Tzara.[22]

Dadaists showed their contempt for art (one art historian calls Dada "the first anti-art movement on record"[23]) by producing works that were deliberately senseless, purposeless, chaotic, and apparently devoid of artistic value. Marcel Duchamp's *Bicycle Wheel* is an example, as is his *Mona Lisa* with a mustache. Despite the Dadaists' nihilistic aims and "calculated irrationality," says the art historian H. W. Janson, "there was also liberation, a voyage into unknown provinces of the creative mind." Thus, Duchamp's painting with the nonsense title *Tu m'* was "dazzlingly inventive [and] far ahead of its time."[24]

Dada ended as a formal movement in 1924 and was succeeded by surrealism. Surrealists inherited from Dada a contempt for reason. They stressed fantasy and made use of Freudian insights and symbols in their art to reproduce the raw state of the unconscious and to arrive at truths beyond reason's grasp. To penetrate the interior of the mind, said André Breton, a French surrealist

Harlequin's Carnival (1924), by Joan Miró (1893–1983). In one of the first surrealist paintings, Miró makes visible an inner world of fantasy and humor populated by an array of imaginary creatures. (Albright-Knox Art Gallery/Art Resource, N.Y.

© 2011 Successió Miró/Artists Rights Society [ARS], New York/ADAGP, Paris.)

poet, the writer should "write quickly without any previously chosen subject, quickly enough not to dwell on and not to be tempted to read over what you have written."[25] Writing should not be dictated by the intellect but should flow automatically from the unconscious. Surrealists tried to portray the world of fantasy and hallucination, the marvelous and the spontaneous. Breton urged artists to live their dreams, even if it meant seeing "a horse galloping on a tomato." In the effort to break through the constraints of rationality so that they might reach a higher reality—that is, a "surreality"—leading surrealists such as Max Ernst (1891–1976), Salvador Dalí (1904–1989), and Joan Miró (1893–1983) used unconventional techniques and depicted an external world devoid of logic and normal appearances.

Artists, like writers, expressed a social conscience. George Grosz combined a Dadaist sense of life's meaninglessness with a new realism to depict the moral degeneration of middle-class German society. In *After the Questioning* (1935), Grosz, then living in the United States, dramatized Nazi brutality; in *The End of the World* (1936), he expressed his fear of another impending world war. Käthe Kollwitz, also a German artist, showed a deep compassion for the sufferer: the unemployed, the hungry, the ill, and the politically oppressed.

In a series of paintings, *The Passion of Sacco and Vanzetti* (1931–1932), American artist Ben Shahn showed his outrage at the execution of two radicals. William Gropper's *Migration* (1932) dramatized the suffering of the same dispossessed farmers described in Steinbeck's novel *The Grapes of Wrath*. Philip Evergood, in *Don't Cry Mother* (1938–1944), portrayed the apathy of starving children and their mother's terrible helplessness.

In his etchings of maimed, dying, and dead soldiers, German artist Otto Dix produced a powerful visual indictment of the Great War's cruelty and suffering. Service in the German army during World War I made Max Beckmann acutely aware of violence and brutality, which he expressed in *The Night* (1918–1919) and other paintings. Designated a "degenerate artist" by the Nazis, Beckmann went into exile. In *Guernica* (1937), Picasso memorialized the Spanish village decimated by Nazi saturation bombing during the Spanish Civil War. *White Crucifixion* (1938) by Marc Chagall, a Russian-born Jew who had settled in Paris, depicted the terror and flight of Jews in Nazi Germany.

Communism: "The God That Failed"

The economic misery of the Depression and the rise of Fascist barbarism led many intellectuals to find a new hope, even a secular faith, in Communism. They considered the Soviet experiment as a new beginning that promised a better future for all humanity. These intellectuals praised the Soviet Union for supplanting capitalist greed with socialist cooperation, replacing a haphazard economic system marred by repeated depressions with one based on planned production, and providing employment for everyone when joblessness was endemic in capitalist lands. Equating socialism with humanitarianism and capitalism with injustice, they believed that the Soviets were reorganizing society for the benefit of humanity. The American literary critic Edmund Wilson said that in the Soviet Union one felt at the "moral top of the world where the light never really goes out."[26] The British political theorists Sidney and Beatrice Webb declared that there was no other country "in which there is actually so much widespread public criticism and such incessant reevaluation of its shortcomings as in the USSR."[27] To these intellectuals, it seemed that in the Soviet Union a vigorous and healthy civilization—a "workers' paradise"—was emerging and that only Communism could stem the tide of Fascism. Many of these deluded people, ignoring or refusing to

recognize the reality of Stalin's terror, continued to embrace the Soviet system. For others, however, the attraction was shortlived. Sickened by Stalin's purges and terror, the denial of individual freedom, and the suppression of truth, they came to view the Soviet Union as another totalitarian state and Communism as another "god that failed."

One such intellectual was Arthur Koestler. Born in Budapest of Jewish ancestry and educated in Vienna, Koestler worked as a correspondent for a leading Berlin newspaper chain. He joined the Communist Party at the very end of 1931 because he "lived in a disintegrating society thirsting for faith," was moved by the suffering caused by the Depression, and saw Communism as the "only force capable of resisting the onrush of the primitive [Nazi] horde."[28] Koestler visited the Soviet Union in 1933, experiencing firsthand both the starvation brought on by forced collectivization and the propaganda that grotesquely misrepresented life in Western lands. Although his faith was shaken, he did not break with the party until 1938, in response to Stalin's liquidations.

In *Darkness at Noon* (1941), Koestler explored the attitudes of the Old Bolsheviks who were imprisoned, tortured, and executed by Stalin. These dedicated Communists had served the party faithfully, but Stalin, fearful of opposition, hating intellectuals, and driven by megalomania, denounced them as enemies of the people. The leading character in *Darkness at Noon*, the imprisoned Rubashov, is a composite of the Old Bolsheviks. Although he is innocent, Rubashov, without being physically tortured, publicly confesses to political crimes that he never committed.

Rubashov is aware of the suffering that the party has brought to the Russian people.

> *In the interests of a just distribution of land we deliberately let die of starvation about five million farmers and their families in one year. . . . [To liberate] human beings from the shackles of industrial exploitation . . . we sent about ten million people to do forced labour in the Arctic regions and the jungles of the East, under conditions similar to those of antique galley slaves. . . . To settle a difference of opinion, we know only one argument: death. . . . Our poets settle discussions on questions of style by denunciations to the*

ANGEL OF HEARTH AND HOME, BY MAX ERNST (1891–1976). Ernst formed part of the transition from Dada to surrealism. His paintings expressed a profound anxiety. André Breton called him "the most magnificently haunted mind in Europe." (Art Resource, N.Y. © 2011 Artists Rights Society [ARS], New York/ADAGP, Paris.)

Secret Police. . . . The people's standard of life is lower than it was before the Revolution, the labour conditions are harder, the discipline is more inhuman. . . . Our Press and our schools cultivate Chauvinism, militarism, dogmatism, conformism and ignorance. The arbitrary power of the Government is unlimited, and unexampled in history. Freedom of the Press, of opinion and of movement are as thoroughly exterminated as though the proclamation of the Rights of Man had never been. We have built up the most gigantic police apparatus, with informers made a national institution, and with the most refined scientific system of physical and mental torture. We whip the groaning masses of the country towards a theoretical future happiness, which only we can see.[29]

Pained by his own complicity in the party's crimes, including the betrayal of friends, Rubashov

questions the party's philosophy that the individual should be subordinated and, if necessary, sacrificed for the good of the regime. Nevertheless, Rubashov remains the party's faithful servant. True believers do not easily break with their faith. By confessing to treason, Rubashov performs his last service for the Revolution. For the true believer, everything—truth, justice, and the sanctity of the individual—is properly sacrificed to the party.

Reaffirming the Christian Worldview

By calling into question core liberal beliefs—the essential goodness of human nature, the primacy of reason, the efficacy of science, and the inevitability of progress—World War I led thinkers to find in Christianity an alternative view of the human experience and the crisis of the twentieth century. Christian thinkers, including Karl Barth, Paul Tillich, Reinhold Niebuhr, Christopher Dawson, Jacques Maritain, and

T. S. Eliot, asserted the reality of evil in human nature. They assailed liberals and Marxists for holding too optimistic a view of human nature and human reason, postulating a purely rational and secular philosophy of history, and anticipating an ideal society within the realm of historical time. Reinhold Niebuhr (1892–1971), a leading American Protestant theologian, declared in 1941: "The utopian illusions and sentimental observations of modern liberal culture are really all derived from the basic error of negating the fact of original sin."[30] For these thinkers, the Christian conception of history as a clash between human will and God's commands provided an intelligible explanation of the tragedies of the twentieth century. Karl Barth (1886–1968), the Swiss-German Protestant theologian, called for a reaffirmation of the Christ who inspires faith, the uniqueness of Christianity, and the spiritual power of divine revelation. The true meaning of history, he said, is not to be found in the liberals' view of the progress of reason and freedom or in the Marxist conception of economic determinism. Rather, it derives from the fact that history is the arena in which the individual's faith is tested.

Jacques Maritain (1882–1973), a leading French Catholic thinker, denounced core elements of the modern outlook: the autonomy of the individual, the autonomy of the mind, and a nonreligious humanism. He urged that the Christian philosophy of Thomas Aquinas be revived, for he believed that it successfully harmonized faith and reason. Maritain argued that humanism, which held that human beings by themselves alone can define life's purpose and create their own values, has utterly failed. Without guidance from a transcendental source, reason is powerless to control irrational drives, which threaten to degrade human existence. Without commitment to God's values, we find substitute faiths in fanatic and belligerent ideologies and unscrupulous leaders.

A strong advocate of political freedom, Maritain stressed the link between modern democracy and the Christian Gospels, which proclaimed "the natural equality of all men, children of the same God and redeemed by the same Christ . . . [and] the inalienable dignity of every soul fashioned in the image of God." He insisted that "the democratic state of mind and . . . the democratic philosophy of life requires the energies of the Gospel to penetrate secular existence, taming the irrational to reason."[31] These energies would control the human propensity for self-centeredness, wickedness, and hatred of others. To survive, secular democracy must be infused with Christian love and compassion.

The English Catholic thinker Christopher Dawson (1889–1970) stressed the historic ties between Christianity and Western civilization. He wrote in 1933: "If our civilization is to recover its vitality, or even to survive, it must . . . realize that religion is . . . the very heart of social life and the root of every living culture."[32]

In 1934, the British historian Arnold Toynbee (1889–1975) published the first three volumes of his monumental work, *A Study of History*, in which he tried to account for the rise, growth, breakdown, and disintegration of civilization. Underlying Toynbee's philosophy of history was a religious orientation, for he saw religious prophets as humanity's greatest figures and the world's major religions as humanity's greatest achievement. Toynbee attributed the problems of Western civilization to its breaking away from Christianity and embracing "false idols," particularly the national state, which, he said, had become the object of Westerners' highest reverence.

Toynbee regarded nationalism as a primitive religion, inducing people to revere the national community rather than God. This deification of the parochial—tribal or local—community intensified the brutal side of human nature and provoked wars among people sharing a common civilization. To Toynbee, Nazism was the culmination of the worst elements in modern European nationalism, "the consummation . . . of a politico-religious movement, the pagan deification and worship of parochial human communities which had been gradually gaining ground for more than four centuries in the Western world at large."[33] The moral catastrophe of Nazism, he said, demonstrates the inadequacy of liberal humanism, for the Enlightenment tradition proved a feeble barrier to the rise and spread of Nazism. The secular values of the Enlightenment, divorced from Christianity, cannot restrain human nature's basest impulses. For the West to save itself, said Toynbee, it must abide by the spiritual values of its religious prophets.

THE NIGHT (1918–1919), BY MAX BECKMANN (1884–1950). Max Beckmann's paintings gave expression to the disillusionment and spiritual unease that afflicted postwar Germany. When the Nazis included his works in the Degenerate Art Exhibition (1937), he left the country. In *The Night*, Beckmann, himself a veteran of the front, depicts brutal men engaging in terrible violence.

(Erich Lessing/Art Resource, N.Y. © 2011 Artists Rights Society [ARS], New York/VGBild-Kunst, Bonn.)

Reaffirming the Ideals of Reason and Freedom

Several thinkers tried to reaffirm the ideals of rationality and freedom that totalitarian movements had trampled. In *The Treason of the Intellectuals* (1927), Julien Benda (1867–1956), a French cultural critic of Jewish background, castigated intellectuals for intensifying hatred between nations and classes. "Our age is indeed the age of the intellectual organization of political hatreds," he wrote. Intellectuals who stir up hatred between nations, said Benda, do not pursue justice or truth but proclaim that "even if our country is wrong, we must think of it in the right." They scorn outsiders, extol harshness and action, and proclaim the superiority of instinct and will to intelligence; or they "assert that the intelligence to be venerated is that which limits its activities within the bounds of national interest." The logical end of this xenophobia, said Benda prophetically, "is the organized slaughter of nations and classes."[34]

José Ortega y Gasset (1883–1955), descendant of a Spanish noble family, gained international recognition with the publication of *The Revolt of the Masses* (1930). According to Ortega, European civilization, the product of a creative elite, was degenerating into barbarism because of the growing power of the masses, for the masses lacked the mental discipline and the commitment to reason needed to preserve Europe's intellectual and cultural traditions. Ortega did not equate the masses with the working class and the elite with the nobility; an attitude of mind, not a class affiliation, distinguished the "mass-man" from the elite.

The mass-man, said Ortega, has a commonplace mind and does not set high standards for himself. He is inert until driven by an external compulsion. He does not enter into rational dialogue with others, defend his opinions logically, or accept objective standards. Faced with a problem, he "is satisfied with thinking the first thing he finds in his head" and "crushes . . . everything that is different, everything that is excellent, individual, qualified, and select. Anybody who is not like everybody, who does not think like everybody, runs the risk of being eliminated."[35] Such intellectually vulgar people, declared Ortega, cannot understand or preserve the processes of civilization. The Fascists exemplify this revolt of the masses, for "under fascism there appears for the first time in Europe a type of man who . . . simply shows himself resolved to impose his opinions. This is the new thing: the right not to be reasonable, the 'reason of unreason.'" The danger lay in "the masses . . . having decided to rule society without the capacity for doing so."[36] Rejecting reason, the massman glorifies violence: the ultimate expression of barbarism. If European civilization is to be rescued from Fascism and Communism, said Ortega, the elite must sustain civilized values and provide leadership.

A staunch defender of the Enlightenment tradition, Ernst Cassirer (1874–1945), a German philosopher of Jewish lineage, emigrated after Hitler came to power, eventually settling in the United States. Just prior to Hitler's triumph, Cassirer wrote of the need to uphold and reenergize that tradition: "The age which venerated reason and science as man's highest faculty cannot and must not be lost even for us. We must find a way not only to see that age in its own shape but to release again those original forces which brought forth and molded this shape."[37]

In his posthumous work, *The Myth of the State* (1946), Cassirer described Nazism as the triumph of mythical thinking over reason. The Nazis, said Cassirer, cleverly manufactured myths—of the race, the leader, the party, the state—that disoriented the intellect. Germans who embraced these myths surrendered their capacity for independent judgment, leaving themselves vulnerable to manipulation by the Nazi leadership. Cassirer warned:

> *In politics we are always living on volcanic soil. We must be prepared for convulsions and eruptions. In all critical moments of man's social life, the rational forces that resist the rise of old mythical conceptions are no longer sure of themselves. In these moments the time of myth has come again. For myth has not been really vanquished and subjugated. It is always there, lurking in the dark and waiting for its hour and opportunity. This hour comes as soon as the other binding forces of man's social life . . . lose their strength and are no longer able to combat the demonic mythical powers.*[38]

To contain the destructive powers of political myths, Cassirer urged strengthening the rational-humanist tradition and called for the critical study of political myths, for "in order to fight an enemy you must know him."[39]

Like Cassirer and many other German-Jewish intellectuals, Erich Fromm (1900–1980), a social theorist and psychoanalyst, settled in the United States after the Nazis took power. In *Escape from Freedom* (1941), Fromm explained the triumph of Nazism within the wider context of European history. During the Middle Ages, said Fromm, the individual derived a sense of security from a structured social system, which clearly defined the roles of clergy, lords, and serfs, and from a Christian worldview, which made life and death purposeful. Modern Westerners have lost this sense of security. Dwelling in impersonal cities, threatened by economic crises, no longer comforted by the medieval conception of life's purpose, they are often tormented by doubts and overwhelmed by feelings of aloneness and insignificance. People try to overcome this "burden of freedom" by surrendering themselves to a person or power that they view "as being overwhelmingly strong"; they trade freedom for security by entering into "a symbiotic relationship that overcomes . . . aloneness."[40] Because modern industrial society has made the individual feel powerless

Jean Paul Sartre and Simone de Beauvoir. Existentialism was a major philosophical movement of the twentieth century. Sartre and de Beauvoir were two of its principal exponents. (©Georges Pierre/Sygma/Corbis.)

and insignificant, concluded Fromm, Fascism is a constant threat. Fromm would meet the challenge of Fascism by creating social conditions that lead the individual to be free yet not alone, to be critical yet not filled with doubts, to be independent yet feel an integral part of humankind.

George Orwell (1903–1950), a British novelist and political journalist, wrote two powerful indictments of totalitarianism: *Animal Farm* (1945) and *1984* (1949). In *Animal Farm*, based in part on his experiences with Communists during the Spanish Civil War, Orwell satirized the totalitarian regime built by Lenin and Stalin in Russia. In *1984*, Orwell, who was deeply committed to human dignity and freedom, warned that these great principles are now permanently menaced by the concentration and abuse of political power. "If you want a picture of the future, imagine a boot stamping on a human face forever," says a member of the ruling elite as he tortures a victim in the dungeons of the Thought Police.[41]

Existentialism

Intellectual Background

The philosophical movement that best exemplified the anxiety and uncertainty of Europe in the era of world wars was **existentialism**. Like writers and artists, existentialist philosophers were responding to a European civilization that seemed to be in the throes of dissolution. Although existentialism was most popular after World War II, expressing the anxiety and despair of many intellectuals who had lost confidence in reason and progress, several of its key works were written prior to or during the war.

What route should people take in a world where old values and certainties had dissolved, where universal truth was rejected and God's existence denied? How could people cope in a society where they were menaced by technology, manipulated by impersonal bureaucracies, and overwhelmed by feelings of anxiety? If the universe is devoid of any overarching meaning, what meaning could one give to one's own life? These questions were at the crux of existentialist philosophy.

Nineteenth-Century Forerunners

Three nineteenth-century thinkers—Søren Kierkegaard (see Chapter 23), Fyodor Dostoevsky (see Chapter 27), and Friedrich Nietzsche (see Chapter 27)—were the principal forerunners of existentialism. Their views of reason, will, truth, and existence greatly influenced twentieth-century existentialists.

Kierkegaard. A Danish religious philosopher and Lutheran pastor, Kierkegaard held that self-realization as a human being comes when the individual takes full responsibility for his or her life. The individual does so by choosing one way of life over another. In making choices, said Kierkegaard, the individual overcomes the agonizing feeling that life in its deepest sense is nothingness.

Twentieth-century existentialists took from Kierkegaard the idea that an all-consuming dread is the price of existence. "I stick my finger into existence," said Kierkegaard; "it smells of nothing. Where am I? What is this thing called the world? Who is it who has lured me into the thing, and now leaves me here? Who am I? How did I come into the world? Why was I not consulted?"[42] The sense that we live in a meaningless world drives us to the edge of the abyss. This overwhelming dread can cause us to flee from life and to find comfort in delusions. But it can also spark courage since it is an opportunity to make a commitment. For both Kierkegaard and twentieth-century existentialists, the true philosophical quest is a subjective experience: the isolated individual, alone and without help, choosing a way of life to which he or she is deeply committed. Only in this way does the individual become a whole person. Kierkegaard's dictum that "it is impossible to exist without passion"—that our actions matter to us—is at the heart of existentialism.

Dostoevsky. Although existentialist themes pervade several of Dostoevsky's works, it is in *Notes*

from Underground (1864) that he treats explicitly the individual's quest for personal freedom, identity, and meaning and the individual's revolt against established norms—themes that are crucial to the outlook of twentieth-century existentialists.

Nietzsche. Friedrich Nietzsche was an important forerunner of existentialism for several reasons. He stated that philosophical systems are merely expressions of an individual's own being and do not constitute an objective representation of reality; there is no realm of being that is the source of values. Nor does religion provide truth, for God is dead. And, asked Nietzsche, is not this godless world absurd? Nietzsche held that modern Westerners had lost all their traditional supports. To overcome nothingness, said Nietzsche, individuals must define life for themselves and celebrate it fully, instinctively, and heroically. Nietzsche's insistence that individuals confront existence squarely, without hypocrisy, and give it meaning—their own meaning—was vital to the shaping of existentialism.

Basic Principles

Existentialism does not lend itself to a single definition, for its principal theorists did not adhere to a common body of doctrines. For example, some existentialists were atheists, like Jean Paul Sartre, or omitted God from their thought, like Martin Heidegger; others, like Karl Jaspers, believed in God but not in Christian doctrines; still others, like Gabriel Marcel and Nikolai Berdyaev, were Christians; and Martin Buber was a believing Jew.

That there are no timeless truths that exist independently of and prior to the individual human being and that serve as ultimate standards of virtue is a core principle of existentialism. Existence—our presence in the here-and-now—precedes and takes precedence over any presumed absolute values. The moral and spiritual values that society tries to impose cannot define the individual person's existence. Our traditional morality rests on no foundation whose certainty can be either demonstrated by reason or guaranteed by God. There are simply no transcendent absolutes; to think otherwise is to surrender to illusion. It is the first principle of

Charlie Chaplin

Charles Spencer (Charlie) Chaplin was born in London in 1889 to music hall entertainers. His mother, Hannah Chaplin, taught young Charles the art of pantomime. Touring the United States with an English company, he was hired by Mack Sennet to act in the popular Keystone Comedies. Insightful, intelligent, musical, and artistic, Chaplin transformed silent film comedy, which was largely slapstick, into an art form.

(Henry Guttmann/Hulton Archive/Getty Images.)

In *The Tramp* (1915), Chaplin played a gentleman tramp, the character with which he would always be identified. The "little tramp" wore baggy pants, a derby, fingerless gloves, a shabby dress coat, handled a bamboo cane with great dexterity, and shuffled as he walked. Critics applauded Chaplin's skill as both actor and director in *The Kid* (1921), which also starred the six-year-old Jackie Coogan. The interaction between the little tramp and the young boy, who had been abandoned, brought tears and smiles to audiences. It also revealed Chaplin's social conscience. Abandoned by his alcoholic father, he knew poverty as a youth.

Chaplin's skill as a social commentator was demonstrated in two classic works: *Modern Times* (1936) and *The Great Dictator* (1940). In *Modern Times*, Chaplin satirized labor in the modern mechanized factory. In one memorable scene, Charlie is tightening nuts on a conveyor belt when the boss orders a speedup. Desperately trying to increase his pace, Charlie moves hyperactively and spasmodically. His mind is also affected. When he sees a secretary wearing a dress with ornaments resembling the nuts that he had been turning, Charlie chases her, determined to apply his wrench to the nut-like ornaments. In *The Great Dictator*, Chaplin mocked Mussolini and Hitler and expressed outrage at German anti-Semitism. He made the film, he said, for "the return of decency and kindness."

After World War II, Chaplin continued to act and direct, but his later works—*Monsieur Verdoux* (1947), *Limelight* (1952), and *A King in New York* (1957)—were not well received. Identified with leftist causes, Chaplin was refused reentry into the United States in 1952. Twenty years later, he returned to the United States and received an honorary Academy Award. In 1975, he was knighted by Queen Elizabeth II. He died at the end of 1977.

existentialism, said Jean Paul Sartre (1905–1980), the prominent French existentialist, that we must choose our own ethics, define ourselves, and give our own meaning to our life.

Existentialists held that reason alone is an inadequate guide to living, for people are more than thinking subjects who approach the world through critical analysis. They are also feeling and willing beings, who must participate fully in life and experience existence directly, actively, and passionately. Only in this way does one live wholly and authentically. Thought must not merely be abstract speculation but must have a bearing on life; it must be translated into deeds.

For existentialists, human nature is not fixed or constant; each person is like no other. Self-realization comes when one affirms one's own uniqueness. One becomes less than human when one permits one's life to be determined by a mental outlook—a set of rules and values—imposed by others.

Existentialists maintained that we are alone in a universe that is indifferent to our expectations and needs, and death is ever stalking us. Awareness of this elementary fact of existence evokes a sense of overwhelming anxiety and depression. Existence is essentially absurd. There is no purpose to our presence in the universe. We simply find ourselves here; we do not know and will never find out why. Compared with the eternity of time that preceded our birth and will follow our death, the short duration of our existence seems trivial and inexplicable. And death, which irrevocably terminates our existence, testifies to the ultimate absurdity of life. But we are free. We must face squarely the fact that existence is purposeless and absurd. In doing so, we can give our life meaning. It is in the act of choosing freely from among different possibilities that the individual shapes an authentic existence. There is a dynamic quality to human existence; the individual has the potential to become more than he or she is. Thus Albert Camus (1913–1960), another prominent French thinker who held that neither religion nor philosophy can tell us what is right or wrong, did urge living by values that advance human dignity and warm human relations; he insisted that we must find life-enhancing alternatives to the nihilistic conclusion that life is meaningless and valueless.

THE MODERN PREDICAMENT

The process of fragmentation that had begun in European thought and the arts at the end of the nineteenth century accelerated after World War I. Increasingly, philosophers, writers, and artists expressed disillusionment with the rational-humanist tradition of the Enlightenment. They no longer shared the Enlightenment confidence in reason's capabilities or in human goodness, and they viewed perpetual progress as an illusion.

For some thinkers, the crucial problem was the great change in the European understanding of truth. Since the rise of philosophy in ancient Greece, Western thinkers had believed in the existence of objective, universal truths: truths that were inherent in nature and applied to all peoples at all times. (Christianity, of course, also taught the reality of truth as revealed by God.) It was held that such truths—the natural rights of the individual, for example—could be apprehended by the intellect and could serve as a standard for individual aspirations and social life. The recognition of these universal principles, it was believed, compelled people to measure the world of the here-and-now in the light of rational and universal norms and to institute appropriate reforms. Philosophy had the task of reconciling human existence with the objective order.

During the nineteenth century, the existence of universal truth came into doubt. A growing historical consciousness led some thinkers to maintain that what people considered truth was merely a reflection of their culture at a given stage in history—their perception of things at a specific point in the evolution of human consciousness. These thinkers, called *historicists,* held that universal truths were not woven into the fabric of nature. There are no natural rights of life, liberty, and property that constitute the individual's birthright; there are no standards of justice or equality that are inherent in nature and ascertainable by reason. It was people, said historicists, who elevated the beliefs and values of an age to the status of objective truth. The normative principles—the self-evident truths proclaimed by Jefferson—that for the philosophes constituted a standard for political and social reform and a guarantee of human rights were no longer linked to the natural order, to an objective reality that could be confirmed by reason. As Hannah Arendt noted, "We certainly no longer believe, as the men of the French Revolution did, in a universal cosmos of which man was a part and whose natural laws he had to imitate and conform to."[43]

This radical break with the traditional attitude toward truth contributed substantially to the crisis of European consciousness that marked the first half of the twentieth century. Traditional values and beliefs, either those inherited from the Enlightenment or those taught by Christianity, no longer gave Europeans a sense of certainty and security. People were left without a normative order to serve as a guide to living—and without such a guide might be open to nihilism. For if nothing is fundamentally true—if there are no principles of morality and justice that emanate from God or can be derived from reason—then it can be concluded, as Nietzsche understood, that everything is permitted. Some scholars interpreted Nazism as the culminating expression of a nihilistic attitude grown ever more brutal.

By the early twentieth century, the attitude of Westerners toward reason had also undergone a radical transformation. Some thinkers, who had placed their hopes in the rational tradition of the Enlightenment, were disillusioned by reason's inability to resolve the tensions and conflicts of modern industrial society. Moreover, the growing recognition of the nonrational—of human actions determined by hidden impulses—led to doubts that reason plays the dominant role in human behavior. The intellect did not seem autonomous and self-regulating but instead seemed subject to the rebellious demands of unconscious drives and impulses. Men's and women's propensity for goodness, their capacity to improve society, and their potential for happiness seemed severely limited by an inherent irrationality. Indeed, civilization itself seemed threatened by people's instinctual needs, as Freud had proclaimed.

Other thinkers were critical of reason. They attacked reason for fashioning a technological and bureaucratic society that devalued and crushed human emotions and stifled individuality; these thinkers insisted that human beings cannot fulfill their potential, cannot live wholly, if their feelings are denied. They agreed with D. H. Lawrence's critique of rationalism: "The attribution of

rationality to human nature, instead of enriching it, now seems to me to have impoverished it. It ignored certain powerful and valuable springs of feeling. Some of the spontaneous, irrational outbursts of human nature can have a sort of value from which our schematism was cut off."[44]

These thinkers pointed out that reason was a double-edged sword: it could demean, as well as ennoble and liberate, the individual. They attacked all theories that subordinated the individual to a rigid system. They denounced positivism for reducing human personality to psychological laws, and Marxism for making social class a higher reality than the individual. Rebelling against political collectivization, which regulated individual existence according to the needs of the corporate state, they assailed modern bureaucracy and technology. These creations of the rational mind, they claimed, had fashioned a social order that devalued and depersonalized the individual, denying people an opportunity for independent growth and a richer existence. According to these thinkers, modern industrial society, in its drive for efficiency and uniformity, deprived people of their uniqueness and reduced human beings to cogs in a mechanical system.

Responding to the critics of reason, other philosophers maintained that it was necessary to reaffirm respect for the rational tradition, first proclaimed by the ancient Greeks and given its modern expression by the Enlightenment philosophes. Reason, said these thinkers, was indispensable to civilization. What they advocated was broadening the scope of reason to accommodate the insights into human nature offered by the romantics, Nietzsche, Freud, modernist writers and artists, and others who explored the world of feelings, will, and the subconscious. They also stressed the need to humanize reason so that it could never threaten to reduce a human being to a thing.

In the decades shaped by world wars and totalitarianism, intellectuals raised questions that went to the heart of the dilemma of modern life. How can civilized life be safeguarded against human irrationality, particularly when it is channeled into political ideologies that idolize the state, the leader, the party, or the race? How can the individual human personality be rescued from a relentless rationalism that reduces human nature and society to mechanical systems and seeks to regulate and organize the individual as it would any material object? Do we, as human beings, have the moral and spiritual resolve to use properly the technological and scientific creations of modern civilization, or will they devour us?

Do the values associated with the Enlightenment provide a sound basis on which to integrate society? Can the individual find meaning in what many came to regard as a meaningless universe? World War II gave these questions a special poignancy.

❖   ❖   ❖

NOTES

1. Quoted in Barbara Tuchman, *The Guns of August* (New York: Macmillan, 1962), 440.

2. Sigmund Freud, "Thoughts for the Times on War and Death," in *Standard Edition of the Complete Psychological Works of Freud*, ed. James Strachey (London: Hogarth Press, 1957), 14:275, 278.

3. Quoted in Hans Kohn, "The Crisis in European Thought and Culture," in *World War I: A Turning Point in Modern History*, ed. Jack J. Roth (New York: Knopf, 1967), 28.

4. Quoted in Franklin L. Baumer, "Twentieth-Century Version of the Apocalypse," *Cahiers d'Histoire Mondiale (Journal of World History)* 1 (January 1954): 624.

5. Quoted in William McNeill, *Arnold J. Toynbee: A Life* (New York: Oxford University Press, 1989), 152.

6. Baumer, "Apocalypse," 624.

7. Erich Maria Remarque, *All Quiet on the Western Front*, trans. A. W. Wheen (Boston: Little, Brown, 1929), 224.

8. W. B. Yeats, "The Second Coming," in *Collected Poems of W. B. Yeats* (New York: Macmillan, 1956), 184–185.

9. T. S. Eliot, "The Waste Land," in *Collected Poems, 1909–1962* (New York: Harcourt, Brace, 1970), 67.

10. Carl Gustav Jung, *Modern Man in Search of a Soul*, trans. W. S. Dell and Cary F. Baynes (New York: Harcourt, Brace, 1933), 231, 234–235.

11. Nicholas Berdyaev, *The Fate of Man in the Modern World* (Ann Arbor Michigan: University of Michigan Press, 1961), 16, 27–28.

12. E. M. Forster, "Post-Munich," in *Two Cheers for Democracy* (New York: Harcourt, Brace and World, 1951), 21.

13. Oswald Spengler, *The Decline of the West*, trans. Charles F. Atkinson (London: Allen and Unwin, 1926), 40.

14. Franz Kafka, *The Trial*, trans. Willa and Edwin Muir (New York: Knopf, 1957), 7.

15. Angel Flores, ed., *The Kafka Problem* (New York: Gordian Press, 1975), xxi.

16. Thomas Mann, "An Appeal to Reason," excerpted in *Sources of the Western Tradition*, 8th ed., ed. Marvin Perry (Boston: Wadsworth, Cengage Learning, 2012), vol. 2, 349–350.

17. Thomas Mann, "Schopenhauer," in *Essays of Three Decades*, trans. H. T. Lowe-Porter (New York: Knopf, 1968), 409.

18. D. H. Lawrence, *Women in Love* (New York: Penguin Books, 1979), 215.

19. Harry T. Moore, ed., *The Collected Letters of D. H. Lawrence* (New York: Viking, 1962), 1:180.

20. Quoted in Peter Childs, *Modernism* (London: Routledge, 2000), 65.

21. Tristan Tzara, "Lecture on Dada (1922)," trans. Ralph Mannheim, in *The Dada Painters and Poets*, ed. Robert Motherwell (New York: Wittenborn, Schultz, 1951), 248, 250.

22. Ibid., 251.

23. Edward Lucie-Smith, in Donald Carrol and Edward Lucie-Smith, *Movements in Modern Art* (New York: Horizon Press, 1973), 49.

24. H. W. Janson, *History of Art*, 2nd ed. (Englewood Cliffs, N.J.: Prentice-Hall, 1977), 661.

25. André Breton, *What Is Surrealism?* trans. David Gascoyne (London: Faber and Faber, 1936), 62.

26. Quoted in David Caute, *The Fellow Travellers* (New York: Macmillan, 1973), 64.

27. Ibid., 92.

28. Richard Crossman, ed., *The God That Failed* (New York: Bantam Books, 1951), 15, 21.

29. Arthur Koestler, *Darkness at Noon* (New York: Macmillan, 1941), 158–159.

30. Reinhold Niebuhr, *The Nature and Destiny of Man* (New York: Charles Scribner's Sons, 1941), 1:273.

31. Jacques Maritain, *Christianity and Democracy* (New York: Charles Scribner's Sons, 1944), 44, 62.

32. Quoted in C. T. McIntire, ed., *God, History, and Historians* (New York: Oxford University Press, 1977), 9.

33. Arnold J. Toynbee, *Survey of International Affairs, 1933* (London: Oxford University Press, 1934), 111.

34. Julien Benda, *The Betrayal of the Intellectuals*, trans. Richard Aldington (Boston: Beacon Press, 1955), 21, 38, 122, 162.

35. José Ortega y Gasset, *The Revolt of the Masses* (New York: Norton, 1957), 18, 63.

36. Ibid., 73.

37. Ernst Cassirer, *The Philosophy of the Enlightenment*, trans. Fritz C. A. Koelln and James P. Pettegrove (Boston: Beacon Press, 1955), xi–xii.

38. Ernst Cassirer, *The Myth of the State* (New Haven, Conn.: Yale University Press, 1946), 280.

39. Ibid., 296.

40. Erich Fromm, *Escape from Freedom* (New York: Avon Books, 1965), 173, 246.

41. George Orwell, *1984* (New York: Harcourt, Brace, 1949; paperback, New American Library, 1961), 220.

42. Quoted in T. Z. Lavine, *From Socrates to Sartre: The Philosophic Quest* (New York: Bantam Books, 1984), 322.

43. Cited in Harry S. Kariel, *In Search of Authority* (Glencoe, Ill.: Free Press, 1964), 246.

44. Cited in Anthony Arblaster, *The Rise and Decline of Western Liberalism* (Oxford: Basil Blackwell, 1984), 81.

Chapter 31

World War II: Western Civilization in the Balance

Hitler and his aides in front of the Eiffel Tower in 1940; after military successes in Belgium and Holland, the German forces overcame France. Hitler (center, right) saw the fall of France as a proof of the invincibility of the Reich and a predestined reversal of the humiliation felt by Germans at their defeat in World War I. (© SZ Photo/Scherl/The Image Works.)

- **The Aftermath of World War I**
- **The Road to War**
- **The Nazi Blitzkrieg**
- **The New Order**
- **Turning the Tide**
- **The Legacy of World War II**

Focus Questions

1. What were Hitler's foreign policy aims?

2. Why did Britain and France pursue a policy of appeasement? With what effect?

3. What factors contributed to the German victory over Poland? Over France?

4. Why was Britain able to win the air battle in the summer of 1940?

5. Why was Germany unable to conquer Russia?

6. What was the nature of the New Order that the Nazis established in conquered. Why were the Jews marked for extermination?

7. What factors led to the defeat of the Nazis?

8. In your opinion, what is the meaning of the Holocaust for Western civilization? For Jews? For Christians? For Germans?

9. What is the legacy of World War II?

From the early days of his political career, Hitler dreamed of forging in Central and Eastern Europe a vast German empire that would bring the millions of Germans living there under the rule of the Third Reich. He believed that only by waging a war of conquest against Russia could the German nation gain the living space and security it required and, as a superior race, deserved. War was an essential component of National Socialist racist ideology, which postulated an eternal struggle between races and the shaping of a New Order in Europe based on race; war also accorded with Hitler's temperament. For the former corporal from the trenches, the Great War had never ended. Hitler aspired to political power because he wanted to mobilize the material and human resources of the German nation for war and conquest. Whereas historians may debate the question of responsibility for World War I, few would deny that World War II was Hitler's war. Most would concur with the assessment of French historian Pierre Renouvin:

> It appears to be an almost incontrovertible fact that the Second World War was brought on by the actions of the Hitler government, that these actions were the expression of a policy laid down well in advance in Mein Kampf, and that this war could have been averted up until the last moment if the German government had so wished.[1]

Western statesmen had sufficient warning that Hitler was a threat to peace and the essential values of Western civilization. In the 1920s, Hitler had openly proclaimed his commitment to a war of revenge and expansion, and in the 1930s he scrapped the Versailles treaty and openly prepared for such a conflict. But Western statesmen, not fully grasping Hitler's ruthlessness and ideological obsession with creating a German racial empire and underestimating his Machiavellian cunning in foreign policy, failed to rally their people and take a stand until Germany had greatly increased its capacity to wage aggressive war.

Chronology 31.1 ❖ The Road to World War II

1931	Japan invades Manchuria
March 1935	Hitler announces German rearmament
October 1935	Italy invades Ethiopia
1936–1939	Spanish Civil War
March 7, 1936	Germany remilitarizes the Rhineland
October 1936	Berlin–Rome Axis is formed
November 1936	German–Japanese anti-Communist pact
July 1937	Japan invades China
March 13, 1938	Anschluss with Austria, which becomes a German province
September 1938	Munich Agreement: Britain and France approve Germany's annexation of Sudetenland
1939	Franco establishes a dictatorship in Spain
March 1939	Germany invades Czechoslovakia
April 1939	Italy invades Albania
May 22, 1939	Pact of Steel between Hitler and Mussolini
August 23, 1939	Nonaggression pact between Germany and Russia
September 1, 1939	Germany invades Poland
September 3, 1939	Britain and France declare war on Germany

THE AFTERMATH
OF WORLD WAR I

World War I showed that Germany was the strongest power on the European continent. In the east, the German army triumphed over Russia. In the west, Britain and France could have hoped for no more than a deadlock without the aid of the United States. The Treaty of Versailles weakened Germany but did not permanently cripple it.

In the decade after the war, responsibility for preserving the peace settlement rested essentially with France. The United States had rejected the treaty and withdrawn from European affairs; Soviet Russia was consolidating its Revolution; and Britain, burdened with severe economic problems, disarmed, and traditionally hostile to Continental alliances, did not want to join with

France in holding Germany down. France sought to contain Germany by forging alliances with the new states of Eastern Europe, which the French hoped would serve as a substitute for alliance with a now untrustworthy Communist Russia. Thus, in the 1920s, France entered into alliances with Poland, Czechoslovakia, Romania, and Yugoslavia. But no combination of small Eastern European states could replace Russia as a counterweight to Germany. Against Hitler's Germany, the French alliance system would prove useless.

In the area of international relations, a feeling of hope prevailed during the 1920s. The newly created League of Nations provided a supranational authority to which nations could submit their quarrels. At the Washington Naval Conference (1921–1922), the leading naval powers—the United States, Britain, France, Italy, and Japan—agreed not to construct new battleships or heavy cruisers for a ten-year period and established a ratio for these large ships among them. It was hoped that avoiding a naval arms race would promote international peace.

In the Locarno Pact (1925), Germany, France, and Belgium agreed not to change their existing borders, which meant, in effect, that Germany had accepted both the return of Alsace and Lorraine to France and the demilitarization of the Rhineland—two provisions of the Versailles treaty. The Locarno Pact held the promise of a détente between France and Germany. But it was only an illusion of peace, for Germany gave no such assurances for its eastern border with Czechoslovakia and Poland, France's allies.

Other gestures that promoted reconciliation followed. In 1926, Germany was admitted to the League of Nations, and in 1928 the Kellogg-Briand Pact renouncing war was signed by most nations. The signatories condemned war as a solution for international disputes and agreed to settle quarrels through peaceful means. But because the pact contained no clauses for its enforcement, this agreement, too, fostered only the illusion of peace.

Nevertheless, between 1925 and 1930, hopes for reconciliation and peace were high. Recovery from the war and increased prosperity coincided with the easing of international tensions. As evidence of the new spirit of conciliation, France and Britain withdrew their forces from the Rhineland in 1930, four years ahead of the time prescribed by the Versailles treaty.

THE ROAD TO WAR

Hitler's Foreign Policy Aims

After consolidating his power and mobilizing the nation's will, Hitler moved to implement his foreign policy objectives: the destruction of the Versailles treaty, the conquest and colonization of Eastern Europe, and the domination and exploitation of racial inferiors. In some respects, Hitler's foreign policy aims accorded with the goals of Germany's traditional rulers. Like them, Hitler sought to make Germany the preeminent power in Europe. During World War I, German statesmen and generals had sought to conquer extensive regions of Eastern Europe, and in the Treaty of Brest-Litovsk, Germany took Poland, Ukraine, and the Baltic

states from Russia. But Hitler's racial nationalism—the subjugation and annihilation of inferior races by a master German race—marked a break with the outlook of the old governing class. Germany's traditional conservative leaders had considered but not revoked the civil rights of German Jews and had sought to Germanize, not enslave, the Poles living under the German flag.

In foreign affairs, Hitler demonstrated the same blend of opportunism and singleness of purpose that had brought him to power. Here, too, he displayed an uncanny understanding of his opponents' weaknesses; and here, too, his opponents underestimated his skills and intent. As in his climb to power, he made use of propaganda to undermine his opponents' will to resist. The Nazi propaganda machine, which had won the minds of the German people, became an instrument of foreign policy. Nazi propaganda tried to win the support of the 27 million Germans living in Europe and the Americas, outside the borders of the Reich proper. To promote social and political disorientation in other lands, the Nazis propagated anti-Semitism on a worldwide basis and tried to draw international support for Hitler as Europe's best defense against the Soviet Union and Bolshevism. The Nazi anti-Communist campaign "convinced many Europeans that Hitler's dictatorship was more acceptable than Stalin's and that Germany—'the bulwark against Bolshevism'—should be allowed to grow from strength to strength."[2]

As Hitler had anticipated, the British and the French backed down when faced with his violations of the Versailles treaty and threats of war. Haunted by the memory of World War I, Britain and France went to great lengths to avoid another catastrophe—a policy that had the overwhelming support of public opinion. Moreover, Britain suffered from a bad conscience regarding the Versailles treaty. Woefully unprepared for war from 1933 to 1938 and believing that Germany had been treated too severely, Britain was amenable to making concessions to Hitler. Although France had the strongest army on the Continent, it was prepared to fight only a defensive war—the reverse of its World War I strategy. France built immense fortifications, called the Maginot Line, to protect its borders from a German invasion, but it lacked a mobile striking force that could punish an aggressive Germany. The United States, concerned with the problems of the Great Depression and standing aloof from Europe's troubles, did nothing to strengthen the resolve of France and Britain. Because both France and Britain feared and mistrusted the Soviet Union, the grand alliance of World War I was not renewed. There was an added factor: suffering from a failure of leadership and political and economic unrest that eroded national unity, France was experiencing a decline in morale and a loss of nerve. It consistently turned to Britain for direction.

British statesmen championed a policy of appeasement: giving in to Germany in the hope that a satisfied Hitler would not drag Europe through another world war. British policy rested on the disastrous illusion that Hitler, like his Weimar predecessors, sought peaceful revision of the Versailles treaty and that he could be contained through concessions. This perception was as misguided as the expectation of Weimar conservatives that the responsibility of power would compel Hitler to abandon his National Socialist radicalism. Some British appeasers, accepting the view that Nazi propaganda cleverly propagated and exploited, also regarded Hitler as a defender of European civilization and the capitalist economic order against Soviet Communism.

In *Mein Kampf*, Hitler had explicitly laid out his philosophy of racial nationalism and *Lebensraum* (living space). As dictator, he had established a one-party state, confined political opponents to concentration camps, and persecuted Jews. But the proponents of appeasement did not properly assess these signs. They still believed that Hitler could be reasoned with. Appeasement, which in the end was capitulation to blackmail, failed. Germany grew stronger and the German people more devoted to the führer. Hitler did not moderate his ambitions, and the appeasers did not avert war.

The Breakdown of Peace

To realize his foreign policy aims, Hitler required a formidable military machine. Germany had to rearm. The Treaty of Versailles limited the size of the German army to 100,000 volunteers; restricted the navy's size; forbade the production of military aircraft, heavy artillery, and tanks; and disbanded the general staff. Throughout the 1920s, Germany evaded these provisions, even entering into a secret arrangement with the Soviet Union to establish training schools for German pilots and tank corpsmen on Russian soil.

In March 1935, Hitler declared that Germany was no longer bound by the Versailles treaty. Germany would restore conscription, build an air force (which it had been doing secretly), and strengthen its navy. The German people were ecstatic over Hitler's boldness. France protested but offered no resistance. Britain negotiated a naval agreement with Germany, thus tacitly accepting Hitler's rearmament.

A decisive event in the breakdown of peace was Italy's invasion of Ethiopia in October 1935. Mussolini sought colonial expansion and revenge for the defeat that the African kingdom had inflicted on Italian troops in 1896. The League of Nations called for economic sanctions against Italy, and most League members restricted trade with the aggressor. But Italy continued to receive oil, particularly from American suppliers. Believing that the conquest of Ethiopia did not affect their vital interests and hoping to keep the Italians friendly in the event of a clash with Germany, neither Britain nor France sought to restrain Italy despite its act of aggression against another member of the League of Nations. The Fascists claimed they were civilizing a backward African nation. In the process, tens of thousands of Ethiopians perished, victims of saturation bombing, poison gas, and mistreatment in concentration camps into which they had been herded.

Mussolini's subjugation of Ethiopia discredited the League of Nations, already weakened by its failure to deal effectively with Japan's invasion of the mineral-rich Chinese province of Manchuria in 1931. At that time, the League formed a commission of inquiry and urged nonrecognition of the puppet state of Manchukuo created by the Japanese, but the member states did not restrain Japan. The invasion of Ethiopia, like the invasion of Manchuria, showed the League's reluctance to use force to resist aggression.

On March 7, 1936, Hitler marched troops into the Rhineland, violating both the Versailles treaty and the Locarno Pact. German generals had cautioned Hitler that such a move would provoke a French invasion of Germany and reoccupation of the Rhineland, which the German army, still in the first stages of rearmament, could not repulse.

ICELAND

Germany and Italy
Italian possessions in Africa before 1935
German aggressions, 1935–1939
Italian aggressions, 1935–1939

0   200   400 Km.
0   200   400 Mi.

NORWAY

SWEDEN

FINLAND

Baltic Sea

ESTONIA

LATVIA

Moscow

North
Sea

DENMARK

Memel
Danzig
EAST
PRUSSIA

LITHUANIA

SOVIET UNION

IRELAND

GREAT
BRITAIN

London

NETHERLANDS

Berlin

POLISH
CORRIDOR

Warsaw

ATLANTIC
OCEAN

Brussels
BELGIUM

Paris

LUXEMBOURG

RHINELAND
1936

GERMANY

Weimar

Nuremberg

Munich

SUDETENLAND
1938

Prague
CZECHOSLOVAKIA
1939

Vienna

POLAND

FRANCE

SWITZERLAND

AUSTRIA
1938

HUNGARY

ROMANIA

SPAIN
(Civil War, 1936–1939)

Madrid

Barcelona

PORTUGAL

ITALY

Rome

YUGOSLAVIA

BULGARIA

Black
Sea

ALBANIA
1939

GREECE

TURKEY

Mediterranean Sea

AFRICA

LIBYA

ERITREA

ETHIOPIA
1935–1936

IT. SOMALILAND

AFRICA

But Hitler gambled that France and Britain, lacking the will to fight, would take no action.

Hitler had assessed the Anglo-French mood correctly. Britain was not greatly alarmed by the remilitarization of the Rhineland. After all, Hitler was not expanding the borders of Germany but only sending soldiers to Germany's frontier. Such a move, reasoned British officials, did not warrant risking a war. France viewed the remilitarization of the Rhineland as a grave threat. It deprived France of the one tangible advantage that it had obtained from the Treaty of Versailles: a buffer area. Now German forces could concentrate in strength on the French frontier, either to invade France or to discourage a French assault if Germany attacked Czechoslovakia or Poland, France's eastern allies. France lost the advantage of being able to retaliate by invading a demilitarized zone.

Three factors explain why France did not try to expel the twenty-two thousand German troops that occupied the zone. First, France would not act alone, and Britain could not be persuaded to use force. Second, the French general staff overestimated German military strength and thought only of defending French soil from a German attack, not of initiating a strike against Germany. Third, French public opinion showed no enthusiasm for a confrontation with Hitler.

The Spanish Civil War of 1936–1939 was another victory for Fascism. Nazi Germany and Fascist Italy aided Franco (see "Liberalism and Authoritarianism in Other Lands" in Chapter 29); the Soviet Union supplied the Spanish Republic. The republic appealed to France for help, but the French government feared that the civil war would expand into a European war. With Britain's approval, France proposed the Nonintervention Agreement. Italy, Germany, and the Soviet Union signed the agreement but continued to supply the warring parties. By October 1937, some sixty thousand Italian "volunteers" were fighting in Spain. Hitler sent between five thousand and six thousand men and hundreds of planes, which proved decisive.

◀ *Map 31.1* GERMAN AND ITALIAN AGGRESSIONS, **1935–1939** German aggression from 1936 to 1939 included the militarization of the Rhineland (1936), Anschluss with Austria (1938), and the dismemberment of Czechoslovakia (1938–1939).

By comparison, the Soviet Union's aid was meager. Viewing the conflict as a struggle between democracy and Fascism, thousands of Europeans and Americans volunteered to fight for the republic.

Without considerable help from France, the Spanish Republic was doomed, but Prime Minister Léon Blum continued to support nonintervention. He feared that French intervention would cause Germany and Italy to escalate their involvement, bringing Europe to the edge of a general war. Moreover, supplying the republic would have dangerous consequences at home because French rightists were sympathetic to Franco's conservative-clerical authoritarianism. In 1939, the republic fell, and Franco established a dictatorship, imprisoning or banishing to labor camps more than 1 million Spaniards and executing another 200,000.

The Spanish Civil War provided Germany with an opportunity to test weapons and pilots. It also demonstrated that France and Britain lacked the determination to fight Fascism, and it drew Mussolini and Hitler closer together. In October 1936, Mussolini sent his foreign minister to meet with Hitler in Berlin. The discussions bore fruit, and on November 1 Mussolini proclaimed that a Rome–Berlin "Axis" had been created.

One of Hitler's aims was the incorporation of Austria into the Third Reich. The Treaty of Versailles expressly prohibited the union of the two countries, but in *Mein Kampf* Hitler insisted that an Anschluss was necessary for German Lebensraum. In February 1938, under intense pressure from Hitler, Austrian chancellor Kurt von Schuschnigg promised to accept Austrian Nazis in his cabinet and agreed to closer relations with Germany. Austrian independence was slipping away, and increasingly, Austrian Nazis undermined Schuschnigg's authority. Seeking to gain his people's support, Schuschnigg made plans for a plebiscite on the issue of preserving Austrian independence. An enraged Hitler ordered his generals to draw up plans for an invasion of Austria. Hitler then demanded Schuschnigg's resignation and the formation of a new government headed by Arthur Seyss-Inquart, an Austrian Nazi.

Believing that Austria was not worth a war, Britain and France informed the embattled chancellor that they would not help in the event of a German invasion. Schuschnigg then resigned, and Austrian Nazis began to take control of the

THE FALL OF FRANCE. French civilians of Marseilles show the shock of defeat in 1940. Hitler's army accomplished what the German generals of World War I had planned but not brought about: the defeat of France. The might of motorized warfare had prevailed over the French army and its outmoded World War I methods. (© Bettmann/Corbis.)

government. Under the pretext of preventing violence, Hitler ordered his troops to cross into Austria, and on March 13, 1938, Austrian leaders declared that Austria was a province of the German Reich.

Many Austrians welcomed the Anschluss, including the archbishop of Vienna, who ordered all churches in the capital to display the Nazi flag and to ring their bells in honor of Hitler's arrival in the city. The idea of a Greater Germany appealed to their Pan-German sentiments, and they hoped that Hitler's magic would produce economic recovery. Moreover, depriving Jews of their rights, property, and occupations had widespread appeal among traditionally anti-Semitic Austrians. The Viennese celebrated by ringing church bells,

waving swastika banners, and spontaneously beating, robbing, and humiliating Jews, including tearing Torah scrolls, shearing the beards of rabbis, and forcing whole families to scrub sidewalks. The Austrians' euphoria over the Anschluss and their sadistic treatment of helpless Jews astonished many observers, including the German occupiers.

Czechoslovakia: The Apex of Appeasement

Hitler obtained Austria merely by threatening to use force. Another threat would give him the Sudetenland of Czechoslovakia. Ethnic Germans, numbering some 3.25 million, predominated in the Sudetenland. The region contained key industries and strong fortifications; since it bordered Germany, it was also vital to Czech security. Deprived of the Sudetenland, Czechoslovakia could not defend itself against a German attack. Encouraged and instructed by Germany, the Sudeten Germans, led by Konrad Henlein, shrilly denounced the Czech government for "persecuting" its German minority and depriving Sudeten Germans of their right to self-determination. The Sudeten Germans agitated for local autonomy and the right to profess the National Socialist ideology. Behind this demand was the goal of German annexation of the Sudetenland and the destruction of Czechoslovakia.

While negotiations between the Sudeten Germans and the Czech government proceeded, Hitler ordered his generals to prepare for an invasion of Czechoslovakia. Fighting between Czechs and Sudeten Germans heightened the tensions. Seeking to preserve peace, Prime Minister Neville Chamberlain (1869–1940) of Britain offered to confer with Hitler, who then extended an invitation.

Britain and France held somewhat different positions toward Czechoslovakia, the only democracy in Eastern Europe. In 1924, France and Czechoslovakia had concluded an agreement of mutual assistance in the event that either was attacked by Germany. Czechoslovakia had a similar agreement with Russia, but with the provision that Russian assistance depended on France's first fulfilling the terms of its agreement. Britain had no commitment to Czechoslovakia. Some British officials, swallowing Hitler's propaganda, believed that the Sudeten Germans were indeed a suppressed minority entitled to self-determination. They also thought that the Sudetenland, like Austria, was not worth a war that could destroy Western civilization. Hitler, they said, only wanted to incorporate Germans living outside of Germany; he was only carrying the principle of self-determination to its logical conclusion. Once these Germans lived under the German flag, Hitler would be satisfied. In any case, Britain's failure to rearm adequately between 1933 and 1938 weakened its position. The British chiefs of staff believed that the nation was not prepared to fight and that it was necessary to sacrifice Czechoslovakia to buy time.

Czechoslovakia's fate was decided at the Munich Conference in September 1938, attended by Chamberlain, Hitler, Mussolini, and Prime Minister Édouard Daladier (1884–1970) of France. The Munich Agreement called for the immediate evacuation of Czech troops from the Sudetenland and its occupation by German forces. Britain and France then promised to guarantee the territorial integrity of the truncated Czechoslovakia. Both Chamberlain and Daladier were praised by adoring crowds in their respective countries for keeping the peace. Hitler considered these Western leaders "little worms."

Critics of Chamberlain have insisted that the Munich Agreement was a tragic blunder. Chamberlain, they say, was a fool to believe that Hitler could be bought off with the Sudetenland. Hitler regarded concessions by Britain and France as signs of weakness; they only increased his appetite for more territory. Second, argue the critics, it would have been better to fight Hitler in 1938 than a year later, when war actually did break out. In the year following the Munich Agreement, Britain increased its military arsenal, but so did Germany, which strengthened western border defenses; built submarines, heavy tanks, and planes; and trained more pilots.

Had Britain and France resisted Hitler at Munich, it is likely that the führer would have attacked Czechoslovakia. But the Czech border defenses, built on the model of the French Maginot Line, were formidable. The Czechs had a sizable number of good tanks, and the Czech people were willing to fight to preserve their nation's territorial integrity. By itself, the Czech army could not have defeated Germany. But while the main elements of the German army were battling the Czechs, the French, who could mobilize a hundred divisions, could have broken through the German West Wall, which was defended by only five regular and four reserve divisions; then they could have invaded the Rhineland and devastated German industrial centers in the Ruhr. (Such a scenario, of course, depended on the French overcoming their psychological reluctance to take the offensive, which was doubtful given the attitude of the French general staff.) And there was the possibility, although probably a slim one given Stalin's reluctance to risk a war with Germany, that the Soviet Union would have fulfilled its agreement and come to Czechoslovakia's aid.

After the annexation of the Sudetenland, Hitler plotted to extinguish Czechoslovakia's

Chronology 31.1 ❖ World War II

September 27, 1939	Poland surrenders
November 1939	Russia invades Finland
April 1940	Germany attacks Denmark and Norway
May 10, 1940	Germany invades Belgium, Holland, and Luxembourg
May 27–June 4, 1940	British and French troops are evacuated from Dunkirk
June 22, 1940	France surrenders
August–September 1940	Battle of Britain
September 1940	Japan begins conquest of Southeast Asia
October 1940	Italian troops cross into Greece
April 6, 1941	Germany attacks Greece and Yugoslavia
June 22, 1941	Germany launches offensive against Russia
December 7, 1941	Japan attacks Pearl Harbor: on December 11 Germany declares war on the United States
1942	Tide of battle turns in the Allies' favor: Midway (Pacific Ocean), Stalingrad (Soviet Union), and El Alamein (North Africa)
April–May 1943	Uprising of Jews in Warsaw ghetto
September 1943	Italy surrenders to Allies, following invasion
June 6, 1944	D-day: Allies land in Normandy
August 1944	Paris is liberated; Poles rise up against German occupiers
January 1945	Soviet troops invade Germany
March–April 1945	Allies penetrate Germany
May 7, 1945	Germany surrenders unconditionally
August 1945	United States drops atomic bombs on Hiroshima and Nagasaki; Soviet Union invades Manchuria; Japan surrenders

existence. He encouraged the Slovak minority in Czechoslovakia, led by a Fascist priest, Josef Tiso, to demand complete separation. On the pretext of protecting the Slovak people's right of self-determination, Hitler ordered his troops to enter Prague. In March 1939, Czech independence came to an end.

The destruction of Czechoslovakia was of a different character than the remilitarization of the Rhineland, the Anschluss with Austria, and the annexation of the Sudetenland. In all these previous cases, Hitler could claim the right of German self-determination, Woodrow Wilson's grand principle. The occupation of Prague and the end of Czech independence, though, showed that Hitler really sought European hegemony. Outraged statesmen demanded that the führer be deterred from further aggression.

Poland: The Final Crisis

After Czechoslovakia, Hitler turned to Poland, demanding that the free city of Danzig be returned to Germany and that railways and roads, over which Germans would enjoy extraterritorial rights, be built across the Polish Corridor, linking East Prussia with the rest of Germany. Poland refused to restore the port of Danzig, which was vital to its economy. The Poles would allow a German highway through the Polish Corridor but would not permit Germany extraterritorial rights. France informed the German government that it would fulfill its treaty obligations to aid Poland. Chamberlain also warned that Britain would assist Poland.

On May 22, 1939, Hitler and Mussolini entered into the Pact of Steel, promising mutual aid in the event of war. The following day, Hitler told his officers that Germany's real goal was the destruction of Poland. "Danzig is not the objective. It is a matter of expanding our living space in the east, of making our food supplies secure. . . . There is therefore no question of sparing Poland, and the decision remains to attack Poland at the first suitable opportunity."[3] In the middle of June, the army presented Hitler with battle plans for an invasion of Poland.

Britain, France, and the Soviet Union had been engaged in negotiations since April. The Soviet Union wanted a mutual-assistance pact, including joint military planning, and demanded bases in Poland and Romania in preparation for a German attack. Britain was reluctant to endorse these demands, fearing that a mutual-assistance pact with Russia might cause Hitler to embark on a mad adventure that would drag Britain into war. Moreover, Poland would not allow Russian troops on its soil, fearing Russian expansion.

At the same time, Russia was conducting secret talks with Nazi Germany. Unlike the Allies, Hitler could tempt Stalin with territory that would serve as a buffer between Germany and Russia. Moreover, a treaty with Germany would give Russia time to strengthen its armed forces. On August 23, 1939, the two totalitarian states signed a nonaggression pact, which stunned the world. A secret section of the pact called for the partition of Poland between the two parties and Russian control over Latvia and Estonia (later the agreement was amended to include Lithuania). By signing such an agreement with his enemy, Hitler had pulled off an extraordinary diplomatic coup: he blocked the Soviet Union, Britain, and France from duplicating their World War I alliance against Germany. The Nazi–Soviet Pact

was the green light for an invasion of Poland, and at dawn on September 1, 1939, German troops crossed the frontier. Two days later, when Germany did not respond to their demand for a halt to the invasion, Britain and France declared war on Germany.

THE NAZI BLITZKRIEG

Germany struck at Poland with speed and power, implementing tactical concepts of a mobile armored offensive worked out by German military planners between the wars. The German air force, the Luftwaffe, destroyed obsolete Polish planes, struck railways to hamper Polish mobilization, attacked tanks, pounded defense networks, and bombed Warsaw, terrorizing the population. Racing across the flat Polish terrain, panzers (tanks) opened breaches in the Polish defenses, and mechanized columns overran the foot-marching Polish army, trapping large numbers of soldiers. The Polish High Command could not cope with the incredible speed and coordination of German air and panzer attacks. By September 8, the rapidly moving Germans advanced to the outskirts of Warsaw which was mercilessly bombed. On September 17, Soviet troops invaded Poland from the east. On September 27, Poland surrendered. In less than a month, the Nazi **blitzkrieg** (lightning war) had vanquished Poland.

The Fall of France

For Hitler, the conquest of Poland was only the prelude to a German empire stretching from the Atlantic to the Urals. When weather conditions were right, he would unleash a great offensive in the west. Meanwhile, the six-month period following the defeat of Poland was nicknamed the "phony war," for the fighting on land consisted only of a few skirmishes on the French–German border. Then, in early April 1940, the Germans struck at Denmark and Norway. Hitler wanted to establish naval bases on the Norwegian coast from which to wage submarine warfare against Britain and to ensure delivery of Swedish iron ore to Germany through Norwegian territorial waters.

Denmark surrendered within hours. A British–French force tried to assist the Norwegians, but the landings, badly coordinated and lacking in air support, failed. The Germans won the battle of Norway. But the Norwegian campaign produced two positive results for the Allies: Norwegian merchant ships escaped to Britain to be put into service; and Winston Churchill (1874–1965), who had opposed appeasement, replaced Chamberlain as British prime minister. (The German victory in Norway eroded Chamberlain's support in the House of Commons, and he was forced to give up the helm.) Dynamic, courageous, and eloquent, Churchill had the capacity to stir and lead his people in the struggle against Nazism.

On May 10, 1940, Hitler launched his offensive in the west with an invasion of neutral Belgium, Holland, and Luxembourg. While armored forces penetrated Dutch frontier defenses, airborne units seized strategic airfields and bridges. On May 14, after the Luftwaffe had bombed Rotterdam, destroying the center of the city and killing many people, the Dutch surrendered.

A daring attack by glider-borne troops gave Germany possession of two crucial Belgian bridges, opening the plains of Belgium to German panzer (tank) divisions. Believing that this was the main German attack, French troops rushed to Belgium to prevent a German breakthrough, but the greater menace lay to the south, on the French frontier. Meeting almost no resistance, German panzer divisions had moved through the narrow mountain passes of Luxembourg and the dense Forest of Ardennes in southern Belgium. On May 12, German units were on French soil near Sedan. Thinking that the Forest of Ardennes could not be penetrated by a major German force, the French had only lightly fortified the western extension of the Maginot Line. The failure to counterattack swiftly was a second mistake. The best elements of the Anglo-French forces were in Belgium, but the Germans were racing across northern France to the sea, which they reached on May 20, cutting the Anglo-French forces in two.

The Germans now sought to surround and annihilate the Allied forces converging on the French seaport of Dunkirk, the last port of escape. But probably fearing that German tanks would lose mobility in the rivers and canals around Dunkirk, Hitler called them off just as the troops prepared to take the port. Instead, he ordered the Luftwaffe to finish off the Allied troops, but fog and rain prevented German planes from operating at full strength, and British pilots inflicted heavy losses on the attackers. The Allies took advantage of this breathing space to tighten their defenses and prepare for a massive evacuation. While the Luftwaffe bombed the beaches, some 338,000 British and French troops were ferried across the English Channel by destroyers, merchant ships, motorboats, fishing boats, tugboats, and private yachts. Abandoning their equipment on the beaches, the British saved their armies to fight another day. Hitler's decision to hold back his tanks made the "miracle of Dunkirk" possible.

Meanwhile, the battle for France was turning into an even worse disaster for the French. Whole divisions were cut off or in retreat, and millions of refugees in cars and carts and on motorcycles and bicycles fled south to escape the advancing Germans. On June 10, Mussolini also declared war on France. With authority breaking down and resistance dying, the French cabinet appealed for an armistice, which was signed on June 22 in the same railway car in which Germany had agreed to the armistice ending World War I.

How can the collapse of France be explained? France had somewhat fewer pilots and planes, particularly bombers, than Germany, but many French planes never left the airfields. France had planes, but the High Command either did not use them or did not deploy them properly. In contrast, the German air force was an integral part of an offensive operation, providing support for advancing tanks and infantry and bombing behind enemy lines. As for tanks, the French had as many as the Germans, and some were superior, but they were spread among the infantry divisions, unlike the Germans who concentrated their tanks in large formations in order to drive through enemy lines. Nor was German manpower overwhelming. France met disaster largely because its military leaders, unlike the Germans, had not mastered the psychology and technology of motorized warfare. French generals had planned for a long war of attrition, a repeat of World War I; they could not cope with the German blitzkrieg.

Map 31.2 WORLD WAR II: THE EUROPEAN ▶ THEATER By 1942, Germany ruled virtually all of Europe from the Atlantic to deep into Russia. Germany's defeat at Stalingrad in Russia and El Alamein in North Africa were decisive turning points. (© 2016 Cengage Learning.)

Legend:

- Hitler's Greater Germany
- Allied with Germany
- Occupied by Germany and its allies
- Advances by Allied forces
- Major battle

SOVIET UNION

Caspian Sea

Volga R.

Stalingrad

Russian Front, Dec. 1941

Russian Front, Nov. 1942

SYRIA

TRANS-JORDAN (Br. Mandate)

TURKEY

• Moscow

• Tula

Dnieper

Ankara •

LEBANON

PALESTINE (Br. Mandate)

Suez Canal

Cairo •

Smolensk •

Russian Front, Spring 1944

Kiev •

UKRAINE

Black Sea

Yalta •

Cyprus

Alexandria •

Nile R.

El Alamein (Summer 1942)

EGYPT

L. Ladoga

Leningrad

FINLAND

Helsinki •

• Pinsk

Russian Front, Feb. 1945

Warsaw •

Posen •

POLAND

Krakow •

Bucharest •

ROMANIA

Sofia •

BULGARIA

HUNGARY

Budapest •

Athens •

GREECE

Crete

Mediterranean Sea

Stockholm •

Baltic Sea

Riga •

SWEDEN

SLOVAKIA

CZECHOSLOVAKIA

Vienna •

AUSTRIA

YUGOSLAVIA

ALBANIA

Monte Cassino (May 1944)

Italian Front, Feb. 1945

ITALY

Rome •

Anzio •

Salerno (Sept. 1943)

Sicily (July 1943)

Malta

LIBYA

NORWAY

Oslo •

DENMARK

Copenhagen •

Berlin •

Elbe R.

GERMANY

SWITZERLAND

Bologna •

Rommel defeated in Tunisia (May 1943)

Tunis •

TUNISIA

North Sea

GREAT BRITAIN

Battle of Britain (Fall 1940)

London •

Dunkirk •

NETHERLANDS

Antwerp •

Rotterdam •

BELGIUM

Bastogne •

Sedan •

Rhine R.

Battle of the Bulge (Dec. 1944)

Western Front, Feb. 1945

FRANCE

Vichy •

VICHY FRANCE (Occupied Nov. 1942)

NORTHERN IRELAND

IRELAND

English Channel

Invasion of Normandy (June 6, 1944)

Paris •

NORMANDY

ATLANTIC OCEAN

Madrid •

SPAIN

PORTUGAL

Lisbon •

Gibraltar (Gr. Br.)

SP. MOROCCO

Algiers •

ALGERIA (Vichy France)

Casablanca (Nov. 1942)

FRENCH MOROCCO

0 200 400 Km.

0 200 400 Mi.

801

"The French commanders, trained in the slow-motion methods of 1914 to 1918, were mentally unfitted to cope with Panzer pace, and it produced a spreading paralysis among them," says the British military expert Sir Basil H. Liddell Hart.[4] Put succinctly, the French were badly outgeneraled. One also senses a loss of will among the French people, a consequence of internal political disputes dividing the nation, poor leadership, the years of appeasement and lost opportunities, and German propaganda, which depicted Nazism as irresistible and the führer as a man of destiny. It was France's darkest hour.

According to the terms of the armistice, Germany occupied northern France and the coast, some 60 percent of the country. The French military was demobilized, and the French government, now located at Vichy, in the south, and headed by Marshal Henri Philippe Pétain, the hero of World War I, would collaborate with the German authorities in occupied France, even to the point of passing racial laws and deporting Jews, including two thousand orphans under the age of six, to Nazi murder factories. The leaders of Vichy and their supporters, many of them prominent intellectuals and anti-Dreyfusards in their youth, shared in the antidemocratic, anti-Marxist, and anti-Semitic tradition of those conservatives who had arrayed themselves against the Third French Republic since the late nineteenth century. Refusing to recognize defeat, General Charles de Gaulle (1890–1970) escaped to London and organized the Free French forces. The Germans gloried in their revenge, and the French wept in their humiliation. The British gathered their courage, for they now stood alone.

The Battle of Britain

Hitler expected that, after his stunning victories in the west, Britain would make peace. The British, however, continued to reject Hitler's peace overtures, for they envisioned only a bleak future if Hitler dominated the Continent. "The Battle of Britain is about to begin," Churchill told his people. "Upon this battle depends the survival of Christian civilization. . . . If we fail, then . . . all we have known and cared for will sink into the abyss of a new Dark Age."[5]

With Britain unwilling to come to terms, Hitler proceeded in earnest with invasion plans.

A successful crossing of the English Channel and the establishment of beachheads on the English coast depended on control of the skies. Marshal Hermann Göring assured Hitler that his Luftwaffe could destroy the British Royal Air Force (RAF), and in early August 1940, the Luftwaffe began massive attacks on British air and naval installations. Virtually every day during the "Battle of Britain," weather permitting, hundreds of planes fought in the sky above Britain. "Never in the field of human conflict was so much owed by so many to so few," said Churchill of the British pilots, who rose to the challenge. On September 15, hundreds of German planes made an all-out effort to destroy the British air force. The RAF, with virtually every available fighter plane seeing action, shot down sixty aircraft, convincing Hitler that Göring could not fulfill his promise to destroy British air defenses, and on September 17 the führer postponed the invasion of Britain "until further notice." The development of radar by British scientists, the skill and courage of British fighter pilots, the unwillingness of Germany to absorb more losses in planes and trained pilots, and the ability of British industry to replenish losses saved Britain in its struggle for survival. After a succession of spectacular victories, Nazi Germany had suffered its first defeat.

With the invasion of Britain called off, the Luftwaffe concentrated on bombing English cities, industrial centers, and ports in the hopes of eroding Britain's military potential and undermining civilian morale. Every night for months, the inhabitants of London sought shelter in subways and cellars to escape German bombs while British planes rose time after time to make the Luftwaffe pay the price. British morale never broke during the "Blitz."

Britain, by itself, had no hope of defeating the Third Reich. What ultimately changed the course of the war were Germany's invasion of the Soviet Union on June 22, 1941 and Japan's attack on the United States on December 7, 1941. With the entry of these two powers, a coalition was created that had the human and material resources to reverse the tide of battle.

The Invasion of Russia

Hitler conceived a conflict with the Soviet Union as an ideological-racial war of annihilation. The Germans would destroy the Soviet system that

GERMAN ATROCITIES. The invading Germans treated the Russian people, whom they regarded as racial inferiors, in a savage manner. They deliberately starved to death Russian prisoners of war and engaged in atrocities against civilians. Here Russians are looking for relatives and friends among seven thousand Crimean villagers slaughtered by the Germans. (© Dmitri Baltermants/The Dmitri Baltermants Collection/Corbis.)

threatened the very life of the fatherland, take control of and settle the fertile Russian plains with Germans, and exploit, enslave, or exterminate racial enemies. German expansion in the East could not wait for the final defeat of Britain. In July 1940, Hitler instructed his generals to formulate plans for an invasion of Russia. On December 18, Hitler set May 15, 1941, for the beginning of Operation Barbarossa, the code name assigned for the blitzkrieg against the Soviet Union. But problems of training and equipping the vast force and events in the Balkans, however, forced Hitler to postpone the date to the latter part of June.

Seeking to make Italy a Mediterranean power and to win glory for himself, Mussolini had ordered an invasion of Greece. In late October 1940, Italian troops stationed in Albania—which

Italy had occupied in 1939—crossed into Greece. The poorly planned operation was an instant failure; within a week, the counterattacking Greeks advanced into Albania. Hitler feared that Britain, which was encouraging and aiding the Greeks, would use Greece to attack the oil fields of Romania, which were vital to the German war effort, and to interfere with the forthcoming invasion of Russia. Another problem emerged when a military coup overthrew the government of Prince Paul in Yugoslavia, which two days earlier had signed a pact with Germany and Italy. Hitler feared that the new Yugoslav government might gravitate toward Britain. To prevent any interference with Operation Barbarossa, the Balkan flank had to be secured. On April 6, 1941, the Germans struck at both Greece and Yugoslavia. Yugoslavia was quickly overrun, and Greece, though aided by fifty thousand British, New Zealander, and Australian troops, fell at the end of April.

For the war against Russia, Hitler assembled a massive force: some 4 million men, 3,300 tanks, and 2,000 planes. Evidence of the German buildup abounded, but a stubborn Stalin ignored these warnings. Desperate to avoid war with Nazi Germany, Stalin would take no action that he feared might provoke Hitler. Consequently, the Red Army was vulnerable to the German blitzkrieg. In the early hours of June 22, 1941, the Germans launched their offensive over a wide front. Raiding Russian airfields, the Luftwaffe destroyed twelve hundred aircraft on the first day, most of them on the ground, a clear example of Stalin's failure to heed warnings provided by an effective Soviet spy network. The Germans drove deeply into Russia, cutting up and surrounding the disorganized and unprepared Russian forces. Contributing to the rout was the poor quality of Russian commanders, a consequence of Stalin's purge of Red Army officers, many of them trained and competent professionals, a few years earlier.

The Russians suffered terrible losses. In a little more than three months, 2.5 million Russian soldiers were killed, wounded, or captured, and 14,000 tanks destroyed. Amid the chaotic retreat, soldiers were deserting by the thousands. Describing the war as a crusade to save Europe from "Jewish-Bolshevik subhumans," German propaganda claimed that victory was assured.

But there were also disquieting signs for the Nazi invaders. The Russians, who had a proven capacity to endure hardships, fought doggedly and courageously for the motherland in what Soviet propaganda stressed was a great "patriotic war," and the government would not consider capitulation. At first, many Russians, particularly in Ukraine, welcomed the German invaders, who they hoped would liberate them from Stalin's tyranny. But German ruthlessness against the local population, whom Nazi ideology marked for exploitation and servitude, strengthened the resolve of the Russian people. The knowledge that Russian prisoners of war were dying in huge numbers, victims of beatings and deliberate starvation, fueled a deep hatred for the German invaders. Moreover, soldiers who deserted, retreated without specific orders, or displayed a

defeatist attitude faced execution or assignment to penal battalions sent on suicide missions behind German lines. Russian reserve strength was far greater than the Germans had estimated. Increasing the Red Army's strength was the drafting of hundreds of thousands of prisoners from labor camps and the recruitment of hundreds of thousands of women, who saw action as artillery and anti-aircraft gunners, fighter pilots, tank personnel, and snipers.

And in an extraordinary feat of organization, within five months the Soviets dismantled 1,523 industrial facilities along with a huge number of workers and moved them east beyond the Ural Mountains and far beyond the reach of the Luftwaffe. Employing modern production methods, acquired in large measure from American technical assistance provided before the war, by early 1942 the Soviets were producing three times as many combat planes and four times as many tanks as the Germans.

The Wehrmacht (German army), far from its supply lines, ran short of fuel, vehicles, and spare parts and had to contend with primitive roads that turned into seas of mud when the autumn rains came. One German general described the ordeal: "The infantryman slithers in the mud, while many teams of horses are needed to drag each gun forward. All wheeled vehicles sink up to their axles in the slime. Even tractors can only move with great difficulty. A large portion of our heavy artillery was soon stuck fast. . . . The strain that all this caused our already exhausted troops can perhaps be imagined."[6] Compounding the supply problem were attacks behind German lines by Russian partisans determined to inflict pain on the hated invaders. Conditions no longer favored the blitzkrieg.

Early and bitter subzero weather hampered the German attempt to capture Moscow. Without warm uniforms, tens of thousands of Germans suffered from frostbite; without antifreeze, guns did not fire. The Germans advanced to within twenty miles of Moscow, but on December 6 a Red Army counterattack forced them to postpone the assault on the Russian capital. The Germans were also denied Leningrad, which since September had been almost completely surrounded and under constant bombardment. During this epic siege, which lasted for two and a half years, the citizens of Leningrad displayed extraordinary courage in the face of famine, disease, and shelling that cost nearly 1 million lives, more than the combined losses of Britain and the United States for the entire war.

By the end of 1941, Germany had conquered vast regions of Russia but had failed to bring the country to its knees. There would be no repetition of the collapse of France. Moreover, by moving machinery and workers east far beyond the German reach, the Soviets were able to replenish their military hardware, which was almost totally destroyed during the first six months of the war. Driven by patriotic fervor—and by fear of the omnipresent NKVD (The People's Commissariat for Internal Affairs) agents searching for malingerers—Russian factory workers, many of them the wives and daughters of soldiers, toiled relentlessly and heroically. Soon they were producing more planes and tanks than Germany. The Russian campaign demonstrated that the Russian people would make incredible sacrifices for their land and that the Nazis were not invincible.

THE NEW ORDER

By 1942, Germany ruled virtually all of Europe, from the Atlantic to deep into Russia. Some conquered territory was annexed outright; other lands were administered by German officials; in still other countries, the Germans ruled through local officials sympathetic to Nazism or willing to collaborate with the Germans. On this vast empire, Hitler and his henchmen, who regarded the war as a racial struggle, imposed a New Order designed to serve the interests of the "master race."

Exploitation and Terror

"The real profiteers of this war are ourselves, and out of it we shall come bursting with fat," said Hitler. "We will give back nothing and will take everything we can make use of."[7] The Germans systematically looted the countries they conquered, taking gold, art treasures, machinery, and food supplies back to Germany and exploiting the industrial and agricultural potential of non-German lands to aid the German war economy. Some foreign businesses and factories were confiscated by the German Reich; others produced

what the Germans demanded. Germany also requisitioned food from the conquered regions, significantly reducing the quantity available for local civilian consumption. German soldiers were fed with food harvested in occupied France and Russia; they fought with weapons produced in Czech factories. German tanks ran on oil delivered by Romania, Germany's satellite. The Nazis also made slave laborers of conquered peoples. Some 7 million people from all over Europe were wrested from their homes and transported to Germany. These forced laborers, particularly the Russians and Poles, whom Nazi ideology classified as a lower form of humanity, lived in wretched, unheated barracks and were poorly fed and overworked; many died of disease, hunger, and exhaustion. Many of Germany's most prominent firms collaborated in the enslavement of foreign workers. The ransacking of occupied lands, the expropriation of Jewish property throughout Europe, and the exploitation of foreign laborers kept Germans largely prosperous and content until the last year of the war.

The Nazis ruled by force and terror. The prison cell, the torture chamber, the firing squad, and the concentration camp symbolized the New Order. In the Polish province annexed to Germany, the Nazis jailed and executed intellectuals and priests, closed all schools and most churches, and forbade Poles from holding professional positions. In the region of Poland administered by German officials, most schools above the fourth grade were shut down. Himmler insisted that it was sufficient for Polish children to learn "simple arithmetic up to five hundred at the most; writing of one's name; a doctrine that it is a divine law to obey the Germans and to be honest, industrious, and good."[8] The Germans were particularly ruthless toward the Russians. Soviet political officials were immediately executed; many prisoners of war were herded into camps and deliberately starved to death. In all, the Germans took prisoner some 5.5 million Russians, of whom more than 3.5 million perished, primarily from starvation. These prisoners of war were supervised not by the notorious SS, who ran the extermination camps, but by the regular army, the Wehrmacht, whose officers made deliberate decisions to starve Russian prisoners, a notorious criminal act committed by a professional army.

German soldiers routinely abused innocents: they stripped Russian peasants of their winter clothing and boots before driving them into the freezing outdoors to die of cold and starvation, slaughtered large numbers of hostages, burned whole villages to the ground in reprisal for partisan attacks, and deported massive numbers of people for slave labor. To the German invaders, drenched in Nazi ideology, the Russians were "Asiatic bestial hordes" led by sinister "subhuman" Jews who aimed to destroy Germany. Recent studies, largely by German historians, dispel the myth that the Wehrmacht, which represented a cross-section of German society, had "clean hands," that the Nazi leadership and the SS were solely responsible for the criminal deeds committed by German forces. These studies reveal how committed many Wehrmacht officers were to Nazi ideological aims, how willing they were to propagate Nazi ideology among the troops, how ideologically devoted many rank-and-file soldiers were to Nazism, and how implicated both officers and ordinary soldiers were in war crimes, including the extermination of the Jews.

The Holocaust

Against the Jews of Europe, the Germans waged a war of extermination. The task of imposing the "Final Solution of the Jewish Problem" was given to Himmler's SS, and they fulfilled these grisly duties with fanaticism and bureaucratic efficiency. In exterminating the Jewish people, the Nazis believed they were righteous and courageous and serving a higher good—the defense of the sacred Volk.

Regarding themselves as idealists who were writing a glorious chapter in the history of Germany, the SS tortured and murdered with immense dedication. The minds of the SS were dominated by the mythical worldview of Nazism, as the following tract issued by SS headquarters reveals.

Just as night rises up against the day, just as light and darkness are eternal enemies, so the greatest enemy of world-dominating man is man himself. The sub-man—that creature which looks as though biologically it were of absolutely the same kind, endowed by Nature

with hands, feet and a sort of brain, with eyes and mouth—is nevertheless a totally different, a fearful creature, is only an attempt at a human being, with a quasi-human face, yet in mind and spirit lower than any animal. Inside this being a cruel chaos of wild, unchecked passions: a nameless will to destruction, the most primitive lusts, the most undisguised vileness. A sub-man—nothing else! . . . Never has the sub-man granted peace, never has he permitted rest. . . . To preserve himself he needed mud, he needed hell, but not the sun. And this underworld of sub-men found its leader: the eternal Jew![9]

Special squads of SS—the *Einsatzgruppen*, trained for mass murder—followed on the heels of the German army into Russia. Entering captured villages and cities, they rounded up Jewish men, women, and children; herded them to execution grounds; and slaughtered them with machine-gun and rifle fire at the edge of open trenches, which sometimes were piled high with thousands of victims, including severely wounded people, who would suffocate to death when the pit was filled with earth. Aided by Ukrainian, Lithuanian, and Latvian auxiliaries, along with contingents from the Romanian army, the Einsatzgruppen massacred some 1.3 million Jews; the commanders kept meticulous records of each *Aktion*. Units of the Wehrmacht actively participated in the rounding up of Jews and sometimes in the shootings. Despite the denials of staff officers after the war, evidence from their own files reveals that they knew fully well that the extermination of the Jews was state policy that units of the Wehrmacht were helping to implement.

In Poland, where some 3.3 million Jews lived, the Germans established ghettos in the larger cities. Jews from all over the country were crammed into these ghettos, which were sealed off from the rest of the population. The German administration deliberately curtailed the food supply, and many Jews died of malnutrition, disease, and beatings. In the ghettos, the Polish Jews struggled to maintain community life and to preserve their spirit. They established schools (forbidden by the German authorities), prayed together (also forbidden), organized social services, and kept hidden archives so that future ages would have a historical record of their ordeal.

The mass killings by gunfire posed problems for the Germans. These murders were too public, whereas the Germans wanted to keep the Final Solution as secret as possible. Furthermore, the face-to-face killing of civilians, including women and children, could be too hard on the psyche of the personnel charged with carrying out such orders, although it often wasn't. To overcome these problems, the Germans transformed concentration camps, originally established for political prisoners, into killing centers, and they also built new ones for this purpose.* Jews from all over Europe were rounded up—for "resettlement," they were told. The victims dismissed rumors that the Germans were engaged in genocide. They simply could not believe that any nation in the twentieth century was capable of such evil.

Jammed into sealed cattle cars, eighty or ninety to a car, the victims traveled sometimes for days, without food or water, choking from the stench of vomit and excrement and shattered by the crying of children. Disgorged at the concentration camps, they entered another planet.

> *Corpses were strewn all over the road; bodies were hanging from the barbed-wire fence; the sound of shots rang in the air continuously. Blazing flames shot into the sky; a giant smoke cloud ascended about them. Starving, emaciated human skeletons stumbled forward toward us, uttering incoherent sounds. They fell down right in front of our eyes gasping out their last breath.*
>
> *Here and there a hand tried to reach up, but when this happened an SS man came right away and stepped on it. Those who were merely exhausted were simply thrown on the dead pile. . . . Every night a truck came by, and all of them, dead or not, were thrown on it and taken to the crematory.*[10]

SS doctors quickly inspected the new arrivals, "the freight," as they referred to them. Rudolf Höss, the commandant of Auschwitz—the most notorious of the murder factories—described the procedure.

> *The way we selected our victims was as follows. . . . Those who were fit to work were sent into the camp. Others were sent immediately to the extermination plants. Children of tender years were invariably exterminated since by reason of their youth they were unable to work. . . . We endeavored to fool the victims into thinking that they were to go through a delousing process. Of course, frequently they realized our true intentions, and we sometimes had riots and difficulties due to that fact. Very frequently women would hide their children under clothes, but of course when we found them we would send the children in to be exterminated.*[11]

The naked bodies, covered with blood and excrement and intertwined with one another, were piled high to the ceiling. To make way for the next group, a squad of Jewish prisoners emptied the gas chambers of the corpses and removed gold teeth, which, along with the victims' hair, eyeglasses, clothing, and jewelry, were carefully collected and shipped back to Germany for the war effort. Later, the bodies were burned in crematoriums specially constructed by I. A. Topf and Sons of Erfurt. The chimneys vomited black smoke, and the stench of burning flesh permeated the entire region. Jewish leaders in the United States and Britain, who got word of the killings, pleaded with the Allies to bomb the rail lines to Auschwitz and the gas chambers, but the Allies did nothing. The killing process went on relentlessly. Between 1.1 million and 1.5 million people died in Auschwitz—90 percent of them Jews. Non-Jewish victims included political prisoners and Soviet prisoners of war.

Auschwitz was more than a murder factory. It also provided the German industrial giant I. G. Farben, which operated a factory adjoining the extermination facilities, with slave laborers, both Jews and non-Jews. The working pace at the factory and the ill treatment by guards were so brutal, reported a physician and inmate, that "while working many prisoners suddenly stretched out flat, turned blue, gasped for breath, and died like beasts."[12]

---

*Some 2.5 million to 3 million Jews were gassed in Nazi death factories built in Poland—Chelmno, Treblinka, Sobibur, Belzec, Lublin, Majdanek, and Auschwitz-Birkenau, the largest.

Concentration Camp Survivors. Thousands of emaciated and diseased inmates of German concentration camps died in the weeks after liberation by the Allies. These camps will forever remain a monument to the capacity of human beings for inhumanity. (© Topham Picturepoint/The Image Works.)

Auschwitz also allowed the SS, the elite of the master race, to shape and harden themselves according to the National Socialist creed. The SS relished their absolute power over the inmates. A survivor recalls seeing SS men and women amuse themselves with pregnant inmates. The unfortunate women were "beaten with clubs and whips, torn by dogs, dragged by the hair, and kicked in the stomach with heavy German boots. Then, when they collapsed, they were thrown into the crematory—alive."[13] By systematically overworking, starving, beating, terrorizing, and humiliating the inmates, by making them live in filth and sleep sprawled all over one another in tiny cubicles, the SS deliberately sought to strip prisoners of all human dignity, to make them appear and behave as subhuman, and even to make them believe that they were subhuman, as the National Socialist ideology asserted. This daily brutalization and humiliation of Jewish inmates produced a psychological distance between the SS and their victims. No sympathy could be felt for people who were frequently depicted as less than human, as repulsive lice and vermin. Tormenting and murdering Jews also reinforced the SS's own sense of superiority and feelings of power.

Many concentration camp inmates went mad or committed suicide; some struggled desperately, defiantly, and heroically to maintain their humanity. When prisoners, exhausted, starved, diseased, and beaten, became unfit for work, which generally happened within a few

Profile

Hans and Sophie Scholl

In February 1943, Hans Scholl, age twenty-five, a medical student, and his twenty-two-year-old sister, Sophie Scholl, who was studying biology and philosophy, were executed by the Nazis for high treason. The Scholls belonged to the White Rose, a small group of idealistic students at the University of Munich who urged passive resistance to the National Socialist regime. The White Rose hoped that if more Germans were aware of the Nazi regime's inhumane character, they would withdraw their loyalty.

The Scholls had once been enthusiastic members of the Hitler Youth, but over the years they grew increasingly disillusioned with Nazism. Their outlook was shaped by their anti-Nazi father, by a commitment to the German humanist tradition best represented by Schiller and Goethe, and by Kurt Huber, a professor of philosophy and psychology at their university, who spoke to trusted students of a duty "to enlighten those Germans who are still unaware of the evil intentions of our government." Hans was also swayed by the persecution of Jews he had witnessed when he was in transport through Poland to the Russian front.

On walls in Munich, the Scholls painted signs: "Down with Hitler" and "Freedom." Stowing their anti-Nazi leaflets in luggage, the students traveled by railroad to several German cities to drop them off. The following excerpts come from three of the White Rose's four leaflets.

Who among us has any conception of the dimensions of shame that will befall us and
our children when one day the . . . most horrible of crimes—crimes that infinitely outdistance every human measure—reach the light of day? (First leaflet)

Our present "state" is the dictatorship of evil. . . . [I]t is your right—or rather, your moral duty—to eliminate this system. (Third leaflet)

We are trying to achieve a renewal from within of the severely wounded German spirit. This rebirth must be preceded, however, by the clear recognition of all the guilt with which the German people have burdened themselves, and by an uncompromising battle against Hitler. (Fourth leaflet)*

On February 18, 1943, Hans and Sophie were spotted dropping leaflets in the university by the building superintendent, who reported them to the Gestapo. On February 23, Hans, Sophie, and Christoph Probst, also a medical student, were executed. Several days before she died, Sophie stated: "What does my death matter if through us thousands of people will be stirred to action and awakened?" Hans's last words, "Long live freedom," echoed through the prison. Students at the University of Munich loudly proclaimed their approval when the Nazi rector of the university told them of the executions. Kurt Huber and other members of the group were executed on July 13, 1943.

---

*Inge Scholl, *Students Against Tyranny*, trans. Arthur R. Schultz (Middletown, Conn.: Wesleyan University Press, 1970), 36, 56, 73, 81–82.

months, they were sent to the gas chambers. Perhaps the vilest assault on human dignity ever conceived, Nazi extermination camps were the true legacy of National Socialism, and the SS, the true end product of National Socialist indoctrination and idealism.

The SS were often ideologues committed to racist doctrines, which, they believed, were supported by the laws of biology. According to these laws, Jews were unworthy of life. A Jewish physician-inmate at Auschwitz asked one of the Nazi doctors who selected Jews for the gas chamber how he could reconcile extermination with the Hippocratic oath he took to preserve life. The Nazi replied:

> Of course I am a doctor and I want to preserve life. And out of respect for human life I would remove a gangrenous appendix from a diseased body. The Jew is the gangrenous appendix in the body of mankind.[14]

The SS were true believers driven by a utopian vision of a new world order founded on a Social Darwinist fantasy of racial hierarchy. To realize this mythic vision of ultimate good, the Jews, whom Nazi ideology designated as less-than-human but also immensely evil, powerful, and dangerous enemies of humanity, had to be destroyed. The defense of Germany required their extermination. These SS saw themselves as a moral elite dedicated to serving the fatherland. Assisting the SS was an army of bureaucrats, transportation employees, town officials, local police, and others involved in deporting Jews to the death camps. Many of these Germans and collaborators in occupied lands were ordinary people doing their duty as they had been trained, following orders the best way they knew how. They were morally indifferent bureaucrats, concerned with techniques and effectiveness, and careerists and functionaries seeking to impress superiors with their ability to get the job done. These people quickly adjusted to the routine of mass murder. And many of these "ordinary people," sharing in the Nazi vision, were willing, if not dedicated, participants in genocide.

Thus, as Konnilyn G. Feig observes, the thousands of German railway workers "treated the Jewish cattle-car transports as a special business problem that they took pride in solving so well."[15] The German physicians who selected Jews for the gas chambers were concerned only with the technical problems and efficiency, and those doctors and scientists who performed unspeakable medical experiments on Jews viewed their subjects as laboratory animals, as the following correspondence between an I. G. Farben plant and the commandant of Auschwitz testifies.

> In contemplation of experiments of a new soporific drug we would appreciate your procuring for us a number of women. . . .

> We propose to pay not more than 170 marks a head. If agreeable, we will take possession of the women. We need approximately 150. . . . Received the order of 150 women. Despite their emaciated condition, they were found satisfactory. . . . The tests were made. All subjects died. We shall contact you on the subject of a new load.[16]

The German industrialists who worked Jewish slave laborers to death considered only cost-effectiveness in their operations. So, too, did the firms that built the gas chambers and the furnaces, whose durability and performance they guaranteed. An eyewitness reports that engineers from Topf and Sons experimented with different combinations of corpses, deciding that "the most economical and fuel-saving procedure would be to burn the bodies of a well-nourished man and an emaciated woman or vice versa together with that of a child, because, as the experiments had established, in this combination, once they had caught fire, the dead would continue to burn without any further coke being required."[17] Höss, the commandant of Auschwitz, who exemplified the bureaucratic mentality, noted that his gas chambers were more efficient than those used at Treblinka because they could accommodate far more people. The Germans were so concerned with efficiency and cost that—to conserve ammunition or gas and not slow down the pace from the time victims were ordered to undress until they were hurried into the chambers—toddlers were taken from their mothers and thrown live into burning pits or mass graves.

When the war ended, the SS murderers and those who had assisted them returned to families and jobs, resuming a normal life, free of remorse and untroubled by guilt. "The human ability to normalize the abnormal is frightening indeed," observes the sociologist Rainer C. Baum.[18] Mass murderers need not be psychopaths. It is a "disturbing psychological truth," notes Robert Jay Lifton, that "ordinary people can commit demonic acts."[19]

There have been many massacres during the course of world history. And the Nazis murdered many non-Jews in concentration camps and in reprisal for acts of resistance. What is unique about the **Holocaust**—the extermination of European Jewry—was the Nazis' determination to murder without exception every single Jew who came within their grasp, and the fanaticism, ingenuity, cruelty, and systematic way—industrialized mass murder—with which they pursued this goal. Despite the protests of the army, the SS murdered Jews whose labor was needed for the war effort, and when Germany's military position was desperate, the SS still diverted military personnel and railway cars to deport Jews to the death camps.

The Holocaust was the fulfillment of Nazi racial theories. Believing that they were cleansing Europe of worthless life and a dangerous race that threatened Germany, Nazi executioners performed their evil work with dedication, assembly-line precision, and moral indifference— a gruesome testament to human irrationality and wickedness. Using the technology and bureaucracy of a modern state, the Germans killed approximately 6 million Jews: *two-thirds* of the Jewish population of Europe. Some 1.5 million of the murdered were children; almost 90 percent of Jewish children in German-occupied lands perished. Tens of thousands of entire families were wiped out without a trace. Centuries-old Jewish community life vanished, never to be restored. Burned into the soul of the Jewish people was a wound that could never entirely heal. For generations to come Germans would be compelled to reflect on this most shameful period in their history. Written into the history of Western civilization was an episode that would forever cast doubt on the Enlightenment conception of human goodness, rationality, and the progress of civilization.

Resistance

Each occupied country had its collaborators— including many government officials, business elite, and right-wing intellectuals—who welcomed the demise of democracy, saw Hitler as Europe's best defense against Communism, approved of Nazi measures against Jews, and profited from the confiscation of Jewish property and the sale of war materiel. In nearly every country occupied by or allied to Nazi Germany, local government officials and the police willingly assisted the Germans in rounding up, hunting down, and deporting Jews to the extermination camps. In Lithuania, the local population was responsible for murdering more than half of the country's 140,000 Jewish

victims (95 percent of Lithuania's Jewish population perished). Thousands of Ukrainians, Latvians, Lithuanians, and Estonians served in the murder squads and as concentration camp guards.

Each occupied country also produced a resistance movement that grew stronger as Nazi barbarism became more visible and prospects of a German defeat more likely. The Nazis retaliated by torturing and executing captured resistance fighters and killing hostages—generally, fifty for every German killed.

In Western Europe, the resistance rescued downed Allied airmen, radioed military intelligence to Britain, and sabotaged German installations. Norwegians blew up the German stock of heavy water needed for atomic research. The Danish underground sabotaged railways and smuggled into neutral Sweden almost all of Denmark's eight thousand Jews just before they were to be deported to the death camps. The Greek resistance blew up a vital viaduct, interrupting the movement of supplies to German troops in North Africa. After the Allies landed on the coast of France in June 1944, the French resistance delayed the movement of German reinforcements and liberated sections of the country. Belgian resistance fighters helped to capture the vital port of Antwerp.

The Polish resistance, numbering some 300,000 at its height, reported on German troop movements and interfered with supplies destined for the Eastern Front. In August 1944, with Soviet forces approaching Warsaw, the Poles staged a full-scale revolt against the German occupiers. The Poles appealed to the Soviets, camped ten miles away, for help. Thinking about a future Russian-dominated Poland, the Soviets did not move. After sixty-three days of street fighting—and the massacre of Polish hostages—remnants of the Polish underground surrendered, and the Germans methodically destroyed what was left of Warsaw.

Russian partisans numbered several hundred thousand men and women. Operating behind the German lines, they sabotaged railways, destroyed trucks, and killed scores of thousands of German soldiers in hit-and-run attacks.

The mountains and forests of Yugoslavia provided excellent terrain for guerrilla warfare. The leading Yugoslav resistance army was headed by Josip Broz (1892–1980), better known as Tito. Moscow-trained, intelligent, and courageous, Tito organized the partisans into a disciplined fighting force, which tied down a huge German army and ultimately liberated the country from German rule.

Jews participated in the resistance movements in all countries and were particularly prominent in the French resistance. Specifically Jewish resistance organizations emerged in Eastern Europe, but they suffered from shattering hardships. They had virtually no access to weapons. Poles, Ukrainians, Lithuanians, Romanians, and other peoples of Eastern Europe with a long history of anti-Semitism gave little or no support to Jewish resisters—at times, they even denounced them to the Nazis or killed them on their own. For centuries, European Jews had dealt with persecution by complying with their oppressors, and they had unlearned the habit of armed resistance that their ancestors had demonstrated against the Romans. The Germans responded to acts of resistance with savage reprisals against other Jews, creating a moral dilemma for any Jew who considered taking up arms. Nevertheless, revolts did take place in the ghettos and concentration camps. In the spring of 1943, the surviving Jews of the Warsaw ghetto, armed only with a few guns and homemade bombs, fought the Germans for several weeks.

Italy and Germany also had resistance movements. After the Allies landed in Italy in 1943, bands of Italian partisans helped liberate Italy from Fascism and the German occupation. In Germany, army officers plotted to assassinate the führer. On July 20, 1944, Colonel Claus von Stauffenberg planted a bomb at a staff conference attended by Hitler, but the führer escaped serious injury. Some five thousand relatives of the conspirators and people thought to harbor anti-Nazi sentiments were arrested, many of them tortured. After show trials in which the accused were vilified and degraded, two hundred were executed in exceptionally barbarous fashion. Suspended from meat hooks, the condemned were slowly strangled in front of cameras. SS leaders observed the film of these excruciating death scenes, but it is doubtful that Hitler ever saw it. In the following months, and particularly when defeat was certain, the Nazis murdered thousands of these political prisoners. Historians believe that at the time of the bomb plot the overwhelming number of civilians and officers opposed the conspirators, whose action they regarded as high treason, particularly during wartime.

TURNING THE TIDE

The Japanese Offensive

While Germany was subduing Europe, its ally, Japan, was extending its dominion over areas of Asia. Seeking raw materials and secure markets for Japanese goods and driven by a **xenophobic** nationalism, Japan in 1931 had attacked Manchuria in northern China. Quickly overrunning the province, the Japanese established the puppet state of Manchukuo in 1932. After a period of truce, the war against China was renewed in July 1937. Japan captured leading cities, including China's principal seaports, and inflicted heavy casualties on the poorly organized Chinese forces, obliging the government of Jiang Jieshi (Chiang Kai-shek) to withdraw to Chungking in the interior.

In 1940, after the defeat of France and with Britain standing alone against Nazi Germany, Japan eyed Southeast Asia—French Indochina, British Burma and Malaya, and the Dutch East Indies. From these lands, Japan planned to obtain the oil, rubber, and tin vitally needed by Japanese industry and enough rice to feed the nation. Japan hoped that a quick strike against the U.S. fleet in the Pacific would give it time to enlarge and consolidate its empire. On December 7, 1941, the Japanese struck with carrier-based planes at Pearl Harbor in Hawaii. Taken by surprise—despite warning signs—the Americans suffered a total defeat: the attackers sank 17 ships, including 7 of 8 battleships; destroyed 188 airplanes and damaged 159 others; and killed 2,403 men. The Japanese lost only 29 planes. After the attack on Pearl Harbor, Germany declared war on the United States. Now the immense American industrial capacity could be put to work against the Axis powers—Germany, Italy, and Japan. American factories produced planes, tanks, and ships at a pace and scale that astonished both friend and foe. The American arsenal supplied Britain and the Soviet Union with badly needed equipment.

Defeat of the Axis Powers

By the spring of 1942, the Axis powers held the upper hand. The Japanese Empire included the coast of China, Indochina (Vietnam),

Thailand, Burma, Malaya, the Dutch East Indies (Indonesia), the Philippines, and other islands in the Pacific. Germany controlled Europe almost to Moscow. When the year ended, however, the Allies seemed assured of victory. Three decisive battles—Midway, Stalingrad, and El Alamein—reversed the tide of war.

At Pearl Harbor, the Japanese had destroyed much of the American fleet. Assembling a mighty flotilla (eight aircraft carriers, eleven battleships, twenty-two cruisers, and sixty-five destroyers), Japan now sought to annihilate the rest of the United States' Pacific fleet. In June 1942, the main body of the Japanese fleet headed for Midway, eleven hundred miles northwest of Pearl Harbor; another section sailed toward the Aleutian Islands, in an attempt to divide the U.S. fleet. But the Americans had broken the Japanese naval code and were aware of the Japanese plan.

On June 4, 1942, the two navies fought a strange naval battle; it was waged entirely by carrier-based planes, for the two fleets were too far from each other to use their big guns or even to see each other. Demonstrating marked superiority over their opponents and extraordinary courage, American pilots destroyed 4 aircraft carriers and downed 322 Japanese planes. The battle of Midway cost Japan the initiative. With American industrial production accelerating, the opportunity for a Japanese victory had passed.

After being stymied at the outskirts of Moscow in December 1941, the Germans renewed their offensive in the spring and summer of 1942. Hitler's goal was Stalingrad, the great industrial center located on the Volga River; control of Stalingrad would give Germany command of vital rail transportation and access to the oil fields of the Caucasus. The battle of Stalingrad was an epic struggle in which Russian soldiers and civilians contested for every building and street of the city. In this urban battlefield, scarred by mile after mile of destroyed buildings and mountains of rubble, the combatants were separated by mere yards, snipers lurked in the maze of ruins, and tough Russian soldiers stealthily and ceaselessly attacked at night with bayonets and daggers; here the blitzkrieg, which had brought the Germans immense success in their earlier offensives, did not apply. Ironically, massive German bombing raids, which had left almost every

structure in ruins, provided the Russian fighters with perfect cover from which to harass the enemy. Superior German technical skills and generalship were of no value in close-quarter combat in basements and sewers and amid the rubble and skeletons of buildings. So brutal was the fighting that at night half-crazed dogs sought to escape the city by swimming across the river. One German soldier wrote in his diary at the end of December: "The horses have already been eaten. . . . The soldiers look like corpses or lunatics looking for something to put in their mouths. They no longer take cover from Russian shells; they haven't the strength to walk, run away and hide."[20]

A Russian counterattack in November, planned by General (later Marshal) Georgi Zhukov, who had successfully defended Moscow the previous year, caught the Germans in a trap. Not believing that the Russians had sufficient reserve armies and tanks or the competence to launch a massive counteroffensive, German commanders were taken by surprise. With his soldiers exhausted and desperately short of food, medical supplies, weapons, and ammunition, Friedrich Paulus, commander of the Sixth Army, urged Hitler to order a withdrawal before the Russians closed the ring. The führer refused, persuaded, in part, by the pompous Hermann Göring's assurance that his Luftwaffe would be able to supply the beleaguered army by air. It was an empty promise; the lack of available transport planes and terrible winter weather, which limited the number of flights and hampered maintenance crews who had to work outdoors on primitive Russian airfields, doomed the airlift. After suffering tens of thousands of additional casualties, their position hopeless, the remnants of the Sixth Army surrendered on February 2, 1943. Some 260,000 German soldiers had perished in the battle of Stalingrad, and another 110,000 were taken prisoner. Russian morale soared.

The Soviet High Command, which had performed terribly in the early days of the German offensive, distinguished itself at Stalingrad. At the battle of Kursk in July 1943, Russian military leaders again demonstrated an increasing ability to master the technique of modern warfare. Analyzing correctly that the Germans would attack the Kursk salient, Zhukhov turned the area

Japanese Empire, 1931
Japanese Empire, 1942
Extent of Japanese expansion
Allied advances

SOVIET UNION

ASIA

MONGOLIA

MANCHURIA

Peiping
(Beijing)

KOREA

Hiroshima

Shanghai

Nagasaki

JAPAN

Tokyo

CHINA

Taiwan

Okinawa
1945

Iwo Jima
1945

PACIFIC OCEAN

Midway 1942

BURMA

Hong
Kong

Mariana Is.

Wake

Hawaiian Is.
Pearl Harbor

THAILAND

FRENCH
INDOCHINA

Manila

Philippine Is.

Leyte 1944

Saipan

Guam
1944

Marshall
Is.

MALAYA

Singapore

Borneo

Caroline Is.

Tawara
1943

Gilbert Is.

Sumatra

Dutch East Indies

New
Guinea

Solomon Is.

Java

INDIAN OCEAN

Guadalcanal
1942

AUSTRALIA

Brisbane

0   500   1000 Km.

0   500   1000 Mi.

into a fortress. Immense numbers of heavy artillery, mines, antitank ditches, tanks, and planes, including dive-bombers equipped with cannons capable of destroying tanks, were set in place. A huge reserve force was positioned to repair breaches opened by panzer attacks. The operation, which included an epic tank battle, had depleted the German military of all its reserves on the Eastern Front. "Soviet success at Kursk . . . was the most important single victory of the war," concludes one military historian. "It was the point at which the initiative passed to the Soviet side. . . . The German front in the east was forced . . . to fall back along its entire length. . . . There was a long way to go to take the fight into Europe and to reach Berlin, but Kursk had unhinged the German front irreversibly."[21]

In January 1941, the British were routing the Italians in North Africa. Hitler assigned General Erwin Rommel (1891–1944) to halt the British advance. Rommel drove the British out of Libya and, with strong reinforcements, might have taken Egypt and the Suez Canal. But Hitler's concern was with seizing Yugoslavia and Greece, and preparing for the invasion of Russia. At the beginning of 1942, Rommel resumed his advance, intending to conquer Egypt. The British Eighth Army, commanded by General Bernard L. Montgomery, stopped him at the battle of El Alamein in October 1942. The victory of El Alamein was followed by an Anglo-American invasion of northwestern Africa in November 1942. By May 1943, the Germans and Italians were defeated in North Africa.

After securing North Africa, the Allies, seeking complete control of the Mediterranean, invaded Sicily in July 1943 and quickly conquered the island. Mussolini's fellow Fascist leaders turned against him, and the king dismissed him as prime minister. In September, the new government surrendered to the Allies, and in the following month, Italy declared war on Germany.

◀ *Map 31.3* WORLD WAR II: THE PACIFIC THEATER The battle of Midway was a major turning point in the Pacific theater. The map also shows the island-hopping of the Americans that brought them closer to Japan. The battles of Iwo Jima and Okinawa were particularly brutal. (© 2016 Cengage Learning.)

Italian partisans, whose number would grow to 300,000, resisted the Germans, who were determined to hold on to central and northern Italy. At the same time, the Allies fought their way up the peninsula. The fighting in Italy, vicious and costly, would last until the very end of the war. Captured by partisans, Mussolini was executed on April 28, 1945, and his dead body, hanging upside down, was publicly displayed.

On June 6, 1944, called D-day, the Allies landed on the beaches of Normandy in France. The invasion force that crossed from England that day consisted of 155,000 soldiers and more than 7,000 vessels, including warships, minesweepers, cargo ships, and landing craft—the greatest armada in history. Some 3,700 fighter planes guarded the ships and covered the invasion beaches; another 1,400 transport planes carried parachute battalions or towed gliders filled with infantry equipment. Although they suspected an imminent landing, the Germans did not think that it would occur in Normandy, and they dismissed June 6 as a possible date because weather conditions were unfavorable. The success of D-day depended on securing the beaches and marching inland. On some beaches, the soldiers struggled ashore in the face of intense enemy fire. At Omaha Beach, the Americans almost did not make it. Landing craft packed with soldiers were destroyed by German mines. Weighed down by heavy equipment, men drowned as they were tossed by high waves; others were killed or wounded by machine-gun fire before reaching the beach. Much of the heavy armor was lost. Those who stumbled ashore hugged the embankment and sheltered themselves behind whatever barrier they could find to escape the German guns firing from the cliffs. Traumatized by the ferocious German fire and the wounded and the dead surrounding them, and often leaderless, the soldiers, many of them facing combat for the first time, seemed paralyzed. But amid the chaos, the men began to advance.

Having established beachheads, the Allies rushed more men and supplies into battle. Still believing that Normandy was only a feint, that the main attack would be directed at Pas de Calais—a deception skillfully promoted by Allied intelligence in the months before the invasion—the

Historical Division, War Department: *Omaha Beachhead*

Ultimately the success of the Allied invasion of France, D-day, depended on what happened during the first few hours. If the Allies had failed to secure beachheads, the operation would have ended in disaster. As the following reading illustrates, some of the hardest fighting took place on Omaha Beach, which was attacked by the Americans. This extract, published in 1945, comes from a study prepared in the field by the Second Information and Historical Service attached to the First Army and by the Historical Section, European Theater of Operations.

The outstanding fact about these first two hours of action is that despite heavy casualties, loss of equipment, disorganization, and all the other discouraging features of the landings, the assault troops did not stay pinned down behind the sea wall and embankment. At half-a-dozen or more points on the long stretch, they found the necessary drive to leave their cover and move out over the open beach flat toward the bluffs. Prevented by circumstance of mislandings from using carefully rehearsed tactics, they improvised assault methods to deal with what defenses they found before them. In nearly every case where advance was attempted, it carried through the enemy beach defenses. . . .

Various factors, some of them difficult to evaluate, played a part in the success of these advances. . . . But the decisive factor was leadership. Wherever an advance was made, it depended on the presence of some few individuals, officers and noncommissioned officers, who inspired, encouraged, or bullied their men forward, often by making the first forward moves. On Easy Red a lieutenant and a wounded sergeant of divisional engineers stood up under fire and walked over to inspect the wire obstacles just beyond the embankment. The lieutenant came back and, hands on

hips, looked down disgustedly at the men lying behind the shingle bank. "Are you going to lay there and get killed, or get up and do something about it?" Nobody stirred, so the sergeant and the officer got the materials and blew the wire. On the same sector, where a group advancing across the flat was held up by a marshy area suspected of being mined, it was a lieutenant of engineers who crawled ahead through the mud on his belly, probing for mines with a hunting knife in the absence of other equipment. When remnants of an isolated boat section of Company B, 116th Infantry, were stopped by fire from a well-concealed emplacement, the lieutenant in charge went after it single-handed. In trying to grenade the rifle pit he was hit by three rifle bullets and eight grenade fragments, including some from his own grenade. He turned his map and compass over to a sergeant and ordered his group to press on inland. . . .

Col. George A. Taylor arrived in the second section at 0815 and found plenty to do on the beach. Men were still hugging the embankment, disorganized, and suffering casualties from mortar and artillery fire. Colonel Taylor summed up the situation in terse phrase: "Two kinds of people are staying on this beach, the dead and those who are going to die—now let's get the hell out of here." Small groups of men were collected without regard to units, put under charge of the nearest noncommissioned officer, and sent on through the wire and across the flat, while engineers worked hard to widen gaps in the wire and to mark lanes through the minefields.

Question for Analysis

1. How did officers manage to rally the shaken and demoralized soldiers?

Omaha Beachhead, prepared by the Historical Division, War Department (Washington, D.C.: U.S. Government Printing Office, 1945); 58–59, 71.

Germans continued, in what was a fatal blunder, to hold back their crack reserves. Adding to the Germans' woes was the destruction of the French transportation system by Allied planes just before the invasion. German troops sent to fortify the defenses at Normandy met delay after delay. Aided by control of the air, the Allies overwhelmed the German defenders. By the end of July, they had built up their strength in France to 1.5 million soldiers. In the middle of August, Paris rose up against the German occupiers and was soon liberated, and in the weeks that followed the Germans were evacuating France.

After their heady victories in France, Allied commanders thought that Germany was virtually finished, that the war would be over before the end of the year. But Germany mobilized its remaining manpower and regrouped its divisions that had been shattered in France. And through a herculean effort, the German armaments industry continued to function at a high level, despite massive Allied bombardments. In the autumn, the Allied advance halted as the revamped German forces inflicted heavy casualties on the Allies in southern Holland, the German border city of Aachen, and the Huertgen Forest, on the German-Belgian border. Nevertheless, as winter approached, the situation looked hopeless for Germany. Brussels and Antwerp fell to the Allies; Allied bombers were striking German factories and carpet-bombing German cities in terror raids that took a horrendous toll of life. The air war eroded Germany's industrial potential; devastated the transportation system, preventing supplies from reaching the fronts; and caused civilian morale to plummet. Desperate, Hitler made one last gamble. In mid-December 1944, he launched an offensive to split the Allied forces and regain the vital port of Antwerp. The Allies were taken by surprise in the battle of the Bulge, but a heroic defense by the Americans at Bastogne, an important road junction, and a few days of clear weather that permitted Allied bombing of German supply lines, helped stop the German offensive. German losses in Hitler's failed gamble proved insurmountable. With its reserve strength now depleted beyond restitution and its industrial capacity eroded by Allied bombings, Germany lacked the manpower, tanks, planes, and fuel to forestall an

Allied assault into its heartland from the west or to turn back the Red Army in the east.

In June 1944, the Russians launched a major offensive, advancing into the Baltic states, Poland, and Hungary. Yet German soldiers continued to fight with remarkable skill and determination, inflicting proportionately more casualties than they suffered. They were driven by a fanatic dedication to Hitler and Nazi ideology, loyalty to their comrades and the endangered fatherland, pride in the tradition of German arms, and fear of both vengeful Russians, and the SS and other special units that were executing "defeatists."

By February 1945, the Russians stood within one hundred miles of Berlin. Also in February, the Allies in the west were battling the Germans in the Rhineland, and on March 7, 1945, American soldiers, seizing a bridge at Remagen that the Germans had failed to destroy, crossed the Rhine into the interior of Germany. By April 1945, British, American, and Russian troops were penetrating into Germany from east and west. From his underground bunker near the chancellery in Berlin, a physically exhausted and emotionally unhinged Hitler engaged in wild fantasies about new German victories. In late April, the Red Army's spearhead pushed into Berlin, which Hitler had ordered defended "to the last man and the last shot." The greatly outnumbered defenders—army remnants, elderly recruits, and fanatical Hitler Youth—fought tenaciously block by block. As the Russians stormed through the devastated city, SS squads hunted down and lynched deserters and ordinary soldiers for the flimsiest of reasons. In the battles to reach and take Berlin, the Russians suffered more than 300,000 dead and wounded. German casualties were also in the hundreds of thousands, many of them civilians. Hundreds of thousands of Berliners fled west to escape revengeful Russians who murdered, mutilated, raped, burned, and looted in indiscriminate acts of savagery, rage, and vengeance. On April 30, 1945, with the Russians only blocks away, the führer took his own life. In his last will and testament, Hitler again showed his vile obsession with Jews. "It is not true that I or anybody else in Germany wanted war in 1939. It was wanted and provoked exclusively by those international

HIROSHIMA AFTER THE ATOMIC BOMB. The mass destruction of Hiroshima ushered in a new age. Nuclear weapons gave humanity the capacity to destroy civilization. (© Bettmann/Corbis.)

statesmen who either were of Jewish origin or worked for Jewish interests."[22] On May 7, 1945, a demoralized and devastated Germany surrendered unconditionally.

After the victory at Midway in June 1942, American forces attacked strategic islands held by Japan. American troops had to battle their way up beaches and through jungles tenaciously defended by Japanese soldiers, who believed that death was preferable to the disgrace of surrender. They fought to the last man and often killed themselves when confronted with the dishonor of falling into enemy hands. In March 1945, twenty-one thousand Japanese perished on Iwo Jima; another 100,000 died on Okinawa in April 1945 as they contested for every inch of the island. On August 6, 1945, the United States dropped an atomic bomb on Hiroshima, killing more than seventy-eight thousand people and demolishing

60 percent of the city. President Harry S. Truman said that he ordered the atomic attack to avoid an American invasion of the Japanese homeland, which would have caused hundreds of thousands of casualties.

Truman's decision has aroused considerable debate. Some analysts say that dropping the bomb was unnecessary, that Japan, deprived of oil, rice, and other essentials by an American naval blockade and defenseless against unrelenting aerial bombardments, was close to surrender and had indicated as much. It has been suggested that with the Soviet Union about to enter the conflict against Japan, Truman wanted to end the war immediately, thus depriving the USSR of an opportunity to extend its influence in East Asia. On August 8, Russia did enter the war against Japan, invading Manchuria. After a second atomic bomb was dropped on Nagasaki on August 9, the Japanese asked for peace.

THE LEGACY OF WORLD WAR II

World War II was the most destructive and murderous war in history. The total war waged by the combatants erased the distinction between soldiers and civilians, who were victims of reprisals, genocide, slave labor, and aerial bombardment of cities. Estimates of the number of dead range as high as 50 million, including some 25 million Russians—one in three Russians lost a father—who sacrificed more than the other participants in both population and material resources. (In comparison, the United States suffered 400,000 service deaths.)

Material costs were staggering. Everywhere cities were in rubble; bridges, railway systems, waterways, and harbors destroyed; farmland laid waste; livestock killed; coal mines wrecked. Homeless and hungry people wandered the streets and roads. Europe faced the gigantic task of rebuilding. Yet Europe did recover from this material blight, and with astonishing speed.

The war produced a vast migration of peoples unparalleled in modern European history. In accordance with an agreement made with Russia at a conference at Yalta in February 1945, Britain and America compelled some 2 million Russian prisoners of war, slave laborers, and those who had been recruited into the German army to return to the Soviet Union—Stalin regarded them all as traitors—many against their will. Ten percent of these deportees were executed and 70 percent sent to Stalin's labor camps. The Soviet Union annexed the Baltic lands of Latvia, Lithuania, and Estonia, forcibly deporting many of the native inhabitants into central Russia. The bulk of East Prussia was taken over by Poland, and Russia annexed the northeastern portion. Millions of Germans fled the invading Russians, who, bent on revenge for the misery the Nazis had inflicted on their kin and country, committed numerous atrocities, including indiscriminate killing and mass rape, before Soviet authorities ended the mayhem. Millions more Germans were driven out of Poland, Czechoslovakia, Yugoslavia, Romania, and Hungary, places where their ancestors had lived for centuries, by vengeful Eastern Europeans. Moreover, leaders in these countries, driven by nationalist aspirations, welcomed an opportunity to rid their nations of an ethnic minority, particularly since so many of these Germans had aided the Nazi occupiers. During 1945–1946, some 12 to 13 million Germans were driven westward. Expelled from their homes, often with only a few minutes' warning, they had to leave almost everything behind. Those herded into internment camps were brutalized by Polish and Czech guards who relished the opportunity to torment Germans. Hundreds of thousands died from malnutrition, disease, exposure, mistreatment, and suicide. Ironically, the German expellees who managed to start a new life in West Germany escaped the Communist dictatorships imposed on the Czechs and Poles who had expelled them, often with great cruelty.

After the war many German war criminals went into hiding, changed their identity, lied about their wartime record, or fled to other countries, particularly in South America. A substantial number of escapees, including major war criminals involved in mass murder, were aided by Austrian, German, and Croatian clerics, some of them important figures at the Vatican. They provided fleeing Nazis with safe houses, money, and forged documents. With the Cold War looming, Nazi war criminals escaped justice by working with American, British, and Soviet intelligence services that protected them. Thousands of East European collaborators, including those who had participated in mass murder, hid their past and found asylum in the United States, Canada, Australia, and Britain. Nevertheless, over the years in Germany and other countries a significant number of war criminals were indicted, imprisoned, and some executed. During 1945–1946, twenty-two leading Nazis stood trial at Nuremberg before the International Military Tribunal, comprised of representatives of the United States, Great Britain, the Soviet Union, and France. The court sentenced twelve to death by hanging and one in absentia; seven were given jail sentences from ten years to life; and three were acquitted.

The war produced a shift in power arrangements. The United States and the Soviet Union emerged as the two most powerful states in the world. The traditional Great Powers—Britain, France, and Germany—were now dwarfed by these superpowers. The United States had the atomic bomb and immense industrial might—its economy, previously suffering from the Great Depression, boomed during the war; the Soviet Union had the largest army in the world and was extending its dominion over Eastern Europe. With Germany defeated, the principal incentive for Soviet–American cooperation evaporated.

After World War I, nationalist passions intensified. After World War II, Western Europeans progressed toward unity. The Hitler years convinced many Europeans of the dangers inherent in extreme nationalism, and fear of the Soviet Union prodded them toward greater cooperation.

Buried in the rubble of German towns and cities was the lure of militarism and expansionism that had fueled two world wars—another good sign for the future. But it would take a generation for many Germans to come to terms with the suffering their country had brought to Europe. In the war's immediate aftermath, Germans forged a selective memory regarding the Nazi past. When they spoke of victims, suffering, and war crimes, they referred to Allied carpet-bombing of their cities, the barbaric behavior of invading Russian soldiers, the expulsion of millions of Germans from Eastern European countries, and the plight of German prisoners of war still languishing in Soviet prison camps. Or they saw themselves as innocent victims of a totalitarian state, erasing from memory their adulation of Hitler, their enthusiastic support of his vision of a Europe dominated by Germany, and their broad involvement in the war effort, including the plundering of occupied lands and the criminal war against the Jews. In the late 1960s, Germans began to confront their past more honestly and continued to do so in succeeding generations.

Women in the belligerent countries served in the armed forces, and in the Soviet Union they were actively involved in combat. Some 2,000 Soviet women fought as snipers, some with great effectiveness. Soviet women also flew fighter planes and drove tanks, and some 200,000 fought with partisans. Women were active in the resistance movements in occupied Europe, and some were captured, tortured, and killed by the Nazis. Britain also planted female spies in occupied France, some of whom fell victim to the Nazis.

In the United States and Britain, women volunteers performed such noncombat duties as flight testing, ferrying planes to different bases, driving ambulances, serving as telegraphers and mechanics, and caring for the wounded in hospitals. Thousands of nurses served in the different branches of service. The role of British women in tracking incoming German planes proved invaluable in the Battle of Britain.

In both the United States and Britain, with men going off to war, large numbers of women—many of them housewives—worked in factories creating armaments needed for the war effort. While some 70 to 75 percent of American women chose to remain at home, that same percentage of British women was employed. When the war ended, many American women were forced to give up their jobs to provide work for the returning soldiers and resumed being housewives, a role that they and their husbands often preferred. Nevertheless, the new possibilities created by the war gave women more confidence in their abilities and in time helped spark a women's movement that pressed for equal opportunity in employment and education.

World War II accelerated the disintegration of Europe's overseas empires. The European states could hardly justify ruling over Africans and Asians after they had fought to liberate European lands from German imperialism. Nor could they ask their people, exhausted by the Hitler years and concentrating all their energies on reconstruction, to fight new wars against Africans and Asians pressing for independence. In the years just after the war, Great Britain surrendered India, France lost Lebanon and Syria, and the Dutch departed from Indonesia. In the 1950s and 1960s, virtually every colonial territory gained independence. In those instances where the colonial power resisted independence for the colony, the price was bloodshed.

The consciousness of Europe, already profoundly damaged by World War I, was again grievously wounded. Nazi racial theories showed that even in an age of sophisticated science, the mind remains attracted to irrational beliefs and mythical imagery. Nazi atrocities proved that people will torture and kill with religious zeal and machinelike indifference. This regression to mythical thinking and savagery bears out Walter

Lippmann's contention that "men have been barbarians much longer than they have been civilized. They are only precariously civilized, and within us there is the propensity, persistent as the force of gravity, to revert under stress and strain, or under temptation, to our first natures."[23] And the behavior of German intellectuals also contained a painful lesson, says German historian Karl Dietrich Bracher: "The intellectuals who supported the Nazis in one way or another all document that the mind can be temporarily seduced, that people can be bribed with careers and fame, that thinking people, especially, are tempted by an irrational cult of action and are peculiarly susceptible to 'one-dimensional' answers and promises of salvation."[24]

The Nazi assault on reason and freedom, the core ideals of Western civilization, demonstrated anew the precariousness of that civilization. This assault would forever cast doubt on the Enlightenment conception of human goodness, secular rationality, and the progress of civilization through advances in science and technology.

The Holocaust was heightened irrationality and organized evil on an unprecedented scale. Auschwitz, Treblinka, Sobibor, and the other death factories represent the triumph of human irrationality over reason—the surrender of the mind to a bizarre racial mythology that provided a metaphysical and pseudoscientific justification for mass murder. They also represent the ultimate perversion of reason. A calculating reason manufactured and organized lies and demented beliefs into a structured system with its own inner logic and employed sophisticated technology and administrative techniques to destroy human beings spiritually and physically. Science and technology, venerated as the great achievement of the Western mind, had made mass extermination possible. The philosophes had not foreseen the destructive power inherent in reason. The historian Omer Bartov poses this disturbing question about the failure of reason and the Western humanist tradition:

> *What was it that induced Nobel Prize-winning scientists, internationally respected legal scholars, physicians known throughout the world for their research into the human body and their desire to ameliorate the lot of humanity,*

> *to become not merely opportunist accomplices, but in many ways the initiators and promoters of this attempt to subject the human race to a vast surgical operation by means of mass extermination of whole categories of human beings? What was there (or is there) in our culture that made the concept of transforming humanity by means of eugenic and racial cleansing seem so practical and rational?*[25]

Both the Christian and the Enlightenment traditions had failed the Germans and many other Europeans. And Hitler's supporters had betrayed civilization, as Joachim Wieder, a German officer and veteran of Stalingrad, concluded after the war:

> *By means of a destructive battle against universal educational and cultural powers of classic antiquity, humanism, and Christianity, an anti-intellectual political religion of power had successively extracted the German people from the best of the commonly-held European body of human thought and thereby also out of the commitment to the objective concepts of truth, compassion, and justice.*[26]

And "what is both historically unique and persistently disturbing about the Holocaust," notes Bernhard Schlink, a prominent German novelist, "is that Germany, with its cultural heritage and place among civilised nations, was capable of those kinds of atrocities. It elicits troubling questions: if the ice of culturally-advanced civilisation upon which one fancied oneself safely standing, was in fact so thin at that time, then how safe is the ice we live upon today?"[27]

Auschwitz marked a rupture in the progressive development of European civilization. It demonstrated that against the forces of mythical thinking, fanaticism, and the human being's propensity for evil, our rational faculties, so admired by the philosophes of the Enlightenment and their liberal heirs, have limited power. Some intellectuals, shocked by the irrationality and horrors of the Hitler era, drifted into despair. To these thinkers, life was absurd, without meaning; human beings could neither comprehend nor control it. In 1945, only the naïve could have faith in continuous progress or believe in the essential goodness of the individual. The future envisioned by the philosophes seemed more distant than ever. Nevertheless, this profound disillusionment was tempered by hope. Democracy had, in fact, prevailed over Nazi totalitarianism and terror. Moreover, fewer intellectuals were now attracted to antidemocratic thought. The Nazi dictatorship convinced many of them, even some who had wavered in previous decades, that freedom and human dignity were precious ideals and that liberal constitutional government, despite its imperfections, was the best means of preserving these ideals. A year before he perished at Normandy, a young British soldier wrote to a friend in words that would aptly describe the sentiments of many skeptical liberal-democrats immediately after the war: "To . . . admit any hope of a better world is criminally foolish, as foolish as it is to stop working for it."[28]

To be sure, immediately after the war, many Europeans gravitated to the Left, believing that Communists, who had been very active in resistance movements against the Nazis and Fascists, would overcome social injustice. However in the decades to come more disclosures of Communist oppression and ineptitude would greatly weaken Marxism's appeal. The future for Western civilization belonged to liberal and (social) democracy, its institutions and values for which the West had fought and sacrificed in World War II.

Finally, World War II saw major advances in weaponry, none more significant than the atomic bomb, that made war more lethal. That states now possess nuclear weapons capable of destroying one another, and even civilization and the planet, is another ever-present, ever-terrifying legacy of World War II.

NOTES

1. Pierre Renouvin, *World War II and Its Origins* (New York: Harper and Row, 1969), 167.

2. Z. A. B. Zeman, *Nazi Propaganda* (New York: Oxford University Press, 1973), 109.

3. *Documents on German Foreign Policy, 1918–1945*, vol. 6 (London: Her Majesty's Stationery Office, 1956), series D, no. 433.

4. Basil H. Liddell Hart, *History of the Second World War* (New York: Putnam, 1970), 73–74.

5. Winston S. Churchill, *The Second World War: Their Finest Hour* (Boston: Houghton Mifflin, 1949), 2:225–226.

6. Quoted in William L. Shirer, *The Rise and Fall of the Third Reich* (New York: Simon and Schuster, 1960), 860.

7. *Hitler's Secret Conversations, 1941–1944*, with an introductory essay by H. R. Trevor Roper (New York: Farrar, Straus and Young, 1953), 508.

8. Quoted in Gordon Wright, *The Ordeal of Total War* (New York: Harper Torchbooks, 1968), 124.

9. Quoted in Norman Cohn, *Warrant for Genocide* (New York: Harper Torchbooks, 1967), 188.

10. Judith Sternberg Newman, *In the Hell of Auschwitz* (New York: Exposition, 1964), 18.

11. *Nazi Conspiracy and Aggression* (Washington, D.C.: U.S. Government Printing Office, 1946), 6:787–789.

12. Quoted in Joseph Borkin, *The Crime and Punishment of I. G. Farben* (New York: Free Press, 1978), 143.

13. Gisella Perl, *I Was a Doctor in Auschwitz* (New York: International Universities Press, 1948), 80.

14. Quoted in Robert Jay Lifton, *The Nazi Doctors* (New York: Basic Books, 1986), 16.

15. Konnilyn G. Feig, *Hitler's Death Camps* (New York: Holmes and Meier, 1979), 37.

16. Quoted in Erich Kahler, *The Tower and the Abyss* (New York: George Braziller, 1957), 74–75.

17. Quoted in Steven T. Katz, "Technology and Genocide: Technology as a 'Form of Life,'" in *Echoes from the Holocaust*, ed. Alan Rosenberg and Gerald E. Meyers (Philadelphia: Temple University Press, 1988), 281.

18. Rainer C. Baum, "Holocaust: Moral Indifference as the Form of Modern Evil," in *Echoes from the Holocaust*, 83.

19. Lifton, *The Nazi Doctors*, 5.

20. Richard Overy, *Why the Allies Won* (New York: Norton, 1995), 82.

21. Ibid., 96.

22. Excerpted in George H. Stein, ed., *Hitler* (Englewood Cliffs, N.J.: Prentice-Hall, 1968), 84.

23. Walter Lippmann, *The Public Philosophy* (Boston: Little, Brown, 1955), 86.

24. Karl Dietrich Bracher, *Turning Points in Modern Times*, trans. Thomas Dunlap (Cambridge, Mass.: Harvard University Press, 1995), 198.

25. Omer Bartov, *Germany's War and the Holocaust: Disputed Histories* (Ithaca, N.Y.: Cornell University Press, 2003), 136.

26. Joachim Wieder, *Stalingrad: Memories and Assessments*, trans. Helmut Bogler (London: Arms and Armor, 1993), 87.

27. Bernhard Schlink, *Guilt About the Past* (Toronto: House of Anansi, 2009), 29.

28. Paul Fussell, ed., *The Norton Book of Modern War* (New York: W. W. Norton, 1991), 381.

Part Seven

The Contemporary World

1940

1950

1960

1970

1980

1990

2000

Politics and Society

Yalta agreement (1945)
United Nations established (1945)
Marshall Plan for recovery of Europe (1947)
Cold War starts (1947)
State of Israel established (1948)
North Atlantic Treaty Organization (NATO)
  established (1949)
Division of Germany (1949)
Triumph of Communism in China (1949)

Korean War (1950–1953)
The Warsaw Pact established (1955)
Hungarian Uprising suppressed (1956)
European Economic Community (EEC)
  established (1957)
Sputnik launched: space age begins (1957)

U2 incident (1960)
Berlin Wall built (1961)
Cuban missile crisis (1962)
Vietnam War (1963–1973)
Prague Spring quashed (1968)
Social rebellion throughout the West (late 1960s)

Détente in East–West relations (1970s)
Soviet invasion of Afghanistan (1979)

Gorbachev becomes leader of Soviet Union (1985)
Explosion at Chernobyl nuclear power plant
  (1986)
Peaceful overthrow of Communist governments
  in Eastern Europe (1989)
Berlin Wall demolished (1989)

Reunification of Germany (1990)
Charter of Paris for a New Europe (1990)
Official end of Cold War (1990)
Persian Gulf War (1991)
Yugoslav federation breaks up and civil war
  begins (1991)
Collapse of Soviet Union (1991)
European Union ratifies the Maastricht Treaty (1993)
Dayton Agreement ends civil war in former
  Yugoslavia (1995)

Terrorist attack on World Trade Center (2001)
U.S.-led war in Iraq; fall of Saddam Hussein (2003)

Thought and Culture

Koestler, *Darkness at Noon* (1940)
Hemingway, *For Whom the Bell Tolls* (1940)
Camus, *The Stranger* (1942)
von Hayek, *The Road to Serfdom* (1944)
Sartre, *Existentialism and Humanism* (1946)
Wiener, *Cybernetics* (1948)
Orwell, *1984* (1949)
de Beauvoir, *The Second Sex* (1949)

Camus, *The Rebel* (1951)
Discovery of DNA by Crick and Watson (1951–1953)
Djilas, *The New Class* (1957)
Chomsky, *Syntactic Structures* (1957)
Grass, *The Tin Drum* (1959)
Snow, *The Two Cultures and the Scientific Revolution* (1959)

Carson, *Silent Spring* (1962)
Friedman, *Capitalism and Freedom* (1962)
Pope John XXIII, *Pacem in Terris* (Peace on Earth) (1963)
McLuhan, *Understanding Media* (1964)
Arendt, *The Origins of Totalitarianism* (1966)
Levi-Strauss, *The Savage Mind* (1966)
Berlin, *Four Essays on Liberty* (1969)

Rawls, *A Theory of Justice* (1971)
Solzhenitsyn, *The Gulag Archipelago* (1974–1978)
Wilson, *Sociobiology* (1975)
Lyotard, *The Postmodern Condition* (1979)

Creation of the Internet (1983)
Berger, *The Capitalist Revolution* (1986)
Dawkins, *The Blind Watchmaker* (1986)
Gorbachev, *Perestroika* (1987)
Grossman, *Life and Fate* (1988)

Havel, *Living in Truth* (1990)
Fukuyama, *The End of History and the Last Man* (1992)
Huntington, *The Clash of Civilizations and the
  Remaking of the World Order* (1998)
Hawking, *A Brief History of Time* (1998)

Levitt and Dubner, *Freakonomics: A Rogue Economist
  Explores the Hidden Side of Everything* (2005)

Chapter 32

Europe After World War II: Recovery and Realignment, 1945–1989

Berlin Wall. The Berlin Wall, swiftly erected by the East German Communist regime in 1961, divided the city of Berlin for twenty-eight years. (© Bettmann/Corbis.)

- The Cold War
- Decolonization
- Building a New Europe: Unity and Recovery
- The Soviet Bloc

Focus Questions

1. What were the origins of and key developments in the Cold War?
2. What do you consider the most important changes that took place in Western Europe in the decades after World War II?
3. What conditions made possible the "revolution" of 1989 in Eastern Europe?
4. What are the main problems confronting the European Union?
5. What factors led to the collapse of Communism and the end of the Cold War?
6. What is the historical significance of Communism's collapse?

At the end of World War II, Winston Churchill described Europe as "a rubble heap, a charnel house, a breeding ground for pestilence and hate."[1] Millions had perished. Industry, transportation, and communications had come to a virtual standstill; bridges, canals, dikes, and farmlands were ruined. Ragged, worn people picked among the rubble and bartered their valuables for food.

Europe was politically cut in half, for in pursuing Hitler's armies, Soviet troops had overrun Eastern Europe and penetrated into the heart of Germany. Europe's future now depended on two countries, the United States and the Soviet Union, which soon became embroiled in a bitter cold war. The Soviet Union, exhausted by World War II and anxious about security, imposed Communist dictatorship on Eastern Europe, while the United States, virtually unharmed by the war, used its wealth and power to help rebuild Western Europe. Henceforth, the United States stood out as the heir to and guardian of the Western tradition, a political giant come into its own.

THE COLD WAR

Origins

The Cold War (the American financier Bernard Baruch coined the phrase in 1947) stemmed from the incompatible ideologies and political ambitions of the United States and the Soviet Union. The wartime coalition of the United States, Britain, and the Soviet Union was based solely on temporary political expediency—the need to defeat Nazi Germany. Most Americans and Britons long considered the Communist system repressive and inefficient and feared its spread to Western Europe, and the Soviet Union had a profound distrust for Western capitalist states, particularly Germany, which in both world wars had invaded Russia. To establish a security buffer against Germany and seizing an opportunity for geopolitical expansion, Stalin annexed border regions and established subservient Communist governments throughout Eastern Europe.

Milovan Djilas: *The New Class: An Analysis of the Communist System*

In 1956, Milovan Djilas (1911–1995), a Yugoslav Communist and political commentator who traveled to Moscow during and after the war, wrote The New Class, *an early and devastating critique of the Communist system, where, he said, government bureaucrats constitute a privileged "exploiting and governing class."*

Earlier revolutions, particularly the so-called bourgeois ones, attached considerable significance to the establishment of individual freedoms immediately following cessation of the revolutionary terror . . . The final results of earlier revolutions were often greater legal security and greater civil rights. This cannot be said of the Communist revolution . . .

In contrast to earlier revolutions, the Communist revolution, conducted in the name of doing away with classes, has resulted in the most complete authority of any single new class. Everything else is sham and an illusion. . . .

The new class may be said to be made up of those who have special privileges and economic preference because of the administrative monopoly they hold. . . .

The mechanism of Communist power . . . leads to the most refined tyranny and the most brutal exploitation. The simplicity of this mechanism originates from the fact that one party alone, the Communist Party, is the backbone of the entire political, economic, and ideological activity. The entire public life is at a standstill or moves ahead, falls behind or turns around according to what happens in the party forums. . . .

. . . Communist control of the social machine . . . restricts certain government posts to party members. These jobs, which are essential in any government but especially in a Communist one, include assignments with police, especially the secret police; and the diplomatic

As the Red Army fought its way west in 1944–1945, Eastern European Communists, trained in the Soviet Union, followed. The Baltic states (Lithuania, Latvia, and Estonia), seized after the Nazi–Soviet Pact of 1939 and then lost to Hitler, were reincorporated into the Soviet Union. The Soviet Union also annexed part of East Prussia; Ruthenia in eastern Czechoslovakia, whose population was predominantly Ukrainian; parts of Romania; and eastern Poland, for which the Poles were compensated with German territory, including much of East Prussia. Elsewhere, Stalin respected, at least outwardly, the national sovereignty of the occupied countries by ruling through returning native Communists and whatever sympathizers he could find. Stalin knew that in free elections Communists had little chance of winning and that left to their own devices these countries would assert their independence. First, negative historical memories colored the views of Eastern Europeans. For example, Russia had ruled Poland repressively for over a century and then had invaded eastern Poland in 1939, deported hundreds of thousands of Poles to desolate regions of the USSR, massacred thousands of Polish officers and other elites, and allowed the Nazis to crush the Warsaw Uprising in 1944. Second, many Eastern European peoples, in particular the Czechs and Hungarians, were traditionally oriented toward Western Europe. Equally important, Soviet-style systems were economically inefficient and politically repressive. Yet the Soviet leadership felt a desperate need for allies both as a security buffer and to legitimize their political system. Thus, military force was required to keep them in line.

and officers corps, especially positions in the information and political services. In the judiciary only top positions have until now been in the hands of Communists. . . .

Only in a Communist state are a number of both specified and unspecified positions reserved for members of the party. The Communist government, although a class structure, is a party government; the Communist army is a party army; and the state is a party state. More precisely, Communists tend to treat the army and the state as their exclusive weapons.

The exclusive, if unwritten, law that only party members can become policemen, officers, diplomats, and hold similar positions, or that only they can exercise actual authority, creates a special privileged group of bureaucrats. . . .

A citizen in the Communist system lives oppressed by the constant pangs of his conscience, and the fear that he has transgressed. He is always fearful that he will have to demonstrate that he is not an enemy of socialism, just as in the Middle Ages a man constantly had to show his devotion to the Church. . . .

. . . Tyranny over the mind is the most complete and most brutal type of tyranny; every other tyranny begins and ends with it. . . .

History will pardon Communists for much, establishing that they were forced into many brutal acts because of circumstances and the need to defend their existence. But the stifling of every divergent thought, the exclusive monopoly over thinking for the purpose of defending their personal interests, will nail the Communists to a cross of shame in history. . . .

Question for Analysis

1. How did Milovan Djilas characterize the "new class"? How did it wield its power? What role did the Communist Party play?

Milovan Djilas, *The New Class: An Analysis of the Communist System* (New York: Frederick A. Praeger, 1957), pp. 27, 36, 39, 70, 72–73, 132.

Yugoslavia alone successfully defied Stalin under the leadership of Marshal Tito, who had led the Yugoslav resistance movement against Nazi occupation. A hardened Communist, Tito was also a Yugoslav patriot who resisted Soviet occupation of his country. Backed by his people, he pursued an independent course. Yet even in Yugoslavia Communist rule could only be maintained by force and terror. As President Ronald Reagan asserted in 1982, "the regimes planted by totalitarianism have had more than 30 years to establish their legitimacy. But none—not one regime—has yet been able to risk free elections. Regimes planted by bayonets do not take root."[2]

Local populations, and their supporters in Western European lands, viewed the Soviet domination of Eastern Europe as a calamity. But the Western peoples were unwilling to risk another war. Now wartime cooperation between the former allies was replaced by the suspicion and hostility of the Cold War. For the next forty-five years, the Continent would be divided into two camps of opposing ideologies. In Churchill's famous words, "From Stettin in the Baltic to Trieste in the Adriatic, an iron curtain has descended across the Continent."[3]

American leaders believed they had the responsibility of rallying Western Europe and the world against Communist threats to freedom and the free market. Significantly, the three main Axis powers—(West) Germany, Italy, and Japan—embraced democratic principles and sided with the United States and its allies in their hostility to Communism and Soviet expansion. The rapid growth of Communist

Chronology 32.1 ❖ Postwar Timeline

1945	United Nations founded; Red Army occupies Eastern Europe; Stalinization begins.
1946	Iron Curtain speech; Italian monarchy ends; Greek Civil War (until 1949)
1947	Truman Doctrine and Marshall Plan inaugurated; UK grants Indian independence: decolonization accelerates
1948	Tito's Yugoslavia breaks with the Soviet Union; National Health Service established in UK: rise of European welfare state
1949	NATO formed; Berlin Airlift; division of Germany
1950–1953	Korean War
1953	Stalin dies
1955	Allied occupation of Austria ends; Warsaw Pact formed
1956	Khrushchev's secret speech on Stalin's crimes; Hungarian Uprising crushed
1957	*Sputnik* launched: space age begins; EEC established
1961	Berlin Wall built, dividing the city of Berlin
1962	Cuban missile crisis
1963–1973	Vietnam War
1964	Khrushchev ousted; Brezhnev and Kosygin installed as leaders in USSR
1968	Czechoslovakia's "Prague Spring": Dubček's "socialism with a human face" crushed by Soviet troops
1971	Détente in East–West relations
1974	Portuguese dictatorship ends
1975	Spanish dictatorship ends
1979	Soviet Union invades Afghanistan
1980	Solidarity trade union formed in Poland
1982	Brezhnev dies, succeeded by Andropov (d. 1984) and Chernenko (d. 1985)
1985	Gorbachev becomes leader of USSR
1989	Year of liberation in Eastern Europe
1990	Reunification of Germany; Charter of Paris for a New Europe: official end of the Cold War; apartheid system begins to decline
1991	Persian Gulf War; Yeltsin elected Russian president; collapse of Soviet Union; Yugoslav federation breaks up and civil war begins
1993	Czechoslovakia splits into Czech Republic and Slovakia; European Union ratifies Maastricht Treaty
1994	South Africa elects multiracial government; war breaks out between Russia and Chechnya
1995	Dayton Agreement ends civil war in Bosnia
1996	Yeltsin reelected president of Russia; truce ends hostilities in Chechnya
1999	NATO invades Kosovo; Russia again attacks Chechnya
2000	Vladimir Putin elected president of Russia
2001	Terrorist attack on World Trade Center; War on Terrorism in Afghanistan
2003	United States and Britain crush regime of Saddam Hussein

parties with allegiance to the Soviet Union throughout non-Soviet-occupied Europe remained a gnawing worry.

Cold War Mobilization

In March 1947, fearing Soviet penetration into the eastern Mediterranean, President Truman proclaimed the Truman Doctrine: "It must be the policy of the United States to support free peoples who are resisting attempted subjugation by armed minorities or by outside pressures."[4] The Truman Doctrine was the centerpiece of the new policy of *containment,* of holding Soviet power within its then-current boundaries. U.S. military and economic support soon went to Greece and Turkey. Thus, a sharp reversal took place in American foreign policy; prewar American isolation gave way to worldwide vigilance against any Soviet effort at expansion.

The policy of containment drew heavily on the views of George Kennan, a prominent diplomat who wrote in 1947,

> Soviet society may well contain deficiencies which will eventually weaken its own total potential. This would of itself warrant the United States entering with reasonable confidence upon a policy of firm containment, designed to confront the Russians with unalterable counter-force at every point where they show signs of encroaching upon the interests of a peaceful and stable world.

He added prophetically that "the United States has it in its power to increase enormously the strains under which Soviet policy must operate, to force upon the Kremlin a far greater degree of moderation and circumspection than it has had to observe in recent years, and in this way to promote tendencies which must eventually find their outlet in either the break-up or the gradual mellowing of Soviet power."[5]

In June 1947, the United States took a major step toward strengthening the West. Secretary of State George C. Marshall announced an impressive program of economic aid, formally called the European Recovery Program but widely known as the Marshall Plan. By 1952, when the plan terminated, it had supplied Europe with a total of $13.15 billion in aid—a modest pump-priming for the subsequent record upswing in U.S., Western European, and even global prosperity. Western Europe recovered, and the United States gained economically strong allies and trading partners.

In 1948, Stalin, seeking greater control in East Germany, cut off access to West Berlin. In response, the United States and British Commonwealth organized a massive, nearly yearlong airlift of supplies to the city, preserving the Western outpost in East Germany.

A key element of America's containment policy was the establishment of the North Atlantic Treaty Organization (NATO) in 1949. NATO linked the armed forces of the United States, Canada, Portugal, Norway, Iceland, Denmark, Italy, Britain, France (which withdrew from 1963 to 2009), Belgium, the Netherlands, and Luxembourg. Greece and Turkey soon joined; West Germany was included in 1956, and Spain in 1982. In response to NATO, the Soviet Union formed the Warsaw Pact (1955), consisting of the armed forces of the Soviet Union and its European satellites.

Military alliances and forces were backed up by ever more powerful armaments. Sooner than expected, in 1949, the Soviet Union exploded its own atomic device. Thereafter, drawing on the most sophisticated science and technology, the arms race escalated to hydrogen bombs (in 1952–1953) and intercontinental ballistic missiles (ICBMs), which ended America's geographical invulnerability.

The U.S.–Soviet rivalry extended into outer space. In 1957, the Soviet government sent the first *sputnik* (satellite) into orbit around the earth, shocking complacent Americans into a keen awareness of their vulnerability. For some years, the Soviet Union remained ahead in the prestigious field of space exploration, sending the first astronaut, Yuri Gagarin, into orbit in 1961. The United States established their preeminence in 1969 by landing a man on the moon.

Korean War. In June 1950, war broke out in Korea, a country divided in 1945 between

MARSHALL PLAN AID. Because much of Europe lay in rubble at the conclusion of World War II, the U.S. Congress approved the European Recovery Program (the official name of the Marshall Plan) in 1948. The earliest aid went toward agricultural assistance and housing construction to alleviate malnutrition and homelessness.

(© Bettmann/Corbis.)

a pro-Soviet Communist regime in the north and a pro-American regime in the south. Eager to restore Korean national unity and mistakenly assuming U.S. nonintervention, the North Korean army invaded South Korea with Soviet and Chinese Communist support, because the leaders of neither country thought the United States would intervene. Immediately, however, the United States gained UN backing (the USSR was temporarily boycotting that body) for a war against North Korea. Under the command of General Douglas MacArthur, South Korean and U.S. troops, assisted by a token force from other U.N. members, fought their way north toward the Chinese border. Joining the conflict, China dispatched troops—"volunteers," as they were called—to drive back the approaching enemy.

Forced to retreat, General MacArthur's troops eventually withdrew from North Korea. Peace was restored in 1953, with the division of Korea reaffirmed. South Korea evolved into a thriving democracy with a sophisticated economy and high standard of living. North Korea retained a ruthless Communist dictatorship and has one of the lowest standards of living on earth.

The Korean War was immensely costly: 36,568 Americans died in action; some 600,000 Chinese troops and more than 2 million Korean soldiers and civilians also perished. President Truman's decision not to use nuclear weapons and Russia's decision not to send troops indicated a tacit, though far from certain, understanding that a "hot" war between the superpowers was unthinkable.

Map 32.1 WESTERN EUROPE AFTER 1945 To counter the Communist threat from the Soviet Union, Western European countries cooperated for their mutual protection. The majority joined NATO for security against Communist attack, and six formed the Common Market (the forerunner of the European Union) to facilitate trade and economic integration. (© 2016 Cengage Learning.)

DECOLONIZATION

World War II, in which many colonial soldiers loyally fought for their masters, stirred up demands among non-Western peoples for an end to Western colonial rule and for political independence. After all, freedom and self-determination were prominent Allied war slogans. In the international climate of opinion after World War II, European colonial empires were viewed as racist

N. KOREA 1948   From Japan

S. KOREA 1948

PHILIPPINES 1946

N. VIETNAM 1954

S. VIETNAM 1954 Unified 1975

CAMBODIA (KAMPUCHEA) 1954

LAOS 1954

SINGAPORE 1965

MALAYSIA 1963

BURMA 1948

INDONESIA 1949

BANGLADESH 1971

INDIA 1947

SRI LANKA (CEYLON) 1948

PAKISTAN 1947

YEMEN (South Yemen 1967)

DJIBOUTI 1977

KUWAIT 1961

IRAQ 1932

JORDAN 1946

SYRIA 1946

CYPRUS 1960

LEBANON 1943

ISRAEL 1948

MALTA 1964

TUNISIA 1957

EGYPT 1922

SUDAN 1956

SOMALIA 1960

UGANDA 1962

KENYA 1963

TANZANIA 1964

MALAWI 1964

MOZAMBIQUE 1975

MALAGASY REP. (MADAGASCAR) 1960

MAURITIUS 1968

LIBYA 1951

CHAD 1960

CENTRAL AFRICAN REP. 1960

ZAIRE 1960

RWANDA 1962

BURUNDI 1962

ZAMBIA 1964

ZIMBABWE 1980

SWAZILAND 1968

LESOTHO 1968

BOTSWANA 1966

NAMIBIA 1990

ANGOLA 1975

SOUTH AFRICA 1910

NIGER 1960

MALI 1960

ALGERIA 1962

MOROCCO 1956

MAURITANIA 1960

WESTERN SAHARA (Morocco)

SENEGAL 1960

GAMBIA 1965

GUINEA-BISSAU 1974

GUINEA 1958

SIERRA LEONE 1961

LIBERIA

IVORY COAST 1960

BURKINA FASO 1960

GHANA 1957

TOGO 1960

BENIN 1960

NIGERIA 1960

CAMEROON 1960

GABON 1960

EQUATORIAL GUINEA 1968

REPUBLIC OF CONGO 1960

GREAT BRITAIN

PORTUGAL

FRANCE

NETH.

BELGIUM

ITALY

INDIAN OCEAN

ATLANTIC OCEAN

Date is year independence was achieved.
Shading indicates former ruler.

Great Britain

France

Netherlands

Italy

Belgium

Portugal

United States

0   500   1000 Km.

0   500   1000 Mi.

834

oppressors of Africans and Asians. Moreover, the European colonial powers were exhausted by the war. A mighty groundswell of decolonization, inspired by the ideals of the United Nations, eventually propelled African and Asian lands into independent statehood—over 50 from 1945 to 1975.

Although America's leaders generally supported the movements for independence—for example, liberating the Philippines in 1946—they feared that the newly independent states might fall under Soviet influence or even domination and thus shift the international balance of power. To counter this threat, the United States offered economic and technical aid throughout the developing world and occasionally intervened militarily. The Soviet leaders similarly provided economic and especially technical and military aid. Thus, developing countries were often counted in one or the other "camp" of the Cold War. Following the Bandung Conference of 1955, numerous "Third World" countries joined the "nonaligned movement," of which China claimed to be the primary leader.

Turmoil After Independence: Civil War and Dictatorship

Decolonization sparked many brutal struggles of building modern states among peoples ill prepared for this effort. For example, in 1960 the Belgians pulled out of the Congo, leaving behind some thirty Congolese university graduates to fill four thousand administrative posts.

Most former African colonies, divided by historic, ethnic, and tribal animosities, fell into civil war or dictatorships headed by ruthless and corrupt leaders who used their power for personal enrichment. Thus Mobuto Sese Seko, who ruled mineral-rich Zaire for thirty-two years, amassed one of the world's largest fortunes while poverty raged among his people. True, some newly independent countries such as Tunisia and Kenya

JOMO KENYATTA (c. 1894–1978). Imprisoned by the British for his opposition to colonial rule, he became the leader of independent Kenya in 1963. Under his slogan, Harambee (pulling together), he built a strong, stable government and a capitalist-oriented economy. In this image, Kenyatta wears a leopard skin over his Western-style suit. (Keystone/Getty Images.)

made a transition to stability. For decades, most African countries suffered economic stagnation, political oppression, and deadly factional violence.

Former Asian colonies also suffered hardships. In 1947, Britain partitioned India into two countries, Hindu India and Muslim Pakistan. The ensuing sectarian frenzy produced several 100,000 civilian deaths, many of them victims of massacres, and over 10 million displaced persons. The animosity persisted. In 1971, Bangladesh, supported by India, fought a bloody war of liberation from Pakistan which was compelled to grant it independence. The United States was drawn into a particularly brutal postimperial conflict in Vietnam.

◀ *Map 32.2* **FORMER EUROPEAN COLONIES**
Agitation for independence started after World War I, reaching a crescendo in the 1960s and giving birth of dozens of new countries.

BOGGED DOWN IN VIETNAM. Americans defended South Vietnam against a threatened takeover by Communist North Vietnam. Between 1964 and 1973, U.S. involvement in the unsuccessful Vietnam War polarized U.S. public opinion over its morality.

(AP Images/Henri Huet.)

The Vietnam War

From the U.S. perspective, the biggest challenge arose in Vietnam, where the Communist regime in the north threatened to take over South Vietnam. The threat had started with the partition of the country in 1954. From the north, the authoritarian regime of Ho Chi Minh (1890–1969), backed by indigenous nationalism and Soviet aid, cast its shadow over an inept and oppressive south. Providing South Vietnam with the stability and strength needed to resist Communist infiltration required increasing U.S. aid—including troops to fight off the Communist guerrillas, the Vietcong. If the Communists prevailed, the argument ran,

all the other countries in East and Southeast Asia emerging from colonial rule would fall like dominoes. Under President Lyndon B. Johnson, who assumed office in 1963, U.S. intervention in South Vietnam became the undeclared Vietnam War.

The U.S. government shipped to Vietnam nearly half a million soldiers, equipped with the latest weaponry and electronic equipment. Yet victory eluded them. The North Vietnamese government and its people withstood the cruelest punishment of bombs and chemical weapons ever inflicted. Nor was South Vietnam spared; virtually every South Vietnamese family saw relatives killed or maimed and their livelihoods ruined.

As domestic opposition to the war increased and Vietcong resistance held firm, President Richard M. Nixon, elected in 1968, initiated negotiations with North Vietnam, while U.S. forces put pressure on the enemy by attacking Communist bases and supply routes in neighboring Cambodia and Laos. Civilians were bombed more fiercely than in World War II. In 1973, by agreement with North Vietnam, the United States withdrew its forces. In 1975, the North Vietnamese swept aside the weak South Vietnamese army and unified the country under a Communist dictatorship. Ho Chi Minh had triumphed against the mightiest nation in the world. Tragically, the Communist regime sent perhaps 2 million citizens to "reeducation camps" where well over 100,000 died, and more than 2 million "boat people" fled the country as the economy collapsed.

In the wake of the American withdrawal, Cambodian Communists—the Khmer Rouge—seized power under their leader, Pol Pot. He drove more than 2 million people from the capital city of Phnom Penh and other cities to the countryside and tried to establish a new order based on ideologically regimented rural communes. The result was genocide in which well over 1 million people perished.

Soviet geopolitical success in winning client states in the developing world frightened voters in the West who elected as their leaders such determined anti-Communists as Margaret Thatcher in 1979 and Ronald Reagan the following year. Presumably the billions of rubles lavished on international relations in distant lands might have been better spent strengthening the weak Soviet economy.

Map 32.3 Southeast Asia and the Vietnam War The Vietcong used the Ho Chi Minh Trail to infiltrate South Vietnam. (© 2016 Cengage Learning.)

Building a New Europe: Unity and Recovery

Historically, a rough balance of power among autonomous states and extraordinary political and technological dynamism had cursed Europe with incessant warfare. Now, however, two ruinous world wars and the clear Soviet threat made some form of Western European unity attractive, if not imperative.

In 1951, the chief Continental consumers and producers of coal and steel, the two items most essential for rebuilding Western Europe, created the European Coal and Steel Community (ECSC). Its six members, France, West Germany, the Netherlands, Belgium, Luxembourg, and Italy, intended to put the Ruhr industrial complex, the heart of German industrial power, under international control, thereby promoting cooperation and reconciliation as well as economic strength.

Emboldened by the success of the ECSC, in 1957 the six countries established the European Economic Community (EEC), or the Common Market, a free-trade zone aimed at improving living conditions among member states. In 1973, Great Britain, Ireland, and Denmark joined the original members in what was now called the European Community (EC); in 1981, Greece and in 1986, Spain and Portugal became members. The EC constituted the world's largest single trading bloc, conducting more than one-fifth of the world's commerce. In this framework of growing cooperation, the major countries of Western Europe experienced a political and economic revival, which contributed to Western superiority in the Cold War.

A most striking fact of recent history in the West has been the unprecedented economic advance. Between the early 1950s and the late 1970s, production in Western Europe and the United States surpassed all previous records. The rapid postwar economic boom suffered a setback in the 1970s due in part to the drastic increase in oil prices imposed by the Organization of Petroleum Exporting Countries (OPEC). Economic growth returned throughout the 1980s, though unemployment remained high, even in West Germany, the strongest country economically.

Stimulated by the expansion of U.S. multinational corporations into Western Europe and by the opportunities offered by the European Community, many European companies came to be dominated by gigantic private and public enterprises tied to other parts of the world.

Boosted by rising standards of living and by U.S. power, the overall trend of political life in the West since World War II has been toward constitutional democracy. Although Spain and Portugal retained their prewar dictatorships until the mid-1970s and Greece for a time wavered between democracy and dictatorship, by the late 1970s even these countries had conformed to the common pattern.

Great Britain and France

Impoverished by the war and forced to give up nearly all its overseas colonies, Great Britain lost its leading role in world politics after World War II. British sea power was replaced by the American navy and air force. The postwar Labor

THE IRON LADY. Margaret Thatcher greeting her supporters upon her landslide victory in June 1983. The first woman prime minister of the UK, Thatcher espoused influential ideas of governance and political economy that came to be known as Thatcherism. (Uppa/Photoshot/ZUMA Press/Newscom.)

government, allied with powerful trade unions, provided Britons with a measure of economic security through social programs and extensive government control over important branches of the economy, though these very policies undermined economic efficiency and output.

In 1979, at a low point in the economy, the voters elected a Conservative government, led by Margaret Thatcher, Britain's first woman prime minister. She dominated English politics for the next decade, fighting inflation and rigorously encouraging individual initiative and free enterprise. During the Thatcher years, the British economy improved, and London regained its former luster as a financial center. Her ideas for economic and

social reform gave rise to an "ism": "Thatcherism," something no other British Prime Minister accomplished.

Across the English Channel, France, liberated from German occupation, was reorganized democratically under the Fourth Republic and soon achieved respectable economic growth, despite frequent changes of cabinet (twenty-six in twelve years). Decolonization caused political turmoil, especially in Algeria, where French settlers and soldiers were determined to thwart independence, resulting in a long and bloody conflict.

In 1958, the agitation to keep Algeria under French control, supported in certain army circles, reached a dangerous point. To prevent a right-wing coup aided by the army, General Charles de Gaulle stepped forward. He had been the leader of the Free French forces in World War II and president for a brief period after the war ended. De Gaulle established the Fifth Republic, with a strong executive authority, and sought to raise the country again to prominence by building its nuclear strength, making France independent of NATO, and renewing French influence in Africa. In 1962, he arranged a cease-fire in Algeria, allowing it to achieve independence. In 1968, demonstrations by students and workers demanding educational reform and social justice, which were supported by the Communist Party, greatly alarmed de Gaulle. He quickly called a general election, in which a frightened electorate gave him a landslide victory. However, unable to revise the constitution in his favor, he resigned in 1969.

The Fifth Republic continued under a government firmly based on a stable centrist majority, flanked by two radical parties. On the left, the Communist Party gradually lost credibility because of its loyalty to Moscow. On the extreme right, the ultranationalist *Front National* gained electoral strength in the early 1980s, stirring up hatred against the increasing number of Muslim immigrants from North Africa.

Amid the economic and political uncertainties of the times, François Mitterrand, a moderate socialist who became president in 1981, maintained the Gaullist tradition. His country was the fourth largest economy in the world and the third largest nuclear power. All along, France was a leading architect of European unity without surrendering its French character. Social welfare spending increased dramatically in all the leading Western European countries but especially in France, where by 2009 it consumed over 30 percent of GDP.

Italy and Germany

Italy became a democratic republic in 1946. Its government, however, was weak and unstable with frequent changes of cabinet. A long peninsula stretching out into the Mediterranean, the country offered a sharp contrast between north and south. The north was efficient and prosperous; the south, backward and infiltrated by the Mafia. Centered in Sicily, the Mafia was a source of political corruption and even occasional terror against the government.

Division also characterized the political parties, from Communists to Christian Democrats. The Italian Communists, relatively free from corruption, well organized, and oriented toward Europe rather than Moscow, usually gained a quarter of the vote. On the other hand, the Christian Democrats—allied with the Vatican and constituting the majority party—were poorly disciplined, like the other non-Communist parties and beset with corruption. Yet the Italian economy proved to be a surprising success, despite the fact that the government was perennially in debt and unemployment ran high, especially in the south.

In 1945, its cities in ruins, Germany had been defeated, occupied, and branded as a moral outcast. Divided among the four occupying powers—the United States, Britain, France, and the Soviet Union—the German nation was politically shattered. Extensive eastern lands were lost to Poland and the Soviet Union; some territory was returned to France. By 1949, two new and chastened Germanys had emerged. West Germany (the Federal Republic of Germany), formed from the three western zones of occupation, faced the hostile, Soviet-dominated East Germany (the German Democratic Republic). The former capital city of Berlin, inside East Germany, was similarly divided into western and eastern zones of occupation. West Germany thus became the crucial frontier of the Cold War, where spies confronted each other in secret and Western prosperity was showcased to the Soviet bloc.

The Cold War proved a boon to the West Germans; it contributed to their integration into the emerging new Europe and to the reduction of old hatreds. The West Germans, along with the Western armed forces stationed on their soil and most importantly the U.S. nuclear deterrent, were in a strategic position to help defend Western Europe against the vastly more powerful Soviet conventional forces. Moreover, German industrial expertise was indispensable for rebuilding the Western European economy. On this basis, West Germany (far larger than its Communist counterpart to the east and the most populous of all Western European countries) began to construct a new political identity.

Profile

Simone de Beauvoir

Simone de Beauvoir (1908–1986) was a prominent writer, feminist, left-wing activist, and leading member of the circle of existentialists that flourished in France after World War II. She received a conventional Catholic upbringing but repudiated religion in her teens. At the Sorbonne, where she was an outstanding student of philosophy, she met Jean Paul Sartre, the formulator of existentialism (see Chapter 30), with whom she formed a committed but open union that lasted until his death in 1980. Sartre encouraged de Beauvoir's writing, which she combined with teaching philosophy; after 1943, she devoted herself solely to her writing, which displayed her incisive intellect and keen wit. In her life and work, she exemplified the existentialist principle that we alone must provide the foundations for our existence, unaided by divine intervention, and are responsible for the consequences of our freedom.

The Second Sex (1949), her best-known work, is a treatise on sexual politics, specifically on how social pressures have relegated women to a secondary status in Western culture.

> *One is not born, but rather becomes, a woman. No biological, psychological, or economic fate determines the figure that the human female presents in society; it is civilization as a whole that produces this creature, intermediate between male and eunuch, which is described as feminine.**

De Beauvoir advocated meaningful careers and autonomous lives for women, free of dependence on others for their sense of identity. The book brought her both admiration and notoriety (no previous writer had discussed women's bodies so graphically); it became a primer for the international women's movement.

The Coming of Age (1972), de Beauvoir's other polemical work, attacked the conspiracy of silence over Western society's indifference to and treatment of the elderly. Her three volumes of autobiography provide, apart from personal interest, a panorama of French political and intellectual life throughout half a century. She was also a novelist and won the prestigious Goncourt Prize for *The Mandarins* (1954). A *roman à clef*, it depicted the role played by post–World War II existentialists in political activity.

Simone de Beauvoir lived a full life according to her principles and was committed to causes in which she believed. She was a pacifist in the 1930s and in the 1950s was openly opposed to France's war in Algeria and the atrocities committed by French officers. Her predominant commitment was to feminism and social change, on which she wrote and lectured tirelessly; she helped launch the French Women's Liberation Movement and fought for abortion rights for French women. Nearly three decades after her death, she is still celebrated as a feminist icon.

---

*Simone de Beauvoir, *The Second Sex*, trans. and ed. H. M. Parshley (London: Jonathan Cape, 1953), 295.

The architect of the new West Germany was Konrad Adenauer, its chancellor from 1949 to 1963 and a Christian Democrat. He sought to restore respect for Germany in cooperation with the leading states of Western Europe and the United States. As a patriot, he reestablished a cautious continuity with the German past. He also had Germany shoulder responsibility for the crimes Nazi regime and assume the payment of indemnifications and pensions to the Jewish victims and survivors of the Nazi era, as well as the payment of reparations to the state of Israel, which had been established in 1948 and where many survivors had settled. Under Adenauer's guidance, the West Germans also rebuilt their economy, leading in the 1950s to the German "economic miracle." As a result, democracy put down roots among the West German people, strengthening their solidarity with their former Western European enemies. West Germany was admitted to NATO in 1957 and, together with East Germany, to the United Nations in 1972. It joined France in promoting the European Community.

After the Adenauer era, German voters shifted from center-right to center-left. The Social Democrat Chancellor Willy Brandt (1969–1974) took the initiative for an "opening toward the East," which helped relax tensions between the superpowers. Generous financial support, backed by all the major Western powers, boosted the sagging Eastern Bloc economies. Social welfare spending in Germany also nearly doubled. At the same time, West German prosperity and a generous admission policy attracted ambitious immigrants, many from Turkey, into the booming economy. The German political system remained a contest between two main parties, with numerous smaller contestants joining them in forming coalition governments, including the Greens (founded in 1980), which advocated environmental protection and opposed nuclear power in all its forms. In 1982, the voters switched again, electing the leader of the Christian Democratic Union, Helmut Kohl, chancellor. He served for sixteen years and played a prominent role in integrating Western Europe and strengthening the Cold War alliance against Soviet Communism.

THE SOVIET BLOC

Stalin's Last Years

For the Soviet Union, World War II was another cruel landmark in the long succession of wars, revolutions, and crises that had afflicted the country since 1914. Despite the military victory, the USSR remained a closed society and a police state. The liberation many soldiers had hoped for as a reward for their heroism did not occur.

Corrupted by unlimited power and unrestrained adulation, his authority reinforced by success in the war, Stalin displayed in his last years an unrelenting ruthlessness. He kept the largely anti-Soviet populations in Eastern Europe in check with brute force and local propaganda machines, rebuilt the Soviet Union by neglecting the production of consumer goods, sent well over 1 million returning Soviet soldiers and prisoners of war to concentration camps for fear of their disloyalty, and poured vast resources into military development. Stalin's indomitable ambition, undiminished by age (he was sixty-six in 1945), was to build up Soviet power in his lifetime, whatever the human cost. More Five-Year Plans and more terror were needed.

Thus, the Soviet Union slid from war into peace, staggering through the hardships and hunger of the war's aftermath (a famine during 1946–1947 ended some 1 million lives), mourning its dead, and desperately short of men. Planning, much selfless hard work, manpower released from the army, and resources requisitioned from all occupied territories brought industrial production back to prewar levels within three years—no mean achievement.

In his last years, Stalin withdrew into virtual isolation, surrounded by a few fawning and fearful subordinates, and his paranoia worsened. Before he died, he "recognized" a plot among the doctors, most of them Jews, who treated him and other senior officials and personally issued orders for their torture (which killed one of them) and trial. A murderous campaign against Jews was averted only when on March 5, 1953, the failing dictator died of a stroke. His advisers sighed with relief, but many people wept. To them, Stalin was the godlike savior of the nation. The human costs of his regime were immense, but of his achievements in raising Soviet power there can be no doubt.

Khrushchev

After Stalin's death, leadership was assumed by a team headed by Nikita Khrushchev, who ruled from 1954 to 1964 and breathed fresh air into Soviet life. Khrushchev was the driving force behind the "thaw" that emptied the forced-labor camps—ironically and sadly increasing criminality in society and thus social discontent—and allowed most of the nationalities forcibly resettled during the war to return to their native regions. In a secret speech at the Twentieth Party Congress in February 1956, Khrushchev attacked Stalin himself. His audience gasped with horror as he recited the facts: "Of the 139 members and candidates of the Party Central Committee who were elected at the 17th Congress (1934), 98 persons, i.e., 70 percent, were arrested and shot."[6] Khrushchev denounced terror, though he failed to reveal statistics compiled for him that during 1937–1938 alone, 681,692 people had been executed. De-Stalinization was aimed to shift the country away from terror and raise Khrushchev's authority but without discrediting the Party. It was a fine line to walk. Indeed, the revelations had a powerful impact in the West (where the speech was smuggled out and published in full), discrediting the Soviet government, disillusioning formerly loyal supporters of Moscow, and contributing to the emergence of the independently oriented and reform-minded Eurocommunist movement. In Eastern Europe the speech provoked open revolt (see next section).

In foreign policy, Khrushchev professed to promote peace. Yet he also made some provocative moves. The U.S.S.R. threatened Western access to West Berlin in 1958, detonated a massive 50-megaton hydrogen bomb in 1961, and authorized the building in August 1961 of the infamous "Berlin Wall" aimed to stop the massive flight of East Germans to West Germany. Khrushchev also withdrew all Soviet advisers from China in 1960 as relations between the two Communist powers had deteriorated. His most adventurous policy culminated in the Cuban missile crisis. In 1959, the dictatorship of Fulgencio Batista had been toppled by Fidel Castro (b. 1927), a left-wing revolutionary who turned Cuba into a Communist-style dictatorship. After an American attempt to overthrow him in 1961—the bungled Bay of Pigs operation—Castro was ready to turn his country into an outpost of Soviet power. Khrushchev planned to exploit this foothold in the Western Hemisphere by installing Soviet nuclear missiles in Cuba. Although the United States had stationed nuclear weapons in Turkey, within easy reach of Soviet targets, the reverse situation—a major Soviet threat close to home—alarmed the country. President John F. Kennedy demanded that Khrushchev withdraw the Soviet missiles from Cuba. The Cold War confrontation threatened to turn into a hot nuclear war. However, Khrushchev backed down—a move that contributed to his fall from power two years later.

Eager to prod his country toward full Communist development, Khrushchev pressed for reforms in industry, agriculture, and party practices. His ceaseless reorganizations, impatient manner, and extravagant promises antagonized wide sections of the state and party administration. In October 1964, while he was on vacation, his comrades in the Politburo ousted him for "ill health" or, as they later added, his "hare-brained schemes." He was retired and allowed to live out his years in peace.

Khrushchev was succeeded by a leadership team, among whom Leonid Brezhnev (1906–1982) gradually rose to the fore. Under his leadership, the government of the USSR turned from a personal dictatorship into an oligarchy: the collective rule of a privileged minority. Brezhnev's style stressed management rather than command. Soviet officials breathed more easily, and Soviet society in turn grew less authoritarian. "A little deal" was unofficially instituted whereby citizens could engage in underground economic and countercultural activities so long as they avoided politics. The widespread attitude of "they pretend to pay us, and we pretend to work" undermined economic output. The country opened cautiously to the outside world. For instance, young people were allowed some access to Western styles of music and dress. More issues of state policy were opened to public debate, and more latitude was granted to artistic expression. Interest in religion revived.

There were, however, limits to official leniency. Any public questioning of the Communist system or its leaders, even in literary allusion, could land one in prison or (later) in a mental institution, beginning with the trial of the "dissident" writers Andrei Sinyavsky and Yuli Daniel during 1965-1966. Yet the dissident movement gained strength. It received a powerful boost from the Helsinki accords, signed in 1975, which recognized the existing Eastern European borders, and so was favored by Moscow, but also guaranteed human rights within them and thus "gradually became a manifesto of the dissident and liberal movement," in the words of the Soviet Ambassador to Washington, Anatoly Dobrynin.[7]

Changes in Eastern Europe

Realizing that continued repression of the satellite countries would provoke trouble, Stalin's successors began to relax their controls there, too.

Soviet tanks in Budapest, Hungary, November 1956. On October 30, 1956, Soviet tanks left Budapest but returned a week later and crushed the Hungarian Uprising, leaving as many as 1,500 civilians dead. (AFP/Getty Images.)

Eastern Europe's Communist rulers adapted their own forms of industrialization, collectivization of agriculture, and dictatorship. The history of the region after 1953 was thus a series of experiments to determine what deviations from Soviet practice in domestic politics and what measure of self-assertion in foreign policy the Kremlin would tolerate. For example, in June 1953 the workers of Berlin in the German Democratic Republic (East Germany) staged an uprising, gaining some concessions, though the Communist Party (here called the Socialist Unity Party) continued to rule with an iron fist.

No event proved more crucial than Khrushchev's attack on Stalin in 1956. It set off a political earthquake throughout the bloc, discrediting Stalinists and encouraging moderates, reviving cautious discussions among intellectuals, and even arousing visions of national self-determination.

The first rumbles of protest were heard in June 1956 in Poland—the largest and most troublesome of the satellite countries. The crisis came to a head in October: would Poland revolt, inviting invasion by the Red Army, or would Khrushchev ease Soviet control? The Soviet boss yielded in return for a Polish pledge of continued loyalty to the Soviet Union. Thereafter, Poland breathed more freely, affirming its Catholicism as a cornerstone of its national identity.

Although the "Polish October" ended peacefully, events moved to a brutal showdown in Hungary. On October 20, 1956, anti-Soviet feeling boiled

Legend:

- German territory to Poland
- Acquired by Soviet Union, 1939–1945
- Soviet satellites
- Communist, nonsatellite nation
- "Iron Curtain" after 1950

Scale: 0 200 400 Km. / 0 200 400 Mi.

ICELAND

IRELAND — Dublin

GREAT BRITAIN — London

NORWAY — Oslo

SWEDEN — Stockholm

FINLAND — Helsinki

SOVIET UNION — Moscow, Leningrad

Gulf of Finland

Volga R.

ESTONIA

LATVIA

LITHUANIA

BELORUSSIA

UKRAINE — Kiev

Dnieper R.

CRIMEA

MOLDAVIA

Baltic Sea

DENMARK — Copenhagen

Gdansk (Danzig)

POLAND — Warsaw

Vistula R.

EAST GERMANY — Berlin

Hamburg

Elbe R.

WEST GERMANY — Bonn, Munich, Hamburg

NETHERLANDS — Amsterdam

BELGIUM — Brussels

LUX.

FRANCE — Paris

Seine R.

Rhône R.

Rhine R.

SWITZERLAND

CZECHOSLOVAKIA — Prague

AUSTRIA — Vienna

HUNGARY — Budapest

ROMANIA — Bucharest

BULGARIA — Sofia

Danube R.

YUGOSLAVIA — Belgrade

ALBANIA — Tirane

GREECE — Athens

ITALY — Rome

Po R.

Corsica

Sardinia

Sicily

SPAIN — Madrid

PORTUGAL — Lisbon

Ebro R.

TURKEY — Ankara

Istanbul

IRAN

IRAQ

SYRIA

Black Sea

Caspian Sea

Adriatic Sea

Mediterranean Sea

North Sea

ATLANTIC OCEAN

over in an uprising in Budapest, forcing Soviet troops to withdraw from the country. A moderate Communist government called for Western-style political democracy and Hungary's withdrawal from the Warsaw Pact. Thoroughly alarmed, the Soviet leaders struck back. On November 4, 1956, Soviet troops reentered Hungary and crushed all opposition, leaving up to 1,500 civilians dead.

But the bold uprising left its mark. The new Communist leader of Hungary, János Kádar, was a moderate. With Khrushchev's approval, he built a pragmatic regime of consumer-oriented "goulash Communism" that granted considerable opportunity to private enterprise. Kádar's regime also allowed non-Communists to participate extensively in public affairs. Relaxation and decentralization of planning made possible in the 1970s a remarkable increase in economic prosperity. The Hungarian experiment became the envy of the other Soviet Bloc countries, though by contrast with Western Europe the standard of living remained abysmally low.

After 1956, Soviet leaders permitted modest social and economic evolution in the Eastern Bloc countries. In Czechoslovakia in 1968, a new group of Czech Communists, led by Alexander Dubček, sought to liberalize their regime to include non-Communists, permit greater freedom of speech, and rid the economy of the rigidities that for so long had impeded prosperity. Their goal was "socialism with a human face": a Communist Party supported by public goodwill rather than by the secret police.

This program panicked the Soviet Bloc leaders. On August 21, Warsaw Pact troops carried out a swift and well-prepared occupation of Czechoslovakia but failed to break the rebellious will of its reformers. While Soviet tanks rumbled through Prague, the Czechoslovak Communist leaders

◀ *Map 32.4* Eastern Europe After 1945 During and after World War II the Soviet Union extended its rule halfway across Europe. Repressive Communist governments in Eastern Europe were controlled by Moscow. Yugoslavia, though a Communist state, defied Moscow and established links to Western Europe and the United States.

(© 2016 Cengage Learning.)

met secretly but defiantly. Nonetheless, the revolt ended in failure. The party was purged, all reforms were canceled, and the country was reduced to abject hopelessness. A cry of moral outrage resounded around the world.

Turning Point of Soviet Power

Soviet power seemed to be increasing internationally. The new countries emerging from colonial rule in Asia and Africa offered seductive opportunities for Communist expansion, and by the late 1970s, the Soviet navy and nuclear arsenal were fast approaching the USA in quantity if not quality. Closer to home, however, the empire was showing strain.

Polish industrial workers, theoretically the real masters in Communist regimes, took the lead in pressing for freedom and a better standard of living. When a Polish cardinal became Pope John Paul II in 1978, patriotism surged. In 1980, workers, under the leadership of an electrician named Lech Walesa, succeeded, with the blessing of the church, in forming an independent labor union. Called Solidarity, the union engaged in numerous strikes. In 1981, matters came to a head: some of Solidarity's more radical members spoke of bringing free elections to Poland. In December, a military dictatorship, formed under General Wojciech Jaruzelski, imposed martial law. Walesa and other leaders of Solidarity were arrested, and protesting workers were dispersed by force.

The Gorbachev Years

Brezhnev died in 1982; his immediate successors, chosen by agreement among top party officials, were old men who survived in office only for a short time. Former KGB chief Yuri Andropov (aged sixty-eight), in poor health from the start, died in early 1984. He was replaced by Konstantin Chernenko, a man of Brezhnev's generation, likewise in poor health, who lasted until early 1985. In March 1985, Mikhail Gorbachev (b. 1931) took over, representing a younger and more sophisticated age group, whose members had started their careers in the calmer times after Stalin's death.

Self-confident, energetic, and articulate, Gorbachev was keenly aware of his country's problems and eager to confront them. Life expectancy was in decline, and infant mortality was rising. Alcoholism was rife. Air and water pollution were at catastrophic levels. Economic growth had stagnated or even stalled. The Soviet Union produced scarcely any consumer goods that could be sold on the international market. Rigid, centralized planning stifled innovation. The country lagged in the design and production of computers, which had huge implications for military technology.

Gorbachev began his term in office with ideas for reform. The Soviet workforce, he believed, was lazy, unmotivated, and overly prone to drinking. His first major policies therefore called for "acceleration," aimed at increasing worker productivity, and an anti-alcohol campaign. The government closed distilleries and uprooted vineyards. The population simply turned to moonshine and dangerous substitutes like eau de cologne.

Gorbachev also hoped to effect a complete restructuring (*perestroika*) of the political and economic system, though without unleashing individual entrepreneurship and other market forces or undermining the Communist Party's monopoly of power. Gradually, he recognized that the political system with its entrenched bureaucratic interests was stymying his reforms. To loosen up administrative rigidity, local officials and entrepreneurs in agriculture, industry, and consumer services were granted more autonomy, though in practice bureaucrats often hindered these efforts.

His advisors then advocated encouraging a public discussion of problems as a means to "light a fire under the bureaucracy." Thus *glasnost*, or openness, was proclaimed in January 1986. This policy was dramatically put to the test in late April 1986 when, because of staff misjudgment, a reactor at the nuclear power plant at Chernobyl exploded, spewing dangerous radiation high into the atmosphere; poisonous fallout covered much of Europe. It was by far the worst nuclear accident ever experienced. At first, the Soviet government, following its usual pattern, downplayed its significance.

The tragedy nevertheless spurred Gorbachev to promote *glasnost* in earnest. He let all the problems of Soviet society, hitherto kept under cover, be openly discussed: corruption, abuse of power, the privileges of the elites, ecological destruction,

and disregard for legality. Domestic news began to depict Soviet reality more accurately. There was also a new candor about the Soviet past. During the seventieth anniversary of the Bolshevik Revolution, Gorbachev asserted that "the guilt of Stalin . . . for the wholesale repressive measures and acts of lawlessness is enormous and unforgivable."[8] Gorbachev then assured Soviet citizens that they should not hesitate to speak out freely. Academics, writers, and artists responded enthusiastically. As contacts with the outside world increased, Western ideals, culture, and respect for human rights entered Soviet minds as never before.

Yet the rigid Communist system was not easy to reform. Economic output and per capita consumption continued to fall. To drum up more support for change, Gorbachev advocated "the democratization of society." This involved shifting power away from the Communist Party and toward an elective Congress of People's Deputies. For the first time since 1917, citizens had the right to choose among more than one candidate. The electoral system was still stacked against non-Communists, only 12 percent of whom were elected during the election of 1989. Even so, and contrary to his own wishes, Gorbachev had mobilized popular opposition not only to the entrenched Communist bureaucrats but to himself as well.

The End of the Cold War

Gorbachev also sought to ease international tensions. Above all, the high cost of the Cold War impeded the reforms that his socialist country so urgently needed. In the spirit of *glasnost*, Gorbachev frankly admitted that the adverse prospects of his country's economy forced him to advocate not only "normal international relations" but also an end to the arms race. Pressure from foreign leaders, especially Ronald Reagan, Margaret Thatcher, and Pope John Paul II, who tirelessly challenged Soviet Communism in both word and deed, lent urgency to Gorbachev's agenda. Reagan took seriously Soviet treaty violations, launched an arms race the Soviets could ill afford, furnished logistical support to anti-Communist groups inside the Soviet Bloc like the Polish trade union

MIKHAIL GORBACHEV AND RONALD REAGAN, 1988. A life-long anti-Communist, Ronald Reagan differed from most Western observers in believing the Soviet system was doomed to collapse. Constant American diplomatic, strategic, moral, and clandestine pressure during his administration helped fulfill this expectation. (SGranitz/WireImage/Getty Images.)

Solidarity, supplied military aid to the mujahideen in Afghanistan and other anti-Communist militants in the Third World, invaded the Caribbean island of Grenada to dislodge Cuban forces, and insisted on building the Strategic Defense Initiative ("Star Wars"), an ultra-sophisticated missile defense system the Soviets could not hope to match.

By early 1989, Gorbachev withdrew the Soviet army from Afghanistan, admitting that the 1979 invasion to preserve the Communist regime had been a mistake. He allowed Eastern Europe to throw off Soviet domination and halted support for Marxist regimes in the Third World. Unilaterally demobilizing sizable units of the Red Army in 1988, he also stopped nuclear testing. At summit meetings—with President Reagan and later with President George H. W. Bush—Gorbachev successfully negotiated strategic reductions of the nuclear arsenals of the United States and the Soviet Union.

The Collapse of Communism

1989: The Year of Liberation.   Resentful of Communist domination and growing economic hardships, in 1989 and 1990 Eastern Europeans demanded democratic reforms. Faced with a rising tide of popular discontent, Communist leaders resigned or agreed to reforms. People around the world cheered the opening of a new era in Eastern Europe.

In Poland, public pressure had forced General Jaruzelski to end his dictatorship and appoint a civilian government. Struggling with a deteriorating economy, Jaruzelski legalized the highly popular Solidarity union in 1989. Permitted to run against Communist Party candidates in a free election, Solidarity won an overwhelming victory. The once jailed Solidarity members now sat in the Polish parliament next to their former jailers. In December 1990, Lech Walesa, the leader of Solidarity, was elected president.

Encouraged by events in Poland, Hungary abolished its Communist bureaucracy in May 1989. By the end of the year, a multiparty system was in place, with two non-Communist parties, the Democratic Forum and the Alliance of Free Democrats, competing for leadership. Hungary had shaken off Soviet domination and embraced the ideals of democracy and free enterprise.

An even more momentous upheaval occurred in 1989 in East Germany. More than 340,000 people voted for freedom and prosperity with their feet, escaping to West Germany across the recently opened borders of Hungary and Czechoslovakia. Far larger numbers took to the streets in protest against the regime. Hoping to restore calm, Party Secretary Erich Honecker's colleagues deposed their sickly, old, hard-line boss, but antigovernment demonstrations continued. On November 6, when almost a million demonstrators crammed the streets of East Berlin, the Communist government resigned. On November 9, in an explosion of patriotic fervor, the Berlin Wall was breached; tens of thousands of East Germans flocked into West Berlin, where they were welcomed with flowers and champagne. Liberated East Germany was soon reunited with West Germany, with Gorbachev's approval.

In Bulgaria, the dramatic events in Berlin led to the resignation of Tedor Zhivkov, the longest-serving Communist dictator in the Soviet Bloc and an opponent of reform. Bulgaria had joined the quest for democratic government and private enterprise.

While democratic reforms triumphed elsewhere, Romania's Nicholae Ceausescu, long bent on pursuing his own dictatorial course and hostile to Gorbachev's reforms, ruthlessly enforced his own rule, ordering his soldiers to shoot into a crowd of antigovernment demonstrators. But popular resentment was too powerful to contain, and even the army turned against the dictator. On December 25, 1989, Ceausescu and his wife were hastily tried and executed. The most hardened symbol of Communist rule, defying to the last the common trend toward democratic freedom, had ignominiously fallen.

Faced with massive demonstrations in Prague and urged by Gorbachev himself to institute democratic reform, Czechoslovakia's Communist leaders resigned on November 24, 1989. Václav Havel, a leading dissident writer and outspoken advocate of democracy who had been jailed for his views, was chosen president on December 25.

Shocked by the news of Ceausescu's execution and Havel's election, the Yugoslav Communist Party caved in. Its central committee suggested the formation of a multiparty system, which was fully adopted in January 1990.

Except for Albania, where the Communist Party held on until free elections in February 1991, all of Eastern Europe had liberated itself from Soviet domination—a breathtaking change, accomplished unexpectedly within a single year. Viewed as a whole, events in Eastern Europe had taken a surprisingly peaceful course, prompted by

Map 32.5 Post–Cold War Europe and the ▶ Former Soviet Union Instead of the stark postwar division of Europe into three blocs—Western Europe, Eastern Europe, and the Soviet Union— the continent is now a patchwork of independent countries, some with new names. Russia remains the largest country, but the former Soviet Republics on Russia's eastern and southern borders gained independence. Within Europe, East and West Germany have reunited, while Yugoslavia and Czechoslovakia have split up. (© 2016 Cengage Learning.)

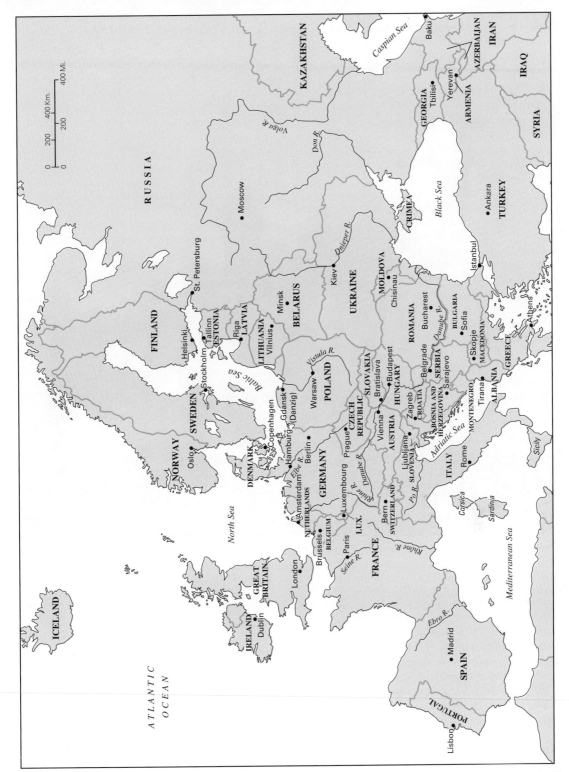

ATLANTIC OCEAN

ICELAND

GREAT BRITAIN
London

IRELAND
Dublin

North Sea

NORWAY
Oslo

SWEDEN
Stockholm

FINLAND
Helsinki

St. Petersburg

RUSSIA
Moscow

KAZAKHSTAN

Caspian Sea

Baltic Sea

DENMARK
Copenhagen

Gdansk (Danzig)

ESTONIA
Tallinn

LATVIA
Riga

LITHUANIA
Vilnius

Minsk
BELARUS

Volga R.

Don R.

GEORGIA
Tbilisi

AZERBAIJAN
Baku

IRAN

ARMENIA
Yerevan

IRAQ

Hamburg
Berlin

NETHERLANDS
Amsterdam

Brussels
BELGIUM

Paris

Seine R.

Elbe R.

GERMANY

Prague
CZECH REPUBLIC

Warsaw

POLAND

Vistula R.

Dnieper R.

Kiev

UKRAINE

MOLDOVA
Chisinau

CRIMEA

Black Sea

Istanbul

TURKEY
Ankara

SYRIA

Luxembourg
LUX.

Danube R.

Rhine R.

SWITZERLAND
Bern

FRANCE

Rhône R.

SLOVAKIA
Bratislava

Vienna
AUSTRIA

Budapest
HUNGARY

Ljubljana
SLOVENIA

Zagreb
CROATIA

Po R.

ROMANIA
Bucharest

Belgrade
SERBIA

BOSNIA AND HERZEGOVINA
Sarajevo

Danube R.

BULGARIA
Sofia

Skopje
MACEDONIA

GREECE

Athens

ITALY
Rome

MONTENEGRO
Tirana
ALBANIA

Adriatic Sea

Corsica

Sardinia

Sicily

Mediterranean Sea

Ebro R.

SPAIN
Madrid

PORTUGAL
Lisbon

400 Km.
400 Mi.
200
200
0
0

849

THE WALL CAME TUMBLING DOWN. The Berlin Wall, symbol of the division of Germany, was breached in November 1989. Young people excitedly clambered onto the partially demolished wall while East and West Berliners thronged the streets. (© Regis Bossu/Sygma/Corbis.)

a number of favorable factors. First, a weakening of censorship had enabled citizens to perceive the vastly higher standard of living in the free and democratic West. Second, led by intellectuals and clergy, the people united against repression, foreign domination, and economic misery. Finally, Gorbachev had been willing to let the satellite peoples go their own way. The revolutionary changes of 1989 constituted an overwhelming victory for Western forms of government and ways of life.

Most of the East European Communist leaders would have fought to keep power, if only their Soviet chief had given them military support. Why did Gorbachev abandon them? He wanted what most Soviet citizens longed for: "a normal life in a normal country." He cared about international criticism of his government's use of violence in the political sphere. He believed in the ideals of the self-determination of peoples and the popular will. Above all he still believed in Soviet-style socialism and its capacity for both peaceful reform and continued popular support.

The Disintegration of the Soviet Union.

The transformation and spiritual rebirth that Gorbachev wanted for the Soviet Union did not occur. In October 1990, he conceded that "unfortunately, our society is not ready for the procedures of a law-based state. We don't have that level of political culture, those traditions. All that will come in the future."[9] Meanwhile, the Soviet Union was experiencing a breakdown of effective government, economic collapse, corruption, and spiraling crime. Especially threatening were nationalist movements in regions inhabited by non-Russian minorities. These included Latvians, Lithuanians, and Estonians in the Baltic region; Armenians and Georgians in the Caucasus; and Moldavians and Ukrainians in the southwest. In response to the mounting crisis, the "democrats," most strongly represented in Moscow and Leningrad among the young generation open to Western ways, pressed, under Boris Yeltsin's guidance, for speedy Westernization, including a multiparty system and a market economy. On the opposite side, the Communist hard-liners prepared to revive the old system, relying on the army and the security forces to restore order and hold the country together. In August 1991, they staged a coup, seeking to depose Gorbachev as president of the Soviet Union. Their aim was to re-establish the Communist dictatorship.

However, the conspirators, all of them high officials appointed by Gorbachev, grossly misjudged the people's revulsion against the Communist Party. The KGB's vanguard forces defected to Yeltsin, elected president of the Russian Federation in June 1991, who led a fervent popular protest at a risk to his life. The emotional outburst in favor of democracy quickly spread from Moscow to other cities, and the coup collapsed within three days. The chief victim of the coup, apart from its leaders, was the Communist Party, now repudiated by Gorbachev himself and swept aside by public fury. Racked by the deteriorating economy and the growing nationalist sentiments among the various ethnic groups, the Soviet Union fell to pieces. The Baltic nations—Lithuania, Latvia, and Estonia—established their independence shortly after the failed coup, and a new Commonwealth of Independent States, consisting of eleven former republics of the collapsed Soviet Union, was proclaimed in December 1991, and Gorbachev, the last leader of the Soviet Union, resigned as president of a now-defunct country. Boris Yeltsin became the informal leader of the commonwealth. Its ideology discredited, its economy shattered, and its government transformed into a confederation of sovereign states, the Soviet Union had collapsed as a major force in world affairs. Only one superpower remained.

The Death of an Ideal?

The sudden and unexpected collapse of Communism in Eastern Europe in 1989 seemed to discredit Marxism irrevocably. Reformers in Eastern European lands liberated from Communist oppression expressed revulsion for the socialist past and a desire to regenerate their countries with an infusion of Western liberal ideals and institutions. Havel, the newly elected president of a free Czechoslovakia, expressed this disillusionment with the past and hope for a new democratic future:

> *The worst of it is that we live in a spoiled moral environment. We have become morally ill because we are used to saying one thing and thinking another. We have learned not to believe in anything, not to care about each other, to worry only about ourselves. . . . The previous regime, armed with a proud and intolerant ideology, reduced people into the means of production. . . . Many of our citizens died in prison in the 1950's. Many were executed. Thousands of human lives were destroyed.*[10]

Marxism had become a failed ideology propped up only by force in the few surviving Communist regimes. "Scientific socialism," which claimed to have deciphered the essential meaning and direction of history, is neither scientific nor relevant to current needs. It is merely another idea that was given too much credence and is now ready to be swept into the dustbin of history. Political theorist Francis Fukuyama suggests that the decline of Communism and the end of the Cold

War reveal a larger process at work, "the ultimate triumph of Western liberal democracy":

> *The twentieth century saw the developed world descend into a paroxysm of ideological violence, as liberalism contended first with the remnants of absolutism, then bolshevism and Fascism, and finally an updated Marxism that threatened to lead to the ultimate apocalypse of nuclear war. But the century that began full of self-confidence in the ultimate triumph of*

> *Western liberal democracy seems at its close to be returning full circle to where it started . . . to an unabashed victory of economic and political liberalism. The triumph of the West, of the Western idea, is evident first of all in the total exhaustion of viable systematic alternatives to Western liberalism. . . . What we may be witnessing . . . is the end point of mankind's ideological evolution and the universalization of Western liberal democracy as the final form of government.*[11]

NOTES

1. Quoted in Walter Laqueur, *Europe Since Hitler* (Baltimore: Penguin Books, 1970), 118.

2. Quoted in Melvyn P. Lefler, *For the Soul of Mankind: The United States, the Soviet Union, and the Cold War* (New York: Hill and Wang, 2007), 340.

3. Winston S. Churchill, "Sinews of Peace: Address, March 5, 1946," *Vital Speeches of the Day*, March 15, 1946, 3.

4. "The Truman Doctrine," in *Major Problems in American Foreign Policy: Documents and Essays*, ed. Thomas G. Paterson (Lexington, Mass.: Heath, 1978), Vol. 2, 290.

5. Richard D. Heffner, ed., *A Documentary History of the United States*, 7th ed. (New York: Signet, 2002), 366–68.

6. Nikita S. Krushchev, in *The Crimes of the Stalin Era: Special Report to the 20th Congress of the Communist Party of the Soviet Union*, annotated by Boris I. Nicolaevsky (New York: The New Leader, 1956), 20.

7. Quoted in John Lewis Gaddis, *The Cold War: A New History* (New York: Penguin Books, 2005), 190.

8. Gorbachev's speech at the seventieth anniversary of the Bolshevik Revolution, quoted in *The New York Times*, November 3, 1987, A3.

9. Quoted in Anthony Lewis, "Et Tu Eduard," *The New York Times*, December 21, 1990, A39.

10. *The New York Times*, January 2, 1990, A13.

11. Francis Fukuyama, "The End of History," *The National Interest* (Summer 1989), 3–4.

Chapter 33

The Troubled Present

The destruction of the World Trade Center's twin towers by members of Al Qaeda, a terrorist organization headed by Osama bin Laden, mobilized the United States to take the offensive against international terrorism. (AP Images/Carmen Taylor.)

- ■ **The Post–Cold War World**
- ■ **New and Old Problems: Muslim Immigration and the Resurgence of Anti-Semitism**
- ■ **Culture Clash, Terrorism, and War**
- ■ **Our Global Age: Promise and Problems**
- ■ **Reaffirming the Core Ideals of the Western Tradition**

Focus Questions

1. How did the collapse of Communism impact politics in Eastern Europe and Russia?

2. What are the problems and perils of the European Union?

3. What tensions surround Muslim immigration to Europe?

4. What are the reasons for the surge of anti-Semitism in contemporary Europe?

5. What are the motivations and goals of radical Muslims? How should Europe and the United States respond to radical Islam?

6. The euphoria with which Westerners first greeted the Arab Spring has waned. Why?

7. What are the West's roles in the contemporary world?

8. In your opinion, what are the reasons to be optimistic about current world conditions? To be pessimistic?

9. What are the essential ideals of the Western tradition? In your opinion, how can these ideals best be preserved?

Since 1989, momentous events have changed the world. The superpower polarization of world politics ended, and a new, multicentered, unstable world order has emerged. Western civilization and its ideals have fostered transcultural worldwide modernity. At the same time, however, traditional cultural diversity still simmers. The end of the Cold War introduced a new uncertainty into human affairs. On the one hand, global interdependence promotes peaceful cooperation and extraordinary innovation and prosperity; on the other, it gives rise to a clash of cultural traditions.

THE POST–COLD WAR WORLD

Post-Communist Russia

Throughout the 1990s and into the twenty-first century, the Russian Federal Republic has been struggling to bring its political and economic systems into conformity with the Western model while coping with its loss of territory and superpower status. The collapse of the Soviet Union revealed Russia to be a weak, poorly developed society beset by profound problems.

Yeltsin's "Shock Therapy." Marred by mismanagement, waste, and lack of incentives, the Soviet economic system had failed miserably in comparison with Western capitalism. In order to reform the economy and improve the standard of living of the Russian people, which lagged far behind living standards in Western lands, President Yeltsin, emerging in 1990 as the leader of the new Russia, adopted policies in 1992 to transition from a state-run economy to private ownership and a capitalist market system. This "shock therapy" in many ways proved a disaster. The chief beneficiaries of privatization were often either former inefficient managers or well-connected party elites. Several of these managers and officials amassed wealth by unscrupulous means. Industrial decline, the withdrawal of government subsidies, and ruinous inflation reduced millions of people dependent on pensions to hand-to-mouth subsistence. Many working

Pope John Paul II

Pope John Paul II, who died in April 2005, earned the tribute and respect of Catholics and non-Catholics throughout the world. Born Karol Jozef Wojtyla in Poland in 1920, he was an excellent student with a flair for languages. At secondary school, young Karol also distinguished himself in athletics and theater. At the time of the German invasion of Poland in 1939, Wojtyla was attending Jagiellonian University in Krakow. When the Nazis closed down the university, he worked in a stone quarry and then in a factory. Leaving the factory job in 1942, he studied secretly for the priesthood in the home of Krakow's archbishop and was ordained in 1946, a year and a half after the war had ended. During the next several years, he earned two doctorates in philosophy and theology, one in Rome and the other in Poland, where he taught social ethics. In 1964, he became archbishop of Krakow, was elevated to the College of Cardinals in 1967, and in 1978 became John Paul II, the first non-Italian pope since 1523.

Several distinguishing features characterized Pope John Paul's twenty-six-year pontificate. He journeyed to more than 120 countries to advance spiritual renewal and interfaith relations. As part of his holy mission, he condemned war and violence repeatedly. In Ireland, he told the violent Catholic and Protestant factions: "On my knees I beg you to turn away from the path of violence and return to the ways of peace." He protested violations of human rights around the world; denounced oppressive Communism; attacked the greed, materialism, and economic injustice fomented by capitalism; and publicly repented for the acts of injustice and intolerance committed by the church in the past two thousand years.

He reached out to non-Catholic Christians, Muslims—no other pope had visited a mosque—Buddhists, and Jews. In dramatic fashion, John Paul continued the work of the post-Holocaust church in improving Jewish–Catholic relations. He reaffirmed the Jewish roots of Christianity; condemned anti-Semitism as a sin "against God and man" and lamented past Christian behavior toward Jews; prayed in the synagogue in Rome (the first pope ever to do so); and established full diplomatic relations with Israel and made an official visit to that country, including moving stops at the Western Wall, Judaism's holiest site, and Yad Vashem, Israel's Holocaust memorial, where he paid his respects to the Jewish victims of Nazi persecution. As a young man, he had witnessed Nazi brutality against Jews.

Historians credit John Paul for aiding the collapse of Communism in Eastern Europe. Soon after his election to the papacy, he visited his native Poland, where huge crowds of admirers turned out to see him. His words— "The exclusion of Christ from the history of man is an act against man"—buoyed the spirits of the intensely Catholic population, giving them hope that the spiritual would prevail over atheistic Communism, which, he said, treats people "merely as means of production." His visit helped give rise to Solidarity, a labor movement that challenged Poland's Communist rulers.

On certain questions, John Paul was extremely conservative—strongly opposing abortion, contraception, premarital sex, homosexuality, same-sex unions, and the ordination of women, and insisting on the inviolability of celibacy for priests. Liberal Catholics faulted the pope's prohibition against condoms, which they felt were necessary for family planning and for protection against AIDS. They also maintained that it was time for the church to admit women to the priesthood and for the church to make celibacy optional. Finally, his papacy came under criticism for its slowness in confronting the problem of sexual abuse by priests.

Russians also sank into poverty as real wages plummeted some 40 percent from 1992 to 1998. Workers often had to wait two to six months for their paychecks, and unemployment soared.

With popular unrest mounting and facing opposition from Communist hard-liners, Yeltsin was forced to slow his liberalization of the economy; the social costs—public confusion over bewildering changes, a sharp decline in the standard of living, and the loss of productivity leading to shortages—were too high. "No more experiments," advised slogans spray-painted on walls. In October 1993, during a confrontation with the legislature, dominated by Communists who resisted reform, Yeltsin ordered military forces to shell the parliament building. The old Communist guard was definitively removed from politics, but hopes for a truly democratic Russia were dashed.

Adding to the intractable problems of the new Russia were soaring crime and corruption. Yeltsin consolidated his power by making alliances with a small group of businessmen, the "oligarchs," who had grown wealthy by acquiring former state-owned enterprises at extremely low prices. They plundered the firms for assets, concentrating Russia's wealth in their own hands. As law enforcement deteriorated, organized crime became a major force in Russian life.

The oligarchs financed Yeltsin's bid for reelection as president in 1996 despite his suffering a heart attack during the election campaign. At age sixty-six and in frail health, Yeltsin could no longer provide effective leadership for his vast, fragmented country, and in 1997, he frankly acknowledged the difficulties that he and his country faced: "After creating a new political system, we failed to outfit it with new tools of government, and we ourselves did not learn to govern in a new way."[1]

Nevertheless, by permitting the oligarchs to buy up the major state enterprises, Yeltsin smashed Soviet central planning. It would be impossible in these circumstances to reinstate Communism in Russia. Yet many key enterprises, including banks and the media, were now controlled by unscrupulous oligarchs. In return for their support of Yeltsin, they became an inner political circle in the Kremlin, controlling the country's policies. No wonder Russians began to feel that the government itself had been privatized.

In August 1998, the dysfunctional banking system precipitated a second currency collapse, wiping out Russians' savings and livelihoods. Among the casualties were many of the oligarchs. Some were ruined by the collapse of their banks, others went abroad, and the remainder backed out of public life. Suddenly their political influence, which had been paramount since 1995, diminished dramatically, and a new generation of businessmen began to emerge. The default had other long-term positive effects. It wiped out inflationary rubles, drove up the cost of imports, and thus stimulated domestic production.

Before the recovery could set in, however, on New Year's Eve 1999, Yeltsin resigned the presidency—the first Russian leader to give up power voluntarily. Yeltsin made appalling mistakes, but he was determined to go down in history as the man who made the restoration of Communism in Russia impossible. It was no mean achievement.

Putin: Clamping Down.　Yeltsin's chosen successor, Vladimir Putin, was determined to make his mark as a strongman during his short term as Yeltsin's prime minister by reopening the war in Chechnya, a small Islamic enclave in the Caucasus, at war for centuries with the conquering Russians. After two years of ruthless fighting, at great political damage to Yeltsin, the defeated Russian armies had withdrawn in 1996, leaving the burden of the final settlement of Chechnya's independence to the future. The war resumed in 1999 when Chechen rebels invaded neighboring Dagestan (a predominantly Muslim region that is part of Russia) in an effort to establish a united independent Islamic state in the Caucasus. At the same time, a terrorist attack on apartment buildings in Russian cities killed more than three hundred people and maimed many more. Putin put the blame for the attack on Chechens and stormed into the Caucasus to force the invaders out of Dagestan. The Chechen capital, Grozny, was devastated; ironically, the main victims were elderly Russian residents, the rebels having already escaped to the mountains. Russian troops took control of the war-devastated Caucasus region, but the Chechen leaders remained at large and continued guerrilla attacks on Russian soldiers.

Vladimir Putin became president of Russia at a time when modest economic stability was beginning to emerge, thanks in large part to a spike in the prices of oil and natural gas, Russia's chief exports. During his first two terms in office (1999–2008), Russia's GDP grew roughly 7 percent annually. His main objective was to establish a strong centralized state. To this end, he reigned in the oligarchs, dismembering an oil group and absorbing their property into the state-controlled oil and gas company. This spectacular government takeover sent a chill through the energy sector of the economy and alarmed foreign investors, who worried that property rights might exist only at the whim of the Russian government. But Putin's popularity increased among people resentful of the oligarchs' wealth and pleased by strong economic growth. New elites grew fabulously rich—buying up luxurious homes in posh European neighborhoods, funneling billions into offshore accounts, and sending their children to English boarding schools. Yet they had to eschew politics.

Putin steadily increased government control of the national television networks, which became pliant servants of the government. The press, radio, and Internet retained more independence, though various forms of intimidation eroded freedom of expression—in the 2000s, numerous journalists, including at least a dozen high profile figures, were murdered, presumably on orders from the government—eroded freedom of expression. These developments drew criticism from Western countries, which had hoped that Russia would follow a democratic path in allowing a free media and encouraging discussion and criticism of political issues.

The Chechen conflict continued in the background, springing dramatically onto the front pages in October 2002 when pro-Chechen terrorists seized a theater in Moscow in the middle of a performance. In the resulting counterattack, all the hostage takers and 129 hostages were killed by an inept gas attack on the theater by Russian authorities. The worst terrorist attack in Russia took place on the first day of the new school year in 2004. Chechen fighters seized a school in Beslan in the Caucasus and held hundreds of children, parents, and teachers hostage. More than three hundred hostages died, many of them children, when Russian special forces attacked the hostage takers. Again, preserving the lives of citizens was less important than affirming state power to Putin, who denounced the Chechen seizure as part of global Islamic terrorism.

Despite the clear influence of Islamic extremism, the principal goal of the Chechen fighters was independence from Russia. This aim clashed with Putin's ideal of a strong Russian state: for intensively multiethnic Russia to grant independence to any region or nationality would weaken the fabric of the fragile country. His tough, efficient image shaken by the well-planned Chechen attack, Putin moved to reassert his authority: "[Terrorists] strive for the breakup of the state, for the ruin of Russia[.] I am sure that the unity of the country is the main prerequisite for victory over terror," he declared, making it clear that unity meant control from the top.[2]

Exhausted by years of turmoil, many Russians supported Putin; they appreciated his strong leadership and welcomed his imposed order. Others saw it as authoritarianism triumphing over Russia's nascent democracy. Indeed, Putin's immediate associates in the Kremlin were drawn from the *siloviki*, former security officials who shared his hard-line law-and-order orientation and had no patience for the checks, balances, and uncertainties of democracy.

The Russian constitution limits the president to two consecutive terms in office. Long before Putin's term was up in March 2008, Western Kremlin watchers began to speculate about his successor. In the fall of 2007, he moved to continue his power by appointing obscure minister Dimitri Medvedev as his prime minister and grooming him as his successor. Putin further announced that he would lead his party, United Russia, in the December 2007 election; its victory gave him a seat in the lower house of Parliament, from which he then became prime minister. Though well within the terms of the democratic constitution, it was a cynical maneuver. Putin was reelected overwhelmingly to the presidency in 2012. As public protests and discontent grew, especially after major demonstrations in December 2011, Putin pushed for still greater central control over society. The small opposition parties were furious, but powerless to intervene.

Putin has sought to restore Russia's power and influence lost in the decades after the breakup of the Soviet Union. For Putin, "the demise of the Soviet Union was the greatest geopolitical catastrophe of the century."[3] He has deliberately stirred nationalist—and anti-American—sentiments among the Russian people, repeatedly curtailed natural gas deliveries to Europe and other trading partners, and invaded neighboring Georgia (in August 2008). In late 2013, Putin strongly pressured Ukraine, formerly part of the USSR, to reject a pathway to membership in the European Union. Mass protests broke out in November, then turned bloody in February 2014, forcing the pro-Kremlin president, Viktor F. Yanukovich, to flee the capital. An interim government was formed. On the 27th, the Russian government seized the Crimean Peninsula, home to Russia's Black Sea Fleet. A majority of Crimea's population is Russian, many of whom identify more with Russia than Ukraine. Russia also temporarily massed troops on its border with eastern Ukraine and, where 30–40 percent of the population in several provinces are native Russian speakers. Pro-Russian activists attacked government buildings and clashed with authorities in numerous cities of eastern and southern Ukraine, seizing control of several at least temporarily and leaving dozens dead on both sides. Western leaders scrambled to diffuse tensions, bolster the shaky Ukrainian economy, and forestall further Russian incursions.

The gap between Russia and the West remains enormous. Russia has vast natural resources, a well-educated population, the world's eighth largest economy, and the ninth biggest population. Yet it is riddled with crime and corruption; it is burdened with a crumbling infrastructure and desperate rural poverty. Russia, in tsarist times "the breadbasket of Europe," is still a net importer of agricultural and food products, though output has increased in the past decade. While huge exports of energy products and raw materials have fueled massive economic growth, an expansion of the middle class, and a current-account surplus, Russia exports few finished goods. Ethnic and racial prejudice remains virulent and widespread. Russia's health and social services are in crisis due to increasing heart attacks, strokes, and illnesses caused by excessive smoking, drug addiction, alcoholism, drug-resistant tuberculosis, and AIDS: a physically weakened and diminished workforce could undermine Russia's further development.

Unrealistic optimism at the time of the Soviet collapse that Russia would emerge as a free, democratic, and market-oriented state changed to pessimism. Building a democratic civic society took centuries in the West; Russia cannot achieve that in one generation. Moreover, the Communist legacy, with its bureaucratic inefficiency, stifling of individual initiative, and repression, still weighs heavily on the country.

Central and Eastern Europe After 1989

After a century of war, occupation, and dictatorship, hopes ran high in the former Soviet satellite countries of Central and Eastern Europe. Poland, Hungary, and the Czech Republic were closest to Western political and economic ideals and eager to move toward full democracy and market economies. Poland achieved a quick but painful transition to a free-market economy; Czechoslovakia followed a similar course. Hungary, the most enterprising of the Communist countries, loosened its economy further. Yet people were unprepared for an open market economy and suspicious of capitalism. Everywhere inflation, unemployment, outdated industrial enterprises, and ignorance of market conditions held down economic development.

After 1995, the economic prospects began to improve with the help of Western aid. Thanks to increasing trade and economic integration with Western Europe, twelve former Soviet bloc countries joined NATO beginning in 1999 and from 2004 to 2013 eleven entered the European Union (discussed later in the chapter).

In the 1990s, the former Yugoslavia became the most troubled region of Europe. Cobbled together after World War I as an artificial state composed of sharply different ethnic groups dominated by Serbia, Yugoslavia was torn apart by nationalist ambitions set off by the collapse of the Soviet Union. In July 1991, Slovenia seceded; Croatia and Bosnia attempted to follow in 1992, ending Serbian domination. Because there were large Serbian populations in both Croatia and Bosnia, Yugoslav president Slobodan Milosevic, a Serb nationalist, refused to give up control and unleashed the Serb army, augmented by Bosnian Serbs, on the two countries. Ethnic hatred exploded, centered on Bosnia, a splintered mountainous region. Its major ethno-religious groups—43 percent Muslim, 17 percent Catholic Croat, and 31 percent Orthodox Serb—were

MUSLIM MILITANTS IN BRITAIN DISPLAY THEIR HATRED OF THE WEST.
Demonstrations against the West, Israel, and Jews have been frequent occurrences
in Muslim lands and Europe. On September 11, 2011, the tenth anniversary of
9/11, Muslim militants demonstrated outside the U.S. embassy in London. They
brandished placards that expressed hatred of the United States and their desire
to extend Islamic power throughout the globe. (Ummah means the Muslim
nation; an emirate is a Muslim state which the demonstrators hope to establish
in Britain.) (CARL COURT/AFP/Getty Images.)

scattered in multiethnic communities; there were
few ethnically consolidated areas.

Muslims, Croats, and Serbs ruthlessly fought
each other. The Bosnian Serbs, hoping to join with
Serbia in a Greater Serbia, conquered 70 percent
of Bosnia, conducting a brutal "ethnic cleansing"
of Muslims while subjecting Sarajevo, Bosnia's
capital, to bloody bombardment. All sides, but
most of all the Serbs, committed heinous
atrocities, including systematic mass murder of
Muslims, provoking moral outrage. A UN force—
not a Europe-led coalition—of sixty thousand
peacekeepers vainly tried to halt ethnic cleansing
by Serbs.

In August 1995, Croatia went on the offensive
to drive Serbs out of its territory, and NATO used
its air force for the first time in its fifty-year history,

against the Bosnian Serbs. In November 1995, the
United States stepped forward, in negotiations
held in Dayton, Ohio, to promote peace. The
Dayton Agreement proposed a Bosnian government equally shared by Muslims, Croats, and
Serbs. While analysts praised NATO's operation
to end the outrageous inhumanities of the Bosnian
civil war, they were critical of both NATO and the
United States for their delay in taking action.

In 1998, violence erupted between Serbs and
ethnic Albanians in the Yugoslav province of
Kosovo. This is a sacred place for Serbs, the site
of Orthodox shrines and of the battle of Kosovo
in 1389, in which the Ottoman Turks defeated
the Serbs, ruling Kosovo until 1912. The Serbs
regard the battle as the birth of the Serb nation.
Ethnic antagonism has persisted between Serbs

and the predominantly Muslim Albanians who form 90 percent of the population of 2 million. In 1998, President Milosevic, seeking to shore up his power by manipulating Serbian nationalist feelings, sent Serbian forces to crush Albanian separatists fighting for an independent Kosovo.

Forced expulsions and massacres of innocent villagers led NATO to intervene. Milosevic refused to allow a NATO peacekeeping force into Kosovo, despite a threat of NATO air strikes, launched against Serbia in March 1999 (amid vociferous Russian protests). Carrying the practice of ethnic cleansing to a new level of brutality, Serbian special forces terrorized and murdered Albanians, systematically burned villages, confiscated valuables, and drove hundreds of thousands of Albanian refugees into neighboring lands, creating a massive humanitarian crisis.

The unrelenting NATO bombardment of Serbia, expected to be brief and decisive, continued for eleven weeks—so too did the ethnic cleansing of Kosovo—until Milosevic capitulated. Eventually the Kosovo Albanians were allowed to return to their ravaged country. A NATO-led force of four thousand troops remained in Kosovo into 2014 to assist with relief efforts, prevent revenge attacks on the remaining Serb population, and ensure Kosovo's autonomy.

The UN International Criminal Tribunal for the Former Yugoslavia indicted President Milosevic and Bosnian Serb and Croatian leaders and military commanders on charges of genocide and crimes against humanity. Milosevic went on trial in 2002 but died in 2006 before sentencing.

After the war, the former Yugoslavia, mired in poverty and dependent on foreign aid, consisted only of a dysfunctional federation of Serbia, Montenegro, and Kosovo. Even so, Western investment and gradual economic development enabled these now independent states to be considered candidates or potential candidates for membership in the European Union, along with Bosnia and Herzeginivia and the Republic of Macedonia, two other lands that had been part of Yugoslavia (see next section).

The European Union

After the end of World War II, six Western European nations began a slow process of economic, political, and cultural integration. The collapse of Soviet power supplied a sudden jolt for accelerating this trend. In 1991, in the Dutch city of Maastricht, the members of the European Community, now twelve in number, negotiated the Maastricht Treaty, designed to shape Europe into a unified economic and political force. By 1993, the member states had ratified the treaty and the European Community became the European Union. In 1999, eleven members adopted a common monetary unit, the euro; by 2009 the Eurozone had expanded to seventeen countries with several more scheduled to join, starting with Latvia in 2014. The euro is the second most heavily traded currency and the world's second reserve currency. In the new Europe, goods, labor, capital, and services move freely between countries. Citizens of its member states feel more and more at home traveling and working throughout the union, typically speaking English as the lingua franca.

Despite an increasing number of Euroskeptics—those who oppose European integration for nationalistic and pragmatic reasons—there has been no lack of European countries eager to join the EU. On May 1, 2004, the European Union accepted ten new members, eight of which had been former Communist countries—the Czech Republic, Estonia, Hungary, Latvia, Lithuania, Poland, Slovakia, and Slovenia—together with Cyprus and Malta. They were followed in 2007 by Romania and Bulgaria and by Croatia in 2013, for a total of 28 members. Several candidates await consideration for entry, including Muslim Turkey. This ambitious enlargement of the EU marked the historic reintegration of a continent that had been divided for forty-five years by the iron curtain. With 500 million inhabitants, it is the world's biggest economic and trading bloc. All the new members had made progress toward a market economy and had demonstrated acceptable standards of democracy and human rights. However, the new countries are much poorer than previous entrants to the EU and naturally hope to increase their prosperity thanks to EU economic assistance.

Many Europeans worried about the future of their countries. Were they surrendering their identity, along with their sovereignty, to the EU? Were Europeanization and globalization (the latter frequently defined as "American imperialism") going to change irrevocably their national status? Many Europeans do not identify with the EU, personified by remote Eurocrats headquartered in Brussels, Belgium. An unelected European Commission makes the decisions, but the weak elected European Parliament in Strasbourg became a focus of anti-European sentiment in May 2014, when voters handed roughly one-third of seats to Euroskeptics. On the positive side, since a large part of EU governance involved generous subsidies to member countries, especially to their agricultural sectors, most citizens were fairly content with this arrangement.

The global financial meltdown of 2008 made it difficult for the EU member countries to maintain their heavy government spending, which on average exceeded 50 percent of GDP in 2009. Unemployment soared in several countries. Investor confidence fell markedly. Increased borrowing costs further drove up budget deficits. During the next few years, Greece, Portugal, Ireland, and Cyprus received huge bailouts from the Economic and Monetary Union (EMU), with Germany paying the lion's share. Many richer Europeans resented having to rescue their poorer neighbors, whom they considered wasteful spenders. Drastic budget cuts were implemented throughout Europe, sparking protests and even violence.

Nevertheless, as late as fall 2013 most economies of the EU remained in the doldrums, with overall Eurozone unemployment hovering at 12 percent and joblessness among the young hitting from 28 percent in Ireland to 56 percent in Spain for those twenty-four and younger and from 16 percent in Ireland to 41 percent in Greece for those aged twenty-five to thirty. All Europeans expect generous cradle to grave social welfare programs, yet their aging (and even declining) populations and slower growing productivity will make paying for them more and more difficult. Resolving this dilemma consumed much political attention throughout Europe.

The three largest and most influential countries in the European Union are France, Germany, and the United Kingdom. France and Germany, with populations of 62 million and 83 million, respectively, have traditionally set the agenda for the EU. France and the UK are nuclear powers. The latter, with a population of 60 million, maintains a special relationship with the United States.

In the United Kingdom, the Tory John Major succeeded Prime Minister Margaret Thatcher in 1990. He maintained an uncertain majority in Parliament, increasingly troubled by political scandals, but his economic policies were fairly successful. Most important, he kept Britain out of the eurozone. In the election of 1997, the Labor party, revitalized by Tony Blair, its young and lively leader, scored an impressive victory. He moved Labor to the political center, endorsing a pro-business policy, limiting benefits for the poor, and jettisoning Labor's old working-class/state-ownership image. Building on Major's accomplishments, these policies helped stimulate the economy. Blair also pursued constitutional reforms, devolving power to Scotland and Wales and reforming the House of Lords, where members now serve not by aristocratic right but by accomplishments in public life.

Blair achieved a remarkable success in Northern Ireland, where Protestants and Catholics had long been at war with each other. In 1998, after three difficult years, he helped end the conflict and create an elected assembly. It was a huge gamble that terrorists and bigots, who had fought each other for decades, could act rationally together. Following a suspension of the Northern Ireland Assembly in 2002, the two sides agreed to try again and in 2007 pledged to work together in the administration of Northern Ireland.

Prime Minister Blair, despite strong opposition in Britain, supported the United States–led invasion of Iraq in 2003 and committed forces to the coalition. He saw his country as an important bridge between the EU and America—a stance that became increasingly unpopular both in his own country and within the EU. He resigned in mid-2007 and was succeeded by Gordon Brown, his chancellor of the Exchequer. Brown worked to rebuild the Labor Party, which had become badly splintered during Blair's last years; to continue the constitutional and social reforms of his predecessor; and to appease Euroskeptics in his own party and in the country at large. He was also less supportive of the Iraq War and removed all but a small contingent of troops in 2009. Following disappointing election results in May 2010, Brown resigned.

Queen Elizabeth asked David Cameron, a Conservative, to form a government. Since no party had won a clear majority, he entered into a coalition with the left-leaning Liberal Democrats. A major theme of his administration has been to roll back what he considered profligate social spending by previous Labor governments. Political scandals, austerity policies, and Britain's poor economic performance (until 2013), however, weakened public support for Cameron. His support for a gay marriage bill, which became law in July 2013, set many in his party against him. Yet his demand to renegotiate Britain's membership in the EU and promise to submit that membership to a popular vote in 2017, should the Tories win reelection in 2015, enjoyed broad support.

Most French believe in their country's exceptionalism: a nation profoundly rooted in the past, but capable of rapid adaptation and innovation. Like all Europeans, they believe in economic equality and fairness. More than most Europeans, who work on average far less than Americans, the French idealize "taking the time to live." These themes shaped the policies of all French politicians, whether of Right or Left.

The moderate conservative, Jacques Chirac, succeeded Socialist François Mitterrand in 1995, continuing the tradition of a strong, centralized state with generous welfare benefits. Chirac had no viable opposition, apart from Jean-Marie Le Pen, an anti-immigration, anti-globalization, anti-Semitic, racist candidate of the far Right, who qualified (with 18 percent of the vote) for a presidential runoff election against Chirac in 2002. Most French people were pleased that Le Pen was soundly defeated in the runoff.

In 2004, President Chirac was at the center of a storm that divided the 6 million Muslims living in France. A law banned the wearing of symbols of religion in France's traditionally secular schools; it was aimed primarily at the headscarves worn by Muslim girls. This reaffirmation of the secular nature of the French state and its insistence on cultural uniformity was at odds with the policies of other EU countries, which have accepted multiculturism and tolerate headscarves in schools.

President Chirac refused French support for the unpopular Iraq War, which won him support in France. His chief foreign policy concern was cooperation with Germany in creating an effective EU that balanced French and German aspirations

and served as a French-led counterweight to the United States.

In 2007, Nicolas Sarkozy succeeded the aging Chirac. He was hyperkinetic and blunt-talking (even frequently insulting), a flashy politician in the limelight rather than the typically distant French president, and a vocal advocate of economically conservative ideas who nevertheless bashed capitalism. Most citizens never really warmed to him. He cut taxes, reduced red tape for employers, increased spending on research and development, diminished central control over his country's universities, raised the minimum retirement age from sixty to sixty-two pushed through a law allowing workers to put in more than 35 hours per week, declined to fill many vacant civil service jobs, slashed government spending, and engineered a significant decline in greenhouse gas emissions. He appointed a Muslim immigrant woman minister of justice (the first woman ever in France) but deported thousands of undocumented Roma (formerly called gypsies). In 2009, Sarkozy reintegrated France into the command structures of NATO and in 2011 spearheaded NATO's intervention in Libya (see page 868), which proved highly successful. Yet his main mission in office—to grow the economy—failed, in large part because of the euro crisis. High unemployment, slow economic growth, and a series of political scandals drove down his popularity. His 2012 budget proposed big tax increases and more spending cuts. By then, most citizens strongly disliked Sarkozy.

In May 2012, the French elected the Socialist François Hollande as president. Running as an "ordinary politician," he was politically inexperienced, especially compared to Sarkozy. Amid anti-business policies, increased taxes, and government spending at 57 percent of GDP, the economy continued to stagnate. By mid-2013, he was advocating spending cuts, increased worker productivity, and competitiveness, to the horror of his leftist supporters. A reformist socialist at heart, he nevertheless refused an open break with the radical Left. His approval rating sank to 19 percent in early 2014 amid revelations of an illicit affair and unemployment climbing to 11.1 percent—a record low for any modern French leader. Commentators spoke increasingly of a French malaise.

Germans are proud of the peaceful reunification of West and East in 1990, their leading role in the EU, and their status as the fourth biggest world economy. A dual educational system in which most young people combine learning at school and on the job, an abundance of efficient small and medium businesses, and a strong business–labor partnership were the envy of Europe. At the same time, the undying memory of Germany's role in World War II and the Holocaust continues to haunt the nation.

Reunification, engineered by the Christian Democrat Helmut Kohl, required huge investments into what had been the Communist German Democratic Republic. The path was thorny. Having no experience with democracy, most of the 17 million former East Germans were somewhat disillusioned with unification. When Communist-era factories closed, unemployment surged to 25 percent. Among the jobless, racist neo-Nazis and skinheads multiplied, lashing out violently against "outsiders"—predominantly Turkish immigrants and Jews—whom they regarded as parasites harmful to the national character. The relocation of the German capital from Bonn to Berlin, the traditional German capital city; high-tech development; and booming economic growth alleviated these problems, though GNP per person remained under three-quarters the western level as late as 2008.

Kohl's conservative chancellorship ended in 1998, when the Germans elected Social Democrat Gerhard Schröder, a former Marxist. He formed a coalition with the Greens, who scaled down their environmental and pacifist radicalism. Schröder sent combat forces to Kosovo in 1999—the first German military deployment since the World War—and Afghanistan in 2001 (some three thousand troops remained in early 2014). Like Chirac, however, he vociferously denounced the impending Iraq War, which helped him win reelection in 2002.

In 2003, when German unemployment stood at 11.6 percent, Schröder announced Agenda 2010. It promised employers more flexibility in hiring and firing workers, liberalized the rules for part-time and temporary employment, curtailed unemployment benefits, and created incentives for the unemployed to accept available jobs. This was a radical shift for his party, which two decades before had stood for unions and social justice. Joblessness slid from over 15 percent in 2005 to under 10 percent in 2012. His supporters on the Left were often unsure of whether to embrace or repudiate his policies.

These positive results were too late to prevent voters in 2005 electing Angela Merkel, Germany's first woman chancellor and a former scientist who grew up in East Germany. Fixing the crisis of the eurozone has been her chief goal; and pressing for dramatic structural reform, the means. A workaholic stateswoman of enormous talent, she became the most powerful political figure in Europe, perhaps second in the world only to Barack Obama. Germany began to regain its confidence. Merkel rejected an EU proposal to impose a quota for women company directors and supported an initiative to increase subsidies to mothers who stay home with their children, but promoted numerous women to mid-level positions in her government. By early 2014, unemployment had fallen to 5 percent, compared to 12 in the Eurozone. Among the major European countries, only Germany had kept its perfect AAA credit rating.

Despite its troubles, Europe remains a transformative region. Its leaders peacefully and productively integrated over two dozen countries formerly racked by perennial warfare—a unique historical achievement. It boasts the world's highest-energy particle collider, the best and most extensive high-speed rail network, the most important financial center (London), and four of the five most energy-efficient countries (along with Japan). Europe is the second biggest producer of cars (after China) and is home to the second biggest airplane manufacturer (Airbus) and second biggest exporter (Germany). Europe vies with the United States in aerospace technology. In 2004, researchers at the University of Manchester isolated grapheme, a two-dimensional (one-atom-thick) material, which is extremely lightweight, strong, and also highly conductive—a material that looks set to revolutionize electronics and manufacturing industries. Thus, many analysts are optimistic about the future of the European economy.

The United States is the undisputed leader in military affairs (the EU countries spend less than half as much on defense as the United States), in science and technological innovation, and perhaps in cultural vibrancy. Yet despite ongoing economic problems, most Europeans view their model of society as superior to that of America. They emphasize that in the EU there are more comprehensive social welfare programs, including national health care, free and inexpensive higher education, lots of paid vacation (yet high economic efficiency), and early retirement with generous government pensions. And, they point out that, unlike Americans, Europeans have no capital punishment and neither a love of guns nor excessive religiosity. In fact, their biggest problem stems, in the eyes of many Europeans, from overly religious immigrants.

NEW AND OLD PROBLEMS: MUSLIM IMMIGRATION AND THE RESURGENCE OF ANTI-SEMITISM

Among the problems that have burdened Europe in the first decade of the twenty-first century are the threat of terrorism by radical Islamists; the failure of millions of Muslim immigrants to integrate into European society; and a resurgence of anti-Semitism. The issue of terrorism is discussed in the next section.

Muslim Immigration

In the 1950s and 1960s, Western Europe's booming economy created a demand for cheap labor that was met by an influx of millions of Muslims from Turkey, Pakistan, and North Africa. In succeeding decades, additional millions of Muslim immigrants from the Middle East and sub-Saharan Africa, many of them illegal, settled in various European lands. Like other immigrants, they sought to join relatives, find economic opportunities, or escape from oppressive regimes. Several of these countries, including France, Germany, Britain, Belgium, Holland, Spain, and Denmark, now have substantial Muslim populations. While some Muslims have achieved success in business and academia, many Muslims remain profoundly alienated from European society and at odds with its values. European liberal democracy, which espouses religious freedom, equal rights for women, separation of church and state, and freedom of expression, noticeably conflicts with many facets of Islamic society.

In describing the failure of Muslim integration, analysts refer to the demands of some Muslim groups that they be governed by their own religious law, sharia, rather than the law of the land. They also cite the perpetuation in Europe by some Muslims of cultural mores that sanction polygamy, forced marriages between young girls and much older men, wife-beating, and so-called honor killings of "wayward" females, and require women to keep their bodies and faces hidden from view; the high crime rate among Muslims—in Britain Muslims are 2 percent of the population, but more than 8 percent of the prison population; the high rate of dependency on social welfare; and the emergence of extremist Islamist cells in European lands that have participated in several terrorist acts—much of the planning for 9/11 took place in Hamburg, Germany. British commentators have raised a difficult question. In the past, they say, immigrant Jews and recently Sikhs and Hindus have thrived in Britain, even when confronted with prejudice. Why, they ask, is the integration of Muslim immigrants in Western society so fraught with problems?

In the fall of 2005, the suburbs of Paris and scores of other French cities were convulsed by two weeks of rioting—nearly nine thousand cars were set afire, and schools, shops, and churches burned to the ground—by young Muslim males from the bleak housing projects inhabited principally by North African immigrants. That the great majority of rioters were not recent immigrants, but had been born in France, was particularly distressing to officials, for the French government prided itself on creating a uniform French identity that superseded ethnic and religious origins. Whatever the aspirations of the government, many French citizens remain resentful of North African immigrants, whom they view as an alien minority that, unlike other immigrants, has failed to integrate into French society. They point to the immigrants' preference for native cultural traditions, the high cost of welfare payments they receive, and the high crime rate among them—Muslims, about 10 percent of the nation, constitute more than 50 percent of France's prison population. Numerous commentators, however, interpreted the riots as a rebellion by a resentful underclass

Contemporary Art

After World War II, myriad styles emerged or continued to develop. The best known of them was abstract expressionism. Art historians cite the realities of the post–World War II era—the aftermath of the atom bomb, the Cold War—as the impetus for a number of movements or subgroups of abstract expressionism. The artists shared an outlook that championed individuality and espoused the freedom to express themselves purely through the use of color and abstract, nonrepresentational forms. As the century progressed, each artist asserted even more freedom of expression, leading to a proliferation of styles. Artists were also subject to an ever more critical audience. Viewers felt freer in their ability to criticize art and in their efforts to understand the artists and the work they had created.

The most famous abstract expressionist, whose style is known as action painting, was Jackson Pollock (1912–1956). He completed his first action painting in 1950. Pollock poured and splattered his colors on the canvas instead of applying them with a brush or palette knife. He used a liquid paint that he dripped onto huge unstretched canvases spread on the floor. By positioning the canvas on the floor below him, Pollock felt closer to it—he became part of the painting. Able to walk around the canvas, Pollock worked on it from all sides. As he painted, there emerged a harmony, an easy, rhythmic give and take between artist and painting, from which the painting acquired a life of its own. His *Convergence* (1952) (Figure 1) may at first seem to be merely an accident, a canvas used as a drop cloth. But each application of color was made in a controlled and studied manner. The artist knew exactly what he was doing every time he dripped, sprayed, or splattered his

1. Jackson Pollock, *Convergence*, 1952.

2. Joan Mitchell (1925–1992), *Untitled*, 1964–1965. Öl auf Leinwand, 161.9 × 113.7 cm. (akg-images/© Estate of Joan Mitchell.)

3. Jasper Johns, *Three Flags*, 1958. (encaustic on canvas) (Fiftieth Anniversary Gift of the Gilman Foundation, Inc., The Lauder Foundation, A. Alfred Taubman, an anonymous donor, and Purchase 80.32 © Jasper Johns/Licensed by VAGA/New York.)

canvas. One might say that his paintings have a tactile, kinesthetic quality that is evident in the linear, agitated shapes on the canvas, virtually reflecting the motion of Pollock's body as he worked on the canvas below him.

Joan Mitchell is considered a leading figure in the Abstract Expressionist movement and was one of a few female artists to gain critical acclaim in the mid-twentieth century. Born in Chicago in 1925, Mitchell was educated at the School of the Art Institute of Chicago, but spent most of her adult life in France; she died in 1992 in Paris. Her paintings give an "impression" of nature, most specifically landscape. However, rather than representing a specific place, they convey the atmospheric effect of an imagined or remembered landscape.

In her early years, Mitchell was influenced by the bright colored compositions of Vincent Van Gogh, Paul Cézanne, and Wassily Kandinsky. In the early 1960s, moving away from dazzling colors, she utilized dark, moody hues to express something

rudimentary and primitive. She began to produce paintings of particular depth and intensity soon after her move from New York to Paris. Mitchell referred to these works as "My black paintings— although there's no black in them." In fact, her palette is straight from nature, made up of earthy greens, cerulean blues, browns, and oranges that give the paintings the moodiness of landscape.

An example of this transition in her painting style is *Untitled*, 1964–1965 (Figure 2). Like most of her work, this painting is abstract but references landscape and natural forms and forces. The dark blue and green center forms a dense mass, expressing something distinctly primordial, out of which oozes drips and slashes of paint. There is a striking physicality to this work. Mitchell flung and squeezed paint onto the canvas, spilling and smearing it across the surface. She used an array of paint applications, from broad strokes and drips as well as softer, gentler gestures to express this dark terrain.

Within a few years Mitchell's abstract compositions changed again as she began to explore the subject of sunflowers. The images created during this later period employ vivid colors and sweeping brushstrokes and explode with new energy, tension, and urgency. While they do not much resemble the plants themselves, Mitchell continued to communicate through them an internal as well as external landscape.

Abstract expressionism spawned its own antagonists. Pop art was a reaction against nonrepresentational abstract art, which pop artists thought was pretentious and overly serious. Pop

4. David Smith, *Cubi XIX*, 1964. (The Tate Gallery, London/Art Resource, NY. Licensed by VAGA/New York; Art © Estate of David Smith.)

The work of sculptors during the second half of the twentieth century reveals both continuity with the sculpture of the pre–World War II period and radical change. Sculptors began to experiment. The major movement from the 1970s was minimalism—simple, symmetrical sculpture made of modern materials that engaged the viewer and, by implication, spurned depicting the human body.

One of the most important minimalist sculptors was David Smith (1906–1965), who flourished during the abstract expressionist era. Smith began to sculpt in metal in 1933. During the 1950s and early 1960s, he produced several series of sculptures, including his Cubi series, inspired by cubism. *Cubi XIX* (Figure 4), made in 1964, is representative of the series. All the cubis are constructed of monumental cubes, cubic rectangles, and cylinders, which Smith himself constructed out of polished and brushed stainless steel. The carefully balanced cubis are meant to be displayed outdoors, where they capture and reflect every change in the natural light.

The most famous architect of the early twenty-first century is Frank O. Gehry (b. 1929). His work is found not only in the United States but also in Japan and several European countries. Gehry's view of architecture has evolved out of his profound interest in painting and sculpture, and his friendships with contemporary artists. His theory of architecture embodies the conviction that architecture is an art form among art forms, like painting and sculpture, expressive of human feeling. Known for his innovative use of materials, Gehry is famous for the way he twists, turns, and bends metal into shapes that affect the emotions. One of his most recent ventures, the Guggenheim Museum at Bilbao, Spain (Figure 5), was opened in 1997.

Gehry's Guggenheim Museum is a perfect illustration of his ability to elevate architecture to the rank of an expressive artistic form not bound by the stultifying rules that consigned previous architectural works to the status of mechanically produced, redundant, boxlike forms. The Bilbao Guggenheim itself is a work of art, a form of sculptural architecture. The building consists of organically interrelated contrasting shapes composed of a multiplicity of materials, ranging from limestone and glass to titanium. It houses nineteen galleries with thirty-six thousand square feet of exhibition space. It not only attracts numerous visitors— 1.3 million in its inaugural year—but also provides the city of Bilbao with a dramatic architectural

artists were influenced by earlier movements that ridiculed the notion of "art for art's sake," scoffed at the idea of the unique art object, and presented readymade objects such as bicycle wheels and urinals as works of art. The phrase *pop art* was first used in England in the late 1950s to signify paintings that exalted postwar consumerism and celebrated popular culture.

Foremost among the early painters in the pop art movement in the United States was Jasper Johns (b. 1930). Largely self-taught as an artist, in 1954 he began to paint common objects such as targets, maps, and especially flags. Four years later, he executed one of his most famous paintings: *Three Flags* (Figure 3) is literally three canvases superimposed on each other, creating a reverse perspective, in which the smallest flag moves into the space of the viewer. *Three Flags* is simultaneously a painting and a relief sculpture. The ambiguous meaning of the painting was hotly debated at the time. Was it a realistic representation of the American flag, was it subtle satirical derision of it, or was some esoteric meaning implicit in its seemingly naïve obviousness?

5. Guggenheim Museum in Bilbao, Spain. (Steve Vidler/Superstock.)

centerpiece that has had the intended effect of reinvigorating the Basque region's recession-plagued economy and revitalizing its cultural life.

Lucian Freud (1922–2011), grandson of Sigmund Freud, fled Nazi Germany with his Jewish parents and settled in England soon after Hitler came to power. Called Britain's "greatest living figurative painter," he is most celebrated for his realistic portraits of intimate acquaintances who were part of his life—fellow artists, friends, lovers, and immediate family—but his work also includes portraits of supermodel Kate Moss, Queen Elizabeth II, and dogs, for which he had a fascination. Freud wrote that his object in painting was "to move the senses by giving an intensification of reality." He wants the picture to combine a careful representation of life with an "obsession with his subject" that reveals his intense feelings. Critics point out that Freud imposes his own consciousness on his subjects. Freud's numerous nude paintings are never idealized; rather, he seems to relish depicting his subject's vulnerability and imperfections—scars, bluish veins, blemishes, fleshy folds, pale skin, emaciated bodies. Freud once described his paintings as "a kind of truth-telling exercise" that gets beneath the skin.

Freud's portrait of Queen Elizabeth II (Figure 6), which exemplifies his intense and psychologically penetrating style, drew both praise and criticism. Some critics said the painting depicted the queen, no longer a young woman, as "brave, honest, stoical and, above all, clear sighted." Others described the portrait as "extremely unflattering," unworthy of an English monarch.

6. Lucian Freud, *Portrait of Queen Elizabeth II*, 2001. (Alpha/ZUMAPRESS/Newscom.)

FRENCH MUSLIMS PROTEST HEADSCARF BAN. Thousands of Muslims take to the streets of Paris to protest the government's proposed law to ban Muslim headscarves, Jewish skull caps, and large Christian crosses from public schools in order to keep education secular and avoid religious strife. France's 6 million Muslims have remained a culturally separate minority, sometimes hostile to the host country. (AP Images/Laurent Rebours.)

protesting discrimination, segregation, poverty, and a staggering unemployment rate—as much as 40 percent—for young Muslim males.

Faced with what is perceived as a rapidly growing, unassimilable Muslim minority that is hostile to Western values, lives in isolated communities, often does not speak the host nation's language, and recruits and finances terrorists, Europe is experiencing a backlash against Muslim immigrants and multiculturalism. An increasing number of Europeans now say that the premise of multiculturalism—assigning equal value to and tolerating Islamic traditions—was a mistake, for several of these traditions undermine democracy and fragment the nation. There is the fear that extremist right-wing political parties will capitalize on this wave of anti-immigrant sentiment that is sweeping across Europe.

Increasingly governments are introducing tighter immigration laws and are deporting Muslim radicals. They are also trying to work with moderate Muslims who support integration into European society and value Europe's liberal-democratic tradition. However, successful integration, say some commentators, is a two-way street. It is necessary that European society also address the socioeconomic problems burdening Muslims, overcome racist attitudes toward immigrants, and recognize the fact that many Muslims do work and pay taxes, respect the laws of their adopted country, and reject extremism; most importantly, Muslims must be made to feel that their religion is not being attacked and insulted. For many years to come, Europeans will be confronted with—or tormented by—the question of Islam's place in their countries.

Resurgence of Anti-Semitism

In the decades following the Holocaust, overt anti-Semitism appeared to have receded in Western Europe. The outbursts of the traditionally anti-Semitic far Right did not greatly affect the surviving Jews and their descendants, who represented a model of successful integration. In recent years, however, there has been a significant upsurge of anti-Semitic incidents in European lands, including physical assaults, even murder; the firebombing of Jewish synagogues, schools, and homes; and the desecration of Jewish cemeteries with Nazi symbols. In several lands, Jews report that they avoid going out in public with anything that would identify them as Jews. Fearful of verbal torment and physical attacks on their children in French public schools, the overwhelming majority of Jewish parents enroll their children in private schools. Denis MacShane, a Labor member of Parliament who in 2007 chaired a committee of British parliamentarians that studied anti-Semitism in Britain, concluded that "hatred of Jews has reached new heights in Europe."[4] Similar conclusions were reached by the U.S. State Department and the Parliamentary Assembly of the Council of Europe.

Many anti-Semitic incidents, but not all, have been initiated by the growing number of Muslims residing in Western Europe. "It is Islamism [Muslim extremism] that has unleashed new twenty-first century anti-Semitism," observes MacShane, "and it is impossible to discuss the problem without dealing with Islamism."[5] The creation of Israel on what is perceived as inviolable Muslim land and the Jewish state's ongoing conflict with the Palestinians have stirred the cauldron of Jew-hatred in the Arab and Muslim world. Now reaching epidemic proportions, anti-Semitism has become a principal theme in the Middle Eastern media and a motivation for attacks on Jews by Muslims living in Europe. As Cardinal Tucci, the director of Vatican Radio, stated in November 2003: "Now in the whole Muslim world, in the media, the radio, television, in schools, a whole system inciting to anti-Semitism exists. It is the worst anti-Semitism that can be imagined after Nazi anti-Semitism, if not its equal."[6]

Contemporary Muslim anti-Semitism borrowed considerably from traditional European anti-Semitism—Christian, nationalist, and Nazi. Like the Nazis, much of the Muslim world perceives Jews as a criminal people that threatens all humanity, blames the Jews for their misfortunes, and holds out the image of a utopian future once Israel is eradicated and the Jews eliminated. As in Nazi Germany, the media in the Arab and Muslim world are often filled with repulsive caricatures of Jews—dark, stooped, sinister, hook-nosed, devil-like creatures—many of them taken from Nazi media. In Arab sermons and classrooms and on the Internet, Jews are often referred to as "accursed," "descendants of apes and pigs," "the scum of the human race," "the rats of the world," "bacteria," "vampires," "usurers," and "whoremongers."

Reminiscent of Nazi propaganda, no accusation against Jews is too absurd not to be included in the litany of Jewish evil propagated in the Muslim media, and not just by extremists. Hamas, the radical Palestinian organization that rules Gaza, maintains that Jews were responsible for the French Revolution, the Russian Revolution, both world wars, and the atomic bombing of Hiroshima and Nagasaki. Osama bin Laden maintained that Jews, "in accordance with their religion, believe that human beings are their slaves and that those who refuse [to recognize this] should be put to death."[7] The Arab media have even revived the outrageous medieval blood libel that Jews are required to murder non-Jewish children in order to obtain their blood for making unleavened bread for Passover. Holocaust denial is widespread in the Middle East; so too is celebrating Hitler's mass murder of Jews. A columnist for *Al-Akhbar*, considered a moderate newspaper sponsored by the Egyptian government, gives "thanks to Hitler of blessed memory," for taking revenge against Jews—although Muslims "do have a complaint against him for his revenge on them was not enough."[8] And Dr. Ahmed Abu Halabiyah, Rector of Advanced Studies at the Islamic University of Gaza, is more representative than unique—similar sentiments are frequently voiced in the Arab media: "The Jews . . . must be butchered and must be killed. . . . It is forbidden to have mercy in your hearts for the Jews in any place and in any land, make war on them anywhere that you find yourself. Any place that you meet them, kill them."[9]

Propagated over the Internet and by radical imams in mosques throughout Europe, this demonization of the Jew has incited Muslim youth in Europe to acts of intimidation, physical assault, and vandalism against Jews; it has also led to organized campaigns of vilification of Jews on college campuses. On a positive note, in some European lands, Muslim and Jewish organizations are engaged in interfaith dialogue, and some Muslim intellectuals and religious leaders have condemned anti-Semitic outbursts.

In addition to the anti-Semitic incidents initiated by Muslims residing in various European lands, analysts have pointed to the ongoing Jew-hatred of the far Right, and a rather new phenomenon, a growing and insidious anti-Semitism afflicting the Left.

As in the past, European anti-Semitism remains a bulwark of the far Right, traditionally hostile to the Enlightenment's legacy of reason, political freedom, and tolerance. Principally extreme nationalists, racists, Fascists, and neo-Nazis, they propagate Holocaust denial and Jewish conspiracy theories—Jews invented a "Holocaust hoax" in order to extract compensation from Germany; Jews control the world's media and finances and are conspiring to dominate the planet; Jews are the real power behind the U.S. government; Jews are a threat to the nation.

During the Nazi era and for decades before, the Left—liberals, socialists, trade unionists, and intellectuals, including many academics—had been the strongest defenders of Jews against their detractors and oppressors. But now the distinguishing feature of the new anti-Semitism is its adoption by a New Left who employ anti-Semitic language and imagery—linking the Star of David with the swastika, a recognized symbol of evil—to express their support of the Palestinians and to delegitimize Israel; for them, Israelis are today's Nazis and Israel is a criminal state that should disappear.

Many Europeans are concerned about the revival of anti-Semitism. They recognize that Jew-hatred and the irrational myths associated with it, which undermine rational thinking and incite barbaric violence, transcend a purely Jewish concern. They threaten the core values of Western civilization, as Nazism so painfully demonstrated.

CULTURE CLASH, TERRORISM, AND WAR

On September 11, 2001, nineteen Muslim Arabs, most of them from Saudi Arabia, hijacked four planes: two of them they crashed into the World Trade Center in New York, bringing down both towers; a third plane rammed into the Pentagon in Washington, D.C., causing severe damage; the fourth plane, apparently headed for the White House, crashed in a field in Pennsylvania when passengers heroically attacked the hijackers. In all, almost three thousand people perished in the worst terrorist attack in history. The meticulously planned operation was the work of Al Qaeda, an international terrorist network of militant Muslims, or Islamists, as they call themselves. In 1998, Al Qaeda was responsible for the deadly bombings of the American embassies in Kenya and Tanzania, which killed hundreds, and in 2000 it detonated a bomb next to the U.S. destroyer *Cole* in the harbor of Aden, costing the lives of seventeen American sailors.

The leader of Al Qaeda, Osama bin Laden, scion of an immensely wealthy Saudi family, operated from Afghanistan with the protection of the radical fundamentalist Taliban, who ruled the country, transforming it into a repressive regime based on a rigid interpretation of Islamic law. In particular, the Taliban imposed oppressive rules for women, permitting beatings by male relatives, prohibiting females from working, barring them from schools, and demanding that they wear a garment—the burqa—that covered them from head to foot. Violators could be severely beaten, imprisoned, or executed.

When Taliban leaders refused to turn bin Laden over to the United States, President George W. Bush, supported by an international coalition, launched a military campaign whose ultimate goal was the destruction of international terrorism. Local Afghan forces opposed to the Taliban, assisted by American air power—which proved decisive—defeated the Taliban in a few weeks. But the new democratically elected government, backed by American and NATO troops, continues to face immense problems: local warlords who defy central authority, a resurgence of Taliban fighters—many of them coming from the

United Nations Secretary-General: Ending Violence Against Women, "the Systematic Domination of Women by Men"

In October 2006 the United Nations released the Secretary-General's in-depth study of violence against women, which concluded that "the pervasiveness of violence against women across the boundaries of nation, culture, race, class and religion points to its roots in patriarchy—the systematic domination of women by men." Excerpts from the study follow.

A number of key means through which male dominance and women's subordination are maintained are common to many settings. These include . . . control over women's sexuality and reproductive capacity; cultural norms and practices that entrench women's unequal status; State structures and processes that legitimize and institutionalize gender inequalities; and violence against women. Violence against women is both a means by which women's subordination is perpetuated and a consequence of their subordination.

Violence against women serves as a mechanism for maintaining male authority. When a woman is subjected to violence for transgressing social norms governing female sexuality and family roles, for example, the violence is not only individual but, through its punitive and controlling functions, also reinforces prevailing gender norms . . .

When the State fails to hold the perpetrators accountable, . . . [it] sends a message to society that male violence against women is both acceptable and inevitable. As a result, patterns of violent behaviour are normalized. . . .

Cultural justifications for restricting women's human rights have been asserted by some States and by social groups within many countries claiming to defend cultural tradition. . . . [R]eligious "fundamentalisms" in diverse geographic and religious contexts [have] become a serious challenge to efforts to secure women's human rights. . . .

Femicide [the murder of women] takes place in many contexts . . . [including] the protection of family "honour". For example, crimes committed in the name of "honour", usually by a brother, father, husband or other male family member, are a means of controlling women's choices, not only in the area of sexuality but also in other aspects of behaviour, such as freedom of movement. . . .

Crimes against women committed in the name of "honour" may occur within the family or within the community. . . . UNFPA estimated that 5,000 women are murdered by family members each year in "honour killings" around the world. . . .

Trafficking is a form of violence against women that takes place in multiple settings and usually involves many different actors including families, local brokers, international criminal networks and immigration authorities. Trafficking in human beings takes place both between and within countries. The majority of the victims of human trafficking are women and children, and many are trafficked for purposes of sexual exploitation.

Question for Analysis

1. According to the UN study, what means are used to maintain male dominance and female subordination?

Ending Violence Against Women: From Words of Action, Study of the Secretary-General, October 9, 2006.

lawless tribal regions of neighboring Pakistan—and a country impoverished by years of warfare and misrule.

Afghan officials, many of them corrupt and inefficient, generally owe their prime loyalties to family and tribe and not to the nation. American and coalition forces succeeded in killing and capturing numerous midlevel Taliban leaders and forcing Taliban fighters out of key population centers. Lack of security continues to plague the Afghan people. To promote instability, the Taliban deliberately target for assassination local Afghan officials and police, and virtually anyone cooperating with the Americans. Suicide bombings and homemade explosives placed at roadsides and in cars have caused the death of American soldiers and Afghan civilians.

After more than twelve years of conflict—the longest war in American history—Americans have grown increasingly disenchanted with the war, and President Barack Obama, who took office in 2009, started pulling out troops in 2011 when the United States had 101,000 troops in the country. In May 2014, President Obama announced a new timetable for the withdrawal of American forces from Afghanistan. By the end of 2014, American troops would be reduced from 32,000 to 9,800. By the end of 2016, a vestigial force would remain to protect the American embassy in Kabul and to assist the Afghans with security matters, including the training of security forces, which still have trouble conducting complex missions against a resilient Taliban without American assistance. During this scaled down presence, only a small number of American soldiers will still be engaged in lethal counterterrorism operations. Analysts fear that the pullout of American forces could make Afghanistan vulnerable to the same terrorist violence and political instability that have plagued Iraq since the departure of American forces; this is a principal reason why America is not carrying out an immediate total withdrawal. But Afghanistan's future remains very precarious. Reflecting the feelings of most American, President Obama said: "We have to recognize Afghanistan will not be a perfect place, and it is not America's responsibility to make it one."

Bin Laden and other Arabs from Morocco to Yemen devoted to a militant Islam had fought in Afghanistan to drive out the Soviets. During that

A Culture Clash. The Niqab worn by this Muslim woman on a street in Brussels covers the body from head to toe, leaving only a slit for the eyes. Maintaining that such dress demeans women, Europeans are increasingly urging banning it outside the home. (Julien Warnand/AFP/Getty Images.)

conflict, bin Laden and his cohorts drew up plans for the creation of an Islamic world-state governed by Islamic law, a revival of the medieval caliphate. They wanted to drive Westerners and Western values out of Islamic lands and impose a narrow, intolerant version of Islam on the Muslim world. Thus they view their struggle against the United States as a jihad or holy war against the infidel; the followers of bin Laden are zealots who are convinced that they are doing God's will. Recruits for suicide missions are equally convinced that they are waging holy war against the enemies of God and their centers of evil, for which they will be richly rewarded in Paradise. In 1998, bin

Laden called "on every Muslim who believes in Allah and wishes to be rewarded to comply with Allah's order to kill the Americans and plunder their money wherever and whenever they find it . . . to launch the raid on Satan's U.S troops and the devil's supporters allying with them."[10]

To be sure, the actions of bin Laden and his followers violated core Islamic teachings against killing civilians. At the same time, however, terrorists find religious justification for their actions in Islamic tradition. The early followers of Muhammad, says historian Bernard Lewis, divided the world

> into two houses: the House of Islam, in which a Muslim government ruled and Muslim law prevailed, and the House of War, the rest of the world . . . ruled by infidels. Between the two, there was to be a perpetual state of war until the entire world either embraced Islam or submitted to the rule of the Muslim state. . . . For Osama bin Laden, 2001 marks the resumption of the war for the religious dominance of the world that began in the seventh century. For him and his followers, this is the moment of opportunity. Today America exemplifies the civilization that embodies the leadership of the House of War, and it . . . has become degenerate and demoralized, ready to be overthrown.[11]

After September 11, several terrorist operations in Europe and the United States were thwarted, including attempts to explode an airplane headed for Detroit and to plant an explosive device in Times Square. But terrorists, either loosely or directly affiliated with Al Qaeda, succeeded in other operations in several countries, most of them suicide bombings that killed and wounded many innocents. In July 2005, Muslim suicide bombers killed more than fifty people and injured seven hundred in a terrorist attack on London's transit system. A year later British security foiled a terrorist plot to blow up several transatlantic flights departing from Heathrow airport that would have killed more people than had perished on September 11. That the planners and perpetrators of these attacks were British citizens terrorizing their fellow citizens distressed analysts; they feared that the millions of Muslims dwelling in Europe were potential recruits for extremist Islamic groups,

including Al Qaeda, engaged in holy war against the West and that European cities would become targets of fanatical suicide bombers. Likewise, U.S. officials are disconcerted by a number of terrorist attempts on American soil by Islamic radicals who are American citizens. (To be sure, the overwhelming number of American Muslims are loyal citizens and do not support terrorism.)

A tenacious United States, and other countries with varying degrees of determination and effectiveness, have combated militant Islam. The tracking down, capture, and killing of Al Qaeda leaders, at times by using sophisticated unmanned drones, and rigorous international efforts to destabilize Al Qaeda's vast financial network had weakened the terrorist organization. Then on May 1, 2011, President Barack Obama announced that a superbly orchestrated operation by the CIA and Navy Seals killed bin Laden—not in a cave in Pakistan's remote tribal lands, where it was generally thought he was hiding, but in a large, specially built compound with tall security fences topped with barbed wire in an upscale section of a town 70 miles from Pakistan's capital Islamabad.

But the death of bin Laden does not mean the end of Al Qaeda or Islamist terrorism. With Al Qaeda located in numerous countries across the Middle East and Africa, international terrorism remains a threat to world stability. Moreover, throughout the globe there are many affiliated, but independent, Islamist groups and freelancers that are inspired by bin Laden's ideology. Like bin Laden, these offshoots regard Muslims as victims of Western exploitation and believe that their faith demands that they fight and conquer nonbelievers.

A horrific example of terrorism by freelancers that shocked the American people occurred during the running of the famed Boston Marathon in April 2013. Two Muslim brothers, refugees from the region where Russia is battling Chechen separatists (see page 853), had lived for several years in the United States, which had granted their family asylum (and education and welfare); one brother had become a naturalized citizen. After embracing Islamic extremism, they planted explosives near the finish line of the race, crowded with spectators. The attack left three people dead and some 260 injured, sixteen of whom, including children, lost legs or feet. One brother died in a fierce gun battle with police and the other is awaiting trial after recovering from serious wounds.

Despite the seizure of Al Qaeda's assets, local cells continue to receive substantial funds from wealthy Arab donors, from contributions from the faithful purportedly for charitable causes, and from the tens of millions paid by European governments for the release of their kidnapped citizens. But terrorist undertakings do not necessarily require great sums of money. The bombing in Bali, Indonesia, which killed 202 people including 88 Australians, cost less than $35,000; the London subway bombings less than $500; and the September 11 attacks under $500,000. And Al Qaeda, with local support, has set up training camps in the remote, tribal areas of Pakistan, and the mountains and deserts of Yemen. Worsening the threat are jihadist sites on the Internet that inflame young Muslims and instruct them in preparing and planting explosives.

The events of September 11 may have signaled a new type of warfare for a new century. Free and open societies like the United States are vulnerable to attack, less from states that are deterred by America's might—as in the Cold War—than from stateless conspiratorial groups employing modern computers, communications, and difficult-to-trace financial operations to organize and finance terrorism. Such groups are not deterred by America's arsenal. And there is the fearful prospect that a rogue state will supply these groups with biological, chemical, and eventually nuclear weapons to wage war by proxy.

It was just such a fear that led President Bush in March 2003 to order an invasion of Iraq. The war was supported by Great Britain, which provided military assistance, but France, Germany, and Russia strongly opposed the decision. In about three weeks, U.S. and British forces, in an awesome display of operational planning and precision weaponry and suffering minimal casualties, destroyed Iraq's military hardware and decimated its armies. The victorious coalition forces uncovered torture chambers, where "enemies" of Hussein's regime were brutalized, and mass graves, where thousands were slaughtered at the tyrant's command. In December 2003, Saddam Hussein was captured. Put on trial by Iraqi authorities and found guilty of crimes against humanity, Saddam was executed by hanging at the end of December 2006.

But vexing problems remained. Could the United States install a democratic regime in a country torn by ethnic, religious, and tribal hatreds; where some Iraqis regarded the Americans as hated occupiers; and where democratic traditions and attitudes were largely lacking?

The United States declared that it had invaded Iraq to overthrow a ruthless dictator who had used poison gas against Iranian forces and Kurdish rebels in the 1980s and was now feverishly amassing an arsenal of biological and chemical weapons and was also seeking a nuclear capability. Now there was a danger that Hussein would supply these weapons of mass destruction (WMD) to be used against Americans. However, American intelligence—and the intelligence of other countries—was faulty. When no such weapons were found in the months after Iraq's defeat, critics in several lands accused the United States of pursuing a reckless foreign policy.

After crushing the Iraqi army, coalition forces still faced insurgency principally from Sunni Muslims who had received favored treatment under Saddam—the ruling elite were virtually all Sunnis. The insurgents also targeted Shi'ite Muslims, who constitute the majority of the population and had been cruelly oppressed by Saddam. By murdering Shi'ite clerics, pilgrims, and worshipers and bombing their mosques, market places, cafes, and funerals, the insurgents hoped to trigger a sectarian conflict that would make the new Iraq ungovernable. After reaching a peak in 2006 and 2007, the sectarian violence eased due to the intervention of the government and coalition forces.

By the end of 2011, President Obama had withdrawn American forces from Iraq. More than 4,450 American soldiers died in the seven-and-a-half-year conflict, and there were more than 160,000 Iraqi civilian fatalities and some 1.5 million had fled the country. When it pulled its troops out, the United States declared that Iraq was on track to becoming a stable democracy, but once American troops left, the Iraqi government had great difficulty controlling the insurgency and renewed religious violence, which increased the death toll and made daily life insecure. Sunni militants, who regard Shi'ites as heretics, felt marginalized and maltreated under the Shi'ite-led government. Determined to wrest power from the Sunnis who had dominated the region for hundreds of years, prime minister Nuri al-Malaki purged Sunnis from government positions and the military. Reacting to these policies, Sunnis carried out murderous attacks mainly in crowded Shi'ite areas that killed some 8,000 in 2013.

Many Sunni militants are members of the radical Islamic State of Iraq and Syria (ISIS), a jihadist terrorist organization which vowed to create a caliphate, an Islamic religious state, that would span Sunni-dominated regions of Syria and Iraq. Intending to rule with Taliban-like rigor in areas under its control, ISIS has already banned soccer and music and requires women to wear the veil. In late spring 2014, ISIS seized vast areas of Iraq. The American-trained Iraqi army, which greatly outnumbered the insurgents, collapsed; fleeing troops left behind stores of American-supplied arms, including heavy equipment. Even Sunnis who do not want their lives regulated by Islamist extremists, sided with ISIS, so hateful are they of the Shi'ite-led government. ISIS jihadists are considered more brutal and fanatic than Al Qaeda; they have crucified and beheaded opponents and slaughtered hundreds of captured Shi'ite prisoners in a mass execution (they posted gruesome photos and videotapes of these atrocities online).

In June, 2014, ISIS declared that the territory it controlled constituted a revived caliphate—the Islamic empire that had ruled over Muslim lands for centuries. ISIS called on all jihadist organizations worldwide to swear loyalty to the new caliph, the head of Isis. By June 2014, when this book went to press, it seemed that Iraq was fragmenting into three autonomous regions, each dominated either by Sunnis, Shi'ites, or Kurds? Only the Kurds have responsible leaders who share Western values. With zealous Shi'ites forming armed militias, would Iraq be convulsed by an all-out war marked by religious fanaticism and reciprocal atrocities? President Obama declared that the United States would not get embroiled in combat in Iraq; it would only provide three hundred military advisers to help train Iraqi security forces. But, how will the United States respond if the state established by ISIS, which is itself an offshoot of Al Qaeda, becomes a terrorist training ground and sanctuary?

Many analysts conclude that the Iraqi and Afghan conflicts demonstrate once more the immense difficulty of transplanting Western democratic values and institutions to regions whose history and cultural traditions do not easily mesh with democracy and whose prime allegiances to sect and ethnic group impede a sense of citizenship in a pluralistic state. And they point to a larger concern: these costly and unpopular wars—some six thousand American fatalities and expenditures of more than 1.5 trillion dollars—illustrate the limitations of American power. The American military had demonstrated the ability to wage successful counterterrorism campaigns, but, say some analysts, it should not be entrapped into nation-building, an amorphous objective fraught with uncertainty that is beyond the capacity of the military, or, indeed, of the U.S. government.

In early 2011, a wave of popular protest against autocratic rulers—what has been called the "Arab Spring"—swept across the Arab world, a region where democracy has been dismissed as an impossible dream. Many of the participants were alienated youth clamoring for jobs and political freedom. Long ruling strongmen were forced out in Tunisia and Egypt and protests resounded in Algeria, Yemen, Bahrain, Jordan, Syria, and Libya. In Libya, there was open rebellion against Muammar el-Qaddafi's forty-year tyranny. To protect Libyan civilians, NATO, including the United States, provided air support for the rebels, who killed Qaddafi. The death of the tyrant produced tribal conflicts and rival militias rather than democracy, and southern Libya has become a haven for jihadists.

In Syria, President Bashar-al Assad's police and army used lethal force against peaceful protesters, killing many. For more than three years a vicious civil war has raged in Syria; more than 150,000 people have perished and some 2 million have fled the violence and increasingly crumbling economy, creating a severe refugee problem in neighboring countries; millions more, seeking to escape the guns, have left their homes searching for safety in other areas of Syria creating still another humanitarian crisis. What began as a political protest against Assad's tyrannical rule has also become a sectarian conflict between Sunnis and the minority Alawites, an offshoot of Shia Islam. Assad, who is an Alawite, depends on his coreligionists for support. The Assad regime also draws money, weapons, and military operatives from Shi'ite Iran, and has been significantly strengthened by Shi'ite volunteers from Iraq and by thousands of trained fighting men from Hezbollah, a militant Lebanese Shi'ite organization, which the United States has blacklisted as a terrorist organization. And Russia continues to supply the Syrian government with arms. In mid-2014, it did not appear that the insurgents could topple Assad. In August 2013, the Assad regime used poison gas to regain control over Sunni suburbs of Damascus, killing an estimated one thousand civilians, including several hundred children, who died painfully. Enraged by this inhuman act that violated international law against the use of chemical weapons, President Obama threatened a limited punitive strike and American warships with missile weapons moved closer to Syria. Assad and the United States accepted a Russian proposal to turn Syria's stockpile of chemical weapons over to international authorities for destruction and, acting quickly, both foreign powers reached an agreement that called for the removal or destruction of Syria's chemical weapons by the middle of 2014.

Because it held the promise of constructive change and the advancement of human rights, Western policy makers were euphoric over the democratic thrust in the Arab world. But the euphoria soon faded. There is now fear that the secular and democratic movement is being usurped by well-organized radical Islamists and jihadists who are poised and eager to exploit any instability and breakdown of authority and to establish authoritarian theocratic regimes that seek to foist a rigid interpretation of Islamic law and hatred of the West. For example, in free elections in 2011 and 2012, the Egyptian people voted into power the Muslim Brotherhood, an anti-Western party that ultimately seeks to impose strict religious rule. Distressed by soaring unemployment, a bankrupt treasury, food shortages, and inept and authoritarian Brotherhood leadership that perverted democracy in its attempt to monopolize power, virtually a million demonstrators called for the resignation of Mohamed Morsi, the Muslim Brotherhood president. In the summer of 2013, the Egyptian military ousted Morsi and in mass shootings security forces killed more than a thousand Morsi supporters protesting the coup and then jailed most of the leaders of the Brotherhood, including Morsi, and seized its assets. In succeeding months the military-backed government designated the movement a terrorist organization and outlawed. In its attempt to suppress opposition, the new government has engaged in human rights violations.

And in Syria, Sunni extremists, several thousand of them volunteers from numerous lands who see themselves as holy warriors, have joined the civil war; many are members of ISIS which has succeeded Al Qaeda as the most formidable terrorist group in the Arab world. It is believed that 3,000 Westerners, including more than seventy Americans, are among the jihadist volunteers; analysts worry that they will return to Europe and America as battle-hardened terrorists. The failure of the Arab Spring demonstrates how little the ethic of tolerance—the acceptance of different peoples and different viewpoints—pervades Arab society.

OUR GLOBAL AGE: PROMISE AND PROBLEMS

Globalization

In the twenty-first century, globalization continues relentlessly; the world is being knit ever closer together by the spread of Western ideals, popular culture (particularly American), free-market capitalism, and technology. Government officials and professional people all over the world dress in Western clothes. Women follow Western fashions in dress and makeup. People line up to eat at McDonald's, see a Hollywood movie, or attend a rock concert. Everywhere people are eager to adopt the latest technology that originated in the West but is now also manufactured in other, particularly Asian, lands. Advanced technology intensifies the means of communication, not only through television and radio but also with faxes, e-mail, cell phones, and the Internet. Breakthroughs in information technology have enabled companies to place production and research facilities in different lands and yet maintain direction and control with instant communication. And it allows individuals all over the world to communicate with each other instantly and inexpensively. These developments promote shared interests among individuals and businesses, some of them multinational corporations, throughout the globe, reducing the importance of national frontiers. All these factors combined are reshaping Western and non-Western societies in a relentless adjustment that holds great promise.

World Poverty and Exploding Population

Generally globalization has enhanced economic growth and improved the standard of living for hundreds of millions throughout the globe. But hundreds of millions are still mired in poverty. According to the World Bank, some 1.1 billion people live in extreme poverty, defined as struggling to survive on less than one dollar a day. Another 1.6 billion live on less than two dollars a day. Each year 8 million people—some 20,000 a day—perish because they lack safe drinking water, proper nutrition, bed nets to protect them from malaria-carrying mosquitos, adequate hospitals, and life-saving drugs. Poverty particularly persists in countries ruled by corrupt elites who use political power to amass personal fortunes. In 2010 UN officials reported that 925 million people were undernourished. Despite these unpleasant images of human suffering, poverty rates continue to decline. From 1990 to 2010 almost a billion people were lifted out of extreme poverty; most successful has been China whose accelerated economic growth rescued 680 million people from dire poverty between 1981 and 2010. It is hoped that continued economic growth and better income distribution will by 2030 rescue another billion people from extreme poverty.

The spread of Western science, medicine, and humanitarianism and economic progress have produced an unprecedented population explosion worldwide. For countless millennia the world's population remained almost stationary, slowly beginning to grow in the eighteenth century. In 1900, the world's population reached 1.6 billion. Fifty years later, it reached 2.5 billion, and by the year 2000, it skyrocketed to 6.1 billion. Despite immense losses of life in two world wars, totalitarian terror, ethnic conflicts, local famines, and other calamities, the world's population nearly quadrupled within a century. And in 2011, it passed seven billion. A spiraling population places immense pressure on the earth's resources and exacerbates both national and international problems. (The world's population continues to increase; the United States remains relatively stable and several European countries have a below-replacement birth rate, that is, fewer births than deaths.)

Transmitting Democracy

The hopes analysts held that the dissemination of democratic institutions around the globe would reduce conflicts and advance human rights have somewhat diminished. The ideals of individual liberty, political democracy, religious and cultural freedom, and increasingly female equality, all historical accomplishments of Western civilization, do exert a powerful influence worldwide. But, unlike technology, these ideals and practices, which evolved from the history and traditions of the West, are often difficult to transmit to non-Western nations. This is particularly true in countries that are riven by ethnic and religious divisions which preclude a willingness to tolerate and cooperate with citizens holding different beliefs and practicing different traditions—a fundamental requirement of a pluralistic democratic society. While some countries, particularly in Asia, have established working democracies, across the globe we see democratically elected governments routinely dismissing constitutional limitations on their power and divesting citizens of constitutionally guaranteed rights. These fraudulent democracies maintain the outer form of democracy—parliaments and elections—but in reality they are contemporary forms of dictatorship, often led by a power-hungry despot. Even more depressing, we see people willingly supporting parties and leaders hostile to democratic principles and human rights—religious toleration and equal rights for women, for example—that conflict with deeply ingrained cultural traditions. John Agresto explains the cultural barriers impeding the implementation of democracy in the Arab world.

> Yet it is the character of a culture that shapes the aspirations of its citizens and the nature of its democracy. A culture in which there is little religious or intellectual freedom, where adherence to the commands of imams or religious scholars is sacrosanct, a culture that believes its duty before God is to punish dissent, kill apostates, and exterminate God's supposed enemies, a culture in which there is no deep acceptance of difference—such cultures will produce illiberal souls who are hardly strong candidates to form a truly liberal and free democracy.[12]

Human Rights

For decades human rights movements throughout the globe have pressed for eliminating abuses that violate human dignity. Due to their efforts many developing countries have instituted legal reforms protecting the rights of their citizens. But despite gains, human rights violations, particularly against the poor and women (see Primary Source, page 864) persist, especially in developing lands. In these countries, abusers of the poor often have no fear of the routinely corrupt police, or of a public justice system that is unsympathetic to the plight of the powerless. In many developing lands it is difficult to overcome cultural traditions that confine women to a subordinate position. Gang rapes in India and the Congo are not uncommon. The attempted assassination by the Taliban in Pakistan of Malala Yousafzai, a young female student, for advocating education for girls created an international furor. Regarding girls' schools as symbols of Western decadence, since 2009 Taliban militants in northwestern Pakistan have bombed more than eight hundred schools. In April, 2014, an extremist Muslim group in Nigeria called Boko Haram—in the Hausa language the name means "Western education is a sin"—set fire to a girls' school and kidnapped more than three hundred girls, some fifty of whom managed to escape. The terrorist leader called the girls slaves and threatened to sell them. Boko Haram's ultimate aim is to establish in Nigeria a pure Islamic state governed by sharia.

Analysts of human rights are growing increasingly concerned with escalating religious persecution in recent years. We discussed the resurgence of anti-Semitism earlier in the chapter. In Myanmar, mobs responding to the spreading of hatred by Buddhist monks against the Muslim minority have terrorized Muslim communities destroying and killing. (Fueling the hostility is the fact that many Muslims are Rohingya, a despised alien ethnic group.). It is estimated that more than 100,000 Muslims, too fearful to return to their villages, are confined to camps that foreign aid workers describe as outdoor jails, and medical care has been deliberately curtailed causing deaths. In India thousands of Muslims fleeing from Hindu violence are also living in dreadful makeshift shelters. The persecution of Christians in Muslim lands, where Christians have been historically regarded as infidels, has increased dramatically. Churches, religious symbols, and the distribution of the Bible are prohibited in Saudi Arabia, and Christians congregating in homes to pray risk being flogged and jailed. Iranian police, at times, raid the homes of Christian converts and imprison them. In 2013, numerous churches were torched and bombed in the Muslim world, including one in Peshawar, Pakistan, that killed 85 Christians and injured 120. In Egypt, radical Muslims, incensed over the army's ouster of Mohamed Morsi, the Muslim Brotherhood president, turned on Coptic Christians whose Egyptian roots go back to the early days of Christianity; more than 80 Coptic Christian churches were torched and looted and scores of Christians were killed or maimed. Bombings on Christmas day in the Christian district of Baghdad, Iraq's capital, killed thirty-seven people, some during a church service; it is not uncommon for Muslim militants to target Christian churches during Christmas and Easter. In Kenya, Nigeria, Mali, Iraq, and Syria, Christians have been kidnapped, raped, murdered, and forcibly converted to Islam.

Faced with the vandalizing of their churches and violent attacks that kill and maim, hundreds of thousands of Christians have fled Muslim lands—in a few years the Christian population of Iraq has fallen from more than 1 million to less than 500,000. Christian spokespersons have lamented the failure of Muslim clergy in both Muslim and non-Muslim lands—with some exceptions—to denounce strongly the anti-Christian behavior of their coreligionists.

Warfare

The world remains burdened with conflicts. In recent years civil wars have caused horrific suffering in several lands. Strife in the Congo left some 3.8 million people dead between 1998 and 2003. More than two decades of warfare in southern Sudan cost 2 million lives before a peace treaty was signed between the government and the rebels in 2005. The actions of Arab militias against blacks in Sudan's Darfur region has been called genocidal; despite the peace treaty, state-supported militias still prey in Darfur, killing helpless civilians and driving hundreds of thousands into refugee camps.

Despite what appears to be a grim picture, in actual fact, the early twenty-first century, says sociologist Joshua S. Goldstein, "has seen fewer war deaths than any decade in the past 100 years." There are fewer civil wars today than in 1990 and since the Korean War, which ended some sixty years ago, great powers have not taken up arms against each other. To be sure, since 9/11 the United States has been engaged in several long wars, but, says Goldstein, "they are far smaller and less lethal. America's decade of war since 2001 has killed about 6,000 U. S. service members, compared with 58,000 in Vietnam and 300,000 [battle fatalities; 400,000 including all fatalities] in World War II."[13]

Most frightening for the future is the development of weapons of mass destruction by states that do not share Western democratic values. North Korea, a ruthless Communist dictatorship, possesses nuclear weapons; so too does Pakistan, which is afflicted with political instability and Taliban insurgents. Iran, headed by Islamic fundamentalists who have financed and provided military assistance to terrorist organizations, is moving ahead with plans to develop nuclear energy that, despite denials, will no doubt include nuclear weapons. It is feared that a nuclear Iran might supply its militant and terrorist clients with nuclear weapons and seek to dominate its Arab neighbors, totally transforming the Middle East. (There is fierce hostility between Iranians, who are Persian and Shi'ites, and Arabs, who are predominantly Sunni.) Most concerned is Israel whose destruction Iran's leaders have repeatedly called for.

Its economy devastated by the crippling sanctions imposed by the United States and its supporters, in late 2013, Iran reached an interim agreement with the United States, Britain, France, Germany, Russia, and China. While the agreement curbed Iran's nuclear enrichment program for six months, its nuclear infrastructure remained essentially intact. In return, some sanctions were lifted—but most remained in place. Critics of the agreement argued that since the accord did not dismantle Iran's nuclear infrastructure, Iran would still be able to build a nuclear weapon in a relatively short time if its leadership decided to do so. The Obama administration regarded the freeze as an interim accord, a first stage designed to halt Iran's race to build a nuclear weapon; a soon to come broader agreement, it believed, would put an end to Iran's nuclear weapons capacity.

Hopeful Signs

There are hopeful signs for the future. Democracy has replaced repressive regimes in Central and East Europe. It is hoped that recent events in Ukraine will not revive the Cold War which the world believed had ended with the breakup of the Soviet Union. Compared to the generation born in the early twentieth century, people are healthier, live longer and better, and the death rate for children under five has plummeted. Impressive economic growth in many lands, including South and East Asia and now Africa, has significantly broadened the middle class and reduced poverty, a testament to the effectiveness of the free market, although worldwide repercussions are still felt from the financial crisis of 2008 caused largely by wild speculation in the American mortgage market. The past decade has seen an astonishing turnaround in Africa. Famine, civil war, dictatorships, and death from AIDS and malaria are receding and the economy is booming. Real income per person in the last ten years has soared by an extraordinary 30 percent, whereas it had contracted by 10 percent in the previous twenty years. And, in parts of Africa, after decades of brutal political violence which took the lives of millions, Africans, including fighters engaged in ethnic struggles and civil wars, have grown weary of war and are putting down their weapons. NATO, the United Nations, and the African Union have provided security forces to quell violent conflicts in several regions.

In the West, in recent decades women have made extraordinary educational, economic, and political progress, rising to positions of power in governments and major corporations and in some parts African and Asian lands, despite the persistence of deeply embedded cultural traditions, women have also risen to prominence.

Advances in science and technology hold great promise for the future. In medicine surgical transplants and new antibiotics are saving lives, and the mapping of the human genome enables the medical field to understand the structure and function of our genes, knowledge that provides new insights for the prevention and curing of disease. Abounding in every area—communications, transportation, agriculture, manufacturing, sanitation, energy, astronomy—scientific and technological breakthroughs are transforming the way we live and work, often for the better. Look at what the worldwide Internet has accomplished! No doubt, as numerous analysts have commented, these achievements could also have troubling, if not, dangerous effects—pollution that ravages the environment; nuclear weapons that can destroy civilization; automation that deprives workers of jobs; the cell phone and e-mail which provide terrorists with instant communication; and Internet videos with which Islamist radicals seek to win recruits, call for jihad, and provide instructions for building and deploying bombs.

How can peaceful global interdependence be advanced, given the persistent cultural and political differences that divide the world, promoting hatred and inciting violence? Can the present generation of Western peoples, above all Americans, help shape the development of the global community in accordance with the highest ideals of Western civilization?

REAFFIRMING THE CORE IDEALS OF THE WESTERN TRADITION

In recent years, modern Western civilization, whose core values were articulated during the Enlightenment, has come under severe attack from several quarters, including religious thinkers, intellectuals loosely called postmodernists, advocates of the poor and oppressed, and militant Muslims. Some religious thinkers deplore the modern age for its espousal of secular rationality, the central legacy of the Enlightenment. These thinkers argue that reason without God degenerates into an overriding concern for technical efficiency—an attitude of mind that produces Auschwitz, Stalin's labor camps, weapons of mass destruction, and the plundering and polluting of the environment. The self without God degenerates into selfish competition, domination, exploitation, and unrestrained hedonism. Human dignity conceived purely in secular terms does not

permit us to recognize the *thou* of another human being, to see our neighbor as someone who has been dignified by God; and removing God from life ends in spiritual emptiness and gnawing emotional distress. These critics of the Enlightenment tradition urge the reorientation of thinking around God and transcendent moral absolutes. Without such a reorientation, they argue, liberal democracy cannot resist the totalitarian temptation or overcome human wickedness.

Postmodernists argue that modernity founded on the Enlightenment legacy, which once was viewed as a progressive force emancipating the individual from unreasonable dogmas, traditions, and authority, has itself become a source of repression through its own creations: technology, bureaucracy, consumerism, materialism, the nation-state, ideologies, and a host of other institutions, procedures, and norms. Aversion to a technoscientific culture and to its methodology leads postmodernists to devalue the principle of objectivity in the social sciences and to give greater weight to the subjective, to feelings, intuition, and fantasy, to the poetry of life. Postmodernists contend that the evaluation of data and reasoned arguments, no matter how logical they seem, reveal only personal preferences and biases. In their view, science has no greater claim to truth than does religion, myth, or witchcraft. In a world marked by cultural diversity and individual idiosyncrasies, there are no correct answers, no rules that apply everywhere and to everyone. Moreover, like those who point out the dangers of reason not directed by spiritual values, postmodernists argue that reason fosters oppressive governments, military complexes, and stifling bureaucracies. Nor has it solved our problems.

Expressing disdain for Western humanism, which ascribes an inherent dignity to human beings, urges the full development of the individual's potential, and regards the rational, self-determining human being as the center of existence, postmodernists claim that humanism has failed. The humanist vision of socialist society ended in Stalinism, and liberal humanism proved no more effective a barrier to Nazism than did Christianity. In our own day, they ask, has the rational humanist tradition been able to solve the problems of overpopulation, worldwide pollution, world hunger, poverty, and war that ravage our planet? Closer to home, has reason coped successfully with urban blight, homelessness, violence, racial tensions, or drug addiction? Moreover, postmodernists contend that the Western tradition, which has been valued as a great and creative human achievement, is fraught with gender, class, and racial bias. In their view, it is merely a male, white, Eurocentric interpretation of things, and the West's vaunted ideals are really a cloak of hypocrisy intended to conceal, rationalize, and legitimate the power, privileges, and preferences of white, European, male elites.

People who identify with victims of exploitation, discrimination, and persecution throughout the globe also attack the Western tradition. They point to the modern West's historic abuses: slavery, imperialism, racism, ethnocentrism, sexism, class exploitation, and the ravaging of the environment. They accuse Westerners of marginalizing the poor, women, and people of color by viewing them as the "other." Furthermore, they condemn the West for arrogantly exalting Western values and achievements and belittling, or even destroying, indigenous peoples and cultures. Finding Western civilization intrinsically flawed, some critics seek a higher wisdom in non-Western traditions—African, Asian, or Native American.

Radical Muslims, who were responsible for or applaud the September 11 terrorist attacks, view Western civilization as a threat to traditional Islam and plot its destruction. Their vision of an Islamic society based on a strict interpretation of the Koran clashes head-on with core principles of Western democracy—separation of church and state, religious toleration, protection of basic rights, and female equality.

Defenders of the Enlightenment heritage argue that this heritage, despite its flaws, still has a powerful message for us. They caution against devaluing and undermining the modern West's unique achievements: the tradition of *rationality*, which makes possible a scientific understanding of the physical universe and human nature, the utilization of nature for human betterment, and the identification and reformation of irrational and abusive institutions and beliefs; the tradition of *political freedom*, which is the foundation of democratic institutions; the tradition of *inner freedom*, which asserts the individual's capacity for ethical autonomy, the ability and duty to make moral choices; the tradition of *humanism*, which regards individuals as active subjects, with both the right and the capacity to realize their full human potential; the tradition of *equality*, which demands equal treatment under the law; and the tradition of *human dignity*, which affirms the inviolable integrity and worth of the human personality and is the driving force behind what is now a global quest for social justice and human rights.

The modern struggle for human rights—initiated during the Enlightenment, advanced by the French Revolution, and embodied in liberalism—continues in the contemporary age. Two crucial developments in this struggle are the civil rights movement in the United States and the feminist movement. Spokespersons for these movements have used ideas formulated by Western thinkers in earlier struggles for liberty and equality. Thus, one reason for the success of Martin Luther King's policy of direct action was that he both inspired and shamed white America to live up to its Judeo-Christian and democratic principles. Though written more than thirty years ago, the insights of the French social theorist Jacques Ellul still apply.

> *The essential, central, undeniable fact is that the West was the first civilization in history to focus attention on the individual and on freedom. . . . The West, and the West alone, is responsible for the movement that has led to the desire for freedom. . . . Today men point the finger of outrage at slavery and torture. Where did that kind of indignation originate? What civilization or culture cried out that slavery was unacceptable and torture scandalous? Not Islam, or Buddhism, or Confucius, or Zen, or the religions and moral codes of Africa and India! The West alone has defended the inalienable rights of the human person, the dignity of the individual. . . . The West attempted to apply in a conscious, methodical way the implications of freedom. . . . The West discovered what no one else had discovered: freedom and the individual. . . . I see no other satisfactory model that can replace what the West has produced.*[14]

The roots of these ideals are ultimately found in the West's Greek and Judeo-Christian heritage, but it was the philosophers of the Enlightenment who clearly articulated them for the modern age. To be sure, these ideals are a goal, not a finished achievement, and nothing should make Westerners more appreciative of the preciousness of these ideals and more alert to their precariousness than examining the ways they have been violated and distorted over the course of centuries. It is equally true that every age has to rethink and revitalize this tradition in order to adapt it to the needs of its own time.

Therefore, it is crucial in this age of globalism, with its heightened sense of ethnic and cultural diversity, that Westerners become sensitized to the histories and traditions of all cultures. But it is equally crucial in an era of global interdependence and tension that Westerners continuously affirm and reaffirm the core values of their heritage and not permit this priceless legacy to be dismissed or negated. As the history of the twentieth century demonstrates, when we lose confidence in this heritage, we risk losing our humanity, and civilized life is threatened by organized barbarism.

❖   ❖   ❖

Notes

1. Boris Yeltsin, "Yeltsin Addresses Parliament on the State of the Nation," *Current Digest of the Post-Soviet Press*, April 9, 1997, 1.

2. Quoted in Steven Lee Myers, "Opponents Call Putin's Overhaul Plan a Step Back," *The New York Times*, September 14, 2004, 1A.

3. http://www.nbcnews.com/id/7632057/ns/world_news/t/putin-soviet-collapse-genuine-tragedy/#.UhS20haqnFc

4. Denis MacShane, "The New Anti-Semitism," *The Washington Post*, September 4, 2007, A17.

5. Denis MacShane, *Globalising Hatred: The New Antisemitism* (London: Weidenfeld & Nicolson, 2008), xi.

6. Quoted in Bat Ye'or, *Eurabia: The Euro-Arab Axis* (Madison, N.J.: Fairleigh Dickinson University Press, 2005, 2006), 240–241.

7. Quoted in Raymond Ibrahim, ed. and trans., *The Al Qaeda Reader* (New York: Broadway Books, 2007), 277.

8. Quoted in Gabriel Schoenfeld, *The Return of Anti-Semitism* (San Francisco: Encounter Books, 2004), 13.

9. Quoted in Itamar Marcus and Barbara Crook, "Kill a Jew—Go to Heaven: The Perception of the Jew in Palestinian Society," *Jewish Political Studies Review*, vol. 17, nos. 3–4 (Fall 2005), 127. Copyright © 2005 Jerusalem Center for Public Affairs. Reprinted with permission.

10. From www.fas.org/irp/world/para/docs/980223-Fatwa.htm.

11. Bernard Lewis, "Revolt of Islam," *The New Yorker*, November 19, 2001, 52, 62.

12. John Agresto, "Was Promoting Democracy a Mistake?" *Commentary*, December 2012, Vol. 134: No 5.

13. Joshua S. Goldstein, "Think Again War," *Foreign Policy*, October 2011, 53.

14. Jacques Ellul, *The Betrayal of the West*, trans. J. O'Connell (New York: Seabury, 1978), 17–19, 29.

Index

A Lifetime of Adventure awaits the diving enthusiast.   Photo by Bob Evans

Many of the exercises and systems shown in this manual will not be found in any other. This is a manual developed from ideas and concepts of the Professional Instructor. He is a man who is teaching all the time and makes diving his vocation. By exchanging ideas with other full time professionals through clinics and through a central clearing house, these ideas and systems were tested and proven into this New Concept of Teaching Safe Scuba.

FOREWORD

For the first time in the recorded history of man, it is now possible for any person in reasonably good health to easily venture into a totally new environment, the underwater world. To be able to do so, requires a certain amount of basic training. The purpose of this manual is to help acquaint the beginner with the fundamental knowledge and practical skills necessary to safely enjoy this most unusual and exciting activity.

If your cup of tea is photography, the underwater world offers a mute challenge to record on film the changing moods and seasons of the sea with all its rare and exotic plant and animal life.

Hunting? No need to spend thousands for a safari to some remote corner of the globe to hunt for a trophy. The giant Black Sea Bass and Grouper are worthy adversaries for any sportsman. These wily monsters with the latent power of a charging water buffalo offer a real challenge. To venture into their domain, learn their habits, stalk them through the giant kelp forests, around coral heads, in and out of caves, through the tangled steel girders of an off-shore drilling rig, and ultimately impale them on a slender shaft of steel is a thrill unequaled. These fish, in one form or another, exist in the temperate waters of all the seas and are easily available to all of us.

On the prosaic side, but equally available, are all of

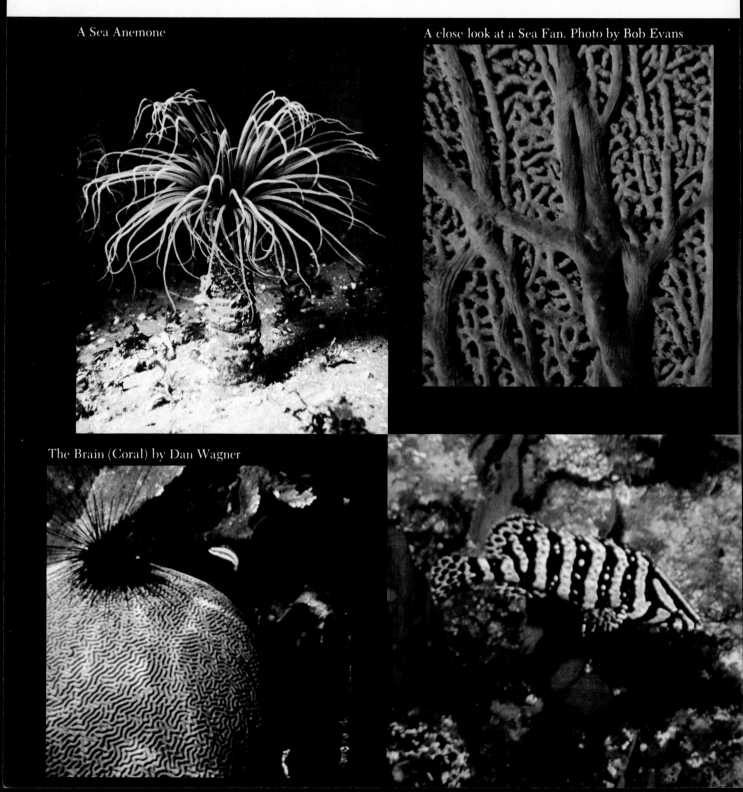

A Sea Anemone

A close look at a Sea Fan. Photo by Bob Evans

The Brain (Coral) by Dan Wagner

the tasty denizens of the deep. The accomplished diver can literally "feed the family" from the sea. Lobsters, crabs, oysters, clams, scallops, abalone, conch, and mussels are but a few of the delicacies stored away in nature's largest food depository, the sea.

At the other end of the hunting spectrum are the divers who collect marine specimens. Armed with a transparent plastic weapon aptly named a "slurp gun," they prowl the mountains, valleys, and forests of the underwater world, collecting — or trying to collect — tiny marine specimens to enhance their home aquariums or to supply commercial collectors. Since many of these tiny fellows are very valuable, it is possible to develop an additional source of income from this activity. It is an interesting

hobby and one in which the whole family can participate. While Dad and Mom are out diving in the kelp beds, the kiddies can wade around in the tide pools with a dip-net and plastic jar. Hand in hand with collecting marine tropicals is the fascinating pursuit of shell collecting.

Are you a rock hound? Is your hobby prospecting or geology? Clever divers have developed six foot long slurp guns (really light weight dredges) for extracting alluvial value from river and stream beds. These highly efficient dredges in the hands of experienced diver-prospectors or diver-geologists — have taken thousands of dollars worth of gold, diamonds, and minerals daily from rivers and streams of the world. Many divers who know nothing

This diver positions his dredge at a 17th Century wreck site. Photo by Bob Marx.

A Spiny Lobster. Photo by Bob Evans.

Gold coins recovered by treasure team. Photo by Bob Marx.

of prospecting or geology team up with a prospector or geologist, and form a profitable partnership, either as a business or as a hobby.

How about marine archeology? Consider the thrill of the discovery of the remains of some ancient temple of a forgotten civilization that has been slumbering on the bottom of the sea for centuries. Or the careful cleaning of the site of the sinking of a slave-powered galley loaded with precious wares bound for some now unknown trading center. Will it be an amateur diver-archeologist who finally proves the existence of the fabled continent of Atlantis? Who knows? Amateurs have contributed considerably to the small amount of knowledge in this fascinating, new field.

Some divers find the lure of treasure diving irresistible. From ancient galleons loaded with a king's ransom to modern day ships, every vessel that goes to the bottom of the sea takes with it something of value. Equipped with SCUBA, almost anyone can find a wreck somewhere to explore.

On the more practical side, learning to SCUBA dive can be the first step to a career underwater. There is a growing demand for technicians and scientists who are trained divers. The diving industry itself offers many challenging careers in the fields of instruction, sales, management, design, and engineering.

Last, but not least, is the large group of purists who dive for the sheer joy of diving. The sensation of "weightlessness" can only be truly experienced by divers in "inner-space" or astronauts in "outer-space." A visit to the floor of the sea with its changing terrain — sometimes as austere as a moonscape, sometimes a lush tropical garden inhabited by weird plants and animals — can be likened to a trip to a planet in the far reaches of outer space.

The passport to this fascinating "Last Frontier" on our planet lies in the hands of your Professional SCUBA Diving Instructor. SCUBA diving is fun. It is easy. It is safe. It does, however, require complete and thorough understanding of the fundamental rules for safe diving. Upon completion of your course, you will be awarded your license to learn . . . your Basic Certification Card.

Welcome to the Underwater World of Adventure.

The fish hang in the current in the clear water of a fresh water river. Photo by Elgin Ciampi.

Welcome to the
Underwater World of Adventure.

SAFE SCUBA

by WILLIAM "BILL" HOGAN

TABLE OF CONTENTS

Acknowledgements

The author wishes to thank the many Professional Instructors from all across the country and others who helped make this book possible. In particular, I am indebted to: *GORDON BATEMAN* M.D. Orthopedic Surgeon in private practice and former U.S. Navy Diving Medical Officer for his review and comments on Diving Physiology.

KEVIN MURPHY, C.P.O. (Ret.) UDT Seal Team & U.S. Navy Diving Instructor for his review of the entire manuscript.

JOHN GAFFNEY, Executive Director of the National Association of Skin Diving Schools who co-ordinated the systems used in the teaching manual of NASDS and this book and for his excellent guidance and constant encouragement.

ROY BRIZZ, the artist and photographer who designed and illustrated the book and who photographed the diving exercises.

The alert reader will notice that a few photographs depict divers who are not wearing buoyancy compensators or safety vests. By modern teaching methods, these divers would be considered poorly trained or unsafe. These photographs were taken prior to the development of good vests and were selected for their beauty or instructional value.

The fish eye camera lens gives a comic effect to the California Garibaldi. Photo by Bob Evans.

BASIC EQUIPMENT

In sport diving, as in any sport that involves the use of equipment, it is extremely important that the novice be carefully fitted with equipment that is comfortable, functional, safe, and of a proven design that will make the transition to the underwater world easy. Good quality basic equipment is inexpensive and any novice wishing to excel in diving should not consider cheap, ill-fitting equipment. Indeed, any beginner with inferior equipment is actually penalizing himself. Adjusting to the underwater environment requires that the novice be relaxed and at ease, a very difficult thing to do when an ill-fitting pair of fins is cramping one's feet, or a mask is constantly leaking.

The beginning diver should seek the advice of a professional equipment counselor or instructor when selecting his equipment. It takes a professional to judge which equipment is best for the kind of diving and the area that the diving will take place in. This will assure the beginning diver of the right equipment for his own special requirements.

FINS

Fins are of two types, open heel or full foot (closed heel). They are available in giant or regular size, in all foot pocket sizes. If the full foot model is chosen, fixe palmes or a similar device should be purchased for use in the surf or fast current. Fins should be of good quality, comfortable fit and of giant size when possible. With some beginners it is advisable to start with regular size fins and progress to the giants as their ability to use fins increases.

Jet Type Fins

Duckfeet

Full Foot

Fixe Palmes

Venturi Type

MASKS

Plain Mask

Masks are made in a variety of shapes to accommodate all size faces. Some are equipped with purge valves and/or equalizing devices. Purge valves are used to clear masks of water easily and equalizers are used for equalizing pressure through the Eustachian tubes to inner ear, as pressure develops when diver is descending. A mask of good quality that fits comfortably, doesn't leak water, has both a purge valve and equalizing pad (or "nose grabber") is recommended. All quality masks have tempered glass and non-corrosive hardware.

3 window

Mask with Purge and Equalizer

Wide View

Mask with purge

SNORKEL

In general, snorkels are either permanently molded in a "J" shape or have a straight section with a corrugated extension that forms a "J" when snorkel is in use. Both types are available with or without a clearing valve located somewhere near the mouthpiece. As a general rule, the larger the diameter of the snorkel, the more difficult it is to clear of water unless a clearing valve is provided.

Snorkels, like masks, come in a variety of sizes and shapes. A good snorkel should be made of a flexible material rigid enough to stay erect and yet pliable enough to bend rather than become entangled in kelp or seaweed. Since the snorkel is a very important factor in safe diving, it should be carefully chosen to fit comfortably. Rigid plastic snorkels with or without ping-pong balls or "amateur" closing valves should not be used. They do not work. They are not safe.

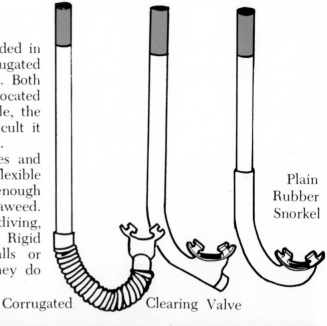

Plain Rubber Snorkel

Corrugated   Clearing Valve

Photo by Omer Nielson

INFLATABLE VEST

A good inflatable vest will have a readily accessible CO_2 cartridge or air valve. It will also have an oral inflator with a smooth operating, positive closing purging valve and valve locking ring. The harness of the vest should be attached to the material of the vest in such a way that any stress on the harness will not damage the vest. Inflatable vests are a result of product development in the field of diving safety. The first type of diving inflatable was a ball-like bladder that the diver carried on his belt. It was also activated by CO_2 cartridges. The next step was aviator's safety vests such as described above. The final step is a Buoyancy Compensator vest designed strictly for diving. A description of this type of vest will be found in a following chapter.

A diver drifting through the kelp beds off the coast of California. Photo by Chuck Nicklin

GLOVES

Divers the world over have found the use of gloves to be essential. Warm water diving requires protection from coral growths while cold water diving demands protection from both the cold and abrasion. A variety of gloves are available ranging from common garden gloves to five fingered neoprene gloves. Since the five fingered gloves are designed for diving, they are more desirable.

Enlightened instructors agree that gloves should be worn in every training session in order to accustom the novice diver to their use in open water diving.

SURFACE FLOAT

A surface float can be a boat, innertube, surf mat, or a paddleboard. It is used to transport the diver and/or his equipment to and from the diving area. It is also a handy platform from which to dive and to display the "Diver Down Flag." The flag should be displayed from a staff at least three feet high, whether diving from a float or a boat. In some areas, the law requires the flag to be displayed when diving. The most important function of the float however, is to provide a resting place for the diver.

Mat.

Tube,

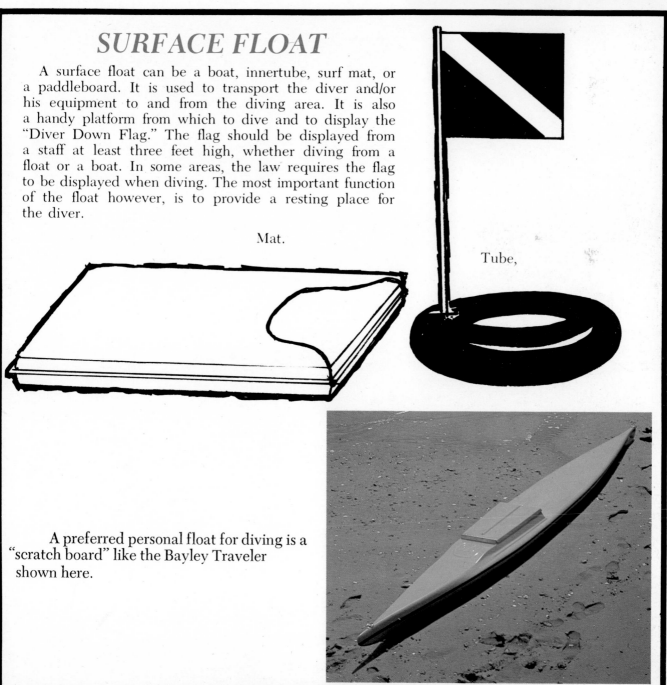

A preferred personal float for diving is a "scratch board" like the Bayley Traveler shown here.

EXTERNAL EAR CANAL

MIDDLE EAR   STIRRUP

HAMMER   INNER EAR

ANVIL

EAR DRUM

AUDITORY NERVE

COCHLEA

EUSTACHIAN TUBE

ear

CHAPTER TWO

USE OF BASIC EQUIPMENT

Swimming Requirements — In learning to dive, as in any aquatic activity, the ability to swim well is a desirable prerequisite. It has been discovered, however, that a relatively weak or physically handicapped swimmer can be a safe diver when supplied with basic equipment (fins, mask, snorkel, buoyancy compensator vest, and surface float) and properly trained and completely aware of his or her limitations.

In general, it is desirable for the beginning diver to be able to demonstrate the following water skills without the use of swim aids:

1. Swim 200 yards any style, without stopping, in a reasonable length of time.
2. Tread water for 3 minutes, 30 seconds with hands out of water.
3. Float five minutes with as little hand and foot motion as possible.
4. Swim underwater twenty yards.
5. Retrieve ten pound weight from ten feet of water.

Students should be able to fulfill these requirements before the end of the course.

"Equalizing" Pressure — As the diver descends, water pressure causes mask to squeeze the face and produce an unpleasant sensation in the region of the eyes. Pressure can be equalized by exhaling into mask through the nostrils, thereby making air pressure inside the mask more or less equal to water pressure outside the mask. And so it goes with pressure on the ear drums and sinuses— by sealing nostrils and blowing gently, air pressure more or less equal to outside water pressure is transmitted to sinuses and ear drums. If difficulty in equalizing is encountered, swallowing, moving the jaws and ascending a few feet will sometimes do the trick. Satisfactory equalizing is experienced when both ears either squeak, pop, or click and both ear drums feel full.

Since the greatest change in pressure is encountered from sea level to 33 feet, novice divers will immediately become aware of the effects of pressure. At 33 feet, pressure is doubled from 14.7 psi to 29.4 psi, and one cubic foot of air is compressed to one-half cubic foot. On any dive, including dives at pool depths, if pain is encountered and you cannot equalize, surface immediately and discuss problem with your instructor. Do not, under any circumstances, descend further when pain is felt; damage to the ear drum may occur. Do not use ear plugs when diving. Pressure can force the plug against the ear drum causing damage; or unequal pressures between the ear plug and the inner ear will result in the ear drum rupturing outward.

SINUS AND TEETH

The sinuses are cavities in the bones of the face and head. (See sketch.) They are connected through the nose and lined with the same membrane. The sinuses are affected by pressure, or lack of it, very much the same as the middle ear.

Pressure differentials from inside the sinus cavities to the outside can cause a sinus "squeeze." That is, if the pressure outside the sinus cavity is greater than inside, the body will attempt to make up the difference by filling the air spaces with swollen tissue, fluid, and blood. Warning of an impending squeeze is felt when a "wedging" sensation takes place in the sinus areas. If the 'wedging" sensation does not disappear do not descend further because tissue damage can occur without pain.

Air may be trapped in a sinus by a mucous plug blocking the opening. Upon ascending, the volume will expand causing internal rupture. This condition is known as a "reverse block."

To avoid sinus problems when diving, never dive with a cold or hay fever. If difficulty is encountered in equalizing, use a decongestant to open passages. If the problem persists, see a doctor.

A toothache can occur from the same mechanisms previously described involving middle ear and sinuses. A minute pocket of air beneath a filling, inlay, or dental cap is linked to air in the mouth by such a tiny hole that rapid equalization of pressure is impossible. The area of relatively reduced pressure beneath the filling may produce excruciating pain. Obviously, the filling should be replaced or capped to prevent future episodes.

STOMACH OR "GUT" SQUEEZE

Air or gas trapped in the stomach or intestines will compress and expand easily when subjected to pressure changes. This is due to the flexible properties of these organs. This condition usually produces only slight, temporary discomfort. It is wise however, to refrain from eating or drinking gas producing foods prior to diving.

MASK SQUEEZE

When a mask squeeze takes place, the partial vacuum or negative pressure under the mask causes rupture of the tiny blood veins in the eyes. This can be prevented by exhaling through the nose into the face mask when pressure is felt.

SUIT SQUEEZE

Air, when trapped in the wrinkles of a dry suit, will cause welts and blisters on a diver's body. Since this occurs only on deep dives, the average SCUBA diver will not be affected. It usually will not happen when using a "wet" suit unless the suit is improperly made.

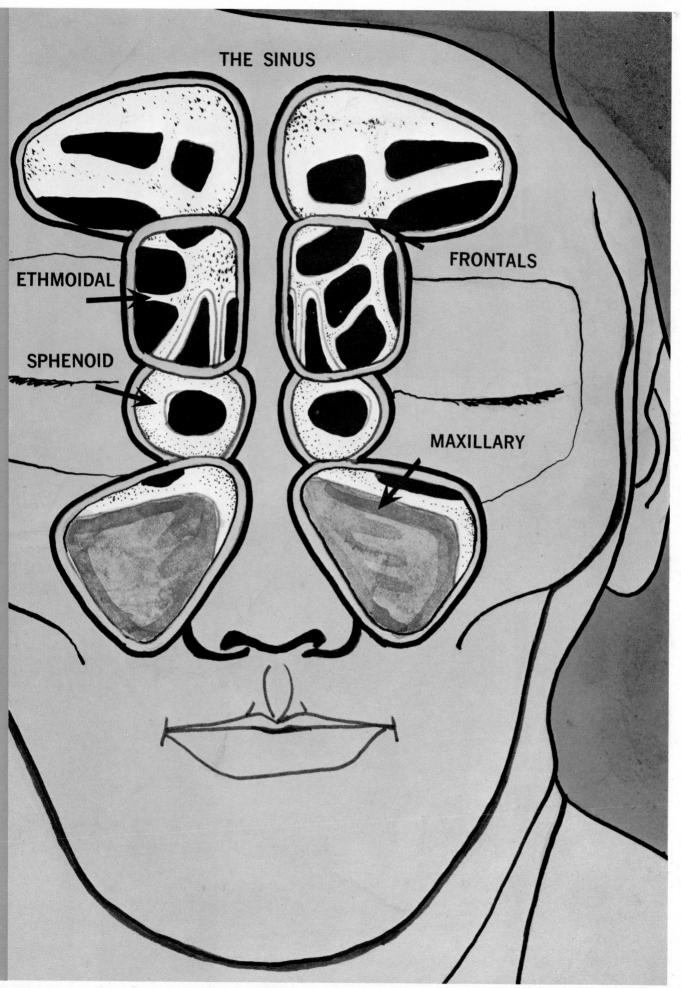

THE SINUS

ETHMOIDAL

SPHENOID

FRONTALS

MAXILLARY

MASK PRACTICE
Shallow Water

Adjust the mask strap to hold the mask comfortably on the face. Defog the mask by rubbing the glass inside and out with saliva or Spectraramar Beris, then rinse.

1. Clear plain mask of water.
2. Clear purge valve mask of water.
3. Exchange mask underwater with buddy and clear.

This picture illustrates the diver clearing a purge type mask by simply tilting his head forward to trap water in the purge valve, holding the top or face of the mask and exhaling through the nose forcing the water out of the non-return valve.

This picture illustrates the diver clearing a non-purge type mask. The diver presses firmly on the top of the mask, tilts head back and/or to the side, exhales sharply through the nose forcing the water out the mask skirt.

Exchanging and clearing masks underwater

Divers in this series of pictures are exchanging the two types of masks to become familiar with the features of each for their personal selection.

Deep Water

1. Equalize pressure with plain mask.
2. Equalize pressure with equalizer mask.
3. Retrieve and clear plain mask from bottom before surfacing.

Equalizing pressure with plain mask

By sealing the nostrils with the mask skirt and blowing gently, the diver equalizes pressure in the sinus and ears.

Equalizing pressure with an equalizer mask

Equalizing pressure is easy when using a mask designed for this purpose.

Retrieving and clearing mask underwater

This exercise demonstrates the divers ability to retrieve and replace his mask should it be lost in open water.

1

MASK AND SNORKEL PRACTICE

1. Attach the snorkel to the mask strap and adjust to a comfortable position on the face.
2. Practice breathing through the snorkel out of the water.
3. Practice breathing through the snorkel with the face mask in the water.
4. Float on the surface face down and breathe through the snorkel.
5. Make repeated surface dives holding breath and clearing or popping snorkel upon return to the surface.

Rest position

In this position, the diver can rest, relax and breathe through either his snorkel or regulator between dives.

2

Clearing snorkel *Clearing or "popping" the snorkel is best accomplished by exhaling sharply. After clearing the snorkel, inhale tentatively to determine if any water remains in the snorkel. If so, clear by repeated short, quick puffs before attempting to inhale.*

FINS

Fins are an extension of the legs and create extra power regardless of the type of stroke used. It has been found however, that a modified flutter kick with knees and ankles slightly relaxed produces the most power for most divers. All strokes should be practiced, since the ability to change strokes reduces the possibility of leg cramps on a long swim. Other strokes used are: scissor, reverse scissor, dolphin. The frog kick is not generally used because it is very inefficient. The arms are not used when swimming with fins.

Dolphin kick

Flutter kick

INFLATABLE VEST

The inflatable vest is used to offset negative buoyancy created by objects the diver has picked up, or simply when the diver wants to rest on the surface. It can be inflated orally, or by use of compressed air or CO_2. It is also used to compensate negative buoyancy created when an exposure suit compresses due to pressure at depth. This subject will be covered fully in the SCUBA section.

Diver resting with vest inflated

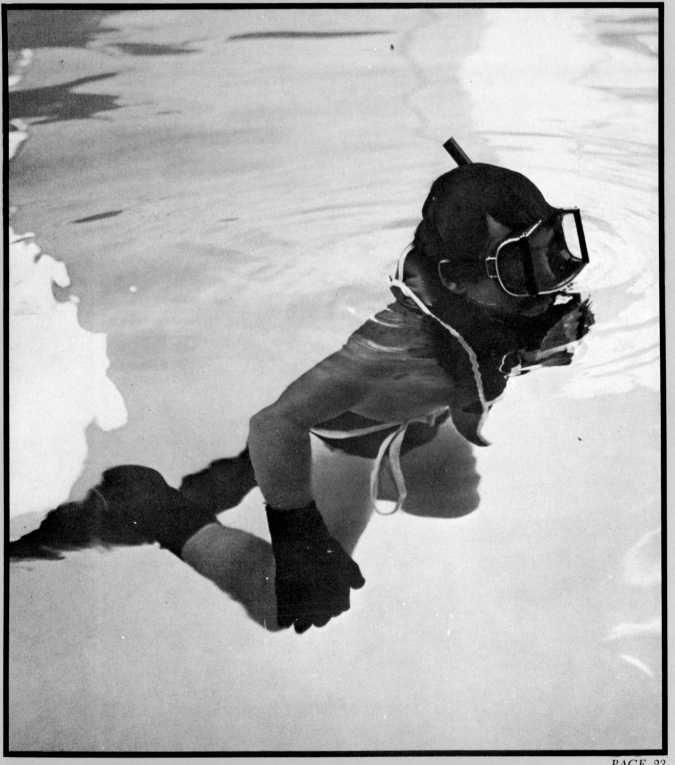

SURFACE DIVES

PIKE DIVE

The most popular surface dive used by divers is the pike, or jackknife. It allows the diver to go deeper, faster, with less effort. It is executed from a face down position with body floating or in a swim stroke by:

1. Reaching downward to touch toes.
2. Hinging at hips and raising feet above surface.
3. Allowing legs to slip into water following hips in a smooth arc.

FOR SAFE ASCENTS, ALWAYS LOOK UP, HOLD ONE ARM EXTENDED ABOVE YOUR HEAD AND TURN 360 DEGREES WHILE ASCENDING. IF POSSIBLE, STOP BRIEFLY AND LISTEN BEFORE SURFACING.

Rest position

2

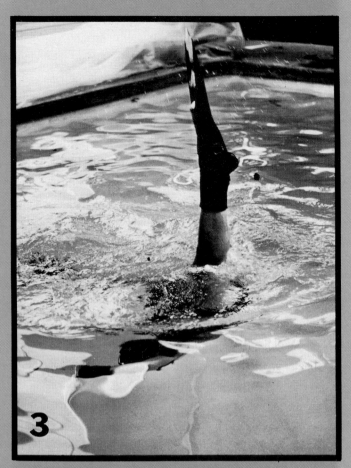

3

Jackknife

Power kick to gain depth

4

5

Returning to surface, arm extended, looking up

SURFACE DIVES

The kelp dive is executed from a vertical position. The diver submerges, then jackknifes underwater and swims off. To go deeper before jackknifing, use a strong scissor kick to raise the body out of the water, thereby using additional weight to force the body deeper. As the name implies, this dive is commonly used in kelp.

KELP DIVE

Turn.
Raise body out of water.
Submerge.
Jackknife.
Swim off.

Rest position

Kick and turn

Strong kick raises the body out of the water

Descent   **Swim off**

WATER ENTRIES

IMPORTANT:

1. On all entries, hold mask firmly in position to prevent dislodging.
2. Before executing entry, make sure water entry area is unoccupied.

Giant stride — Step off deck in wide stride position. After entering water, bring fins together rapidly. This action, when properly executed, will place diver in vertical position with head out of water. (Note: Execute from no higher than three feet.)

Feet together — Same as giant stride, but with feet together. Used from heights greater than three feet.

Front roll — Executed by rolling forward into the water with head tucked well down.

Back roll — Executed by backward roll into the water.

Open water entries—all of the aforementioned entries are acceptable open water entries from a boat, ladder, or dock. Entries from the shore offer an infinite number of possibilities and situations, depending upon the locale. They will be covered by the instructor for the area involved.

CHAPTER THREE

Physical Requirements For Scuba Diving

The physical exertion required when SCUBA diving varies considerably, depending upon the locale and the interests of the individual diver. The middle aged sportsman who anchors his boat in a quiet, shallow cove for an afternoon of diving will end his day relaxed and comfortable, having expended about as much energy as he would in a game of golf. Some individuals offer sharp contrast to this leisurely approach. In the course of a day's outing they will arise at the crack of dawn, drive fifty miles to a diving spot, carry several loads of equipment down a cliff which requires the dual capabilities of a pack mule and a mountain goat, wade out over a rocky bottom, swim a quarter mile through the surf (laden with equipment), empty one or more air tanks, fill a game bag, return through the surf, across the rocks, up the cliff and off for home. This diver will end his day having expended as much energy as an Olympic cross country runner.

Obviously, common sense must be employed by the individual diver in choosing the type of diving compatible with his physical condition.

A properly trained sixty year old can enjoy diving within his limitations just as much — often more — than the eighteen year old sportsman. DIVING *IS* A SPORT FOR EVERYONE.

While the various types of swim aids will help keep the diver safe in the water, they should not be relied upon as a substitute for physical condition. A diver should know his physical limitations and stay well within them.

The usual exercises, with emphasis on running, will help to condition the individual for the more strenuous types of SCUBA diving.

Anyone with a history of trouble in the following areas should have his physician's approval before SCUBA diving:

1. Heart ailments.
2. Sinus.
3. Asthma.
4. Lungs.
5. Ear or mastoid infections.
6. Diabetes.
7. Epileptic seizures.

Diving is a sport for everyone if you know your limitations.

This lady finds just studying small fish in 20 feet
of water an exciting experience. Photo by Bill Hardy.

CHAPTER FOUR *Scuba Diving Physics*

The air we breathe, whether it is "free" or compressed, is composed of a combination of the following gases:

1. Oxygen—Colorless, odorless, tasteless. Is capable of supporting life alone. Approximately 20% by volume.
2. Nitrogen — Colorless, odorless, tasteless. Inert and incapable of supporting life. Approximately 79% by volume.
3. Carbon Dioxide—Colorless, has acid taste and odor in high concentrations. Approximately .03% by volume.
4. Rare Gases—Traces only. Of no particular consequence or interest. Approximately 1% by volume.

The air we breathe has weight. At sea level this weight is measured at 14.7 p.s.i. and is called one atmosphere of absolute pressure. Each additional 14.7 p.s.i. is considered one more atmosphere absolute. Thus, 29.4 p.s.i. is two atmospheres absolute and 44.1 p.s.i. is three atmospheres absolute, and so on. The word "absolute" indicates total pressure as distinguished from "water pressure" which is total pressure minus the atmospheric pressure present at the surface.

The water we dive in has weight, and since it is practically incompressible, this weight is measured as pressure at 0.445 p.s.i. per foot of depth for salt water, and 0.432 p.s.i. per foot of depth in fresh water. Thus, one additional atmosphere is experienced for every 33 feet of salt water or 34 feet of fresh water. (See fig. 1)

With every foot of descent, pressure increases .445 p.s.i. At 99 feet (4 atmospheres absolute, three atmospheres water pressure) the pressure has increased to 58.8 p.s.i. or four times that encountered on the surface.

As SCUBA divers we are interested in the behavior of these gases when subjected to varying conditions of pressure, volume and temperature. Specific laws have been formulated concerning the actions of gases under these varying conditions.

BOYLE'S LAW—At constant temperature, the volume of a gas varies inversely with the pressure put upon it.

That is, if the pressure on a gas is doubled, its original volume is decreased by one half. Concurrently, its original density is doubled. (See fig. 2)

EFFECTS OF PRESSURE

Fig. 1.

INCREASING PRESSURE

Figure 2

DALTON'S LAW—In a mixture of gases each gas exerts a pressure proportionate to the percentage of the total gas which it represents.

For easy figuring, let us say that air is composed of 80% nitrogen and 20% oxygen. Normal atmospheric pressure is 14.7 p.s.i. Therefore, at the surface the partial pressure of nitrogen is 80% of 14.7 p.s.i. or 11.76 p.s.i. The partial pressure of oxygen is 20% of 14.7 p.s.i. or 2.94 p.s.i. As depth increases, partial pressures increase proportionately. The effects of partial pressures will be discussed in the following chapter.

HENRY'S LAW—The components of a mixture of gases in contact with a liquid will dissolve in direct proportion to their partial pressures.

In other words, at two atmospheres of pressure, twice as much gas can be dissolved in a liquid; at three atmospheres, three times as much, and so on. Conversely when the partial pressure of a gas absorbed in a liquid is decreased by one half, a corresponding liberation of one half of the gas from the liquid will occur. Henry's Law will be discussed further in the following chapter.

CHAPTER FIVE
Scuba Diving Physiology

This is a portable Decompression Chamber. This means it can be moved by a crane.

PART I.

MECHANICAL OR DIRECT EFFECTS OF PRESSURE ON THE AIR SPACES AND CELLS OF THE BODY.

The normal human lungs at sea level contain between four and five pints of air. After a forceful exhalation, two to three pints of air remain in the lungs and air passages. This is known as residual air. At full capacity, the lungs contain about ten pints. Consider a SCUBA diver with full lungs at 33 feet (two atmospheres absolute). His lungs contain ten pints of compressed air at 29.4 p.s.i. (See Boyle's Law.) The lungs are composed of very delicate tissues and are not capable of containing pressure. With full lungs, the critical amount of pressure is equivalent to about four feet of water. In other words, once the lungs are expanded to maximum size, an ascent of only four feet more could result in damage. IF THE DIVER WERE TO ASCEND RAPIDLY, HOLDING HIS BREATH, THE TEN PINTS OF AIR WOULD EXPAND TO TWENTY AND HIS LUNGS WOULD RUPTURE. THIS WOULD ALLOW AIR TO ENTER THE BLOOD STREAM AND/OR OTHER PARTS OF THE BODY AND ONE OR MORE OF THE FOLLOWING PHYSIOLOGICAL EFFECTS WOULD TAKE PLACE:

1. AIR EMBOLISM
    a. Cause — Air bubble or bubbles entering blood stream are pumped by the heart to the brain.
    b. Effect — Sooner or later the air bubble gets "stuck" thereby shutting off blood circulation to affected portion of the brain. Lack of circulation results in unconsciousness and sometimes breathing stops.
    c. Symptoms — Bloody froth at the mouth, respiratory difficulty, numbness in extremities, dizziness, loss of consciousness and bluish discoloration.
    d. Treatment — Immediate recompression and medical attention. Speed is essential. Death can result in severe cases even after prompt treatment. If a recompression chamber is not readily available, elevate victim's legs and keep his head down to keep any more air from going to the brain and administer oxygen if available. If the victim is not breathing, artificial respiration should be given.

2. SPONTANEOUS PHEUMOTHORAX
    a. Cause — Air pocket forms outside the lung and is contained by the rib cage.
    b. Effect — Expanding air in chest cavity causes collapse of lung.
    c. Symptoms — Pain in chest, shortness of breath, irregular pulse, distension of neck veins and bluish discoloration of the skin.
    d. Treatment — Recompression and medical attention.

3. MEDIASTINAL EMPHYSEMA
    a. Cause — Air is forced into the tissue spaces in the middle of the chest.
    b. Chest pains, difficulty in breathing and swallowing, shock.
    c. Treatment — Recompression if indicated by doctor.

4. SUBCUTANEOUS EMPHYSEMA
    a. Cause — Same as mediastinal emphysema.
    b. Effect — Air lodges under the skin in the neck region.
    c. Symptoms — Swelling of the neck and the air beneath the skin produces a characteristic crackling sensation upon pressure as the tiny bubbles slide about and burst under one's fingers.
    d. Treatment — Recompression and medical attention.

If the above effects sound grim to you, all you have to remember to avoid them is NEVER, NEVER, NEVER, HOLD BREATH WHILE SCUBA DIVING AND DEVELOP YOUR BREATHING HABITS.

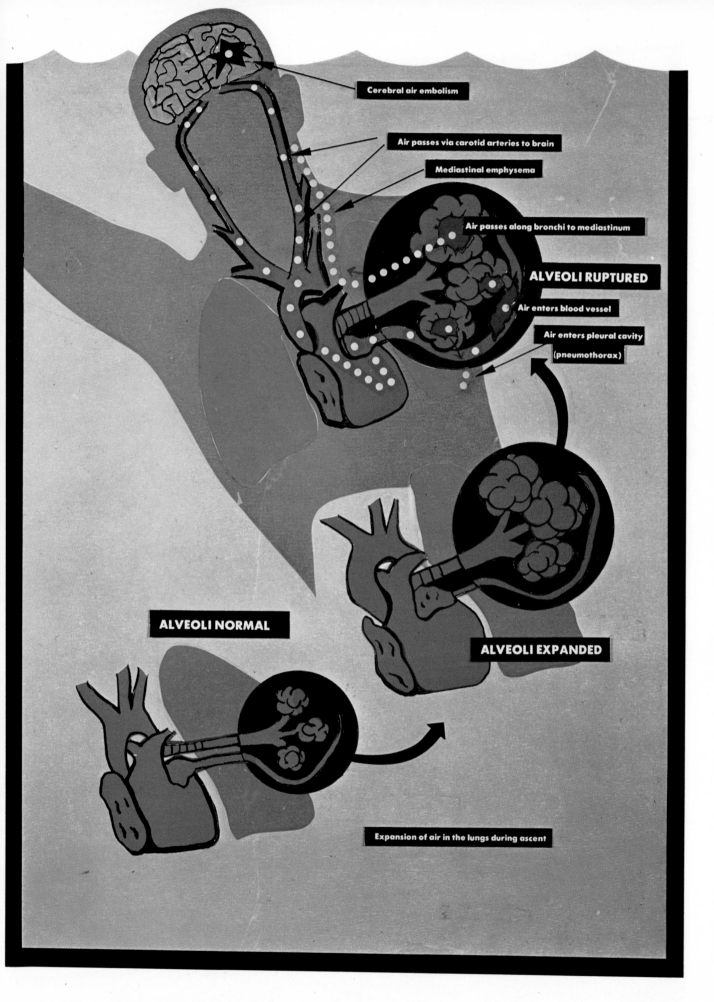

Cerebral air embolism

Air passes via carotid arteries to brain

Mediastinal emphysema

Air passes along bronchi to mediastinum

ALVEOLI RUPTURED

Air enters blood vessel

Air enters pleural cavity (pneumothorax)

ALVEOLI NORMAL

ALVEOLI EXPANDED

Expansion of air in the lungs during ascent

LEARN YOUR HABITS
SNORKEL DIVING
DO NOT HYPERVENTILATE

NORMAL CO2   NEEDS TO BREATHE

AFTER HYPERVENTILATING   NEEDS TO BREATHE

PASS OUT FROM ANOXIA

Most novice divers are able to make dives of very short duration only, usually twenty to forty seconds. This situation will change as experience increases and physical condition improves.

Hyperventilation — Hyperventilation is the practice of clearing CO2 from the lungs by forced breathing with emphasis on exhalation. This process enables the diver to hold his breath longer and thereby extend the length of his dive. It is not a recommended practice for the novice diver because it can cause a change in the body chemistry, resulting in unconsciousness.

IF YOU MUST PRACTICE EXTENDED BREATH HOLDING AND HYPERVENTILATION, DO IT OUT OF THE WATER.

PART II
Indirect Effects Of Pressure

Indirect effects of pressure are defined as the physiological effects which take place as a result of the gas or combination of gases the diver breathes under pressure.

CAISSON'S DISEASE OR THE "BENDS" — Caisson's Disease, the "bends," or Decompression Sickness, as it is sometimes called, is a diving ailment that is directly related to the use of compressed air as a breathing medium. Nitrogen comprises approximately 79% of the air we breathe and is somewhat soluble in the blood at surface pressure. As the partial pressure of nitrogen increases with depth (Dalton's Law) it becomes highly soluble, goes into the bloodstream and is carried to all the tissues of the body. There it remains at the same partial pressure as the nitrogen in the lungs. The depth and the time spent at the depth govern the amount of nitrogen which goes into solution. The amount varies to some small degree with the individual, depending upon body weight, fat content, and the condition of the individual's respiratory and circulatory systems. When a diver goes deep enough and stays long enough, the dissolved nitrogen in his blood and tissues returns to the gaseous state in the form of bubbles if he ascends too rapidly for the lungs to remove this excess nitrogen. These bubbles are carried by the bloodstream to all parts of the body and lodge in the joints, causing circulation blockage in the brain and spinal cord. A common analogy is carbonated beverages in which the CO_2 is dissolved under pressure when the bottle is capped —(Henry's Law)— and bubbles off as soon as the cap is removed. Instead of being carbonated, the diver's bloodstream is nitrogenated. He is, however, deprived of the benefit of a cap to keep the nitrogen from bubbling off when the pressure is released. Using this analogy further, if the bottle cap is loosened only slightly, and the CO_2 is allowed to bleed off gradually, bubbles will not form. In the case of the diver this is accomplished by ascending slowly at a rate that will allow the excess nitrogen to be eliminated from the system through the lungs. This is called decompression. The rules for decompression have been worked out in a set of tables.

These tables show timed stops at various depths to allow the body to eliminate nitrogen. Contrary to popular belief, there is no margin of safety in the tables. *As a matter of fact, if the tables are followed religiously, a minimum of 5% incidence of the bends will take place.*

If the bends occur, "recompression" is necessary. This should take place only in a Recompression Chamber with trained personnel in attendance. A case of the bends is recompressed according to the "Treatment Tables," which are completely different from the Decompression Tables. Recompression should never be attempted in the water, as additional damage is sure to occur.

Diving is fun; recompression is not. Recompression is

No Decompression Units

Depth (Feet)	Bottom Time (Minutes)
Less than (33)	(No Limit)
35	310
40	200
50	100
60	60
70	50
80	40
90	30
100	25
110	20
120	15
130	10
140	10
150 to 190	5

usually painful and always expensive. The easiest way to avoid the possibility of the bends and resulting decompression is to stay within the limits of the "No Decompression Table". Beginners should limit their diving to the 30 to 40 foot range, thereby avoiding the possibility of decompression. Remember, even on a thirty foot dive, the rate of ascent cannot exceed the standard of sixty feet per minute.

Actually, diving in the shallower depths has many advantages besides eliminating the possibility of the bends. In these depths the air supply lasts longer, visibility is usually better, and it is the dwelling place for most of the sea life which interest the sport diver.

If you must make dives which require decompression, understand the Repetitive Dive tables, use a decompression computer, keep a spare tank and regulator handy for emergencies, and know the location of the nearest Recompression Chamber. If decompression is required and the diver is out of air, an ascent to the surface for a quick change of tanks with an immediate descent to the proper depth is acceptable.

Decompression dives are in the realm of advanced diving and as such are thoroughly covered in the Open Water Program.

SYMPTOMS OF THE BENDS — Most of the symptoms listed below will appear within one hour after the dive. As a general rule, others will show up within, but never after, twenty-four hours. The rule is: IF ANY OF THE FOLLOWING SYMPTOMS APPEAR AFTER DIVING, THE AFFECTED DIVER SHOULD BE RUSHED TO THE NEAREST RECOMPRESSION CHAMBER FOR TREATMENT.
1. Severe pain in joints, muscles and bones. This is the most common symptom.
2. Itching, burning, tingling or numbness of the skin.
3. A rash with mottled skin and deep pain.
4. Dizziness and nausea.
5. Paralysis.
6. Convulsions.
7. Shortness of breath.
8. Loss of speech or hearing or visual disturbances.
9. Unconsciousness.

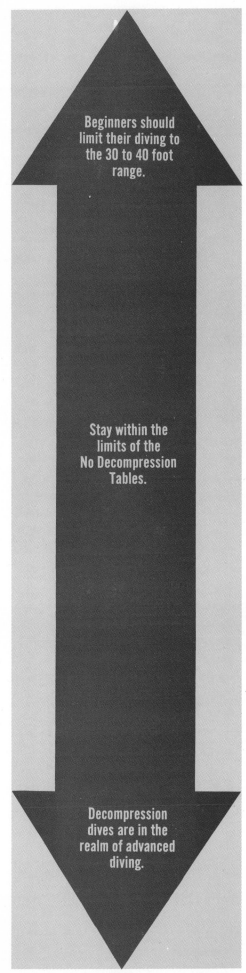

Beginners should limit their diving to the 30 to 40 foot range.

Stay within the limits of the No Decompression Tables.

Decompression dives are in the realm of advanced diving.

U.S. Navy Standard Air Decompression Table

GENERAL PRINCIPLES OF DIVING

Repetitive Dive Procedure

A dive performed within 12 hours of surfacing from a previous dive is a repetitive dive. The period between dives is the surface interval. Excess nitrogen requires 12 hours to be effectively lost from the body. These tables are designed to protect the diver from the effects of this residual nitrogen. Allow a minimum surface interval of 10 minutes between all dives. For any interval under 10 minutes, add the bottom time of the previous dives to that of the repetitive dive and choose the decompression schedule for the total bottom time and the deepest dive. Specific instructions are given for the use of each table in the following order:

(1) The *No-Decompression Table* or the *Navy Standard Air Decompression Table* gives the repetitive group designation for all schedules which may precede a repetitive dive.

(2) The *Surface Interval Credit Table* gives credit for the desaturation occurring during the surface interval.

(3) The *Repetitive Dive Timetable* gives the number of minutes of residual nitrogen time to add to the actual bottom time of the repetitive dive to obtain decompression for the residual nitrogen.

(4) The *No-Decompression Table* or the *Navy Standard Air Decompression Table* gives the decompression required for the repetitive dive.

U.S. NAVY STANDARD AIR DECOMPRESSION TABLE

Instructions for Use

Time of decompression stops in the table is in minutes.

Enter the table at the exact or the next greater depth than the maximum depth attained during the dive. Select the listed bottom time that is exactly equal to or is next greater than the bottom time of the dive. Maintain the diver's chest as close as possible to each decompression depth for the number of minutes listed. The rate of ascent *between* stops is not critical for stops of 50 feet or less. Commence timing each stop on arrival at the decompression depth and resume ascent when the specified time has lapsed.

For example—a dive to 82 feet for 36 minutes. To determine the proper decompression procedure: The next greater depth listed in this table is 90 feet. The next greater bottom time listed opposite 90 feet is 40. Stop 7 minutes at 10 feet in accordance with the 90/40 schedule.

For example— a dive to 110 feet for 30 minutes. It is known that the depth did not exceed 110 feet. To determine the proper decompression schedule: The exact depth of 110 feet is listed. The exact bottom time of 30 minutes is listed opposite 110 feet. Decompress according to the 110/30 schedule unless the dive was particularly cold or arduous. In that case, go to the schedule for the next deeper and longer dive, i.e., 120/40.

(FORMERLY TABLE 1–5, 1963 DIVING MANUAL)

TABLE 1–10.—*U.S. Navy Standard Air Decompression Table*

Depth (feet)	Bottom time (min)	Time to first stop (min:sec)	50	40	30	20	10	Total ascent (min:sec)	Repetitive group
40	200						0	0:40	(*)
	210	0:30					2	2:40	N
	230	0:30					7	7:40	N
	250	0:30					11	11:40	O
	270	0:30					15	15:40	O
	300	0:30					19	19:40	Z
50	100						0	0:50	(*)
	110	0:40					3	3:50	L
	120	0:40					5	5:50	M
	140	0:40					10	10:50	M
	160	0:40					21	21:50	N
	180	0:40					29	29:50	O
	200	0:40					35	35:50	O
	220	0:40					40	40:50	Z
	240	0:40					47	47:50	Z
60	60						0	1:00	(*)
	70	0:50					2	3:00	K
	80	0:50					7	8:00	L
	100	0:50					14	15:00	M
	120	0:50					26	27:00	N
	140	0:50					39	40:00	O
	160	0:50					48	49:00	Z
	180	0:50					56	57:00	Z
	200	0:40				1	69	71:00	Z
70	50						0	1:10	(*)
	60	1:00					8	9:10	K
	70	1:00					14	15:10	L
	80	1:00					18	19:10	M
	90	1:00					23	24:10	N
	100	1:00					33	34:10	N
	110	0:50				2	41	44:10	O
	120	0:50				4	47	52:10	O
	130	0:50				6	52	59:10	O
	140	0:50				8	56	65:10	Z
	150	0:50				9	61	71:10	Z
	160	0:50				13	72	86:10	Z
	170	0:50				19	79	99:10	Z
80	40						0	1:20	(*)
	50	1:10					10	11:20	K
	60	1:10					17	18:20	L
	70	1:10					23	24:20	M
	80	1:00				2	31	34:20	N
	90	1:00				7	39	47:20	N
	100	1:00				11	46	58:20	O
	110	1:00				13	53	67:20	O
	120	1:00				17	56	74:20	Z
	130	1:00				19	63	83:20	Z
	140	1:00				26	69	96:20	Z
	150	1:00				32	77	110:20	Z
90	30						0	1:30	(*)
	40	1:20					7	8:30	J
	50	1:20					18	19:30	L
	60	1:20					25	26:30	M
	70	1:10				7	30	38:30	N
	80	1:10				13	40	54:30	N
	90	1:10				18	48	67:30	O
	100	1:10				21	54	76:30	Z
	110	1:10				24	61	86:30	Z
	120	1:10				32	68	101:30	Z
	130	1:00			5	36	74	116:30	Z
100	25						0	1:40	(*)
	30	1:30					3	4:40	I
	40	1:30					15	16:40	K
	50	1:20				2	24	27:40	L
	60	1:20				9	28	38:40	N
	70	1:20				17	39	57:40	O
	80	1:20				23	48	72:40	O
	90	1:10			3	23	57	84:40	Z

GENERAL PRINCIPLES OF DIVING

TABLE 1–10.—*U.S. Navy Standard Air Decompression Table*—Continued

Depth (feet)	Bottom time (min)	Time to first stop (min:sec)	50	40	30	20	10	Total ascent (min:sec)	Repetitive group
100—Continued	100	1:10			7	23	66	97:40	Z
	110	1:10			10	34	72	117:40	Z
	120	1:10			12	41	78	132:40	Z
110	20						0	1:50	(*)
	25	1:40					3	4:50	H
	30	1:40					7	8:50	J
	40	1:30				2	21	24:50	L
	50	1:30				8	26	35:50	M
	60	1:30				18	36	55:50	N
	70	1:20			1	23	48	73:50	O
	80	1:20			7	23	57	88:50	Z
	90	1:20			12	30	64	107:50	Z
	100	1:20			15	37	72	125:50	Z
120	15						0	2:00	(*)
	20	1:50					2	4:00	H
	25	1:50					6	8:00	I
	30	1:50					14	16:00	J
	40	1:40				5	25	32:00	L
	50	1:40				15	31	48:00	N
	60	1:30			2	22	45	71:00	O
	70	1:30			9	23	55	89:00	O
	80	1:30			15	27	63	107:00	Z
	90	1:30			19	37	74	132:00	Z
	100	1:30			23	45	80	150:00	Z
130	10						0	2:10	(*)
	15	2:00					1	3:10	F
	20	2:00					4	6:10	H
	25	2:00					10	12:10	J
	30	1:50				3	18	23:10	M
	40	1:50				10	25	37:10	N
	50	1:40			3	21	37	63:10	O
	60	1:40			9	23	52	86:10	Z
	70	1:40			16	24	61	103:10	Z
	80	1:30		3	19	35	72	131:10	Z
	90	1:30		8	19	45	80	154:10	Z
140	10						0	2:20	(*)
	15	2:10					2	4:20	G
	20	2:10					6	8:20	I
	25	2:00				2	14	18:20	J
	30	2:00				5	21	28:20	K
	40	1:50			2	16	26	46:20	N
	50	1:50			6	24	44	76:20	O
	60	1:50			16	23	56	97:20	Z
	70	1:40		4	19	32	68	125:20	Z
	80	1:40		10	23	41	79	155:20	Z
150	5						0	2:30	C
	10	2:20					1	3:30	E
	15	2:20					3	5:30	G
	20	2:10				2	7	11:30	H
	25	2:10				4	17	23:30	K
	30	2:10				8	24	34:30	L
	40	2:00			5	19	33	59:30	N
	50	2:00			12	23	51	88:30	O
	60	1:50			3	19	26	62	112:30	Z
	70	1:50			11	19	39	75	146:30	Z
	80	1:40	1	17	19	50	84	173:30	Z
160	5						0	2:40	D
	10	2:30					1	3:40	F
	15	2:20				1	4	7:40	H
	20	2:20				3	11	16:40	J
	25	2:20				7	20	29:40	K
	30	2:10			2	11	25	40:40	M
	40	2:10			7	23	39	71:40	N
	50	2:00		2	16	23	55	98:40	Z
	60	2:00		9	19	33	69	132:40	Z
	70	1:50	1	17	22	44	80	166:40	Z
170	5						0	2:50	D
	10	2:40					2	4:50	F
	15	2:30				2	5	9:50	H
	20	2:30				4	15	21:50	J
	25	2:20			2	7	23	34:50	L
	30	2:20			4	13	26	45:50	M
	40	2:10		1	10	23	45	81:50	O
	50	2:10		5	18	23	61	109:50	Z*
	60	2:00	2	15	22	37	74	152:50	Z
	70	2:00	8	17	19	51	86	183:50	Z
180	5						0	3:00	D
	10	2:50					3	6:00	F
	15	2:40				3	6	12:00	I
	20	2:30			1	5	17	26:00	K
	25	2:30			3	10	24	40:00	M
	30	2:30			6	17	27	53:00	N
	40	2:20		3	14	23	50	93:00	O
	50	2:10	2	9	19	30	65	128:00	Z
	60	2:10	5	16	19	44	81	168:00	Z
190	5						0	3:10	D
	10	2:50				1	3	7:10	G
	15	2:50				4	7	14:10	I
	20	2:40			2	6	20	31:10	K
	25	2:40			5	11	25	44:10	M
	30	2:30		1	8	19	32	63:10	N
	40	2:30		8	14	23	55	103:10	O
	50	2:20	4	13	22	33	72	147:10	Z
	60	2:20	10	17	19	50	84	183:10	Z

*See table 1–11 for repetitive groups in no-decompression dives.

(FORMERLY TABLE 1–7, 1963 DIVING MANUAL)

Table 1–12.—*Surface Interval Credit Table for air decompression dives*

[Repetitive group at the end of the surface interval (air dive)]

Z	O	N	M	L	K	J	I	H	G	F	E	D	C	B	A
0:10/0:22	0:23/0:34	0:35/0:48	0:49/1:02	1:03/1:18	1:19/1:36	1:37/1:55	1:56/2:17	2:18/2:42	2:43/3:10	3:11/3:45	3:46/4:29	4:30/5:27	5:28/6:56	6:57/10:05	10:00/12:00*
O	0:10/0:23	0:24/0:36	0:37/0:51	0:52/1:07	1:08/1:24	1:25/1:43	1:44/2:04	2:05/2:29	2:30/2:59	3:00/3:33	3:34/4:17	4:18/5:16	5:17/6:44	6:45/9:54	9:55/12:00*
	N	0:10/0:24	0:25/0:39	0:40/0:54	0:55/1:11	1:12/1:30	1:31/1:53	1:54/2:18	2:19/2:47	2:48/3:22	3:23/4:04	4:05/5:03	5:04/6:32	6:33/9:43	9:44/12:00*
		M	0:10/0:25	0:26/0:42	0:43/0:59	1:00/1:18	1:19/1:39	1:40/2:05	2:06/2:34	2:35/3:08	3:09/3:52	3:53/4:49	4:50/6:18	6:19/9:28	9:29/12:00*
			L	0:10/0:26	0:27/0:45	0:46/1:04	1:05/1:25	1:26/1:49	1:50/2:19	2:20/2:53	2:54/3:36	3:37/4:35	4:36/6:02	6:03/9:12	9:13/12:00*
				K	0:10/0:28	0:29/0:49	0:50/1:11	1:12/1:35	1:36/2:03	2:04/2:38	2:39/3:21	3:22/4:19	4:20/5:48	5:49/8:58	8:59/12:00*
					J	0:10/0:31	0:32/0:54	0:55/1:19	1:20/1:47	1:48/2:20	2:21/3:04	3:05/4:02	4:03/5:40	5:41/8:40	8:41/12:00*
						I	0:10/0:33	0:34/0:59	1:00/1:29	1:30/2:02	2:03/2:44	2:45/3:43	3:44/5:12	5:13/8:21	8:22/12:00*
							H	0:10/0:36	0:37/1:06	1:07/1:41	1:42/2:23	2:24/3:20	3:21/4:49	4:50/7:59	8:00/12:00*
								G	0:10/0:40	0:41/1:15	1:16/1:59	2:00/2:58	2:59/4:25	4:26/7:35	7:36/12:00*
									F	0:10/0:45	0:46/1:29	1:30/2:28	2:29/3:57	3:58/7:05	7:06/12:00*
										E	0:10/0:54	0:55/1:57	1:58/3:22	3:23/6:32	6:33/12:00*
											D	0:10/1:09	1:10/2:38	2:39/5:48	5:49/12:00*
												C	0:10/1:39	1:40/2:49	2:50/12:00*
													B	0:10/2:10	2:11/12:00*
														A	0:10/12:00*

Repetitive group at the beginning of the surface interval from previous dive

Instructions for Use

Surface interval time in the table is in *hours* and *minutes* (7:59 means 7 hours and 59 minutes). The surface interval must be at least 10 minutes.

Find the *repetitive group designation letter* (from the previous dive schedule) on the diagonal slope. Enter the table horizontally to select the surface interval time that is exactly between the actual surface interval times shown. The repetitive group designation for the *end* of the surface interval is at the head of the vertical column where the selected surface interval time is listed. For example, a previous dive was to 110 feet for 30 minutes. The diver remains on the surface 1 hour and 30 minutes and wishes to find the new repetitive group designation: The repetitive group from the last column of the 110/30 schedule in the Standard Air Decompression Tables is "J." Enter the surface interval credit table along the horizontal line labeled "J." The 1-hour-and-30-minute surface interval lies between the times 1:20 and 1:47. Therefore, the diver has lost sufficient inert gas to place him in group "G" (at the head of the vertical column selected).

*NOTE.—Dives following surface intervals of *more* than 12 hours are not considered repetitive dives. *Actual* bottom times in the Standard Air Decompression Tables may be used in computing decompression for such dives.

(FORMERLY TABLE 1-6, 1963 DIVING MANUAL)

TABLE 1-11.—*No-decompression limits and repetitive group designation table for no-decompression air dives*

Depth (feet)	No-decompression limits (min)	Repetitive groups (air dives)													
		A	B	C	D	E	F	G	H	I	J	K	L	M	N	O
10	-----------	60	120	210	300	-----	-----	-----	-----	-----	-----	-----	-----	-----	-----	-----
15	-----------	35	70	110	160	225	350	-----	-----	-----	-----	-----	-----	-----	-----	-----
20	-----------	25	50	75	100	135	180	240	325	-----	-----	-----	-----	-----	-----	-----
25	-----------	20	35	55	75	100	125	160	195	245	315	-----	-----	-----	-----	-----
30	-----------	15	30	45	60	75	95	120	145	170	205	250	310	-----	-----	-----
35	310	5	15	25	40	50	60	80	100	120	140	160	190	220	270	310
40	200	5	15	25	30	40	50	70	80	100	110	130	150	170	200	-----
50	100	----	10	15	25	30	40	50	60	70	80	90	100	-----	-----	-----
60	60	----	10	15	20	25	30	40	50	55	60	-----	-----	-----	-----	-----
70	50	----	5	10	15	20	30	35	40	45	50	-----	-----	-----	-----	-----
80	40	----	5	10	15	20	25	30	35	40	-----	-----	-----	-----	-----	-----
90	30	----	5	10	12	15	20	25	30	-----	-----	-----	-----	-----	-----	-----
100	25	----	5	7	10	15	20	22	25	-----	-----	-----	-----	-----	-----	-----
110	20	-----	-----	5	10	13	15	20	-----	-----	-----	-----	-----	-----	-----	-----
120	15	-----	-----	5	10	12	15	-----	-----	-----	-----	-----	-----	-----	-----	-----
130	10	-----	-----	5	8	10	-----	-----	-----	-----	-----	-----	-----	-----	-----	-----
140	10	-----	-----	5	7	10	-----	-----	-----	-----	-----	-----	-----	-----	-----	-----
150	5	-----	-----	5	-----	-----	-----	-----	-----	-----	-----	-----	-----	-----	-----	-----
160	5	-----	-----	-----	5	-----	-----	-----	-----	-----	-----	-----	-----	-----	-----	-----
170	5	-----	-----	-----	5	-----	-----	-----	-----	-----	-----	-----	-----	-----	-----	-----
180	5	-----	-----	-----	5	-----	-----	-----	-----	-----	-----	-----	-----	-----	-----	-----
190	5	-----	-----	-----	5	-----	-----	-----	-----	-----	-----	-----	-----	-----	-----	-----

Instructions for Use

I. No-decompression limits:

This column shows at various depths greater than 30 feet the allowable diving times (in minutes) which permit surfacing directly at 60 feet a minute with no decompression stops. Longer exposure times require the use of the Standard Air Decompression Table (table 1-10).

II. Repetitive group designation table:

The tabulated exposure times (or bottom times) are in minutes. The times at the various depths in each vertical column are the maximum exposures during which a diver will remain within the group listed at the head of the column.

To find the repetitive group designation at surfacing for dives involving exposures up to and including the no-decompression limits: Enter the table on the *exact or next greater depth* than that to which exposed and select the listed exposure time *exact or next greater* than the actual exposure time. The repetitive group designation is indicated by the letter at the head of the vertical column where the selected exposure time is listed.

For example: A dive was to 32 feet for 45 minutes. Enter the table along the 35-foot-depth line since it is next greater than 32 feet. The table shows that since group D is left after 40 minutes' exposure and group E after 50 minutes, group E (at the head of the column where the 50-minute exposure is listed) is the proper selection.

Exposure times for depths less than 40 feet are listed only up to approximately 5 hours since this is considered to be beyond field requirements for this table.

(FORMERLY TABLE 1-8, 1963 DIVING MANUAL)

TABLE 1–13.—*Repetitive dive timetable for air dives*

Repetitiv groups	Repetitive dive depth (ft) (air dives)															
	40	50	60	70	80	90	100	110	120	130	140	150	160	170	180	190
A	7	6	5	4	4	3	3	3	3	3	2	2	2	2	2	2
B	17	13	11	9	8	7	7	6	6	6	5	5	4	4	4	4
C	25	21	17	15	13	11	10	10	9	8	7	7	6	6	6	6
D	37	29	24	20	18	16	14	13	12	11	10	9	9	8	8	8
E	49	38	30	26	23	20	18	16	15	13	12	12	11	10	10	10
F	61	47	36	31	28	24	22	20	18	16	15	14	13	13	12	11
G	73	56	44	37	32	29	26	24	21	19	18	17	16	15	14	13
H	87	66	52	43	38	33	30	27	25	22	20	19	18	17	16	15
I	101	76	61	50	43	38	34	31	28	25	23	22	20	19	18	17
J	116	87	70	57	48	43	38	34	32	28	26	24	23	22	20	19
K	138	99	79	64	54	47	43	38	35	31	29	27	26	24	22	21
L	161	111	88	72	61	53	48	42	39	35	32	30	28	26	25	24
M	187	124	97	80	68	58	52	47	43	38	35	32	31	29	27	26
N	213	142	107	87	73	64	57	51	46	40	38	35	33	31	29	28
O	241	160	117	96	80	70	62	55	50	44	40	38	36	34	31	30
Z	257	169	122	100	84	73	64	57	52	46	42	40	37	35	32	31

Instructions for Use

The bottom times listed in this table are called "residual nitrogen times" and are the times a diver is to consider he has *already* spent on bottom when he *starts* a repetitive dive to a specific depth. They are in minutes.

Enter the table horizontally with the repetitive group designation from the Surface Interval Credit Table. The time in each vertical column is the number of minutes that would be required (at the depth listed at the head of the column) to saturate to the particular group.

For example: The final group designation from the Surface Interval Credit Table, on the basis of a previous dive and surface interval, is "H." To plan a dive to 110 feet, determine the residual nitrogen time for this depth required by the repetitive group designation: Enter this table along the horizontal line labeled "H." The table shows that one must *start* a dive to 110 feet as though he had already been on the bottom for 27 minutes. This information can then be applied to the Standard Air Decompression Table or No-Decompression Table in a number of ways:

(1) Assuming a diver is going to finish a job and take whatever decompression is required, he must add 27 minutes to his actual bottom time and be prepared to take decompression according to the 110-foot schedules for the sum or equivalent single dive time.

(2) Assuming one wishes to make a quick inspection dive for the minimum decompression, he will decompress according to the 110/30 schedule for a dive of 3 minutes or less (27+3=30). For a dive of over 3 minutes but less than 13, he will decompress according to the 110/40 schedule (27+13=40).

(3) Assuming that one does not want to exceed the 110/50 schedule and the amount of decompression it requires, he will have to start ascent before 23 minutes of actual bottom time (50−27=23).

(4) Assuming that a diver has air for approximately 45 minutes bottom time and decompression stops, the possible dives can be computed: A dive of 13 minutes will require 23 minutes of decompression (110/40 schedule), for a total submerged time of 36 minutes. A dive of 13 to 23 minutes will require 34 minutes of decompression (110/50 schedule), for a total submerged time of 47 to 57 minutes. Therefore, to be safe, the diver will have to start ascent before 13 minutes or a standby air source will have to be provided.

The boat is anchored in 28 feet of water.

A TYPICAL DIVE

On his first dive, the diver descends to 30 feet and spends 10 minutes spearing an elusive blackfish.

He then descends to 60 feet and captures a lobster. Time, 25 minutes. His submersible gauge tells him it is time to return to the surface for an air refill.

HALF TIMES

Half times are an easy way to understand the absorption of nitrogen into the bloodstream.

Throughout the human body, tissues absorb nitrogen at different rates. To simplify this explanation, let's discuss a dive.

Starting on the surface we are breathing air at about 15 pounds per square inch. About 80% of this air is nitrogen. 80% of 15 p.s.i. is what? Answer — 12 p.s.i. That means that on the surface we have 12 p.s.i. of nitrogen going through our bloodstream. Therefore, on the surface our tissues are 100% saturated with nitrogen at 12 p.s.i.

Different tissues in the body absorb nitrogen at different rates. We will call them 5, 10, and 20 minute tissues and so forth. Fatty tissues are the slowest, especially in the areas of poor blood supply.

We are now going down to 100 feet. At 100 feet what pressure are we breathing ? Answer — About 60 p.s.i. What percentage of that is nitrogen? Answer — Still 80%. So now the 12 p.s.i. nitrogen in our bloodstream has changed to 48 p.s.i.

As the pressure increases, nitrogen has a "Driving Force" pushing the nitrogen into our tissue. This is equal to the difference between the pressure in our tissue at any particular time and the pressure in our bloodstream at the same time.

The easiest way to calculate absorption is in

He spends 41 minutes on the surface.

On his second dive, he returns to 60 feet briefly,
then ascends to 40 feet for a look around.
Time spent, 10 minutes.

He then descends to 100 feet and
stays for 15 minutes.

What is his decompression?

whole time increments, or every 5, 10, or 20 minutes. We absorb one half of the "Driving Force" for each time increment. For example, after 5 minutes at 100 feet the 5 minute tissue has absorbed an additional 18 p.s.i. of nitrogen. If we add that 18 to the 12 already in the tissue, the pressure of nitrogen has changed to 30 p.s.i. The other tissues are still loading up, but they can't be calculated yet.

After 10 minutes, the 10 minute tissue has changed to 30 p.s.i. as the 5 minute tissue did previously. Of course, the 5 minute tissue has changed to 39 p.s.i. of nitrogen. Remember, the "Driving Force" changes every time the p.s.i. of

After 20 minutes, the 20 minute tissue has now changed to 30. The 10 minute tissue to 39 and the 5 minute tissue has changed twice again to 43½ and 45¾. Simple, isn't it!

Keep in mind that as sport divers, we are constantly changing depth which changes the "Driving Force." If we are diving on the tables, it is almost impossible to recalculate our time and depth accurately.

NITROGEN NARCOSIS. Nitrogen narcosis, "Rapture of the Deep," or depth drunkeness, as it is sometimes called, is a condition which begins to affect most divers at a depth of around one hundred feet. However, some individuals are susceptible in shallower depths. As has been pointed out previously, the greater the depth, the greater the partial pressure of nitrogen, and the larger the amount of this gas dissolved in the blood and tissue fluids. This excessive amount of dissolved nitrogen in the system causes a sense of "well being" or euphoria sometimes accompanied by dizziness similar to that which follows the consumption of alcohol. This similarity has produced a rule of thumb known as "Martini's Law." At 50 feet, the effect of nitrogen is the same as that produced by one martini on an empty stomach. At 100 feet, the effect is that of two martinis and so on.

The exact cause of nitrogen narcosis is unknown; however it disappears when a shallower depth is attained. There are no after effects.

Diving to the depths that produce marked symptoms of nitrogen narcosis is in the realm of an expert Open Water diver and should not be attempted by the novice.

MARTINI'S LAW

50 Feet

200 Feet

300 Feet

OXYGEN POISONING — Despite the fact that oxygen is life supporting, certain harmful effects occur when pure oxygen is used as a breathing medium under pressure (depth). Although there are individual variations, the following symptoms can occur when pure oxygen is used at depths of thirty-three feet or more: nausea, muscular twitchings, vertigo, visual disturbances, confusion, numbness, sensations of abnormality, convulsions, and finally unconsciousness. *TO AVOID ALL OF THIS NEVER USE PURE OXYGEN FOR DIVING.*

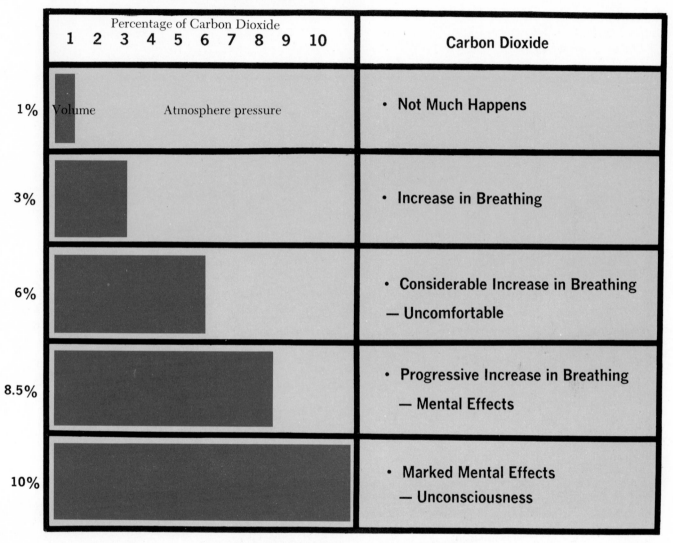

Percentage of Carbon Dioxide 1 2 3 4 5 6 7 8 9 10	Carbon Dioxide
1% Volume Atmosphere pressure	• **Not Much Happens**
3%	• **Increase in Breathing**
6%	• **Considerable Increase in Breathing** **— Uncomfortable**
8.5%	• **Progressive Increase in Breathing** **— Mental Effects**
10%	• **Marked Mental Effects** **— Unconsciousness**

CARBON DIOXIDE POISONING. Carbon dioxide poisoning is not likely to occur when using SCUBA because of the very small amount of dead air space in the regulator. It can, however, occur if "skip breathing" or breath holding is practiced at any appreciable depth. Symptoms are: shortness of breath, nausea, headache, visual disturbances and sometimes unconsciousness, which is called "shallow water blackout." Treatment: Return to the surface and breathe surface air. Administer artificial respiration if necessary. *DO NOT SKIP BREATHE.*

CARBON MONOXIDE POISONING. To avoid Carbon Monoxide poisoning all gasoline or diesel powered air compressors should be inspected to assure that exhaust fumes are not being compressed. Carbon monoxide is a poisonous gas which is tasteless, odorless and colorless. Symptoms are: cherry colored lips and fingernails, headache, excessive fatigue and sometimes coma. Treatment includes breathing surface air, oxygen if available, and artificial respiration if necessary.

CHAPTER SIX
EQUIPMENT

Scuba diving is a dynamic, growing sport and industry. Changes and refinements in equipment take place constantly. For this reason, the beginning diver or for that matter, the experienced diver should rely heavily on the professional instructor or equipment counselor for advice before purchasing any scuba equipment.

PURE AIR...

On _____, your air was tested under specification directed by the National Association of Skin Diving Schools, Scripps Institution of Oceanography, and U.S. Naval Requirements.

OXYGEN _____
Carbon Monoxide _____
Carbon Dioxide _____
Dust, Oil and Water _____
Odor _____

This meets or exceeds all requirements for compressed air used in S.C.U.B.A. diving.
Yours for safe diving

JOHN GAFFNEY
EXECUTIVE DIRECTOR

VISUAL **I**NSPECTION **P**ROTECTION ©

THIS CYLINDER HAS BEEN INSPECTED BY A MEMBER OF THE NATIONAL ASSOCIATION OF SKIN DIVING SCHOOLS AND SHOWS NO SIGNIFICANT RUST OR CORROSION. THIS INSPECTION IS ONLY VALID FOR THE CALENDAR YEAR—

1974

AIR CYLINDER — Often called "tank" or "bottle," it supplies the diver with air. It is manufactured of chrome moly steel to withstand extremely high pressures. Marking on the neck of the cylinder identifies manufacturer, rated pressure, serial number, and test date. For example, WK is the initial of the manufacturer, D.O.T. (formerly ICC) 3AA2250 is rated pressure, 240678 is serial number, and 1 69 is the test date and the symbol of the test station. If the test date is followed by a plus sign, the cylinder can be filled to a ten percent overload for the first five years after the initial test. Cylinders are required by law to be tested for metal fatigue and stamped every five years. However it has been discovered that because of the possibility of internal corrosion, diving cylinders could become fatigued in less than that time. Consequently, they should be inspected internally at least once per year. For this reason, the Visual Inspection Program ("VIP") was instituted across the country by concerned diving schools. A fully charged diving cylinder has the latent power of a small "bomb" and if significant internal corrosion is present, it could explode at any time. For this reason, *all diving cylinders should be internally inspected annually and so marked by a pro dive store/school participating in the "VIP" program.*

Air cylinders are attached to the diver by means of a harness or back pack. A back pack is preferable because it is more comfortable and keeps the cylinder in proper position on the diver. All harnesses and back packs should be equipped with a quick release buckle which can be operated by either hand.

A cylinder is equipped with a valve to allow the correct amount of air to escape through the regulator as the diver needs it. Valves are of two types, no reserve or "K" valves, and reserve or "J" valves. A "K" valve is simply an on-off valve. It is to be used for shallow water diving. A "J" valve is a manually operated valve which provides the diver with a reserve supply of air of 300 to 600 pounds, depending upon the valve. After the air supply is depleted, both types of valves will provide air on ascent due to the reduction of ambient pressure. This air should not be relied upon as "reserve" air but strictly as "emergency" air. *DO NOT TAMPER WITH THE VALVE. IT SHOULD BE SERVICED BY TRAINED PERSONNEL ANNUALLY. NEVER USE OIL ON HIGH PRESSURE VALVES.*

Air cylinders should always be handled carefully, and when transported should be padded or blocked to prevent movement. If the cylinder is to be stored, it should be in an upright position with at least two hundred pounds of air pressure. Never empty tank and leave the valve open because it can be contaminated. Never fill tank with oxygen or any other gas.

NEVER HAVE YOUR TANK FILLED IF YOU HAVE ANY DOUBTS ABOUT THE PURITY OF THE THE AIR. PRO DIVE STORE / SCHOOLS PROUDLY DISPLAY THEIR "CLEAN AIR CERTIFICATES."

Air cylinder

Reserve valve (J)

Standard valve (K)

BACK PACKS

You can not learn to be a safe diver with an "Open Water Checkout." This is an outdated concept still used by many other programs. To feel comfortable in open water, the student diver should enroll in the NASDS Open Water Program. This is a continuation of the basic class giving the novice diver instruction in the Open Water Classroom.

REGULATORS: The regulator supplies the diver with air on demand at "ambient" or surrounding water pressure. Naturally, the deeper the diver goes, the greater the air pressure necessary. Regulators are classified as single or two stage, depending on the method by which it reduces the high pressure air in the cylinder to ambient pressure. Single stage regulators reduce the pressure in one step from high to ambient. These units have two hoses.

REGULATORS

Two stage regulators reduce the pressure in two steps, producing an intermediate level of pressure or second stage at a pressure usually around one hundred pounds. The second stage further reduces this pressure to ambient. Through design, pressure to the second stage is always at ambient plus the intermediate pressure setting. Two stage regulators are available in either the two hose or the single hose design. On one hose regulators the first stage is located at the tank and the second stage is located at the mouthpiece.

DO NOT TAMPER WITH THE REGULATOR. IT SHOULD BE SERVICED BY TRAINED PERSONNEL ANNUALLY. NEVER USE OIL ON REGULATORS.

WEIGHT BELT. The weight belt is worn to offset buoyancy caused by the exposure suit and/or the diver's natural buoyancy. All weight belts should have a non-corrosive quick release buckle easily operated by either hand. For deep dives a contracting weight belt is desirable.

PRESSURE GAUGES. Two types are available. One is submersible and gives the diver a constant reference to the amount of air remaining in the cylinder. It is an invaluable aid for computing air consumption while in the water. Topside, it can also be used to check air pressure in any cylinder. The submersible gauge is attached to, or is part of the first stage of a regulator.

The non-submersible pressure gauge is used for checking air pressure in cylinders out of the water.

EXPOSURE SUITS. In the early days of sport diving, individuals with low tolerance for cold water were responsible for the development of the "dry suit." Patterned somewhat like commercial divers' dress, the dry suit was made from thin sheet rubber. It was made oversize to allow the wearing of woolens inside to provide insulation and warmth. It worked, and in extremely cold water it is still in use.

The "wet suit" is made from foam neoprene rubber and, as the name implies, its user gets wet. The diver is insulated from the cold water by the thickness of the foam rubber. To prevent water circulation and the loss of heat, the wet suit must fit somewhat like a second skin, but not so tight as to be uncomfortable nor so loose as to permit water circulation.

In addition, it should fit comfortably around the neck as excess pressure on the carotid artery may cause black out. For these reasons, it is usually desirable for the wet suit to be custom tailored to the individual diver.

An example of a wet suit is shown on the opposite page.

Photo by Chuck Nicklin

BUOYANCY COMPENSATOR VESTS

The concept of the buoyancy compensator is directly related to the progressive teaching developments of the members of the National Association of Skin Diving Schools. Buoyancy compensator vests are available with an oral inflator or with an oral inflator and mechanical inflator.

Buoyancy compensators are invaluable safety aids when using SCUBA. Before entering the water, the vest should be inflated. Once in the water, air can be "valved off" for descent (see opposite page) or to provide sufficient buoyancy for snorkeling on the surface. Underwater, the diver can compensate for loss of buoyancy by simply putting the equivalent of a breath or two of air in the vest orally or mechanically. With proper use of the buoyancy compensator the diver can maintain neutral buoyancy with little or no effort.

Due to the large volume of air contained in buoyancy compensator vests, it is possible, on ascent, to accelerate beyond control if the expanding air is not "valved off" at the proper rate. Air is "valved off" by raising the hose over head and opening the oral valve as descending. A watch and a depth guage should be used to check the rate of ascent. On the surface, the buoyancy compensator vest should be inflated for the return trip to the beach or boat.

BUOYANCY COMPENSATOR

The mechanical inflator is connected to the low pressure port on the first stage of a single hose regulator. By pushing a button the diver can inflate the vest from air in his tank.

The At-Pac is a buoyancy compensator with an oral and mechanical inflator in combination with the weight belt and back pack.

Using the "Diver's Elevator", the diver holds his B.C. hose over his head. The water pressure forces the air out of his vest allowing him to effortlessly descend to his area of neutral buoyancy.

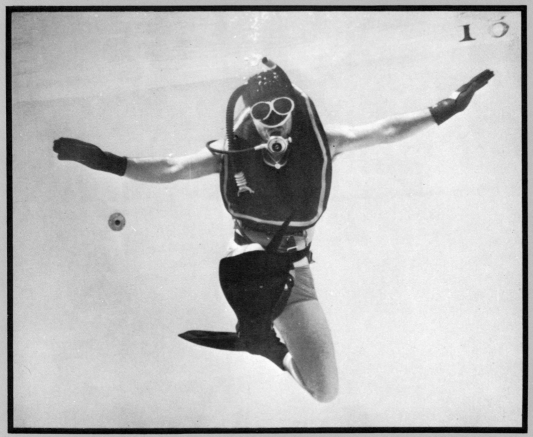

Proper inflation of the Buoyancy Compensator Vest or At-Pac results in perfect buoyancy control.

DIVING INSTRUMENTS

Depth (feet)	No-decompression limits (min)	Repetitive groups (air dives)													
		A	B	C	D	E	F	G	H	I	J	K	L	M	N
10	--------	60	120	210	300	----									
15	--------	35	70	110	160	225	350								
20	--------	25	50	75	100	135	180	240	325	----					
25	--------	20	35	55	75	100	125	160	195	245	315	----	----		
30	--------	15	30	45	60	75	95	120	145	170	205	250	310	----	
35	310	5	15	25	40	50	60	80	100	120	140	160	190	220	270
40	200	5	15	25	30	40	50	70	80	100	110	130	150	170	200
50	100	----	10	15	25	30	40	50	60	70	80	90	100	----	
60	60	----	10	15	20	25	30	40	50	55	60	----			
70	50	----	5	10	15	20	30	35	40	45	50	----			
80	40		5	10	15	20	25	30	35	40	----				
90	30		5	10	12	15	20	25	30	----					
100	25		5	7	10				25	----					
110	20			5	----										
120	15			5	----										
130	10			5	----										
140	10				----										
150	5														
160	5														
170	5														
180	5														
190															

Decompression Computer

The Decompression Computer is an instrument that records the rate that nitrogen goes into the bloodstream and tissues of the diver. This information is transmitted to the dial of the instrument and the required decompression is reflected. The decompression meter accurately calculates repetitive dives and has a six hour memory zone. Since sport divers knowingly or unknowingly are on the repetitive tables when diving, this instrument is a necessity when Scuba diving.

Compass

For accurate navigation underwater, a compass should have a large face with a luminous dial for easy reading and should also have a lubber line and a movable bezel. Small compasses that do not work when tilted slightly should be avoided. Like all instruments, compasses allow the diver to PLAN HIS DIVE AND DIVE HIS PLAN thus eliminating hard work and long swims.

Depth Gauges

Depth gauges are of three types i.e: capillary, bourdon tube, and oil filled.

The capillary and bourdon tube types reflect the depth by allowing water to enter the gauge and exert pressure which is measured on the face of the gauge.

The oil filled type is completely sealed and has a flexible case which is sensitive to water pressure. The oil filled type is superior because it is sealed from its environment.

Diving Watches

A good diving watch is a necessity when Scuba diving in order to keep track of time to avoid decompression or to plan for decompression. A good diving watch has a bezel and/or other devices for reflecting elapsed time.

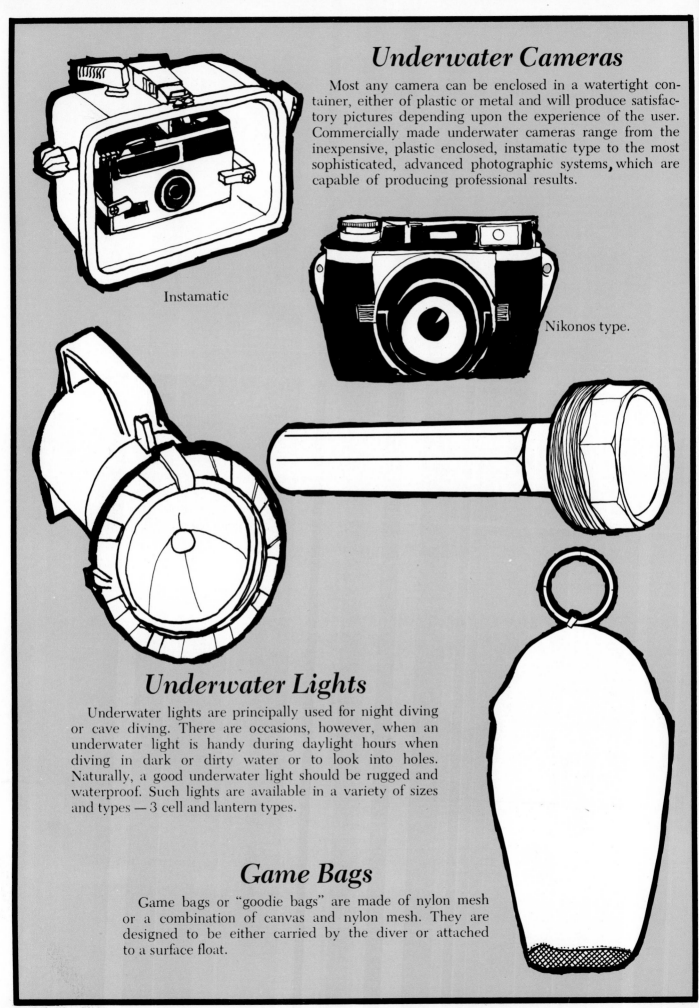

Underwater Cameras

Most any camera can be enclosed in a watertight container, either of plastic or metal and will produce satisfactory pictures depending upon the experience of the user. Commercially made underwater cameras range from the inexpensive, plastic enclosed, instamatic type to the most sophisticated, advanced photographic systems, which are capable of producing professional results.

Instamatic

Nikonos type.

Underwater Lights

Underwater lights are principally used for night diving or cave diving. There are occasions, however, when an underwater light is handy during daylight hours when diving in dark or dirty water or to look into holes. Naturally, a good underwater light should be rugged and waterproof. Such lights are available in a variety of sizes and types — 3 cell and lantern types.

Game Bags

Game bags or "goodie bags" are made of nylon mesh or a combination of canvas and nylon mesh. They are designed to be either carried by the diver or attached to a surface float.

Gear Bags

A well designed gear bag will be large enough to contain a complete diving outfit with the exception of the tank and back pack. Most are made of naugahyde or a similar material with noncorrosive fasteners. All personal equipment should be well marked with rubber paint for easy identification.

Subject: Sheepshead. Photo by Chuck Nicklin

Rubber

Spearfishing Guns

Spearfishing is one of the most exciting activities available to sport divers. Depending on the type of game to be hunted, the weapon can vary from simple hand spear or Hawaiian sling to the complex magnum charged power head. After a few hours of practice, most beginners can become as adept as an old timer in the use of underwater spearguns.

Hawaiian Sling

Power Head.

Pneumatic

Hand Spear

Diving Knives

A knife used for diving should be made of non-corrosive metal and have a serrated section on the blade for cutting rope or kelp. Since a knife is used as a tool and not a weapon, a metal knob on the end of the handle makes a good hammer. The blade should be of sufficient thickness so that the knife can be used for prying without damage to the blade. Floating knives are not desirable because of the problem of retrieving them from the surface when underwater. All good diving knives have sheaths that can be used on the belt or on the leg. When diving in kelp, it is a good idea to wear the knife on the inside of the leg to avoid entanglement.

The Chase. Photo by Omer Nielson

SPEARFISHING RULES

1. Never load the gun out of the water.

2. Unload your weapon before coming out of the water.

3. Be sure of what you are shooting at in dirty water.

4. Treat your weapon as you would a firearm.

SAFE SCUBA HABITS

In the past, SCUBA courses were a prescribed length of time, at the end of which, a student either "passed" or "failed." Enlightened Professional Instructors questioned this system for years and finally a new concept in SCUBA instruction was developed. This manual is the quintessence of their thousands of hours of teaching experience. Aside from the number of hours of classroom lecture necessary to impart the information required for a clear understanding of the technical aspects of diving, it was found that students could progress through the practical portion of the course as rapidly as they could learn FOUR HABITS FOR SAFE DIVING. They follow:

1. BREATHE ALL THE TIME. Breathing all the time must be an automatic habit before you are a safe diver. The best method is a deep inhalation and a long, slow exhalation.
2. COME UP SLOWLY. The proper rate of ascent is 60 feet per minute.
3. MAINTAIN CONTROL. To maintain control in any emergency, stop, think, get control, and take action.
4. PLAN YOUR DIVE AND DIVE YOUR PLAN. (Know your limitations). Think about your dive. Are you feeling good? How far do you have to swim? Which way is the current? How long a dive do you plan?

As soon as a student has mastered the above habits and the other practical and written exercies required, he has completed the basic course and is ready to continue on in the Open Water Program and master the advanced open water techniques. Because of dissimilarity of experience and backgrounds, students learn at different rates. Therefore, the length of a Basic Scuba Course can vary considerably depending upon the individual, however it has been found that *anyone* can learn to dive, provided he wants to and is given the proper amount of instruction.

Blowing little bubbles

This diver is illustrating the cardinal rule for safe scuba diving. When the regulator is out of your mouth, always *blow little bubbles.*

Drop weight belt

Last on first off
Know where the quick release buckle is and how to use it. When dropping the weight belt it should be held well out from the body to avoid entanglement with the legs or other equipment.

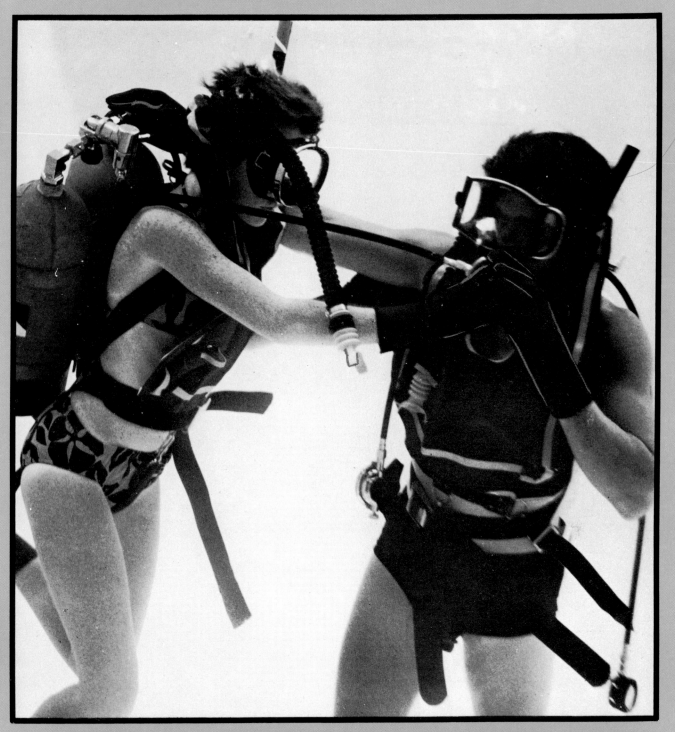

Buddy breathing side by side

Under actual diving conditions in case of an equipment failure or depletion of air the decision to buddy breathe should be made only if one's buddy is a competent and experienced diver. Remember, upon ascent, pressure changes result in additional air being available to the diver. A free ascent from reasonable depths presents no problems so long as the diver exhales continuously and his rate of ascent does not exceed 60 feet per minute. Caution: Always blow bubbles while ascending during buddy breathing.

BREATHING

Unfortunately for divers, the human breathing system is not designed to utilize all of the air that is inhaled. We only use a small percentage of the available oxygen before exhaling, and further, our plumbing is such that we waste the last quart of air we take in, which is the first quart of air we exhale. This air is not exposed to lung tissues and is lost in the tubes through which we inhale.

On any given dive, our time is limited by the number of cubic feet of air we have with us. Therefore, our problem is to get the maximum amount of time from our available air by breathing efficiently and SAFELY.

It has been found that if we breathe shallow and move two quarts of air in and out, we waste one half of every breath we take. One quart in the tubes, one quart in the lungs. On the other hand, if we breathe deeply and move four quarts of air in and out, we waste only one-quarter of every breath we take. One quart in the tubes, three quarts in the lungs.

RIGHT LUNG

EFFICIENTLY

So the proper way to breathe when using SCUBA is to take a deep breath on every inhalation. Don't overdo this, simply breathe deeply.

The next step is to get as much oxygen as is possible out of the air we have inhaled without holding our breath. This is achieved in the following manner. Immediately after a deep breath, we begin to exhale tiny bubbles and continue to do so until the desire to breathe is felt. This is the CO2 level rising in our system and we should respond to this by finishing the exhalation and taking another deep breath.

A good, safe diver will develop a pattern to his breathing. This can be observed by watching his bubbles. An unsafe diver will take a breath and hold it. He is the one who will get into trouble if an emergency develops. So the rule is: Breathe all the time with a deep inhalation and a long, slow exhalation.

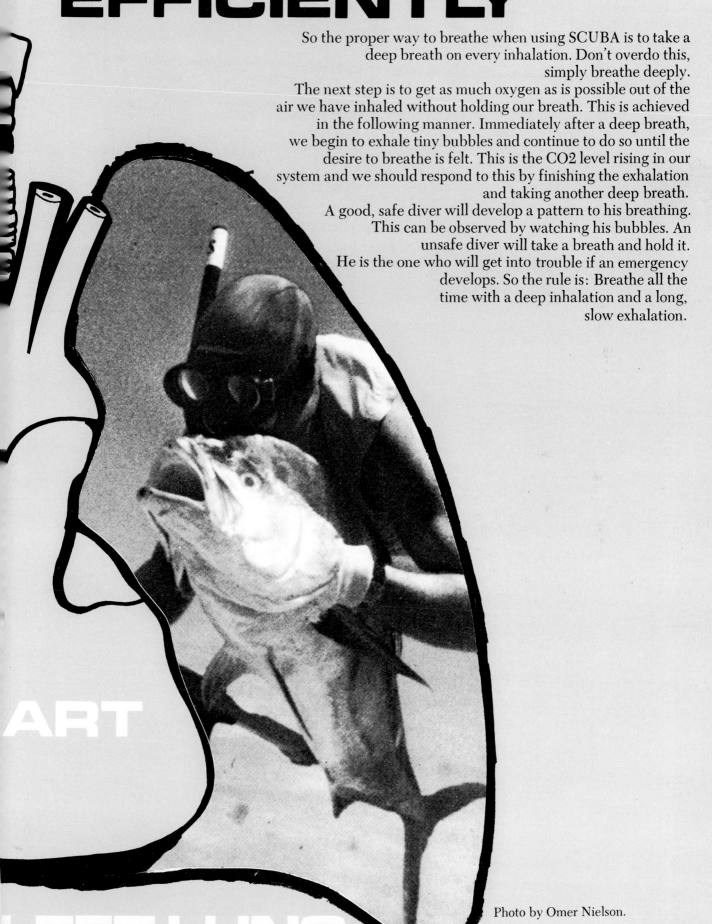

ART

LEFT LUNG

Photo by Omer Nielson.

PAGE 65

Buddy Diving

Through all phases of diving instruction students will be paired off with a buddy. Many of the exercises in the pool and open water require the help of a buddy. After the completion of Basic and Open Water training, it is a good idea to continue the habit of buddy diving. No matter how proficient a diver may become, there can be occasions when the presence of a buddy can spell the difference between a safe dive and a diving accident. Besides, diving is more fun when it is shared with another person!

Her buddy hurries to give her a hand with this rare piece of Purple Coral. Photo by Bill Hardy.

CHAPTER SEVEN

Scuba Exercises

Having mastered the use of the mask, fins and snorkel at the beginning of this course, the novice diver will find the use of SCUBA extremely easy. Some of our exercises with SCUBA are merely review. These include surface dives and water entries. Other exercises are to condition the beginning diver's mind and body (reflexes) to react automatically to any situation or emergency underwater. These exercises include weight control, clearing mask of water, clearing hoses and mouthpiece of water, swimming underwater without mask, switching from snorkel to mouthpiece and vice versa while swimming on the surface, swimming underwater without fins, buddy breathing, defense position, breathing from the tank valve, and changing regulators underwater while buddy breathing. All of these exercises are of a practical nature and are designed to teach the novice diver control, skill, and safe habits. Once mastered, these exercises prepare the novice for supervised open water diving.

PUTTING THE TANK ON IN THE WATER.
The easiest way to put the tank on is the way you will do it in open water, over your head. To do this, hold the tank in front of you, pack up, valve pointing toward your stomach. Put your arms through the straps, just past your elbows. The regulator should be hanging free and the waist straps off to either side. Take a breath, duck underwater and put the tank on over your head. Now buckle the waist straps.

WATER ENTRIES

Feet together

Giant stride

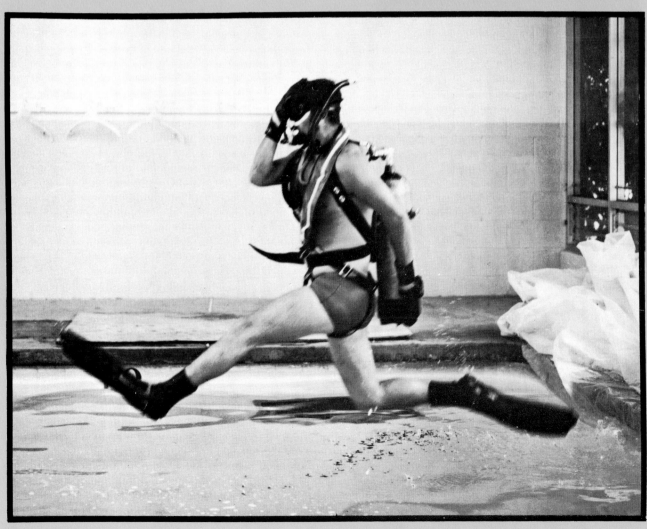

WATER ENTRIES

Front roll

Back roll

Sitting down entry from dock or boat

The diver sits erect on the dock and turns while balancing himself with his hands. He enters the water with a wide stride kick to hold him away from the dock and to remain on the surface.

1

2

3

4

Jackknife

Power kick to gain depth

PIKE DIVE

5

Rest position

Strong kick raises the body
out of the water

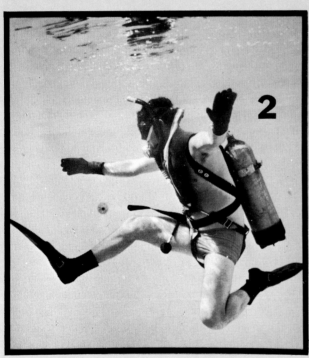

Kick and turn

KELP DIVE

Descent

Weight control

Proper inflation of the Buoyancy Compensator Vest results in perfect buoyancy control.

Clearing mask without purge valve

Clearing two hose regulators of water

Two hose regulators require a special method of clearing when flooded. The mouthpiece must be removed from the mouth and raised in order to cause the air to flow and clear the inhale hose of water.

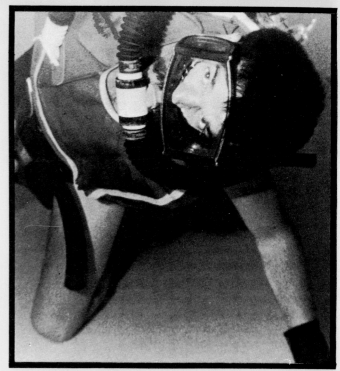

After air supply is established, the diver must roll on his left side and exhale to clear water from the exhaust hose.

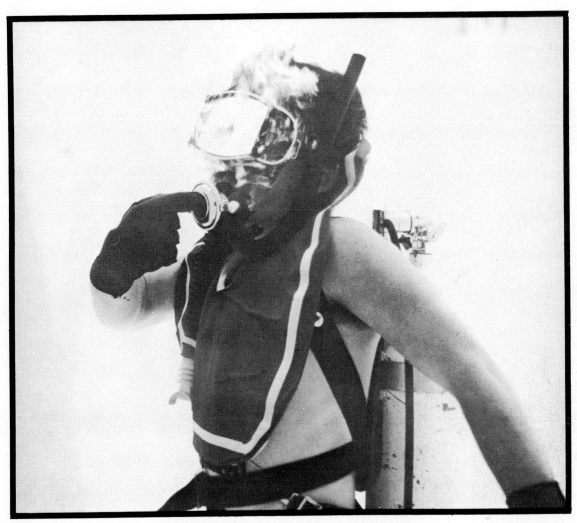

Clearing one hose regulator of water

Exhalation will clear regulator

Pushing exhaust button clears regulator

Swishing is the technique used when the lungs are empty and the exhaust button cannot be reached. By working the jaws in a chewing motion, water is pumped out of the regulator and air supply regained.

Underwater swim without mask

This exercise prepares the diver to function underwater if the mask is lost.

Underwater swim without fins

This exercise prepares the diver to make a safe, normal ascent in the event one or both fins are lost.

Switching from snorkel to regulator on surface

This is excellent practice for clearing the snorkel and regulator of water. It also accustoms the diver to having small amounts of water in the mouth from time to time.

Defense position

This position demonstrates control and the divers ability to think underwater. It can be used if entangled underwater or as a defense against a menace.

Sharing air or buddy breathing with a competent diver

These divers are under control and sharing air while making a slow ascent. They are holding on to each others back pack or tank and passing the regulator back and forth. Note that the mouthpiece is not inserted all the way into the mouth and that the divers are blowing small bubbles when not using the regulator. The correct method for holding the regulator is either lightly in the hand or by the swivel between the hose and the second stage.

1

The diver removes the tank by releasing the *harness and pulling his tank around the right* shoulder.

2

The tank is then held in position between the legs while removing the regulator.

Sharing air during the exercise

Attaching regulator to tank while sharing air.

SHARING AIR
WHILE CHANGING
REGULATOR
AND REPLACING IT.

Clearing the regulator at the end of the exercise

The purpose of this whole exercise is to demonstrate control in the use of the equipment and the ability to think and perform a task underwater. It is a prelude to performing the same exercise in open water during the Open Water Program.

Sharing air while removing and replacing mask

Removing the mouthpiece

Removing the mask

Replacing the regulator

Replacing the mask and clearing of water

This complete exercise demonstrates control, familiarity with equipment and the ability to to do a task with eyes, nose and mouth exposed to the water. Note the divers blowing little bubbles when not using the regulator.

Breathing off the tank valve is a simple maneuver with a little practice. This exercise teaches the diver control over the glottis as well as
control over breathing and equipment.

Divers should always help each other on and off with their equipment to prevent tiring.

PRE-DIVE EQUIPMENT CHECK

Prior to the dive and the donning of equipment, the following equipment check should be made:
1. *Check cylinder pressure.*
2. *Inspect all quick release buckles for ease of operation.*
3. *Attach regulator to cylinder and check for air leaks.*
4. *Check operation of regulator.*
5. *Inflate buoyancy control vest orally and check for leaks. Inspect CO2 cartridge or air mechanism and cartridges.*
6. *Inspect exposure suit and mend if necessary.*
7. *Inspect mask straps, snorkel adjustment and fin straps.*
8. *Inspect buddy to locate both weight belt buckle and tank release buckle.*
9. *Plan your dive. Dive your plan.*

CHAPTER EIGHT
Marine Life

The sea abounds with creatures that are harmless, interesting and beautiful. There are a few, however, which possess armament in the form of teeth or spines, coupled with unpredictable or aggressive behavior patterns. These creatures are to be avoided.

The Kaleidoscope. Photo by Jim Hodges.

Sharks

SHARKS. Despite the fact that there are virtually no records of sharks attacking a fully submerged diver, it is wise to avoid large sharks at all times. If you encounter sharks, leave the water as soon as possible. If immediate exit is impractical, remain submerged and appear aggressive. Banging on the air cylinder with knife handle or rock and shouting into the water has been effective in driving sharks away. When diving in an area where dangerous sharks are known to exist, be extremely cautious with speared fish or blood in the water, as these conditions seem to attract them.

Killer Whales

KILLER WHALES. Killer whales are very rarely seen underwater by divers and there are no recorded attacks. However, due to their size, speed, intelligence, and voracious appetites, divers should leave the water immediately if killer whales are sighted in the area.

Eels

EELS. Moray, Conger, and Spotted eels are all of the same family and their behavior patterns are usually the same. They live in caves or holes and are rarely aggressive. If disturbed, they will bite. Their bite is not poisonous but is extremely susceptible to infection. Divers should never stick their hands into a hole or cave without a preliminary inspection for the presence of an eel. Eels are sometimes attracted by divers taking abalone. It is prudent to give the abalone to the eel if he insists. Eels are speared by many divers as they are excellent food. If speared, they should be handled with caution.

Not all sharks are dangerous. Shown here is a Shovelnose Shark. Below is a Horned Shark. Photos by Bob Evans.

The Moray Eel may bite if you take his food or poke your hand in his mouth. Photo by Bob Evans.

The Wolf Eel lives in the waters of Washington, Oregon and Northern California. He has teeth capable of biting should you stick your hand in his mouth. Photo by Don Bloye.

STING RAYS. When sting rays strike it is a purely defensive action. A painful encounter can be avoided by shuffling one's fins or feet while wading in shallow water. This action disturbs the ray, causing him to swim away. A wound from a sting ray should have immediate medical attention.

(Left) This bat ray has a stinger on it's tail like most rays. Avoid the stinger. Photo by Bob Evans.

(Below) This puffer fish could be dangerous if you didn't use gloves to handle him or you stuck your finger in his mouth. Photo by Geza Kremples.

(Left) A couple of Rock Fish. These fellows have sharp spines that might cause problems if you didn't handle them carefully while spearfishing. Photo by Bob Evans.

(Top) This "meanie" is a sculpin and he has spines that could cause problems. Simply take care while handling. Photo by Bob Evans.

SEALS Seals are usually playful in the water although the males tend to be aggressive near rookeries. If an aggressive male appears it is wise to leave the water.

JELLY FISH. Avoid touching because their sting is painful. When diving in an area where large concentrations of jelly fish are present, wear protective clothing.

All types of Jelly Fish can cause problems if they touch you when you are NOT wearing protective clothing (wet suit, warm water diving apparel, etc.). Photo by Bob Evans.

(Below) Male Seals may become aggressive during the mating season.

Photo by Joe Jordan

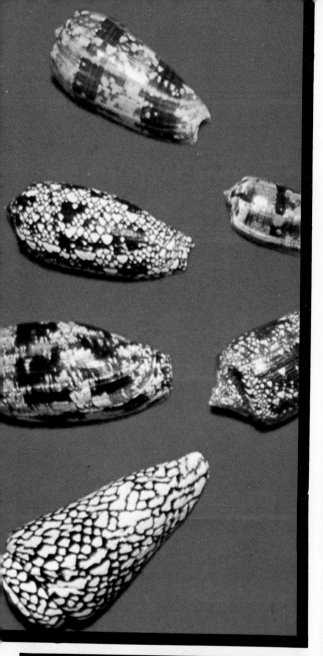

SEA URCHINS, BARNACLES, TUBEWORMS, SHELL LIFE, CORAL, ETC. Wear protective clothing and gloves when diving in areas where these types of sea life are present.

Finally, do not touch or disturb any sea life you cannot identify.

The shells shown (top left) are Cone shells. Some are poisonous and should be handled with care. Keep your skin away from any of the soft parts of the body. Photo by Joe Jordan.

(Top) The Most Dangerous Animal In The Sea. The sea urchin causes more problems than any single creature in the sea. It has sharp needles. Be careful when handling or stepping on them. Photo by Bob Evans.

(Left) Here are collectors items. These are safe to handle. Photo by Omer Nielson.

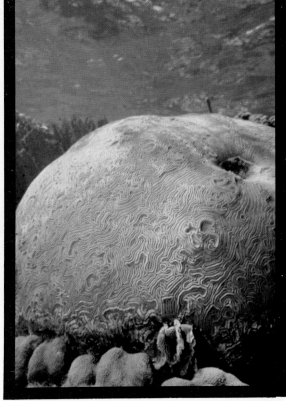

(Left) The Sea's Jungle, a Kelp Garden. Photo by Bob Evans.

(Below) This is Brain Coral. Some coral may give the diver a "burn". This is Fire Coral and the burn will go away in a short time.

KELP DIVING. The forests of kelp with their corridors, passageways, and overhead canopies are excellent areas for diving. When diving in kelp, be cautious to avoid entanglement, because projecting parts of diving gear tend to gather kelp stalks. If you become entangled, keep a cool head and methodically cut or break the kelp stalks. If it is necessary to surface in the kelp bed, select an area of relatively clear water. When submerging, use a kelp dive to avoid entanglement.

At ease in a slight swell and chop. This diver knows his limitations and his equipment. Photos by Bob Evans.

(Below) The surge moves over a section of rock creating a strong current.

CHAPTER NINE

Currents And Waves

The understanding of the actions of currents and waves is important to divers, as this knowledge can make the difference between an easy, fun-filled dive or a difficult, tiring one. The following sketches illustrate various wave and current patterns. A few minutes spent in relating this information to a specific diving area will always result in a better dive.

SMALL DEEP COVE

ROCKY COVE

Before making an entry in any type of surf condition, the surf should be studied carefully and entries and exits planned for areas where the wave action is the lightest.

SMOOTH SLOPING BOTTOM

Waves breaking well out from the beach once and continuing in an even pattern indicate a gradual sloping bottom. The diver should watch the wave patterns and enter and exit during the lull in the breaks or when smaller waves are breaking.

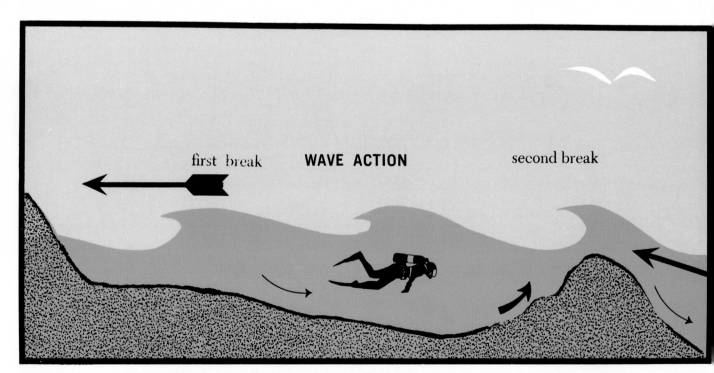

OFFSHORE REEF OR SANDBAR

A double break indicates an offshore reef. Usually deeper water exists between the breaks. Once past the first break, the diver should continue underwater until well past the second break.

POINT OR JETTY

Entry and exit should be made on the sheltered side of the point or jetty.

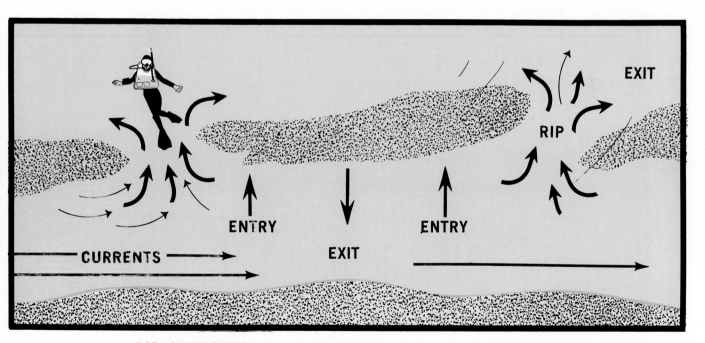

RIP CURRENTS

Rip currents are caused by water flowing seaward through a gap in a bar or reef. This causes a strong outward current which disperses rapidly beyond the area of the reef. Rip currents can usually be identified by watching for a gap in the breaker line which indicates the outgoing current. As the above illustration shows it is best to make entries and exits in the fringe areas of the rip. If inadvertently caught in a rip, make certain your Buoyancy Compensator Vest is inflated, relax and ride it out to calm water. Experienced divers frequently use rip currents for an easy trip out.

A WORD ABOUT THE NASDS
EXCLUSIVE UNDERWATER PHOTOGRAPHY COURSE.

The pictures shown here are actual pictures taken by NASDS divers after they have concluded the NASDS Underwater Photography Course. This course is designed in the same matter as your NASDS basic and Open Water diving programs. By using simplified methods that have been tested and proven by experts from every part of the United States and Canada, you are insured of being able to take underwater pictures you can be proud of in a very short time. No longer does the diver have to spend years of trial and error learning secrets on what makes a good photographer. If underwater photography interests you, ask your instructor when the next class starts.

Photos by Ron Benedict

Hints on Currents and Waves

1. When diving off a boat, swim upcurrent and return to the boat with the current. Utilize your buoyancy compensator.
2. Avoid long swims against a heavy current. It is better to swim ashore and walk back to point of entry. Utilize your buoyancy compensator.
3. Determine current action and take advantage of it when entering and leaving the water. Use caution with rips.
4. Make entries and exits during "lull" between sets of waves.
5. Do not attempt to dive when surf is high or sea is extremely rough.
6. Always inflate buoyancy control vest for swim back to boat or beach.
7. Use caution when handling spear gun in the surf.
8. **Do not attempt surf diving without proper instruction. It is covered thoroughly in the Open Water Program.**

This diver has taken a compass heading back to where she started the dive and will have avoided a long swim. Photo by Dan Wagner.

The AQUARIUS #1 during a five day NASDS diving vacation. Photo by Bill Hardy.

Handling the surge the NASDS way. The divers back into the open water holding hands to support each other. Photo by Bill Walters.

Almost all lectures are delivered at the diving site. The Open Water Program teaches practical diving techniques. This group is learning the Open Water Program in Port Austin, Mich.

A Word About The Open Water Program

Jon Johnson lectures his Open Water group at the edge of a sink hole in Florida.

The NASDS Open Water Program is designed to facilitate the transition from novice to accomplished diver. It is programmed to meet the regional diving requirements for each area of the country. Depanding upon locale, the following subjects are covered.

1. Night diving.
2. Deep diving.
3. Surf diving.
4. Wreck diving.
5. Underwater navigation.
6. Kelp diving.
7. Cave diving.
8. Ice diving.
9. Swift and dirty water diving.

In order to enjoy the underwater world completely, it is recommended that all novice divers participate in their regional Open Water Program.

These divers are learning the NASDS Open Water Program from the dive Boat, AQUARIUS No. 1, the NASDS diving yacht.

Tony Zimos, one of the world's leading instructors is shown teaching a class at the NASDS Instructors College. This is a 10 week vocational college to train full time instructors for member store/schools. You can get more details of this exciting life time career from your NASDS member school.

First Aid For Divers

ARTIFICIAL RESPIRATION. The most effective method of artificial respiration for diving victims is mouth to mouth. It should be started immediately while victim is in the water and continued until victim recovers or competent medical help is available. The breathing rate for adults is approximately 12 cycles per minute and for children approximately 20 cycles per minute. Never attempt to give an unconscious diver air by pushing the purge button on a single hose regulator. This could result in a lung rupture.

FIRST AID KIT FOR DIVERS. Any complete first aid kit is adequate for the diver with the following additions: Sun tan lotion, alcohol, salt tablets, motion sickness pills, and decongestant pills.

Hal Watts gives mouth to mouth resusitation to instructional candidates at a recent Clinic. It is every divers duty to understand how to do this effectively. Photo by Bill Hardy.

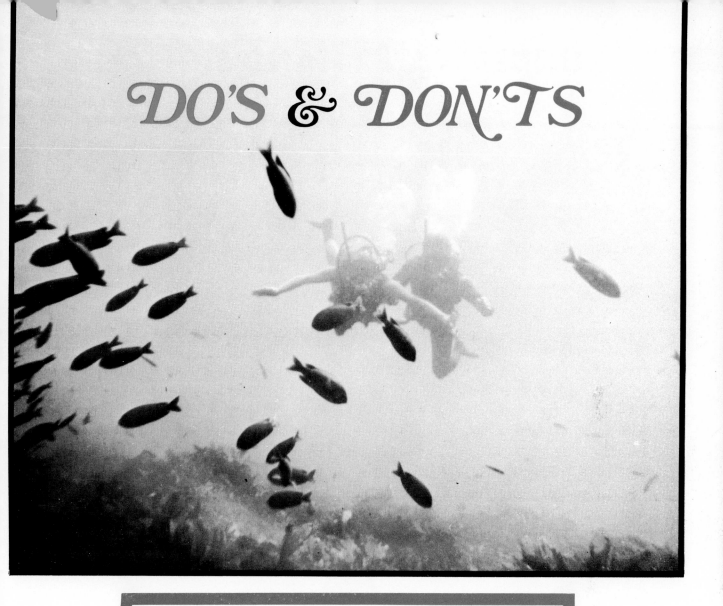

DO'S & DON'TS

Common Sense Rules Of Diving

1. Know your physical limitations and stay well within them when diving. Avoid fatigue.
2. Get good equipment and keep it in good condition. Check it before each dive.
3. Avoid decompression dives. If you must make decompression dives, know the tables or use a decompression meter.
4. Never hold breath while SCUBA diving. Exhale continuously on emergency ascent.
5. If snorkel diving, avoid excessive hyperventilation and do not push your limit on breath holding.
6. Dive with a buddy.
7. Fly the "Diver's Flag" when diving.
8. Never dive after drinking alcoholic beverages or with a hangover.
9. Plan your dive. Do not dive if surf is high or sea is rough. Have a beach party instead.
10. Remember that your Basic SUCBA Certification is a *license to learn*. To become a proficient diver, join the NASDS Open Water Program. You will enjoy your diving more.

UNDERWATER HAND SIGNALS

GIVE ME AIR!
POINT TO REGULATOR

HOLD EVERYTHING!
RAISE CLOSED FIST

"EARS NOT CLEARING"

"EASY"
"SLOW DOWN"
"BE CAREFUL"
FLAT PALM FACING DOWN
MOVES UP AND DOWN FROM ELBOW

"CUT"
INDEX AND SECOND FINGER
MAKE SCISSORS MOTION

"AIR SUPPLY LOW"
CLENCH FIST POUND ON CHEST

QUESTION?
ONE OR BOTH HANDS HELD PALM UP

"IS EVERYTHING O.K.?"
"O.K."
INDEX FINGER AND THUMB FORM
CIRCLE

"YES"
"NO"
NOD OR SHAKE HEAD

"ALERT TO DANGER"
"DANGEROUS"
"SHARK"
ARM MAKES CIRCULAR MOTION —
UP TOWARDS SELF AND PUSH AWAY.

"WATCH ME"
POINT TO SELF

"COME HERE"
PALM TOWARDS SELF, MOVES BACK
AND FORTH FROM WRIST

"STAY BACK OR GET AWAY"
ARMS MOVE BACK AND FORTH

"TALK"
THUMB AND FINGERS OPEN AND
CLOSE

"GO THAT WAY"
INDEX FINGER EXTENDED, MOVE IN
DESIRED DIRECTION

"UNDER"
"OVER"
"AROUND"

"SIZE — LONG OR SMALL"
"MANY OR FEW"
PALMS FACE EACH OTHER AND
INDICATE SIZE

"YOU LEAD, I'LL FOLLOW"
"STAY BESIDE ME"

"STAY THERE"
"HOLD STILL"
"WAIT"
FLAT PALM EXTENDED TOWARD
PARTNER

"I NEED AIR"
POINT TO MOUTHPIECE

"HURRY"
"FASTER"
"HARDER"
FIST CLENCHED, WHOLE ARM MOVES
UP AND DOWN

"LOOK"
"THAT OBJECT"
INDEX FINGER EXTENDED POINTS TO
OBJECT

"ABALONE"
FINGERS TOGETHER IN CUP SHAPE

"LOBSTER"
"CRAB"
FINGERS SPREAD IN CUP SHAPE

"WHAT TIME"
"WHAT DEPTH"
POINT TO WRIST

ASSISTANCE!
ARM STRAIGHT
OPEN HAND

ASSISTANCE!
EMERGENCY!
WAVE HAND

AIR LOW!
FIST ON CHEST

"ASSEMBLE HERE"
ARM EXTENDED
MOVES IN CIRCULAR MOTION

"ANYTHING OVERHEAD"
FLAT PALM MOVES BACK AND FORTH
OVERHEAD

"FISH"
HAND MOVES IN WAVE-LIKE
MOVEMENT

"EVERYBODY"
MOVE ARM FROM ELBOW IN FRONT OF SELF

"SHIP"
"BOAT"
INDEX FINGER AND THUMB OF EACH HAND PUT TOGETHER TO FORM TRIANGLE

"QUESTION"
PALM UP

"TELL HIM"
"TELL THEM"
USE 'TALK' MOTION THEN INDICATE TO WHOM WITH INDEX FINGER

"GO BACK"
"BACK TO STARTING POINT"
MOTION OVER SHOULDER WITH INDEX FINGER POINTING

"THIS DEPTH"
FLAT PALM DOWNWARD, MOVES SIDE TO SIDE FROM ELBOW

OUT OF AIR!
FLAT HAND ACROSS THROAT

"THIS SPOT"
"RIGHT HERE"
INDEX FINGER POINTS TO CENTER OF PALM

"WHICH DIRECTION"
CLENCH FIST THUMB EXTENDED, MOVE HAND SIDE TO SIDE FROM WRIST

ATTENTION!
BANG ON TANK WITH KNIFE OR ROCK

"LOOK AT . . ."
"LOOK AROUND"
FLAT PALM DOWNWARD, HAND ON BROW

"I AM COLD"

LOOK! (THAT WAY)
POINT FOREFINGER

LET'S GO! (THIS WAY)
POINT WITH THUMB (ALL
DIRECTIONS)

OK!!??
(BOTH QUESTION AND ANSWER)
MAKE CIRCLE WITH FOREFINGER AND
THUMB

YOU GO! (THAT WAY)
FLAT HAND MOVING — PALM DOWN

TRAVEL

One of the most interesting pursuits for the accomplished SCUBA diver is exploring different waters with different conditions from those found in his own locale. Throughout the United States there are many opportunities for unusual diving experiences. Consider gold diving in Northern California or collecting marine specimens in the warm waters around the Florida Keys. How about spearing giant jewfish beneath the oil rigs of the Gulf Coast? Or exploring the beauty of a kelp forest in California? A dive under the ice high in the mountains of Colorado is an adventure. Wreck diving in the Great Lakes can result in the finding of an artifact of historical significance or perhaps, a ships bell that will serve as a conversation piece in the home of the lucky diver who recovered it.

All across the country, wherever diving is possible, there is an NASDS member to serve the visiting diver. He can be depended upon to offer all of the services normally expected from a diving specialist. In addition, and most important, he can furnish advice and special instruction when necessary for the type of diving in his locale. Use him!

Just outside the continental limits of the United States is a region which holds a special fascination for those who love the sea. The Gulf of California or Mar de Cortez (which is its first and proper name) is formed by the mainland of Mexico on the East and by the one thousand mile long peninsula of Baja California on the West. Starting with the upper reaches of the Sea of Cortez with its colder waters and moving Southward through the raging Midriff area where the cold and warm waters mix causing waterspouts, tidal bores, and a fantastic conglomeration of sea life, and extending hundreds of miles South to the placid, warm, gin clear waters of La Paz and finally meeting the Pacific Ocean at Cabo San Lucas, Mar de Cortez offers the diver the total

The first part in a co-operative recreational system for NASDS qualified divers is the diving yacht, AQUARIUS #1. See your Pro School for more details.

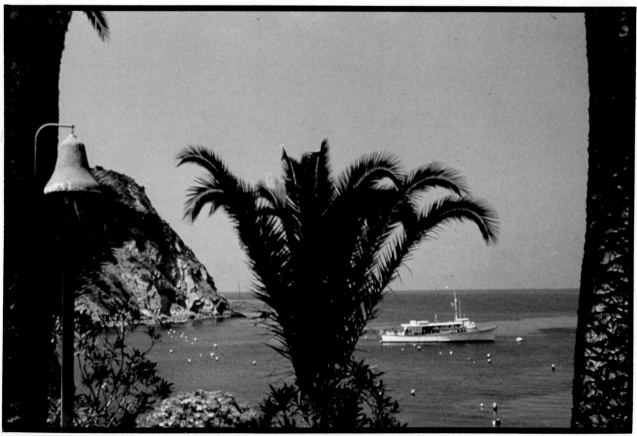

spectrum of salt water diving experience. In addition, Baja California, with its remote tropical beaches, unhurried way of life and hospitable people, makes a visit to this part of the world an unforgetable adventure. Baja is only a few hours away from anywhere in the United States.

From the Caribbean on our Eastern doorstep it is a short hop to the South Atlantic or Africa, the Indian Ocean, the Mediterranean or most any place the inquisitive diver has a mind to explore. Indeed, this is one of the great attractions in diving. In no other sport is such a variety of conditions available to the enthusiast. The diver has over ⅘ths of the earth's surface to explore. He may discover a new kind of fish or a new sea shell. He can photograph sights seen by no other man. In short, the world is his personal oyster.

Photo by Bob Evans

This beautiful beach is only 2½ hours from Los Angeles. It is the site of the first diving resort for NASDS divers. It is located below La Paz, Baja California, Mexico under the sponsorship of Club Aquarius.

Around the world in many of these remote areas, diving resorts are in operation, and many more are in the process of being established now. Because of the weight restrictions on air travel a diving resort should furnish tanks, weight belts and air as part of their "package." There are some other travel rules to consider. The owner of the resort you choose must be a specialist in high pressure air, diving equipment and an expert in the type of diving he can offer you. Some areas prohibit spearfishing and encourage photography. This could be very discouraging if your trip was planned around spearfishing. NASDS members are travel specialists who can make arrangements to send you to the area that will be best suited for your particular needs. Usually they will have two or three special trips planned to areas that are truly "different." Consult with your NASDS member before making any diving vacation plans.

RECIPES

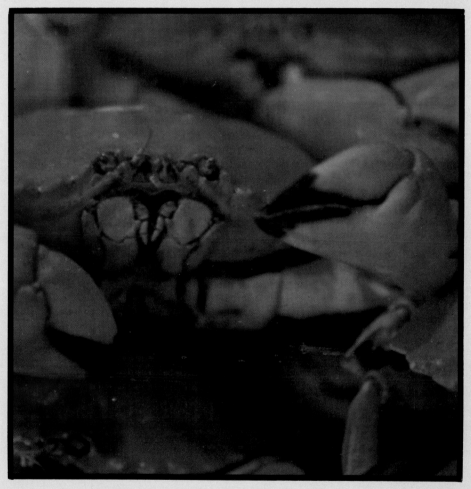

There are many thousands of fine recipes for preparing fish and shellfish. Unfortunately only a few of these delicious, nutrious offerings can be presented in a publication such as this. One of the finest cookbooks written for divers is "Bottoms Up Cookery". Published by Fathom Enterprises.

Other excellent sources for recipes are cookbooks published by Sunset and Life Magazines.

The nutritive value of fish and shellfish is well known, and the accomplished diver can provide many fine meals for his family and friends. As a matter of fact, the diver is the only sportsman who can literally take his choice of many seafood delicacies that are not available in the markets.

RECIPES

SMOKING FISH THE EASY WAY

Smoked fish is a delicacy that most everyone enjoys and one that very few people have time to prepare. What modern home or apartment has a handy smoke house as an appliance? This recipe produces smoked fish with the flavor and quality that one would expect from an authentic, outdoor smoke house. Generally speaking, fish with a high oil content are best for smoking. These include, but are not limited to, Bonita, Mackeral, Albacore, Yellowtail, Tuna and Barracuda. Don't be afraid to experiment. Clean the fish and cut out the backbone, leaving the skin on. Cut up in chunks for smoking. Prepare a salt brine by mixing 1 cup of salt to one-half gallon of water. Soak the fish for thirty minutes in the brine. Take out and drain. Preheat oven to 400°. Place fish in open pan or on aluminum foil, baste three times with a mixture of one part liquid smoke to three parts of soya sauce while baking. Bake until done. (White all the way through or flaky).

PHOTOS BY ROY BRIZZ

STEAMED CLAMS A LA JOYCE

- 10 lbs. Little Neck clams
- 2 medium onions
- 1 stick margarine
- 1 Tbs. dry vermouth
- 1 cup diced celery
- 2 tsp. garlic salt
- 1 Tbs. ground pepper
- ½ glass water (cover while cooking)
- 1 tsp. parsley
- 1 clove garlic

Saute onions, celery, garlic salt, pepper and garlic in half of the margarine. Add parsley. Wash clams thoroughly. Place clams over mixture. Add remaining margarine. Pour water and vermouth over clams. Seal clam pot and steam on medium flame for 10 minutes. Clam must be open. Serves four. Garnish and flavor with ground pepper.

FILET OF FLOUNDER, PATRICIA

- 4 flounder filets
- 2 tblsp corn oil
- 2 onions
- 1 large fresh tomato
- 1 tsp. lemon juice
- ¼ glass tomato sauce
- 1 cup flour

In an enamel or teflon pan, sauté onions and tomatoes. Cut into quarters. When partially cooked, remove from pan and set aside. Dip filets in flour and add to pan. Cover with onion and tomato mixture. Add lemon juice, tomato sauce and water to cover fish. Cook over low flame 30 minutes, basting with sauce frequently. Remove to heated platter. Serves four.

LOBSTER CLAMBAKE

- 12 dozen hard shell clams (more or less, depending upon type and size)
- 6 live lobsters
- sea weed
- 1 tarpaulin

As a rule, one large lobster and a dozen or so clams will satisfy the appetite of the diver who has spent the better part of an afternoon diving for the ingredients. Dig a large hole in the sand and line it with rocks. Place a few rocks in the bottom and build a big fire that will produce fiery red coals. When the fire is reduced to coals and the rocks are hot, cover with a light layer of seaweed. Then a layer of lobsters, next a layer of seaweed, then a layer of clams, then a layer of seaweed. Continue alternate layers of seaweed and clams until enough has been placed in the "bake" to satisfy all of the hungry appetites. The final covering of seaweed should be thick. Cover with canvas tarpaulin securely held down by rocks. Bake until clam shells begin to open. Beer and potato chips compliment this hearty, outdoor meal.

Note: If lobsters are out of season, use clams only.

BAKED LINGCOD

- 1 whole lingcod (4 lbs.)
- 4 slices bacon
- 6 small whole potatoes
- ½ lb. sliced mushrooms
- ½ cup flour
- 1½ tsp. salt
- ⅛ tsp. pepper
- pinch of cayenne
- ⅛ tsp. basil
- 1½ cups dry Rhine wine
- 6 sprigs mint

Clean fish, remove head if desired, wipe with damp cloth and cut four, two inch gashes across one side.

Sprinkle fish with mixture of flour, salt, pepper, cayenne and basil. Place fish in shallow baking dish and lay bacon slices in gashes. Pour wine around fish. Pre-heat oven to 350° and bake for thirty minutes. Add potatoes and mushrooms, baste with wine and juices in pan, bake until done. (Approx. thirty minutes.) When done, place on pre-heated platter and pour remaining fluid on fish. Serve immediately on pre-heated plates. Garnish with mint springs. Serves six.

Note: Try this recipe with any whole fish.

CATFISH IN BROWN BUTTER

- 3 lbs. catfish
- ¼ lb. butter
- 2 tsp. salt
- ¼ tsp. pepper
- 12 sprigs parsley
- 2 tsp. chopped fresh mint
- 2 Tbs. flour

Clean the fish, skin it, wipe with damp cloth and dust lightly with flour.

Melt butter in sauce pan and brush fish lightly with part of it. Sprinkle fish with chopped mint. Broil four minutes in pre-heated broiling pan two inches below flame. Baste with melted butter and broil four minutes more.

Meanwhile, fry parsley sprigs four minutes in butter over low flame. Place broiled fish on pre-heated platter, add salt & pepper. Garnish with butter and hot parsley sprigs. Serve immediately on pre-heated dishes. Serves six.

LEMON SOLE

- 4 lemon sole filets
- ½ cup corn oil
- 1 lemon
- 1 egg
- 1 tsp. flour
- 1 glass water

Heat corn oil in saucepan. Dip lemon sole in flour. Fold and put in oil. Add one glass of water with juice from fresh lemon. Cover and cook 15 minutes over low flame. Beat egg well. Heat juice from filet with egg mixture until it thickens, stirring constantly. When thick, pour over fish. Serves four.

PHOTOS BY ROY BRIZZ

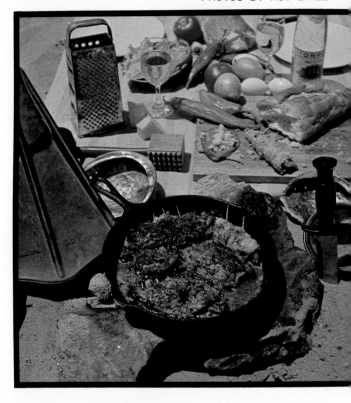

ABALONE A LA BRUHA

Ingredients: abalone, ortega chili, jack cheese, eggs, condensed milk or cream, fritos, ritz crackers, salt & pepper, butter.

Remove abalone from the shell in the usual manner. Slice it into ½ inch steaks. Pound it with a tenderizing hammer until tender but firm. Take your Ortega Chili and open it with a center cut, laying the chili over the abalone steak. Grate a large bar of Jack Cheese and spread liberally over the chili and steak.

Prepare an egg batter from eggs, cream or condensed milk. Make a mixture of Fritos and Ritz Crackers (½ and ½), salt and pepper (white pepper), using a pinch of each.

Prepare a deep frying pan with hot oil and two patties of butter. Now everything is ready. Roll the abalone over the Ritz and Frito mixture and roll it into a roll, using two tooth picks to hold it together.

Drop it into the hot frying pan and cook as fast as possible until the roll is brown. Turn over and cook the other side the same way.

Serve with white wine, salad and side dish of crab or lobster cocktail.

INTERESTING READING

U.S. Navy Diving Manual "Navships" 250-538
Superintendent of Documents
U.S. Government Printing Office
Washington, D.C.

"The Complete Goggler"
Guy Gilpatric
Dodd, Mead & Company
New York, N.Y.

"The Skin Diver"
Elgin Ciampi
Ronald Press Co.
New York, N.Y.

"Free Diving"
Demitri Rebikoff
E. P. Dutton & Co.
New York, N.Y.

"Underwater Photography Simplified"
Jerry Greenberg
Seahawk Products

"The Silent World"
J. Y. Costeau
Harpers & Brothers
New York, N. Y.

"Diving to Adventure"
Hans Hass
Doubleday & Company
Garden City, N.Y.

"Lady with a Spear"
Eugene Clark
Harper & Brothers
New York, N.Y.

"The Blue Continent"
Folco Quilici
Rinehart & Co.
New York, N.Y.

"4,000 Years Under the Sea"
Phillipe Diolé
Julian Messner Inc.
New York, N.Y.

"Peter Freuchens Book of the Seven Seas"
Julian Messner Inc.
New York, N.Y.

"Bottoms Up Cookery"
Fathom Enterprises
Palos Verdes, Calif. 90274

"Underwater Medicine"
Stanley Miles
J. B. Lippincott Co.
Philadelphia, Pa.

"Physiology and Medicine of Diving and Compressed Air Work"
P. B. Bennett and D. H. Elliott
Williams and Wilkens Co.
Baltimore, Maryland

"Decompression from Non-Saturated Dives"
copy of lecture by H. R. Schreiner
Biological Research Department
Union Carbide Corp.
Linde Division Research Lab.
Tonawanda, N.Y.

Photo by Chuck Nicklin

GLOSSARY

Absolute Pressure — Indicated gauge pressure plus 14.7 pounds. True pressure.

Ambient Pressure — Pressure of surrounding water including air pressure above it.

Breathing Air — Compressed air that is free of contaminants.

Buoyancy — In water, the upward force exerted on an immersed or floating object.

Buoyancy Compensation — The act of controlling buoyancy underwater or on the surface.

Currents — A horizontal movement of water.

Cylinder — Compressed air tank.

Decompression — To release from pressure or compression.

Density — The weight of anything per unit of volume.

Eel Grass — Long, green grass that grows along the coast in rocky areas.

Exhale — To breathe out.

Gauge Pressure — Instrumental indication of change in pressure from the normal atmospheric level.

Half Times — A method for calculating the rate at which tissue absorbs and releases nitrogen.

Hemorrhage — Any discharge of blood from blood vessels.

Inhale — To breathe into the lungs.

Kelp — Various large brown seaweeds.

Longshore currents — Movement of water parallel and close to the shore.

Narcosis — A state of arrested activity or stupor.

Nausea — A sickness of the stomach causing a desire to vomit.

Partial Pressure — The effect of a gas exerting its share of the total pressure in a given volume.

Physics of Diving — The science of matter and motion as related to the activity of diving.

Physiology of Diving — The organic process and phenomena dealing with life and functions of man underwater.

Recompression — The treatment for various types of diving sickness in a recompression chamber using the treatment tables.

Reef — A shallow area caused by rocks, sand, coral or any other objects.

Regulator — A device which upon demand, delivers air to the diver at a pressure equal to ambient pressure.

Rip current — A strong current flowing seaward.

Rupture — Bursting, breaking apart as an ear drum under unequalized pressure.

Sand Bar — A body of sand built up by the action of currents or waves.

SCUBA — Self-contained underwater breathing apparatus.

Skin Diving — Diving without the use of scuba.

Surf — Waves breaking upon the shore.

Surge — A great rolling swell of water, a violent rising and falling.

Symptoms — Perceptible changes in body or function which may indicate disease or injury.

Tanks — Compressed air cylinders.

Toxic — Poisonous.

Valve — A device that can be opened and closed which regulates the flow of air in one direction.

Volume — Space measured by cubic units.

NAME _____ STUDENT No. _____

HOMEWORK ASSIGNMENT CLASS No. 1

1. When is your Mid-term dive?

2. What features do you consider desirable in a mask, and why?

3. Why do you need fins?

4. Why is a snorkel such a valuable piece of equipment?

5. What items of equipment must you furnish for your basic class?

6. Why do you want to be a diver?

7. What did you choose to let a professional teach you as opposed to teaching yourself?

8. Have you read your Dear Student letter in your Student Folder? If not, do it now.

9. List 3 advantages of purchasing your basic equipment from a pro store as opposed to a discount or mail order store.

10. How do you rate yourself as a swimmer?
    A. Poor
    B. Good
    C. Average
    D. Above Average

USE BACK OF PAGE FOR ADDITIONAL SPACE

NAME _____ STUDENT No. _____

HOMEWORK ASSIGNMENT CLASS No. 2

1. Draw and describe a divers flag.

2. Define the term squeeze as applied to diving.

3. List the air spaces in the body where a squeeze may occur.

4. At a depth of 66 feet in salt water, the pressure on a diver is equivalent to _____ atmospheres.

5. What is an eustachian tube and its purpose?

6. How may you avoid a thoratic squeeze?

7. What is the best way to extend your time underwater on breath-holding dives?

8. What are the two types of surface dives? When are each most applicable?

9. When surfacing, what is the first part of your body to emerge?

10. Describe the proper way to use your fins (kick as described by your instructor).

USE BACK OF PAGE FOR ADDITIONAL SPACE

NAME _____ STUDENT No. _____

HOMEWORK ASSIGNMENT CLASS No. 3

1. The function of your scuba equipment is to:
   A.
   B.
   C.

2. The gas we use to fill our tanks is _____ and is comprised of _____ % _____ and _____ % _____ primarily.

3. What would probably happen to you if you hold your breath and swim to the surface after breathing compressed air underwater? Why?

4. What is the first rule of diving?

5. Describe the most efficient way for a human to breathe from a limited air supply.

6. In what three ways may you determine a safe rate of ascent?

7. What is neutral buoyancy? How do you achieve neutral buoyancy?

8. Describe three ways to clear your regulator.

9. Have you made your counseling appointment yet? When?

10. If you have to leave your tank unattended, what is the safe way?

USE BACK OF PAGE FOR ADDITIONAL SPACE

HOMEWORK ASSIGNMENT CLASS No. 4

1. Why should you consider your buoyancy compensator your most important piece of equipment?

2. Give a short version of your idea of a good diving buddy.

3. The cardinal rule in any unusual situation is:
   1.
   2.
   3.

4. You are at 60′ depth, your buddy is 30′ away upstream against a fairly strong current, you discover you have a loss of air supply, what do you do and how?

5. In a situation that requires you to share your buddy's air, from which side should you approach and why?

6. You and your buddy are sharing air with a regular rhythm, the regulator is being passed as fast as practical yet you feel air starved, what should you do?

7. You are swimming back to the beach and discover you are being swept parallel to your destination by an along-shore current, how do you overcome this situation?

8. You are diving from a boat (with crew) anchored in a slight current, how do you plan your dive?

9. What, thus far, is your opinion of cave diving?

10. You've trailered your 16′ boat to the Keys with a competent buddy. You meet two well-trained divers who want you to take them night diving, should you? Why?

USE BACK OF PAGE FOR ADDITIONAL SPACE

NAME _____ STUDENT No. _____

HOMEWORK ASSIGNMENT CLASS No. 5

1. Define air embolism, its cause, symptoms and treatment in detail.

2. What is the only way to protect yourself from air embolism?

3. What is the maximum safe rate of ascent?

4. At what pressure does oxygen become toxic to the average human? In what ways may a diver elevate his oxygen pressure to a dangerous level?

5. Describe the cause and prevention of carbon dioxide narcosis (shallow water blackout).

6. Describe the cause and prevention of nitrogen narcosis.

7. In what ways can you determine the difference between bends and air embolism?

8. What effect will being cold, tired, overweight or the recent consumption of alcohol have on a diver's nitrogen absorption?

9. How does a wet suit warm you?

10. What is the first aid treatment for the bends?

USE BACK OF PAGE FOR ADDITIONAL SPACE

NAME _____ STUDENT No. _____

HOMEWORK ASSIGNMENT CLASS No. 6

1. Why is knowing your surface air consumption important?

2. You just made a 10 minute swim at 20 feet in salt water and used 300 psi of air, what is your surface rate of consumption?

3. When is the only time you use Table 1-10?

4. What are the two most important factors governing any dive deeper than 33' salt water?

5. You have just completed a dive to 90' for 30 minutes and discovered you've left a valuable piece of equipment on the bottom. Its recovery will require a bottom time of 12 minutes. What is the minimum surface interval you must wait before you can recover the equipment without decompressing?

6. Why is a decompression computer safer than the tables for most sport divers?

7. What is residual nitrogen? Where did it come from? Where does it go?

8. After a 20 minute dive to 80' you sit 3 hours. Then make a 20 minute dive to 90'. What is your repetitive group at the end of the 1st dive, at the end of the sit, and at the end of the 2nd dive?

9. You and your buddy are in a strange part of the country for the first time with your equipment and want to go diving. Briefly describe your preliminary actions.

10. In what ways will owning your own equipment make you a safer diver?

USE BACK OF PAGE FOR ADDITIONAL SPACE

HOMEWORK ASSIGNMENT CLASS No. 7

1. What is the most important maintenance you yourself perform for your regulator?

2. Is an adjustable second stage a desirable feature?

3. When, if ever, would you want an octopus?

4. What are the most important features to look for in a depth gauge?

5. How often do you plan to dive once you've completed your training?

6. How do you plan to obtain your equipment: A. Borrow B. Steal C. Rent D. Buy for Cash E. Buy on Time   F. Count on Gifts   G. Other (Explain)

7. How often must you have your tank Hydrostated?   VIPed?

8. Do you desire more open water training such as the Open Water Course?

9. Do you desire to join a diving club?

10. Which do you consider the best tank for yourself, aluminum or steel? Doubles (any size) or a single? Why?

USE BACK OF PAGE FOR ADDITIONAL SPACE

TRIP SIGN CONFIRMATION

NAME_____

ADDRESS_____

CITY_____ STATE_____ ZIP_____

PHONE OFF._____ RES._____

NAME AND NO. OF TRIP_____

DEPARTURE DATE:_____

READ CAREFULLY:

ALL RESERVATIONS MUST BE IN OUR OFFICE 30 DAYS BEFORE TRIP DEPARTURE. A FEE MUST ACCOMPANY EACH RESERVATION OR PERSON ON TRIP. THERE IS NO REFUND ON THE DEPOSIT. TOTAL FEE MUST BE PAID 15 DAYS BEFORE DEPARTURE DATE AND IS REFUNDABLE EXCEPT FOR DEPOSIT. I HAVE READ THE ABOVE AND AM IN AGREEMENT WITH ITS CONTENTS.

SIGNATURE_____

YOU MUST BE NASDS CERTIFIED AND A CLUB AQUARIUS MEMBER.

TRIP WILL BE CANCELLED 7 DAYS IN ADVANCE IF 8 PEOPLE DO NOT GO.

NOTES

This is our diving yacht, the AQUARIUS No. 1 (above), located in La Paz, Mexico. It has bunks for 28 people, a compressor, and complete galley.

When you take lessons at an NASDS member school you are getting more than the finest teaching program in diving. Your school is also an expert in diving travel and local activities. Your membership money to Club Aquarius is used to buy facilities for you to use. This protects your investment in your equipment and your sport. Shown here are just a few of the facilities Club Aquarius NASDS divers have already built to insure that your diving days are fun days.

Club Aquarius bought this quarry in North Carolina to make sure that NASDS divers would be able to dive the year round on the East Coast. As we continue to grow, we will be buying more springs and more quarries. On page 107 of this textbook you see ten acres of beachfront property for our diving resort in Baja California, Mexico. Ask your instructor how you can participate.

This is our diving yacht, the AQUARIUS No. 2, located in Honduras. It is 158 feet long, carries 35 divers, and has complete facilities to give you the dive of a lifetime.